Psychology

Philip G. Zimbardo
Stanford University

Ann L. Weber
University of North Carolina at Asheville

 HarperCollins*CollegePublishers*

Acquisitions Editor: Meg Holden
Developmental Editor: Arlene Bessenoff
Project Coordination, Text and Cover Design: Proof Positive/Farrowlyne
    Associates, Inc.
Cover Illustration: "La Tristesse du Roi" by Henri Matisse
Photo Researcher: Roberta Knauf
Production Manager: Willie Lane
Compositor: Proof Positive/Farrowlyne Associates, Inc.
Printer and Binder: R. R. Donnelley & Sons Company
Cover Printer: The Lehigh Press, Inc.

PSYCHOLOGY

Library of Congress Cataloging-in-Publication Data

Zimbardo, Philip G.
        Psychology/Philip G. Zimbardo, Ann L. Weber.
            p.   cm.
        Includes bibliographical references and indexes.
        ISBN 0-06-501340-9 (student paperback edition)
        ISBN 0-06-502348-X (student hardcover edition)
        ISBN 0-06-501416-2 (instructor's edition)
        1. Psychology.   I. Weber, Ann L.   II. Title.
BF121.Z53   1994
150—dc20
                                                        93-39548
                                                        CIP

94 95 96 97 9 8 7 6 5 4 3 2 1

Dedication

Dedicated with love and thanks to our spouses,

Christina Maslach and John Quigley,

for tolerantly pretending that we did not exist

and taking care of the Significant Other details in our lives

(such as our homes, children, cat, and friends)

while we concentrated (not forever—we promise!)

on producing this wonderful book.

Brief
Contents

Detailed Contents

Chapter 1

Mind, Behavior, and Science

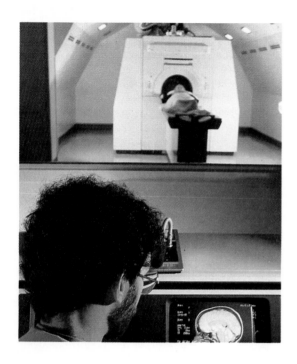

Chapter 2

Biopsychology

Chapter 3

States of Mind

Chapter 4

Psychological Development

Free Copy
Not For Student Use

Chapter 5

Sensation and Perception

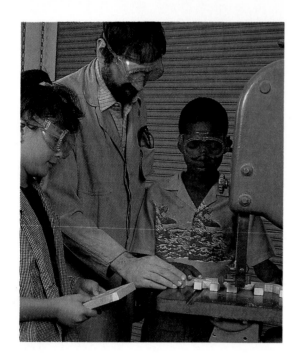

Chapter 6

Learning

Chapter 7

Cognitive Processes

Chapter 8

Motivation and Emotion

Chapter 9

Stress, Coping, and Health

Chapter 10

Personality

Chapter 11

Individual Differences

Chapter 12

Social Psychology

Chapter 13

Psychopathology

Chapter 14

Psychotherapies

Preface

To the Instructor

Psychology has a long past but a short history—millennia of fascination with human nature culminating in a scientific discipline that is but a little more than a century old. Our book represents a marriage of that scientific tradition with the immediacy and vitality of teaching what we know about the human condition. Our goal is to present an enriched view of psychological knowledge that combines the basic, accumulated wisdom from scientific psychology with the contemporary views of human nature that emerge from the study of human diversity.

We started out to create an "essential" version of the popular text, *Psychology and Life* (thirteenth edition) by Philip G. Zimbardo. *"Psych and Life"* is the oldest continuously selling textbook in all of psychology. We imagined a brief text that would be distinct from its progenitor in two dimensions: it would be comprehensive but shorter than *Psychology and Life* and more accessible to a wider range of students through its language, special pedagogical features, and rich examples and explanations. As we worked, the book surpassed our original ideas and took on a life of its own. We kept the essential content, but reduced the *level* of detail. We maintained its wisdom, but added new perspectives. We also retained its "voice" in speaking directly to student-readers, but made it speak authoritatively yet gently to a broader range of readers. We continually asked, "What does an introductory psychology student need to know about our field? How can we present that information in ways that are irresistibly inviting and readily accessible?"

We relied on our common values to help us shape the text. We both love teaching and especially enjoy teaching the introductory psychology course. We share a love of our work, a delight in psychology's diversity, a commitment to basic research, and an appreciation of exchanging ideas. Our colleagues and students provided continuous input. Experienced reviewers—instructors like yourself from schools that span the spectrum of instruction in psychology—offered us detailed feedback at each stage in the development of our manuscript.

In developing the text, we concentrated on three areas: *key written features; revised organization;* and *intensified pedagogy.* We will examine each dimension briefly before we present the resources *Psychology* offers you. The second part of this preface, directed specifically at students, provides strategies designed to help them get the most out of the study time they put into reading this book.

Key Features

The key written features of *Psychology* are designed to provide current coverage of the latest research and applications, encourage students to think critically about the material they read, and present a cross-cultural perspective so that they can appreciate how behaviors differ depending on one's cultural orientation. The key features of the text are as follows:

Up-to-Date Research and Applications. Through in-text examples, boxed features, and chapter-opening vignettes, *Psychology* presents the reader with information and illustrations based on cutting-edge research, current events, and public controversy. Examples of up-to-date coverage include:

- a review of the latest brain-scanning technology (Chapter 2).
- a consideration of how claims of what some call "false memory syndrome" have affected criminal investigation, psychotherapy, and family relations (Chapter 7).
- a focus on coping with the loss of close relationships (Chapter 12).
- a close look at eating disorders, a type of behavioral problem with which many college students are personally acquainted (Chapter 13).

Critical Thinking. Every chapter of *Psychology* has an extended discussion of how a specific topic might affect the student reader's own thoughts and life. These shaded sections, titled **"Time Out for Critical Thinking,"** are meant to be read in the context of the text, without interrupting the flow of the student's comprehension. Each critical thinking feature includes questions designed to provoke self-reflection or discussion. Topics included in "Time Out for Critical Thinking" include:

- ethical implications of the choices made available by recent advances in genetics (Chapter 2).
- the responsibility for helping youth at risk (Chapter 4).
- the impact of individual values on decision making (Chapter 7).
- the process of violating norms (Chapter 12).

Additional critical thinking questions are posed throughout the text. All critical thinking items are flagged with an arrow to emphasize points for concentrated analysis.

Cross-cultural Perspectives. Nine of the fourteen chapters in *Psychology* feature boxed discussions that examine issues in cultural diversity and cross-cultural psychology relevant to the focus of the chapter. The boxes were developed by **Richard Brislin**, Professor at the East-West Center at the University of Hawaii. Cross-cultural perspectives focus on the following:

- accepting cultural diversity (Chapter 1).
- cross-cultural research on moral development (Chapter 4).
- culture shock (Chapter 9).
- a discussion of six cultural "universals in therapy" (Chapter 14).

 In addition, a cross-cultural perspective is woven into discussions throughout the text. All cross-cultural discussions are identified by a globe that appears in the margin.

In Focus: Research, Theory, and Application. "In Focus" boxes present more detailed discussions of selected topics in two boxed essays for each chapter. Each essay in *Psychology* focuses on classic or contemporary research, the development and uses of theory, or the practical or professional applications of chapter topics. Examples of these essays include the following:

- a *research* focus reviews the phenomenon of "Learned Helplessness" (Chapter 6).
- a *theory* focus explores "The Mating Game," as understood by evolutionary psychologists (Chapter 8).
- an *application* focus presents strategies for "Living with AIDS" (Chapter 9).

The Organization of *Psychology*

In organizing the text, we strove to develop a book of a manageable size that tells a comprehensive yet comprehensible story of psychology. Here are the most noticeable distinctions in the sequence of topics in *Psychology*:

- Chapter 1, **Mind, Behavior, and Science**, includes the basics of *psychological research* in addition to psychology's definition, history, and current perspectives. This chapter covers the context of discovery and the context of justification, as well as an overview and rationale for the major psychological research methods and advice to readers on "becoming a wiser research consumer."

- Chapter 2, **Biopsychology**, concentrates on neuropsychology, evolutionary psychology, and a basic introduction to the biology of behavior. The traditional view of the "behaving brain" is supplemented with the new view of the "responsive brain" that is continually modified by external stimulation and its own actions. The chapter reviews and explains major connections and findings regarding behavior genetics.

- Chapter 3, **States of Mind**, combines a new understanding of the nature of consciousness in psychology with a survey of alterations of states of mind induced naturally and through special techniques and drugs.

- Chapter 4, **Psychological Development**, encompasses *both* the topical and chronological approaches to development, acknowledging the distinctions of these two perspectives. The chapter examines childhood, adolescence, adulthood, and old age, while covering in some depth major facets of life span development—cognition, language, socialization and attachment, transitions, moral development, and mortality.

- Chapter 5, **Sensation and Perception**, combines these two vast but interrelated topics. The chapter maintains a level of detail that introductory students may be expected to master. Practical and relevant examples of how art and illusions utilize perception principles are presented in ways that students can appreciate.

- Chapter 6, **Learning**, reviews core areas of behavioristic psychology while presenting a modern view of biological and cognitive constraints on learning.

- Chapter 7, **Cognitive Processes**, unites in a single chapter the structures of thinking (such as concepts and schemas), the uses of thinking (such as reasoning and decision making), and remembering (including the three stages of sensory, working, and long-term memory), as well as forgetting (including mnemonics, and "false memories").

- Chapter 8, **Motivation and Emotion**, unites these often linked subjects, examining shared processes as well as differences between the two in behavior, research, and theory. Human sexuality is given more coverage than is typical in most introductory psychology texts.

- Chapter 9, **Stress, Coping, and Health**, includes often neglected material on biology and emotion in the contexts of wellness and illness.

- Chapter 10, a rich chapter on **Personality**, examines the history and usefulness of the concept of personality, reviews the major personality theories, *and* briefly explains the forms and purposes of personality assessment.

- Chapter 11, **Individual Differences**, enhances basic coverage of testing with some background on the *perspective* of work in individual differences, especially as a complement to the situational perspective of social psychology.

- Chapter 12, **Social Psychology**, focuses on three issues that are the most valuable lessons of this field's innovative research: the power of the situation; the construction of social reality; and using our knowledge to solve social problems. Because the topic of social psychology is integrated into the rest of "normal" psychology, and its perspective is compared to that of individual differences, the chapter follows **Personality** instead of coming at the end of the book—as in other texts.

- The last chapters of the text focus on the material that most students begin this course assuming psychology is all about—abnormal behavior and therapy. Chapter 13 examines **Psychopathology**, organizing clinical material around DSM-III-R (and the forthcoming DSM-IV) categories; Chapter 14 looks at all the major **Psychotherapies**, including biomedical treatments for behavioral and mental disorders.

Pedagogical Support

No textbook "teaches itself." Students always learn better with the encouragement and instruction of an accessible, interested person—you. However, that interaction can be enhanced by effective pedagogical supports. Here's a summary of the teacher's aids we have built into *Psychology:*

- **Opening Case.** Each chapter opens with a real-life vignette designed to grab student attention and vividly depict the relevance of the chapter's topic.
- **Preview Questions.** At the beginning of each chapter a set of "Preview Questions" prepares students for the material that follows. Throughout the chapter, numbered icons indicate where the reader can find the answer to each question.
- **Marginal Glossary.** A running glossary, listed in the margins, provides definitions of key terms. Definitions of these terms are placed as close as possible to where the terms appear in the text.
- **Summing Up.** Interim summaries conclude each major section within a chapter, recapping main points before the student moves on to the next section.
- **Multicultural Icons.** In addition to signaling cross-cultural boxes, icons guide the reader to specific, in-text discussions of cultural issues related to chapter topics.
- **Sectional Summaries.** Beginning each **Chapter Review** is a brief summary of major-heading sections. Each sectional summary opens with a recap of the "Preview Questions," to prompt the student to review what she or he has learned.
- **Key Terms and Major Contributors.** The key terms and names of major contributors introduced in each chapter section are listed with page references after each sectional summary. They are cited in the text in bold-faced type for ease of identification.
- **Practice Tests.** A Practice Test at the end of each chapter consists of ten multiple-choice items designed to provide students with a quick self-test of their comprehension of major concepts and applications. Correct answers and full explanations are provided in the **Appendix.**
- **If You're Interested . . .** Readers interested in knowing more about each chapter's topics and issues are provided with a brief annotated list of relevant books and videos. Entries have been culled from the authors' favorites, as well as from student and reviewer recommendations.
- **End-of-Text Glossary.** Key terms and definitions from chapters' marginal glossaries are assembled in alphabetical order in an end-of-text glossary with page references.
- **References.** Because students might best use the "References" in their own research and writing, the section lists all references cited in the text.
- **Name Index and Subject Index.** These indexes catalog the names, concepts, terms, and topics covered in the text, and give page references.
- **Mastery Tests.** A perforated section at the end of the text includes short tests—20 multiple-choice items and five short-answer items per chapter—

to be used by instructors as in-class assessments, take-home assignments, or for other purposes. Correct answers are provided in the Instructor's Manual.

- **Art Program.** The tables, graphs, figures, and photographs that illustrate the text have been developed to ensure that the art is clear, vivid, and contemporary in feel. Expanded captions and labels complement and support the text.

Support Materials

A good textbook is only one part of the package of educational materials that makes an introductory psychology course more engaging to students and more gratifying for instructors. The introductory psychology course is one of the most difficult courses to teach because it surveys an enormous range of topics, from many different levels of analysis, and must overcome students' initial misconceptions about psychology learned from mass media "pop psych."

To make it easier for you and more worthwhile for your students, HarperCollins has worked with us to prepare a valuable collection of ancillary materials.

- **Instructor's Manual** (ISBN #0-06-501418-9) by Glenda Smith and text co-author Phil Zimbardo. This comprehensive, up-to-date teacher's resource features chapter outlines, lecture notes referenced to chapter preview questions, discussion questions, in-class experiments and demonstrations, biographical profiles, student handouts, and tips for effective teaching. Original time lines put key figures and important developments in psychology in historical perspective. The manual includes a section on how to teach concept mapping, to support that topic in the **Study Guide and Workbook**; a detailed bibliography; and references to media that can be used in the classroom.
- **Test Bank** (ISBN #0-06-501419-7) by Jeffrey Parsons. This file contains approximately 3,000 multiple-choice, true-false, statement-completion, and essay items. Questions are balanced for a range of difficulty and content: 25 percent are applied, 25 percent factual, and 50 percent conceptual in nature. Items also reflect sensitivity to nonnative English speakers. Each question is referenced to a text page and Preview Questions. One item per Preview Question also appears in the student **Study Guide and Workbook**, and is keyed in the test item file. The Test Bank content has been assessed by outside reviewers as well as text authors. A national testing development service has also analyzed the Test Bank for accuracy and comprehension.
- The **Study Guide and Workbook** (ISBN #0-06-501417-0) by Peter Gram was developed with the assistance of Ann Weber and Phil Zimbardo. Each chapter begins with a concept map of major topics, followed by an exploded chapter outline featuring lots of room for note-taking and personal mnemonics. **Key Terms** from the text's marginal glossary are presented in a flash-card format for student review. **Preview Questions** are explored via the SQ3R method. All exercises and features lead the student back to the text. Two sets of multiple-choice **Practice Quizzes** with answers (and, for the first set, explanations) and page references are included. One question per preview question also appears in the **Test Bank.** Special material is provided on *concept mapping*, making visual connections among key concepts and theories in each chapter. Each chapter concludes with a student-generated lexicon of **Words Worth Review**, an extended glossary of words other than key terms worth readers' review. The **Study Guide and Workbook** also contains work-

sheets and procedural materials that are coordinated with a set of original experiments and demonstrations (developed and class tested by Zimbardo) found in the **Instructor's Manual**.

- **How to Write Psychology Papers** (ISBN #0-06-501798-6) by Les Parrott III guides students step-by-step through the process of writing psychology papers. The book gives students directions, confidence, and the ability to maintain a sense of the big picture as they are writing.
- **Thinking Critically About Research on Sex and Gender** (ISBN #0-06-501621-1) by Paula J. Caplan and Jeremy B. Caplan offers students the right level of support to learn about—and make sense of—the varied research in the field. The text unveils a revolutionary approach to understanding sex and gender research—one that puts students in touch with the practical meaning behind research and its vital effects on daily life.
- **Industrial and Organizational Psychology Supplement for Introductory Psychology** (ISBN #0-67-399317-5) by Sherri Lind Hughes. This stand-alone supplement provides students with a thorough look at I/O psychology. This "mini-text" covers industrial and organizational psychology, including discussions of recruitment and selection, training, motivation, and job satisfaction. Detailed references and cases are also included.

Personal Acknowledgments

Many experts and teachers of introductory psychology shared their constructive criticism with us on every chapter and feature of our text. We acknowledge them in alphabetical order below and hope they will see their valued input in much that is good in *Psychology*.

Larry M. Anderson, Kwantlen College
Doug Bonesteel, Sheridan College
Peter Gram, Pensacola Junior College
Richard A. Griggs, University of Florida
Charles Halcomb, Wichita State University
Stephen Hamilton, Mount San Antonio Community College
Christine Hollmann, Ohio University
James A. Johnson, Sam Houston State University
Connie Lanier, Central Piedmont Community College
Richard A. King, University of North Carolina, Chapel Hill
Gail Knapp, C.S. Mott Community College
Mary-Louise Kean, University of California, Irvine
Harold L. Mansfield, Fort Lewis College
Robert F. Massey, Seton Hall University
Lillie McCain, C.S. Mott Community College
Edward R. Mosley, Passaic County Community College
Elliot Palefsky, Armstrong State College
David Perkins, College of St. Elizabeth
Bobby J. Poe, Belleville Area College
Cornelius P. Rea, Douglas College
Steven Richman, Nassau Community College
Marc Riess, Middlebury College
Manly N. Spigelman, University of Winnipeg
Frank J. Vaccaro, Hofstra University
Anthony A. Walsh, Salve Regina University

Composing this book has been a life lesson in social support: We relied on our friends and colleagues for help and understanding that was well beyond the call of duty—and we cultivated new friends among helpful colleagues and students. **Helen J. Gilbart of St. Petersburg Junior College** reviewed the text for readability. Her astute observations and excellent suggestions helped us to ensure that the material is accessible to our student readers. Throughout our collaboration our patient, vigilant Muse has been **Arlene Bessenoff**, surely the finest Developmental Editor ever to bless our efforts as writers. **Meg Holden**, Psychology Editor, was always there for us, with enthusiastic input and organizational acumen. **Marcus Boggs**, Editor in Chief, and **Art Pomponio,** Director of Development, provided ongoing wisdom, direction, and support. **Evelyn Owens** has been the wise shepherdess of the supplements flock of materials, finding great authors for them, and overseeing the complex interrelations between each of them and our text. **Paula Soloway** of HarperCollins and **Kathleen Ermitage** of Proof Positive/Farrowlyne Associates, Inc., intelligently guided our manuscript through each stage of the production process. The new art program owes much to the sensitivity and aesthetic values of the design group at Proof Positive/Farrowlyne Associates, Inc., photo researcher **Roberta Knauf** of HarperCollins, and the meticulous checking by **Ray Noonan**. We are also indebted to **Barbara Cinquegrani**, Director of Marketing, and **Mark Paluch**, Marketing Manager, for their hard work in promoting and marketing the text.

Especially helpful to Ann Weber at critical moments were the following Asheville denizens: **Dr. Tracy Brown, Dr. Allan Combs, Dr. Lisa Friedenberg,** and **Dr. Gary Nallan**, all of the Department of Psychology, UNC at Asheville; **Araby Greene**, Public Services Librarian at D. Hiden Ramsey Library, UNC at Asheville; and the talented professionals at WaldenBooks in Biltmore Square, especially Manager **Richard Huffine,** Assistant Manager **Tony Cable**, and staff members **Anthony Sutton** and **Ken Weaver**. Finally, Ann Weber wishes to thank her cherished friend and mentor, **John H. Harvey** of the University of Iowa Psychology Department, and her beloved partner and spouse, **John Quigley**, for their support, encouragement, and abiding affection.

Phil Zimbardo publicly expresses his joy at discovering in his new coauthor not only a talented writer/psychologist, but a wonderful, funny, and lifelong friend.

Ann Weber says the feeling is sincerely mutual.

To the Student

The course you are beginning and the text you are reading together represent a *journey* of sorts. Your teacher is your tour director, this text your tour book, and we authors serve as your local tour guides. Why set out on this journey in the first place? Because your destination is to change your life and your world view by beginning to understand the most fascinating wonders of the universe: the human brain, the human mind, and the behavior of all living creatures (especially your own). Psychology is about understanding the seemingly mysterious processes that give rise to our innermost thoughts, complex feelings, and pivotal actions.

Get the most out of this experience, whether this will be your first of many psychology courses, or possibly the last for some time. Following are some general guidelines and specific tips on how to use this book to get the benefit—and the grade—you deserve for your performance and effort in appreciating *Psychology*.

Study Strategies

1. *Set aside sufficient time* to do assigned reading and review your class notes. This text contains much new technical information, many principles to learn, and a challenging glossary of terms you will have to memorize and use. To master this material, you will need at least *three hours reading time per chapter*.

2. *Keep a record of your study time* for this course. Plot the number of hours (in half-hour intervals) you study at each reading session. Chart your time investment on a cumulative graph, adding each new study time to your previous total on the y-axis and each study session to the x-axis (baseline). The graph will provide visual feedback of your progress and show you when you have not been hitting the books as you should.

3. *Be active and space your studying.* Optimal learning occurs when the learner is actively involved with the material. Read attentively, listen mindfully to lectures, ask questions, create examples, and paraphrase the words you read or hear as you take notes. In the text, underline brief key sections, write notes to yourself in the margins, and summarize points you expect to be covered on class tests. Find a study partner among your classmates, and take turns explaining concepts and processes to each other. As we ourselves have discovered, teaching is the best way to learn!

   Research in psychology tells us that it is best to space out your studying efforts, scheduling brief but regular sessions to read and review, rather than cramming just before tests. If you let yourself fall behind, it is difficult to catch up on the information in introductory psychology during that last-minute panic.

4. *Get study-centered.* Find a place with minimal distractions where you can study. Reserve that location for reading, writing, and course review—and nothing else (no food, television, or socializing). Soon you will find that this place is so completely associated with course work that you already "feel" like studying when you arrive at your study center.

5. *Encode reading for future testing.* To benefit from a text like **Psychology**, you must feel alert and focus your attention. What you remember from reading the text depends on your deliberate efforts to remember, especially as you prepare for tests. Such efforts begin with *encoding*—putting the information you read into a form that is suitable for retrieving it for later use or tests. To encode what you read, you must *summarize* key points, *rehearse* sections of material (sometimes aloud), and ask *questions* about content you expect to be tested on.

How will you be tested? Try taking the teacher's perspective. Imagine the kinds of questions you would ask—and then try to answer them yourself. Remember to provide different kinds of answers for essay, short-answer, or multiple-choice questions. These different answers require different approaches to studying. Decide whether you should focus on big ideas or small details. Essays and fill-ins require an ability to *recall*—to produce information from memory; multiple-choice and true-false tests rely on your *recognition* skills— your ability to match test materials with previously learned information. Your instructor is your best guide (and your ally) in determining how best to study for examinations in your course.

Take the **Practice Tests** at the end of each chapter, and check on both the answers and their explanations at the back of the text—prior to in-class examinations. Also regularly take the **Mastery Tests** found at the back of the book, which are similar in content, form, and difficulty to the tests in the test bank from which your teacher is likely to compose in-class tests. Answers are available in your teacher's Instructor's Manual, so ask for them to check on your progress.

Study Tactics

1. *Review the chapter outline as it appears in the detailed table of contents.* The chapter outline shows you the main topics covered, their sequence, and their relationship, giving you an overview of what is to come. Skim through the pages of the chapter before you begin reading seriously, to get an idea of what you will read and how it will be presented.

2. *Ask yourself the Preview Questions.* Each chapter opens with Preview Questions (PQs), keyed to the ideas presented in the chapter's major sections. Examine each cluster of questions, and each individual PQ, and flip through the chapter to locate the answers—marked by PQ "icons."

3. *Jump to the end of the chapter for the Chapter Review.* The Chapter Review includes a recap of the PQs, followed by sectional summaries of the preceding chapter. The main points in each section are summarized and followed by lists of the key terms and major contributors cited in that section.

4. *Skim through the chapter,* reading lightly, and turning the pages at an even pace, to get the gist of its contents. Don't stop or take notes, and read as quickly as you can (one hour maximum time allowed).

5. *Finally, dig in* and master the material, by actively reading, underlining, taking notes in a separate notebook, making marginal notes to yourself, questioning, rehearsing, and paraphrasing as you go (two hours minimum time expected). Read the opening case, as well as the boxed special sections: "In Focus" and "Cross-cultural Perspectives," which are also included in the test bank questions.

Special Features to Use

1. The **Opening Case** that begins each chapter was written to grab and focus your attention. Taken together, these cases present a wide range of vivid, personalized material about people in different types of behavior settings. Each opener illustrates a central theme of the chapter, and the cases are often referenced later in the chapter.

2. At the end of each major section within a chapter is an interim summary, called **Summing Up**. These summaries review the key points presented in the section and explain the relationships between concepts. Be sure that you understand the ideas in the Summing Up unit of the current section before you move ahead.

3. **Key Terms** and **Major Contributors** appear in boldface type to help you keep track of the people and ideas central to psychology. They are listed again, with page numbers, at the end of each sectional summary in the Chapter Review, in order of their original appearance.

4. The **References** section, also at the end of the text, gives essential bibliographic information on every book, journal article, or other source used to document some point made in the text. This is a valuable resource in case you wish to know more, or look up specific information for your own research and interest. In the text, when a name and date are set off in parentheses—(**Zimbardo, 1990**)—this *citation* is your clue to finding the rest of the information in the "References" section. Citations with more than two authors list the senior author followed by **et al.**, the Latin abbreviation for "and the others."

5. The **Name Index** and **Subject Index**, appearing at the end of the text, provide you with an alphabetized listing of people cited in the text, all terms, and subject matter, along with page references.

6. Finally, your studying and test performance are likely to be enhanced by using the **Study Guide and Workbook** to accompany *Psychology*. The Study Guide was prepared to give students a boost in studying more efficiently and taking tests more effectively. The Study Guide contains *concept maps* to guide you through the many concepts and connections each chapter introduces. It also provides helpful tips—from senior author Dr. Peter Gram—as well as practice tests, flash cards, outlines, and suggestions for creatively using and reviewing the material.

We sincerely appreciate the opportunity your teacher has given us by choosing *Psychology* for your course. We urge you to *use this book:* Carry it with you, scribble in it, flip through it when you are waiting in line somewhere, dog-ear the pages you want to reread, refer to it for ideas, names, or details.

Enough packing for the trip. It's time to get started. Please begin reading your first assignment in what we trust will become one of your favorite courses and most enjoyable intellectual journeys.

Phil Zimbardo

Ann Weber

About the Authors . . .

After more than 35 years of teaching, Phil Zimbardo still gets excited about teaching Introductory Psychology to large lecture classes at Stanford University. Numerous awards for distinguished teaching attest to the impact he has had on his students and colleagues. This influence as a mentor goes beyond direct contact in the classroom by virtue of his authorship of one of the most widely read texts in psychology, *Psychology and Life,* as well as through the prize-winning television series, *Discovering Psychology,* which he created, wrote, and hosted. Although writing texts and teaching about psychology are Phil's main priorities, he has managed to find time to do some provocative and influential research on shyness, violence, prisons, time perspective, and madness. His wife, Christina Maslach, is also a professor of psychology at the University of California, Berkeley; they live in San Francisco with their teenaged daughters, Zara and Tanya. Son Adam is studying to become a psychotherapist.

Like Phil Zimbardo, Ann Weber is a social psychologist who is enthusiastic about introducing psychology to her students. Since attending college at the Catholic University of America and doing graduate work at The Johns Hopkins University, she has taught for over 15 years at the University of North Carolina at Asheville, the official liberal arts university of the UNC system, where she is Professor of Psychology. Ann's commitment to teaching has taken several forms, including newsletter columns, journal articles, text supplements, and conference presentations on teaching, as well as her regular courses in introductory psychology, social psychology, and the psychology of close relationships. Ann's research and other writing focus on close relationship loss, and the "accounts" or stories people formulate in grieving and coping with such experiences. Originally from Maryland, Ann lives in the mountains of western North Carolina with her husband, John Quigley, and their cat, Minerva. She loves her work, and hopes her excitement about this book will be contagious.

Psychology

Philip G. Zimbardo, Stanford University
Ann L. Weber, University of North Carolina at Asheville

For years, Phil Zimbardo has been considered one of the most influential textbook authors in the field; his book, *Psychology and Life,* has maintained success through thirteen best-selling editions. Zimbardo's knack for combining sound scholarship and real-life issues, and his thorough integration of classic and cutting-edge research, have demonstrated his ability to respond both to the changes in psychology and the demands of students and professors nationwide. Now, written in response to their latest request—a more concise, less expensive, paperback introduction to psychology—comes *Psychology,* co-authored by Ann Weber. Here, of course, is Zimbardo's hallmark method of presenting psychology in an interesting and meaningful way with updated examples and applications. Yet in *Psychology,* the subject is more accessible and engaging than ever. Outstanding pedagogy, a phenomenal art program, and a well integrated supplements package ensure comprehension, high-interest, and a true student-centered focus.

Chapter
4

Psychological
Development

Chapter-Opening Previews and Cases

Previews—written in question form—raise key questions that are answered in each chapter. Designed to pique students' interest, opening cases introduce real-world situations to illustrate basic themes in the material that follows, and are integrated into the chapter discussions as appropriate.

◆ **Preview Questions**

1. What are the two approaches developmental psychologists use to understand psychological change? What are the arguments in the nature-nurture debate? How does maturation contribute to psychological development? What position do stage theories take on continuity?

2. How have conceptions of childhood changed in recent centuries? What factors affect language acquisition in childhood? What are the major stages in Piaget's theory of cognitive development? Which processes and behaviors change in social and emotional development?

3. Which tasks must be accomplished during adolescence? How are the tasks and cognitive processes of adulthood different from those of adolescence? What are the psychological meanings associated with old age?

1984. The two tiny figures in buntings are not quite three weeks old. They lie in their crib on their stomachs, in mirror image positions—a small fist inches from each mouth, one head turned to the right, the other to the left. Nicole wakes up first. She lies there, quite content, listening to her mother in the kitchen. Ten minutes later, Alexis awakens. Almost immediately, she begins to howl. The babies' mother runs in from the kitchen, picks up Alexis, and reaches for a clean diaper.

Nicole and Alexis are genetically identical twins, the products of a fertilized ovum that split sometime in the first two weeks of prenatal life. Because of their positions on the placenta, Nicole was always first to get the nutrients that support prenatal growth. Thus, at birth she weighed 4 pounds; Alexis weighed a little less. Although no one can tell the girls apart when they are dressed identically, there are important differences between the babies.

1985. Much to her mother's dismay, Alexis starts climbing on chairs as soon as she learns to crawl. Nicole follows in a couple of days. Alexis takes her first step on her first birthday. Friends and relatives clap and cheer. Nicole watches. In less than a week, she is walking too. After her morning Cheerios™, Alexis sits in her daddy's lap and opens her mouth wide for bites of his scrambled eggs. She never seems to get enough. When anyone offers eggs to Nicole, she turns away and grimaces. She sticks to Cheerios.

1986. When Alexis and Nicole are 19 months old, their mother goes away for four days. This is the first time she has left her daughters for more than a day. The girls accompany their father to the hospital where their mother and a newborn baby, Mikey, are waiting. Nicole greets heer mom with a big smile and a hug, as though nothing has left her daughters for more than a day. The girls accompany their father to the hospital where their mother and a newborn baby, Mikey, are waiting. Nicole greets her mom with a big smile and a hug, as though nothing has happened. Alexis looks away, fidgets, and shows little emotion.

1987. Both girls are wild about clothes. Sometimes they empty their drawers and closet and put on several layers of socks, blouses, skirts, and hats. Then they stand before their mother's full-length mirror and admire their fashions. Alexis claims pink and green are her favorite colors and is very possessive about them. Nicole likes purple, but allows Alexis to wear "her color" if she wants.

Nicole likes sleeping alone, while lexis often gets anxious if she feels she has lost track of her sister—even in her sleep. Sometimes Alexis wakes up in the night

---

2 *Categorizing into Concepts* The categories we form, which are mental representations of related items that are grouped in some way, are called concepts. Concepts are the building blocks of thinking, enabling us to organize knowledge in systematic ways. Concepts may represent *objects, activities,* or *living organisms.* They may also represent *properties,* (such as *red* or *large*), *abstractions* (such as *truth* or *love*) and *relations* (such as *smarter than*) (Smith & Medin, 1981). As mental structures, concepts cannot be observed directly, but must be discovered through research or invented by psychological theories.

A basic task of thinking is concept learning or concept formation—identifying the stimuli properties that are common to a class of objects or ideas. The mind lives by the principle of cognitive economy, minimizing the amount of time and effort required to process information. We learn not only features that form concepts, such as the colors of traffic lights, but also *conceptual rules* by which these features are related. For example, consider traffic light rules: If red, stop; if yellow, slow down and prepare to stop; if green, go. It is amazing how many conceptual rules we learn, store, retrieve on demand, and use to direct our interactions with people and the environment (Haygood & Bourne, 1965).

Critical Features Versus Prototypes What is the unit of information that is stored in memory when we form a concept? Psychologists have not yet agreed on the unit. Currently, two competing theories attempt to account for the form in which information is stored.

The **critical feature** approach suggests that we store definitions or lists of critical features that are necessary and sufficient conditions for a concept to be included in a category. A concept is a member of the category if (and only if) it has every feature on the list. For example, a FAX (facsimile) machine has a telephone connection, receiver, number keypad, and paper dispenser. If you encounter an elaborate machine that looks like a FAX but has no way of dispensing paper for messages, it may be some kind of telephone but you cannot categorize it as a FAX machine.

The **prototype** approach suggests that categories are structured around an ideal or most representative instance, called a *prototype* (Rosch, 1973). A concept is classified as a member of a category if it is more similar to the prototype of that category than it is to the prototype of any other category. A stimulus might not fit precisely within the limits of a stored category but would still be classified as belonging to the category if its variation from the prototype was within an acceptable range. For example, although the fonts illustrated on this page are very different, we still recognize them as belonging to the same category—the letter *Z.*

Which approach—critical feature or prototype—best explains typical human thinking? In fact, we seem to use them both, each for different kinds of concepts. For example, the concept *mammals* is defined as "vertebrates that nurse their young." Organisms possessing these critical features qualify as mammals, while those which lack them do not. But the critical features approach does not work as well with the concept of *birds.* The dictionary defines a *bird* as "a warm-blooded vertebrate with feathers and wings." When you think of a bird, what example do you imagine? If you are like most people, you are more likely to think of typical birds like robins, blue jays, and sparrows; you are less likely to imagine atypical members of the class, such as ostriches or penguins. These birds may qualify for membership, but they don't seem to "belong" to the concept as well as the typical examples. Thus bird is a fuzzy concept; it has no well-defined boundaries between members of its class (Zadeh, 1965). To correct this fuzziness, you probably define the concept not only by critical features (such as feathers) but by ideas about typical members of the category.

A concept is a mental event that represents a category or class of objects. The concept of *flower* encompasses many different flowers.

critical feature Quality that is a necessary and sufficient condition for including a concept in a category.

prototype Most representative example of a category.

Numbered Icons

Numbered Icons throughout each chapter alert readers to where the questions raised in the **Chapter-Opening Previews** are answered.

Marginal Glossary

This running glossary ensures that terms are defined as soon as they appear in the text.

consciousness Awareness of the general condition of your mind, of particular mental contents, or self-awareness.

The Nature of Consciousness

Think of *consciousness* as the front page of the mind and *attention* as the lead story. Awareness is the knowledge that the story is in the newspaper of your mind. Ordinary waking consciousness includes the immediate mental experiences comprising your perceptions, thoughts, feelings, and desires at a given moment—all the mental activity on which you are focusing your attention. You are conscious of what you are doing and of the *fact* that you are doing it. This experience of watching ourselves from a privileged "insider's" position leads to a *sense of self.* Together these mental activities form the *contents* of consciousness—all the experiences we are consciously aware of at a particular moment.

But there is more to consciousness than its contents. We also use the term *consciousness* to refer to a general *state of mind* rather than to its specific contents. In sum, **consciousness** can mean that you are aware of the general condition of your mind, aware of particular mental contents, or self-aware.

Functions of Consciousness

An evolutionary perspective reminds us that consciousness must be highly adaptive to be part of our behavior today. The general functions of consciousness are to aid our survival and to enable us to construct both personal realities and culturally shared realities. For example, imagine waking up to find yourself in a strange bed, being examined by white-coated strangers who tell you, "You've been in an accident, but you're in a hospital, and you're going to be all right." Your conscious abilities will enable you to organize your thoughts ("Was I alone?") and recognize new information ("A hospital is a place where I will get medical care").

From a biological perspective, consciousness is probably perceiving and reacting to available perceptual information. Thus you know when you are awake, and what you can see, hear, or feel. At the second level, consciousness relies on symbolic knowledge to free us from the constraints of real objects and present events—it gives us *imagination.* At this second level, you can think *about* what you see, hear, or feel. The top level of consciousness is **self-awareness**, cognizance that personally experienced events have an *autobiographical* character. Thus you know that it is *you* who is seeing, hearing, or feeling—not someone else giving you second-hand information. Self-awareness gives us our sense of personal history and identity. When you reflect on events and tell others about them, your memories of what you have experienced become part of your unique personality.

self-awareness Cognizance that personally experienced events have an autobiographical character.

Structures of Consciousness

Were you aware of your heartbeat just now? Probably not; control of your heartbeat is part of *nonconscious processes.* Were you thinking about your last vacation or the author of *Hamlet?* Again, probably not; control of such thoughts is part of *preconscious memories.* Were you aware of background noises, like a clock ticking or traffic on nearby streets? You couldn't be and still pay attention to this chapter, because awareness of nonrelevant stimuli is part of *subconscious awareness.* Finally, are you aware of how some of your early life experiences, and present desires and impulses affect what you say and do? According to psychodynamic analysis, powerful *unconscious* forces block awareness of these emotions. Let us examine these distinctions more carefully.

nonconscious processes Information that is not represented in consciousness or memory but that still influences fundamental bodily or mental activities.

Nonconscious processes. **Nonconscious processes** involve information that is not represented in consciousness or memory but that still influences fundamental bodily or mental activities. The regulation of blood pressure is an example of a nonconscious process: physiological information is detected and

Endocrine communication sustains not only slow an[d] but also critical responses. When you encounter a str[ess] such as the loud sound of an alarm or the cry of a per[son], mone adrenaline is released into the bloodstream, e[nabling] quick defensive action—for "fight or flight." Your hea[rt] tense up, and you are driven to take whatever acti[on] makes sense.

Because influence of hormones is diverse but s[pecific] called "the messengers of life" (Crapo, 1985). The [secre]-tory" sites in the body produce chemicals that influence a variety of bodily processes. **Table 2.1** outlines the major glands and their hormonal targets.

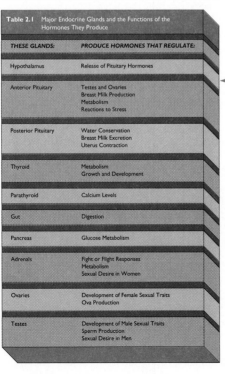

THESE GLANDS:	PRODUCE HORMONES THAT REGULATE:
Hypothalamus	Release of Pituitary Hormones
Anterior Pituitary	Testes and Ovaries Breast Milk Production Metabolism Reactions to Stress
Posterior Pituitary	Water Conservation Breast Milk Excretion Uterus Contraction
Thyroid	Metabolism Growth and Development
Parathyroid	Calcium Levels
Gut	Digestion
Pancreas	Glucose Metabolism
Adrenals	Fight or Flight Responses Metabolism Sexual Desire in Women
Ovaries	Development of Female Sexual Traits Ova Production
Testes	Development of Male Sexual Traits Sperm Production Sexual Desire in Men

Table 2.1 Major Endocrine Glands and the Functions of the Hormones They Produce

Effective Graphics

All graphs, tables, and illustrations give *Psychology* a truly contemporary feel. Graphs have been designed to provide clear, expressive information for students. Tables are attractive and easy to read.

Multicultural Icons

These icons call attention to coverage of multicultural material or issues.

Empirical evidence and expert opinion strongly suggest that hypnosis can exert a powerful influence on many psychological and bodily functions (Bowers, 1976; Burrows & Dennerstein, 1980; E. Hilgard, 1968, 1973). One of the most common and undisputed values of hypnosis is its effect on pain. Our minds can amplify pain stimuli through anticipation and fear; we can also diminish the psychological component of pain with hypnosis. Pain control is accomplished through a variety of hypnotic suggestions: distraction from the pain stimulus, imagining the part of the body in pain as nonorganic (made of wood or plastic) or as separate from the rest of the body, taking one's mind on a vacation from the body, and distorting time in various ways. Hypnosis has proven especially valuable to surgery patients who cannot tolerate anesthesia, to extreme burn patients, to mothers in natural childbirth, and to cancer patients learning to endure the pain associated with the disease and its treatment. Moreover, self-hypnosis enables patients to control their pain whenever it arises.

Meditation

Many religious and traditional psychologies of the East work to direct consciousness away from immediate worldly concerns, external stimulation, and action. They seek to achieve an inner focus on the mental and spiritual self. **Meditation** is a form of consciousness change designed to enhance self-knowledge and well-being by reducing self-awareness. During meditation, a person focuses on and regulates breathing, assumes certain bodily positions (yogic positions), minimizes external stimulation, and either generates specific mental images or frees the mind of all thought.

To view meditation as an altered state of consciousness may reflect a particularly Western world view. For example, Asian views of the mind are diametrically different from those of most Western cultures. Buddhism teaches that the visible universe is an illusion of the senses; the world is nothing but mind; and the individual's mind is part of the collective, universal mind.

 Cross-cultural Perspective   Cross–Cultural Psychology

Another approach to research in psychology takes as a starting point that behavior in all parts of the world should be investigated. Cross-cultural psychologists argue that if psychologists pay too little attention to people from various ethnic groups in different countries, then they run the risk of developing explanations of behavior that are too narrow (Triandis, 1989; Berry, et. al., 1992; Brislin, 1993). Cross-cultural psychologists argue further that too many accepted principles of behavior are based on research with a very limited number of people. These research participants are often Caucasian, young, male, middle-class and articulate when interacting with psychologists. To make sure that explanations of behavior are not limited to this select population, many psychologists recommend that greater attention be given to people from very diverse backgrounds. The concept "culture" has been especially central to the thinking of these psychologists.

Culture refers to concepts, values and assumptions about life that provide guidance for various behaviors that people choose to follow. These guidelines for behavior are often widely accepted by people who live in the same part of their country and who speak the same language. These assumptions about life and guidelines for behavior are transmitted generation to generation by parents, other older relatives, teachers, and other respected adults. The transmission is rarely explicit. Children are rarely approached by their parents and given lessons in "what our culture tells us we should do." Rather, parents correct their children's mistakes over many years until eventually the children engage in behaviors that need no positive or negative commentary from adults. Or, children observe the behavior of people considered successful in their culture and engage in the same behaviors as these models. Eventually, most children learn the

behaviors necessary for day-to-day living and become accepted members of their culture. If they do not, they become deviants and must accept their culture's punishments for people who engage in unacceptable behaviors. Examples are time in prison for people who steal, or the absence of job promotions for lazy people who are members of a culture where hard work is valued.

The concept that culture provides guidance for behavior is important. Culture does not dictate that a very narrow set of behaviors is acceptable and that all others should be avoided. Rather, culture provides a number of suggestions for proper behavior in various situations. Some of the most memorable examples of culture's influence and of cultural differences occur when people from very diverse backgrounds interact frequently. Such interactions will occur more and more frequently in the future given such major social policies as immigration, the encouragement of international tourism, political asylum for refugees, and the recruitment of culturally diverse students in colleges and universities. Assume that a Caucasian male from the American middle class is attending Protestant church services with an acquaintance who is an African-American from a similar economic background. Are there cultural differences that, if poorly understood, might influence whether or not this acquaintanceship becomes a friendship? The answer is "yes" (Kochman, 1981).

The cultural difference centers on the amount of emotional expressiveness considered appropriate for churchgoers. If the two people attend a church service where most members are Caucasian, the guidance provided by their culture is that highly emotional displays of religious fervor are rare. People pray and sing aloud, but rarely with intense emotions. They listen to the pastor's sermon, but rarely make comments about its content while the pastor is

speaking. T[...] different f[...] attending [...] most memb[...] ethnic back[...] Americans, it is considered very appropriate for people to have very intense emotional experiences during church services. People sing with great fervor. While the pastor speaks, congregation members shout their comments about various parts of the message. During many church services, one or more people faint. This rarely causes a problem, however, since the cultural guidance also includes provision of a nurse at church services. Investigation of culture's influence should include attention to the reasons for observed behaviors. For this example, psychologists should look to history. When slavery was an accepted part of American culture, African-Americans were not allowed to express strong emotions in the presence of Caucasians. Attendance at church provided one of the few opportunities for African-Americans to express themselves freely.

Whenever culture and cultural differences are discussed, psychologists should be careful to keep in mind that there will be individual differences. Not all people will accept the guidance that their culture offers. Some African-Americans will prefer attending church services where emotional expressiveness is low. Some Caucasians join churches where emotional displays are prominent, such as some Fundamental Baptist groups in the American South. Without attention to individual differences, people also run the risk of unhelpful and demeaning stereotypes. For example, this discussion of one cultural difference should not be expanded to a broader statement about the amount of control people have over their emotions. Students of psychology have the challenging task of keeping in mind that cultural differences exist.

"Cross-cultural Perspective" boxes are also featured. Developed by Professor Richard Brislin, a leading cross-cultural psychologist on the faculty of the University of Hawaii, these features focus on the importance of diversity and multicultural issues in the study of psychology. Boxes discuss topics such as "Cross-cultural Research on Moral Development" and "Culture and Perception."

The adolescent stage is a time in which independence and self-definition replace childhood dependence on parents and other adults. In American society adolescence has no clearly defined beginning or end. It can extend for more than a decade, through the teens to the mid-20s, until adult roles begin. The legal system defines adult status according to age; but different legal ages exist for different "adult" activities, such as drinking alcohol in public, driving, engaging in sex, marrying without parental consent, joining the military, and voting (see "Time Out for Critical Thinking: Youth at Risk"). Similarly, social events, such as graduation from high school (or college, or graduate school), moving out of the family home, the establishment of financial independence, and marriage, have been used to mark the beginning of adulthood.

➡ TIME OUT... FOR CRITICAL THINKING

Youth at Risk

Historical analysis is encouraging in that it reveals that treatment of children and adolescents has continually improved over the centuries. However, many current indicators suggest that the 1980s were terrible for youth in many families and that conditions will worsen in the 1990s. More American children are likely to be poor, pregnant, in jail, hungry, homeless, suffering from psychological problems, or dead from violence and preventable diseases. Lawmakers, health care professionals, and others stress that major reforms are needed to institute and coordinate better health care, welfare programs, and social policy.

- Who is responsible for the well-being of troubled and endangered children and adolescents? If their parents cannot or will not care for them, on whom—or on what institutions—does this charge fall?
- Even if your life is insulated from personal contact with these young people at risk, how does their presence in society, and their worsening plight, affect your country, your community, and your family?
- What questions would you like to ask, in order to better understand and cope with the problem of youth at risk? How can developmental psychology begin to answer these questions?
- Once we have answers—then what? How should information and discovery be translated into policy?

By mulling over these questions you will discover that an understanding of development can give you insight not only into your own life, but into the people and events in your own community and society.

Tasks of Adolescence

Although many issues are important in adolescence, we will focus on three developmental tasks that commonly confront adolescents in Western society: coming to terms with physical maturity and adult sexuality; redefining social roles, including achieving autonomy from parents; and deciding upon occupational goals. Each of these issues is a component of the central task of establishing an integrated identity. Consistent with Erikson's (1968) description of the social context of identity, each of these issues p...
which young people define themselves in relation to o...

Physical maturation. The first concrete indic...
hood is the pubescent growth spurt. Two to three ye...
growth spurt, **puberty**, or sexual maturity, is rea...
begins with the production of live sperm (usually abo...

"Time Out for Critical Thinking" Sections

Appearing once in each chapter, these study tools ask students to reflect on the ethical and abstract implications of the subject matter covered.

An additional grammatical skill that children need to acquire is using *morphemes*, the structural units or building blocks of words. We use morphemes such as -'s, -ed, and -ing to mark certain kinds of meaning, such as possession (*Maria's*), past tense (*danced*), and continuing action (*laughing*). It is apparent that children test and try out the use of grammatical morphemes—and sometimes their hypotheses are wrong. A common error is overregularization, applying a rule too widely and creating incorrect forms. Once children learn the part-tense rule (adding -ed to the verb), they often add -ed to all verbs, forming words such as *hitted* and *breaked*. As children learn the rule for plurals (adding the sound -s or -z to the end of a word), they again overextend the rule, creating words such as *foots* and *mouses* (*see Figure 4.6*). To researchers, such mistakes are evidence that language learning depends on acquiring *general rules of grammar*, rather than just imitating what adults say (Slobin, 1979). For developmental psychologists interested in language acquisition, the common errors of childhood offer exciting glimpses into the complex mental processes that underlie all human speech.

Cognitive Development

In reading about language acquisition, you may have the impression that children's minds are bursting with thoughts and ideas long before they have the words to express them. For example, if you have ever had contact with a toddler going through the naming explosion, you have seen that children have an insatiable appetite for the labels of things they know. Clearly, long before they have the vocabulary, babies and young children see and think about the world.

➡ How and when do children begin to reason, think, plan strategies, and solve problems? Cognitive development is the study of the processes and products of the mind as they emerge and change over time. Do children know objects still exist even when they can't see them? Do they know that it is possible to believe in ideas that aren't true and that people have desires and dreams—but objects do not? Developmental psychologists want to know the way children think and what they think.

There are two dominant views on the nature of the human cognitive system. *The information-processing approach* uses computer information-processing as the model for how people think and deal with information. The *cognitive-development view* originates from the pioneering work of the late Swiss psychologist **Jean Piaget**. For nearly 50 years, he observed children's intellectual development. Piaget's training in biological methods of observation helped him investigate human cognition as a form of biological adaptation. Piaget saw the human mind as an active biological system that seeks, selects, interprets, and reorganizes environmental information to fit with or adjust to its own existing mental structures.

Piaget began his quest to understand the nature of the child's mind by carefully observing the behavior of his own three children. He would pose problems to them, observe their responses, slightly alter the situations, and once again observe their responses. Piaget used simple demonstrations and sensitive interviews to generate complex theories about early mental development.

In their short early lives, children learn to transform specific information about concrete events into general, abstract concepts. How does their thinking develop in this way? There are three key components of Piaget's approach to cognitive development: schemes; assimilation and accommodation; and the four stages of cognitive growth.

Although an infant will begin to suck a bottle just the way he or she sucked a breast (assimilation), the infant will soon discover that some changes are necessary (accommodation). The child will make an even greater accommodation in the transitions from bottle to straw to cup.

Critical Thinking Icons

These icons alert students to critical thinking questions that are raised within text discussions.

"In Focus" Boxes

These three types of boxes—"In Focus: Research," "In Focus: Theory," and "In Focus: Application" highlight various methods, ideas, and real-life issues in psychology. Boxes cover such timely issues as the ethics of human and animal research, ageism in our society, and the latest technology used to "see" the brain.

ETHICAL ISSUES IN HUMAN AND ANIMAL RESEARCH

Respect for the basic rights of humans and animals who participate in psychological research is a fundamental obligation of all researchers. To guarantee that these rights are honored, special committees oversee every research proposal, imposing strict guidelines issued by the U.S. Department of Health and Human Services. Psychology departments at universities and colleges, hospitals, and research institutes each have review panels that approve and reject proposals for human and animal research. The American Psychological Association (1982) has established detailed guidelines for ethical standards for researchers. We will review several of the most common ethical concerns and the guidelines developed to address them: informed consent; risk/gain assessment; intentional deception; debriefing; and animal research.

Informed Consent

Typically all research with human subjects begins with a description of the procedures, risks, and benefits each subject might experience. After they receive this information, subjects are asked to sign statements indicating that they have given their informed consent to participate, and they know that they can leave an experiment whenever they wish. Subjects are also invited to contact the experimenters for further information.

Risk/Gain Assessment

The risk to subjects of most psychological experiments is minimal (e.g., eye strain from focusing on visual stimuli), but some procedures can be upsetting or disturbing (e.g., emotional reactions, damage to self-image, or social pressures). Subjects' physical and psychological well-being is a priority of all research, so these risks must be minimized, explained, and safeguarded by precautions. The same procedures apply to animal research, where humane and considerate treatment is essential.

Intentional Deception

For some kinds of research, advance explanations make unbiased

study impossible. Informed subjects may be too self-conscious to behave in a natural or genuine way. For example,

if a subject is told that an experiment examines how people deal with extreme frustration, anticipating trouble may lead the subject to cope better—or perhaps worse—than usual. In such cases subjects are usually deceived with a cover story that distorts the true nature or purpose of the experiment. For example, subjects may be told that the experiment focuses on problem-solving strategies; this half-truth omits any mention of frustration, and avoids alarming subjects in advance. After the experiment, all subjects are debriefed by being given a full and honest account of the experiment's true purpose and assumptions.

Advocates of such limited deception argue that most subjects enjoy participation and, when debriefed, accept having been deceived. But critics argue that this does not excuse deception, which violates every subject's basic right of informed consent. Most researchers seek compromise by avoiding designs that would require deception, minimizing deception when it is used, and debriefing all subjects thoroughly after their participation.

Debriefing

In debriefing, the researcher provides as much information as possible about the study after it is completed,

and makes certain no subject departs with any remaining confusion, discomfort, or embarrassment. If subjects were deceived or misled, the deception and its rationale are completely explained, and all questions are answered. Ultimately, subjects have the right to withdraw their data if they feel abused or misused in any way.

Animal Research

In recent years, concern over the care and treatment of animals used in psychological and biomedical research has led to the development of strict guidelines that researchers must follow to obtain funding and approval. Laboratory facilities must be well maintained, use qualified staff, and monitor animals' health and well-being. Pain and discomfort must be minimized, and the least stressful treatments applied whenever possible.

The debate over animal testing and research goes beyond issues of ethics. It centers on society's recognition of the contributions that animal and human research makes every day to the health and well-being of all species, notably in drugs for humans and veterinary medicine for domestic animals. At present, animal researchers subscribe to higher standards of care and concern than most keepers of companion animals (pets) and farm animals. Attitudes about animal research may also be complicated by images of "cute" creatures (e.g., dogs, cats, mice) versus those regarded with less sympathy (e.g., slugs, worms, rats).

Ultimately all citizens must keep themselves informed about the total costs and benefits—to humans and to animals—of animal research. Taking uninformed actions to end such research would be both unnecessary and self-defeating. In a democracy, as in scientific endeavors, rational information should guide decisions.

Functionalism had been developed by the American p
Dewey applied this perspective when seeking ways
practices. Functionalism emphasized adaptation to t
organism's practical goal. The functionalists believe
thought or behavior, one should ask what function
what its structure contained. James agreed that psy
explaining rather than controlling behavior and menta

Evolutionism: Natural Selection of Mind and Behavior

Darwin's theory of evolution pushed humans out of the spotlight by giving them a common ancestry with other animals.

Until 1859, there was no coherent scientific account of why we exist and where we came from. The religious doctrine of creationism asserted that all species, including humans, were divinely created as separate, unchanging types. In 1859, however, Charles Darwin's theory of evolution by natural selection gave biology the central tool it needed to understand how complex organisms come to exist. Organisms born with advantageous features are more likely to survive and procreate, passing on these inherited characteristics to successive generations. Over time, natural forces select the fittest species to survive and develop.

According to **evolutionism**, all species are ever-changing as successful features survive and are passed on. Useless or interfering features become handicaps in the competition for survival. For example, universal psychological processes--like the ability to learn and change--are assumed to give a species an edge over less flexible creatures. Nature (inherited tendencies) and nurture (life experience) work together, since personal experiences interact with inherited abilities in determining individual survival. Just as functionalism questions the adaptive value of a particular behavior, evolutionism questions the adaptive value of patterns of behavior and mental processes in the history of entire species.

SUMMING UP

Three historically important approaches to the study of psychology are structuralism, functionalism, and evolutionism. Structuralism had its origins in early laboratory research on the elements that make up the structure or contents of the human mind. The structuralist school of psychology emerged from Wundt's studies that used introspection to investigate how the mind organizes the experiences of the senses. Titchener carried this approach to the United States, where it was attacked as reductionistic, simplistic, and mentalistic.

Functionalism, developed by Dewey and James, emphasized the function or purpose of any behavioral act. It assumed that the purpose of behavior was to enable each organism to adapt to its environment.

Evolutionism, proposed by Darwin, is the scientific account of how species have survived and are related through natural selection processes. It too focuses on how organisms adapt to the challenges of changing environments, but its time frame is millions of years rather than a human lifetime.

CURRENT PSYCHOLOGICAL PERSPECTIVES

In this section we outline the perspectives, or conceptual approaches, that dominate contemporary psychology. Each perspective defines a different area that is important in the study of psychology. These approaches contain points of view and assumptions that influence what will be studied and how it will be

Interim Summaries

These summaries follow almost every first-level heading. They give students timely reviews of main ideas before asking them to understand subsequent material.

Grouped by sections in each chapter are:

Chapter Reviews are organized around the major themes in each chapter. They help students focus their study efforts.

The **Key Terms and Major Contributors** summarizes, at a glance, those important terms and major names in psychology that appeared in the preceding chapter. Page references from the chapter are included.

CHAPTER REVIEW

Perspectives on Development *What are the two approaches developmental psychologists use to understand psychological change? What are the arguments in the nature-nurture debate? How does maturation contribute to psychological development? What position do stage theories take on continuity?*

Developmental psychologists study those processes that accompany aging throughout the life span. They evaluate the contributions of nature and nurture in contributing to human development. Physical maturation interacts with environmental experience to determine individual functioning and performance. Development can be viewed from a chronological or topical perspective—as either a continuous or discontinuous (stage) process.

Key Terms	Major Contributors
developmental psychology	Locke, John
chronological age	Rousseau, Jean
developmental age	Itard, Jean Marie
chronological approach	Kagan, Jerome
topical approach	Blass, Elliott
nature-nurture controversy	
maturation	
constitutional factors	
temperament	
developmental stages	
critical period	

The Developing Child *How have conceptions of childhood changed in recent centuries? What factors affect language acquisition in childhood? What are the major stages in Piaget's theory of cognitive development? Which processes and behaviors change in social and emotional development?*

Developmental research is influenced by the historically recent view of the child as person. The tasks and processes of childhood include learning language—from the early predisposition to babble and utter words to acquiring the rules of grammar. Cognitive development as theorized by Piaget is based on developmental schemes, a balance between assimilation and accommodation, and four developmental stages: sensorimotor, preoperational, concrete operational and formal operational thinking. Socialization begins with attachment and establishes the child's connections with family, friends, and society. For Erikson, childhood development involves c rises of trust, autonomy, initiative, and competence.

Key Terms	Major Contributors
normative investigations	Chomsky, Noam
longitudinal design	Fernald, Anne
cross-sectional design	Piaget, Jean
sequential design	Bowlby, John
habituation	Harlow, Harry
dishabituation	Erikson, Erik
phonemes	
language acquisition device (LAD),	
motherese	
grammar	

PRACTICE TEST

Chapter 4: Biopsychology

For each of the following items, choose the single correct or best answer. Correct answers, explanations, and page references appear in Appendix B.

1. In studies of developmental psychology, the usual independent variable is _____ while the usual dependent variable is _____.
   A.. time; affect or ability
   B. age; behavior
   C. sensory input or information; aging
   D. children; intelligence or aptitude

2. "The mind at birth is merely a blank slate. Life experience writes on the slate. Thus all we are is a result of our experiences and education." This statement best reflects the opinions of _____ .
   A. John Locke
   B. Jean Rousseau
   C. Jean Piaget
   D. Erik Erikson

3. Which of the following is true of the physical abilities of the newborn infant?
   A. At birth babies already have prejudices favoring particular tastes and smells and disliking others.
   B. Just moments after birth a neonate turns in the direction of a voice or reaches out an exploring hand.
   C. While babies are born legally blind, they soon learn to detect large objects and high-contrast patterns.
   D. All of the above.

4. A developmental researcher arranges to track the progress of a 30-member kindergarten class over the next ten years. maintaining contact with the children's teachers and families in order to test tem annually. This ambitious plan illustrates the use of a _____ research design.

   A. sequential
   B. longitudinal
   C. cross-sectional
   D. None of the above.

5. Which of the following utterances illustrates overregularization in language development?
   A. "Babababa."
   B. "Me gots two foots and two handses."
   C. "Drink milk, all gone."
   D. "Want cookie."

6. "Hey! That's not fair," complains Judi. "Tonio has moreice cream than me." Actually, both Judi and Tonio received a single scoop, but Tanio has stirred his around so it seems to fill the dish, while Judi's scoop is more compact. Jude's complaint indicates that she has not yet acquired the concept of _____ that affects how children think about the physical properties of things.
   A. object permanence
   B. egocentrism
   C. conservation
   D. animistic thinking

7. Harry Harlow conducted landmark studies of the behaviors of baby monkeys who separated from their mothers and had access only to mother "dummies" in their cages. Harlow's work confirmed that _____ .
   A. contact comfort and physical touch are important for healthy early development
   B. the "cupboard theory of attachment" is essentially true for both humans and nonhumans
   C. genuine attachment is only possible with the infant's biological mother
   D. nonhuman infants will imprint on and restrict social behavior to the first visually prominent thing they see after birth

IF YOU'RE INTERESTED...

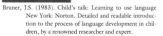

Bruner, J.S. (1983). Child's talk: Learning to use language New York: Norton. Detailed and readable introduction to the process of language development in children, by a renowned researcher and expert.

Gilligan, C. (1982). In a different voice: Psychological theory and women's development. Cambridge, MA: Harvard University Press. Short and readable book by the author of much of the gender controversy in moral development theory; includes brief summary of Kohlberg's original research strategy and early findings.

"Ordinary People." (Video: 1980, color, 123 minutes). Directed by Robert Redford; starring Donald Sutherland, Mary Tyler Moore, Judd Hirsch, and Timothy Hutton. Well-done film of Judith Guest's novel about a family's deterioration after the death of their son, especially in terms of its effects on the surviving adolescent boy.

"Stand by Me." (Video: 1986, color, 87 minutes). Directed by Rob Reiner; starring Wil Wheaton, River Phoenix, Corey Feldman, Kiefer Sutherland, Richard Dreyfuss. Based on Steven King's story. "A grim discovery lies at the center of this mostly nostalgic reflection on boyhood adventures and friendships."

Practice Tests

Featured at the end of each chapter, these tests provide students with opportunities to review the material just studied. Annotated answers appear at the end of the text.

The **"If You're Interested"** feature provides print and video resources for students and instructors seeking further information. Items suggested by reviewers are included.

Psychology

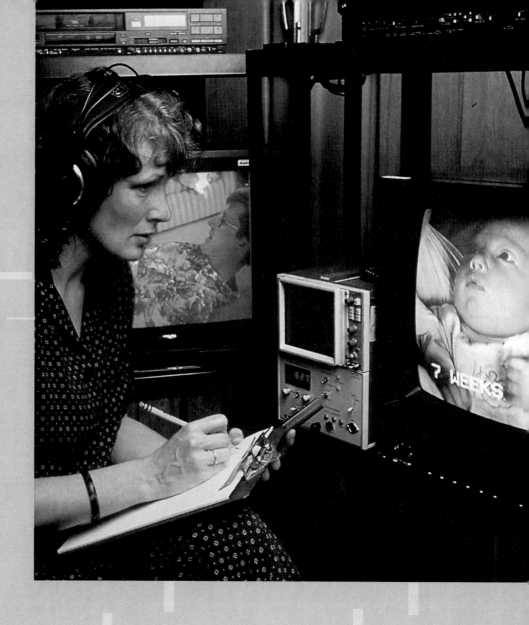

Chapter 1 **Mind, Behavior, and Science**

 **Preview Questions**

1. What is psychology? How is psychology related to other disciplines? What are the distinctive goals of psychology?

2. What is meant by the statement that "Psychology has a long past, but its real history is short"? What was the first formal approach to the study of psychology? How did later approaches differ?

3. Which perspectives or conceptual approaches are currently considered most useful to psychologists? What differences emerge when you compare these perspectives to each other?

4. Why do you need to understand scientific research in order to learn about psychology? How can you use such an understanding in becoming a wiser research consumer?

As the runners lined up to start the 1986 NCAA 10,000-meter championship race, Kathy O. was the odds-on favorite. She had broken high-school track records in three distances and recently set a new American collegiate record for the 10,000-meter race. Her parents, always supportive fans, watched from the sidelines. Kathy got off to a slow start, but she was only a few paces behind the leaders. Her fans knew she could soon catch up. But this time Kathy didn't bolt to the lead as she had in the past. Instead, she veered away from the other runners. Without breaking her stride, she ran off the track, scaled a 7-foot fence, raced down a side street, and jumped off a 50-foot bridge. Ten minutes later, her coach found her on the concrete flood plain of the White River. She had two broken ribs and a punctured lung, and she was paralyzed from the waist down. Not only would she never run again, she might never walk again.

What happened to Kathy? Why did she quit the race and nearly self-destruct? As a star athlete and premed student on the dean's list, Kathy had everything going for her. She had been valedictorian of her high-school class. Teachers and coaches described her as sweet, sensible, diligent, courteous, and religious. Nobody understood her behavior. It didn't make sense.

Kathy's father thought the tragedy "had something to do with the pressure that is put on young people to succeed." Teammates felt the pressure may have come from within Kathy herself. "She was a perfectionist," said one of them. Determined to excel at everything, Kathy had studied relentlessly, even during team workouts.

How did Kathy explain her actions? She told an interviewer that she was overcome by the terrifying fear of failure as she began falling behind in the race. "All of a sudden . . . I just felt like something snapped inside of me." She felt angry and persecuted. These negative reactions were new to Kathy, and they made her feel as if she were someone else. "I just wanted to run away," she recalled. "I don't see how I climbed that fence . . . I just don't feel like that person was me. I know that sounds strange, but I was just out of control. . . . I was watching everything that was happening and I couldn't stop" (UPI, 12/22/86).

The case of Kathy O. raises fascinating questions for psychology. There are different fields of psychology that differ in the way they might focus on such a case. Personality, social, and developmental psychologists might ask how athletic ability, intelligence, parental support, competition, motivation to achieve, and personality traits combined to make Kathy a superstar in the first place. Clinical psychologists would want to know why something "snapped" inside Kathy at this race, why feelings of anger were so foreign to her, and why she felt persecuted. Those who study the nature of consciousness would try to understand Kathy's perception that she was outside herself, unable to stop her flight toward self-destruction. Health psychologists and those who work in the area of sports psychology might try to identify signs of stress and clues in earlier behaviors that could have signaled an impending breakdown. Psychologists who emphasize the biological basis of behavior might consider the role of brain and hormonal factors in her sudden, abnormal reaction. Are there any circumstances under which *you* might quit as Kathy O. did?

We may never completely understand what motivated Kathy's behavior, but psychology provides (1) the tools, *research methods,* and (2) the "instructions," *theories* about the causes of behavior, for exploring basic questions about who we are and why we think, feel, and act as we do. Psychologists are challenged to make sense of cases (such as Kathy's) that violate ordinary conceptions about human nature. Psychologists' motivation is not only intellectual curiosity, but also a desire to discover how to help people prevent such tragedies in the future.

Introduction

Welcome to the start of our exciting journey into the realms of the human mind. There are many paths that we must travel to understand "the nature of human nature." We will journey through the inner spaces of the brain and mind and the outer dimensions of human behavior. Between those extremes, we shall investigate events and experiences that you take for granted, such as how you perceive your world, communicate, learn, think, remember, and even sleep. We will also try to understand how and why we dream, fall in love, feel shy, act aggressively, and become mentally ill.

Psychology holds the key to a general understanding of how human beings function. As you discover what psychologists know about people in general, you can apply that knowledge to change your own behavior, and the behavior of other people, for the better. Ideally, you will also perceive ways to change society, since efforts to resolve many of the urgent problems of our time benefit from a psychological perspective.

The first goal of *Psychology* is to provide a comprehensive survey of what psychologists have discovered about the workings of the brain, mind, and behavior. The second goal is to show how that knowledge is applied in our everyday lives, and how it can be used to enhance many aspects of the human condition. By the end of our journey, if you have put in the time and effort necessary to qualify as a novice psychologist, you too will discover the fascination of "people watching." Maybe you will also accept the role of being a source of psychological knowledge, and even comfort, to others.

A scientific quest for understanding will be foremost in our journey. We want to know why we think, feel, and behave as we do. What makes each of us different from all other people? Yet why do we often behave so alike in some situations? One of America's great writers, Ralph Waldo Emerson, commented on the complexity of human beings:

> All persons are puzzles until at last we find in some word or act the key to the man, to the woman: straightway all their past words and actions lie in light before us.

Psychology: Definitions, Goals, and Tasks

In this section we will look at some formal definitions of psychology and establish what psychology is all about. We will also see how psychology compares to other disciplines that analyze behavior, the brain, and the mind. Then we will preview the five general goals that guide the research and practice of professional psychologists.

Definitions

psychology The scientific study of the behavior of individuals and their mental processes.

Psychology is formally defined as the scientific study of the behavior of individuals and their mental processes. A basic question that psychology asks is this: What is the nature of human nature? Psychology answers this question by looking at *processes* that occur within individuals as well as within the physical and social environment. Let's examine each aspect of the definition of psychology—scientific, behavioral, individual, and mental.

The *scientific* aspect of psychology requires that psychological conclusions are based on evidence collected following the principles of the scientific method. Instead of relying on a conclusion that "makes sense," seems logical, or is personally satisfying, the scientist is trained to use a particular method in answering questions. The **scientific method** consists of a set of orderly steps used to analyze and solve problems. The scientific method relies on *empirical evidence*—information (data) gathered directly by the senses of the observer. Unbiased methods are used to make observations, collect data, and formulate conclusions to verify information.

scientific method A set of orderly steps used to analyze and solve problems by relying on objective research data; also an open-minded yet cautiously skeptical attitude toward evidence and conclusions.

For example, when you have a bad cold, will your eating habits affect your recovery? You have probably heard the adage, "Feed a cold, starve a fever"; if you follow this advice, you will eat more than usual. Alternatively, you might follow the advice that instructs you to "stay in bed, drink lots of water, and eat nothing." Instead of relying on folk wisdom, you could use the scientific method by trying out one strategy and observing the results. If skipping meals during your last cold seemed to help you recover, then do the same for your next cold; if it seemed to make you worse, then try the opposite strategy and eat more than usual. By trying one strategy and observing the results, you can learn from experience from empirical evidence.

behavior Observable action; the means by which organisms adjust to their environment.

Behavior is the means by which organisms adjust to their environment. Behavior is action. The subject matter of psychology is largely the observable behavior of humans and other species of animals. Psychologists observe how an individual functions, what the individual does, and how the individual goes about doing it within a given behavioral setting and social context. Note that the subject of psychological analysis is usually an individual—for example, a newborn baby, a college student, or a widowed grandmother—although the subject might also be an animal learning a new task or responding to a change in the environment. The individual might be studied in its natural habitat or in the controlled conditions of a research laboratory.

As the field of psychology has matured, it has become clear that psychologists cannot directly investigate *mental processes,* the workings of the human mind. Many of our human activities are really private, internal events: thinking, planning, reasoning, creating, and dreaming. Many psychologists believe that mental processes represent the most important aspect of psychological inquiry. Although such processes are difficult to study, their importance has led to the development of new research techniques, which we will discuss later in the text.

Ties to Other Disciplines

Psychology is unique because of its ties with so many different areas of knowledge. As one of the *social sciences,* psychology draws from economics, political science, sociology, and cultural anthropology. Some psychologists are especially interested in the similarities and differences in the behavior from all parts of the world. These cross-cultural psychologists draw from the contributions of colleagues in anthropology. (See "Cross-cultural Perspective: Accepting the Importance of Diversity" on page 20.) Because it systematically analyzes behavior, along with its causes and consequences, psychology is a *behavioral science.* Other behavioral sciences, such as education and environmental design, rely on psychology for the principles that are applied in training people or shaping their surroundings. Psychologists share many interests with researchers in biological sciences, especially with those who study brain processes and the biochemical bases of behavior. As part of the emerging area of *cognitive science,* psychologists' questions about how the human mind works are related to research and theory in computer science, artificial intelligence, and applied mathematics. As a *health science,* psychology seeks to improve the quality of our individual and collective well-being.

While the remarkable breadth and depth of modern psychology is a source of delight to those who become psychologists, it often makes the field a difficult challenge to the student exploring it for the first time. There is much more to the study of psychology than you probably expect, and there will be many valuable ideas that you can take away from this introduction to psychology.

The Goals of Psychology

The goals of the psychologist conducting basic research are to describe, explain, predict, and control behavior. The applied psychologist has a fifth goal—to improve the quality of human life. Most applied psychologists are able to conduct their own basic research, scientifically studying particular problems in order to solve them. The process of accomplishing one goal and moving on to the next is ideally a natural, flowing experience, energized by the psychologist's interest in the question being studied.

Describing What Happens. The first task in psychology is to observe behavior carefully and to describe it objectively. Because every observer has personal biases, prejudices, and expectations, it is difficult to prevent subjectivity from distorting the data. *Data* are reports of observations (*data* is the plural form and *datum* is the singular). For example, the prices of specific items in a local grocery store are data that can help you decide where to shop.

behavioral data Reports of observations about the behavior of organisms and the conditions under which the behavior occurs or changes.

Behavioral data are reports of observations about the behavior of organisms and the conditions under which the behavior occurs or changes. The specific behavior that is being observed and measured is termed the *response.* A response is triggered by an environmental condition known as a *stimulus* (the plural of *stimulus* is *stimuli*). When you are startled by the sudden, loud ringing of a telephone in a quiet room, the ringing is the stimulus that causes your startled response.

Psychologists look for consistent, reliable relationships between stimuli and responses. They also look for relationships between sets of particular responses, such as a pattern of helping one's friends and a pattern of contributing to charitable causes. Psychologists identify and study these relationships to understand something about the person or organism making the responses or about the underlying process that causes or relates responses and stimuli.

Because of our prior experiences, both personal and cultural, we often see in data what we *expect* to see. Consider how expectations about gender can alter the way American parents perceive their children. When parents of newborn infants (less than 24 hours old) were asked to describe their babies, they gave very different descriptions depending on the baby's sex. Compared to sons, daughters were rated softer, smaller, weaker, more delicate, and more awkward. Objective measures were then made of the infants' weight, length, state of health, and other attributes relevant to the subjective descriptions. According to these objective criteria, there were no actual differences between the boys and the girls (Rubin et al., 1974). Within 24 hours of a child's birth, the parents have already begun to see "what is expected to be" rather than "what is." We find ways to distort what others do in order to make their actions conform to our beliefs and prejudices.

An objective description of behavior includes only external features that others can perceive. You cannot say whether this couple is happy or sad without making an inference about an inner state.

Even professional observers may fall prey to this tendency to let their own perspectives prevent objective observation. However, two procedures help them maintain objectivity. The first safeguard requires that observations be made under carefully controlled and clearly described conditions so that other researchers may repeat the conditions of the experiment. The second requires precise, unambiguous definitions of responses and stimuli so that behavioral data are described, measured, and reported in a consistent fashion. This practice also allows independent observers to repeat the experiment and provides a common basis for understanding the results.

It is not as simple as you might think to describe events objectively. For example, how would you describe the actions of the couple in the photo? In an objective description you would note gestures, facial expressions, objects, people, and actions being performed. But if you say that a person is showing anger, fear, arrogance, or timidity, you are inferring inner states, not simply describing behavior that you can see. Your descriptions of behavior (your data) must include only external features that can be perceived equally by all, such as what a person said, what movements were made, what score a person got, or how many people indicated agreement with a decision. In objective description, the key is to avoid making judgments about traits and attributes that cannot be seen directly.

Explaining What Happens. While *descriptions* must come from perceivable information, *explanations* deliberately go beyond what can be observed impartially. We began this chapter by asking for an explanation of why Kathy O. quit the race and nearly destroyed her life. Fans of mystery stories, after figuring out who did it, want to understand the reason why.

In many areas of psychology, the central goal is to find regular patterns in behavioral and mental processes. Psychologists want to discover "how behavior works." Understanding such behaviors involves finding out how certain stimuli cause observed responses and discovering relationships between sets of responses.

Correct explanations may also come from research that systematically evaluates alternative views about a psychological event. There is no better path to understanding than that of informed imagination. Sometimes researchers make an *inference*—a logical or reasonable judgment not based on direct observation—about a process that is happening inside an animal or human being. Often, this inference helps make the observed behavior more understandable. For example, if your cat is meowing more than usual and pawing at your ankles, and you notice her food dish is empty, you may make an inference: "She must be hungry! No wonder she was trying to get my attention."

Psychologists make inferences about **intervening variables**—inner, unseen conditions (such as emotions like anger and motives like hunger) that are assumed to function within living creatures. Psychologists conceive of intervening variables to link observable stimulus input with measurable response output.

Psychological explanations often center on sources of motivation that might account for observed behavior. For example, one explanation for Kathy O.'s behavior may be that a cumulative buildup of pressures to achieve and succeed led her to believe that anything less than perfection was failure. For Kathy, winning was everything. When she thought she was losing the race, she felt frustrated and ashamed, and her self-image declined. Running away from the scene of her perceived failure and attempting to kill herself might have been impulsive reactions to these overpowering emotions and motivations. A very different explanation could be generated from a biological perspective. For example, perhaps Kathy was suffering from an undetected physical problem such as a brain tumor.

Any proposed explanation depends on one's perspective and available evidence, but the proposition needs to be checked against systematically collected

intervening variables Hypothetical conditions that are assumed to function as the links between observable stimulus input and measurable response output.

data that support it or rule out alternative explanations. For example, if "starving" yourself the last time you had a cold only made you feel worse, you could assume that eating normally during your next cold will make you feel better; however, this is also only an assumption, and it could prove to be wrong.

Predicting What Will Happen. Predictions in psychology are statements about the likelihood that a certain behavior will occur or that a given relationship will be found. When differing explanations are put forward to account for some behavior or relationship, they are usually judged by how well they can make accurate and comprehensive predictions.

When you meet someone you like, you may ask friends for "references" so that you can be sure he or she will treat you fairly. Before you pay someone to tutor you, you expect to see evidence that this person is a competent and experienced teacher. These examples highlight our need to know what will happen in the future. Because our well-being and even our survival depend on making accurate predictions about situations that could be dangerous or favorable, we strive to make and find reliable predictions. A scientific prediction is based upon an understanding of the ways events relate to each other, and it suggests what mechanisms link those events to certain predictors, which are signs of future occurrences. Scientific predictions must be worded precisely enough so that they can be tested and disconfirmed if the evidence is not supportive.

A common form of prediction is based on the assumption that people's past actions are a good indicator of their future behavior. If you lack knowledge of a particular individual's past record, you might consider the past behavior of similar people who were in the same situation. This is a *base rate* prediction. A **base rate** is a statistic that identifies the normal frequency, or probability, of a given event. When you are trying to predict what someone is likely to do in a new situation, the base rate is a very helpful datum.

Predictions in psychology also usually recognize that most behavior is influenced by a combination of factors. Some influences come from within the individual, others are unique to the individual's personality or disposition, and still others are external factors, which are conditions of the environment or situation. Any of these may be "the key" to predicting behavior, although they are more likely to work in some combination. What made Kathy O. suddenly "snap" and take drastic action? Perhaps it was not a single problem or threat that was too much for Kathy, but rather a unique combination of her past training, recent pressures, and momentary fear of failure in this particular race.

A *causal prediction* in psychology specifies that some behavior will be changed by the influence of a given stimulus variable. Psychologists often want to know if a particular stimulus always causes a person to make a certain response. A researcher could manipulate (that is, vary or change) stimulus conditions and observe their influence on the subject's response. (Any such condition, event, or process that changes or varies is called a **variable**.) Is your new roommate always this grouchy after getting a phone call from home, or do all phone calls have that effect? By having different people call, or by observing your roommate's responses after various phone conversations, you can learn which conditions cause grouchiness and which do not.

The stimulus condition that can vary independently of other variables in the situation is known as the **independent variable.** Any variable whose values are the results of changes in one or more independent variables is known as a **dependent variable.** In the example of the grouchy roommate, the independent variable includes the different telephone callers, while the dependent variable is your roommate's mood—whether he or she is grouchy after talking on the phone. The independent variable is the predictor, and the dependent variable is the *predicted response.* Typically, a situation in which a stimulus causes a response is known as an S → R relationship.

Controlling What Happens. For many psychologists, control is the central, most powerful goal. Control means making behavior happen or not happen:

base rate A statistic that identifies the most common frequency or probability of a given event.

independent variable The stimulus condition that can vary independently of other variables in the situation; presumed to predict or influence behavior.

dependent variable Any behavioral variable whose values result from or depend upon changes in one or more independent variables.

starting it, maintaining it, or stopping it, and influencing its form, strength, and rate of occurrence. A causal explanation of behavior is convincing if it can create conditions under which the behavior can be controlled.

The ability to control behavior is important not only because it validates scientific explanations, but also because it provides psychologists with methods of helping people improve their lives. Many psychologists optimistically believe that virtually any undesired behavior pattern can be modified by the proper intervention. *Intervention* occurs when new conditions or circumstances are introduced, and it may require the aid of an outsider like a teacher or therapist. Such attempts at control are at the heart of all programs of psychological treatment or therapy.

Serious ethical issues can arise, however, when one person tries to control another person's behavior. Not too long ago, psychotherapists attempted to "cure" homosexual men of their alleged sickness by applying *aversive* treatments—pain or discomfort—to discourage their "sick" behavior. That "treatment" stopped once the scientifically accepted conception of homosexuality was changed from one of sexual *deviance* to one of sexual *preference*. Until recently, therapists with the best of intentions intervened in the lives of gay men in ways that would be considered unethical, if not illegal, today.

It is interesting to note that understanding, rather than control, tends to be the ultimate goal of psychologists in many Asian and African countries (Nobles, 1972). Control may be a value in Western societies that biases psychological research and practice. Being in control is especially important to most notions of masculinity, and most of the founders and early shapers of psychological science were men. If women had been more prominent than men in developing modern psychology, values other than control might have prevailed in shaping professional psychology.

Improving the Quality of Life. Many of the findings of psychology are applied to solve human problems. Psychology enriches life in profound ways that shape many fundamental ideas and perspectives underlying so-called common-sense knowledge. "In Focus: Professional Psychology" on page 10 describes how psychologists perform diverse tasks and the varied settings and roles in which they work. Knowing what psychology is and what psychologists do prepares you to investigate the origins of the discipline. We will begin with a history of the ideas that form the intellectual foundation of psychology.

SUMMING UP

Psychology has four main goals: (1) to describe objectively the behavior of individuals; (2) to develop an understanding of the causes and consequences of that behavior using explanations based on both the best available evidence and creative imagination; (3) to predict whether, when, how, and in what form a given behavior will occur; and (4) possibly to control a behavior by making it start, stop, or vary in some predictable way. A fifth and more practical goal is to improve the quality of individual lives and human society.

Psychology's Historical Foundations

"Psychology has a long past, yet its real history is short," wrote one of the first experimental psychologists, Hermann Ebbinghaus (1908). Scholars have long asked important questions about how people perceive reality, the nature of consciousness, and the origins of madness. Not until recently have there been adequate answers for such questions about human nature. The roots of modern psychology lie in ancient Greece. In the fifth and fourth centuries B.C., the classical philosophers Socrates, Plato, and Aristotle began rational dialogues

In Focus:

PROFESSIONAL PSYCHOLOGY

Most psychologists work in academic settings such as universities, colleges, and medical schools. The principal employment setting for many other psychologists is business, government, hospitals, or clinics. Those in private practice may treat clients in their offices or conduct personal consulting services for private firms.

The majority of psychologists concentrate on the diagnosis and treatment of severe emotional and behavioral problems. *Clinical psychologists* tackle problems of mental illness, juvenile delinquency, drug addiction, criminal behavior, mental disability, and marital and family conflict. *Counseling psychologists* are similar to clinical psychologists, but they often work on problems of a less severe nature, and the treatment they provide is usually shorter in duration. *Community psychologists* work in community settings delivering social and psychological services to the poor, minorities, immigrants, and the growing number of homeless people in American cities.

Researchers in *biological psychology* study the biological bases of behavior, feelings, and mental processes.

Specialists in *neuroscience* study mechanisms that link the brain to behavior. *Psychopharmacologists* investigate the effects of drugs on behavior and thought.

Experimental psychology primarily uses experimental methods to work with both human and animal subjects in the quest for general laws of psychology that apply to all species.

Cognitive psychologists focus their research on consciousness and mental processes, such as thinking and communicating, remembering and forgetting, and making decisions and solving problems. *Psycholinguistics* involves a particular study of the psychology of language.

Developmental psychology focuses on how human functioning changes over time, identifying the factors that shape behavior from birth to death. *Personality psychology* concentrates on the ways individuals differ from each other, despite similar concerns and development. *Social psychology* reverses this orientation, focusing on the common situations and social contexts that influence human behavior despite individual differences.

Industrial psychology and *organizational behavior* examine the relationships between people and jobs. A subcategory of industrial psychology is *human factors psychology*, which studies the interaction between worker, machines, and work environment.

Further specialization can be found among many areas of applied psychology. *Educational* and *school psychologists* study ways to improve the learning process, both by applying learning theory and working with students in the school environment. *Environmental psychologists* work with architects, city planners, and environmental designers to meet the needs of users and residents. *Health psychologists* collaborate with medical researchers to understand how different life-styles and behavior patterns affect health and stress. *Forensic psychologists* apply psychological knowledge to human problems in the field of law enforcement. Finally, *sports psychologists* analyze the performance of athletes and use psychological principles in training them to achieve peak performance.

---

about how the mind works, the nature of free will, and the relationship of individual citizens to their community state.

Later, as the doctrines of the Roman Catholic Church spread throughout Europe, theologians taught that the mind and soul had free will (God's gift to humans) and were not subject to the natural laws and principles that determined the actions of physical bodies of all other creatures. There could be no scientific psychology until this assumption was challenged.

The formal start of modern psychology can be traced to only a century ago, relatively recently in terms of human history. In 1879, in Leipzig, Germany, **Wilhelm Wundt,** probably the first person to refer to himself as a *psychologist,* founded the first formal laboratory devoted to experimental psychology. In the late 1880s German physicists, physiologists, and philosophers began to challenge the notion that the human organism is special in the great chain of being, demonstrating that natural laws determine human actions. Hermann von Helmholtz, trained as a physicist, conducted simple but revealing experiments on perception and the nervous system. At about the same time, another German, Gustav Fechner, began to study how physical stimulation is translated into sensations that are experienced psychologically. Like Wundt, Helmholtz and Fechner advocated **determinism,** the doctrine that

determinism Doctrine that physical, behavioral, and mental events are not random but rather are determined by specific causal factors.

In 1897, Wilhelm Wundt (center) founded the first formal laboratory devoted to experimental psychology. He's shown here in his laboratory in Leipzig in 1912.

William James (1842–1910)

physical, behavioral, and mental events are determined by specific causal factors. Determinism is essential to science because it assumes that complex realities can be understood if they are investigated and their causes identified.

Ideas and intellectual traditions from both philosophy and natural science converged to give rise to the development of the new field of psychology. In 1890, a young Harvard philosophy professor who had studied medicine and had strong interests in literature and religion developed a uniquely American psychological perspective. **William James,** brother of the great novelist Henry James, wrote a two-volume work, *The Principles of Psychology,* which many experts consider to be the most important psychology text ever written.

These early writers and their works were just the beginning of a continuing fascination with the science of psychology. Today the rapid pace of technology has led to an explosion of new ideas and applications, but if we look closely we see it has been an "orderly" explosion. Modern concepts of thought and behavior have descended from earlier ideas, some of which were organized into influential "schools" of psychology. Each school influenced the training and thinking of generations of scholars whose work shaped what psychology is today. Three of the most historically significant schools of psychology are structuralism, functionalism, and evolutionism. To appreciate the richness and usefulness of modern psychology, we must first understand the development of these three approaches.

Structuralism: The Contents of the Mind

When psychology became a laboratory science organized around experiments, its unique contribution to knowledge was established and recognized. In Wundt's laboratory, the data were collected through systematic, objective procedures, so that independent observers could repeat the results of these experiments. An emphasis on experimental methods, a concern for precise measurement, and statistical analysis of data characterized Wundt's psychological tradition.

When European-trained psychologist **Edward Titchener** brought Wundt's psychology to the United States, he also advocated that psychology study consciousness. Titchener wondered how the elements of mental life could be studied. The method of choice at that time was *introspection,* a sys-

structuralism The study of the structure of mind and behavior, including elements and components.

tematic examination of one's own thoughts and feelings about specific sensory experiences. Titchener emphasized the "what" of mental contents rather than the "why" or "how." His approach came to be known as **structuralism,** the study of the structure of mind and behavior.

Structuralism was based on the presumption that all human mental experience could be understood as the combination of simple events or elements. You may have made this assumption yourself if you have ever enjoyed a new food and wondered aloud, "This is good. What's in it?" This appealing model—that one can understand something by studying its ingredients—is especially popular in physical sciences such as biology and chemistry. You have structuralistic ideas about psychology if you think that some experiences are "made of" combinations of thoughts, emotions, or motives. Early critics of structuralism attacked it as too simplistic in reducing psychological experiences to basic sensations. It was also criticized as too mentalistic, placing too much faith in verbal descriptions of internal, mental processes.

Functionalism: Minds with a Purpose

functionalism School that gave primary importance to learned habits that enabled organisms to adapt to their environment and to function effectively.

evolutionism Theory that all species are ever-changing as successful features survive and are passed on genetically to successive generations.

Emerging as the champion of American psychology, William James agreed with Titchener that the study of consciousness must be central to psychology. However, James disagreed with the structuralist search for elements and contents. James argued that consciousness was an ongoing stream, a property of mind continually interacting with the environment. Human consciousness facilitated one's adjustment to the environment; thus, the *functions* of mental processes, not the contents of the mind, were significant. **Functionalism** gave primary importance to learned habits that enabled organisms to adapt to their environment and to function effectively.

Functionalism had been developed by the American philosopher **John Dewey.** Dewey applied this perspective when seeking ways to improve educational practices. Functionalism emphasized adaptation to the environment as every organism's practical goal. The functionalists believed that in order to understand a thought or behavior one should ask what *function* or purpose it served, not what its *structure* contained. James agreed that psychology must focus on explaining rather than controlling behavior and mental processes.

Evolutionism: Natural Selection of Mind and Behavior

Darwin's theory of evolution changed the way humans think of themselves by giving them a common ancestry with other animals—however, not pleasing to all people.

Until 1859, there was no coherent scientific account of why humans exist and where we came from. The religious doctrine of *creationism* asserted that all species, including humans, were divinely created as separate, unchanging types. In 1859, however, Charles Darwin's theory of evolution by natural selection gave biology the central tool it needed to understand how complex organisms come to exist. Organisms born with advantageous features are more likely to survive and procreate, passing on these inherited characteristics to successive generations. Over time, natural forces select the fittest species to survive and develop.

According to **evolutionism,** all species are ever-changing as traits that help organisms survive are passed on. Useless or interfering features become handicaps in the competition for survival. For example, universal psychological processes, such as the ability to learn and change, are assumed to give a species an edge over less flexible creatures. Nature (inherited tendencies) and nurture (life experience) work together, since personal experiences interact with inherited abilities in determining individual survival. Just as functionalism questions the adaptive value of a particular behavior, evolutionism questions the adaptive value of patterns of behavior and mental processes in the history of entire species.

SUMMING UP

Three historically important approaches to the study of psychology are structuralism, functionalism, and evolutionism. Structuralism had its origins in early laboratory research on the elements that make up the structure, or contents, of the human mind. The structuralist school of psychology emerged from Wundt's studies that used introspection to investigate how the mind organizes the experiences of the senses. Titchener carried this approach to the United States, where it was judged as reductionistic, simplistic, and mentalistic.

Functionalism, developed by Dewey and James, emphasized the function or purpose of any behavioral act. This school assumed that the purpose of behavior was to enable each organism to adapt to its environment.

Evolutionism, proposed by Darwin, is the scientific account of how species have survived and are related through natural selection processes. This school also focuses on how organisms adapt to the challenges of changing environments, but its time frame is millions of years rather than a human lifetime.

Current Psychological Perspectives

In this section we will outline the perspectives, or conceptual approaches, that dominate contemporary psychology. Each perspective defines a different area that is important in the study of psychology. These approaches contain points of view and assumptions that influence what will be studied and how it will be investigated. A psychologist's point of view determines what to look for, where to look, and which methods to employ.

By combining particular points of view (assumptions about what to study and how to study it) and temporal orientations (past, present, or future), we can identify six broad conceptual models psychologists use to study behavior and mental processes: biological, psychodynamic, behavioristic, cognitive, humanistic, and evolutionary.

These perspectives are *models* in the sense that they draw an analogy between the processes being studied and a system that is already understood. For example, you could use the model of a car to explain that your body "needs repair" because you have been "running on empty" and feel "broken down." Likewise, early psychologists used the analogy of a telephone switchboard as a model for how the human brain uses information. While reading about these six perspectives on psychology, try to identify the model in each that helps you to understand it better.

Biological Approach

The **biological approach** guides psychologists who search for the causes of behavior in the functioning of genes, the brain, the nervous system, and the endocrine system. This approach makes four assumptions: (1) psychological and social phenomena can be understood in terms of biochemical processes; (2) complex behaviors can be understood by analyzing them into smaller, more specific units; (3) all behavior—or behavior potential—is determined by physical structures and largely hereditary processes; and (4) experience can modify behavior by altering these underlying biological structures and processes.

The biological approach to Kathy O.'s behavior would assume that biochemical processes account for her experience. Perhaps the stress of running aggravated an undetected physical disease (such as a thyroid disorder) and interfered with Kathy's ability to control her behavior. The biological approach is also concerned with hereditary factors. While heredity cannot be changed,

biological approach Approach that searches for the causes of behavior in the functioning of genes, the brain, the nervous system, and the endocrine system.

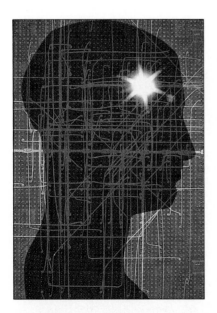

Early psychologists used the analogy of a telephone switchboard as a model for how the brain communicates information.

once these influences are understood, people like Kathy can be helped with medication and other forms of therapy.

Psychodynamic Approach

psychodynamic approach
Approach that views behavior as driven or motivated by powerful mental forces and conflicts.

According to the **psychodynamic approach,** behavior is driven, or motivated, by powerful inner forces. In this view, human actions stem from inherited instincts, biological drives, and attempts to resolve conflicts between personal needs and societal demands to act appropriately. Motivation is the key concept in the psychodynamic model. Deprivation states, physiological arousal, conflicts, and frustrations provide the power for behavior just as coal fuels a steam locomotive. In this model, the organism stops reacting when its needs are satisfied and its drives reduced.

Psychodynamic principles of motivation were most fully developed by Viennese physician **Sigmund Freud** in the late nineteenth and early twentieth centuries. According to Freud's theory, each person is fully determined by a combination of heredity and early childhood experiences. As a child learns to resolve the conflict between personal desires and social restrictions, his or her personality develops. Unresolved conflicts can contribute to long-lasting emotional problems. Freud's model was the first to recognize that human behavior is not always rational or easy to explain. The psychodynamic model can be seen as a cynical view of human nature in its depiction of selfish urges curbed only by strong societal controls. Nonetheless, Freud's ideas have influenced more areas of psychology than those of any other person, and they continue to inspire new forms of research and practice.

Applying the psychodynamic perspective to the case of Kathy O., we might wonder what forces and desires were driving her so hard that she "snapped" and lost control. Perhaps as a child she tried to please her parents or overcome her own feelings of inadequacy by excelling in competition and being a "winner." If she doubted her own ability to keep this up, she might panic or overreact. Kathy's suicidal jump just as she thought she was losing the race might have been a drastic effort to "escape" the disappointment of her parents and the pressures of her life.

Sigmund Freud (1856–1939), shown here in the office of his Vienna home, developed the psychodynamic approach to behavior.

Behavioristic Approach

behavioristic approach Approach that focuses on overt behaviors that can be objectively recorded and manipulated.

Those who follow the **behavioristic approach** are interested in overt behaviors that can be objectively recorded. Behaviorally oriented psychologists focus on specific, measurable responses for their data; examples include blinking an eye, pressing a lever, or saying yes following an identifiable stimulus (such as a light or a bell). These psychologists are not concerned with inferring biochemical processes or unconscious motives.

The main objective of behavioristic analysis is to understand how particular environmental stimuli control particular kinds of behavior. First, behaviorists identify the conditions or stimuli that trigger a response. Next they examine the nature of the response itself to understand, predict, and perhaps control it. Finally, they consider the consequences or impact of the response on the physical and social environment.

According to the behavioristic model, behavior is wholly determined by conditions in the environment. People are neither good nor evil but simply reactive to their environment. Behaviorists further assume that most of what people become is a matter of nurture, not nature.

behaviorism Assertion that only the overt behavior of organisms is the proper subject of scientific study.

conditioning The process of learning and modifying behavior by pairing stimulus events in specific patterns.

Behaviorism asserts that only the overt behavior of organisms is the proper subject of scientific study. **John B. Watson,** the first American behaviorist, was influenced by the work of Russian physiologist **Ivan Pavlov.** Pavlov had discovered the principles of **conditioning,** the process of learning and modifying physical reflexes. Watson saw that if all behavior could be shown to result from learning, new possibilities for changing undesirable behavior would evolve. He believed that mental events could not be studied scientifically, and that introspection was at best an unreliable source of information. Watson established a new direction in psychology—a search for causes in the environment rather than within the individual. He was the first to insist that psychologists study only observable behavior.

If Watson laid the groundwork for behaviorism, Harvard's **B. F. Skinner** was its major architect. Until Skinner's death in 1990, his plans and visions shaped behaviorism for many decades. In Skinner's blueprint, psychology could be described as scientific only if it restricted itself to the study of how behavior operates on the environment and how behavior is changed by the consequences it has on the environment.

The behavioristic model has dominated American psychology for much of this century. Its emphasis on the need for rigorous experimentation and carefully defined variables has influenced most areas of psychology. Although Skinner and his disciples conducted their basic research with animal subjects (mostly pigeons and rats), the principles of behaviorism have been widely applied to human problems.

The behaviorist perspective on Kathy O.'s tragedy is very different from either a search for biochemical influences or an analysis of emotional conflicts. A behaviorist would dismiss any guesses about Kathy's thoughts and feelings as purely speculative. The behaviorist would say that no one could know what was going on in Kathy's head. Instead, it is more sensible and scientific to focus on Kathy's behavior and what might have influenced it. Just before Kathy "snapped," she was falling behind in the race. In past races, how had she behaved when she began to fall behind? Did falling behind usually mean she would lose the race? Had Kathy suffered from parental disapproval or derision by classmates after previous losses? When Kathy failed or suffered disappointment in school or her personal life, did she usually "run away" from the problem? An analysis of Kathy's past behavior and its consequences might reveal an explanation for her recent experience. Perhaps Kathy had recently been overreacting to other disappointments, and when her efforts in this competition began to fail, she sought a quick escape—with tragic results.

Cognitive Approach

cognitive approach View that emphasizes human thought and all the processes of knowing as central to the study of psychology.

The "cognitive revolution" in psychology has emerged over the past three decades as a direct challenge to the limited perspectives of behaviorism. The centerpiece of the **cognitive approach** is human thought and all the processes of knowing: attending, thinking, remembering, expecting, solving problems, fantasizing, and consciousness. From the cognitive perspective, people act because they think, and people think because the natural design of the human brain equips them to do so.

Cognitive psychologists believe that the processing of information about a stimulus is at least as important in determining behavior as is the stimulus itself. Humans are not simply reactive creatures; they also actively choose and create individual stimulus environments. If the volume on your television set suddenly increases, you react by jumping up to adjust it; but you also flip through the channels, looking for something more interesting to watch, rather than passively accepting whatever comes on next. An individual responds to reality as it appears *subjectively* in the individual's inner world of thoughts and imagination, not as it exists in the objective world.

In the cognitive model, some of the most significant behavior emerges from totally new ways of thinking, not from predictable ways used in the past. The ability to imagine options and alternatives enables people to work toward new futures that transcend limited realities. In the cognitive approach, people start life as neither good nor evil, but with the potential, in the form of mental "programs," to be both good and evil. For example, a hungry animal has only limited options for finding food, and it may behave wildly if it is unsuccessful in meeting this need. In contrast, a hungry human can think of many ways to get food. If he or she has money, then shopping, telephoning, and charging food are options. If he or she does not have money, then begging, borrowing, and stealing are alternatives. No one is *forced* to become a thief, and thus everyone is responsible for the choices he or she makes.

The cognitive perspective on the case of Kathy O. invites us to look inside Kathy's head, in a manner of speaking. As the behaviorist model notes, we cannot directly observe inner processes or know what Kathy was thinking. But we are fairly certain that Kathy *was* thinking and that her thoughts had some impact on her behavior. During the race, what was Kathy paying attention to? Did she notice who watched her as she ran, and could she have felt distracted? Did running keep her from thinking clearly, so that her worries about losing the race became overpowering? In the cognitive approach we assume there are connections between what we perceive, think, decide, and do. To understand human action, we must first understand human cognition.

Part of the appeal of the cognitive approach is that it uses the computer processing model to explain human cognition; this model is both popular and practical. This approach promises satisfying explanations for basic psychological questions. Not surprisingly, many psychologists see the new cognitive orientation as the dominant one in psychology today.

Humanistic Approach

humanistic approach View that the main task for human beings is to strive for growth and development of their potential.

Humanistic psychology emerged in the 1950s as an alternative to the pessimism and determinism of both the psychodynamic and the behavioristic models. In the humanistic view, people are active creatures who are innately good and capable of choice. According to the **humanistic approach,** the main task for human beings is to strive for growth and development of their potential. **Figure 1.1** shows one illustration of the humanistic view of human action and potential.

The humanistic psychologist looks for patterns in people's life histories, with a focus on the individual's subjective experience. For example, a humanist would want to know whether you often *felt*—in your subjective view—as

Figure 1.1 A Humanistic Concept of the Self
According to humanistic psychologists, the main task for human beings is to strive for growth and development of their potential. In this view, the self is compared to the possible self, and one's strengths and weaknesses are evaluated subjectively, not necessarily in a realistic or objective way.

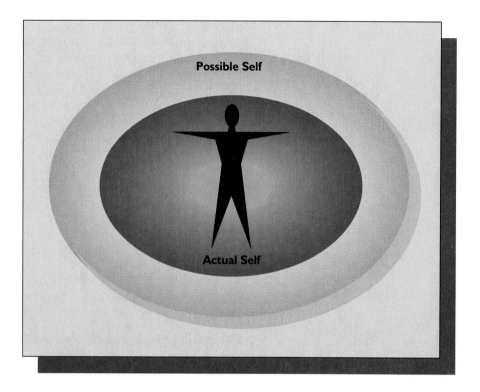

though you were an unattractive and unloved child. This is more important than an outsider's objective view as to whether you were an unattractive and unloved child. It is your personal view of the events in your life that will provide understanding; yours is the only view that has any reality.

Humanistic psychologists deal with the whole person, practicing a *holistic* approach to human psychology. They believe that true understanding requires integrating the mind, body, and behavior of the individual with social and cultural forces.

From a humanistic perspective, Kathy's actions would be seen as the outcome of Kathy's own view of herself and her world. The humanistic approach would focus on the interplay of different values that influence Kathy's perspective and decisions. Who does she think she is, who does she want to be . . . and why?

The humanistic approach expands the realm of psychology beyond the confines of science to include valuable lessons from literature, history, and the arts. In this manner, psychology becomes a more complete discipline that balances scientific empiricism (which has a reliance on sensory evidence) with the nonempirical, imaginative approaches of the humanities (Korn, 1985).

Evolutionary Approach

evolutionary approach Approach that assumes that human mental abilities, like physical abilities, evolved over millions of years to serve particular adaptive purposes.

The concept of behavioral and mental *adaptiveness* is the basis for the **evolutionary approach.** This approach assumes that human mental abilities, like our physical abilities, evolved over millions of years to serve particular adaptive purposes. Recent advances in evolutionary theory have clarified researchers' understanding of adaptive behavior. Adaptive behavior does not mean promoting the good of the species or even of the individual. It means only one thing: promoting the replication of the genes carried in the individual and in the individual's offspring and relatives. Behaving adaptively can include sacrificing oneself for one's children or one's siblings, or helping others who may return that help in the future.

Humans spent 99 percent of their evolutionary history as hunter-gatherers living in small groups during the Pleistocene era. After identifying the adaptive problems that these evolving protohumans faced, evolutionary psychologists generate inferences about the sorts of mental mechanisms, or psychological adaptations, that might have evolved to solve those problems.

Evolutionary psychology differs from other perspectives most fundamentally in its temporal focus on the extremely long process of evolution as a central explanatory principle. The "applied side" of evolutionary psychology strives to use knowledge about our evolved tendencies to help us direct those tendencies in the ways we choose rather than being directed blindly by them (Cosmides & Tooby, 1987).

Was Kathy O.'s tragedy a case of adaptive behavior gone awry? Consider what you might do if you felt horribly threatened. If a predator were about to attack you, you would probably flee or look for an escape route. But what if the threat were *inside* you—how could you run from yourself? If Kathy became overwhelmed with fear and anger as she began to fall behind in the race, she may have had the impulse to run away from the race, from herself, and from life. A runner as swift as Kathy might well succeed in escaping from an external predator; however, the inherited impulse to flee has not yet adapted to the many psychological threats that confront modern humans.

Comparing Psychological Perspectives

Most psychologists are eclectic in their everyday work in the discipline: They apply the most useful concepts and strategies from all six models, weaving them together in unique combinations. For example, in advising a client who wishes to quit smoking, a psychologist might concentrate on changing the client's habits (a behaviorist focus) while considering whether smoking reflects a basic insecurity or nervousness (a psychodynamic view of motivation) and whether the client sees his own smoking as one way to "live my life the way *I* want to live it" (a humanistic nod to subjective reality).

There are also cultural factors. Far more people smoke in some countries than in others (such as Japan, Korea, France, Turkey). In such countries, the person who asks to be seated in a non-smoking section of a restaurant is considered odd. In contrast, the same request has recently become very reasonable in most parts of the United States.

Table 1.1 presents a more direct comparison of the six approaches to modern psychology. For each approach, consider its distinctive view of human nature, what the model proposes as the determinants of behavior, and what the approach studies both generally and specifically. Can all six approaches examine the same behaviors and processes? Which elements and approaches do you find particularly appealing or sensible?

SUMMING UP

We've reviewed the six major approaches that psychologists adopt in studying human and animal behavior and the mental and biological processes that underlie that behavior. Each approach takes a unique perspective on what is most important in psychology, what should be investigated, and how.

The biological, psychodynamic, cognitive, and humanistic approaches emphasize inner processes. Each approach focuses on very different internal factors and mechanisms. The behavioristic approach focuses on external or environmental determinants of behavior. In one sense, the evolutionary approach is based on inner determinants—inherited adaptive tendencies. But in another sense, it emphasizes the environmental challenges that our ancestors faced and survived in order to pass on their genes to us. Cultural influences must also be considered to understand human behavior completely and accurately. No one approach is better than the others; they form an array of different angles that reflect the diversity of modern psychology.

Table 1.1   Comparison of Six Approaches to Modern Psychology

APPROACH	VIEW OF HUMAN NATURE	DETERMINANTS OF BEHAVIOR	FOCUS OF STUDY	PRIMARY RESEARCH APPROACH STUDIES
Biological	Passive Mechanistic	Heredity Biochemical processes	Brain and nervous system processes	Biochemical basis of behavior and mental processes
Psycho-dynamic	Instinct-driven	Heredity Early experiences	Unconscious drives Conflicts	Behavior as overt expression of unconscious motives
Behavioristic	Reactive to stimulation Modifiable	Environment Stimulus conditions	Specific overt responses	Behavior and its stimulus causes and consequences
Cognitive	Creatively active Stimulus reactive	Stimulus conditions Mental processes	Mental processes Language	Inferred mental processes through behavioral indicators
Humanistic	Active Unlimited in potential	Potentially self-directed	Human experience and potentials	Life pattern Values Goals
Evolutionary	Adapted to solving problems of the Pleistocene era	Adaptations and environmental cues for survival	Evolved psychological adaptations	Mental mechanisms in terms of evolved adaptive functions

Psychological Research

Before we examine what researchers have found in the major areas of psychology, we need to identify the ways psychologists gather data about behavior and mental processes. Like it or not, you are a daily consumer of mass media reports on research findings; some of these are valuable, some are worthless, and others are confusing and misleading. You will become a wiser consumer of research-based conclusions as you develop your understanding of *how* psychological research is conducted and *why* the scientific view of knowledge dictates such methods. Let's turn now to how psychologists know *what* they know.

Recall that psychology is the scientific study of the behavioral and mental functioning of individuals. It is scientific because it uses the principles and

Cross-cultural Perspective   Accepting the Importance of Diversity

Another approach to research in psychology takes as a starting point the idea that behavior in all parts of the world should be investigated. Cross-cultural psychologists argue that if psychologists pay too little attention to people from various ethnic groups in different countries, they run the risk of developing explanations of behavior that are too narrow (Triandis, 1989; Berry et al., 1992; Brislin, 1993). Cross-cultural psychologists argue further that too many accepted principles of behavior are based on research with a very limited number of people. These research participants are often Caucasian, young, male, middle class, and articulate when interacting with psychologists. To make sure that explanations of behavior are not limited to this select population, many psychologists recommend that greater attention be given to people from diverse backgrounds. The concept of "culture" has been especially central to the thinking of these psychologists.

Culture refers to concepts, values, and assumptions about life that provide guidance for various behaviors that people may choose to follow. These guidelines for behavior are often widely accepted by people who live in the same part of their country and who speak the same language. These assumptions about life and guidelines for behavior are transmitted generation to generation by parents, older relatives, teachers, and other respected adults. The transmission is not usually explicit. Children are rarely approached by their parents and given lessons in "what our culture tells us we should do." Rather, parents correct their children's mistakes over many years until eventually the children engage in behaviors that need no positive or negative commentary from adults. Or, children observe the behavior of people considered successful in their culture and engage in the same behaviors as these models. Eventually, most children learn the behaviors necessary for day-to-day living and become

accepted members of their culture. If they do not, they become deviants and must accept their culture's punishments for unacceptable behaviors. Examples are time in prison for people who steal, or the absence of job promotions for inactive people who belong to a culture where hard work is valued.

The concept that culture provides guidance for behavior is important. Culture does not dictate that a very narrow set of behaviors is acceptable and that all others should be avoided. Rather, culture provides a number of suggestions for proper behavior in various situations. Some of the most memorable examples of culture's influence and of cultural differences occur when people from very diverse backgrounds interact frequently. Such interactions will occur more and more frequently in the future given such major social policies as immigration, the encouragement of international tourism, political asylum for refugees, and the recruitment of culturally diverse students in colleges and universities.

Assume that a Caucasian male from the American middle class is attending Protestant church services with an acquaintance who is an African American from a similar economic background. Are there cultural differences that, if poorly understood, might influence whether or not this acquaintanceship becomes a friendship? The answer is "yes" (Kochman, 1981).

The cultural difference centers on the amount of emotional expressiveness considered appropriate for churchgoers. If the two people attend a church service where most members are Caucasian, the guidance provided by their culture is that highly emotional displays of religious fervor are rare. People pray and sing aloud, but rarely with intense emotions. They listen to the pastor's sermon but rarely make comments about its content while the pastor is speaking. The cultural guidance is different for African Americans attending church services

where most members are from their same ethnic background. For most African Americans, it is considered appropriate for people to have very intense emotional experiences during church services. People sing with great fervor. While the pastor speaks, congregation members shout their comments about various parts of the message. During some church services, one or more people faint. This rarely causes a problem, however, since the cultural guidance also includes provision of a nurse at church services. In investigating the influence of culture it is important to study the reasons for observed behaviors. For an investigation of different cultural behaviors at church, psychologists should look to history. When slavery was an accepted part of American culture, African Americans were not allowed to express strong emotions in the presence of Caucasians. Attendance at church provided one of the few opportunities for African Americans to express themselves freely.

Whenever culture and cultural differences are discussed, psychologists should be careful to keep in mind that there will be individual differences. Not all people will accept the guidance that their culture offers. Some African Americans will prefer to attend services at churches where emotional expressiveness is low. Some Caucasians join churches where emotional displays are prominent, such as some Fundamental Baptist groups in the American South. Without paying attention to individual differences, people also run the risk of holding unhelpful and demeaning stereotypes. For example, this discussion of one cultural difference should *not* be expanded to a broader statement about the amount of control people have over their emotions. Students of psychology face the challenge of not only keeping in mind that cultural differences exist, but also of knowing that there will always be exceptions due to the complexities of individuals.

empirical investigation Research that relies on sensory experience and observation as research data.

◆4

context of discovery Initial phase of research during which an investigator comes up with a new idea or a different way of thinking about phenomena.

theory A body of interrelated principles used to explain or predict some psychological phenomenon.

"We plan to determine once and for all if there really ARE any cultural differences between them."

practices of the scientific method. **Empirical investigation** in any field requires the use of the scientific method to observe, measure, and experiment. Even if you never do any scientific research in your life, mastering information on psychological research will be useful. You can improve your *critical thinking skills* by learning how to ask the right questions about behavior and how to evaluate the answers you find.

The Context of Discovery

The research process in psychology, as in all empirical sciences, can be divided into two major categories that usually occur in sequence: getting an idea and then testing it. The **context of discovery** is the initial phase of research during which observations, beliefs, information, and general knowledge lead someone to come up with a new idea or a different way of thinking about phenomena.

Theories, Hypotheses, and Paradigms. Psychological research focuses on four sets of concerns: (1) the *stimulus events* that cause a particular response to start, stop, or change in quality or quantity; (2) the *structure* of behavior that links certain actions in predictable, orderly ways to other actions; (3) the relationships between *internal* psychological processes or physiological mechanisms and *observable* behavior patterns; and (4) the *consequences* that behavior has on the individual's social and physical environment.

For example, in 1959 two social psychologists, Elliot Aronson and Judson Mills, conducted a classic study of group initiation. The researchers wondered whether a member's loyalty to a group could be strengthened by a difficult initiation. They invited college women to join group discussions about sex, a daring topic in the late 1950s. Before being permitted to join the group, each woman was required to prove her ability to discuss the subject freely by reading a word list aloud to a male organizer. Some women were given a word list that included common terms that were easy to read; others were given a list containing embarrassing obscenities and slang. All "passed" the initiation and were asked to "listen in" on a group discussion in progress. Although the discussion was scripted to be a disappointing bore, only the women who had read the easy list found it uninteresting. The women who had struggled through the difficult list insisted they enjoyed listening to the discussion and looked forward to joining. This elegant experiment confirmed the researchers' guess: The more severe their initiation, the greater the loyalty members will feel to the group.

In this example, the *stimulus event* was the list a subject was asked to read; the *structure* of her behavior linked her experience reading the list to her feelings about joining the group. Her inner desire to justify having performed a difficult task to join the group *caused* her to feel greater loyalty to it. Finally, feeling loyal led her to insist that a boring discussion sounded *interesting to her*. (The process assumed to intervene between the stimulus event was called *cognitive dissonance*, about which we will say more in Chapter 12.)

Researchers begin with the assumption of determinism, the idea that all events (physical, mental, and behavioral) result from specific causal factors. Researchers also assume that behavior and mental processes follow set patterns of relationships that can be discovered and revealed through research.

Psychological theories, in general, attempt to understand how brain, mind, behavior, and environment function and how they may be related. Any particular **theory** focuses on a more specific aspect of this broad conception, using a body of interrelated principles to explain or predict some psychological phenomenon. For example, in the study by Aronson and Mills summarized above, the researchers relied on a theory that humans seek consistency and meaning, and when experiences seem not to make sense, people will try to "do the right thing." The women whose initiation had been easy rightly judged the overheard discussion to be boring, but those who had suffered in order to join

hypothesis A tentative and testable explanation of the relationship between two or more events or variables.

the group developed loyal attitudes about group action so they could justify their own choices.

The value of a theory is often measured in terms of the new ideas, or hypotheses, that can be derived from it and tested. A **hypothesis** is a tentative and testable explanation of the relationship between two or more events or variables. A *variable* is any factor that changes, or varies, in size or quality. Mood may be a variable, for example, since people's moods may vary from one situation to another. Test performance is another variable, since a person's score may vary from one test to the next. In the Aronson and Mills study, the variables were the difficulty of the lists the women were asked to read (easy or difficult) and how they rated the brief group discussion they overheard (boring or interesting). The researchers' hypothesis was their expectation that women who read the easy list would find the discussion boring, while those who read the difficult list would think the discussion had been interesting.

Since a hypothesis is a testable explanation of the relationship between variables, it may be a guess based on observations, or it could be a hunch about how ideas go together. An instructor may have a hypothesis about how varying teaching techniques will cause changes in students' test scores. The instructor may have formed this hypothesis by observing students; ideas about better teaching techniques are also generated from research in educational psychology.

paradigm A model of the functions and interrelationships of a process; a "way of thinking" about the world and how to study it.

Finally, our understanding of a complex process is also aided by using the correct paradigm. A **paradigm** is a model of the functions and interrelationships of a process, a "way of thinking" about the world and how to study it. Entire fields of knowledge, including psychology, can change directions when new paradigms challenge existing ones. When paradigms shift, revolutions of knowledge usually follow (Kuhn, 1970).

Before a new theory, hypothesis, or paradigm makes a difference in science, it has to undergo an "ordeal of proof." Most often this happens when researchers publish (make public) their findings, and other scholars investigate whether they find the same patterns in their own data. This process of publication and communication moves scientific research into the public eye, where ideas are tested and proven.

Research Biases. The hardest part of doing research is remaining objective, or free from bias. Most of your ideas and beliefs are probably colored by bias because they are influenced by your opinions or values. A variety of biases have been found to distort people's impressions of collected data. *External influences* such as one's culture or the media can influence people to accept a particular world view. *Personal bias* distorts estimating or evaluating processes as a result of personal beliefs, attributes, or past experiences. *Observer bias* operates when one's biases act as "filters" through which some events are noticed or seen as meaningful while others are not. It must be kept in mind that researchers themselves were raised in certain cultures, and that they are members of ethnic groups and particular social classes. They also have been exposed to certain gender role expectations. These background factors can all affect the way that researchers observe and interpret events in their lives.

Expectancy bias can affect observations of behavior by triggering reactions to the events being observed. Researchers sometimes expect to find specific outcomes, and being only human, they may see what they expect to see rather than remain objective. Unfortunately, if one is not alert to the possibility of expectancy bias, it may seem as though the observed events are being "discovered" instead of *created* by the observer's expectations.

Finally, *placebo biases* operate when people strongly want to believe a treatment is proving successful. Believing in the treatment may make an ineffective treatment appear effective. For example, many people may claim to feel better after taking a *placebo* such as a sugar pill. In those cases where the outcome involves a subjective judgment about results (how well you feel or whether your pain has been relieved), the desire for a drug or therapeutic method to work may be enough to achieve the desired result (see Roberts et al., 1993).

The Context of Justification

The **context of justification** is the second phase of research in which results are prepared for useful communication with other scientists. Psychologists face a difficult challenge when they try to get accurate data and reliable evidence that will generate valid conclusions. They rely on one ally to succeed: the scientific method. As we mentioned at the beginning of the chapter, scientific method is a general set of procedures for gathering and interpreting evidence in ways that limit errors and yield dependable conclusions. The scientific method also demands special attitudes and values on the part of research scientists.

Scientific Attitudes and Values. Scientists are motivated by a curiosity about the unknown and the uncertain. Since the truth may be disguised, the scientific method demands a critical and skeptical attitude toward any conclusion until it has been duplicated repeatedly by independent investigators. By remaining somewhat open-minded, scientists keep the truth "provisional"—subject to revision after new discoveries—but agree to evaluate phenomena they may personally doubt or suspect. For example, instead of rejecting any possibility that psychic processes like ESP (extrasensory perception) really exist, scientists collect evidence on which to base judgments.

Secrecy is banned from the research procedure because all data and methods must eventually be open for *public verifiability.* Other researchers must have the opportunity to review the data and conclusions and then attempt to replicate the results. Thus science is not a set of rules but rather a process of asking, observing, explaining, testing, and retesting explanations of reality.

Scientific knowledge is based on respect for empirical evidence obtained through controlled observation and careful measurement. In the realm of science, when good data clash with the opinions of experts, the data win. Science is a way of knowing; it is not a hierarchy of experts. You do not need a special degree to act like a scientist, but you *do* need to make a commitment to objectivity.

Objectivity Safeguards. Since subjectivity must be minimized in the data collection and analysis phases of scientific research, procedural safeguards are used to increase objectivity. These safeguards begin with keeping complete *records* of observations and data analyses in a form that other researchers can understand and evaluate. As a result, most scientific reports are written in a similar form and published by organizations of scientists. These reports communicate ideas to the entire scientific community and open those ideas to criticism.

A second safeguard is *standardization.* **Standardization** means using uniform, consistent procedures in all phases of data collection. All subjects should receive the same instructions and be treated in the same way. By applying a standard treatment for all participants in the course of study, researchers ensure they will have the same basic experiences.

A third safeguard involves standardizing the meaning of concepts, known as *operationalization.* An **operational definition** of a concept defines that concept in terms of how it is measured or what operations produce it. For example, an operational definition of the letter grade A in one psychology class might be "90% or higher of all test points possible." This definition tells you that this instructor calculates each student's total performance percentage to determine whether or not that person's work deserves an A.

Operational definitions are especially important because many psychological processes are popular issues and everyday concerns. For example, if a new drug promises to reduce anxiety, you need to know whether the drug manu-

How would you characterize the behavior of the girl in this picture? She may appear shy to you. Shyness can be operationalized in many different ways, including looking down, being silent, or standing apart from others. Shyness also can be operationalized in terms of ratings made by the child's parents, teachers, peers, or self-reports.

facturer's definition of anxiety is the same as yours. For you, "anxiety" may mean occasional nervousness before being evaluated or judged. But for the pharmaceutical company, "anxiety" could mean a set of symptoms experienced by patients in psychiatric hospitals. A drug developed to reduce that kind of anxiety may be inappropriate for you.

Researchers must also safeguard objectivity by *avoiding bias.* As we explained earlier, bias from external influences, personal beliefs, observers' perspectives, and human expectations can all distort data. To control, if not totally eliminate such biases, researchers use various *control procedures* to test hypotheses in ways that are fair and error-free. One control strategy is to keep subjects uninformed, or **blind,** about the purpose of the study; this makes them less likely to perform to researchers' expectations. An even better strategy is to employ uninformed testers to observe uninformed subjects, called the **double-blind control.** Similarly, when placebo effects might occur, researchers employ a **placebo control** and compare those who received actual treatment with those who received only attention or a "dummy drug." For example, to test whether a new drug will help people sleep, some subjects will be given the drug in tablet form while others are given an identical tablet that does not contain the drug (a placebo). If the drug is effective, those given the placebo will not sleep better or faster; if it is not effective, subjects' sleeping experiences will all be similar.

Finally, researchers must be careful to consider all possible influences on the behavior being studied. As discussed earlier in the text, the *independent variable* is the factor assumed to influence the behavior or mental process of interest, the *dependent variable.* If another factor—called a **confounding variable**—could be confused with the independent variable, it should be eliminated or controlled by keeping it the same ("constant"). For example, a teacher gives some students essay tests and others multiple-choice tests on the same material. Which students do you think will do better? Unfortunately, the essay students were all in early morning classes, while the multiple-choice students were in late afternoon classes. Because the time difference is confounded with the test difference, test performance cannot be clearly explained. The teacher should have kept the conditions as similar as possible, with the test type as the only difference, so that other explanations could be ruled out.

Psychological Research Methods

Research begins with an objective definition and a precise description of the process of interest. The goal of this first phase is to discover the relevant factors and determine how to measure or manipulate them. After this phase, the researcher wants to know which variables are related to one another, to what extent they are correlated, and whether they can be used to make accurate predictions. To find out if one variable is *causally* related to another, researchers turn to a special kind of investigation that relies on experimental methods. In this section we will outline some basic methods of psychological measurement that use *descriptive research* techniques, and we'll examine how psychologists use *correlational* and *experimental* methods.

Psychological Measurement. Because psychological processes are so varied and complex, they pose major challenges to researchers who want to measure them. The first challenge is to access the psychological phenomenon one wants to understand. A second challenge is to find the right measure, or the best *outcome variable,* to assess the psychological phenomenon described in the theory or hypothesis.

All attempts at measurement use some procedure to assign numbers to, or *quantify,* different levels, sizes, intensities, or amounts of a variable. Assigning numbers to variables increases the precision of scientific communication procedures and results.

blind   Uninformed about the purpose of a research study.

double-blind control   A control strategy that employs both uninformed experimenters and uninformed subjects.

placebo control   A control strategy where researchers compare those who received actual treatment with those who received only attention or a "dummy drug."

confounding variables   Factors that could be confused with the independent variable in a research study and thus distort the results.

"Find out who set up this experiment. It seems that half of the patients were given a placebo, and the other half were given a different placebo."

Psychologists use three important methods of descriptive measurement: self-reports, behavior analysis, and physiological measures. **Self-report measures** are verbal answers, either written or spoken, to questions posed by researchers. When you tell a poll-taker your age, occupation, and political preferences, you are providing a self-report. Self-reports cannot be obtained from preverbal or language-limited populations, and their accuracy is unreliable if respondents try to present themselves in socially desirable ways. Nonetheless, self-report measures such as questionnaires, surveys, and interviews are popular because they are often convenient and easy to obtain.

Behavioral measures are used to study overt actions and observable and recordable actions. Direct observations of subjects being studied or tested and naturalistic observations of subjects in their normal environments are useful ways to investigate many phenomena, especially when first identifying important variables and effects. For example, to study how college students form close relationships, you should begin by going where they go and watching them meet, make contact, and interact—but not in a laboratory.

Finally, **physiological measures** are often made to gather information about less observable processes like brain activity. For example, the *electroencephalogram (EEG)* is one apparatus for recording the electrical activity of the brain. The patterns of waveforms it records provide clues about which parts of the brain are involved in various activities. Physiological measures are difficult to obtain since they are *invasive* (they intrude on subjects' awareness and can change their behavior) and require sophisticated equipment and operation. Brain waves do not "lie" as people do when they are verbally responding to a questionnaire, but it is far easier to collect people's voluntary answers to questions than to harness them to so-called "lie detectors."

Correlational Methods. Psychologists use correlational methods when they want to determine to what extent two variables, traits, or attributes are related. Is intelligence related to creativity? Are optimists healthier than pessimists? These are correlational questions.

To determine the precise degree of correlation that exists between two variables, psychologists use two sets of scores to compute a statistical measure known as the **correlation coefficient** (r). When two variables are totally (100 percent) correlated, their correlation coefficient is +1.0; if they are negatively correlated—one increases as the other decreases—their coefficient is

self-report measures Verbal answers to researchers' questions.

behavioral measures Techniques used to study overt, observable, and recordable actions.

physiological measures Data based on subjects' biological responses to stimuli.

correlation coefficient A statistical measure used to determine the precise degree of correlation between two variables; symbolized as r.

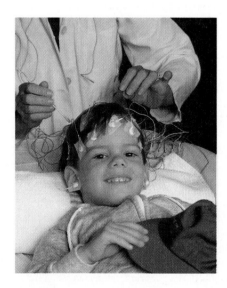
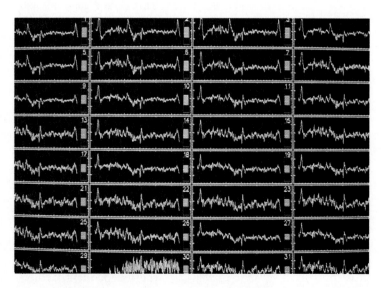

By connecting subjects to EEG, scientists can study the activity of the brain.

−1.0. If two variables are not correlated at all either positively or negatively, their correlation is zero (0).

For example, your grades in related courses might be strongly correlated: Probably your grades in a Painting course and those in a Drawing course have a correlation higher than +0.5. In contrast, your grades in unrelated courses, such as Painting and Basic Accounting, might be +0.15. Finally, the relationship between the number of hours you spend studying per week and the mistakes you make on tests should be negative because the *more* hours you study, the *fewer* mistakes you make. This correlation might be −0.20.

After data are collected, the correlation coefficient would be computed first to see whether two variables are related in any way. Later research would specify "any relationship" in greater detail. A strong correlation (approaching either −1.0 or +1.0) indicates that two sets of data vary together in a systematic way. The correlation does not ensure that one of them *causes* the other. It is very important to note that correlation does *not* imply causation. The correlation could reflect any one of several cause-and-effect possibilities or none whatsoever.

To clarify the difference between correlation and causation, consider this problem: How could you explain a positive correlation between religiousness and racism? One explanation might be that religiousness *causes* one to be racist. Another might be that racist attitudes *cause* people to follow certain religions. And one other explanation could be that a third set of influences (such as political conservatism) could be causing both religiousness *and* racism. The fact that the two are correlated does not "prove" that one caused the other; both may be related results of other, unmeasured influences.

An advantage of correlational studies is that they can establish relationships between variables that cannot be studied directly. Instead of assigning subjects to become religious or racist or politically conservative, correlational researchers study people who already describe themselves in these terms. However, by lumping respondents together in groups and taking sets of measurements, we lose the ability to make accurate predictions about individuals. Knowing that there is a correlation between heavy smoking and lung cancer does not equip us to predict whether a particularly heavy smoker, like your roommate, will develop lung cancer or remain healthy.

As convenient and informative as initial correlational research can be, it does not prove causality and cannot be as accurate or specific as most researchers wish. For those qualities, one must conduct experimental research.

Experimental Methods. Suppose you want an attractive classmate to like you. You notice that this person is smiling at you now, and you realize you are wearing a new cologne. Could the cologne be making you more attractive and *causing* this classmate to smile? If you are curious, you might start noticing days this individual does and does not glance your way. You might link that behavior to other factors: whether you're wearing cologne, what the weather is like, who else is around, and so on. Such a correlational study—one that examines how existing variables (cologne, weather, a person's smiling behavior) are related—can indicate whether these events might be connected. But as we have seen, correlation alone cannot confirm that wearing cologne causes your dream person to smile at you. For that you must conduct an experiment. Experimental methods are used to discover causal relationships between variables specified by the hypothesis being tested.

controlled experiment Observations of specific behavior made under systematically varied conditions, in which subjects have been randomly assigned to experimental and control (non-treatment) conditions.

Control. In a **controlled experiment**, observations of specific behavior are made under systematically varied conditions. An experimenter manipulates a stimulus and measures its effects on one or more behavioral outcomes. The behavior or experience that the experimenter predicts will change, as a result of the independent variable, is called the *dependent variable*. The experimenter observes or measures the dependent variable to discover whether it really does "depend" on the independent variable. All other conditions except the independent variable are held constant or controlled to prevent confounding (confusing them with the independent variable). Thus *control* is an essential ingredient of a useful experiment. Controlling other conditions allows the experimenter to concentrate on how the independent variable specifically affects the dependent variable.

To apply scientific control to your cologne/smiling question, you begin with a hypothesis: Perhaps the cologne is attractive to the person you like, whom we'll call *X*. Does the cologne *cause X* to smile at you? To find out, you must wear the cologne randomly on some days but not on others. Cologne (either present or absent) represents the independent variable. In addition, every day you must observe the person's smiling behavior; this is the dependent variable. You must also take into account the influence of other factors, such as the weather. For instance, if you wear cologne only on sunny days but not on rainy days, it will not be clear if the smiling behavior depends on cologne or on sunshine.

Random Assignment. A second essential ingredient of experimentation is **randomization**. Research subjects must be randomly assigned by chance procedures either to an **experimental condition** (exposed to the independent variable or treatment) or to a **control condition** (not exposed to the experimental treatment). "Random" means that before assignment, every subject has an equal chance of ending up in any of the conditions, experimental or control.

randomization Assignment of subjects so that every subject has an equal chance of ending up in any of the conditions, experimental or control.

experimental condition Condition in which research subjects are exposed to the independent variable or treatment in a controlled experiment; contrasted with control condition.

control condition Condition in which research subjects are not exposed to the experimental treatment in a controlled experiment; contrasted with experimental condition.

After the behavior or experience of each group is measured, the results from the experimental subjects can be compared to the results from the control subjects to determine whether there are meaningful differences. (A nonrandom assignment might involve letting subjects choose which of two testing times to attend, or assigning friendly subjects to one tester and unfriendly ones to the other. If this were done, and differences were later found between subject groups, the experimenter could not be certain the differences were caused by the independent variable rather than by the testing time or the friendliness of the subjects.)

Application: Does Frustration Cause Aggression? Consider how the experimental concepts we have just discussed are applied in the following example. A researcher wants to learn whether feeling frustrated will make people more aggressive. In experimental terms, she wants to study whether *frustration* (the independent variable) will cause or affect *aggression* (the dependent variable). First she must choose her subject population, the people she will observe in drawing her conclusions. Because she is a college student, she decides to study the behavior of several classmates, instead of the behavior of children, soldiers, or many other types of people who experience frustration and aggression.

frustration State assumed to exist when goal-directed activity is blocked in some manner.

Next, she must *operationally define* frustration. **Frustration** is conceptually defined as the experience of being blocked or prevented from reaching a goal. What operation can the experimenter perform in order to make her subjects feel frustrated? College students have many different goals, and many obstacles can interfere with reaching them. The experimenter chooses a familiar form of frustration: waiting in line. She recruits classmates to complete written assignments that require them to look up a journal article, photocopy the article, and answer questions about the article and the assignment. She promises to reward subjects only if they complete their work within a time limit. Unbeknownst to her subjects, however, she arranges for them to find either short lines or long lines of people waiting to use the library's photocopy machine. The operational definition of "high frustration" is "joining a long line to use the photocopier," because subjects trying to meet the deadline will be frustrated—blocked from achieving their goal—by losing time while they wait in line. In the "low frustration" condition, subjects will find no line or only a short line at the photocopy machine, causing them only a minimal delay.

aggression Physical or verbal behavior with the intent to hurt or destroy.

debriefing Procedure conducted with subjects at the end of an experiment, in which researcher explains hypothesis, reveals deception, and provides emotional support.

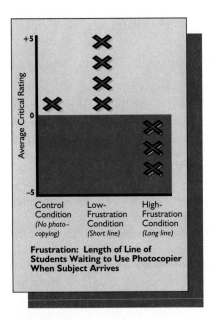

Figure 1.2 Does Frustration Cause Aggression?
In a hypothetical experiment subjects are exposed to either a control condition, a low-frustration condition, or a high-frustration condition. Later, all subjects are invited to rate their assignment as either positive or negative. If frustration causes aggression, those in the high-frustration condition will rate the assignment more negatively than those in the low-frustration or control conditions.

Frustration (the independent variable) is presumed to cause aggression (the dependent variable). Now the student researcher must operationally define aggression. **Aggression** is behavior intended to harm someone. There are many kinds of harm, ranging from constructuve criticism to destructive, violent action. The researcher chooses a relatively "safe" form of aggression: criticizing the assignment. After each subject has photocopied the article and completed the written assignment, he will receive a questionnaire inviting him to rate the experience on scales such as "worthless-worthwhile," "boring-interesting" and "unpleasant-pleasant."

Finally, the researcher randomly assigns her volunteer subjects to the one of two experimental conditions of the independent variable: waiting in a long line, or waiting in a short line. She also assigns some subjects to a control condition, in which they are not required to make photocopies at all. When students in the "long line" ("high frustration") condition go to the library, the researcher has *confederates* (people who are working with her) pose as fellow students waiting in line to use the photocopier. No confederates join the line when students in the "short line" ("low frustration") condition go to the library.

At the end of the assignment, all students turn in their essays and complete the questionnaire, including criticizing the assignment. If frustration causes aggression, then students who waited in the long line will offer more critical (aggressive) judgments than either short-line subjects or control subjects. Because subjects were randomly assigned to the three treatments, it must be the experience of waiting or not waiting in line-not differences between the students themselves—that causes differences in how negative their ratings are in criticizing the assignment. **Figure 1.2** illustrates the relationship the researcher expects to find among the data she collects.

Obtaining the results does not end the experiment! The experimenter owes each subject an explanation of what really took place—deliberately manipulating the photocopier line to create frustration—as well as a chance for the subject to complain, discuss the experience, and ask questions. In this process, known as **debriefing,** the experimenter explains the research hypothesis and the justification for having deceived and frustrated subjects. It is especially important to make sure that no subject leaves the experiment feeling confused, upset, or embarrassed. Valuable research is impossible without the assistance and cooperation of volunteer subjects. All researchers are obligated to provide such explanations to subjects in order to obtain their *informed consent* (see "In Focus: Ethical Issues in Human and Animal Research").

Critiquing the Experimental Method. There are limits and disadvantages to psychologists relying on the experimental method. First, during an experiment, behavior is often studied in an artificial environment, the *laboratory,* where the situation and conditions are controlled so heavily that behavior is a distortion of what would occur naturally. Second, research subjects typically know they are in an experiment and are being tested and measured. They may react to this awareness by trying to please the researcher, guess the purpose of the research, or behave in a different way than if they were unaware of being monitored. An experiment is a simplified version of reality, and at times it is too simplified to tell us much about real life. Third, some people challenge experimental research on ethical grounds. The "In Focus" box provides a more detailed look at the ethical issues raised by research.

Becoming a Wiser Research Consumer

Books, magazines, tabloids, and television "infomercials" frequently promise that your life can be improved if you will follow the simple rules of a program, technique, course, or miraculous treatment that can be purchased "for a limited time only!" How can you tell the difference between a deceptive claim and

Research

ETHICAL ISSUES IN HUMAN AND ANIMAL RESEARCH

Respect for the basic rights of humans and animals who participate in psychological research is a fundamental obligation of all researchers. To guarantee that these rights are honored, special committees oversee every research proposal, imposing strict guidelines issued by the U.S. Department of Health and Human Services. Psychology departments at universities and colleges, hospitals, and research institutes each have review panels that approve and reject proposals for human and animal research. The American Psychological Association (1982) has established detailed guidelines for ethical standards for researchers. We will review several of the most common ethical concerns and the guidelines developed to address them: informed consent; risk/gain assessment; intentional deception; debriefing; and animal research.

Informed Consent

Typically all research with human subjects begins with a description of the procedures, risks, and benefits each subject might experience. After they receive this information, subjects are asked to sign statements indicating that they have given their *informed consent* to participate, and they know they can leave an experiment whenever they wish. Subjects are also invited to contact the experimenters for further information.

Risk/Gain Assessment

In most psychological experiments, the risk to subjects is minimal (for example, eye strain from focusing on visual stimuli). Some procedures, however, can be upsetting or disturbing because they involve emotional reactions or social pressures. Subjects' physical and psychological well-being is a priority of all research, so these risks must be minimized, explained, and safeguarded by precautions. The same procedures apply to animal research, where humane and considerate treatment is essential.

Intentional Deception

For some kinds of research, advance explanations make unbiased study impossible. Informed subjects may be too self-conscious to behave in a natural or genuine way. For example, if a subject is told that an experiment examines how people deal with extreme frustration, anticipating trouble may lead the subject to cope better (or perhaps worse) than usual. In such cases subjects are usually deceived with a cover story that distorts the true nature or purpose of the experiment. For example, subjects may be told that the experiment focuses on problem-solving strategies; this half-truth omits any mention of frustration, and it avoids alarming subjects in advance. After the experiment, all subjects are debriefed by being given a full and honest account of the experiment's true purpose and assumptions.

Advocates of such limited deception argue that most subjects enjoy participation and, when debriefed, accept having been deceived. But critics argue that this does not excuse deception, which violates every subject's basic right of informed consent. Most researchers seek compromise by (1) avoiding designs that would require deception, (2) minimizing deception when it is used, and (3) debriefing all subjects thoroughly after their participation.

Debriefing

During debriefing, the researcher provides as much information as possible about the study after it is completed, making certain that no subject departs with any remaining confusion, discomfort, or embarrassment. If subjects were deceived or misled, the deception and its rationale are completely explained, and all questions are answered. Ultimately, subjects have the right to withdraw their data if they feel abused or misused in any way.

Animal Research

In recent years, concern over the care and treatment of animals used in

psychological and biomedical research has led to the development of strict guidelines that researchers must follow to obtain funding and approval. Laboratory facilities must be maintained properly, use qualified staff, and monitor animals' health and well-being. Pain and discomfort must be minimized, and the least stressful treatments must be applied whenever possible.

The debate over animal testing and research goes beyond issues of ethics. It centers on society's recognition of the contributions that animal and human research make every day to the health and well-being of all species, notably in drugs for humans and veterinary medicine for domestic animals. Today, animal researchers subscribe to higher standards of care and concern than most keepers of companion animals (pets) and farm animals. Attitudes about animal research may also be complicated by images of "cute" creatures (such as dogs, cats, and mice) versus those regarded with less sympathy (such as slugs, worms, and rats).

Ultimately, all citizens must keep themselves informed about the total costs and benefits of animal research to humans *and* to animals. Taking uninformed actions to end such research would be both unnecessary and self-defeating. In a democracy, as in scientific endeavors, rational information should guide decisions.

Psychology is often misrepresented in media such as talk shows and self-help books.

a genuine breakthrough? (See "Time Out for Critical Thinking.") You must become an informed consumer of psychological research. Our society is rich in information, and we are surrounded by claims of truth, false "commonsense" myths, and biased conclusions that serve special interests. To be a responsible citizen you must hone your critical thinking skills and assess the believability of claims made about "what research shows."

Although it plays an increasing role in our everyday lives, psychology is often misrepresented in media such as talk shows and self-help books. Professional psychologists are challenged to keep the public accurately informed about what the discipline has to offer. A major goal of formal education is to help the learner understand how the world functions and how to separate superstition and faulty thinking from fact and reason. In general, the more formal education a person has, the less that person believes in miracles, the occult, and the paranormal. However, national surveys of public opinion reveal that for many of the 25 million American adults without high-school diplomas, the world is a confusing and threatening place that operates in incomprehensible ways. They feel that they are controlled by fate and can do little to control their lives. It follows that such people are inclined to believe in lucky numbers, cosmic signs, omens, horoscopes, and mystical forces. Many believe that "scientific researchers have a power that makes them dangerous." Even more agree that "the only way we can know what is going on is to rely on leaders and experts who can be trusted" (J. D. Miller, 1987). Such beliefs are sometimes shared by educated people, indicating that our schools fail to provide the conceptual framework for separating superstition and science fiction from scientific understanding and fact.

The multimillion-dollar *pseudoscience industry* sells diverse products to the legions of "true believers" who are prepared to accept the unexplained, the unevaluated, and the unproven. The hucksters and hawkers who seek to sell their wares ("simple" solutions to personal unhappiness, political turmoil, or economic injustice) may offer their own leadership as a substitute for rational systems. Since unfounded authorities can mislead and betray our trust, we must cultivate an open-minded skepticism about others who would totally restructure our view of reality.

Psychology is inevitably a part of your real world. Every day you address the same issues psychologists do: You ask questions about your own behavior and that of other people, you seek answers in your theories or observations of what "authorities" say, and you check out the answers against the evidence available to you. As part of your formal education, psychology will help you make wiser decisions based on the evidence collected. Some of these decisions are the everyday ones about which products to buy or services to use. Others are more substantial and affect your entire life-style and perhaps even the life of this planet.

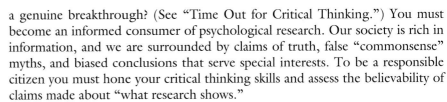

➡ TIME OUT . . . FOR CRITICAL THINKING

As a preview of coming events, here are some general rules to learn and apply in becoming a more sophisticated shopper in the supermarket of knowledge. Evaluate each one, and consider ways to incorporate these strategies in your own life. As you progress through chapters to come, flip back to this checklist occasionally and review these practical guidelines.

- How can you avoid the assumption that correlation is causation?

- Can you define critical terms and key concepts operationally so that there can be consensus about their meanings?

- Consider first how to disprove a theory, hypothesis, or belief before seeking confirming evidence or justification. What is the advantage of this process?

- Be wary of personal testimonials and case studies that don't offer objective data or comparative base rates and that have special conditions associated with their success or failure. Why are such appeals unreliable?

- How might you search for alternative explanations to the obvious ones proposed, especially when the explanations benefit the proposer?

- Could your own personal biases be distorting your perceptions of reality?

- Know the gender, cultural background, ethnicity, and social class background of the person making the claims. Why is this important?

- Why should you be suspicious of simple answers to complex questions or single causes and cures for complex effects and problems?

- Question any statement about the effectiveness of some treatment, intervention, or roduct by finding the comparative basis for the effect. To what is it being compared?

- Be cognitively flexible. Although you recognize that most conclusions are tentative and not certain, how can you keep yourself open to change and revision?

- Why is it a fallacy to explain social and psychological problems in terms of the people alleged to cause them rather than the situations that influence their behavior?

- Do you have the courage to challenge authority that is unjust, uses personal opinion in place of evidence for conclusions, and is not open to constructive criticism?

SUMMING UP

Our beliefs, motives, and expectations can influence our interpretation of reality. Our conclusions are often subject to personal biases, observer biases, expectancy biases, and placebo biases. Psychologists use scientific theories, testable hypotheses, and creative paradigms to unravel the mysteries of mind and behavior.

Psychological researchers use the scientific method to test ideas developed within the context of discovery. The scientific method encourages curiosity, open-minded skepticism, and a reliance on empirical data. The scientific method also establishes a set of procedures to increase objectivity and reduce errors and bias in research-based conclusions. Good research depends on standardizing the administration of all parts of a study, operationally defining key terms, and using control procedures to safeguard against confounding variables.

To describe and communicate research results, psychologists quantify measures of behavior and mental processes. Variables are measured by various techniques, each with both advantages and disadvantages: verbal self-reports, overt behavioral responses, and physiological responses.

After describing the variables of interest, researchers use correlational and experimental methods to understand, predict, and control behavior.

Correlational methods are best for the early stages of research; they help us discover which variables are related and how strongly they are related. Experimental methods are designed for testing hypotheses about the causal relationship between two variables. Correlational studies use sets of scores or other data to quantify the degree of relationship, generating a correlation coefficient. Strong correlations often allow for predictions of behavior, but these cannot be used as proof of causation, since correlated variables can be related in many different ways. The essential parts of conducting a controlled experiment are (1) systematically varying the independent variable; (2) controlling extraneous variables; (3) randomly assigning subjects to conditions; (4) standardizing testing procedures; and (5) precisely measuring behavioral outcomes.

With better knowledge of psychological research you will understand how information is collected and how to apply it. Honing your critical thinking skills will enable you to become a wiser consumer of research information. The pseudoscience industry presents ideas to the public with little or no explanation or proof of validity. Everyone can become a wiser and better protected research consumer by understanding research techniques, developing a skeptical but open-minded perspective, and insisting on standards for evidence and justice.

CHAPTER REVIEW

1 Psychology: Definitions, Goals, and Tasks   *What is psychology? How is psychology related to other disciplines? What are the distinctive goals of psychology?*

Psychology is the study of the behavior and mental processes of individuals. The scientific goals of psychology are to describe, predict, explain, and help control behavior. An applied goal is to help improve human functioning. The objective data that psychology uses are observable stimuli and responses. Behavior is a function of the characteristics of the individual and the stimulus. The context of the stimulus also affects behavioral outcome.

Key Terms

psychology, p. 5
scientific method, p. 5
behavior, p. 5
behavioral data, p. 6
intervening variables, p. 7

base rate, p. 8
independent variable, p. 8
dependent variable, p. 8

2 Psychology's Historical Foundations   *What is meant by the statement that "Psychology has a long past, but its real history is short"? What was the first formal approach to the study of psychology? How did later approaches differ?*

Structuralism emerged from the work of Wundt and Titchener. It emphasized the structure of the mind and behavior built from elemental sensations. Functionalism, developed by Dewey and James, emphasized the purpose behind behavior. Evolutionism, developed by Darwin, focuses on how organisms adapt to the challenges of changing environments over millions of years and pass on their genes to subsequent generations.

Key Terms	Major Contributors
determinism, p. 10	Wilhelm Wundt, p. 10
structuralism, p. 12	William James, p. 11
functionalism, p. 12	Edward Titchener, p. 11
evolutionism, p. 12	John Dewey, p. 12

3 Current Psychological Perspectives

Which perspectives or conceptual approaches are currently considered most useful to psychologists? What differences emerge when you compare these perspectives to each other?

Each of the six approaches to studying psychology differs in its view of human nature, the determinants of behavior, the focus of study, and the primary research approach. The biological perspective studies relationships between behavior and brain mechanisms. The psychodynamic perspective looks at behavior as driven by instinctive forces, inner conflicts, and unconscious motivations. The behavioristic perspective stresses mental processes that intervene between stimulus and response. According to the cognitive perspective, all human action is based on thinking, a process for which the brain is naturally designed. The humanistic perspective emphasizes an individual's capacity to make rational choices. Finally, the evolutionary perspective looks at human mental abilities as having evolved as adaptations for survival in the environment.

Key Terms	Major Contributors
biological approach, p. 13	Sigmund Freud, p. 14
psychodynamic approach, p. 14	John B. Watson, p. 15
behavioristic approach, p. 15	Ivan Pavlov, p. 15
behaviorism, p. 15	B. F. Skinner, p. 15
conditioning, p. 15	
cognitive approach, p. 16	
humanistic approach, p. 16	
evolutionary approach, p. 17	

4 Psychological Research

Why do you need to understand scientific research in order to learn about psychology? How can you use such an understanding in becoming a wiser research consumer?

In the discovery phase of research, observations, beliefs, and information lead to a new way of thinking about a phenomenon. External or internal biases can distort the discovery phase. In the justification phase, ideas are tested and either disconfirmed or proven. Researchers use the scientific method, and they must maintain objectivity by keeping complete records, standardize procedures, make operational definitions, minimize biases, and control error. A reliable result is one that can be repeated in similar conditions by independent investigators.

Descriptive research techniques include self-reports, behavior analysis, physiological measures, questionnaires, surveys, interviews, and psychological tests. Correlational research determines whether and how much two variables are related. Experimental methods determine causal relationships between variables specified by the hypothesis being tested. Respect for the rights of human and animal subjects is the obligation of all research, and various ethical guidelines provide safeguards for the protection of subjects. Becoming a wise research consumer involves learning how to think critically and knowing how to evaluate claims about what research shows.

Key Terms

empirical investigation, p. 21
context of discovery, p. 21
theory, p. 21
hypothesis, p. 22
paradigm, p. 22
context of justification, p. 23
standardization, p. 23
operational definition, p. 23
blind, p. 24
double-blind control, p. 24
placebo control, p. 24
confounding variable, p. 24
self-report measures, p. 25
behavioral measures, p. 25

physiological measures, p. 25
correlation coefficient, p. 25
controlled experiment, p. 26
randomization, p. 27
experimental condition, p. 27
control condition, p. 27
frustration, p. 27
aggression, p. 28
debriefing, p. 28

PRACTICE TEST

Chapter 1: Mind, Behavior, and Science

For each of the following items, choose the single correct or best answer. Correct answers, explanations, and page references appear in the Appendix.

1. Because psychology is a science, psychological principles must be based on _____ .
   A. rational speculation
   B. recognized philosophical traditions
   C. the evidence of data gathered by the senses
   D. each observer's subjective interpretation of events

2. In determining whether to admit a new student, most colleges consider an applicant's secondary school records. This illustrates that a common form of prediction is based on the assumption that people's _____ are a good indicator of their future behavior.
   A. past actions
   B. personality profiles
   C. drives and motives
   D. family relationships

3. For many psychologists, _____ is the central, most powerful goal of the discipline. This may reflect a bias distinctive among Western world cultures.
   A. explanation
   B. control
   C. prediction
   D. healing

4. Although psychology has been characterized as having a "long past," it has a short history. Its origins are usually traced to the late 19th century, when _____ established the first psychological laboratory.
   A. Wilhelm Wundt
   B. William James
   C. Edward Titchener
   D. John B. Watson

5. "To understand consciousness or behavior, you must focus on the probable purpose of a specific action." This statement best reflects the perspective of _____ .
   A. functionalism
   B. structuralism
   C. behaviorism
   D. evolutionism

6. According to the _____ perspective in psychology, behavior and personality are the result of inner tensions and unconscious conflicts created when one's selfish wishes are restricted by societal controls.
   A. biological
   B. humanistic
   C. behavioristic
   D. psychodynamic

7. According to the evolutionary approach in modern psychology, human behavior has evolved in the direction of ever greater _____ .
   A. integration of mind, body, behavior, and culture
   B. adaptation and genetic survival
   C. information processing
   D. conflict between the individual and society

8. Which of the following psychological specialties is *not* concerned with delivering services and treatment in the solution of personal and social problems?
   A. community psychology
   B. counseling psychology
   C. social psychology
   D. clinical psychology

9. In psychological research, a _____ is a tentative and testable explanation of the relationship between two events or variables.
   A. hypothesis
   B. theory
   C. model
   D. paradigm

10. A researcher compares the reactions of two randomly divided groups of children attending a summer camp. One group is told scary stories every night before bedtime. The other group listens to a variety of stories that are funny or interesting but never frightening. At the end of one week, the researcher finds that those who heard frightening stories prefer more group activities than the children who did not hear frightening stories. Which of the following statements about this research is *not* true?
    A. The experimental group was the group that heard the frightening stories.
    B. The type of stories is the independent variable.
    C. Preference for group activities is the dependent variable.
    D. This is an example of a correlational investigation.

IF YOU'RE INTERESTED . . .

Career encounters in psychology. (Video: 1991, color, 30 minutes).

  Several psychologists with diverse careers describe their work in this American Psychological Association documentary.

Colman, A. M. (1987). *Facts, fallacies, and frauds in psychology.* London: Hutchinson.

  Short, readable, and fascinating review of myths and realities in psychological theory and research.

Eysenck, H. J. (1988). *Fact and fiction in psychology.* Baltimore: Penguin Books.

  Engaging review of what is and is not known in the realm of scientific psychology, written by one of its most articulate ambassadors to popular culture.

Fancher, R. E. (1990). *Pioneers of psychology* (2nd ed.). New York: W. W. Norton & Co.

  Collected brief biographies of the men and women who established and developed psychology as a scientific discipline.

Gay, P. (1988). *Freud: A life for our time.* New York: W. W. Norton & Co.

  The definitive biography by the foremost Freud historian of our day, told sympathetically and yet realistically.

Hilgard, E. R. (1987). *Psychology in America: A historical survey.* New York: Harcourt Brace Jovanovich.

  An interesting reference work that describes the historical context, lives, and personal endeavors that distinguished psychology in research, academia, and professional practice in the United States.

Hunt, M. (1993). *The story of psychology.* New York: Doubleday.

  A fascinating history of the lives and times of the "Magellans of the mind," from ancient philosophy to modern research.

Stanovich, K. E. (1989). *How to think straight about psychology* (2nd ed.). Glenview, IL: Scott, Foresman.

  Very practical handbook for surviving and thriving by using what you know about psychological research and applications.

Woods, P. (1987). *Is psychology the major for you?* Washington, D.C.: American Psychological Association.

  Everything you ever wanted to know about how and why to major in psychology—and what kind of life and career you might expect after college.

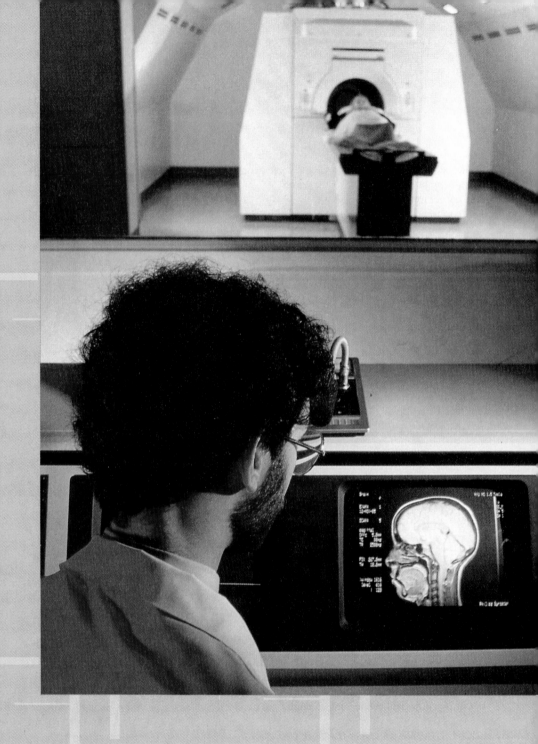

Chapter 2 **Biopsychology**

1. According to Charles Darwin's theory of evolution, how does the environment influence species' biology? How can human development be better understood through genetics?

2. How has modern science influenced the link between psychology and biology? What are the three layers or structures of the brain, and how do their functions account for human behavior?

3. What are the body's two communication systems? How is the organization of the nervous system related to behavior and experience?

4. What does research indicate about the connection between the cerebral hemispheres and consciousness? What do researchers mean when they talk about our "two brains"? Why can the human brain be described as "responsive"?

Five-and-a-half weeks before her twins were due, Christine felt the first sharp pains of labor. Her husband drove her to the hospital where, for 16 hours, the two of them followed the breathing instructions they had learned in their natural-childbirth class. Then a fetal monitor showed that the heartbeat of one of the babies was weakening. Doctors quickly performed a cesarean section. Within minutes, Nicole (4 pounds) and Alexis (3 pounds 14 ounces) had entered the world.

Immediately after birth, Nicole and Alexis joined half a dozen other babies in the Neonatal Intensive Care Unit. For two-and-a-half weeks, electronic devices monitored their vital signs. Experienced nurses tended to their physical needs and held them frequently. Christine spent a good part of each day with her babies, holding and rocking them and feeding them her breast milk from bottles, awaiting the day when she could actually breast-feed them. Wearing diapers barely the size of cocktail napkins, the twins looked fragile and unfinished. With no layers of baby fat, every little rib in their bodies showed.

Had Nicole and Alexis been born 20 years earlier, their first few weeks of life would have been quite different. Until the late 1970s, prematurely born infants were touched as little as possible. Parents and medical personnel feared that any unnecessary contact with the outside world might harm the babies. Fortunately for Nicole and Alexis, we now know better.

Research with infant rats and humans has led scientists to conclude that brain functioning can be altered by touch, and that touch is essential for normal growth and development of newborns. Biologist **Saul Schanberg** found that when rat pups were removed from their mothers, the levels of an enzyme important for growth decreased dramatically (Schanberg et al., 1990). The longer they were deprived of maternal contact, the less responsive the pups became. The effects of maternal deprivation could be reversed in only two ways: by returning them to the mother, who immediately started licking them, or by having a researcher vigorously stroke them with a small paintbrush to mimic the mother's massaging. Schanberg (1990) concluded that "the need for a mother's touch is really brain based. It isn't just nice to have it. It's a requirement for the normal development and growth of the baby."

Complementing this research with animals are current studies by psychologist **Tiffany Field,** who collaborated with Schanberg (Field & Schanberg, 1990) to conduct studies of prematurely born human infants. Her research team randomly selected 20 preemies to receive periodic massages throughout the day, while 20 others received normal hospital treatment in the intensive care unit, which did not

Tiffany Field (*Discovering Psychology,* 1990, Program 3)

include massages. According to Field, "The premature babies who were massaged for 45 minutes a day for ten days before they were discharged gained 47 percent more weight than the babies who did not get massaged. They were more active. They were more alert." Eight months later, the massaged babies had maintained their weight advantage and were also more advanced in motor, cognitive, and emotional development (Field, 1990). This research is being extended and replicated in larger samples of preemies in order to establish the effects of human touch on biological and psychological health.

In the United States, more than a quarter of a million infants are born prematurely each year. Those who are touched and cuddled leave the hospital several days sooner than they would have otherwise, reducing health-care costs by about $3,000 per child. Unfortunately, not all hospitals apply what scientists have learned about the positive effects of early touch on development. If they did, the lives of thousands of children would be improved, and billions of dollars would be saved each year—two very practical benefits of this basic research.

When Nicole and Alexis left the hospital, they were still rather small, but they were developing so well that the doctors felt confident they would be alright. At home, the babies shared a crib in the living room, where relatives and friends who remarked on their tiny size were encouraged to pick them up gently and cuddle them. Christine and her husband were acutely aware that such physical stimulation is apparently critical for optimal development of the brain and, in turn, the mental and physical processes that the brain controls.

Introduction

When fully matured, the adult brain weighs only 3 pounds, less than Nicole and Alexis did at birth. Even though it weighs little and is made up of the same basic chemical molecules found throughout the universe, the brain is the most complex structure in the known universe. This biocomputer contains more cells than there are stars in our entire galaxy; it contains over 100 billion nerve cells designed to communicate and store information. This biochemical structure holds the basis for communicating all the information that is possible for the brightest of us to know or the most sensitive of us to experience.

The human brain has developed over millions of evolutionary years. The brain is the subject of study for a new breed of researchers in the rapidly emerging field of *neuroscience,* in which several disciplines work together to understand the functioning of the nervous system. The psychologists in neuroscience also work as researchers in *biopsychology,* a rapidly growing area of psychology that studies the relationship among biology, behavior, and environment. Biopsychologists seek to identify the biochemical mechanisms that underlie the actions of all living creatures, and they want to explain how these components cooperate to produce all the complex forms of human action. Ultimately, the questions biopsychologists want to answer are these: How does the human mind emerge from this mass of tangled organic tissue? How does the biological machinery of the brain and nervous system become the basis for intelligent life? How can a series of on-off electrical impulses within the brain's nerve cells be the stuff of which our dreams, thoughts, feelings, motives, and actions are made?

It may seem strange to *use* your brain in order to *understand* your brain. This conscious aspect of one's mind—the sense of self that looks out at the world and in at its own thoughts and mortality—seems to exist independently of its biology. We may even think of the body as mere flesh, "inferior" to the sophisticated realm of the higher mind. But when brain cells are destroyed by disease, drugs, and accidents, we are dramatically reminded of the biological basis of the human mind. In such cases, we are forced to recognize the physical matter from which sensation and language, learning and memory, passion and pain, and human reason and madness spring forth.

In this chapter, we will first examine how evolution and heredity determine our biology and behavior. Next, we will consider what research reveals about the workings of the brain. Finally, we will see that external stimulation can actually modify the brain, changing both its structure and how it functions. You may find this material more challenging than the rest of *Psychology* since it involves the terms and operations of anatomy. You will also probably find that the results are worth the challenge: Understanding your biological nature will help you to appreciate how the brain, mind, behavior, and environment interact to create the unique experience of being human—your humanity.

Evolution, Brain, and Behavior

How did this marvelous piece of biology called the brain come to be, and why are the brains of all species, although similar, so different? The first question requires us to consider **evolution,** the theory that over time, organisms originate and adapt to their unique environments. The second leads to a review of **heredity,** the biological transmission of traits from parents to offspring.

evolution   The theory that over time organisms originate and adapt to their unique environments.

heredity   The biological transmission of traits from parents to offspring.

Human Evolution

About 50 years before Wilhelm Wundt established psychology's first experimental laboratory, **Charles Darwin,** a new college graduate, set sail on a five-year cruise that would have an enormous impact upon his life and upon the history of science. In 1831 the *H.M.S. Beagle,* an ocean research vessel, left England to survey the coast of South America. During the trip, Darwin studied every life form and fossil he encountered, building on this evidence to write his most famous book, *On the Origin of Species,* published in 1859. It was in this work that Darwin set forth science's grandest theory: the *evolution* of life on this planet.

Darwin's observations convinced him that some natural mechanism influenced the breeding of organisms from one generation to the next, so that species ultimately either (1) adapted to their environments or (2) failed to adapt and became extinct. Specifically, plants' and animals' characteristics (such as physical size, coloring, and abilities) are either favored by the forces of nature and preserved, or they are not favored and consequently end up being destroyed. The result of this process over time, claimed Darwin, "would be the formation of a new species" (Darwin, 1887).

natural selection   The theory that the forces of nature *select* the organisms—and the features of those organisms—that will survive, reproduce, and pass their advantageous traits to the next generation.

Natural Selection.   Darwin called his theory—that some members of a species tend to produce more offspring than others—the theory of **natural selection.** The forces of nature *select* the organisms (and the features of those organisms) that will survive, reproduce, and pass their advantageous traits to the next generation. Organisms that have adapted well to their environment, whatever it happens to be, will produce more offspring than those less well adapted. Over time, those organisms that possess traits more favorable for survival will become more numerous than those organisms that do not possess those traits. In evolutionary terms, an individual's success is measured only by the number of offspring he or she produces. For example, while many people in the world need corrective lenses to see, they are outnumbered by people who have good vision. Presumably this is because long ago, before glasses were invented, good vision was important for survival, and parents with excellent vision produced more offspring and protected them better than people with worse vision. Regardless of the other qualities and personalities involved, the genes for good vision helped the individual who possessed them to be an evolutionary success.

Charles Darwin (1809–1882)

phenotype Observable features by which individuals are recognized.

genotype Genetic structure inherited from one's parents.

bipedalism The ability to walk upright.

encephalization Increases in brain size.

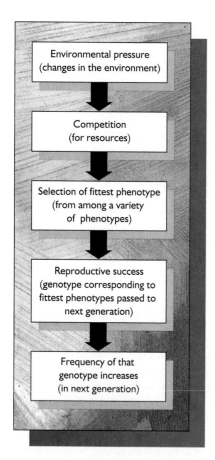

Figure 2.1 How Natural Selection Works
Environmental changes create competition for resources among species members. Only those individuals possessing characteristics instrumental in coping with these changes will survive and reproduce. The next generation will have a greater number of individuals possessing these genetically based traits.

Variation and Competition. Although the environment is the driving force behind natural selection, it is not the only factor. Two other factors, variation and competition, also play key roles.

Variation refers to differences in biological and psychological traits among individuals within a given population. Some people are big and strong; others are intelligent; and still others are big, strong, and intelligent. Features by which individuals are recognized make up the **phenotype.** The phenotype is the outward expression of an individual's **genotype,** the genetic structure inherited from one's parents. Genotypes determine the extent to which the environment can influence an organism's development and behavior. Any organism's phenotype is determined by only one process: the interaction of the organism's genotype with the environment. For example, imagine two sisters who have inherited a similar genotype for light hair. One works outdoors, where the sun bleaches her hair lighter, and the other sister works indoors, so they end up with different phenotypes. Ultimately, natural selection operates at the level of the genotype; if the phenotype is not well adapted to an environment, then neither is the particular genotype that gave rise to it.

Now consider how environmental conditions contribute to *competition* in the natural selection process. Suppose that a particular species of animal occupies a *habitat* (a set of food resources and living conditions) with only one edible plant. Sudden climate changes wipe out much of that plant, and the animals that feed on it are threatened with extinction. A few of them, however, have an inherited tendency (their genotype) to behave in more creative, exploratory ways (the phenotype); they try other sources of food, including plants and insects they formerly avoided. The animals that lack this inherited tendency go hungry and die seeking the increasingly scarce plant they prefer. Ultimately, environmental competition favors the adventurous phenotype and the genotype that causes it. The omnivorous creatures survive the drastic weather, thrive, procreate, and eventually outnumber the picky eaters. The first stage of this process can already be seen in the changing food habits of grizzly bears in the Northwest American forests. Faced with shortages of traditional food supplies, some bears have turned to a new diet of moths. Moths are high in nutritional value and plentiful at certain times of the year. The adventurous eaters, as well as their offspring, are more likely to survive than those bears who restrict their diet to familiar but scarce foods.

Environmental competition has sharpened the *selective advantage* of particular genetically based variations among organisms. Trace this example through **Figure 2.1,** which depicts a simplified model of natural selection through the processes of variation and competition.

The Human Advantage. How has natural selection shaped the selective advantages of human biology and behavior? Consider how our life-style, with all of its conveniences and luxuries, is the result of the natural selection of certain genotypes passed along to us from our ancient ancestors. Social and biological scientists now know that, in the evolution of our species, natural selection favored two adaptations: *bipedalism* and *encephalization.* **Bipedalism** refers to the ability to walk upright, and **encephalization** refers to increases in brain size. Together these two adaptations made possible the rise of human civilization. They are responsible for most, if not all, of the other major advances in human evolution, including cultural development (see **Figure 2.2**).

The ability to walk upright made humans better able to explore and relocate than other species. Increases in brain size—especially in certain kinds of brain tissue—led to increased capacity for complex thinking, reasoning, remembering, and planning. Ultimately, only intelligent bipedal humans survived to reproduce and roam the earth's varied habitats.

After bipedalism and encephalization, perhaps the other most important evolutionary milestone for our species was the advent of *language* (see

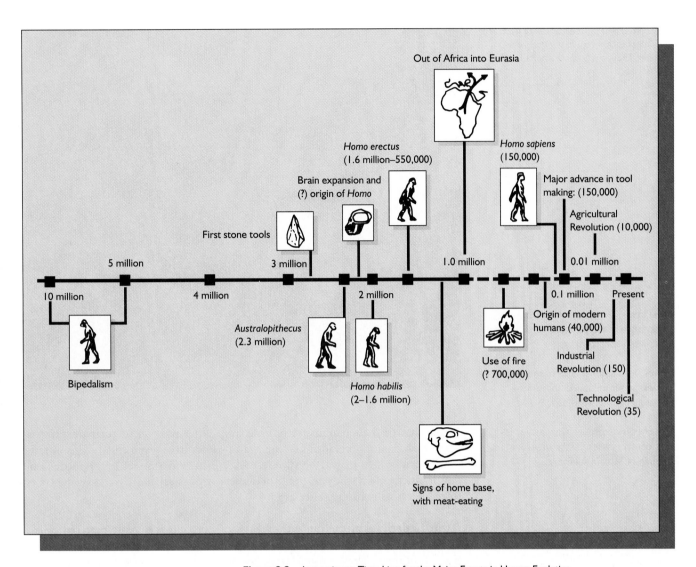

Figure 2.2 Approximate Time Line for the Major Events in Human Evolution
Bipedalism freed the hands for grasping and tool use. Encephalization provided the capacity for higher cognitive processes such as abstract thinking and reasoning. These two adaptations probably led to the other major advances in human evolution.

Diamond, 1990). The capacity for language, of course, stemmed directly from encephalization. Language makes possible interactions as simple as instructions for tool use or as complex as historical documentation. Language is the basis for *cultural evolution*, the tendency of cultures to respond adaptively to environmental change through learning and to transmit knowledge across generations.

The marvelous piece of biology that is the human brain exists because it was favored by natural selection in our ancestors' quest for survival. Our brains differ from those of other species for much the same reason (Harvey & Krebs, 1990). The earliest humans lived and survived in an environment different from those of other species, so their brains evolved differently to meet the needs of that environment.

Genes and Behavior

Despite a similar heritage, children are different from their parents. One reason is that children grow up and live in different environments than their parents did. Another difference is that children possess a unique combination of genes

Genotype coding for the capacity to learn and think abstractly has made cultural evolution possible. These are Native American petroglyphs (rock carvings).

genetics The study of heredity—the inheritance of physical and psychological traits from ancestors.

genes Functional units of the chromosomes; genes influence heredity by directing protein synthesis.

sex chromosomes Chromosomes that contain genes for the development of male or female anatomy.

We have significant genetic similarities to our parents, making us like them in many ways.

unlike that of their parents. A mother and father pass on to their offspring a part of what past generations of their family lines have given them. This inheritance results in a distinct biological blueprint and timetable for individual development. The study of the inheritance of physical and psychological traits from ancestors is called **genetics.**

Brain Genetics. In the nucleus of each of our cells is genetic material called DNA (deoxyribonucleic acid). DNA contains the instructions for the production of proteins. These proteins regulate the body's physiological processes and the expression of phenotypic traits: body build, physical strength, intelligence, and many behavior patterns. DNA is organized into tiny units called **genes** that are found on rodlike structures, known as *chromosomes.*

At the moment you were conceived, you inherited 46 chromosomes from your parents—23 from your biological mother and 23 from your biological father. Each of these chromosomes contains thousands of genes. How do these genetic arrangements contribute to the kind of person you are? The **sex chromosomes** contain genes for development of male or female anatomy. An XX combination in this pair codes for femaleness; you inherited an X chromosome from your biological mother. An XY combination codes for maleness; you inherited either an X (if you are female) or a Y (if you are male) from your biological father. Your genotype (XX for female or XY for male) determines your biological gender and its development, including changes in body structure and chemistry throughout your lifetime. But how much more are you influenced by the *meaning* of being male or female in the social world? Have people treated you differently because you are the gender you are? Obviously, yes! Your self-concept, aspirations, and relationships would all be different if you had been born the other sex. In this way, you may begin to understand that your psychology—how you get along in the world—is rooted in your biology.

But your biology does not define your destiny because your genotypes only set your *potential.* Being tall doesn't mean you must play basketball. Being female may give you the option of bearing children, but doing so is a matter of choice. Physical strength can be determined by exercise or the lack of it. Intellectual growth depends both on genetic potential and educational

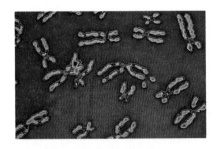

Normal pairs of human chromosomes.

human behavior genetics New field that unites geneticists and psychologists interested in determining the genetic basis of behavioral traits and functioning, such as intelligence, mental disorders, and altruism.

developmental disabilities Genetically based disorders that affect the development of some behavior or process.

experiences. Genes interact with the environment to produce the person you finally become.

Genetics and Psychology. The task for psychologists is to determine which environments help people develop their full potential. Consider, for example, people with Down's syndrome. *Down's syndrome* is caused by an extra chromosome in the 21st pair (resulting in three chromosomes instead of two). It is characterized by impaired psychomotor and physical development as well as mental retardation. Without intervention from mental health professionals, people with Down's syndrome depend almost wholly on others to fulfill their basic needs. However, special educational programs can train persons with this disorder to care for themselves, hold simple jobs, and establish some personal independence. The behavior of persons with Down's syndrome can be modified through training.

As this example shows, the disciplines of psychology and genetics have an important relationship. Together they seek to understand how genes influence behavior and to determine how environmental variables (such as training programs, diet, and social interactions) can modify genetically influenced behavior. **Human behavior genetics** is a relatively new field uniting geneticists and psychologists interested in determining the genetic basis of behavioral traits and functioning, such as intelligence, mental disorders, and altruism (Fuller, 1982; Plomin & Rende, 1991). Psychologists working in the field of **developmental disabilities** design programs to improve the quality of life for individuals born with genetically based disorders.

Genetic research over the past two decades has brought us to a threshold of understanding once thought impossible. We may soon be able to map all of the human genes and use that knowledge to improve the human condition by gigantic leaps (Delisi, 1988). *Genetic mapping* is the attempt to decipher the DNA code for each of our estimated 100,000 genes. Once scientists know which genes give rise to which traits, they will be able to conduct more accurate diagnostic tests for genetically based disorders. In the past 20 years, the genes involved in juvenile diabetes, certain cancers, arthritis, and blindness have been identified. Identifying defective genetic coding is the first step in developing effective intervention and treatment programs. (See "Time Out for Critical Thinking.")

As we learn more about genes and their relationship to behavior and psychological disorders, psychologists will likely be called on to provide further guidance about how that knowledge can best be used (Wingerson, 1990). Ultimately we will probably discover that most genetic links to psychology are based in the structure and function of the brain, where we will turn our attention in the next section.

➡️ *TIME OUT* . . . FOR CRITICAL THINKING

Science and technology are making it possible to prevent or at least predict genetic disorders by identifying individuals who are at risk. For example, Tay-Sachs disease causes massive neurological damage to afflicted infants, who usually die before age 4. Diagnostic tests can warn couples of their risk for bearing children with this disorder, allowing them to make an informed decision about whether and how to become parents.

Is our ability to foretell such risk a complete advantage over our ancestors? Should we only have children if we are sure they will be healthy? Is it irresponsible not to have our genes tested if there is a chance our children will suffer? Consider how you might answer each of the following ethical dilemmas, and discuss your answers with others:

- If parents know that their children might be born severely disabled, would it be responsible for them to have children?

- If you knew you carried a gene that might give your own children a fatal illness, would you have children?

- If you knew you might carry such a gene, would you want to be tested? Would it be fair to require you to be tested before conceiving children?

- How important is it to you to have children? Is there an important difference between having biological children and raising children you have not biologically parented?

SUMMING UP

Species originate and change over time because of natural selection, which is the tendency of some organisms to produce more offspring than others due to the interaction of phenotypic traits with the environment. Changes in environmental conditions can create competition for resources. This competition can favor organisms who vary in specific ways from others. In human evolution, natural selection has favored bipedalism (walking upright) and encephalization (increased brain development). Language and culture are important outcomes of these developments.

The basic unit of evolution is the gene, a tiny package of DNA found on chromosomes. Genotypes set the potential range of phenotypes, which are traits that are also influenced by the environment. Psychologists and geneticists work together to understand how genes influence behavior and how life can be improved in spite of or because of these influences.

The Brain and Behavior

Long before Darwin's voyage aboard the *Beagle,* scholars debated the role of the nervous system in everyday life. One of the most important figures to address this question was the French philosopher **René Descartes** (1596-1650). Descartes proposed the idea that the human body is an "animal machine" that can be understood scientifically. He believed that natural laws could be discovered through empirical observation. He raised *physiological* questions about body mechanics and motion, speculating about the forces that control human action. Basically, Descartes argued that human action is a mechanical reflex to environmental stimulation. Although religious doctrine at that time taught that humans were divinely endowed, Descartes' idea of reflexive behavior implied that humans behaved like other animals. He moderated this radical idea by adding the idea of a rational soul that guides human decisions and actions.

Modern scientific psychology recognizes that it is the brain—not the heart or a soul—that guides human behavior. Descartes' ideas that human behavior can be scientifically studied and that the body contributes to that behavior eventually led to modern brain research. Other milestones in this endeavor were reached in the 19th century as medical researchers identified the components of the nervous system and some of their basic functions. In more recent times, technological innovations such as the electron microscope and the brain scan have led to an explosion in developing theories and conducting tests of how the brain works. **Figure 2.3** displays the quality and detail possible with five brain-scanning techniques: SPECT, PET, EEG, SQUID, and MRI. What we know today about the brain and nervous system is a result of the quest begun by Descartes in the 17th century. "In Focus: Eavesdropping on the Brain" highlights modern technology's contribution to brain research.

René Descartes (1596–1650)

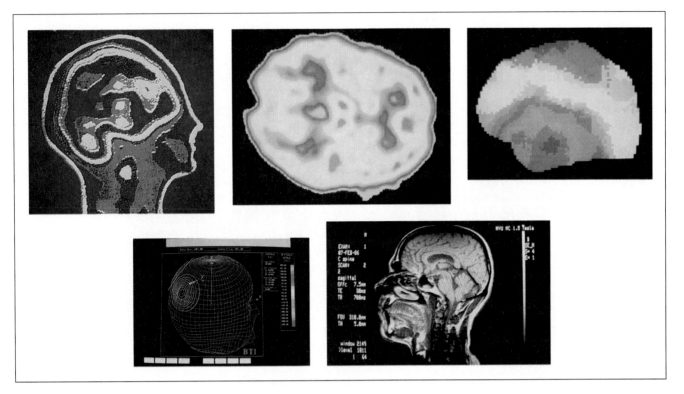

Figure 2.3   Windows on the Mind?
Five brain scanning devices. Top, from left: SPECT, PET, EEG. Bottom, from left: SQUID, MRI. Each scanning and recording device has strengths and weaknesses. PET accurately tracks brain activity, but it cannot distinguish structures less than half an inch apart. MRI cannot detect activity, but it can distinguish structures that are less than one-tenth of an inch apart.

Brain Structures and Functions

The formation and separation of the brain into divisions occurs in a similar way for many species. However, the higher the species is on the evolutionary scale, the larger and more complex the brain becomes and the more sophisticated the functions it can perform. In the human brain, the genetic instructions lead to a remarkably precise, efficient system of communication and computation unmatched by any other species.

The brains of human beings have three interconnected layers, each corresponding to different epochs in our evolutionary history (MacLean, 1977). In the deepest recesses of the brain, in a region called the *central core,* are structures involved primarily with autonomic processes such as heart rate, breathing, swallowing, and digestion. Enveloping the central core is the *limbic system,* which is involved with emotional and sexual behaviors as well as with eating, drinking, and aggression. Wrapped around these two "primitive" brains is the pinnacle of human evolution: the *cerebral cortex.* For each of us, the universe of the human mind exists in this region, just beneath the scalp. Without the cerebral cortex we would be no different from the lowliest animal species. With it, we can design new ways to challenge the limits imposed by heredity on our human nature. Within the cerebral cortex, sensory information is integrated, precise bodily movements of the mouth and hands are controlled, and abstract thinking and reasoning are facilitated (see **Figure 2.4** on page 48). Let us examine more closely the structure and function of each layer of the brain.

The Central Core.   The **central core** is found in all vertebrate species. It contains five structures that collectively regulate the internal state of the body (see **Figure 2.5** on page 49). The **medulla,** located at the very top of the

central core   Area of the brain that contains five structures that collectively regulate the internal state of the body.

medulla   The center for breathing, waking, sleeping, and the beating of the heart. Nerve fibers connecting the brain and the body cross over at the medulla.

Application

EAVESDROPPING ON THE BRAIN

Neuroscientists have four ways of plumbing the depths of the brain to uncover its secrets: (1) studying patients suffering from brain damage; (2) chemically or electrically producing lesions at specific brain sites; (3) electrically stimulating and recording brain activity; and (4) using computer-driven scanning devices to "photograph" the brain. Each technique serves two functions: First, it produces new knowledge about the structure, organization, and biochemical basis of normal brain functions; and second, it diagnoses brain disease and dysfunctions and then clinically evaluates therapeutic effects of specific treatments.

Brain Damage

In September 1848, a 25-year-old railroad worker named Phineas Gage sustained a horrible head injury when a construction explosion blasted an iron rod through his face and head. Astoundingly, he recovered from this injury and lived another 12 years. Gage's injury has become part of the annals of brain science because he was a *psychologically* changed man. Those who knew him remarked that he had gone from being an efficient and capable manager to behaving in irresponsible, fitful, and even profane ways. In essence, he was no longer himself. Had the site of his injury—the front and top of his brain—been the "residence" of his "old self"?

At about the same time that Gage was convalescing from his injury, **Paul Broca,** a French neurosurgeon, was studying the brain's role in language. His first laboratory research in this area involved an autopsy of a man whose name was derived from the only word he had been able to speak, "Tan." Broca found that the left front portion of Tan's brain had been severely damaged. Broca discovered that damage to the same region of the brain resulted in similar language impairments. He concluded that language ability depended on the functioning of structures in a specific region of the brain.

Lesions

Some researchers were not content just to study the effects of accidental

Phineas Gage

brain damage on behavior. The problem with studying accidentally damaged brains, of course, is that researchers have no control over the location, extent, or context of the damage. Researchers began, with considerable deliberation and skill, to destroy sections of the brains of otherwise intact animals (typically rats) and then to systematically measure the outcomes. **Lesions** are carefully inflicted injuries to specific brain areas. Early neuroscientists believed this was a good strategy, despite the ethical concerns that seem obvious to us today.

Researchers create three types of lesions: They either surgically remove specific brain areas, cut the neural connections to those areas, or destroy those areas by applying intense levels of heat, cold, or electricity. (Laser surgery can also be used.) Comparisons of the behavior between lesioned and nonlesioned animals has dramatically affected the development of brain science. For example, suppose that a rat were unable to run a recently learned maze after a specific part of its hippocampus had been lesioned. This would be evidence that learning and memory are processed in the lesioned structure.

Electrical Stimulation and Recording

Before the Canadian neurosurgeon **Wilder Penfield** operated on the brain of a patient suffering from epileptic seizures, he made a map of the cortex (outermost brain tissue) so that he

could localize the origin of the seizures and leave unharmed other areas vital to the patient's functioning. He used an **electrode** (a thin wire passing mild electrical current) to test the results of stimulating different specific sites. Probing a certain area might stimulate a particular body movement, sensory experience, emotion, or memory (Penfield & Baldwin, 1952). In the mid-1950s, Walter Hess pioneered the use of electrical stimulation to probe structures deeper in the brain. Deeply placed electrodes were found to stimulate elaborate sequences of behavior and emotional activity. In the context of Penfield's earlier brain-mapping work, Hess's findings indicated that there are many "start/stop" brain centers located throughout the brain.

Other neuroresearchers discovered another application of the new electrode technology. Instead of electrically stimulating the brain, they used electrodes to record the electrical activity of the brain as it responded to environmental stimulation. Electrodes positioned over the surface of the head can transmit signals about the brain's electrical activity to a machine called an electroencephalograph. This machine produces an **electroencephalogram (EEG),** an amplified tracing of the activity. An EEG is used to study the brain during states of arousal. It has been particularly useful in helping researchers study processes involved in sleeping and dreaming. Clinicians also use it to diagnose abnormalities in brain activity.

Brain Scans

The most exciting technological innovations for studying the brain are machines originally developed to help neurosurgeons detect brain abnormalities, such as tumors or damage caused by strokes or diseases. These machines, called brain scanners, produce images of different regions of the living brain. Research using brain scans does not require surgery or other intrusive procedures that may damage brain tissue.

Five brain scanning devices are currently used by researchers and clinicians. The process of computerized

lesions   Carefully inflicted destruction of tissue at specific brain areas.

electrode   A thin wire passing mild electrical current, usually into a brain site.

electroencephalogram (EEG)   An amplified tracing of the brain's electrical activity used to study the brain during states of arousal.

CT scanning   The process of computerized tomography, which creates a computerized image of X-rays passed through various angles of the brain.

PET scan   Positron emission tomography used to measure neural functioning by tracking the movement of radioactive substances in the active regions of the brain.

MRI   Magnetic resonance imaging process used to reveal whether brain cells are functioning normally by using radio waves to glimpse the effects of magnetic pulses of energy.

SPECT   Single-photon emission computerized tomography, used as a brain scanning process that tracks cerebral blood flow, which is a sign of activity in specific brain areas.

SQUID   Superconducting quantum interference device which senses tiny changes in the brain's magnetic fields that depict the pattern of neural activity in a three-dimensional portrait.

spinal cord, is the center for breathing, waking, sleeping, and the beating of the heart. Nerve fibers connecting the brain and the body cross over at the medulla, so that the left side of the body is linked to the right side of the brain and the right side of the body is connected to the left side of the brain.

Directly above the medulla is the **pons,** which is involved in dreaming and in waking from sleep. The **reticular formation** is a dense network of nerve cells situated between the medulla and pons. It serves as the brain's sentinel, arousing the cerebral cortex to attend to new stimulation and keeping the brain alert even during sleep.

Nerve fibers run from the reticular formation to the spinal cord, the limbic system, and a central core structure called the **thalamus.** The thalamus is a relay station that receives sensory information and channels it to appropriate areas of the cerebral cortex. For example, the thalamus relays visual information from the eyes to the visual cortex at the back of the brain.

The last major structure within the central core is the **cerebellum,** which is attached to the brain stem at the base of the skull. The cerebellum organizes bodily motion, controls posture, and maintains equilibrium. Your ability to walk, run, and dance reflects the functioning of the cerebellum. Consider the common functions and properties of all central core structures: the medulla, pons, reticular formation, thalamus, and cerebellum are all involved in the *coordination* of arousal, information, and physical movement.

The Limbic System.   The central core is found in all vertebrates, but only mammals are equipped with the more recently evolved limbic system. The **limbic system** processes motivated behaviors, emotional states, and certain kinds of memory. Since motivation, emotion, and memory are essential to individual survival, you can see why psychologists consider the limbic system to be part of the "animal brain," a set of structures very similar to those found in simpler species. It also regulates body temperature, blood pressure, and blood-sugar level. The limbic system is comprised of three structures: the hippocampus, amygdala, and hypothalamus (see **Figure 2.6** on page 49).

The **hippocampus,** which is the largest of the limbic system structures, plays an important role in memory, especially in long-term storage of information (Galluscio, 1990). Damage to the hippocampus does not impair the learning of new information, but it does impair the ability to remember it. Evidence for the hippocampus's role in memory is derived mostly from clinical research, notably from studies of H.M., perhaps psychology's most famous subject. When he was 27, H.M. underwent surgery in an attempt to reduce

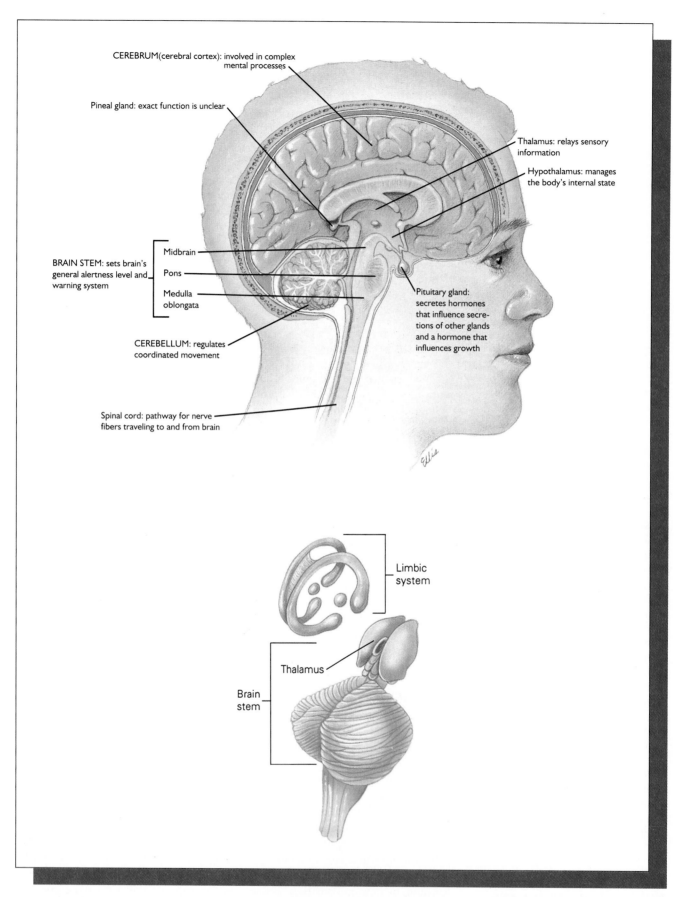

Figure 2.4 The Central Core, Limbic System, and Cerebral Cortex
From an evolutionary perspective, the central core is the oldest part of the brain; the limbic system evolved next; and the cerebral cortex is the most recent achievement in brain evolution.

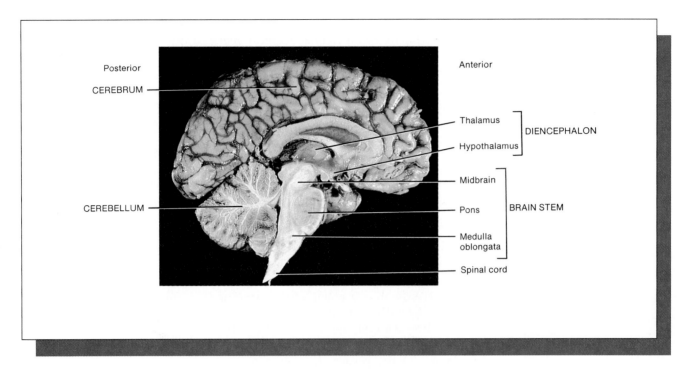

Figure 2.5   The Structures of the Central Core
The structures of the central core are primarily involved with basic life processes: breathing, pulse, arousal, movement, balance, and rudimentary processing of sensory information.

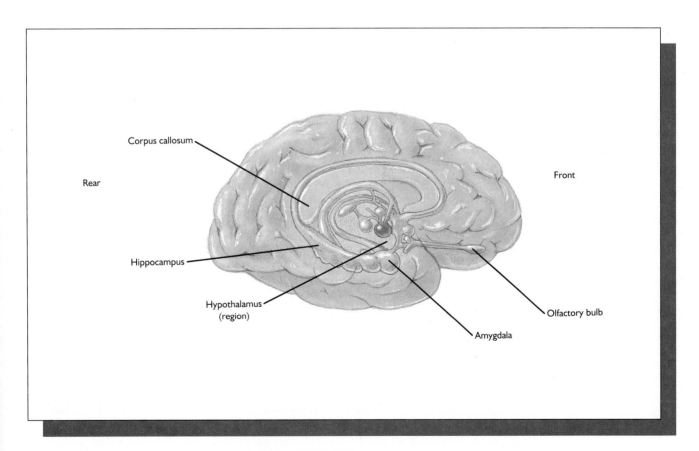

Figure 2.6   The Limbic System
The structures of the limbic system, which are present only in mammals, are involved with motivated behavior, emotional states, and memory processes.

pons   Part of the brain involved in dreaming and waking from sleep.

reticular formation   Dense network of nerve cells situated between the medulla and pons that arouses the cerebral cortex to attend to new stimulation and keeps the brain alert.

thalamus   Relay station that channels incoming sensory information to the appropriate area of the cerebral cortex, where that information is then processed.

cerebellum   Structure of the brain at the base of the skull, which organizes bodily motion, posture, and equilibrium.

limbic system   Brain system that processes motivated behaviors, emotional states, and certain kinds of memory.

hippocampus   Limbic system structure that is involved in memory.

amygdala   Limbic system structure involved in aggression, eating, drinking, and sexual behaviors.

hypothalamus   Limbic system structure that regulates the physiological processes involved in motivated behavior (including eating, drinking, temperature regulation, and sexual arousal).

homeostasis   The body's internal balance or equilibrium.

cerebral cortex   Area of the brain that regulates the brain's higher cognitive and emotional functions.

cerebral hemispheres   Two nearly symmetrical halves of the cerebral cortex.

corpus callosum   Thick mass of nerve fibers that connects the two hemispheres of the cerebral cortex.

the frequency and severity of his epileptic seizures. During the operation, parts of his hippocampus were accidentally removed. As a result, H.M. could only recall the very distant past; his ability to put new information into long-term memory was gone. Long after his surgery, he continued to believe he was living in 1953, which was the year the operation was performed. It appears that hippocampal damage has similar effects on memory in humans, monkeys, and rats, although *how* similar cannnot be determined because the species are studied via different methods (Squires, 1992).

The **amygdala** is known best for its role in aggression, although it is also involved in feeding, drinking, and sexual behaviors. Studies with several animal species, including humans, have shown that cutting parts of the amygdala has a calming effect on otherwise mean-spirited individuals, while electrically stimulating the amygdala triggers aggressive behavior.

The **hypothalamus** is one of the smallest structures in the brain, yet it plays a vital role in many of our most important daily actions. It is composed of several bundles of neurons that regulate physiological processes involved in motivated behavior (including eating, drinking, temperature regulation, and sexual arousal). For example, when your body is "running low" on nutrients, it is the hypothalamus that sends signals to make you feel hungry and then eat. The hypothalamus also regulates the activities of the endocrine system, which secretes hormones. The hypothalamus basically maintains **homeostasis,** the body's internal balance or equilibrium.

The uniquely mammalian limbic system structures (the hippocampus, amygdala, and hypothalamus) all function to maintain *balance,* both within the body and between the individual and the environment.

The Cerebral Cortex.   In humans, the **cerebral cortex** makes up two-thirds of the brain's total mass. It regulates the brain's higher cognitive and emotional functions. The cerebral cortex is divided into two nearly symmetrical halves, the **cerebral hemispheres,** each mediating different cognitive and emotional functions. The *left cerebral hemisphere* is associated with spontaneous use of language (both written and spoken), integration of complex movement, memory for words and numbers, and anxiety and positive emotions. The *right cerebral hemisphere* mediates memory for music and geometric patterns, facial recognition, and feelings of negative emotions. The two hemispheres are connected by a thick mass of nerve fibers, collectively referred to as the **corpus callosum.** This pathway sends messages back and forth between the hemispheres.

The Four Lobes.   Neuroscientists have mapped each hemisphere using two important landmarks as their guides. The deep *central fissure* divides each hemisphere vertically, while the *lateral fissure* divides each one horizontally (see **Figure 2.7**). These vertical and horizontal divisions create four areas, or brain lobes, in each hemisphere. Each of these lobes serves specific functions. The *frontal lobe,* above the lateral fissure and in front of the central fissure, is involved with motor control and cognitive activities, such as planning, deciding, and pursuing goals. Accidents that damage the frontal lobes can have devastating effects on human action and personality, as in the case of Phineas Gage (See "In Focus: Eavesdropping on the Brain"). The *parietal lobe* controls incoming sensory information and is located directly behind the central fissure, toward the top of the head. The *occipital lobe,* at the back of the head, is the major destination for visual information. The *temporal lobe,* on the side of each cerebral hemisphere, is where auditory information is processed. No one lobe controls any specific function alone. For example, when you do something as simple as answering a ringing telephone, you hear it in your temporal lobes, visually locate it in your occipital lobes, grasp and handle the receiver with the help of your parietal lobes, and engage in conversation with processes in your frontal lobes. The brain's structures

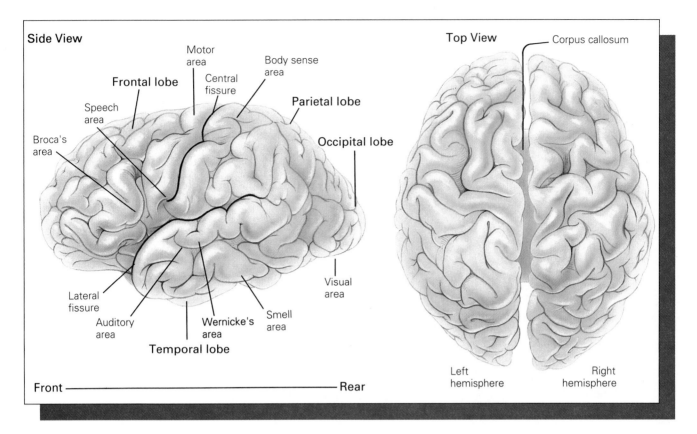

Side View

Frontal lobe

Speech area

Broca's area

Motor area

Central fissure

Body sense area

Parietal lobe

Occipital lobe

Lateral fissure

Auditory area

Wernicke's area

Smell area

Visual area

Temporal lobe

Front ——————————————— Rear

Top View

Corpus callosum

Left hemisphere

Right hemisphere

Figure 2.7 The Cerebral Cortex
Each of the two hemispheres of the cerebral cortex has four lobes. Different sensory and motor functions have been associated with specific parts of each lobe.

work in concert to perform their functions, although specific structures appear to be necessary for specific activities, such as vision, hearing, language, and memory.

The Cortical Functions. The actions of the body's voluntary muscles, of which there are more than 600, are controlled by the **motor cortex,** located just in front of the central fissure in the frontal lobes. As you can see in **Figure 2.8** (on the next page), the upper parts of the body receive far more detailed motor instructions than the lower parts. In fact, the two largest areas of the motor cortex are devoted to the fingers (especially the thumb) and to the muscles involved in speech; this reflects the importance of manipulating objects and talking in human activity. Remember that commands from one side of the brain are directed to muscles on the opposite side of the body. So, the motor cortex in the right hemisphere of your brain controls the muscles in your left foot.

The **somatosensory cortex** is located just behind the central fissure in the left and right parietal lobes. This part of the cortex processes information about temperature, touch, body position, and pain. Similar to the motor cortex, the upper part of the somatosensory cortex relates to the lower parts of the body, and the lower part relates to the upper parts of the body. Most of the somatosensory cortex area is devoted to the lips, tongue, thumb, and index fingers—the parts of the body that provide the most important sensory input (see Figure 2.8). Similar to the motor cortex, the right half of the somatosensory cortex communicates with the left side of the body and the left half with the right side of the body.

Auditory information is processed in the **auditory cortex,** which is in the two temporal lobes. The auditory cortex in *each* hemisphere receives informa-

motor cortex Part of the cortex that controls the actions of the body's voluntary muscles.

somatosensory cortex Part of the cortex that processes information about temperature, touch, body position, and pain.

auditory cortex Part of the cortex that processes auditory information.

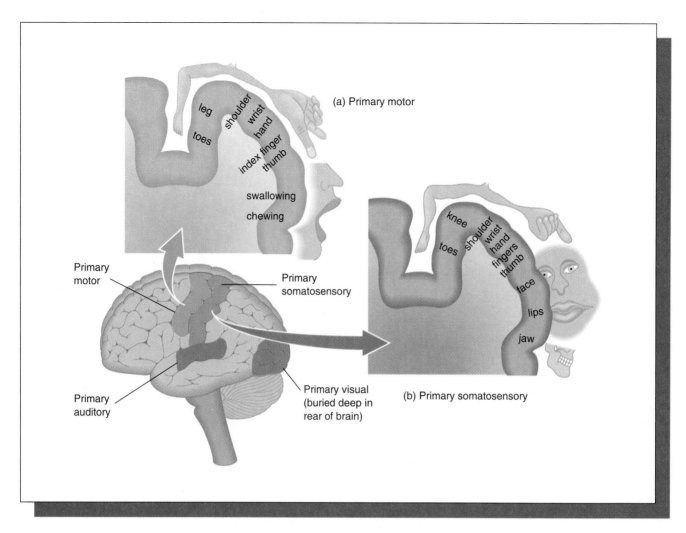

(a) Primary motor

leg
shoulder
wrist
hand
toes
index finger
thumb

swallowing

chewing

Primary
motor

Primary
somatosensory

Primary
auditory

Primary visual
(buried deep in
rear of brain)

knee
shoulder
wrist
hand
toes
fingers
thumb
face
lips
jaw

(b) Primary somatosensory

Figure 2.8 The Motor Cortex

Different parts of the body are more or less sensitive to environmental stimulation and brain control. Sensitivity in a particular region of the body is related to the amount of space in the cerebral cortex devoted to that region. In this figure, the body is drawn so that size of body parts is relative to the cortical space devoted to them. The larger the body part in the drawing, the greater its sensitivity to environmental stimulation and the greater the brain's control over its movement.

visual cortex Part of the cortex that processes visual input.

association cortex Part of the cortex where processes such as planning and decision-making occur.

tion from *both* ears. One area of the auditory cortex is involved in the production of language and a different area is involved in language comprehension. Visual input is processed at the back of the brain in the **visual cortex,** located in the occipital lobes. Here the greatest area is devoted to input from the center part of the retina at the back of the eye, the area that transmits the most detailed visual information.

Not all of the cerebral cortex is devoted to processing sensory information and commanding the muscles to action. In fact, the majority of it is involved in integrating information. Processes such as planning and decision making are believed to occur in all the areas of the cortex *not* labeled in Figure 2.7, or the **association cortex.** Animals on higher rungs of the evolutionary ladder have more of their cortexes devoted to association areas than lower animals do. This difference in the relative size of association areas reflects a physiological, structural difference among animals, but it also reflects a behavioral difference. For example, humans, at the top of the evolutionary ladder, show greater flexibility in behavior. This flexibility is due to the fact that proportionately more of the human cortex is devoted to association areas.

Descartes' speculation that natural laws govern the human body and that the brain contributes to behavior laid the foundation for modern neuroscience. Modern neuroscientists use four methods to study brain-behavior relationships: studying patients with brain damage, producing lesions at specific brain sites, electrically stimulating and recording brain activity, and using computerized scanning to photograph the brain. These methods have permitted neuroscientists to make important discoveries about how the brain processes information, generates thoughts, and coordinates complex behavior.

The brain is divided into three integrated layers: the central core, the limbic system, and the cerebral cortex. The central core is the oldest part of the human brain and is chiefly responsible for coordinating life-sustaining functions. Encircling the central core is the limbic system, which is involved in balance, motivation, and emotion. The cerebral cortex, surrounding the central core and limbic system, accounts for most of the brain's mass and is divided into two roughly symmetrical halves called hemispheres. Different lobes of the cortex initiate movement or process different kinds of environmental stimulation. But the brain functions as an integrated whole; no one brain region operates independently of the others.

The Biology of Behavior

Our bodies actually have two distinct and highly complex communication systems. One system, the **endocrine system,** is a network of glands that manufacture and secrete chemical messengers called **hormones** into the bloodstream (see **Figure 2.9**). The other system, the **nervous system,** is a massive network of nerve cells that rapidly relays messages to and from the brain using different kinds of chemical messengers called **neurotransmitters.** These systems work together to trigger various types of individual human action.

The Endocrine System

Hormones, secreted directly into the bloodstream by the endocrine glands, are involved in a wide array of bodily functions and behaviors. They influence body growth, sexual development, arousal, mood, and metabolism (the body's rate of energy use). Endocrine glands are stimulated in three ways: by chemical levels in the bloodstream, other hormones, or nerve impulses from the brain. Hormones are then secreted into the blood, which pumps them to their targets. Hormones influence the body's chemical regulation only at genetically receptive sites.

Endocrine communication sustains not only slow and continuous processes, but also critical responses. When you encounter a stressor or an emergency (such as the loud sound of an alarm or the cry of a person in distress) the hormone adrenaline is released into the bloodstream, energizing your body for quick defensive action—for "fight or flight." Your heart pounds, your muscles tense up, and you are driven to take whatever action your brain tells you makes sense.

Because the influence of hormones is diverse but specific, they have been called "the messengers of life" (Crapo, 1985). The different hormone "factory" sites in the body produce chemicals that influence a variety of bodily processes. **Table 2.1** outlines the major glands and their hormonal targets.

The hypothalamus, a small limbic system structure at the base of the brain, is in charge of the endocrine system. The hypothalamus is an important relay station among other parts of the brain, the endocrine system, and the central

endocrine system A network of glands that manufacture and secrete chemical messengers called hormones into the bloodstream.

hormones Chemical substances secreted into the bloodstream.

nervous system A massive network of nerve cells that relays messages to and from the brain.

neurotransmitters Chemical messengers that relay messages to and from the brain.

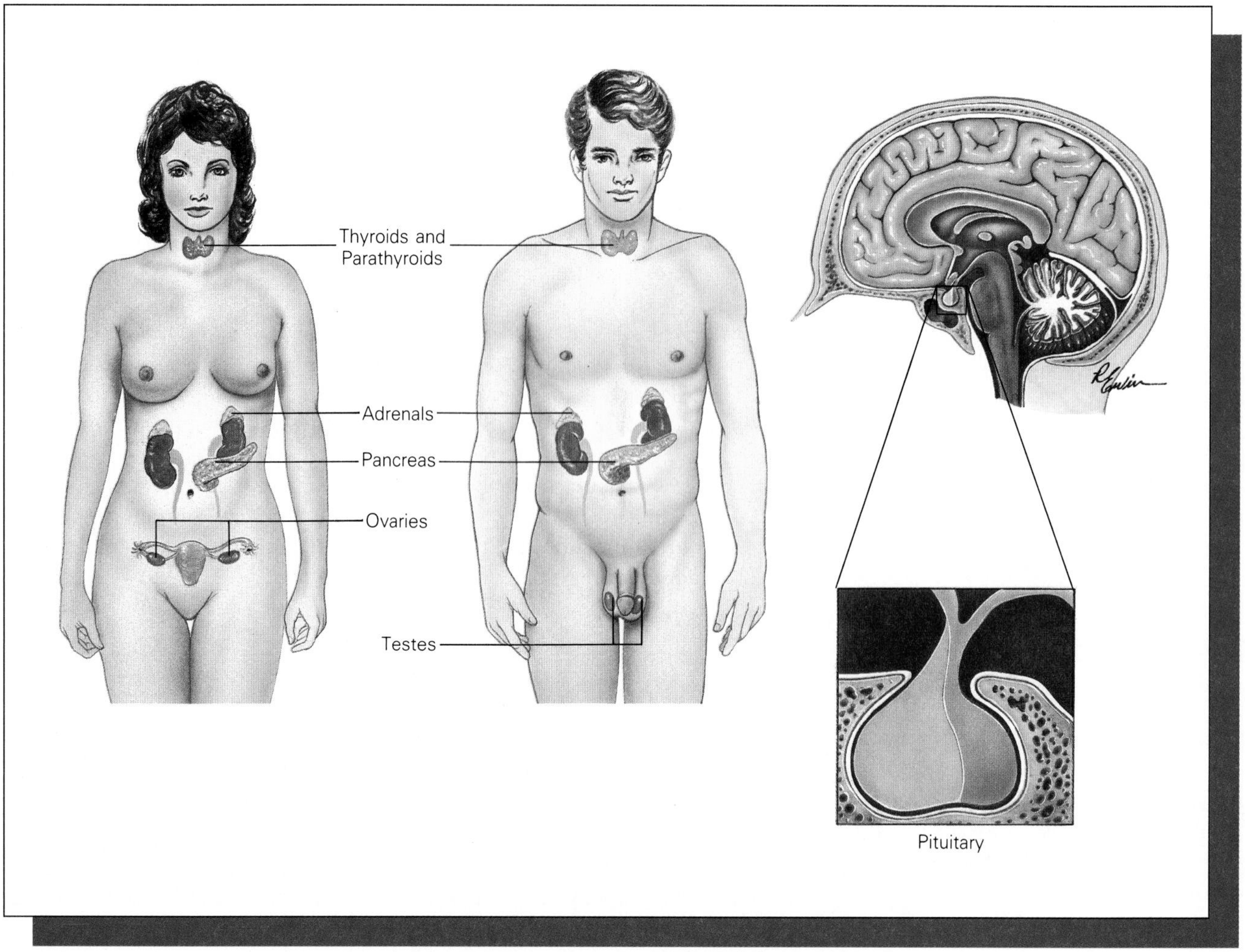
Thyroids and
Parathyroids
Adrenals
Pancreas
Ovaries
Testes
Pituitary

Figure 2.9 Endocrine Glands in Females and Males
The pituitary gland is shown at the far right; it is the master gland that regulates the glands shown at the left. The pituitary gland is under the control of the hypothalamus, an important structure in the limbic system.

nervous system. Specialized cells in the hypothalamus receive messages from other brain cells commanding it to release a number of different hormones to the *pituitary gland,* where they either stimulate or inhibit the release of other hormones.

pituitary gland Gland that secretes hormones that influence the secretions of all other endocrine glands, as well as a hormone that influences growth.

The **pituitary gland** is often called the "master gland," because it secretes hormones that influence the secretions of most other endocrine glands, as well as a hormone that influences growth.

The Nervous System

The body's other communication system, the nervous system, is more extensive and acts more quickly than the endocrine system. The nervous system is composed of billions of highly specialized nerve cells, or neurons, that are organized either into densely packed clusters (nuclei) or pathways (nerve fibers). The nuclei make up the brain, and they process information; the nerve fibers and the brain together make up the nervous system.

Organization of the Nervous System. The nervous system is subdivided into two major subsystems: the **central nervous system (CNS)** and the **peripheral**

Table 2.1 Major Endocrine Glands and the Functions of the Hormones They Produce

THESE GLANDS:	PRODUCE HORMONES THAT REGULATE:
Hypothalamus	Release of Pituitary Hormones
Anterior Pituitary	Testes and Ovaries Breast Milk Production Metabolism Reactions to Stress
Posterior Pituitary	Water Conservation Breast Milk Excretion Uterus Contraction
Thyroid	Metabolism Growth and Development
Parathyroid	Calcium Levels
Gut	Digestion
Pancreas	Glucose Metabolism
Adrenals	Fight or Flight Responses Metabolism Sexual Desire in Women
Ovaries	Development of Female Sexual Traits Ova Production
Testes	Development of Male Sexual Traits Sperm Production Sexual Desire in Men

central nervous system (CNS)
Subsystem of the nervous system composed of all the neurons in the brain and spinal cord.

peripheral nervous system (PNS)
Subsystem of the nervous system composed of all the neurons forming the nerve fibers that connect the CNS to the rest of the body.

nervous system (PNS). The CNS is composed of all the neurons in the brain and spinal cord; the PNS is made up of all the neurons forming the nerve fibers that connect the CNS to the rest of the body. **Figures 2.10** and **2.11** (on the next page) show the relationship of the CNS to the PNS.

The CNS integrates and coordinates all bodily functions, processes incoming neural messages, and sends out commands to different parts of the body, depending upon the environmental situation. For example, if the scene contains a predator, your legs are signalled to run; if it contains a friend, your arms are signalled to reach out, and your voice is signalled to speak. The CNS sends and receives neural messages through the *spinal cord,* a trunk line of neurons

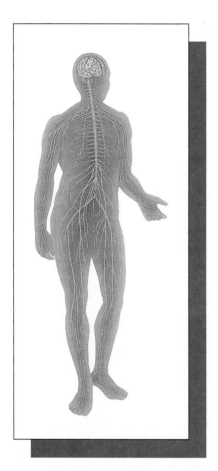

Figure 2.10 Physical Organization of the Human Nervous System
The sensory and motor nerve fibers that constitute the peripheral nervous system are linked to the brain by the spinal cord.

somatic nervous system Subdivision of the PNS that regulates the actions of the body's skeletal muscles.

autonomic nervous system (ANS) Subdivision of the PNS which sustains basic life processes.

Figure 2.11 Hierarchical Organization of the Human Nervous System
The central nervous system is composed of the brain and the spinal cord. The peripheral nervous system is divided according to function: The somatic nervous system controls voluntary actions, and the autonomic nervous system regulates internal processes. The autonomic nervous system is subdivided into two systems: The sympathetic nervous system governs behavior in emergency situations, and the parasympathetic nervous system regulates behavior and internal processes in routine circumstances.

that connects the brain to the PNS. The trunk line is housed in a hollow portion of the backbone called the spinal column. The spinal cord also coordinates the activity of the left and right sides of the body and is responsible for simple, swift reflexes that do not involve the brain. For example, an organism whose spinal cord has been severed from its brain can still withdraw its limb from a painful stimulus. Though normally the brain is notified of such action, the organism can complete the action without directions from the brain. Damage to the nerves of the spinal cord can result in paralysis of the legs or trunk, as seen in paraplegic individuals. The extent of paralysis depends on how high up on the spinal cord the damage occurred: the higher up the site of damage, the greater the extent of the paralysis.

Despite its commanding position, the CNS is isolated from any direct contact with the outside world. The PNS provides the CNS with information from sensory receptors, such as those found in the eyes and ears, and relays commands from the brain to the body's organs and muscles. The PNS is actually composed of two subdivisions of nerve fibers (see **Figure 2.11**). The **somatic nervous system** regulates the actions of the body's skeletal muscles. For example, when you type a message on a keyboard, the movement of your fingers is regulated by the somatic nervous system. As you plan what to say, your brain sends signals about which fingers to use on which keys, and your fingers return feedback about their position and movement. If you strike the wrong ke**e,** the somatic nervous system informs the brain, which issues a correction so you can quickly delete the error and hit the right ke**y.**

The other subdivision of the PNS is the **autonomic nervous system (ANS),** which sustains basic life processes. *Autonomic* means self-regulating or independent. The ANS operates constantly, regulating bodily processes we don't usually control consciously, such as respiration, digestion, and arousal. It works during sleep, and sustains life processes during anesthesia and coma. The autonomic nervous system deals with survival matters of two kinds: responding to threats and maintaining bodily functions. The autonomic nervous system is subdivided into the sympathetic and parasympathetic nervous system, which work together "in opposition" (see **Figure 2.11**). The **sympathetic division** governs responses to stress in emergencies, when action must be quick and powerfully energized. This is the "fight or flight" response

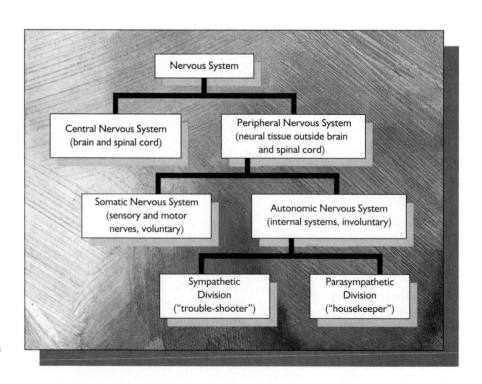

sympathetic division   Division of the ANS that governs responses to stress in emergencies.

parasympathetic division   Division of the ANS that monitors the routine operation of the body's internal functions, and returns it to calmer functioning after sympathetic arousal.

neuron   Nerve cell specialized to receive, process, and/or transmit information to other cells within the body.

system. It energizes you to respond to a stressor quickly by either fighting what threatens you or taking flight from what you cannot fight. In contrast, the **parasympathetic division** monitors the routine operation of the body's internal functions; this division returns the body to calmer functioning after sympathetic arousal. The separate duties of the sympathetic and parasympathetic nervous systems are illustrated in **Figure 2.12.**

The Neuron.   To interact with the world, we depend more on the nervous system than on the endocrine system. Exactly how does the nervous system permit us to sense and respond to the world outside our bodies? To answer this question, we will begin by discussing the structure and function of the neuron, the basic unit of the nervous system. The **neuron** is a cell specialized to receive, process, and/or transmit information to other cells within the body. Neurons vary in shape, size, chemical composition, and function. Over 200 different types have been identified in mammal brains, but all neurons have the same basic structure (see **Figure 2.13** on the next page). The human brain has a fixed number of neurons, and this stability may be essential for the *continuity*

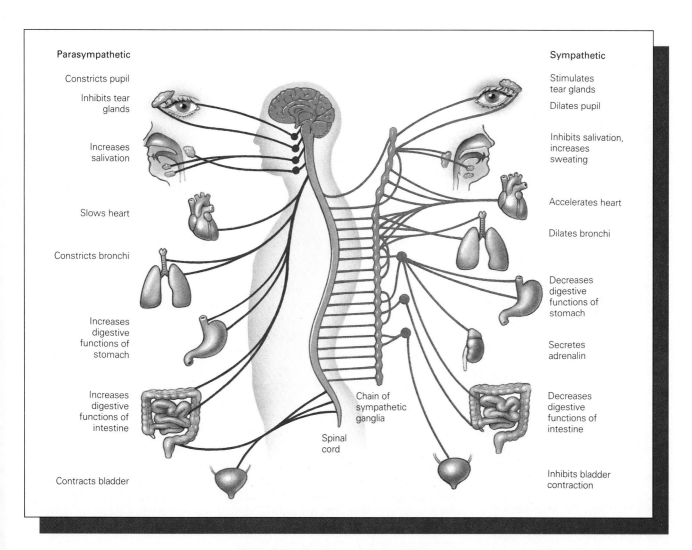

Parasympathetic

Constricts pupil

Inhibits tear glands

Increases salivation

Slows heart

Constricts bronchi

Increases digestive functions of stomach

Increases digestive functions of intestine

Contracts bladder

Sympathetic

Stimulates tear glands

Dilates pupil

Inhibits salivation, increases sweating

Accelerates heart

Dilates bronchi

Decreases digestive functions of stomach

Secretes adrenalin

Decreases digestive functions of intestine

Inhibits bladder contraction

Chain of sympathetic ganglia

Spinal cord

Figure 2.12   The Autonomic Nervous System
The parasympathetic nervous system, which regulates day-to-day internal processes and behavior, is shown on the left. The sympathetic nervous system, which regulates internal processes and behavior in stressful situations, is shown on the right. Note that on their way to and from the spinal cord, the nerve fibers of the sympathetic nervous system innervate, or make connections with, ganglia, which are specialized clusters of neuron chains.

Figure 2.13 Two Different Kinds of Neurons
Note the differences in shape and dendritic branching.

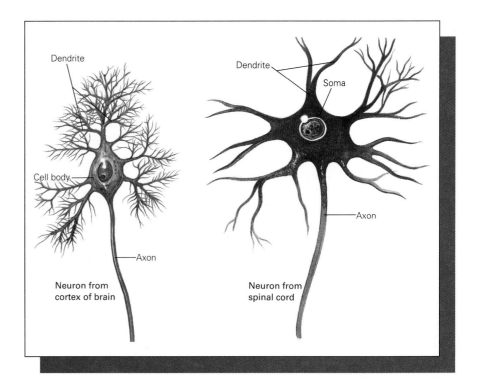

Dendrite

Cell body

Axon

Neuron from cortex of brain

Dendrite

Soma

Axon

Neuron from spinal cord

dendrites   Branched fibers that extend outward from the cell body and take information into the neuron.

soma   The cell body containing the nucleus of the cell and the cytoplasm that sustains its life.

axon   A single, extended fiber that conducts information about stimulation along its length, usually from neuron cell body to terminal buttons.

terminal buttons   Swollen, bulblike structures, located at the far end of the axon, through which stimulation passes to nearby glands, muscles, or other neurons.

law of forward conduction   Principle that neurons transmit information in only one direction: from the dendrites through the soma to the axon to the terminal buttons.

sensory neurons   Also called *afferent neurons*, nerve cells that carry messages from sense receptor cells toward the central nervous system.

motor neurons   Also called *efferent neurons*, nerve cells that carry messages away from the central nervous system toward the muscles and glands.

interneurons   Neurons that relay messages from sensory neurons to other interneurons or to motor neurons.

of learning and memory over a long lifetime (Rakic, 1985). However, human neurons die in astonishing numbers—about 10,000 will die every day of your life. Fortunately, because we start out with so many neurons, we will lose less than 2 percent of our original supply in 70 years.

The Structure of a Neuron. Neurons typically take in information at one end and send out messages from the other. The part of the cell that receives incoming signals consists of branched fibers called **dendrites,** extending outward from the cell body. The dendrites receive stimulation from other neurons or sense receptors.

The cell body, or **soma,** contains the nucleus of the cell and the cytoplasm that sustains its life. The soma integrates information about the stimulation received from the dendrites (or in some cases received directly from another neuron) and passes it on to a single, extended fiber, the **axon.**

The axon conducts this information along its length, which can be several feet long in the spinal cord and less than a millimeter in the brain. At the far end of an axon are swollen, bulblike structures called **terminal buttons,** through which stimulation passes to nearby glands, muscles, or other neurons.

Neurons transmit information in only one direction: from the dendrites through the soma to the axon to the terminal buttons; this is known as the **law of forward conduction** (see **Figure 2.14**).

Types of Neurons. In general, there are three major classes of neurons: sensory neurons, motor neurons, and interneurons. **Sensory neurons,** also called afferent neurons (from a Latin term meaning "carrying toward"), carry messages from sense receptor cells toward the central nervous system. Receptor cells are highly specialized sensory neurons that are sensitive to light, sound, or other stimuli.

Motor neurons, also called efferent neurons (meaning "carrying from"), carry messages away from the central nervous system toward the muscles and glands.

Sensory neurons rarely communicate directly with motor neurons. Instead, they rely on the **interneurons** that make up most of the billions of neurons in

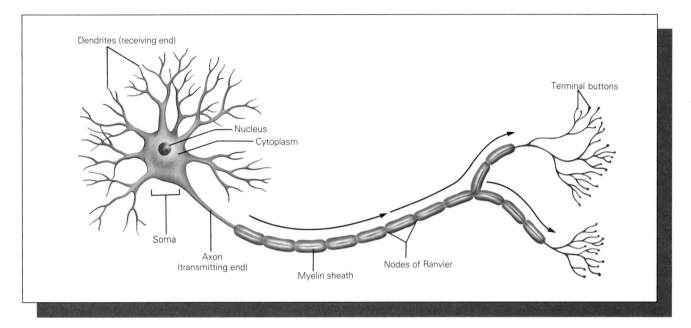

Dendrites (receiving end)

Nucleus

Cytoplasm

Terminal buttons

Soma

Axon
(transmitting end)

Myelin sheath

Nodes of Ranvier

Figure 2.14 The Major Structures of the Neuron
The neuron receives nerve impulses through its dendrites. It then sends the nerve impulses through its axon to the terminal buttons, where neurotransmitters are released to stimulate other neurons.

the brain. Interneurons relay messages from sensory neurons to other interneurons or to motor neurons. For every motor neuron in the body there are as many as 5,000 interneurons in the great intermediate network that forms the computational system of the brain (Nauta & Feirtag, 1979).

Interspersed among the brain's vast web of neurons are about ten times as many glial cells, or **glia.** The word *glia* is derived from the Greek word for "glue," hinting at a major function of glia: They bind neurons to each other (without actually touching). Glial cells also form a fatty insulating cover, the *myelin sheath,* around some types of axons, which greatly speeds the conduction of nerve signals.

glia Cells that bind neurons to each other.

Neurotransmission. You may wonder why you need to understand the nervous system function in such great detail. After all, this is psychology—not an advanced physiology course. Neural activity, however, is the biological medium in which behavior, thinking, and emotion all occur. Changes in nervous system activity lead to changes in how people behave, think, and feel. This text includes this information to help you understand the basic terms and operations of the biology of psychology.

The Neural Impulse. The nervous system uses electrochemical signals to process and transmit information. A single neuron's electrical activity changes when electrically charged particles called *ions* flow through the membrane that separates the cell's inside from the outside environment.

The neuron and its environment both contain ions (atoms of sodium, chloride, calcium, and potassium) that are either positively or negatively charged. The membrane separating the inner cell from the outer environment determines the cell's *polarity,* which is its electrical charge relative to the outside. An inactive, *polarized* nerve cell has a slightly more negative voltage inside relative to outside.

The cell membrane is not a perfect seal, so ions "leak" in and out of the neuron. The polarized balance is maintained with powerful transport mechanisms that pump certain ions in and others out, keeping neurons inactive but "ready" (Kalat, 1984).

When a neuron is stimulated by another neuron's impulse or by sensory stimulation, it becomes less negatively charged, or *depolarized,* and begins to produce its own electrical signals. In this depolarized state, the cell membrane is more easily permeated by ions flowing into and out of the cell body. In the jargon of neuroscience, the neuron is said to be "firing."

As a neuron fires, the inner cell becomes relatively more *positive* relative to the outside environment: It becomes fully depolarized. After firing, the transport mechanisms in the membrane restore the ionic balance that returns the neuron to a state of readiness once more.

Synaptic Transmission. The neural impulse travels the length of the neuron along the axon, finally arriving at the terminal buttons—where there is no direct physical connection to the next destination. No two neurons ever touch; they are always separated by a gap at their near-junction, the **synapse.** Firing sets off activity at the synapse. This begins a remarkable sequence of events called **synaptic transmission,** in which information is relayed from one neuron to another across the synaptic gap (see **Figure 2.15**).

As the neural impulse proceeds, small packets called *synaptic vesicles* move from within the cell to the inner membrane of the terminal buttons. Each vesicle contains **neurotransmitters,** biochemical substances that stimulate other neurons. The vesicles rupture, spilling their contents into the synaptic gap, and the neurotransmitters attach themselves to the receiving neuron.

synapse Space between neurons that provides a junction for information transfer.

synaptic transmission Process in which information is relayed from one neuron to another across the synaptic gap.

neurotransmitters Biochemical substances that stimulate other neurons and the endocrine system.

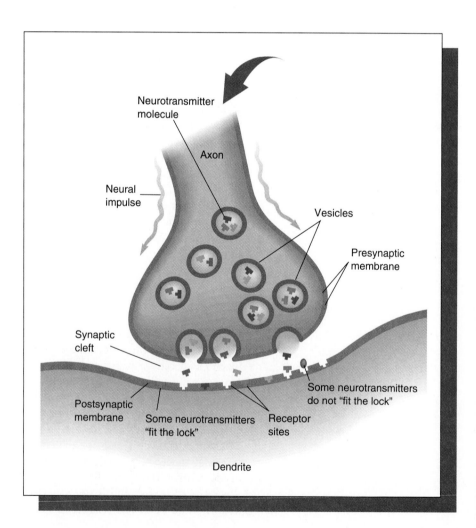

Figure 2.15 Synaptic Transmission
The action potential in the presynaptic neuron causes neurotransmitters to be released into the synaptic gap. Once across the gap, they stimulate receptor molecules embedded in the membrane of the postsynaptic neuron. Multiple neurotransmitters can exist within the same cell.

If the neurotransmitters are sufficiently stimulated, the receiving neuron will experience a change (either being excited into firing or inhibited from firing). Thus the impulse "message" will be relayed, cell to cell, until the message is completed.

Neurotransmitters. Since all nervous system activity depends on synaptic transmission, let's take a closer look at neurotransmitters. More than 60 different chemical substances are known or suspected to function as neurotransmitters in the brain. In particular, researchers have studied six neurotransmitters that play an important role in daily brain functioning. These are acetylcholine, GABA, dopamine, norepinephrine, serotonin, and the endorphins.

Acetylcholine is found in both the central and peripheral nervous systems. In the brain, it appears to be associated with memory processes.

A chemical called gamma-amino butyric acid, abbreviated GABA, is affected by a variety of depressants, chemical compounds that reduce central nervous system activity. These depressants may cause sedation or reduction of anxiety by increasing levels of GABA active at synapses (Paul et al., 1986).

Both *dopamine* and *norepinephrine* have been found to play important roles in psychological disorders such as schizophrenia and mood disturbances. Norepinephrine is also apparently involved in some forms of depression. Levels of dopamine that are higher than normal have been found in persons with schizophrenia, leading researchers to develop treatments that might decrease brain levels of dopamine.

Another important neurotransmitter is *serotonin*. All serotonin-producing neurons are located in the brain stem, which is involved with arousal and many autonomic processes. Hallucinogenic drugs such as LSD (lysergic acid diethylamide) appear to have profound effects on these serotonin neurons by influencing the way they receive impulse transmission (Jacobs, 1987). Hallucinogens produce vivid, bizarre, and sometimes long-lasting sensory experiences.

Finally, the *endorphins* are a group of chemical substances that change or modify the activity of a neuron receiving an impulse transmission. Endorphins were discovered during experiments in the early 1970s on morphine, a powerful sedative drug (Pert & Snyder, 1973). Apparently, the brain produces its own morphinelike substances, including the endorphins, which play an important role in the experience of emotion, pain, and pleasure. Endorphins have been called the "keys to paradise"; can you see why?

Volume Transmission. Is it possible for information to leave the structured circuits of neurons and closely linked synapses to travel to receptors in distant parts of the brain? If you think of neuronal circuits as railroad networks that require trains of information to stay on track, then it would seem impossible. Instead of the railroad model, think of communication in the brain as being like a radio broadcast in which signals are picked up by any properly tuned receptor. A new theory of how the brain transmits information proposes two types of cerebral communication: (1) the traditional, swift relaying of messages across synapses and (2) a slower diffusion of messages in the fluid-filled space between the cells of the brain. In the second process, called *volume transmission,* remote cells are influenced by neurons that release chemical signals into the brain's extracellular space (Agnati et al., 1992).

Volume transmission is a complement, not an alternative, to synaptic transmission. For fast, precise signalling, as in reading and understanding these words, you rely on efficient neurotransmission across the synapses of intimately related neurons. However, new research reveals that neurons also release chemical signals that are not necessarily detected by neighboring cells but are picked up by distant cells (see **Figure 2.16** on the next page). This medium of communication works similar to the way glands release hormones into the bloodstream; the process is slower than neuronal communication but has longer-lasting effects.

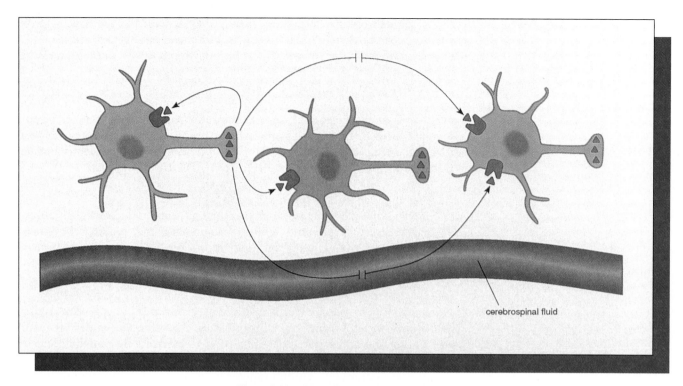

Figure 2.16 Volume Transmission in the Brain
Chemical signals in the volume-transmission mode of intercellular communication can travel various distances through the extracellular spaces of the brain. Neuroactive substances (*red triangle*) can affect the neuron that releases the signal (*blue*), a neighboring neuron (*orange*) or a distant neuron (*green*). Chemical signals can also travel large distances in the cerebrospinal fluid.

Volume transmission distributes information to a general region of sensitive brain cells, rather than only a specific set of neurons in a circuit. Because of this, volume transmission influences the general activity level of these neural connections instead of determining their specific activity. In this way, the release of chemical signals into the extracellular spaces of the brain may serve to regulate an individual's alertness and mood. Current research on volume transmission has two areas of focus: (1) studying the interaction with synaptic transmission and (2) identifying the properties of the spaces between neurons that provide the medium for the slow, general messages.

SUMMING UP

The endocrine and nervous systems function as communications systems. Controlled by the hypothalamus, the endocrine's slow-acting glands produce and secrete hormones into the bloodstream, influencing body growth, sexual development, metabolism, digestion, and arousal.

The nervous system is composed of billions of neurons and is divided into two major subdivisions: the CNS (the brain and spinal cord) and the PNS (all the neurons connecting the CNS to the body). The PNS is further divided into the somatic nervous system, which regulates the skeletal muscles, and the autonomic nervous system, which governs basic living functions. The sympathetic division of the autonomic nervous system springs into action during times of stress and emergency, and the parasympathetic division operates under more routine circumstances.

The neuron, the basic unit of the nervous system, receives, processes, and relays information to other cells, glands, or muscles. Sensory neurons send messages toward the CNS; motor neurons channel messages from the CNS; and interneurons relay information between neurons. Glial cells help bind neurons together and perform other basic duties for the cell and the synapse.

When a neuron depolarizes, or "fires," information is relayed in one direction: from the dendrites to the soma and through the axon to the terminal buttons. Neurotransmitters are released into the synaptic gap and may be taken up by the receiving neuron, which is either excited (turned on) or inhibited (turned off). Of more than 60 known neurotransmitters, six have been studied very closely to identify their specific brain and behavioral functions.

In volume transmission, neural impulses release not only fast-acting synaptic transmissions but also slower-moving chemical messages to more distant cells. Volume transmission influences general neural activity, and may affect alertness and mood. Current research is examining how volume transmission works and interacts with synaptic transmission.

The Biology of Consciousness

The nervous system is the basis for all of our conscious experience. Anything that changes how the nervous system operates also changes normal consciousness—usually for the worse. In the next chapter, we will focus our attention on the realm of consciousness and the mind, but first we will take a closer look at the links between the biological processes of the nervous system and the human experience of consciousness.

cerebral dominance Tendency of each hemisphere of the brain to dominate the control of different functions.

The Cerebral Hemispheres

The cerebral cortex is the part of the brain responsible for consciousness. Each hemisphere appears to be involved in regulating different aspects of conscious experience. Here are some findings of some research investigating the cerebral hemispheres:

- Patients suffering strokes that paralyze the right side of their bodies often develop speech disturbances.
- Patients suffering strokes that damage the left hemisphere often develop problems using and understanding language. (Recall Paul Broca's early findings).
- The left hemisphere is usually slightly larger than the right one.

Though the two hemispheres appear to be physically similar, both clinical and experimental evidence clearly indicates dissimilarity in their functions. In fact, each hemisphere tends to dominate the control of different functions. This tendency is called **cerebral dominance.**

Although the brain typically functions in an integrated and harmonious, or holistic, fashion, some actions and processes are more under the control of the right hemisphere, while others are left-hemisphere dominant.

Much of our knowledge about cerebral dominance comes from observing people who have suffered brain damage on one side or whose cerebral hemispheres could not communicate with each other (see **Figure 2.17**). Patients with right-hemisphere damage are more likely to have perceptual and attentional problems, which can include serious difficulties in spatial orientation. For example, they may feel lost in a previously familiar place or be unable to fit geometric shapes together.

In general, studies of healthy individuals have shown that the left side of the brain is more involved in controlling verbal activities, and the right side is more important in directing visual-spatial activities. However, the two hemispheres often make different contributions to the same function. Both hemispheres contribute to language and memory functions, to perceptual-cognitive functions, and to emotional functions (see **Figure 2.18** on the next page).

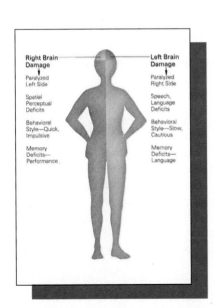

Figure 2.17 The Effects of Damage to One Side of the Brain

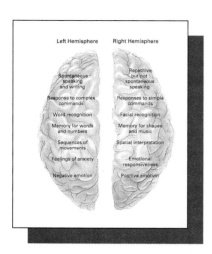

Figure 2.18 Specialization of the Cerebral Hemispheres

The differences between the hemispheres are hard to detect except in the cases of rare surgical patients. Generally, each hemisphere seems to *complement* rather than oppose the other. "In Focus: One Brain or Two?" examines in greater detail how researchers have discovered this relationship, and what it implies about human consciousness.

Our Responsive Brain

It is one thing to recognize that the brain controls behavior and our mental processes, but it is quite another to understand *how* it serves all those functions that we take for granted when it functions normally. It is also important to understand what happens when the brain doesn't work properly.

We began our study of the biology of behavior with the example of how touch can have a biological effect in transforming the growth of premature infants. (For more on the effects of touch, see Brown, 1984, and Gunzenhauser, 1990). This positive effect of physical stimulation on bodily growth is mediated by changes in brain functioning. The massaged babies gained more weight than the unstimulated control infants (despite similar formula and calorie intake), they became more physically active, and their sleep patterns changed. Stimulated babies apparently release more of several neurotransmitters. Deprivation of contact with the mother shuts down the growth hormone, and in turn, massaging the infants can maintain the brain's release of the hormone (Field & Schanberg, 1990). This example provides a clear case in which external stimulation profoundly modifies the brain's functioning. It has also been found that therapeutic touch profoundly improves the mental and physical health of the elderly (Fanslow, 1984). Psychologists have concluded that physical touch between people who care about each other not only symbolizes affection but also achieves real biological benefits.

New research is demonstrating that the brain is a *dynamic* system capable of changing both its functions and its physical structure in response to various kinds of stimulation and environmental challenges (Fernald, 1984; Sapolsky, 1990). Because of such research, a new perspective is developing about the nature of the brain. In addition to the *behaving brain* that controls behavior, we now recognize the *responsive brain* that is changed by the behavior it generates and by environmental stimulation. The capacity for its own internal modification makes the complex human brain the most dynamic, responsive system on the planet (Rosenzweig, 1984b).

SUMMING UP

The cerebral cortex is the basis of consciousness. The cerebral cortex is divided into two halves, or hemispheres, connected by the corpus callosum. Although the hemispheres are physically symmetrical, their functions are not. Language (memory for words and numbers, word recognition), feelings of anxiety, and negative emotions are regulated by the left hemisphere. The right hemisphere controls spatial interpretation, facial recognition, and positive emotions.

The two hemispheres can be physically disconnected by surgically severing the corpus callosum. When one split-brain hemisphere receives information, the other hemisphere is neither aware of that stimulation nor of the kind of cognitive activities that are taking place in the other hemisphere. Thus severing the corpus callosum creates two brains, each capable of independent functions.

Recent research emphasizes the responsive nature of the brain. Stimulation and experience interact dynamically with the nervous system, so that the process of adapting to the environment is ongoing and personally distinctive.

In Focus:

Research

ONE BRAIN OR TWO?

The existence of two cerebral hemispheres, each with apparently different functions, raises an intriguing question: Would each half of the brain be able to act as a separate conscious mind if it were somehow separated from the other? A treatment for severe epilepsy has provided the chance to investigate this possibility. In this procedure, surgeons sever the corpus callosum, a bundle of about 200 million nerve fibers that transfers information back and forth between the two hemispheres (see **the figure below left**). The goal of this surgery is to prevent the violent electrical rhythms that accompany epileptic seizures from crossing between the hemispheres (Wilson et al., 1977). The operation is usually successful, and a patient's subsequent behavior in most circumstances appears normal. Patients who undergo this type of surgery are often referred to as *split-brain patients*.

What gave researchers the idea that the two hemispheres may be able to function independently? Early studies of hemispheric differences focused on the way the brain combines infor-

mation from two-sided sources. For example, when sensory input from the eyes is registered by the receptors, it automatically goes to the opposite side of the brain (right visual field to left hemisphere; left field to right hemisphere). However, the information is shared by both hemispheres through the corpus callosum. So when split-brain patients can coordinate input from both eyes, they can function without problems. But when they receive special tasks that present separate information to each eye or each hand, the behavior of the split-brain patients is far from normal, as we shall see below.

The first split-brain operations on human patients were performed by neurosurgeon William Van Wagener in the early 1940s (Van Wagener & Herren, 1940). Over a decade later, experimenters cut the corpus callosum in animals and then trained the subjects in visual discrimination tasks with one eye covered. When the eye patch was switched to the other eye, the animals took as long to learn the tasks as they had the first time. The one side of the brain had not learned anything from

the experience of the other side (Myers & Sperry, 1958).

To test the capabilities of the separated hemispheres of epileptic patients, **Roger Sperry** (1968) and **Michael Gazzaniga** (1970) devised situations that could allow visual information to be presented separately to each hemisphere (see **the figure below right**). The researchers found that the left hemisphere was superior to the right hemisphere in problems involving language or requiring logic and sequential or analytic processing of concepts. The left hemisphere could "talk back" to the researchers while the right hemisphere could not. Communication with the right hemisphere was achieved by confronting it with manual tasks involving identification, matching, or assembly of objects—tasks that did not require the use of words. The right hemisphere turned out to be better than the left at solving problems involving spatial relationships and at pattern recognition. However, it could only add up to 10 and was about at the level of a 2-year-old in the use and comprehension of word combinations.

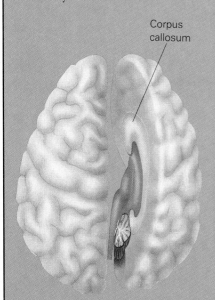

The Corpus Callosum
The corpus callosum is a massive network of nerve fibers that channels information between the two hemispheres. Severing the corpus callosum impairs this communication process.

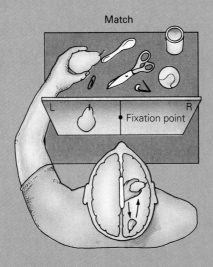
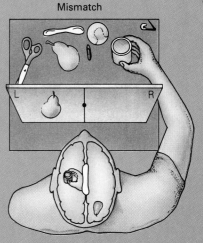

Coordination Between Eye and Hand
Coordination between eye and hand is normal if a split-brain patient uses the left hand to find and match an object that appears in the left visual field because both are registered in the right hemisphere. However, when asked to use the right hand to match an object seen in the left visual field, the patient cannot do so because sensory messages from the right hand are going to the left cerebral hemisphere, and there is no longer a connection between the two hemispheres. Here the cup is misperceived as matching the pear.

The two hemispheres also seemed to have different "styles" for processing the same information. For example, on matching tasks, the left hemisphere matched objects analytically and verbally—by similarity in function. The right hemisphere matched things that looked alike or fit together to form a whole pattern.

The brain is designed to function as a whole with a vast, precise communication network integrating both hemispheres. When the hemispheres are disconnected, the result is two separate brains and a *duality of consciousness*. Each hemisphere can respond independently and simultaneously when stimuli are presented separately to each side. When stimuli are presented to only one side, responses are either emotional or analytic, depending on which hemi-sphere has the task of interpreting the message. Because it lacks language competence, the disconnected right hemisphere has limited and vastly inferior visual-spatial skills as compared to the cognitive skills of the left hemisphere.

We must be cautious about generalizing such findings from split-brain patients into a basic view of the way that normal brains function. Does the brain function holistically as a uniform central command system, or is it organized according to specialized functions for each hemisphere? A number of investigators propose that the human mind is neither a single entity nor a dual entity but rather a confederation of multiple mind-modules. Each of these "miniminds" is specialized to process almost automatically a specific kind of information, such as spelling or arithmetic. The input from these many separate modules is then synthesized and coordinated for action by central, executive processors (Fodor, 1983; Hinton & Anderson, 1981; Ornstein, 1986).

Other neuroscientists and psychologists are skeptical about the importance and validity of hemispheric specialization. These investigators still suspect that any asymmetries can be explained in terms of specialized processes located in each hemisphere (Efron, 1990). Ideally, the debate between these two views of the brain will generate a fuller understanding of how the brain works so effectively. The debate may also provide insights into why the human brain sometimes fails to function rationally.

CHAPTER REVIEW

Evolution, Brain, and Behavior *According to Charles Darwin's theory of evolution, how does the environment influence species' biology? How can human development be better understood through genetics?*

Species originate and change over time because of natural selection. In human evolution, bipedalism and encephalization were responsible for subsequent advances, including language and culture. The basic unit of evolution is the gene. Genes determine the range of effects that environmental factors can have in influencing the expression of phenotypic traits.

Key Terms
evolution, p. 39
heredity, p. 39
natural selection, p. 39
phenotype, p. 40
genotype, p. 40
bipedalism, p. 40
encephalization, p. 40
genetics, p. 42
genes, p. 42
sex chromosomes, p. 42
human behavior genetics, p. 43
developmental disabilities, p. 43

Major Contributors
Schanberg, Saul, p. 37
Field, Tiffany, p. 37
Darwin, Charles, p. 39

2 The Brain and Behavior
How has modern science influenced the link between psychology and biology? What are the three layers or structures of the brain, and how do their functions account for human behavior?

Neuroscientists use four methods to research the relationship between the brain and behavior. They study brain-damaged patients, produce lesions at specific brain sites, electrically stimulate and record brain activity, and use computerized devices to scan the brain.

The brain consists of three integrated layers: the central core, limbic system, and cerebral cortex. The central core is responsible for breathing, digestion, and heart rate. The limbic system is involved in long-term memory, aggression, eating, drinking, and sexual behavior. The cerebral cortex consists of two hemispheres, and different areas of the cortex process different kinds of stimulation, form associations, or initiate movement.

Key Terms
central core, p. 45
medulla, p. 45
lesions, p. 46
electrode, p. 46
electroencephalogram (EEG), p. 46
CT scanning, p. 47
PET scan, p. 47
MRI, p. 47
SPECT, p. 47
SQUID, p. 47
pons, p. 47
reticular formation, p. 47

thalamus, p. 47
cerebellum, p. 47
limbic system, p. 47
hippocampus, p. 47
amygdala, p. 50
hypothalamus, p. 50
homeostasis, p. 50
cerebral cortex, p. 50
cerebral hemispheres, p. 50
corpus callosum, p. 50
motor cortex, p. 51
somatosensory cortex, p. 51
auditory cortex, p. 51
visual cortex, p. 52
association cortex, p. 52

Major Contributors
Descartes, René, p. 44
Broca, Paul, p. 46
Penfield, Wilder, p. 46

3 The Biology of Behavior
What are the body's two communication systems? How is the organization of the nervous system related to behavior and experience?

The endocrine system produces and secretes hormones into the bloodstream. Hormones help regulate growth, primary and secondary sexual characteristics, metabolism, digestion, and arousal. The hypothalamus stimulates the pituitary gland to initiate a chain of hormonal releases.

The brain and the spinal cord make up the central nervous system (CNS). The peripheral nervous system (PNS) is composed of the somatic nervous system, which regulates the body's skeletal muscles, and the autonomic nervous system (ANS), which regulates basic life processes. The sympathetic division of the ANS is active during stress, while the parasympathetic division operates under routine circumstances.

The neuron, the basic unit of the nervous system, receives, processes, and relays information to other cells, glands, and muscles. Sensory neurons receive messages and send them toward the CNS, while motor neurons channel messages away from the CNS to muscles and glands. Interneurons relay information from sensory neurons to other interneurons or motor neurons.

A neuron "fires," or depolarizes, when it is stimulated to allow ions to permeate across the cell membrane. Neurotransmitters are released into the synaptic gap. Once across the gap, they lodge in the receiving neuron, where they may either excite or inhibit that cell's firing.

Key Terms

endocrine system, p. 53
hormones, p. 53
nervous system, p. 53
neurotransmitters, p. 53
pituitary gland, p. 54
central nervous system (CNS), p. 55
peripheral nervous system (PNS), p. 55
somatic nervous system, p. 56
autonomic nervous system (ANS), p. 56
sympathetic division, p. 56
parasympathetic division, p. 57
neurons, p. 57
dendrites, p. 58

soma, p. 58
axon, p. 58
terminal buttons, p. 58
law of forward conduction, p. 58
sensory neurons, p. 58
motor neurons, p. 58
interneurons, p. 58
glia, p. 59
synapse, p. 60
synaptic transmission, p. 60
neurotransmitters, p. 60

4 The Biology of Consciousness *What does research indicate about the connection between the cerebral hemispheres and consciousness? What do researchers mean when they talk about our "two brains"? Why can the human brain be described as "responsive"?*

The cerebral cortex is the part of the brain responsible for consciousness. Language, analytical thinking, and negative emotions are regulated by the left hemisphere, while the right hemisphere controls spatial interpretation, visual and musical memory, and positive emotions. If the hemispheres are surgically severed, each functions independently of the other and is not aware of stimulation or cognitive activities that affect the other.

The behaving brain initiates and controls behavior. The responsive brain's functions and structure are changed by stimulation from the environment and from its own behavior. Research indicates that the brain's functioning is modified in profound ways by external stimulation, showing that the brain is a dynamic system, responsive to environmental stimulation and capable of self-modification.

Key Terms

cerebral dominance, p. 63

Major Contributors

Sperry, Roger, p. 65
Gazzaniga, Michael, p. 65

PRACTICE TEST

Chapter 2: Biopsychology

For each of the following items, choose the single correct or best answer. Correct answers, explanations, and page references appear in the Appendix.

1. Studies conducted by Tiffany Field and Saul Schanberg show that when premature infants are _____ on a regular basis, they gain more weight and are more active and alert than babies who are not.

   A. read to by their parents
   B. gently massaged
   C. kept in a quiet, unstimulating environment
   D. physically restrained

2. _____ is the factor in natural selection represented by individuals' different phenotypes and genotypes.
   A. Environment
   B. Competition
   C. Variation
   D. None of the above

3. Human beings' capacity for _____ stemmed from the development of _____ in the course of our evolution.
   A. bipedalism; encephalization
   B. language; bipedalism
   C. language; encephalization
   D. culture; bipedalism

4. The idea that the brain contributes in important ways to behavior, which can be scientifically studied, was originally developed by _____.
   A. René Descartes
   B. Wilder Penfield
   C. Paul Broca
   D. Charles Darwin

5. A researcher surgically destroys a minute section of brain tissue in a living animal and later observes the animal's ability to learn and retain new information. This demonstrates the use of _____ in conducting brain research.
   A. lesioning
   B. CT scanning
   C. the EEG
   D. MRI

6. Which of the following statements identifying the locations of important brain structures is true?
   A. The hypothalamus is part of the limbic system.
   B. The medulla is part of the central core.
   C. The occipital lobe is part of the cerebral cortex.
   D. All of the above.

7. _____ is an example of behavior controlled primarily by the autonomic nervous system.
   A. Typing a sentence accurately on a keyboard
   B. Solving a mathematical problem
   C. Breathing and swallowing while asleep
   D. None of the above

8. During a neural impulse, a neuron "fires" when _____.
   A. it is physically contacted by a another cell that is transmitting the signal
   B. it undergoes a change in its electrical charge relative to the outside environment
   C. it spasmodically contracts, releasing powerful chemicals directly into the bloodstream
   D. signals entering at the axon travel the length of the cell and exit through the dendrites

9. The left hemisphere of the cerebral cortex is more involved than the right hemisphere in experiences such as _____.
   A. recognizing and appreciating visual stimuli
   B. enjoying and appreciating music
   C. using spoken and written language
   D. understanding spatial relationships

10. The brain is characterized as "responsive" because we recognize that _____.
    A. it dictates every action and experience with specialized control centers
    B. it is a closed system, communicating with other biological processes but not with the outside environment
    C. every brain cell has a single, unvarying function
    D. its functioning is modified in profound ways by external stimulation

IF YOU'RE INTERESTED . . .

Awakenings. (Video: 1990, color, 121 minutes). Directed by Penny Marshall; starring Robin Williams, Robert DeNiro, and Julie Kavner.

   The film based on the research and experiences of Oliver Sacks, a clinical neurologist studying the relationship between brain and behavior.

Gazzaniga, M. (1985). *The social brain: Discovering the networks of the mind*. New York: Basic Books.

   An invitation to the layperson to review the findings of modern brain research and their implications, by one of the pioneers of split-brain research.

Restak, R. (1984). *The brain*. Toronto: Bantam.

   A highly readable introduction to the brain by a noted researcher and science writer.

Sacks, O. (1985). *The man who mistook his wife for a hat, and other clinical tales*. New York: Summit Books.

   A fascinating series of clinical stories about patients with neurological disorders that had extraordinary effects on their lives.

Chapter 3   **States of Mind**

Preview Questions

1. Why is psychology's modern conception of the mind considered a new form of dualism? How can consciousness be described in terms of different functions, levels, and structures?

2. What is daydreaming? How does it resemble fantasy? What is the rhythm underlying sleep? Why do we sleep? How do different psychological theories explain dreaming?

3. Which processes and experiences are considered to be extended states of consciousness? How is a hypnotized subject's state of mind different from normal consciousness? What are some consequences of meditation? What causes one to experience hallucinations? How do different classes of psychoactive drugs alter consciousness? What part has consciousness played in human evolution?

"One hundred, 99, 98, 97. . . ." Karen counted as the anesthetic flowed from the needle into her vein. Geometric patterns oscillated wildly before her. "Ninety-two, 91, 9. . . ." Darkness descended. Sensation and awareness shut down. Karen's surgery began.

Karen hadn't worried about this operation—it was only minor surgery to remove a cyst in her mouth. Minutes into the operation, however, the surgeon exclaimed, "Why, this may not be a cyst at all. It may be cancer!" Fortunately, the biopsy proved him wrong. In the recovery room the surgeon told Karen, who was still groggy and slightly nauseous, that everything was fine; the operation was a complete success.

That night, Karen felt anxious and had trouble falling asleep. She started crying for no apparent reason. Finally, when she did fall asleep, she dreamed about a puppy she couldn't get because of her allergy to dogs. Karen awoke feeling sad and was depressed all day. At first, she attributed her bad mood to her dream. But when all attempts to restore her usual good spirits failed and her depression worsened, Karen sought professional help.

A therapist hypnotized Karen and asked her to lift her hand if something was disturbing her. Karen's hand rose, and the therapist suggested that she report what was disturbing her. Karen exclaimed, "The cyst may be cancerous!"

Karen's depression lifted after she received assurances that the cyst was benign. Consciously, Karen had not understood the source of her anxiety. But even in an unconscious, anesthetized state, some part of her mind had understood the surgeon's words. The dire meaning of that information became psychologically traumatic to Karen.

Karen's case is not unusual. Increasing evidence indicates that patients who are fully anesthetized and have no conscious recall of their operations may still hear what is going on during their surgery. Our hearing sensitivity appears to remain on alert even under adequate anesthesia. The reasons for this auditory alertness may be deeply rooted in our evolutionary history: Animals in the open had to respond swiftly to sounds of possible danger even when asleep. Whatever the reason, highly specialized cells in the auditory nerve make signals passing along it exceptionally clear and hard to block out with anesthetics. Because of this sensitivity, even casual remarks in the operating room can be dangerous. "I think they can kill people, if you want to know the truth," said a researcher in the department of anesthesiology at a California medical center. "I've seen cardiac arrests during surgery that can't be explained except by comments made around the operating table" (Rymer, 1987, p. 19).

Physicians and psychologists are intrigued by research findings on the capacity of anesthetized patients to learn and remember auditory information experienced during an operation. Such recall seems to occur despite patients' insistence of amnesia when they are conscious (Bennett, 1992). Although not all research supports the operation of memory under general anesthesia, most recent, controlled experiments support several important conclusions (Ghoneim & Block, 1992). Patients under general anesthesia may not be oblivious to their operative experiences, partly because there is no adequate way to measure the depth of anesthesia while a patient is unconscious. Patients also perform well on experimental tasks that measure implicit memory of information presented to them during anesthesia (Block et al., 1991; Khilstrom et al., 1990). More important for patients' health are findings that unfavorable comments voiced about them during anesthesia may harm them, as in Karen's case (Blacher, 1987; Eich et al., 1985; Levinson, 1967). On the positive side, therapeutic suggestions during anesthesia may improve patients' postoperative recovery, as shown by reduced use of morphine and earlier discharge (Evans & Richardson, 1988; McLintock et al., 1990).

Introduction

Karen's case introduces us to the complexities of human consciousness. Her ordinary state of conscious awareness was altered in many ways: by drugs, by sleeping and dreaming, and by hypnosis. Her waking thoughts and moods were influenced by memories and subtle impulses, such as her frustrated desire for a puppy and her fear of cancer. Even when Karen's body was immobilized by a general anesthetic, her brain was still subconsciously processing environmental stimuli.

➡ What is ordinary conscious awareness? Can unconscious mental events influence our thoughts, emotions, and actions? How and why does consciousness change, and how can we intentionally change our states of mind?

Our search for answers to these questions puts the human mind in the spotlight. In the previous chapter we began to explore the relationship between brain and behavior. In this chapter we continue that exploration by first reflecting on the relationship between brain and mind. Next, we will analyze the nature of consciousness. Then we will shift to the regular mental changes we experience every day of our lives. Finally, we will look at how special techniques and experiences can alter consciousness both dramatically and deliberately.

The Nature of Consciousness

Our early ancestors traced the causes of human actions to their *anima*, or inner life force, and the operation of outer spiritual forces (divine and demonic) that they believed existed in nature. They assumed that an individual's spirit, or soul, was separate from the body; they also assumed that the soul controlled the person. When the spirit left, the person could do nothing, and the body died. If evil spirits entered a person's body, they could cause disease or bizarre behavior. Puncturing the person's skull allowed these evil spirits to escape. Although archaeological evidence indicates that many "patients" survived this primitive brain surgery, such a drastic procedure was obviously based on a strong conviction of the power of spirits to rule the body. Over the centuries, philosophers have debated the relationship between the brain and the mind—the sources of all action and thoughts. The "In Focus: The Mind-Body Problem" examines this debate.

Trephination—perforating the skull with a sharp instrument—was long thought to be a means of treating mental disorders. The process was originally believed to drive out the evil spirits causing the disturbance.

THE MIND–BODY PROBLEM

The relationship between the brain and the mind has long perplexed serious thinkers and defied easy solutions. On one side of the debate are those who hold that the *mind* does not exist: They believe the term is merely a popular way to refer to what the brain does. It is only the *brain*, they say, that thinks about the brain's activities, just as a computer's diagnostic programs check on its own circuits and functioning. The opponents of such a view believe that mind is more than just a convenient term for thoughtful reflection. They argue that mind and consciousness are central to what it means to be human.

The mind–body problem has perplexed humans for much of recorded history, but it was first systematically considered in the writings of the ancient Greek philosopher Plato (427? – 347? B.C.).

Plato was one of the first Greek philosophers to try to distinguish between mind and body. In his view, the mind and its mental processes were absolutely distinct from the physical aspects of body and brain. Plato gave the mind a special position. He believed that the mind went beyond the physical world of the senses to consider abstractions and "ideal realities." He speculated that the mind survived the death of the body. Plato's view became known as *dualism*. **Dualism** proposes that the mind is fundamentally different from and independent of the brain: The mind and brain are two distinct but interwoven aspects of human nature.

With the rise of the Roman Empire, philosophical analyses of such matters were set aside in favor of military, legal, and technological matters. The ideas of Plato and other Greek thinkers were further suppressed by the spread of Christianity, which insisted that belief in the nonphysical soul was a matter of uncontested faith and not open to debate. It was not until the Renaissance that a renewed appreciation for scientific, rational inquiry sparked efforts to understand the nature of the mind.

In the mid-1600s, the French philosopher and mathematician **René Descartes** advanced the radical new theory that the body was an "animal machine." This meant that the body's workings could be studied scientifically by reducing all sensations and actions to their underlying physical components. In this *mechanistic approach*, animal behaviors and some basic human behaviors are reflex reactions to physical energies

exciting the senses. It follows from Descartes' theory that since the body is a machine, it cannot be subject to moral principles; therefore, other human behaviors (for example, reasoning, decision making, and thinking about oneself) are based on the operation of the soul, or human mind. Descartes's dualistic view enabled him to resolve the dilemmas he faced as a devoutly religious Catholic (who believed in the spiritual soul), a rational thinker (who believed in the ephemeral mind), and a scientific observer (who believed in the mechanistic view of perception and reflex actions).

In opposition to dualism is **monism,** which proposes that mind and brain are one and that mental phenomena are nothing but the products of the brain. Monists contend that the mind and its mental states are reducible, in principle, to brain states; that is, all thought and action have a physical, material base (Churchland, 1986). If monism is accurate, then thoughts, ideas, and dreams are part of the same bodily reality that gives rise to breathing, digesting, and walking. The monistic view of human nature holds that the processes of the mind will eventually be fully explained by the laws that govern all matter. If we accept the monistic view, we may have difficulty accepting the idea that we *are* what our bodies *do*, rather than a supernatural soul or spirit wrapped in a mortal shell. Because our ideas about the meaning of life are entwined with what we believe about nature, the study of the mind always sparks controversy and debate.

---

dualism Theory that the mind is fundamentally different from and independent of the brain: the mind and the brain are two distinct but interwoven aspects of human nature.

monism Theory that mind and brain are one—that mental phenomena are the products of brain activity.

Psychology's Conception of the Mind

Throughout psychology's short history, there has been an ongoing, vigorous tug-of-war between scholars with two distinct conceptions of the mind: **dualism** and **monism** (see the "In Focus" box). When psychology gradually emerged as distinct from philosophy in the late 1800s, it became "the science of the mind." Wilhelm Wundt and E. B. Titchener advocated using introspection in their structuralist analysis of the mind. William James asserted on the first page of his 1890 classic text, *The Principles of Psychology,* that "psychology [is] the description and explanation of 'consciousness' as such."

John B. Watson's objective behaviorism dismissed introspection and stream of consciousness studies as unscientific, emphasizing instead direct observations of behavior. In the three decades that behaviorism dominated American psychology (from the 1930s to the 1960s), the discipline focused solely on external behavior.

In the 1960s, cognitive psychologists and psycholinguists studying thought and communication examined the workings of the mind and its products. Humanistic psychologists, who focus on the processes of self-knowledge and self-actualization, made their entire discipline the study of the human mind.

The emergence of brain sciences led biologically oriented psychologists to support the monist position. They believed the mind and the brain to be identical. But if the mind is indistinct from the brain's biological processes, then consciousness must also be eliminated from psychologists' interest.

This narrow view of consciousness was challenged by the research of Roger Sperry and Michael Gazzaniga. In their independent investigations, Sperry and Gazzaniga found that surgically disconnecting the cerebral hemispheres created a duality of conscious experience in patients (see Chapter 2). Out of this research came a new perspective, called the **emergent-interaction theory** of mind-brain relationships. This theory asserts that brain activities give rise to mental states, but that these mental states are not the same as and not reducible to brain states. On the contrary, brain and mind *interact,* so just as the brain acts on the mind, the mind influences the brain to govern, rule, and direct neural and chemical events. Ultimately, the conscious mind exerts decisive causal influence over the brain in directing and controlling behavior.

This new form of dualism is compatible with the perspectives of most psychologists. This view fuses science with our common experience, as Roger Sperry (1976, 1987) concludes:

> The mind has been restored to the brain of experimental science. . . . Scientific theory has become squared finally with the impression of common experience: we do in fact use the mind to initiate and control our physical actions. (1987, p. 166)

It is not possible (either scientifically or logically) to prove or disprove the existence of the mind. The mind is by definition something we each experience subjectively. While we are aware of the *products* of mind and consciousness, such as thoughts and ideas, we cannot perceive the *processes* that give rise to our attention, awareness, and personal experience of consciousness. So, accepting the existence of one's own mind remains a matter of faith.

Research Approaches. In Chapter 2 we examined several techniques that researchers use to study the brain. In this section we will look at the strategies that researchers apply in studying the mind. Modern researchers use a new variation of *introspection* as an exploratory procedure to map the workings of the mind. Subjects are asked to speak aloud as they work through puzzles, operate unfamiliar machines, or carry out other complex tasks. They report in as much detail as possible the sequence of thoughts they experience as they work. Their reports, called **think-aloud protocols,** are used to document the mental strategies that subjects use and to analyze their awareness of using them (Ericsson & Simon, 1984; Newell & Simon, 1972).

In the **experience-sampling method,** subjects wear electronic pagers. They write down or tape-record what they are feeling and thinking whenever the pager signals. A radio transmitter activates the pager at various random times each day for a week or more (Emmons, 1987; Hurlburt, 1979). Subjects may also be asked to respond to questions, such as "How well were you concentrating?" Researchers thus keep a running record of people's thoughts, awareness, and attention as they go about their everyday lives (Csikszentmihalyi, 1990).

emergent-interaction theory
Theory that brain activities give rise to mental states, but these mental states are not the same as and not reducible to brain states.

think-aloud protocols Reports used to document the mental strategies of subjects and analyze their awareness of using them.

experience-sampling method
Research technique where subjects wear electronic pagers and record what they are feeling and thinking whenever the pager signals.

In one type of experience-sampling study, subjects are signaled by electronic pagers. As soon as they can do so, they pause amid their activities and record what they were thinking and feeling when they were signaled.

dichotic listening task Experiment where a subject listens through stereo earphones to two different channels of input while being instructed to *attend* to just one channel.

In the **dichotic listening task,** a subject listens through stereo earphones to two different channels of input while being instructed to *attend* to just one channel (Broadbent, 1954). The subject is required to repeat the input aloud as it enters the attended ear—that is, to "shadow" it while ignoring the input to the other ear. Not surprisingly, subjects do not remember information presented to the unattended ear. They don't even notice major changes in that input, such as when the tape is played backwards or the language changes. They *do* notice changes in pitch—as when a speaker's voice switches from male to female (Cherry, 1953)—and special signals, such as their own names. Obvious physical features of the unattended message are apparently perceived at a *subconscious* level of awareness, but the meaning does not get processed into consciousness (Lackner & Garrett, 1973).

These and other new techniques allow psychological researchers to explore the secret world of other people's consciousness. This same goal motivated Wundt, Titchener, and James a century earlier to begin their exploration of consciousness and establish the science of psychology.

The Nature of Consciousness

Think of consciousness as the front page of the mind and attention as the lead story. Awareness is the knowledge that the story is in the newspaper of your mind. Ordinary waking consciousness includes the immediate mental experiences comprising your perceptions, thoughts, feelings, and desires at a given moment—all the mental activity on which you are focusing your attention. You are conscious of what you are doing and of the fact that you are doing it. This experience of watching ourselves from a privileged "insider's" position leads to a *sense of self.* Together these mental activities form the *contents* of one's consciousness.

But there is more to consciousness than its contents. We also use the term *consciousness* to refer to a general *state of mind* rather than to its specific contents. In sum, **consciousness** can mean you are (1) aware of the general condition of your mind, (2) aware of particular mental contents, or (3) self-aware.

consciousness Awareness of the general condition of one's mind, awareness of particular mental contents, or self-awareness.

Functions of Consciousness. An evolutionary perspective reminds us that consciousness must be highly adaptive to be part of our behavior today. In general, consciousness functions to aid our survival and enable us to construct both personal realities and culturally shared realities. For example, imagine waking up to find yourself in a strange bed, being examined by white-coated strangers who tell you, "You've been in an accident, but you're in a hospital, and you're going to be all right." Your conscious abilities will enable you to organize your thoughts ("Was I alone?") and recognize new but culturally meaningful information ("A hospital is a place where I will get medical care").

From a biological perspective, consciousness probably evolved because it helped individuals make sense of environmental information and use that information to plan the most appropriate and effective actions. How does this work? First, consciousness restricts attention, controlling what we notice and think about. It allows us to attend to only what is "relevant" and rule out anything unessential or trivial. Second, consciousness helps us *select* and store personally meaningful stimuli from the flow of all this relevant input. Third, it makes us stop, think, consider alternatives based on past knowledge, and imagine various consequences. For example, as part of your morning routine, you restrict attention to certain tasks, such as showering and dressing. You probably rule out other tasks, such as calling friends and writing letters. You also notice and remember weather announcements on the radio, consider which clothes are appropriate for the weather conditions, and imagine the consequences of your choices. For all these reasons, consciousness gives us great potential for flexible, appropriate responses to the changing demands in our lives (Ornstein, 1986; Rozin, 1976).

Levels of Consciousness.   Psychologists identify three different levels of consciousness: (1) a basic level of awareness of the world; (2) a second level of reflection on what we are aware of; and (3) a top level of awareness of ourselves as conscious, reflective individuals (Hilgard, 1980; Natsoulas, 1981; Tulving, 1985). See **Figure 3.1** for one view of the levels of consciousness.

At the basic level, consciousness is being aware that we are perceiving and reacting to available perceptual information. Thus you know when you are awake, and what you can see, hear, or feel. At the second level, consciousness relies on symbolic knowledge to free us from the constraints of real objects and present events; it gives us *imagination*. At this second level, you can think about what you see, hear, or feel. The top level of consciousness is called **self-awareness,** cognizance that personally experienced events have an *autobiographical* character. Thus you know that *you* are seeing, hearing, or feeling. You realize that you are not receiving input from someone else. Self-awareness gives us our sense of personal history and identity. When you reflect on events and tell others about them, your memories of what you have experienced become part of your unique personality.

Structures of Consciousness.   Were you aware of your heartbeat just now? Probably not; control of your heartbeat is part of *nonconscious processes*. Were you thinking about your last vacation or about the play *Hamlet*? Again, probably not; control of such thoughts is part of *preconscious memories*. Were you aware of background noises, like a clock ticking or traffic on nearby streets? You couldn't be and still pay attention to this chapter, because awareness of nonrelevant stimuli is part of *subconscious awareness*. Finally, are you aware of how some of your early life experiences, as well as present desires and impulses, affect what you say and do? According to psychodynamic analysis, powerful *unconscious* forces block awareness of these emotions. In the following sections, we will examine these distinctions more carefully.

Nonconscious Processes.   **Nonconscious processes** involve information that is not represented in consciousness or memory but that still influences fundamental bodily or mental activities. The regulation of blood pressure is an

self-awareness   Cognizance that personally experienced events have an *autobiographical* character.

nonconscious processes   Information that is not represented in consciousness or memory but that still influences fundamental bodily or mental activities.

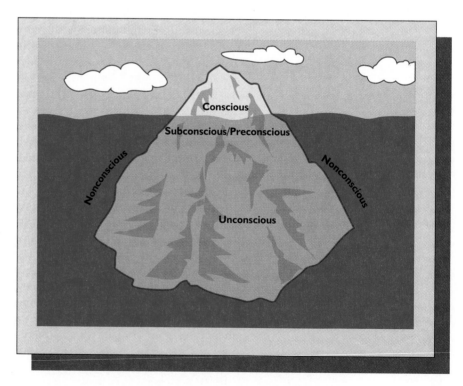

Figure 3.1   Levels of Consciousness
The iceberg metaphor for levels of consciousness. If conscious experience were represented as an iceberg, conscious processes would be located above the surface, while the Unconscious would be submerged. Subconscious and preconscious processes would both lie beneath the surface but are accessible through special attention and recall. Nonconscious processes influence bodily functions but never become accessible to consciousness.

example of a nonconscious process: Physiological information is detected and changes are acted on continually without our awareness.

Preconscious Memories. Memories accessible to consciousness only after something calls our attention to them are **preconscious memories.** Preconscious memories function in the backgrounds of our minds until they are needed or stimulated, until something interferes with our usual performance, or until we are trying to teach others tasks that we consider automatic, like tying shoelaces.

preconscious memories Memories accessible to consciousness only after something calls attention to them.

Subconscious Awareness. We put much of the stimulation around us out of our minds in order to focus attention on a small part of it. Nevertheless, a great deal of stimulation gets registered and evaluated at some level below that of conscious awareness. **Subconscious awareness** involves processing information not currently in consciousness but retrievable from memory by special recall or attention-getting procedures. Much research indicates that we are influenced by stimuli not perceived consciously (Kihlstrom, 1987). In addition, much cognitive processing seems to occur automatically, without awareness or effort, as when we correctly navigate a familiar route to work or school without apparent thought (Uleman & Bargh, 1989).

subconscious awareness The processing of information not currently in consciousness but retrievable from memory by special recall or attention-getting procedures.

In the case that opened this chapter, Karen's depression was the result of a subconscious process; once it was brought into her consciousness by hypnotic therapy, she could recognize it and deal with it appropriately.

The Unconscious. In common speech, we use the term *unconscious* to refer to someone who has fainted, is comatose, or is under anesthesia. In psychology, however, the term has a special meaning. Within psychoanalytic theory, developed by **Sigmund Freud,** the **Unconscious** refers to mental processes that keep out of conscious awareness any information that would cause extreme anxiety. Such processes are assumed to stem from the need to *repress* traumatic memories and taboo desires. For example, a young child who is sexually molested by a family member may repress her awareness of being attacked. Buried in her unconscious for years, these memories might surface only when she is older and emotionally equipped to face the reality of having been such a victim.

Unconscious Mental processes that keep out of conscious awareness any information that would cause extreme anxiety.

According to Freud, although the content of painful memories is repressed (put out of consciousness), the strong feelings associated with the thoughts still remain and show up in various forms. Much adult behavior is influenced by unconscious processes that originate in early life. Long before the incest victim is able to retrieve clear memories of being abused, she may find herself avoiding people who resemble her attacker; she might also feel uncomfortable with her own sexual feelings as she matures. Freud argued that unconscious associations and reminders of repressed trauma can shape our behavior even if we have no awareness or recognition of these thoughts.

SUMMING UP

Psychology's conception of consciousness has been influenced by the continuing debate over the relationship between mind and body. Dualism considers them separate; monism postulates they are one. A new form of dualism, the emergent-interaction theory, proposes that brain activities create mental states, and that brain and mind interact.

Consciousness aids our survival in several ways. By restricting input, selectively storing relevant information, and using knowledge to plan future actions, consciousness allows us to make intentional, flexible responses Research designed to observe these private events of consciousness employs

From a very young age, children experiment with ways to change consciousness.

daydreaming Mild form of consciousness alteration, in which attention shifts away from the immediate situation.

Daydreaming is common among people of all ages. It provides a means of transcending time and space.

new variations on introspection, such as think-aloud protocols and experience sampling. The dichotic listening task detects the effects on consciousness of attentional focus.

There are at least three different levels of consciousness: a basic level of world awareness; a level of reflection about what we are aware of; and a top level of self-consciousness. Structures of consciousness include nonconscious processes that regulate bodily functions, preconscious memories, subconscious awareness, and the Unconscious, which is hypothesized to be both the process that represses thoughts and the storehouse for all those repressed thoughts.

Everyday Changes in Consciousness

➡ Watch children stand on their heads or spin around to make themselves feel dizzy. Why do they do it? It seems that "human beings are born with a drive to experience modes of awareness other than the normal waking one; from very young ages, children experiment with techniques to change consciousness" (Weil, 1977, p. 37).

As they grow older, some people continue these mind experiments by taking drugs that alter ordinary awareness, including legal drugs such as alcohol, tobacco, and caffeine. Other individuals change their consciousness through specific behaviors or experiences. Even without making such special efforts, we all undergo a change of consciousness every time we daydream, sleep, and dream.

Daydreaming

Daydreaming is a mild form of consciousness alteration. When we daydream, attention shifts away from the immediate situation or task to thoughts that are elicited almost automatically, either deliberately or when triggered by some stimulus. Daydreams include fantasies and thoughts about current concerns. Daydreaming occurs when people are alone, relaxed, engaged in a boring or routine task, or just about to fall asleep (Singer, 1966, 1975).

Do you daydream? In one sample of 240 respondents—ages 18 to 50, with some college education—96 percent reported daydreaming daily. Young adults, ages 18 to 29, reported the most daydreaming; there was a significant decline with age (Singer & McCraven, 1961).

Experts believe that daydreaming serves valuable functions and that it is often healthy for children and adults alike (Klinger, 1987). Current research using the experience-sampling method suggests that most daydreams dwell on practical and current concerns, everyday tasks, future goals (trivial or significant), and interpersonal relationships. Daydreaming reminds us to make plans, helps us solve problems, and gives us creative opportunities for a time-out.

What triggers daydreams? Usually the stimulus is a cue from the environment or our own thoughts. We may also deliberately initiate daydreams to relieve the tedium of a boring lecture or job or to prepare ourselves for a particular task.

One research method on this subject is a daydream questionnaire, developed by **Jerome Singer,** the most influential pioneer in modern daydreaming research, and his colleague, John Antrobus. Their research reveals that daydreamers differ from one another in three ways. They vary in (1) the number of vivid, enjoyable daydreams they regularly have, (2) the proportion of their daydreams that are ridden with guilt or fear, and (3) the ease with which they are distracted or can maintain their attention (Singer & Antrobus, 1966).

Fantasy is one aspect of daydreaming. When we *fantasize,* we are not necessarily escaping from life. Instead, we may be confronting the mysteries of life and working through difficulties with wonder and respect. Regardless of how realistic or pertinent to our lives our fantasies may be, daydreams are rarely as vivid and compelling as night dreams.

Sleep and Dreaming

About one-third of your life is spent sleeping, with your muscles in a state of "benign paralysis" and your brain humming with varied activity. We take this daily dramatic alteration of consciousness for granted because it generally happens spontaneously.

We slip in and out of different states of consciousness as a natural consequence of light cycles and patterns of wakefulness and sleep. These ordinary fluctuations in consciousness are part of the rhythm of nature.

circadian rhythms Patterns that repeat approximately every 24 hours.

Circadian Rhythms. All creatures are influenced by nature's rhythms; humans are attuned to a time cycle known as **circadian rhythms,** patterns that repeat approximately every 24 hours. An individual's circadian rhythm corresponds to daily changes in the physiological activities of his or her nervous system. Arousal levels, metabolism, heart rate, body temperature, and hormonal activity ebb and flow according to the ticking of this internal clock. But the clock the body uses to measure time is not the same clock we use to keep our daily appointments. Instead of a precise 24-hour schedule, the biological clock controlling circadian rhythms apparently operates on a 25-hour cycle. Perhaps this is why many of us have difficulty falling asleep at night sometimes (we are not quite sleepy enough) and why we are so reluctant to rise in the morning (we are not yet fully awake).

Upset Rhythms. Circadian rhythms are sensitive to environmental change. Anything that throws off our biological clocks affects how we feel and act. When people fly across many time zones, they may experience *jet lag,* a condition whose symptoms include fatigue, irresistible sleepiness, and subsequent unusual sleep-wake schedules. Jet lag occurs because the internal circadian rhythm is disrupted by the new temporal environment. Traveling eastbound creates greater jet lag than traveling westbound, because our biological clocks can adjust and lengthen more readily than shorten. It is easier to stay awake a bit longer than it is to fall asleep a bit sooner.

rapid eye-movement (REM) Eye movements that occur at periodic intervals during sleep.

non-REM sleep (NREM) The time when a sleeper is not showing REM.

The Rhythms of Sleep. About one-third of circadian rhythm is devoted to the period of quiescence (vegetative inactivity) called *sleep.* With the development of the electroencephalogram (EEG), researchers could record brain activity during this quiescence without disturbing the sleeper. They found that brain waves change in form, first at the onset of sleep, and then in further systematic, predictable changes during the entire period of sleep (Loomis et al., 1937).

The next significant discovery in sleep research was that bursts of **rapid eye-movement (REM)** occur at periodic intervals during sleep (Aserinsky & Kleitman, 1953). The time when a sleeper is not showing REM is known as **non-REM sleep (NREM).** During a study, sleepers were awakened and asked to describe their mental activity during REM sleep and NREM sleep. The NREM reports were filled with brief descriptions of ordinary daily activities, similar to waking thoughts. But most of the REM reports were qualitatively different; they were vivid, fanciful, bizarre scenes from incomplete plots—in essence, dreams. Rapid eye-movements (REM) are reliable behavioral signs that a sleeper's mental activity is centered around dreaming—as if the sleeper's eyes were darting about to keep track of visual scenes on some private viewing screen.

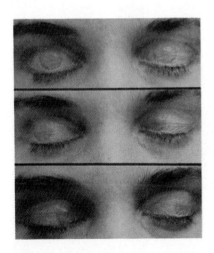

This double exposure photograph shows the rapid eye movements associated with dreaming.

The Sleep Cycle. Imagine that you are preparing to sleep. As you undress, an EEG records that your brain waves are moving along at a rate of about 14 cycles per second (cps). Once you are comfortably in bed, you relax and your

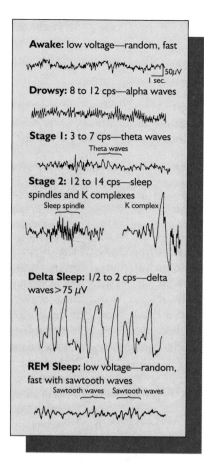

Figure 3.2 EEG Patterns Reflecting the Stages of a Regular Night's Sleep

brain waves slow down to a rate of about 8 to 12 cps. Soon you are asleep, and the EEG shows further changes. In fact, over the course of the night, your sleep cycle crosses several stages, each of which shows a distinct EEG pattern. In Stage 1 sleep, the EEG shows brain waves of about 3 to 7 cps. During Stage 2, the EEG is characterized by *sleep spindles*—minute bursts of electrical activity of 12 to 16 cps. In the next two stages (3 and 4), you enter a very deep state of relaxed sleep. Your brain waves slow to about 1 to 2 cps, and your breathing and heart rate decrease. In Stage 5, the electrical activity of your brain increases; your EEG looks very similar to those recorded during stages 1 and 2. You experience REM sleep during Stage 5, when your eyes move rapidly back and forth and you begin to dream (see **Figure 3.2**).

REM and NREM. It takes about 90 minutes to progress through the first four stages of sleep (NREM sleep). Stage 5 sleep lasts for about 10 minutes. Over the course of a night's sleep, you pass through this 100-minute cycle four to six times. With each cycle, the amount of time you spend in deep sleep (Stages 3 and 4) decreases, and the amount of time you spend in REM sleep increases. During the last cycle (Stage 5), you may spend an hour in REM sleep. See **Figure 3.3** for the pattern of sleep through the average night.

If you were deprived of REM sleep for a night, you would have more REM sleep than usual the next night. (Perhaps we need sleep only to get REM sleep rather than to rest.) REM sleep can also play a role in the maintenance of mood and emotion, and it may be required for storing memories and fitting recent experiences into networks of previous beliefs or memories (Cartwright, 1978; Dement, 1976).

Duration. How long must you sleep? This is an intriguing question—since sleep may be as much a *habit* as it is a *need*. Research shows that the length of nocturnal sleep depends on many factors. Two basic factors include (1) a *genetic need* for sleep which is different for each species and, most importantly

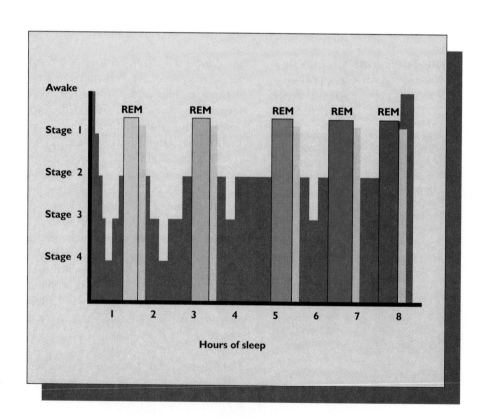

Figure 3.3 Stages of Sleep
A typical pattern of the stages of sleep during a single night includes deeper sleep in the early cycles but more time in REM in the later cycles.

for humans, (2) *volitional* determinants—that is, *wanting* to sleep. People actively control sleep length in a number of ways, such as staying up late and using alarm clocks. Sleep duration is also controlled by circadian rhythms, so that time asleep may depend on one's personal peak times for REM.

There are other factors that account for variations in amount of sleep. Individuals who sleep longer than average are found to be more nervous, worrisome, artistic, creative, and nonconforming. Short sleepers tend to be more energetic and extroverted (Hartmann, 1973). Strenuous physical activity during the day increases the amount of time spent in the slow-wave sleep of Stage 4, but it doesn't affect REM time (Horn, 1988). Mental problems seem to have the effect of extending REM sleep. One study of individuals depressed about divorce found their sleep was often disrupted with REM periods starting too early or lasting too long, and their dreams were often "stuck in the past" (Cartwright, 1984).

Finally, sleep duration varies over one's lifetime. As **Figure 3.4** shows, we begin life by sleeping at about 16 hours per day, with half that time devoted to REM. Young adults typically sleep 7 to 8 hours, with 20 percent REM. By old age, we sleep very little, with only 15 percent of sleep in REM.

Why Sleep? Apparently there is an evolutionary basis as well as a biological need for sleep. There are two general functions of sleep: to *conserve* and to *restore*. Researchers suggest that sleep evolved because it enabled animals to *conserve* energy at times when there was no need to forage for food, search for mates, or work (Allison & Cicchetti, 1976; Cartwright, 1982; Webb, 1974). Sleep also enables the body to engage in "housekeeping" functions and to *restore* itself in several ways. During sleep, neurotransmitters build up to compensate for the quantities used in daily activities, and postsynaptic receptors return to their optimal level of sensitivity (Stern & Morgane, 1974).

Francis Crick (Nobel Prize winner who unraveled the structure of DNA) and mathematician Graeme Mithison propose a different function for sleep. They believe that sleep and dreams help the brain to flush out the day's accumulation of unwanted and useless information. Dreams may also serve to

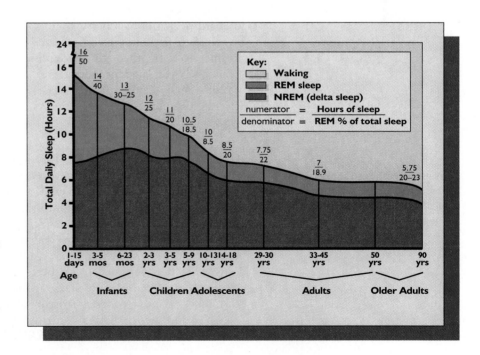

Figure 3.4 Patterns of Human Sleep over a Lifetime
The graph shows changes with age in total amounts of daily REM and NREM sleep and percentage of REM sleep. Note that the amount of REM sleep decreases considerably over the years, while NREM diminishes less sharply.

reduce fantasy and obsession, thereby minimizing bizarre connections among our many memories (Crick & Mithison, 1983).

William Shakespeare proposed a somewhat more elegantly stated hypothesis: "Sleep knits up the ravelled sleeve of care." During sleep, unravelled material—loose ends of information—may be integrated or eliminated. According to sleep researcher Ernest Hartmann, "In the morning, sleep has done its thing. If you're in good shape your sleeve has been restored for the next day's wear" (*Discovering Psychology,* 1990, program 13).

Because sleep has definite functions, and is not merely a state of being "not awake," people become concerned when their sleep is disrupted or inadequate. "In Focus: Sleep Disorders" discusses several distinct types of sleep disorders, each traceable to different factors and treatable in different ways.

 Dreaming. During every ordinary night of your life, you experience the most bizarre event staged by the human mind—the dream. Vivid, colorful, completely nonsensical hallucinations characterized by complex miniplots that transform time, sequence, and place occupy the theater of your sleep. Dreamers may feel as if they are behaving in unusual—or impossible—ways. They may talk, hear, and feel sexually excited, but they cannot smell, taste, or feel pain. Dreams are probably best characterized as theater of the absurd—chaotic dramas that appear illogical when analyzed in the rational mindset of our waking hours.

Freud called dreams "the royal road to the Unconscious," rich with clues to an individual's mental life. Once only the province of prophets, psychics, and psychoanalysts, dreams have become a vital area of study for scientific researchers. Dream research got its impetus from sleep laboratory findings that correlated rapid eye-movements, unique EEG patterns, and the sleeper's report of having dreamed.

Although dreams are primarily REM phenomena, some dreaming (of a different quality) also takes place during NREM periods. Dreaming associated with NREM states has less of a story-like quality and has little sensory imagery. Subjects also recall a much higher percentage of REM dreams than NREM dreams (Freeman, 1972).

Freudian Dream Analysis. Sigmund Freud made the analysis of dreams the cornerstone of psychoanalysis with his classic book *The Interpretation of Dreams* (1900). In the Freudian perspective, dreams have two main functions: to guard sleep and to serve as sources of wish fulfillment. Dreams guard sleep by relieving psychic tensions created during the day, and by allowing the dreamer to work through unconscious desires. To the therapist who uses dream analysis to understand and treat a patient's problems, dreams reveal the patient's unconscious wishes, the fears attached to those wishes, and the characteristic defenses the patient employs to handle the resulting psychic conflict between the wishes and the fears.

Activation-Synthesis Theory. The Freudian view is facing its severest challenge from a biologically based theory. This model, the **activation-synthesis theory,** states that all dreams begin with random electrical discharges from deep within the brain. The signals emerge from the brain stem, and then stimulate higher areas of the brain's cortex. This *activation* involves purely biochemical energy. There are no logical connections and no coherent patterns to these random bursts of electrical signals. However, the brain handles this strange event by doing what it is designed to do best: It tries to make sense of all input it receives, to impose order on chaos, and to *synthesize* separate bursts of electrical stimulation into a coherent story by creating a dream.

The proponents of this controversial theory, **Robert McCarley** and **J. Allen Hobson** (1977), argue that REM sleep furnishes the brain with an

activation-synthesis theory Theory that all dreams begin with random electrical discharges from deep within the brain.

In Focus:

Application   SLEEP DISORDERS

For millions of Americans, sleep disorders pose a persistent, serious burden that can disrupt marriages, interfere with careers, and even result in death. It is estimated that more than 100 million Americans get insufficient sleep. Of those working night shifts, more than half nod off at least once a week on the job. Some of the world's most serious accidents—Three Mile Island, Chernobyl, Bhopal, and the Exxon Valdez disaster—have occurred during late evening hours. People have speculated that such accidents occur because key personnel fail to function optimally as a result of insufficient sleep (Dement, 1976). Some types of sleep disorders are biological, while others are more psychological. Here we review four different sleep problems: insomnia, narcolepsy, sleep apnea, and daytime sleepiness.

Insomnia

When people are dissatisfied with the amount or quality of their sleep, they are suffering from **insomnia.** This chronic failure to get adequate sleep is characterized by an inability to fall asleep quickly, frequent arousals during sleep, and/or early morning awakening (Bootzin & Nicasio, 1978). Insomnia is a complex disorder caused by a variety of psychological, environmental, and biological factors (Borkovec, 1982). When insomniacs are studied in sleep laboratories, the objective quantity and quality of their actual sleep varies considerably, and ranges from disturbed sleep to normal sleep. Research has revealed that many insomniacs who complain of lack of sleep actually show completely normal patterns of sleep. This condition is described as *subjective insomnia.* Equally curious is the finding that some people who show detectable sleep disturbances report no complaints of insomnia (Trinder, 1988). The discrepancies may result from differences in the way people recall and interpret a state of light sleep.

Narcolepsy

Narcolepsy, a sleep disorder found in dogs and humans, is characterized by a periodic compulsion to sleep during the daytime. It is often combined with *cataplexy*—a total loss of mus-

cle control brought on by emotional excitement that causes the afflicted to fall down suddenly. When they fall asleep, narcoleptics enter REM sleep almost immediately. This rush to REM causes them to experience vivid hallucinations or images of their dreams that break into daytime consciousness. Because narcolepsy runs in families, scientists assume the disease has a genetic basis.

Narcoleptics can adapt to their condition by recognizing the nature of their disease and by working with social support groups. In the United States, about 10 of every 10,000 individuals are afflicted with the disease; many of these people remain undiagnosed long after they first notice its symptoms (Guilleminault et al., 1989; Joyce, 1990).

Sleep Apnea

Sleep apnea is an upper respiratory sleep disorder in which the person stops breathing while asleep. When this happens, the blood's oxygen level drops and emergency hormones are secreted, causing the sleeper to awaken, to begin breathing again, and then to fall back to sleep. While most of us have a few apnea episodes a night, someone with sleep apnea disorder can have hundreds of such cycles every night. Sleep apnea is frequent in premature infants who sometimes need physical stimulation to start breathing again. Because of their underdeveloped respiratory system, these infants must remain attached to moni-

tors in intensive care nurseries as long as the problem continues.

Sometimes apnea episodes frighten the sleeper, but often they are so brief that the sleeper fails to attribute accumulating sleepiness to them (Guillemenault, 1989). Delay in recognizing the nature of the problem can cause sufferers—and their families and coworkers—to mistakenly interpret unusual daytime behavior as laziness or neglect, when the behavior is traceable to a nighttime disorder.

Daytime Sleepiness

Sleepiness is a common problem, an inevitable consequence of not getting enough nocturnal sleep. However, *excessive daytime sleepiness* is a persistent problem that qualifies as a sleep disorder because it is a physiological state not remedied by simply getting more sleep. About 4 to 5 percent of the general population surveyed reports excessive daytime sleepiness (Roth et al., 1989). This sleepiness causes diminished alertness, delayed reaction times, and impaired performance of motor and cognitive tasks. Nearly half the patients with excessive sleepiness report automobile accidents, and more than half have had job accidents—some serious.

You may wonder if it is an exaggeration to call sleepiness a disorder. Can't boring lectures, overheated rooms, heavy meals, or monotonous tasks cause daytime sleepiness? No, say the experts. These conditions only unmask the presence of physiological sleepiness; they do not cause it (Roth et al., 1989). Although the cause of daytime sleepiness is not simply insufficient sleep—tension, worry, depression, and agitation are often responsible—learning how to get longer, more restful sleep can reduce its undesirable symptoms.

Do *you* need help with a chronic sleep disorder? The following organizations offer assistance to individuals who suffer from persistent sleep problems:

American Sleep Disorders Association
685 2nd Street, SW
Rochester, Minnesota 55902

Sleep Disorders Center, TD-114
Stanford University School of Medicine
Stanford, California, 94305

insomnia Chronic failure to get adequate sleep characterized by an inability to fall asleep quickly, frequent arousals during sleep, and/or early morning awakening.

narcolepsy Sleep disorder characterized by a periodic compulsion to sleep during the daytime.

sleep apnea Upper respiratory disorder in which the person stops breathing while asleep.

internal source of activation—when external stimulation is turned down—to promote the growth and development of the brain. Dream content results from random stimulation, not unconscious wishes. Hobson (1988) claims that meaning is added as a "brainstorm afterthought." When meaningless activations are synthesized, dreams seem familiar and meaningful.

The activation-synthesis approach helps explain many of the mysteries of sleep we posed earlier. The "stuff" of dreams may be a brain chemical, *acetylcholine,* which is turned on by one set of neurons in the brain stem during REM. Those neurons are "on" only when the others, which trigger the release of *serotonin* and *norepinephrine,* are "off." Those two brain chemicals are necessary to store memories. We forget some 95 percent of our dreams because they are only stored temporarily in our short-term memory. They cannot be "printed" to more permanent memory because serotonin and norepinephrine are shut off during the dream. Our dreams are vivid but devoid of smells and tastes because only visual neurons are stimulated by the electrical discharges during REM. We dream with such rich, vivid images because the brain uses symbols and metaphors to store higher-order knowledge; the dream is simply utilizing this storehouse of material to find some preexisting meaning in the madness of chaotic brain discharges.

Recently, Hobson's research team injected Carbachol, a drug that mimics the action of acetylcholine into the brain stems of cats. Not only did this drug trigger the flow of special brain waves (PGO waves) from the brain stem to the occipital cortex (where the dreams are visualized), but the cats' REM sleep increased by 300 percent! This technique of generating REM sleep allows researchers to study how REM sleep is related to various forms of behavioral and mental functioning. Hobson believes that his findings "have opened the door to the molecular biology of sleep," and closed it on the psychoanalytic theory of dreams (see Bianchi, 1992).

It appears, then, that we humans are so good at making sense out of things, we even do it in our sleep. By better understanding the mechanisms of dreaming, we can enhance our knowledge of waking aspects of imagery and conscious thought processes (Antrobus, 1991).

SUMMING UP

Everyday changes in consciousness include daydreaming, sleeping, and night dreaming. Daydreaming is a common, mild consciousness alteration that shifts attention away from a current situation to practical personal concerns, future goals, or fantasies.

Many changes in consciousness correspond to the body's circadian rhythm and to physiological and neural activities. Daily stresses, physical exertion, and traveling across time zones are examples of the kinds of activities that can disrupt circadian rhythms.

For all of us, sleep represents an important change in consciousness. Sleep is characterized by a reliable series of changes in the brain's electrical activities. We cycle through five stages of sleep several times each night. Stage 5 or REM sleep is significant because of the corresponding heightened electrical activity that occurs in the brain and because dreams occur primarily in this stage. Sleep serves two functions: to conserve energy and to restore resources used by the nervous system. In the standard sleep cycle, REM and NREM follow a predictable, alternating pattern throughout the night. Sleep duration is determined by a genetic sleep need and volitional factors. Sleep disorders are surprisingly common and costly to individuals and society. The major types of sleep disorders are insomnia, narcolepsy, sleep apnea, and daytime sleepiness.

Dreams are the most common variations of consciousness. Vivid dreaming occurs during REM sleep, which is brought on by nerve cell signals in the brain stem. Dreams are influenced by age and experience. In Freudian interpretation, dreams are disguised manifestations of unconscious wishes. A competing activation-synthesis theory argues that dreams are biologically based, caused by random activation of the brain stem's nerve discharges. The mind then tries to make sense of and synthesize the associated sensations and memories into a coherent story.

Extended States of Consciousness

Sleep and dreams are generally satisfying alternatives to consciousness that sometimes make it difficult to rise in the morning and start the waking day. But fantasies and dreams may not be "enough." In every society, people have been dissatisfied with such ordinary transformations of their waking consciousness. They have developed practices that enable them to experience extended states of consciousness. Psychological researchers and therapists have also developed procedures for deliberately altering states of consciousness. Such procedures include training people to control their dreams and using hypnosis or meditation to modify ordinary mental and emotional processes.

Hypnosis

Most people find hypnosis fascinating. This section will explore the following questions: What is hypnosis, what are its important features, and what are some of its valid psychological uses?

hypnosis An induced alternate state of awareness characterized by deep relaxation and heightened suggestibility.

Hypnosis is a term derived from *Hypnos,* the name of the Greek god of sleep. Sleep plays no part in hypnosis, except that the subject often appears to be in a deeply relaxed, sleeplike state. If a subject were actually asleep, he or she would not respond to hypnosis. There are many different theories about what hypnosis is and how it works. In a broad sense, hypnosis is an alternate state of awareness induced by a variety of techniques and characterized by the special ability some people have to respond to suggestion with changes in perception, memory, motivation, and sense of self-control (Orne, 1980). In the hypnotic state, the subject experiences heightened responsiveness to the hypnotist's suggestions, and often feels that his or her behavior is performed without intention or any conscious effort.

The questions surrounding hypnosis have made it a mysterious and fascinating subject. As a form of popular entertainment, stage hypnotists frequently amaze their audiences with the feats of memory and concentration their voluntary subjects perform. Remember that the same qualities that make hypnosis intriguing and entertaining may also be employed with qualified, professional guidance in self-help and therapy. Individuals who are able to reach deep levels of hypnosis may find it easier to concentrate their attention, focus their imagination, or change their own behavior in a desired direction. However, as we will discuss, not everyone can achieve the same levels of hypnosis.

Hypnotizability. The most dramatic stage performances of hypnosis give the impression that the power of hypnosis lies with the hypnotist. However, the real star is the person who is hypnotized; the hypnotist is more like an experienced guide showing the way. Some individuals can even practice self-hypnosis, or *autohypnosis,* without an hypnotic operator.

hypnotizability The degree to which an individual is responsive to standardized hypnotic suggestions.

The single most important factor in hypnosis is a participant's ability or "talent" to become hypnotized. **Hypnotizability** is the degree to which an

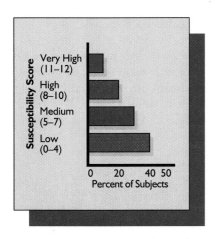

Figure 3.5 Level of Hypnosis at First Induction
The graph shows the results for 533 subjects hypnotized for the first time. Hypnotizability was measured on the Stanford Hypnotic Susceptibility Scale which consists of 12 items.

meditation A form of consciousness change designed to enhance self-knowledge and well-being by reducing self-awareness.

individual is responsive to standardized suggestions to experience hypnotic reactions. There are *individual differences* in this susceptibility—varying from no responsiveness to any suggestion to total responsiveness to virtually every suggestion. A highly hypnotizable person may respond to suggestions to change motor reactions, experience hallucinations, have amnesia for important memories, and become insensitive to powerful, painful stimuli.

Figure 3.5 shows the percentage of college-age subjects at various levels of hypnotizability the first time they were given a hypnotic induction test. High scorers are more likely than low scorers to experience pain relief as a result of hypnosis (*hypnotic analgesia*) and to respond to hypnotic suggestions to have perceptual distortions of various kinds. For example a hypnotist may "test" a new subject's acceptance of suggestion by saying, "Your right hand is lighter than air," and observing whether the subject "allows" his or her arm to float upward.

Hypnotizability is not the result of gullibility or conformity, and it is not an attempt at role playing or a reaction to the social demands of the situation (Fromm & Shor, 1979). Hypnotizability is a unique cognitive ability—a special aspect of the human imagination. It develops early in life along with the sense of being able to become completely absorbed in an experience. A hypnotizable person is one who is capable of deep involvement in the imaginative-feeling areas of experience, such as reading fiction or listening to music. A hypnotizable person can be hypnotized by anyone he or she is willing to respond to, while someone unhypnotizable will *not* respond to the tactics of even the most skilled hypnotist.

Altered Reality. It is necessary to maintain a scientific skepticism about the claims made about hypnosis, especially when such claims are based on individual case reports or research that lacks proper control conditions (Barber, 1969). Researchers disagree about the psychological mechanisms involved in hypnosis (Fromm & Shor, 1979). Some argue that hypnosis is simply heightened motivation (Barber, 1976); subjects are not entranced but aroused to channel more energy to suggested attention and activities. Others believe that hypnosis is only social role playing, a kind of *placebo response* of trying to please the hypnotist (Sarbin & Coe, 1972).

Empirical evidence and expert opinion strongly suggest that hypnosis can exert a powerful influence on many psychological and bodily functions (Bowers, 1976; Burrows & Dennerstein, 1980; E. Hilgard, 1968, 1973). One of the most common and undisputed values of hypnosis is its effect on pain. Our minds can amplify painful stimuli through anticipation and fear; we can also diminish the psychological component of pain with hypnosis. Pain control is accomplished through a variety of hypnotic suggestions: (1) distracting (the subject) from the painful stimulus, (2) imagining the part of the body in pain as nonorganic (made of wood or plastic) or as separate from the rest of the body, (3) taking one's mind on a vacation from the body, and (4) distorting time in various ways. Hypnosis has proven especially valuable to surgery patients who cannot tolerate anesthesia, to extreme burn patients, to mothers in natural childbirth, and to cancer patients learning to endure the pain associated with the disease and its treatment. Moreover, self-hypnosis enables patients to control their pain whenever it arises.

Meditation

Many religions and traditional psychologies of the Eastern world (Asian cultures) direct consciousness away from immediate worldly concerns and external stimulation. They seek to achieve an inner focus on the mental and spiritual self. **Meditation** is a change in consciousness designed to enhance self-knowledge and well-being by reducing self-awareness. During meditation,

In this demonstration of hypnotic control, the hypnotized student reports feeling no pain from the ice water (Dr. Mark Oster on faculty of Adler School of Professional Psychology, Chicago).

a person focuses on and regulates breathing, assumes certain bodily positions (yogic positions), minimizes external stimulation, and either generates specific mental images or frees the mind of all thought.

To view meditation as an altered state of consciousness may reflect a particularly Western world view. For example, Asian cultures' beliefs about the mind are very different from the beliefs of Western cultures. Buddhism teaches that the visible universe is an illusion of the senses; the world is nothing but what the mind creates; and the individual's mind is part of the collective, universal mind. Excessive mental activity distracts one from focusing on inner experience and allowing mind to rise above sensory experience. Meditation is a life-long exercise in discovering how to remove the mind from distractions and illusions, thus allowing it to roam freely and discover wisdom. To become an enlightened being, a Buddhist tries to control bodily yearnings, stop the ordinary experiences of the senses and mind, and discover how to see things in their truest (most real) light. In contrast, the Western scientist views meditation as an *altered* (changed) or *alternate* form of experience and behavior. What exactly are the effects of meditation?

One consequence of meditation is mental and bodily relaxation. Meditation reduces anxiety, especially in those who function in stress-filled environments (Benson, 1975; Shapiro, 1985). Meditative practices can function as more than valuable time-outs from tension. When practiced regularly, some forms of meditation can heighten consciousness, achieve enlightenment by enabling the individual to see familiar things in new ways, and free perception and thought from the restrictions of automatic, well-learned patterns. When practiced regularly, meditation is said to lead to *mindful awareness* in one's daily life. Awareness of the routine activity of breathing especially creates a sense of peace. One of the foremost Buddhist teachers of meditation, Nhat Hanh (1991), recommends awareness of breathing and simple appreciation of our surroundings and minute daily acts as paths to psychological equilibrium.

The practice of using meditation to achieve peace of mind, a sense of connectedness with the world, and spiritual awakening requires neither group participation nor a group leader. Any individual who is sufficiently motivated to modify the standard operating procedures of his or her consciousness can effectively practice meditation. While researchers dispute whether its effects are measurable, advocates claim wide-ranging benefits and little or no risk (Holmes, 1984).

Hallucinations

hallucinations Vivid perceptions that occur in the absence of objective stimulation.

Under unusual circumstances, a distortion in consciousness occurs during which the individual sees or hears things that are not really present. **Hallucinations** are vivid perceptions that occur in the absence of objective stimulation; they are mental constructions of an individual's altered reality. Hallucinations differ from *illusions,* which are perceptual distortions of real stimuli and are experienced by most people. For example, for most people, the flashing lightbulbs on a theater marquee look like a single light zooming around the edge of the sign. Perceiving stationary lights to be moving is a common illusion, the *phi phenomenon* (see Chapter 5). But if you "see" lights around people where there are no such lights, you are experiencing a hallucination.

Hallucinations can occur during high fever, epilepsy, and migraine headaches. They also occur in cases of severe mental disorders when patients respond to private mental events as if they were external sensory stimuli. Hallucinations have been associated with heightened arousal states and religious ecstasies as well (see "Time Out for Critical Thinking"). In some cultures and circumstances, hallucinations are interpreted as mystical insights that confer special status on the visionary. So, in different settings, the same vivid perception of direct contact with spiritual forces may be devalued as a sign of mental illness or respected as a sign of special gifts.

Hallucinations may be induced by psychoactive drugs, such as peyote and LSD (lysergic acid diethylamide), as well as by withdrawal from alcohol in severe cases of alcoholism. For the most part, however, chemically induced hallucinations are not regarded as "true" hallucinations because they are direct physical effects of the drug on the brain rather than part of a new view of reality that a person creates psychologically.

The complex functioning of the brain requires constant external stimulation. When it lacks such stimulation, the brain manufactures its own. Some subjects, when kept in a special environment that minimizes all sensory stimulation, show a tendency to hallucinate. *Sensory isolation* "destructures" the environment and may force subjects to try to restore meaning and stable orientation to a situation. Hallucinations may be a way of reconstructing a reality in accordance with one's personality, past experiences, and the demands of the present experimental setting (Zubeck et al., 1961; Suedfeld, 1980).

> ## ➡ *TIME OUT . . . FOR CRITICAL THINKING*
>
> Many episodes of altered states of consciousness are reported following overstimulating experiences, such as mob riots, religious revival meetings, prolonged dancing (such as that done by the religious sect of dervishes), extreme fright or panic, trance states, and moments of extreme emotion.
>
> Meditation, prayer, fasting, and spiritual communication all contribute to a *religious experience.* For William James, the religious experience constituted a unique psychological process (James, 1917). He believed that religious experience is characterized by a sense of oneness and relatedness of events, of realness and vividness of experience, and an inability to communicate the nature of the whole experience in ordinary language. For many

people, intense religious experiences are clearly not part of ordinary consciousness.

For example, the beliefs and practices of the Holy Ghost People of Appalachia enable them to do some remarkable things. At church services they handle deadly poisonous snakes, drink deadly poison, handle fire, and speak in imaginary languages. Considering such behavior, how would you answer the following questions?

- Is religious experience a kind of supernatural event? Why are superhuman feats sometimes considered "proof" of religiousness or holiness?

- How can an experience be religious without involving "ecstasy" or other forms of altered consciousness?

- What is the difference between a religious experience and an event that is merely difficult to explain?

- Why might some faiths require believers to prove their commitment by taking risks or inducing altered states of consciousness?

The Holy Ghost People of Appalachia and other religious sects engage in such practices as snakehandling to prove faith and achieve changes in consciousness. Rayford Dunn was bitten on the hand by a cottonmouth moments after this picture was taken in Kingston, Georgia. Although he behaved normally afterward—going out to eat, and returning to church the next day to handle snakes again—some believers have died from poisonous snake bites.

You can probably think of examples of the way different religious traditions explain or use altered states of consciousness to support the participation of believers. Consciousness is a mystery of human nature that has long been pondered in most religions.

Psychoactive Drugs

Since ancient times, people have taken drugs to alter their perception of reality. Individuals throughout the world take drugs to relax, cope with stress, avoid the unpleasantness of current realities, feel comfortable in social situations, or experience an alternate state of consciousness. In 1954, the publication of Aldous Huxley's *The Doors of Perception* popularized the use of drugs to alter

psychoactive drugs Chemicals that affects mental processes and behavior by temporarily changing conscious awareness.

The line between substance use and abuse is easy to cross for many who become addicted.

tolerance Lessened effect of a drug following continued use.

physiological dependence A process in which the body adjusts to and requires presence of a substance, in part because neurotransmitters are depleted by the frequent presence of the drug.

consciousness. Huxley took mescaline as an experimental treatment of his own consciousness. He wanted to test the validity of poet William Blake's assertion in *The Marriage of Heaven and Hell* (1793): "If the doors of perception were cleansed every thing would appear to man as it is, infinite. For man has closed himself up, till he sees all thro' narrow chinks of his concern."

A few decades after Huxley's book appeared, nearly 55 percent of American high-school seniors (in annual surveys of over 16,000 students) have reported using one or more illegal drugs in their senior year (Johnston et al., 1989). Although this figure has declined steadily since 1982 (to about 38 percent in 1987), the number of adolescents addicted to drugs has reached epidemic proportions.

Dependence and Addiction. **Psychoactive drugs** are chemicals that affect mental processes and behavior by temporarily changing conscious awareness. Once in the brain, they may attach themselves to synaptic receptors, blocking or stimulating certain reactions. Drugs profoundly alter the brain's communication system, affecting perception, memory, mood, and behavior. With certain drugs, continued use lessens the effect on the nervous system; greater dosages are required to achieve the same effect. Such reduced effectiveness with repeated use is called **tolerance.**

Hand-in-hand with tolerance goes **physiological dependence**—a process in which the body adjusts to and becomes dependent on the substance, in part because neurotransmitters are depleted by the frequent presence of the drug. **Addiction** is the tragic outcome of tolerance and dependence. A person who is addicted requires the drug in his or her body and suffers painful **withdrawal symptoms** (shakes, sweats, nausea, and in the case of alcohol withdrawal, even death) if the drug is not present.

When an individual finds the use of a drug so desirable or pleasurable that a *craving* or persistent hunger develops, with or without addiction, the individual has a **psychological dependence.** Psychological dependence can occur with any drug—including caffeine and nicotine. In extreme cases, a person's life-style comes to revolve around drug use so that his or her capacity to function is limited or impaired. In addition, the expense of maintaining an illegal drug habit often drives an addict to robbery, assault, prostitution, or drug peddling. One of the gravest dangers currently facing addicts is the threat of infection with HIV (the virus that causes AIDS) by sharing hypodermic needles. Intravenous drug users can unknowingly inject themselves with drops of bodily fluid from others with HIV.

Varieties of Psychoactive Drugs. **Table 3.1** summarizes common psychoactive drugs. We will discuss some of the effects and characteristics common to each category of substances.

Hallucinogens. Drugs known as **hallucinogens** or **psychedelics** produce the most dramatic changes in consciousness. These drugs alter perceptions of the external environment and inner awareness. They often create hallucinations and blur the boundary between self and the external world. For example, an individual experiencing hallucinogenic effects might listen to music and suddenly feel she is producing the music or that the music is coming from within herself. Hallucinogenic drugs, such as LSD, act in the brain at specific receptor sites for the chemical neurotransmitter serotonin (Jacobs, 1987). The four most commonly known hallucinogens are *mescaline* (from cactus plants), *psilocybin* (from a mushroom), and *LSD* and *PCP*, which are synthesized in chemical laboratories. Young people are most likely to abuse PCP, or *angel dust.* PCP produces a strange dissociative reaction in which the user becomes insensitive to pain, becomes confused, and feels apart from her surroundings.

Table 3.1 Psychoactive Drugs: Uses, Duration, and Dependencies

	MEDICAL USES	DURATION OF EFFECT (HOURS)	DEPENDENCE	
			PSYCHO-LOGICAL	PHYSIO-LOGICAL
Opiates (Narcotics)				
Morphine	Painkiller, cough suppressant	3–6	High	High
Heroin	Under investigation	3–6	High	High
Codeine	Painkiller, cough suppressant	3–6	Moderate	Moderate
Hallucinogens				
LSD	None	8–12	None	Unknown
PCP (Phencyclidine)	Veterinary anesthetic	Varies	Unknown	High
Mescaline (Peyote)	None	8–12	None	Unknown
Psilocybin	None	4–6	Unknown	Unknown
Cannabis (Marijuana)	Nausea associated with chemotherapy	2–4	Unknown	Moderate
Depressants				
Barbiturates (e.g., Seconal)	Sedative, sleeping pill, anesthetic, anticonvulsant	1–16	Moderate–High	Moderate–High
Benzodiazepines (e.g., Valium)	Antianxiety, sedative, sleeping pill, anticonvulsant	4–8	Low–Moderate	Low–Moderate
Alcohol	Antiseptic	1–5	Moderate	Moderate
Stimulants				
Amphetamines	Hyperkinesis, narcolepsy, weight control	2–4	High	High
Cocaine	Local anesthetic	1–2	High	High
Nicotine	Nicotine gum for cessation of smoking habit	Varies	Low–High	Low–High
Caffeine	Weight control, stimulant in acute respiratory failure, analgesic	4–6	Unknown	Unknown

addiction Physical state in which withdrawal occurs if a certain drug is not present in the body.

withdrawal symptoms Painful physical symptoms experienced when, after addiction, level of drug is decreased or drug is eliminated.

psychological dependence Pervasive desire to obtain or use a drug; not based on physical addiction.

Cannabis. **Cannabis** is a drug often classified as a hallucinogen but differs in many ways from other substances. The active ingredient in the cannabis plant is *THC,* found in both the plant's dried leaves and flowers *(marijuana)* and in the solidified resin of the plant *(hashish).* The experience derived from inhaling THC depends on its dose—small doses create mild, pleasurable highs, and larger doses result in long hallucinogenic reactions. The positive effects reported by regular users include changes at a sensory and perceptual level—notably, euphoria, well-being, and distortions of space and time. However, depending on the social context and other factors, the effects may be negative—fear, anxiety, and confusion. Because motor coordination is impaired with marijuana use, those who work or drive under its influence suffer more industrial and auto accidents (Jones & Lovinger, 1985).

Opiates. Drugs such as *morphine, heroin,* and *codeine* that suppress physical sensation and response to stimulation are known as **opiates.** All highly addic-

hallucinogens (psychedelics) Drugs that alter perceptions of the external environment and inner awareness.

cannabis Drug, derived from hemp plant, whose psychoactive effects include altered perception, sedation, pain relief, and mild euphoria.

opiates Class of drugs, derived from opium, that suppresses physical sensation and response to stimulation.

depressants Drugs that slow down the mental and physical activity of the body by inhibiting CNS transmission of nerve impulses.

tive, opiates are derived from *opium,* an extract of the unripe seedpods of the opium poppy. Morphine and codeine have analgesic (pain-relieving) properties; morphine has long been used in post-surgical medicine, and codeine is employed as a cough suppressant. Heroin is a derivative of morphine, originally developed as a medicine by the Bayer Company of Germany in the late nineteenth century, but abandoned because of its undesirable side effects. The initial effect of an intravenous injection of heroin is a rush of pleasure; feelings of euphoria supplant all worries and awareness of bodily needs. There are no major changes in consciousness, but serious addiction is likely once a person begins to inject heroin. To avoid withdrawal, a heroin user takes the drug at least twice daily. The use of this drug has been blamed for a high proportion of property crime in cities and cultures worldwide.

Depressants. **Depressants** include *barbiturates* (usually prescribed for sedation), *benzodiazepines* (tranquilizers such as Valium), and most notably *alcohol.* These drugs tend to depress (slow down) the mental and physical activity of the body by inhibiting or decreasing the transmission of nerve impulses in the central nervous system. High dosages of barbiturates induce sleep but reduce the time spent in REM sleep. Overdoses of barbiturates lead to loss of all sensations, and coma. More deaths are caused by overdoses of barbiturates, taken either accidentally or with suicidal intent, than by any other poison (Kolb, 1973).

The benzodiazepines (or minor tranquilizers) are much safer to use than barbiturates, and are most commonly prescribed to treat anxiety. Benzodiazepines calm a patient without causing sleepiness or sedation. Because benzodiazepines are so widely prescribed, they may be overused and abused, causing such symptoms as increased anxiety, muscle twitching, and sensitivity to sound and light during withdrawal. Overdoses of benzodiazepines may cause muscle incoordination, slurred speech, weakness, and irritability.

Alcohol was one of the first psychoactive substances used extensively by our ancestors. Under its influence, people become silly and talkative, abusive, or quietly depressed. In small dosages, alcohol can induce relaxation and slightly improve an adult's reaction speed. However, the body breaks down alcohol at the rate of only one ounce per hour, and greater amounts consumed in short periods overtax the central nervous system. When the level of alcohol in the blood reaches 0.15 percent, an individual experiences gross negative effects on thinking, memory, and judgment along with emotional instability and motor incoordination.

Advertisers in the United States spend millions of dollars annually to create ads depicting the social and personal benefits of drinking beer and whiskey. Alcohol-related automobile accidents are the leading cause of death among people between the ages of 15 and 25. When the amount and frequency of drinking alcohol interferes with job performance, impairs social and family relationships, and creates serious health problems, the diagnosis of *alcoholism* is appropriate. Physical dependence, tolerance, and addiction all develop with prolonged heavy drinking.

Stimulants. Users of **stimulants** such as *amphetamines* and *cocaine* seek three major effects: increased self-confidence, greater energy and alertness, and euphoria. Heavy users experience frightening hallucinations and develop beliefs that others are out to harm them, a thought pattern known as a *paranoid delusion.* Special dangers of cocaine use include both euphoric highs and very depressive lows, which lead users to increase the frequency and dosage of use beyond their own control.

In the 1980s, a particularly destructive street drug appeared called *crack,* a highly purified form of cocaine. It produces a swift high that wears off quickly. Because crack is sold in small, inexpensive quantities, this drug is readily avail-

stimulants Drugs that increase CNS activity, speeding up both mental and physical activity.

able to the young and the poor, and is destroying social communities. Despite the well-publicized deaths of prominent people from crack overdoses, there is little evidence that its use is declining.

Two stimulants that we rarely think of as psychoactive drugs are *caffeine* and *nicotine*. Within 10 minutes, two cups of strong coffee or tea administer enough caffeine to profoundly affect the heart, blood, and circulatory functions. They can also disturb sleep. Is it accurate or fair to think of commonplace, legal substances like coffee or tobacco as "drugs?" For example, is nicotine really addictive? Definitely. Like all addictive drugs, nicotine mimics natural chemicals released by the brain. These chemicals stimulate receptors that make us feel good whenever we have done something right—a phenomenon that aids our survival. Unfortunately, nicotine teases those same brain receptors into responding as if it were good for us to be smoking, chewing tobacco, or using snuff.

By short-circuiting our brains, nicotine shortens our lives as well. The total negative impact of nicotine on health is greater than that of all other psychoactive drugs combined, including heroin, cocaine, and alcohol. The U.S. Public Health Service attributes 350,000 deaths annually to cigarettes. While smoking is the leading cause of preventable sickness and death, it is both legal and actively promoted—$2.7 billion are spent annually on its advertising and promotion. Although antismoking campaigns have been somewhat effective in reducing the overall level of smoking in the United States, some 54 million Americans still smoke. Of the million people who start smoking each year, the majority are under 14, female, and members of a racial minority (Goodkind, 1989).

The Question of Consciousness

Why do we have a conscious mind, and why do we sometimes try to alter it? The evolution of the human brain permitted survival of those of our forebears who could cope with a hostile environment, even when their sensory and physical abilities were not adequate. Humans became capable of *symbolic representation* of the outer world and of their own actions—enabling them to remember, plan, predict, and anticipate (Craik, 1943). *Homo sapiens*' complex brain was able to model its world, to imagine how present realities could be transformed into alternative scenarios.

The capacity to deal with objective reality in the here-and-now was expanded by the capacity to bring back lessons from the past (memory) and to imagine future options (foresight). A brain that can deal with both objective and subjective realities needs a mechanism to keep track of the focus of attention. That part of the brain is the conscious mind.

Human intelligence and consciousness evolved as a result of competition with the most hostile force in the evolutionary environment—*other humans*. Thus the human mind may have evolved as a consequence of the extreme sociability of our ancestors. Close-group living created new demands for cooperative as well as competitive abilities with other humans. Natural selection favored those who could think, plan, and imagine alternative realities that could promote both bonding with kin and victory over adversaries (Lewin, 1987).

If the mind is the sum of the integrative mental activities to which brain processes give rise, then consciousness is the mind's *active construction of incoming information into a coherent, stable, organized pattern of symbols*. This construction makes sense of a confusing world, imposes order on chaos, and finds meaning in nonsensical events (Johnson-Laird, 1983).

Why do we become dissatisfied with our everyday working minds and seek to alter our consciousness? Perhaps, at times, we all long to reach beyond the confines of ordinary reality (Targ & Harary, 1984). The human need to expand consciousness is the mental equivalent of learning to walk although it is easier to crawl and of seeking the uncertainty of freedom instead of settling for the security of the status quo. Extending our consciousness broadens the universal experience of what it means to be a thoughtful human being.

SUMMING UP

Extended states of consciousness include hypnosis, meditation, and drug-induced states of mind. Hypnosis is a fascinating and mysterious alternate state of awareness. Hypnosis is induced by suggestions from a hypnotist that affect perceptions, thoughts, motives, and self-control. Hypnosis is often applied for relieving pain.

Meditation is a reduction in self-awareness with an enhancing effect on self-knowledge and well-being. While meditation is viewed by some cultures as a natural extension of personal experience, it is viewed by Western culture as an altered state of consciousness. Although there is dispute about its effectiveness, some argue that meditation offers a completely self-controlled route to peace of mind and spiritual awakening.

Hallucinations are an unusual effect of some distortions in consciousness. An hallucination is a vivid perception that occurs without corresponding physical stimulation. Hallucinations may be brought on by some psychoactive drugs, psychological disorders such as schizophrenia, or excessive sensory isolation.

Religious experiences may induce altered states as a result of individuals' unusual beliefs or actions. The mind-body connection may include resistance to pain or injury, changes in perception, and speaking in imaginary languages.

Psychoactive drugs are substances that temporarily affect thoughts and behaviors. Hallucinogens such as LSD and cannabis distort perception and performance. Opiates such as heroin suppress physical sensation and responsiveness. Depressants—including barbiturates, benzodiazepines, and alcohol—slow down the body's rate of activity. Stimulants such as amphetamines, cocaine, caffeine, and nicotine can increase self-confidence, heighten energy, and improve mood. Psychoactive drugs offer their effects at a high price, which may include health risk, damage to performance and relationships, psychological dependence, and physiological addiction.

Consciousness evolved as symbolic representation offered humans improved chances for survival. Memory, foresight, planning, and imagination all provided a selective advantage for our ancestors in competition with the environment and each other.

1 The Nature of Consciousness
Why is psychology's modern conception of the mind considered a new form of dualism? How can consciousness be described in terms of different functions, levels, and structures?

Consciousness is an awareness of the mind's functioning and its contents. Psychologists use many varied research techniques to study different aspects of consciousness. These include think-aloud protocols, experience sampling, and dichotic listening tasks.

A continuing debate in psychology and philosophy has centered on the relationship between mind and body. Dualism considers them separate; monism postulates that they are one. The emergent-interaction approach offers a reconciliation of the two views by proposing that brain activities give rise to mental states that are emergent properties of the brain's organization, and that brain and mind interact.

Consciousness evolved because it aids our survival. There are three levels of consciousness: a basic awareness of the world; a reflection on what we are aware of; and self-awareness. The structure of consciousness includes nonconscious processes, preconscious memories, subconscious awareness, the Unconscious, and conscious awareness.

Key Terms
dualism, p. 73
monism, p. 73
emergent-interaction theory, p. 74
think-aloud protocols, p. 74
experience-sampling method, p. 74
dichotic listening task, p. 75
consciousness, p. 75
self-awareness, p. 76
nonconscious processes, p. 76
preconscious memories, p. 77
subconscious awareness, p. 77
Unconscious, p. 77

Major Contributors
Descartes, René, p. 73
Freud, Sigmund, p. 77

2 Everyday Changes in Consciousness
What is daydreaming? How does it resemble fantasy? What is the rhythm underlying sleep? Why do we sleep? How do different psychological theories explain dreaming?

Ordinary alterations of consciousness include daydreams, sleep, and dreams. Daydreaming is the common experience of shifting from the immediate situation to other thoughts. The length of sleep for humans is determined by genetic and volitional factors. The fifth stage of sleep, REM, is signaled by rapid eye-movements and accompanied by vivid dreaming. About one-fourth of sleep is REM, coming in 4 or 5 separate dream episodes. Sleep disorders are more common than usually recognized, especially among overactive people. Insomnia, narcolepsy, and sleep apnea can be modified with medical and psychological therapy.

Freud proposed that dream content is unconscious material stimulated by the day's events. The activation-synthesis dream theory challenges Freud's psychodynamic approach with a purely biological explanation.

Key Terms
daydreaming, p. 78

Major Contributors
Singer, Jerome, p. 78

circadian rhythms, p. 79
rapid eye movement (REM), p. 79
non-REM sleep (NREM), p. 79
activation-synthesis theory, p. 82
insomnia, p. 83
narcolepsy, p. 83
sleep apnea, p. 83

McCarley, Robert, p. 82
Hobson, J. Allen, p. 82

 Extended States of Consciousness *Which processes and experiences are considered to be extended states of consciousness? How is a hypnotized subject's state of mind different from normal consciousness? What are some consequences of meditation? What causes one to experience hallucinations? How do different classes of psychoactive drugs alter consciousness? What part has consciousness played in human evolution?*

Hypnosis is an alternate state of consciousness characterized by the ability of hypnotizable people to respond to suggestions from the hypnotist with changes in perception, motivation, memory, and self-control. Pain control is a major benefit of hypnosis.

Meditation changes conscious functioning by ritual practices that divert attention from external concerns to inner experience that may enhance self-knowledge.

Hallucinations are vivid perceptions that occur in the absence of objective stimulation. Psychoactive drugs affect mental processes by temporarily changing consciousness as they modify processes in the central nervous system. Among the psychoactive drugs that alter consciousness are hallucinogens (for example, cannabis), opiates (for example, heroin), depressants (for example, alcohol), and stimulants (for example, cocaine and nicotine).

Because consciousness evolved as an aid to survival, our desire to extend our states of mind may be a natural consequence of being imaginative creatures.

Key Terms

hypnosis, p. 85
hypnotizability, p. 85
meditation, p. 86
hallucinations, p. 88
psychoactive drugs, p. 90
tolerance, p. 90
physiological dependence, p. 90
addiction, p. 90

withdrawal symptoms, p. 90
psychological dependence,
  p. 90
hallucinogens (psychedelics),
  p. 90
cannabis, p. 91
opiates, p. 91
depressants, p. 92
stimulants, p. 92

PRACTICE TEST

Chapter 3: States of Mind

For each of the following items, choose the single correct or best answer. Correct answers, explanations, and page references appear in the Appendix.

1. According to _____ , the activities of the brain give rise to mental states that are not the same as brain activities and cannot be reduced to biochemical events. Instead, mind and brain interact and influence each other.
   A. early dualism
   B. monism
   C. emergent-interaction theory
   D. activation-synthesis theory

2. A research subject wears headphones that channels a spoken monologue into her right ear while her left ear receives a familiar popular song. This demonstrates use of the _____ method of consciousness research.
   A. experience-sampling
   B. think-aloud protocol
   C. dichotic listening
   D. classical introspection

3. Which of the following is *not* one of the basic functions of consciousness cited by your text?
   A. restricting attention to what is relevant
   B. relinquishing control to enhance self-awareness
   C. selective attention and memory
   D. imagining and considering alternatives

4. Which of the following choices correctly pairs an example of an experience or process with its appropriate level of consciousness?
   A. Unconscious: Repressing sexual attraction to someone
   B. Subconscious: Regulation of glucose level in blood
   C. Nonconscious: Remembering how to tell time
   D. None of the above.

5. Rapid eye movements are reliable behavioral signs that _____ .
   A. one has achieved a genuine meditative state
   B. a subject is very low in hypnotizability
   C. one is in Stage 4, the deepest level of sleep
   D. a sleeper's mental activity is centered on dreaming

6. _____ is a sleep disorder characterized by brief interruptions when the sleeper stops breathing, wakens, resumes breathing, and falls back asleep.
   A. Apnea
   B. Narcolepsy
   C. Insomnia
   D. None of the above.

7. Which of the following statements about hypnosis is true?
   A. Hypnosis is actually a form of NREM sleep.
   B. Anyone can be hypnotized if the hypnotist knows the most effective techniques to use.
   C. The less intelligent or educated a person is, the more hypnotizable he or she will be.
   D. None of the above.

8. One of the most common explanations for the popularity of meditation is that with regular practice its users
   _____ .
   A. have increased energy levels and alertness
   B. experience hallucinations and delusions
   C. have less self-awareness and self-consciousness
   D. feel more physically and mentally relaxed

9. Which of the following is a condition that would lead one to experience hallucinations?
   A. sensory isolation
   B. use of the drug mescaline
   C. withdrawal from alcohol in severe alcoholism
   D. All of the above.

10. Three major effects sought by users of _____ are increased energy and alertness, increased self-confidence, and euphoria.
    A. stimulants
    B. depressants
    C. opiates
    D. hallucinogens

IF YOU'RE INTERESTED . . .

Altered States. (Video: 1980, color, 102 minutes). Directed by Ken Russell; starring William Hurt, Blair Brown, Bob Balaban, Charles Haid.

> Very loosely based on Paddy Chayefsky's novel of the same name. A scientist experiments with sensory deprivation, primal consciousness, and mind expansion. Good for imagery, not information.

Borbely, A. (1986). *Secrets of sleep.* New York: Basic Books.

> An intriguing review of sleep research and its applications.

Bowers, K. S. (1983). *Hypnosis for the seriously curious, 2nd edition.* New York: Norton.

> As its title promises, a volume written to inform the reader who is more than a layperson, less than a scholar in what is known—and not yet known—about hypnosis.

Freud. (Video: 1962, B&W, 120 minutes). Directed by John Huston; starring Montgomery Clift, Susannah York.

> A popularized film biography of the founder of psychoanalysis. Features fascinating dream sequences with classic psychoanalytic symbolism and interpretation.

Hobson, J. A. (1988). *The dreaming brain.* New York: Basic Books.

> For an alternative to traditional Freudian dream theory, consider Hobson's presentation of his own research and theory about the nature and "meaning" of dreams.

Ornstein, R. E. (1986). *The psychology of consciousness, 3rd edition.* New York: Viking Penguin.

> Challenging but accessible introduction and review of the subject of consciousness by one of its foremost researchers and writers.

Chapter 4 **Psychological Development**

1. What are the two approaches developmental psychologists use to understand psychological change? What are the arguments in the nature-nurture debate? How does maturation contribute to psychological development? What position do stage theories take on continuity?

2. How have conceptions of childhood changed in recent centuries? What factors affect language acquisition in childhood? What are the major stages in Piaget's theory of cognitive development? Which processes and behaviors change in social and emotional development?

3. Which tasks must be accomplished during adolescence? How are the tasks and cognitive processes of adulthood different from those of adolescence? What are the psychological meanings associated with old age?

1984. The two tiny figures in buntings are not quite three weeks old. They lie in their crib on their stomachs, in mirror image positions—a small fist inches from each mouth, one head turned to the right, the other to the left. Nicole wakes up first. She lies there, quite content, listening to her mother in the kitchen. Ten minutes later, Alexis awakens. Almost immediately, she begins to howl. The babies' mother runs in from the kitchen, picks up Alexis, and reaches for a clean diaper.

Nicole and Alexis are genetically identical twins, the products of a fertilized ovum that split sometime in the first two weeks of prenatal life. Because of their positions on the placenta, Nicole was always first to get the nutrients that support prenatal growth. Thus, at birth she weighed 4 pounds; Alexis weighed a little less. Although no one can tell the girls apart when they are dressed identically, there are important differences between the babies.

1985. Much to her mother's dismay, Alexis starts climbing on chairs as soon as she learns to crawl. Nicole follows in a couple of days. Alexis takes her first step on her first birthday. Friends and relatives clap and cheer. Nicole watches. In less than a week, she is walking too. After her morning Cheerios™, Alexis sits in her daddy's lap and opens her mouth wide for bites of his scrambled eggs. She never seems to get enough. When anyone offers eggs to Nicole, she turns away and grimaces. She sticks to Cheerios.

1986. When Alexis and Nicole are 19 months old, their mother goes away for four days. This is the first time she has left her daughters for more than a day. The girls accompany their father to the hospital where their mother and a newborn baby, Mikey, are waiting. Nicole greets her mom with a big smile and a hug, as though nothing has happened. Alexis looks away, fidgets, and shows little emotion.

1987. Both girls are wild about clothes. Sometimes they empty their drawers and closet and put on several layers of socks, blouses, skirts, and hats. Then they stand before their mother's full-length mirror and admire their fashions. Alexis claims pink and green are her favorite colors and is very possessive about them. Nicole likes purple, but allows Alexis to wear "her color" if she wants.

Nicole likes sleeping alone, while Alexis often gets anxious if she feels she has lost track of her sister—even in her sleep. Sometimes Alexis wakes up in the night. "I had a bad dream," she cries. "I lost 'Cole and I couldn't find her anywhere." Together or apart, they sleep in identical, sometimes mirror-image, positions.

When the girls work at their little table, Alexis scribbles intently on sheets of paper, "writing" letters and stories that she later dictates to her mother. Nicole is more interested in three-dimensional art projects: She sculpts Play-Doh™ into intricate shapes and makes collages out of miscellaneous objects she finds. Nicole still sucks her thumb and likes to stay close to her Mom. She also loves to climb on the tire swing in the backyard, and she begs to be pushed "higher, higher." Alexis prefers to watch.

1990. Although Alexis sometimes eats up to three times as much as Nicole, the girls' weight never differs by more than 4 ounces. (Nicole is heavier.) Nicole loves fruits and vegetables. Alexis prefers eggs and meat. Nicole takes violin lessons and practices every day. Alexis would like to take lessons too, but she doesn't want to practice. While Nicole practices, Alexis reads. She can read anything, even the instructions for the family's new laptop computer. When Nicole picks up a book, she looks first at the pictures and then reads each word carefully.

On vacation, Alexis likes to sleep with her aunt and grandma. Nicole prefers to stay with her mother. When Nicole is nearby, Alexis is theatrical and outgoing, but on her own, Alexis seems more withdrawn. Nicole is more self-contained than Alexis and seems less dependent on social approval. Alexis reacts immediately and intensely to everything that happens, with her emotions seemingly just beneath her skin. Nicole is more likely to watch and wait passively, not revealing what she is feeling.

At the end of each day, the girls brush their teeth (which grew at the same time but on opposite sides of their mouths). After listening to a bedtime story, Alexis and Nicole climb into their beds and curl up in identical mirror-image positions. Their parents wonder which aspects of their future development will be identical and which will be shaped by the unique experiences they will have in school and outside the home.

Introduction

Although Alexis and Nicole developed from the same egg and sperm, the preceding excerpts from their baby book illustrate how very different they were three weeks after birth. The book also describes the unique personality traits and behaviors each was exhibiting six years later. How is it possible that two people with identical origins could develop so differently?

This chapter begins our study of **developmental psychology,** the branch of psychology that is concerned with the changes in physical and psychological functioning that occur from conception across the entire life span. The task of developmental psychologists is to find out how organisms change over time. They study the ages and stages of development at which different abilities and functions first appear and observe how those functions are modified.

In studies of development, the usual independent variable is *age;* the dependent variable is the behavior studied at various ages. Age is really an indicator of underlying physiological and psychological processes that are presumed to be taking place and causing, or making possible, the changes in observed behavior. Psychologists distinguish between **chronological age**—the number of months or years since birth, which is usually used as the independent variable—and **developmental age**—the chronological age at which most children show a particular level of physical or mental development. For example, a 3-year-old child who has verbal skills typical of most 5-year-olds is said to have a developmental age of 5 for verbal skills.

This chapter presents a vast amount of information, spanning both the individual lifetime and the complexity of human experience. We begin by considering *how* to think about psychological development. Later we will examine the processes that develop from birth to death, and how these processes interact.

Perspectives on Development

➡ To understand the complexity of development, imagine attempting to describe your life in 25 words or less. Try to capture all that makes you unique, unusual, and yet similar to other people.

developmental psychology The branch of psychology that is concerned with the changes in physical and psychological functioning that occur, from conception across the entire life span.

chronological age The number of months or years since birth.

developmental age The chronological age at which most children show a particular level of physical or mental development.

How well can you perform this "simple" task? Where do you begin? What do you include or exclude? In some ways you *are* much like other people: You were born, have matured, and will die someday. In other ways you are distinctive: Perhaps you matured socially earlier than your friends, and are more self-confident and popular than the others. Or maybe you are not quite the scholar or athlete that some people become. The story of your development has two subplots: the *order* of the events in your lifetime, and the *processes or tasks* that together make up your life experience.

These two subplots are reflected in the way we explain and unfold developmental psychology. By focusing on the orderly sequence of development over time, developmental psychologists use the **chronological approach** to understand behavior and mental processes. This is the more common structure of lessons in developmental psychology. Texts that take the chronological approach first examine infancy, then childhood, then adolescence, and finally adulthood and old age. For each major period of life, the chronological approach "lumps together" the many different tasks and experiences that may be involved in the individual's experience. The chronological approach captures the *continuity* of growth: You are always growing, changing, and developing.

The alternative subplot focuses on the various lifelong processes of development, without categorizing them by time. As you develop, so do your many skills and talents, such as cognitive abilities, social relationships, moral reasoning, and physical maturation. The **topical approach** to developmental psychology examines each topic or task as a distinct, lifelong process. For example, your pattern of forming relationships with others—starting with parents and family members, then friends, intimate partners, and colleagues—is related to other processes (such as cognitive development), but is also distinct from them. The topical point of view considers each topic separately instead of lumping them all together for a particular period of life. The topical approach to developmental psychology captures the *complexity* and richness of your many life experiences.

These two perspectives on development can be complementary instead of contradictory. In this chapter we will balance our consideration of these two approaches. We will first review the major developmental processes topically, and then we will consider their progress in each of the four major periods of the life span: infancy and childhood, adolescence, adulthood, and old age.

The Nature–Nurture Controversy

To what extent is human behavior determined by heredity (nature), and to what extent is it a product of learned experiences (nurture)? The **nature–nurture controversy** is a long-standing debate among philosophers, psychologists, and educators over the relative importance of heredity and learning. To appreciate one of the classic elements in this controversy, we must go back to a curious discovery that began in the year 1800.

At the end of the eighteenth century, the science of "mental medicine," an early version of modern psychology, began to capture the interest of learned people. These people debated the true nature of the human species. On one side of the debate was the belief that the human infant is born without knowledge or skills. Experience, in the form of human learning, etches messages on the blank tablet, or *tabula rasa,* of the infant's unformed mind. This view crediting human development to experience is called *empiricism,* proposed by British philosopher **John Locke.** What directs human development is the stimulation people receive as they are *nurtured*.

Among the scholars opposing empiricism was French philosopher **Jean Rousseau.** He argued the *nativist* view that *nature,* what we bring into the world, shapes development. People at birth are "noble savages," unsophisticated but innocent, and likely to be spoiled or corrupted by contact with society (Cranston, 1991).

chronological approach
Understanding of behavior and mental processes by focusing on the orderly sequence of development over time.

topical approach Approach to developmental psychology that examines each topic or task as a distinct, lifelong process.

nature-nurture controversy A long-standing debate among scholars over the relative importance of heredity and learning.

Victor, the Wild Boy of Aveyron

The nature-nurture debate was intensified by the discovery in 1801 of a wild boy who had apparently been raised by animals in the forests around the village of Aveyron, France. This 12-year-old, uncivilized, *feral* (wild) child, who became known as the Wild Boy of Aveyron, was thought to hold the answers to these profound questions about human nature.

A young doctor, **Jean Marie Itard,** tried to civilize and educate the Wild Boy of Aveyron, whom he named Victor. At first, Itard's intensive training program seemed to work. Victor became affectionate and well-mannered and learned to follow instructions. After five years, however, his progress stopped, and the teacher reluctantly ended the experiment (Itard, reprinted, 1962).

Did nature or nurture fail in this case? Perhaps Victor had been abandoned as an infant because he was developmentally disabled. If that were so, training would have only limited success. If not, would modern training procedures have helped the boy develop more fully than Itard's methods?

Today, thanks to research, we know that the extreme positions of Locke and Rousseau do injustice to the richness of human behavior. Almost any complex action is shaped both by an individual's biological inheritance and by personal experience, including learning. Heredity and environment have a continuing influence on each other: Each makes possible advances on the other, but each also limits the other's contributions.

As we discussed in Chapter 2, heredity sets a range of potential; experience determines where in that range any individual will be. For example, your heredity determines how tall you can grow; how tall you actually become depends partly on nutrition, an environmental factor. **Figure 4.1** illustrates how the genetic potential (genotype) for height interacts with environmental support for different groups of children. In this as in other examples (such as intelligence), *nature and nurture interact.* Nature provides the raw materials, and nurture affects how genes "play out" their potential. Although the debate continues, investigators today are more interested in *how* heredity and environment interact to contribute to development than in the relative importance of each.

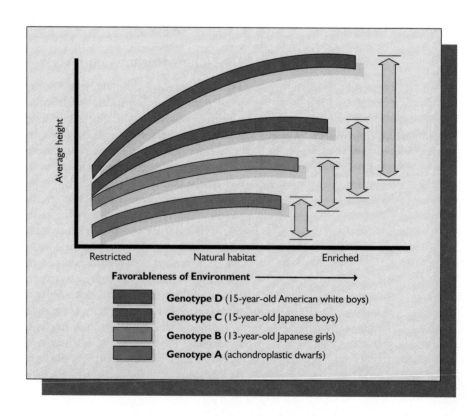

Figure 4.1 Reaction Ranges for Height as a Function of Environment

Maturation

Your body build, behavior, and development were all determined, to some extent, at the moment the genetic material in sperm and egg cells of your parents united. Your genetic inheritance imposes certain constraints, but it also makes possible certain behaviors that are not possible for members of other species. The blueprint provided by the genes directs the physical development of an organism in a predictable sequence. The blueprint is also responsible for the appearance of certain behaviors at roughly the same time for all normal members of a species, although there are some cultural variations.

Some basic survival behaviors, such as sucking, are unlearned. Others follow inner promptings but need a bit of refinement, which comes through experience. For example, most children sit without support by 7 months of age, pull themselves up to a standing position a month or two later, and walk soon after their first birthday. Once the underlying physical structures are sufficiently developed, proficiency in these behaviors requires only a minimally adequate environment and a little practice. On the other hand, these behaviors can't be accelerated by earlier efforts. They seem to "unfold from within," following an inner, genetically determined timetable that is characteristic for the species.

maturation Systematic changes occurring over time in bodily functioning and behavior, influenced by physical factors that are the same for all members of a species.

Maturation refers to the process of growth typical of all members of a species who are reared in the species' usual environment. Maturation includes the systematic changes in bodily functioning and behavior, which are influenced by genetic factors, chemical factors (for example, nutrition), and sensory factors that are the same for all members of a species (for example, gravity).

The characteristic maturational sequences of physical and mental growth are determined by the interaction of biology and environment that is normal for a given species. For example, in the sequence for locomotion, as shown in **Figure 4.2,** a child learns to walk without special training. Development of

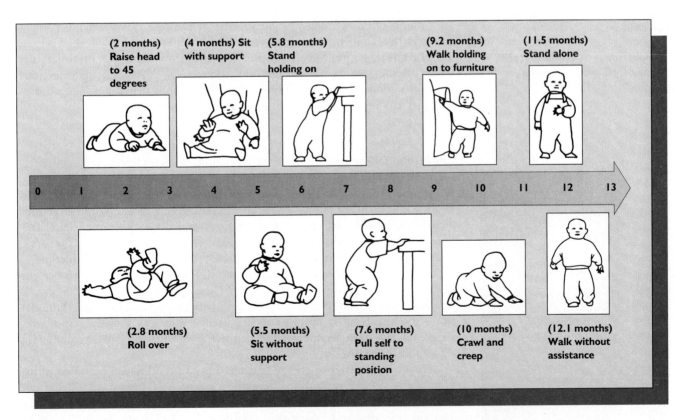

Figure 4.2 Maturational Timetable for Locomotion
The development of walking requires no special teaching. It follows a fixed time-ordered sequence that is typical of all physically capable members of our species. In cultures where there is more stimulation, children begin to walk sooner (Shirley, 1931).

The Native American use of back cradles delays the age at which infants learn to walk. However, the development of walking in Native American infants will follow the same time-ordered sequence as in other infants.

constitutional factors   Basic physical and psychological tendencies that remain fairly constant throughout a person's lifetime.

temperament   Individual's specific manner of behaving or reacting.

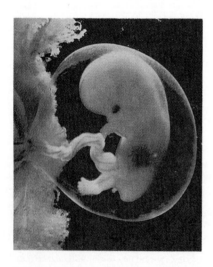

As the brain grows in the developing fetus, it generates 250,000 new neurons per minute.

walking follows a fixed, time-ordered sequence that is typical of all physically capable members of our species. In cultures where there is more physical stimulation, children begin to walk sooner.

Genetic factors are believed to instigate the maturational changes that make an individual ready for new experiences and learning. However, certain kinds of experience may influence physiological functioning and thus biological development (Gottleib, 1983). The influence of maturation is most apparent in early development, but it continues throughout life. The interaction between genetic factors and experience is the basic issue in the nature-nurture controversy. Different aspects of development follow different maturational timetables.

Physical Growth.   The heartbeat is the earliest behavior of any kind. It begins in the *prenatal period,* before birth, when the embryo is about three weeks old and a sixth of an inch long. Responses to stimulation have been observed as early as the sixth week, when the embryo is not yet an inch long. Spontaneous movements are observed by the eighth week (Carmichael, 1970; Humphrey, 1970).

After the eighth week the developing embryo is called a *fetus.* The mother feels fetal movements in about the sixteenth week after conception. In the sixteenth week, the fetus is about 7 inches long (the average length at birth is 20 inches). As the brain grows prenatally, it generates new neurons at the rate of 250,000 per minute, reaching a full complement of over 100 billion neurons by birth (Cowan, 1979). This cell proliferation and migration of neurons to their correct locations takes place prenatally, while the development of the branching processes of axons and dendrites largely occurs after birth (Kolb, 1989). The sequence of brain development, from 25 days to nine months, is shown in **Figure 4.3.**

The neural tissue of the brain (the total mass of brain cells) grows at an astonishing rate, increasing by 50 percent in the first two years, 80 percent above birth size in the next two years, and leveling off by about 11 years of age. In contrast, genital development follows a very different timetable. Genital tissue shows little change until the teenage years, and then develops rapidly to adult proportions. **Figure 4.4** shows the systematic, though different, patterns of growth for neural and genital tissues, compared with overall body growth.

Constitutional Factors.   By birth, or soon after, one's endowment of genetically determined characteristics and the influences of our early environment interact to determine an individual's **constitutional factors.** Constitutional factors include a person's basic physical and psychological tendencies. Examples include body build and predisposition to certain illnesses (physiological factors) and **temperament** or personality style (psychological factors). Constitutional factors remain fairly consistent throughout a person's lifetime.

Harvard researcher **Jerome Kagan** has shown that about 10 to 15 percent of infants are "born shy" or "born bold" (Kagan & Snidman, 1991; Kagan & Reznick, 1986). The infants differ in sensitivity to physical and social stimulation—the shy baby is more easily frightened and less socially responsive. People are less likely to interact and be playful with the shy baby, accentuating the child's initial disposition.

However, experience and special training can modify the way a constitutional factor is expressed. When developmental psychologists speak of *environmental* effects, they often mean factors such as culture, childrearing methods, parental attitudes, and educational opportunities that shape the child's development. For example, if a shy baby's parents recognize the child's withdrawal and gently play with her and encourage her to interact, the child may become more outgoing than her temperament would otherwise have predicted.

Figure 4.3 The Development of the Human Brain

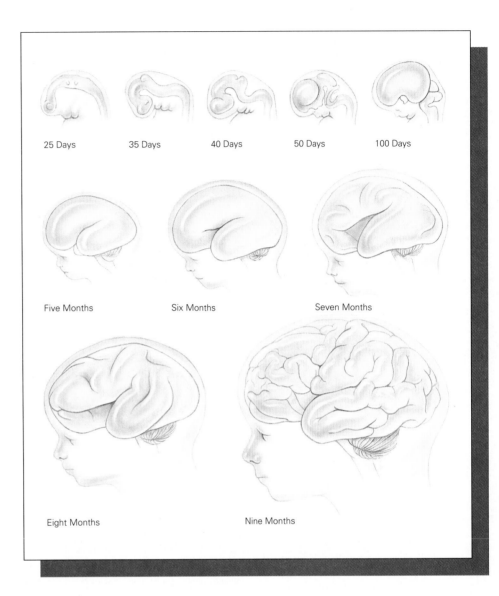

25 Days   35 Days   40 Days   50 Days   100 Days

Five Months   Six Months   Seven Months

Eight Months   Nine Months

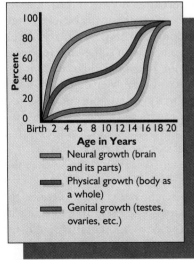

Figure 4.4 Growth Patterns Across the First Two Decades of Life as Related to Percent of Maximum
Neural growth occurs very rapidly in the first year of life. It is much faster than overall physical growth. By contrast, genital maturation does not occur until adolescence.

Sensory Development. William James, the foremost American psychologist at the turn of the century, believed that the human infant was a totally helpless and confused organism. After the tranquility of life in the womb, the infant was suddenly assailed by bursts of stimulation—the world was "one great blooming, buzzing confusion." In 1928, John Watson, the founder of behaviorism, described the human infant as "a lively, squirming bit of flesh, capable of making a few simple responses." As recently as 1964, one medical textbook author proclaimed that the newborn could not focus its eyes or respond to sounds and did not possess consciousness.

These individuals were more wrong than they could begin to imagine. For the past two decades, accumulating research has pointed to an inescapable conclusion: Babies come into the world with the ability to perform all sorts of amazing mental and perceptual feats. Moments out of the womb, infants begin to reveal that they are precocious, sophisticated, and friendly. A few minutes after birth, a newborn's eyes are alert. She turns in the direction of a voice and searches inquisitively for the source of preferred sounds, or stretches out an exploratory hand.

Babies are also born with prejudices. For example, as early as 12 hours after birth, they show distinct signs of pleasure at the taste of sugar water or vanilla. Infants smile when they smell banana essence, and prefer salted to unsalted cereal (Bernstein, 1990; Harris et al., 1990). But they recoil from the

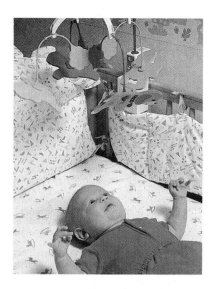

Early on, infants can perceive large objects that display a great deal of contrast.

taste of lemon or shrimp or from the smell of rotten eggs. Their hearing functions even before birth, so they are prepared to respond to certain sounds when they are born. They prefer female voices, are attentive to clicking sounds, fall asleep to the beating of a heart, and recognize their mothers' speech a few weeks after birth.

Vision is less well developed than the other senses at birth; indeed, babies are born "legally blind" with a visual acuity of about 20/500. Good vision requires that a great many photoreceptor cells function in the eye's retina. At birth, not enough of these connections are laid down. These immature systems develop very rapidly and the baby's visual abilities soon become evident (Banks & Bennett, 1988). Early on, infants can perceive large objects that display a great deal of contrast. A 1-month-old child can detect contours of a head at close distances; at 7 weeks the baby can scan the interior features of his caregiver's face, and as the caregiver talks the baby can scan his or her eyes. As early as 2 months, the baby begins to see color—differentiating patterns of white, red, orange, and blue. At 3 months, the baby can perceive depth and is well on the way to enjoying the visual abilities of adults.

Babies apparently start life already equipped with remarkable know-how, and they can use many of their senses to take in and react to information. As "In Focus: Are Babies Prewired for Survival?" shows, they might be thought of as prewired "friendly computers," well suited to respond to adult caregivers and to influence their social environments.

Continuity and Change

An important issue in developmental psychology is the extent to which development is characterized by *continuity* or *discontinuity.* Some psychologists believe that development is essentially continuous. According to this view, we become more skillful in thinking, talking, or using our muscles in much the same way that we become taller—through the cumulative action of the same continuing processes.

developmental stages   Periods during which physical or psychological functioning differs from earlier or later functioning.

In contrast, other psychologists see development as a succession of reorganizations—behavior is different in different *age-specific life periods,* such as infancy, childhood, and adolescence. In this view, while development itself is continuous, particular aspects of it are discontinuous. For example, newborns are not perceived as less dependent on the mother than they were before birth; they are *as* dependent but in different ways. Psychologists who believe development is discontinuous theorize about **developmental stages,** different levels of development. They believe different behaviors appear at different ages or life periods because different underlying processes are operating then. A *stage* is a period of time when psychological functions are observably changed. You may have heard parents dismissing a child's misbehavior or stubbornness as "just going through a stage." Developmental stage theories are more precise than these "commonsense" ideas, although they have similar expectations that stages are temporary and focused on specific tasks or experiences.

A stage progresses toward an assumed goal—a state or ability that the individual must achieve (Cairns & Valsinger, 1984). Different individuals may experiences stages in the same order but at different rates. Stage theories are models of development in which every individual progresses by engaging in one central task or challenge at a time. In the developmental research we review in this chapter, two themes recur among stage theories: *cognitive development* (including language and moral reasoning) and *social development* (including emotions, attachment, and relationships). As you read about and evaluate each stage theory, consider the many different forms of behavior and the tensions between continuous and discontinuous processes.

critical period   A sensitive time in an organism's development when it will acquire a particular behavior if certain stimuli and experiences occur.

The concept of *critical periods* is related to stages of development. A **critical period** is a sensitive time in an organism's development when the organism will acquire a particular behavior if certain stimuli and experiences occur. If

Research ARE BABIES PREWIRED FOR SURVIVAL?

How do babies organize their early experiences and what can they do? These questions are at the core of an explosion of research on the *infancy period*, which lasts for about the first 18 months of life while the child is incapable of speech. (The Latin meaning of the word *infancy* is *incapable of speech*.) Much of this research is focused on the *neonate*, the newborn baby up to a month old (see table below for an outline of the early stages of child development).

Responding and Adapting

Even within the first hours of life, a newborn infant, given an appropriate stimulus, is capable of a variety of responses. If placed upon the mother's abdomen, the baby will usually make crawling motions. The baby will also turn its head toward anything that strokes its cheek—a nipple or a finger—and begin to suck it. Sucking is the only behavior that is common to all mammals (Blass & Teicher, 1980). *Sucking* is an exceedingly complex, but already highly-developed, behavior pattern. Most babies know how to do it from the start.

Sucking is an adaptable behavior that can be changed by its *consequences*. For example, the sweeter the fluid, the more continuously and forcefully an infant will suck (Lipsitt et al., 1976).

Infants apparently come into the world preprogrammed to like and seek pleasurable sensations, such as sweetness, and to avoid or escape unpleasant stimulation, such as loud noises, bright lights, strong odors, and painful stimuli.

Elliott Blass (1990) and his research team at Johns Hopkins University started studying the abilities of newborn babies with baby rats. They wanted to know how newborn rats, which are blind and deaf, learn to find their mother's nipple. Smell is the key—baby rats move toward a familiar odor when they search for a nipple. When the mother's nipple is washed, making it lose its odor, the rats don't attach.

The researchers began studying human newborns after their studies with rats. They taught newborns 2 to 48 hours old to *anticipate* the pleasurable sensation of the sweet taste of sucrose.

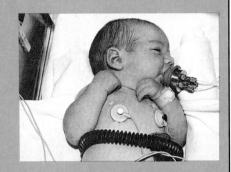

Infant with Lipsitt sucking device

When they stroked the baby's forehead and gave it the sugar water, it extended its tongue and became calm. Soon, just stroking alone would cause the baby to turn its head in the direction from which the sweet fluid was delivered—in anticipation of good times past. What do you predict happened when the stroking was not followed by sucrose? The babies got upset. Almost all (seven of eight) newborns cried when the sweets failed to show up, while few cried (1 of 16) in the control group not conditioned to expect sucrose after stroking. It is as if the babies were responding emotionally to a violation of a reliable relationship that had been established (Blass, 1990).

It seems that babies start to build up their knowledge of the world by observing relations between connected sensory events. Through interactions of inherited tendencies and learned experiences, babies can become competent survivors able to learn vast amounts of information.

Interacting Socially

Babies are designed to be sociable. They prefer human voices to other sounds and human faces to most other patterns (Fantz, 1963). At only a week old, some babies can distinguish their mothers' voices from the voices of other women (Carpenter, 1973).

Babies not only respond to, but also interact with, their caregivers. High-speed film studies of this interaction reveal a remarkable degree of *synchronicity*—close coordination between the gazing, vocalizing, touching, and smiling of mothers and infants (Martin, 1981;

Stages in Early Life-Span Development

STAGE	AGE PERIOD	SOME MAJOR CHARACTERISTICS
Prenatal Stage	Conception to birth	Physical development
Infancy	Birth at full term to about 18 months	Locomotion; rudimentary language; social attachment
Early Childhood	About 18 months to about 6 years	Well-established language; gender typing; group play; ends with "readiness" for schooling
Late Childhood	About 6 years to about 13 years	Many cognitive processes become adult except in speed of operation; team play

Trevarthen, 1977). Babies respond and learn, but they also send out messages to those willing to listen to and love them. The feelings of mothers and infants are also matched in a socially dynamic fashion (Fogel, 1991). A 3-month-old infant may laugh when its mother laughs and frown or cry in response to her display of negative emotion (Tronick et al., 1980).

Developmental psychologists are becoming more impressed with how precocious (smart for their age) babies are. Babies seem to come equipped to accomplish three basic tasks of survival: sustenance (feeding), maintenance of contact with people (for protection and care), and defense against harmful stimuli (withdrawing from pain or threat). These tasks require perceptual skills, ability to understand experiences, and basic thinking skills (von Hofsten & Lindhagen, 1979).

stimulus conditions are not met, however, the individual will not develop the behavior and will have difficulty doing so later. Experiments have confirmed that critical periods for certain behaviors occur in both animals and humans. For example, when dogs and monkeys are raised in isolation for a few months after birth, they lack contact with their species during a critical period of social development. Even if they are then reared with other normal animals, they behave in abnormal ways throughout the rest of their lives (Scott, 1963). For example, a female adult rhesus monkey who was initially reared in isolation will not react appropriately to signals for mating, and if she gives birth, she will not give her baby normal maternal care.

SUMMING UP

Developmental psychologists study the processes and changes that accompany different ages and stages of human development, from conception through infancy and childhood and throughout the entire life span. The chronological perspective on development presents these changes in terms of their sequence, while the topical presentation characterizes development in terms of distinct underlying processes.

The nature-nurture controversy is an ongoing, but continuing, debate about which is more vital to human development—what we bring into the world or what the world brings to us. Current wisdom suggests that nature and nurture always interact to determine any complex behavior.

Physical growth and abilities follow a genetically based timetable of maturation, but early chemical and sensory factors also play a role in maturation. Environmental inputs can modify genetically inherited predispositions. The three sensory systems that are well developed at or soon after birth are hearing, smell, and touch. Vision develops more slowly.

Infants are born with active minds and many abilities that enable them to survive by getting nourishment, defending against harm, and making social contact with adult caregivers.

While some developmental psychologists argue that development is continuous over time, others take the discontinuity view that specific functions are different at different age periods. The proponents of discontinuity outline a series of sequential stages that all children must experience to achieve optimal performance. Related to stage theory is the concept of critical periods—time periods during which infants in some species are especially sensitive to influential environmental stimuli.

The Developing Child

Developmental psychologists generally portray the child as an isolated entity for professional study. On the other hand, proponents of historical analysis study individual development in a social, economic, and political context (Furstenberg, 1985). The cultural meaning of childhood powerfully influences our understanding and treatment of children. In this section we will examine first *how* children are understood and studied. We then consider the specific development of children's language, thought, relationships, and feelings.

Perspectives on Childhood

Developmental psychology requires both a view of the child as a person and a research strategy appropriate for studying young people. In this section we first review the history of the concept of childhood, and then consider how it is possible to study infants and children in objective, informative ways.

Changing Conceptions of Childhood. Prior to the sixteenth century, children above 6 years of age were considered small adults and were expected to perform accordingly if possible. Parents and employers had virtually unlimited power over children, who might be abused, abandoned, sold as slaves, or mutilated (McCoy, 1988; Pappas, 1983).

From the sixteenth through the eighteenth centuries, children were considered *chattel,* family property useful for getting work done and contributing to household income. Infant and child mortality was high, and adults generally considered young children to be interchangeable and replaceable. Children's individual identities were not acknowledged; all that mattered was their ability to contribute to family livelihood.

When nineteenth century industrialization reduced the need for children as cheap labor, the concept of childhood was extended to include *adolescence*— a term used to keep young people out of the competitive job market (Krett, 1977). Eventually, children began to be treated as *valuable* and also as *vulner-*

"Infanta Margarita" [1660], Diego Velázquez, The Prado, Madrid.

"The Grace" [1740], Jean-Baptiste Siméon Chardin, The Louvre, Paris.

For most of human history, children were regarded as property—chattel—to be traded (for example, married off or exchanged) or used (for family work), and as small adults rather than developing persons. Such perceptions are obvious in these paintings of both aristocratic and common children, dressed and coached to conform to adult expectations.

able property by parents, schools, and society. During the 1800s, people began to realize that many conditions were threatening to children. These concerns led to child labor laws, compulsory education, and juvenile court systems.

During the first half of the twentieth century, children became valued as "potential persons." Child-oriented family life emerged, as did institutions like developmental psychology and juvenile courts. But not until the second half of this century did the emerging status of *child as person* afford children legal rights, including protection from abuse and neglect, due process in juvenile courts, and self-determination. Children are today recognized as competent persons worthy of considerable freedom (Horowitz, 1984).

➡ At this point in history, further advances in securing the person status of children require greater contribution by psychologists. As a science, psychology can provide empirical evidence of children's readiness or capacities for making independent choices, and can develop the best practices to achieve such self-determination in a supportive, protective environment. For example, when is a child old enough to decide which of his divorced parents he wants to live with? And should children be permitted to follow religious beliefs their parents disagree with? Psychology can provide powerful insights for investigations into these sorts of questions.

➡ *Developmental Research.* How do we know what babies can do, feel, and think? Developmental psychologists observe, compare, and test children at different ages. Here we examine four types of investigative designs, each with advantages and disadvantages: normative investigations; longitudinal designs; cross-sectional designs; and sequential designs. Researchers also use the infant's physical reactions as indicators of internal processes. Each method generates the evidence on which modern developmental psychology rests.

normative investigations A type of investigation in which researchers describe a characteristic of a specific age or developmental stage.

Normative Investigations. **Normative investigations** describe a characteristic of a specific age or developmental stage. By systematically testing individuals of different ages, researchers can determine developmental landmarks, such as those listed in **Table 4.1**. The data provide *norms*—standard patterns of development or achievement—based on observations of many children, indicating the average age at which the behaviors were performed. Thus a child's performance can be compared to the standard for the typical individual at the same age. A child who is found to be behind the norm for a particular ability—slow to begin walking or talking, for example—might be given special assistance to catch up to her peers.

longitudinal design A type of investigation in which researchers repeatedly observe and test the same individuals over time.

Longitudinal Investigations. In the **longitudinal design,** researchers repeatedly observe and test the same individuals often for many years. Because the subjects lived through the same socioeconomic period, age-related changes cannot be confused with variations in differing societal circumstances. For example, a researcher may study the behavior of a class of first-graders every few months as they proceed through elementary school. If these different children experience the same changes at the same times, such developments are probably caused by their age rather than by coincidence or societal changes.

Unfortunately, the results of longitudinal designs can be generalized only to a very limited group: those of the same generation as the original subjects. Longitudinal design is also costly because it is difficult to keep track of subjects over extended time periods in a mobile society, and data are easily lost because of subject attrition.

cross-sectional design A type of investigation in which groups of subjects of different chronological ages are observed and compared at a given time.

Cross-sectional Designs. Because longitudinal designs are not always practical, most research on development uses a **cross-sectional design** in which groups of subjects of different chronological ages are observed and compared simultaneously. A researcher can then draw conclusions about behavioral differences

Table 4.1 Norms for Infant Mental and Motor Development (based on the Bayley Scales)

ONE MONTH

Responds to sound
Becomes quiet when picked up
Follows a moving person with eyes
Retains a large easily grasped object placed
    in hand
Vocalizes occasionally

TWO MONTHS

Smiles socially
Engages in anticipatory excitement (to feeding,
    being held)
Recognizes mother
Inspects surroundings
Blinks to object or shadow (flinches)
Lifts head and holds it erect and steady

THREE MONTHS

Vocalizes to the smiles and talk of an adult
Searches for sound
Makes anticipatory adjustments to lifting
Reacts to disappearance of adult's face
Sits with support, head steady

FOUR MONTHS

Head follows dangling ring, vanishing spoon,
    and ball moved across table
Inspects and fingers own hands
Shows awareness of strange situations
Picks up cube with palm grasp
Sits with slight support

FIVE MONTHS

Discriminates strange from familiar persons
Makes distinctive vocalizations (e.g., pleasure,
    eagerness, satisfaction)
Makes effort to sit independently
Turns from back to side
Has partial use of thumb in grasp

SIX MONTHS

Reaches persistently, picks up cube deftly
Transfers objects hand to hand
Lifts cup and bangs it
Smiles at mirror image and likes frolicking
Reaches unilaterally for small object

SEVEN MONTHS

Makes playful responses to mirror
Retains two of three cubes offered
Sits alone steadily and well
Shows clear thumb opposition in grasp
Scoops up pellet from table

EIGHT MONTHS

Vocalizes four different syllables (such as
    da-da, me, no)
Listens selectively to familiar words
Rings bell purposively
Attempts to obtain three presented cubes
Shows early stepping movements (prewalking
    progression)

This table shows the average age at which each behavior is performed up to 8 months. Individual differences in rate of development are considerable, but most infants follow this sequence.

that may be related to those age differences. In experiments using cross-sectional designs, those in the experimental group receive a particular treatment while those in the control group (with the same age distribution) are not exposed to the independent variable. Researchers can thus investigate an entire age range at one time.

The disadvantages of cross-sectional design come from the fact that subjects of different ages grow up in different eras and conditions. Thus differences discovered among them may be due to those living circumstances rather than to their ages. For example, a study conducted today comparing 10-year-olds and 18-year-olds will find differences; but are those differences due to the mere eight-year difference in subject's ages—or to the fact that the older subjects were children in a world that had already changed by the time the younger ones were born? Thus cross-sectional studies cannot really distinguish between age effects and those of one's environment—the events, places, and relationships that shape one's life.

sequential design A type of investigation in which subjects who span a certain, small age range are grouped according to their birth years and observed repeatedly over several years.

Sequential Investigations. **Sequential design** combines the best features of cross-sectional and longitudinal approaches. In a sequential design, subjects span a specific and small age range, are grouped according to their birth years, and, are observed repeatedly over several years. By studying children whose ages will overlap in the course of study, a researcher can avoid the confounding problems of cross-sectional designs and the strategic difficulties of longitudinal work.

Internal Processes. Modern developmental researchers observe what infants can do and then infer the meaning, that certain patterns (internal processes) of behavior have for those infants. Infants move their eyes to look at certain things, reach out to touch objects, and suck liquids. Researchers use these simple behaviors as signals of the infants' abilities, capacities, and psychological states.

One of the most useful research paradigms is that of *habituation*. If an infant looks at one stimulus more than another, this is an indication that the infant can perceive the difference between them. Babies soon stop responding if they get too much of the same stimulus. Such a decrease in response to any repeatedly presented event is known as **habituation,** a basic response process found in most species and especially evident in newborns. **Dishabituation** occurs when, after habituating—no longer responding—to a familiar stimulus, the infant responds to a new stimulus, revealing that the baby perceives it to be different. Researchers use the babies' looking time and reaching as dependent measures of attention, preference, or perceptual ability. In addition to recording these simple responses such as smiling, crying, and sucking, special devices can chart electrical brain activity, pupil dilation, or heart rate. Each of these responses tells the researcher something about the babies' responses to different events.

habituation Decrease in response to any repeatedly presented event.

dishabituation Recovery from habituation; occurs when novel stimuli are presented.

But how can we know what a baby is thinking, or what babies already know about the world when they can't tell us? Developmental psychologists are finding ways for babies to indicate the state of their worldly knowledge. A baby's smiles and stares can reveal much about the baby's mind, when the testing situation is arranged so that those reactions indicate mental processes. For example, when a baby expects a certain event to occur, it will look less long and smile less at the event than it will for an unexpected, surprising event. By comparing the length of time that a baby stares at an expected event with the length of time the baby stares at an unexpected event, we can begin to understand what the baby must know in order to produce that difference. For example, a baby sees one object added to a second, and then a screen is dropped to block the objects from view. When the screen is quickly raised, revealing three objects, the baby stares longer at them than at the first two objects. This is taken to mean that the baby has developed a basic sense of numbers or addition, long before any formal arithmetic training. A similar research approach is being used to show that babies of only 3 or 4 months have already developed some sense of basic laws of physics, such as recognizing that solids cannot pass through solids. In demonstrating this perceptual ability, infants stare longer at "impossible" events than at "possible" ones, showing surprise when they view toy cars that seem to pass through obstacles on a hidden track (Baillargeon, 1986).

The joys from the mother-child bond help offset the daily struggles for survival faced by poor mothers the world over.

Acquiring Language

Infants know no language at all, yet in only a few years virtually all young children become fluent speakers of any language they hear spoken and have the opportunity to speak. What makes infants such adept language learners? Infants appear to be born with important language-learning abilities. As we shall see, this innate readiness for learning language is only part of the answer; social factors in conversational language and children's cognitive ability to learn new rules also play major roles in language acquisition.

Inborn Language Readiness. While the ability to learn language is biologically based—that is, we are born with an innate language capacity—there is no universal language. The predisposition to learn language is thus remarkably flexible as well as strong (Meier, 1991). Four factors are especially important in language mastery by children: high social interest; abilities to perceive speech and then to produce it; and finally their language acquisition device.

Social Interest. Infants are social beings. Studies show that infants prefer stimuli that have many rounded contours and edges and that move and emit sounds—in other words, objects that look and act similar to people. Such perceptual preferences indicate an interest in interacting and communicating with others. Without this interest in social interaction, there would be no motivation for children to learn language.

Speech Perception. Except for children being born with hearing deficits, all infants can hear many of the sound contrasts that languages use to distinguish between different meanings. In English, *bit* and *pit* have different meanings. We know that they are different words because we can hear the difference between *b* and *p*, which are different **phonemes**, or minimal, meaningful sound units. There are about 45 distinct phonemes in English. Using the habituation paradigm to study perception of speech sounds in infants from 1 to 4 months of age, researchers have shown that newborns can distinguish all the English phonemes. Moreover, recent studies have shown that infants can hear sound differences that their parents can't. In this sense, infants are "super-equipped," and ready to deal with more sounds than a given language is likely to contain, since no language uses all of the speech sound contrasts that can be made. A well-known example is the lack of differentiation in Japanese between the English sounds *r* and *l*. Native speakers of Japanese often have a very hard time hearing the difference between these sounds when they study English. The inability of Japanese speakers to differentiate between the "l" and "r" sounds leads to ethnic jokes. For instance, instead of saying "long legs" a comic imitating a Japanese user of English would say "rong regs." A similar situation exists in the pronunciation by Chicanos of the "j" sound for "y," which might result in the same comic saying, "He went to Jale University."

Speech Production. In addition to the ability to perceive speech sounds, infants have a biological predisposition to make certain sounds that they will later use in speaking. The basic apparatus for speech production (the vocal tract) is inborn. Moreover, well before they begin to use true words, infants *babble,* making speechlike sounds, such as "mamama" or "beebee." The age of onset of babbling seems to be biologically determined. Some linguists have argued that babblings are the direct precursors of speech sounds. They suggest that a baby babbles all sounds in all languages, and the repertoire is eventually narrowed down to those sounds found in the language he or she learns (Mowrer, 1960). This view is not entirely accurate because infants do not babble certain speech sounds (consonant clusters such as *str* in *strong* and *xth* in *sixth*). In addition, some sounds (*r* and *l,* for example) are present in babbling but not in a child's first words. Babbling allows children to practice making sounds, grouping the sounds into sequences, and adding intonation (Clark & Clark, 1977).

phonemes Smallest meaningful units of sound in a language.

LAD: Language Acquisition Device. Many theorists have agreed that, in addition to innate abilities, there is a biologically based **language acquisition device** (LAD) that plays a major role in children's language learning. Psycholinguist **Noam Chomsky** (1965, 1975) argues that children are born with biologically predetermined mental structures that facilitate the comprehension and production of speech. LAD helps children understand the grammar of language, making it easier for them to discover grammatical patterns and relationships.

There are three lines of evidence for LAD. First, virtually all human beings learn language very quickly. Second, they do so based on input that does not provide enough information to allow them to learn how to extract grammatical rules. Finally, feedback from caregivers is not sufficient to teach children grammatical rules.

Caregivers tend to correct children's utterances on the basis of the *truth value* of their content rather than on their accurate grammatical quality. If a child says, "One, two, I have two foots!" the caregiver may respond enthusiastically, "That's right! You really know how to count now." The caregiver is unlikely to say, "No, silly, you have two FEET, not two foots!" However, when children utter a grammatically correct but factually incorrect sentence, they are likely to be corrected. Thus neither learned imitation nor parental correction can explain grammatical development very well. Moreover, many aspects of language emerge and evolve at particular periods—critical language acquisition periods—that correspond more closely with physical and cognitive maturation than with particular learning experiences (Lenneberg, 1969).

Communication Skills. Without language you cannot communicate abstract ideas, but by using nonverbal gestures you can indicate you are hungry or tired. Similarly, preverbal infants use nonverbal means to communicate. They cry when distressed and coo and smile when pleased. At first, infant communication relies greatly on caregivers as interpreters, but over time, children take on more of the communication burden. Caregivers work to keep their infants' interest and to introduce them to language. When adults speak to infants and young children they use a special form that differs from adult speech: an exaggerated, high-pitched intonation known as **motherese.** This serves a number of functions: getting and holding infants' attention, communicating affect (emotion), and signalling turn-taking in parent-infant dialogues.

Variations in motherese offer flexibility and instruction. Motherese intonations contain affective messages without words. Caregivers use rising intonation to engage babies' attention, falling intonation to comfort them, and short staccato bursts as prohibitions. Research by **Anne Fernald** and her colleagues shows that parents in many different cultures use these patterns and babies understand them, even if they are not in their native tongue (Fernald et al., 1989). For example, in the 1987 film *Three Men and a Baby,* one of the three bachelors entertains the baby girl who has been left on their doorstep by reading the newspaper's sports page to her—but he does so in a lilting, high-pitched voice, instead of the more matter-of-fact style he might use to read to an adult.

Caregivers work to introduce their infants to language by engaging them in simple "training" dialogues. At first these are very one-sided; caregivers do the talking, but pause at certain points to let infants respond. Caregivers accept anything the babies do—even burping or sneezing—as a valid response.

As babies get older, caregivers become more demanding conversational partners. At first, caregivers require that babies verbalize, then that they use actual words, and finally that they use words relevant to the topic at hand. This pattern of gradually increasing demands on the child and decreasing caregiver support is called *scaffolding.* Young children rely less on their caregivers as interpreters of communication. Eventually, children use their first words for making assertions and requests; they seem to use their very first words to communicate messages to others (Greenfield & Smith, 1976). For example, a child

Anne Fernald

who knows the word *cookie* (or something that sounds similar) will not usually utter the word when she is alone, but will say it when others are present—using the word socially to ask for a cookie or point to a cookie, rather than merely rehearsing her speech. In some cultures, other people besides the parents take on the role of language teacher. For example, older siblings and cousins often have the responsibility for looking after toddlers. As part of their efforts, they expose the toddlers to the language of their culture and give the toddlers practice in communicating with others (Rogoff, 1990).

Children must acquire additional skills and knowledge to become fully competent communicators Adult language users coordinate many different kinds of information to communicate effectively. They know the "rules" of verbal exchange—how to partake in conversations, take turns talking and listening, and make contributions relevant. Adult speakers communicate successfully by using devices such as body language, intonation, and facial expressions. They also use feedback that they get from listeners, and are able to take the perspective of the listener. Children must master these skills to become successful communicators.

grammar A language's set of rules about how to combine—and not combine—words, word units, and order to make understandable sentences.

Learning Words. Acquiring a basic vocabulary is an important project for children in their first few years of life. Despite the challenges of understanding others and acquiring language, young children are excellent word learners. By the age of 6, the average child is estimated to understand 14,000 words (Templin, 1957). Assuming that most of these words are learned between the ages of 18 months and 6 years, this works out to about nine new words a day, or almost one word per waking hour (Carey, 1978). The cumulative growth of a child's vocabulary is shown in **Figure 4.5.**

Children develop vocabulary and grammar through three initial stages: the *one-word stage,* the *two-word stage,* and *telegraphic speech.* During the one-word phase, children use only one word at a time, usually concrete nouns or verbs. Children use them to *name* objects that move, make noise, or can be handled such as, "mama", "ball," and "dog." Children sometimes *overextend* words, using them incorrectly to cover a wide range of objects, such as using the word *dog* to refer to all animals.

At around 18 months, children's word learning often takes off at an amazing rate. At this age, children might point to every object in a room and ask, "What's that?" Researchers have called this phase the *naming explosion* because children begin to acquire new words, especially names for objects, at a rapidly increasing rate.

Learning the names for objects is only the first stage of language learning. As children grow older, they begin to express more abstract meanings, going beyond their physical world to talk about their psychological world. For example, around the age of 2, children begin to use words such as *dream, forget, pretend, believe, guess,* and *hope,* as they talk about internal states (Shatz et al., 1983). They also use words such as *happy, sad,* and *angry* to refer to emotional states. Finally, after cognitive advances that occur later in childhood, they understand and use abstract words such as *truth, justice,* and *idea.*

As their vocabularies grow, children combine their new words in utterances of two or more words. It is in these two-word and telegraphic stages that they first develop grammar.

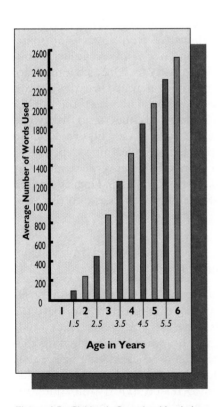

Figure 4.5 Children's Growth in Vocabulary The number of words a child can use increases rapidly between the ages of 18 months and 6 years. This study shows children's average vocabularies at intervals of six months. (*Source:* B. A. Moskovitz, "The Acquisition of Language," *Scientific American,* Inc. All rights reserved. Reprinted by permission.)

Acquiring Grammar. Adult users of language know how to combine words into meaningful larger units. Combining words greatly increases the number of meanings and complexity we can express. For example, "I was talking to her when she saw him" and "She was talking to him when I saw her" use exactly the same words but have completely different meanings. **Grammar** is a language's set of rules about combining words, word units, and order to make understandable sentences. Different languages use considerably different rules about grammatical combinations.

When and how do children acquire grammar? After the naming explosion between 18 months and 2 years, children begin to use their one-word utterances in sequence to convey more complex meanings. By combining words into two-word utterances, children can communicate more than simple identification. At this *two-word stage,* children from widely differing language communities tend to use two-word utterances to divide the world into similar linguistic categories. For instance, ten children speaking different languages (English, Samoan, Finnish, Hebrew, and Swedish) were found to talk mostly about three categories: movers, movable objects, and locations (Braine, 1976). When Tanya kicks a ball, for example, the mover is Tanya and the movable object is ball. Tanya then puts the sequence into words: "Tanya ball."

After two words, sequence size continues to increase. In early multiword sentences, children's speech is *telegraphic*—filled with short, simple sequences that use content words but omit plurals, tense endings, and function words like *the* and *of.* For example, "Ball hit Evie cry" is a telegraphic message.

In addition to learning how to fill out the full grammatical form of sentences, children must learn how to put words together. In English, this means recognizing and using the familiar order of actor-action-object, as in "The lamb followed Mary." This becomes complicated when alternative orders—such as "Mary was followed by the lamb"—convey the same meaning. Children must also learn how to rearrange elements of statements to form questions and negatives. To make a sentence negative, young children may simply put a no in front of it: "No the sun is shining." Later they learn where to insert the negative: "The sun is not shining."

An additional grammatical skill that children need to acquire is using morphemes, the structural units or building blocks of words. We use morphemes such as -'s, -ed, and -ing to mark certain kinds of meaning, such as possession (Maria's), past tense (danced), and continuing action (laughing). It is apparent that children test and try out the use of grammatical morphemes—and sometimes their hypotheses are wrong. A common error is **overregularization,** applying a rule too widely and creating incorrect forms. Once children learn the past-tense rule (adding -ed to the verb), they often add -ed to all verbs, forming words such as "hitted" and "breaked." As children learn the rule for plurals (adding the sound -s or -z to the end of a word), they again overextend the rule, creating words such as "foots" and "mouses" (see **Figure 4.6**). To researchers, such mistakes are evidence that language learning depends on acquiring general rules of grammar, rather than just imitating what adults say (Slobin, 1979). For developmental psychologists interested in language acquisition, the common errors of childhood offer exciting glimpses into the complex mental processes that underlie all human speech.

overregularization Applying a grammatical rule too widely and creating incorrect forms.

Cognitive Development: Piaget's Theory

In reading about language acquisition, you may have the impression that children's minds are bursting with thoughts and ideas long before they have the words to express them. For example, if you have ever had contact with a toddler going through the naming explosion, you have seen that children have an insatiable appetite for the labels of things they know. Clearly, long before they have the vocabulary, babies and young children see and think about the world.

➡ How and when do children begin to reason, think, plan strategies, and solve problems? **Cognitive development** is the study of the processes and products of the mind as they emerge and change over time. Do children know objects still exist even when they can't see them? Do they know that it is possible to believe in ideas that aren't true and that people have desires and dreams—but objects do not? Developmental psychologists want to know the way children think and what they think.

cognitive development The study of the processes and products of the mind as they emerge and change over time.

Figure 4.6 What's a child to do—or say? Although regular English nouns are made plural by adding an "s," many common words (such as *feet, sheep, geese, mice, women, men,* and *children*) have irregular plurals. Even adults have problems keeping track of words like *data, stimuli, criteria,* and *phenomena*—using these forms as if they were singular, although they are all plural.

There are two dominant views on the nature of the human cognitive system. The *information-processing approach* uses computer information-processing as the model for how people think and deal with information. The *cognitive-development view* originates from the pioneering work of the late Swiss psychologist **Jean Piaget.** For nearly 50 years, he observed children's intellectual development. Piaget's training in biological methods of observation helped him investigate human cognition as a form of biological adaptation. Piaget saw the human mind as an active biological system that seeks, selects, interprets, and reorganizes environmental information to fit with or adjust to its own existing mental structures.

Piaget began his quest to understand the nature of the child's mind by carefully observing the behavior of his own three children. He would pose problems to them, observe their responses, slightly alter the situations, and once again observe their responses. Piaget used simple demonstrations and sensitive interviews to generate complex theories about early mental development.

In their short early lives, children learn to transform specific information about concrete events into general, abstract concepts. How does their thinking

Although an infant will begin to suck a bottle just the way he or she sucked a breast (assimilation), the infant will soon discover that some changes are necessary (accommodation). The child will make an even greater accommodation in the transitions from bottle to straw to cup.

schemes In Piaget's theory, cognitive structures that develop as a child learns to adapt sensorimotor sequences to environmental conditions.

develop in this way? There are three key components of Piaget's approach to cognitive development: schemes; assimilation and accommodation; and the four stages of cognitive growth.

Schemes. Infant cognition involves sensorimotor intelligence—a hands-on approach to sensing and doing—rather than symbolic representation. Sensorimotor intelligence consists of **schemes**—mental structures or programs that guide sensorimotor sequences, such as sucking, looking, grasping, and pushing. Schemes are enduring abilities and dispositions used to carry out specific kinds of action sequences that aid the child's adaptation to its environment—with little or no "thought." For example, as an infant's hand touches an object like a pencil, the fingers curl around it in a grasp—the infant appears to do this all at once, instead of first closing one finger, then another, and so on, until the pencil is completely enclosed. At first, these sensorimotor sequences depend on the physical presence of objects that can be seen or handled. Later, mental structures incorporate more and more *symbolic representations* of outer reality. As this occurs, the child performs more complex mental operations (Gallagher & Reid, 1981; Piaget, 1977). For example, a toddler sees the string attached to a favorite pull-toy, but not the toy itself, so she pulls the string to "bring" the toy out of hiding and close enough to touch. She must be able to imagine the toy and remember that the string is attached to it, before she can use a pulling scheme to gain access to it.

Assimilation and Accommodation. According to Piaget, there are two basic processes at work in cognitive growth: assimilation and accommodation. In assimilation, the new is changed to fit the known; in accommodation, the known is changed to fit the new.

Assimilation modifies new environmental information to fit into what is already known. A baby reflexively knows how to suck from a nipple, for example, and will try to use the same technique on new objects—sucking on a sugary finger, for example, or messily slurping at the rim of a cup.

In contrast, **accommodation** restructures or modifies the child's existing schemes so that new information can fit in better. Consider the transitions a baby must make from sucking at mother's breast, to sucking from a bottle, sipping through a straw, and drinking from a cup. The initial sucking response is a reflex action present at birth, but it must be modified to *accommodate* new vessels.

In adapting to a bottle, an infant still uses many parts of the sequence unchanged (assimilation), but must grasp and suck somewhat differently than before and simultaneously hold the bottle (accommodation). For Piaget, cognitive development results from the constant interweaving of assimilation and accommodation. Assimilation keeps and adds to existing abilities and lessons already learned, while accommodation results from new problems posed by the environment. These *discrepancies* between the child's old ideas and new experiences are an important motivator of changes in cognitive development. Assimilation and accommodation are needed in balance. Through these two processes, children's behavior and knowledge become less dependent on concrete external reality and more reliant on abstract thought.

Stages of Cognitive Development. There are four qualitatively different Piagetian stages of cognitive growth: the *sensorimotor stage* (infancy), the *preoperational stage* (early childhood), the *concrete operational stage* (middle childhood), and the *formal operational stage* (adolescence). Distinct styles of thinking emerge at each stage in this progression from sensory reaction to logical thought. All children progress through these stages in the same sequence, although one child may take longer to pass through a given stage than another.

assimilation A process that modifies new environmental information to fit into what is already known.

accommodation A process that restructures or modifies the child's existing schemes so that new information is better understood.

object permanence The perception that objects exist independently of one's own actions or awareness.

egocentrism Self-centered focus; the inability to distinguish mental from physical worlds.

centration Thought pattern characterized by inability to take into account more than one factor at a time.

conservation The understanding that physical properties of an object do not change when nothing is added or taken away, even though its appearance changes.

Piaget proposed that the typical 6-month-old will attend to an attractive toy (top photo), but will quickly lose interest if a screen blocks the toy from view (bottom photo). He mistakenly believed that the average 6-month-old lacked object permanence.

Sensorimotor Stage. (Birth to age 2) Many new cognitive achievements appear during the first two years of a child's life. In this section, we will examine only two main trends: Changes in how the infant interacts with its environment, and the infant's understanding of object permanence.

During the first year of life, the sensorimotor sequences are improved, combined, coordinated, and integrated. They become more varied as the infant tests different aspects of the environment and discovers that actions can have an effect on external events. But in the sensorimotor period, the child is tied to the immediate environment and motor-action schemes, lacking the cognitive ability to represent objects symbolically.

The most important lesson acquired in infancy is the ability to form mental representations of absent objects. There is a vast mental difference, for example, between *pointing* to the toy one wants and *knowing* it must be somewhere so that it can be sought or asked for. By the end of the second year, the child has developed this understanding. **Object permanence** refers to the perception that objects exist independently of one's own actions or awareness. I may not be able to *see* the doll, but I know that there *is* a doll that I can find and play with. Object permanence develops gradually during this first stage of cognitive development and is solidly formed before age 1 (Flavell, 1985).

Preoperational Stage. (From 2 to 7 years of age) The big cognitive advance in the next developmental stage is the ability to represent objects mentally that are not physically present. Representational thought becomes fully functioning in the preoperational stage. Except for this development, Piaget characterizes the preoperational stage according to what the child can't do, such as solve problems using logical operations. Three of the most interesting features of the child's mind in this period are egocentrism (self-centered focus), the inability to distinguish mental from physical worlds, and centration (focus on only central features of objects). Because of **egocentrism,** children cannot take another person's perspective, seeing the world only in terms of themselves and their own position. Young children also engage in *animistic thinking,* imagining that inanimate objects have life and mental processes—as when a child who has banged her head on a tabletop complains about the "bad table." Finally, **centration** involves being too focused on a single perceptual quality to be able to notice or understand an event. For example, a thirsty child may insist on having a "big glass" of juice rather than drinking a larger serving from a cup, merely because the narrow glass is tall and transparent, while the cup seems short ("littler") and its contents cannot be seen.

Concrete Operational Stage. (From 7 to 11 years of age) At this stage, the child is capable of *mental operations* but still cannot reason abstractly. He or she depends heavily on concrete sensory impressions to make choices and judgments—for example, seeing ice-cream colors before identifying a favorite flavor. In this stage children begin to break through their centration, looking past a single compelling feature to take other features into account.

For example, most 7-year-olds have mastered the concept of **conservation:** The idea that physical properties do not change when nothing is added or taken away, even though their appearance changes. A string of red beads is *not* longer than an identical string of blue beads, even though the red beads are stretched out in a line while the blue beads lie in a small pile. They may *look* different, but this does not mean that they *are* different in length or number of beads.

Although children learn to use logic and inference to solve concrete problems, the symbols they use in reasoning are still symbols for concrete objects and events and not abstractions. The limitations of their thinking are shown in the familiar game of Twenty Questions, the goal of which is to determine the identity of an object by asking the fewest possible questions of the person who thinks up the object. A child of 7 or 8 usually sticks to very specific questions,

This 5-year-old girl is aware that the two containers have the same amount of colored liquid. However, when the liquid from one is poured into a taller container, she indicates that there is more liquid in the taller one. She has not yet grasped the concept of conservation, which she will understand by age 6 or 7.

such as "Is it a bird?" or "Is it a cat?" Children at the concrete operational stage usually don't ask abstract questions, such as "Does it fly?" or "Does it have hair?"

Formal Operational Stage. (From about age 11 on) In this final stage of cognitive growth, thinking becomes abstract. Adolescents can see that their particular reality is only one of several imaginable realities. They begin to ponder deep questions of truth, justice, and existence. Most young adolescents have acquired all the mental structures needed to go from being naive thinkers to experts. Adolescents and adults approach the Twenty Questions game in a way that demonstrates their ability to use abstractions and to adopt an information-processing strategy that is not merely random guesswork. They impose their own structures on the task, starting with broad categories and then formulating and testing hypotheses in light of their knowledge of categories and relationships. Their questioning moves from general categories ("Is it an animal?") to subcategories ("Does it fly?") and then to specific guesses ("Is it a bird?") (Bruner et al., 1966).

Modern Perspectives. Piaget's theory of the dynamic interplay of assimilation and accommodation is generally accepted as a valid account of the way a child's mind develops. Piaget's *stage* approach to cognitive development is the model used by many developmental psychologists to understand how other mental and behavioral processes develop.

While challenging Piaget's approach, contemporary researchers have come up with different ways to study the development of the child's cognitive abilities. Their research has shown that children are much more intellectually sophisticated at each stage than Piaget had found. Investigators also challenge Piaget's theory of the sensorimotor foundations of thought (J. Mandler, 1990) and turn more to information-processing models of cognitive development (Siegler, 1986). This research benefits from the use of superior technology, more valid index variables, and cross-sectional experimental research designs involving many children. Some of this work has refined concepts originally introduced by Piaget. For example, preoperational children may actually *understand* some of the same concepts as children at the concrete operational stage, but they may still lack the memory or language skills to *perform* accordingly. For example, a 5-year-old child who has watched her father prepare breakfast before can watch him and understand what he is cooking, but may not be able to describe it to her visiting grandmother, or express why she likes her pancakes "the way Daddy fixes them."

Other contemporary researchers have rejected Piaget's stage approach altogether, in favor of the *information-processing approach* that likens the child's mind to a computer. In this view children are, like adults, constantly taking in information about the world. But unlike adults, children are restricted by limited memory capacity; as they overcome these limitations, their cognitive functioning visibly improves. Developmental research is not a closed book; researchers continue to force the field to rethink long-cherished ideas about the child's mind and how it grows.

Social and Emotional Development

A child who is competent in language and cognitive skills would still be deficient without appropriate social and emotional reactions and capabilities. Children's basic survival depends on forming meaningful, effective relationships with other people. Children need to learn the rules that their society uses for governing its members' social and political interactions. They must be in touch with their own feelings and respond to the feelings of others.

Smiling is one way that young children can have an impact on their social environment. We smile not only as a sign of positive feelings, but also because

Is a child's mind like a computer? Some technophobic parents may think so when they themselves are unable to decipher "computerese"—but watch in amazement as their young children relate to computer technology with no such fear.

socialization The life-long process of shaping an individual's behavior patterns, values, standards, skills, attitudes, and motives to conform to those regarded as desirable in a particular society.

attachment The intense, enduring, social-emotional relationship between a child and a parent or other regular caregiver.

imprinting Primitive learning in which some infant animals follow and form an attachment to the first moving object they see and hear.

Konrad Lorenz, the researcher who pioneered in the study of imprinting, graphically demonstrates what can happen when young animals become imprinted on someone other than their mother.

we have an audience who expects such a facial expression (Fridlund, 1990). The delight a parent takes in a baby's first smile represents the beginning of lifelong social lessons.

Socialization and Attachment. **Socialization** is the life-long process of shaping an individual's behavior patterns, values, standards, skills, attitudes, and motives to conform to those regarded as desirable in a particular society (Hetherington & Parke, 1975). Many people and institutions exert pressure on the individual to adopt socially approved values. Of these, the family is the most influential shaper and regulator of socialization. The family helps the individual form basic patterns of responsiveness to others; these patterns, in turn, form the basis of the individual's habitual style of relating to other people.

Infant Attachment. Social development begins with the establishment of a close emotional relationship between a child and a parent or other regular caregiver. This intense, enduring, social-emotional relationship is called **attachment.** Attachment behaviors appear to occur instinctively in many species. One example is **imprinting,** the demonstration of social actions (such as following and nestling) specifically to the first moving object or individual the infant sees. A baby chick hatched by a mother duck will form an attachment to this surrogate parent, staying close to her and following her right up to the water's edge when she and her ducklings go for a swim.

The imprinting tendency is an innate predisposition, but the organism's environment and experience determine what form it will take. Human infants and human caregivers may have similar instinctive attachment patterns. However, biological research indicates that hormonal influences do not dictate parental feelings or actions. Human babies are not mobile enough to use their own locomotion to get closeness or attention from a caregiver. Babies *can emit* signals—such as smiling, crying, and vocalizing—to promote responsive behavior (Campos et al., 1983). Who can resist a baby's smile? According to **John Bowlby** (1973), an influential theorist on human attachment, infants will form attachments to individuals who consistently and appropriately respond to their signals.

Once established, secure attachment has powerful, lasting, beneficial effects; it provides a psychological home base from which an individual can explore the physical and social environment. Secure attachment to valued adult models who offer dependable social support enables the child to learn a variety of prosocial behaviors (taking turns, sharing, cooperating), to take risks, to venture into new situations, and to seek and accept intimacy in personal relationships. For example, a securely attached toddler may behave shyly at first when meeting new children, but will soon feel safe and brave enough to move away from the parent and get acquainted with the newcomers.

Attachment Research and Theory. The power of attachment has inspired several theories to explain how it is established and developed. The evolutionary explanation for attachment assumes that infants who formed close attachments to parents or other caregivers and got the support and protection they needed were more likely to survive and pass their genes on to future generations than infants without such attachments. Attached infants are less at risk for being killed by predators, getting lost, suffering exposure or hunger, or receiving injuries from members of their own species.

Sigmund Freud and others have argued that babies become attached to their parents because the parents provide them with food—their most basic physical need. This is the "cupboard theory" of attachment. **Harry Harlow** (1965) did not believe that the cupboard theory completely explained the motivation for and importance of attachment. He set out to test the cupboard theory of attachment, guessing that infants might also become attached to

contact comfort Reassurance derived from physical touch and access of caregiver.

psychosocial dwarfism Syndrome in which children's normal development is inhibited by traumatic living conditions.

psychosocial stages According to Erikson, successive developmental crises that focus on an individual's orientation to self and others.

One of Harlow's monkeys and its artificial terry cloth mother. Harlow found that the contact comfort mothers provide is essential for normal social development.

those who provide "contact comfort." Harlow separated macaque monkeys from their mothers at birth and placed them in cages where they had access to two artificial "mothers": a wire one and a terry cloth one. Harlow found that the baby monkeys nestled close to the terry cloth mother and spent little time on the wire one. They did this even when only the wire mother gave milk! The baby monkeys also used the cloth mother as a source of comfort when frightened and as a base of operations when exploring new stimuli. The infant monkeys became attached to and actually preferred the mother that provided **contact comfort** over the one that provided food (Harlow & Zimmerman, 1958).

Observations of human infants have also demonstrated the critical value of contact comfort. Many studies have shown that a lack of close, loving relationships in infancy affects physical growth and even survival. In family environments marked by emotional detachment and hostility, children are found to weigh less and to have retarded bone development. They begin to grow when they are removed from the hostile environment, but their growth again becomes stunted if they are returned to it—a phenomenon known as **psychosocial dwarfism** (Gardner, 1972). Negative environments, however, affect not only physical development but also social development. For example, a child from an emotionally detached family background may become an adult who is uncomfortable expressing caring feelings for others.

Stress, trauma, neglect, and inadequate contact in early life can slow physical, mental, and social development, producing lasting handicaps (Kagan & Klein, 1973). For example, adults who, as children, saw their own parents abuse each other are more likely to become either abusers or victims of domestic violence in their own families—a *cycle of violence* that can endure for generations (Gelles, 1980; O'Leary, 1988). Yet there are almost always some children who are resilient to the consequences of severe life stress and deprivation, who somehow transcend their traumatic early life experiences (Garmezy, 1976; Skolnick, 1986). Why? The presence of strong attachment relationships in these children's lives may be part of the answer. A close interactive relationship with loving adults is a child's first step toward healthy physical growth and normal socialization.

Psychosocial Stages of Development: Erikson's Theory. As a middle-aged immigrant to America, **Erik Erikson** (1963) became aware of conflicts he faced because of his new status. Erikson's awareness caused him to reflect on the many such conflicts all individuals face in the continuing process of development. His reflection resulted in a new way of thinking about human development. Erikson saw human development as a sequence of conflicts and challenges that emerge at many stages in the life course, from infancy to old age. **Psychosocial stages** are successive orientations toward oneself and toward others that influence personality growth across the entire life span. Each stage requires a new level of social interaction; success or failure in achieving such interaction can change the course of subsequent development in a positive or negative direction.

Erikson identified eight psychosocial stages characterizing development throughout life. At each stage, a particular conflict comes into focus, as shown in **Table 4.2.** Although the conflict continues in different forms, it must be sufficiently resolved at a given stage if an individual is to cope successfully with the conflicts of later stages.

Trust versus Mistrust. For example, in the first stage, an infant needs to develop a basic sense of trust in the environment through interaction with caregivers. Trust is a natural accompaniment to a strong attachment relationship with a caregiver who provides food, warmth, and the comfort of physical closeness. A child whose basic needs are not met, who experiences inconsistent handling, lack of physical closeness and warmth, and the frequent absence of a car-

Table 4.2 Erikson's Psychosocial Stages

APPROXIMATE AGE	CRISIS	ADEQUATE RESOLUTION	INADEQUATE RESOLUTION
0–1½	Trust vs. mistrust	Basic sense of safety	Insecurity, anxiety
1½–3	Autonomy vs. self-doubt	Perception of self as agent capable of controlling own body and making things happen	Feelings of inadequacy to control events
3–6	Initiative vs. guilt	Confidence in oneself as initiator, creator	Feelings of lack of self-worth
6–puberty	Competence vs. inferiority	Adequacy in basic social and intellectual skills	Lack of self-confidence, feelings of failure
Adolescent	Identity vs. role confusion	Comfortable sense of self as a person	Sense of self as fragmented; shifting, unclear sense of self
Early adult	Intimacy vs. isolation	Capacity for closeness and commitment to another	Feeling of aloneness, separation; denial of need for closeness
Middle adult	Generativity vs. stagnation	Focus of concern beyond oneself to family, society, future generations	Self-indulgent concerns; lack of future orientation
Later adult	Ego-integrity vs. despair	Sense of wholeness, basic satisfaction with life	Feelings of futility, disappointment

ing adult, may develop a pervasive sense of mistrust, insecurity, and anxiety. This child will not be prepared for the second stage which requires the individual to be adventurous.

Autonomy versus Self-doubt. With the development of walking and the beginning of language, a child's exploration and manipulation of objects (and sometimes people) expands. With these activities should come a comfortable sense of autonomy and of being a capable and worthy person. Excessive restriction or criticism at this stage may lead to self-doubts. Demands beyond the child's ability—such as attempting toilet training too early—can discourage efforts to persevere in mastering new tasks. Such demands also can lead to stormy scenes of confrontation, disrupting the supportive parent-child relationship. The 2-year-old who demands the right to do something without help is acting out of a need to affirm his or her autonomy and adequacy.

Initiative versus Guilt. Toward the end of the preschool period, a child who has developed a basic sense of trust is now a person who can initiate intellectual and motor tasks. For example, a child in this stage wants to do things for himself, such as pour a glass of juice, choose what to wear, or get dressed. Caregivers' responses to these self-initiated activities either encourage the freedom and self-confidence needed for the next stage or produce guilt and feelings of incompetence.

Competence versus Inferiority. During the elementary-school years, the child who has successfully resolved the crises of the earlier stages is ready to go beyond random exploration to systematically develop competencies. School and sports offer arenas for learning intellectual and motor skills, and peer interaction offers the chance to develop social skills. Successful efforts in these pursuits lead to feelings of competence.

Some youngsters, however, become spectators rather than performers, or they experience discouraging failure that leaves them with a sense of inferiority. Such children will find it more difficult to face continuing challenges and crises of psychosocial development.

Erikson's formulation has been widely accepted, because it looks at the life cycle as a whole, putting both changes and overall continuity into perspective. The first four stages are part of a child's socialization; the last four are landmarks in an adult's continuing socialization. We will look at these last four stages in the next section as we examine the forces that shape adolescence, adulthood, and old age.

SUMMING UP

Ideas about childhood have changed dramatically over recent centuries. The child today is considered a complete if immature person. Researchers have studied the behavior of infants through normative investigations—comparing individuals to age standards and focusing on studies of overt behaviors, including reflexive and deliberate responses to stimuli.

Children are master language learners, coming into the world prepared to use language and supported by social contact and cognitive abilities to solve problems. Children may also have a language acquisition device—an innate mental structure limiting the possible choices and sequences employed in communicating. Experience and practice enable children to learn the rules of grammar. Language development begins with preverbal babbling, continuing through one-word and two-word stages and telegraphic speech. Psycholinguists study children's errors to understand the relationship between thought and language.

Through careful observations, Piaget formulated significant views about how the infant's mind develops. His key ideas include the development of schemes, the balance between assimilation and accommodation, and the four stages of cognitive development: sensorimotor, preoperational, concrete operational, and formal operational thinking.

Socialization is the process of acquiring social standards and motives appropriate to our culture. Socialization begins with infantile attachment to a caregiver. Failure to make this attachment leads to numerous physical and psychological problems. Erikson believed that socialization takes place in a series of psychosocial stages from infancy to old age.

Adolescence and Adulthood

Psychological development spans the entire course of life. Though the childhood years are formative, we have a remarkable capacity for change across the entire life span (Brim & Kagan, 1980). The long-term effects of early infant and childhood experiences are highly variable and continue to be influenced by later experiences (Henderson, 1980; Simmel, 1980).

Most early theorists who influenced the study of individual development focused only on early life periods. They assumed that the burden of development is carried on only through adolescence; after that the person and the psyche were set for life and would experience only a few more important changes. Contemporary research is challenging such notions. Out of this research has emerged the basic premise of **life-span developmental psychology:** Personality, mental functioning, and other vital aspects of human nature continue and change throughout the entire life cycle.

We continue our examination of lifelong changes, by concentrating first on the context of adolescence. We then pick up where we left off—with Erikson's psychosocial stages of development—and review the continuing tasks and challenges of adult development.

Adolescence

Adolescence is commonly defined as the stage of life that begins at the onset of *puberty,* when sexual maturity, or the ability to reproduce, is attained. However, it is not very clear where adolescence ends and adulthood begins. Variations among cultures account for much of the difficulty in defining the span of adolescence. Although the physical changes that take place at this stage are universal, the social and psychological dimensions of the adolescent experience depend on the cultural context. For example, if you enter your teen years in a culture that celebrates puberty as the start of adult status and rewards you with the power to make responsible choices, you will have a very different experience from someone whose culture condemns teenagers as confused troublemakers who worry their parents and threaten their society.

Transitions and Initiations

Most nonindustrial societies do not identify an actual adolescent stage as we know it. Instead, many such societies have *rites of passage* or **initiation rites.** These rituals usually take place around puberty and serve as a public acknowledgment of the transition from childhood to adulthood. The rites vary widely from extremely painful ordeals to periods of instruction in sexual and cultural practices or periods of seclusion involving survival ordeals. For example, in tribal cultures, the young person may be asked to take a meditative journey alone—or submit to symbolic scarring or circumcision surrounded by friends and family. A subtler rite of passage for many teenagers in our society is qualifying for a driver's license. Whatever form they take, such rites are usually highly dramatic and memorable ceremonies in which young initiates symbolically give up their childhood roles and accept the full privileges and responsibilities of adulthood.

In many traditional societies, then, the period of adolescence as a transition between childhood and adulthood lasts for only the few hours or the few months of the rite of passage. Once individuals have passed through that period, there is no ambiguity about their status—they are adults and the ties to their childhood have been severed. In our society there are few transition rituals to help children clearly mark their new adolescent status or for adolescents to know when they have become young adults.

The adolescent stage is a time in which independence and self-definition replace childhood dependence on parents and other adults. In American society adolescence has no clearly defined beginning or end. It can extend for more than a decade, through the teens to the mid-20s, until adult roles begin. The legal system defines adult status according to age; but different legal ages exist for different "adult" activities, such as drinking alcohol in public, driving,

life-span developmental psychology
Study of personality, mental functioning, and behavior as they develop and change throughout the entire life cycle.

adolescence The stage of life that begins at the onset of puberty and continues until adulthood.

initiation rites Rituals (or rites of passage) that usually take place around puberty and serve as a public acknowledgment of the transition from childhood to adulthood.

Many cultures have initiation rites that signal a child's passage into adulthood. Shown at the top is a *bar mitzvah,* a Jewish ceremony marking a boy's 13th birthday. The middle photo records the puberty rites of the White Mountain Apaches of Arizona. At bottom is the initiation ceremony of a young Lamaist monk.

engaging in sex, marrying without parental consent, joining the military, and voting (see "Time Out for Critical Thinking"). Similarly, social events, such as graduation from high school (or college, or graduate school), moving out of the family home, the establishment of financial independence, and marriage, have been used to mark the beginning of adulthood.

➡ *TIME OUT . . .* FOR CRITICAL THINKING

Historical analysis is encouraging in that it reveals that treatment of children and adolescents has continually improved over the centuries. However, many current indicators suggest that the 1980s were terrible for youth and many families and that conditions will worsen in the 1990s. More American children are likely to be poor, pregnant, in jail, hungry, homeless, suffering from psychological problems, or dead from violence and preventable diseases. Lawmakers, health care professionals, and others stress that major reforms are needed to institute and coordinate better health care, welfare programs, and social policy.

- Who is responsible for the well-being of troubled and endangered children and adolescents? If their parents cannot or will not care for them, on whom—or on what institutions—does this charge fall?

- Even if your life is insulated from personal contact with these young people at risk, how does their presence in society, and their worsening plight, affect your country, your community, and your family?

- What questions would you like to ask, in order to better understand and cope with the problem of youth at risk? How can developmental psychology begin to answer these questions?

- Once we have answers—*then* what? How should information and discovery be translated into policy?

By mulling over these questions you will discover that an understanding of development can give you insight not only into your own life, but into the people and events of your own community and society.

Tasks of Adolescence. Although many issues are important in adolescence, we will focus on three developmental tasks that commonly confront adolescents in Western society: coming to terms with physical maturity and adult sexuality; redefining social roles, including achieving autonomy from parents; and deciding upon occupational goals. Each of these issues is a component of the central task of establishing an *integrated identity.* Consistent with Erikson's (1968) description of the social context of identity, each of these issues presents a different way in which young people define themselves in relation to others.

Physical Maturation. The first concrete indicator of the end of childhood is the *pubescent growth spurt.* Two to three years after the onset of the growth spurt, **puberty,** or sexual maturity, is reached. Puberty for males begins with the production of live sperm (usually about age 14 in the United States), while for girls it begins at **menarche,** the onset of menstruation (between ages 11 and 15).

Part of achieving a personal identity involves coming to terms with one's physical self by developing a realistic, yet accepting image of physical appear-

puberty Attainment of sexual maturity (ability to reproduce).

menarche The onset of menstruation in women.

body image The way one views one's appearance.

ance. Attractiveness influences the way we view each other at all ages (Hatfield & Sprecher, 1986), and during adolescence one becomes increasingly focused on appearance. The term **body image** refers to the way one subjectively views one's appearance. This image is dependent not only on measurable features, such as height and weight, but also on other people's assessments and on cultural standards of physical beauty. During adolescence, dramatic physical changes and heightened emphasis on peer acceptance (especially peers of the opposite sex) can intensify concern with one's body image.

Approximately 44 percent of American adolescent girls and 23 percent of boys claimed that they "frequently felt ugly and unattractive" (Offer et al., 1981a). In another study, physical appearance was the biggest source of concern for a group of 240 high-school students (Eme et al., 1979). Girls' self-concepts are particularly tied to perceptions of their physical attractiveness, while boys seem more concerned with their physical prowess, athletic ability, and effectiveness in achieving goals (Lerner et al., 1976). These differences probably mirror a cultural preoccupation with female beauty and male strength—an inevitable source of concern since not all adolescents can embody the cultural ideals of attractiveness. Over time, adolescents seem to become more accepting of their appearances. Nonetheless, the attainment of acceptable body images can be a difficult task.

Sexuality. A new awareness of sexual feelings and impulses accompanies physical maturity. In one large study of American adolescents, the majority of adolescent males and females said that they often think about sex (Offer et al., 1981a). Although they think about sex, many adolescents still lack adequate knowledge or have misconceptions about sex and sexuality. Sex is a topic parents find difficult to discuss with children, so adolescents tend to be secretive about sexual concerns, making information and communication even more difficult. The development of a sexual identity that defines sexual orientation and guides sexual behavior thus becomes an important task of adolescence.

In early adolescence, masturbation is the most common expression of sexual impulses (Bell et al., 1981; Hass, 1979; Sorensen, 1973). Homosexual experiences are also common in adolescence; 14–17 percent of teenage boys and half that many girls report some homosexual experiences (Hass, 1979; Sorensen, 1973; Wyatt et al., 1988), though most of these individuals ultimately choose a heterosexual orientation. Exclusively homosexual feelings are much more difficult to resolve during adolescence. While most gays and lesbians first become aware of their sexual orientation in early adolescence, many do not attain positive sexual identities until their middle or late 20s (Riddle & Morin, 1977). The time lag undoubtedly reflects the relative lack of social support for homosexual orientation and exemplifies the importance of society's role in all aspects of identity development.

The proportion of adolescents engaging in sexual intercourse has risen substantially in the last 20 years. At least half of all young people have engaged in intercourse before age 18, and about 75 percent have done so by the age of 20 (Chilman, 1983; London et al., 1989).

There is evidence that the initial sexual experiences of males and females differ substantially. The vast majority of females become sexually involved with individuals whom they love. In contrast, for most adolescent males, personal relationships appear to be less important than the sexual act itself—the average male reports no emotional involvement with his first sexual partner (Miller & Simon, 1980).

Developing a sexual identity involves more than recognizing and accepting one's own sexual orientation and gaining sexual experience. Adolescents must develop and then rely on personal values to guide their sexual activity. They may have to reassess values—their own and others'—they have never questioned before. Those who choose to become sexually active are challenged to conduct their sexual relationships in a responsible fashion. This means considering the consequences of one's actions as well as being sensitive to the needs of one's partner and oneself. Can the young individual develop a personally meaningful sexual ethic—and act upon it? This requires being realistic and understanding, balancing impulses with intelligence, and may take many years to complete, but it is in adolescence that the foundations of a healthy sexual identity are established.

Social Identity. Erikson believes that the essential crisis of *adolescence* is discovering one's true *identity* amid the confusion of playing many different roles for different audiences in an expanding social world. Resolving this crisis helps the individual develop a sense of a coherent self. Failure to resolve the crisis adequately may result in a self-image that lacks a central stable core. Resolution of the identity crisis is both a personal process and a social experience.

Several factors influence the move toward self-identity. Family ties become stretched as the adolescent spends more time outside the home. In American society, the adolescent experiences less structure and adult guidance, is exposed to new values, and develops a strong need for peer support and acceptance. Adolescents talk to their peers four times as much as adults talk to theirs (Csikszentmihalyi et al., 1977). With their peers, adolescents refine their social skills and try out different social behaviors, gradually defining their social identities, the kind of people they choose to be, and the sorts of relationships they will pursue.

As the need for close friendships and peer acceptance becomes greater, anxiety about the possibility of rejection increases. As a result, young adolescents may choose the "safe" route of conformity—going along with their friends to avoid weakening those relationships. Females may be especially concerned with personal relationships, but less likely than males to give in to group pressure to behave antisocially (Berndt, 1979).

Loneliness becomes significant during adolescence. Between 15 and 25 percent of adolescents report feeling very lonely (Offer et al., 1981a). Similarly, shyness reaches its highest level in early teenage years as the desire for social acceptance markedly increases (Zimbardo, 1990).

The dual forces of parents and peers at times exhibit conflicting influences on adolescents, fueling the separation from parents and increasing identification with peers. But generally parents and peers serve complementary functions and fulfill different needs in adolescents' lives (Davis, 1985). For example, adolescents look to their families for structure and support, while they look to their friends for acceptance and approval. Ultimately, identity development involves establishing independent commitments that are sensitive to both parents *and* peers.

Occupational Choice. According to Erikson, deciding upon a vocational commitment is the hallmark of adolescent identity formation. The question, "What are you going to be when you grow up?" reflects the common assumption that what you *do* determines what you *are*. Selecting an occupation involves tasks central to all aspects of identity formation—appraising abilities and interests, developing alternatives, and making choices. Through vocational choice, adolescents can differentiate themselves from others while showing their acceptance of social values. For example, a high-school senior can plan to attend college—conforming with friends and fulfilling family wishes—but may choose to major in a nontraditional discipline to express unique personal goals and talents. The resulting sense of continuity and connectedness to one's social environment is critical to achieving a sense of consistent individual identity.

While many factors affect vocational interests and achievement, the clearest factor is socioeconomic background. Adolescents from families of higher socioeconomic status are more likely to pursue and complete education beyond high school and to aspire toward and achieve higher levels of success. Middle-class and upper middle-class parents encourage higher achievement

According to Erikson's social identity stage, adolescents must define their identities as individuals even as they seek the comfort and feeling of belonging that comes from being with friends and family. One compromise might be to experiment with different norms—such as clothing or hair styles—within the security of supportive relationships with companions, cliques, or romantic partners.

motivation in their children, model greater career success, and supply the economic resources unavailable to poorer children.

Educational and occupational choices made in later adolescence can profoundly affect future options. But perhaps occupational identity is best understood within the context of the entire life cycle. Success in adulthood can be measured by flexibility and a willingness to explore new directions—based on the self-confidence developed by successfully negotiating the demands of adolescence.

Adulthood

➡ The transition from adolescence to young adulthood is marked by decisions about advanced education, vocation, intimate relationships, and marriage. What are the tasks of adulthood and what form does psychological development take over the course of adulthood? How might one's experiences in childhood and adolescence affect the choices made in adulthood?

Tasks of Adulthood. Several developmental theories deal with the tasks of adulthood. According to Freud, adult development is driven by two basic needs: *love and work*. Abraham Maslow (1968) described these needs as *love* and *belonging* which, when satisfied, develop into the needs for *success* and *esteem*. Other theorists describe these basic needs as *affiliation* or *social acceptance* needs and *achievement* or *competence* needs.

Erikson's Psychological Stages. In Erikson's theory, the last three of the eight lifelong stages are crises of adulthood. The crisis of young adulthood is intimacy versus isolation; that of mid-life is generativity versus stagnation. We discuss the final crisis, ego-integrity versus despair, when we discuss old age in the following section.

Intimacy Versus Isolation. The essential crisis for the *early adult* (see **Table 4.2**) is to resolve the conflict between *intimacy* and *isolation*—to develop the capacity to make full emotional, moral, and sexual commitments to other people. Making those commitments requires compromising personal preferences, accepting responsibilities, and yielding some privacy and independence. Failure to resolve this crisis leads to isolation and the inability to connect to others in meaningful ways. (We will see throughout *Psychology* that much research supports the conclusion that anything that *isolates* us from sources of social support—isolates us from a reliable network of friends and family—puts us at risk for a host of physical ills, mental problems, and even social pathologies.)

Erikson described **intimacy** as the capacity to make a full commitment—sexual, emotional, and moral—to another person. Intimacy, which can occur in both friendships and romantic relationships, requires openness, courage, ethical strength, and usually some sacrifice and compromise of one's personal preferences.

Erikson perceived young adults as consolidating clear and comfortable senses of their identity (the crisis of adolescence) in preparation for embracing the risks and potentials of intimacy. For example, how can you know what it means to love someone and seek to share your life with that person until you first know—because you know yourself—who you are and what you want to do with your life? However, the sequence from identity to intimacy that Erikson described may not accurately reflect present-day realities. The trend in recent years has been for young adults to live together before marrying, so they tend to marry later in life than people did in the past. Many individuals today must struggle with identity issues (for example, career choices) at the same time they are dealing with intimacy issues.

Today, marriage, as the prototype of the successful resolution of the search for intimacy, often occurs more than once. In fact, married adults are now

intimacy The capacity to make a full commitment—sexual, emotional, and moral—to another person.

In recent years, growing tolerance for divorce has led many adults to change their ideas about traditional marriage. Communication and affection between modern spouses has also changed—improving over earlier times. Shown here on their wedding day are Ril and Sayoko Bandy with Ril's children from a previous marriage.

In the stage of generativity versus stagnation, the crisis of middle adulthood is a struggle between the desire for security and the desire for freedom. An individual who seeks a more meaningful, fulfilling existence risks losing much of what is stable in his or her life. In contrast, one who clings to a safe routine risks becoming stagnated, stuck in the slow lane, or in a traffic jam, while others have some place to go and many ways to get there.

"It just doesn't look like the usual case of midlife crisis, Dr. Elmark."

divorcing at a rate four times greater than adults did 50 years ago. Divorce and separation lead many adults to reexamine their ideas and hopes for intimacy at later points in the life cycle. Spouses have had high—unrealistically high—expectations of each other and about what constitutes an ideal marriage and family structure (Cleek & Pearson, 1985). However, there is evidence that communication and affection between modern spouses is substantially better than it was in earlier times (Caplow, 1982).

Generativity versus Stagnation. The next major opportunity for growth, Erikson's second adult stage, is the *generativity* crisis of *adult midlife.* People in their 30s and 40s move beyond a focus on self and partner toward broader commitments to family, work, society, and the world. Those who haven't resolved earlier crises of identity and intimacy may experience a mid-life crisis. Such people remain self-indulgent, question past choices, yearn for one last fling—and pursue freedom at the expense of security.

Those who meet the challenges of identity and intimacy successfully usually move on to *generativity.* This is a commitment beyond oneself to family, work, society, or future generations—a crucial challenge of one's 30s and 40s. A crisis that develops at this middle stage of life is the struggle between the desire for *security* and the desire for *freedom.* In traditional marriages, many women have given up much more personal freedom and autonomy than men in exchange for the hope of security, which may be but illusory and short-lived. For example, a woman may conclude that she has sacrificed too much freedom for security, and she may seek a change by attending school or pursuing a career. Or a man may worry that working hard and staying free have cost him the chance to have a family or form friendships, and he may decide to devote more time to the people in his life.

Adult Transitions. Adults are continually exploring options for security, commitment, work, and social acceptance, while seeking greater change and opportunity. Life-span researcher **Daniel Levinson** (1978, 1986) outlines the chronological periods in adulthood that correspond to critical transitions in life structures. As **Table 4.3** shows, adulthood transitions involve periods of questioning, choice, and change.

For men, the 20s seem to be a period of hope, optimism, independence, and responsible action. Early in their 30s, men may reassess their lives, questioning basic directions set in their 20s and either affirming them or taking new directions. The late 30s are often a time of consolidation and satisfaction. Between 40 and 50 a mid-life crisis may occur, when past choices and present commitments are questioned. Life is half over: Has freedom been sacrificed for security? Has intimacy been traded for career success? Men become concerned about genuine identity, and in adapting may renew commitments, make changes, or seek to resign themselves to unfulfilling choices.

All of this is well and good in the effort to understand *men,* perhaps. What about women? In general, less is known about the adult personality development of women, although more is being learned. In light of changing sex roles over the last few decades, a central issue for adult women is the integration of occupational and family aspirations. Women express greater uncertainty about vocational choice than men. Among women who worked exclusively as homemakers, one study found feelings of social isolation, frustration, and guilt for not pursuing goals their education had prepared them for (Sheehy, 1976). Other research has found that women who have families and work outside the home tend to be more satisfied with their lives than either single working women or married homemakers (Crosby, 1982). Nonetheless, meeting the demands of both work and family is a daunting challenge for most of us. We are fortunate to be living in a time when roles are changing, rather than under the "doctrine of two spheres—the work world for husbands, that of home and children for wives—that ruled only a generation ago (Hatfield and Rapson,

Table 4.3 Levinson's Stages of Adulthood

Ages 17 to 22	*Early Adult Transition* Leave adolescence, make preliminary choice for adult life.
Ages 22 to 28	*Entering the Adult World* Initial choices in love, occupation, friendship, values, life-style.
Ages 28 to 33	*Age 30 Transition* Change in life structure. Either a moderate change or, more often, a severe and stressful crisis.
Ages 33 to 40	*Settling Down* Establish a niche in society, progress on a timetable, in both family and career accomplishments.
Ages 40 to 45	*Mid-life Transition* Life structure comes into question. Usually a time of crisis in the meaning, direction, and value of each person's life. Neglected parts of the self (talents, desires, aspirations) seek expression.
Ages 45 to 50	*Entering Middle Adulthood* Choices must be made and a new life structure formed. Person must commit to new tasks.
Ages 50 to 55	*Age 50 Transition* Further questioning and modification of the life structure. Men who did not have a crisis at age 40 are likely to have one now.
Ages 55 to 60	*Culmination of Middle Adulthood* Build a new life structure. Can be time of great fulfillment.
Ages 60 to 65	*Late Adult Transition* Reappraisal of life. Moments of pride in achievement are interspersed with periods of despair.
Ages 65 to 80	*Late Adulthood* Make peace with oneself and others. Fewer illusions, broader perspective on life.
Age 80 plus	*Late Late Adulthood* Final transition. Prepare for death.

1993). We are less fortunate with regard to our social institutions that have been reluctant to accommodate changes that would allow women to succeed in their jobs and permit men to become more involved in caring for their families.

Many political messages during the 1992 Presidential campaign forced us to recognize how much a woman's development is influenced by society's norms and the laws that determine what is possible, acceptable, or punishable. Politicians and their spouses on each side of the debate defined the role of the "good woman" in maintaining either "family values" or "feminism," and in their response to the issues of abortion and equal rights for both sexes. For example, televangelist Pat Robertson, a former candidate for the presidency and a major force in preparing the 1992 Republican Convention platform, said of the proposed equal rights amendment: "It is about a socialist, anti-family political movement that encourages women to leave their husbands, kill their children, practice witchcraft, destroy capitalism, and become lesbians" (quoted in *Newsweek*, 9/7/92, p. 15). How do such political comments influence individuals' decisions about their own roles and choices?

Anatomical differences between males and females are generally magnified by social roles and rules. For example, women on the average have less upper body strength than men—a distinction that has been used to exclude women from combat infantry and military advancement. But why would an ability to lift slightly less than men disqualify women for positions as combat pilots, where little or no heavy lifting is required? Men and women's different experiences thus result from tradition, stereotyping, and prejudice in addition to any actual physical differences. Adult personality development may continue to progress differently for men and women because the sexes have thus far been socialized differently—men urged toward *separateness,* and women toward *attachment.* Each pattern is one-sided, so that in mid-life many adults move in alternate directions, seeking greater balance (Gilligan, 1982).

Adult Thinking. Adults' thinking differs from adolescents' in several distinctive ways. Learning from experience, adults are more focused and channeled in specific directions. They must take into account more divergent perspectives and personalities than they considered as adolescents. They must negotiate disputes, make compromises, and strike bargains.

Recall that for Piaget the final stage of cognitive development is *formal operational thought,* which enables one to reason logically, think abstractly, and consider hypotheses in solving problems. However, most adults' everyday, practical problems occur in ambiguous, unstructured social and work relationships. Formal thought is too limiting and rigid to deal with so many half-truths and unknowns. Adult life requires a more dynamic, less abstract way of thinking that can accept inconsistencies and contradictions. This practical, world-wise, adult cognitive style is termed **postformal thought** (Basseches, 1984; Labovie-Vief, 1985). For example, a child or adolescent might avoid taking classes with a disliked teacher, but an experienced adult knows too well that it may not be possible to avoid a disliked boss or supervisor. Instead, one balances the boss's bad qualities with insight into good ones ("She may not be very friendly, but she's honest") and acceptance of simple realities ("I love my job and want to keep it, so I should try to get along with my boss"). Postformal thinking is itself an ongoing, developing process, unfolding from a data-collecting approach in adolescence and early adulthood to more responsible decision making in mid-life and finally to the wisdom of later life (Schaie, 1982).

Moral Development. One of the hallmarks of adult thinking is the development of higher levels of moral reasoning. **Morality** is a system beliefs, values, and underlying judgments about the rightness or wrongness of human acts. Parents and society want children to become adults who accept their moral value system and whose behavior is guided by their moral principles. As we shall consider, however, there is an important difference between moral understanding and moral behavior.

postformal thought   A more dynamic, less abstract way of thinking that can accept inconsistencies and contradictions.

morality   A system of beliefs, values, and underlying judgments about the rightness or wrongness of human acts.

The best-known psychological approach to moral development was created by **Lawrence Kohlberg** (1964, 1981), who based his theory on Piaget's work. Each stage in Kohlberg's theory of *moral reasoning* is based on a different standard of moral judgment. **Table 4.4** summarizes the seven stages proposed by Kohlberg.

Kohlberg theorizes that an individual attains the same stages in the same order in all cultures. The acquisition of these stages parallels the stages of Piaget's theory of cognitive development in its movement from concrete, egocentric targets to more other-oriented, abstract ideals of right and wrong. The lowest level of moral reasoning is based on self-interest, while higher levels center on social good, regardless of personal gain. Not all people attain stages 4 to 7; many adults never even reach stage 5, and few go beyond it. The cosmic orientation of Stage 7 is very rare; Kohlberg presents it as an ideal upper limit.

Research suggests real-world limits to Kohlberg's theory. The higher stages have not been found in all cultures. In our own culture they appear to be associated with education and verbal ability—experiences which should not necessarily be prerequisites for moral judgment (Rest & Thoma, 1986).

Kohlberg's stages of moral reasoning have generated considerable controversy. Especially controversial is Kohlberg's early claim that women generally lag behind men in moral development and stop at a less advanced level than men do. **Carol Gilligan** (1982) proposes that this finding—that women's morality is less fully developed than that of men's—can be explained by the fact that Kohlberg's coding scheme is biased in favor of men. His original work was based on observations of boys only. Gilligan believes that women develop *differently*, not *less* morally. She proposes that women's moral devel-

Table 4.4 Kohlberg's Stages of Moral Reasoning

LEVELS AND STAGES	REASONS FOR MORAL BEHAVIOR
I PRECONVENTIONAL MORALITY	
Stage 1 Pleasure/pain orientation	To avoid pain or not to get caught
Stage 2 Cost-benefit orientation; reciprocity—an eye for an eye	To get rewards
II CONVENTIONAL MORALITY	
Stage 3 Good child orientation	To gain acceptance and avoid disapproval
Stage 4 Law and order orientation	To follow rules, avoid censure by authorities
III PRINCIPLED MORALITY	
Stage 5 Social contract orientation	To promote the society's welfare
Stage 6 Ethical principle orientation	To achieve justice and avoid self-condemnation
Stage 7 Cosmic orientation	To be true to universal principles and feel oneself part of a cosmic direction that transcends social norms

According to researcher Carol Gilligan, women may more greatly value connectedness to others, while men learn to value independence. Advertising may take advantage of such cultural values by promising their fulfillment if a consumer will buy specific products.

opment is based on a standard of *caring for others* and progresses to a stage of self-realization, whereas men base their reasoning on a standard of *justice*.

Additional questions concern Kohlberg's decision to study moral *reasoning* instead of moral *action*. Critics believe that what people *say* and what they *do* when faced with moral choices often differ (Kurtines & Grief, 1974). If we want to understand moral development more completely, we must consider what it is that motivates people to behave honestly, cooperatively, or altruistically. Researchers investigating the roots of morality suggest that inner emotions, especially *empathy*, motivate the child to behave morally (Hoffman, 1987). Children may experience empathy at very young ages, and some researchers believe that empathy may be an innate response like sucking or crying.

empathy The condition of feeling someone else's emotion.

Empathy is the condition of feeling someone else's emotion. Feeling another's distress may trigger a sympathetic response. Many psychologists now believe such helpful and positive behaviors signal the beginning of moral development. When a 4-year-old gently hands her favorite toy to her unhappy little brother, because she feels sorry for him and wishes to cheer him up, this simple gesture indicates a significant leap in her social and cognitive functioning. Empathy may well represent part of the foundation for future moral behavior.

We seem to need a new theory of moral development, one that integrates patterns of moral reasoning with the motives and social conditions that can prompt helpful and altruistic acts (Zahn-Waxler & Radke-Yarrow, 1982). (See "Cross-cultural Perspective: Cross-cultural Research on Moral Development.")

Old Age

At the beginning of this century, only 3 percent of the U.S. population was over 65. Today that figure is about 13 percent, and when the baby-boom generation reaches old age, nearly a quarter of our population will be in this oldest group. By the year 2030 (when today's college students will be around 60 years old) it is projected that more than 80 million Americans will be over 60 years of age. That is more than the number expected to be under 20 years of age—a dramatic reversal of all previous demographics (Pifer & Bronte, 1986). With such drastic changes in our society's age distribution, it is more essential than ever to understand the nature of aging as well as the abilities and needs of the elderly.

Cross-cultural Perspective   Cross-cultural Research on Moral Development

Psychologists who study the effects of culture on behavior frequently begin their investigations with human conditions faced by individuals all over the world: for example, how everyone must find enough food to live or how human beings must be dependent on others during infancy since they cannot take care of themselves. Another universal human condition people face is how to pursue individual goals along with those of others. For example, should a person accept a challenging and higher-paying job in a city 2000 miles away if it means leaving the care of an elderly parent to professionals in a nursing home? Doing so might achieve the person's own goals of prestige and advancement; however, these achievements will interfere with the elderly parent's desire for frequent interactions with her child. Some people may turn down the high-paying job because they feel that they have an obligation to their parent. This sacrifice of personal achievement is more likely to be found among some cultural groups than others. Psychologists interested in moral development have asked whether or not the concept of "obligation to others" has been given enough attention in the development of Kohlberg's seven stages (Snarey, 1985; Miller, et al., 1990).

Many cross-cultural psychologists have argued that culture provides a great deal of guidance when issues arise involving personal goals that may conflict with group goals (Triandis, 1989; Schwartz, 1990; Hofstede, 1991). In individualistic countries, such as the United States, Canada, and Australia, people are socialized to place a high value on their own goals. This does not *always* mean that people will ignore the wishes of others, but it does mean that cultural norms encourage people to think carefully about their own desires when making decisions. In collectivist

countries—such as Japan, Hong Kong, and Colombia—people are socialized to think carefully about the wishes of others and to be attentive to their needs. People are encouraged to consider the wishes and needs of others when setting their own goals. At times, this will mean setting aside one's own goals because of a higher priority placed on the needs or desires of others in one's group. For example, many graduate students in the United States are from collectivist countries in Asia. Some of these students could have started their graduate studies years ago, but they had to take care of obligations to others at home. When they were finally able to consider leaving their countries and coming to the United States, they had to obtain approval from extended family members. Uncles, aunts, grandparents, and sometimes cousins were consulted. This consultation took place because any one person looks upon herself or himself as a group member. These other group members must be kept in mind in the pursuit of one's own goals. Students from Asia, as well as Asian Americans, study a great deal and place great emphasis on good grades because when one person does well, the entire group is honored. For the same reason, when one person does poorly, the entire group may feel a sense of shame.

Cultural guidance with regard to individualism and collectivism contributes to an understanding of Kohlberg's stages of moral development. Consider this moral dilemma: A man's wife is dying. He needs to buy a very expensive drug for her. The drug will probably save the woman. But the man does not have money to buy the drug. So he breaks into a drugstore and steals the drug. Should he have done that? Why or why not?

From a cross-cultural perspective, it is clear that Kohlberg is from an indi-

vidualist culture. Consequently, in developing the scoring system for the seven stages of moral development, he emphasized the reasoning of people with an individualistic orientation toward moral dilemmas. This reasoning places an emphasis on the individual's own view of the dilemma and his or her arguments about justice, rights, and the dignity of humans. But has this emphasis on the arguments of individuals downplayed the cultural guidance people receive in collectivist cultures? Consider the moral conclusion of a Maisan village leader in Papua, New Guinea: "If nobody helped him [save his dying wife] and so he [stole to save her], I would say *we* had caused that problem" (Snarey, 1985, p. 225). Future work on moral development must include the reasoning of people who start their thinking by considering the needs and responsibilities of the collective community.

Cross-cultural psychologists do not want to discard the contributions of psychologists who do most of their research within one country. Rather, they recognize the contributions of researchers such as Kohlberg but at the same time recommend that theories be expanded and revised to take cultural issues into account. In this regard, cross-cultural psychologists make recommendations similar to those of researchers active in women's studies. The text notes that Carol Gilligan has challenged Kohlberg's research because there is inattention to the value of *caring for others*. That value, more commonly reported among women than men, alters responses to some of the moral dilemmas posed in the Kohlberg test situation. Theories in psychology will continue to be improved as the importance of diversity becomes central to the work of various researchers.

In Erik Erikson's theory of lifelong psychosocial development, awareness of one's mortality and changes in one's body, behavior, and social roles sets the stage for *late adulthood*. The crisis at this stage is the conflict between *ego-integrity* and *despair*. Resolving the crises at each of the earlier stages prepares the older adult to resolve the crisis of late adulthood—to look back without regrets and to enjoy a sense of wholeness. When previous crises are unresolved, aspirations remain unfulfilled, and the individual experiences futility, despair, and self-deprecation. The individual then fails to solve the crisis at this final developmental stage as well.

➡ In this section, then, consider that Erikson's characterization of old age is as a time of challenge. There is a job to be done, a crisis to be confronted. What are the tasks of old age, and what resources and limitations must we confront as we look ahead to the autumn of our lives? We first review research approaches to aging and then consider the diverse changes that accompany aging. Finally we consider the psychological meaning of facing the end of life.

Research Approaches to Aging. As you learn about psychological research on aging, you will most often be interested in data on *age changes*—the way people change as they grow older. In contrast, most studies report *age differences*—the way people of different ages differ from one another—because cross-sectional research designs are more common than longitudinal research. Cross-sectional age difference studies sometimes do and sometimes do *not* reflect age changes. They may instead represent differences between people born at different times in history, rather than differences in what the same people at different chronological ages can do.

If a study compares individuals of different age groups, it informs us only of differences or similarities between young people and elderly people. If instead a study compares assessments of the same group of individuals over time, it can inform us about *how people change or remain the same as they age.* This is what we really want to know—so be sure to interpret data on aging cautiously, because a study's design may limit how it can be interpreted. Find out whether a particular study employed longitudinal (same group over time) or cross-sectional (different groups, all at once) design.

New Perspectives on Aging. What does aging mean? From a biological perspective, aging typically means decline—energy reserves are reduced, cells decay, and muscle tone diminishes. From a psychological perspective, however, aging is not synonymous with decline. Many aspects of the human condition improve with age. A lifetime's accumulation of experience may finally culminate in wisdom. Theories of aging are models of balance or trade-off: In old age, a person may *lose* energy reserve but *gain* an ability to control emotional experiences and thereby conserve energy. Thus we can expect two kinds of changes—gains and losses—as we grow older (Baltes, 1987). What then would be a good strategy for dealing with life's changes? Perhaps successful aging consists of making the most of gains while minimizing the impact of losses. While this general strategy may be universal, each individual's adaptations will take on different forms.

➡ Many elderly people have discovered particular strategies that help them age successfully. For example, older adults can remain both active and close to people by doing volunteer work in the community, joining clubs and classes, or spending time with grandchildren. What about those who experience trouble or personal difficulty in aging? In our youth-centered society, many beliefs about growing old are based more on folklore than on sound empirical evidence (see "In Focus: Ageism and the Myths of Aging"). What happens if people arrive at old age believing these myths? Might there be a way to generate more positive approaches to growing old? Consider yourself a consultant of sorts: How might you suggest ways to live well by taking advantage of remaining abilities and gains, while minimizing the impact of losses? Do you

In Focus:

AGEISM AND THE MYTHS OF AGING

Ageism is prejudice against older people. Ageism leads to discrimination that limits the opportunities of the elderly, isolates them, and fosters their negative self-images. Our society values growth, strength, and physical appearance and worships youthfulness. The enemy—aging—is marked by signs of decline and weakness (Butler & Lewis, 1982). Even undergraduate psychology texts are guilty of ageism. A survey of 139 texts written over the past 40 years reveals that many texts failed to cover the period of late adulthood or presented stereotypical views of the elderly (Whitbourne & Hulicka, 1990). A more dramatic instance of ageism is shown in the personal experiences of a reporter who deliberately "turned old" for a while.

Pat Moore disguised herself as an 85-year-old woman and wandered the streets of over 100 American cities to discover what it means to be old in America. Clouded contact lenses and earplugs diminished her vision and hearing; bindings on her legs made walking difficult; and her taped fingers had the dexterity of arthritic ones. This "little old lady" struggled to survive in a world designed for the young, strong, and agile. She couldn't open jars, hold pens, read labels, or climb up bus steps. The world of speed, noise, and shadows frightened her. When she needed assistance, few ever offered it. She was ridiculed for being old and vulnerable and was even violently attacked by a gang of adolescents (Moore in *Discovering Psychology*, 1990, Program 18).

At left is Pat Moore; in the photo on the right, she is disguised as an elderly woman (*Discovering Psychology*, 1990, Program 18).

Perhaps prejudice against the elderly is based in part on our own fear of becoming ill or unable to be independent. While old age increases susceptibility to illness, it is crucial to distinguish changes associated with normal aging from those associated with disease or illness. This distinction is not as simple as it sounds. At one time, it was a commonly held myth that anyone would become senile if he or she lived long enough. Today most severe cognitive deficits are attributed to age-related diseases—some of which are avoidable or treatable—rather than to natural conse-

quences of aging. Is it true that "You can't teach an old dog new tricks," "Old people lose their sexuality," and "Old people are typically abandoned by their children"? A few myths about aging are partially borne out by scientific data, but most are not.

The boundaries between what we consider normal age changes and the effects of disease and illness are changing as our medical knowledge expands. We now know that most cognitive abilities do not show major or significant decline under ordinary circumstances of aging.

ageism Prejudice against older people.

think that people in other cultures, where the wisdom of older people is respected, might have advice to give to memebers of youth-oriented cultures such as the middle-class United States and Canada?

The Changes of Age. Some of the most obvious changes that occur with age affect people's physical appearances and abilities. As we grow older, we can expect our skin to wrinkle, our hair to thin and gray, and our height to decrease an inch or two. Our hearts and lungs operate less efficiently, so we expect decreased physical stamina. We can also expect some of our senses to dull. These changes occur and develop gradually, so we have ample opportunity to gauge them and try to adjust.

Vision. The vast majority of people over 65 experience some loss of visual ability. Without corrective lenses, half of the elderly would be considered legally blind. The lenses in our eyes become rigid and discolored as we age, and this can affect both distance and color vision. Most normal visual changes in old age can be aided with corrective lenses. An elderly person may find glasses helpful for night driving or bifocals useful for close work such as reading.

Hearing. Hearing loss is common among those 60 and older. The average elderly person has difficulty hearing high frequency sounds. Elderly people can have a hard time understanding speech—particularly that spoken by high-pitched voices. Hearing loss that remains undetected or denied can have far-reaching implications (Maher & Ross, 1984; Manschreck, 1989). An elderly person may think that those around him are whispering so he won't be able to hear them converse. If this is how someone makes sense of his or her ability to understand other people's speech, it is easy to see how mild paranoia can develop. Hearing loss can trigger a process of inaccurately explaining others' behavior, and blaming evil intentions when one's faulty ears are the real culprits. Hearing loss is more easily corrected early on with the help of *hearing aid therapy* than it is later with psychotherapy. Hearing aids can compensate for much hearing loss. Speaking in lower tones, enunciating clearly, and reducing background noise can also help older people understand speech better.

Sexual Functioning. One myth about aging is that elderly people can't or shouldn't be sexual. Belief in such a myth can be a greater obstacle than physical limitations to experiencing satisfying sex in old age. There is no age—for women or for men—at which orgasm ceases. During old age, sex loses its reproductive functions but not its capacity to provide pleasure. Sex is one of life's "healthy pleasures," and regular practice will only enhance successful aging since it provides arousal, aerobic exercise, fantasy, and social interaction (Ornstein & Sobel, 1989). Sexuality is one clear domain where experience and experimentation can compensate for minor physical changes or general losses in physical stamina.

Intelligence. One of the great fears about aging is that it is accompanied by the loss of cognitive abilities. Is this fear justified? There is little evidence that general cognitive abilities decline among the healthy elderly. The majority of us will experience more difficulty forming new associations, and we acquire new information more slowly by the time we are in our 70s or 80s, but we undergo no dramatic changes in thinking and remembering.

There is even evidence that some aspects of intellectual functioning are superior in older people. Psychologists are now exploring age-related gains in **wisdom**—expertise in the fundamental pragmatics of life (Baltes, 1990). Individuals also vary greatly in their later life intellectual performance. Elderly people who pursue high levels of environmental stimulation, including both formal and informal education, tend to maintain high levels of cognitive abilities. It appears that *disuse,* rather than decay, may be responsible for isolated deficits in intellectual performance. "Use it or lose it" is the motto of the wise elderly.

Memory. A common complaint among the elderly is the feeling that their ability to remember things is not as good as it used to be. Memory difficulties appear primarily in that part of the memory system known as *short-term* (or *working*) *memory,* in which new memories are processed and stored for less than a minute (Poon, 1985). Aging does not seem to diminish *long-term memory* (access to knowledge or information about events that occurred long ago). For example, an elderly person may have to ask a newcomer's name once or twice before finally remembering it, but will have no trouble remembering the names of long-known friends or celebrities.

wisdom Knowledge, practical experience, and judgment.

This elderly woman shares her experiences with a classroom of young children.

Elderly people who pursue high levels of environmental stimulation tend to maintain higher levels of cognitive abilities.

Theories of memory changes related to aging are being vigorously investigated at this time. The hope is to improve both our general understanding of the nature of human memory and the aging process as well as to develop strategies and procedures for preventing memory impairment.

Social Changes. One unfortunate consequence of living a long life is that you can expect to outlive some of your friends and family members. When you consider the reduced mobility associated with some aspects of aging, it is not surprising that people become less socially active in old age. One early explanation of this behavior assumed that the elderly voluntarily withdrew from society in symbolic preparation for death (Cumming & Henry, 1961). This *disengagement theory* suggested that the weakened emotional attachments of the elderly were general, universal, and inevitable.

The disengagement view of social aging has been largely discredited for a number of reasons. First, not all social contact is limited; older people maintain contacts with family and old friends. Maintaining a single intimate relationship can make a marked difference in personal health, as can living with a beloved pet (Siegel, 1990). Second, disengagement also falsely implies emotional detachment—a problem that does *not* characterize older persons' relationships and may even be a problem that is more intense in younger years.

One theory suggests that, as people age, they become more selective in choosing their social partners. They sift through their various relationships and keep only those that are most rewarding. Such *selective social interaction* may also be a practical way to regulate emotional experiences and conserve physical energy (Carstensen, 1987, 1991).

Psychopathology. The incidence rates for most functional mental disorders appear to be *lowest* after age 65, with the exception of perhaps depression and the dementias, such as Alzheimer's disease (Kay & Bergmann, 1982). The normal course of aging does not necessarily or usually entail worsened mental health. Depression has long been assumed to be the most common psychological disorder among the elderly. Depression presents a major problem for many older people, and it is the number one reason for psychiatric hospitalization in old age. Depression often accompanies the dependence and helplessness

Alzheimer's disease Chronic, organic brain disorder, characterized by gradual loss of cognitive abilities and memory, and deterioration of personality.

caused by many illnesses. This is true at any age, but perhaps older adults expect some degree of dependence in old age.

Alzheimer's disease is the most common form of dementia, characterized by gradual loss of memory and deterioration of personality. It is a chronic organic brain syndrome that afflicts about 5 percent of Americans over 65 and 20 percent of those over 80. The causes of Alzheimer's disease are not yet known and there is no known cure. In advanced stages, people with Alzheimer's disease may become completely mute and inattentive, even forgetting the names of their spouses and children. In these final stages, Alzheimer patients can become incapable of caring for themselves, lose memory for who they are, and eventually die.

At Life's End. While medical advances cannot prevent death, they have changed our manner of dying. Chronic illnesses now constitute the major causes of death. Thus for most people, dying will be a lengthy process. Preparing for one's own death—and the deaths of others—is a part of life that psychologists want to understand so that they may help people cope with it.

Dying a Good Death. According to some theorists, notably **Elisabeth Kübler-Ross,** all dying patients go through the same series of *emotional stages* (Kübler-Ross, 1969, 1975). The first is *denial,* which may actually help a person maintain hope by avoiding overwhelming grief. In the second stage, *anger,* one reacts against the loss of personal control over events and plans. The third stage is *bargaining,* when, for example, a dying person might hope to negotiate with God in exchange for a little more time. The fourth stage is *depression,* from an anticipated or actual turn for the worse. The final stage is *acceptance;* with time and emotional support, people can work through their anguish and calmly accept their own impending deaths. Kübler-Ross believes that, if people accept their own death, it is easier for them to die in peace and dignity—essentially to "die the good death."

Other researchers studying the reactions of dying people have observed more fluidity and complexity than this fixed-stage model suggests. Denial, anger, and depression may reappear at different times during the dying process, depending on the context of the death and the nature of the illness or trauma (Kastenbaum, 1986). Nonetheless, Kübler-Ross's work provides useful insights into the psychology of dying. It has helped health care professionals compassionately assist the dying through this ultimate life transition.

Bereavement. The impact of death does not end when a person dies. Family and friends cope with their own feelings of grief and bereavement for months or even years after the death of someone close to them. Loss of one's longtime spouse can be particularly traumatic; it actually substantially increases the chances of illness and mortality. Compared to the general population, widows and widowers have twice as many diseases as those of the same age who are single or married (Stroebe et al., 1982). Because women typically live longer, and marry men older than themselves, they are more likely to lose a spouse. Yet there is some evidence that the stress of losing a spouse is harder on men than on women. Married women are more likely than their husbands to maintain broader social networks, so the loss of a partner has a different meaning and social consequence to widows than widowers.

Some investigators have identified distinct *stages of mourning* (Kalish, 1985). The first stage, *shock,* is followed by the *longing* phase of desire to be with the deceased. The third major reaction is the *depression* stage, with despair sometimes combined with anger and confusion. The last stage of mourning is the *recovery* phase, as death is at last put into a meaningful perspective.

These women, newly widowed, have joined a support group to help them with their losses.

Family and friends cope with feelings of grief and bereavement long after the death of someone close to them. Top, IRA funeral; bottom, a burial in Romania.

Memories of the deceased individual can live on in all those who were somehow touched by his or her presence. It is in this sense that we can say that the human life cycle is never ending.

SUMMING UP

Adolescence is a vaguely defined period between childhood and adulthood, often marked by the onset of puberty. The central psychosocial crisis of adolescence is identity versus role confusion. Most adolescents are satisfied with their lives but overconcerned about their appearance and social acceptance. Adolescents must develop a personal identity by accepting their sexuality, forming comfortable social relationships with family and peers, and choosing an occupation.

The central concerns of adulthood are organized around two groups of needs: love (intimacy) and work (generativity). Adult thought shows the emergence of postformal thinking. Moral reasoning in adults shows a clear stage model of development at the lower levels but not for hypothetical higher levels. There is some controversy about gender effects in moral reasoning, and the distinction between moral thought and moral action.

The crisis of old age is integrity versus despair. Successful aging is characterized by optimizing one's functioning in areas of personal priority and compensating for losses by using substitute behaviors. Age-related declines in sensation, sexuality, cognitive functioning, and social experience are exaggerated by myths of old age, and vary greatly among individuals. Most people will die in old age from chronic illnesses of long duration. Kübler-Ross suggests that dying involves stages of denial, anger, bargaining, depression, and finally acceptance. Bereavement and mourning may also develop in stages, offering insight into responses to one's own and others' deaths.

CHAPTER REVIEW

Perspectives on Development *What are the two approaches developmental psychologists use to understand psychological change? What are the arguments in the nature-nurture debate? How does maturation contribute to psychological development? What position do stage theories take on continuity?*

Developmental psychologists study those processes that accompany aging throughout the lifespan. They evaluate the contributions of nature and nurture in contributing to human development. Physical maturation interacts with environmental experience to determine individual functioning and performance. Development can be viewed from a chronological or topical perspective—as either a continuous or discontinuous (stage) process.

Key Terms
  developmental psychology, p. 100
  chronological age, p. 100
  developmental age, p. 100
  chronological approach, p. 101
  topical approach, p. 101

Major Contributors
  Locke, John, p. 101
  Rousseau, Jean, p. 101
  Itard, Jean Marie, p. 102
  Kagan, Jerome, p. 104
  Blass, Elliott, p. 107

2 The Developing Child *How have conceptions of childhood changed in recent centuries? What factors affect language acquisition in childhood? What are the major stages in Piaget's theory of cognitive development? Which processes and behaviors change in social and emotional development?*

Developmental research is influenced by the historically recent view of the child as person. The tasks and processes of childhood include learning language—from the early predisposition to babble and utter words to acquiring the rules of grammar. Cognitive development as theorized by Piaget is based on developmental schemes, a balance between assimilation and accommodation, and four developmental stages: sensorimotor, preoperational, concrete operational and formal operational thinking. Socialization begins with attachment and establishes the child's connections with family, friends, and society. For Erikson, childhood development involves crises of trust, autonomy, initiative, and competence.

Key Terms

Major Contributors

3 Adolescence and Adulthood *Which tasks must be accomplished during adolescence? How are the tasks and cognitive processes of adulthood different from those of adolescence? What are the psychological meanings associated with old age?*

Adolescent development begins at puberty and centers on the identity crisis. Adolescents must also develop sexual, social, and occupational directions and roles. Adult development centers on the crises of intimacy and then generativity, implying concerns with personal relationships, work, and life meaning. The crisis of old age involves integrity in the fact of declining abilities. Successful aging requires a balance of realistic limitations with compensation and optimal functioning. At the end of life we face issues of our own as well as others' death.

Key Terms

life-span developmental
    psychology, p. 125
adolescence, p. 125
initiation rites, p. 125
puberty, p. 126
menarche, p. 126
body image, p. 127
intimacy, p. 129
postformal thought, p. 132
morality, p. 132
empathy, p. 134
ageism, p. 137
wisdom, p. 138
Alzheimer's disease, p. 140

Major Contributors

Levinson, Daniel, p. 130
Kohlberg, Lawrence, p. 133
Gilligan, Carol, p. 133
Moore, Pat, p. 137
Kübler-Ross, Elisabeth,
    p. 140

PRACTICE TEST

Chapter 4: Psychological Development

For each of the following items, choose the single correct or best answer. Correct answers, explanations, and page references appear in the Appendix.

1. In studies of developmental psychology, the usual independent variable is _____ while the usual dependent variable is _____ .
   A. time; affect or ability
   B. age; behavior
   C. sensory input or information; aging
   D. children; intelligence or aptitude

2. "The mind at birth is merely a blank slate. Life experience writes on the slate. Thus all we are is a result of our experiences and education." This statement best reflects the opinions of _____ .
   A. John Locke
   B. Jean Rousseau
   C. Jean Piaget
   D. Erik Erikson

3. Which of the following is true of the physical abilities of the newborn infant?
   A. At birth babies already have prejudices favoring particular tastes and smells and disliking others.
   B. Just moments after birth a neonate turns in the direction of a voice or reaches out an exploring hand.
   C. While babies are born legally blind, they soon learn to detect large objects and high-contrast patterns.
   D. All of the above.

4. A developmental researcher arranges to track the progress of a 30-member kindergarten class over the next ten years, maintaining contact with the children's teachers and families in order to test them annually. This ambitious plan illustrates the use of a _____ research design.
   A. sequential
   B. longitudinal
   C. cross-sectional
   D. None of the above.

5. Which of the following utterances illustrates overregularization in language development?
   A. "Babababa."
   B. "Me gots two foots and two handses."
   C. "Drink milk, all gone."
   D. "Want cookie."

6. "Hey! That's not fair," complains Judi. "Tonio has more ice cream than me." Actually, both Judi and Tonio received a single scoop, but Tonio has stirred his around so it seems to fill the dish, while Judi's scoop is more compact. Judi's complaint indicates that she has not yet acquired the concept of _____ that affects how children think about the physical properties of things.
   A. object permanence
   B. egocentrism
   C. conservation
   D. animistic thinking

7. Harry Harlow conducted landmark studies of the behaviors of baby monkeys who were separated from their mothers and had access only to mother "dummies" in their cages. Harlow's work confirmed that _____ .
   A. contact comfort and physical touch are important for healthy early development
   B. the "cupboard theory of attachment" is essentially true for both humans and nonhumans
   C. genuine attachment is only possible with the infant's biological mother
   D. nonhuman infants will imprint on and restrict social behavior to the first visually prominent thing they see after birth

8. For Erikson, the psychosocial crisis of _____ is addressed by skill development and social interaction during the elementary school years, when children must explore their abilities, talents, and peer relationships.
   A. trust versus mistrust
   B. autonomy versus doubt
   C. competence versus inferiority
   D. identity versus role confusion

9. The briefest summary of the concerns and crises of adult development might simply be _____ .
   A. identity
   B. intimacy
   C. love and work
   D. mortality

10. In old age, the loss of _____ has often been associated with feelings of paranoia and social isolation.
    A. sexual functioning
    B. one's spouse
    C. hearing
    D. intellectual abilities

IF YOU'RE INTERESTED . . .

Bruner, J. S. (1983). *Child's talk: Learning to use language.* New York: Norton.

Detailed and readable introduction to the process of language development in children, by a renowned researcher and expert.

Gilligan, C. (1982). *In a different voice: Psychological theory and women's development.* Cambridge, MA: Harvard University Press.

Short and readable book by the author of much of the gender controversy in moral development theory; includes brief summary of Kohlberg's original research strategy and early findings.

Ordinary People. (Video: 1980, color, 123 minutes). Directed by Robert Redford; starring Donald Sutherland, Mary Tyler Moore, Judd Hirsch, and Timothy Hutton.

Well-done film of Judith Guest's novel about a family's deterioration after the death of one son, especially in terms of its effects on his surviving adolescent brother.

Rymer, R. (1993). *Genie: An abused child's flight from silence.* New York: Harper Collins.

Powerful story of the efforts to teach Genie to talk and function normally after she had grown up in total neglect without any language or social training. Can the best of scientific instruction overcome the critical-period barriers? What are the trade-offs between using Genie for this unusual "natural experiment" and her quest to be a normal human being?

Stand by Me. (Video: 1986, color, 87 minutes). Directed by Rob Reiner; starring Wil Wheaton, River Phoenix, Corey Feldman, Kiefer Sutherland, Richard Dreyfuss.

Based on Stephen King's story "The Body." A grim discovery lies at the center of this mostly nostalgic reflection on boyhood adventures and friendships.

Chapter 5 **Sensation and Perception**

Preview Questions

1. What are the dual functions of our sensory systems? At what point in visual processing is light energy converted into neural information? Why are sound stimuli interpreted as signaling action in the environment? Which of our other senses is considered the most primitive, and why?

2. What is the task of perception? Why is attention considered a vulnerable process? What quality of perception is produced by organizational processes? In our perceptions, how do we experience continuity over time and across situations?

One night in late 1965, a United Airlines Boeing 727 started a steady descent to Chicago's O'Hare Airport from an altitude of 22,000 feet. Nineteen miles off the shore of Lake Michigan, the plane plunged into the lake.

One month later, also at night, an American Airlines Boeing 727, preparing to land at Kentucky's Boone County Airport, followed the thread of the Ohio River toward the runway which began at the river's steep south bank. The plane never touched down. It crashed into the bank, 12 feet below the runway.

One night in early 1966, an Al Nippon Airlines Boeing 727 headed toward Tokyo Bay. The pilot could see the lights of Tokyo and Yokohama clearly. He requested and received permission to approach using visual cues rather than relying exclusively on the plane's instruments. The pilot had not even let down the wheels or extended the flaps when, six-and-a-half miles from the runway, the plane dove into Tokyo Bay at a speed of 240 knots.

Preliminary analyses of these and other similar cases showed that all the accidents occurred at night, under clear weather conditions, with the planes flying over a dark area of water or land. In every case, irregular patterns of light (as opposed to grids of neatly intersecting lines of street lights) in the distance had been visible to the pilots.

In a way, the design of the new Boeing 727 was partly responsible for the accidents, because the plane was so *well* engineered. In earlier, less stable models, feedback from vibrations and sounds and kinesthetic sensations would have warned the pilots that they were descending too rapidly. However, more than an improved design caused the accidents.

Using a flight simulator, engineering psychologist **Conrad Kraft** found that an error in the pilot's visual perception was responsible for each accident. Pilots making a visually guided approach over a dark terrain relied on the relatively constant visual angle between their planes and the distant light patterns to determine their altitudes. If they were approaching flat terrain, their altitude estimates were generally correct, but if the terrain sloped upwards, with the farthest lights higher than the closer ones, even the most experienced pilots descended to dangerously low altitudes. With no visual information from the "dark hole" below them, the pilots overestimated their distance from the ground and inappropriately adjusted their descent angles.

Why didn't the pilots also use their altimeters—instruments that measure elevation? When landing an airplane, a pilot must monitor several functions simultaneously—speed, engine power, altitude, direction—while responding to air traffic controller directions and watching for other aircraft. With all of these responsibilities, especially when visibility is good, pilots may fail to check their altimeters.

After Dr. Kraft solved the mystery of the accidents, commercial airlines around the world informed pilots of the conditions under which they might misjudge altitude on approach to landing. Psychologists like Dr. Kraft study perception in order to learn how the body's major sensory systems help (and sometimes trick) us in gathering information about the environments in which we live and work (Kraft, 1978).

Introduction

Are humans doomed to make costly mistakes in sensing and perceiving the world? Perhaps our abilities are adequate for a simpler kind of life, but our limitations become apparent when we try to fly, move at incredible speeds, or keep up with increasingly sophisticated technology. How exactly do we sense the world around us? And how do we organize and interpret the many stimuli coming from all our senses into our brain? Is it realistic to hope we can identify and correct mistakes like pilot error?

This chapter deals first with **sensory processes**—those systems associated with the sense organs and peripheral aspects of the nervous system that put us in direct contact with sources of stimulation. *Sensation* gets the show started, but *perception* is necessary to make the performance meaningful and interesting, and most importantly, to enable us to respond effectively to our experiences.

Most of the time, sensing and perceiving occur so effortlessly, continuously, and automatically that we take them for granted. They typically give us an accurate view of reality. The perceptual distortion experienced by the ill-fated pilots is one exception to this rule. By examining patterns of both human perceptual error and flawless functioning, we will learn how we sense—and *make* sense—of our complicated, challenging world.

sensory processes Sense organ functions that put the nervous system in direct contact with sources of stimulation.

Sensation

Sensation involves the basic elements of experience—the processes of detecting sensory input. Beyond sensation are higher-level activity processes of the central nervous system, the *perceptual processes*—identification, interpretation, integration, and classification of sensory experience. In this section, we will consider the features of sensory processing that are common to all of our senses. We then examine the functioning of specific **sensory modalities** such as vision and hearing.

sensory modalities Separate sensory systems that take in information.

sensuality State or quality of appreciating sensory pleasures.

Sensory Knowledge of Our World

➥ Before we begin our journey into the world of sensation, we should reflect on the dual functions of our senses: *survival* and *sensuality*. Our senses help us survive by sounding alarms of danger, priming us to take swift action to ward off hazards, and by directing us toward agreeable sensations—such as tasty foods, which are healthy, and sexual touch, which promotes procreation. Our senses also provide us with sensuality. **Sensuality** is the quality of being devoted to the gratification of the senses; it entails enjoying the experiences that are appealing to the eye, the ear, touch, taste, and smell. How does the brain—locked in the dark, silent chamber of the skull—experience the blaze of color in a Van Gogh painting, the booming melody of Beethoven's Ninth Symphony, the refreshing taste of watermelon on a hot day, and the pain of illnesses that afflict us all? Our senses do more than make contact with our world; they involve us in the richness of life. Bear in mind, therefore, that we can judge sensation not only by its accuracy—how perfectly it represents reality to us—but also by the sensual pleasure it affords us in even the simplest experiences.

Ordinarily, our experience of external reality is relatively accurate and error-free; it has to be if we are to survive. All species have developed some

Your first author appears to defy the laws of gravity by floating in air. This perceptual illusion is created by the mirror reflection of the right side of his body which obscures the fact that his left leg is planted firmly on the ground (*Discovering Psychology*, 1990, Program 7).

sensation Process of converting physical energy into stimulation of receptor cells (for example, converting light energy into visual stimulation).

perception Processes that organize sensory information and interpret it in terms of its environmental origins.

kind of specialized *information-gathering apparatus.* Humans lack the acute senses that other species have perfected, such as the vision of hawks, the hearing of bats, or the sense of smell of rodents. Instead, we have developed complex sensory organs and additional neural apparatuses that enable us to process a wider range of more complex sensory input than any other creature. **Sensation** is the process by which a stimulated *receptor* (or sensory neuron) creates neural impulses that result in a feeling or awareness of conditions inside or outside the body. **Perception** is the elaboration, interpretation, and assignment of meaning to these sensory experiences. The boundaries between sensation and perception are not distinct. Most psychologists treat sensation as a primitive experience generated by the activities of receptors responding to sensory data, and they treat perception as a higher-level interpretation of sensation.

Although our perceptual system has worked remarkably well to enable our species to survive and prosper in a varied range of environments, its occasional failures (as in the opening example of pilot error) remind us of the mystery and vulnerability of our information-gathering strategies. This is one of the reasons that the study of sensation and perception has had a prominent place since the early history of experimental psychology. We saw in Chapter 1 that Wundt (1896, 1907) proposed that sensations and feelings are the elementary processes from which complex experiences are built. E. B. Titchener (1898) brought this view to the United States, giving sensation a central place in his introspective examination of the contents of consciousness. Introspection was later replaced by a broader cognitive approach to sensation that focused on how the processing of stimuli guides the perceiver's behavior (Coren & Ward, 1989).

➡ Sensory psychologists work with physiologists, biologists, geneticists, and neurologists to map the process by which physical energy from the external world is transformed into sensations that result in our ten senses: vision, hearing, smell, taste, touch, warmth, cold, equilibrium, kinesthesis (movement), and pain. Consider how different these qualities are from each other. How are physical stimulations transformed into such a powerful variety of experiences? Consider for a moment how your life would change if you were deprived of any of those senses.

To hunt small flying objects at night, bats rely on the sensory system of echolocation, a kind of sonar. Bats emit high-frequency sounds that bounce off insects, revealing their locations so the bats can find and eat them.

From Physical Energy to Mental Events. Stimulus energy arrives at our sensory receptors as physical energy. It is then converted into electrochemical signals that the nervous system can transmit. This stimulus energy is physical energy coded by our nervous system. When the signal reaches the cerebral cortex, we have a sensation of a particular type, such as seeing that a cat's eyes are orange, or feeling the cat's soft, thick fur. The study of sensation is the study of the translation of physical energy into neural processes.

Transduction is the process that converts one form of physical energy, such as light, to another form, such as neural impulses. Although the essence of this conversion remains a mystery, research has taught us a great deal about how and where this happens and what physical and psychological processes affect it.

All sensory systems share at least three components: a *stimulus detector unit,* consisting of a specialized sensory receptor neuron; an *initial receiving center,* where the convergent information from different detector units is assembled by neurons at this level; and one or more *secondary receiving/integrating centers,* where neurons receive and process information from groups of the initial receiver neurons. The interaction of a variety of these secondary centers generates perception.

The trigger for any sensing system is the detection by a sensory neuron of an environmental event, or *stimulus.* This stimulus detector converts the physical form of the sensory signal into a *nerve impulse,* which then codes the sensory event into cellular signals that can be processed by the nervous system. These cellular signals travel along the sensory neuron to the receiving center specialized for each form of sensation. At this stage, information is extracted about the basic qualities of the stimulus, such as its size, intensity, shape, and distance. The secondary processing centers receive this information. They then combine the information into complex codes that are passed on to the neurons in specific areas of the cerebral cortex. The **afferent systems** (sensory systems) process information coming *into* the brain. (*Afferent* comes from the Latin *ad* meaning "toward" + *ferens* meaning "carrying.") The motor systems process information *going out* of the brain to muscles and glands; these processes are known as **efferent systems** (from *ex* meaning "out" and *ferens* meaning "carrying").

Table 5.1 summarizes the stimuli and receptors for each category of the human senses. As you review this list, consider the enormous versatility of human receptors—the neurons that specialize in detecting and transforming stimuli as different as pungent odors, faint lights, and gravity.

Psychophysics. How bright must a warning light be in the dashboard of your car so that it appears twice as bright as the other lights? Such practical questions often arise when people are making decisions about safety regulations and product design. To answer them, we must measure the intensity of sensory experiences. This task is accomplished by relating these psychological experiences to an amount of physical stimulation. **Psychophysics** studies correlations between physical stimuli and the behavior or mental experiences the stimuli evoke. Psychophysics represents the oldest field of the science of psychology (Levine & Shefner, 1981). Psychophysics literally maps physical reality onto psychological reality, tracing differences in matter as they become differences in mind.

The most significant figure in the history of psychophysics was the German physicist, **Gustav Fechner** (1801–1887) who taught at the University of Leipzig (along with Wilhelm Wundt). Fechner (who coined the term *psychophysics*) studied how to relate the intensity of a physical stimulus, such as the volume of sound (measured in physical units), to the magnitude of the sensory experience, such as loudness (measured in psychological units) (Fechner, *Elements of Psychophysics,* 1860). Fechner's psychophysical techniques measure

transduction Transformation of one form of energy into another (for example, tranformation of vibration energy into neural impulses later interpreted as sound).

afferent systems Sensory systems that process information coming into the brain.

efferent systems Motor systems or systems that process information from the brain to muscles and glands.

psychophysics Study of correspondence between physical stimulation and psychological experience.

Table 5.1 Human Sensory System: Fundamental Features

SENSE	STIMULUS	SENSE ORGAN	RECEPTOR	SENSATION
Sight	Light waves	Eye	Rods and cones of retina	Colors, patterns, textures
Hearing	Sound waves	Ear	Hair cells of the basilar membrane	Noises, tones
Skin sensations	External contact	Skin	Nerve endings in skin (Ruffini corpuscles, Merkel disks, Pacinian corpuscles)	Touch, pain, warmth, cold
Smell	Volatile substances	Nose	Hair cells of olfactory epithelium	Odors (musky, flowery, burnt, minty)
Taste	Soluble substances	Tongue	Taste buds of tongue	Flavors (sweet, sour, salty, bitter)
Equilibrium	Mechanical and gravitational forces	Inner ear	Hair cells of semi-circular canals and vestibule	Spatial movement gravitational pull

the strength of sensations experienced by an alert, normal organism in response to stimuli of different strengths.

Classic research in psychophysics has examined two approaches to sensory thresholds: *absolute thresholds* and *difference thresholds*. More recent research has developed an alternate approach to understanding sensation: the theory of *signal detection*. The following discussion considers all three approaches.

Absolute Thresholds. What is the smallest, weakest stimulus energy that an organism can detect? How dim can a light be, for instance, and still be visible? These questions refer to the **absolute threshold** for different types of stimulation—the minimum amount of physical energy needed to produce a sensory experience. If while stargazing you point out a faint star to a friend who never reports seeing it, the star's light is above your absolute threshold (you can see it) but below that of your friend (who cannot).

According to the classical view of absolute thresholds, stimuli below the threshold produce no sensation; stimuli above it do. However, because a stimulus does not become clearly detectable at a specific point, a person's absolute threshold is more accurately defined as the intensity at which the stimulus is detected *half* of the time over many trials. **Table 5.2** on the next page shows absolute threshold levels for several familiar natural stimuli.

Signal Detection Theory. The **theory of signal detection** (TSD) is an alternative to the classical psychophysics approach to absolute thresholds (Green &

absolute threshold Minimum amount of physical energy needed to stimulate a sensory system.

theory of signal detection (TSD) Theory that a perceptual judgment combines sensation and decision-making processes.

Table 5.2 Approximate Thresholds of Familiar Events

SENSE MODALITY	DETECTION THRESHOLD
Light	A candle flame seen at 30 miles on a dark clear night
Sound	The tick of a watch under quiet conditions at 20 feet
Taste	One teaspoon of sugar in 2 gallons of water
Smell	One drop of perfume diffused into the entire volume of a 3-room apartment
Touch	The wing of a bee falling on your cheek from a distance of 1 centimeter

Swets, 1966). Signal detection theory emphasizes the process of making a *judgment* about the presence or absence of stimulus events. Whereas classical psychophysics conceptualized a single absolute threshold, TSD identifies two distinct processes in sensory detection: (1) an initial *sensory process,* which reflects the subject's sensitivity to the strength of the stimulus (the *signal strength*); and (2) a subsequent separate *decision process,* which reflects the subject's response biases. Why would a subject's response be biased? Experience and expectations may lead a subject to be "too ready" to say, "Yes, I heard something" or "No, there was nothing there." Nervousness, hope, fantasy, and desire can all predispose you to detect "something" that wasn't there—or completely miss something that *was*. These biases are sources of confusion or *noise* in the system and lead to inaccurate estimates of the signal. A subject's task is to identify the signal accurately, resisting the biases of the background noise.

For example, suppose your date for tonight is supposed to call to confirm at 4:00 p.m. Arriving home, perspiring from your exercise run, you notice the time is 3:45 p.m. This gives you 15 minutes to shower before the phone call, so you dash into the bathroom and turn on the water. In the shower, you become aware of all the ringing, phone-like sounds you can possibly hear. Is that the phone—could your date be calling a bit early—or is it just the normal pinging of water on tile? If you overreact and run to the phone, you may track water everywhere for no reason. But if you ignore the "ringing," you could miss your only chance to confirm your date, and you *did* promise to be home to get the call.

In this example, the *signal* is the ringing of the telephone: It either rings (signal "on") or it does not ("off"). Your response is your decision: You either jump out of the shower to answer the phone ("yes") or you decide you are imagining things and ignore the phone-like sounds ("no"). The *noise* includes the auditory confusion of splashing water and the increased sensitivity of expecting a phone call at about this time. Your task is to recognize when the phone really rings and answer it in time—and *not* to make the mistake of answering a nonringing phone or ignoring a real call. As you may know from experience, this "simple" task is not so easy.

Figure 5.1 shows the four possible consequences of combining these two signal situations ("on" or "off") with your two response options ("yes" or "no"). If you recognize a real signal despite the noise, you score a *hit;* if you fail to recognize it, you score a *miss.* Responding "yes" when the signal was "off" qualifies as a *false alarm;* accurately concluding that there was no signal counts as a *correct rejection.*

What does TSD offer that was missing in classical psychophysics? The critical factor seems to be human judgment. The theory of signal detection states that any stimulus event (signal or noise) produces some neural activity in the sensory system. In deciding whether a stimulus was present, the observer compares the sensory experience with a personal standard. For example, perhaps you know that your telephone rings loudly enough for you to hear it even when you are in the shower. If the sound you thought you heard was not that loud, you will *judge* it to be noise, not a signal; you will *decide* not to respond.

The TSD approach now dominates modern psychophysics. It provides a model of decision making that can be used in other contexts as well. (Many everyday decisions involve different rewards for every "hit" and correct rejection and penalties for every "miss" and false alarm). However, decisions are likely to be biased by the schedule (system) of anticipated gains and losses. Such a detection matrix is called a *payoff matrix.* The size and nature of these gains and losses influence your response biases. For example, if you judge it would be worse to miss your date's call than to track water through the house while hurrying to the telephone, your payoff matrix favors guessing "yes"— even risking a false alarm—rather than more conservatively guessing "no."

Difference Thresholds. Suppose you are watching television on the one night you don't have to study while your roommate busily prepares for an early morning exam. Your roommate asks you to "turn it off or something" to eliminate the distraction. You want to comply but you also want to hear the rest of the program. What is the least amount you can lower the volume to prove your good intentions to your roommate while still keeping the volume audible? Your ability to make judgments like this one depends on the **difference**

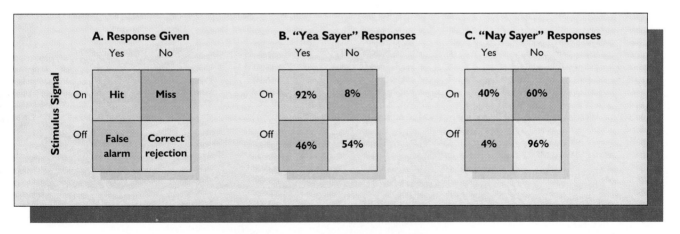

Figure 5.1 The Theory of Signal Detection
Matrix A shows the possible outcomes when a subject is asked if a target stimulus occurred on a given trial. Matrices B and C show the typical responses of a *yea sayer* (biased toward saying "yes") and a *nay sayer* (biased toward saying "no").

threshold—the smallest physical difference between two stimuli that can still be recognized as a difference.

If you turn the volume knob as little as possible, your roommate might complain, "I don't hear any difference" or "You haven't turned it down enough." By "enough," your roommate probably means his or her difference threshold. Even if you adjusted the volume downward, the difference might not be large enough to detect. If *you* hear the difference, it exceeds your own difference threshold; if your roommate can hear the difference, it exceeds his or hers. Suppose you start adjusting the volume and ask your roommate to "say when"—to stop you when the adjustment is "enough." This amount of change in the signal is the **just noticeable difference** (JND).

Research on the JND for different senses has yielded some interesting glimpses of how human detection works. If you have the television volume turned up very high, the JND for the next-lower volume will be large as well: You will have to turn the knob or press the remote control button several times to make the difference noticeable. In contrast, if you already have the volume set to a very low level, so that you can barely hear it if you listen carefully, a minute adjustment lower will probably be noticeable "enough." In other words, the JND is high when the stimulus intensity is high, and low when the stimulus intensity is low.

This relationship—that the size of the JND depends on the intensity of the stimulus—was first established in 1834 by a colleague of Fechner, **Ernst H. Weber** (pronounced VAY-ber). **Weber's law** states that the JND between stimuli is *a constant fraction of the intensity of the standard stimulus*. In equation form, Weber's law is expressed as $\Delta I/I = k$: The noticeable change in a stimulus's intensity (ΔI or "delta I"), when divided by that background intensity (I), equals a constant (k). This means that, for a given sense (for example, vision, taste), the JND for a particular quality (for example, brightness, salty concentration) is always the same fraction or proportion of the background intensity. **Table 5.3** identifies Weber's constant—the fraction of background intensity that a stimulus change must be to be just noticeable—for several human senses.

Table 5.3 Weber's Constant Values for Selected Stimulus Dimensions	
STIMULUS DIMENSION	**WEBER'S CONSTANT**
Sound frequency	.003
Light intensity	.01
Odor concentration	.07
Pressure intensity	.14
Sound intensity	.15
Taste concentration	.20

What does Weber's law mean for your understanding of human sensation? It means that our senses, in translating physical stimuli so our minds can experience them, send information about *relationships*. Our senses compare signals to backgrounds and send us combined messages, not precise pictures of signals alone. For humans, the *meaning* of what we sense begins in the relationships between stimuli and background. You can show the effects of background on stimulus change with a simple demonstration. Obtain a three-way lamp and a lightbulb with equal wattage increments, such as a 50-100-150 watt bulb. In a dark room, switching the light on (to 50 watts) will unmistakably increase brightness. Changing from 50 to 100 watts will seem like a huge increase, because adding 50 watts to a 50-watt background causes a 50/50 or 100 percent jump in brightness. But the last 50-watt increase, changing from 100 to 150 watts, will appear only slightly brighter, because adding 50 more watts to a 100-watt background causes only a 50/100 or 50 percent increase. Your brain does not calculate signal wattage, but rather leaves you with the impression that you have been shortchanged by the 100-150 watt switch, because your sensory systems always compare signals to backgrounds.

Sensory Adaptation. In addition to being determined by the meaning and relationships of stimuli, sensation is also critically determined by *change*. The main role of our stimulus detectors is to announce changes in the external world. Thus our senses are ultimately novelty detectors. Our receptors bring each new event into the total pool of information we use to interpret the momentary status of our sensory field. If not for a specially evolved function of all sensory systems—*adaptation*—this great quantity of new incoming stimuli would overwhelm our ability to deal with old sensations. **Sensory adaptation** is the diminishing responsiveness of sensory systems to prolonged stimulus input. More simply, we cease to notice stimulation that does not change in intensity or some other quality. For example, you do not realize—until you read these words and consider their meaning—that you have already adapted to the press of furniture against your body at this moment; until you focus attention there, you do not "feel" the chair against your posterior, the upholstery at your back, or the pillow under your neck. In a similar way, you do not notice the tension of socks or hose on your legs and feet, the concentration of cologne near your own nose, or the unvarying drone of an air conditioner. As long as these streams of stimulation remain relatively constant, your attention is diverted to other sensations. However, any shift in the signals you are receiving—for example, if the air conditioner suddenly becomes louder or higher-pitched—will rivet your sensory attention once more because the signals have changed. (See "Time Out for Critical Thinking" on the next page.)

The process of adaptation reveals the dynamic and vital nature of sensation. As our response to old stimuli fades quickly over time, we are continually refreshed by the vibrant world of sensory impressions around us. Sensory adaptation is another application of sensory *comparisons* that adjust to stimulation over time. Some of our sensory systems are so efficient at adapting to extreme conditions that we may not realize how extreme those conditions are. When you're at a noisy party, you may not realize that you and your companions are shouting; in the morning your sore throat will remind you how screaming strains your voice. Similarly, after watching a film in a dark theater in the afternoon, you may emerge feeling blinded by an overcast day and momentarily paralyzed by discomfort that—under normal conditions—would not even warrant sunglasses.

sensory adaptation Loss of responsiveness in receptor cells after stimulation has remained unchanged.

Vision

Now that we have considered the purposes of sensation, we will explore its processes in several bodily sensory systems, especially vision and hearing.

Sensory adaptation is a form of living proof that we are "programmed" to notice and respond to change. How does this change-orientation make sense for our survival? When environmental conditions are familiar or continuous, we probably need not monitor them as vigilantly as when circumstances are novel or sudden. Consider how you might interpret the following sensations:

- As you begin your walk home from campus, the sky seems to cloud over and darken in a matter of minutes, and the still air whips into a brisk wind. What should you do? Why is this important?

- You are babysitting a friend's two young children for an hour. While you change the baby's diaper, you can hear the toddler chattering to her doll. Suddenly her voice becomes shrill and loud. What might this mean?

- At lunch with your sweetheart, you become aware that the conversation is going nowhere. Your usually cheerful partner is uncharacteristically quiet. When you ask what might be wrong, you hear "Oh, nothing." How should you respond?

In each case, a change might actually signal a threat—to your comfort, to someone's safety, or to your relationship. How do you react to change in your life? Do changes tend to irritate and surprise you, or are you usually able to adapt to them? Can you see how routines, patterns, and familiar territory provide a stable background so you can learn ideas and experiences to add to them?

Vision is the most complex, highly developed, and important sense for humans and most other mobile creatures. Animals with good vision have an enormous evolutionary advantage. Good vision helps us detect goals, threats, and changes in our physical environment and adapt our behavior accordingly. With specialized instruments we can even enhance our visual detection to see distant galaxies or microscopic life forms. Not surprisingly, vision is the most studied of all the sense modalities.

The Human Eye and Brain. After light is detected by our eyes, it is converted to neural impulses and sent for further processing to and through the brain. Here we will review the pathways of visual processing and the qualities of visual sensation.

The Structures of the Eye. The eye is the camera for the brain's motion pictures of the world (see **Figure 5.2**). Like a camera, the eye gathers and focuses light. Light first enters the *cornea,* a transparent bulge on the front of the eye that is filled with a clear liquid called the *aqueous humor;* next it passes through the *pupil,* an opening in the opaque, ringed muscle that is the *iris.* The iris controls the amount of light that enters the eye, by either relaxing to constrict the pupil (and shut out light) or contracting to dilate the pupil (and let more light in). To focus a camera, we move its lens closer to or further from the object viewed. To focus the eye, neural signals change the shape of the eye's rubbery, bean-shaped crystalline *lens,* thinning it to focus on distant objects and thickening it to focus on near ones.

At the back of a camera body, photosensitive film records the variations in light that have passed through the lens. Similarly, in the eye, light travels

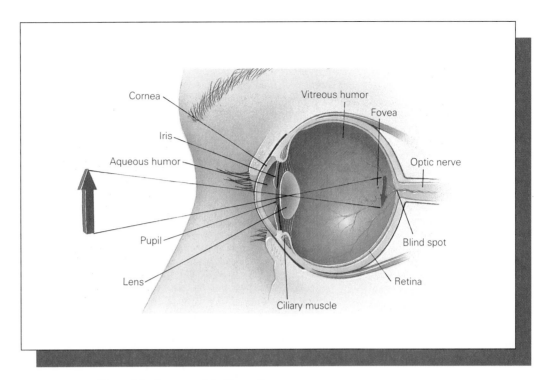

Figure 5.2 Structure of the Human Eye

retina Layer of cells at the back of the eye containing photoreceptors.

through the thick, translucent vitreous humor, finally striking the **retina**, a thin sheet of neurons that lines the rear wall of the eyeball.

How exactly does the camera of the eye "snap" pictures of our dynamic, living world? We look with our eyes but we *see* with our brains. The eye gathers light, focuses it, and sends a neural signal on its way for subsequent processing into a visual image. The eye's critical function is this last task: To convert the information about the world from light waves into neural signals the brain can process. This transduction happens in the **retina**—the "film" at the back of the eye—where visual information is also first integrated. The retina is a layered structure interweaving five types of neurons: (1) the receptor cells, called the *rods* and *cones,* (2) the *bipolar neurons,* (3) the *ganglion cells,* (4) the *horizontal* cells, and (5) the *amacrine* cells.

photoreceptors Light-sensitive cells in the retina that convert light energy to neural responses.

Photoreceptors absorb light energy and convert it into neural responses. Intriguingly, the rods and cones are positioned at the rearmost layer of the retina. Light rays must make it through the maze of preceding neurons to the very back of the retina to trigger photoreception. The transformed (now neural) impulse is then relayed *forward* to the other neurons of the retina before being channeled via nerve fibers to the brain (see **Figure 5.3** on the next page).

rods Photoreceptors abundant in periphery of retina that detect presence/brightness of light and function best in dimness.

Why *two* kinds of photoreceptors? Because we sometimes function in darkness and sometimes in bright light, nature has provided two different ways of processing light stimuli with two distinct types of receptor cells (named roughly for their shape). The 125 million thin **rods** "see in the dark" and report what they detect in black and white. The seven million fat **cones** "view" the bright, color-filled day, each specialized to detect either blue, red, or green hues. In the very center of the retina is a small region called the **fovea** that contains nothing but densely packed cones—it's rod-free. The fovea is the area of our sharpest vision—both color and spatial detail are most accurately detected there.

cones Photoreceptors concentrated in and near the fovea of the retina that detect wavelength (color) and function best in bright light.

fovea Central focal region of retina, densely packed with cones, that provides sharpest vision.

The retina's bipolar and ganglion cells gather the responses of many nearby receptors. Each **bipolar cell** has a single branching dendrite and a single axon, creating two "poles." These cells combine impulses from many receptors

bipolar cell Nerve cell, with one dendrite and one axon, that combines impulses from many receptors and transmits them to ganglion cells.

Figure 5.3 Retinal Pathways
This is a stylized and greatly simplified diagram showing the pathways that connect three of the layers of nerve cells in the retina. Incoming light passes through all these layers to reach the receptors at the back of the eyeball which are pointed away from the source of light. Note that the bipolar cells gather impulses from more than one receptor cell and send the results to several ganglion cells. Nerve impulses (blue arrow) from the ganglion cells leave the eye via the optic nerve and travel to the next relay point.

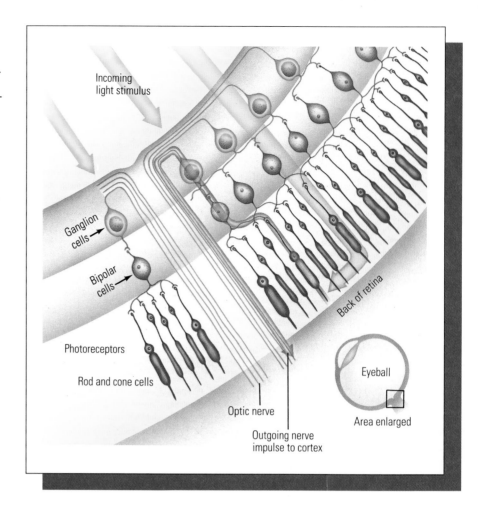

Incoming
light stimulus

Ganglion
cells →

Bipolar
cells →

Back of retina

Photoreceptors

Rod and cone cells

Eyeball

Optic nerve

Area enlarged

Outgoing nerve
impulse to cortex

ganglion cell   Nerve cell that integrates impulses from many bipolar cells into a single rate of firing.

optic nerve   Bundled axons of ganglion cells carrying information from the eye to the brain.

visual cortex   Region of occipital lobes in back of brain where visual information is processed.

and send the results to ganglion cells. Each **ganglion cell** combines the impulses from many bipolar cells into a single rate of firing. The axons of the ganglion cells contain nerve fibers that, bundled together, make up the **optic nerve,** which carries visual information from the eye to the brain. As the optic nerve exits the eye, it leaves a small but measurable area of the retina without a corresponding layer of photoreceptors; this area is the *blind spot.* You do not normally experience blindness there because what one eye "misses" the other eye registers, and the brain "fills in" the information that is most likely missing. To find your own blind spot, examine **Figure 5.4,** and follow the caption's instructions for two revealing exercises.

Pathways to the Brain. At the back of the brain is a special area for processing the neural coded information coming from the eyes. This area in the occipital cortex is known as the primary **visual cortex.** Here the brain "sees" what the eyes have "collected." Research has revealed how visual information is routed and analyzed, cell by cell, from eye to brain.

Nerve impulses leaving the retina project to several different parts of the brain. The bundled axons of the ganglion cells forming the optic nerve first travel to the base of the brain, where they come together in the *optic chiasma,* an X-shaped intersection named for the Greek letter *chi,* resembling our X (see **Figure 5.5**). At the chiasma, half of each eye's bundled fibers cross to the other side toward the back of the brain. Visual information is subsequently divided between two waystations: The *lateral geniculate nucleus* (LGN), which recognizes patterns, and the *superior colliculus,* which identifies their locations.

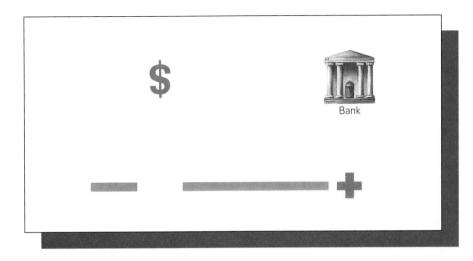

By the time visual information reaches the visual cortex, important analyses have worked to determine *what* you are seeing and *where* you are seeing it.

Seeing Color. A remarkable feature of the human visual system is that our experiences of form, color, position, and depth are based on processing the same sensory information in different ways. Physical objects and beams of light seem to have the marvelous property of being painted with color, but the red Valentines, green fir trees, blue oceans, and rainbows that you see are actually

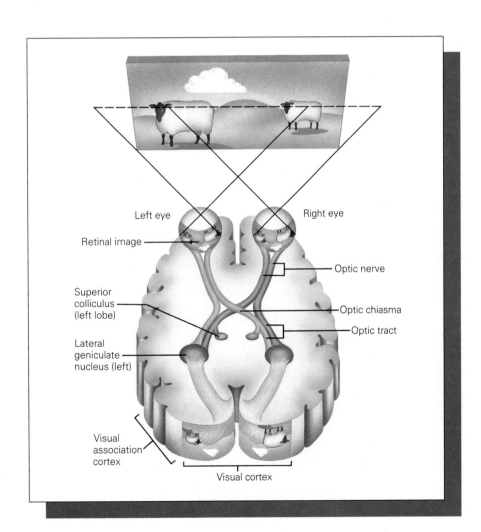

Figure 5.5 Pathways in the Human Visual System
The diagram shows the way light from the visual field projects onto the two retinas and shows the routes by which neural messages from the retina are sent to the two visual centers of each hemisphere.

Sir Isaac Newton (1642–1727)

hue Perceived color, corresponding to wavelength of light.

saturation Perceived purity or vividness of color.

brightness Perceived intensity of light.

complementary colors Colors opposite each other on the color circle.

Isaac Newton showed that white light passing through a prism yields a rainbow of all colors of the spectrum.

colorless. Despite appearances, color does not exist in the objects you see; it only exists in the mind.

Color is a psychological property of your sensory experience, created when your brain processes the information coded in the light source. Although the processes involved are fairly complex, color vision is one of the best understood aspects of our visual experience.

Wavelengths and Hues. **Sir Isaac Newton,** who in the seventeenth century discovered the laws of motion and of gravity, also discovered that when white light passes through a prism it separates into a rainbow of colors: The *visible spectrum.*

Visible light is a kind of energy that our sensory receptors can detect. The light we see is a small portion of a physical dimension called the *electromagnetic spectrum,* which also includes X-rays, microwaves, radio waves, and TV waves. Because we have no receptors sensitive to these light waves, we need special detection instruments to help us convert them into the signals we use.

All electromagnetic energy travels through distance—even through a vacuum-like, airless space—and can be described in terms of its *wavelength,* determined by its speed or frequency. Wavelengths of visible light are measured in *nanometers* (*nm*—billionths of a meter). Visible light ranges from short, high-frequency waves (400 nm at the violet end of the spectrum) to long, low-frequency waves (700 nm at the red end). White sunlight combines all these wavelengths in equal amounts, but a prism can separate them into their distinctive wavelengths. Light is described physically by particular wavelengths; colors exist only in your visual experience.

All experiences of color can be described in terms of three basic dimensions of our perception of light: hue, saturation, and brightness. **Hue** refers to the essential color of a light. **Saturation** is the purity and vividness of color sensations. Undiluted colors have the most saturation; muted, muddy, and pastel colors have intermediate amounts of saturation; and grays have zero saturation. Finally, **brightness** is the intensity of light. White has the most brightness, while black has the least. When colors are analyzed along these three dimensions, a remarkable finding emerges: Humans are capable of visually discriminating among about 5 million different colors! However, most people can identify only 150 to 200 colors.

How is it that all colors combine to form white light? To answer this, refer to the *color circle* in **Figure 5.6,** which arranges similar hues side by side in a continuous circle. Their order mirrors the order of hues in the spectrum. The four unique hues—red, yellow, green, and blue—are equally spaced, and colors located opposite each other are **complementary colors.**

Afterimages. After you stare at a brightly colored object for a while and then turn away to look at a blank surface, you will see the object's complementary color as a *visual afterimage.* Since seeing is sometimes believing, try the Patriotism Test in **Figure 5.7** on page 162 before continuing.

Afterimages (or aftereffects) may be negative or positive. *Negative afterimages* are the opposite or the reverse of the original experience, as in the flag example; they are more common and last longer. *Positive afterimages* are caused by a continuation of the receptor and neural processes following stimulation; they are rare and brief. An example of positive afterimages occurs when you blink after you look at a flashbulb light.

Color Blindness. Not everyone sees colors in the same way; some people are born with a color deficiency. *Color blindness* is the partial or total inability to distinguish colors. (The negative afterimage effect of viewing the green, yellow, and black flag in Figure 5.7 will not work if you are color-blind.)

There are different forms of color-blindness. People with one form called *color weakness* can't distinguish pale colors, such as pink or tan. Most color

Any two unique hues yield the complement of a third color, but the combination of the three wavelengths produces white light.

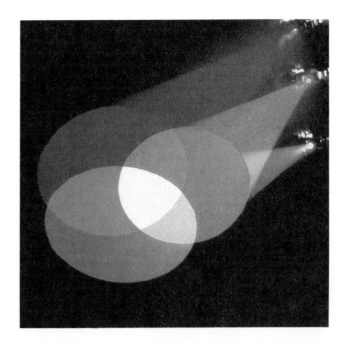

blindness involves trouble distinguishing red from green, especially at weak saturations. Those who confuse yellows and blues are rare—about one or two people per thousand. Rarest of all are those who see no color at all and see only variations in brightness. Only about 500 cases of this total color blindness have ever been reported. To see whether you have a major color deficiency, look at **Figure 5.8** on the next page and note what you see. If you see the number 26 in the dot pattern, your color vision is probably normal. If you see something else, you are probably at least partially color blind.

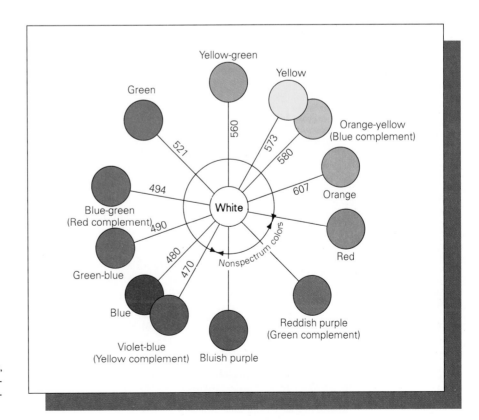

Figure 5.6 The Color Circle
Colors are arranged by their similarity. Complementary colors are placed directly opposite each other. Mixing complementary colors yields a neutral gray or white light at the center. The numbers next to each hue are the wavelength values for spectral colors, those colors within our region of visual sensitivity. Nonspectral hues are obtained by mixing short and long spectral wavelengths.

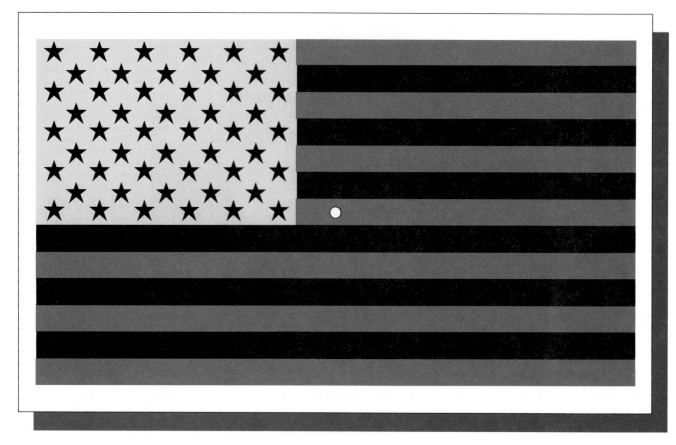

Figure 5.7 Color Afterimages: The Patriotism Test
Stare at the dot in the center of the green, black, and yellow flag for at least 30 seconds. Then fixate on the center of a sheet of white paper or a blank wall. Try this aftereffect illusion on your friends.

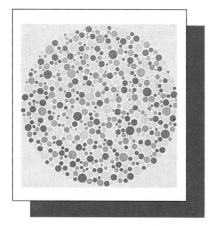

Figure 5.8 The Ishihani Color Blindness Test
A person who cannot discriminate between red and green colors will not be able to identify the number hidden in the figure. What do you see? If you see the number 26 in the dot pattern, your color vision is probably normal.

From Attention to Action. Normal visual experience is a challenging process of picking and choosing. With so many signals coming in and competing for processing in the brain, how can we resist confusion and focus on what is important? How are the objects of our attention chosen and how are our eyes and hands directed to move them? The ordinary ability of many animals—especially humans—to reach out, grasp, and manipulate perceived objects is a feat of biological engineering that is unmatched by state-of-the-art robots. Apparently, we are able to perform these feats because of specialized cells in the central nervous system. Some cells help direct our attention to certain objects, others help move the eyes to the object of most interest, and still others help generate limb movements to grasp and manipulate objects.

In the first stage of processing, *figure-ground separation* occurs. The visual system analyzes the scene for *edges,* and for *contrasts* to distinguish figures (distinct objects or shapes) from their ground (background elements). In the second stage of visual processing, specific objects or special features of forms are selected for more careful analysis. This is the *attentional stage* of perception, which operates by focusing on one or two objects at a time. While attention at a *psychological level* facilitates behavioral responses and access to memory (discussed later in this chapter), attention at this *neurophysiological level* can have powerful effects on the responses of individual neurons. For example, while driving toward an unfamiliar intersection, you rely on your attention processes to pick out the crucial sign—such as the one that directs traffic to the interstate highway—and ignore irrelevant signs (for example, the road you know you are on) and predictable stimuli (for example, normal traffic behind you, stable weather conditions).

Once attention focuses the brain's information processing system on the object, a number of other processes are called into play. *Gaze control* directs eye movement to scrutinize the target; *limb movement control* directs arms, hands, and mouth toward the target; and *body movement control* directs the body toward targets out of reach and away from feared targets. These actions are largely controlled by neurons in the *motor cortex*. Neurons here have been shown to begin discharging impulses before the first muscle activity starts to move the limbs. Thus, as soon as you detect an interstate sign for a left turn, you can begin moving your eyes, hands, and feet in ways that will signal your plans, slow your vehicle, and steer into the turn lane.

Researchers are developing models of the neural networks involved in visually guided movement. Their challenging task is to demonstrate how one's accumulated *experience*—learning and memory—adjusts and maintains the consistency between sensory input maps and the motor output maps. These models will increase our basic understanding of how we are able to act so accurately on the basis of what we perceive. They will also have practical use in assisting patients suffering from problems of visual-movement impairments (Wise & Desimone, 1988). For instance, many people who suffer partial paralysis can be trained to drive safely once they determine limits on their movements and legal restrictions on where and when they can operate a vehicle.

Hearing

Although vision is the most investigated of our senses, the study of hearing is also of great psychological importance. Like vision, hearing provides us with reliable spatial information over extended distances. However, hearing may be even more important than vision in orienting us toward distant events. We often hear stimuli before we see them, and we often have readier access to sound than to vision. For example, you can remain seated in your room, studying for tomorrow's test and seeing only the words on the page, and your sense of hearing will still inform you about traffic outside your window, footsteps in the hall, and voices at the door. You may take for granted your ability to use these cues to determine what time it is, who is nearby, and what you should do.

Besides orienting us, hearing plays a crucial role in our understanding of spoken language; it is the principal sensory modality for human communication. The importance of hearing and the tragedy of its loss is captured in the following eloquent description:

> The world will still make sense to someone who is blind or armless or minus a nose. But if you lose your sense of hearing, a crucial thread dissolves and you lose track of life's logic. You become cut off from the daily commerce of the world, as if you were a root buried beneath the soil (Ackerman, 1990, p. 175).

You may better understand the details of the process of sensing sound if you first appreciate its value in human experience. Take a moment to reflect on the power of hearing in your life and the lives of those around you. Then move on to the next section, where we review how sound is first sensed and then understood.

 The Physics of Sound. Actions create sounds because they cause objects to vibrate. The vibrational energy is transmitted to the surrounding medium—usually air—as the vibrating objects push the molecules of the medium back and forth. Resulting changes in pressure spread outward in the form of sound waves traveling at a rate of about 1100 feet per second. Sound cannot travel in a true vacuum (such as outer space) because there is no medium there to move or vibrate.

Changes in air pressure travel in *sine waves,* energy changes that unfold in time or space (see **Figure 5.9** on the next page). Frequency and amplitude are

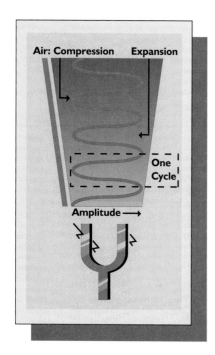

Figure 5.9 Sound Waves

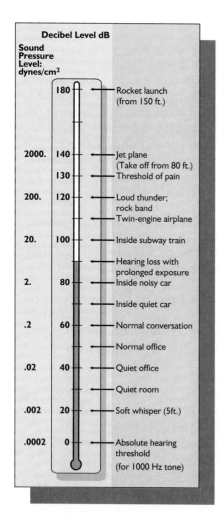

Figure 5.10 Loudness of Familiar Sounds

the physical properties of a sine wave that determine how it sounds to us. *Frequency* measures the number of cycles the wave completes in a given amount of time; it is usually expressed in cycles per second (cps) or **hertz (Hz)**. *Amplitude* measures the physical strength of the sound wave (shown in its peak-to-valley height); it is defined in units of sound pressure or energy.

A *pure tone*—such as that made by a tuning fork—is the sound produced by a single sine wave. A pure tone has only one frequency and one amplitude. Most sounds are produced not by pure tones but by complex waves containing a combination of frequencies and amplitudes. We hear different qualities of sounds (clarinet versus piano, for example) because most sounds contain different combinations of frequencies and amplitudes.

The Psychology of Hearing. The three dimensions of sound that we experience are pitch, loudness, and quality.

Pitch. **Pitch** is the highness or lowness of a sound determined by the sound's frequency; high frequencies produce high pitch, and low frequencies produce low pitch. The full range of human sensitivity to pure tones extends from frequencies as low as 20 cps to frequencies as high as 20,000 cps.

Just as the visual system "specializes" in sensing color, the auditory system is particularly adept at detecting and distinguishing pitch. As reviewed in "In Focus: Theories of Pitch Perception" on page 167, two distinct theories have been proposed—and reconciled—to account for pitch perception.

Loudness. The **loudness** or physical intensity of a sound is determined by its amplitude; sound waves with large amplitudes are experienced as loud and those with small amplitudes as soft. People can hear sounds across a wide range of loudness. The auditory system is sensitive enough to hear the tick of a wristwatch at 20 feet; this is the system's absolute threshold. If it were more sensitive, we would hear the blood flowing in our ears. At the other extreme, a jet airliner taking off 100 yards away is so loud that it is painful. When we compare the two sounds in terms of physical units of sound pressure, the jet produces a sound wave with more than a billion times the energy of the ticking watch.

Because the range of hearing is so great, physical intensities of sound are usually expressed in ratios rather than absolute amounts; loudness is measured in units called **decibels** (dB). **Figure 5.10** shows the loudness of some representative natural sounds in decibel units. It also shows the corresponding sound pressures for comparison. Notice that sounds louder than about 90 dB can produce hearing loss, depending on how long one is exposed to them.

Timbre. The **timbre** (pronounced TAM-b'r) of a sound reflects the quality of complexity of its sound wave. A complex sound can be analyzed as a sum of many different pure tones, each with a different amplitude and frequency. **Figure 5.11** shows the complex waveforms that correspond to several familiar sounds. The graph in the figure shows the sound spectrum for middle C on a piano—the range of all the frequencies actually present in that note and their amplitudes. The human ear analyzes complex waves by breaking them down into their simpler component waves.

The sounds that we call *noise* contain many frequencies that are unrelated systematically to each other. For instance, the static noise you hear between radio stations contains energy at all audible frequencies; you perceive it as having no pitch because it has no frequency common to all components.

The Physiology of Hearing. How does the physiological activity of the auditory system give rise to the psychological experience of sound? For people to hear, four basic *energy transformations* must take place.

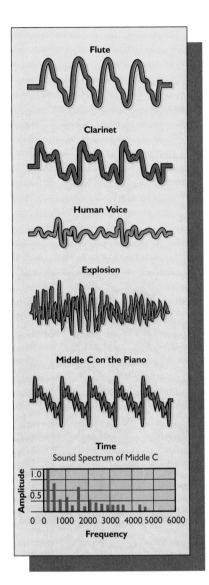

Figure 5.11 Waveforms of Familiar Sounds Below the complex waveforms of five familiar sounds is the sound spectrum for middle C on the piano. The basic wavelength is produced by the fundamental, in this case at 256 cycles, but the strings are also vibrating at several higher frequencies that produce the jaggedness of the wave pattern. These additional frequencies are identified in the sound spectrum.

hertz (Hz)   Unit of sound frequency, also expressed as *cycles per second (cps)*.

pitch   Perceived frequency of sound.

loudness   Perceived intensity or amplitude of sound energy.

decibels (dB)   Units of physical intensity of sound.

timbre   Perceived complexity of sound wave.

1. *Airborne sound waves must get translated into fluid waves within the cochlea of the ear.* In this first transformation, vibrating air molecules enter the ears (see **Figure 5.12** on the next page). Some sound enters the external canal of the ear directly and some enters after having been reflected off the *external ear,* or *pinna.* When the sound wave reaches the end of the canal, it encounters and sets in motion a thin membrane called the *eardrum,* or *tympanic membrane.* The eardrum transmits the vibrations from the outer ear into the middle ear, a chamber that contains the three smallest bones in the human body: the *hammer,* the *anvil,* and the *stirrup.* This series of bones mechanically transmits and concentrates the vibrations to the primary organ of hearing, the *cochlea,* located in the *inner ear.*

2. *The fluid waves must then stimulate mechanical vibrations of the basilar membrane.* This second transformation occurs in the cochlea, where the airborne sound wave becomes "seaborne." The cochlea is a fluid-filled, coiled tube with a thin tissue known as the **basilar membrane** running through its core. The stirrup vibrates against the oval window at the base of the cochlea and sets the inner fluid in wave motion. The fluid wave causes the basilar membrane to move similarly, bending the membrane's tiny hair cells.

3. *These vibrations must be converted into electrical impulses.* The bending of the hair cells stimulates sensory nerve endings. These transform the mechanical vibrations of the basilar membrane into neural activity.

4. *Finally, the impulses must travel to the auditory cortex.* Nerve impulses leave the cochlea in a bundle of fibers called the **auditory nerve.** These fibers meet in the brain stem, with stimulation from each ear traveling to both sides of the brain. Auditory signals ultimately proceed to the **auditory cortex**—which is in the temporal lobes of the cerebral hemispheres—for higher-order processing.

If the auditory system seems complicated, you might think of it as a sensory "relay race." Sound waves are first funneled in by the outer ear, then transferred from tissue to bone in the middle ear. Mechanical vibrations become waves in the inner ear, and finally these waveforms trigger neural impulses to the brain. This series of steps ingeniously transforms commonplace vibrations and shifts in air pressure into experiences as exquisite and varied as music, doorbells, whispers, shouts—and psychology lectures.

Our Other Senses

Of all our senses, vision and hearing have been studied the most because they are the most important; however, our survival depends on many other senses as well. To conclude our discussion of sensation, we will briefly review (1) the processes that enable us to sense position and movement, (2) smell, (3) taste, (4) the skin senses, and (5) pain.

Position and Movement.   To move around purposefully in our environment we need constant information about where our limbs and other body parts are in relation to each other and to objects in the environment. Without this knowledge, even our simplest actions would be hopelessly uncoordinated. The **vestibular sense** tells us how our bodies—especially our heads—are oriented in the world with respect to gravity. It also tells us when we are moving or how our motion is changing. The receptors for this information are tiny hairs in the inner ear, which are triggered when the pull of gravity on surrounding fluid signals information about body position and orientation.

The **kinesthetic sense** (also called *kinesthesis*) provides constant sensory feedback about what the body is doing during motor activities. Without it, we could not coordinate most of the voluntary movements we make so effortlessly. Receptors for kinesthetic information can be found in the joints and in the

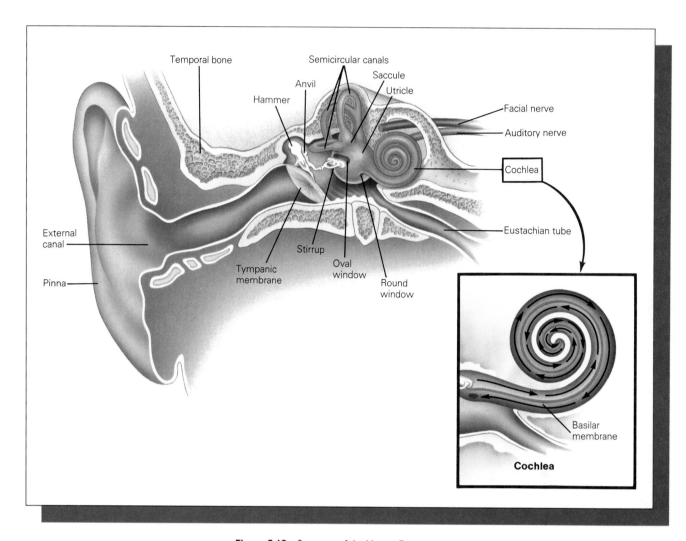

Temporal bone

Semicircular canals

Saccule

Utricle

Anvil

Hammer

Facial nerve

Auditory nerve

Cochlea

External canal

Eustachian tube

Pinna

Stirrup

Tympanic membrane

Oval window

Round window

Basilar membrane

Cochlea

Figure 5.12 Structure of the Human Ear

Sound waves are channeled by the external ear, or pinna, through the external canal, causing the tympanic membrane to vibrate. This vibration activates the tiny bones of the inner ear—the hammer, anvil, and stirrup. Their mechanical vibrations are passed along from the oval window to the cochlea where they set in motion the fluid in its canal. Tiny hair cells lining the coiled basilar membrane within the cochlea bend as the fluid moves, stimulating nerve endings attached to them. The mechanical energy is then transformed into neural energy and sent to the brain via the auditory nerve.

basilar membrane Thin membrane (tissue) that runs through the cochlea; hair cells on the basilar membrane are activated by sound (vibration) energy.

auditory nerve Bundle of axons from inner-ear cells carrying sound information to the brain.

auditory cortex Area of temporal lobes in brain that receives and processes sound information.

vestibular sense Sense of body orientation with respect to gravity.

kinesthetic sense Sense of body position and movement of body parts relative to each other (also called *kinesthesis*).

muscles and tendons. We sometimes take kinesthetic information for granted and make automatic adjustments in our movements. But we do not necessarily know our own limits! If you have ever injured yourself while exercising or physically working, you know that healthy action depends both on understanding how your body works and on paying attention to the signals it may be sending to you.

Smell. The sense of smell or *olfaction* involves a sequence of biochemical activities that trigger neural impulses. Odors, in the form of chemical molecules, interact with receptor proteins on the membrane of tiny hairs in the nose. Once initiated, these nerve impulses convey odor information to the **olfactory bulb,** located just above the receptors and just below the frontal lobes of the cortex. The brain center that specializes in processing information about smell is the *rhinencephalon,* one of the primitive parts of the brain. Smell may be our most primitive sense, having evolved before other senses were differentiated. Smell signals go directly to the brain's smell center, rather than being relayed indirectly through the thalamus like other sensory information.

Theory THEORIES OF PITCH PERCEPTION

We "read" a rich amount of information in the pitches of the sounds we hear. Can you imagine music without the high-pitched delicacy of strings, or the low-pitched soul of bass? The pitch of a voice gives us clues about the age and gender of the speaker. A change to a higher pitch warns us of alarm, while a lowering of pitch might mean calm—or the end of a speech. Two distinct theories have been proposed to explain how the auditory system converts sound waves into sensations of pitch: *place theory* and *frequency theory.*

Place theory was initially proposed by **Hermann von Helmholtz** in the 1800s and was later modified, elaborated, and tested by **Georg von Békésy,** who won a Nobel prize for this work in 1961. **Place theory** proposes that pitch perception depends on which part of the receptor is stimulated. When sound waves are conducted through the inner ear, the basilar membrane moves. Different frequencies produce maximum movement at different specific *places* on

the membrane. For high-frequency tones, the wave motion is greatest at the base of the cochlea, while for low-frequency tones, the greatest motion is at the apex of the basilar membrane. Thus in place theory, perception of pitch depends upon the specific place on the basilar membrane where the greatest stimulation occurs. Different places may represent specific codes in the nervous system's processing of sound.

The alternative view, **frequency theory,** explains pitch by the timing of neural responses. It hypothesizes that neurons fire only at a particular point in each sound wave. Their firing rate is determined by a tone's frequency. This *rate of firing* is the code for pitch. Thus pitch is a matter of time, not place.

The place and frequency theories of pitch perception were long thought to be in direct conflict. Recently, it has become clear that both are correct, each accounting for only a portion of the audible frequency range. Frequency theory accounts well for coding frequencies

below about 5000 Hz; place theory accounts well for perception of pitch at frequencies above 1000 Hz. Between 1000 and 5000 Hz both mechanisms can operate. The two pitch theories have proven to be compatible. Each offers good explanations of parts of the puzzle. A complex sensory task is divided between two systems that, together, offer greater sensory precision than either system alone could provide.

Our auditory system seems designed for greatest precision within the 1000 and 5000 Hz range of sounds. What is the evolutionary significance of this range? Not coincidentally, the frequency of human speech has a considerable overlap with this range. The shape of the auditory canal magnifies sounds within the range of human speech. Thus the auditory system may well have evolved especially for hearing the human voice.

---

olfactory bulb   Brain site of olfactory processing, below frontal lobes, where odor-sensitive receptors send their signals.

place theory   Explanation for pitch perception; claims that different frequencies produce maximum neural activity at different locations on the basilar membrane, and that pitch is neurally coded for these different places.

frequency theory   Explanation for pitch perception; claims that neural firing rate along basilar membrane is caused by a tone's frequency, and that pitch is neurally coded for different firing rates.

pheromones   Chemical signals released by organisms to communicate with other members of their species.

Smell presumably evolved as a system for detecting and locating food (Moncrieff, 1951). It is also used for detecting potential sources of danger. In addition, smell can be a powerful form of active communication. Members of some species (for example, insects such as ants and termites, and vertebrates such as dogs and cats) communicate with each other by secreting and detecting chemical signals called *pheromones.* **Pheromones** are chemical substances used as communication within a given species to signal sexual receptivity, danger, territorial boundaries, and food sources. Humans primarily seem to use the sense of smell in conjunction with taste to seek and sample food, but there is some evidence that humans may also secrete and sense sexual pheromones. Consider the value—and power—of smell in your own emotional experiences. Are there fragrances that you have found particularly attractive? Have certain scents ever seemed to disgust you? How difficult has it been for you to change such basic responses—if you have even tried to do so? Our reactions to certain olfactory experiences may be too automatic to override or change. And smelling is also remembering. When we study memory, we will see that memory for certain smells is remarkably accurate and long-lasting. Aren't there some aromas that you instantly recognize as part of your own childhood?

Taste.   When you eat, the senses of taste and smell work together closely. When you have a cold, food seems tasteless because your nasal passages are blocked and you can't smell the food. The subtle distinctions you detect in flavors are really signalled by smell; your sense of taste or *gustation* is far less precise in its sensitivity. There are only four true, or primary, taste qualities: sweet,

Wine tasters are able to make subtle and complex taste distinctions. They rely on smell as well as taste.

taste buds Receptors for taste, located primarily on upper side of the tongue.

skin senses Sensory systems for processing reception and experience of pressure, warmth, and cold.

sour, bitter, and salty (saline). These qualities define your *taste space*—like a color wheel for flavors—in which the primary tastes are positioned at the corners of a prism. **Figure 5.13** shows the mouth locations where primary tastes are concentrated.

The taste receptor cells are gathered in the **taste buds,** clustered in very small mucous-membrane projections called *papillae.* These are distributed throughout the mouth cavity, particularly on the upper side of the tongue, as shown in **Figure 5.14.** Sensitivity to sweetness is greatest at the tip of the tongue; sensitivity to sourness is greatest on the edges; and sensitivity to bitterness is greatest at the back. Sensitivity to saltiness is spread over the whole surface.

Taste is important to survival. Even when you are too young to know what's good for you, you know what you like—and what you don't like. Taste sensitivity is exaggerated in infants and decreases with age. Many elderly people who complain that food has lost its taste really mean that they have lost much of their sensory ability to detect differences in the taste and smell of food.

The Skin Senses. The skin is a remarkably versatile organ. It protects us against surface injury, holds in body fluids, and helps regulate body temperature. The skin also contains nerve endings that—when they are stimulated by contact with external objects—produce sensations of pressure, warmth, and cold. These sensations are the **skin senses,** and we could not survive without them.

The skin's sensitivity to pressure varies tremendously over the body. For example, we are ten times more accurate in sensing the position of stimulation on our fingertips than the position of stimulation on our backs. Our sensitivity is greatest where we need it most—on our faces, tongues, and hands. Precise sensory feedback from these parts of the body permits effective eating, speaking, and grasping.

One aspect of skin sensitivity plays a central role in human relationships, emotions, and sexuality: *touch.* Through touch we communicate our desire to give or receive comfort, support, love, and passion. Touch is the primary stimulus for sexual arousal in humans. It is also essential for healthy development. In Chapter 2, Tiffany Field's research showed how massaging helps premature

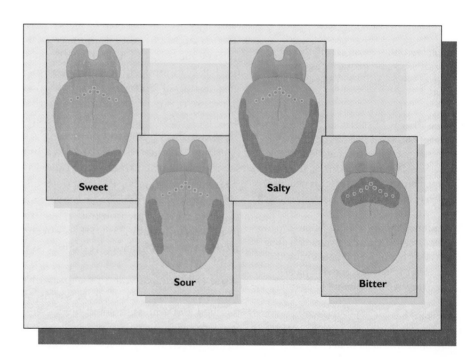

Figure 5.13 Taste Space
Shown are the four primary tastes. Although different parts of the tongue and mouth are more sensitive to one taste or another, individual taste receptors seem to respond to all tastes in varying proportions.

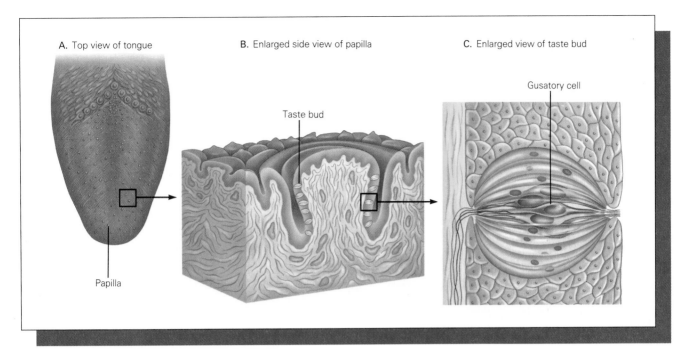

A. Top view of tongue   **B.** Enlarged side view of papilla   **C.** Enlarged view of taste bud

Gusatory cell

Taste bud

Papilla

Figure 5.14 Receptors for Taste
Part A shows the distribution of the papillae on the upper side of the tongue. Part B shows a single papilla enlarged so that the individual taste buds are visible. Part C shows one of the taste buds enlarged.

babies to survive and develop. Deprivation of touch stimulation has been shown to stunt the growth of rat babies and human children. The practical message is clear: touch those you care about often and encourage others to touch you—it not only feels good, it's healthy for you and for them (Lynch, 1979; Montague, 1986).

Pain. The final sense we will examine is the most puzzling of all—our sense of pain. Pain is the universal complaint of the human condition. About one-third of Americans are estimated to suffer from persistent or recurring pain (Wallis, 1984). Depression and even suicide can result from the seemingly endless nagging of chronic pain.

pain Bodily sensation of noxious stimuli intense enough to threaten or cause tissue damage.

Pain is the body's response to stimulation from *noxious stimuli*—those that are intense enough to cause tissue damage or threaten to do so. The pain response is complex, involving a remarkable interplay between biochemistry, nerve impulses, and psychological and cultural factors. Pain is itself unpleasant, so it is more than a mere signal of danger; pain acts as a window into our experience of being hurt or damaged. "It is always more than a distressing sensation. It is useful to think of pain as a person's emotional experience of a distressing sensation; thus, morale and mood can be as important as the intensity of the feeling itself in determining the degree of pain" (Brody, 1986, p. 1).

Acute pain is sharp or sudden stimulation. It is studied experimentally in laboratories with paid volunteers who experience varying degrees of a precisely regulated stimulus, such as heat applied briefly to a small area of the skin. This procedure can test a subject's *tolerance* for pain and measure responses to it without causing any tissue damage. *Chronic pain* (prolonged or enduring sensation) is typically studied in hospital research clinics as part of the treatment program designed to find new ways to alleviate such pain.

You might think that it would be nice never to experience pain. Actually, such a condition would be deadly. People born with congenital insensitivity to pain do not feel what is hurting them, but their bodies often become scarred

The sensation of pain may not be directly related to the intensity of the stimulus. Individuals taking part in religious rituals, such as walking on a bed of coals, are able to block out pain.

and their limbs often become deformed from injuries that they could have avoided if their brains were able to warn them of danger. In fact, because of their failure to notice and respond to tissue-damaging stimuli, they tend to die young (Manfredi et al., 1981). Pain serves as an essential defense signal; it warns us of potential harm. It helps us to survive in hostile environments and to cope with sickness and injury.

Much research points to the conclusion that the pain one feels is affected by the following: (1) the meaning one attaches to the experience, (2) culturally learned habits, (3) social support and attention, and (4) learned gender roles (Weisenberg, 1977). Because pain is in part a psychological response, it can be modified by treatments that use mental processes, such as hypnosis, deep relaxation, and thought-distraction procedures. The way you perceive your pain, how you communicate it to others, and even the way you respond to pain-relieving treatments may reveal more about your psychological state—about the kind of inferences you are making—than about the intensity of the pain stimulus. What you perceive may be different from, and even independent of, what you sense—as we will see in our study of the psychology of perception.

SUMMING UP

Sensation involves all the sensory processes that put us in direct contact with the physical energies of our world. Translating physical energy of stimuli into neural impulses via transduction is the process that produces sensation. Psychophysicists look at the measurable relationships between psychological responses and physical stimuli.

The determination of absolute thresholds (minimum stimulation that activates the senses) is vital to the study of sensation. The theory of signal detection explains sensation as involving both physical stimulation and decision making. Difference thresholds are minimally detectable changes in stimuli; the just noticeable difference (JND) between two stimuli is a constant fraction of the background stimulus intensity, according to Weber's law. Sensory adaptation enables receptors to fade out responsiveness to prolonged stimulation in preparation for processing new signals.

The visual system is the most thoroughly studied of any sensory system. In the eye, light energy is converted to neural impulses by photoreceptors (rods and cones) in the retina, and then integrated by ganglion and bipolar cells, before it is transmitted to the visual cortex via the optic nerve. The optic nerves meet at the optic chiasma before one pathway proceeds to the superior colliculus for location processing and another passes through the lateral geniculate nucleus (LGN) for pattern identification.

The stimulus for color is the wavelength of light within the visible spectrum. Color sensations differ in hue, saturation, and brightness. Fatigue in photoreceptors creates negative afterimages in the stimulus's complementary color—its color-circle opposite. Color blindness involves a deficiency in distinguishing or detecting colors.

Visual processing begins with figure-ground separation before going on to the attentive analysis of objects and features. Motor coordination is then adjusted so that vision and movement work together.

Hearing is produced by sound waves that vary in frequency, amplitude, and complexity. Our sensations of sound vary in pitch, loudness, and timbre. Place theory and frequency theory have been proposed to account for precise pitch perception. The human auditory system may have evolved to specialize in dealing with human speech. Sound waves travel into the outer ear, transfer from tissues to the bones in the middle ear, and then transform into fluid waves in the inner ear. Vibrations stimulate tiny hair cells in the inner ear to generate nerve impulses that travel to the auditory cortex.

Other senses are also important to human experience and survival. The vestibular sense processes information about body orientation. The kinesthetic sense provides continuous feedback about bodily movement and position. Smell (olfaction) may be the most primitive sense, processing chemical information directly to the brain, and powerfully influencing basic behaviors like eating and sexual interaction. Taste (gustation) works closely with smell for subtler sensations, since receptors in the taste buds sense only the primary tastes of sweet, sour, bitter, and salty. The skin senses are concentrated in the most sensitive bodily regions—our faces, tongues, hands, and genitals. These senses are responsible for sensitivity to touch, which is so important to sexuality, health, and basic survival. Our sense of pain is essential to our survival, warning us of acute threats and chronic conditions that endanger our wellbeing. Like all the senses, pain interacts with other information and is a function of individual psychological functioning and expectations.

Perception

➡ How do we organize and interpret the many sources of stimulus input coming from all of our sensory systems into our brain? How do we form mental representations of external objects and events taking place? To begin to understand the tasks of perception, try this experiment: Shut this book, rotate it, and open it again. Hold the book at arm's length and then move it toward your face. Consider—and check on—this question: Did any images in the book change shape or size? Probably not, but why are you so sure? According to the sensory information from your retina there were many objects moving and changing. How can you be so confident that the movement was a function of your body or eyes and not a property of the objects you saw? These questions go beyond our ability to *detect* information about the world, and into the nature of our ability to *understand* it.

We might say that the role of perception is to make *sense* of sensation. Making sense requires more than processing sensory input to create a personal understanding of our experienced physical world. Perception involves many different mental processes: synthesizing elements into combinations; judging sizes, shapes, distances, intensities, and pitches; distinguishing the unknown from known features; remembering past experiences; comparing different stimuli; and associating perceived qualities with appropriate ways of responding to

percept The experienced outcome of the process of perception.

perception Processes that organize sensory information and interpret it in terms of its environmental origins.

identification and recognition Two processes in which meaning is assigned to percepts.

distal stimulus Object in environment that is source of external stimulation; contrasted with *proximal stimulus*.

proximal stimulus Sensory system's impression of external stimulation, for example, image on the retina; contrasted with *distal stimulus*.

bottom-up processing Processing in which incoming stimulus information is perceived as coming from sensory data and is sent upward to the brain for analysis and interpretation.

top-down processing Processing in which perceiver's past experience, knowledge, expectations, motivation, and background influence analysis and interpretation of perceived stimuli.

When sensory and perceptual processes do not work together in perceptual synthesis, the world appears to be fragmented and disjointed.

them. Every action of perception then becomes a series of very complex *computational* problems to be solved by the perceiving person's brain.

The task of perception is to extract *sensory input* from the environment and organize it into stable, meaningful *percepts*. A **percept** is what is perceived—the experienced outcome of the process of perception (the psychological product of perceptual activity). Perception must discover what features of the world are *invariant*—fixed and unchanging—by using varying information collected by a perceiver in motion. Consider how challenging it is to sort through overwhelming or confusing sensations in search of clear, reliable information about the real world. We will first discuss how perception discerns what is real, and then consider the perceptual tasks of attention, organization, and identification.

Reality, Ambiguity, and Distortion

The term *perception*, in its broad usage, means the overall process of grasping the nature of objects and events in the external environment—to sense them, understand them, identify and label them, and to prepare to react to them. We can understand the process of perception best if we divide it into three stages: sensation, perception, and identification/recognition of objects.

Sensation is the first stage in which physical energy—such as light and sound—is *transduced* or changed into neural activity that codes information about the nature of the stimulation, as we have just discussed.

Perception, in its narrow usage, refers to the next stage in which an internal representation of an object is formed and a percept of the external stimulus is developed. The representation provides a working description of the perceiver's external environment. For example, the sensory pattern of three straight lines could be recognized as the percepts 1–1, H, Δ, or III, depending on the context. Perception involves *synthesis* (integration and combination) of simple sensory features, such as colors, edges, and lines, into the percept of an object that can be recognized later.

Identification and recognition (the third stage) assigns meaning to the percepts. Circular objects may "become" baseballs, coins, clocks, oranges, and moons. People may be identified as friend or foe, pretty or ugly, movie star or rock star. At this stage, the perceptual question ("What does the object look like?") changes to a question of identification ("What is this object?") and to a question of recognition ("What is the object's function?").

Perception and the combined processes of identification and recognition work so swiftly that they seem to act as one process in our everyday lives. However, they are conceptually different from one another. By dividing the global process of perception into the stages of sensation, perception, and identification/recognition, we begin to see the different parts of this complex process. Throughout the rest of this chapter we will use perception in its narrow sense—that of going beyond sensory information to provide a meaningful awareness and knowledge of the world of objects, actors, and episodes. Thus, we will focus on the second and third steps in the overall perceptual process.

Stages of Perception. Imagine that you are the person in section A of **Figure 5.15.** You are seated in a furnished room; light reflected by objects in the room enters your eye, forming an image on your retina. In section B of **Figure 5.15** you can see what would appear to your left eye as you sat in the room. How does this retinal image compare with the environment that produced it?

One important difference is that the retinal image is *two-dimensional* whereas the environment it represents is *three-dimensional*. Compare the shapes of the physical objects out there in the world with the shapes of their corresponding retinal images. The shapes in **Figure 5.15** that you "know" are really rectangular do not necessarily *appear* rectangular to your eyes. As you see in section C of Figure 5.15, only the window, viewed straight on, is perceived as an intact rectangle. The other shapes are distorted into trapezoids, or

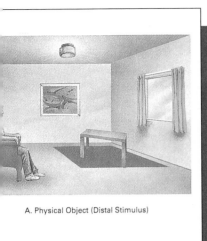

A. Physical Object (Distal Stimulus)

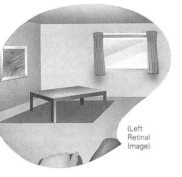

(Left
Retinal
Image)

B. Optical Image (Proximal Stimulus)

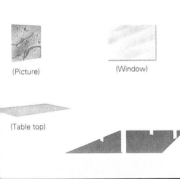

(Picture)   (Window)

(Table top)

Figure 5.15 Interpreting Retinal Images

Figure 5.16 Distal and Proximal Stimulus
The distal stimulus is the pattern or external condition that is sensed and perceived. The proximal stimulus is the pattern of sensory activity that is determined by the distal stimulus. As illustrated here, the proximal stimulus may resemble the distal stimulus, but they are separate events.

partially blocked by other objects. On reflection, it is amazing that you are able to see and recognize these shapes when their retinal images are so distorted and different from each other.

The differences between a physical object in the world and its optical image on your retina are so profound and important that psychologists distinguish between them as two different stimuli for perception. The physical object in the world is called the **distal stimulus** (distant from the observer) and the optical image on the retina is called the **proximal stimulus** (proximate or near to the observer), as shown in **Figure 5.16.** What you *perceive* corresponds to the *distal stimulus*—the "real" object in the environment. The stimulus that generated your sensory information is the *proximal stimulus*—the image on the retina. The major task of perception is to determine the distal stimulus based on information contained in the proximal stimulus.

There is more to perceiving a scene, however, than determining the *physical properties* of the distal stimulus. You see objects as familiar and meaningful: a window, a picture, a table, and a rug. Besides accurately perceiving the shapes and colors of the objects, you *interpret* them in terms of your past experience with similar objects. This process of identification and recognition is part of what you do automatically and almost constantly as you go about perceiving your environment.

To illustrate the distinction among the three stages in perceiving, let's examine one of the objects in the scene from **Figure 5.15:** the picture hanging on the wall. In the *sensory stage*, this picture corresponds to a two-dimensional trapezoid in your retinal image. In the *perceptual stage*, you see this trapezoid as a rectangle turned away from you in three-dimensional space. In the *recognition stage*, you recognize this rectangular object as a *picture*.

Figure 5.17 on the next page is a flow chart illustrating this sequence of events. The processes that take information from one stage to the next are shown as arrows between the boxes. Taking sensory data into the system by receptors and sending it upward for extraction and analysis of relevant information is called **bottom-up processing.** At the same time, however, the opposite process is also occurring; **top-down processing** involves a perceiver's past experience, knowledge, expectations, memory, motivations, cultural background, and language in the interpretation of the object of perception. The two types of processes usually interact as we perceive our environment.

Reality and Ambiguity. A primary goal of perception is to get an accurate "fix" on the world—to recognize predators, prey, possible danger, and plea-

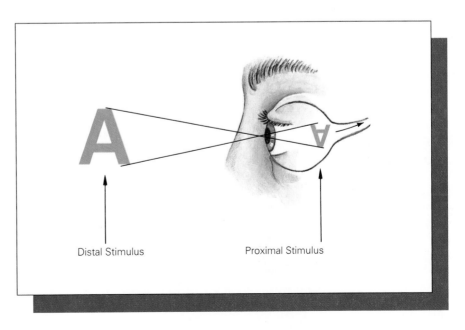

Distal Stimulus   Proximal Stimulus

Figure 5.17 Sensation, Perception, and Identification/Recognition Stages
The diagram outlines the processes that give rise to the transformation of incoming information at the stages of sensation, perception, and identification/recognition. Bottom-up processing occurs when the perceptual representation is derived from the information available in the sensory input. Top-down processing occurs when the perceptual representation is affected by an individual's prior knowledge, motivations, expectations, and other aspects of higher mental functioning.

illusion Demonstrably incorrect experience of a stimulus pattern, shared by others in the same perceptual environment.

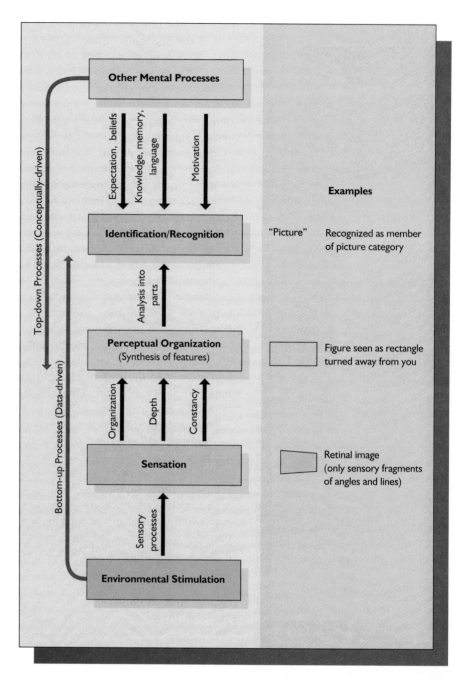

sure, and to behave appropriately. Survival depends on accurately perceiving the environment, but the environment is not always easy to "read." Take a look at the photo of black and white splotches in **Figure 5.18.** What is it? Try to extract the stimulus figure from the background: A Dalmatian taking a walk. The dog is hard to find because it blends with the background.

The world is filled with ambiguous data that lead to uncertainty and sometimes danger. Experience teaches you not to trust appearances entirely and to use judgment as well as sensory cues. When something or someone seems "too good to be true," you may suspect a lie or a trap, and proceed with caution.

When your senses deceive you into experiencing a stimulus pattern in a manner that is demonstrably incorrect, you are experiencing an **illusion.** Typically, illusions become more common when the stimulus is *ambiguous,* information is missing, elements are combined in unusual ways, and familiar patterns are not apparent. As reviewed in "In Focus: The Lessons of Illusions," research on perceptual illusions can illuminate processes that normally resist distorted or deceptive conclusions.

Figure 5.18 Ambiguous Picture

Several prominent modern artists fascinated with the visual experiences created by ambiguity have used perceptual illusion as a central artistic device in their work. Consider the three examples of art shown here. "Gestalt Bleue" by Victor Vasarely produces depth reversals like those in the Necker cube, with corners that alternately project and recede. In "Sky and Water" by M. C. Escher, you can see birds and fishes only through the process of figure-ground reversal, as in the vase/faces illusion. Finally, surrealist Salvador Dali's "Slave Market with the Disappearing Bust of Voltaire" reveals a more complex ambiguity in which the viewer must reorganize a whole section of the scene in order to perceive the "hidden" bust of the French philosopher and writer Voltaire. Although it might be difficult at first for some to "find" the picture-in-the-picture, once you have seen Voltaire you will find him obvious every time you look. This discovery underscores the determination of human perception to make sense of the world and to stick with the best interpretation we can make.

Illusions are an inescapable aspect of the subjective reality we each construct with our personal experiences, learning, and motivation. People can

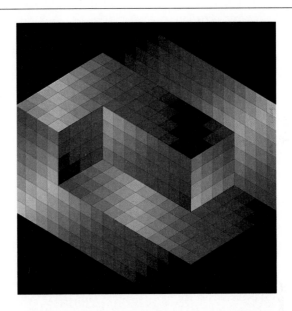

Paintings by Victor Vasarely (top), M. C. Escher (left), and Salvador Dali. Top: "Gestalt Bleue"; bottom left: "Sky and Water"; bottom right: "Slave Market with the Disappearing Bust of Voltaire."

In Focus:

THE LESSONS OF ILLUSIONS

Psychologists who study perception love ambiguities and the illusions they generate. Since the first scientific analysis of illusions was published by **J. J. Oppel** in 1854, thousands of articles have been written about illusions in nature, sensation, perception, and art. Oppel's study included a simple array of lines that appeared longer when divided into segments than when only the end lines were present:

||||||||||||||||||||| versus | |

Oppel called his work the study of *geometrical optical illusions*. Illusions point out the discrepancy between percept and reality—between the marvelously complex sensory and perceptual processes that are evolution's masterpiece and the ease with which they can be fooled by a simple arrangement of lines. Illusions can demonstrate the distinctions between sensation, perception, and identification and can help us understand some fundamental properties of perception (Cohen & Girgus, 1978).

First examine an illusion that works at the sensation level: the black-and-white *Hermann grid*. As you stare at the center of the grid, dark, fuzzy spots appear at the intersections of the white bars. Focus closely on one intersection; the spot vanishes. As you shift focus, you transform the spots into little dancing dots. How do you do that? The answer lies in the way receptor cells in your eyes interact with each other. The firing of certain ganglion cells in the retina prevents or *inhibits* the firing of adjacent cells. Because of this inhibiting process, you see dark spots—*not white* areas—at white intersections just outside your focus. Even though you *know* the squares in the Hermann grid are black and the lines are white, your knowledge cannot overcome the illusion, which operates at the more basic, sensory level. Illusions at the sensory level generally occur because a pattern stimulates receptor processes in an unusual way that generates a distorted image.

To study illusions at the level of *perception*, psychologists rely on ambiguous figures—stimulus patterns that can be seen in two or more distinct ways.

The Hermann Grid
This Hermann Grid has two ganglion cell receptive fields projected on it. It is an example of an illusion at the sensory stage.

Ambiguity is an important concept in understanding perception because it shows that a *single image* at the level of sensation can result in *multiple interpretations* at the perceptual and identification levels.

Figures A and B on p. 177 show three examples of ambiguous figures. Each figure is accompanied by two unambiguous but conflicting interpretations. Look at each image until you can see its two interpretations. Once you have seen both interpretations, your perception will flip back and forth between them as you look at the ambiguous figure. This perceptual *instability* of ambiguous figures is one of the most important characteristics of such figures. The vase/faces and the Necker cube are examples of ambiguity in the perception stage. You have two different perceptions of objects in space relative to you, the observer. The ambiguous alternatives are different physical arrangements of objects in three-dimensional space, both resulting from the same stimulus image. Because your perceptual system cannot recognize both alternatives simultaneously, it has focused on certain features to decide how to synthesize the elements.

The duck/rabbit figure is an example of ambiguity in the recognition stage. You perceive the figure as one physical shape but ambiguity arises when you try to determine what it represents and how to classify the figure with the mixed information available. Transforming ambiguity and uncertainty about the environment into a clear interpretation is a fundamental property of normal human perception. Our perceptual system must meet the challenges of a world filled with variability and change.

Perceptual illusions make us aware of two considerations: the active role the mind plays in structuring our view of the world, and the effects of *context* on the way we perceive stimuli within it. Examine the classic illusions in the third figure. These illusions occur because the central nervous system does not simply record events. Instead, the system involves complex processes for detecting, integrating, and interpreting information about the world in terms of what we already know and expect. Thus, what we "see" goes beyond present physical stimulus properties. These processes usually occur effortlessly and they help us decode the world around us, but this does not mean that they are simple or error-free. When cues or context mislead us, for example, we may easily "fall for" even a familiar illusion.

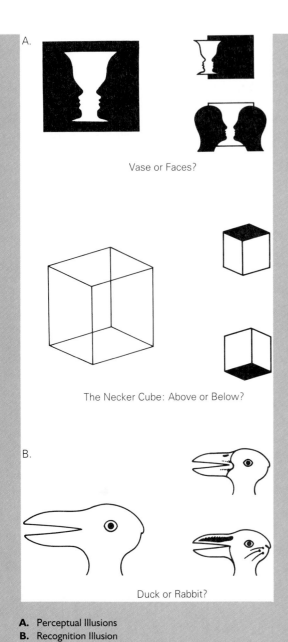

Vase or Faces?

The Necker Cube: Above or Below?

B.

Duck or Rabbit?

A. Perceptual Illusions
B. Recognition Illusion

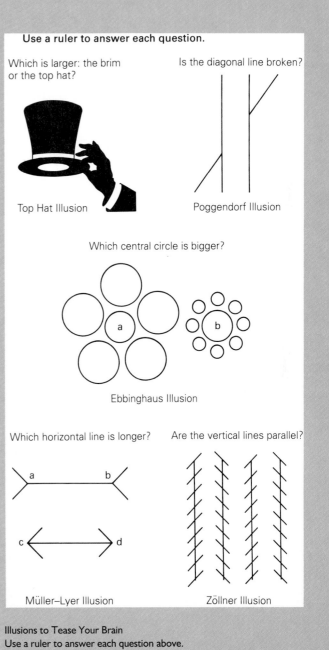

Use a ruler to answer each question.

Which is larger: the brim or the top hat?

Top Hat Illusion

Is the diagonal line broken?

Poggendorf Illusion

Which central circle is bigger?

a
b

Ebbinghaus Illusion

Which horizontal line is longer?

a   b

c   d

Müller–Lyer Illusion

Are the vertical lines parallel?

Zöllner Illusion

Illusions to Tease Your Brain
Use a ruler to answer each question above.

even control illusions to achieve desired effects. Architects and interior designers use principles of perception to make spaces seem larger or smaller than they really are. A small apartment becomes more spacious when it is painted in light colors and sparsely furnished. Set and lighting designers in movies and theatrical productions purposely create illusions on film and on stage. Many of us make everday use of illusion in our choices of cosmetics and clothing (Dackman, 1986). Light-colored clothing and horizontal stripes can make our bodies seem larger while dark-colored clothing and vertical stripes can make our bodies seem slimmer. Illusions also appear in more tragic contexts, as we noted in our opening case about pilot error. In continually trying to resolve the discrepancy between the distal (real) stimulus and the proximal (sensed) stimulus, we establish personal perceptions that guide our decisions and behavior—for better or for worse.

Explaining Perception. We can divide theoretical explanations of how perceptual processes work into four categories: (1) experience-based inference; (2) Gestalt principles; (3) environmental adaptation; and (4) the artificial-intelligence (AI) approach. These views have shaped the way researchers explore perception and how psychologists apply their conclusions.

Inferring from Experience. For almost a century the dominant model among perception theorists was the approach established by Hermann von Helmholtz. In 1866 Helmholtz argued for the importance of *experience* in perception. According to his theory, an observer uses prior knowledge of the environment to make sense of the proximal stimulus. Based on this experience, the observer makes inferences—reasonable guesses or hunches—about what these sensations mean. Ordinarily these inferences are fairly accurate, but as we have seen, confusing sensations and ambiguous arrangements can create perceptual illusions and erroneous conclusions. Helmholtz's theory proposes that we learn how to interpret sensations on the basis of our experience with the world; our interpretations are, in effect, *hypotheses* about our perceptions. For example, a baby learns that faces always possess certain features (eyes, nose, mouth) in certain arrangements (two eyes near the top of the face, mouth near the bottom), and that the right-side up arrangement is better for communicating than upside-down or sideways.

The Gestalt Approach. Founded in Germany in the second decade of this century, **Gestalt psychology** maintained that psychological phenomena could be understood only when viewed as organized, structured *wholes* and not when broken down into primitive perceptual elements (by introspective analysis). The German word **Gestalt** (pronounced guh-SHTAHLT) roughly means *form, whole, configuration,* or *essence.* It challenged the views of the structuralists and behaviorists by arguing that the whole is more than the sum of its parts. For example, a particular melody is perceived as a whole tune even though it is composed of separate notes. Gestalt psychologists argued further that we perceive the world of objects as whole units because our brain is organized to function that way—to coordinate incoming stimuli into meaningful arrays. We organize sensory information according to meaningfulness because this method is the simplest, most economical way to package sensory input within our nervous systems.

Environmental Adaptation. Whereas Helmholtz's theory credits the power of experience and Gestalt theory credits the brain with the power to determine meaning, an alternative view proposed by **James Gibson** argues that innate sensory processes enable an observer to make accurate sense of the world. Gibson (1966, 1979) searched for aspects of the proximal stimulus that provide information about the distal stimulus. Gibson believed that the answer to the question "How do we learn about our world?" is simple: As our senses

Gestalt psychology School of psychology that maintains that psychological phenomena can only be understood when viewed as organized, structured wholes, not when broken down into component elements.

Gestalt German word, meaning *whole configuration,* from which the name for *Gestalt psychology* is derived.

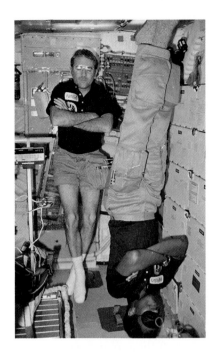

Psychologists have researched the effects of environment on perception in order to design space capsules that have pleasant sensory qualities.

come into contact with the environment, they directly detect its invariant properties. For example, since sensory experiences always bring in new shapes, sizes, patterns, and combinations, why are we not confused most of the time? Luckily, our sensory systems are well adapted to make sense of our environment. Sensations may be different from varying perspectives, but these differences are not random. Our sensory systems are tuned to detect the stable, unchanging properties of stimuli. This result has evolved to exist in our environment because such sensory abilities are critical to our survival (Palmer, 1981). For example, we learn that ice is always cold to the touch. If someone hands us a glass cube that looks like ice, we revise our perspective. The cube is smooth and slick, but our perception tells us it is fake ice.

According to Gibson and others, our sensory and perceptual abilities evolved in ancestors who were on the move, seeking sustenance, shelter, and companionship in a changing environment (Gibson, 1979; Pittenger, 1988; Shaw & Turvey, 1981; Shepard, 1984). Gibson proposed that perception could best be understood by analyzing the environment to which it had adapted. For Gibson, perceiving is a process of *actively exploring* our environment and adjusting our actions to it, not passively waiting and taking in whatever we might receive. Thus we are equipped, by our well-evolved perceptual abilities, to make accurate judgments about our world. We are generally so good at doing our perceptual jobs, it is difficult to trick us with illusions in the real world. Only in artificial or extreme conditions are we deprived of the information we need to draw the right conclusions.

The AI Approach. According to proponents of the *artificial intelligence* or **AI approach,** a complete theory of perception addresses three levels: the *hardware* or physiological mechanisms of perceptual processes; the *rules* that specify perceptual processes; and the *task* of perception, or analysis of physical properties that give us this access to the world (Banks & Krajicek, 1991). These three levels are not yet integrated into a complete theory of perception. Neuroscientists concentrate on the first level, the hardware of perception. Followers of Gibson work on the third level, the study of perceptual tasks. Most of the work on the second level—the operational rules of perception—is done by researchers in the AI field. These researchers may study, for example, the perceptual processes of nonhuman animals, or of thinking machines like computers. In particular, AI models focus on two main issues: the mechanisms by which information in the stimulus is picked up, and the inferences and judgments observers make to arrive at their perceptual interpretations (Bennett et al., 1989). (See "Cross-cultural Perspective: Culture and Perception" on page 181.)

Current approaches to explaining perception incorporate the best of these four approaches: inference from experience, Gestalt, environmental adaptation, and AI. New theories emphasize the importance of past experience and environmental adaptiveness, the power of simplicity and economy in perceptual organization, and the value of the AI approach in developing testable models of the functional properties of the process of perceiving.

AI approach Artificial intelligence approach to studying cognitive processes that studies perception at three levels of analysis: neurophysiological mechanisms, perceptual processes, and perceptible properties of the world.

Attentional Processes

➡ When your teacher encourages you to pay *attention,* exactly what does this mean? You are aware that *attention* is something you can control voluntarily—that you can *choose* to pay attention, or not. Probably you've discovered that, when you pay attention, you comprehend information better and get more details. And you certainly have discovered that sometimes, even when you try, you cannot pay attention; you are distracted. **Distraction** means you are unable to focus your perceptual processing on the stimuli that are relevant to the task at hand. Attention appears to be critical for effective perception and thought, yet it is a vulnerable process.

distraction Inability to perceptually process available stimuli due to interference.

Attention appears to serve different purposes for perception, cognition, and consciousness. Some researchers now believe that we have several kinds of attention, each with its own mechanisms and functions (Posner, 1990). Different methods of studying attention may lead to different conclusions about how it works. We'll briefly review what research has already suggested about attentional processes, and consider what this reveals about the nature of perception.

Preattentive Processing. Even though conscious memory and recognition of objects require attention, complex processing of information does go on without our awareness and without attention. For example, even if you are attentive in reading this passage, you would probably notice certain qualities and changes in the background stimuli you are now ignoring. If your favorite song were played now on the radio, you would recognize that experience before directing your attention there. This earlier stage of processing is called **preattentive processing** because it operates on sensory inputs before we attend to them—as they first come into the brain from the sensory receptors.

Attention is important for integrating features into composites that we recognize as whole units (based on experiments by Beck, 1982; Julesz, 1982; and Treisman, 1988). When asked to locate boundaries between regions of a scene, subjects report that the boundaries "pop out" when they are defined by a difference in a single simple feature, such as color, curved versus straight line shape, or orientation of lines (vertical versus horizontal), as shown in panel A of **Figure 5.19**. The boundaries of red and blue and of V's and O's in panel B are distinct. In contrast, the boundaries between red V's or blue O's and red O's or blue V's in panel C must be sought out with more mental effort. While boundaries based on a single feature emerge *preattentively,* boundaries defined by a combination of features do not, since combining features requires attention.

Functions of Attention. Psychologists have proposed several important functions for attention within the complex interrelated processes of perceiving, responding, and consciously remembering sensory and perceptual information. Research has identified three possible functions of attention: (1) as a *sensory filter;* (2) as *response selection;* and (3) as a *gateway to consciousness.*

Attention may act as a *sensory filter* by selecting some part of sensory input for further processing. British psychologist **Donald Broadbent** introduced the modern version of this view in his 1958 book, *Perception and Communication.* Broadbent was the first to compare the mind to a *communications channel* like a telephone line or computer link that actively processes and transmits information. The amount of information the channel can handle accurately at any one time is severely limited. Therefore, people must focus on one source of information at a time.

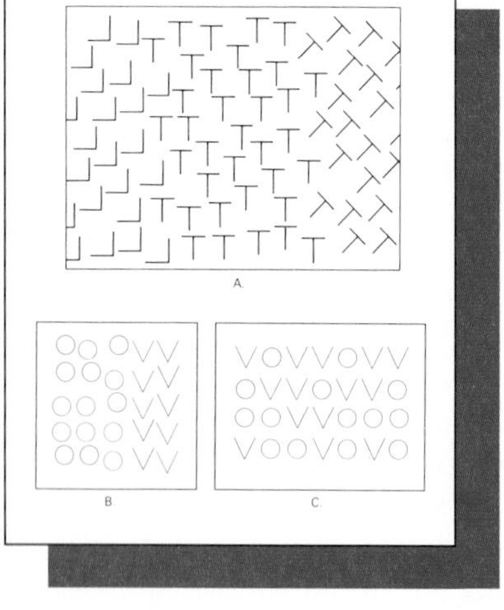

Imagine listening to a lecture while people on both sides of you are engaged in conversations. What do you hear, understand, and remember? You will probably be able to stay tuned to the lecturer if the material is interesting or important. But if the lecture is boring and irrelevant to your goals, and if either of the conversations is particularly intriguing, you'll most likely tune out the lecture and tune into the alternative stimuli. You cannot listen carefully to all three sources of input simultaneously or even to two of them at once. You must *selectively attend* to only one at a time if you are to fully understand and remember anything.

Broadbent conceived of attention as a *selective filter* that deals with the overwhelming flow of incoming sensory information by blocking out the unwanted sensory input and passing on specific desired input. Since the mind has a *limited capacity* to carry out complete processing, attention filters out some information and allows other information to continue. The filter theory of attention asserts that the selection occurs early in the process, before the input's meaning is accessed.

preattentive processing Processing that operates on sensory inputs from receptors before they are attended to.

Figure 5.19 Locating Boundaries Between Regions of a Scene

Both Hermann von Helmholtz and James Gibson pointed to the importance of experience in explaining perception. Cross-cultural psychologists have argued that since people in various cultures around the world have very different everyday experiences, there should be differences in people's perception of some objects and events. One of the most important and influential contributions of cross-cultural psychology has been the development of strong arguments to support a relationship between culture and perception (Segall, et al., 1966). People's responses to visual illusions have played an important part in many cross-cultural investigations (Deregowski, 1980). Consider the following two figures:

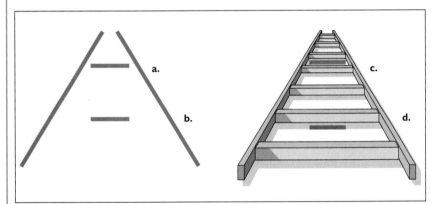

These are versions of the Ponzo illusion. The question for respondents looking at the left-hand figure is: "Which line is longer, the one on top (marked "a") or the one on the bottom (marked "b")?" The same question is asked about the right-hand figure, where the top line is marked "c" and the bottom line is marked "d." In actuality, all four lines are of the same length. Many readers of this book, however, will report that the top lines are longer than the bottom lines. People make a perspective correction about the size of objects by considering cues for apparent distance when making these judgments. In their everyday experiences, all readers of this book have learned that objects far away from themselves look smaller than they actually are. For example, a friend who is 6 feet tall looks much shorter when seen 100 yards in the distance. Yet people

don't conclude that their 6-foot friend has suddenly shrunk. Rather, they recognize that the person is far away and take this fact into account when making conclusions about his real height. People do this so often that the perceptual process (called "size constancy") is applied without conscious awareness.

Consider what some of the cues are that people use in making judgments about objects that are distant from themselves. One cue is converging lines. When people look down a long corridor, the hallway seems to converge in the distance. Yet people have learned from their everyday experiences that hallways don't converge in the distance. That fact that hallways *seem* to converge is a cue to distance.

Other opportunities to see objects converge in the distance occur when people look down railroad tracks (as pictured in the figure on the right) or a long, flat super highway. In the Ponzo illusion, many readers of this book will judge the top line as longer because they are making an unconscious perceptual cue. They are applying the knowledge (which most often helps them make good decisions) that converging lines indicate distance. Objects at a distance are bigger than they appear. Consequently, they apply this knowledge to judgments about the figures; however, in this instance their judgments are incorrect.

Note that "many readers of this book" refer to some of the people who would view these illusions. Many readers are from cultures where they will have had extensive experience with converging lines as a cue to distance.

But what about people from cultures where individuals have had far less experience with this distance cue? Will they be as susceptible to the Ponzo illusion? The answer is "no."

Research has been carried out on the Pacific Island of Guam where there are no railroad tracks (Brislin, 1974; 1993). Roads are winding, and so there are few opportunities to see them converge in the distance. There are several long runways for jet airplanes, but safety considerations mean that few people have the opportunity to stand at one end and look into the distance. There are buildings with corridors, but fewer than in most medium-sized cities given the high costs of air conditioning for buildings large enough to have long hallways. People who have spent their entire lives on Guam, then, have fewer opportunities to learn the strong perceptual cue that converging lines indicate distance. They will not be so familiar with this cue such that they will unconsciously apply it when viewing two-dimensional figures that employ the cue as a major feature.

As predicted, adult respondents in Guam were less susceptible to the Ponzo illusion than were respondents from Pennsylvania. People in Pennsylvania were chosen under the assumption that their perceptual experiences would be typical of individuals in a highly industrialized nation such as the United States. Respondents from Guam were less likely to report that the top lines in the figures were longer—when they were, in actuality, slightly shorter. In addition, children 12 years of age and younger were less susceptible to the illusion in both Guam and Pennsylvania. The data from children also support the argument that people's *experiences* affect their perception. Children have had less time to learn strong perceptual cues such as converging lines. Consequently, they will be less likely to use this cue when presented with drawings such as those used to measure susceptibility to the Ponzo illusion. Can you think of other differences in cultural experiences that might affect one's perceptions?

Selection theory was challenged by research that showed how some subjects perceived things they would have been unable to if attention totally filtered out all ignored material. For example, subjects sometimes noticed their own names or other personally relevant information in the message they had been ignoring (Cherry, 1953). Personal interest or special meaning can apparently "pull" attention over to the nonattended channel. These findings forced researchers to conclude that attention is more flexible than filter theory postulated. **Anne Treisman** subsequently proposed that ignored information may get some partial higher-level, meaningful analysis, although this analysis may not reach consciousness (Treisman, 1964b; Norman, 1968). Attention is still necessary to guarantee that sensory fragments will be meaningfully organized. This modified view of feature selection is now more widely accepted.

Another function of attention is to *select responses*. Look at **Figure 5.20.** As the caption instructs, try to read the red letters in each column while disregarding the overlapping green letters. Is one column harder to read than the other? Why should there be a difference?

In the first column, there is no relationship between the green letters and the red letters. But in the second list, starting with the second letter, each red letter is the same as the green *letter* above it—the one you just *ignored*. Several experiments show that subjects take longer to read the second list because the ignored letters are first processed and then suppressed. The second encounter with each such letter requires the reader to "undo" the suppression, and this slows one's reading of the list overall (Tipper & Driver, 1988; Driver & Tipper, 1989). Of course, you were not conscious of processing, suppressing, and then "unsuppressing" your attention to the letters in the second list. Just because something did not enter consciousness does not mean it was not processed completely. The *late selection* view hypothesizes that all sensory inputs may be processed completely without attention (Deutsch & Deutsch, 1963; Driver & Tipper, 1989). According to this view, attention is limited not in handling input but in producing output or responses. Selection of responses, or *late selection,* occurs particularly when the stimuli are few and familiar and have been processed many times before in the past (Posner, 1986).

Finally, a third function of attention may be to control what is *allowed into consciousness*. When we select something to attend to, either because of its striking characteristics or its relevance to a goal, we inevitably ignore many other possibilities. Attention is the bridge that carries pieces of the external world—the pieces selectively focused on—to the subjective world of consciousness (Carver & Schneider, 1981; Posner, 1982, 1986).

As you pay attention to these words, you lose the meaning of background voices and other stimuli in your surroundings—until you momentarily refocus your attention on them to make sure you don't miss anything important. Information that does not reach consciousness can be stored—and may influence later behavior—but people have difficulty explicitly remembering such material (Jacoby et al., 1989; Richardson-Klavehn & Bjork, 1988; Schacter, 1989). Only conscious processing allows new ideas to be developed about the "attended to" material (Baddeley, 1986; Mullin & Egeth, 1989; Nissen & Bullemer, 1987).

Attentional Mechanisms. Now that we have examined the functions of attention, we will focus on how it works. In principle, there are two possible ways for attention to perform its tasks. First, attention may *facilitate* processing stimuli—selecting responses to stimuli, or consciously accessing *relevant* information. For example, attention may work by helping you "zoom in" on what you need to perceive. Second, attention may hinder undesired processing; it may *inhibit* processing, responding to, or consciously accessing *irrelevant* information. In this sense, attention may "block out" irrelevant or uninformative stimuli. Most researchers believe that attention employs both these mechanisms, perhaps at different times or for different tasks (Posner, 1990). These

Figure 5.20 A Test of Your Attentional Mechanisms

First read aloud the red letters in column one as quickly as possible, disregarding the green. Next, quickly read the red letters in column two, also disregarding the green. Which took longer?

Some people are very confident in their ability to attend to more than one stimulus at the same time.

automaticity Apparently effortless, involuntary processing conducted without intention.

Once you learn how to roller skate you don't need to think about how to do it. This routinizing makes your supply of mental energy go further when attending to other events.

two mechanisms function through the processes of *resource allocation* and *automaticity*.

Resource Allocation. We allocate more attentional resources to demanding stimuli than to any other stimuli. Consider the techniques advertisers regularly employ to capture your attention. The sound tracks that accompany television commercials are often louder than the regular programs, because advertisers know that people tend to tune out anything familiar or predictable. Commercials are played louder than other programs so they will command your attention. This works because we allocate our attentional resources to the more demanding stimuli.

Both unfamiliar stimuli and physiological conditions can direct our attention. Hunger makes us notice advertisements for food or conversations about restaurants. Listening to a charismatic speaker, watching an exciting movie, or reading an absorbing novel can capture and restrict your attention.

When people do two or more things at once, attention focused on one task hurts performance on the other (Navon, 1979; Hirst et al., 1980). Can two people have a conversation if one is reading a newspaper? Probably not, since to really listen, the reader must stop reading, which "tunes out" the speaker. Thus, some researchers refer to attention as a *limited processing resource* (Kahneman, 1973; Navon & Gopher, 1979). Each task uses up a certain amount of the limited supply. Allocating more resources to one task will diminish performance on others.

The ability to perform two tasks at the same time without interference requires that the tasks do not use the same pool of resources. When you try to do two things at once to save time, make sure the tasks you choose don't compete with each other for the same perceptual resources. You may be able to jog and listen to music at the same time, but you cannot study for a test while you sing.

Automaticity. Psychologists studying attention are greatly interested in highly practiced cognitive and motor tasks, such as typing, reading, or riding a bicycle. Learning such tasks requires a great deal of concentrated effort, but with practice, performance of the tasks becomes automatic. **Automaticity** takes place when task performance meets one or more of the following conditions: (1) performance becomes seemingly effortless; (2) it can be conducted without any conscious attention; and (3) other tasks can be performed at the same time without interference (Logan, 1980; Shiffrin & Schneider, 1977).

➡ The *Stroop task* is a good illustration of automaticity in reading. In this task, a subject must name the ink color of a word without reading the word itself. A Stroop task is shown in Figure **5.21** on page 184. Follow the instructions given. You will probably discover that you cannot stop yourself from reading the word, even though reading it interferes with the task of naming the ink color. In the Stroop task, reading satisfies two out of three criteria for automaticity—it is carried out without attention and it appears to be effortless. However, the last criterion is violated—it does interfere with naming the ink color. The Stroop task is a reminder not to take automaticity for granted; tasks may seem automatic in many ways, yet they still make measurable demands on our attention. Can you recall other experiences in which you have found that your actions or abilities seemed automatic—but only up to a point?

Organizational Processes

As we have discussed, attention focuses effort and resources in perception. Our discussion will now explore what is known about several kinds of processes that transform sensory information into perception of real-world objects. We will examine vision because vision has been more intensively studied than the other modalities, and it is easier to provide visual demonstrations on the printed page.

perceptual organization Putting sensory information together to create coherence.

Imagine how confusing the world would be if we could not put together and organize the information available from the output of our millions of retinal receptors. Processes of **perceptual organization** put sensory information together to give us the perception of coherence. For example, your percept of the two-dimensional geometric design in section A of **Figure 5.22** is probably three diagonal rows of figures, one each of squares, arrowheads, and diamonds. This may not seem remarkable, but consider all the organizational processing that you must perform to see the design in this way. Many of the organizational processes we will discuss in this section were first described by Gestalt theorists who argued that perception depends on laws of organization, or simple rules by which we perceive shapes and forms.

Region Segregation. Consider your initial sensory response to section A of **Figure 5.22.** Your retina is composed of many separate receptors; your eye responds to this stimulus pattern with a mosaic of millions of neural responses coding the light falling on your retina. (This mosaic pattern is represented in section B of **Figure 5.22**). The first task of perceptual organization is to segregate the pattern into meaningful regions. The primary information for this region segregation process comes from color and texture. An abrupt change in color or texture signifies a boundary between two regions. Finding these boundaries is the first step in organizational processing.

figure Object-like region in forefront of visual field, distinguished from *ground*.

ground Background areas of visual field against which figures stand out.

subjective contours Edges or boundaries perceived in proximal stimulus that do not exist in distal stimulus.

closure Organization process leading to perception of incomplete figures as complete.

Figure and Ground. As a result of region segregation, the stimulus in section A of **Figure 5.22** has now been divided into ten regions: nine small dark ones and a single large light one. Another organizational process divides the regions into figures and background. A **figure** is an object-like region in the forefront, and **ground** is the backdrop against which the figures stand out. In section A of **Figure 5.22,** you probably see the dark regions as figures and the light region as ground. (You could also reverse this interpretation, like the vase/faces illusion, by imagining the circle as a white sheet with dark cutouts.) When you perceive a region as a figure, boundaries between light and dark are interpreted as edges or contours belonging to the figure, and the ground seems to extend and continue behind these edges.

The tendency to perceive a figure as being in *front* of a ground is very strong. In fact, you can even get this effect in a stimulus when the perceived figure doesn't actually exist! In **Figure 5.23,** you probably perceive a fir tree shape against a ground of red circles on a white surface. But of course there is no fir tree shape; the figure consists only of three solid red shapes and a black-line base. You see the illusory white triangle in front because the wedge-cuts in the red circles seem to be the corners of a solid white triangle. To see an illusory six-pointed star, look at **Figure 5.24** on page 186. Here, the nonexistent "top" triangle appears to blot out parts of red circles and a black-lined triangle—when in fact none of these figures is depicted completely!

PURPLE	BLUE	RED
GREEN	YELLOW	ORANGE
RED	BLACK	BLUE
ORANGE	GREEN	BROWN
BLUE	YELLOW	PURPLE

Figure 5.21 The Stroop Task
Perform the following two tasks:
1. Time yourself as you read aloud all the words, ignoring the colors in which they are printed.
2. Time yourself as you read the colors, ignoring what the words say.
   You probably did the first task quickly and effortlessly, with little or no thought. The second required your full conscious attention because you had to deal with cognitive interference.

Contours and Closure. In **Figures 5.23** and **5.24,** there seem to be three levels of organization: the pure white triangle—superimposed on red circles and black lines—*and* a larger white surface behind everything else. Perceptually you have divided the white area into two regions: the illusory triangle and the background. Where this division occurs you perceive **subjective contours** that exist not in the distal stimulus but only in your subjective experience.

Your perception of the white triangles demonstrates another powerful organizing process: *closure.* **Closure** makes you see incomplete figures as complete and supplies the missing edges beyond gaps and barriers. Humans have an innate tendency to perceive stimuli as complete and balanced even when pieces are missing.

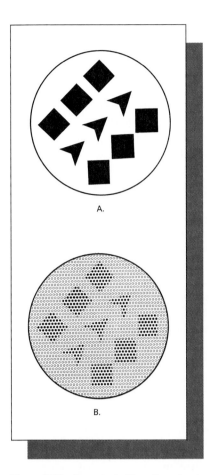

Figure 5.22 Percept of a Two-dimensional Geometric Design
What is your percept of the geometrical design in A? B represents the mosaic pattern that stimulus A makes on your retina.

perceptual grouping   Process of perception in which sets of stimuli are judged to belong together; focus of several Gestalt princples of perception.

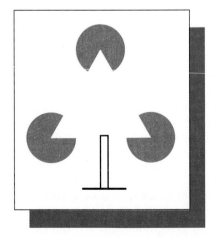

Figure 5.23 Subjective Contours That Fit the Angles of Your Mind

Principles of Perceptual Grouping.   In **Figure 5.25** on the next page, a six-by-six array of circles (section A) is presented in six variations (sections). Section B seems to be made up of horizontal rows, while C looks more like vertical columns. In section D, the color is varied to show alternating rows of light and dark, while in E the size of the circles is varied to show columns or large and small circles. In section F the circles become tiny quadrangles—alternately oriented so you read them down or across. Finally in section G some columns of circles seem as though they could be moving while the alternate columns are stationary. How does your visual system accomplish this **perceptual grouping,** the perception that sets of stimuli belong together?

The problem of grouping was first studied extensively by Gestalt psychologist **Max Wertheimer** (1923). Wertheimer presented subjects with arrays of simple geometric figures. By varying a single factor and observing how it affected the way people perceived the structure of the array, he was able to formulate a set of laws of grouping. **Figure 5.25** illustrates several of these laws.

For example, in sections B and C, the circles are spaced somewhat closer to each other, vertically and horizontally, so that the closer circles seem to "belong" together. These groupings illustrate Wertheimer's **law of proximity**: All else being equal, the nearest (most proximal) elements are grouped together.

The rows in section D are either dark or light; the columns in E are either large or small circles. The shapes in section F are all tiny oblongs, but some belong in horizontal rows and others in vertical columns. Our tendency to perceive things as belonging together because they share common features reflects the **law of similarity.**

When elements in the visual field are moving, similarity of motion also produces a powerful grouping. The **law of common fate** states that, all else being equal, elements moving in the same direction and at the same rate are grouped together. If the dots in every other column of section G were moving upward, as indicated by the blurring, you would group the image into columns because of their similarity in motion. You get this effect at a ballet when several dancers move in a pattern different from the others.

The Gestalt grouping laws operate only when two or more elements are simultaneously present in a visual field. According to the Gestaltists, the whole stimulus pattern somehow determines the organization of its own parts; in other words, the *whole percept* is different from the mere collection of its *parts.* Gestalt psychologists believed that all of these grouping laws are particular examples of one general principle—the **law of Prägnanz** ("meaningfulness"), which argues that the simplest organization requiring the least cognitive effort will always emerge. The most general Gestalt principle may be that we perceive the simplest organization that fits the stimulus pattern—the *minimum principle of perception.*

Identification and Recognition

The perceptual processes described so far provide reasonably accurate knowledge about physical properties of the distal stimulus—the position, size, shape, texture, and color of three-dimensional things in a three-dimensional world. With just this knowledge and some basic motor skills, you would be able to walk around without bumping into objects, manipulate objects that are small and light enough to move, and make accurate models of the objects that you perceive. However, you would not know what these objects were and whether you had seen them before. Your experience would resemble a visit to an alien planet where all the objects were new to you; you would not know what to eat, what to put on your head, what to run away from, or what to approach.

To get information about the objects you perceive, you must be able to identify or recognize them as something you have seen before and as members

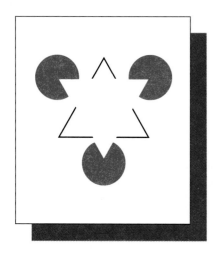

Figure 5.24 Subjective Contours That Fit the Angles of Your Mind

set Temporary readiness to perceive or react to stimulus in a particular way.

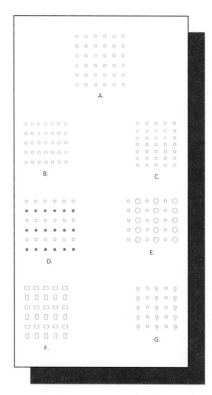

Figure 5.25 Grouping Phenomena
We perceive each array from B through G as being organized in a particular way, according to different Gestalt principles of grouping.

of the meaningful categories that you know from experience. Identification and recognition attach meaning to percepts.

Bottom-Up and Top-Down Processes. Identifying objects implies matching what you see against your stored knowledge. The processes of bringing in and organizing information from the environment are called *data-driven* or bottom-up processes, because they are guided by sensory information—the raw data of direct experience. For example, if you see something up in a tree as you walk by, but cannot make out what it is, your inspection of the tree is a data-driven effort, determined by the information you collect. Sensations of visual features and perceptions of organized objects are largely the result of such bottom-up processes.

In contrast, processes that originate in the brain and influence the selection, organization, or interpretation of sensory data are called *conceptually driven* (or hypothesis-driven) or top-down processes. For example, your experience teaches you that the mysterious object in the tree is more likely to be a bird or squirrel than a doll or catcher's mitt. Abstract thoughts, prior knowledge, beliefs, values, and other mental processes control the way incoming stimulation is managed and even what qualifies as relevant (review **Figure 5.17**). The importance of top-down processes can be illustrated by drawings called *droodles* (Price, 1953, 1980). Without the labels, these drawings are meaningless, but once identified, their meaning is obvious (see **Figure 5.26**).

Identification and recognition give our experiences continuity over time and across situations. The third stage of perception is a process in which memory, analysis, expectation, motivation, personality, and social experience all interact to help us understand what is being perceived. This stage adds *conception* (mental activity) to perception, and *meaning* to facts.

Contexts and Expectations. Have you ever had the experience of seeing people you knew in places where you didn't expect to see them, such as in a different city or an unusual social group? It takes much longer to recognize them in such situations, and sometimes you aren't even sure that you really know them. The problem is not that they look different but that the *context* is unfamiliar; you didn't *expect* them to be there. Once you have identified the context, you have expectations about what objects you are likely and unlikely to see nearby (Biederman, 1989).

Perceptual identification depends on your expectations as well as on objects' physical properties. *Object identification is a constructive, interpretive process.* Depending on what you already know, where you are, what else you see around you, and your expectations from context, the identification you make will vary. Read the following words.

THE CAT

They read *THE CAT*, right? Now look again at the middle letter of each word. Physically, these two letters are exactly the same, yet you perceived the first as an *H* and the second as an *A*. Why? Clearly, your perception was affected by what you know about words in English. The context provided by *T__E* makes an *H* highly likely and an *A* unlikely, whereas the reverse is true of the context of *C__T* (Selfridge, 1955).

Perceptual Set. Another aspect of the influence of context and expectation on your perception (and response) is *set*. **Set** is a temporary readiness to perceive or react to a stimulus in a particular way. A *perceptual set* is a readiness to detect a particular stimulus in a given context. For example, a new mother is perceptually set to hear the cries of her child. Often, a perceptual set leads you to see an ambiguous stimulus as the one you are expecting.

law of proximity   Grouping law that asserts that nearest stimuli are grouped together.

law of similarity   Grouping law that asserts that stimili are grouped together on the basis of common elements.

law of common fate   Grouping law that asserts that elements moving in the same direction and at the same rate are grouped together.

law of Prägnanz   Gestalt principle of meaningfulness, which asserts that the simplest organization requiring the least cognitive effort will emerge.

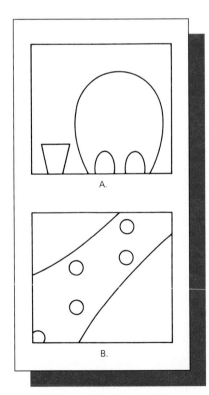

Figure 5.26   Droodles
Do you see a woman bending over while washing the floor (A) and a giraffe's neck (B)? Each of these figures can be seen as representing something familiar to us, although this perceptual recognition usually does not occur until some identifying information is provided.

Read quickly through the series of words that follow in row 1. Then do the same with row 2. Do the words in row 1 lead you to read D?CK differently than at the end of row 2?

1. FOX; OWL; SNAKE; TURKEY; SWAN; D?CK

2. BOB; RAY; DAVE; BILL; TOM; D?CK

Perceptual set is created by the meanings of words read prior to the ambiguous stimulus.

Labels are another context that can create perceptual set for an ambiguous figure. Look carefully at the picture of the woman in **Figure 5.27** on page 188; have a friend examine **Figure 5.28** on the next page. Next, together look at **Figure 5.29** on the page after that: What does each of you see? Did prior exposure to the same picture with a specific label affect either perception of the ambiguous image? People can easily develop different views of the same target after prior conditions have created different sets. Similarly, sets can influence social attitudes and bias how we interpret some part of our world.

Social and Personal Factors.   We each bring a unique history, personal experiences, needs, coping styles, and personality to our perception of the world. These social characteristics affect our initial data-collection as well as later interpretation, especially when the stimulus is ambiguous or unclear.

There are many ways in which social variables may influence perception. Broad cultural influences set basic, accepted social categories that determine standards for beauty, fear, appropriateness, or unacceptability. Socially learned attitudes can function as anchors or standards by which new inputs are often evaluated (Deregowski, 1980). This principle is illustrated in the case of a student who participates in a study-abroad program as you will see described in Chapter 7. For example, a child whose family has traveled the world may have learned to view new foods as interesting and worth trying, while one who has never explored beyond the confines of his or her own small town may regard unusual foods with suspicion and distaste.

On the other hand, we may copy others' reactions if we find ourselves in novel circumstances. A student who is new in a grade school, for example, may not know whether a particular substitute teacher is good or bad news, so the student imitates the reactions of classmates as they groan and complain in unison. The way one person classifies objects and events in the environment can thus be influenced by the ways similar people classify them. We humans are social creatures that depend on others for much of our information in life.

Individual differences also distinguish our perceptions of the world. For example, psychologists have linked one personality dimension—*leveling versus sharpening*—to a variety of perceptual tasks. Leveling and sharpening are two poles on the dimension of *cognitive style*. Levelers tend to smooth over what seems irregular, novel, or unusual. They omit details and are more likely to miss subtle differences. Levelers' perceptions are dominated by similarities apparently because their perceptual processing is too much influenced by memory of what has gone before. By contrast, when sharpeners are given a task with a sequence of gradually changing stimuli, they see each display's elements as independent of what went before; they exaggerate the details. Sharpeners tend to perceive the elements of a situation more accurately than do levelers, but by focusing on details they can lose sight of the big picture. When summarizing a movie, a leveler may simplify the story and leave out minor details, while a sharpener may reveal so many subplots and characters that you have difficulty following the story.

Perception as a Constructive Process.   The top-down effects of expectations, personality, and social influence all highlight the same important fact: Perceptual experience in response to a stimulus event is a response of the whole person. In addition to the information provided when your sensory receptors are stimulated, your final perception depends on who you are, whom you are with, and what you expect, want, and value.

The interaction of top-down and bottom-up processes also means that perception is an act of *constructing reality* to fit one's assumptions about how reality probably is or should be. If perceiving were completely *data-driven,* we would all be bound to the same mundane, concrete reality of the here-and-now. We would register experience but not profit from or be changed by it later. For example, without the lessons of experience to help you interpret the world, you could not make assumptions about new perceptions. Before using the shower in a hotel room, for example, you would have to study all the bathroom fixtures and controls to learn how to operate them.

If processing in perception were completely conceptually driven (*hypothesis-driven*), however, we would each be lost in our fantasy worlds of what we expect and hope to perceive. Your perceptions of someone you love, for example, might never be grounded in reality, since you would only see what you wished to see. A proper balance between the two extremes of data-driven and hypothesis-driven construction achieves the basic goal of perception: to experience what is out there in a way that best serves our needs as biological and social beings living in and adapting to our physical and social environment.

Creative Perception

Because of our ability to go beyond the sensory gifts that evolution has bestowed on our species, we can become more creative in the way we perceive the world. Who shall our role model be? Not a perfectly programmed, computerized robot with exceptional sensory acuity. Even in science fiction and fantasy, such robotic characters come to lament their lack of human playfulness. Instead, our role model for creative perception ought to be someone like the late, great, modern artist Pablo Picasso (1881-1973). Picasso's genius was in part attributed to his talent for "playful perception." He could free himself from the bonds of perceptual sets, and see not the old in the new but the new in the old, the novel in the familiar, and the unusual figure concealed within the ground.

Perceptual creativity involves experiencing the world in ways that are imaginative, personally enriching, and fun (as illustrated in Herbert Leff's original work, 1984). You can achieve perceptual creativity by consciously directing your attention and full awareness to the objects and activities around you. Become more flexible in what you allow yourself to perceive and think; remain open to alternative responses to situations in your life.

We conclude this rather formal presentation of the psychology of perception by proposing eleven suggestions for playfully enhancing your powers of perception:

1. Imagine everyone you meet is really a machine designed to look humanoid. Are some more convincing than others?
2. Notice all wholes as ready to come apart into separately functioning pieces. Could they all make it on their own?
3. Imagine that your mental clock is hooked up to a video recorder that can rewind, fast forward, and freeze time. Which buttons would you press, and why?
4. Recognize that most objects around you have a "family resemblance" to other objects. Do some objects even seem to have "family trees"?
5. View the world from the point of view of an animal or a home appliance. How would *you* look from such a perspective?
6. Consider one new use for each object you view (for example, a tennis racket could be used to drain cooked spaghetti). Why didn't you think of these before?

Figure 5.27 A. Young Beauty

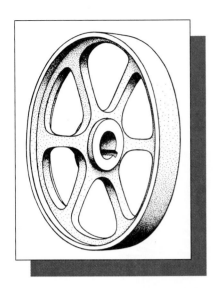

Is this figure possible?

7. Suspend the law of causality so that events just happen, while coincidence and chance rule over causes and effects. How does this view of the world make you feel?
8. Dream up alternative meanings for the objects and events in your life. Do any of these alternatives make sense?
9. Discover something really interesting about activities and people you used to find boring. Were you hasty or unfair in your earlier judgment?
10. Surprise yourself—and others: Violate some of the assumptions about what you would and wouldn't do (without engaging in a dangerous activity). Could this be the "real" you?
11. Recall a disagreement you had recently with a member of the opposite sex. Take his or her position and generate a set of convincing arguments.

SUMMING UP

Perception extracts sensory input from external energy sources and organizes it into stable, meaningful percepts. The proximal stimulus is the pattern of neural activity triggered in a receptor, while the distal stimulus is the real source of the stimulation. The process of perception can be divided into three stages: sensation; perception (organization and combination of sensory information); and identification/recognition. Perception is usually accurate but can fail when sensory data are confusing or inaccurate or when perceptual patterns are ambiguous. Explanations of perception have included four theories: (1) Helmholtz's view that human experience educates perceptual inference; (2) the Gestalt view that brain processes organize stimulus details into meaningful units; (3) Gibson's view that perception is a natural process shaped by evolutionary adaptation to the environment; and (4) the AI approach focusing on the stages and processes of stimulus interpretation.

Attention divides stimulation into that which is processed and that which is not. Preattentive processing registers simple stimulus features. Attention itself serves several functions: filtering early sensations; selecting appropriate responses; and processing stimuli into consciousness. Attention serves these functions by inhibiting irrelevant processing and facilitating appropriate processing. Attention also manages our limited mental resources. High levels of practice enable us to perform tasks with automaticity—tasks such as effortless processing, minimal attention, and noninterference from concurrent tasks.

Perceptual organization puts sensory information together to form coherent scenes. Sensory detection of changes in color or texture results in region segregation. Figure-ground separation distinguishes between objects and backgrounds. Illusory contours can emerge in figure-ground separation and also illustrate the principle of closure—the tendency to perceive images as whole and balanced. Separate figures may be perceived as a group if they are close together (the law of proximity), like each other (the law of similarity), or move together (the law of common fate). An underlying principle of these grouping laws is the principle of Prägnanz (meaningfulness)—the simplest configuration is that which will emerge.

Identification and recognition processes attach meaning to percepts. These processes involve both bottom-up (data-driven) and top-down (conceptually driven) analysis and interpretation. Identification is also constructed on the basis of the context of the stimulus and one's expectations about it. Expectations can create a perceptual set or readiness to make specific inferences. Socially learned attitudes and personality differences also contribute to the process and products of identification and recognition. Clearly, both bottom-up and top-down processing must interact and balance to produce the most meaningful and adaptive perceptions.

Figure 5.28 B. Old Woman

An appreciation of perception can be applied in making your own experience more creative. By challenging assumptions and adopting a playful perspective you can improve the flexibility and openness of your own perceptual experience.

Figure 5.29 C. Now What Do You See?

CHAPTER REVIEW

◆ **Sensation** *What are the dual functions of our sensory systems? At what point in visual processing is light energy converted into neural information? Why are sound stimuli interpreted as signaling action in the environment? Which of our other senses is considered most primitive, and why?*

Sensation is the first stage in the process of perception. It transduces the physical energy of stimuli into neural codes. Psychophysics investigates psychological responses to physical stimuli. To study sensation, researchers measure absolute thresholds, difference thresholds, and just noticeable differences between stimuli. Signal detection theory views sensation as a process of both sensitivity and judgment.

In the visual system, photoreceptors convert light energy into neural impulses, which are then transferred to the brain's visual cortex via the optic nerve. The superior colliculus processes stimulus location, while the lateral geniculate nucleus processes pattern recognition. Color sensation is stimulated by light wavelength and distinguished according to hue, saturation, and brightness.

Hearing is produced by sound waves distinguished by frequency, amplitude, and complexity. Sound waves travel from the outer ear to the middle ear; they are transformed into neural signals in the inner ear. Signals travel from the cochlea to the auditory cortex. Pitch perception has been explained by both place theory and frequency theory.

The vestibular sense processes information about bodily motion, and the kinesthetic sense detects signals about body position and coordination. Olfaction (smell) and gustation (taste) respond to the chemical properties of stimuli. Olfaction is accomplished by odor-sensitive cells deep in the nasal passages. Taste receptors are distributed throughout the mouth in taste buds. The skin senses detect pressure, temperature, and touch. Pain is the body's response to potentially harmful stimuli. Pain is in part a psychological response that can be modified by treatments emphasizing mental processing and distraction.

Key Terms

sensory processes, p. 148
sensory modalities, p. 148
sensuality, p. 148
sensation, p. 149
perception, p. 149
transduction, p. 150
afferent systems, p. 150
efferent systems, p. 150
psychophysics, p. 150
absolute threshold, p. 151
theory of signal detection (TSD), p. 151
difference threshold, p. 154
just noticeable difference (JND), p. 154
Weber's law, p. 154
sensory adaptation, p. 155
retina, p. 157
photoreceptors, p. 157
rods, p. 157
cones, p. 157
fovea, p. 157
bipolar cell, p. 157
ganglion cell, p. 158
optic nerve, p. 158

visual cortex, p. 158
hue, p. 160
saturation, p. 160
brightness, p. 160
complementary colors, p. 160
hertz (Hz), p. 164
pitch, p. 164
loudness, p. 164
decibels (dB), p. 164
timbre, p. 164
basilar membrane, p. 165
auditory nerve, p. 165
auditory cortex, p. 165
vestibular sense, p. 165
kinesthetic sense, p. 165
olfactory bulb, p. 166
place theroy, p. 167
frequency theory, p. 167
pheromones, p. 167
taste buds, p. 168
skin senses, p. 168
pain, p. 169

Major Contributors

◆2 Perception

What is the task of perception? Why is attention considered a vulnerable process? What quality of perception is produced by organizational processes? In our perceptions, how do we experience continuity over time and across situations?

Our perceptual systems actively organize and interpret information. Research on illusions provides clues about normal perceptual processes. The task of perception is to determine what the distal stimulus is, based on information in the proximal stimulus. At the perceptual level, brain processes organize sensations into coherent images; at the identification level, percepts are compared with memory and tested for recognition. Perception involves three stages: sensation, perceptual organization, and identification/recognition. Ambiguity can arise when the same sensory information is organized into different percepts.

Attention refers to our ability to select part of the sensory input and disregard the rest. Attention may function to select features early in processing, later in processing, or for providing access to consciousness. Attention may work by suppressing irrelevant material or facilitating processing of relevant material. Our ability to pay attention to several simultaneous stimuli is limited, and depends on whether tasks compete for the same resources or involve automaticity.

Organization processes in perception segregate percepts into regions and organize them into figure-ground distinctions. We tend to see contours separating figures, and to see incomplete figures as wholes. Gestalt principles explain grouping by proximity, similarity, and common fate—all indications of meaningfulness.

The final stage of perception involves identification and recognition. Percepts are given meaning through processes that draw on cognitive (top-down) processes, context and expectation, perceptual set, cultural and personal factors. Ultimately perception depends on who we are, what we know and expect, and the nature of the sensory stimulus.

Key Terms

PRACTICE TEST

Chapter 5: Sensation and Perception

For each of the following items, choose the single correct or best answer. Correct answers, explanations, and page references appear in the Appendix.

1. _____ is the process that converts one form of physical energy, such as sound waves, to another form, such as neural impulses.
   A. Sensory adaptation
   B. Psychophysics
   C. Transduction
   D. Kinesthesis

2. Marcus borrows his brother Jared's car, although Jared has warned him "the engine has been acting up lately." Nervous about breaking down far from home, Marcus makes frequent stops during his road trip. He imagines he can hear ominous noises that might signal engine trouble. Which of the following best explains why Marcus hears things that might not be there?
   A. classical absolute threshold theory
   B. the theory of signal detection
   C. the law of Prägnanz
   D. Weber's law

3. Which of these visual structures adjusts to focus on near or distant stimuli?
   A. lens
   B. ganglion cells
   C. lateral geniculate nucleus
   D. visual cortex

4. Place theory and frequency theory are alternative explanations for the sensation of _____ .
   A. the hue created by a light's wavelength
   B. the pitch of sound
   C. the timbre of sound
   D. different olfactory stimuli

5. _____ may be our most primitive sense, since it is processed in the oldest part of the brain and has basic connections to survival and interaction with other creatures.
   A. Vision
   B. Kinesthesis
   C. The vestibular sense
   D. Olfaction

6. After sensation and perception, the third stage in the process of perception is responsible for which of the following accomplishments?
   A. transforming physical energy into neural coding
   B. assigning meaning to percepts
   C. synthesizing sensory features into recognizable patterns
   D. distinguishing between different regions and features

7. _____ is more commonly experienced when the stimulus is ambiguous, information is missing, elements are combined in unusual ways, or familiar patterns are not apparent.
   A. An illusion
   B. A false alarm
   C. Closure
   D. A correct rejection

8. The approach that characterizes perception as a natural process shaped by evolution and adaptation our environment is attributed to _____ .
   A. Hermann von Helmholtz
   B. James Gibson
   C. Gestalt psychology
   D. artificial intelligence

9. Liza is attending a crowded party and trying to overhear a conversation between two strangers who are talking about her. She pretends to smile at other people and watch the party while she strains to eavesdrop. She will most likely lose track of the conversation and pay attention to a new stimulus if _____ .
    A. something interesting happens across the room
    B. someone addresses her in a loud voice
    C. someone addresses her in a calm whisper
    D. she realizes she recognizes one of the strangers

10. Although the markings in the ceiling tile are of all different shapes and sizes, you notice that the larger, darker spots seem to be floating against a background made up of the smaller, lighter ones. Which principle of perceptual grouping explains this distinction?
    A. the law of similarity
    B. the law of proximity
    C. the law of common fate
    D. the principle of closure

IF YOU'RE INTERESTED . . .

Ackerman, D. (1990). *A natural history of the senses.* New York: Vintage.

Diane Ackerman's bestselling collection of provocative and powerful essays on smell, touch, taste, hearing, vision and synethesia—experiencing one sense's stimuli in another (that is, hearing color or feeling a fragrance).

Gregory, R. L. (1970). *The intelligent eye.* New York: McGraw-Hill.

An eye's-eye view of visual perception, reviewing illusions, ambiguities, and constancies. Rich with illustrations and examples.

Gregory, R. L. (1990). *Eye and brain,* 4th edition. Princeton, NJ: Princeton University Press.

Latest edition of Gregory's classic, highly readable text on the eye-brain connection and the basics of visual perception.

Matlin, M. W. (1983). *Perception.* Boston: Allyn and Bacon.

Good overview text of the tasks and processes of perception.

The miracle worker. (Video: 1962, B&W, 107 minutes). Directed by Arthur Penn; starring Patty Duke, Anne Bancroft, Victor Jory, Inga Swenson.

Powerful movie, an adaptation of William Gibson's play about Helen Keller, blind and deaf since infancy, and her awakening to sensation, perception, and language through the efforts of her teacher, Anne Sullivan.

Shepard, R.N. (1990). *Mindsights.* New York: W. H. Freeman.

Warren, R. M. (1982). *Auditory perception: A new synthesis.* New York: Pergamon.

Academic review of research and theories of hearing.

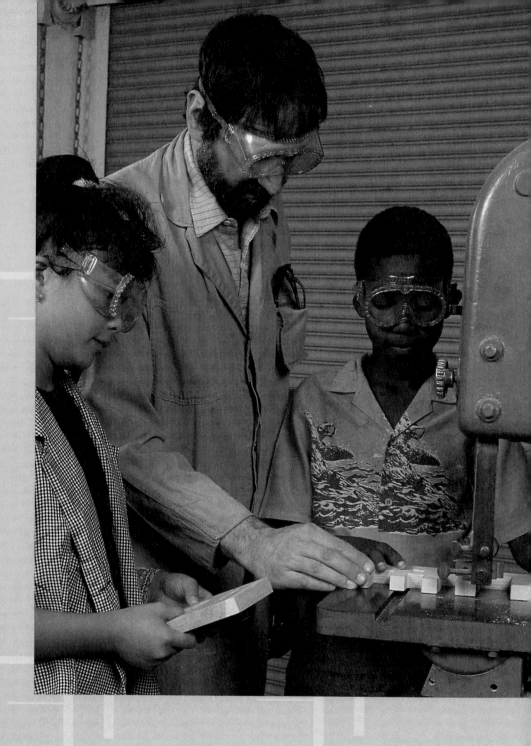

Chapter 6

Learning

1. How is learning different from other changes in behavior? How is the behavioristic view of learning distinct from other perspectives?

2. How does Pavlovian conditioning change reflexive behavior? What are the basic processes of classical conditioning?

3. What does the law of effect explain? What do behavior analysts do? What makes an experience rein-forcing? Why are reinforcers and punishers considered the power brokers of operant conditioning?

4. How do biological factors affect species' ability to learn? What evidence suggests that organisms learn even when they are not reinforced? Does learning theory have any practical applications?

A woman we'll call Nora is reflecting on her past relationships as she chats with her girlfriends over brunch. "It's true I've been happy with my partner for more than ten years," she admits, "but I wasn't always so happy—or so smart." Nora tells a story to show how far she's come. When she was a senior in college years ago, Nora had a boyfriend who made her feel sad and insecure. "He was an interesting guy, not great-looking but really confident. He was a musician and I was very impressed with his talent," Nora confesses. "I think he really cared for me at first, but he couldn't stop looking around. He was always chasing after other women, afraid he'd miss out on something if he made a commitment to me—or to *anyone.*" One day Nora caught him in a lie: After he had denied seeing anyone else, he turned up with a date at the same out-of-town concert Nora was attending with her girlfriends. "After that, I had no trouble writing him off, as if I really *knew* there was no hope. We just parted ways and I never pursued him again." But the memory is still vivid—sometimes more than others. "He always wore the same cologne—Brut™—and too much of it. I got so I couldn't stand the fragrance, no matter who was wearing it. I once rejected a perfectly wonderful guy just because I couldn't get past the bad feelings I associated with his cologne, the same one my old boyfriend always wore."

It isn't unusual to associate feelings with sensory experiences, especially scents like the cologne worn by someone you loved—or hated. As we saw in the last chapter, smell may be our most primitive sense, linking whiffs of stimulation with judgments about survival, satisfaction, and pain. Normally we might not worry about the connections we form between such stimuli and experiences, except when, as Nora reflects, we miss out on some "perfectly wonderful" opportunity because old associations are so hard to change.

"Some years later, I took advantage of some old associations to help me get over a painful breakup," Nora continues. "I'd been dumped by this guy, Hal, for another woman. Our time together had not always been rosy, but naturally when *he* rejected *me,* all I could think of was how much I wanted him back. I saw a therapist and she told me to imagine him treating me badly, so I didn't just associate him with good times. That helped a little. Then she suggested I imagine Hal in some ridiculous situation, one where he'd seem more like a person, less like a god. Hal was always such a neat freak, I imagined him with potato salad dumped on his head. He would never laugh at himself in such a situation, he would be so uptight and worried about how he 'looked.' Whenever I felt sorry for myself and nostalgic about Hal, I would force myself to picture him with the potato salad on his head. It would make me laugh and realize we really weren't right for each other. It seemed to speed up the process of falling out of love. So I got on with my life. And when I met my current partner, I had learned a few things about how to make intelligent decisions about love—I had learned how to be happy."

Social scientists suggest that falling in love involves two views of another person—the *real* person you interact with and the *ideal* image you have in your mind about that person. If the ideal is more attractive than the real person, it may not be "love" but an illusion, similar to your perception of ambiguous stimuli like those we examined in the last chapter. Similarly, if an ideal image lures you into love in the first place, perhaps a less-than-ideal image can help you find a way *out* of a love that ends or doesn't work. This is one of the recommendations Debora Phillips makes in her 1978 book, *How to Fall Out of Love.* By picturing a lost love in an exaggerated, humorous situation—a neatnik coping with a mess, or a pompous expert wearing nothing but diapers—you can learn to let go of impossible, idealistic fantasies about the relationship.

Some learned associations are strangely resistant to change—such as Nora's association of old anger and dislike with the scent of Brut™ cologne. But it is possible for us to take control of other learned associations to move away from unrewarding behavior patterns and relationships and move toward new, constructive responses to the people and situations in our lives.

Introduction

Nora talks about love as if it were learned. Does that make sense? Literature, poetry, folk wisdom, and popular music convey that romantic love is not something we can consciously control. Instead, it just "happens"; you are "struck by the thunderbolt," the "chemistry" is just right, or you just "really connect" with another person. Otherwise, we might argue, why do we sometimes fall for the wrong people? Why can't we make ourselves love those who would be good to us, instead of pursuing hopeless attachments or repeating unhealthy patterns again and again?

The answer may lie in the nature of human learning. Our complex species has fewer basic inborn instincts that control our behavior than any other species. Animals lower on the developmental continuum deal with their environmental challenges by relying on **fixed-action patterns.** Fixed-action patterns are unlearned sets of responses stimulated in a given species by a specific environmental event or object. Humans are remarkably adaptive to diverse environments, challenges, and circumstances. In order to be flexible, our behavior must rely primarily on lessons acquired through *experience* rather than built-in patterns of action. The flexibility we develop as a result of learning accounts for problems (such as not knowing what to do in new situations) as well as solutions (such as avoiding competition by not being attracted to the same people as everyone else). Learning explains why people in the same society, who have learned similar lessons, would be alike in many ways. It also explains the wide variety of behaviors among individuals who grow up with different family structures and personal values.

Learning About Learning

Psychologists have long been interested in *conditioning*—the ways in which environmental contexts, specific stimuli, and behavior become associated with one another. Although the study of conditioning is historically rooted in the study of animal behavior, research since the 1970s has shown that conditioning applies equally well to humans.

Researchers have focused on two basic types of learning: classical conditioning and operant conditioning. In classical conditioning, two *stimuli* become associated so that the occurrence of one reliably predicts the occur-

fixed action pattern Unlearned set of responses triggered within a given species by a specific stimulus.

rence of the other. In our opening example, Nora associated the scent of Brut™ cologne with her boyfriend's presence—and the pain and anger he had caused her. Later she deliberately associated a silly image with thoughts of another man to ease her recovery from a doomed past relationship.

In operant conditioning, behavior becomes associated with its *consequences*. This may explain why people fall in love in the first place. According to one theory (Byrne, 1971), attraction forms when you associate a particular person with rewards. If one individual provides you with rewarding experiences such as agreement, support, affection, and passion, you will naturally learn to desire his or her presence and contact. We may even form bad relationships in the same way we form bad habits, by becoming so attached to the benefits of a particular person that our behavior is hard to change after it ceases to be rewarding or healthy.

In this chapter, we will examine the ways researchers have studied classical and operant conditioning and the conclusions they have drawn about how we learn what to do to survive and prosper. We will further examine evidence that shows the complex nature of what we assume to be simple kinds of learning. First, consider the significance of learning from an *evolutionary perspective*. Learning is influenced by experience; that is, nature does not bequeath us a fixed tendency to learn only certain things. Instead, we inherit a *capacity* for learning. Whether and how much that capacity is realized depends on the individual. We all have similar capacities for learning, but we learn different things to different degrees because our life experiences are ultimately unique.

Our capacity for learning separates us from our fellow creatures. Some creatures, such as reptiles and amphibians, do not benefit much from interactions with the environment. For those creatures, life is a series of rigid stimulus-response patterns. Their survival depends on living in a relatively *constant habitat* in which their responses to specific environmental events get them what they need or protect them from what they must avoid. The behavior of animals higher on the evolutionary ladder, such as monkeys and humans, is less influenced by genetic factors. Such behavior is based on greater *plasticity*, or variability, in learning.

Learning may seem to reflect the democratic ideal that people can shape their lives by their actions and that they are not limited by biology or family history. People can aspire to better lives, regardless of their origins. This optimistic view of learning is unique to psychology in the United States; psychologists in other countries do not have such an optimistic view. These psychologists believe that learning may be linked to the development of maladaptive behaviors, such as superstitions, phobias, and irrational beliefs. The opening case showed how even affairs of the heart may thus be influenced by applying conditioning principles to change irrational behavior. Nora described how she recovered from a painful breakup by learning to associate humorous images with an ex-boyfriend, thus overcoming her irrational, romantic expectations. The psychology of learning is at the heart of much that is human nature—for better or for worse.

Defining Learning

Learning is a process that results in a relatively permanent change in behavior or behavior potential. That process is based on experience. Let's consider each of these learning criteria in turn: *behavior* or behavior potential; relatively *permanent* change; a process based on *experience*.

A Change in Behavior or Behavior Potential. Learning is not observed directly but is inferred from changes in observable behavior. Learning is apparent from improvements in your **performance,** but performance may not show everything that has been learned. For example, if test questions seem unfair or you feel anxious, you may perform poorly despite having learned the material.

learning Process based on experience that results in a relatively permanent change in behavior or behavior potential.

performance External behavior that reveals that learning has occurred, although it may not reveal all that has been learned.

Further, learning may affect your *potential for behavior* more than your immediate behavior. An inspiring course or a powerful lecture can increase your appreciation for art or your understanding of cultural history in ways that are not apparent in measurable actions. Nonetheless, you have learned attitudes and values that will affect the choices you make—for leisure, literature, or other commitments—for years to come.

Although learning is inferred from changes in observable behavior, we should be careful not to infer learning from *all* changes in behavior or behavior potential. Sometimes behavioral changes occur for reasons other than learning. Some changes are due to physical maturation or brain development; other changes occur because of disease, brain damage, or drugs. Similarly, if your motivation level is unusually high or low, you may perform in ways that you have not actually learned. For example, an athlete who has been training for an upcoming competition may find that the arousal caused by performing in public increases her stamina and skill in ways she was unable to accomplish during practice. Because such "one-shot" achievements are not actually learned, the new behavior cannot be sustained when conditions return to normal.

A Relatively Permanent Change. To qualify as learned, a change in behavior or behavior potential must be relatively permanent. Once you learn to swim, you will probably always be able to do so. Some changes in behavior, however, are transitory and not learned. Reflexive behavior (for example, an eyeblink, a kneejerk) results when the nervous system is stimulated; this behavior is neither learned nor lasting. Conversely, much of what you know is forgotten or changed by later lessons; thus learned changes may not last forever. However, learning always involves *memory* for what has been learned, so that on subsequent occasions you can recall or do again what you learned before.

A Process Based on Experience. Learning can take place only through experience. Experience includes taking in information and making responses that affect the environment. Some lasting changes in behavior require a combination of experience and maturational readiness. For example, a child is ready to crawl, stand, walk, and run according to a specific timetable. No amount of training or practice will produce those behaviors before the child has matured sufficiently. In this case, changes in behavior are based on experience rather than on inborn factors that occur without specific transactions with the environment.

Under most circumstances, learning can be said to have taken place when the three criteria we have outlined exist (listed on page 199). However, sometimes it is not obvious to the person or observers that these conditions are present. Learning of a broad rather than specific nature—such as adopting a value system of respect for authority or love of one's country—is very difficult to measure. Finally, what constitutes experience varies from person to person. These exceptions or extensions of the definition of learning highlight the need for researchers to be precise when determining the conditions associated with different types of learning. Originally, psychologists began their investigation of learning with careful observations of behavior and the influences that account for behavior change.

Analyzing and Modifying Behavior

Much of modern psychology's view of learning finds its roots in the work of **John B. Watson** (1878–1958). As you might recall from Chapter 1, Watson founded the school of psychology known as *behaviorism*. For nearly fifty years, the behaviorist tradition dominated American psychology. In perhaps his most influential work, *Psychology from the Standpoint of a Behaviorist*, Watson (1919) argued that introspection—verbal reports of sensations, images, and feelings—

John B. Watson (1878–1958)

was *not* an acceptable means of studying behavior because it was too subjective. The subject matter of psychology should be *observable behavior*. In Watson's words, "States of consciousness, like the so-called phenomena of spiritualism, are not objectively verifiable and for that reason can never become data for science" (Watson, 1919, p. 1).

B. F. Skinner (1904–1990) began his graduate study in psychology at Harvard after reading Watson's 1924 book *Behaviorism*. During his career, Skinner pioneered a new brand of behaviorism known as *radical behaviorism*. Skinner challenged early behaviorist theories that considered internal states and mental events to be legitimate *causes of behavior* (Skinner, 1990). In Skinner's view, mental events, such as thinking and imagining, do not cause behavior. Rather, they are examples of behavior that are caused by environmental stimuli.

Suppose that we deprive a pigeon of food for 24 hours, place it in an apparatus where it can peck at a lever to obtain food, and find that it soon does so. Skinner would say that the bird's behavior is explained by food deprivation, an event that was manipulated environmentally. It adds nothing to our account to say that the bird pecked the lever because it was "hungry" or because it "wanted" to get the food. The animal's behavior can be explained by an *environmental* event—deprivation. The subjective feeling of hunger, which cannot be directly observed or measured, does not cause the behavior but results from deprivation. Similarly, the lever-pecking behavior (with its consequence of getting food) results from the initial deprivation followed by the environmental *consequences* of the animal's actions.

The commonsense explanation for the pigeon's behavior is that it is hungry so it does whatever it can to get its food. The Skinnerian explanation is that food deprivation causes an internal state that makes getting the food highly rewarding, so the pigeon learns to press the lever. These two explanations may seem like the same story in different language—one familiar, one laden with jargon—but they are really different ways of *viewing* behavior. While the commonsense perspective makes vague assessments about how the pigeon "feels," the behaviorist approach carefully maps stimulus events that the organism perceives and the consequences that follow its responses.

Although the behavioristic position has yielded many valuable explanations of human nature, we will see that it has been challenged by other psychologists who insist on keeping a thinking brain and a rational mind in control of the behaving body.

SUMMING UP

Learning may be defined as a relatively permanent change in behavior or behavior potential based on experience. Our capacity for learning depends upon both our genetic heritage and the nature of our environment. The study of learning has been dominated by the behavioristic approach as represented in the work of Watson and Skinner.

Classical Conditioning

classical conditioning Form of learning in which two stimuli become associated so that one acquires the power to elicit the same behavioral response as the other.

In the story that began our chapter, Nora recalled how she associated the scent of a particular men's cologne with an old boyfriend, and involuntarily responded with bad feelings and dislike whenever she encountered it. Nora had learned to associate an "innocent" stimulus (the cologne) with a powerful stimulus (the painful memory of her old boyfriend). This connection is known as **classical conditioning,** a form of basic learning in which one stimulus or event predicts the occurrence of another stimulus or event. The organism learns a new *association* between two stimuli—a neutral stimulus (that did not previously elicit the response) and a more powerful stimulus (that elicits the response by itself). Following conditioning, the formerly neutral stimulus develops the power to elicit a response that is very similar to the original response. This simple pairing of events has profound implications in everyday life as well as in psychological theory.

Pavlov's Discovery

The Russian physiologist **Ivan Pavlov** (1849–1936) is credited with discovering the basic principles of classical conditioning. He began to formulate the tenets of classical conditioning while conducting research on digestion, research for which he won a Nobel Prize in 1904.

Pavlov had devised a technique to study digestive processes in dogs. He implanted tubes in their glands and digestive organs to divert bodily secretions to containers outside their bodies; he then measured and analyzed those secretions. Pavlov's assistants put meat powder into the dogs' mouths to trigger these processes. After repeating this procedure a number of times, Pavlov observed an unexpected behavior in his dogs—they salivated *before* the powder was put in their mouths! They would start salivating when they saw the food or the assistant who brought it. Any stimulus that regularly preceded the presentation of food came to elicit salivation. Quite by accident, Pavlov had discovered that learning may result from two stimuli becoming associated with each other.

To Pavlov, this finding did not make sense physiologically. What is the survival value, for example, in getting ready to eat at the sound of footsteps? Why should a new stimulus be added to an already effective, existing stimulus-response sequence? Pavlov turned his attention to understanding these "psychic secretions"—automatic responses triggered by mental ("psychic") events rather than environmental stimuli. He abandoned his work on digestion and, in so doing, changed the course of psychology forever (Pavlov, 1928).

The behavior Pavlov studied was the reflex. A **reflex** is an unlearned response, such as salivation, pupil contraction, knee jerks, or eye blinking, that is naturally elicited by specific stimuli that have biological relevance for the organism. Simply put, a reflex is an elicited behavior that promotes biological adaptation to a changing environment. For example, salivation helps digestion. After conditioning, organisms make reflexive responses to new stimuli that have no original biological relevance.

To discover what was causing his dogs to salivate, Pavlov knew that he would have to manipulate various aspects of his experimental setting and observe what effects, if any, would follow. His strategy was elegant and simple. He first placed a dog in a restraining harness. At regular intervals, a tone was sounded and the dog was given a bit of food. The dog's first reaction to the tone was only an *orienting response:* The dog pricked its ears and moved its

reflex Unlearned response elicited by specific stimuli that are biologically relevant to the organism.

To study classical conditioning, Pavlov placed his dogs in a restraining apparatus. The dogs were then presented with a neutral stimulus, such as a tone. Through its association with food, the neutral stimulus became a conditional stimulus, eliciting salivation.

head to locate the source of the sound. But with *repeated pairings* of the tone and the food, the orienting response stopped, and salivation began. This phenomenon could be replicated under controlled conditions. A neutral stimulus (such as the tone) when paired with another, more relevant stimulus (such as food) will eventually elicit a response very similar to the original reflex (such as salivation). The same kind of conditioning occurs in kitchens everywhere when a pet owner uses an electric can opener to open dog or cat food and the pet runs into the room, ready to eat.

Figure 6.1 illustrates the main features of Pavlov's classical conditioning procedure. Any stimulus that naturally elicits a reflexive behavior is called an **unconditional stimulus** (UCS) because learning is *not* a necessary *condition* for the stimulus to control the behavior. The behavior elicited by the unconditional stimulus is called the **unconditional response** (UCR). During conditioning trials, a neutral stimulus, such as a tone, is repeatedly paired with the unconditional stimulus so that it predictably follows the neutral stimulus. After several trials, the tone is presented alone and elicits the same response as the UCS does—salivation.

In these trials, the tone stimulus acquires some of the power to influence behavior that was originally limited to the unconditional stimulus. After conditioning, the neutral stimulus paired with the unconditional stimulus is called the **conditional stimulus** (CS) because its power to elicit behavior is *conditional* upon its association with the UCS. The reflexive behavior elicited by the CS is called the **conditional response** (CR), the same behavior triggered by a new stimulus. In other words, nature provides us with natural UCS-UCR connections, but the learning created by classical conditioning creates the new CS-CR connection.

unconditional stimulus (UCS) In classical conditioning, the stimulus that elicits an unconditional response.

unconditional response (UCR) In classical conditioning, the response elicited by an unconditional stimulus without prior learning.

conditional stimulus (CS) In classical conditioning, previously neutral stimulus that comes to elicit the conditional response.

conditional response (CR) In classical conditioning, response elicited by previously neutral stimulus that has become associated with the unconditional stimulus.

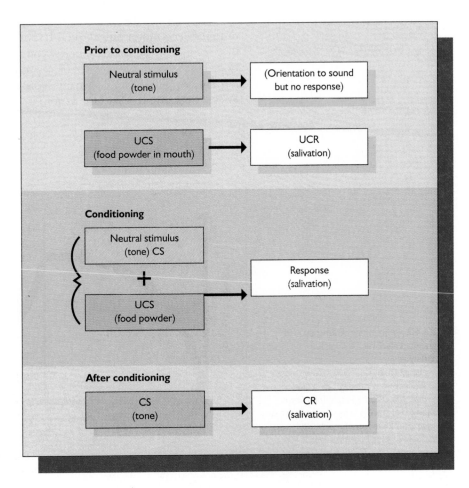

Figure 6.1 Basic Features of Classical Conditioning
Before conditioning, the unconditional stimulus (UCS) naturally elicits the unconditional response (UCR). A neutral stimulus, such as a tone, has no eliciting effect. During conditioning, the neutral stimulus is paired with the UCS. Through its association with the UCS, the neutral stimulus becomes a conditional stimulus (CS) and elicits a conditional response (CR) that is similar to the UCR.

Pavlov's careful laboratory experiments showed how otherwise neutral stimuli could come to exert powerful control over reflexive behavior. His research uncovered a number of important processes involved in classical conditioning, most of which are still being studied by modern psychologists. Classical conditioning is also called *Pavlovian conditioning,* due to Pavlov's discovery of the phenomena of conditioning and his dedication to tracking down the variables that influence it. In the next section, we will examine the processes and conditions essential to classical conditioning.

Basic Processes

What conditions are optimal for classical conditioning? The answers provide clues to the fundamental processes underlying learning. We will first identify how the conditioned association is acquired, then how it is extinguished and sometimes spontaneously recovered. After we distinguish between the processes of stimulus generalization and discrimination, we will analyze the conditions essential to effective classical conditioning.

Acquisition. Under most conditions, the CS and UCS must be paired at least several times before the CS reliably elicits a CR. **Acquisition** refers to the process at the beginning of a classical conditioning experiment by which the CR is first elicited and gradually increases in frequency over repeated trials. Panel 1 in **Figure 6.2** shows the acquisition phase of a hypothetical experiment. At first, very few CRs are elicited by the CS. With continued CS-UCS pairings, however, the CR is elicited with increasing frequency, and a conditional response is acquired by the organism.

In conditioning (as in telling a good joke) *timing* is critical. The CS and UCS must be presented close enough in time so that the organism perceives them as being related. The range of time intervals between the CS and UCS that will produce the best conditioning depends upon the response being conditioned. For motor and skeletal responses, such as eye blinks, a short interval of a second or less is best. For visceral responses, such as heart rate and salivation, longer intervals of 5 to 15 seconds work best. Conditioned fear usually requires longer intervals of many seconds or even minutes to develop (see "In Focus: Learning to Fear" for a more detailed discussion).

acquisition Stage of classical conditioning when conditional response is first elicited by the conditional stimulus.

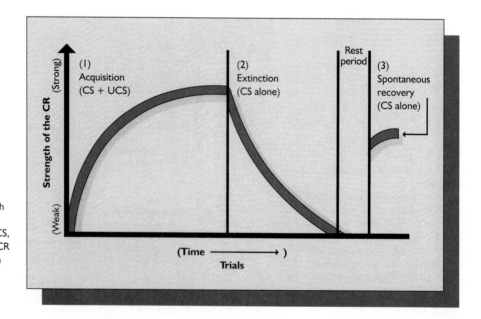

Figure 6.2 Acquisition, Extinction, and Spontaneous Recovery in Classical Conditioning
During acquisition (CS + UCS), the strength of the CR increases rapidly. During extinction, when the UCS no longer follows the CS, the strength of the CR drops to zero. The CR may reappear after a brief rest period, even when the UCS is still not presented. The reappearance of the CS is called "spontaneous recovery."

In Focus:

LEARNING TO FEAR

Pavlov's conditioning with meat powder is an example of *appetitive conditioning*—conditioning in which the UCS is of positive value to an organism. However, classical conditioning may also involve an aversive, painful UCS. Aversive conditioning occurs when the CS predicts the presentation of an aversive UCS, such as an electrical shock. An organism's natural response to such stimuli is reflexive behavior that reduces the intensity of the UCS or removes it entirely. If you touch something painfully hot, for example, you jerk your hand away reflexively, preventing any further pain or damage. Through its association with the UCS, the CS also comes to elicit such avoidant responses when it is presented later independently of the UCS.

Aversive conditioning studies have shown that the organism learns not only a specific conditional muscle response but also a *generalized fear reaction*. The subject learns a specific response to a stimulus and reevaluates the previously neutral stimulus as affectively negative. Withdrawal from the negative stimulus is accompanied by reactions of the autonomic nervous system, such as changes in heart rate and respiration. These changes become part of an overall conditional fear response.

Interestingly, when strong fear is involved, conditioning may take place after only *one* pairing of a neutral stimulus with the UCS. Traumatic events in our lives that may occur only once can condition us to respond with strong physical, emotional, and cognitive reactions that are highly resistant to extinction. Conditional fear is often easy to acquire and difficult to extinguish.

Psychologists John B. Watson and Rosalie Rayner conducted a classic study of conditional fear in a human being

with an infant named Albert. Using techniques that would not be likely to receive approval from research review committees today, Watson and Rayner (1920) trained Albert to fear a white rat he had initially liked by pairing its appearance with an aversive UCS—a loud gong struck just behind him. The unconditional startle response and the emotional distress to the noxious noise was the basis of Albert's learning to react with fear to the appearance of the white rat. His fear was developed in just seven conditioning trials. The emotional conditioning was then extended to behavioral conditioning when Albert learned to escape from the feared stimulus. The infant's learned fear then generalized to other furry objects, such as a rabbit, a dog, and even a Santa Claus mask (Harris, 1979)!

We now know that conditioned fear is highly resistant to extinction. Even if the overt components of muscle reaction eventually disappear, the reactions of the autonomic nervous system continue. This leaves an individual vulnerable to arousal by the old signals, sometimes without awareness of why the reaction is occurring. Thus you may find yourself feeling nervous "for no reason" or fearing that a new food will "make you sick" because of long-forgotten associations in your past experience. And some people have lifelong fears of snakes or other, generally harmless, creatures without even remembering the reason.

Conditional fear reactions may persist for years, even when the original frightening UCS is never again experienced, as shown in the following study: During World War II, the signal used to call sailors to battle stations aboard U.S. navy ships was a gong sounding at the rate of 100 rings a minute. To personnel

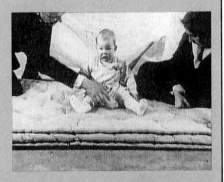

John Watson and Rosalie Rayner conditioned Little Albert to fear small, furry objects (*Discovering Psychology*, 1990).

on board, the sound was associated with danger; thus, it became a CS for strong emotional arousal. Fifteen years after the war, a study was conducted on the emotional reactions of hospitalized navy and army veterans to a series of 20 different auditory stimuli. Although none of the sounds were current signals for danger, the sound of the old "call to battle stations" still produced strong emotional arousal in the navy veterans who had previously experienced that association. Their response to the former danger signal, as determined by galvanic-skin-response measures, was significantly greater than that of the army veterans (Edwards & Acker, 1962).

All of us retain learned readiness to respond with fear, joy, or other emotions to old signals that aren't appropriate or valid in our current situation. When we are unaware of their origins, these once reasonable fear reactions may be interpreted as anxiety, and we get more upset because we seem to be reacting irrationally without adequate cause or reason (Dollard & Miller, 1950).

Conditioning occurs most rapidly when the CS stands out against the many other stimuli that are also present. Thus, a stimulus will be more readily noticed the more *intense* it is and the more it *contrasts* with other stimuli. In general, the feature of the CS that most facilitates conditioning is its *informativeness*—its reliability in predicting the onset of the UCS (Rescorla, 1972; Rescorla & Wagner, 1972). In the opening example of this chapter, Nora associated her feelings toward her boyfriend with the distinctive fragrance of his cologne—not with such characteristics as his hair color or the sound of his voice that might resemble other people she encountered. In real life, as in the conditioning laboratory, the key to developing a strong conditional response is to increase the signal-to-noise ratio of the CS by making it stronger than all other competing events—background stimuli or irrelevant noise.

Extinction and Spontaneous Recovery. Once a conditional response is acquired, does it last forever? When the UCS no longer follows the CS, the CR becomes weaker over time and eventually stops occurring. When the CR no longer occurs in the presence of the CS (and absence of UCS), **extinction** is said to have occurred (see Figure 6.2, Panel 2). Conditional responses, then, are not necessarily a permanent aspect of the organism's behavioral repertoire. However, the CR will reappear in a weak form when the CS is presented alone again (see Figure 6.2, Panel 3). Pavlov referred to this sudden reappearance of the CR after a rest period (or time-out) without further exposure to the UCS as **spontaneous recovery**. For example, years after Nora thought she had overcome her association of Brut™ cologne with memories of an unpleasant relationship, she found herself recoiling from a new acquaintance simply because he was wearing Brut™. She had spontaneously recovered the previously extinguished conditional response.

Stimulus Generalization. Once a CR has been conditioned to a particular CS, similar stimuli may also elicit the response. For example, if conditioning was to a high frequency tone, a lower tone may also elicit the response. A child bitten by a big dog is likely to respond with fear even to smaller dogs, or to all furry animals. This automatic extension of responding to stimuli that have never been paired with the original UCS is called **stimulus generalization**. The more similar the new stimulus is to the original CS, the stronger the response will be. When response strength is measured for each of a series of increasingly dissimilar stimuli along a given dimension, as shown in **Figure 6.3**, a *generalization gradient* or slope is found.

Important stimuli rarely occur in exactly the same form every time in nature. Thus, stimulus generalization operates as a similarity safety factor by extending the range of learning beyond the original specific experience. With this feature, new but comparable events can be recognized as having the same meaning or behavioral significance despite apparent differences. For example, a predator can make a different sound or be seen from a different angle and still be recognized and responded to quickly.

Stimulus Discrimination. Though stimuli similar to the original CS may elicit a similar response, it is possible for an organism to respond only to one particular CS and not respond to other stimuli, regardless of how similar they are. **Stimulus discrimination** is the process by which an organism learns to respond differently to stimuli that are distinct from the CS on some dimension (for example, differences in hue or in pitch). Early in conditioning, stimuli similar to the CS will elicit a similar response, though not quite as strong. As discrimination training proceeds, the responses to the other, dissimilar stimuli weaken: The organism gradually learns which "event signal" predicts the onset of the UCS and which signals do not.

For example, if the sound of a telephone ringing on a television show is similar to the sound actually made by your own telephone, you may automatically move to answer it before you realize your mistake. Most of the time, however, a televised phone will sound noticeably different from your phone, so that you can discriminate between the "real thing" and the television version.

extinction In learning, the weakening of a conditioned association in the absence of unconditional stimulus or reinforcer.

spontaneous recovery Reappearance of an extinguished conditional response after a rest period.

stimulus generalization Making conditional responses to similar stimuli that have never been paired with the unconditional stimulus.

stimulus discrimination In conditioning, responding differently to stimuli that differ from the conditional stimulus.

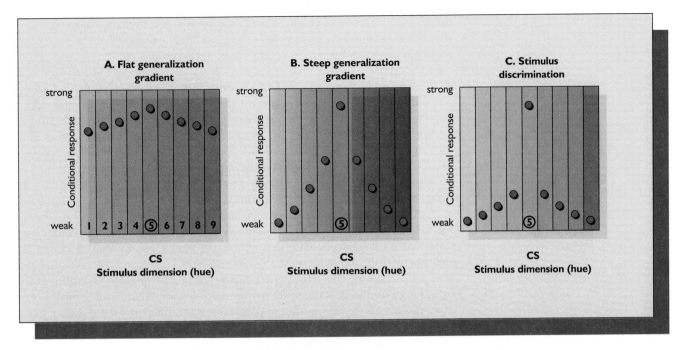

Figure 6.3 Stimulus Generalization Gradients
After conditioning to a medium green stimulus, the subject responds almost as strongly to stimuli of similar hues, as shown by the flat generalization gradient in panel A. When the subject is exposed to a broader range of colored stimuli, responses grow weaker as the color becomes increasingly dissimilar to the training stimulus. The generalization gradient becomes very steep, as shown in panel B. The experimenter could change the generalization gradient shown in panel A to resemble the one in panel C by giving the subject discrimination training. In this case, the medium green stimulus would be continually paired with the UCS but stimuli of all other hues would not.

For optimum adaptation, an organism's initial tendency to generalize all somewhat similar stimuli must give way to discrimination among them—responding only to those that are followed by the UCS. Ideally, conditioning is a process in which *discrimination* ultimately wins over *generalization;* but it is a balancing act between these two counteracting tendencies of being overselective and overresponsive.

Conditions for Conditioning. Pavlov's work helps us understand significant everyday behavior. "In Focus: Learning to Fear" examines the processes whereby fear and avoidance might be learned. Many of the emotions we experience and many of our attitudes can be explained by classical conditioning. Not surprisingly, real-life conditioning must occur in circumstances that are quite different from the neat system that makes up the laboratory environment. Modern research on classical conditioning has refined the earlier understanding of how it occurs. Researchers recognize that real-life conditioning depends on a connection or *contingency* between the associated stimuli, and on how *informative* stimuli appear to be.

Contingency. In his original conceptualization, Pavlov argued that to create a CS-CR connection, the two stimuli—the CS and the UCS—must occur close together in time, or be *temporally contiguous.* Work by **Robert Rescorla** (1966), however, has further indicated that the learner (human or animal) must also see the UCS as *contingent* on the CS. That is, if you are to form a connection between a powerful stimulus and a neutral stimulus, the UCS that causes the reaction must seem to be contingent on—reliably signalled by—the CS. In a sense, learning creatures are always scanning their environments to detect useful signals. If certain sights, smells, or sounds reliably signal danger, they will be identified and responded to more readily than signals that are only randomly associated in time with the meaningful stimuli.

Information. Further work by **Leon Kamin** (1969) has revealed that a learner will only form a CS-CR connection if the CS seems to provide unique information about the UCS. Some experiences are signalled not by a single stimulus but by a series of stimuli. Do you pay attention to *all* of them? According to Kamin, no: You learn to respond particularly to the stimuli that provide important *information* about the environment.

For example, if you ride a subway along the same route every day, you learn the sequence of sights and sounds that signal that your stop is coming up and it's time to rise and move toward the doors. One regular signal might be the familiar visual patterns of the tunnels and stations, such as the colors and signs that always precede your destination. Another regular signal, of course, is the conductor's announcement. When you notice these reliable signals, you may stop reading the newspaper, tense your leg muscles, assemble your belongings, and look for a route to the nearest door. After several trips, however, you may find you ignore the conductor's announcement and do not even hear his voice: It adds no *information* to what you can already detect from the telltale visual signals that trigger your reaction of preparing to disembark.

Classical conditioning, then, is much more complex than Pavlov originally theorized. Simply pairing a neutral stimulus with a UCS will not result in classical conditioning. For a neutral stimulus to become a CS, the UCS must be *contingent* on the CS's appearance, and the CS must provide distinctive *information* about the UCS. The power of any particular neutral stimulus to become a CS thus depends on the presence of other stimuli that could also serve as potential signals; the true signal must stand out as the "figure" that carries the vital information for predicting the future based on past associations.

SUMMING UP

A widely used procedure for investigating learning—especially about relationships between stimulus events in the environment—is classical conditioning. In this procedure, developed by Pavlov, a biologically significant stimulus, called an unconditional stimulus (UCS), elicits a reflex, called an unconditional response (UCR). A neutral stimulus that is then paired repeatedly with the UCS becomes a conditional stimulus (CS), which elicits a similar response, called the conditional response (CR).

If the UCS no longer follows the CS, extinction or disappearance of the CR occurs. After a rest period, spontaneous recovery may occur; the CR partially returns when the CS is presented alone again. Stimuli similar to the CS also elicit the CR; this phenomenon is called stimulus generalization. If these stimuli are not followed by the UCS, stimulus discrimination occurs; the organism stops responding to the irrelevant stimuli and responds only to the original CS.

For classical conditioning to occur, two criteria must be met. First, there must be a contingency relationship between the CS and UCS; the CS must reliably predict the occurrence of the UCS. Second, the CS also must be informative. Classical conditioning is a powerful means by which we learn to respond emotionally to a host of desirable or fearful stimuli.

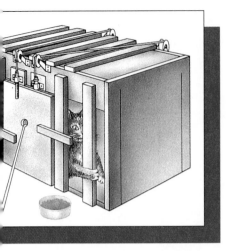

Figure 6.4 A Thorndike Puzzle Box
To get out of the puzzle box and obtain food, Thorndike's cat had to manipulate a mechanism that would release a weight that would then pull the door open.

law of effect Basic law of learning that states that the power of a stimulus to evoke a response is strengthened when the response is followed by a reward and weakened when it is not followed by a reward.

Operant Conditioning

At about the same time that Pavlov was using classical conditioning to induce Russian dogs to salivate to the sound of a bell, **Edward L. Thorndike** (1898) was watching American cats trying to escape from puzzle boxes (see **Figure 6.4**). He reported his observations and his inferences about the kind of learning taking place in his subjects:

> When put into the box, the cat shows evident signs of discomfort and develops an impulse to escape from confinement. It tries to squeeze through any opening; it claws and bites at the bars or wire; it thrusts its paws out through any opening and claws at everything it reaches. . . . The cat that is clawing all over the box in [its] impulsive struggle will probably claw the string or loop or button so as to open the door. And gradually all the other unsuccessful impulses will be *stamped out* and the particular impulse leading to the successful act will be *stamped in* by the resulting pleasure, until, after many trials, the cat will, when put in the box, immediately claw the button or loop in a definite way. (Thorndike, 1898, p. 13)

According to Thorndike's procedure, learning was an association not between two stimuli (as in the experience of Pavlov's dogs) but between stimuli in the situation and a response that a subject learned to make—a *stimulus-response* (S-R) *connection*. Thorndike believed that responses repeatedly followed by rewards brought satisfaction and were strengthened or stamped in; nonrewarded responses were weakened or stamped out. Thorndike's conditioning procedure allowed an animal to respond freely, but only one of its responses would have a satisfying consequence.

The Law of Effect

According to Thorndike's "connectionist" theory, the learning of reinforced S-R connections occurs gradually and automatically in a mechanistic way as the animal experiences the consequences of its actions through blind *trial-and-error*. Gradually, the behaviors that have satisfying consequences increase in frequency; they eventually become the dominant response when the animal is placed in the puzzle box. Thorndike referred to this relationship between behavior and its consequences as the **law of effect.**

The law of effect has an important conceptual parallel to *natural selection* in evolution (Skinner, 1981). For both, the environment acts as the agent of selection. In natural selection, the environment determines which genes become more frequent in future populations. Similarly, the law of effect describes how environmental changes produced by behavior increase the frequency of that behavior in the future. Behaviors leading to satisfying or rewarding consequences are selected; they are likely to occur more frequently in the future than behaviors leading to unsatisfying or punishing consequences. For example, if you find that as you go to bed punching up your pillow makes your sleep more comfortable, you are likely to repeat the pillow-punching behavior more frequently, even when you sleep in a different bed with a different pillow.

While Thorndike created his theories based on animal learning, he also believed that the law of effect was applicable to human learning. His ideas had a major impact on the educational psychology of his time, even though he believed that learning involved trial-and-error without conscious thought. Your own early education may have included methods of practicing skills or memorizing information, in the expectation that such repeated efforts would improve your general ability to learn. However, Thorndike found that the study of animal learning was easier and allowed greater control over relevant variables than did the study of human learning. In most cases, his ultimate

hope was that this basic research with simpler animals would shed more light on the mysteries of human learning—on how we have learned the many *habits* that form our behavioral repertoires.

Behavior Analysis

B. F. Skinner embraced Thorndike's view that environmental consequences influenced the responses that preceded them, but he rejected all assumptions about *satisfaction* and about S-R *habits* being learned. Essentially, Skinner

B. F. Skinner is shown at work building a scale model of a Skinner box, a small cage for housing an animal. The experimenter is in control of the subject's physical environment.

rejected any interpretation that resorted to inferences about an organism's intentions, purposes, or goals. What an animal wanted was not important. Skinner refused to make inferences about what happens inside an organism. For example, while approaching food and eating it can be observed and recorded, desire for food or pleasure at receiving it cannot.

To analyze behavior experimentally, Skinner developed operant conditioning procedures in which he manipulated the consequences of an organism's behavior in order to see what effect it had on subsequent behavior. An **operant** is any behavior that is *emitted* by an organism and can be characterized in terms of the observable effects it has on the environment. Literally, *operant* means *affecting the environment,* or *operating* on it (Skinner, 1938). Unlike classically conditioned behaviors, operants are *not elicited* by specific stimuli as classically conditioned behaviors are. Pigeons peck, rats search for food, babies cry and coo, some people gesture while talking, and others stutter or say "like" and "you know" frequently. The probability of these behaviors occurring in the future can be increased or decreased by manipulating the effects they have on the environment. Operant conditioning, then, modifies the probability of different rates of operant behavior as a function of the environmental consequences they produce.

Behavior analysts manipulate contingencies of reinforcement to study behavior. Usually, this manipulation occurs within the highly controlled environment of a special apparatus invented by Skinner—the *operant chamber* (Baron et al., 1991).

In many operant experiments, a *cumulative recorder* is used to record the animal's responding and delivery of reinforcers. Each response "steps" a pen vertically across paper that is being rotated outward by a small moving drum. The greater the animal's response rate, the steeper the line drawn by the pen. Delivery of reinforcers is denoted by tiny hash marks drawn downward from this line.

Reinforcement

Significant events that can strengthen an organism's responses—if they are only delivered in connection with those responses—are called *reinforcers.* If an

An operant conditioning laboratory.

This porpoise has been trained through operant conditioning to leap over hurdles at Marine World.

attractive classmate only seems to smile at you when you offer help, and you volunteer your help more and more often as a result, this winsome smile is a reinforcer. Reinforcers are always defined empirically—in terms of their effects on changing the probability of a response. Reinforcers in operant conditioning situations differ from unconditional stimuli in classical conditioning situations because of the variations between the procedures used in each form of conditioning and not because of any special properties of the stimuli themselves.

A **reinforcement contingency** is a consistent relationship between a response and the changes in the environment that it produces. For example, the consistent relationship between your classmate's reinforcing smile and your offers of help shows that you see the smile as *contingent on* your willingness to help, but you need to be conscious of the contingency for it to work.

Using Skinner's work as a foundation, modern behavior analysts seek to understand behavior wholly in terms of reinforcement contingencies. Their primary goal is to understand complex behavior in terms of the reinforcement contingencies that teach and maintain it. By identifying the key properties of reinforcement as described below, behavior analysts apply their understanding of reinforcement contingencies to a wide variety of everyday situations—including programming learning in schools, modifying behavior in therapy, and even training porpoises and whales in zoos.

Increasing Responses. While the term *reinforcement* technically includes all processes of changing behavior, it is used most often to describe the contingencies that *increase* behavior. In this sense, behavior analysts have identified both positive reinforcers—which work when they are presented—and negative reinforcers—which work when they are removed or prevented.

Positive Reinforcers. Any stimulus that is contingent upon a behavior and increases the probability of that behavior over time is a **positive reinforcer.**

reinforcement contingency
Consistent relationship between a response and the changes it produces in the environment.

positive reinforcer Stimulus, received after a response, that increases the probability of that response.

Delivering a positive reinforcer contingent upon a response is *positive reinforcement*. A food pellet positively reinforces a rat to press a lever. Getting a laugh positively reinforces a human to tell a joke. Your obvious attention positively reinforces your professor to lecture.

Behavior that produces desirable consequences is reinforced and repeated. We can use this principle to identify what is desirable for those organisms that cannot communicate their desires. For example, newborn infants have been shown to learn a response (sucking on an artificial nipple) that gives them the opportunity to hear their mothers' voices instead of the voice of another female. The evidence shows that newborns can discriminate between speakers and that they prefer their own mothers' voices, and that operant conditioning can be used to assess the perceptual and motivational capacities of all organisms that cannot tell us in words. (DeCasper & Fifer, 1980).

Negative Reinforcers. Any stimulus that when removed, reduced, or prevented increases the probability of a given response over time is a **negative reinforcer.** The removal, reduction, or prevention of a negative reinforcer following a response is called *negative reinforcement*. Using an umbrella to prevent getting wet during a downpour is a common example of a behavior that is maintained by negative reinforcement. You avoid the negative reinforcer, rain, by using an umbrella. An automobile seat-belt buzzer also serves as a negative reinforcer; its annoying sound stops when the driver buckles up.

To distinguish between positive and negative reinforcement, try to remember the following: Both positive and negative reinforcement *increase* the probability of the response that precedes them. Positive reinforcement increases response probability by presenting a positive stimulus following a response; negative reinforcement does the same by removing, reducing, or preventing a negative stimulus following a response. As we saw in the umbrella example, staying dry is a positive stimulus that positively reinforces you to use an umbrella; the rain is a negative stimulus that negatively reinforces you to use an umbrella.

Decreasing Responses. Positive and negative reinforcement explain how new behaviors are acquired and old ones maintained. Suppose, however, that you wanted to *eliminate* an existing operant. How would you do it?

Extinction. One way to eliminate an existing operant would be to use **operant extinction,** a procedure in which delivery of a positive reinforcer is withheld. If the behavior does not produce any consequences, it returns to the level it was before operant conditioning; in other words, it is *extinguished*. For example, smiling and nodding are behaviors that may reinforce your professor to look at you often. Withholding these reinforcers will decrease the probability of the professor looking at you as often. Have you ever had the experience of dropping a few coins into a vending machine and getting nothing in return? If you kicked the machine and your soda or candy came out, kicking would be reinforced. However, if your kicking produced no soda or candy but only a sore foot, kicking would quickly be extinguished.

An unwanted response is extinguished only if all reinforcers can really be withheld. Complete withholding is difficult outside the laboratory where many aspects of one's environment are not under the control of readily identifiable reinforcers. Extinction is thus more likely to occur when withholding of reinforcers is combined with positive reinforcement to increase the probability of the desired response. A child who throws tantrums in public to get his parents' attention is most likely to stop such misbehavior if it doesn't work any more (an example of extinction—as hard as that may be when parents are distressed at the child's display in public!) and when the child discovers that other, more socially approved behaviors (such as asking a question politely) do elicit attention (positive reinforcement).

negative reinforcer Stimulus that increases the probability of a response when it is terminated or avoided after that response.

operant extinction Withholding a positive reinforcer to extinguish an operant behavior.

Kicking a vending machine would be reinforced if candy or soda came out as a result.

The punishment of the pain resulting from touching a hot stove decreases the probability that the child will do it again.

punisher Aversive stimulus that decreases the probability of the preceding response.

Punishment. Punishment is another technique for decreasing the probability of a response. Any stimulus that is made contingent upon a response and decreases the probability of that response over time is called a **punisher.** *Punishment* is the delivery of a punisher following a response. Touching a hot stove, for example, produces pain that punishes the preceding action (or response) so that you are less likely next time to touch the stove. Responses that are punished immediately tend to decrease in frequency; however, responses that produce delayed aversive consequences are only suppressed. When a formerly punished response no longer produces aversive consequences, it tends to increase in frequency to prepunishment levels.

For example, immediately spanking a child for playing with matches will probably suppress the dangerous behavior. But if the child learns to play with matches only in times and places where she will not be caught, she may eventually play with them just as much as ever—out of sight of those who would punish her. (See "Time Out for Critical Thinking.")

Although punishment and negative reinforcement are closely related, they differ in important ways. By definition, punishment always *decreases* a response or *reduces* its probability of occurring again. In contrast, negative reinforcement is defined as always *increasing* the response's probability of recurring. For example, some people get severe headaches after drinking caffeinated beverages. The headache is the stimulus that *punishes* and reduces the behavior of drinking caffeinated products. However, once they have the headache, people will often take pain-relieving medication to eliminate it. Pain relief is the stimulus that *negatively reinforces* such drug-taking behavior.

➡ TIME OUT . . . FOR CRITICAL THINKING

A word of caution is in order regarding the *use* and *abuse* of punishment in family and institutional settings. To eliminate undesired behaviors, it is always preferable to reinforce the alternative, desired behavior than it is to punish the undesired behavior. When reinforcement cannot or does not stop the negative action swiftly enough and punishment is the only alternative, psychological research shows that punishment should meet the following conditions:

- Punishment should be swift and brief.

- It should be administered immediately after the response occurs.

- It should be limited in intensity.

- It should be specific to the person's behavior, and never to the person's character.

- It should be limited to the situation where the response occurs.

- The punishment should not give mixed messages to the person being punished.

- Finally, effective punishment consists of *penalties* (such as the loss of privileges) instead of physical *pain*. (Walters & Grusec, 1977)

Given such an extensive checklist, it is doubtful that most old-fashioned disciplinarians would meet these requirements. Are the consequences of punishment—such as verbal or physical assaults—serious enough that we should rethink such cultural beliefs as "Spare the rod, spoil the child"? Research consistently argues that they are. Using punishment to control human behavior indicates that authority figures do not understand how to positively motivate or reward those in their power. Punishers can "go overboard" and abuse their victims, especially children. It causes physical harm, emotional scars, and hatred of the punisher. Worst of all, the punished person learns that aggression is an acceptable means of controlling others (Bongiovanni, 1977; Hyman, in Schmidt, 1987).

Considering the difficulty of making punishment effective (using the preceding seven-point list) and the tragedy of ineffective punishment, can you think of alternative strategies for reducing or eliminating each of the following problem behaviors?

- A five-year-old hides in a closet to experiment with matches because her parents have warned her not to play with them.

- A second-grade boy who is big for his age repeatedly teases and hits smaller classmates.

- A girl in junior high school fails to pay attention, and annoys other students by asking them questions when they are supposed to be working quietly.

- In a government office, an employee who does careful work progresses more slowly than everyone else and always misses deadlines.

- A friend of yours is chronically late or forgetful—making plans to meet you but always showing up late or not at all.

Finally, think about the types of punishment you have received during your life. Were they effective? Did some punishments cause regrettable side effects? Would other strategies have taught or shaped you differently? In what ways did punishment change you?

Applying Reinforcement

Reinforcers and punishers are the power brokers of operant conditioning; they change or maintain behavior. Contingent reinforcement strengthens responding; contingent punishment suppresses responding. Noncontingent stimuli have little effect on behavior; if your behavior does not seem to be a condition for the good or bad things that befall you, you are unlikely to change it.

Unlike most other species, humans can learn even when behavioral consequences are long delayed rather than immediate. You typically get your grade on an exam days after you have studied for and taken the test, but if the feedback is positive, your response (studying for the next test) is likely to be strengthened. Although your test score is the reinforcer of your interest in testing situations, just taking the test and being able to respond quickly and confidently to some items will reinforce the way you usually study.

Conditioned Reinforcers. In operant conditioning, neutral stimuli paired with primary reinforcers, such as food and water, can become **conditioned reinforcers** for operant responses. They can then come to serve as ends in themselves. Human behavior is influenced by a wide variety of conditioned reinforcers. Money, grades, praise, smiles of approval, gold stars, and various kinds of status symbols are among the many potent conditioned reinforcers that can influence our learning and behavior.

Virtually any stimulus can become a conditioned reinforcer by being paired with a primary reinforcer. In an early study, simple tokens were used as conditioned reinforcers with animal learners.

In an early study, chimps were trained to learn how to solve problems with edible raisins as primary reinforcers. Then tokens were delivered along with the

conditioned reinforcers In operant conditioning, a formerly neutral stimulus that has become a reinforcer.

Inedible tokens can be used as conditioned reinforcers with animals. In one study, chimps deposited tokens in a "chimp-o-mat" in exchange for raisins.

Premack principle Principle developed by David Premack that a more preferred activity can be used to reinforce a less preferred activity.

shaping Also *training by successive approximations,* operant learning technique in which a new behavior is produced by reinforcing responses that approach the desired performance.

schedules of reinforcement In operant conditioning, patterns of delivering and withholding reinforcement.

partial reinforcement effect Principle that behavioral responses acquired through intermittent reinforcement resist extinction more than those continuously reinforced.

raisins. When only the tokens were presented, the chimps continued working for their "money" because they could later deposit their hard-earned tokens in a "chimp-o-mat" designed to exchange tokens for the raisins (Cowles, 1937).

In some mental institutions, *token economies* have been set up based on these principles. Desired behaviors (grooming or taking medication, for example) are explicitly defined, and token payoffs are given by the staff when these behaviors are performed. Tokens can later be exchanged by the patients for a wide array of rewards and privileges (Ayllon & Azrin, 1965; Holden, 1978). These systems of reinforcement are especially effective in promoting patients' self-care, maintenance of their environment, and positive interactions with others. However, systems of behavior modification that rely on token reinforcement have been criticized as resorting to materialistic values instead of humanistic ones. Another criticism is that for any token economy to work, the patients or clients must first be deprived of all basic resources, so that earning tokens gets them the bare necessities of life. Thus it is a strategy that only works with the relatively poor and deprived.

Preferred Activities. In the laboratory positive reinforcers are usually substances such as food or water. However, outside the laboratory there are many more behavior reinforcers in operation. For example, when you have several chores to do, you probably prefer some over others. If you have been putting off work on a psychology paper, you may find you "want" to write a return letter to a friend or do your laundry instead. People who exercise regularly might use a daily run or fitness class as a "reward" for getting other tasks done. Grade-school teachers have even found that children will learn to sit still if such behavior is reinforced with permission to run and scream (Homme et al., 1963).

The principle that a more preferred activity can be used to reinforce a less preferred one is called the **Premack principle**—so named after its discoverer **David Premack** (1965). He found that water-deprived rats learned to increase their running in an exercise wheel when the running was followed by an opportunity to drink. Other rats that were not thirsty but exercise-deprived would learn to increase their drinking when that response was followed by a chance to run.

According to the Premack principle, a reinforcer may be any event or activity that is valued by the organism. The Premack principle is often used by parents and teachers to get children to engage in low-probability activities. For a socially outgoing child, playing with friends can reinforce the less pleasant task of finishing homework first. For a shy child, reading a new book can be used to reinforce the less preferred activity of playing with other children. The valued activity can be used as a reinforcer and thus increase the probability that the individual will engage in an activity that is not valued. Over time, there is the possibility that less-favored activities will become more valued as exposure to them leads individuals to discover their intrinsic worth. For example, the once-shy child might eventually enjoy playing with others.

Shaping. Reinforcing behavior only once or twice in the presence of a discriminative stimulus is usually not sufficient to produce learning. So-called *one-trial learning* is unusual enough in most species to warrant this special label. In the laboratory, behavior analysts train new behaviors with a method called *shaping* or *training by successive approximations,* which means reinforcing any responses that successively approximate (resemble or come close to) and ultimately match the desired response.

Shaping is a procedure for changing behavior in small steps that successively approximate the desired end performance. When shaping begins, any element of the target response is reinforced. When this element occurs regularly, only responses more like the final goal response are reinforced. By reinforc-

Animals can learn to do some surprising things, with a little help from their human friends and the application of operant conditioning techniques. Water skiing, anyone?

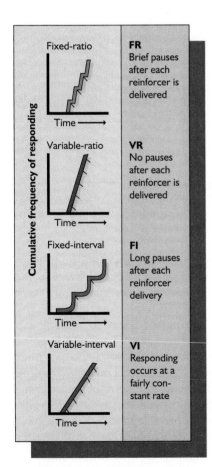

Figure 6.5 Reinforcement Schedules
These different patterns of behavior are produced by four simple schedules of reinforcement. The hash marks indicate when reinforcement is delivered.

ing more and more specific versions of the target behavior, an experimenter can shape this higher-level action.

Suppose that you wish to train an animal, such as a rat, to press a lever in an operant chamber. The rat has learned to use its paws in many ways, but it probably has never pressed a lever before. First, you deprive the rat of food for a day, to make food a valuable reinforcer. Next, you teach it to eat food from the food hopper in an operant chamber. When the rat is properly motivated and trained to find food, you can begin the shaping process. You start by delivering food only when the rat behaves in specific ways, such as leaning toward the lever. Next, food is delivered only as the rat moves closer to the lever. Soon the requirement for reinforcement is actually to touch the lever. Finally, the rat must depress the lever to trigger food delivery. Now the rat can be left on its own; it has learned—one step at a time—that it can produce food by pressing the lever.

The possibilities of shaping suggest that humans and nonhumans alike will search for ways to respond to new situations in their environments. "In Focus: Learned Helplessness" on page 218 considers the consequences of discovering that none of your responses is effective—a condition known as *learned helplessness.*

Schedules of Reinforcement. Sometimes when you raise your hand in class the teacher calls on you, and sometimes not. Some slot machine players continue to put coins in even though the reinforcers (the payoff) are delivered rarely. Obviously, behavior is not always followed by reinforcement or punishment. **Schedules of reinforcement**—patterns of delivering the consequences of behavior—have marked effects on how rapidly learning occurs and how resistant learned responses are to extinction.

There is a legendary story about the way the young B. F. Skinner accidentally discovered the first schedule of reinforcement. One weekend Skinner was secluded in his laboratory with not enough of a food-reward supply for his hard-working rats. He economized by giving the rats pellets after every two responses rather than after each one. From the rats' points of view, half the time they responded they got reinforcers and half the time they did not. The rats still acquired the operant response, although more slowly than usual. Later, when these animals underwent extinction training—their responses were followed by no pellets at all—they continued to respond longer and more vigorously than did rats who had gotten payoffs after every response. This **partial reinforcement effect**—a more durable response—is now a widely established principle: Responses acquired under schedules of partial reinforcement are more resistant to extinction than those acquired with continuous reinforcement (Bitterman, 1975). To keep a learned response going for a long time in the absence of rewards, researchers deliver reinforcement during training occasionally but not continuously.

For example, if you could only learn new behavior if you were reinforced *every time* you performed in the desired way, teaching or coaching you would be a very expensive and exhausting proposition. Teachers and coaches are therefore relieved to know that they may deliver only partial reinforcement—occasionally but not *always* saying "Good work!" or "Nice try"—and still encourage steady effort. As illustrated in **Figure 6.6** and discussed below, different reinforcement schedules have different effects on behavior.

Fixed-Ratio (FR) Schedules. In *fixed-ratio schedules,* the reinforcer comes after the organism has emitted a fixed number of responses. When reinforcement follows one response, the schedule is called an *FR-1 schedule.* If the first 24 responses are unreinforced but reinforcement follows every twenty-fifth response, the schedule is an *FR-25 schedule.* The FR-1 schedule, or *continuous reinforcement schedule,* is the most efficient for rapidly shaping an animal to acquire a new response. FR schedules generate high rates of response because there is a direct correlation between responding and reinforcement—the more

If reinforcement increases desirable responses while punishment suppresses undesirable responses, what happens when the individual gets punished arbitrarily regardless of the response? Imagine that, after years of raising your hand in classes to get teachers' attention, you take a class in which the teacher makes fun of you for raising your hand, suggesting that you must think you are in elementary school. The teacher never calls on you, no matter how you signal your desire to be called on. What do you do? One simple answer is that you give up—you stop trying to get the teacher's attention. Because environmental consequences do not seem to be related in any contingent or meaningful way to what you do, you stop trying to control them. This passive resignation that follows prolonged, noncontingent, inescapable punishment is termed **learned helplessness.**

Learned helplessness was discovered by **Martin Seligman** and **Steven Maier** (1967) in a study on dogs who received painful, unavoidable shocks. Some of the dogs could escape the shocks by learning to press a switch that stopped the shock (negative reinforcement). However, others continued to get shocked no matter what response they made (noncontingent punishment). In the next phase, each dog was put into a shuttlebox (a two-part cage). The dogs could escape the shocks on the grid floor by jumping over the small hurdle between the two compartments of the box. Just before a shock was given, a tone sounded (the conditional stimulus). Some of the dogs—those who had learned to escape before by pressing the switch—soon learned that tone reliably predicted shock; these dogs escaped to the safe side of the box as soon as the tone signal came on. The dogs who had been exposed previously to noncontingent punishment, however, did not escape the painful shocks, even when it was possible and easy to do so. Instead, they crouched, barked, or shook with fear; they seemed to have given up.

The passively resigned dogs' impaired performance included three common characteristics: *motivational deficits*—they were slow to initiate known actions; *emotional deficits*—they appeared rigid, listless, frightened, and distressed; and *cognitive deficits*—they demonstrated poor learning in new situations where simple new responding would be reinforced. Even when these dogs were repeatedly dragged over the hurdle to the safe side of the box, they did not learn to jump over on their own (Maier & Seligman, 1976).

There are some obvious parallels between learned helplessness in animals and depression in humans (Seligman, 1975). However, in the case of humans, we must consider cognitive factors—the ways in which they interpret situations of noncontingency. Do humans attribute failure to personal factors or to situational features? How important is it for them to have a sense of control over their outcomes (Abramson et al., 1978)? We will answer these questions in Chapter 13 when we investigate clinical depression.

---

learned helplessness Pattern of not responding to noxious stimuli after an organism learns its behavior has no effect.

"FR 25! Pass it on!"

responses the more often reinforcement is delivered. When workers get paid once after making or selling a given total number of units, FR schedules are in operation.

Variable-Ratio (VR) Schedules. In *a variable-ratio schedule,* the number of responses required for reinforcement varies from one reinforcer delivery to the next. A VR-10 schedule means that *on the average* reinforcement follows every tenth response; but it might come after only one response or after twenty responses. Variable-ratio schedules generate the highest rate of responding and the greatest resistance to extinction, especially when the VR value is large. A pigeon on a VR-110 schedule will respond with up to 12,000 pecks per hour and will continue responding for hours with no reinforcement. Gambling would seem to be under the control of VR schedules. The response of dropping coins in slot machines is maintained by the payoff that is delivered only after an unknown, variable number of coins has been deposited. VR schedules leave us guessing when the reward will come; we gamble that it will be after the next response and not much later.

Fixed-Interval (FI) Schedules. On a *fixed-interval schedule,* a reinforcer is delivered for the first response made after a fixed period of time has elapsed. On an FI-10 schedule, the subject, after receiving any one reinforcer, will have to wait at least 10 seconds before another response is reinforced. Other responses in between, before the time interval has elapsed, have no programmed consequences; they do not count toward reinforcement. Immediately after each reinforced response, the animal makes few if any responses; it takes a time out without making meaningful responses. As time passes, the animal responds more and more until, eventually, it is payoff time.

Human examples of fixed-interval schedules often involve waiting until a deadline before taking critical action. For example, soldiers in boot camp must pass inspection in order to earn weekend leave. The purpose of such a contingency is to train recruits always to keep their belongings orderly and prepared. However, most troops soon learn they safely can leave their gear in a disorderly heap all week, as long as they clean it up just in time for inspection. Threats of surprise inspections or, for students, pop quizzes, are designed to keep the desired behavior on a more consistent response level.

Variable-Interval (VI) Schedules. With *variable-interval schedules,* reinforcement is delivered to the first response made after a variable period of time has elapsed since the last reinforcement. On a VI-20 schedule, reinforcers are delivered, on the average, once every 20 seconds. Thus, a response after 10 seconds is sometimes followed by a reinforcer, but sometimes 30 seconds must pass before a response is reinforced. Responses during the intervening interval have no effect on reinforcement. This schedule generates a low but stable response rate; extinction is gradual and much slower than under fixed-interval schedules. There is a steady decline in responding without reinforcement, but subjects trained under a long VI schedule continue to respond for long periods. In one case, a pigeon pecked 18,000 times during the first 4 hours after reinforcement stopped and required 168 hours before its responding extinguished completely (Ferster & Skinner, 1957).

SUMMING UP

Drawing from his research on cats in puzzle boxes, Thorndike formulated his law of effect: Behavior that produces "satisfying" outcomes tends to be repeated. Skinner incorporated the law of effect into his study of operant conditioning. Emitted behaviors are called operants because they operate on or change the environment. Skinner's analytic approach centers on manipulating contingencies of reinforcement and observing the effects on behavior. A positive reinforcer is any stimulus that, when made contingent upon a behavior, increases the probability of that behavior over time. A negative reinforcer is any stimulus that, when removed, reduced, or prevented following a response, increases the probability of that response over time. Two ways to reduce or eliminate behavior are extinction, which is the withholding of a positive or negative reinforcer, and punishment, which is the delivery of an aversive stimulus contingent upon responding.

Primary reinforcers are biologically important stimuli that function as reinforcers even though an organism may have had no previous experience with them. Conditioned reinforcers are learned; for humans, these reinforcers include money, praise, and status symbols. Behavior may be shaped by successively reinforcing closer approximations of the desired response. Partial or intermittent reinforcement leads to greater resistance to extinction than continuous reinforcement. Behavior is affected by schedules of reinforcement that may be fixed or that vary in the number of responses or in the temporal patterning of reinforcers. On ratio schedules, reinforcers are delivered after a certain number of responses that may be constant (fixed) or irregular (variable). On interval schedules, reinforcers are delivered after a specified interval of time that may also be fixed or variable.

When punishment is not contingent on behavior but occurs regardless of what the organism does, a state of learned helplessness may emerge. The learned helplessness syndrome includes the triad of deficits in motivation, emotion, and cognition; it also has parallels to states of human depression.

Learning, Biology, and Cognition

The bulk of research on animal learning has focused on arbitrarily chosen responses to conveniently available stimuli in artificial laboratory environments. The laboratory approach was adopted purposely by researchers who believed that the laws of learning they uncovered would be powerful general principles of behavior for all organisms and all types of learning. Critics have argued that traditional behavior theory did not do justice to the conception of humans as controllers of their own lives. Personal autonomy, inner directedness, or reason-based actions had no rightful place in this view of learning (Schwartz & Lacey, 1982).

Centuries ago, English philosopher David Hume (1771) first proposed the contemporary view that all human and animal learning can be accounted for by similar principles of association. Hume reasoned that a given theory of human action would be more believable "if we find that the same theory is requisite to explain the same phenomena in all other animals" (Hume, 1977/1951, p. 104). In other words, a theory that only "works" for humans but not for other creatures cannot be much of a theory.

The appealing simplicity of such a view has come under attack in the last three decades as psychologists have discovered certain *constraints,* or limitations, on the generality of the findings regarding conditioning. Some constraints are imposed by the biological makeup of the organism and the environmental habitats to which particular species must normally adapt (Leger, 1991). Other constraints are imposed by the fact that animal learners can think, reason, interpret, and attribute meaning and causality to stimulus events and to behavior. These cognitive processes serve to make conditioning less mechanical and more flexible than originally believed—making possible more complex kinds of learning than those envisioned in the simpler views of conditioning.

Biological Constraints on Learning

To fit a given ecological niche, each species must develop certain behaviors that aid survival. For instance, birds living on steep cliffs must make nests so that their eggs will not roll out; the offspring of birds that make the wrong kind of nests die and fail to pass on their genes. Different species may have different capacities for learning in a given situation—notably the habitat in which their species usually functions. Some relationships between CSs and UCSs, or behavior and its consequences, may be more difficult for some organisms to learn than others, depending on their relevance to those organisms' survival.

Biological constraints on learning are limitations on learning imposed by a species' genetic endowment. These constraints can apply to the animal's sensory, behavioral, and cognitive capacities. The fact that there are such constraints suggests that the principles of conditioning cannot be universally applied to all species across all situations and that not all reinforcement contingencies work equally well to produce learning in any given species. Two areas of research, on species-specific behavior and taste-aversion learning, show that behavior-environment relations can be *biased* by an organism's genotype.

Species-Specific Behavior. You have seen animals performing tricks on television, or in live displays and exhibits. Some animals play baseball or table tennis and others drive tiny race cars. For years, **Keller** and **Marion Breland** used operant conditioning techniques to train thousands of animals from many different species to perform a remarkable array of such behaviors. The Brelands believed that they could apply general principles derived from laboratory research using virtually any type of response or reward to control animal behavior outside the laboratory.

biological constraints on learning
Limitation on an organism's capacity to learn that is caused by inherited capabilities of the species.

Keller and Marion Breland used operant conditioning techniques to train thousands of animals from many different species to perform a remarkable array of behaviors. At some point after their training, however, some of their animals began to "misbehave." This experience convinced the Brelands that, even when animals have learned to make operant responses perfectly, the newly "learned behavior drifts toward instinctual behavior" over time.

instinctual drift Tendency over time for learned behavior to relapse and resemble instinctual behavior.

At some point after their training, however, some of their animals began to "misbehave." For example, a raccoon was trained, after great difficulty, to pick up a coin, put it into a toy bank, and collect an edible reinforcer. The raccoon, however, would not immediately deposit the coin. Later, when there were two coins to be deposited, conditioning broke down completely—the raccoon would not give up the coins at all. Instead, it would rub the coins together, dip them into the bank, and then pull them back out. Such behavior seems strange until you consider that raccoons often engage in rubbing and washing behaviors as they remove the outer shells of a favorite food, crayfish.

This experience convinced the Brelands that, even when animals have learned to make operant responses perfectly, the newly "learned behavior drifts toward instinctual behavior" over time. They termed this tendency **instinctual drift** (Breland & Breland, 1951, 1961). The animals' behavior is understandable if we consider the species-specific tendencies imposed by an inherited genotype—for example, that raccoons naturally rub objects together before eating them. These tendencies override the temporary changes in behavior brought about by operant conditioning. In fact, the inherited behavioral pattern is incompatible with the operant conditioning task. The animals' misbehaviors were a manifestation of natural, biologically significant relationships interfering with learning a new sequence of behaviors.

Taste-Aversion Learning. When we were children, both of your authors had bad experiences with distinctive foods. One of us got sick after eating pork and beans in the grade-school lunchroom. The other had been ill and experienced worsening nausea after eating home-made fried apples. In both cases, we attributed our sickness to the distinctive smell and taste of the food, not to any other possible environmental cause or preexisting condition. And for both of us, the very smell or appearance of the "culprit" food triggered reactions of nausea and avoidance.

Our experience with these biases is not strange. Humans and many other animals readily form an association between illness and a small class of likely causes—food. Did we learn this bias or is it a part of the genetic endowment?

taste-aversion learning Biological constraint on learning in which an organism learns in one trial to avoid a food when eating it is followed by illness.

Taste-aversion learning, or the tendency to associate a substance's taste with illness caused by eating that substance, represents a genetic bias in learning. Indeed, studies of taste aversion seem to violate the usual principles of conditioning but make sense when viewed as part of a species' adaptiveness to its natural environment.

Experimental Evidence. Suppose that a rat eats poisoned bait, and many hours later becomes ill but survives. After only this one pairing—and despite the long interval (up to 12 hours) between tasting the food (CS) and experiencing poisoned-based illness (UCS)—the rat learns to avoid other foods with that specific flavor. No principle in classical conditioning can adequately explain such one-trial learning and why such a long CS-UCS interval is effective in eliciting a CR.

Interestingly enough, other stimuli present at the same time are not avoided later—only those associated with *taste,* as shown in a study by **John Garcia,** the psychologist who first discovered the phenomenon of taste-aversion learning. According to Garcia's work with his colleague Robert Koelling (1966), in particular species of animals there are some CS-UCS combinations that can be classically conditioned—and some that cannot be learned. For example, the experimental rats learned an association between the flavor of the bait and a later illness; they did not learn to associate the flavor with a simultaneous pain. Similarly, they learned to associate sound and light cues with a shock-produced pain, but did not connect these sensory cues with illness (see **Figure 6.6**). (It is tempting to take off the behaviorist hat and infer that this probably makes "sense" to the rat, since drinking can cause illness while something that involves light and noise can cause pain—but not vice versa.) Garcia and Koelling's results suggest that rats have an inborn bias to associate particular stimuli with particular consequences.

bait shyness Unlearned aversion to novel foods or to familiar foods in novel environments or conditions.

Even without conditioning, most animals show **bait shyness,** an unlearned reluctance to sample new foods or even familiar food in a strange environment. Of all the stimuli available to them, animals seem to use the sensory cues—of taste, smell, or appearance—that are most adaptive in their natural environments to respond to potential edible or dangerous foods. Evolution has provided organisms with a survival mechanism for avoiding foods that are toxic and thus illness-producing, and perhaps all unfamiliar foods are responded to as potentially toxic until proven otherwise. In a sense, only "fools rush in" where animals fear to eat.

Applications of Taste Aversion. The principles of conditioned food aversion have been applied to treating a diverse range of subjects, from coyotes to cancer patients. To stop coyotes from killing sheep (and sheep ranchers from shooting coyotes), John Garcia and his colleagues put toxic lamb burgers wrapped in sheep fur on the outskirts of fenced-in areas of sheep ranches. The

The coyote is showing species-specific disgust responses to the carcass of prey after having been exposed to taste-aversion conditioning.

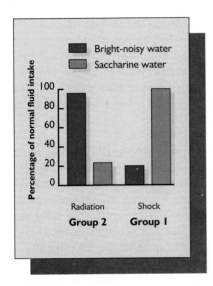

Figure 6.6 Inborn Bias
Results from Garcia and Koelling's study (1966) showed that rats possess an inborn bias to associate certain cues with certain outcomes. Rats avoided saccharine-flavored water when it predicted illness but not when it predicted shock. Similarly, rats avoided the "bright-noisy water" when it predicted shock but not when it predicted illness.

observational learning Learning new responses by watching another individual's behavior.

coyotes who ate these lamb burgers got sick, vomited, and developed an instant distaste for lamb meat. Their subsequent disgust at the mere sight of sheep makes them back away instead of attack them (Garcia, 1990).

Cancer patients often develop aversions to normal foods in their diets to such an extent that they become anorexic and malnourished. In part, their aversions are a serious consequence of their chemotherapy treatments, which produce nausea and often follow meals. Researchers are working to prevent the development of aversions to nutritive foods—necessary in the diets of children with cancer—by arranging for meals not to be given just before the chemotherapy and by presenting the children with a "scapegoat" aversion. They are given candies or unusually flavored ice cream before the treatments so that the taste aversion becomes conditioned only to those special flavors. Extension of this practical solution to cancer may be a lifesaver for some cancer patients (Bernstein, 1988).

Some instances of conditioning, then, depend on the way an organism is genetically predisposed toward stimuli in its environment (Barker et al., 1978). What any organism can—and cannot—learn in a given setting is to some extent a product of its evolutionary history.

Cognitive Influences on Learning

Despite Skinner's insistence on building a psychology of learning based solely on observable events, cognitive processes are significant in many kinds of learning. *Cognition* is any mental activity involved in the representation and processing of knowledge. Cognitive activities include thinking, remembering, perceiving, and using language. Because these processes cannot be observed, their involvement in learning must be inferred in a variety of research discoveries.

Observational Learning. Unless you enjoy taking risks, chances are that you look before you leap into new ventures and uncertain situations. Recognizing the right cues enables you to behave appropriately and avoid embarrassment. Much social learning occurs in situations where learning would not be predicted by traditional conditioning theory, because a learner has made no active response and has received no tangible reinforcer. The individual has simply watched another person exhibiting behavior that was reinforced and later behaved in exactly the same way; or the individual observed behavior that was punished and refrained from that behavior. **Observational learning** is the type of learning that occurs when someone uses observations of another person's actions and their consequences to guide his or her future actions.

A classic demonstration of observational learning occurred in the laboratory of **Albert Bandura.** After watching adult models of behavior punching, hitting, and kicking a large plastic BoBo doll, the children in the experiment later showed a greater frequency of the same behaviors than did children in control conditions who had not observed the aggressive models (Bandura et al., 1963). Subsequent studies showed that children imitated such behaviors just from watching filmed sequences of models, even when the models were cartoon characters.

There is little question now that we learn much—both prosocial (helping) and antisocial (hurting) behaviors—through observation of models. This capacity to learn from watching as well as from doing is extremely useful. It enables us to acquire large, integrated patterns of behavior without going through tedious trial-and-error. Observational learning also enables us to profit from the mistakes and successes of others. Our ability to learn from *others'* lessons saves us the redundancy and frustration of having to "reinvent the wheel" every time we encounter a dilemma we have seen others face.

As you might expect, much psychological research has been directed at assessing the behavioral impact that TV's modeled behavior has on viewers (Huston, 1989; Williams, 1986). In controlled laboratory studies, the two major effects of filmed violence were a reduction in emotional arousal and distress at viewing violence (conditions resulting in *psychic numbing*) and an increase in the likelihood of engaging in aggressive behavior (Murray & Kippax, 1979).

Cognitive Maps. Psychologist **Edward C. Tolman** (1886–1959) was among the first to demonstrate the importance of cognitive processes in learning. He accepted the behaviorists' idea that psychologists must study observable behavior, but he created many situations in which mechanical, one-to-one associations between specific stimuli and responses could not explain the behavior that he observed. Tolman (1948) claimed that learning probably involved two components: a **cognitive map,** or inner representation of the learning situation as a whole, and an *expectancy* about the consequences of one's actions.

Tolman and his students performed a series of studies on *place learning*. They demonstrated that, in a maze, when an original goal-path is blocked, an animal will take the shortest detour around the barrier, even though that particular response was never previously reinforced (Tolman & Honzig, 1930). **Figure 6.7** shows the arrangement of one such maze. Rats behaved as if they were responding to an internal cognitive map, rather than blindly exploring different parts of the maze through trial-and-error. More recent experiments on cognitive maps in rats, chimpanzees, and humans have confirmed Tolman's earlier findings (Menzel, 1978; Moar, 1980; Olton, 1979). Organisms learn the general layout of their environment by exploration, even if they are not reinforced for learning particular paths.

Tolman's results showed that learning is neither blind nor simple. Conditioning includes the learning of expectancies, predictions, and judgments—cognitive factors—as well as learning about other facets of the total behavioral context (Balsam & Tomie, 1985). For example, a student using a computer hears thunder and realizes a storm is brewing. Knowing that electrical storms can cause disruptions in power, she saves the file to prevent the loss

cognitive map Mental representation of physical space.

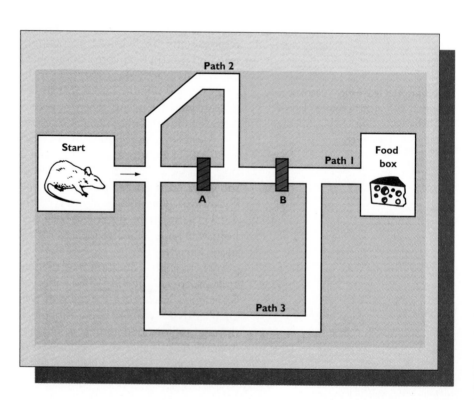

Figure 6.7 Use of Cognitive Maps in Maze Learning
Subjects preferred the direct path (path 1) when it was open. With a block at A, they preferred path 2. When a block was placed at B, the rats usually chose path 3. Their behavior seemed to indicate that they had a cognitive map of the best way to get the food.

From top to bottom: Adult models aggression; boy imitates aggression; girl imitates aggression.

of her data. This precaution may not turn out to be necessary, but experience has taught her to use available information (for example, signs of a storm) to form expectations and predictions (for example, the computer could lose power, she might lose her file) and take appropriate action (for example, save the file).

In the past two decades, there has been a significant shift among psychologists from the behavioral viewpoint toward cognitive approaches to learning. At the same time, there has been an increased recognition of the significance of evolutionary and neurological processes in learning (Garcia & Garcia y Robertson, 1985; McGaugh et al., 1985; Thompson, 1986).

Learning More About Learning. Our understanding of how humans and animals learn has come a long way from the early studies of Pavlov, Thorndike, and Skinner. Researchers are exploring the basic principles of conditioning and learning in many exciting new directions. The search for the biological bases of learning and the interest in the cognitive dimension of human learning have expanded. The new evolutionary perspective adds another dimension. We are also witnessing a wider, practical utilization of learning theory in psychotherapy—including programs for stress reduction and health management. Learning theory has been applied in homes, sports arenas, businesses, supermarkets, industry, transit systems, television, and school systems (Krasner, 1985).

SUMMING UP

Research has uncovered constraints that limit the possibilities of human and animal learning. For some types of animals, only certain actions—species-specific behavior—can be observed. In some cases, learned sequences of behavior are disrupted by instinctual drift, a tendency to behave in original, unlearned patterns. Another constraint is demonstrated by taste aversion—humans' and animals' ability to connect consequences (like illness) only with "likely" stimuli (like food) rather than other conditions.

Cognitive influences on learning include the ability to learn by observing others and the capacity to develop cognitive maps. Research on observation learning confirms that humans learn from a variety of live and fictional models, including depictions on television. Tolman's work with rats learning to run mazes confirms that even simple creatures can learn from experience to form internal models to guide later behavior. Research on learning continues to explore new models and generate new applications to human and nonhuman experience.

CHAPTER REVIEW

1   Learning About Learning   *How is learning different from other changes in behavior? How is the behavioristic view of learning distinct from other perspectives?*

The capacity for learning depends on genetic heritage and environmental influences. The study of learning has been dominated by behaviorism. Behaviorists believe that learning can be explained by the processes involved in classical and operant conditioning.

Key Terms
    fixed action patterns, p. 198
    learning, p. 199
    performance, p. 199

Major Contributors
    Watson, John B., p. 200
    Skinner, B. F., p. 201

2   Classical Conditioning   *How does Pavlovian conditioning change reflexive behavior? What are the basic processes of classical conditioning?*

Classical conditioning, discovered by Pavlov, is widely used for investigating relationships between stimulus events. In classical conditioning, an unconditional stimulus (UCS) stimulates an unconditional response (UCR). A neutral stimulus paired with the UCS becomes a conditional stimulus (CS) that elicits a similar response, called the conditional response (CR). Extinction occurs when the UCS no longer follows the CS. In stimulus generalization, stimuli that are similar to the CS elicit the CR. For classical conditioning to occur, there must be a contingent relationship between the CS and UCS. The CS must be informative as well as predictive.

Key Terms
    classical conditioning, p. 201
    reflex, p. 202
    unconditional stimulus (UCS), p. 203
    unconditional response (UCR), p. 203
    conditional stimulus (CS), p. 203
    conditional response (CR), p. 203
    acquisition, p. 204
    extinction, p. 206
    spontaneous recovery, p. 206
    stimulus generalization, p. 206
    stimulus discrimination, p. 206

Major Contributors
    Pavlov, Ivan, p. 202
    Rescorla, Robert, p. 207
    Kamin, Leon, p. 208

3   Operant Conditioning   *What does the law of effect explain? What do behavior analysts do? What makes an experience reinforcing? Why are reinforcers and punishers considered the power brokers of operant conditioning?*

Thorndike's law of effect states that satisfying outcomes tend to be repeated. Skinner's behavior analytic approach centers on manipulating contingencies of reinforcement and observing the effects on behavior. There are two kinds of reinforcers: negative and positive. Withholding a reinforcer (until the behavior is extinguished) and punishment are the two ways of eliminating a behavior.

Primary reinforcers are stimuli that function as reinforcers even when an organism has not had previous experience with them. Conditioned reinforcers are learned. Complex responses may be learned through shaping. Partial or intermittent reinforcement leads to greater resistance to extinction than does continuous reinforcement. Behavior is affected by schedules to reinforcement that may be varied or fixed and delivered in intervals or in ratios.

Key Terms

law of effect, p. 209
operant, p. 211
reinforcement contingency,
    p. 212
positive reinforcer, p. 212
negative reinforcer, p. 213
operant extinction, p. 213
punisher, p. 214
conditioned reinforcers, p. 215
Premack principle, p. 216
shaping, p. 216
schedules of reinforcement, p. 217
partial reinforcement effect, p. 217
learned helplessness, p. 218

Major Contributors

Thorndike, Edward L.,
    p. 209
Premack, David, p. 216
Seligman, Martin, p. 218
Maier, Steven, p. 218

4 Learning, Biology, and Cognition *How do biological factors affect species' abilities to learn? What evidence suggests that organisms learn even when they are not reinforced? Does learning theory have any practical applications?*

Several lines of research evidence suggest that learning is constrained by genetic heritage and cognitive abilities. The species-specific repertoires of different organisms, adaptive in their natural environments, make some CS-UCS and response-reinforcement connections easier to learn than others. Further evidence of biological constraints on learning is found in instinctual drift and taste aversion. Cognitive influences on learning are shown in observational learning—learning from the actions of models—and the development of internalized cognitive maps. Research has led to a better understanding of learning, with many applications outside of the laboratory in everyday life.

Key Terms

biological constraints on learning,
    p. 220
instinctual drift, p. 221
taste-aversion learning, p. 222
bait shyness, p. 222
observational learning, p. 223
cognitive map, p. 224

Major Contributors

Breland, Keller, p. 220
Breland, Marion, p. 220
Garcia, John, p. 222
Bandura, Albert, p. 223
Tolman, Edward C., p. 224

PRACTICE TEST

Chapter 6: Learning

For each of the following items, choose the single correct or best answer. Correct answers, explanations, and page references appear in the Appendix.

1. According to the evolutionary perspective on learning theory, humans have probably inherited _____ .
   A. a capacity for learning that is uniquely shaped by experience
   B. a natural tendency to engage in simple, adaptive behaviors but not to conduct more complex activities
   C. self-protective abilities but not social skills
   D. no talents, tendencies, or capacities that would explain our ability to acquire behavior change

2. Much of modern psychology's view of learning finds its roots in the work of _____ , emphasizing the analysis of behavior.
   A. Wilhelm Wundt
   B. William James
   C. Sigmund Freud
   D. John B. Watson

3. A cat is fed a steady diet of canned food, served twice every day. Her human companion notices that in a short time the cat has learned to run to her food dish and look for the expected contents almost every time she hears the electric can opener running. In this demonstration of classical conditioning, the _____ is the UCS.
   A. sound of the can opener
   B. food dish
   C. cat food
   D. running behavior

4. For an organism to learn a conditioned association between two stimuli, the UCS must seem to _____ .
   A. predict the CS
   B. be predicted by the CS
   C. be independent of the CS
   D. None of the above.

5. According to Thorndike's law of effect, behavior is strengthened or not strengthened as a result of its _____ .
   A. consequences in the organism's environment
   B. association with stimuli similar to those that have triggered it
   C. purpose in the organism's efforts to survive
   D. level of complexity in the organism's repertoire

6. A _____ is a consistent relationship between a response and the changes in the environment that it produces.
   A. behavior potential
   B. behavior analysis
   C. reinforcement contingency
   D. conditioned reinforcer

7. "The best part of going to the beach," your friend exclaims as you start your vacation, "is getting away from all the stress of work and school." If this is true, then your friend's behavior has been influenced by _____ .
   A. positive reinforcement
   B. negative reinforcement
   C. extinction
   D. punishment

8. For punishment to be most effective, it should meet all *except which* of the following conditions?
   A. It should be swift and brief.
   B. It should be extremely intense.
   C. It should not give mixed messages.
   D. It should be focused on the response.

9. According to the Premack principle, a reinforcer can be anything that _____ .
   A. changes behavior from its past norms
   B. rewards rather than penalizes behavior
   C. becomes associated with an unconditional stimulus
   D. is valued by the organism, such as an activity

10. Instinctual drift and taste aversion are both examples of _____ .
    A. learned helplessness
    B. fear conditioning
    C. spontaneous recovery
    D. biological constraints on learning

IF YOU'RE INTERESTED . . .

Brubaker. (Video: 1980, color, 132 minutes). Directed by Stuart Rosenberg; starring Robert Redford, Yaphet Kotto, Jane Alexander, David Keith, Morgan Freeman.

Interesting melodrama based on true story of a prison warden trying to reform the practices of a corrupt Southern system. Some interesting images of how behavior might—and might not—change.

Clockwork Orange, A. (Video: 1971, color, 137 minutes). Directed by Stanley Kubrick; starring Malcolm McDowell, Patrick Magee, Adrienne Corri, Aubrey Morris, James Marcus.

Fascinating, disturbing film based on Anthony Burgess's novel about a futuristic society's efforts to reform a violent criminal by applying conditioning techniques.

Phillips, D. and Judd, R. (1978). *How to fall out of love.* New York: Fawcett Popular Library.

Interesting and surprisingly useful introduction to behavior modification applied to overcoming painful loss. Some techniques—such as thought-stopping and positive image building—can be applied to almost any intentional behavior change program. Numerous examples.

Seligman, M. E. P. (1991). *Learned optimism.* New York: Alfred A. Knopf.

A program for a healthy, positive lifestyle, proposed by the original researcher of learned helplessness. Includes self-assessment techniques and programs for escaping pessimism and acquiring optimistic, constructive life skills.

Skinner, B. F. (1976). *Walden two.* New York: Macmillan.

Skinner's dramatic proposal for using principles of reinforcement to govern and shape community life.

Chapter 7 **Cognitive Processes**

1. What experiences and abilities are included in human cognitive processes? How do we study cognition, if these processes cannot be directly observed? How accurate is human memory? What is the "information processing view" of memory?

2. What is a concept, and why is concept-formation considered to be among the most basic abilities of thinking organisms? How do we use schemas and scripts to guide our everyday thinking? When do we rely on mental images instead of words?

3. Is one kind of thinking more useful than another? How is deductive reasoning different from inductive reasoning? What are the most efficient strategies for solving problems, arriving at judgments, and making decisions?

4. What three processes are necessary for remembering? What are the three memory systems? How can we improve our memories? Why do we sometimes forget?

When Edith Eva Eger was 16, her world turned upside down. She and her family were suddenly arrested and interned in Auschwitz, a Nazi concentration camp in Poland. Shortly after they arrived at Auschwitz, Edith's mother was sent to the gas chamber. Before she was taken away, she urged Edith and her sister to live their lives fully: "Remember," she said, "what you put inside your brain, no one can take away" (Eger, 1990, p. 6).

In the horror-filled existence of concentration camp life, Edith found that the basic logic of the world was reversed. The notions of good behavior she had learned growing up "were replaced by a kind of animal quiver, which instantly smelled out danger and acted to deflect it." Matters of life and death were decided as casually as flipping a coin—you could be sent to the "showers of death" for having a loosely tied shoelace.

After years of being brutalized, the camp inmates longed for freedom, yet, paradoxically, also dreaded it. When their liberators arrived, some prisoners "rushed forward but most retreated and even returned to their barracks."

Edith was a fortunate survivor. She later married, emigrated to the United States, and became a clinical psychologist. In her sixties, Dr. Eger needed to understand the twisted reality of the camps and she returned to Auschwitz. "I came to mourn the dead and celebrate the living. I also needed to formally put an end to the denial that I had been a victim and to assign guilt to the oppressor" (Eger, 1990, p. 6). For many years, Edith Eger had denied the horrible truths of her camp experiences, but eventually denial was unacceptable to her. By reliving the events of her incarceration and forcing herself to think about the meaning of that horror, Dr. Eger believes she has become better able to help others understand events that seem inexplicable in the context of their everyday lives.

The fundamental human desire to comprehend the nature of one's existence that motivated Dr. Eger was eloquently described by another survivor of Auschwitz, Italian writer Primo Levi. He reports, "It might be surprising that in the camps one of the most frequent states of mind was curiosity. And yet, besides being frightened, humiliated, and desperate, we were curious: hungry for bread and also to understand. The world around us was upside down and somebody must have turned it upside down . . . to twist that which was straight, to befoul that which was clean" (Levi, 1985, p. 99).

Edith took her mother's last words to heart. No one can take away what she has "put inside her brain." By becoming a psychotherapist, Dr. Eger chose a career in which she helps others cope with personal realities that defy rational explanation. Noting that today's college students have little knowledge of the Holocaust, she hopes "that some day, when they are ready, my grandchildren will have the curiosity to ask their grandmother questions about the time when the world was upside down. So that if it starts tilting again, they and millions of others can redress it before it is too late" (Eger, 1990, p. 9).

Introduction

Philosopher René Descartes said, "*Cogito ergo sum*"—I think, therefore, I am. Dr. Eger's story forces us to add the postscript, "I am human, therefore *I must think.*" Even in the hell of a concentration camp, the human mind insists on knowing the *why* of such evil. We appear to be driven by a basic need to understand the nature of our existence and to try to comprehend the causes of our thoughts, feelings, and actions. We have looked at consciousness, perception, and learning. Now we will examine how humans think, reason, judge, remember, and solve life's many problems and puzzles.

Overview of Cognitive Processes

Only humans have the capacity to go beyond the perception of what is here and now to think about what was, will be, might be, and should be. Thinking provides the context for perception, the purposes for learning, and the meaning for memories. Thoughts developed in the inner universe of our minds enable us to form abstract working models of our physical and social worlds. We then use these personal mental representations of reality to reshape and sometimes improve aspects of those worlds (Hunt, 1982).

The study of thinking is the study of all the higher mental processes. **Cognition** is a general term for all forms of knowing. As **Figure 7.1** shows, these forms of knowing include attention, memory, thinking and problem solving, perception, and pattern recognition.

cognition Processes of knowing, including attending, remembering, and reasoning; contents of cognitive processes, including concepts and memories.

A cognition is a bit of information, a thought unit, or an idea. Cognition includes both contents and processes. The contents of cognitive processes are concepts ("apples"), facts ("Apples grow on trees"), propositions ("You can make applesauce from fresh apples"), rules ("Add liquid to the apples so the applesauce doesn't burn"), and memories ("Grandma's house smelled like cinnamon when she made fresh applesauce"). Some *cognitive processes* mentally represent the world around us, such as those that classify information and interpret experiences; others are internally focused, such as those in our dreams

Figure 7.1 The Domain of Cognitive Psychology

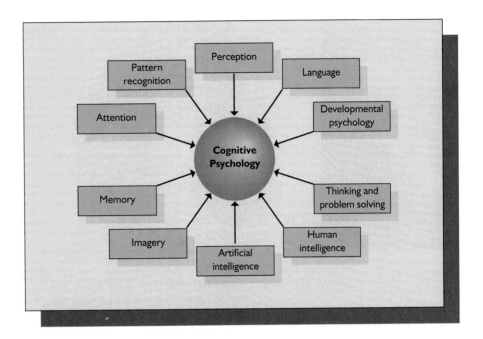

and fantasies. Knowledge-based processes of the mind make sense of the neurally coded signals coming from the eye and other sensory systems.

We will begin by analyzing the ways in which researchers try to measure the inner, private processes involved in cognitive functioning. We will then outline some of the models and basic ideas of information processing that are used to account for the ways we think, reason, and remember; in short, the way we come to understand ourselves. Finally, we will examine basic topics in cognitive psychology that are generating much excitement among researchers and those who are applying this knowledge to education and other areas: including reasoning, problem solving, decision making, judging, and remembering.

Studying Cognition

cognitive psychology The scientific study of mental processes and mental structures.

Cognitive psychology is the scientific study of mental processes and mental structures. Cognitive psychologists investigate the ways people take in, transform, manipulate, and transmit information.

Although it seems obvious that thinking and using knowledge should occupy a central position in psychology, it was not always so. During the decades when psychology was entrenched in *behaviorism,* the discipline focused on examining the organism's behavioral reactions to the external world. A *science of the mind* developed in the 1950s when researchers and scholars from different fields began to seek an understanding of the ways the mind processes information and gives observed behavior its direction, meaning, and coherence. The shift in focus from behaviorism to cognition began with the convergence of three significant approaches to human thought involving computers, communication, and children.

Historical Development. The modern conception of a computer as a general-purpose logic machine with built-in intelligence that is able to operate flexibly on internal instructions came from the vision of a brilliant young mathematician, **John Von Neumann.** In 1945, he compared the electronic circuits of a new digital computer to the brain's neurons and the computer program to the brain's memory. Psychological researchers **Herbert Simon** and **Allen Newell** were the first to develop computer programs to simulate human problem solving, thereby also providing new ways of studying mental processes (Newell, Shaw, & Simon, 1958).

Noam Chomsky

cognitive science   An interdisciplinary field that studies the variety of systems and processes that manipulate information.

cognitive model   An explanatory metaphor that describes how information is detected, stored, and used by people and machines.

information-processing model
Model that proposes that thinking and all other forms of cognition can be understood by analyzing them into parts.

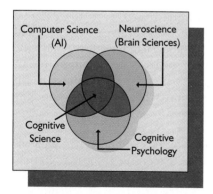

Figure 7.2 The Domain of Cognitive Science
The domain of cognitive science occupies the intersection of cognitive psychology, computer science (artificial intelligence) and neuroscience.

Around the same time, developmental psychologist **Jean Piaget** was pioneering a successful way to infer the mental processes children go through to understand physical realities (Piaget, 1954). As we saw in Chapter 4, Piaget's notion of stages of cognitive development was based on observations of the mental tasks that children of different ages could perform.

Finally, and also at about the same time, linguistic researcher **Noam Chomsky** studied language as part of a unique cognitive system for comprehending and producing symbols (Chomsky, 1957). Chomsky postulated that an innate *language acquisition device (LAD)* made it possible for young children to understand the basic rules of grammar in the absence of any formal education or systematic reinforcement.

These three new approaches to human thought involving computers, children, and communication boosted the scientific legitimacy of research on all forms of higher mental processes. Since then, cognitive theory has developed into the foundation of the psychology of the 1990s (Mayer, 1981; Solso, 1991).

Cognitive Science. **Cognitive science** is an interdisciplinary field that studies the variety of systems and processes that manipulate information. **Figure 7.2** shows that cognitive science draws on the three overlapping disciplines of cognitive psychology, computer science, and neuroscience (Farah, 1984). Cognitive science also receives input from philosophy, economics, and cultural anthropology. Cognitive science seeks to explore the classic questions of Western thought: What is knowledge, and how is it represented in the mind (Gardner, 1985)?

Researchers who study how information is represented and processed build *conceptual models* to help them understand cognitive processes. A **cognitive model** is an explanatory metaphor that describes how information is detected, stored, and used by people and machines. Cognitive models are useful ways of thinking about specific phenomena because they can guide new research and make sense of existing knowledge. However, regardless of how correct a model may seem, it must withstand the "data test," which allows for new empirical research to modify or discard the model.

The basic approach taken by most cognitive psychologists is represented by the **information-processing model.** This model proposes that thinking and all other forms of cognition can be understood by organizing them into component parts. Incoming information goes through a series of simpler to more complex stages. As the information passes through all of the brain systems, different subsystems break down the complex input to be decoded, simplified, and understood on its own terms. Then these subsystems respond appropriately—with thoughts, memories, feelings, and often actions.

You might think of cognition as an assembly line process, building from primitive stages, such as basic sensations and perception, to more complex stages, such as naming, classifying, reasoning, and problem solving. However, the human mind works on parallel paths simultaneously. The mind can also make remote associations between thought units, and come up with novel concepts and links between them that have never before been processed.

The shift from behaviorist models to the information approach has permitted psychologists to study cognitive processes that are not directly observable. As we discuss in "In Focus: How We Measure the Mind," researchers have been creatively challenged to develop methods of accessing and examining these inner workings of our mind. They study what is going on in the secret world of private experiences by discovering ways to externalize the internal and to measure and map the mind.

Investigating Memory

Memory is the mental capacity for storing experiences and then recalling or recognizing those events. For most cognitive psychologists, **memory** is an

HOW WE MEASURE THE MIND

If thinking is an internal, subjective process that only you can experience, how can it be studied scientifically? Psychologists have developed a number of general approaches and specific methods to assess that which is not directly observable. These approaches and methods all try to "measure the mind." Some of the techniques currently used include introspection, think-aloud protocols, behavioral observation, measuring reaction time, and error analysis.

Introspection and Think-Aloud Protocols

As we saw in Chapter 1, *introspection* was developed by Wilhelm Wundt in the late 1800s. It involved training people to analyze the contents of their own consciousness into component parts, such as sensations, images, and feelings. However, the introspective approach provided no clues about the actual sequences of mental processes in life situations. When the introspections of two people differed in the same situation, there was no empirical way to resolve the discrepancy between them. Moreover, many mental processes are not even available for conscious inspection. For example, in the five seconds or so that it took you to read that last sentence, you identified the letters and words, retrieved the stored meaning of each of them, and comprehended the meaning of the sentence. You even began to store that unit of information under different retrieval labels for ready access should it appear on a test. Do you know *how* you did *what* you just did so efficiently?

Introspection can be used to supplement other methods, but it can never work as a technique for studying cognition. Recently, however, researchers have found a way to use introspection as an *exploratory procedure* to help map out more precise research. As they work on tasks, experimental subjects describe what they are doing and why. Researchers use their reports, called **think-aloud protocols,** to infer the mental strategies the subjects employed to do the task and the ways the subjects represented knowledge.

Think-aloud protocols show how people *actually* proceed instead of how a purely logical approach assumes they *ought* to behave. Such protocols have been collected in a wide variety of studies; they have proven especially useful in studying the cognitive processes involved in problem solving. For example, one study that investigated how people plan shopping trips found that shoppers were not logical and organized but rather opportunistic, switching among several simultaneous trains of thought to discover relevant information (Hayes-Roth & Hayes-Roth, 1979).

Behavioral Observation

A basic task of much psychological research is to infer internal states and processes from observations of external behavior. If we know the context in which the behavior occurred, we can theorize about the affective, motivational, or cognitive determinants of that behavior. Crying at a funeral is evidence of grief, while crying at a prize ceremony is evidence of great joy.

A direct test of the acquisition of an early kind of symbolic understanding observed the behavior of children as they searched a room for a hidden object. Researchers wanted to determine at what age a child comes to understand that a model represents or symbolizes something else. Researcher Judy DeLoache (1987) devised an ingenious hide-and-seek problem for toddlers to solve. First a child had to retrieve a hidden miniature object from a scale model of a room. Next the child had to find a full-size object in its corresponding hiding place in the real environment. Children aged 2 1/2 did the first task as well as 3-year-olds, but not the second task. Apparently the 6-month older children had developed the ability to represent their environment symbolically, and use this representation to learn from experience and conduct a systematic search.

Measuring Reaction Time

The elapsed time between the presentation of some stimulus or signal and a subject's response to it is known as **reaction time.** Cognitive psychologists use reaction time to assess mental responses on different tasks. They then infer underlying differences in the thought processes involved in generating those responses, with slower reaction times indicating more complex mental processing. Adopting the principle that complex mental processes take more time, researchers today use reaction time to infer the occurrence of various cognitive processes. Reaction time reflects experience and familiarity. For example, runners decrease their reaction time when they practice fast starts at the sound of a starting pistol.

Analyzing Errors

Cognitive psychologists assume that errors, such as reaching an incorrect conclusion or remembering something incorrectly, are probably not random but reflect systematic properties of the thought processes involved. Analysis of thought errors can give us clues about these properties. Sigmund Freud (1904) pioneered the analysis of speech errors—slips of the tongue—to detect latent sexual or hostile impulses. For example, a competitor pretending to like you might say, "I'm pleased to *beat* you" instead of "I'm pleased to *meet* you." In such cases the true intention slips past the conscious censor we all use to suppress socially inappropriate thoughts.

Current researchers believe that some slips arise merely from lapses of attention to the specifics of what is being said; others reveal a mental competition between similar verbal choices. People often say, "I'd be *interesting* in . . ." instead of the correct "I'd be *interested* in. . . ." The sentence structure allows the two suffixes to be exchanged if the person's attention is not focused.

memory   Mental capacity to store and later retrieve previously experienced events.

think-aloud protocols   Reports of mental processes subjects make while working on tasks.

reaction time   Time elapsed between stimulus presentation and organism's response; used to measure time required by mental processes.

remembering   Retaining or recalling experiences.

Psychologists suggest that units of information are stored in our brains as memories in much the same way that bits of information are stored in a computer's data bank.

active mental system that receives, encodes, modifies, and retrieves information. Memory also refers to *what* is retained—the total body of remembered experience as well as a specific event that is recalled. We use the term **remembering** to mean either *retaining* or *recalling experiences.*

Unlike photographs or written records, memories are rarely exact copies of earlier experiences. What you remember is influenced by many factors—some operating at the time of the original event, others operating when you're storing the information for later use, and still others operating when you're recalling the original information. Your memories can be affected by your physical health, attention, emotions, and prejudices. For example, when you feel sick, you may be more likely to remember previous illnesses and unhappy times. The net effect of the many influences on your memory is that you remember a collage of the events you experience, second-hand descriptions of events, expectations, and even fantasies. In fact, your most vivid memories may actually be distortions of what really happened. Instead of thinking of your memory as a video log of objectively recorded events, think of it as a library of your personal history. Memories help you define yourself, connect your present thoughts and actions to your roots, and prepare you for a meaningful future.

The scientific study of memory began with the work of researcher **Hermann Ebbinghaus,** who published his first significant study in 1885. Ebbinghaus examined *verbal* memory by having a subject (frequently himself) memorize meaningless syllables. The syllables (such as CEG or DAX) were pronounceable but were not recognizable words. Since the stimuli had no meaning, remembering them could not be influenced by previous learning or associations. Ebbinghaus thus hoped to obtain a "pure" measure of memory.

For many decades, psychologists followed Ebbinghaus's lead and studied verbal learning by observing subjects who learned word-like stimuli *uncontaminated by meaning.* The study of memory for *meaningful* material was neglected until the 1950s when theorists began to use computers to simulate psychological processes in memory, language, and reading. Researchers noted that by removing the meaning from material to be remembered, Ebbinghaus had "thrown out the human baby with the bath water of impure memories." Today, the study of how we remember, distort, and forget meaningful information has become an important branch of memory research. Modern theorists favor the *information-processing view* of memory, which identifies distinct mental processes that transform sensory stimuli, thoughts, and feelings into remembered bits of information.

Modern psychologists view the mind as an information-processing *system.* These psychologists find it helpful to talk about mental processes in the language of computer programming because it enables them to break down complex processes into simpler subprocesses or stages.

How helpful is it to compare the human brain with a computer? According to psychologists, information can be stored in both, although mental operations are more complex and subtle than computer operations. A digital computer processes information in codes made up of only two alternating signals: "on" (1) and "off" (0). In contrast, the brain uses codes of changing electrochemical signals—and can process many different messages simultaneously, instead of one sequence at a time. In sum, the brain can engage in *parallel processing* of multiple messages, while computers rely primarily on *serial processing,* digesting only one piece of information at a time.

Humans and computers also differ in the stability of their memories. A computer does not spontaneously add to or modify its stored memories, whereas the trillions of synapses (neural connections) in the brain permit processing far more complex than that provided by any computer (Sinclair, 1983). On the other hand, the brain's memory units are not as stable and unchanging as those of computer memory. The very act of recalling information changes a human memory in some way.

Clearly there are significant differences between a computer and the human brain. Nonetheless, borrowing from computer science has helped researchers formulate hypotheses about remembering and forgetting that can be tested experimentally on humans.

SUMMING UP

One basic function of the human mind is to create abstract representations of the physical and social worlds in which we live. The study of cognitive psychology includes looking at the mental processes and mental structures that enable us to think, reason, make inferences and decisions, solve problems, and use language. Cognition is the general term for all forms of knowing. Cognitive psychologists generally use an information-processing approach to analyze information in components that are processed in stages or sequences. Cognitive psychology has come to replace behaviorism as the core area of U.S. psychology. It began to emerge in the 1950s with the triple developments of digital computers; the study of knowledge development in children; and the analysis of language acquisition as an innate system for manipulating symbols.

Cognitive science is a new interdisciplinary field of study that utilizes the expertise of cognitive psychologists and researchers of neuroscience and computer science to study the way the brain and mind use knowledge to guide thought and action. Cognitive researchers employ a variety of techniques to test their models and hypotheses, including introspection and think-aloud protocols, behavioral observation, reaction time, and error analysis. Think-aloud protocols are introspective methods that require subjects to verbalize their thoughts as they work on a cognitive task. Behavioral observations are used to index internal processes as revealed by search behavior, facial expressions, and attentional focus. The reaction time technique assumes that greater cognitive complexity is reflected in longer reaction times, and error analysis is used to study cognitive and linguistic rules that are violated when a speech error is made.

Early investigations of memory were conducted by Hermann Ebbinghaus, who focused on the learning of meaningless material. More recently, researchers have applied the analogy of computer operations to the capacities and features of memory. In this view, memory is part of an information-processing system, and though human memory is complex it can be studied and tested experimentally.

The Structures of Thinking

Human thought processes are at the upper end of the information-processing sequence, building on the more fundamental components of lower-order cognitions, such as pattern recognition and perceptual analysis. What happens when we reach that ultimate stage of information processing called *thinking*? **Thinking** is a complex mental process of forming a new representation by transforming available information. That transformation involves the interaction of many mental activities, such as inferring, abstracting, reasoning, imagining, judging, problem solving, and, at times, creativity. From the perspective of cognitive psychology, thinking has three general features:

thinking Mental process that transforms available information to form a new mental representation.

1. Thinking occurs in the mind but is inferred from observable behavior.
2. Thinking is a process that manipulates knowledge in a person's cognitive system.
3. Thinking is directed toward finding solutions to problems facing the individual (Mayer, 1983).

As we store information from our encounters with people and things, we build mental representations—models in our minds—of their features. We also

A concept is a mental event that represents a category or class of objects. The concept of *flower* encompasses many different flowers.

concept   Mental representation of categories of items or ideas, based on experience.

cognitive economy   Minimizing time and effort required to process information.

critical feature   Quality that is a necessary and sufficient condition for including a concept in a category.

develop generalizations based on specific experiences, such as "It is safer to approach a stranger who is smiling than one whose expression is angry." Thinking relies on a variety of mental structures. These structures include concepts, schemas, scripts, and visual imagery. Let's examine how we utilize each of them to form thoughts.

Concepts

You have probably had the experience known as *déjà vu* (from the French for "already seen"), the sensation that something you are perceiving now is also part of a memory of the past—that "this has happened before." Perhaps you visit a new place that seems oddly familiar, or have a social conversation that seems repetitive. But what would it be like to experience the opposite sensation, what comedian George Carlin calls "vujà dé," the feeling that "none of this has ever happened before"? Imagine that every object or event looked truly new to you and seemed unrelated to anything you had ever experienced before. On the one hand, you would certainly maintain a fresh view of the world. However, you would also lose information vital for survival and happiness; you could not distinguish between sources of danger and pleasure, friends and foes, or fantasy and reality. In a world of perpetual novelty with no way to classify information, you could not build on one experience to behave more effectively in the next one.

Fortunately, you do have the capacity to treat new stimuli as instances of familiar, remembered categories. This ability to *categorize individual experiences*—to take the same action toward them or give them the same label—is regarded as one of the most basic abilities of thinking organisms (Mervis & Rosch, 1981).

Categorizing into Concepts.   The categories we form, which are mental representations of related items that are grouped in some way, are called **concepts.** Concepts are the building blocks of thinking, enabling us to organize knowledge in systematic ways. Concepts may represent *objects, activities,* or *living organisms.* They may also represent *properties,* (such as *red* or *large*), *abstractions* (such as *truth* or *love*) and *relations* (such as *smarter than*) (Smith & Medin, 1981). As mental structures, concepts cannot be observed directly, but must be discovered through research or invented by psychological theories.

A basic task of thinking is concept learning or concept formation—identifying the stimuli properties that are common to a class of objects or ideas. The mind lives by the principle of **cognitive economy,** minimizing the amount of time and effort required to process information. We learn not only features that form concepts, such as the colors of traffic lights, but also *conceptual rules* by which these features are related. For example, consider traffic light rules: If red, stop; if yellow, slow down and prepare to stop; if green, go. It is amazing how many conceptual rules we learn, store, retrieve on demand, and use to direct our interactions with people and the environment (Haygood & Bourne, 1965).

Critical Features Versus Prototypes.   What is the unit of information that is stored in memory when we form a concept? Psychologists have not yet agreed on the unit. Currently, two competing theories attempt to account for the form in which information is stored.

The **critical feature** approach suggests that we store definitions or lists of critical features that are necessary and sufficient conditions for a concept to be included in a category. A concept is a member of the category if (and only if) it has every feature on the list. For example, a FAX (facsimile) machine has a telephone connection, receiver, number keypad, and paper dispenser. If you encounter an elaborate machine that looks like a FAX but has no way of dispensing paper for messages, it may be some kind of telephone but you cannot categorize it as a FAX machine.

prototype Most representative example of a category.

The **prototype** approach suggests that categories are structured around an ideal or most representative instance, called a *prototype* (Rosch, 1973). A concept is classified as a member of a category if it is more similar to the prototype of that category than it is to the prototype of any other category. A stimulus might not fit precisely within the limits of a stored category but would still be classified as belonging to the category if its variation from the prototype was within an acceptable range. For example, although the fonts illustrated on this page are very different, we still recognize them as belonging to the same category—the letter *Z*.

Which approach—critical feature or prototype—best explains typical human thinking? In fact, we seem to use them both, each for different kinds of concepts. For example, the concept *mammals* is defined as "vertebrates that nurse their young." Organisms possessing these critical features qualify as mammals, while those which lack them do not. But the critical features approach does not work as well with the concept of *birds*. The dictionary defines a *bird* as "a warm-blooded vertebrate with feathers and wings." When you think of a bird, what example do you imagine? If you are like most people, you are more likely to think of *typical* birds like robins, blue jays, and sparrows; you are less likely to imagine atypical members of the class, such as ostriches or penguins. These birds may qualify for membership, but they don't seem to "belong" to the concept as well as the typical examples. Thus *bird* is a fuzzy concept; it has no well-defined boundaries between members of its class (Zadeh, 1965). To correct this fuzziness, you probably define the concept not only by critical features (such as feathers) but by ideas about typical members of the category.

Many of our concepts in everyday life are like this. We can identify clusters of properties that are shared by different instances of a concept, but there may be no one property that all instances show. We consider some instances as more representative of a concept—more typical of our mental prototype—than others.

Research studies show that people respond more quickly to typical members of a category than to its more unusual ones (their reaction times are faster). For example, reaction time to determine whether a robin is a bird is shorter than reaction time to determine whether an ostrich is a bird, because robins resemble the prototype of a bird more than ostriches do (Kintsch, 1981; Rosch et al., 1976). A prototype is formed on the basis of frequently experienced features. These features are stored in memory, and the more often they are perceived the stronger their overall memory strength is. Thus, the prototype can be rapidly accessed and recalled.

The police use the general principle of the prototype when they help witnesses identify criminal suspects. They prepare a prototype face made of plastic overlays of different facial features (from a commercially prepared "identi-kit"). The witness then is asked to modify the prototype model until it is most similar to the suspect's face. Psychological researchers have used the overlay technique to study memory for prototypes. In a typical exercise, subjects study a series of "exemplar faces" that vary from a prototype.

In one study (Solso & McCarthy, 1980), subjects were shown a set of 12 exemplar faces made from three prototype faces. Then they saw a second group of faces: some of the original exemplar faces, some new ones that were made to differ from the prototype, and the original prototype face, which they had never seen. The subjects' task was to rate their confidence in having seen each face before, during the first presentation. Three results clearly emerge, as seen in the chart in Figure 7.3 on the next page.

Recall confidence was equally high for all the old items. The new items were accurately identified as unfamiliar, but false confidence in a feeling of having seen them was greater as the items more resembled the prototype. Finally,

Different fonts all express the same underlying concept—the last letter of the alphabet.

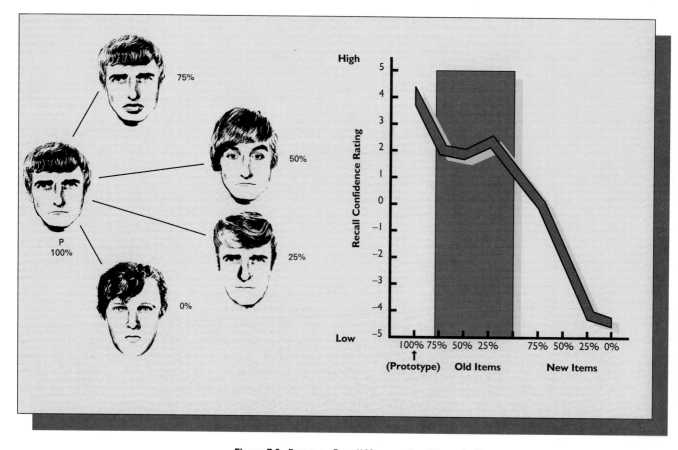

Figure 7.3 Prototype Face (100-percent) and Exemplar Faces
The 75-percent face has all the features of the prototype face except the mouth; the 50-percent face has different hair and eyes; the 25-percent face has only the eyes in common; and the 0-percent face has no features in common. Subjects were least confident about recalling faces with fewer features in common with previously seen (old) faces. Ironically, they were most confident about recalling the prototype face—which they had never previously seen.

pseudomemory Form of memory in which one confidently believes a new stimulus was experienced previously because several of its features have been remembered.

the highest level of confidence was for the prototype face itself—although the subjects had never seen it before.

The subjects' reaction here is known as **pseudomemory** (pronounced SUE-doe-memory), recall of a *new* stimulus because its attributes were stored in memory (Solso & McCarthy, 1981).

Hierarchies and Basic Levels. Concepts are often organized in *hierarchies,* from general to specific, as seen in **Figure 7.4.** The broad category of *animal* has several subcategories, such as *bird* and *fish,* which in turn are subdivided into their specific forms, such as *canary, ostrich, shark,* and *salmon.* The animal category is itself a subcategory of the still larger category of *living beings.* These concepts and categories are arranged in a hierarchy of levels, with the most general and abstract at the top and the most specific and concrete at the bottom. They are also linked to many other concepts—some birds are *edible,* some are *endangered,* some are *national symbols.*

basic level Optimal level of categorization for an object to be mentally represented; level most quickly accessed by memory and most efficiently used.

Psychologists have identified a level in such hierarchies at which people best categorize and think about objects. That level—the **basic level**—can be retrieved from memory most quickly and used most efficiently. For example, the chair at your desk belongs to three obvious levels in a conceptual hierarchy: *furniture, chair,* and *desk chair.* The lower level category, *desk chair,* would provide more detail than you generally need, whereas the higher level category, *furniture,* would not be precise enough. When spontaneously identifying it, you would be more likely to call it a *chair* than a *piece of furniture* or a *desk chair.* It is now believed that our dependence on basic levels of concepts is another fundamental aspect of thought.

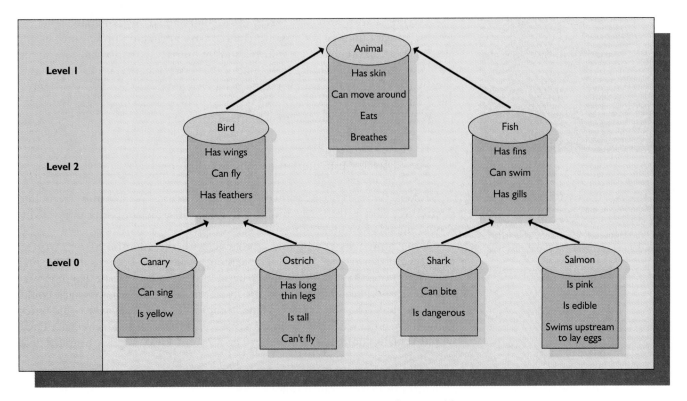

Level 1

Level 2

Level 0

Animal

Has skin

Can move around

Eats

Breathes

Bird

Has wings

Can fly

Has feathers

Fish

Has fins

Can swim

Has gills

Canary

Can sing

Is yellow

Ostrich

Has long
thin legs

Is tall

Can't fly

Shark

Can bite

Is dangerous

Salmon

Is pink

Is edible

Swims upstream
to lay eggs

Figure 7.4 Hierarchically Organized Structure of Concepts

Schemas and Scripts

schema Collected knowledge and expectations about a topic.

Much of what we know seems to be stored as **schemas**—general conceptual frameworks or clusters of knowledge and preconceptions regarding certain objects, people, and situations. Schemas are "knowledge packages" that provide expectations about the features we will find in future examples of various concepts and categories. For example, for a student, the term *registration day* probably conjures up a schema that includes scenes of hassle, long lines, delay, and frustration. For a political candidate, however, the schema for *registration day* might include feelings of nervousness and excitement and scenes of photographers, large crowds, and campaign posters.

Making Inferences. Schemas include expectations about the features and effects that are typical of particular concepts or categories. New information, which is often incomplete or ambiguous, makes more sense when we can relate it to existing knowledge in our stored schemas. So we may say that schemas enable us to make inferences about missing information. What can you infer about the statement, "Tanya was upset to discover, upon opening the basket, that she'd forgotten the salt"? With no further information, you can infer a great deal about this event that is not explicit in the description. Salt implies that the basket is a picnic basket. The fact that Tanya is upset that the salt is missing suggests that the food in the basket is food that is usually salted, such as hardboiled eggs or vegetables. You automatically know what other foods might be included and, equally important, what definitely is not—everything in the world that is larger than a picnic basket and anything that would be inappropriate to take on a picnic—from a boa constrictor to bronze-plated baby shoes. The body of information you now have has been organized around a "picnic-basket" schema. By relating the statement about Tanya to your preestablished picnic-basket schema, you understand the statement better.

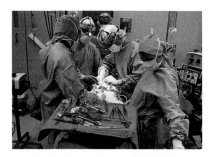

Drawing on a schema can lead individuals to change information so that it becomes consistent with their *schema-based expectations*. In one experiment, after subjects related a given story to their schema for hospital surgery, they "remembered" labels from their schema that were not present in what they had read.

script A cluster of knowledge about sequences of interrelated, specific events and actions expected to occur in a certain way in particular settings.

According to researchers **David Rumelhart** and **Don Norman,** schemas are the primary units of meaning in the human information-processing system (1975). We comprehend new information by integrating consistent new input with what we already know. If we find a discrepancy between new input and already stored schemas, we overcome it by changing what we know or ignoring the new input.

What do the following sentences mean to you?

- The notes were sour because the seam was split.
- The haystack was important because the cloth ripped.

Taken alone, these sentences make little sense. What notes are being referred to, what is the seam, and how does a split seam cause sour notes? Why should ripped cloth make a haystack important?

Now, how does your thinking change with the addition of two words: *bagpipes* and *parachute*? Presto! The sentences suddenly become understandable. The notes were sour because the seam in the bag of the bagpipe was split. If you were falling from a plane in a torn parachute, the haystack could save your life. The sentences became comprehensible when you could integrate them into what you already knew—into appropriate schemas. They would remain confusing to anyone who did not know what a bagpipe or a parachute was.

Thinking is a *constructive process* in which we draw on our existing mental structures to make as much sense as possible out of new information. We construct our subjective reality and personal world views of all the information we process. Once we interpret information as belonging to a particular schema, we may unwittingly change the information in our internal representation of it. To see how this transformation can occur, read the following passage:

> Chief Resident Jones adjusted his face mask while anxiously surveying a pale figure secured to the long gleaming table before him. One swift stroke of his small, sharp instrument and a thin red line appeared. Then the eager young assistant carefully extended the opening as another aide pushed aside glistening surface fat so that the vital parts were laid bare. Everyone stared in horror at the ugly growth too large for removal. He now knew it was pointless to continue.

Stop! Without looking back, please complete the following exercise:
Circle below the words that appeared in the passage:

patient	scalpel	blood	tumor
cancer	nurse	disease	surgery

In the original study, most of the subjects who read this passage circled the words *patient, scalpel,* and *tumor.* Did you? However, none of the words were there! Interpreting the story as a medical story made it more understandable, but also resulted in inaccurate recall (Lachman et al., 1979). Once the subjects had related the story to their schema for hospital surgery, they "remembered" labels from their schema that were not present in what they had read. Drawing on a schema not only gave the subjects an existing mental structure to tie the new material to but also led them to change the information to make it more consistent with their *schema-based expectations.*

Scripts as Event Schemas. We have schemas not only about objects and environmental events but also about persons, roles, and ourselves. These schemas help us to decide what to expect or how people should behave under specific circumstances. An event schema or **script** is a cluster of knowledge about sequences of interrelated, specific events and actions expected to occur in a certain way in particular settings. We have scripts for going to a restaurant, using the library, listening to a lecture, and going on a first date. Some scripts in other cultures differ from ours, such as the scripts that govern exchanging gifts, attending funerals, and ways to treat women. In Japan, for example, giving money is almost always an appropriate wedding present. Choosing a wedding gift is thus an extremely easy task. This contrasts sharply with the United States, where many types of wedding gifts are appropriate and people often spend a great deal of time thinking about a "good" gift. Cultural distinctions in scripts emerge in everyday life as well as on special occasions. For example, during the Persian Gulf War, American women stationed in Arab locales discovered that many behaviors they might take for granted at home—such as walking unescorted in public, wearing clothing that showed their faces and legs, or driving a car—were considered scandalously inappropriate by citizens of their host country. To maintain good relations, these servicewomen had to change their habits and plans to accommodate local customs. As explored on the next page in "Cross-cultural Perspective: Understanding Diverse Others," the rules that govern different cultures may have developed from distinct ways of viewing the world.

When all people in a given setting follow similar scripts, they feel comfortable because they have comprehended the "meaning" of that situation in the same way and have the same expectations of each other (Abelson, 1981; Schank & Abelson, 1977). When all people do not follow similar scripts, however, they are made uncomfortable by the script "violation" and may have difficulty understanding why the scene was "misplayed." The discomfort we experience when scripts "clash" may signal trauma or danger. For example, in a case of date rape, the rapist's script tells him that when she says "no" she means "yes," and that she wants to be physically overpowered so she won't feel responsible for agreeing to sex. In contrast, the victim's script tells her that "no" means "no," that the rapist's assault is his wish, not hers, that he wants not intimacy but power, and that the experience is violent, not passionate.

We have trouble comprehending situations that do not fit scripted patterns. When we encounter new information that challenges or contradicts existing expectations, we feel discomfort and tension. One reason why relatively unprejudiced people do not interact with members of other ethnic groups (for example, Caucasian Americans with African Americans) is that people do not understand each others' scripts. When scripts clash, people can say, "I tried to interact, but it was so awkward that I don't want to try again" (Brislin, 1993). One way to reduce such discrepancies is to keep learning—to enlarge and change our schemas to *accommodate* new ideas. The reward for such mental flexibility is an easier understanding and acceptance of diversity and novelty. For example, if the computer you are using malfunctions, striking it is more likely to break it than fix it. But if you experiment by typing different keys, you may succeed in restarting the program—and learn a handy solution for future computer problems.

The penalty for mental rigidity, by contrast, is continual frustration in trying to fit new experiences into narrow, old molds, and merely making "special exceptions" for events that break the rules, without ever changing the schemas or scripts themselves. Returning to the computer example, if every time you encounter a difficulty you hit the same keys—or punch the machine—you doom yourself to frustration and damage expensive equipment in the process.

During the Persian Gulf War, American women stationed in Arab locales discovered that many behaviors they might take for granted at home—such as walking unescorted in public, wearing clothing that showed their faces and legs, or driving a car—were considered scandalously inappropriate by citizens of their host country.

Imagery and Cognitive Maps

Do you think only in words or do you sometimes think in pictures and spatial relationships? Although you may not actually store visual memories in visual codes, you clearly are able to use imagery in your thinking. *Visual mental imagery* is a review of information previously perceived and stored in memory. It takes place in the absence of appropriate immediate sensory input and relies

Cross-cultural Perspective   Understanding Diverse Others

Assume that you have a good friend named Mary, and she asks you for help with a problem she has been having in her college studies. You and Mary went to high school together. During your junior and senior years, you were in the same classes in both science and social studies. You liked your teachers because they introduced a variety of activities. Sometimes the teachers gave formal lectures, but they also allowed group discussions and introduced various real-life problems that were relevant to the concepts learned in class. The teachers, especially in the social studies classes, also encouraged students to develop their own projects and gave credit for community service activities. They encouraged students to disagree with ideas presented in the textbooks and with their own teachers' positions, if students could defend their ideas with sound arguments.

Mary went to a different college than you did, and she took advantage of her school's study abroad program. She is now spending a year in Spain and is enrolled in a series of courses much like those taken by any Spanish student attending college. Mary's Spanish is quite good. She had four years in high school and an intensive, advanced course in college. From Spain, she writes to you:

I can't figure out what's going on in my classes. I thought I knew what professors did from my experiences in America, but here they just lecture all the time—there is no opportunity for class discussions. Forget about having one's own opinion on anything! The professors seem to think that they know it all and that students have nothing to contribute! The professors even assign topics for our term papers—we can't even suggest our own topics! And students better not ask about an extension on handing in a paper because they want to do more thinking about a topic—deadlines are really strict! I know you are taking psychology now; I sure wish I had taken it at my school before I came here. Can

you give me any insight as to what is going on, maybe something you learned in psychology? I know you can't change things for me here, but maybe you can at least help me understand the professors' behavior. If I can understand them, maybe I'll be more sympathetic. I sure am frustrated now!

Does cross-cultural research in psychology allow you to make some suggestions in your return letter to Mary? The answer is "yes." As discussed in the section "Accepting the Importance of Diversity: Cross-cultural Psychology" in Chapter 1, culture provides guidance for behavior. In that section, the guidance provided by the concepts *individualism* (pursuit of own goals) and *collectivism* (attention to others' goals) was discussed. Another concept that is very helpful when analyzing cultural differences is "uncertainty avoidance." The Dutch psychologist Geert Hofstede (1986, p. 308) argues that uncertainty avoidance "defines the extent to which people within a culture are made nervous by situations that they perceive as unstructured, unclear, or unpredictable, situations which they try to avoid by maintaining strict codes of behavior and a belief in absolute truths."

A lack of structure, clarity, and predictability (in short, uncertainty) are issues that everyone in the world faces. For example, nobody can predict exactly what they will be doing ten years from now, especially in this fast changing world. Different cultures have developed ways of dealing with uncertainty. Some cultures, called "high uncertainty avoidant," have many rules that guide behavior. Such cultures also avoid uncertainty by having widely accepted views of truth. If many people accept a certain set of "facts" as true, they can turn to these facts when challenged by any of life's problems. Other cultures, called "low uncertainty avoidant," have fewer strict rules and less rigidity concerning views of absolute truths. People in these cultures also recognize uncertainty in their futures. However, they prefer to believe that flexible rules and multiple

approaches to discovering truth will provide better preparation for the future.

Can these insights, developed by Hofstede (1986, 1991), be applied to Mary's complaints? Spain is a high uncertainty avoidant country. Other high uncertainty avoidant countries to which many students travel for study abroad opportunities, include Greece, Belgium, France, Israel, and Italy. High uncertainty avoidance leads to strict rules in the classroom, precise objectives for courses, and norms that enforce the expectation that the professor is the source of knowledge. Students are not expected to have their own opinions or to make suggestions about course content. In low-uncertainty avoidant countries, such as the United States, Canada, and Sweden, professors are allowed to say "I don't know" and to accept suggestions from students. Professors are also far more tolerant of students who take opposing views; professors often view disagreements as intellectually stimulating.

A knowledge of culture and cultural differences won't always solve problems immediately. Mary will face the same issues in her classes whether or not she understands concepts such as uncertainty avoidance! And to make matters more complex, there will always be exceptions to generalizations about culture and cultural differences. Mary may learn about a particular professor in Spain, for example, who encourages group discussions. But if the stress indicated in her letter becomes severe, an understanding of the reasons for her problems can help her make general adjustments to her life in another culture.

In the text, the importance of "knowledge packages" is introduced. There is no one package of knowledge concerning what college professors should do. Different cultures present different knowledge packages concerning topics such as classroom structure, lectures, and disagreements with students. Concepts such as uncertainty avoidance help us understand differences in the knowledge packages people encounter in different cultures.

on internal representations of events and concepts in visual forms. For example, answer the following question:

What shape are a German shepherd's ears?

If you answered correctly, how did you know that information? You probably have not memorized the shapes of dog ears, or ever expected to be quizzed about such knowledge. To answer that a German shepherd has pointed ears, you probably consulted a visual image of a German shepherd stored in your memory. Many psychologists believe that visual thought differs from verbal thought in the ways information is processed and stored (Kosslyn, 1983; Paivio, 1983).

Visual thought adds complexity and richness to our thinking, as do forms of thought that involve the other senses (sound, taste, smell, and touch). Visual thinking can be useful in solving problems in which relationships can be grasped more clearly in diagram form than in word form. Visual thought, for example, is useful in spatial or geographical relationships.

cognitive map Mental representation of physical space.

A cognitive representation of physical space is called a **cognitive map.** Learning theorist **Edward C. Tolman** was the first to hypothesize that people form mental maps of their environment as they learn their way through life's mazes, and these internal maps guide their future actions toward desired goals (see Chapter 6). Cognitive maps help people get where they want to go, and they enable them to give directions to others. By using cognitive maps, people can move through their homes with their eyes closed or go to familiar destinations even when their usual routes are blocked (Hart & Moore, 1973; Thorndyke & Hayes-Roth, 1978). If you found the main door to the psychology classroom building locked, your cognitive map would tell you where to look for the back door or side entrance.

Mental maps seem to reflect our subjective impressions of physical reality. The maps often mirror the distorted view we have developed about the world from our personal or culturally egocentric perspective. A case in point is world-scale cognitive maps. If you were asked to draw a world map, where would you begin and how would you represent the size, shape, and relations between various countries? This task was given to nearly 4,000 students from 71 cities in 49 countries as part of an international study of the way people of different nationalities visualize the world. The goal of the study was to broaden understanding of cultural differences and to promote world peace.

Among other information, the study found that the majority of maps had a Eurocentric world view—Europe was placed in the center of the map and the other countries were arranged around it (probably due to the dominance for many centuries of Eurocentric maps in geography books). However, the study also yielded many instances of culture-biased maps, such as the one by a Chicago student in **Figure 7.5** and that of an Australian student in **Figure 7.6** (both maps are on the next page). In addition, American students did poorly on this task, misrepresenting the placement of countries, while students from the former Soviet Union and Hungary made the most accurately detailed maps (Saarinen, 1987). This suggests that cultural differences—perhaps in education or world view—have an impact on geographical thinking.

SUMMING UP

Thinking is a higher-order mental process that goes beyond the information given by sensory processing. Thinking transforms available information into new abstract representations. Human thought relies on many types of mental structures. One of the most basic abilities of thinking organisms is categorizing individual experiences. Concepts, the building blocks of thinking, are mental representations that group related items in particular ways. We form concepts

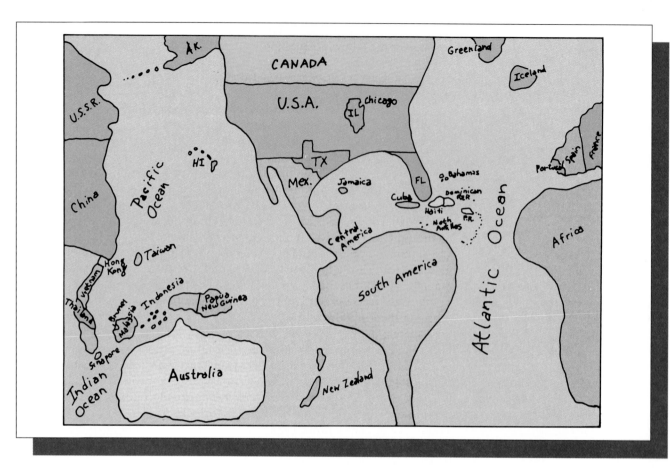

Figure 7.5 Chicagocentric View of the World   How does this compare with your view of the world?

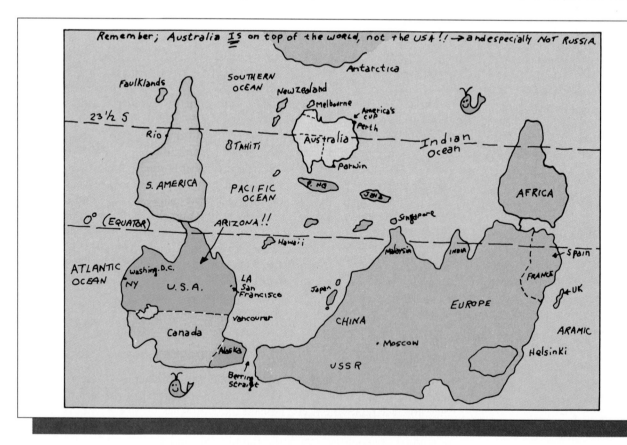

Figure 7.6 An Australiocentric View of the World   Now who's down under?

by identifying those properties that are common to a class of objects or ideas. We store the critical features of well-defined concepts in order to identify their members. For concepts with ill-defined boundaries, we seem to store the prototypical or the most average instance of the concept. We respond to prototypes more quickly and recall them with more confidence than nonprototypical instances. Concepts are often arranged in hierarchies, from general to specific, and there is an optimal level of describing a complex concept—called the basic level—to which we respond most effectively.

Other mental structures that guide thinking are the knowledge packages of schemas and scripts. Schemas are collections of information about objects; scripts are schemas for experiences and events. These mental structures help to encode and store information in memory and also to form expectations about appropriate attributes and effects of concepts. Scripts are event schemas—organized knowledge about expected sequences of action in given settings. In addition to these verbal thinking structures, we rely on visual imagery that adds further richness to thinking. Cognitive maps are cognitive representations of physical space, and they help us learn our way around and represent our personal and cultural worldviews. Taken together, these mental structures form the basis of how we think so efficiently.

The Uses of Thinking

Our thoughts range between two extremes: the autistic and the realistic. **Autistic thinking** is a personal, idiosyncratic process involving fantasy, daydreaming, unconscious reactions, and ideas that cannot be tested against reality. This type of individualized thought is part of most creative acts. However, when it generates delusions and hallucinations, autistic thinking can be evidence that the individual has lost touch with reality and suffers from some type of mental illness.

In contrast, **realistic thinking** requires that ideas fit into the reality of situational demands, time constraints, operational rules, and personal resources. Thinking realistically involves frequent checks on reality and tests that measure the appropriateness and correctness of one's ideas against some acceptable standard.

Reasoning is a process of realistic, goal-directed thinking in which conclusions are drawn from a set of facts. In reasoning, information from the environment and stored information are used in accordance with a set of rules (either formal or informal) for transforming information. There are two types of reasoning: deductive and inductive.

Deductive Reasoning

Deductive reasoning is drawing a conclusion that follows logically according to established rules from two or more statements, or premises. More than 2,000 years ago, Aristotle introduced the form of deductive reasoning known as the **syllogism,** which has three components: a major premise, a minor premise, and a conclusion. He also developed rules for syllogistic reasoning. If these rules are adhered to, the conclusion will be drawn *validly* from the premises. Consider the following example:

Major premise:	All people are thinking creatures.
Minor premise:	Descartes was a person.

autistic thinking Distinctive, personal cognition involving fantasy, daydreaming, unconscious processes, and untestable ideas.

realistic thinking Fitting one's ideas to situational demands, time limits, rules of operation, and accurate evaluation of one's personal resources; contrasted with *autistic thinking*.

reasoning Realistic thinking process that draws a conclusion from a set of facts; goal-directed thinking.

deductive reasoning Drawing a conclusion intended to follow logically from two or more statements (premises).

syllogism Form of deductive reasoning with a major premise, a minor premise, and a logical conclusion.

Valid conclusion: Therefore, Descartes was a thinking creature.
Invalid conclusion: Therefore, all thinking creatures are Descartes.

If the conclusion is not derived by the rules of logic it is *invalid,* as shown in the second conclusion of the example. You immediately knew the second conclusion was invalid—evidence that deductive reasoning is a fundamental part of reasoning ability (Ripps, 1983).

Cognitive psychologists study the errors people make in logic and syllogistic reasoning to understand their mental representations of premises and conclusions (Johnson-Laird & Byrne, 1989). Some errors occur because the individual's personal beliefs about the premises and conclusions get in the way of logic. People tend to judge as valid those conclusions with which they agree and as invalid those with which they don't agree (Janis & Frick, 1943).

Inductive Reasoning

Inductive reasoning uses available evidence to generate a conclusion about the likelihood of something. When you reason inductively, you construct a hypothesis based on limited evidence and then test it against other evidence. The hypothesis is not drawn from the logical structure of the argument as in deductive reasoning. Rather, inductive reasoning requires leaping from data to decisions. These inferential leaps are accomplished by integrating past experience, perceptual sensitivity, weighted value of the importance of each element of evidence, and a dash of creativity. Most scientific reasoning is inductive.

After solving a difficult mystery, fictional detective Sherlock Holmes frequently explains to his companion Dr. Watson that his conclusions were based on observation and "deduction." Wrong! In fact, Holmes's solutions involve shrewd *induction:* piecing together bits of data—clues in the case, and his own vast general knowledge—into a compelling web of evidence that eventually explains the manner and perpetrator of the crime. In our lives, inductive reasoning plays a key role in helping all of us solve many of the problems we face. If you misplace your keys, for example, you use inductive reasoning to search your memory and review the evidence—"I set my umbrella down there," "I remember the phone was ringing as I opened the door"—to retrace your steps and find your missing keys (still in the lock, right where you left them).

Problem Solving

Problem solving is a basic part of our everyday existence. We continually encounter problems that require solutions: how to manage work and tasks within a limited time frame, how to succeed at a job interview, how to break off an intimate relationship, how to conserve energy, or how to avoid sexually transmitted diseases. For psychologists, **problem solving** is thinking that is directed toward solving specific problems. Such thinking moves from an initial state to a goal state by means of a set of mental operations.

Many problems are discrepancies between what you know and what you need to know. When you solve a problem, you reduce that discrepancy by finding a way to get the missing information. To get into the spirit of problem solving yourself, try the problems in **Figure 7.7** (the answers are on page 250, as depicted in **Figure 7.8**).

In information-processing terms, a problem has the following three parts:

1. *An initial state.* The initial state of the problem includes the incomplete information with which you start. Perhaps that information corresponds to some unsatisfactory set of conditions in the world.

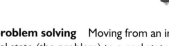

inductive reasoning   Drawing a conclusion about the probability of an event or condition based on available evidence.

problem solving   Moving from an initial state (the problem) to a goal state (the solution) by means of a set of mental operations.

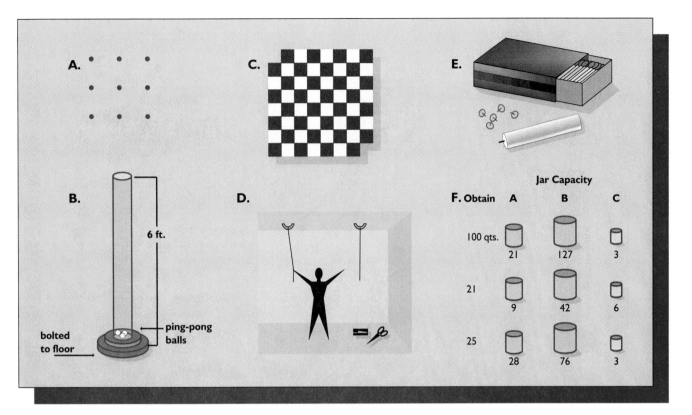

Figure 7.7 A. Can You Solve It?

A. Can you connect all the dots in the pattern by drawing four straight, connected lines without lifting your pen from the paper?

B. A prankster has put 3 ping-pong balls into a 6-foot long pipe that is standing vertically in the corner of the physics lab, fastened to the floor. How would you get the ping-pong balls out?

C. The checkerboard shown has had 2 corner pieces cut out, leaving 62 squares. You have 31 dominoes, each of which covers exactly 2 checkerboard squares. Can you use them to cover the whole checkerboard?

D. You are in the situation depicted and given the task of tying 2 strings together. If you hold one, the other is out of reach. Can you do it?

E. You are given the objects shown (2 candles, tacks, string, matches in a matchbox). The task is to mount a lighted candle on the door. Can you do it?

F. You are given 3 "water-jar" problems. Using only the 3 containers (water supply is unlimited), can you obtain the exact amount specified in each case?

2. *A goal state.* Your goal is the set of information or state of the world you hope to achieve.

3. *A set of operations.* These are the steps you must take to move from an initial state to a goal state (Newell & Simon, 1972).

Together, these three parts define the problem space. You can think of solving a problem as walking through a maze (the problem space) from where you are (the initial state) to where you want to be (the goal state), making a series of turns (the allowable operations).

A common real-life problem might be having to pay an unexpected bill. In the *initial state* of this problem, you receive a bill for a necessary service—such as a car repair or doctor's visit—but you did not anticipate paying the bill right away. Your *goal* is to pay the bill without upsetting your budget or sacrificing other expenses you had hoped to cover. Some problem-solving *operations* (such as borrowing money from your own savings account) are easier or more acceptable than others (asking your parents for a loan or writing a bad check). By using the best operations, you hope to move from your initial state to your goal state—to pay the bill without doing anything wrong or creating new problems for yourself.

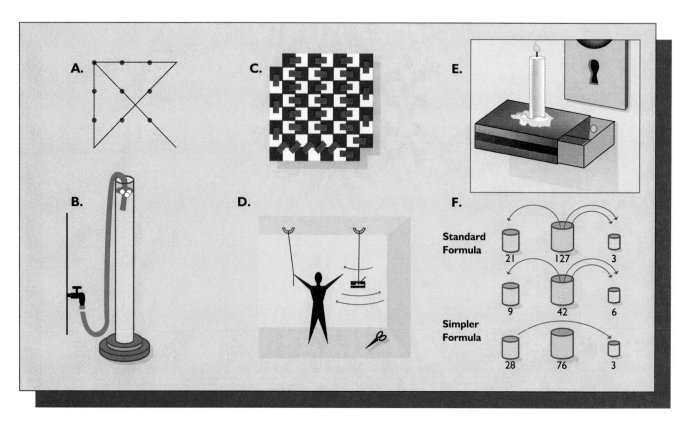

Figure 7.8 B. Solutions to the Problems

Understanding the Problem. Setting up an internal representation of the problem space—specifying all the elements in it—is not an automatic process. This task often requires finding the appropriate schema from previous similar tasks or situations. However, existing schemas can be restricting when the new problem calls for a new solution.

If you solved the problems in **Figure 7.7,** you recognized the importance of an accurate internal representation of the problem space. To connect the nine dots, you had to realize that nothing in the instructions limited you to the area of the dots themselves. To get the Ping-Pong balls out of the pipe, you had to realize that the solution did not involve reaching into the pipe. In the checkerboard problem, you had to realize that you could use the domino at any angle to cover any two squares, regardless of their color. To connect the two strings, you had to see one of the tools on the floor as a weight. To mount the candle on the door, you had to alter your usual perspective and perceive the matchbox as a platform instead of as a container and you had to perceive the candle as a tool as well as the object to be mounted on the door.

Mental Sets. The last two problems show a phenomenon called *functional fixedness* (Duncker, 1945; Maier, 1931). **Functional fixedness** is a mental block that hinders problem solving and creativity by making it hard to perceive a new function for an object that was previously associated with some other purpose. Functional fixedness would prevent you, for example, from seeing that a knifeblade can be used as a screwdriver, and that metal pliers can be used as a hammer. When your thinking is functionally fixed, you put your conceptual "blinders" on and use only your familiar schemas; this shows again the power of schemas to guide or misguide perception of reality. For example, seeing the matchbox as a platform and the candle as a tool are examples of overcoming functional fixedness.

functional fixedness Inability to perceive a new use for an object associated with a different purpose; limits problem solving and creativity.

Another kind of mental rigidity may have hampered your solution of the water-jar problem. If you had discovered in the first two problems the conceptual rule that B − A − 2(C) = the answer, you probably tried the same formula for the third problem and found it didn't work. Actually, simply filling jar A and pouring off enough to fill jar C would have left you with the right amount. If you were using the other formula, you probably did not notice this simpler possibility—your previous success with the other rule would have given you a *mental set*. A **mental set** is a preexisting state of mind, habit, or attitude that can enhance the quality and speed of perceiving and problem solving under some conditions, but inhibit or distort the quality of our mental activities at times when old ways of thinking and acting are nonproductive in new situations. Much problem solving involves "breaking set"—temporarily giving up your reliance on past learning and mental habits to fully explore the present stimulus array so that you can see all your options from a new perspective. For example, when a snowstorm blocked roads and downed power lines in a mountain town, citizens had to think of their fireplaces as stoves and their icy porches as temporary refrigerators, until electricity was restored.

Another approach to problem solving contrasts *descriptive thinking*—how computers and people solve problems—with *prescriptive thinking*—how people *ought* to solve problems (Levine, 1987). People need to be taught ways to avoid pitfalls in reasoning and to be sensitive to perceptual sets and biases. They also need to adhere to the following prescriptive principles for solving problems:

- *Formulate a plan.* Make it sufficiently concrete to be action-oriented and sufficiently abstract to generalize beyond specific, limited applications.
- *Work in an organized way.*
- *Work, at first, with simpler versions of complex problems.*
- *Mentally rehearse taking the right action.* Visual imaging can be especially helpful for learning motor habits.
- *Engage yourself in the problem.* Inform yourself, and work up enthusiasm for solving it. Give it time and energy.
- *Set yourself up for success.* Anticipate challenges as part of your situation, not as part of yourself. Don't assume you are disadvantaged or inadequate because of prejudices like "I'm not good at numbers," "men aren't good listeners," or "women can't use machinery."

Table 7.1 offers additional tips for improving your cognitive skill functioning.

Search Strategies: Algorithms Versus Heuristics. Once you know the problem space, you have defined the problem but you haven't yet solved it. Solving the problem requires using the operations that get you from the initial state to the goal state. If a problem is like a maze, you must still decide on a strategy for selecting the right path.

One search strategy is an **algorithm**—a methodical, step-by-step procedure for solving problems that guarantees that eventually, with sufficient time and patience, you will find a solution. For example, there are 120 possible combinations of the letters *otrhs*, but only one combination is an actual word. You could try each combination to find that word: *short*. But for an eight-letter group such as *teralbay*, there would be 40,320 possible combinations (8 × 7 × 6 × 5 × 4 × 3 × 2 × 1). A search of all the combinations would eventually reveal the solution, but the search would be long and tedious. The price of a guaranteed solution is sometimes intense, careful labor.

Luckily, there is an alternate approach that we can use to solve a great many problems every day. We can use a **heuristic,** an informal rule of thumb that provides *shortcuts,* reducing complex problem solving to more simple

mental set Tendency to respond to a new problem in the manner used for a previous problem.

algorithm Problem-solving procedure that guarantees reaching a correct outcome by reviewing every possible strategy.

heuristic Cognitive strategy or "rule of thumb," used as a shortcut to solve a complex mental task.

Table 7.1 Tips for Improving Cognitive Skills

APPLICATIONS OF BASIC PRINCIPLES FOR DEVELOPING YOUR COGNITIVE SKILLS CAN BE SUMMARIZED AS FOLLOWS (ANDERSON, 1981, 1982):	
1. *Space your practice.*	In learning a new skill, practice a short time each day, trying to complete a unit of study or one action pattern at one occasion.
2. *Master the subskills.*	Many skills have component parts. Develop these to the point where they are automatic so you don't have to attend to them. Then start focusing on the next higher level and, finally, on the overall skill.
3. *Internalize an ideal model.*	Observe the correct performance of an expert role model so you can get a good picture of what you are trying to achieve. Then monitor your own performance, noting explicitly how it compares with that of your model.
4. *Seek immediate feedback and use it immediately.*	Get knowledge as quickly as you can about the quality of your performance—if possible while the feeling of your action is still in your working memory. Then try to use the feedback while it is still in your working memory.
5. *Anticipate initial frustrations, setbacks, and plateaus in performance.*	Overcoming them requires persistence, practice, renewed effort, and a sense of one's self-efficacy in achieving preset goals.

judgmental operations. Heuristics are general strategies that have often worked in similar situations in the past and may also work in the present case. Some heuristics have become familiar aphorisms, such as "Consider the source." Others are habits or guidelines that some people find personally effective. For instance, where should you put a note to remind yourself to run early morning errands? If one of the first things you look at every morning is your reflection in the bathroom mirror, the mirror is a good place to post a note to yourself. When you have a problem to solve or a decision to make, a heuristic offers a handy strategy in place of a guaranteed solution.

A heuristic that can help you solve the word jumble of *teralbay* is "Look for short words that could be made from some of the letters, and then see if the other letters fit around them." Using such a strategy, you might generate *ably* (tear*ably?*), *able* (ray*table?*), and *tray* (la*tray*be?). By using this search strategy, you would probably not need to try more than a few of the possibilities before you came up with the solution: *betrayal* (Glass et al., 1979).

Using a heuristic does not guarantee that a solution will be found; using an algorithm, tedious though it might be, does. One way experience helps us become better problem solvers is by teaching us which heuristics have served us well, and when and how to use them. When the "guaranteed solution" route will not be too time-consuming, rely on the algorithm; when this demands time or resources you do not have, go for the heuristic. The previous sentence is itself one kind of heuristic that can guide rational problem-solving strategies.

Judging and Deciding

We live in a world of *uncertainty*. We can never be completely confident in our predictions about how people will behave or how events will unfold. Despite this uncertainty, we are constantly called upon to make personal, economic, and political decisions that have enormous impacts on our lives. Are there accepted guidelines or models for making good decisions? In this section, we will see that decision making is always subjective, often error-prone, and sometimes irrational. In addition, we will see that human intuition can be fallible—at times it leads us to make mistakes. By recognizing the underlying cognitive mechanisms that guide our choices, however, we have an opportunity to improve our decision making skills.

judgment   Process of forming opinions, reaching conclusions, and making evaluations based on available material; the product of the judgment process.

Psychologists often distinguish between judgment and decision making. **Judgment** is the process by which we form opinions, reach conclusions, and make critical evaluations of events and people on the basis of available information. We often make judgments—the product of that process—spontaneously, without prompting. **Decision making,** on the other hand, is the process of choosing between alternatives, selecting and rejecting available options. Judgment and decision making are interrelated processes. For example, you might meet someone at a party, and after a brief discussion and a dance together, you might *judge* the person to be intelligent, interesting, honest, and sincere. You might then *decide* to spend most of your party time with that person and to arrange a date for the next weekend.

decision making   Choosing between alternatives; selecting or rejecting available options.

Judging: Making Sense of the World.   Our everyday world is complicated, and we often must rely on relevant knowledge we accumulated previously to guide our behavior. Unlike Dr. Eger, whose experience in the chaos of a concentration camp had no parallels in her life up to that point, most of the situations in which we find ourselves share basic properties with previous situations we've encountered. The theories we've developed through a wide variety of experiences can help us understand novel events and new information. For example, as a student you have attended a great number of classes, and your memory of these experiences will determine how you behave on the first day of a new class. Using previous knowledge simplifies matters; you do not need to relearn the guidelines for class behavior every time you begin a new course.

inference   Logical assumption or conclusion based, not on direct observation, but on samples of evidence or prior beliefs and theories.

Our judgments are based on **inference,** the reasoning process of drawing a conclusion on the basis of a sample of evidence or on the basis of prior beliefs and theories. We use a variety of *inferential strategies* to simplify the inferences we make. Ordinarily these strategies serve us well. In some circumstances, however, we misapply these strategies to new data. When faced with new information that is inconsistent with previous knowledge, we are often too ready to try to fit such information into an established theory rather than consider the possibility that the theory itself requires revision.

In an ongoing quest for efficiency and economy, we do not always choose strategies that are exhaustive and thorough. People habitually use *mental short-*

cuts to make up their minds quickly, easily, and with maximum confidence (Kahneman et al., 1982). Unfortunately, overuse of shortcuts can lead to systematic errors. In fact, people can be misled by the same cognitive processes that work effectively in most situations. However, it might make more sense to use a mental shortcut that *usually* works than to employ a more ideal approach that *always* yields the correct answer but takes a great deal of time and mental effort.

While it is cognitively efficient to identify a few significant, stable characteristics around which to organize our initial reactions to others, we may form overgeneralized stereotypes based on minimal, faulty, or false information. These stereotypes can influence the way we behave toward other people and, in turn, the way they behave toward us. For example, if you are told that someone you are about to meet is schizophrenic, you are likely to form an emotional impression that differs from the impression you would have formed had you not been given the label—regardless of the person's behavior (Fiske & Pavelchak, 1986).

Why are initial impressions so persistent over time and so resistant to new information and contradictory data? What are the forces that distort the way we interpret the evidence of our senses, the memories we retrieve, and the decisions we make?

The Perseverance of False Beliefs. A child interprets the new by *assimilating* it into known categories and *accommodating* old mental structures to fit this new information. For instance, a toddler used to sucking on bottles' nipples might, when given a new clown doll, suck on its protruding plastic nose. Her early efforts to assimilate the doll's nose into the "suckable" category will cease when the child accommodates "sucking" (adjusts it) to exclude things (like dolls' noses) that "don't give milk." Similarly, the adult mind must decide again and again when new data support or fit old theories, and when old theories must be changed because new data just doesn't fit. By balancing our efforts to assimilate and accommodate, we make the best use of new knowledge while also benefitting from past lessons. For example, after surviving a painful breakup, you may approach new relationships with mistrust, assimilating new people into your old system of fears. But if you meet someone who seems trustworthy, you must drop your guard and accommodate your attitude to give another relationship a chance.

We often continue to persevere in beliefs, theories, and ways of doing things because we assimilate data or new experiences in a *biased* fashion (Ross & Lepper, 1980). Data consistent with our beliefs are given only brief attention and quickly filed away mentally since they meet our expectations. But we pay close attention to data that are incongruent and challenging, and we devote our efforts to reinterpreting and explaining this information within the context of our theories. This process is known as **biased assimilation.** Using current theories to explain new data is a reasonable approach, but what if our earlier beliefs are wrong? In such cases, new information which should help us to correct the mistake may be taken instead as evidence *supporting* the first impression.

Adding to this problem is the fact that we may choose to ask questions in ways that they are bound to yield the answers we want (Snyder & Swann, 1978a). For example, if a job interviewer asks you, "Are you prepared to work hard at this job?" would you be prepared to say "No"—especially if you were desperate for a job? Thus the way we collect information may be biased by our expectations. In addition, we tend to surround ourselves with people who share our biases (Festinger, 1957; Olson & Zanna, 1979). It appears we are quite good at shoring up our opinions once they are in place.

Is there anything wrong with our reliance on such cognitive self-protection? One problem is that our tendency to cling to initial theories can lead to *overconfidence* in the truth of our beliefs, because it causes us to underestimate the probability that these beliefs could be wrong. For example, a prejudiced

biased assimilation Collecting data without careful attention because the information supports one's preexisting beliefs.

employer refuses to hire members of a specific ethnic group because she believes "those people" make unreliable workers. Since she doesn't hire them, she never sees them *or* the high quality of their performance—so she maintains her belief that "those people" are not qualified. Ironically, the consequences of prejudice may keep such biased thinking in place by preventing it from being challenged.

We have a tendency to overestimate our accuracy in making predictions and social judgments. Is this necessarily costly? Researchers still debate whether such overconfidence does more harm than good (Taylor & Brown, 1988). On one hand, an inflated sense of confidence may encourage persistence and help you accomplish feats you might not otherwise take on. On the other hand, overconfidence in your impressions could lead you to trust someone who does not deserve it, to put yourself in jeopardy, or to expose yourself to danger. Unrealistic optimism can get you into trouble by preventing you from seeing the potential error—and danger—in your situation, and from taking preventive action or coping effectively (Weinstein, 1980).

Cognitive Biases. We make decisions based on judgments, and we make judgments based on inferences about the evidence we have. Our use of mental shortcuts can result in **cognitive bias,** systematic error in this sequence of inference, judgment, and decision. At times, these biases are not errors but differences in emphasis or perspective that we bring to a situation we are trying to understand. We often maintain confidence in the validity of our intuitions and, as a result, sometimes ignore or discard objective evidence that is less susceptible to subjective error.

Researchers have identified a number of different biases in judgment. For example, we tend to perceive random events as nonrandom (such as superstitiously whispering to dice before you roll them) and correlated events as causally related (like the belief that a full moon makes people crazy). We also tend to perceive people as causing rather than being victimized by their experiences (as when we accuse a rape victim of "asking for it"). Psychologists study these biases to understand the cognitive strategies people use to make complex judgments.

We have noted that heuristics are mental shortcuts used to solve problems by reducing the range of possible solutions. However, overreliance on heuristics can backfire by making mistakes more likely. For example, perhaps you use a heuristic such as "select the longest answer" when taking one professor's multiple-choice tests. But another professor may write test items in which the longest answer is usually the wrong choice—so your trusty heuristic can hurt you if you apply it in the wrong context.

Two heuristics in particular have been found to cause mistakes when they are overused or relied on to excess. These are the *availability heuristic* and the *representativeness heuristic,* first studied by **Amos Tversky** and **Daniel Kahneman.**

Availability Heuristic. You probably try to make intelligent choices about your own health and safety, and seek to avoid unnecessary risks. Consider what you have learned about various threats to well-being. Do tornadoes kill more people than asthma annually in the United States? And how do accidental deaths compare with fatal diseases? When research subjects were asked such questions about the frequency of different causes of death, they overestimated those that were rare but dramatic (such as tornadoes, accidents), and underestimated those that were more frequent but private and "quieter" (such as asthma, diseases) (Slovic, 1984). In fact, asthma kills 20 times more people than tornadoes, and diseases kill 16 times more than accidents do. How can people's estimates be so far off, especially in matters of life and death?

When we use the **availability heuristic,** we estimate the likelihood of an outcome based on how easily similar or identical outcomes can be brought to

cognitive bias A systematic error in the sequence of inference, judgment, and decision.

availability heuristic Cognitive strategy that estimates probabilities based on personal experience.

Because tornadoes are dramatic, they are covered in news reports. Thus, when asked to estimate the frequency of certain causes of death, research subjects overestimated those causes that were rare but dramatic (for example, tornadoes, accidents), and underestimated those that were more frequent but private and "quieter" (for example, asthma, diseases) (Slovic, 1984).

mind or imagined. This heuristic causes us to judge as more frequent or probable those events that are more readily imagined or retrieved from memory. For example, tornadoes are rare destroyers that merit news coverage in headlines and television. The very rarity of colorful threats makes them newsworthy—just as bad news has more shock value than good news. An event may be mentally available not because it is frequent but because it is vivid or recent. Don't make the mistake of equating mental availability with actual frequency.

Representativeness Heuristic. Another judgmental heuristic that simplifies the complex task of social judgment under uncertain conditions is the **representativeness heuristic.** It is based on the presumption that membership in a particular category implies having the characteristics considered typical of members of that category. When estimating the likelihood that a specific case belongs to a given category, we look to see whether it has the features found in a typical category member. For example, is your new acquaintance Holly a vegetarian? You've invited her to dinner and do not want to offend her by serving her a cooked animal on a plate. Of course you could *ask* Holly her preference, but if that is not an option, you might guess based on what you *do* know about her. Does Holly resemble a "typical" vegetarian? Perhaps you believe that most vegetarians wear (non-leather) sandals, ride bicycles, and support liberal social causes. If Holly fits this description, you might feel safest guessing she must also be a vegetarian. In other words, you might judge that Holly *represents* enough of the characteristics of other vegetarians to belong to the same group.

But is this reasonable? Suppose Holly wears sandals because when the weather is balmy, many people do so. She rides a bicycle like many other students do—although most students are not vegetarians. And suppose that most supporters of liberal social causes are not vegetarians. By ignoring the *base rate information*—the real probabilities that features occur or co-occur in the larger population—you have drawn erroneous conclusions. Holly may in fact be an omnivore like most of your acquaintances, although she will probably accept the cheese pizza and salad you offer her without complaint. The penalty for relying on the representativeness heuristic—judging people or events by what seems to be their "type"—may not be great in all instances, but small "acceptable" mistakes can accumulate over time into larger, painful misjudgments, such as in the numerous misjudgments people make regarding characteristics of minorities.

Availability and representativeness are just two of many heuristics that we use in making judgments about the world every day. The biased judgments that result from these and other rules of thumb can distort our views of reality, and remain compelling even when we know the true state of affairs.

Decision Making. Judgments involve evaluating information about the world, while decisions require making choices. How do people make choices? Classic economic theory starts with the assumption that people act to maximize gain, minimize loss, and allocate their resources efficiently. It assumes that people do the best they can with available information and that most people have the same set of information and act as if they understand and can apply the laws of probability properly. However, people do not always understand and correctly apply the laws of probability, and they are often required to make decisions under *conditions of uncertainty* in which the relevant probabilities are not known (see "Time Out for Critical Thinking").

Research shows that different descriptions of the same decision can result in different choices. In addition, decision makers may be more influenced by risks than by reason.

Decision Frames. A decision frame is the structure or context of a problem's presentation. While preferences between options should be consistent—the same regardless of how a problem is worded, for example—this is often not

---

representativeness heuristic
Cognitive strategy that assigns items to categories based on whether items possess some characteristics representative of the category.

the case. Decisions *are* influenced by the decision frame, even when the alternatives are formally equivalent or technically the same. Consider, for example, the choice between surgery and radiation for treatment of lung cancer. Statistical information about the results of each treatment for previous patients can be presented either in terms of survival rates or mortality rates.

➥ First read the survival frame for the problem and choose your preferred treatment; then read the mortality frame and see if you feel like changing your preference.

Survival Frame

Surgery: Of 100 people having surgery, 90 live through the postoperative period, 68 are alive at the end of the first year, and 34 are alive at the end of five years.
Radiation Therapy: Of 100 people having radiation therapy, all live through the treatment, 77 are alive at the end of one year, and 22 are alive at the end of five years.
Which do you choose: surgery or radiation?

Mortality Frame

Surgery: Of 100 people having surgery, 10 die during surgery or the postoperative period, 32 die by the end of one year, and 66 die by the end of five years.
Radiation Therapy: Of 100 people having radiation therapy, none die during treatment, 23 die by the end of one year, and 78 die by the end of five years.
Which do you choose: surgery or radiation?

You can see that, objectively, the data are identical in both frames. But research subjects faced with both presentations were more likely to choose radiation therapy given the mortality frame (44 percent of them) than given the survival frame (only 18 percent). This framing effect held equally for a group of clinic patients, statistically sophisticated business students, and experienced physicians (McNeil et al., 1982). Presentation matters!

➥ **TIME OUT . . . FOR CRITICAL THINKING**

When we make a decision, we consider the likelihood of various outcomes and how much we value each one. Most of the research on decision making has focused mainly on people's probability estimates and related concepts. Recently, however, psychologists have turned their attention to the value component and have raised some fascinating questions.

One area of particular interest is our ability to predict how much we will like something at a later time or after repeated exposure. Tastes change—later we might not enjoy something that we do now—and so do values. But recent evidence suggests that people are not always accurate predictors of changes in their tastes (Kahneman & Snell, 1990), and that their theories of how tastes change lead them to decisions they later regret.

We can avoid many common pitfalls in decision making by becoming better information processors. Awareness of the power of biases, base rates, heuristics, and decision frames can help you improve your own decision making. Examine your own decision-making "conscience" with these values questions:

- What kind of relationship would you need to have with someone to be willing to die for that person?

- If you could make the world a better place by doing so, would you be willing to make yourself uncomfortable? to experience pain? to move away and leave your friends and family behind forever?

- If you and your best friend were the final contestants in competition for a vast sum of money, would you be willing to let your friend win? In the same situation, do you think your friend would let *you* win?

- Would you be willing to donate hard labor to an important cause if your contribution would always remain anonymous?

- Can you imagine time or circumstances ever *changing* your answers to any of the above questions?

- What processes do you use to make important decisions in your life? Have these strategies worked well so far, or could you improve on them by adding new ideas from this chapter?

SUMMING UP

The extremes of human reasoning are autistic and realistic. Autistic reasoning is personal, individually distinctive, and not validated by external reality. Realistic reasoning is governed by reality constraints. Deductive reasoning involves drawing conclusions from premises on the basis of rules of logic. Inductive reasoning involves inferring a conclusion from evidence on the basis of its likelihood or probability. Scientific hypotheses and testing are typically based on inductive reasoning.

When solving problems, we must define the initial state, the goal state, and the operations that can get us from the first to the second—a difficult task in ill-defined problems. Mental sets such as functional fixedness can hamper creative problem solving until the set is broken. Algorithms ensure an eventual solution if there is one, but are impractical in many cases. Heuristics are mental shortcuts that often help us reach a solution quickly, although they do not guarantee success.

To make sense of uncertainty in our world, we draw inferences on which to base judgments or critical evaluations. By relying on mental shortcuts that usually serve us well, we may become prone to error and bias. Prior beliefs can bias our assimilation of new data. Relying on the availability heuristic involves judging examples to be common simply because they are available in memory. The representativeness heuristic involves judging individual cases in terms of how typical they seem to be of specific categories. Decision making is influenced by the way choices are framed and by the risks people are willing to take.

Remembering

➡ Imagine what it would be like if you suddenly had no memory of your past—no memory of people you have known or of events that have happened to you. Without such "time anchors," how would you maintain a sense of who you are (self-identity)? Suppose you lost the ability to form *new* memories. How would your life be altered?

Research on people suffering from amnesia (memory loss) is just one way psychologists are trying to understand the complex mechanisms of memory. More often, researchers study the way people with normal memories store the enormous amount of information that they acquire, the way people retrieve that information from memory when they need it, and the way people sometimes cannot find what they have stored in their vast memories.

Memory failures raise questions about what memory is and what role it plays in our lives. It is estimated that the average human mind can store 100

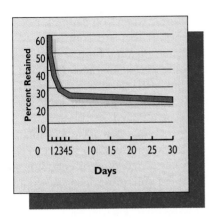

Figure 7.9 Ebbinghaus's Forgetting Curve
The curve shows how many nonsense sylla-bles that the individuals using the savings method can remember when tested over a 30-day period. The curve decreases rapidly and then reaches a plateau.

trillion bits of information, yet, sometimes, we can't recall where we left the car keys, or we forget a promise to call home. We all would like to be able to improve our memories—for trivial information, names, faces, musical tunes, and funny jokes. Some psychologists are engaged in developing techniques for memory enhancement.

As noted earlier, the nineteenth-century researcher Hermann Ebbinghaus was the pioneering force in the experimental investigation of human verbal memory. Ebbinghaus would present nonsense syllables to a human subject, whose task was *serial learning* or memorization of a set of items presented one by one. When he used himself as a subject, Ebbinghaus used *rote learning*, memorization by mechanical repetition, to perform the task. For example, he would begin by examining a list of nonsense syllables—such as POV, KEB, RUZ—and read through the items one at a time until he finished the list. He would then read through the list, again and again, in the same order, until he could recite all the items in the correct order. Then he distracted himself from rehearsing the list by forcing himself to learn many other lists. Finally, instead of trying to recall all the items on the original list, Ebbinghaus measured his memory by seeing how many trials it took him to *relearn* the original list. If he took fewer trials to relearn it than he had to learn it, he had *saved* information from his original study. Using this *savings method*, Ebbinghaus recorded the degree of memory lost after different time intervals. The curve he obtained is shown in **Figure 7.9**. As you can see, he found a rapid initial loss of memory, followed by a gradually declining rate of loss. Ebbinghaus's curve is typical of results from experiments on rote memory of meaningless material found in research laboratories throughout the world.

Modern memory researchers are more interested than Ebbinghaus was in how we remember *meaningful* material in every aspect of our daily lives. Memory raises a variety of issues for psychologists in many different fields. Social psychologists consider how people remember the traits and behaviors of others when forming coherent mental representations of their social environments. Cognitive psychologists need to know how memory affects people's ability to solve problems or reason logically. Developmental psychologists are concerned with when in life memory begins to help a person structure his or her world; they also want to find ways to help the elderly cope with declining memory skills. Since so much of what we do depends on memory, memory has become a separate field of study. Psychologists have come to see that our thoughts and dreams and our sense of identity are defined by our memories of past experiences.

Encoding, Storage, and Retrieval

The ability to recall an experience at a later time requires the operation of three mental processes: encoding, storage, and retrieval. **Encoding** is the translation of incoming stimulus energy into a unique neural code that your brain can process. **Storage** is the retention over time of encoded material. **Retrieval** is the recovery at a later time of the stored information.

Encoding requires that you first select some stimulus event from among the huge array of inputs nearly always available to you. Then you must identify the distinctive features of that experienced event. Is the event a sound, a visual image, or a smell? If it's a sound, is it loud, soft, or harsh? Does it fit with other sounds into some pattern that forms a name, a melody, or a cry for help? Is it a sound you have heard before? During encoding, you try to tag an experience with a variety of labels. Some of these labels are specific and unique—"It's Adam Z." Others put the event into a general category or class—"He's a rock musician." This encoding process is usually so automatic and rapid that you are unaware you are doing it.

A further encoding process relates the new input to other information you already possess or to goals or purposes for which it might later prove relevant.

encoding Converting information into a code that can be communicated.

storage Retaining encoded information over time.

retrieval Recovery of stored information from memory.

elaboration Relating new input to previously acquired information or to relevant goals or purposes.

This process is called **elaboration.** Retention is better when you can link new information with what you already know. Memories that are connected to other information are much more usable than isolated memory units.

Storage retains encoded information over some period of time. Encoded information tends to be lost when it cannot be linked to already stored information, or if it is not periodically practiced or used. The more often some bit of information is rehearsed, the more likely it is to be retained.

Retrieval is the payoff for all your earlier effort. When it works, it enables you to gain access—sometimes in a split second—to information you stored earlier. Can you remember what comes before storage: decoding or encoding? The answer is simple to retrieve now, but will you be able to retrieve *encoding* as swiftly and as confidently when you are tested on this chapter days or weeks from now? To understand the complexity of memory, it is important to consider that some retrieval experiences will be more difficult than others.

Retrieval Methods. You might assume that you either know something or you don't and that any method of testing what you know will give the same results. Not so. The two most common testing methods—recall and recognition—give quite different results.

recall Retrieval method in which one must reproduce previously presented information.

Recall means reproducing the information to which you were previously exposed. "What are the three memory systems?" is a recall question. Recognition means realizing that a certain stimulus event is one you have seen or heard before. **Recognition** is the retrieval method you employ when you answer the following multiple choice question:

recognition Retrieval method in which one must identify present stimuli as having been previously presented.

> Which of the following refers to a rule of thumb?
> A. syllogism
> B. premise
> C. heuristic
> D. algorithm

Recognition is also the method employed when police ask an eyewitness to identify a perpetrator among a lineup of suspects.

Recall questions usually give fewer and less specific cues than recognition questions. There is another important difference between recognition and recall. For recognition, you need simply to match a remembered stimulus against a present perception; both the stimulus and perception are in your consciousness. For recall, however, you must reconstruct from memory something that is not in the present environment and then describe it well enough so that an observer can be sure about what is really in your mind.

Encoding, storage, and retrieval processes take place in each of three basic memory systems. Before we turn to examine what these memory systems do, take a moment to answer the questions that follow:

1. What is your social security number? What is your best friend's?
2. Name the title and authors of this textbook.
3. When did you *first* experience the emotion of guilt? When was the *last* time you told your parents that you loved them?
4. Do you know the difference between iconic and echoic sensory information storage?
5. What is the significance of "rosebud" in the movie *Citizen Kane?*

Was your recall quick and certain on some items and incomplete and vague on others? Was your memory for negative emotional experiences similar to your ability to recall numbers or names? Are there answers you are sure you do not know? Familiarizing yourself with your own memory and retrieval mechanisms will help clarify some of the abstract discussions of the memory types and processes that follow.

Three Memory Systems: Sensory, Working, and Long-Term Memory

Psychologists are fairly confident that, within the overall system of remembering and recalling information, there are three memory systems: sensory memory, working memory, and long-term memory. *Sensory memory* preserves fleeting impressions of sensory stimuli—sights, sounds, smells, and textures—for only a second or two, as when the sound of a television commercial seems to ring in your ears after you turn off the set. *Working memory* includes recollections of what you have recently perceived, such as a phone number you have just looked up; such limited information lasts only up to 20 seconds unless it receives special attention. *Long-term memory* preserves information for retrieval at any later time—up to an entire lifetime. Information in long-term memory constitutes our knowledge about the world, and includes such varied material as the lyrics to your favorite song, and the year that Wilhelm Wundt founded the first experimental laboratory in psychology. (Quiz: When was that? 18__.)

The three memory systems are also thought of as *stages* in the sequence of processing information. The three systems or stages of remembering are conceptual models of the way psychologists believe we process incoming information, retain it, and then later use it. By learning how information is processed in each subsystem, psychologists hope to understand why some conditions help us remember experiences, even trivial ones, while other conditions make us forget even important experiences. **Figure 7.10** shows the hypothesized flow of information into and among these subsystems.

We will first review each of the three memory subsystems: sensory memory, working memory, and long-term memory. Next we will consider the constructive nature of memory. Finally we will turn to explanations for forgetting and "false" remembering.

sensory memory Initial process that preserves brief impressions of stimuli; also **sensory register.**

Sensory Memory. A **sensory memory**—also called a **sensory register**—is an impression formed from input of any of the senses. Sensory memory represents

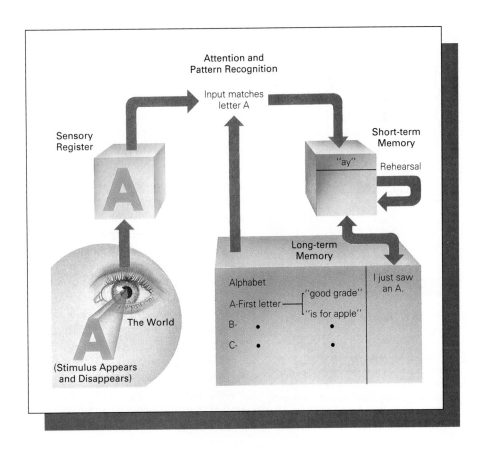

Figure 7.10 A Model of the Human Memory System

icon Visual memory, lasting about one half-second.

echo Auditory memory, lasting several seconds.

working memory Memory processes that preserve recently perceived events or experiences; also *short-term memory*.

short-term memory (STM) See *working memory*.

a primitive kind of memory and a register for each sense; it also holds appropriate incoming stimulus information for a brief interval. A visual memory, or **icon,** lasts about one-half second. An auditory memory, or **echo,** lasts several seconds (Neisser, 1967). You can easily demonstrate the difference between the sensory registers for yourself. When you turn off a radio, the sounds of the music literally echo in your head for a while after the sound is gone, but if you pull down a window shade, the scene outside is gone almost at once.

What would happen if icons and echoes did not occur? Without them, we could see and hear stimuli only at the moment they were physically present, which would not be long enough for recognition to occur. These sensory registers are essential to hold input until it is recognized and passed on for further processing.

Storage of Sensory Memories. Though fleeting, your sensory storage capacity is large—more than all your senses can process at one time. Early researchers underestimated the amount of stimuli that sensory memory could store, because they asked subjects to report entire arrays. Subjects shown a three-by-three array of nine items (such as the one below) for a fraction of a second could only report about four items.

    D J B
    X H G
    C L Y

Researcher **George Sperling** guessed that subjects had a limited ability to *report* all viewed items, but not necessarily to *recall* them. Immediately after flashing stimulus arrays, Sperling gave subjects an auditory signal about which row of letters to report. Asked to give this smaller "partial report," subjects achieved perfect accuracy—no matter *which* row was signalled. Further research confirmed that, although reporting might be limited to about four items, the span of sensory memory was as great as nine items (Sperling, 1960, 1963). However, while sensory memory is quite accurate, the image or *trace* of the stimulus decays very rapidly (see **Figure 7.11**).

In auditory memory as well, more information is available than people can typically report (Darwin et al., 1972). Echoic memories may be necessary to process many subtle, simultaneously presented aspects of speech, such as intonation and emphasis. Would it be better if sensory memories lasted longer so that we would have more time to process them? Not really. New information is constantly coming in, and it must also be processed. Sensory memories last just long enough to give a sense of continuity but not long enough to interfere with new sensory impressions.

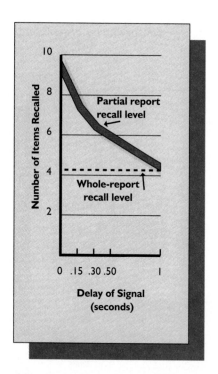

Figure 7.11 Recall by the Partial-Report Method
The solid line shows the average number of items four subjects recalled using the partial-report method, both immediately after presentation and at three later times. For comparison, the dotted line shows the number of items recalled by the whole-report method (Adapted from Sperling).

Working Memory. Working memory—also called **short-term memory (STM)**—occurs between the fleeting events of sensory memory and the more permanent storage of long-term memory. A number of interesting characteristics distinguish this memory-processing phase.

Working memory has a very *limited capacity.* Much less information is stored in this stage than in either of the other two stages. It also has a *short retention duration:* What is stored is lost after about 18-20 seconds unless it is held in consciousness. But working memory is the only memory stage in which conscious processing of material takes place, and material held in it survives as long as it is held in conscious attention—far beyond the 20-second limit when material is held without attention. This is why short-term memory came to be called working memory: Material transferred to it from either sensory or long-term memory (both of them nonconscious) can be worked over, thought about, and organized. For example, after looking up a phone number, you may repeat it to yourself until you dial it, perhaps reciting the numbers aloud, or picturing the digits, to make the number memorable.

Encoding. Information enters working memory as organized images and patterns that are recognized as familiar and meaningful. Verbal patterns entering working memory seem to be held there in *acoustic* form—according to the way they sound—even when they come through an individual's eyes rather than ears. When subjects are asked to recall lists of letters they have just seen, their errors tend to be confusions of letters that *sound* similar—such as D and T—rather than letters that look similar—such as D and O (Conrad, 1964). Acoustic coding may reflect our preference for verbal rehearsal of information.

immediate memory span Brief, limited (between five and nine chunks of information) storage capacity of working memory.

Storage. The limited, brief storage capacity of working memory is called **immediate memory span.** When the items to be remembered are *unrelated,* the capacity of working memory seems to be between five and nine bits of information—about seven (plus or minus two) familiar items, such as letters, words, numbers, or almost any kind of meaningful item. When you try to force more than seven items into working memory, earlier items are lost to accommodate more recent ones. This displacement process is similar to laying out seven 1-foot bricks on a 7-foot table. When an eighth brick is pushed on at one end, the brick at the opposite end is pushed off the table. Human memory seems bound by this "magic number" 7, as discovered by **George Miller** (1956) in repeated studies and demonstrations, subjects worldwide are able to retain—more or less—only about seven meaningful units of information.

chunk Meaningful unit of information.

Processing in Working Memory. There are two important ways to increase the limited capacity of short-term storage so that more of the information there can be transferred into long-term memory. These two methods—*chunking* and *rehearsal*—should be familiar to you since you use them regularly.

A **chunk** is a meaningful unit of information. A chunk can be a single letter or number, a group of letters or other items, or even a group of words or an entire sentence. For example, the sequence 1-9-8-4 consists of four digits that could constitute four chunks—about half of what your working memory can hold. However, if you see the digits as a recent year or the title of George Orwell's novel—*1984*—they constitute only one chunk, leaving you much more capacity for other chunks of information. **Chunking** is the process of recoding single items by grouping them on the basis of similarity or some other organizing principle, or by combining the items into larger patterns based on information stored in long-term memory. When you memorize a seven-digit phone number as two sequences—one of three digits, and one of four—you automatically increase the capacity of your working memory by compacting seven bits of information into two manageable chunks.

chunking Recoding information into a single meaningful unit.

Between looking up a needed telephone number and successfully dialing it, you probably repeat or recite the digits to yourself to keep them in mind. This technique is called **maintenance rehearsal.** Undistracted rehearsal appears to be essential to retaining information in working memory. Rehearsal keeps information in working memory and prevents competing inputs from pushing it out; but maintenance rehearsal is not an efficient way to transfer information to long-term memory.

maintenance rehearsal Active repetition of information to enhance subsequent access to it.

To make sure that information is transferred, you need to engage in **elaborative rehearsal,** a process in which the information is not just repeated but actively analyzed and related to already-stored knowledge. This process happens when you note that the telephone number 358-9211 can also be thought of as *3 + 5 = 8* and *9 + 2 = 11.* This elaboration depends upon having addition rules and summations stored in and transferred from long-term memory. If these rules and summations are in long-term memory, you can find patterns and meanings in otherwise unrelated and meaningless items. The same principle—using meaning to organize information—is used by services whose telephone numbers are memorable words, such as 1-800-FLOWERS for a florist delivery service.

elaborative rehearsal Repetition of incoming information to analyze and relate new material to previously stored knowledge.

A good listener uses the process of chunking while listening to a lecture.

Retrieval from Working Memory. You now know something about how to get approximately seven chunks of information into your working memory, but how do you get them out? Getting them out is the task of *retrieval*. Research by **Saul Sternberg** has indicated that, when subjects review a list of digits in STM to discover whether it contains a specific digit, they review the entire series before answering yes or no. Thus longer lists take longer to review, although both short and long series are exhausted before a subject is sure of the answer.

long-term memory (LTM) Memory processes associated with preserving information for retrieval at any later time; theorized to have unlimited capacity.

Long-Term Memory (LTM). **Long-term memory (LTM)** is the storehouse of all the experiences, events, information, emotions, skills, words, categories, rules, and judgments that have been transferred from sensory and short-term memories. LTM constitutes each person's total knowledge of the world and of the self. Material in long-term memory enables you to solve new problems, reason, keep future appointments, and use a variety of rules to manipulate abstract symbols—so that you can think about situations you have never experienced, or create new words.

Given the amount of information stored in long-term memory, it is a marvel that it is so accessible. You can often get the exact information you want in a split second: Who discovered classical conditioning? Name a play by Shakespeare. Your responses to these requests probably came effortlessly because of several special features of long-term memory: words and concepts have been encoded by their *meanings,* linking them to many other stored items; the knowledge in your long-term memory is stored in an organized order; and many alternative cues can help you retrieve exactly what you want from all that is there.

Types of Long-Term Memory. There are actually two main varieties of long-term memory—procedural and declarative. Each is distinguished by the kind of information it holds.

procedural memory LTM component that stores memory for how things are done.

Procedural memory is the way we remember *how* things get done. It is used to acquire, retain, and employ perceptual, cognitive, and motor skills (Anderson, 1982; Tulving, 1983). Skill memories are memories of *actions,* such as bicycle riding or tying shoelaces. You can consciously recall skill mem-

Participants in a knowledge bowl need to draw on their long-term memories to answer the varied questions they are asked.

ories only during the early phases of performance (right after you first learn the skill). Experts perform tasks requiring advanced skills without conscious recall of the appropriate skill memories. In fact, experts are often unable to consciously think through their tasks without hindering their performance. It's easier to perform the task than describe how to do it.

Unlike procedural memory, **declarative memory**—the way we recall explicit information—involves some degree of conscious effort. Remembering how to drive is a procedural process; recalling directions for driving to a specific location requires declarative memory.

There are two different types of declarative memory: semantic and episodic. **Semantic memory** is the generic, categorical memory that stores the basic *meanings* of words and concepts without reference to their time and place in experience. It more closely resembles an encyclopedia than an autobiography. Among other information, your semantic memory includes generic facts about grammar, musical composition, and scientific principles. The things you know and lessons you learn are stored in semantic memory.

Episodic memory stores autobiographical information—an individual's own perceptual experiences—along with some *temporal coding* (or time tags) to identify when the event occurred and some *content* coding for where it took place. For example, memories of a happiest birthday or of a first love affair are stored in episodic memory.

Successful recall of much of the factual information you have learned in college can also involve episodic memory because you have stored information according to its context, the event or personal symbolism it triggers. In answering a test question, you may remember not only the lecture material that provides the correct answer, but also where you were sitting when you took the notes, and where on the chalkboard the lecturer inscribed the key terms.

Encoding in LTM. Sensory memory encodes brief sensations, and working memory records items in their order of arrival. In contrast, long-term memory stores items according to their meanings, and cross-references them with other stored information. Every item in long-term memory is connected by its meaning to many other indexes for retrieval.

The role that *meaningful organization* plays in long-term storage is demonstrated when you remember the gist or sense of an idea rather than the actual sentence you heard. For example, if you hear the sentence, "Mary picked up the book," and later hear, "The book was picked up by Mary," you might think that the second sentence was the same as the one you heard earlier, because the meaning was the same even though the form was different.

declarative memory Memory for explicit information; also known as *fact memory*.

semantic memory LTM component that stores memory for basic meanings of words and concepts.

episodic memory LTM component that stores autobiographic information coded for reference to a time frame for past occurrences.

We are more likely to store information about the *meanings* of sentences than the exact structures of the sentences (Bransford & Franks, 1971). If you do not understand the meaning of a sentence or paragraph, you will be unable to organize it into a memorable unit of information. As in working memory, chunking and elaborative rehearsal are helpful to LTM because they organize material for storage and make it more meaningful.

Material can usually be meaningfully organized in more than one way. Sometimes you encode by noticing the structure already imposed on the material, such as the different levels of headings in this chapter. Other times you may impose your own organization by outlining the main points and subpoints or by fitting new items into a structure of knowledge you already have. You may also organize material on the basis of relevant personal experiences or physical reminders. For example, you might remember the names of people you met over a year ago by recalling that you all attended a friend's birthday party, and the celebration included games and jokes involving all the guests' names.

mnemonics Strategies or techniques that use familiar associations in storing new information to be more easily retrieved.

Mnemonics: Strategies to Improve Memory. To help yourself remember, you can use special mental strategies called mnemonics (from the Greek word meaning *to remember*). **Mnemonics** are short, verbal devices that encode a long series of facts by associating them with familiar and previously encoded information. Three types of mnemonic strategies have been carefully studied: natural language mediators, the method of loci, and visual imagery.

Natural language mediators are meanings or spelling patterns of words that are already stored in LTM. These can easily be associated with new information. For instance, to remember a grocery list you can concoct a story linking the items: "The cat discovers I'm out of *tuna* so she interrupts me while I'm using the *shampoo* and meows to *egg* me on," and so on. The use of rhyming slogans and rhythmic musical jingles can make it easier to remember material as diverse as brand names and grammar rules (for example, "I before E except after C").

The *method of loci* relies on making places (from the Latin *locus,* "place") for memories. To use the *method of loci* (pronounced LOW-sigh) you would imagine a familiar sequence of places, such as the rooms of your home. When memorizing a series of words or names, you mentally put one in each of those places; to retrieve the series, you examine the places to "see" what you have put in each one. To recall a grocery list, you might imagine seeing a can of *tuna* on your bed, turning to find *shampoo* spilled on the floor, and walking carefully through the hall so as not to step on the *eggs* lying there. More bizarre combinations are easier to remember; a can of tuna in your bedroom will be a more memorable image than tuna in your kitchen. (Bower, 1972)

The method of loci may rely on the mnemonic power of *visual imagery,* one of the most effective forms of encoding. Mental images may work well because they use both verbal and visual memories simultaneously (Paivio, 1968). With visual imagery, you remember words by associating them with vivid, distinctive mental pictures. In the case of the infamous grocery list, for example, you might combine the images of tuna, shampoo, and eggs in a bizarre but memorable way: Picture a *tuna* floating on an enormous fried *egg* in a sea of foamy *shampoo,* for example. Or imagine a politician you dislike eating *tuna* from the can, his hair covered with *shampoo* suds, while you throw *eggs* at him.

Besides these three effective systems, other mnemonic strategies will be familiar to you. You may arrange words in a memorable sing-song organization, such as "Thirty days hath September—April, June, and November." Or you may isolate the initials of the terms to memorize and arrange them into meaningful letter strings, such as using the name Roy G. Biv to remember the visible spectrum's Red, Orange, Yellow, Green, Blue, Indigo, Violet. Acronyms—abbreviations composed of initials—are pronounceable strings of initials very popular among bureaucracies, such as HUD for the Department of

Housing and Urban Development, and RADAR for Radio Detecting and Ranging.

Encoding Specificity. Your method of organizing material in the encoding stage directly affects not only how the material is stored but, equally important, what cues will work when you want to retrieve it. The close relationship among encoding, storage, and retrieval is called the **encoding specificity principle** (Tulving & Thomson, 1973). The better the match between your encoding and later cues, the better your recall will be. For example, if you memorize the word jam in the context of *traffic jam,* you will have trouble recognizing it when the context is changed to *strawberry jam.* If you expect to be given an essay test on material you are studying, you should try to encode it by remembering general information about abstract relationships, concepts, and analysis, because that is probably what you will be asked to retrieve. If you expect multiple-choice questions, you should pay more attention to specific, concrete facts, definitions, and distinctions.

Storage in LTM. Psychologists know that information in LTM is stored in organized patterns, with networks of meaning connecting chunks of knowledge. Because the system is enormously complex, researchers know little about the way all forms of remembered experiences are actually represented in long-term memory. Psychologists have put forth three hypotheses about the ways that people represent ideas and experiences in long-term memory. These three are propositional storage, dual-code memory, and eidetic imagery.

The smallest unit of meaning that people store is called a **proposition.** A proposition is an idea that expresses a relationship between concepts, objects, or events. To express that relationship, the proposition is comprised of a subject and a predicate. "People drink water" and "Grandparents spoil children" are examples of propositions. As you can see, propositions are not facts; they are merely assertions that can be judged true or false. According to some theorists, networks of propositions form the structural building blocks of LTM. These semantic (meaning) networks enable us to locate stored information, alter it, or add to it (Anderson, 1976).

Other investigators believe that people use visual codes in addition to verbal ones for storing memories. This hypothesis is known as the **dual-code model** of memory (Begg & Paivio, 1969; Paivio, 1983). According to this view, sensory information and concrete sentences are more likely to be stored as images, while abstract sentences are coded verbally. Verbal codes cannot act as indexes or reference pegs for visual codes.

Some psychologists have proposed that memory uses different types of codes to represent different types of information (Day, 1986). For example, propositional networks are used to encode test information (Anderson & Bower, 1973), and mental images are used for maps (B. Tversky, 1981). The answer to the debate seems to be that both propositions and images represent information, but at different times and for different processing demands.

Actual images may be stored in memory. We know this because of the phenomenon of photographic memory, known technically as **eidetic imagery.** Research subjects who claim to have eidetic imagery report seeing a whole stimulus picture in front of their closed eyes as if they were experiencing it directly rather than scanning memory for traces of it. Instead of asking subjects to describe pictures they have been shown, researchers now use a more demanding test for eidetic imagery. They show subjects two pictures in succession. Each picture is meaningless by itself, but together they form a meaningful composite. The subjects must hold the two images in visual memory in enough detail so the images will fuse to form a single picture that is not predictable from either part alone. As the test progresses, the pictures become more complex. When tested with this method, only a small number of people qualify as true "eidetikers" (Gummerman et al., 1972; Leask et al., 1969)—only about 5 percent of those studied (Gray & Gummerman, 1975).

encoding specificity principle
Assumption that information retrieval is enhanced if cues received at time of recall are consistent with those present at time of encoding.

proposition Expression of relationship between concepts, objects, or events.

dual-code model (of memory)
Memory coding theory that proposes both visual and verbal codes are used to store information.

eidetic imagery Uncommon memory process by which some individuals can store detailed, whole pictorial representations of scenes or patterns for some periods of time.

retrieval cues Available internal or external stimuli that help in recovering information from memory.

Retrieval from LTM. Some researchers argue that all information encoded in long-term memory is stored there permanently. However, retrieval failures occur when the appropriate retrieval location or pathway for a given memory is forgotten (Linton, 1975). The stimuli available as you search for a memory are known as **retrieval cues.** These cues may be external, such as questions on a quiz (What memory principles do you associate with the research of Sternberg and Sperling?), or generated internally (Where have I met her before?).

Since information is organized in LTM storage, it is not surprising that cues based on *organization* can also help you retrieve what you know. In one study, subjects were given a list of words to memorize for free recall. The words were arranged by categories; a label preceded each category. The category labels were not mentioned in the instructions; subjects were simply told to memorize the words. During the recall test, half the subjects were given the category labels as retrieval cues, while the other subjects were asked only to recall as many items as they could. Recall was much better for the subjects given the category labels as retrieval cues (Tulving & Pearlstone, 1966). Other research has shown that recall is aided by organization, whether the organization is imposed by the experimenter or generated by the subject (Mandler, 1972).

Even with good cues, not all stored content is equally accessible, as you know only too well. In the case of familiar, well-learned information, more aspects of it have been stored and more connections between it and the many different parts of the memory network have been established—so a number of cues can give you access to it. On the other hand, when trying to find the one key that will unlock a less familiar memory, you may have to use special search strategies. For example, to remember the name of someone you met only once, you must recall your impressions of that one meeting. In contrast, to retrieve the name of a more familiar individual, you may be able to imagine several mutual friends all speaking the elusive name.

Constructive Memory

Sometimes what people remember is either more than or different from what they actually experienced. Based on laboratory studies about the way people process and remember meaningful material, psychologists view remembering as a continuation of the active, constructive process of perception. According to this new view, as we organize material to make it meaningful, we frequently add details to make it more complete or change it to make it fit better with other, already existing information in our personal memory store. Psychologist **Jerome Bruner** first noted that when we construct memories we "go beyond the information given" (1973). The study of such constructive processes is guided by the general principle that *how and what you remember is determined by who you are and what you already know.* In other words, what is perceived and remembered is a function of the individual's past history, current values, and future expectations, as well as the nature of the stimulus being committed to memory.

Schemas. Many studies have demonstrated the importance of schemas in helping us organize and remember details. Schemas, you recall, are "knowledge packages" about people and things that shape our perceptions and expec- expectations. They also shape our memories of past experiences. For example, story titles give us schemas that help us make sense of elements in the plot and enable us to remember relevant sections of the story. When the elements don't fit with the title, reconstructive memory has trouble, as seen in the following study: While some subjects read a story titled "Watching a Peace March from the Fortieth Floor," other subjects read the exact same story retitled "A Space Trip to an Inhabited Planet." Most of the story was ambiguous enough to fit under either title, but one sentence fit only the space trip title: "The landing was gentle, and luckily the atmosphere was such that no special suits had to be worn." More than half of those who were given the space trip title remembered this sentence, but only a few who read the "peace march" story remembered it. The titles seemed to have activated different schemas. For one schema, the critical sentence fit, was interpreted as relevant, and was remembered; for the other, it had no meaning and was lost or not retrievable (Bransford & Johnson, 1972).

Similarly, we have people-related schemas that can influence what we perceive and remember about people who are described to us (Cantor & Mischel, 1979). For example, most of us have schemas for Communists, cult leaders, environmentalists, and used-car salesmen. If a person we do not know is described as belonging to one of these categories, our schemas lead us to assume that the person has particular personality characteristics, and they lead us to have an emotional reaction to the person, either approving or disapproving. In addition, when we hear details about someone we do not know, we remember more of the details if we can relate them to an appropriate organizing schema.

When we try to recall information that is not consistent with a schema we have formed about certain individuals, our memory may distort the input to make it more schema-consistent. For example, if we are told that two people are arguing a great deal during their courtship, but a year later we hear that they are happily married to each other, we either forget about their early arguments or we suspect their marriage is not really "happy." Either way, distortion permits a memory consistent with our schema. When the same early information about disagreement is followed by a report of an unhappy marriage, we tend to remember the disagreement quite accurately (Spiro, 1977).

Although it is only recently popular, the study of constructive processes in memory actually began over 50 years ago with British psychologist **Sir Frederic Bartlett,** who described his work in his classic book, *Remembering* (1932). Bartlett focused on the kinds of constructions that take place when people try to remember material that is unfamiliar to them. He observed the way British undergraduates transmitted and remembered simple stories whose themes and wording were taken from another culture. The most famous story was "The War of the Ghosts," an American Indian tale. Bartlett found that the original story was evidently unclear to the subjects because of their lack of cultural understanding. The subjects unknowingly changed details to fit their own schemas so that the story would make sense to them.

Eyewitness Testimony. If memory is reconstructed to fit our schemas, how far should the memory of eyewitnesses be trusted in revealing the truth about criminal events? The ease with which we can be misled into "remembering" false information has been amply demonstrated in the laboratory research of **Elizabeth Loftus** (1979, 1984) and her colleagues. During the research, bright college students with good memories were misled into "recalling" that, "at the scene," a yield sign was a stop sign, a nonexistent barn existed, and a green traffic light was shining red. They might have heard another "witness" report something about a man's mustache when, in fact, the man had no mustache. Although many subjects resisted being misled, a significant proportion integrated the new information into their memory representations and confidently reported the nonexistent mustache, barn, and stop sign as part of what they actually saw "with their own eyes."

This line of research has practical, applied value and also contributes to basic knowledge. The process by which a person perceives an event, encodes that information, and recalls it at a later time is at the heart of psychological interest in learning and memory. Our human capacity for constructive memory not only increases the difficulty of getting accurate eyewitness testimony but also shields people from some truths they do not want to accept. We distort incoming information to fit our prejudices, and remember what we expected rather than what really happened.

Despite its faults, constructive memory is an enormously positive feature of creative minds. More often than not, it helps us make sense of our uncertain world by providing the right context in which to understand, interpret, remember, and act on minimal or fragmentary evidence. Without it, our memories would be little more than second-rate transcription services that could not assign any special significance to our many unique and personal experiences.

Forgetting

We all remember an enormous amount of material over long periods of time. College students can accurately recall details about the births of younger siblings even when those events occurred 16 years earlier (Sheingold & Tenney, 1982). Knowledge in semantic memory (for example, knowing what happened in the year 1066) is retrieved even better than knowledge in episodic memory (recalling where and when you first learned about 1066), regardless of the time that has lapsed since the actual experience of the knowledge. In semantic memory, you will retain generalizations longer than details. However, even well-learned material may be irretrievable over time. We forget much of what we have learned. Why?

In this section we discuss four perspectives on forgetting: decay, interference, retrieval failure, and motivated forgetting. Each approach attempts to explain failures in either storage or retrieval.

Decay. Early psychologists theorized that we forget because we suffer gradual storage loss; the memory traces decay over time, just as batteries lose their charge. It seems plausible that decay is partly responsible for the inability to remember material learned long ago, but all we can say with certainty is that decay is an important factor in sensory memory loss and in short-term memory loss when all maintenance rehearsal is prevented.

In fact, some memories do not seem to become weaker over time. Learned motor skills are retained for many years even with no practice. Once you learn to swim, you never forget how. In addition, trivia and irrelevant information, such as song titles and commercial jingles, seem to persist in memory, as do memories of odors from childhood.

Interference. Interference from other experiences affects both our learning and our retention of new material. **Proactive interference** (*pro* means "forward acting") refers to the phenomenon that occurs when the vocabulary list you learned yesterday interferes with your learning of today's list. The old material has proactively interfered with your efforts to retrieve the new memory. **Retroactive interference** (*retro* means "backward acting") describes what happens when studying today's list interferes with your memory for yesterday's list. Recent material retroactively interferes with your ability to retrieve an older memory.

Three general principles govern interference. First, the greater the *similarity* between two sets of material the greater the interference between them. (Two vocabulary lists in the same foreign language would interfere with each other more than a vocabulary list and a set of chemical formulas.) Second, meaningless material is more vulnerable to interference than meaningful material. (It would be more difficult for you to memorize the nonsense syllables ZAX, QOG, and KIV than the more meaningful TAX, FOG, and GIV). Third, the more difficult the distracting task between learning and recall the more it will interfere with memory of material learned earlier. (Between studying for a test and taking it, you will forget more if you study for another course than if you do your laundry—a simpler and less relevant distraction.)

The most obvious prediction that emerges from interference theory is that information undisturbed by new material will be recalled best. A classic study by Jenkins and Dallenbach (1924) provided support for this hypothesis. Subjects who went to sleep immediately after learning new material recalled it better the next morning than those who spent the same amount of time performing their usual activities after learning.

Retrieval Failure. An apparent memory loss often turns out to be only a failure of retrieval. A question worded a little differently will guide us to the information, or a question requiring only recognition will reveal knowledge that we could not access and reproduce by recall. It seems clear that many failures to remember reflect poor encoding or inadequate retrieval cues rather than loss of memories. Failure to call up a memory is never positive proof that the memory is not there.

Why do we forget the names of many of our high-school classmates or even college teachers when we meet them away from school? When the social context is different from that in which we met those people originally, we have lost the *social-context retrieval cues* we used to form memories for those acquaintances (Reiser et al., 1985). Memories of people are formed around the social contexts in which they were encountered, and only later with more interaction, do we add secondary retrieval cues based on the personality traits and personal attributes of those people (Bond & Brockett, 1987).

Motivated Forgetting. In 1989, 28-year-old Eileen Franklin-Lipsker contacted county investigators with information about a case they had been unable to solve for 20 years in the northern California neighborhood where she had

proactive interference Memory process in which stored information prevents learning similar new information.

retroactive interference Memory process in which newly learned information prevents retrieval of previously stored, similar material.

Eileen Franklin-Lipsker

George Thomas Franklin
(Eileen's father)

repression In Freudian theory, basic defense mechanism that excludes painful thoughts, feelings, or memories from consciousness.

false memory syndrome (FMS) A pattern of thoughts, feelings, and actions based on mistaken or distorted recollection of experiences the rememberer claims to have previously repressed.

grown up. In 1969, Eileen's friend, 8-year-old Susan Nason, had disappeared; after weeks of searching, Susan's remains were finally found, but her killer was never identified or apprehended. Eileen's new information emerged from a long-buried memory of witnessing Susan's rape and murder and recognizing her killer: Eileen's father. After two decades, the horrible events that Eileen had forgotten came flooding back in a brief moment, when she made eye contact with her own daughter and was suddenly reminded of the look in Susie's eyes before she was killed.

Eileen's father had threatened to kill Eileen if she reported Susan's rape and murder. Knowing that this was no idle threat (Eileen later testified her father had molested and beaten her when she was a child), she forgot the horror and trauma of what she had seen. When the memory returned 20 years later, the investigation was re-opened, and Eileen's father was charged on the basis of her testimony.

Newspapers reported that "the testimony of memory experts played a key role in the trial, which some believe may give more credence to other victims of violence who have repressed memories . . ." (Workman, 1990). After less than eight hours of deliberation, the jury found Eileen's father guilty. He was sentenced to life imprisonment by a judge who called him "a depraved and wicked man" (*San Francisco Chronicle,* January 30, 1991).

In cases of psychologically caused amnesia, such as this one, the forgotten material is retained but blocked from retrieval. Not until an effective retrieval cue is experienced does the traumatic memory come flooding back. We sometimes forget because we do not want to remember certain memories that are frightening, painful, or personally degrading.

Sigmund Freud (1923) first perceived memory and forgetting as dynamic processes that enable us to maintain a sense of self-integrity. Research on childhood memories recalled by adults found that, in general, unpleasant events were more often forgotten than pleasant events (Waldvogel, 1948). We all forget some experiences we do not want to recognize as part of us, appointments we do not want to keep, names of people we do not like, and past events that threaten our basic sense of self or security. Freud gave the label **repression** to the mental process by which we protect ourselves from unacceptable or painful memories, pushing them out of consciousness.

Our motivational needs not only prevent retrieval of certain memories but even change the tone and content of memories that we do retrieve. A study of early recollections revealed that many memories judged as traumatic by the researchers were selectively recoded as neutral or even pleasant by the subjects during recall. Evidently, we can reconstruct our early childhood so that we remember the "good old days" not the way they were but the way they should have been (Kihlstrom & Harackiewicz, 1982). Recently, however, cases have come to light that suggest that our knowledge of motivated forgetting might lead people to overinterpret their "memories." "In Focus: False Memory Syndrome" explores this fascinating and disturbing new phenomenon, dubbed the *false memory syndrome*. It seems that, the more we learn about remembering and forgetting, the more complex our picture of human cognitive processes becomes.

SUMMING UP

Memory is the process whereby we take in and later reproduce information. Ebbinghaus originally studied the savings and relearning of meaningless nonsense syllables. The information-processing model permits modern researchers to examine how we remember meaningful information and experiences.

The act of remembering can be divided into three stages: encoding, storage, and retrieval. Retrieval can involve either recall or recognition. The information processing model of memory identifies three memory systems: sensory memory, short-term memory, and long-term memory.

Application   FALSE MEMORY SYNDROME

In December of 1989, Judy Norris and her estranged husband, Albert Norris, received separate notices that their daughter Anne, 24, had a few months earlier filed a $20 million lawsuit against them, alleging years of incest and satanic ritual abuse, from Anne's infancy to about age 16. The Norrises were shocked; they claim that theirs had been an "imperfect but normal" family life, from which Anne had emerged as a bright, attractive honor student in music. In dramatic contrast, Anne's account, supported by her therapist, alleges that she herself was born to baby breeders who supplied satanic cults; that for years the Norrises raped, beat, and sodomized her with broomsticks and hoses; and that they and other cult members ritualistically tortured her with knives, wires, and fishhooks. Telling their side of the story, the Norrises and their other children tearfully deny that any cult existed or that they could tolerate—much less commit—the horrors Anne claims she remembers (Salter, 1993).

In recent years, it has become a familiar story: An adult enters therapy to resolve persistent conflict or unhappiness, and with the therapist's support, revives a long-buried memory of traumatic abuse, incest, or molestation. No longer repressed, the horrible memories are unleashed, and may prompt the individual to take long-delayed action—just as Eileen Franklin-Lipsker charged her own father with sexually assaulting her and murdering her girlfriend (see pages 271–272). In theory, the shock and terror of such childhood experiences causes decades, possibly a lifetime, of amnesia. After recall, the painful memories can be turned into legal evidence for criminal and civil prosecution. *But what if the memories are false?*

This is the question raised by the more than 3,000 families who have registered their stories with the False Memory Syndrome Foundation based in Philadelphia. The **false memory syndrome** is a pattern of thoughts, feelings, and actions based on mistaken or distorted recollection of experiences the rememberer claims to have previously repressed. According to Stephanie Salter, the journalist who wrote the series

Pamela Freyd, director of the False Memory Syndrome Foundation.

"Buried Memories/Broken Families" for the San Francisco *Examiner* (April 4–9, 1993), three common elements appear in the stories of family members who say they have been unjustly accused of harming children:

1. The daughter or son makes the accusations after a period of remoteness during which he or she only vaguely reports being in therapy.
2. After confronting the parents by letter or telephone, the accusing child severs further contact.
3. The parents are condemned by the child's therapist, who typically refuses to meet them or hear their protests that the charges are false.

When an individual—child or adult—accuses a once-trusted family member of rape or assault, whether recent or long ago, subsequent suspicion and concern that it *might* be true can forever alter and even destroy relationships and reputations. Naturally, if the charges are true, the truth must be told to meet the goals of justice and therapy. But how can any outsider know the facts?

Pamela Freyd is herself an accused parent and the director of the False Memory Syndrome Foundation. She notes that on hearing that someone has accused family members of incest or abuse, most people's "kneejerk reaction" is to assume the accused are guilty. After all, why would anyone willingly disrupt her own life and others' lives by falsely claiming to be a victim and making up such lies? Freyd speculates that at least

some of the therapists who help their patients recover memories of childhood traumas actually implant false memories—whether intentionally or not—through hypnotic suggestion, asking leading questions, and broadly defining "incest" and "abuse."

The suggestion that therapists are encouraging troubled individuals to construct false recollections is difficult to make—and harder to have others accept—simply because no one wants to discourage real-life incest victims from remembering, recovering, and seeking reparation. Ellen Bass, author of *The Courage to Heal,* a self-help book for incest survivors, warns that the FMS Foundation (as an organization) may be little better than a "haven" for those who truly have abused and molested children. "People don't want to believe that so many horrible things have happened to so many children," says Bass, in the *Examiner* interview, "It's just too painful" (Salter, 1993, p. A–15).

For most of human history, children and their needs have not been taken seriously. In the enlightened and well-intentioned atmosphere of the late twentieth century, theorists posit that we may have become so attentive to the possibility of child abuse and dirty secrets like incest that we "see it where it doesn't exist" (Salter, p. A-15). Unfortunately, in "private" offenses such as rape and child abuse, the only evidence is often testimony—one person's word against another. How can we know who is telling the truth? Is righting an old wrong worth the risk of ruining innocent lives?

Taking the false memory syndrome seriously means doubting the testimony of at least some self-described victims of horrible crimes. Explaining the decision to write the series—involving four months of work, interviews with more than 140 people, and reviews of more than 4,000 pages of legal and professional documents, Salter concludes, "[W]e believe it is a worthy story and . . . that information is not a weapon but light" (April 4, 1993, p. A-19). What is needed is more talking about the issues involved, objective nonjudgmental listening, and unbiased research.

Sensory memory retains sensory information long enough for it to be processed. Sensory memory—as shown by the visual icon and auditory echo—lasts only briefly but has a large capacity, as shown by Sperling's partial-report procedure. Information decays in about a second but may last longer in sensory memory. Only a fraction of sensory memory can be transferred to short-term memory because of limits in selective attention and familiarity.

Working memory, also called short-term memory (STM), links sensory memory to long-term storage. Working memory has a limited capacity (about seven plus or minus two items) and a brief duration unless actively rehearsed. Its capacity can be increased by chunking and rehearsal.

Material in long-term memory (LTM) may be either declarative (factual) or procedural (how-to) information. Declarative memory includes both semantic (knowledge) and episodic (event-related) knowledge. Most LTM encoding relies on organization strategies. Mnemonics are strategies for associating new information with what is already familiar to aid recall. Evidence shows that LTM is constructive, since new information and context can influence what one is able to remember.

Four theories explain forgetting as caused by decay, interference, retrieval failure, and motivated forgetting. Some memory traces may decay with disuse over time. More likely remembering is blocked by interference from older or newer memories. Retrieval failures occur when cues are lacking or misleading. Some memories may be too painful or traumatic to allow conscious recall, so they are repressed into the unconscious. It may also be possible to misremember supposedly repressed experiences, as alleged by victims of the false memory syndrome.

CHAPTER REVIEW

◆1 Overview of Cognitive Processes
What experiences and abilities are included in human cognitive processes? How do we study cognition, if these processes cannot be directly observed? How accurate is human memory? What is the "information processing view" of memory?

The study of cognitive psychology includes theories and research on the mental processes and structures that enable us to think, reason, make inferences and decisions, and solve problems. Cognitive psychologists generally use an information-processing approach to analyze information into components that are then processed in stages or sequences. Cognitive psychology has replaced behaviorism as the core area of research in American psychology. Cognitive science pools the efforts of psychologists, researchers in the brain sciences, and computer scientists to study how the brain and mind represent and use knowledge.

Key Terms
- cognition, p. 232
- cognitive psychology, p. 233
- cognitive science, p. 234
- cognitive model, p. 234
- information-processing model, p. 234
- memory, p. 234
- think-aloud protocols, p. 235
- reaction time, p. 235
- remembering, p. 236

Major Contributors
- Von Neumann, John, p. 233
- Simon, Herbert, p. 233
- Newell, Allen, p. 233
- Piaget, Jean, p. 234
- Chomsky, Noam, p. 234
- Ebbinghaus, Hermann, p. 236

◆2 The Structures of Thinking
What is a concept, and why is concept-formation considered to be among the most basic abilities of thinking organisms? How do we use schemas and scripts to guide our everyday thinking? When do we rely on mental images instead of words?

Thinking is a higher order mental process that forms new abstract representations by transforming available information. Concepts are the building blocks of thinking; they are formed by identifying properties that are common to a class of objects or ideas. We store well-defined concepts as definitions and fuzzy concepts as prototypes. Concepts are often arranged in hierarchies, ranging from general to specific. Other mental structures that guide thinking include schemas and scripts. We also rely on visual imagery such as mental maps.

Key Terms
- thinking, p. 237
- concepts, p. 238
- cognitive economy, p. 238
- critical feature, p. 238
- prototype, p. 239
- psuedomemory, p. 240
- basic level, p. 240
- schema, p. 241
- script, p. 242
- cognitive map, p. 245

Major Contributors
- Rumelhart, David, p. 242
- Norman, Donald, p. 242
- Tolman, Edward C., p. 245

The Uses of Thinking *Is one kind of thinking more useful than another? How is deductive reasoning different from inductive reasoning? What are the most efficient strategies for solving problems, arriving at judgments, and making decisions?*

Deductive reasoning involves drawing conclusions from premises on the basis of rules of logic. Inductive reasoning involves inferring a conclusion from evidence on the basis of its likelihood or probability. Forming and testing scientific hypotheses typically involves inductive reasoning. In solving problems, we must define the initial state, goal state, and the operations that get us from the initial to the goal state. Heuristics are mental shortcuts that can help us reach solutions quickly.

Decision making is always subjective and prone to error. Awareness of mental traps is the first step in avoiding them. Inferential strategies normally serve us well, but occasionally we misapply these strategies to new data; we may not consider that new data inconsistent with prior knowledge could indicate a need to revise a particular theory. We continue to hold certain beliefs and theories or to persist in certain ways of doing things because we assimilate data or new experiences in a biased way. Cognitive biases are now assumed to generate most apparently irrational decisions. The availability heuristic leads us to estimate an outcome according to how easily similar or identical outcomes can be imagined. The representativeness heuristic is based on the presumption that belonging to a category implies having the characteristics considered typical of all members of that category. People often do not follow normative behavioral rules. Decisions are influenced by the way a problem is framed, even when alternatives are technically the same. People also have attitudes toward risk that influence decision making. Finally, an optimistic bias can influence decisions.

Key Terms
autistic thinking, p. 247
realistic thinking, p. 247
reasoning, p. 247
deductive reasoning, p. 247
syllogism, p. 247
inductive reasoning, p. 248
problem solving, p. 248
functional fixedness, p. 250
mental set, p. 251
algorithm, p. 251
heuristic, p. 251
judgment, p. 253
decision making, p. 253
inference, p. 253
biased assimilation, p. 254
cognitive bias, p. 255
availability heuristic, p. 255
representativeness heuristic, p. 256

Major Contributors
Tversky, Amos, p. 255
Kahneman, Daniel, p. 255

Remembering *What three processes are necessary for remembering? What are the three memory systems? How can we improve our memories? Why do we sometimes forget?*

Cognitive psychologists view remembering as a way of processing information. They view it as a three-stage process in which information that arrives through our senses is encoded, stored, and later retrieved. Three separate memory systems have been proposed: sensory, working, and long-term. Sensory memory has a large capacity but a very short duration. Working memory has a limited capacity (7 ± 2), and lasts only briefly without rehearsal. Long-term memory (LTM) constitutes our total knowledge of the world and of the self; it is nearly unlimited in capacity. Meaningful organization is the key to encoding for LTM. The more specifically material is encoded in terms of expected retrieval cues, the more efficient later retrieval will be. Memory content includes procedural memory, semantic memory, and episodic memory.

Remembering is a constructive and selective process. Schemas play a major role in constructive memory processes. Information or misinformation provided during retrieval can bias recall without our realizing it, making eyewitness testimony unreliable when contaminated by after-the-fact input. Explanations for forgetting include decay, interference, retrieval failures, and motivated forgetting. After repression, memories may surface accurately or, as in the false memory syndrome, the details or facts of personal experiences may be misremembered.

Key Terms

Major Contributors

PRACTICE TEST

Chapter 7: Cognitive Processes

For each of the following items, choose the single correct or best answer. Correct answers, explanations, and page references appear in the Appendix.

1. According to the _____ model of cognition, cognitive processes can best be understood as separate but connected components in a sequence of operations from simpler to more complex.
   A. information processing
   B. organic continuum
   C. procedural
   D. logical

2. As a participant in a cognitive psychology experiment, a student solving a math problem thinks out loud as she tries first one then another approach to finding the answer. This is a modern version of the approach known as _____ .
   A. behavioral observation
   B. reaction time
   C. error analysis
   D. introspection

3. Which of the following statements about thinking is true?
   A. It transforms available information to form new mental representations.
   B. It cannot be inferred from observable behavior.
   C. It stores but does not manipulate one's knowledge.
   D. All of the above.

4. An alien being from another galaxy has landed on the Earth and is overwhelmed by the sensory input it must process. Eventually the alien simplifes its thinking by categorizing sets of experiences and objects according to common features. In other words, the alien learns to form _____ .
   A. memories
   B. schemas
   C. concepts
   D. heuristics

5. A mental _____ outlines the proper sequence in which actions and reactions might be expected to happen in given settings, as when you visit a new grocery store but are still able to shop and complete your purchases although you have never visited this particular location before.
   A. prototype
   B. script
   C. algorithm
   D. map

6. A syllogism is a form of _____ reasoning, in which a conclusion is drawn by applying rules relating a minor premise to a major premise.
   A. inductive
   B. deductive
   C. heuristic
   D. algorithmic

7. In information-processing terms, a(n) _____ has an initial state, goal state, and operations.
   A. prototype
   B. concept
   C. assimilation
   D. problem

8. Mack wants to estimate the total number of miles he will be driving during his vacation, so he carefully and tediously records every point-to-point mileage index in the road atlas between his home town and his destination city. This slow but sure process is an example of a(n) _____ .
   A. prototype
   B. algorithm
   C. mnemonic
   D. syllogism

9. Your abilities to recall how to use a can opener, boot up your computer, address an envelope, and program a VCR are all examples of _____ memory.
   A. procedural
   B. semantic
   C. sensory
   D. constructive

10. Elise used to live in a house with a large kitchen, where all the silverware was stored in a drawer to the right of the sink. Since she moved to her new apartment, she finds that she habitually looks for the silverware in a drawer to the right of the sink—although no such drawer exists. Her behavior reflects forgetting due to _____ .
    A. decaying of the memory trace.
    B. repression.
    C. proactive interference.
    D. retroactive interference.

IF YOU'RE INTERESTED . . .

Benne, B. (1988). *WASPLEG and other mnemonics.* Dallas, TX: Taylor Publishing.

Handy tricks and gimmicks for remembering the seven deadly sins and other lists that might otherwise exceed the limits of memory.

Frankl, V. E. (1984). *Man's search for meaning.* New York: Washington Square Books.

Viktor Frankl's powerful memoir of survival in the Nazi concentration camps, originally published in 1946 to introduce his system of "logotherapy," based on the human need for meaning in life.

Groundhog Day. (Video: 1993, color, 103 minutes). Starring Bill Murray, Andie MacDowell, Chris Elliot.

A cynical television weather announcer is challenged to change his ways when he finds he mysteriously relives the same day over and over—but he alone remembers all the days he has experienced.

Lewis, D. (1983). *Thinking better.* New York: Holt, Rinehart, and Winston.

More a how-to manual on using your head than a text—helpful and encouraging.

Loftus, E. (1980). *Memory.* Reading, MA: Addison-Wesley.

An overview of a fascinating subject by a psychologist distinguished for her research, teaching, and applications of what is known about memory.

Luria, A. R. (1987). *The mind of a mnemonist.* Cambridge, MA: Harvard University Press.

Fascinating true account of a Russian researcher's study of "S" a man capable of recalling even brief experiences in precise detail. A classic chronicle, recently revised.

Nisbett, R. E. and Ross, L. (1980). *Human inferences: Shortcomings of social judgment.* Englewood Cliffs, NJ: Prentice Hall.

Important findings about the errors we make when we rely on thought and decision-making strategies that usually serve us well.

Chapter 8 **Motivation and Emotion**

Preview Questions

1. How does motivation affect behavior? What is the difference between a motive and a drive? Is there any way to influence others' motivation? How is motivation related to emotion?

2. Are there any human instincts? What kinds of behaviors seem to be motivated by drives? How does arousal affect human performance? What is Maslow's needs hierarchy? How can our own expectations and beliefs affect our motivation?

3. What causes hunger? Why is human eating behavior so hard to control? Does the human sex drive operate in the same way as other motives? What experiences and actions affect human sexual behavior? Do people have a drive to achieve? Why don't we all work equally hard to reach our goals?

4. What purpose is served by human emotions? What are the major theories of emotional experience? How did emotions develop in the course of evolution? Do different people express emotions in different ways?

"Mike, let's do El Capitán!"

Many climbers dream of scaling the majestic, domed cliff that rises 3200 feet from California's Yosemite Valley, but only a few succeed. Mark Wellman had more than the normal number of obstacles to overcome. In 1982, a fall from another Yosemite peak had paralyzed both his legs. However, seven years later, Mark announced that he would climb El Capitán.

For six months, 29-year-old Mark strengthened the muscles of his upper body with daily weight training and with many practice climbs, climbing only with his arms. Finally, he was ready to do what most others thought was impossible. In July of 1989, Mark looked up the sheer rock face at its distant summit. His friend Mike Corbett preceded him, placing the ropes that would be Mark's handholds on the arduous ascent. Mark grabbed the first rope and pulled himself up—six inches closer to his ultimate goal. He grasped the next one: another pull-up; another six inches. For a week, Mike placed ropes and Mark did pull-ups—hundreds of pull-ups a day, six inches at a time.

On some afternoons, the temperature topped 100°F. The heat, however, was never as bad as the wind, which gusted fiercely between 11 A.M. and 8 P.M. every day. At times the wind pushed the men ten feet out from the cliff face, but they still persevered (*The New York Times*, 1989).

On the eighth night of their adventure, Mark and Mike tied themselves into their sleeping bags and camped on a narrow ledge. The next morning they would begin their final ascent: 300 feet for Mike; 600 pull-ups for Mark. After a total of more than 7000 pull-ups, Mark's body ached in places he didn't even know existed. But the next day his pain gave way to euphoria as he pulled himself up those last inches—he had made it to the top of the mountain, the crest of El Capitán. He had achieved the impossible.

How did he feel about it? "It's great; it's fantastic. It was a really great, beautiful climb and a really wonderful experience" (*The New York Times*, 1989).

A reporter asked Mike Corbett about his scariest moment. There had been many: the wind had pushed him away from a crucial foothold; one morning he had opened his eyes to see a 3000-foot drop only centimeters from his sleeping bag; once his sweaty palms had caused him to lose his grip on a rock, on the rope, and on his friend (*Los Angeles Times*, 1989).

What motivates someone to try what others deem impossible? Already paralyzed from one fall, why did Mark risk another? What distinguishes him from those of us who, with all limbs functioning, can barely roll out of bed in the morning to hit the snooze button on the alarm clock? What about Mike? What made him take on the major responsibility of helping his friend?

Introduction

➡ Why climb a mountain, *any* mountain? What makes people act as they do? Why do so many of us strive to attain our goals despite the effort, pain, and financial costs involved? On the other hand, why do we procrastinate before starting work on some tasks, or give up and quit too soon on others?

We often use the term *motivation* to represent a variety of complex concepts: "I didn't do well on that test because I didn't like the teacher; he just never got me motivated enough." We hear sports announcers proclaim, "They won because they wanted the win more than their overconfident, undermotivated opponents." As we read detective stories, we try to figure out the hidden motive for the crime, which will provide a clue to the culprit's identity. Millions of faithful soap opera fans glue themselves to their televisions day after day to peer into cauldrons of seething motives—greed, power, and lust—bathed in passion-filled emotions of love, hate, jealousy, and envy.

Emotions are the touchstones of human experience. They enrich our interactions with others and our contacts with nature; they add joy to our existence, significance to our memories, and hope to our expectations. Emotions help to motivate our adaptation to our circumstances.

Contemporary psychologists recognize that human actions are motivated by a variety of needs—from fundamental physiological needs to psychological needs for love, achievement, and spirituality. Even simple biological drives such as hunger may be related to needs for personal control and social acceptance that can become distorted into eating disorders. The first part of this chapter deals with the nature of motivation. Next we will consider the many important functions and forms of human emotion. But first we will consider the relationship between motivation and emotion and their importance to psychology.

Understanding Motivation and Emotion

Motivation is the general term for all the processes involved in starting, directing, and maintaining physical and psychological activities. *Motivation* includes the internal mechanisms involved in *preferring* one activity over another; the *strength* of responses; and the *persistence* of actions toward relevant goals. The highly motivated person seeks out certain activities over others; practices behaviors and perfects skills required to attain the objective; and focuses energy on reaching the goal despite frustrations.

Both the words *motivation* and *emotion* come from the Latin *movere*, meaning "to move." *Action* is the fundamental property of living systems. Evolution favors organisms that can move toward what they need to survive and away from what threatens them. Some appetites escalate into *addictions,* which dominate all other motivational systems. Some aversions become pathological fears and freeze our behavioral options. Between the extremes of frenzied action and immobility lie the motivational currents that shape the flow of our daily lives.

Motivation cannot be seen directly. Behavior, on the other hand, is observable. To explain the observable, behavioral changes we must make inferences—or educated speculations—about the underlying psychological and physiological variables that influenced those changes. These inferences about

motivation Process that starts, directs, and maintains physical and psychological activity, including activity preference, strength, and persistence.

Soap operas focus on basic human motivation, which accounts for their popularity.

drive Biologically instigated motivation.

motive Psychologically and socially instigated motivation, assumed to be at least partially learned.

an individual's goals, needs, wants, intentions, and purposes are formalized in the concept of motivation.

Two terms that researchers frequently use are *drive* and *motive*. **Drive** refers to motivation that is assumed to be primarily biological, such as hunger. **Motive** refers to psychological and social needs that are assumed to be learned through personal experience. Motives can be either *conscious* or *unconscious*, but it is not always easy to distinguish them. For example, can we be sure Mark's painful push to reach the summit was a conscious desire to achieve his goal, or could he have been compensating—unconsciously—for feelings of inadequacy?

Psychologists don't always agree on how motivational terms should be used. For example, some psychologists use the term *need* only in connection with biological demands (the body's need for water or oxygen). But others think *need* is equally appropriate in discussing psychological requirements (as in needs for achievement or power).

Another distinction psychologists make is whether motivation comes from the *person*—an individual's inner qualities—or is the response to outside *situations*—cultural expectations and social pressures. As assumptions vary, so do theorists' explanations of what makes people tick.

The Concept of Motivation

Psychologists have used the concept of motivation for five basic purposes:

1. *To account for behavioral variability.* We use motivational explanations when the *variations* in people's performance in a constant situation cannot be traced to differences in ability, skill, practice, reinforcement history, or chance. For example, motivation explains why you might do a given task well on one day but poorly on another. It also explains variability among different people—the fact that some people do better in competition than others, for example.

2. *To relate biology to behavior.* We are biological organisms with internal mechanisms that automatically regulate our bodily functions so we can survive. States of deprivations trigger these mechanisms which then motivate us—through hunger, thirst, or cold—to act to restore the body's balance. For example, in low temperatures, physical activity and body shivers help to warm you somewhat.

3. *To infer private states from public acts.* There are two ways to respond to someone's behavior: take it at face value or see it as a symptom or overt expression of an underlying emotion or motive. Researchers in cognitive and social psychology are investigating the inferences that people make about what causes behavior, whether it is their own or others'. For example, if the one you love forgets to call you on your birthday, you may see this forgetfulness as a sign of neglect, whereas if *you* are the forgetful one, you may blame your error on the stress of your busy life.

4. *To assign responsibility for actions.* The concept of personal responsibility is basic in law, religion, and ethics. Personal responsibility presupposes inner motivation and the ability to control one's actions. The concept of personal responsibility dissolves without the concept of consciously directed motivation. We call such behavior volitional (willful) or intentional. If we did not hold people personally responsible for their actions, we would not praise them for their successes or punish them for their crimes.

5. *To explain perseverance despite adversity.* Finally, motivational constructs help us understand why organisms can continue to perform consistently despite obvious variations in stimulation. Motivation gets you to work or class on time even when you're exhausted. Motivation helps you persist in playing the game to the best of your ability even when you are losing or suffering and realize that you can't possibly win.

Motivation can explain variability among different people—the fact that some people do better in competition than others, for example. These men are participating in the International Games for the Disabled.

Studying Motivational Concepts

Because motivation is invisible, it is a slippery concept that is hard to define. To be scientifically useful, the concept of motivation must be tied to two factors: external behavioral signs (dependent variables) that can be measured on the output side; and observable conditions or treatments (independent variables) that a researcher can introduce as input. In other words, we need to specify the *stimuli* that create motivation and the *responses* that motivation leads to.

In his classic text, *Purposive Behavior in Animals and Men* (1932), learning theorist **Edward C. Tolman** described motivation as a process that intervenes between stimulus input and response outcome in an organism. Instead of trying to link each separate aspect of some behavior to particular stimulus input, motivational psychologists postulate an overall *intervening variable*—a condition such as hunger, sex, or achievement that develops *between* the stimulus and the response—that connects the causes and the consequences. **Figure 8.1** outlines how motivation as an intervening variable links stimulus input and response output. For example, if the stimulus input is deprivation of food, the intervening variable will be hunger motivation, and the response output will involve searching for food, eating, and bypassing other attractions in favor of a meal.

➡ Think for a moment, before going on, about some of the motives in your life. We sometimes use vivid language to talk about motivation—events or circumstances can "turn you on" or "turn you off," "push your buttons" or "pull your strings," "roll right off your back" or "make you snap." Think of some experiences that you characterize this way. Try to outline the stimulus-response connections of your own experiences.

Identifying Motivated Behavior. Researchers have used many different index variables (indicators) to identify motivation and its strength.

- *Activity level.* The more motivated an organism is in its behavior, the higher its level of activity will be.

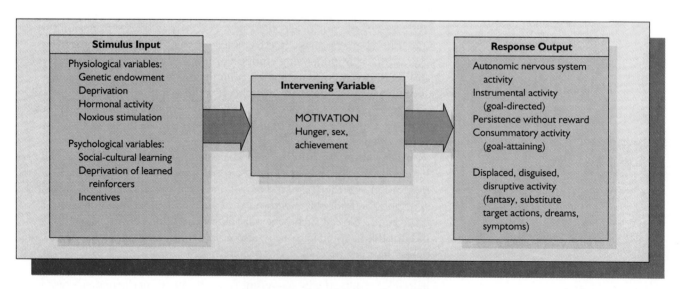

Figure 8.1 Motivation as an Intervening Variable
Any particular motivation, such as hunger, is assumed to be the result of a number of physiological and/or psychological variables. Motivation may lead to one or more of the kinds of response output shown. The intervening variable links the input conditions to the output consequences that are observable, manipulable, or measurable.

- *Rate of learning.* Strong motivation increases the rate of learning, so that strongly motivated students can be observed to learn faster than others.
- *Performance level attained.* Motivation enables one to reach a higher level of performance.
- *Resistance to extinction.* Once learned, a motivated response should be more resistant to extinction—harder to eliminate or discourage—than a less motivated one.
- *Interference with unrelated activities.* Being highly motivated in one direction disrupts attention for and investment of effort into other activities.
- *Choices.* Motivation leads an organism to choose certain tasks, goals, and rewards over others.
- *Consummatory behavior.* Behavior that consummates or satisfies a motive will be stronger than less motivated behavior. For example, an extremely hungry animal will consume more food than one that is only moderately hungry.

Overcoming Obstacles. Another approach to measuring motivation in behavior is to study how many obstacles one overcomes to reach one's goal. For example, a classmate who must work two part-time jobs and live at home in order to pay for college may be understood as more motivated in her studies than someone who has fewer financial obstacles to overcome.

C. J. Warden first experimentally applied obstacles in the study of motivation in the 1920s at Columbia University. In these studies, Warden assessed the relative strengths of various drives by means of an *obstruction box*. This apparatus used an electrified grid to separate a deprived rat from incentives it could see on the other side of the grid. The incentives included food, water, a sexually responsive mate, and the rat's offspring. Behaviorally, drive strength was measured as the number of times the animal would cross the hot grid in a given period of time. **Figure 8.2** shows the typical data obtained with this method.

The motivating effects of thirst and hunger were greatest after a short period of deprivation, but then declined when water or food deprivation became extreme and the animals weakened. This declining response was not found in two cases, however. With sexual contact as a reward, sex-deprived rats kept running at a constant rate (after the first few hours). Mother rats separated from their newborn pups endured the most suffering, running most frequently across the hot grid even with a minimal period of social deprivation. This was interpreted at the time as evidence for the existence of a powerful maternal drive.

Self-Descriptions. Human motivation can be assessed with self-reports and responses to projective tests (for example, interpretations offered of ambiguous patterns). Researchers may ask participants to fill out questionnaires evaluating their own needs, desires, and anxieties. The researchers use the scores as indicators of strength of motivation. These scores can then be correlated with behavioral measures. In other research, subjects create stories about ambiguous pictures, and researchers analyze the content of these themes to reveal different types of needs.

Manipulating Drives. One way to study motivation is to identify different groups of individuals and compare their behavior—such as a group of people who have been deprived of a needed commodity and another group who have not. Such a *correlational study* evaluates the outcomes of existing differences.

Correlational designs can indicate whether a relationship exists between individual differences and motivational states. But researchers often want to learn whether changes in motivation *cause* changes in behavior. To do this

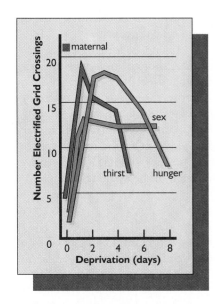

Figure 8.2 Behavioral Assessment of the Relative Strengths of Primary Drives
In reaction to various incentives on the other side, rats crossed an electrified grid in the Columbia obstruction box. Their deprivation level was manipulated by time separated from the goal object. Thirst and hunger performance reached a peak and then declined as the animals became debilitated. Sexual motivation peaked soon and remained steady throughout the study. Mothers separated from their offspring showed the highest level of motivation by enduring the most electric shocks to reach their offspring after only a brief period of deprivation.

they must conduct *experimental research*. In a motivation experiment, a researcher manipulates conditions to induce the motivational state, or make it stronger or weaker. Three procedures for experimental studies are *lesioning, deprivation,* and *stimulation.*

Lesioning, discussed in Chapter 2, is an operation that destroys the specific brain tissue assumed to be vital to motivated behavior. If the operation destroys an area of the brain that triggers or controls motivated action, the subject will exhibit observable changes in behavior. For example, lesioning the part of the brain that triggers eating behavior results in an animal's refusal to eat even when it is deprived of food.

Deprivation involves denying food, water, sexual contact, or specific substances (for example, calcium or salt). Warden's obstruction box studies manipulated drive states through deprivation. For humans, deprivation might involve withholding psychological conditions, such as social contact. For example, people may be motivated to seek out others if they are deprived of social contact (Schachter, 1957).

Finally, *stimulation* involves giving stimuli to an organism to create response tendencies. Aversive stimuli like pain or heat will prompt an animal to escape or flee; pleasant stimulation may arouse certain drives like desire for sexual contact. Researchers have used stimulation such as barriers, unsolvable tasks, and competition to study human motivation.

Lesioning, deprivation, and stimulation are all ways to manipulate drive states that cannot be directly observed.

Incentive Motivation. Whether or not we are internally motivated, some external stimuli can independently move us to action. A beverage ad on TV, an attractive person, the illustrations on a menu, or the aroma of some foods can arouse us to act even when we are not impelled from within by thirst, sex, or hunger. External stimuli that promise rewards are called **incentives.**

incentives External stimuli that arouse motives.

incentive motivation Motivation aroused by external stimuli.

Incentive motivation refers to the activating and energizing effect that stimuli, by promising rewards, can have on us. Although in animal research incentives always involve external stimuli, for humans incentive motivation may be self-induced by mental imagery. Being able to picture your goal, or seeing that it is closer than before, provides incentive motivation. Incentive motivation can also be induced by *negative incentives,* such as fear of developing an addiction to drugs, or feeling ashamed of dropping out of the marathon—or of staggering through its last lap. Consider how positive and negative incentive motivation helped Mark and Mike up the mountain in the opening example.

Explaining Emotion

We noted earlier that the concepts of motivation and emotion are linked by a common root in their word histories: the Latin word *movere,* "to move." Most modern psychologists would agree that we can understand motivation better by also seeking to understand emotion, and vice versa. Emotions are elicited by experiences that are important for our survival and general well-being. Emotional reactions focus attention on these experiences by marking them as special in some way, by recording them more indelibly in memory, and by rousing us to take action. Because emotions involve so many aspects of human functioning, the study of emotions has emerged recently as a central issue in research and theory for a host of psychologists from different backgrounds (Bower, 1981; Frijda et al., 1989; Hoffman, 1986; Lazarus, 1982; Leventhal, 1980; Plutchik, 1980; Zajonc, 1982).

emotion Complex pattern of changes in response to situation perceived as personally significant, including physiological arousal, feelings, thoughts, and behaviors.

Contemporary psychologists generally agree that **emotion** is a complex pattern of bodily and mental changes including physiological arousal, feelings, cognitive processes, and behavioral responses to a personally significant situation (Kleinginna & Kleinginna, 1981). The physiological *arousal* includes neural, hormonal, visceral, and muscular changes (some of which were

Overt behavioral reactions can be action-oriented, such as urging others to make certain responses, or expressive, such as smiling or crying.

described in Chapter 2). The *feelings* include both a general affective state (good-bad, positive-negative) and a specific tone, such as joy or disgust. The *cognitive processes* include interpretations, memories, and expectations. The overt behavioral *responses* include expressive reactions (crying, smiling) and action-oriented responses (screaming for help). Finally, we may perceive the situation as *significant* either consciously or nonconsciously. See **Table 8.1** for a summary of the components of emotion. (See also "Time Out for Critical Thinking.)

Humans are unique in the array of events that trigger our emotions (Hebb, 1980). However, emotions are surprisingly similar among people throughout the world and some emotions can even be expressed in similar ways among other animals. As we ascend the evolutionary scale from simpler organisms to humans, we observe increasing differentiation of the facial muscles used to express emotion and an increasing diversity of emotional behavior. Humans have not evolved *away* from nonrational, primitive emotions but *toward* a combination of intellect and emotion (Scherer, 1984).

In some cases, it is easy to infer a connection between motivations and emotions. For example, when you are unable to relate to others (an important social *motive*) you will probably experience unpleasant *emotions* such as sadness, loneliness, or anger. But in other cases the motive-emotion connection is not as direct or obvious. For example, a food-deprived infant will experience hunger *motivation*. But what is the child's most likely *emotion:* Will she cry out of anger, sadness, or fear? These feelings are not typically associated with hunger, although they are considered basic human emotions.

The ability to *explain* emotion is complicated by individual assessments of *experiencing* emotion. Emotions are subjective experiences that are distinctive

Table 8.1	Physical and Psychological Changes Associated with Emotion	
TYPE OF CHANGE	**DESCRIPTION**	**EXAMPLE**
Physiological Arousal	Neural, hormonal, visceral, and muscular changes	Increased heart rate, blushing
Feelings	Subjective interpretation of affective state	Anger, sadness, happiness
Cognitive Processes	Interpretations, memories, beliefs, expectations	Blaming someone, looking forward to something, believing oneself to be threatened
Behavioral Reactions	Expressing emotion, taking action	Smiling, crying, screaming for help
Significance	Conscious or unconscious perception	Judgment that one is in love; realizing that this is an emergency

and personal for every individual. As such, they defy attempts to describe them in purely objective terms. A brief examination of emotional experience may reveal the possible connections between motivation and emotion—and the challenges researchers face in being scientific about human feelings.

➡ *TIME OUT . . .* FOR CRITICAL THINKING

As mentioned above, both *motivation* and *emotion* are terms related by the central concept of movement or motion. What is it that "moves" you? When you are strongly motivated, we say you are "moved to action." When you are strongly affected by an emotional stimulus, we say you are simply "moved," or that the experience was very "moving." Consider these connections, as you answer the following questions:

- What was the last task you felt strongly motivated to undertake or complete? What accompanying emotions did you feel (such as excitement about feeling energized, exhilaration at reaching a goal, fear of failure, or anxiety about deadline pressures)?

- Which of the following seem to motivate you more: forces that generate positive emotions, or those that create negative emotions? How might your answer depend on the task involved? What are the consequences of having either good or bad feelings accompanying your motivations?

- What was the last particularly strong emotion you felt? What caused it? Did you feel "moved" to act on your feelings in a specific way? What was the consequence of acting—or *not* acting—on such feelings?

- What seems to be the important difference between the concepts of motivation and emotion? Think of a time when you felt strongly motivated but not emotional. Can you likewise feel strong emotion without feeling motivated to act in some way on those feelings? If either case is possible, is something "missing" when motivation lacks emotion? What is missing, and does it matter?

The Physiology of Emotion. Bodily reactions provide the machinery of emotional experience. The body reacts to internal and external stimuli by sending signals that activate or inhibit emotional responses. Research has identified the important roles played by the divisions of the nervous system, hormones, hemispheric differences (between the two sides of the cerebral cortex), and brain biochemistry.

The Reticular Activating System. Physiological reactions begin with the arousal of the brain as a whole by the *reticular activating system* (RAS). Incoming sensory messages pass through it on their way to the brain (Lindsley, 1951; Zanchetti, 1967). This system functions as a general alarm system for the rest of the brain. Strong emotional arousal stimulates physical arousal just as sexual arousal stimulates genital arousal. Your heart races, your respiration goes up, your mouth dries, your muscles tense, and maybe you feel shaky. All of these reactions are designed to mobilize the body for action.

The Autonomic Nervous System. The *autonomic nervous system* (ANS) prepares the body for emotional responses through the action of both its divisions, which act in balance and in response to the nature of arousal. With mild, *unpleasant* stimulation, the *sympathetic* division is more active; with mild, *pleasant* stimulation, the *parasympathetic* division is more active. Physiologically, strong emotions such as fear or anger activate the body's *emergency reaction system,* which swiftly and silently prepares the body for potential danger. The sympathetic nervous system directs the release of hormones from the adrenal glands which in turn lead the internal organs to release blood sugar, raise blood pressure, and increase sweating and salivation. To calm us after the emergency has passed, the parasympathetic nervous system takes over, inhibiting the release of those hormones. We may remain aroused for some time after experiencing a strong emotional activation because some hormones continue to circulate in the bloodstream.

Hormones. Several kinds of studies have shown the influence of *hormones* on emotion. When hormones are administered medicinally or when diseases affect the endocrine glands, changes occur in one's emotional response. Hormone levels in the blood and urine rise during emotional states because hormones are released when one perceives emotional stimuli. *Steroid hormones* act on many different kinds of body tissue, including nerve cells, by causing them to change their excitability rapidly and directly. They can produce euphoria in short-term low doses but depression in long-term high doses (Majewska et al., 1986). Many of the mood changes associated with stress, pregnancy, and the menstrual cycle may be related to the effects that steroid hormones have on brain cells.

Brain Structures. The hormonal and neural aspects of emotional arousal are integrated by two regions of the brain: the *hypothalamus* and the *limbic system.* These structures are old-brain control systems for emotions and patterns of attack, defense, and flight. Lesioning or stimulating parts of the limbic system produces dramatic changes in emotional responding. Tame animals may become killers; prey and predators may become peaceful companions (Delgado, 1969).

In all complex emotions, the cerebral *cortex*—the outermost layers of brain tissue, our "thinking cap"—is involved. The cortex provides the associations, memories, and meanings that integrate psychological and biological experiences. Research suggests there are different emotional centers in the cortex for processing positive and negative emotions. The left hemisphere seems to involve positive emotions, such as happiness, while the right hemisphere influences negative emotions, such as anger (Davidson, 1984). This **lateralization of emotion** in the human brain has been found through EEG analysis of normal subjects' emotional reactions and research relating emotional facial expression to right or left hemisphere brain damage (Ahern & Schwartz, 1985; Borod et al., 1988).

lateralization of emotion Different influences of the two brain hemispheres on various emotions, with the left hemisphere assumed to influence positive emotions (for example, happiness) and the right hemisphere to influence negative emotions (for example, anger).

Biochemistry. The biochemical responses involved in emotional reactions may differ according to the *meaning* we attach to the situations in which the reactions are experienced. Although tears are associated with sorrow, we cry in response to many types of emotional arousal—for example, when we're angry or when we're filled with joy and ecstasy. Of course, tears also flow in response to eye-irritating stimuli. But when researchers compared the biochemistry of emotional tears and irritant tears, they found that emotional tears (generated when subjects watched a sad movie) differ significantly from irritant tears (generated when subjects inhaled the vapor of freshly grated onions). Under emotional conditions, the lacrimal glands which stimulate the tear ducts secrete a greater volume of tears and also produce tears with a higher concentration of protein (Frey & Langseth, 1985). There are no differences between the sexes

Is she crying because she lost the race? No—she just set a new high-school record.

on either of these measures, but an analysis of *reported* emotional crying over a one-month period shows that women cried for emotional reasons more frequently than did men (Frey et al., 1983). See **Figure 8.3** for a summary of this analysis.

Interpreting and Labeling Emotions. Because we attach meaning to emotional experiences, we can sometimes become confused or be mistaken about what we and others are feeling. Consider the following example, a true story. A man had confided to friends that he felt attracted to a new co-worker, and could tell that the feeling was mutual. "Whenever I go into her office to ask her or her boss something, she acts very nervous. She stumbles over her words and drops pencils and things. I'm pretty sure she likes me!" Months later, the two-some—a committed couple now—chatted about their early attraction with friends. "Remember how nervous you were whenever I was around?" he teased her. "Oh, it wasn't *you* that was making me nervous," she corrected, "but since it was my first real job ever, I was always pretty self-conscious whenever my *boss* was around. You only saw me at work in those days, so you jumped to the wrong conclusion—though I'm glad you did!"

As in many joint stories of relationship history, each partner's version of their early days depicts the other's behavior differently. He attributes her nervousness to his attractiveness, whereas she insists it was her boss, not her boyfriend-to-be, who made her jumpy. In fact, they may both be correct. Emotions—our own or others'—can be difficult to interpret accurately. Because arousal symptoms and internal states for different emotions are similar, it is possible to confuse them when they are experienced in ambiguous or novel situations. As this couple's story illustrates, the cognitive processes

Figure 8.3 Episodes of Emotional Crying in a Month

In the first formal investigation of adult crying behavior, 45 male and 286 female subjects judged to be psychiatrically normal kept records of their emotional crying behavior during a month. Duration of episodes for both groups was about six minutes, and the most frequent stimuli for crying involved interpersonal relations and media presentations. A high proportion of both groups said they felt better after crying.

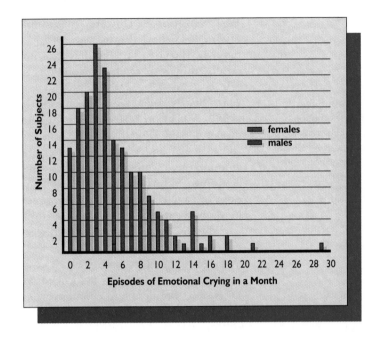

involved go beyond physiological arousal and *interpret* what we are feeling. We *appraise* our physiological arousal in an effort to discover what we are feeling, what emotional label fits best, and what our reaction means in the particular setting in which it is being experienced. For example, if you think you are nervous because you are anxious to do well in your new job, you will make job-relevant changes in your behavior. But if instead you think it is an attractive co-worker who is making you nervous, you will make different changes in your behavior based on this interpretation.

Misattributing Arousal. Typically, the external situation determines your definition of the emotional arousal being experienced, without much need for elaborate interpretation. We can also experience physical arousal from non-emotional sources, such as caffeine, exercise, arousing drugs, or intense heat. When we are aware that these sources are the causal stimuli, we make no emotional interpretation. However, what happens when we do not recognize their direct physiological impact?

We sometimes *misattribute* physically based arousal as emotion-based arousal, mislabeling our physical symptoms as part of a psychological state. Being overheated can become feeling anxious; being physically aroused from exercise can be misinterpreted as being sexually aroused. Psychological researchers have contrived several experiments to illustrate this emotional misattribution. In one study, a female researcher interviewed male subjects who had just crossed one of two bridges in Vancouver, Canada. One bridge was a safe, sturdy structure; the other was a wobbly, precarious bridge. The researcher pretended to be interested in the effects of scenery on creativity and asked the men to write brief stories about an ambiguous picture depicting a woman. She also invited them to call her if they wanted more information about the research. Those men who had just crossed the dangerous bridge wrote stories with more sexual imagery, and four times as many of them called the female researcher as did those who had crossed the safe bridge. To show that arousal was the independent variable influencing the emotional misinterpretation, the researchers also arranged for another group of men to be interviewed 10 minutes or more *after* crossing the dangerous bridge, enough time for their physical arousal symptoms to be reduced. These nonaroused men did not show the signs of sexual interest that the aroused men showed (Dutton & Aron, 1974).

Basic Emotions. Despite the complexity of emotional experience, some researchers believe there is a set of basic emotions that is biologically and experientially distinct. Two models explaining this basic set of emotions are those proposed by Robert Plutchik and by Carroll Izard.

emotion wheel Theorist Robert Plutchik's model of innate emotions, involving eight basic emotions made up of four pairs of opposites: joy-sadness, fear-anger, surprise-anticipation, and acceptance-disgust.

Plutchik's Emotion Wheel. The **emotion wheel** developed by **Robert Plutchik** (1980, 1984) proposes a set of innate emotions. As **Figure 8.4** shows, the model depicts eight basic emotions, made up of four pairs of opposites: joy-sadness, fear-anger, surprise-anticipation, and acceptance-disgust. All other emotions are assumed to be variations, or *blends,* of these basic eight. Complex emotions, shown on the outside of the emotional wheel, result from combinations of two adjacent primary emotions. For example, love is a combination of joy and acceptance, while remorse combines sadness and disgust.

Plutchik proposes that emotions are best separated from each other when they are at high intensities, such as loathing and grief, and least different when they are low in intensity, such as disgust and sadness. He also believes that each primary emotion is associated with an adaptive evolutionary response. Disgust is considered an evolutionary result of rejecting distasteful foods from the mouth, while joy is associated with reproductive capacities.

Izard's Developmental Model. **Carroll Izard** (1977) proposes a slightly different set of basic emotions. His model specifies ten emotions: joy, surprise, anger, disgust, contempt, fear, shame, guilt, interest, and excitement—with combinations of them resulting in other emotional blends (joy + interest or excitement = love).

As we saw earlier, a child's ability to think and to use language follows a built-in timetable of development. The same is generally true of emotional development, if appropriate stimulation is available. Some developments in emotional response may be linked to specific anatomical changes in the brain (Konner, 1977). For example, smiling emerges in infants of all cultures as soon as the necessary nerve pathways mature, one or two months after birth.

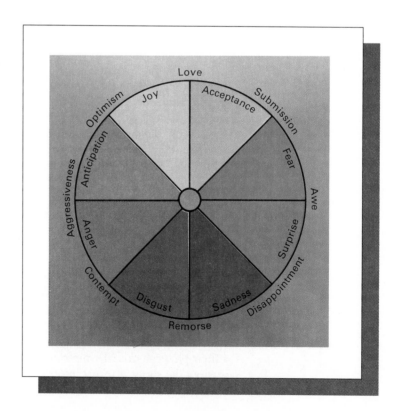

Figure 8.4 The Emotion Wheel
Plutchik's model arranges eight basic emotions within a circle of opposites. Pairs of these adjacent primary emotions combine to form more complex emotions noted on the outside of the circle. Secondary emotions emerge from basic emotions more remotely associated on the wheel.

Izard contends that a newborn is capable of feeling only a generalized positive state, a generalized negative state, and the emotions of interest and sadness (Izard, 1982). A few months later, joy and anger develop. By the age of nine months, shame and fear appear, emotions that require a self-awareness that younger infants do not yet have. Emotional responses may continue to change throughout life, reflecting both physiological and cognitive changes (Mandler, 1984).

SUMMING UP

Motivation is a general concept explaining the processes involved in starting, directing, sustaining, and stopping behavior. It includes mechanisms that affect preferences for goals and activities, response strength, and persistence of patterns of action toward relevant goals. The concept of motivation serves various purposes, such as relating biological and behavioral processes and helping to explain why people persevere despite obstacles and adversity.

When used in research, motivation acts as an intervening variable that links a host of measurable, manipulatable conditions (independent variables) with observable responses (dependent variables). The strength of motivation is measured through variables such as activity level, rate and amount of learning, resistance of a response to extinction, preferences, and consummatory behavior. With humans, self-reports and projective tests assess different types and degrees of motivation. Motivation has been manipulated in research by lesioning, stimulation, and deprivation procedures. Incentive motivation is at work when the organism is aroused by external stimuli of desired goal objects or aversive conditions.

The concept of emotion is related to that of motivation, and equally challenging to study. Emotion is a complex pattern of physical changes, feelings, cognitive appraisal, and behavioral responses. These changes occur in response to situations seen as personally significant. When emotions are ambiguous or novel, arousal may be misattributed to unrelated situations. Some theorists maintain that we possess a set of basic, innate emotions. Plutchik's wheel of emotions includes eight primary emotions that are blended to produce secondary states. According to Izard's theory, emotions develop from early infantile response patterns that have evolved from human survival skills.

Theories of Motivation

Psychologists have sought to explain behavior with a host of different motivational theories. For centuries, philosophers distinguished between human action (presumably guided by reason and free will) and nonhuman action (determined by "brute appetites"). Darwin's theory of evolution challenged this distinction, paving the way for a theory that both human and animal behaviors are driven by instinct. Evolutionary theory inspired psychologists to look at the motivational value of *adapting* to one's environment. This view was embraced by *functionalists,* who introduced the concept of motivation into psychology. These psychologists were concerned with the way the mind functions to promote the organism's well-being.

The *instinct theory* of functional psychologists fell into disfavor for a number of reasons and was replaced in the 1930s and 1940s by *drive theory.* According to drive theory, a passive organism seeking physiological balance is impelled to action by drives. Organisms learn new responses when these actions reduce the intensity of motivating drives. However, drive theory was discarded because it failed to explain actions that increased arousal instead of reducing drives, such as exploring a novel environment.

Some drives, such as curiosity or seeking stimulation, are dedicated to increasing rather than reducing arousal. Development of this concept led to *arousal theory* and the concept of *optimal arousal level*—in which the sources of motivation are variations in individual arousal levels. Arousal theory had weaknesses that limited its utility, but it contributed important ideas to the development of subsequent theories.

Social psychologists from the Gestalt tradition proposed analyzing motivation in terms of the *tension* between a person's current position in life and his or her distant goals. Theories of social cognition (social thinking) emphasize the motivational power of personal beliefs and expectations.

Many of these motivational theories have centered on deficiencies and tensions in otherwise passive humans. In contrast, humanistic theories of self-actualization emphasized *growth motivation*. Humanist Abraham Maslow's description of the hierarchy of human needs portrays human nature as having an imperative for developing to its full potential once basic needs are satisfied.

➡ Keep this background sketch in mind as we examine these five theoretical perspectives on motivation: instinct theory, drive theory, arousal theory, humanistic growth theory, and social-cognitive theory. Which theory best explains your own views about what motivates you and others you know?

Instinct Theory

According to instinct theory, organisms are born with certain built-in tendencies that are essential for the species' survival. Some instinct theorists have seen this biological force as *mechanistic*—determining behavior without purpose and beyond individual control, like a complex reflex. Others believe that instincts allow an organism some choice among different courses of action.

The instinct concept explains the behavior of many nonhumans. Animals engage in regular cycles of activity that enable their species to survive. Salmon swim thousands of miles back to the exact stream where they were spawned, leaping up waterfalls until they come to the right spot, where the surviving males and females engage in ritualized courtship and mating. Fertilized eggs are deposited, the parents die, and in time their young swim downstream to live in the ocean until years later they return to complete their part in the continuing drama. Bees communicate the location of food to other bees, army ants embark on synchronized hunting expeditions, birds build nests, and spiders spin complex webs—exactly as their parents and ancestors did.

Originally, instinct theorists merely described instincts in terms of mysterious inner forces that impelled certain activities. Today, instincts in animals are usually studied as **fixed-action patterns,** unlearned patterns of action triggered by identifiable stimuli. Ethologists study animal behavior and species' natural habitats in detail, over time. Experimental researchers focus on identifying the brain mechanisms that work with environmental cues in producing instinctive behavior. Three functionalist psychologists—William James, William McDougall, and Sigmund Freud—originally explored these patterns of behavior.

William James, writing in 1890, stated his belief that humans rely on even more instincts than lower animals do to guide their behavior. In addition to the biological instincts they share with animals, a host of human social instincts—for example, sympathy, modesty, sociability, and love—come into play. For James, both human and animal instincts were *purposive,* serving important purposes in the organism's adaptation to its environment.

Psychologist **William McDougall** extended this view of the vital role of human instincts. McDougall (1908) defined instincts as inherited dispositions that had three components: a general *energizing* aspect, an *action* aspect, and *goal-directedness*. However, he viewed human nature as basically immoral and egoistic; "moralization" by society was required to bring base individual nature under social control.

Sigmund Freud (1915) had a somewhat different view of instinct, though one that was hardly more flattering to humanity. Freud thought instincts—life

fixed-action patterns In particular species, unlearned set of responses stimulated by specific environmental event or object in the natural habitat.

Salmon swim thousands of miles back to the exact stream where they were spawned.

instincts (such as sexuality) and death instincts (such as aggression)—had neither conscious purpose nor predetermined direction, and that organisms could learn many different means of satisfying them. He believed that instinctive urges exist to satisfy bodily needs, and that these urges create *psychic energy.* This tension drives us toward activities or objects that will reduce the tension. Freud assumed that most instincts operate unconsciously, but that they affect our conscious thoughts and feelings as well as our actions, sometimes putting us in conflict with society's demands. For example, you may have an unconscious urge to make immediate physical contact with an attractive classmate you have just met—but you realize (surely!) that acting on this impulse would not only get you into trouble socially, but also would not be likely to improve your chances for impressing the target of your interest.

Early interest in this subject led to a bulging catalogue of over 10,000 "human instincts" by the 1920s (Bernard, 1924). But these instincts did not exactly *explain* behavior; instead, they provided only new labels or names for unexplained action patterns. Another criticism of instinct theories emerged from the work of cultural anthropologists. Researchers such as Ruth Benedict (1959) and Margaret Mead (1939) found enormous variations from one culture to another; their findings contradicted the assumptions that universal motives govern human behavior. Finally, learning theorists demonstrated that much early behavior is learned rather than inborn. This marked the demise of all instinct theories except Freud's—whose secure place within the body of psychoanalytic theory kept it alive and well supported.

Drive Theory

The concept of motivation as an inner *drive* that determines behavior was introduced by **Robert Woodworth** (1918), another functionalist who had studied with William James. Woodworth defined *drive* in biological terms as energy released from an organism's store; it was *nonspecific energy,* blind to direction. Drive was the fuel of action, called forth by triggering stimuli and available to be channeled into goal-directed activities. Other mechanisms, such as perceptual and learning processes, guided action in appropriate directions.

Drive theory was most fully developed by Yale University theorist **Clark Hull** (1943, 1952). Hull believed that motivation was necessary for learning to occur, and learning was essential for successful adaptation to the environment. Similar to Freud, Hull emphasized the role of *tension* in motivation; he believed that *tension reduction* was reinforcing. In his view, primary drives were biologically based, aroused when the organism was deprived. These drives activated the organism; when they were satisfied, or reduced, the organism ceased acting. For example, food deprivation creates a hunger drive, a biological state of tension. Eating food reduces this tension, so a hungry organism will learn to engage in any behavior that is rewarded with food.

Drive-reduction theory is *homeostatic* because it assumes that an organism is driven to maintain *homeostasis,* a balance among the systems and processes of the body. This homeostatic, drive-reduction theory of motivation and learning was influential until the mid-1950s when it was challenged by new data. These data showed that humans and animals often do things in the *absence* of any apparent deprivation, drives, or drive reduction in order to *increase* stimulation. Both humans and animals play and exhibit exploratory and manipulatory behaviors.

Recall the rats in the Columbia Obstruction Box. Without deprivation of any kind, the animals still crossed the hot grid a few times. They crossed the painful barrier even when there was nothing on the other side—except a novel environment. Later research on curiosity motivation showed that rats deprived of food and water, when placed in a novel environment with plenty of opportunities everywhere to eat or drink, chose to explore instead. Only after they had first satisfied their curiosity did they begin to satisfy their hunger and thirst

(Zimbardo & Montgomery, 1957; Berlyne, 1960; Fowler, 1965). Apparently, for both people and animals, exploring and taking an interest in the world is a rewarding experience in itself.

Arousal Theory

Arousal is a measure of the general responsiveness of an organism to activation of the brainstem's *reticular system*. Arousal theory emerged from several converging sources. One source was the concept of emergency reactions to stress situations. Early research confirmed that certain emotions, such as fear and rage, prepare or motivate us for action when we are faced with danger; these arousal reactions are accompanied by measurable bodily changes. Other research, taking EEG measures of the activity of brain structures, encouraged psychologists to focus on the ways arousal of the brain prepares individuals to respond to stimuli. Finally, a series of studies related performance to motivation level. These lines of research converged to indicate a particular relationship between arousal and performance.

optimal arousal Level of arousal at which people best perform tasks of different levels of difficulty.

Yerkes-Dodson law Correlation between task difficulty and optimal level of arousal; as arousal increases, performance of difficult tasks decreases, while performance of simple tasks increases, to form an inverted-U function.

Performance as a Function of Arousal. For the hungry and thirsty rats in the Columbia Obstruction Box, as motivation increased, the curve of performance first rose and then later declined over time. This pattern, an *inverted U-shaped function*, suggests that too little or too much motivation may impair performance. For example, consider the effects of motivation arousal on your ability to study for an important test. If you are not worried or aroused—for example, if the test seems far off and the course is not important to you—you will not study very hard or perform very well. As your arousal increases, you become more directed and attentive in your studying. But above a certain level of arousal, you may be *too* worried to concentrate; last minute panic may scatter your efforts to study, and cause you to "freeze up" during the test.

The discovery of the *inverted-U relationship* between arousal and performance implies that there is a best or *optimal arousal level* for one's best performance. The concept of **optimal arousal** has been used in several ways. It has been used to identify the way motivational intensity and performance vary with tasks of different difficulty. It has also been used to account for the fact that some people (and animals) will sometimes work to *increase* their arousal, seeking stimulation rather than trying to reduce it.

The Yerkes-Dodson Law. Some tasks are best approached with high levels of motivation and others with more moderate levels. On some tasks, performance is best when motivation is relatively low. The key to the appropriate level of motivation is *task difficulty*. With difficult or complex tasks, the actor reaches the optimal level of arousal at the low end of the motivation continuum. As arousal increases, performance on difficult tasks quickly deteriorates. In contrast, for simple or easy tasks, the optimal level of motivation—the level required to perform most effectively—is greater. One's performance gets better and better as arousal increases, up to a later point when it tapers off. For example, if you are a fairly good typist, you will probably type even better if stimulated by background conversation or music, but when you are first learning to type, even the slight arousal caused by having friends chat in the background may disrupt your concentration and hurt the accuracy and speed of your typing.

Humans and animals often participate in activities to increase stimulation, rather than just to reduce drives.

The **Yerkes-Dodson law** formalizes the relationship between arousal and performance. According to this law, as arousal increases performance of difficult tasks *decreases* while performance of easy tasks *increases* (Yerkes & Dodson, 1908). See **Figure 8.5** for an illustration of this principle. Note that, although the timing of the optimal level is different for simple versus difficult tasks, extreme arousal (low or high) always causes relatively poor performance.

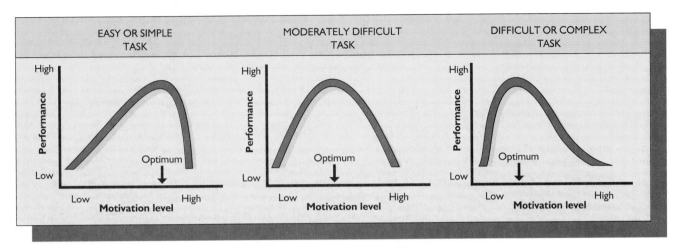

EASY OR SIMPLE TASK	MODERATELY DIFFICULT TASK	DIFFICULT OR COMPLEX TASK

Figure 8.5 The Yerkes-Dodson Law
Performance varies with motivation level and task difficulty. For easy or simple tasks, a higher level of motivation increases performance effectiveness. However, for difficult or complex tasks, a lower level of motivation is optimal. A moderate level of motivation is generally best for tasks of moderate difficulty. These inverted U-shaped functions show that performance is worst at both low and high extremes of motivation.

deficiency motivation Motivation to restore physical or psychological equilibrium (balance).

growth motivation Motivation to help oneself beyond what one has been and done in the past; central to humanistic theories.

Abraham Maslow (*Discovering Psychology*, 1990, Program 12)

What Influences Arousal? There are *individual differences* in the optimal arousal level—variations in how much arousal different people feel or need to function most effectively. Some people seem to need high levels of stimulation or work best in tension-filled settings that would make most people ineffective. They may even pressure themselves to increase the arousal level, knowing that greater arousal will help them succeed. Some individuals are more sensation-seeking than others (Zuckerman, 1983; Zuckerman et al., 1980). Individuals who like a higher level of stimulation relish risky activities such as skydiving or motorcycle racing and may use drugs to intensify sensations. These individuals may be vulnerable to substance addiction or high-risk, destructive behaviors.

Experience affects an individual's response to stimulation. Over time, most events become less stimulating, motivating an individual to seek a greater arousal level in more exciting stimuli (Zuckerman, 1979; Zuckerman, 1983). On the other hand, when arousal is too high, an individual acts to reduce the amount of stimulation (Maddi, 1980). There is some optimal level of arousal for each organism—below it, stimulation is sought and above it, stimulation is avoided. For example, when you feel bored (understimulated), you seek interest or adventure; but when you are exhausted or overwhelmed by people and activity (overstimulated), you retreat to a calm corner for some peace and quiet.

Although arousal theory generated new research perspectives, it didn't hold up as a general theory. This was mainly because different measures of physiological arousal did not correlate well with each other. This suggests that arousal is complex and expressed in many functions and actions, rather than being a single, centralized, driving force. Even restful states—such as REM sleep—involve intense brain activity, not a cessation of such processes.

Humanistic Theory·

Humanistic psychologist **Abraham Maslow**'s (1970) theory of human motivation explains both tension-reducing and tension-increasing actions. Maslow contrasted **deficiency motivation,** in which individuals seek to restore physical or psychological equilibrium, and **growth motivation,** in which individuals do more than reduce deficits as they seek to realize their fullest potential. Growth-motivated people may welcome uncertainty, tension, and even pain if they see it as a way of fulfilling their potential and as a way to achieve their goals. For example, a person who voluntarily suffers for a religious or political purpose accepts pain or humiliation as a necessary part of advancing the cause. Meaningful goals and personal values are worth some sacrifice or pain.

Maslow's Hierarchy of Needs. Maslow's theory holds that our basic needs form a **needs hierarchy**, as illustrated in **Figure 8.6.** Our inborn needs are arranged in a sequence of stages from primitive to advanced. The basic *biological needs*, such as hunger and thirst, are at the bottom of that hierarchy. They must be satisfied before other needs can begin to operate. When biological needs are pressing, other needs are put on hold and are unlikely to influence our actions; but when they are reasonably well satisfied, the needs at the next level—*safety needs*—motivate us. When we are no longer concerned about danger, we become motivated by *attachment needs*—needs to belong, to affiliate with others, to love, and to be loved. If we are well fed and safe and if we feel a sense of social belonging, we move up to *esteem needs.* These include the needs to like oneself, to see oneself as competent and effective, and to do what is necessary to earn the esteem of others. Humans are thinking beings, with complex brains that demand the stimulation of thought. We are motivated by strong *cognitive needs* to know our past, to comprehend the puzzles of our current existence, and to predict the future. The force of these needs enables scholars and scientists to spend their lives in the quest for new knowledge. At the next level of Maslow's hierarchy, comes the human desire for beauty and order, in the form of *aesthetic needs* that give rise to the creative aspect of humanity. At the top of the hierarchy are people who are nourished, safe,

needs hierarchy Abraham Maslow's theoretical sequence of needs motivating human behavior, from the most primitive level to higher needs only satisfied after lower ones are achieved.

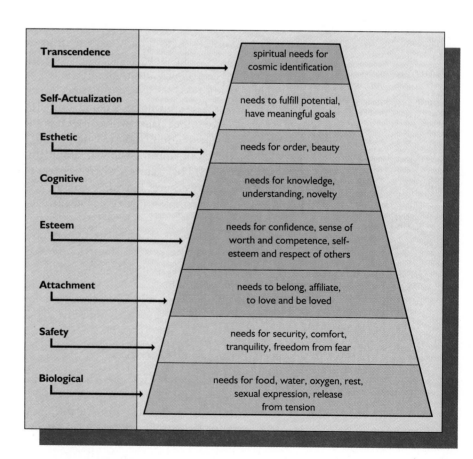

Figure 8.6 Maslow's Hierarchy of Needs According to Maslow, needs at the lower level of the hierarchy dominate an individual's motivation as long as they are unsatisfied. Once these are adequately satisfied, the higher needs occupy the individual's attention.

loved and loving, secure, thinking, and creative. These people have moved beyond basic human needs in the quest for the fullest development of their potential, or *self-actualization*. A self-actualizing person is self-aware, self-accepting, socially responsive, creative, spontaneous, and open to novelty and challenge—among other positive attributes. Maslow's hierarchy includes a step beyond the total fulfillment of individual potential. *Needs for transcendence* may lead to higher states of consciousness and a cosmic vision of one's part in the universe. Very few people develop the desire to move beyond the self to achieve union with spiritual forces.

Maslow's theory is valued more for influencing therapy and education than for stimulating psychological research. For Maslow, the central motivational force for humans is the innate need to grow and actualize one's highest potentials. Such an upbeat approach was welcomed by many psychologists who had wearied of the earlier diet of negative motivational views. Accentuating the positive fit a new orientation toward helping normal people achieve their potential, rather than making disturbed people less able to do so.

Motivation and Projection. Harvard psychologists Henry Murray and David McClelland used a special projective technique called the **Thematic Apperception Test (TAT)** to identify a limited number of human motives that are central in people's lives. In the TAT, subjects are shown a series of ambiguous pictures, and asked to generate a story about each one. In performing this task, a subject must *apperceive* or add interpretations to the limited scene depicted. Motivation researchers found that the stories subjects composed reflected personal needs and concerns. The researchers theorized that this occurs because needy subjects project their needs onto ambiguous stimuli, and weave need-related themes into their interpretations.

Using the TAT, Murray and McClelland uncovered many positive human motives similar to the ones Maslow described. Mingled with positive needs were needs that could demean human nature, such as abasement, self-blame, and humiliation. Many of the story themes centered on needs for power, dominance, and aggression—hardly the stuff of Maslow's higher levels of human potential. Later researchers were thus challenged to develop more comprehensive theories of human motivation.

Social-Cognitive Theories

To understand social-cognitive theories of motivation, consider a particular need state: loneliness. You tend to feel lonely when you think your social contacts are inadequate. But how do we define "inadequate"? Some people seem quite content in their own company, living alone, having contact with only a very few close friends. Others seem to need to be where the action is, in the middle of a happy, close group, in order to feel adequately loved. And still others might forsake all their "mere friends" for a single intimate, romantic relationship. Just as there are many forms of companionship, there seem to be many definitions of loneliness.

Social-cognitive theories of motivation share the concept that human motivation comes not from objective realities but from our *subjective interpretation* of them. What we do is controlled by what we *think* is or was responsible for causing our actions, what we *believe* we can do, and what we *anticipate* will be the outcome of our efforts. In the cognitive approach, these higher mental processes control motivation, rather than physiological arousal or biological mechanisms. This explains why human beings are often more motivated by imagined, future events than by genuine, immediate circumstances.

The Power of Expectations. The importance of *expectations* in motivating behavior was developed by **Julian Rotter** in his *social-learning theory* (1954).

Thematic Apperception Test (TAT)
Projective test in which an individual tells stories about each of a series of ambiguous pictures.

An example of the kinds of ambiguous figures used by Murray and McClelland.

locus of control orientation General belief about whether one's actions are controlled by internal or external factors.

For Rotter, the probability that we will engage in a given behavior (studying or an exam instead of partying) is determined by our *expectation* of attaining a goal (getting a good grade) that follows the activity and by the *personal value* of that goal. Expectation of a future occurrence is based on our past reinforcement history, which in turn has helped us develop a personal sense of *locus of control*. A **locus of control orientation** is a belief that the outcomes of our actions are contingent on what we do *(internal control orientation)* or on events outside our personal control *(external control orientation)*.

We have discussed general theories of motivation. In the next section, we will take a closer look at three very different motives and the behaviors they direct: hunger and eating, sexual motivation, and work and achievement.

SUMMING UP

Psychologists have explored many different theories to understand the nature of motivated behavior, but none have been completely satisfactory. Darwin's ideas inspired instinct theory, which asserted that for both animals and humans, motivation is inborn, mechanistic, and mindless.

Under a critical barrage from all sides, instinct theory gave way to drive theory, which proposed that need-based tension led to learning new, tension-reducing responses. This theory could not account for behavior motivated by arousal-seeking actions such as curiosity and play. Arousal theory dealt with the notion that humans and animals apparently prefer some optimal level of arousal. The Yerkes-Dodson law states that performance is a function of arousal, first increasing toward and then deteriorating beyond an optimal level.

Humanistic approaches to motivation, such as that of Abraham Maslow, postulate a hierarchy of needs arranged from the most basic survival needs to those that are more human, such as social, cognitive, and esthetic needs. As individuals seek to grow in their humanness and reach their fullest potential, other needs come into play, such as those for esteem, actualization, and transcendence. Specific human motives have been identified by projective techniques, in which subjects project their needs onto ambiguous patterns. Social and cognitive psychologists have influenced psychological thinking about motives by emphasizing the power of individual perceptions and the power of beliefs.

Motivated Behaviors

We can develop a solid understanding of human motivation by reviewing research on specific systems of motivated behavior. Among all the biological, social, and personal motives, three have been studied in great detail: hunger, sexuality, and achievement.

Eating

The primary drives, such as hunger and thirst, represent the body's way of keeping its long-running show on the road even when there isn't time for everyone to learn all the roles. Of the body's many homeostatic mechanisms for maintaining internal balance, those involved in hunger motivation are among the more complex. Biological regulation—by certain brain areas, neurotransmitters, hormones, and bodily organs works—with mental, behavioral, and social processes to control motivation to start and stop eating.

Regulation of Eating Patterns. To regulate food intake effectively, organisms must be equipped with mechanisms that accomplish four tasks.

1. Organisms must detect the need for food.
2. They must initiate eating behavior.
3. They must monitor the amount and nourishment of the food eaten.
4. These mechanisms must signal an end to eating when enough food has been consumed.

Researchers have been able to relate these tasks to two levels of bodily processes: *central* brain mechanisms (for example, the hypothalamus or "eating center") and *peripheral* mechanisms (for example, stomach contractions).

Peripheral Cues: Hunger Pangs. How do you *know* you're hungry? Where do sensations of hunger come from? Does your stomach rumble and send out distress signals—pangs and cramps? **Walter Cannon** (1934), a pioneering physiologist believed that sensations created by an empty stomach were the sole basis for hunger. He believed that an empty stomach created disagreeable stimulation, or cramps, triggering activity with a goal of filling the stomach and turning off the hunger pangs.

Cannon tested his *peripheral cues hypothesis* in an interesting demonstration on his student, A. L. Washburn. Washburn trained himself to swallow an uninflated balloon attached to a rubber tube. The other end of the tube was attached to a device that recorded changes in air pressure. Cannon then inflated the balloon in Washburn's stomach. As the student's stomach contracted, air squeezed from the balloon vibrated the recording pen. Washburn's reports of feeling hunger pangs were correlated with periods when his stomach was severely contracted. Cannon thought this proved that stomach pangs were responsible for hunger (Cannon & Washburn, 1912).

Cannon had only established a *correlation,* not a *causal* connection. Although hunger pangs accompanied stomach contractions, maybe something else was causing both responses. Sure enough, later research showed that stomach contractions are not a necessary condition for hunger. You can feel hungry without having stomach pangs, and you can have stomach pangs that you "know" are not from hunger. Surgical patients who have had their stomachs entirely removed still experience hunger (Janowitz & Grossman, 1950), and rats without stomachs still learn mazes when rewarded with food (Pennick et al., 1963). Thus sensations in the stomach play a familiar role in our usual experience of hunger, but they do not explain how the body detects its need for food and becomes motivated to eat.

A Multiple-System Approach. For many years researchers used models of central regulation, trying to identify the brain "hunger centers" responsible for starting and stopping the processes of feeling hungry and eating. However, that view also proved too limited. The current view of hunger and eating uses a more complex biological and psychological model.

The *multiple-system approach* begins by specifying that the brain works with many other systems, biological and psychological, to gather information about energy requirements, nutritional state, acquired hungers, and food preferences, as well as social and cultural demands. For example, your readiness to eat a slice of pizza depends on many factors, including how long it's been since you last ate, what you're hungry for, whether you like pizza, and even what time of day it is (for example, pizza might be acceptable for lunch but not for breakfast). Assembling all these data, the brain sends signals to neural, hormonal, organ, and muscle systems to start or stop food-seeking and eating.

The "Start" Center. The brain region primarily involved in starting and controlling eating is the *lateral hypothalamus* (LH). A separate brain area nearby, the *ventromedial hypothalamus* (VMH), controls cessation or inhibition of eating. This *dual-hypothalamic mechanism*—a "start" center and a "stop" center—together with many inputs and related processes, triggers eating and shuts it down.

Figure 8.7 summarizes many of the factors believed to be involved in the complex regulation of hunger detection, feeding, and satiation. In general, the biological systems respond to an organism's energy needs and nutritional state. The psychological systems account for acquired food preferences and respond to social, emotional, and environmental cues that determine whether eating in general—and specific foods in particular—will be desirable or aversive. We will touch briefly on the features of each factor.

Sugar (as blood sugar or glucose) and fat are your metabolism's energy sources. Evidently, receptors monitor the levels of sugar and fat in the blood. When blood glucose is too low, liver cell receptors send signals to the LH where glucose-detecting neurons respond to this information. When blood glucose levels fall there is an immediate effect on reported hunger in healthy adults. Normally, then, you feel hungry when you are low on nutrients—and need to start looking for energy.

The Set Point. With free access to food, adult animals and humans will maintain a stable body weight over their lifetime at a level consistent for them. Most organisms maintain a tightly controlled balance between intake of nutrition and expenditure of energy. An internal biological scale weighs the fat in

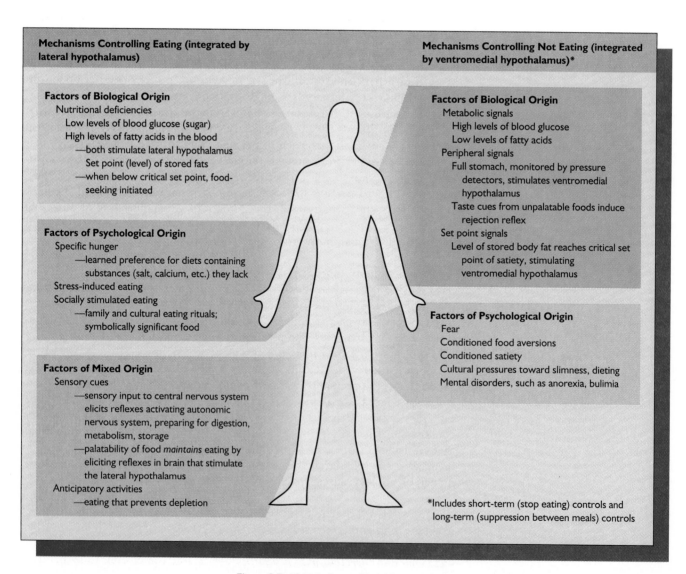

Mechanisms Controlling Eating (integrated by lateral hypothalamus)

Factors of Biological Origin
Nutritional deficiencies
   Low levels of blood glucose (sugar)
   High levels of fatty acids in the blood
      —both stimulate lateral hypothalamus
   Set point (level) of stored fats
      —when below critical set point, food-seeking initiated

Factors of Psychological Origin
Specific hunger
      —learned preference for diets containing substances (salt, calcium, etc.) they lack
Stress-induced eating
Socially stimulated eating
      —family and cultural eating rituals; symbolically significant food

Factors of Mixed Origin
Sensory cues
      —sensory input to central nervous system elicits reflexes activating autonomic nervous system, preparing for digestion, metabolism, storage
      —palatability of food *maintains* eating by eliciting reflexes in brain that stimulate the lateral hypothalamus
Anticipatory activities
      —eating that prevents depletion

Mechanisms Controlling Not Eating (integrated by ventromedial hypothalamus)*

Factors of Biological Origin
Metabolic signals
   High levels of blood glucose
   Low levels of fatty acids
Peripheral signals
   Full stomach, monitored by pressure detectors, stimulates ventromedial hypothalamus
   Taste cues from unpalatable foods induce rejection reflex
Set point signals
   Level of stored body fat reaches critical set point of satiety, stimulating ventromedial hypothalamus

Factors of Psychological Origin
Fear
Conditioned food aversions
Conditioned satiety
Cultural pressures toward slimness, dieting
Mental disorders, such as anorexia, bulimia

*Includes short-term (stop eating) controls and long-term (suppression between meals) controls

Figure 8.7 Multiple-System Model Summarizing Factors Controlling Hunger and Feeding

critical set point Level on an internal, biological scale that alerts the central nervous system about the body's fat content; when fat cell composition drops below this level, the brain triggers eating behavior.

the body and keeps the central nervous system informed. Whenever fats stored in specialized fat cells fall below a certain level, termed the **critical set point,** "eat" signals are sent out (Keesey & Powley, 1975).

This internal set point exerts a major influence on the amount people eat and on their weight. Besides eating to *satisfy* hunger, we eat to *prevent* it. Observations of free-ranging animals in their native habitat suggest that they do the same thing you probably do: eat *before* hunger sets in. Predators invest enormous energy in hunting for prey before hunger weakens them. Similarly, many species gather, store, and hoard food. These strategies *prevent depletion* instead of making up for an existing deficiency (Collier et al., 1972).

The "Stop" Center. Many of the mechanisms that stop eating are similar to those that start it, but they work through the VMH and rely on an opposite set of cues. *Short-term inhibitors* terminate ongoing feeding and *long-term inhibitors* suppress eating activities between meals.

High glucose levels and low levels of free fatty acids in the blood are signals that the set point has been reached. However, even before the brain processes this nutritional information, several peripheral cues signal "stop." Pressure detectors in the stomach signal fullness; if food is bad, unpleasant taste cues can induce a *rejection reflex* (including vomiting).

Like eating, *not* eating is influenced by a host of emotional and learned psychological processes, some occurring at meals and some between meals. For example, humans and animals do not eat when they are fearful. In addition, animals do not eat much of a new food; they'll sample a bit, then wait for several hours before eating more if no illness has developed. This protective reaction is known as *bait shyness* and is observable when pets seem to be finicky.

Situations can also signal "Don't eat." Some cultural influences encourage eating as an important social ritual, while others discourage it. For example, in this culture, ultra-thin fashion models remind women how they are "supposed" to look, an ideal that becomes distorted in two self-destructive eating syndromes: *anorexia* and *bulimia*. These serious disorders, especially prevalent among female college students, involve issues of personal control of one's body and are often linked to self-image and sexual attitudes. "In Focus: Obesity and Dieting" on the next page examines how attitudes about body weight can shape both eating behavior and self-image.

Sexual Motivation

While eating is essential to individual survival, sex is not. Some animals and humans remain celibate for a lifetime without apparent detriment to their daily functioning. But for a species to continue to evolve, it is more important for individuals to reproduce than to survive. Many animals have evolved to breed fast and die young. Evolution does not look kindly upon celibacy and tends to eliminate it very quickly. In general, if there were any inherited tendencies toward celibacy, they would die out—with no offspring to carry them on— while any inherited tendencies toward lust would survive and proliferate.

Sex benefits a breed or a species, so nature makes sexual stimulation intensely pleasurable. (If sex were a chore rather than a pleasure, few would undertake it and the species would die out). A climactic orgasm serves as the ultimate reinforcer for all the costs expended in mating.

Sexual drive is a unique source of motivation in several ways, noted as follows:

- Sex is essential to the survival of the *genes* the individual carries—not to the individual carrying them.
- Sex motivates an unusually wide variety of behaviors and psychological processes.

In Focus:

OBESITY AND DIETING

If you have ever tried to lose weight, you know how difficult it is first to get rid of those "extra" pounds—and then to *keep* them off. Maintaining a constant weight is itself a tricky problem of bodily and behavioral control: to keep one's food intake in line with energy output. Your weight generally reflects the balance between the fuel you take in and the energy you burn in your daily activities. Most people manage to keep a general, if not precise, match between these two factors, so their body weight remains in the healthy range and fluctuates very little over the years.

However, the growing health problem of obesity—body weight at least 20 percent above the healthy ideal for one's age and body structure—indicates the difficulty of maintaining perfect intake/output balance. Over one-fourth of the American population are considered overweight or obese, with attendant risks of heart disease, diabetes, high blood pressure, and some types of cancer. Diets, support groups, and weight-loss plans seem to be a national obsession, but most graduates of such programs gain the lost weight back within five years (Martin, et al., 1991). What regulates the body's link between taking food in and burning it up, and why is weight so difficult to change or regulate?

If the intake/output model of body weight can be relied on, there are two ways to reduce weight: to decrease intake (for example, eat less), and to increase output (for example, to exercise more often and more vigorously). On closer examination, however, we find that body weight is quite complex. For example, body fat is not like other stores of nutrients and tissue, and total body fat may not be subject to regulation in the same way as general weight (Martin et al., 1991). People "programmed" to be obese—who have a built-in tendency to be overweight—have more *fat cells* (adipose tissue) than people of normal weight as a result of either genetic factors or overfeeding at critical periods in

infancy (Brownell, 1982; Sjørstrøm, 1980). Beyond infancy, dieting or overeating changes the *size* of the fat cells, but not their *number*. The number of fat cells a person has remains constant throughout life. Consequently, someone with a large number of fat cells who diets will lose weight and may become skinny. However, the person will still have the same *critical set point* and so will be generally hungry (Nisbett, 1972). The bodies of obese individuals are programmed to be fat and rebel against extreme interventions that try to make them slim. One form of rebellion is the body's adjustment of energy expenditure—the metabolic rate at which the body burns fuel—such that when food is restricted, the metabolism decreases and burns less fuel. As a result, dieting alone can lower one's metabolism but not result in weight loss.

When obese people diet and reach their new reduced weight, their body chemistry becomes disorganized. Fat cells shrink, menstruation may stop, and thyroid hormone levels and white blood cell counts drop, as do blood pressure and pulse rate. These formerly obese individuals complain of intolerance to the cold, and they are obsessed with thoughts about food. Because our culture is filled with external cues to eating—such as restaurant ads and social rituals organized around meals—food-obsessed individuals can be surrounded by temptation beyond their resistance.

Sadly, it tends to be the rule that weight loss from dieting programs is short-term; gradually the body's own weight regulators take over and restore its weight equilibrium (Kolata, 1985). To be effective, any dieting program must include regular exercise, daily monitoring of food intake, systematic record keeping of caloric intake and weight change, techniques for avoiding severe stress, and social (especially family) support. For the obese, dieting is not a question of "mind over matter"; instead, it is a question of biology asserting itself

over psychology. It is true that some people *do* maintain significant weight losses for years—even for the rest of their lives—but generally only through major changes in their habits and lifestyles.

Why do people and sometimes animals overeat in the first place? Stressful stimulation leads to overeating in both human and animal subjects (Antelman et al., 1976; Schachter et al., 1968). In the case of humans, social and cultural factors determine when, how much, how fast, and what people eat. A mother who expresses her love with home-cooked meals may interpret refusal to eat as a rejection. Her children might best show their filial love by chowing down whatever she sets before them.

Humans also may overeat or fast for the *symbolic* value of food—for example, fasting during religious holidays. The charitable organization Oxfam International sponsors an annual day-long fast, after which participants are encouraged to donate the money they *would* have spent on meals to the cause of eliminating world hunger. In this context, food is more than fuel; it is a powerful social, cultural, and personal symbol. Our reactions to it and our ability to control eating habits are influenced by complex combinations of meanings, flavors, values, and preferences. Small wonder that for many people food is the subject of a lifelong love-hate affair.

In Chapter 13 we will discuss the causes and sometimes deadly consequences of becoming one of the "fasting girls"—young women who suffer from a condition known as *anorexia nervosa* (Brumberg, 1988). Inspired by images of ultra-thin models, and fearful they too might be rejected like people who are "too" old, fat, or unattractive, victims of anorexia starve themselves in order to be "acceptably" slim. Literally dying for perfection, individuals with eating disorders may find they have developed a habit and mindset that they can no longer control.

- Sex may develop independently of sexual deprivation.
- Sex can be aroused by almost any stimulus—a touch, a fantasy, or sexual object—that represents or symbolizes the opportunity for mating.

Although Sigmund Freud called attention to the importance of sexual motivation more than a century ago, research psychologists did not follow up on his ideas at that time. Sex did not fit well into the then-prevalent, tension-reduction theory of motivation. Fear and anxiety fit the model better and so received more research attention (Brown, 1961). Psychologists have long ignored systematic study of this powerful human motive primarily because of cultural taboos against dealing openly with sexuality. Even today it may be difficult for some students to read this material in a text without experiencing discomfort or self-consciousness.

Let us first consider some of what is known about the sex drive and mating behavior in lower animals. We will then turn our attention to selected issues in human sexuality.

Nonhuman Sexual Arousal. In nonhuman species, sexual arousal is determined primarily by physiological processes. Animals become receptive to mating largely in response to the flow of hormones controlled by the pituitary gland and secreted from the *gonads,* the sex organs. In males, these hormones are known as *androgens,* and they are continuously present in sufficient supply so that males are hormonally ready for mating at almost any time. However, in the females of many species, the sex hormone *estrogen* is released according to regular time cycles of days or months or according to seasonal changes. Thus, the female is not always hormonally receptive to mating.

Sex hormones act on both the brain and genital tissue and often lead to a pattern of predictable, *stereotyped sexual behavior* for all members of a species. If you've seen one pair of rats in their mating sequence, you've seen them all. The receptive female rat darts about the male until she gets his attention. Then he chases her as she runs away. She stops suddenly and raises her rear, and he enters her briefly, thrusts, and pulls out. She briefly escapes him, and the chase continues—interrupted by 10 to 20 intromissions before he ejaculates, rests a while, and starts the sex chase again. Apes also copulate only briefly (for about 15 seconds). Predators like lions can afford to indulge in long, slow copulatory rituals. But their prey, such as antelope, copulate for only a few seconds, often on the run (Ford & Beach, 1951).

Peripheral stimuli can sensitize or activate innate response patterns. In many species, the sight and sound of ritualized display patterns by potential partners is a *necessary* condition for sexual response. Touch, taste, and smell can also serve as stimulants for sexual arousal. Some species secrete chemical signals called **pheromones** that attract suitors, sometimes from great distances. In many species, pheromones are emitted by the female when her fertility is optimal (and hormone level and sexual interest are peaking). In humans, though, reactions to sex-related odors are quite variable—determined more by *who* is giving off the smell than by any unlearned, irresistible, olfactory properties of the chemical communication (Hopson, 1979).

Sexual Reproduction. From a biological perspective, sexual behavior is the set of responses that results in sexual reproduction. A psychological perspective, however, is focused less on reproduction and more on individual feelings associated with sexual activities. **Sexual reproduction** refers to the production of progeny by sexual means. Some species of fish, lizards, and other animals reproduce by nonsexual means, but they produce offspring fit to survive only in highly stable environments. Sexual reproduction confers the advantage of *genetic variability,* enabling some of the offspring to be genetically prepared to survive in a changing world.

pheromones Chemical signals an organism releases to communicate with other members of the species; often a sexual attractor.

sexual reproduction Production of offspring by means of sexual interaction, so that germ cells (for example, sperm, eggs) combine to form unique genetic combinations.

Mating behavior in the frog improves the chances of each egg being fertilized. The male stimulates the female to release her eggs and almost simultaneously releases his sperm over the egg mass.

Sexual Synchrony. Sexual reproduction requires at least two sexual types: males and females. The female must have large gametes (eggs)—the energy store for the embryo to begin its growth—and the male must produce smaller gametes (sperm) that are specialized for motility (to move into the eggs). This basic sex cell differentiation gets amplified as males and females diverge in physical structure, physiological functions, and behavior. The two sexes must synchronize—bring together—their activity so that gametes meet under the appropriate conditions, resulting in production of viable young. There are at least four elements of sexual synchronization (Adler, 1978):

- A *proper* mate—finding one who is of the same species, is reproductively mature, and has the greatest genetic potential for offspring's well-being.
- The right *place and time*—timing the breeding season so that offspring will be produced when the environment will be most supportive.
- Behavioral *adaptation*—getting "in the mood" through courtship rituals and foreplay.
- *Pregnancy readiness*—in mammals, altering the female's physiological and behavioral state away from sexual receptiveness and *toward pregnancy readiness.*

While hormonal activity is important in regulating sexual behavior among female mammals in other animal species, it has no known effect on sexual receptiveness or gratification in women. In men, the sex hormone testosterone (one of the androgens) is necessary for sexual arousal and performance. Testosterone levels become high enough only after *puberty* when sexual maturation is achieved. Sexual stimulation and orgasm raise the level of this hormone, but so do hostile or anxious mood states. Perhaps this similar effect of sexual stimulation and hostility contributes to many men's association of sex with aggression (Donnerstein, 1980; Donnerstein & Berkowitz, 1981; Donnerstein, Linz & Penrod, 1987; Malamuth, 1984; 1986; 1989).

➡ **Human Sexuality.** How interested are you in sex? How much do you *know* about sex? Interest and knowledge are not the same thing. And interest *without* knowledge can cause serious problems. Before going on with this section, answer each of the following items of a "sexual I.Q." test with either true or false (adapted from *Consumer Reports on Health,* February 1992):

1. No one food or drink has been found to be an effective aphrodisiac.
2. Sexual activity need not end in orgasm to be satisfactory.
3. Impotence—a man's inability to achieve or maintain an erection—usually reflects a psychological problem.
4. For best competitive performance, athletes should refrain from sexual activity the night before a game.
5. The symptoms of sexually transmitted disease are usually noticeably painful or disfiguring.

If you are unsure about your answers to any of the above questions, you have probably sensed the psychological factors—including information and confidence—of sexual experience and behavior. But we won't keep you in suspense; here are the answers: Number 1 is true: No food or beverage has been found to stimulate sexual arousal; although alcohol lowers some people's inhibitions, it actually interferes with both sexual arousal and orgasm. Number 2 is true: While orgasms bring intense pleasure, reaching orgasm is not the "key" to sexual satisfaction, and focusing on orgasm to the exclusion of other sensations can heighten anxiety and diminish performance. Number 3 is false: In most cases, impotence is caused by physiological factors, including side effects of medication and problems with circulatory, hormonal, or nervous system function. Number 4 is false: Sex the night before a competition will not drain

human sexuality Combination of humans' physical characteristics and capacities for sexual behaviors; psycho-sexual learning, values, norms, and attitudes about sexual behaviors.

sexual arousal Motivational state stimulated by physiological and cognitive reactions to erotic stimuli.

Our cultural lessons and life experiences dramatically influence the meaning of sex in our lives.

athletic ability or strength; a good night's sleep will usually restore an athlete's vigor. Number 5 is false: Though most sexually transmitted diseases can cause harm, several may have no noticeable symptoms, though they are infectious.

No matter how you did on this quiz, you will realize that information about human sexual behavior is learned; it does not "come naturally." Our cultural lessons and life experiences dramatically influence the meaning of sex in our lives. Sexuality is far more dependent on psychological factors in humans than it is in animals. As a result, it is also more variable in humans than in other species. **Human sexuality** includes an evolved core of motivations focused on mating for reproduction and pleasure from sexual behavior, along with societal constraints on and inducements toward sexual activities. **Sexual arousal** in humans is the motivational state of excitement and tension brought about by reactions to erotic stimuli. *Erotic stimuli* give rise to sexual excitement or feelings of passion. Sexual arousal induced by erotic stimuli is reduced by sexual activities that are perceived by the individual as satisfying, especially by achieving orgasm.

Scientific Evidence. Scientific investigation of normal human sexual behavior was given the first important impetus by the work of **Alfred Kinsey** and his colleagues beginning in the 1940s (1948, 1953). They interviewed some 17,000 Americans about their sexual behavior. To a generally shocked public these researchers revealed that certain behaviors previously considered rare and even abnormal were actually quite widespread—or at least reported to be. However, it was **William Masters** and **Virginia Johnson** (1966, 1970, 1979) who really broke down the traditional sexual taboo. They legitimized the study of human sexuality by directly observing and recording under laboratory conditions the physiological patterns involved in ongoing human sexual performance. By doing so, they studied not what people said about sex (with obvious problems of response bias) but how they actually reacted—during intercourse and masturbation. It is important to note that Masters and Johnson studied arousal and response only. They did *not* study the psychologically significant initial phase of sexual responding—that of *sexual desire,* the motivation to seek out a sexual partner or to make oneself available for sexual experience.

Four of the most significant conclusions drawn from this research on human sexuality are as follows:

1. Men and women have similar patterns of sexual responding, regardless of the source of arousal.
2. Although the sequence of phases of the sexual response cycle is similar in the two sexes, women are more variable, tending to respond more slowly but often remaining aroused longer.
3. Many women can have multiple orgasms, while men rarely do in a comparable time period.
4. Penis size is generally unrelated to any aspect of sexual performance (except in the male's *attitude* toward having a large penis).

Masters and Johnson found four phases in the human sexual response cycle: excitement, plateau, orgasm, and resolution (see **Figure 8.8,** on p. 308).

- In the *excitement phase,* there are blood vessel changes in the pelvic region. The penis becomes erect, the clitoris swells, and blood and other fluids become congested in the testicles and vagina.
- During the *plateau phase,* a maximum level of arousal is reached. Rapid increases occur in heartbeat, respiration, blood pressure, glandular secretions, and muscle tension.
- During the *orgasm phase,* males and females experience a very intense, pleasurable sense of release from the cumulative sexual tension. Orgasm, characterized by rhythmic genital contractions, culminates in ejaculation

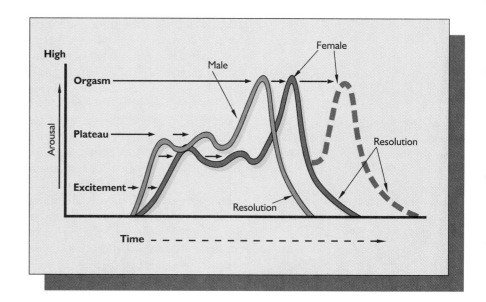

Figure 8.8 Phases of Human Sexual Response
The phases of sexual response in males and females have similar patterns. The primary differences are in the time it takes for males and females to reach each phase and in the greater likelihood that females will achieve multiple orgasms.

of sperm in men, and can involve either clitoral or vaginal sensations in women.

- During the *resolution phase,* the body gradually returns to its normal pre-excitement state, with both blood pressure and heartbeat slowing down. After one orgasm, most men enter a refractory period preventing further orgasm for minutes to hours more. With sustained arousal, women are capable of multiple orgasms in fairly rapid succession.

Sexual arousal can lead to sexual intercourse, which in turn can lead to off-spring. What sorts of sexual passion will evolve for different species and different sexes? If males had adapted to a very different social-sexual environment than females, we would expect them to have very different sexual passions and motivations. As proposed in "In Focus: The Mating Game: Evolution at Work and Play," men and women did evolve in different social-sexual environments, even though we belong to the same species.

Sexual Cues. Masters and Johnson's work demonstrated conclusively that problems in sexual response often have psychological rather than physiological origins that can be changed through therapy. Of particular concern is the inability to complete the response cycle and achieve gratification. This inability is called *impotence* in men and *frigidity* in women. Often the source of the inability is a preoccupation with personal problems, fear of the consequences of sexual activity, or anxiety about having one's sexual performance evaluated. Poor nutrition, fatigue, stress, and excessive use of alcohol or drugs can also diminish sexual drive and performance.

The sequence of sexual activities that may culminate in orgasm can begin with only one unconditioned stimulus and with an endless variety of conditioned stimuli. The unconditioned stimulus is touch. In the form of genital caresses, touch is a universal component of sexual foreplay (Ford & Beach, 1951). Virtually any stimuli that become associated with genital touch and orgasm can become conditioned motivators, whether they are present physically or only in memory or fantasy.

Research suggests that sensations and fantasy during masturbation provide the primal setting for associating virtually any stimulus with pleasurable arousal (Storms, 1980, 1981). Inanimate objects, textures, sounds, visual images, odors—any tangible or imagined stimulus event—can come to elicit arousal through this conditioned association. Through conditioning, some of us learn culturally acceptable sexual orientations, while others learn sexual deviations.

Theory   THE MATING GAME: EVOLUTION AT WORK AND PLAY

Sex. Say the word and you suddenly seem to have everyone's attention. See the word or suggestive pictures in a movie, commercial, or advertisement, and you may find it difficult to turn your attention elsewhere. Sexual innuendos make interactions interesting; sexual references prompt nervous laughter; sexual images can inspire, excite, or alarm us. The human species seems to be obsessed with sex. Why?

An evolutionary perspective suggests that sexual reproduction is essential to the continuation of our species, and that individuals' actions determine whose genes will shape those next generations. In this view, the mating game is "nothing personal," just a matter of following nature's urges to mate and produce offspring. But if this were accurate, wouldn't people be more promiscuous, less discriminating, and far less secretive about sex? If sexual motivation is as basic as eating and drinking, why don't we offer sex as easily as we offer to get someone a soft drink? Why don't television commercials advertise opportunities for sexual contact as glamourously as they encourage us to visit fast-food restaurants?

Obviously, the business of selecting mates and producing children is a very personal and complex process. Consider gender differences in attitudes toward sexuality. Women tend to be somewhat conservative about sexual involvement (for example, more cautious and discriminating) while men tend to be generally more permissive. How did this distinction evolve?

For females, the reproductive environment consists of the behavioral tendencies and abilities of males and of competing females; for males, the reverse holds. The difference comes down to *gametes*—germ cells, in the form of sperm and eggs. Males could reproduce hundreds of times a year if they could find enough willing mates. To produce a child, all they must invest is a teaspoon of sperm and a few minutes of intercourse. But women can reproduce at most about once a year, and each child reproduced then requires a huge investment of time and energy. Males of every species have greater variance in their

reproductive performance: some have no children and some have many.

Thus, eggs are the limited resource, and males compete for opportunities to fertilize them. The basic problem facing male animals is to maximize the number of offspring produced by mating with the largest number of females possible. The basic problem facing *female* animals is to find a high-quality male to insure the best, healthiest offspring from her limited store of eggs. Throughout nature, males strive for *quantity* and females for *quality*. So each sex evolves the emotions and motivations that best solve their respective investment strategy problems.

For some animals, such as primates and humans, offspring take so long to mature and are so helpless while growing that substantial **parental investment** is required (Trivers, 1972). Mothers and fathers must spend time and energy raising the children—unlike fish or spiders which simply lay eggs and depart. Females then have the problem of selecting not just the biggest, strongest, smartest, highest-status, most thrilling male but the most loyal, committed male who will help raise their children.

Then why does commitment seem to be such a problem for modern couples? **David Buss** (1989), an evolutionary psychologist, has suggested that men and women evolved different strategies, emotions, and motivations for *short-term mating* versus *long-term mating*. The male strategy of seducing and abandoning—giving signs of loyalty and commitment and then leaving—is a short-term strategy. The male strategy of staying committed to the female and investing in the offspring is a long-term strategy. The female strategy of attracting a loyal male who will stay to help raise her children is a long-term strategy. There is controversy about whether observable behaviors reflect gender-wide mating strategies—exceptions to every "rule" can be identified. It is wise to remember, then, that sexual motivation is a complex matter involving more (and different) issues than reproduction. Obviously, our nervousness about sex and our attraction to sexual images and ideas is not identical to our interests in having or raising children.

According to the evolutionary approach, as far as reproduction goes, women should be more future-oriented and men more present oriented, because women are looking for potential fathers while men are looking for momentary lovers. All of these arguments depend on the social-sexual environment that existed when humans were evolving. Yet women and men show exactly the patterns predicted by evolutionary psychology across all cultures, even when the modern environment changes the risks and rewards of different mating strategies. Everywhere in the world, sex is considered something that women give away to men, either in exchange for immediate material reward (short-term mating, such as prostitution) or in exchange for long-term commitment and support (marriage). In general, men show a greater desire for a variety of sexual partners and are less discriminating about their mates. This is true even though modern contraception eliminates many of the dangers of short-term mating strategies for women and even though modern economies may allow both men and women to raise children alone. If humans were simply responding rationally to the social-sexual environment, or if social and sexual emotions were learned to fit the current environment, we would expect their emotions and motivations to keep up with technological and social developments. Instead, our evolved mating strategies seem resistant to change.

The human mating game no longer consists of trying to figure out what men and women really want. Men evolved to exploit the reproductive capabilities of women, and women evolved to exploit the reproductive capabilities of men. Although this mutual exploitation evolved for the purposes of reproducing genes, it can give rise to many powerful sexual emotions and experiences. The most important consideration in any discussion of sex, then, is not whether we as a species have overcome our biological past, but how evolution has been able to construct male and female minds that are capable of attracting, seducing, and enjoying each other.

parental investment Time, energy, and resources parents must spend raising their offspring.

Some people learn to become aroused *only* by conditioned stimuli such as the sight of high-heel shoes, young children, or even pain (Rachman, 1966).

In humans, sexuality can be less concerned with meeting physiological need than with satisfying cognitive desires. For most humans, the goal of sexual activity is "the attainment of a cognitive state: the conscious perception of sexual satisfaction. This state depends on a combination of experiences originating in the experiencer's body and in that of the sexual partner" (Davidson, 1980, p. 227). Interpretations of experiences, the meaning of specific sexual events, sexual beliefs and values, and imagination and expectation all play a part in human sexual behavior and satisfaction (Byrne, 1981). Even the subjective experience of orgasm, which has been compared by some to a profound altered state of consciousness (Davidson, 1980), usually depends not only on physical stimulation but on interpersonal factors, such as being in a close, trusting relationship.

Sexual Scripts. Generalized sexual arousal can be channeled into different specific behaviors, depending on how the individual has learned to respond and think about sexual matters. **Sexual scripts** are socially learned programs of sexual responsiveness that include prescriptions, usually unspoken, of what to do; when, where, and how to do it; with whom, or with what to do it; and why it should be done (Gagnon, 1977). Different aspects of these scripts are assembled through social interaction over one's lifetime. The attitudes and the values embodied in one's sexual script define one's general orientation to sexuality.

sexual scripts Socially learned programs of sexual interpretation and responsiveness.

Scripts are combinations of prescriptions generated by social norms (what is proper and accepted), individual expectations, and preferred sequences of behavior from past learning. Your sexual scripts include scenarios of not only what you think is appropriate on your part but also of your expectations of a sexual partner. Differing scripts can create problems of adjustment between partners when they are not discussed or synchronized. For example, there is evidence that touch has different meanings for men and women.

Researchers questioned 40 male and 40 female undergraduates about the meaning they attach to touch, when applied to different parts of the anatomy by a friend. Quite different meanings were found between the sexes. For females, the more a touch was associated with sexual desire, the less it was considered to imply warmth, pleasantness, or friendliness. When a close male friend touches a woman in an area of her body that communicates sexual desire to her, then that is its *only* meaning to her. For males, the same touch is interpreted as having a cluster of meanings: pleasantness, warmth, love, and sexual desire. Misunderstandings can arise when one person's "friendly touch" is perceived by the other as a "sexual advance" (Nguyen et al., 1975). This study suggests that, from the female perspective, male touch without the rituals of courtship and the preliminaries of respect and commitment is interpreted as a sexual advance—for "easy," short-term mating. For males, female touch is interpreted as pleasant in most situations since it is assumed to suggest a willingness to mate.

Sexual scripts include similar roles for the actors within a given culture, socioeconomic class, gender, and educational level. But there are also unique features in each individual's personal script, learned through his or her own history of sexual experience. Because erotic stimuli can be intensely pleasurable while also often strongly prohibited by society and religion, we learn many different ways of responding to the variety of erotic stimuli we experience in society. Here's where we really see the power of conditioned associations. Because any stimulus that has been associated with sexual arousal can become a potent elicitor of later arousal, there are enormous variations in the forms our human sexuality takes.

Sexual scripts within a society can become dangerously confused. *Date rape* is a trauma that illustrates devastating conflict between male and female sexual scripts. In one sample of college women, 57 percent reported having experienced what they thought of as rape (Koss, 1985). The accuracy of this staggering figure is confirmed by surveys of male students. One in every three college men said he would rape a woman if he were sure he would not get caught (Malamuth, 1984). When questioned about their actual experiences, over half the men in another survey admitted to forcing a date to perform some sexual act, and 25 percent admitted to forcing intercourse (Koss & Oros, 1982). Researchers suggest that date rape may be a *result* of confusion over sexual scripts. The female script may lead a woman to give in if a man's behavior is coercive and insistent; the male script may consider some humiliation of a woman acceptable, and may justify rape in light of peer pressure on men to be sexually aggressive (Murnen et al., 1989; Muehlenhard & Cook, 1988). As the brutal realities of date rape are exposed, it is more likely that societies and communities will develop strategies to counter the confused and conflicted sexual scripts that make possible such abuse of intimate relations.

Sexual Orientation. Ever since Alfred Kinsey's first reports, we have known that human sexual orientation is a complex business. For one survey's findings about the variety of sexual behavior found among modern humans, see **Table 8.2** on the next page. Kinsey found a large percentage of men in his sample who had had some homosexual experience, and somewhat smaller percentages for women. Psychologists have become more interested in this important but neglected aspect of human sexual motivation. Cultural and historical studies reveal that human societies vary widely in their attitudes and expressions about homosexuality. In some cultures it is suppressed, while in others it is accepted and even favored over heterosexuality.

Theories about the nature and development of homosexuality reflect the full range of psychological disciplines. Some theories seek to explain the physiological or genetic variations that might produce homosexuality. Other theories focus on the individual's family life or on early learning experiences that might affect one's sexual orientation. Psychoanalytic theory suggested that male homosexuality represented an arrested sexual development that occurred

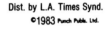

Dist. by L.A. Times Synd.
©1983 Punch Publs. Ltd.

"Now, tell me. What's it like being a sex symbol?"

Table 8.2 Sexual Preferences and Behaviors of Adult Americans, 1989

Random Survey Sample N = 1401

CATEGORY	%/#
I. Sexual Preference	
A. Exclusively heterosexual (since age 18)	91.0%
B. Homosexual or bisexual (since age 18)	6.0
C. Not sexually experienced	3.0
II. Sexual Behavior Reported	
A. Frequency of intercourse (mean)	
1. All adults	57 times/year
2. Men	66
3. Women	51
4. Married	67
5. Separated	66
6. Widowed	8
7. Under age 40	78
8. Under age 50	67
9. Under age 60	46
10. Under age 70	23
11. Over age 70	8
B. Number of sexual partners (mean)	
1. Men (since age 18)	12 partners
2. Women (since age 18)	3
3. People with postgraduate education	13
4. People with college education	8
5. People with less than high-school education	5
C. Abstinence	
1. Overall	22.0%
2. Men	14.0
3. Women	28.0
D. Marital infidelity	1.5
III. AIDS Risk	
A. High risk (5 or more sexual partners, casual partners, male homosexual or bisexual partners)	5.5%
B. Multiple high risk (2 or more of above conditions)	1.3

because the child failed to resolve the Oedipus conflict under the influence of a dominant mother and absent or hostile father (Bieber et al., 1962). However, evidence that parents "cause" homosexuality in this way has been inconclusive (Bell et al., 1981). Attempts to identify physiological causes of homosexuality have likewise been inconclusive. However, it is clear that homosexuality is *not* due to deficient levels of testosterone in adult gay males nor to too much testosterone in adult lesbians (Meyer-Bahlburg, 1977).

Controversial new evidence suggests that sexual orientation may yet be found to be physically determined rather than a lifestyle choice. Neurobiologist **Simon LeVay** (1991) performed autopsies on the brains of 35 victims of AIDS: 19 homosexual men and 16 men who were presumably heterosexual. LeVay found that, in the homosexual men, a segment of the anterior (frontal) hypothalamus—a group of cells called the *third interstitial nucleus*—was less than half the size of the same structure in the heterosexual men. Could a person's basic sexual orientation be influenced in some way by processes involving this neural tissue? Since all subjects were AIDS victims, critics have warned that the tissue size differences might be due to the deterioration caused by that disease. However, the heterosexual victims should have shown such effects as well. LeVay's research raises interesting questions: Do these anatomical differences "cause" sexual orientation? Are these differences inborn, or might they develop later in life? The answers to these questions have implications for human relations and social policies, since *homophobia* (prejudice against gay men and lesbians) is one of the last remaining bases of discrimination in law and public life.

Finally, a cognitive-behaviorist theory suggests that it is early erotic experience that determines sexual orientation (Storms, 1981). Most young children have friendships exclusively with the same sex. If a child begins to masturbate and fantasize relatively early, before having a chance to associate closely with the opposite sex, perhaps sexual pleasure will become associated only with same-sex peers.

Researchers have begun to explore the ways that individual gays and lesbians come to define themselves. Four stages in their self-definition have been outlined (Troiden, 1989):

1. Up through the age of about 12, boys and girls report defining themselves as *different from their peers,* not in sexual feelings but in their activities. Lesbians feel they are less feminine and more physically active than other girls, while gay men prefer solitary activities to typical masculine pursuits.
2. In adolescence, they start to recognize that they are different from their peers in terms of their *sexual feelings.* Forced to consider the possibility that they are not heterosexual, they employ various strategies to deny, change, or cope with this realization.
3. In later adolescence and early adulthood, they attempt to integrate homosexuality into *self-identity.* Crucial experiences to development include positive or negative encounters with other gays or lesbians, and dealing with the stigma of acknowledging one's orientation.
4. The final stage is a fusion of sexual and emotional feelings, allowing the person to see homosexuality as *natural and normal for the self.* Occasional loss of confidence is common, and not all people reach this stage.

These theories are still very much in the early stages of development. In all probability, human sexual orientation does not have any one cause. Some people may be born gay or lesbian, but that does not preclude others from choosing to have homosexual experiences. Cultural variation also reminds us how difficult it is to generalize about homosexuality, and how flexible we humans tend to be about physical possibilities and affairs of the heart.

Achievement Motivation

Sigmund Freud is credited with observing that a healthy life has two goals: love and work. We seek joy and satisfaction not only in pleasure or relationships, but also in a job well done. The desire to achieve one's goals, whether they involve getting an A in psychology or climbing to the top of a steep mountain, is a pervasive psychological motive that empowers a wide variety of human actions. Achievement motives are usually satisfied by the individual's knowledge that he or she has been effective in a personally significant activity. Achievement motives operate at a particular level—high, low, or somewhere in between—whatever the specific task might be, whether it is recognized by praise, or money, or no reward at all. Achievement motives link specific goals, the path to attaining them, planning and effort, and feelings of self-worth. However, in some cases, achievement motives can become so extreme that they lead to limitless aspirations—the desire for perfection, being the best and being "number one" at everything. Another feature of achievement motives is their *future orientation*. The future-oriented person uses cognitive strategies that rely on long-term instrumental steps toward near and distant goals rather than focusing on the potential pleasure of more readily available but less valuable present stimuli (DeCharmes & Muir, 1978; Nuttin, 1985). For example, a future-oriented child, given a dollar by a visiting aunt, will save it as part of her plan to buy an expensive game she wants, while her sister would rather spend her dollar immediately on a much smaller treat.

The Need for Achievement. As early as 1938, Harvard psychologist **Henry Murray** had postulated a "need to achieve" which varied in strength in different people and influenced their tendency to approach success and evaluate their own performances. As discussed earlier in the chapter, Murray and his colleague **David McClelland** used a special technique called the Thematic Apperception Test (TAT) to identify several important human motives. They asked subjects to tell stories in response to a series of ambiguous pictures. These stories, the psychologists believed, would represent "projections" of the respondent's needs, but it is more correct to regard the stories as simply reflecting themes that are important to the storyteller and that come readily to mind.

From subject responses to a series of these TAT pictures, McClelland worked out measures of several human needs. The **need for achievement** was designated as *n Ach.* (pronounced en-ATCH). It reflected individual differences in the extent to which people were concerned about improving their performance, about getting concrete feedback on how well they were doing, and taking personal responsibility for a performance so that they could get satisfaction from doing it well. A great many studies in both laboratory and real-life settings have validated the usefulness of this measure. For example, persistence in working on an impossible task was greater for those with high *n Ach* when the task was announced as difficult rather than easy. Low *n Ach* subjects gave up sooner when they were led to believe the task was difficult, but they persisted for the supposedly easy (actually impossible) task. In other research, high-scoring *n Ach* people were found to be more upwardly mobile than those with low scores; and sons who had high *n Ach* scores were more likely than sons with low *n Ach* measures to advance above their fathers' occupational status (McClelland et al., 1976). **Figure 8.9** shows an example of how a high *n Ach* individual and low *n Ach* individual might interpret a TAT picture.

The need to achieve clearly energizes and directs behavior. It also influences perceptions of many situations and interpretations of our own and others' behavior. Even the economic growth of a society can be related to its encouragement of achievement motivation. McClelland demonstrated (1963) that even the extent to which popular literature in a country is dominated by

need for achievement (*n Ach*)
Concept developed by Henry Murray and David McClelland of basic human drive to meet a wide variety of goals.

Figure 8.9 Alternative Interpretations of a TAT Picture

Story Showing High n Ach
The boy has just finished his violin lesson. He's happy at the progress he is making and is beginning to believe that all his progress is making the sacrifices worthwhile. To become a concert violinist he will have to give up much of his social life and practice for many hours each day. Although he knows he could make more money by going into his father's business, he is more interested in being a great violinist and giving people joy with his music. He renews his personal commitment to do all it takes to make it.

Story Showing Low n Ach
The boy is holding his brother's violin and wishes he could play it. But he knows it isn't worth the time, energy, and money for lessons. He feels sorry for his brother who has given up all the fun things in life to practice, practice, practice. It would be great to wake up one day and be a top-notch musician but it doesn't happen that way. The reality is boring practice, no fun, and a big possibility of becoming nothing better than just another guy playing a musical instrument in a small town band.

intrinsic motivation Desire to engage in activity for its own sake.

extrinsic motivation Desire to engage in activity to achieve external consequences.

achievement themes is related to how hard people strive to improve their performance—particularly in the economic indicators such as more rapid rates of economic growth for a whole country over time. More recently McClelland (1985) has reported a similar finding showing that achievement themes were more prominent in letters to stockholders of Japanese than American automobile companies and that in both countries the higher the achievement motivation content in the letters, the greater the economic success of the company over the following years. McClelland (1961) also found that children in "achieving societies" were more often trained to work harder on their own to master challenging tasks and thus to develop an autonomous achieving lifestyle. In some Protestant countries, where achievement and independence tend to be encouraged, men are trained to be autonomous and success-seeking more frequently than are women. In many countries, even today, women are socialized to be nurturant and supportive rather than achievement-motivated.

Intrinsic Versus Extrinsic Motivation. Motivation to engage in an activity for its own sake, in the absence of external reward, is called **intrinsic motivation.** Things that we do because we simply enjoy doing them—such as playing video games, singing in the shower, doing crossword puzzles, or keeping a secret diary—are intrinsically motivated. Work, too, can be intrinsically motivated when an individual is deeply interested in the job to be done.

Extrinsic motivation is motivation to engage in an activity for some external consequence. In extrinsic motivation, behavior is instrumental (useful) for obtaining something else. In intrinsic motivation, behavior is carried out without a purpose beyond the immediate rewards of doing it. Taking vitamins is extrinsically motivated; eating cream puffs is intrinsically motivated.

➡ Consider what might happen when children are given extrinsic rewards for behavior that they were already motivated intrinsically to produce. Play becomes work when fun activities are given superfluous rewards, as shown in a series of classroom experiments by **Mark Lepper** and his colleagues (Lepper et al., 1973). When an extrinsic reward is given, the motivation becomes extrinsic and the task itself is enjoyed less. When the extrinsic rewards are withdrawn, the activity loses its material value (Deci, 1975; Lepper, 1981; Lepper & Greene, 1978). The moral is *"A reward a day makes work out of play."*

Extrinsic constraints on people, such as evaluation pressure or close surveillance during an activity, seem to have effects on motivation similar to those of rewards. Typically, students in courses where grades are heavily emphasized might find that their motivation, even for their favorite subjects, dwindles after the final exam—they were working only for the grade. Gold stars, grades, and penalties for failure or misbehavior are testament to the (false) belief that schoolchildren are extrinsically motivated and must be given threats or promises of external consequences to learn.

flow Near-ecstatic state achieved by total, present focus on activity, increasing creative ability.

Intrinsically motivating activities have been described as producing a special state of mind called **flow** (Csikszentmihalyi, 1990). Flow experiences are characterized by a pleasurable loss of self-awareness and of any sense of the passage of time, along with a deep concentration on the task rather than its outcome. Flow is inherent in the creative process, and is produced by the motivation of ultimate involvement in the activity and not by its possible outcomes. Going with the flow is the reward for intrinsic motivation. Although some people turn to drugs or alcohol to experience the flow feeling, researchers have found that work produces more of these optimal flow experiences than do leisure-time activities. In fact, one type of flow experience identified by Csikszentmihalyi (1990) is very similar to the goal of *n Ach* as identified by McClelland (1985), namely the intrinsic pleasure obtained from mastering a challenging task or doing something well. Thus McClelland (1985) has argued that the main social motives are developed through learning around a few biologically given, intrinsically satisfying flow experiences.

SUMMING UP

Hunger is the most studied of all drives, but our understanding of all the mechanisms involved is still incomplete. Early researchers mistakenly believed hunger was caused by peripheral cues such as stomach contractions, and later investigators erred by thinking hunger was explained entirely by central processes. A modern multiple-system approach best explains the interworkings of brain structures, hormones, stimulation, and psychological processes. Food-seeking and eating are affected by the activities of the lateral hypothalamus (LH), while cessation or inhibition of eating is influenced by the ventromedial hypothalamus (VMH). Food intake and body weight are regulated according to a set point. Because the number of fat cells determining set point is constant throughout life, diet and weight change may be a constant challenge in the face of cultural standards of weight and appearance.

Sexual motivation is unique in human experience in that it is biologically influenced but not necessary to individual survival. Studies of nonhuman sexual behavior have limited value in understanding human sexual motivation, which is less programmed and more variable. Although only touch is an unconditioned stimulus for sexual arousal, anything associated with it can become a conditioned stimulus. Kinsey's pioneering work on American sexual behavior was followed by Masters and Johnson's investigation of the physiology and psychology of human sexual response. We learn sexual scripts through various experiences and expectations. Conflicts in sexual scripts can lead to misunderstandings and traumas such as date rape. Many theories attempt to explain homosexuality's origins and development, but none is conclusive. Of prime importance is a recognition of the stages of awareness and coping experienced by gay males and lesbians, and of the flexibility and variability possible among human motivational behavior.

Early research by Murray and McClelland identified the value of social motives like the need for achievement in human fantasy and interpretation. Work is also motivated by both extrinsic and intrinsic considerations, with the latter more likely to produce a state of flow. Flow experiences are characterized by a pleasant loss of self-awareness or the sense of time passing, and deep concentration on a task and its outcome.

Emotion

As we discussed at the start of this chapter, emotions are complex experiences composed of physiological and neurological activity, subjectively experienced feelings, and behavioral expressions and responses. The concept of *emotion* is akin to that of *motivation,* yet we make an important distinction between the two. Psychologists view the concept of emotion differently than they view the functions and usefulness of motivational concepts. In this final section, we examine first the functions of emotions, then several theories of emotion, and finally the nature of emotional expression.

The Functions of Emotions

Why do we have emotions? What functions do emotions serve for us? Different theorists point to different functions as central to the role of emotions in human life (Fridja, 1989). Emotions do many things for us. They serve a motivational function by *arousing* us to move and to take action with regard to some experienced or imagined event. Emotions then *direct* and *sustain* our actions toward specific goals that benefit us, such as energizing behavior toward helpful stimulation and away from the harmful. To obtain the love of another person, we may do all in our power to attract, be near, or possess that person. For the love of principle or of country, we may sacrifice our lives. Positive emotions stem from acting in ways that are consistent with our motives (gaining a preferred, rewarding goal), while negative emotions are motive-inconsistent (moving away from preferred goals or toward aversive goals). We feel frustrated when we are unable to act in ways that get us what we want—for example, when a slow-moving vehicle pulls in front of us and prevents us from traveling faster. We feel angry when we are forced to confront a punishing situation—for example, when our boss insists we must work on a day that is a traditional holiday (Roseman, 1984). Emotions help to *organize* our experiences by influencing what we attend to, how we perceive ourselves and others, and the way we interpret and remember various features of life situations (Bower, 1981).

Emotions serve functions other than *amplifying* or intensifying selected life experiences. Emotions also signal that a response is especially significant or that an event has *self-relevance* (Tompkins, 1981). Emotions can give us an *awareness of inner conflicts* when we observe how they can make us react irrationally or inappropriately to a given situation (Jung, 1971).

On a social level, emotions regulate relationships with others, promote prosocial behaviors, and are part of our nonverbal communication system. Emotions serve the broad function of *regulating social interactions;* as a positive social glue, they bind us to some people; as a negative social repellant, they distance us from others (Averill, 1980). Some psychologists go further in arguing that most emotions emerge from and are central to fully experiencing human relationships (DeRivera, 1984).

An ample amount of research points to the impact of emotion on stimulating *prosocial behavior* (Isen, 1984; Hoffman, 1986). When individuals are made to feel good, they are more likely to engage in a variety of helping behaviors. Similarly, when research subjects were made to feel guilty about a misdeed in a current situation, they were more likely to volunteer aid in a future situation, presumably to reduce their guilt (Carlsmith & Gross, 1969).

Finally, the *communication* function of emotion reveals our attempts to conceal from others what we are feeling and intending. We back off when someone is bristling with anger; we approach when someone signals receptivity with a smile, dilated pupils, and a "come hither" glance. Strong, negatively felt emotions are often suppressed out of respect for another person's status or out of concern that they will reveal information being concealed. Much human communication is carried on in the silent language of nonverbal bodily messages (Buck, 1984; Mehrabian, 1971).

Theories of Emotion

Theories of emotion attempt to explain what causes emotions, what are the necessary conditions for emotion, and what sequence best captures the way emotions are built up from the complex interaction of the factors we have discussed. We will review briefly four key theories: the James-Lange theory of body reaction, the Cannon-Bard theory of central neural processes, the Lazarus-Schachter theory of cognitive-arousal, and Darwin's evolutionary theory of emotions.

James-Lange Theory of Bodily Reactions. It is reasonable to assume that when we perceive an emotional stimulus that induces an emotional feeling, it in turn creates a chain of bodily reactions—physiological, expressive, and behavioral. The sight of a beautiful person induces feelings of desire. This physically arouses us, which in turn motivates approach reactions and appropriate displays of passion. This explanation of emotion seems reasonable, but is it the true sequence? A hundred years ago, William James argued, as Aristotle had much earlier, that the sequence was reversed—we feel *after* our body reacts. As James put it, "We feel sorry because we cry, angry because we strike,

This tiger is displaying aggression. The bared teeth and open-jawed roar signal others to flee, submit—or fight. You may find this photograph is powerful enough to arouse an emotional response on your part.

afraid because we tremble" (James, 1890/1950, p. 450). Although contrary to common sense, this view that emotion stems from *bodily feedback* was taken seriously by many psychologists and became known as the **James-Lange theory of emotion.** (Carl Lange [pronounced "LONG-uh"] was a Danish scientist who presented similar ideas in the same year as James.) According to this theory, perceiving a stimulus causes autonomic arousal and other bodily actions that lead to the experience of a specific emotion (see **Figure 8.10**). According to the James-Lange theory, for example, when the object of your affections walks into the room, your perception of this intensely emotional stimulus causes your body to respond: your heartbeat speeds, you blush, your palms feel sweaty. Recognizing your own bodily response, you interpret your emotion: "I'm in love!"

The James-Lange theory assigns the most prominent role in the emotion chain to visceral gut reactions, from actions of the autonomic nervous system that are peripheral to the central nervous system. In this model, then, if you experience no physical reaction to a stimulus, you neither have nor identify an emotional response.

Cannon-Bard Theory of Central Neural Processes. Physiologist **Walter Cannon** (1927, 1929) rejected the James-Lange theory in favor of a focus on the action of the central nervous system. With experimental evidence and logical analysis (Leventhal, 1980), Cannon fired criticism against the James-Lange

James-Lange theory of emotion
Theory, developed independently by William James and Carl Lange, that emotional stimulus triggers behavioral response that sends sensory and motor feedback to the brain and creates feeling of a specific emotion.

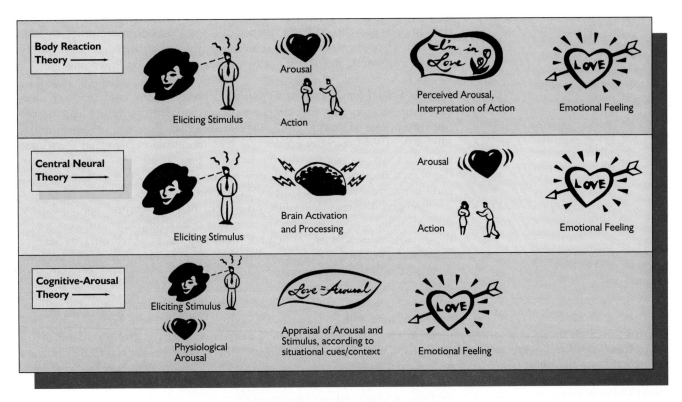

Figure 8.10 Comparing Three Emotion Theories
These classic theories of emotion propose different components of emotion. They also propose different process sequences by which a stimulus event results in the experience of emotion. In body reaction theory (James-Lange), events trigger both autonomic arousal and behavioral action, which are perceived and then result in a specific emotional experience. In central neural theory (Cannon-Bard), events are first processed at various centers in the brain, which then direct three simultaneous reactions of arousal, behavioral action, and emotional experience. In cognitive arousal theory (Lazarus-Schachter), both stimulus events and physiological arousal are cognitively appraised at the same time according to situational cues and context factors, with the emotional experience resulting from the interaction of arousal and appraisal.

theory. He (and other critics) raised four major objections. First, visceral activity was irrelevant for emotional experience; animals in experiments continued to respond emotionally even after their viscera were separated surgically from the CNS. Second, visceral reactions are similar across different arousal situations; the same heart palpitations accompany aerobic exercise, lovemaking, and fleeing danger—but the reactions do not lead to the same emotion from perceiving feedback on how one is responding. Third, many emotions cannot be distinguished from each other simply by their physiological components; they "look the same" under the skin. Finally, ANS responses are typically too slow to be the source of split-second elicited emotions.

According to Cannon, emotion requires that the brain intercede between the input and output of stimulation and response. Signals from the thalamus get routed to one area of the cortex to produce emotional feeling and to another for emotional expressiveness. Another physiologist, **Philip Bard,** also concluded that visceral reactions were not primary in the emotion sequence. Instead, an emotion-arousing stimulus has two simultaneous effects, causing both bodily arousal via the sympathetic nervous system and the subjective experience of emotion via the cortex. The views of these physiologists were combined in the **Cannon-Bard theory of emotion.** An emotional stimulus produces two concurrent reactions, arousal and experience of emotion, which do not cause each other (see **Figure 8.9**). In the Cannon-Bard theory, the sudden sight of the one you love prompts two parallel reactions: you experience a bodily response (heartrate increase, perspiration) and *at the same time* your brain interprets what you feel as "love."

Strong evidence against the Cannon-Bard theory comes from a recent study of people with spinal cord injuries (Chawlisz et al., 1988). Although their injuries prevented them from perceiving any autonomic arousal, they still reported strong emotions, some even stronger than before their injuries. Clearly, autonomic arousal cannot be a necessary condition for emotion.

Lazarus-Schachter Theory of Cognitive Arousal.

Many contemporary theories of emotion suggest that cognitive processes direct the most adaptive emotional responses (Lazarus, 1987; Leventhal, 1980; Roseman, 1984; Smith & Ellsworth, 1985). Sensory experiences lead to emotion only when the stimuli are cognitively appraised as having personal significance. As we noted earlier, the particular emotion that is felt depends on the way a situation is interpreted and the meaning attributed to it by the individual.

Richard Lazarus, a leading proponent of the cognitive appraisal view, maintains that emotional experience "grows out of ongoing transactions with the environment that are evaluated" (1984, p. 124). According to **Stanley Schachter** (1971), the experience of emotion is the joint effect of physiological arousal and cognitive appraisal, with both parts necessary for an emotion to occur. All arousal is assumed to be general and undifferentiated, and it comes first in the emotion sequence. Cognition serves to determine how this ambiguous inner state will be labeled. This position has become known as the *two-factor theory of emotion* or the **Lazarus-Schachter theory of emotion** (Mandler, 1984; Schachter & Singer, 1962). Organic, visceral factors *interact* with mental factors to produce an emotion. Thus, when there is sympathetic arousal *without* a known, specified source, a person will search the environment for relevant, salient cognitions that can be used to label the arousal and give it emotional meaning (see **Figure 8.9**). According to the Lazarus-Schachter model, as the person you adore approaches your table, your heart palpitates, your mouth becomes dry, and your palms become damp. Noticing these changes, and searching for an explanation, you see that special person. If he or she is the cause of your reaction, you conclude, then "it must be love."

This view of emotion and the ingenious research used to demonstrate it (Schachter & Singer, 1962) drew attention to the role of cognitive interpretations in emotional experience. Also, it showed that independent components

Cannon-Bard theory of emotion
Theory, developed independently by Walter Cannon and Philip Bard, that arousal and emotional experience do not cause each other but are both produced by an emotional stimulus.

Lazarus-Schachter theory of emotion Theory, developed independently by Richard Lazarus and Stanley Schachter, that emotional experience is the joint effect of physiological arousal and cognitive appraisal, which determines how an ambiguous inner state will be interpreted.

of emotion—arousal states and situational cues—could be manipulated experimentally and studied in a laboratory setting. However, some of the specific aspects of the two-factor theory have been challenged. Awareness of one's physiological arousal is *not* a necessary condition for emotional experience. When experimental subjects are exposed to emotion-inducing stimuli after receiving beta-blockers that reduce heart rate, they still experience anxiety or anger even though they have minimal physical feelings (Reisenzein, 1983). In addition, experiencing strong arousal without any obvious cause does *not* lead to a neutral, undifferentiated state, as the two-factor theory assumes. *Unexplained* physical arousal is generally interpreted as *negative*, indicating that something is wrong. However, the search for an explanation tends to be *biased* toward finding stimuli that will explain or justify this negative interpretation (Marshall & Zimbardo, 1979; Maslach, 1979).

We intuitively believe that our feelings and preferences follow cognitions and inferences. An alternate view is that feelings and preferences are *not* necessarily derived from thoughts, but may be immediate reactions to stimuli, independent of cognitive analysis. We enjoy chocolate and hate liver and we are attracted to smiling faces and repulsed by frowns. Such immediate "gut reactions" can occur independently of our reasoning about them.

Darwin's Evolutionary Theory of Emotion. In order to develop a better way of categorizing emotions and investigating how they work, an evolutionary perspective encourages us to look at the situations emotions are designed to handle. Following in Charles Darwin's path, evolutionary psychologists consider the *adaptive* functions of emotions, not as vague, unpredictable, personal states that color how we see the world, but as highly specific, coordinated modes of operation of the human brain. In evolutionary terms, emotions are viewed as inherited, specialized mental states designed to deal with a certain class of *recurring situations* in the world.

Many of the situations that affect an individual's survival and reproduction are not isolated flukes but are part of a repeating pattern or series. Over the history of our species, humans have been attacked by predators, fallen in love, given birth to children, fought each other, confronted their mates' sexual infidelity, and witnessed the death of loved ones—all innumerable times. Any special mode of behavior that could be turned on specifically to help humans deal better with these recurring life situations would tend to be passed on to offspring and proliferate through the species. It would become part of the human emotional repertoire. For example, *sexual jealousy* can be seen as a special mode that is "turned on" to deal with the situation of mate infidelity. Physical arousal increases in preparation for possible violent conflict; motivations to deter or injure the rival and to punish or desert the mate emerge; memories are selectively activated to reanalyze the past relationship, and other reactions emerge to cope with the distressing situation. Evolving humans who had different, less adaptive emotional responses to important life situations did not leave as many offspring, so their nonadaptive responses were not passed on.

If emotions evolved as coordinated systems to deal with specific types of situations, we might expect the features of particular emotions to match the threats and opportunities characteristic of the situations with which they were designed to cope. Emotions evolve to control whatever biological or psychological processes are relevant to dealing with their target situation. This way of thinking can help us understand some aspects of emotion that have puzzled researchers. Rather than asking if every emotion has an opposite (for example, happy versus sad), we can ask if the *situation* corresponding to an emotion has an opposite. Perhaps happiness and sadness are opposite because they are both moods designed to regulate energy expenditure in opposite directions, depending on whether the *environment* is propitious, or favorable (Nesse, 1990). Happiness results when we sense that the environment is rewarding our efforts in situations indicating increased survival or reproductive success. When happy, we generally show more optimism, exuberance, energy, and activity, which is appropriate when these qualities are rewarded with increased species fitness. However, in situations when the environment is not propitious—when it does not reward us—we conserve energy by becoming more passive, and our mood is one of sadness. We wait for the situation to change but we do not take direct action to change it because those actions will not be reinforced. The moods of happiness and sadness may be complementary regulatory processes that match our level of activity to the accommodation of the environment.

Emotional Expression

If one function of emotion is to prepare and motivate a person to respond adaptively to the demands of living, then two specific abilities are essential to coordinate our social behavior: We must be able to effectively *communicate* our emotional feelings, and we need to *decode* the way others are feeling. If, for instance, we can signal that we are angry at someone and are likely to become aggressive, we can often get the person to stop doing whatever is angering us without resorting to overt aggression. Similarly, if we can communicate to others that we feel sad and helpless, we increase our chances of soliciting their aid. By reading the emotional displays of others, we can predict more accurately when to approach and when to avoid them and whether to respond with tenderness or toughness.

Are Facial Expressions Universal? According to **Paul Ekman,** the leading researcher on the nature of facial expressions, all people speak and understand the same "facial language" (Ekman, 1984; Ekman, 1982; Ekman & Friesen, 1975). Ekman and his associates have demonstrated what Darwin first proposed—that the same set of emotional expressions is *universal* to the human species, presumably because they are innate components of our evolutionary heritage. What about the influence of culture on emotion? Culture does play a role in *emotional displays* by establishing social rules for *when* to show certain emotions and for the social *appropriateness* of certain types of emotional displays by given types of people in particular settings. However, people all over the world, regardless of cultural differences, race, sex, or education, express basic emotions in the same way and are able to identify the emotions others are experiencing by reading their facial expressions.

Take the facial emotion identification test in **Figure 8.11** to see how well you can identify these seven universally recognized facial expressions of emotion (Ekman & Friesen, 1986). There is considerable evidence that these seven expressions are recognized and produced worldwide in response to the emotions of *happiness, surprise, anger, disgust, fear, sadness,* and *contempt.*

Cross-cultural researchers ask people from different cultures to identify the emotions associated with a variety of expressions in standardized photographs. They are generally able to identify the expressions associated with the seven listed emotions. Children after age 5 can detect the emotion depicted in stimulus displays about as accurately as college students can.

The Mechanics of Expressing Emotion. Emotion researchers generally agree about which specific *facial muscle movements* are associated with each of the basic emotions (Smith, 1989). Studies that record facial muscle movements while subjects imagine various mood settings show specific patterns of muscle groups that are different for happy, sad, and angry thoughts (Schwartz, 1975). For example, the expression of happiness consists of raised mouth corners (a smile) and tightened lower eyelids. The expression of surprise consists of raised eyebrows, raised upper eyelids that widen the eyes, and an open mouth. The expression of fear is very similar to the expression of surprise, except that, in addition to being raised, the eyebrows are pulled together and lowered back

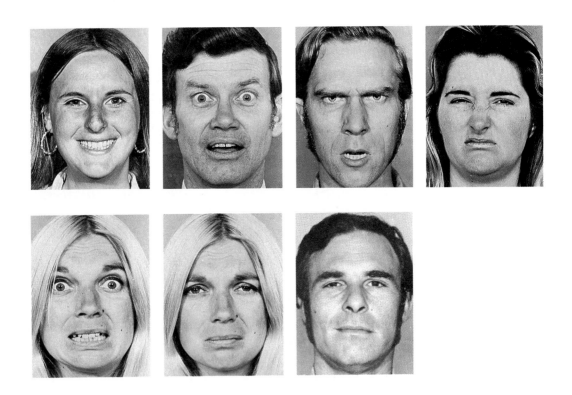

Figure 8.11 What emotion is being expressed by each of these faces? Clockwise, starting at the top left, they show happiness, surprise, anger, disgust, fear, sadness, and contempt.

down slightly into an "eyebrow frown." (The similarity between the two expressions might explain why subjects had such trouble discriminating between them.)

Motives and Emotions. As you read this book, calmly turning the pages, it may be difficult to grasp the power of motivation and emotion. Our words for these concepts may be relatively abstract and distant from your real-life experience. But consider for a moment the power of motivation and emotion, in

Facial expressions convey a universal message. Although their culture is very different, it is probably not hard for you to tell how these people from New Guinea are feeling.

your everyday routine as well as in the crises that punctuate your life. Motivation refers to the engaging forces of behavior—desires, pressures, impulses, and movements that shape your life, carry you along, and even sweep you up in events. Emotion involves the power of your thoughts and the richness of your feelings—your enduring passions, momentary whims, thrills, chills, heated moments, and greatest bliss! Savor your understanding of these human essentials. In the next chapter, we consider the role of motives, emotions, and other processes in determining human health and well-being.

SUMMING UP

Emotions serve many vital functions, such as arousing, directing, and sustaining actions; organizing experience; aiding social communication and social interaction; and motivating prosocial behavior.

Four classic theories of emotion give varying emphasis to peripheral arousal or central brain processing, the sequence by which an external stimulus creates an emotional response, and the involvement of cognitive appraisal and adaption to recurring situations. The James-Lange theory makes visceral arousal feedback the important component in emotion. In the Cannon-Bard theory, brain processing causes both arousal and emotional feelings. Lazarus-Schachter's combined view is a cognitive model that highlights the role of interpreting of arousal and social cues in the stimulus situation. Darwinian evolutionary theory proposes that emotions are inherited response systems that are adaptive in selectively reacting to recurring life situations relevant for reproduction and survival.

Cross-cultural research supports Darwin's hypothesis that the facial expression of emotion is universal, similar for humans and primates and across peoples of different cultures, races, ages and sexes. Cultures vary in the display rules that specify the social appropriateness of showing certain emotions, but seven emotional expressions are universally recognized across cultures, according to Ekman's research.

CHAPTER REVIEW

◆ Understanding Motivation and Emotion *How does motivation affect behavior? What is the difference between a motive and a drive? Is there any way to influence others' motivation? How is motivation related to emotion?*

Motivation is a dynamic concept used to describe the processes directing behavior. Motivational analysis explains how biological and behavioral processes are related and why people pursue goals despite obstacles and adversity. Researchers use motivation as an intervening variable to link stimuli (as independent variables) with responses (as dependent variables). Lesioning, stimulation, and deprivation are three procedures used to manipulate motivation in animal research. External stimuli can arouse incentive motivation.

Emotions are complex patterns of changes composed of physiological arousal, brain function, feelings, cognitive interpretations, behaviors, and expressions. Emotions are usually defined by an external stimulus, but misattributions of emotions—to obvious but incorrect circumstances—are possible.

2 Theories of Motivation *Are there human instincts? What kinds of behaviors seem to be motivated by drives? How does arousal affect human performance? What is Maslow's needs hierarchy? How can our own expectations and beliefs affect our motivation?*

No one theory has been able to explain motivation completely. Instinct theory developed out of the Darwinian revolution. Drive theory and arousal theory followed. Humanistic approaches to motivation postulate a hierarchy of needs leading humans toward self-actualizing action. Social and cognitive psychologists emphasize the power of perception, context, and situations.

3 Motivated Behaviors *What causes hunger? Why is human eating behavior so hard to control? Does the human sex drive operate in the same way as other motives? What experiences and actions affect human sexual behavior? Do people have a drive to achieve? Why don't we all work equally hard to reach our goals?*

Hunger is the most studied of all drives. Early researchers mistakenly theorized that hunger is caused by peripheral cues like stomach contractions. Later theories that hunger is caused by brain processes do not account for all eating behavior. Eating is motivated by complex interactions of brain function, hormones, stimulation, and psychological factors. Food intake and body weight are regulated by a set point, measured by the capacity of fat cells.

Sex is the mechanism for producing offspring and perpetuating genetic heritage. Thus sexual behavior serves the species more than the individual, who must experience sexual motivation in terms of pleasure as well as reproduction. Research on human sexual behavior was begun by Kinsey and continued by Masters and Johnson. Discrepancies in sexual scripts can lead to misunderstandings and violations such as date rape. Thus far, theories of homosexuality are inconclusive, suggesting that sexual orientation is neither a lifestyle choice, a genetic predisposition, nor a result of psychodynamic factors.

Achievement and many types of work are driven by future-oriented motivations. People and societies have different needs for achievement. In the absence of external reward, intrinsic motivation directs our activities; too much extrinsic reinforcement can undermine intrinsic task motivation.

<table>
<tr><td>

Key Terms

critical set point, p. 303
pheromones, p. 305
sexual reproduction, p. 305
human sexuality, p. 307
sexual arousal, p. 307
parental investment, p. 309
sexual scripts, p. 310
need for achievement (*n Ach*), p. 314
intrinsic motivation, p. 315
extrinsic motivation, p. 315
flow, p. 316

</td><td>

Major Contributors

Cannon, Walter, p. 301
Kinsey, Alfred, p. 307
Masters, William, p. 307
Johnson, Virginia, p. 307
Buss, David, p. 309
Levay, Simon, p. 313
Murray, Henry, p. 314
McClelland, David, p. 314
Lepper, Mark, p. 316

</td></tr>
</table>

4 **Emotion** *What purpose is served by human emotions? What are the major theories of emotional experience? How did emotions develop in the course of evolution? Do different people express emotions in different ways?*

Emotions are complex experiences of bodily arousal, subjective interpretation, and behavioral expression. The functions of emotions include arousing, directing, and sustaining action; organizing our experience; amplifying life events; regulating social interactions; and communicating with others. Four theories are the James-Lange theory (emotions are produced by reactions to arousal); the Cannon-Bard theory (that emotions are a concurrent reaction to bodily responses); the Lazarus-Schachter theory (emotions consist of bodily reactions and cognitive interpretations); and Darwin's early proposal that emotions are adaptations to challenging situations. Despite individual and cultural differnences, several emotional expressions appear to be universally recognized. Motivation and emotion are powerful influences on everyday behavior and experience.

<table>
<tr><td>

Key Terms

James-Lange theory of emotion, p. 319
Cannon-Bard theory of emotion, p. 320
Lazurus-Schachter theory of emotion, p. 320

</td><td>

Major Contributors

Cannon, Walter, p. 319
Bard, Philip, p. 320
Lazarus, Richard, p. 320
Schachter, Stanley, p. 320
Ekman, Paul, p. 322

</td></tr>
</table>

PRACTICE TEST

Chapter 8: Motivation and Emotion

For each of the following items, choose the single correct or best answer. Correct answers, explanations, and page references appear in the Appendix.

1. Psychologists have used the concept of motivation for five basic purposes. Which of the following is *not* one of them?
   A. to identify the instincts causing human social behavior
   B. to infer private states from public acts
   C. to explain perseverance despite adversity
   D. to assign responsibility for actions

2. A motivation researcher deprives a test animal of a substance to which it usually has access. She then observes any changes in the animal's behavior when its actions are rewarded with small amounts of the same substance. In this sequence of conditions and events, the animal's motivation for acting is presumed to be accounted for by _____.
   A. a stimulus input
   B. a response output
   C. an intervening variable
   D. an aversive experience

3. Very different theorists such as William James, William McDougall, and Sigmund Freud all shared a common conviction that human motivation is best explained by the concept of _____ , although they differed in their interpretations of this concept.
   A. drive
   B. arousal
   C. control
   D. instinct

4. In Abraham Maslow's needs hierarchy, your desires to have friends and express your love for others are considered part of your _____ needs.
   A. safety
   B. attachment
   C. biological
   D. esteem

5. The sexual behavior of humans is distinct from that of nonhuman animals because, for humans, sex is _____.
   A. more predictable and less variable
   B. essential to survival
   C. not influenced by other motivations
   D. far more dependent on psychological factors

6. Which of the following describes what a subject is asked to do to complete the TAT?
   A. Tell or write a story about each of a series of pictures.
   B. Examine an ambiguous stimulus and list the objects and ideas you associate with it.
   C. Draw in the missing lines in a series of incomplete sketches.
   D. Fill in the blanks among a set of self-descriptive written statements.

7. People who are high in the need for achievement have been found to be more likely to _____.
   A. be upwardly mobile
   B. persist in impossible tasks
   C. work independently
   D. All of the above

8. Marcie enjoys solving mathematics problems because the work is challenging but she performs it well. To encourage her further, her parents promise her a financial reward if she sets a goal of solving even more math problems every week. According to work on intrinsic and extrinsic motivation, the result of this plan will probably be that _____.
   A. Marcie easily achieves her new goal and demands even greater challenges
   B. Marcie generalizes this incentive to other fields, and excels in areas in which she used to do poorly
   C. Marcie loses interest in math and sees it as a chore to be completed in exchange for money
   D. None of the above

9. Research indicates that emotional experience and expression are activated and controlled by the _____.
   A. autonomic nervous system
   B. reticular activating system
   C. limbic system
   D. All of the above

10. According to the _____ theory of emotion, an emotional stimulus simultaneously produces two reactions: physical arousal and the subjective experience of emotion.
    A. James-Lange body reaction
    B. Cannon-Bard central neural processing
    C. Lazarus-Schachter cognitive arousal
    D. Darwin evolutionary function

IF YOU'RE INTERESTED . . .

Fatso. (Video: 1980, color, 94 minutes). Directed by Anne Bancroft; starring Dom Deluise, Anne Bancroft, Candice Azzara, Ron Carey.

Mildly absorbing story of an obese man's efforts to lose weight, amid the humor and hypocrisy of a culture's obsessions with food, looks, and body functions.

McClelland, D. C. (1985). *Human motivation.* Glenview, IL: Scott, Foresman.

Solid text providing an overview of motivation theory and research, by the originator of work on the human need for achievement.

Tavris, C. (1983). *Anger: The misunderstood emotion.* New York: Simon and Schuster.

Fascinating and very readable, a review of myths and images of human anger and aggression, and a critique of research that debunks many of these ideas.

Weinrich, J. D. (1987). *Sexual landscapes: Why we are what we are, why we love whom we love.* New York: Charles Scribner's Sons.

Fascinating review of history, scientific research, and theory on subjects of love, sex, arousal, gender roles, sexual orientation, and courtship.

Chapter 9 **Stress, Coping, and Health**

Preview Questions

1. What is stress? What causes stress in our lives? How do people deal with stressors? How do we react to stress, physically and psychologically?

2. What are the major ways we can cope with the demands that living makes on us? How can we accommodate our thinking to cope better? What environmental adjustments can improve our coping strategies?

3. What model underlies health psychology? How are health, wellness, and illness interrelated in one's life? Which elements are critical to effective health promotion programs? What problems must be overcome in order to recover from illness? How do personality and behavior patterns influence health? Is there anything you can do to increase your own chances of staying healthy?

Lucy went to the hospital to visit Emma, a neighbor who had broken her hip. The first thing Lucy saw when the elevator door opened at the third floor was a clown with an enormous orange nose, dancing down the hall and pushing a colorfully decorated cart. The clown stopped in front of Lucy, bowed, and then somersaulted to the nurses' station. A cluster of patients cheered. Most of them were in wheelchairs or on crutches. When she asked for directions, Lucy learned that Emma was in the "humor room," where the film *Blazing Saddles* was about to start.

Since writer **Norman Cousins** described the role of humor in his recovery from a debilitating and usually incurable disease of the connective tissue, humor has gained new respectability in hospital wards around the country. Cousins, the long-time editor of *Saturday Review,* supplemented his regular medical therapy with a steady diet of Marx Brothers movies and "Candid Camera" film clips, with the cooperation of his physician. Although he never claimed that laughter alone effected his cure, Cousins is best remembered for his passionate support of the notion that, if negative emotions can cause distress, then humor and positive emotions can enhance the healing process (Cousins, 1979, 1983, 1989).

The idea that humor can help in the recovery process caught on even before it had much empirical support. Today, hospitals in Houston, Los Angeles, and Honolulu provide patients with videotapes of comedy films. "Laugh wagons" carrying humorous books and tapes roll through the halls of health centers across the country. At a Catholic hospital in Texas, the nuns are expected to tell at least one joke a day (Cousins, 1989). Nurse Patty Wooten travels the United States in a clown suit, with bedpan and enema bags strapped to her belt, teaching nurses how to use humor to cope with the stresses of health care (*Wellness New Mexico,* 1987). Allen Funt, creator of "Candid Camera," has set up a foundation to distribute his funny videos free to researchers, hospitals, and individual patients, so that humor therapy will be used to treat distress and illness and the effects of such therapy can be studied.

What are the medical benefits of humor? Cousins's doctor found that, according to one measure, his tissue inflammation decreased after only a few moments of robust laughter. This decrease in inflammation was also reflected in Cousins's ability to enjoy two hours of pain-free sleep after ten minutes of hearty laughing (Cousins, 1989). Stanford psychiatric researcher William Fry, Jr., compares laughter to "stationary jogging." Increases in respiration, heart rate, and blood circulation created by laughing bring oxygen to the blood at a rate as much as six times greater than ordinary speech (Fry, 1986). Some biochemical changes, including reductions in the stress hormone *cortisol,* have also been detected (Berk, 1989). Salivary immunoglobulin A, thought to protect the body against certain viruses, increased

psychoneuroimmunology (PNI)
Research specialty that investigates effects of stress on systems and functions of the body, particularly the immune system.

health psychology Field of psychology devoted to understanding how people stay healthy, why they become ill, and how they respond when ill.

stress The pattern of specific and general responses made by an organism to stimulus events that disturb the organism's equilibrium and tax or exceed its ability to cope.

stressor Internal or external stimulus event that induces stress.

Modern society creates a stressful environment whether we are working or playing.

significantly in people who viewed humorous videotapes for 30 minutes. In addition, people who said they used humor to deal with difficult situations in everyday life had the highest baseline levels of this protective substance (Dillon & Totten, 1989).

Cousins significantly enhanced the public's awareness of the relatively new field of **psychoneuroimmunology (PNI),** the study of healing interactions between brain, body, emotions, and the immune system. Researchers hope that advances in this area will help explain the physiological underpinnings of laughter's tonic effect.

Introduction

Feelings, stress, illness, and health are all intertwined in the approach that uses humor to treat physical ailments. As we examined in the last chapter, emotions are the touchstones of human experience, engaging us in the intensity of nature, action, and society. But emotions alone cannot protect us from the extremes and harsh realities of living. If the demands on our biological and psychological functioning are excessive, we may become overwhelmed and unable to deal with the stressors in our daily lives. This chapter will examine how stress affects us and how we can combat it. We will extend these concerns as we look at psychology's most important new area: **health psychology.** Health psychologists investigate how environmental, social, and psychological processes contribute to the development of illness and how these same factors can be utilized to treat and prevent illness.

Stress

Stress is a unique type of emotional experience that has gained considerable attention from psychologists and other scientists. How do common stressors in our society affect our health? How can we cope with stress more effectively?

Our modern industrialized society sets a rapid, hectic, treadmill pace for our lives. We often live in overcrowded conditions, have too many demands placed on our time, worry about our uncertain futures, hold frustrating jobs (or do not have jobs), and have little time for family and fun. Would we be better off without stress? The answer is no! A stress-free life would offer no challenge—no difficulties to surmount, no new fields to master, and no reason to sharpen our wits or improve our abilities. Stress is an unavoidable part of living. Every organism faces challenges from its external environment and from its personal needs; these challenges are life's problems that the organism must solve to survive and thrive.

Stress is the pattern of specific and general *responses* made by an organism to stimulus events that disturb the organism's equilibrium and tax or exceed its ability to cope. Formally defined, a **stressor** is a *stimulus* event—either an internal or external condition—that places a demand on an organism for some kind of adaptive response. The organism's reaction to external stressors is known as **strain.** An individual's response to the need for change is a diverse combination of reactions—physiological, behavioral, emotional, and cognitive. How do psychologists study such a complex stress response? To better understand the concept of stress, researchers have tried to identify its specific components and their interactions.

Have you ever wondered why some people who experience stressful events seem to suffer little or no negative effects, while others are seriously upset by even minor hassles? For example, while stuck in an unexplained traffic jam, you may notice that some drivers calmly daydream or listen to their radios, while others frantically hit their horns or crane their necks for a better view of the obstruction. This difference can be found in people's responses to stress because the effect a stressor has depends both on what it is and what it *means.*

strain Organism's reaction to external stressors.

Stress is a personal matter. How much stress we experience is determined by the quality of the stressor, how it is interpreted, the resources available to deal with the stressor, and the kind of strain this places on us. **Figure 9.1** diagrams the elements of the stress process—stressors, stress, cognitive appraisal (mental evaluation of the situation), resources, and stress responses. (See also "Cross-cultural Perspective: Culture Shock.")

Sources of Stress

Everyone faces stress. Naturally occurring stressful changes are an unavoidable part of life. People close to us get sick, move away, and die. We get new jobs, get fired or laid off, leave home, start college, succeed, fail, begin romances, get married, and break up. In addition to these big life changes, there are routine frustrations, such as traffic jams, snoring roommates, and missed appointments. Unpredictable, catastrophic events, such as earthquakes or major accidents, will affect some of us; and chronic societal problems, such as pollution, crime, prejudice, and homelessness, will pose important sources of stress for others.

Life Changes. Sudden *changes* in our life situations are at the root of stress for many of us. Although change puts spice in our lives, too much change can ruin our health. Even events that we welcome may require major changes in our routines and adaptation to new requirements. Recent studies reveal that one of the most desired changes in a married couple's life, the birth of their first child, is also a source of major stress, contributing to reduced marital satis-

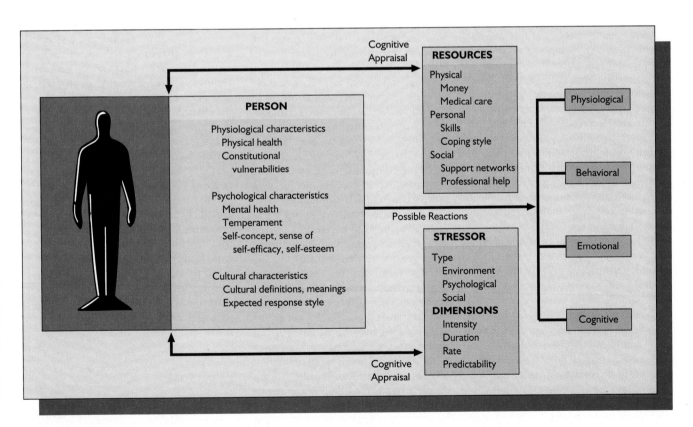

Figure 9.1 A Model of Stress
Cognitive appraisal of the stress situation interacts with the stressor and the physical, social, and personal resources available for dealing with the stressor. Individuals respond to threats on various levels—physiological, behavioral, emotional, and cognitive. Some responses are adaptive and others are maladaptive or even lethal.

faction for many couples (Cowan & Cowan, 1988). On the other hand, stress may result more from anticipating decisions than from making and living with them. For example, a review of research on the psychological responses to

Cross-cultural Perspective   Culture Shock

Many people can point to a part of their culture that they consider *home*. Their feelings of "home" include positive emotions, familiarity, knowledge about ways to satisfy everyday needs, and attachment to others who demonstrate acceptance and affection. Feelings that people have about home often are associated with the length of time they spend in one place. Because time spent in one place is connected to feelings of home, some people may not react positively to the concept of "home." For example, the children of migrant workers or the children of military families may never have lived in one place long enough to consider it home.

For those people who do have strong emotional ties to a home, moves from their familiar surroundings can cause stress. Consider a time in your own life when you were away from home and felt discomfort because of your move. This may have occurred when you first went away to college. It could have occurred in years past when your family relocated due to a job transfer by one of your parents, or when you left home in the summer to attend summer camp or visit distant relatives. What were your feelings? Did you feel lonely, out-of-step with others, frustrated at your inability to satisfy everyday needs, or clumsy because you did not know how to behave in acceptable ways? With these thoughts in mind, consider the following situations.

1. An 18-year-old Navajo female from rural Arizona, who had won awards as a high-school basketball player, begins studies at one of the large state universities on an athletic scholarship.

2. An African-American businessman accepts a vice-presidential position in a large company where 95 percent of the upper-level executives are male Caucasians.

3. A student, very much like Mary in the section "Understanding Diverse Others" (see Chapter 7) participates in a study-abroad program in Europe.

4. An American businesswoman travels to Japan to establish joint trade agreements for the marketing of computer hardware and software.

What do these experiences (including your own) have in common? All of these experiences involve moves away from familiar surroundings and the need to adjust to many new social situations. All of the individuals involved moved on their own, without others who had long shared their respective support groups. When faced with everyday demands such as finding food, housing, and local transportation, these people had only their own resources to help them cope. Often, such individuals feel overwhelmed in their new surroundings and experience high levels of stress (Barna, 1991). *Culture shock* is the term commonly used to describe the stress experienced by people who move to unfamiliar surroundings.

The term "culture shock" was originally coined to explain the intense experiences of people who found themselves on overseas assignments in roles such as diplomats, international students, technical assistance advisers, or businesspeople (Oberg, 1960). Over the last thirty years, the term has expanded to include other types of experiences people have when they move across cultural boundaries *within any one country*. Occasionally, culture shock is used to explain reactions to

the new and the unfamiliar. Examples include going away to college, getting married, or being forced to go on welfare after years of productive employment.

The complaints people have when experiencing culture shock are very similar, whether they are international students, overseas businesspeople, or members of an underrepresented ethnic group (Furnham & Bochner, 1986). Such individuals experience a sense of frustration and helplessness at their inability to meet their everyday needs. They feel lonely and find it hard to meet people and to develop good interpersonal relationships. Victims of culture shock often become suspicious of others and come to believe that others are "out to get them." People also report a predictable set of physical symptoms. They complain of stomachaches, inability to sleep, diarrhea, headaches, lack of sex drive, general feelings of tiredness, mild depression, and a lack of enthusiasm for life.

Many organizations now sponsor programs to help prepare people for life's transitions. Most commonly called "cross-cultural training programs" (Brislin, 1993), one of the goals of such curricula is to introduce people to the various experiences they are likely to encounter. During the programs, participants are commonly told that the experiences associated with "culture shock" are normal and are to be expected. Knowledge of what culture shock is, how frequently it is experienced, and effective coping strategies can aid in reducing people's stress.

abortion reveals that distress is generally greatest *before* the abortion. Severe distress is low for women following the abortion of an unwanted pregnancy or a first-trimester abortion, especially if they have had social support for their decision (Adler et al., 1990).

Some researchers have viewed stress as resulting from exposure to major *life changes* or *life events* (Dohrenwend & Dohrenwend, 1974; Dohrenwend & Shrout, 1985; Holmes & Rahe, 1967). Sometimes people can absorb stress and keep on functioning. Their reactions depend on their resources and the contexts in which stress occurs. If you have the money, time, and friends to help you pick up and go on after a disruption, you will certainly fare better than someone for whom more bad news is the last straw in a series of progressive setbacks being faced alone.

The influence of major life changes on subsequent mental and physical health has been a source of considerable research. It started with the development of the *Social Readjustment Rating Scale* (SRRS), a simple scale for rating the degree of adjustment required by the various life changes that many people experience. To develop the scale, adults from all walks of life identified those life changes that applied to them, and rated the amount of readjustment each one required. Researchers then calculated the total number of **life-change units (LCU)** an individual had undergone during that period, using the units as a measure of the amount of stress the individual had experienced (Holmes & Rahe, 1967).

life-change units (LCU) Measures of stress caused by different kinds of change experienced during a specific time period.

Table 9.1 on the next page shows a modification of this scale for college students. What is your LCU rating? Compare the relative severity of hassles in your life with those of the four groups outlined in **Table 9.2** (students, mothers, general community members, and the elderly on page 335).

Early studies of life changes found support for a relationship between medical problems and the amount of readjustment in life. Patients with heart disease, for example, had higher LCU scores than healthy subjects. Other studies reported that life stress increases a person's overall susceptibility to illness (Holmes & Masuda, 1974), and LCU values are also high for some time after an illness (Rahe & Arthur, 1978).

One problem in interpreting studies that relate stressful life events to illness is that such studies tend to be *retrospective* (backward-looking). That is, both the stress measures and the illness measures are obtained by having subjects recall prior events, and this remembering process may distort and bias the results. For example, subjects who are sick are more likely to remember past negative stressors than subjects who are well. Some *prospective* (looking ahead) studies, following healthy individuals over a period of years, have found significant correlations between accumulated life stress units and later medical problems (Brown & Harris, 1989; Johnson & Sarason, 1979). However, the bulk of current research evidence points to a *weak*, though positive, association between major life events and disease (Brett et al., 1990). Why should this be so? We will see in the next sections that it is your interpretation of the life event that is critical, as well as other variables in the change-disease equation.

Hassles. To what extent do minor irritations pile up and become stressors that affect your health? One view of stress holds that an accumulation of small frustrations more often leads to stress than big, infrequent jolts of change (Weinberger et al., 1987). If you interpret these *hassles* as salient, harmful, or threatening to your well-being, they affect you more than you might imagine (Lazarus, 1984).

In a diary study, a group of white, middle-class, middle-aged men and women kept track of their daily hassles over a one-year period. They also recorded major life changes and physical symptoms. A clear relationship emerged between hassles and health problems: The more frequent and intense the hassles people reported, the poorer was their health, both physical and

Table 9.1 Student Stress Scale

The Student Stress Scale represents an adaptation of Holmes and Rahe's Social Readjustment Rating Scale. Each event is given a score that represents the amount of readjustment a person has to make in life as a result of the change. People with scores of 300 and higher have a high health risk. People scoring between 150 and 300 points have about a 50–50 chance of serious health change within two years. People scoring below 150 have a 1 in 3 chance of serious health change. Calculate your total Life Change Score (LCU) each month of this year and then correlate those scores with any subsequent changes in your health status.

EVENT	LIFE CHANGE UNITS
Death of a Close Family Member	100
Death of a Close Friend	73
Divorce Between Parents	65
Jail Term	63
Major Personal Injury or Illness	63
Marriage	58
Being Fired from Job	50
Failing an Important Course	47
Change in Health of Family Member	45
Pregnancy	45
Sex Problems	44
Serious Argument with Close Friend	40
Change in Financial Status	39
Change of Major	39
Trouble with Parents	39
New Girl- or Boyfriend	38
Increased Workload at School	37
Outstanding Personal Achievement	36
First Quarter/Semester in College	35
Change in Living Conditions	31
Serious Argument with Instructor	30
Lower Grades than Expected	29
Change in Sleeping Habits	29
Change in Social Activities	29
Change in Eating Habits	28
Chronic Car Trouble	26
Change in Number of Family Get-togethers	26
Too Many Missed Classes	25
Change of College	24
Dropping of More than One Class	23
Minor Traffic Violations	20

My 1st Total [ ] (date: ___) My 2nd Total [ ] (date: ___) My 3rd Total [ ] (date: ___)

mental (Lazarus, 1981; 1984). As daily hassles go down, well-being goes up (Chamberlain & Zika, 1990). Although daily stressors have been shown to affect one's mood immediately, people habituate to them so that the negative effects do not carry over to the next day. The exception is cases of interpersonal conflicts (Bolger et al., 1989). As you probably know, a problem in a close

Table 9.2 Severity of Hassles as Perceived and Ranked by Four Groups

In these New Zealand samples, each hassle type differed significantly in severity among the four groups. The ranked perceived severity was almost reversed for student and elderly groups with time pressures most important and neighborhood and health pressures least important for students, while the latter were the most important sources of hassles and time pressures were the least for the elderly. Note the hassle priorities for these mothers who had one or more young children at home and no household help.

HASSLE TYPE	STUDENTS (N = 161)	MOTHERS (N = 194)	COMMUNITY (N = 120)	ELDERLY (N = 150)
Time pressure	1	2	3	4
Future security	2	4	1	3
Finances	3	1	2	4
Household	3	1	2	4
Neighborhood	4	3	2	1
Health	4	3	2	1

relationship—a dispute with a friend or a misunderstanding with a romantic partner—is harder to resolve than frustrations with objects or strangers. These relational stressors threaten to recur until they are dealt with effectively.

Some scholars (such as Gilligan, 1982) feel that problems with close relationships are more stressful for females than for males. Since females place a greater value on "concern for others," they become stressed when their concerns are misunderstood in problematic relationships.

Catastrophe.   When an event is negative, uncontrollable, unpredictable, or ambiguous, the experience is more stressful (Glass, 1977). These conditions hold especially true in the case of *catastrophic events.*

The 1989 World Series was about to begin at San Francisco's Candlestick Park. As people settled into their seats, the band began to play. Suddenly, the entire stadium started to shake violently, the lights went out, and the scoreboard turned black. Sixty-thousand fans became completely silent. They had just experienced a major earthquake. Elsewhere in the city, fires erupted, a bridge collapsed, highways were crushed—and people were dying.

Shortly after the quake, a team of research psychologists began to study how people coped with the catastrophe. Nearly 800 people were chosen randomly from the San Francisco area and from several comparison cities some distance away. These subjects were interviewed at either 1, 2, 3, 6, 8, 16, 28, or 50 weeks after the quake. Subjects completed a ten-minute phone survey about their thoughts, social behavior, and health. Three distinct phases of stress reactions were found among the San Francisco residents. In the *emergency phase* (first three to four weeks), people's social contacts, anxiety, and

When disaster strikes, cries of anguish and grief are a victim's first responses to catastrophic stress. These people are responding to the aftermath of the 1992 Los Angeles riots.

obsessive thoughts about the quake increased. The *inhibition phase* (next three to eight weeks) was characterized by a sudden decline in talking and thinking about the quake, but indirect, stress-related reactions increased, such as arguments and earthquake dreams. In the *adaptation phase* (from two months on), the psychological effects of the catastrophe were over for most people. However, as many as 20 percent of San Francisco area residents remained distressed about the quake even one year later (Pennebaker & Harber, 1991).

A great deal of research on the physical and psychological effects of catastrophic events has been conducted (Baum, 1990). Researchers have found that response to disasters tends to occur in five stages:

1. Typically, there is a period of shock, confusion, and even *psychic numbness,* during which people cannot fully comprehend what has happened.
2. In the next phase, called *automatic action,* people try to respond to the disaster and may behave adaptively but with little awareness of their actions and poor later memory of the experience.
3. In the third stage, people often feel great accomplishment and even a positive sense of communal *effort* toward a shared purpose. Also in this phase, people feel weary and are aware that they are using up their reserves of energy.
4. During the next phase, people experience a *letdown;* their energy is depleted and the impact of the tragedy is finally comprehended and felt emotionally.
5. An extended final period of *recovery* follows, as people adapt to the changes brought about by the disaster (Cohen & Ahearn, 1980).

Knowledge of these typical reaction stages provides a model that can help predict people's reactions when disaster strikes. This model enables rescue workers to anticipate and help victims deal with the problems that arise. Responses to events such as floods, tornadoes, airplane crashes, and factory explosions have all been shown to follow this model of disaster reactions.

Societal Stressors. How do overpopulation, crime, economic recession, pollution, AIDS, and the threat of nuclear war affect our mental well-being? Surveys of the attitudes of students throughout the United States have uncovered a general disquiet and uneasiness about the future (Beardslee & Mack, 1983). Studies in the last decade have shown a significant increase in junior high- and senior high-school students' expressions of fear, helplessness, and anger toward the adult generation. Adults are also worried about the state of the world, but they are also affected by the more immediate concerns of employment and economic security. According to research on the effects of the American economic recession in the early 1970s, many stress-related problems increase when the economy is in a down-swing: Admission to mental hospitals, infant mortality, suicide, and deaths from alcohol-related diseases and cardiovascular problems all increase (Brenner, 1976).

Unemployed men have been found to report more symptoms, such as depression, anxiety, and worries about health, than do those men who are employed—but these symptoms disappear when the men are subsequently reemployed (Liem & Rayman, 1982). According to a recent investigation, high blood pressure among African Americans (long thought to be primarily genetic) appears to be a consequence of chronic stress caused by low status jobs, limited education, fruitless job seeking, and low socioeconomic status (Klag et al., 1991). Hypertension results from frustrations in efforts to achieve basic life goals; it is not linked to genetic factors.

The times and circumstances into which we are born may deal us particularly difficult cards to play. The more we can learn about stress management, the better we may respond to the challenges of our own very stressful lifetimes.

Knowledge of the typical reaction stages can help predict people's reactions when disasters strike, such as the World Trade Center bombing (top) and Hurricane Andrew (bottom).

Dealing with Stress

stress moderator variables
Variables that change the impact of a stressor on a particular reaction.

Variables that change the impact of a stressor on a given type of stress reaction are known as **stress moderator variables.** Moderator variables filter or modify the usual effects of stressors on the individual's reactions. For example, your level of fatigue and general health status are moderator variables that influence your reaction to a given psychological or physical stressor. If you have been up all night studying for an exam, an early-morning disagreement with your roommate will provoke harsher words and leave you feeling more upset than if you had gotten a good night's sleep beforehand. When you're in good shape, you can deal with a given stressor better than when you aren't.

cognitive appraisal Recognition and evaluation of stressor to assess the threat, demand, resources available to deal with it, and appropriate strategies.

Cognitive Appraisal. One major moderator variable, **cognitive appraisal,** plays a central role in defining the stressful situation—what the demand is, how big a threat it is, what resources one has for meeting it, and what strategies are appropriate. Some stressors—such as personal harm or loss—would be experienced as threats by almost everyone. However, many other stressors can be defined in various ways, depending on the circumstances. A situation that causes acute distress for one person may be all in a day's work for another.

Your appraisal of a stressor and of your resources for meeting it can be as important as the stressor itself. For example, you could define a stressor as an interesting new challenge to test yourself against instead of as a threat; you could get psyched up for it instead of feeling anxious. Examinations are stressors for many students, but they can be stimulating challenges for those who are prepared and confident. Your appraisal of a stressor determines your conscious experience of it and your success in meeting its demands.

primary appraisal First stage of cognitive appraisal of stress, in which a situation or its seriousness is evaluated.

Richard Lazarus, a pioneer in stress research and emotion research, has distinguished two stages in our cognitive appraisal of demands. He uses the term **primary appraisal** for the initial evaluation of the seriousness of a demand: What is it? How big? How bad? How enduring? If the demand is considered *stressful,* an individual appraises the potential impact of the stressor by determining whether harm has occurred or is likely to and whether action is required (see **Table 9.3** on the next page). Once a person decides something must be done, **secondary appraisal** begins. The person evaluates the available personal and social resources for dealing with the stressful circumstance and considers the action that is needed (Lazarus, 1976). Appraisal continues as coping responses are tried; if the first ones don't work and the stress persists, new responses are initiated, and their effectiveness is evaluated (Lazarus, 1991). For example, if you were counting on using a friend's computer this weekend to complete a paper due on Monday, you will be stressed to learn that the computer isn't available. During primary appraisal, you change your immediate plans so you will have time to find another computer and finish the work. During secondary appraisal, you review your knowledge of friends and classmates who might have access to another computer, and consider other time-saving strategies that will help you make the deadline.

secondary appraisal Second stage of cognitive appraisal of stress, in which individual evaluates personal and social resources needed to respond and determines action to take.

hardiness Quality resulting from the three C's of health: challenge (welcoming change), commitment (focused involvement in purposeful activity), and control (internal guide for actions).

Hardiness. Psychologist **Suzanne Kobasa** believes a particular personality type is especially effective in diffusing stress. She identified two groups of subjects from a pool of managers working for a big public utility in a large city. The members of one group experienced high levels of stress but were seldom ill, while the members of the second group had high stress and frequently experienced illness (Kobasa et al., 1979). The stress survivors possessed the characteristics of hardiness.

Hardiness involves welcoming change as a *challenge* and not as a threat, having focused *commitment* to purposeful activities, and having a sense of internal *control* over one's actions. These three C's of health—challenge, com-

Table 9.3 Stages in Stable Decision Making/Cognitive Appraisal	
STAGE	*KEY QUESTIONS*
1. Appraising the challenge	Are the risks serious if I don't change?
2. Surveying alternatives	Is this alternative an acceptable means for dealing with the challenge? Have I sufficiently surveyed the available alternatives?
3. Weighing alternatives	Which alternative is best? Could the best alternative meet the essential requirements?
4. Deliberating about commitment	Shall I implement the best alternative and allow others to know?
5. Persevering despite negative feedback	Are the risks serious if I *don't* change? Are the risks serious if I *do* change?

mitment, and control—are *adaptive interpretations* of stressful events (Kobasa, 1984).

While the *hardy personality* has received much attention as a moderator variable in reducing the negative effects of distress, other personality characteristics have also been associated with the concept of stress. Are you a daredevil, mountain climber, or "hot dog" skier? Does your temperament drive you to a life of risk-taking, stimulation, and excitement seeking? If this description fits you, you have a **Type-T personality;** the *T* stands for *thrills.* Psychologist **Frank Farley** (1990) distinguishes between creative Type T's, who are motivated to act constructively, and destructive Type T's, who engage in delinquent behaviors, vandalism, crime, and substance abuse. These are the extremes of the Type-T continuum. Most people fall between the high risk, thrill-seeking types and those who actively avoid any risk. The Type-T personality and its related Type-T behaviors are examples of moderator variables that affect the psychology of stress.

Reacting to Stress

We are a nation on the go; most of us will move a number of times, often considerable distances from our families, friends, and hometowns. Moving involves a host of stressors—loss of the familiar, fear of the unknown, packing and moving, distraction, and getting used to new people and places.

These temporary states of arousal are examples of **acute stress;** they have typically clear onset and offset patterns. In contrast, **chronic stress** is a state of enduring arousal, continuing over time, in which demands are perceived as greater than the inner and outer resources available for dealing with them (Powell & Eagleston, 1983). For example, chronic stress is the problem if your roommate always monopolizes the phone, or if your home requires constant, costly repairs. Whether chronic or acute, these states of arousal are expressed

Type-T personality Behavior pattern of taking risks, seeking thrills, stimulation, and excitement.

acute stress Temporary pattern of arousal, with clear onset and offset.

chronic stress Continuous state of arousal, in which demands are perceived to be greater than resources available to deal with them.

People who engage in risky behavior, such as skydiving, tend to have Type-T personalities.

on several levels as physiological aspects of the stress response and also as psychological stress reactions.

The human brain developed originally as a center for more efficient coordination of action. *Efficiency* involves flexible and often quick, automatic response to changing environmental requirements. This first set of bodily responses occurs when an external threat is perceived. Instant action and extra strength may be needed if the organism is to survive, and automatic mechanisms have evolved to meet this need. A second set of physiological stress reactions occurs when the danger is internal, and the organism is threatened by invading microbes or disease agents that upset normal physiological processes. We will first examine these two response systems—quick emergency reactions versus preventive health-maintenance functions—and then review the physical and psychological experiences of stress response.

Emergency Reactions. In the 1920s, physiologist **Walter Cannon** outlined the first scientific description of the way animals and humans respond to external danger. He found that a sequence of activity is triggered in the nerves and glands to prepare the body for combat and struggle—or for running away to safety. Cannon called this dual-stress response the **fight-or-flight syndrome.** At the center of this primitive stress response is the *hypothalamus,* sometimes referred to as the *stress center* because it controls the autonomic nervous system (ANS) and activates the pituitary gland.

fight-or-flight syndrome   Sequence of internal activities preparing organism for struggle or escape, triggered when a threat is confronted.

The ANS regulates the activities of the body's organs. In stressful conditions, breathing becomes faster and deeper, the heart rate increases, and muscles open the breathing passages to allow more air into the lungs. The ANS sends messages to the smooth muscles to stop bodily functions like digestion that are irrelevant to the emergency at hand. During stress the ANS also gets adrenaline flowing. The spleen releases more red blood corpuscles to aid in clotting if there is an injury; bone marrow makes more white corpuscles to combat possible infection; and the liver produces more sugar, building up body energy. The *pituitary gland* responds to signals from the hypothalamus by secreting hormones vital to the stress reaction. When the body is stressed chronically, increased production of "stress hormones" taxes the immune system. Staying physiologically "on guard" wears down the body's natural defenses. A summary of this physiological stress response is shown in **Figure 9.2** on the next page.

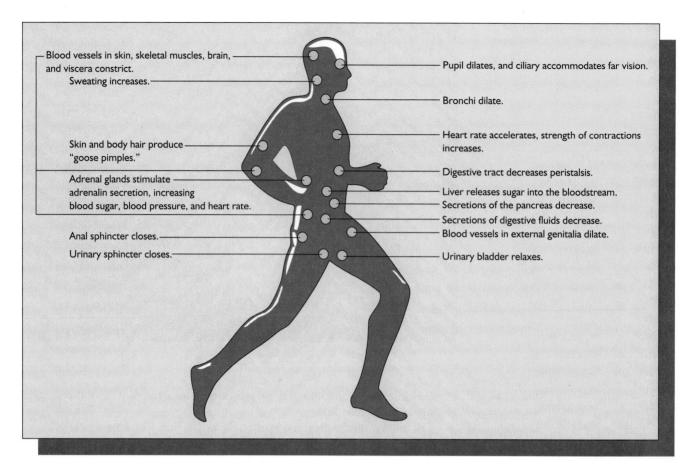

Blood vessels in skin, skeletal muscles, brain, and viscera constrict.

Sweating increases.

Skin and body hair produce "goose pimples."

Adrenal glands stimulate adrenalin secretion, increasing blood sugar, blood pressure, and heart rate.

Anal sphincter closes.

Urinary sphincter closes.

Pupil dilates, and ciliary accommodates far vision.

Bronchi dilate.

Heart rate accelerates, strength of contractions increases.

Digestive tract decreases peristalsis.

Liver releases sugar into the bloodstream.

Secretions of the pancreas decrease.

Secretions of digestive fluids decrease.

Blood vessels in external genitalia dilate.

Urinary bladder relaxes.

Figure 9.2 The Body's Reaction to Stress

The capacity to mobilize the body's active response systems as a way of dealing with *physical stressors* has been valuable to our species for ages. But modern living is dramatically different in its demands on human responsiveness. Ironically, our fight-or-flight focus may backfire in our efforts to face *psychological* stressors. Consider people working on a crisis hot line, taking calls from potentially suicidal strangers. Except for the heightened attentiveness promoted by the ANS, their psychological responses are not adaptive. A hotline volunteer can't run away from the stressor or fight with the caller; the unconditioned fight-or-flight syndrome is out of place. Instead, the volunteer must try to stay calm, concentrate on listening, and make thoughtful decisions. Unfortunately, these interpersonal skills are not enhanced by the stress response. Primitive physical preparations for dealing with external danger are counterproductive for facing many modern-day stressors. Rather than relying on avoidance (flight) or hostility (fight), we must learn new, more adaptive stress responses.

The General Adaptation Syndrome (GAS). The first modern researcher to investigate the effects of continued severe stress on the body was **Hans Selye,** a Canadian endocrinologist. In the late 1930s, Selye reported on the complex responses of laboratory animals to damaging agents such as bacterial infections, toxins, trauma or forced restraint, heat, cold, and so forth. According to Selye (pronounced "SELL-yuh"), there are many kinds of stress-producing agents (stressors) that can trigger the same systematic reaction or general bodily response. All stressors demand *adaptation*—maintaining overall integrity and well-being by restoring equilibrium, or homeostasis. The theory conceptualizes stress as a state within the organism.

Selye described the general physical response to such nonspecific stressors as the **general adaptation syndrome (GAS).** It includes three stages: an alarm reaction, a stage of *resistance,* and a stage of *exhaustion* (Selye, 1956). The GAS is adaptive because, during the stage of resistance, the organism can endure and *resist* further debilitating effects. This stimulated defense against the stressor develops and maintains an intermediate stage of *restoration.* The three stages are shown in **Figure 9.3.**

The general adaptation syndrome has proven valuable in explaining disorders that baffled physicians, some of whom never considered stress as a cause for illness and disease. On the other hand, as a physician, Selye focused on reactions to *physical* stressors among experimental animals, so his theory had little to say about the importance of *psychological* aspects of stress among human beings. In his work with animals, for example, there was no place for recognizing the importance of cognitive appraisal (Mason, 1975).

The Immune System. Earlier in this chapter, we defined *psychoneuroimmunology* (PNI) as the scientific field that investigates the mind-body link, particularly the interaction between stress and the immune system. Our opening case

general adaptation syndrome (GAS)
Pattern of nonspecific bodily mechanisms activated in response to a continuing threat by almost any serious stressor.

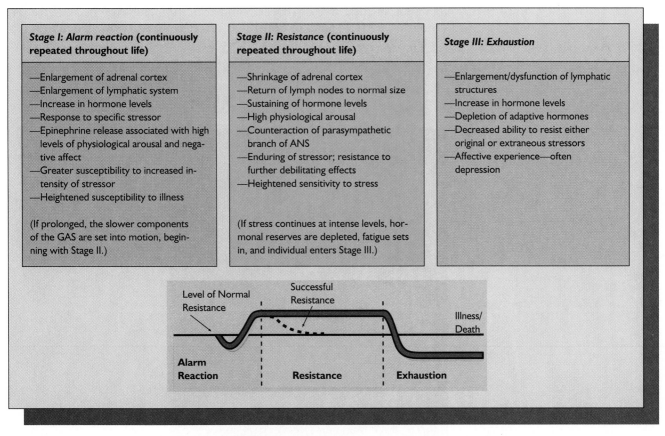

Stage I: Alarm reaction (continuously repeated throughout life)

—Enlargement of adrenal cortex
—Enlargement of lymphatic system
—Increase in hormone levels
—Response to specific stressor
—Epinephrine release associated with high levels of physiological arousal and negative affect
—Greater susceptibility to increased intensity of stressor
—Heightened susceptibility to illness

(If prolonged, the slower components of the GAS are set into motion, beginning with Stage II.)

Stage II: Resistance (continuously repeated throughout life)

—Shrinkage of adrenal cortex
—Return of lymph nodes to normal size
—Sustaining of hormone levels
—High physiological arousal
—Counteraction of parasympathetic branch of ANS
—Enduring of stressor; resistance to further debilitating effects
—Heightened sensitivity to stress

(If stress continues at intense levels, hormonal reserves are depleted, fatigue sets in, and individual enters Stage III.)

Stage III: Exhaustion

—Enlargement/dysfunction of lymphatic structures
—Increase in hormone levels
—Depletion of adaptive hormones
—Decreased ability to resist either original or extraneous stressors
—Affective experience—often depression

Level of Normal Resistance   Successful Resistance   Illness/Death

Alarm Reaction   Resistance   Exhaustion

Figure 9.3 The General Adaptation Syndrome
Following exposure to a stressor, the body's resistance is diminished until the physiological changes of the corresponding alarm reaction bring it back up to the normal level. If the stressor continues, the bodily signs characteristic of the alarm reaction virtually disappear; resistance to the particular stressor rises above normal but drops for other stressors. This adaptive resistance returns the body to its normal level of functioning. Following prolonged exposure to the stressor, adaptation breaks down; signs of alarm reaction reappear, the stressor effects are irreversible, and the individual becomes ill and may die.

showed how humor can enhance health by altering immune functions. Researchers have consistently found a link between stress and declines in indicators of immune activity. The brain can influence the immune system in two ways: through the nerve connections between brain regions and organs in the immune system, and through connections between the endocrine system and immune system. The brain triggers the endocrine system to release hormones; receptors for various hormones are located on white blood cells in the immune system, making the immune system responsive to the action of the endocrine system.

Studies with humans have shown that the quality of interpersonal relationships and their disruption or absence can strongly affect the immune system (Cohen & Syme, 1985; Kiecolt-Glaser & Glaser, 1988). Bereavement and depression also produce *immunosuppression,* suppression or reduction in the function of the immune system. For example, men with wives dying of breast cancer (Schleifer et al., 1983) and recently widowed women (Irwin et al., 1987) are less able to fight disease, and face an increased risk of illness and premature death.

Health psychologist **Judith Rodin** of Yale University has been studying the immune system mechanisms by which psychological variables affect the immune system. She is investigating how providing people (especially the elderly) with an increased sense of personal control improves their health through changes generated in the immune system (Rodin, 1990; *Discovering Psychology,* Program 23). For example, institutional settings like nursing homes and prisons can be humanized if residents are given manageable but meaningful responsibilities, such as choosing how their furnishings will be arranged, or caring for potted plants or small pets (Deci & Ryan, 1987; Pomerleau & Rodin, 1986; Ruback, Carr & Hopper, 1986; Wener, Frazier & Farbstein, 1987).

Judith Rodin (*Discovering Psychology,* 1990, Program 23)

Psychological Responses. Our physiological stress reactions are automatic, predictable, built-in responses over which we normally have no conscious control. However, our psychological reactions are learned; they depend on our perceptions and interpretations of the world and on our capacity to deal with stress. Psychological stress reactions can include behavioral, emotional, and cognitive responses.

Behavioral Patterns. In most psychological studies of stress, the behavior observed as a reaction to a stressor is the key dependent measure. Certain stress-related behaviors, such as muscle tension or spasms, can be directly observed and measured. However, since almost any behavior can be part of a stress response, an observer cannot be sure that a particular action connotes stress. For example, eating sweet desserts can be a behavioral stress response if the person never ate sweets before being diagnosed as a diabetic. An observer would not recognize the significance of the action without knowledge of the person's background.

The behavior of a person who has been confronted with a stressor depends in part on the *level of stress* experienced. Different reaction patterns have been associated with mild, moderate, and severe levels of stress. *Mild stress* activates and intensifies biologically significant behaviors, such as eating, aggression, and sexual behavior. Mild stress makes an organism more alert. It may lead to positive behavioral adjustments, such as becoming better informed, seeking support from others, and learning better attitudes. Continued *unresolved mild stressors* can cause maladaptive behavioral reactions, such as increased irritability, poor concentration, and chronic impatience.

Moderate stress typically disrupts behavior, especially behavior that requires skilled coordination. Giving a speech or playing in a recital are familiar examples of moderate stress situations. For some people, overeating is a typical behavioral response to moderate stress. Overt aggressive behavior can occur, especially in response to frustration. Moderate stress may also produce repetitive, stereotyped actions, such as pacing in circles or rocking back and forth. These repetitive responses are adaptive because they reduce stimulation, but they are also nonadaptive because they are rigid, inflexible, and persistent.

Severe stress inhibits and suppresses behavior and may lead to total immobility. Seligman's research (1975) noted that when dogs' and humans' actions could not prevent painful shocks, they experienced *learned helplessness.* As we reviewed in Chapter 6, individuals may react with helplessness when experience has taught them that their efforts to cope have failed. An injured or traumatized person may be so overwhelmed by pain or grief that she does not react to relatively minor discomforts like hunger or a headache—problems that otherwise healthy people quickly act to solve. Immobility under severe stress may be a defensive reaction, representing "an attempt by the organism to reduce or eliminate the deleterious effects of stress . . . a form of self-therapy" (Antelman & Caggiula, 1980).

Emotional Aspects of Stress. Most stress is acutely uncomfortable, producing only negative emotions and efforts to lessen the discomfort in direct or indirect ways. Stressful life changes that involve loss or separation from friends and loved ones are frequent forerunners of depression. After a breakup, although both partners suffer, the one who was rejected probably feels worse than the one who did the rejecting. Studies show that depression is more likely to result when someone is left behind than when a separation is caused by one's own action (Paykel, 1973).

Rape and incest victims, survivors of plane and serious automobile crashes, combat veterans, and others who have experienced traumatic events may react emotionally with a **posttraumatic stress disorder (PTSD).** PTSD is a delayed stress reaction that recurs repeatedly, even long after the traumatic experience.

posttraumatic stress disorder (PTSD) Reaction in which individual involuntarily reexperiences emotional, cognitive, and behavioral aspects of past trauma.

Victims experience an emotional numbing in relation to everyday events and feelings of alienation from other people. The emotional pain of this reaction can result in various symptoms—such as problems with sleeping, guilt about surviving, difficulty concentrating, and an exaggerated "startle response" (wide-eyed, gasping, surprised behavior displayed when one perceives a sudden threat). Rape victims, for example, may experience a barrage of aftereffects, including feelings of betrayal by people close to them, anger about having been victimized, and fear of being alone or feeling vulnerable (Cann et al., 1981; Baron & Straus, 1985).

The emotional responses of posttraumatic stress can occur in an acute form immediately following a disaster, subsiding over a period of several months. Such responses can also persist, becoming a chronic syndrome called the **residual stress pattern** (Silver & Wortman, 1980). They can also be delayed for months or even years. Clinicians are still discovering veterans of World War II and the Korean War who display residual or delayed posttraumatic stress disorders (Dickman & Zeiss, 1982).

residual stress pattern Chronic pattern in which symptoms of posttraumatic stress disorder persist over time.

Cognitive Effects. Once a stressor has been interpreted as threatening, a variety of intellectual functions may be adversely affected. In general, the greater the stress, the greater the reduction in cognitive efficiency and the more interference with flexible thinking. Because attention is a limited resource, when we focus on the threatening aspects of a situation and on our arousal, we reduce the amount of attention available to cope effectively with the other tasks at

Delayed posttraumatic stress syndrome has been a special problem for Vietnam veterans. Feeling rejected by the American public seemed to heighten their difficulty in adjusting to civilian life. For some, stress was increased by the contrast between that rejection and the welcome received by soldiers returning from the Persian Gulf War.

hand. You may recognize this experience as a sort of "tunnel vision," an inability to see or notice things beyond your immediate focus. Memory is affected too because short-term memory is limited by the amount of attention given to new input, and retrieval of past relevant memories depends on smooth operation of the use of appropriate retrieval cues. Ironically, then, just when you feel under the most pressure to be accurate, you may become forgetful or feel "blocked," as though you were prevented from accessing information you have stored in memory. Similarly, stress can interfere with problem solving, judgment, and decision making by narrowing perceptions of alternatives and by substituting stereotyped, rigid thinking instead of more creative responding (Janis, 1982a). When you feel tense or hurried, you may feel that the answer or choice you seek is "staring right at you," but your preoccupations prevent you from seeing it.

SUMMING UP

Stress is the pattern of reactions an organism makes in response to stressors, stimulus events that tax its ability to cope. Change and the need to adapt to demands are basic causes of stress. Accumulated life changes and the chronic hassles of everyday existence are stressors that affect functioning and health. Studies of natural disasters and catastrophes find evidence of a sequence of stages or phases that marks changing patterns of coping over time. Chronic stressors of society strain us both biologically and mentally.

Appraisal is one of the primary stress moderator variables, filtering and changing the effect of stressors on our experience of stress. Other moderator variables are our resources for dealing with a stressor, certain personal traits such as hardiness, and coping patterns. Cognitive appraisal defines the demand; primary appraisal determines whether the demand is stressful; secondary appraisal evaluates the available personal and social resources and the appropriate actions to take.

Physiological stress reactions are automatic mechanisms facilitating swift emergency action. They lessen sensitivity to pain and provide extra energy for fight or flight. These mechanisms are useful for combating physical stressors, but they can be maladaptive in response to psychological stressors. The general adaptation syndrome is a three-stage pattern of physiological defenses—alarm, resistance, and exhaustion—against continuing stressors that threaten internal well-being. The interaction between body, mind, and environmental stimulation is central to the study of psychoneuroimmunology, which focuses on the impact of psychosocial variables on the immune system.

Psychological stress reactions include behavioral, emotional, and cognitive elements. Mild stress can feel challenging and enhance performance. Moderate stress disrupts behavior and may lead to repetitive, stereotyped actions. Severe stress suppresses behavior and causes dysfunctional reactions. Emotional stress reactions include irritation, anger, and depression. Posttraumatic stress disorders are delayed emotional reactions that prolong the negative consequences of acute stress. Cognitive stress reactions include narrowed attention, rigid thinking, and impaired judgment and memory.

Coping with Stress

coping Means of dealing with a situation perceived to be threatening.

If chronic distress can disrupt our lives (and even cause death), we need to develop ways to manage stress. **Coping** refers to the process of dealing with internal or external demands that are perceived as straining or exceeding an

anticipatory coping Efforts made in advance of a potential stressor to balance perceived demands with available resources.

individual's resources (Lazarus & Folkman, 1984). Coping may be accomplished with actions, feelings, or motives. Sometimes we try to deal with stress before it actually occurs. Such a strategy is called **anticipatory coping** (Folkman, 1984). For example, how would you tell your parents that you are dropping out of school, or break the news to your lover that you are no longer in love? Anticipating stressful situations leads to thoughts and feelings that may be stress-inducing in themselves, as in the cases of tests, interviews, speeches, or blind dates. But anticipatory coping can lead you to better prepare for the actual event when it occurs.

Psychologists have made great advances in conceptualizing and measuring coping (Carver et al., 1989; Folkman et al., 1986; Holahan & Moose, 1987). Measures of coping targeted for particular groups, such as adolescents experiencing similar stressors, may be more useful than more general coping measures designed for the so-called "average" person (Wills, 1986).

Human beings have a tremendous potential for adapting not only biologically over generations, but psychologically, within a lifetime—even within a short period of time if they decide they want to change. In this section, we consider strategies that work, and how we may best use those strategies in our lives.

Coping Strategies

Researchers distinguish between two coping strategies: *problem-solving focus,* in which the goal is to confront the problem directly, and *emotion-regulation focus,* in which the goal is to lessen the discomfort associated with the stress (Billings & Moos, 1982; Lazarus & Folkman, 1984). **Table 9.4** shows several subcategories of these two basic approaches.

Facing up to a problem includes all strategies designed to deal *directly* with the stressor, whether through overt action or through realistic problem-solving activities. We confront a difficult person or run away. We try to win a challenger over with bribes or other incentives. If continually threatened by this person, we might take self-defense training, or notify the "proper authorities." In all these strategies, our focus is on the problem to be dealt with and on the agent that has induced the stress. Such problem-solving efforts are useful for managing *controllable stressors.*

The second approach is useful for managing the impact of more *uncontrollable stressors.* We do not look for ways to change the external stressful situation; instead, we try to change our feelings and thoughts about it. For example, if the "bully" in your life is an unidentified neighbor who blasts his stereo loudly through your dormitory or apartment complex, you might shrug your shoulders and remind yourself that intrusive noise is a fact of life for renters, and there's nothing you can do to permanently solve the problem. This strategy that regulates emotions is a *remedial coping strategy.* It does not eliminate stress at the source, but seeks to remedy your upset feelings by justifying or accepting the status quo.

Table 9.4 Taxonomy of Coping Strategies

PROBLEM-FOCUSED COPING

Change stressor or one's relationship to it through direct actions and/or problem-solving activities	Fight (destroy, remove, or weaken the threat) Flight (distance oneself from the threat) Seek options to fight or flight (negotiating, bargaining, compromising) Prevent future stress (act to increase one's resistance or decrease strength of anticipated stress)

EMOTION-FOCUSED COPING

Change self through activities that make one feel better but do not change the stressor	Somatically focused activities (use of drugs, relaxation, biofeedback) Cognitively focused activities (planned distractions, fantasies, thoughts about oneself) Unconscious processes that distort reality and may result in intrapsychic stress

Included in emotion-focused coping are *ego defense mechanisms,* such as repression, denial of reality, and rationalization. You *repress* when you conveniently forget an upsetting event, such as setting aside an unopened phone bill that you know will be expensive. In *denial,* you acknowledge a stressor but minimize its importance, like when you pretend that a failing course grade might be "improved" with an extra-credit assignment. *Rationalization* involves manufacturing reasons for not taking a problem-solving focus, such as telling yourself "It wouldn't do any good" or "I would only make things worse if I tried to fix things now." We often utilize these defenses without conscious awareness. These mechanisms can protect us from anxieties by enabling us to appraise situations in less self-threatening ways. Such coping strategies are aimed more at self-protection than problem-solving. However, when these mechanisms are overused, they can cause us to distort reality in maladaptive ways (as we will see in Chapter 13, where we review the study of abnormal behavior).

For coping to be successful, resources must match the perceived demand. Successful coping depends on a match between coping strategies and specific features of the stressful event. Thus, the availability of multiple coping strategies would be most adaptive because we are more likely to achieve a match and manage the stressful event. When we know we possess a large repertoire of coping strategies, we feel greater confidence about meeting environmental demands (Bandura, 1986). (See "Time Out for Critical Thinking.")

Researchers and therapists often distinguish between *coping* and *defending*. Coping involves identifying and eliminating the source of stress. In contrast, defending merely lessens the symptoms or reduces their severity, usually only temporarily. For example, if you have a headache, you can defend against the pain by taking a pain reliever; but if the headache recurs, you must consider a more effective way of coping. Finding out what is causing the headaches—perhaps an allergy or chronic work stress—is the first step in solving the problem at the source.

We are often tempted to take defensive action instead of really coping. Why is it so hard to cope? Consider what would be required in each of the following situations if you were to solve the problem rather than merely lessen your symptoms:

- Although you have tried your best, you will not be able to finish a term paper that is due tomorrow. You could defend by pretending to be sick, and use your absence as extra time to complete the work. What are the pros and cons of such a plan?

- An acquaintance who has done you a favor seems to want one in return. You have been avoiding this person for several days, even going out of your way to prevent a meeting. It is getting harder and harder to keep "escaping." Why not just confront this person, once and for all?

- Your car is making strange noises and may be due for a major breakdown. To get around, you could walk and accept rides from friends for a while, but not being able to rely on your car will disrupt your life. On the other hand, if something major is wrong, you probably don't have the money to pay for the necessary repairs. What will you do?

In many cases of stress, we use defense mechanisms and deny that anything is "really" wrong, pretending that the problem is "easy" to solve; or we try to avoid facing it. This strategy can allow anxiety and frustration to build up, so that finally facing up to the problem is more complicated and difficult than it has to be. Although it is not easy to face up to problems, assertiveness and competence can be *learned* in the course of experience. By finding good models to imitate and empowering ourselves with information and skills, we equip ourselves to cope rather than merely defend.

Modifying Cognitions

A powerful way to handle stress more adaptively is to change our evaluations of stressors and our self-defeating cognitions about the way we deal with them. Two ways to cope mentally with stress are reappraising the nature of the stressors and restructuring our ideas about our stress reactions.

Reappraising Stressors. Learning to think differently about certain stressors can help. Relabeling them and imagining them in a less-threatening (perhaps even funny) context are forms of cognitive reappraisal that can reduce stress. If you are worried about giving a speech to a large, forbidding audience, imagine your potential critics sitting there in the nude—a less intimidating, perhaps more self-conscious than critical group. If you are anxious about being shy at a social function you must attend, think about finding someone who is more shy than you and reducing her social anxiety by starting a conversation. You can learn to reappraise stressors by engaging the creative skills you already possess, and by imagining and planning your life in more positive, constructive ways.

Restructuring Cognitions. Two important factors in perceiving stress are an individual's *uncertainty* about impending events and *sense of control* over them (Swets & Bjork, 1990). For a person in a stressful setting, effective coping strategies can provide some or all of four types of control:

1. *Information control*—knowing what to expect
2. *Cognitive control*—thinking about the event differently and more constructively
3. *Decision control*—being able to decide on alternative actions
4. *Behavioral control*—taking actions to reduce the pain or discomfort associated with the event.

These strategies can lead to *cognitive restructuring* and more effective coping. For example, depressed or insecure people often tell themselves that they are no good, that they'll do poorly, and—if something goes well—that it was a fluke or just random luck. "In Focus: Reassessing Stress" (on p. 350) explores two factors in cognitive restructuring: changing cognitions and perceiving control. In a very real sense, stress is ultimately in the mind of the beholder.

The Environment

2

It is especially difficult to cope with stress all alone. Forming alliances with others is necessary for effective coping. Contemporary research shows that being part of a social support network and living and working in a healthy environment lead to an improvement in coping.

social support Resources, materials, sympathy, or information provided by others to help a person cope with stress.

Social Support. **Social support** refers to the resources others provide, giving the message that one is loved, cared for, esteemed, and connected to other people in a network of communication and mutual obligation (Cobb, 1976; Cohen & Syme, 1985). In addition to these forms of *socioemotional support*, other people may provide *tangible support* (money, transportation, housing) and *informational support* (advice, personal feedback, information). Anyone with whom you have a significant social relationship can be part of your social support network in time of need.

Much research points to the power of social support in moderating vulnerability to stress (Cohen & McKay, 1983). When people have other people they can turn to, they are better able to handle job stressors, unemployment, marital disruption, serious illness, and other catastrophes, as well as the everyday problems of living (Gottlieb, 1981; Pilisuk & Parks, 1986). Lack of a social support system clearly increases one's vulnerability to disease and death (Berkman & Syme, 1979). Decreases in social support in family and work environments are related to increases in psychological maladjustment.

Health psychologist **Shelley Taylor** and her colleagues at UCLA studied the effectiveness of different types of social support given to cancer patients. They found that helpfulness depended on who the helper was: patients appreciated information and advice from physicians but not from family members, and they valued a spouse's "just being there" but not a doctor's or nurse's mere presence (Taylor, 1986; Dakof & Taylor, 1990).

Researchers are also trying to determine when sources of support might backfire and actually *increase* the recipient's anxiety. For example, if you prefer to attend a doctor's appointment or college interview alone, your mother's insistence on accompanying you might cause you to feel anxious, not relaxed (Coyne et al., 1988). Too much social support may become intrusive and not helpful in the long run; having one close friend may be as beneficial as having many. A close other who is not supportive may leave you in greater stress than if you were alone. For example, the symptoms of depression are more likely to increase for a married person who cannot communicate well with his or her spouse than for a control subject without a spouse (Weissman, 1987).

REASSESSING STRESS

By telling yourself you will fail in some endeavor or that your success was a lucky accident, you may only doom yourself to disappointment and discouragement. Fortunately, it may be possible to intentionally change this self-defeating cycle. Cognitive-behavior therapist **Donald Meichenbaum** (1977) has proposed a three-phase process to overcome self-defeating thinking.

In Phase 1, people work to develop a greater awareness of their actual behavior, what instigates it, and what its results are. One of the best ways to do this is to keep daily logs or journals. By helping people redefine their problems in terms of their causes and results, logs can increase their feelings of control. In Phase 2, individuals begin to identify new behaviors that negate the maladaptive, self-defeating behaviors—perhaps smiling at someone, offering a compliment, or acting assertively. In Phase 3, after adaptive behaviors are being emitted, individuals appraise their consequences, avoiding the former internal dialogue of put-downs. Instead of telling themselves, "I was lucky the professor called on me when I happened to have read the text," they say, "I'm glad I was prepared for the professor's question. It feels great to be able to respond intelligently in class."

This three-phase approach means initiating responses and self-statements that are incompatible with previous defeatist cognitions. Once they start on this path, people realize that they are changing, and they take full credit for those changes, which in turn promotes further successes. The table below gives examples of coping self-statements that help in dealing with stressful situations.

One of the major variables that promotes positive adjustments is *perceived control* over the stressor, a belief that you have the ability to make a difference in the course or the consequences of some event or experience. If you believe that you can affect the course of the illness or the daily symptoms of the disease, you are probably adjusting well to the disorder (Affleck et al., 1987).

Examples of Coping Self-statements

PREPARATION

I can develop a plan to deal with it.
Just think about what I can do about it. That's better than getting anxious.
No negative self-statements, just think rationally.

CONFRONTATION

One step at a time; I can handle this situation.
This anxiety is what the doctor said I would feel; it's a reminder to use my coping exercises.
Relax; I'm in control. Take a slow deep breath.

COPING

When fear comes, just pause.
Keep focus on the present; what is it I have to do?
Don't try to eliminate fear totally; just keep it manageable.
It's not the worst thing that can happen.
Just think about something else.

SELF-REINFORCEMENT

It worked, I was able to do it.
It wasn't as bad as I expected.
I'm really pleased with the progress I'm making.

However, if you believe the source of the stress is another person whose behavior you cannot influence or a situation that you cannot change, chances increase for a poor psychological adjustment to your chronic condition (Bulman & Wortman, 1977).

In a classic study by Ellen Langer and Judith Rodin (1976), two simple elements of perceived control were introduced into a nursing home environment. Each resident was given a plant to take care of (behavioral control) and asked to choose when to see movies (decision control). Comparison subjects on another floor of the institution had neither sense of control; they were given plants that nurses took care of and they saw

movies at prearranged times. On delayed measures several weeks later and a full year later, those elderly patients who had been given some control over the events in this bleak institutional setting were more active, had more positive moods, and were psychologically and physically healthier than the no-control patients. Most amazing is the finding that, one year later, fewer of those in the perceived control situation had died than those on the comparison floor (Rodin & Langer, 1977; Rodin, 1983). Such research findings have important implications for policies and programs in institutional settings (Rodin, 1986).

The social and psychological dimensions of the environment can also be

Other research focuses on the problems caregivers experience as they attempt to *provide* social support. These problems involve giving support that is intense, long term, unappreciated, or rejected (Coyne, et al., 1988; Kiecolt-Glaser et al., 1987; Schulz et al., 1987). In coming years, more people may be pressed into service as caregivers among their family and friends as a result of societal stressors like rising health-care costs and a depressed economy. Middle-aged adults, for example, may find they must make room for grown children who cannot yet afford to live on their own at the same time they are caring for their own elderly parents. Caught between the demands of two sets of family members, this "sandwich generation" will increasingly need help and advice about how to cope.

The Physical Environment. Psychologists now recognize that, in addition to changing behavior patterns and cognitive styles, stress management should involve restructuring our physical environments to reduce their unhealthy or stress-inducing features.

Psychological researchers in NASA's space program have found that they can help astronauts cope with the stress of long duration space travel by designing the space capsule in ways that make it more relaxing. The capsule is painted in colors found to be most psychologically pleasing—the walls are darker at the bottom to create an illusion of more height and space. Nature pictures of rivers, waterfalls, and mountains are found to be the most effective types of posters for combatting the sense of separation and isolation space travelers experience (*Discovering Psychology*, 1990, Program 24).

Payload specialist and scientist-astronaut Millie Hughes-Fulford is one of NASA's psychological researchers who has studied ways to help astronauts cope with the stress of long duration space travel.

SUMMING UP

Coping strategies are means of dealing with the perceived threat of various types of stressors. Two primary coping categories are problem-focused coping (taking direct actions) and emotion-regulation coping, which is often indirect or avoidant. We can learn to manage stress better by reappraising the nature of stressors and by restructuring our relevant cognitions. Social support is a significant stress moderator. The quality and nature of the source of social support are important components that affect people's evaluations of the sources. At times the best coping strategy entails taking action to restructure the physical and social environments in which we live, study, and work.

Health Psychology

Research on how stress develops and affects human life has piqued psychologists' interests in how behavior and mental processes affect well-being in general. In a 1993 report, the American Medical Association cited criminal violence and bad habits such as legal and illegal drug use as causes for rising health-care costs—estimated at over $42.9 billion annually in direct medical expenses (*San Francisco Chronicle*, February 23, 1993). Acknowledging the importance of such psychological and social factors in health has spurred the growth of a new field. Health psychology is devoted to understanding the ways people stay healthy, the reasons they become ill, and the ways they respond when they do get ill (Taylor, 1990; 1992). Among the many areas of concern for health psychologists are health promotion and maintenance; prevention and treatment of illness; causes and correlates of health, illness, and dysfunction; and improvement of the health care system and health policy information (Matarazzo, 1980).

The Biopsychosocial Model

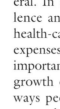

biopsychosocial model New view of body-mind interaction which examines the health consequences of links among factors in the nervous system, immune system, behavior, cognition, and environment.

health Condition in which body and mind are sound and vigorous as well as free from illness or injury.

For all of recorded time, psychological principles have been applied in the treatment of illness and the pursuit of health. Many ancient cultures understood the importance of communal health and relaxation rituals in enhancing the quality of life. Among the Navajo, for example, disease, illness, and well-being have been attributed to social harmony and mind-body interactions. Illness is seen as the outcome of any *disharmony*, and as caused by evil introduced through the violation of taboos, witchcraft, overindulgence, or bad dreams. The illness of any member of a tribe is seen not as his or her individual responsibility (and fault) but rather as a sign of broader disharmony that must be repaired by communal healing ceremonies. This cultural orientation guarantees a powerful social support network that automatically comes to the aid of the sufferer.

Similarly, among the Nyakusa of Tanzania, Africa, any sign of disharmony or social deviance generates a swift communal intervention to set the situation right. Thus, strong anger, the birth of twins, the sudden death of a young person, and illness are all signs of an anomaly because they are unusual events for this tribe. Special tribal rituals are quickly enacted around the person or family in which the discord occurs. One feature of these rituals is evidence of the social acceptance of the person(s) afflicted. For the Nyakusa, medicine is administered not only to effect biological change but to change the habits, dispositions, and desires of people—for psychological cures. Anger in husbands, employers, and police is controlled by a special medicine; other medicine cures thieves of criminal habits and makes men and women more attractive and more persuasive as lovers and leaders (Wilson, 1959).

Traditional Western scientific thinking has relied exclusively on a *biomedical model* that distinguishes between body and mind. According to this model, medicine treats the physical body (*soma*) as separate from the mind (*psyche*); the mind is important only for emotions and beliefs and it has little to do with the reality of the soma. However, researchers are looking at links between the nervous system, the immune system, behavioral styles, cognitive processing, and environmental factors which, in combination, can put us at risk for illness or increase our resistance to stress, trauma, and disease. This view, relatively new in the history of Western medical science, is embodied in the **biopsychosocial model** of health and illness (Engle, 1976).

Comprehending Health and Illness

Health refers to the general condition of the body and mind in terms of their soundness and vigor. Health is not simply the absence of illness or injury but is

This Zambian woman (on the right) is an AIDS widow, shown here with her children and a nurse. Efforts to reduce the spread of AIDS in Zambia have come into conflict with some ancient customs. For example, the brother of a man who has died of AIDS may be expected to marry the widow, thus exposing himself to the disease instead of protecting the family as the tradition originally intended.

more a matter of how well all the body's component parts are working. "To be healthy is to have the ability, despite an occasional bout of illness, to live with full use of your faculties and to be vigorous, alert, and happy to be alive, even in old age" (Insel & Roth, 1985, p. xvii).

Your physical health is linked to your state of mind and the world around you. Health psychologists view health as a complex, dynamic experience. Optimal health, or **wellness,** applies to many domains—physical, intellectual, emotional, spiritual, social, and environmental. When you undertake any activity for the purpose of preventing disease or detecting it in the asymptomatic stage (before the appearance of any symptoms), you are exhibiting *health behavior* (Kasl & Cobb, 1966). A *healthy habit* or behavior pattern is one that operates automatically without extrinsic reinforcement or incentives and contributes directly to your overall health (Hunt et al., 1979).

Is there a difference between illness and illness behavior? **Illness** involves documented pathology, such as biological or physiological damage, cell deterioration, or chemical imbalance. However, if you ever missed a class you didn't really want to go to because you believed you had a stomachache, you were exhibiting *illness behavior.* Whether or not you are really ill, illness behavior (saying "ouch," seeing a physician, or taking medicine, for example) does not necessarily prove the existence of underlying pathology (Taylor, 1990). A growing number of biopsychosocial researchers are calling for the application of behavioral indicators of illness or behavioral outcomes as dependent measures in scientific studies. In other words, researchers need to understand illness behavior—what triggers it, how it is learned, how it affects feelings and other behaviors—and the medical reasons for the illness itself.

wellness Optimal health, including full, active functioning in the physical, intellectual, emotional, spiritual, and social domains.

illness Pathology or damage to the structure or function of bodily systems.

Health Promotion

Behavior is essential to health management. Health psychologists have identified four elements that determine the likelihood of someone engaging in a healthy habit or in changing a faulty one (Bandura, 1986; Janz & Becker, 1984; Rogers, 1984):

1. *The person believes the threat to health is severe.* For example, a heavy smoker must believe she is at risk for a stroke, not just a bad cough.
2. *The person believes her perceived personal vulnerability and/or the likelihood of developing the disorder is high.* The heavy smoker must be convinced that she is already in a high-risk group for stroke, perhaps because of her age or her family's medical history.
3. *The person believes she is able to perform the response that will reduce the threat (self-efficacy).* Once convinced she must quit smoking, the patient must believe she can learn to overcome her smoking habit if she tries.
4. *The response is effective in overcoming the threat.* Finally, the smoker must believe that it is not too late to reduce her risk for stroke, and that quitting her smoking habit can still save her life.

Modifying health behaviors is not a simple matter. Even when health habits change for the better, there is always the threat of **relapse,** or falling back into bad habits. New health habits must be practiced regularly to become automatic. Many people have difficulty putting new resolve and new actions into a standard regime when they remain in the same *behavior setting* that reinforced the unhealthy behavior patterns in the first place. Without changing their environment, ex-convicts, recovered drug addicts, and weight clinic clients often relapse into former ways of behaving even when they have learned new, healthy behaviors—ones that work in other environments.

It may be less difficult to change our unhealthy behaviors if we anticipate rewards. Healthier lifestyles not only reduce the risk of death or debilitation from disease, they also enhance the quality (the enjoyability) of living. A 30-

relapse Reverting to former behavior patterns that have been changed.

year study examined the lifestyle changes and disease histories of more than 15,000 men. The researchers found that men who began moderate exercise programs and quit smoking not only reduced their risk of heart attack and lived longer than men who made no changes, they also worked better, looked better, and claimed to feel better (*San Francisco Chronicle*, February 25, 1993). Health is not only an absence of disease; it reflects the presence of wellness.

The promotion of health and wellness requires national and international efforts that go beyond a focus on the psychology of individuals to systemwide involvement. A general model for health promotion developed by the Canadian government outlines basic health challenges, mechanisms to promote health, and strategies for implementing changes designed to achieve health for all. Similarly, the U.S. Department of Health and Human Services has outlined national public health goals and objectives for the 1990s in its official report, *Healthy People 2000*. The three broad national goals for public health over the next decade are as follows:

1. To increase the span of healthy life,
2. To reduce the disparities in health status among different populations, such as the poor, minorities, and children, and
3. To provide access to preventive health care services for all people.

To meet these general goals, nearly 300 specific objectives have been identified in 22 priority areas outlined in **Table 9.5.** In a comparable national agenda developed prior to 1990, the goals for public health have had reasonably good success, achieving nearly half of the goals set for 1990; but a quarter of them were not met and another quarter could not be evaluated because of inadequate data (McGinnis, 1991). Government policy and social activism can help to reach public health goals, but only individual people can make the choice to live healthier lives.

Psychological Treatments. Many investigators believe that psychological strategies can improve the emotional well-being of individuals. The availability of a biopsychosocial model of health has resulted in increased scientific evidence supporting benefits of psychological treatments for diagnosed illness. A recent study conducted by **David Spiegel,** a research psychiatrist at Stanford University School of Medicine, demonstrates the impact of psychosocial treatment on the course of disease. Breast cancer patients who participated in weekly group support and therapy were found to cope better and survive longer than control subjects who did not participate in such psychotherapy. The patients discussed their personal experiences in dealing with cancer; they could reveal their fears and other strong emotions in an understanding environment. Spiegel's finding indicates that psychological treatments can affect the course of disease, the length of one's life, and the quality of life (Spiegel et al., 1989).

The power of psychological treatments is beginning to affect the recommendations of health professionals. Many health psychologists want medical treatments to be more flexible. For example, many oncologists (cancer specialists) believe the treatment of metastatic cancer should include psychological practices in addition to traditional radiation and chemotherapy. Theirs is a call for flexibility—a medical arsenal augmented by psychological methods—not, as some traditionalists fear, a cry to abandon proven therapies in favor of untried methods.

illness prevention General and specific strategies to reduce or eliminate the risk that one will become sick.

Illness prevention means developing general strategies and specific tactics to eliminate or reduce the risk that people will get sick. The prevention of illness poses a much different challenge in the 1990s than it did at the turn of the century, according to pioneering health psychologist **Joseph Matarazzo** (1984). He notes that, in 1900, the primary cause of death was infectious disease. Health practitioners at that time launched the first revolution in

Table 9.5 Health Objectives for the Year 2000

PRIORITY AREA

HEALTH PROMOTION	PREVENTIVE SERVICES
1. Physical Activity and Fitness	14. Maternal and Infant Health
2. Nutrition	15. Heart Disease and Stroke
3. Tobacco	16. Cancer
4. Alcohol and Other Drugs	17. Diabetes and Chronic Disabling Conditions
5. Family Planning	18. HIV Infection
6. Mental Health and Mental Disorders	19. Sexually Transmitted Diseases
7. Violent and Abusive Behavior	20. Immunization and Infectious Diseases
8. Educational and Community-Based Programs	21. Clinical Preventive Services
HEALTH PROTECTION	**SURVEILLANCE**
9. Unintentional Injuries	22. Surveillance and Data Systems
10. Occupational Safety and Health	
11. Environmental Health	
12. Food and Drug Safety	
13. Oral Health	

American public health. Through the use of research, public education, the development of vaccines, and changes in public health standards (such as waste control and sewage), they were able to reduce substantially the deaths associated with such diseases as influenza, tuberculosis, polio, measles, and smallpox.

To continue advancing the quality of life into the twenty-first century, health practitioners must seek to decrease those deaths associated with lifestyle factors (see **Table 9.6**). Smoking, weight problems, high intake of fat and cholesterol, drug and alcohol abuse, driving without seat belts, and stress contribute to heart disease, cancer, strokes, cirrhosis, accidents, and suicide. Changing the behaviors associated with these *diseases of civilization* will prevent much illness and unnecessary premature deaths. **Figure 9.4** shows the estimated percent of deaths that could be prevented by changes in behavior, early detection, and prevention strategies.

Modifying Lifestyle. What are prevention strategies in the "war on lifestyle"? One approach is to modify lifestyle to change or eliminate poor health habits.

Table 9.6 Leading Causes of Death, United States, 1989

RANK	% OF DEATHS	CAUSE OF DEATH	CONTRIBUTORS TO CAUSE OF DEATH (D—diet; S—smoking; A—alcohol)
1.	34.1	Heart disease	DS
2.	23.1	Cancers	DS
3.	6.8	Strokes	DS
4.	2.3	Accidents: motor vehicles	A
	2.1	Accidents: all others	
5.	3.9	Chronic obstructive lung diseases	S
6.	3.5	Pneumonia and influenza	S
7.	1.8	Diabetes	D
8.	1.4	Suicide	A
9.	1.2	Chronic liver diseases	A
10.	1.1	Homicide	A
11.	1.0	AIDS, HIV disease	

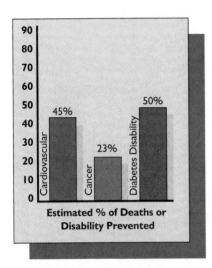

Figure 9.4 Prevention of Death
Changes in behavior, early detection of problems, and intervention could prevent death in many cases.

Familiar examples of this strategy are programs to help people become healthy or stay that way; to quit smoking; to stop using and abusing drugs; to exercise; to lose excess weight; and to be aware of sexually transmitted diseases and how to prevent them. People are more likely to stay well if they practice good health habits such as those listed in **Table 9.7.** In addition, focused research programs have identified strategies that work (and some that don't work) for increasing healthy habits, such as exercise, and reducing specific habits and health hazards, such as heart disease, smoking, and sexually transmitted diseases.

Heart Disease. A major study to prevent heart disease was conducted in three towns in California. The goals of the study were to persuade people to reduce their cardiovascular risk via changes in smoking, diet, and exercise, and to determine which method of persuasion was more effective. In one town, a two-year campaign was conducted through the mass media. A second town received the same two-year media campaign plus a personal instruction program on modifying health habits for high-risk individuals. The third town served as a control group and received no persuasive campaign.

Results showed that the townspeople who had gotten only the mass-media campaign were more knowledgeable about the links between life-style and heart disease, but, as seen in **Figure 9.5,** they showed only modest changes in

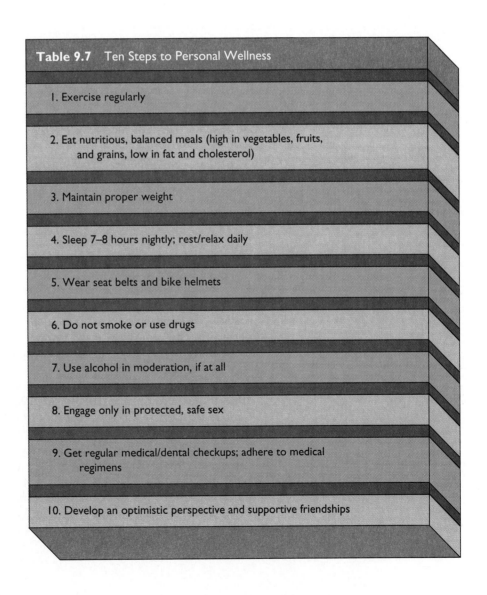

Table 9.7 Ten Steps to Personal Wellness
1. Exercise regularly
2. Eat nutritious, balanced meals (high in vegetables, fruits, and grains, low in fat and cholesterol)
3. Maintain proper weight
4. Sleep 7–8 hours nightly; rest/relax daily
5. Wear seat belts and bike helmets
6. Do not smoke or use drugs
7. Use alcohol in moderation, if at all
8. Engage only in protected, safe sex
9. Get regular medical/dental checkups; adhere to medical regimens
10. Develop an optimistic perspective and supportive friendships

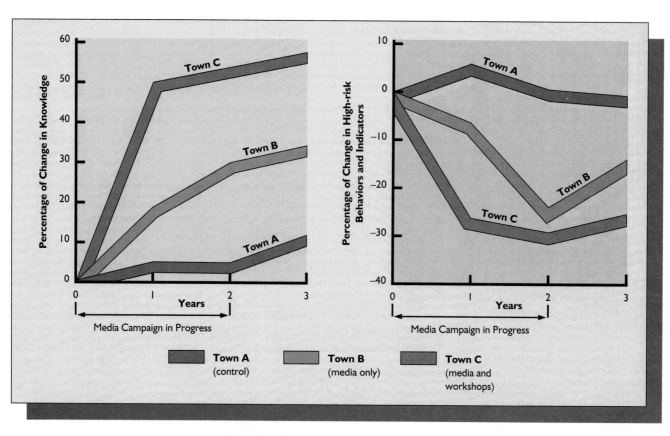

Figure 9.5 Response to Media Health Messages and Hands-on Workshops
Knowledge of cardiovascular disease risk factors was greater among residents of Town B, who were exposed to a 2-year mass-media health campaign, than among residents of Town A, who were not exposed to the campaign. Knowledge gain was greater still when residents of Town C participated in intense workshops and instruction sessions for several months during the media blitz. As knowledge increased, bad health habits (risk behaviors) and signs (indicators) decreased, with Town C leading the way, followed by Town B.

their own behaviors and health status. Personal instruction showed more substantial and long-lasting effects in changing health habits, particularly in reduced smoking (Farquhar et al., 1984; Maccoby et al., 1977).

Conclusions about this research are mixed. The good news is that lifestyle factors can be modified; the bad news is that it is difficult and expensive to do so. Also, mass-media campaigns are not very effective in changing some health behaviors. The campaigns may, however, contribute to long-term changes in social attitudes that support lifestyle changes.

Smoking. Annual U.S. deaths related to smoking climbed to over 400,000 in 1988 from the estimated 188,000 in 1965 and 390,000 in 1985 (National Centers for Disease Control report, 1991). Despite the steady trend toward reduced smoking, 29 percent of Americans continue to smoke. Among the estimated 50 million American pack-a-day smokers, male smokers are 22 times more likely than male nonsmokers to die of lung cancer, and the risk of death from lung cancer is 12 times higher for women smokers than for women nonsmokers. Only 10 percent of smokers initiate this deadly habit after the age of 21. Imagine the gains in the long-term health of society if the 3000 children who start smoking each and every day of the year could be prevented from lighting that first cigarette.

The health benefits of becoming a nonsmoker are immediate and substantial for men and women of all ages. Even heavy smokers who kick the nicotine habit can improve their chances of avoiding disease and premature death due to smoking. Because tobacco is not only a highly addictive drug, but a legal, heavily promoted drug, most tobacco users find it difficult to quit once they have started. The best health policy appears to be either to never start smoking or to join the ranks of the estimated 35 million other Americans who have quit. Because smoking often starts in adolescence, some psychologists have tried to tackle the problem by studying ways to keep teenagers from smoking. The programs that seem to be most successful provide antismoking information in formats that appeal to adolescents; portray a positive image of the nonsmoker as independent and self-reliant; and use peer group techniques, with popular peers serving as nonsmoking role models, who instruct teens to resist peer pressure (Evans et al., 1978).

Exercise. Regular exercise has been established as an important factor in promoting and maintaining health. Major improvements in health are gained from aerobic exercises—such as bicycling, swimming, running, or fast walking—which are characterized by high intensity, long duration, and high endurance. These exercises lead to increased fitness of the heart and respiratory systems, improvement of muscle tone and strength, and other health benefits. But most people do not engage in such exercise consistently. Researchers exploring questions of who exercises regularly and why they exercise have found that people are more likely to exercise regularly if it is easy and convenient to do so. This is one reason that many companies now provide exercise equipment, aerobics classes, or jogging tracks for their employees to use during work breaks.

Sexually Transmitted Diseases. It may be ironic that sex—which keeps our species alive—can be hazardous to our health. Sexually transmitted diseases (STDs) include ancient scourges like syphilis and gonorrhea, as well as more recently identified afflictions such as chlamydia, genital herpes, and AIDS.

The physical intimacy necessary for most transmissions makes it difficult for societies to admit such diseases exist; STDs are not something people acknowledge or discuss casually. It is even more difficult, then, to maintain the objectivity and focus necessary to discuss how to prevent and treat STDs. As examined in "In Focus: Living with AIDS" on the next page, the terror and destructiveness of AIDS may raise social consciousness about all STDs, and stir the need for awareness, education, and tolerance in winning our lives back from illness and fear.

Returning to Health

Treatment focuses on helping people adjust to their illnesses and recover from them. Knowledge about one's treatment is a critical factor in recovery; it is better to know what to expect than to leave it to the doctor. Researchers have found that patients who show the best recovery from surgery are those who received complete information before their operations (Janis, 1958; Johnson, 1983). However, other types of communication between doctor and patient often do not occur as planned.

Following Doctors' Orders. Patients are often given a *treatment regimen,* which might include medications, dietary changes, prescribed periods of bed rest and exercise, and follow-up procedures such as return checkups, rehabilitation training, and chemotherapy. Failing to adhere to treatment regimens is one of the most serious problems in health care (Rodin & Janis, 1982). The rate of **patient nonadherence** is estimated to be as high as 50 percent. The

patient nonadherence Patient's failure to abide by medical guidelines or follow physicians' recommendations for treatment.

LIVING WITH AIDS

A deadly virus is the cause of one of today's most frightening diseases—AIDS. **AIDS** is an acronym for *Acquired Immune Deficiency Syndrome*. While hundreds of thousands are dying from this virulent disease, many more people are living with HIV infection. **HIV** (*Human Immunodeficiency Virus*) is a virus that attacks the white blood cells in human blood, damaging the immune system and weakening the ability to fight other diseases. The individual then becomes vulnerable to infection by a host of other viruses and bacteria that can cause such life-threatening illnesses as cancer, meningitis, and pneumonia. HIV requires direct access to the bloodstream to produce an infection, and the incubation period can be as long as five years. At the moment, the diagnosis of AIDS requires a severe deterioration of the immune system and an episode of a life-threatening infection. Although most of the estimated millions of those infected with HIV do not have AIDS, they must live with the continual stress that this life-threatening disease might suddenly emerge. HIV is generally passed from one person to another either by the exchange of semen or blood during sexual contact, or by the sharing of intravenous needles and syringes used for injecting drugs. The virus has also been passed through blood transfusions and medical procedures in which infected blood or organs are unwittingly given to healthy people.

Unheard of until about a decade ago, AIDS is now a worldwide epidemic growing in frightening proportions in many countries. Since first recording the disease in 1981, the Centers for Disease Control (CDC) had as of December 1991 identified 206,392 active AIDS cases and 133,232 deaths in the United States. The CDC's 1992 estimate was that 1–2 million Americans were currently HIV positive. It has been estimated that the country's 172,000 hospitalized AIDS patients would require medical care costing a total of $5–13 *billion* (Public Health Reports, 1988). Medically, emotionally, and financially, the AIDS epidemic threatens us all.

Who is at risk? Potentially everyone. Although the initial discovery of AIDS in the United States was in the male homosexual community, the disease has spread widely, and AIDS is now found among heterosexuals and homosexuals of both sexes. According to the National Centers for Disease Control Report (November, 1990), as many as 35,000 college students, or one in 500, are estimated to be HIV positive. Given the escalating number of AIDS cases, the anticipated additional burden on the health care system and community health budgets will be unprecedented.

How can the worldwide spread of AIDS be limited? Behavioral intervention programs to modify sexual behavior and drug use have proven difficult and challenging for psychological and public agencies to implement. Four problems seem to make AIDS particularly resistant to intervention:

1. *Misinformation:* Many people still do not understand who is at risk or how behaviors can affect that risk.
2. *Illusion of invulnerability:* Individuals at risk may incorrectly believe they cannot be harmed. Many teenagers often believe it is "safe" to have unprotected sex with young or inexperienced partners.
3. *Pleasure:* The short-term pleasures people associate with sexual behavior and habitual drug use may inhibit their efforts to make long-term changes in behavior.
4. *Value conflicts:* People's beliefs, cultural mythology, and goals may conflict with scientific evidence about risk factors. For example, young, unmarried *Latinas* (Hispanic women) increasingly engage in anal intercourse in order to give in to sexual pressure from boyfriends but retain their technical virginity (under pressure from their conservative culture and religion) by not having vaginal intercourse. It is a deadly compromise: the incidence of AIDS is increasing more among Latino populations than among any other

ethnic group (Emmons et al., 1986; Joseph et al., 1988; Singer et al., 1990). Researchers agree that anal intercourse is the sexual behavior most at risk for HIV transmission.

The only way to protect oneself from being infected with HIV is to change those lifestyle factors that put one at risk. This means making permanent changes in patterns of *sexual behavior* and in use of drug paraphernalia. The safest approach is to abstain from risky behavior—including unprotected or nonmonogamous sex, and intravenous drug use. The only way to prevent infection by HIV is to practice *safe* sex (use condoms during sexual contact and withdraw prior to ejaculation), use sterile needles, and know your HIV status. There is great potential for the media to show young people how to practice AIDS prevention behaviors while developing new healthful social norms and correcting inaccurate perceptions of social norms (Flora, 1991). Celebrities can offer facts to replace fears or unsafe habits, for example, and the characters and plots of popular television programs can model effective ways to

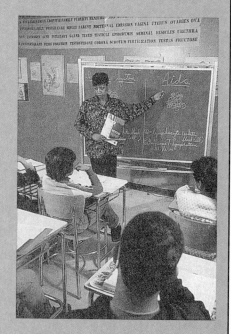

Educating young people about the risk of AIDS is an important step in eliminating the spread of this fatal disease.

AIDS Acquired Immune Deficiency Syndrome, a lethal condition caused by a virus that damages the body's immune system.

HIV Human Immunodeficiency Virus, a virus that attacks white blood cells (T-lymphocytes) in human blood, thus weakening immune system functioning.

culprit seems to be the communication process between doctor and patient. For example, the reason a man fails to follow his doctor's recommendations for diet and medication may not be that he deliberately disregards her advice, but rather that he misunderstood her instructions or could not get clear reassurance from her about his fears.

Patients are more satisfied with health care when they believe the cost of treatment is outweighed by its effectiveness, and when their practitioners communicate clearly, act courteously, and convey caring and support. Some physicians critical of their profession argue that doctors must be taught to care in order to cure (Siegel, 1988). Strategies that social psychologists have developed to help people gain compliance with their orders are also being used to overcome the lack of cooperation between patients and practitioners (Zimbardo & Leippe, 1991). For example, research shows that people are more likely to comply with requests when they feel they have freedom of choice. Therefore, instead of demanding that a patient strictly adhere to one course of treatment, a physician could be more effective by offering the patient several different options, and asking him or her to choose one.

Talking It Out. While good communication between a doctor and a patient is necessary for good health, communication between an individual and his or her peers is also important. Have you ever had a secret too shameful to tell anyone? If so, tell someone—now! That is the conclusion of a large body of research by health psychologist **James Pennebaker** (1991), who has shown that suppressing thoughts and feelings associated with personal traumas, failures, and guilty or shameful experiences takes a devastating toll on mental and physical health. Such inhibition is psychologically hard work and, over time, it undermines the body's defenses against illness. Confiding in others neutralizes the negative effects of inhibition; there are immediate changes in brain wave patterns and skin conductance levels, drops in blood pressure, and improvements in immune functions. This experience of *letting go* often is followed by improved physical and psychological health weeks and months later.

The accounts we keep and relate about our losses and traumas have been found to be an important part of efforts to interact with and explain ourselves to each other. Forming and transmitting such accounts may even reflect a more general human need to tell our stories and be understood by those close to us (Harvey et al., 1990).

Positive Illusions and Well-Being. A surprising result emerging from a considerable body of research is the mental health advantage of maintaining a *distort-*

Confiding in others is beneficial for health and happiness.

ed perception of the self, the world, and the future in the form of *positive illusions* (Taylor & Brown, 1988). When an individual receives negative feedback or is threatened in other ways, adaptive behavior filters such incoming information through self-perceptions that are overly positive, unrealistically optimistic, and exaggerated. These characteristics of human thought promote other criteria of mental health such as the abilities to care about others, be happy and content, and engage in productive and creative work. In other words, while it is important to be realistic, it is healthiest to be somewhat optimistic, even if this requires a slight distortion of the facts. For example, terminally ill patients who believe they can "beat the odds" may be more likely to fight their disease and bring about their own improvements.

Healthy and Unhealthy Patterns

Health psychologists are interested in the causes of illness and injury. While poor health habits are important contributors, personality or individual behavioral styles may also play a causal role (Friedman, 1990).

Personality. Is there a general, negative affective style or "disease-prone personality" that is characterized by depression, anxiety, and even hostility? These negative emotional states do indeed affect coronary disease, asthma, headache, ulcers, and arthritis (Friedman & Booth-Kewley, 1988). Longitudinal studies have also supported the validity of the link between negative emotional states and illness. Chronic negative emotional states tend to produce pathogenic (disease-causing) physiological changes, lead people to practice faulty health behaviors, produce illness behavior, and result in poor interpersonal relationships (Matthews, 1988).

A great deal of research has focused attention on a particular behavioral style called the **Type-A behavior syndrome** (Strube, 1990). The Type-A syndrome is a complex pattern of behavior and emotions that includes being excessively competitive, aggressive, impatient, time-urgent, and hostile. Type-A people are often dissatisfied with some central aspect of their lives, are highly competitive and ambitious, and often are loners. Some of these Type-A characteristics are valued in our society, but in general this behavioral style is very dysfunctional. Type-A businessmen, for example, are stricken with coronary heart disease more than twice as often as men in the general population (Friedman & Rosenman, 1974; Jenkins, 1976). In fact, many studies have shown that people manifesting the Type-A behavior syndrome are at significantly greater risk for all forms of cardiovascular disease (Dembroski et al., 1978; Haynes & Feinleib, 1980). Unfortunately, Type-A behavior patterns have been seen among college and high-school students and even among children in grade school (Thoresen & Eagleston, 1983). More recent research relates Type-A behavior to many subsequent illnesses—allergies, head colds, headaches, stomach disorders, and mononucleosis—in addition to heart disease (Suls & Sanders, 1988; Suls & Marco, 1990). The current focus is on identifying the specific dimensions of the Type-A behavior syndrome, particularly *hostility,* as the personality factor that influences coronary heart disease (Dembroski & Costa, 1987).

Healthy Personal Style. A long-term research program by **Martin Seligman** (1991) and his associates at the University of Pennsylvania indicates that there are healthy benefits to another aspect of personality—*optimism.* Optimistic people have fewer physical symptoms of illness, are faster at recovering from certain disorders, are generally healthier, and live longer than pessimists do (Peterson et al., 1988).

There is more good news. Interventions to reduce Type-A behavior have been successful in most cases (Friedman et al., 1986). The size of the effect is small, but subjects with Type-A negative emotion and subjects with a pes-

Type-A behavior syndrome Pattern of angry, competitive, and perfectionistic behavior in response to stress; assumed to increase risk of coronary heart disease.

Type-A people are often in a hurry, unable to relax, striving intensely for achievement, and especially prone to hostility. In the 1985 film *Wall Street,* Michael Douglas played Gordon Gekko, a Type-A investment banker who was driven by greed.

simistic explanatory style have been found to respond successfully to intervention (Friedman & Booth-Kewley, 1988; Peterson et al., 1988).

A large-scale intervention program with more than 1000 volunteer survivors of a first-time heart attack has found that a behavioral treatment that alters typical Type-A reaction patterns deters a second heart attack and reduces death from other causes as well (Thoresen et al., 1990). Those who had substantially lowered their Type-A behavior had almost a 50 percent lower mortality rate over an eight-year follow-up period than those who did not change substantially.

Caregiver Burnout. This discussion of health psychology concludes with the delivery of health care—involving health institutions, the health professionals who staff them, and the health policies they follow.

job burnout Pattern of symptons —including emotional exhaustion, depersonalizing others, and sense of failure—that afflicts human service professionals.

Providing health care can be an enormously challenging and rewarding career. However, the daily routine of nurses, social workers, emergency room personnel, hospice workers, and other specialists includes dealing with pain, illness, poverty, and death. Even the most enthusiastic health care workers run up against the emotional stresses of working intensely with many people suffering from a variety of personal, physical, and social problems. The special type of emotional stress experienced by these professional health and welfare practitioners has been termed *burnout* by **Christina Maslach,** a leading researcher on this widespread problem. **Job burnout** is a syndrome of emotional exhaustion, depersonalization, and reduced personal accomplishment often experienced by workers in professions that demand high intensity interpersonal contact with patients, clients, or the public. With job burnout, health practitioners begin to lose their caring and concern for patients and may come to treat them in detached and even dehumanized ways. These practitioners begin to feel bad about themselves and worry that they are failures. Burnout is correlated with greater absenteeism and job turnover, impaired job performance, poor relations with coworkers, family problems, and poor personal health (Leiter & Maslach, 1988; Maslach, 1982; Maslach & Florian, 1988).

Several social and situational factors affect the occurrence and level of burnout and, by implication, suggest ways of preventing or minimizing it. For example, the quality of the patient-practitioner interaction is greatly affected by the number of patients for whom a practitioner is providing care—the greater the number, the greater the cognitive, sensory, and emotional overload. Another factor is the amount of direct contact with patients. Longer work hours with continuous direct contact with patients or clients are correlated with greater burnout—especially when the nature of the contact is difficult and upsetting, such as interactions with patients who are dying or who are verbally abusive. The emotional strain of such prolonged contact can be eased by a work schedule that provides chances for a practitioner to withdraw temporarily from such high-stress situations. For example, team contact could replace individual contact, relieving team members of overload in intense cases. Additionally, team members and other coworkers can develop a program for giving positive feedback to professionals for their efforts.

Resolving to Be Healthy

You are probably aware of making many choices that contribute to your distress and lack of optimal health—choices to eat poorly, not to exercise regularly, to commute long distances, to be overly competitive, to work too much, to relax too little, or not to take time to cultivate friendships. What choices are you making, and how do they affect your well-being? Instead of waiting for stress or illness to strike and then reacting to it, set goals and structure your life in ways that forge a healthy foundation. The following guidelines are presented to encourage you to take a more active role in your own life and to create a more positive psychological environment for yourself and others.

1. When searching for the causes of your behavior, consider the current situation and its relation to past situations. Understand the context of your behavior.
2. Never say bad things about yourself. Give yourself and others only *constructive criticism*—what can be done differently next time to get what you want?
3. Compare your reactions, thoughts, and feelings to those of your peers in your current life, so that you can maintain realistic standards and ideals.
4. Develop friendships and communicate with several close friends on a regular basis, people with whom you can share feelings, joys, and worries. Maintain and expand your social support network.
5. Develop a sense of *balanced time perspective* in which you can flexibly focus on the demands of the task, the situation, and your needs. Be future-oriented about work to be done, present-oriented when the goal is achieved and pleasure is at hand, and past-oriented to stay in touch with your roots.
6. Take full credit for your successes and happiness, and share your positive feelings with other people. Keep an inventory of all the qualities that make you special and unique. Know your sources of personal strength and available coping resources.
7. When you feel you are losing control over your emotions, distance yourself from the situation by physically leaving it, role-playing another position, imagining the future to gain perspective on the problem, and talking to a sympathetic listener. Allow yourself to feel your emotions as well as express them, so that you know your own concerns and goals.
8. Remember that failure and disappointment are sometimes blessings in disguise. Learn from every failure. Acknowledge it by saying, "I made a mistake"—and move on.
9. If you cannot help yourself or another person in distress, seek the counsel of a trained specialist in your student health service or community. Check out your local mental health services *before* you need them, and use them without any concern about being stigmatized.
10. Cultivate healthy pleasures; give yourself permission to take time out, relax, meditate, get a massage, fly a kite, blow bubbles, and enjoy things you can do *alone*. Use these opportunities to get in touch with and better appreciate yourself.

As a postscript to end where we began this chapter, take time to laugh with others at yourself, and even at the occasional absurdity of life itself. Discover the weird, invent the bizarre, and appreciate the mundane in all matters. Be playful: The joy that came naturally to you in childhood can be rediscovered, and can continue to enrich the rest of your life.

SUMMING UP

The biopsychosocial model of health links physical well-being with psychological and social functioning. Health is considered a dynamic, complex process; illness is distinguished from illness behavior, which does not necessarily indicate pathology. Behavior change can prevent illness, just as lifestyle change can reduce the diseases of civilization. Research has focused on ways to reduce heart disease, help people quit smoking, encourage regular aerobic exercise, and reduce the risk of contracting sexually transmitted diseases. Returning to health requires adhering to a treatment regimen, revealing one's account of pain or loss, and maintaining positive illusions of well-being. Unhealthy patterns of behavior may result from personality patterns like the Type-A syndrome. In contrast, healthy behavior may rely on optimism and effectively coping with burnout. You can promote your own well-being by resolving to be healthy and acting to stay that way.

CHAPTER REVIEW

◆**1** **Stress** *What is stress? What causes stress in our lives? How do people deal with stressors? How do we react to stress, physically and psychologically?*

Stress can be negative or positive. Stress is studied using a variety of models. At the root of most stress is change and the need to adapt to environmental, biological, physical, and social demands. Cognitive appraisal is a primary process in determining the experience of stress. Physiological stress reactions are regulated by the hypothalamus and a complex interaction of the hormonal and nervous systems. Psychoneuroimmunology is the study of how psychosocial variables affect the immune system. Depending on its severity, stress can be a mild disruption or lead to dysfunctional reactions.

Key Terms

psychoneuroimmunology (PNI), p. 330
health psychology, p. 330
stress, p. 330
stressor, p. 330
strain, p. 330
life-change units (LCU), p. 333
stress moderator variables, p. 337
cognitive appraisal, p. 337
primary appraisal, p. 337
secondary appraisal, p. 337
hardiness, p. 337
Type-T personality, p. 338
acute stress, p. 338
chronic stress, p. 338
fight-or-flight syndrome, p. 339
general adaptation syndrome (GAS), p. 341
posttraumatic stress disorder (PTSD), p. 343
residual stress pattern, p. 344

Major Contributors

Cousins, Norman, p. 329
Lazarus, Richard, p. 337
Kobasa, Suzanne, p. 337
Farley, Frank, p. 338
Cannon, Walter, p. 339
Selye, Hans, p. 340
Rodin, Judith, p. 342

◆**2** **Coping with Stress** *What are major ways we can cope with the demands that living makes on us? How can we accommodate our thinking to cope better? What environmental adjustments can improve our coping strategies?*

Coping strategies either focus on problems (taking direct actions) or attempt to regulate emotions (indirect or avoidant). Social support is a significant stress moderator. Its effectiveness depends on the identity of the helpers and the kind of help they provide. At times, the best coping strategy is to restructure one's work or home environment.

Key Terms

coping, p. 345
anticipatory coping, p. 346
social support, p. 349

Major Contributor

Taylor, Shelley, p. 349
Meichenbaum, Donald, p. 350

3 **Health Psychology** *What model underlies health psychology? How are health, wellness, and illness interrelated in one's life? Which elements are critical to effective health promotion programs? What problems must be overcome in order to recover from illness? How do personality and behavior patterns influence health? Is there anything you can do to increase your own chances of staying healthy?*

Health psychology is a new field that is devoted to treatment and prevention of illness. The biopsychosocial model of health and illness looks at the connections among physical, emotional, and environmental factors in illness. Health promotion represents an important area where community and government policy can help improve everyone's quality of living. Psychosocial treatment of illness adds another dimension to patient treatment. Studies show that the functioning of the immune system improves with this approach to treatment. Illness prevention in the 1990s will focus on lifestyle factors, including weight, nutrition, and risky behavior. AIDS is one of the most threatening illnesses we face today and can be combatted by reducing risky behavior and continuing community education. Your own behavior can provide you with the resources to promote health and happiness.

Key Terms

biopsychosocial model, p. 352
health, p. 352
wellness, p. 353
illness, p. 353
relapse, p. 353
illness prevention, p. 354
patient nonadherence, p. 359
AIDS, p. 360
HIV, p. 360
Type-A behavior syndrome, p. 362
job burnout, p. 363

Major Contributors

Spiegel, David, p. 354
Matarazzo, Joseph, p. 354
Pennebaker, James, p. 361
Seligman, Martin, p. 362
Maslach, Christina, p. 363

PRACTICE TEST

Chapter 9: Stress, Coping, and Health

For each of the following items, choose the single correct or best answer. Correct answers, explanations, and page references appear in the Appendix.

1. Which of the following life events is most likely to cause stress that would put a student's health at risk?
   A. getting married
   B. chronic car trouble
   C. having a serious argument with an instructor
   D. changing his or her major

2. Which of the following experiences would be considered a chronic societal stress?
   A. an earthquake
   B. a jail term
   C. being stuck in traffic
   D. widespread unemployment

3. You are just getting over a bad cold when your steady partner announces a desire to break up and see other people. Your present state of health is an example of a _____ , because it affects how well you can deal with the stress of the breakup.
   A. defense mechanism
   B. moderator variable
   C. cognitive appraisal
   D. life change

4. Malcolm does not get upset when he encounters problems, seeing them as challenges to be overcome rather than threats to his well-being. Which of the following

terms best describes Malcolm's approach to possible stressors?
A. hardiness
B. learned helplessness
C. the Type A personality
D. the Type T personality

5. The fight-or-flight syndrome is governed by the _____ .
A. PTSD
B. PNI
C. ANS
D. GAS

6. Which of the following is *not* a stage in the general adaptation syndrome described by Hans Selye?
A. alarm
B. withdrawal
C. resistance
D. exhaustion

7. Research indicates that, if it can be resolved, _____ stress can actually make an organism more alert, focused, and effective in gathering information and support.
A. mild
B. chronic
C. moderate
D. severe

8. Research showed that nursing home patients had more positive moods, better health, and longer survival compared to others when they were provided with _____ .
A. round-the-clock medical care
B. busy work and entertaining activities
C. responsibilities that gave them perceived control
D. service that relieved them of all aspects of self-care

9. Improving health by reducing incidences of heart disease and smoking, increasing exercise, and preventing sexually transmitted diseases is based on a strategy of waging a "war on _____ ."
A. poverty
B. ignorance
C. lifestyle
D. hunger

10. A good of friend of yours has recently suffered the loss of a close family member. To help your friend cope with this trauma, you should encourage her to _____ .
A. accept others' help with the demands of daily living
B. talk about her loss, even if it is painful to do so
C. keep busy with work and other distractions
D. None of the above.

IF YOU'RE INTERESTED . . .

Cousins, N. (1979). *The anatomy of an illness as perceived by a patient: Reflections on healing and rejuvenation.* New York: Norton.

Norman Cousins' original work, now a classic, on his discoveries and beliefs about the psychology of illness and wellness.

Doctor, The. (Video: 1991, color, 123 minutes). Directed by Randa Haines; starring William Hurt, Elizabeth Perkins, Christine Lahti, Mandy Patinkin.

A sucessful but insensitive surgeon is diagnosed with throat cancer, and must experience life from the patient's perspective. Based on the true story, *A taste of my own medicine,* by Ed Rosenbaum, M.D.

Heartsounds. (Video: 1984, color, 135 minutes). Directed by Glenn Jordan; starring Mary Tyler Moore, James Garner, Sam Wanamaker, Wendy Crewson.

Well-acted portrayal of Martha Weinman Lear's novel, about a woman whose husband, a physician, suffers a series of heart attacks. Outstanding presentation of the stresses and traumas that challenge people, and the strengths that can help us to survive.

Lazarus, R. S. and Folkman, S. (1984). *Stress and coping.* New York: Columbia University Press.

Comprehensive review of the nature of stress and the stages of stress response.

Radner, G. (1989). *It's always something.* New York: Simon and Schuster.

A sad, funny, honest memoir by the late comic actress Gilda Radner, reflecting on her family life, friendships, career, marriage to actor Gene Wilder, and her struggle to overcome, with hope and optimism, the devastation of ovarian cancer.

Chapter 10   **Personality**

1. How is personality defined? How do researchers study it? How do personality theories meet the goals of psychology?

2. What are the six major personality theories? How do they resemble each other? How do they differ?

3. What are the two major approaches to personality assessment? What are the major personality inventories in use today? How are projective tests thought to reveal personality?

In 1923, personal tragedy completely transformed the life of an 18-year-old Texan named Howard. This overprotected college freshman had never made a major decision for himself. When a heart attack killed his father, only two years after the death of his mother, young Howard inherited three-fourths of the interest in the family's lucrative tool company. His uncle and grandparents, who owned the rest of the business, urged Howard to return to school. Despite his reputation as a shy and obedient boy, Howard refused. Within four months, he bought out his relatives' share in the company. By the time Howard was 19, a judge had granted him adult status, giving him full legal control of the million-dollar company (Barlett & Steele, 1979). However, he had no interest in running the family business. Instead, he wanted to become the world's top aviator and most famous motion picture producer. "Then," he told his accountant, "I want you to make me the richest man in the world" (Dietrich & Thomas, 1972, p. 73).

By the time he was 38, Howard Hughes was an American legend. He founded the Hughes Aircraft Company—manufacturer of the first spacecraft to land on the moon. He transformed Trans World Airlines into a $500 million empire. He designed and built airplanes for racing, military, and commercial uses. As a pilot, he broke many aviation records, capping his triumphs with a 1938 round-the-world flight. Ticker-tape parades in New York, Chicago, Los Angeles, and Houston honored his achievement (Drosnin, 1985). But long before that, when he was only 20 years old, he had already reaped national honors producing several films, among them an Academy Award winner. As head of the RKO film studio, Hughes used his power to fuel the 1950s anti-communist purge in Hollywood. Eventually, Howard Hughes realized his ambition—he became the world's richest man.

Despite his incredible public success, Howard Hughes was a deeply disturbed individual. As his empire expanded, he became increasingly disorganized. He began to focus so excessively on trivial details that he accomplished less and less. He became a recluse, sometimes vanishing for months at a time.

Hughes's mishaps as a pilot and driver caused three deaths. On several occasions Hughes himself suffered serious head, face, and, perhaps, brain injuries; treatment for injuries from one near-fatal plane crash led to a lifetime addiction to codeine (Fowler, 1986). His risk-taking extended to the world of finance, where he lost over $100 million of taxpayers', stockholders', and his own money (Dietrich & Thomas, 1972).

As he grew older, Howard Hughes became obsessed with germs. Upon hearing a rumor that an actress he once dated had a venereal disease, he burned all his clothes, towels, and rugs. Eventually, the only people allowed to see him were members of his "Mormon guard," an elite cadre of men who never questioned his often bizarre orders. Those orders included instructions to "wash [themselves] four distinct and separate times, using lots of lather each time from individual bars of soap" (Drosnin, 1985, p. 167). Anything their employer might touch they wrapped in 50-tissue swaths of Kleenex; each box had to be opened with a clean, unused knife.

Paradoxically, the elderly Hughes lived in squalor. He rarely wore clothes or washed, never brushed his teeth, and used an unsterilized needle to inject himself with large doses of codeine. He stayed in bed for days at a time. The richest man in the world slowly starved his 6-foot, 4-inch frame to an emaciated 120 pounds.

In looking at Howard Hughes's childhood for clues to the paradox of his personality, researchers have found many possible links between his early experiences and their later transformation. Like his father, Hughes loved mechanical gadgets. At age 3, he started taking pictures with a box camera. He tinkered in his father's workshop, creating objects out of bits of wire and metal. He was allowed to play in the workshop—as long as he kept it spotless.

Hughes's parents fussed excessively about his health. His quiet, dignified mother devoted herself full-time to him, taking him to the doctor at the slightest provocation.

At 14, his parents sent him to a boarding school in Massachusetts. A developing hearing loss affected his ability to communicate and isolated him from friendships. The highlight of his stay in the East was a ride with his father in a seaplane, which led to a lifelong fascination with airplanes and aviation. Many acquaintances and biographers considered this fascination to be his most enduring passion.

Later, when attending a California school, Hughes spent much of his time alone, riding his horse in the hills and visiting his uncle, a Hollywood screenwriter. At Sunday brunches given by his uncle, Hughes met many stars and movie moguls, as did his father, who had an eye for beautiful women. Hughes began to perceive people as objects to be either avoided or collected. He later would bring teenaged aspiring starlets to Hollywood, put them up in apartments, and, as they waited for stardom, forget about them (Fowler, 1986).

A few years before Hughes's death (in 1976 when Hughes was 70), his former barber reflected on the eccentric billionaire's personality, "I know he has his problems: don't we all? He just operates a little different from the rest of us. Who's to say who's wrong?" (Keats, 1966, p. x).

Introduction

➡ What impressions have you drawn about Howard Hughes's personality from this brief glimpse at his complex life? What type of person was he? What experiences and influences fueled his ambitions and fed his destructive life-style? We are moved to wonder what, if anything, might have led his life story to have a different, happier ending.

Our "psychological autopsy" of Howard Hughes begins with a search for *continuities* between the personality and reaction patterns of the child and the adult. We can trace the roots of his eventual fear of germs to his parents' excessive concern about his health. His own illnesses brought him attention in childhood and care in later life. Thus Hughes received social reinforcement for his concern about health and hygiene. His mechanical inclinations were strongly reinforced by his father, and his early passion for flying was sustained throughout his life. Hughes was isolated from peers as a child and so he never learned to form close human bonds. We see evidence that he identified with his father through shared hobbies, although he later rebelled against his father by living in squalor—a sharp contrast to the elder Hughes's compulsive hygiene. Finally, his personality development suffered adversely from such problems as an early hearing disorder, later brain injury, the early deaths of his parents, national publicity—and untold wealth that got him almost anything he wanted.

➡ If psychologists studied *you*, what portrait of your personality would they draw? What differentiates you from other individuals who function in many of the same situations as you? Rather than viewing personality in hindsight, consider how you may apply what you are learning to understand yourself and others while your personality is still developing.

The Psychology of the Person

personality Unique qualities and distinctive behavior patterns of an individual across time and situations.

Psychologists define personality in many different ways, but common to all of them are two basic concepts: *uniqueness* and *characteristic patterns of behavior*. **Personality** is the complex set of unique psychological qualities that influence an individual's characteristic patterns of behavior across different situations and over time. Investigators in the field of personality psychology seek to discover how individuals differ. They also study the extent to which personality traits and behavior patterns are consistent from one situation or occasion to another.

The field of *personality psychology* attempts to integrate all aspects of an individual's functioning. This integration requires the psychologist to build on the accumulated knowledge of all the areas of psychology we have already discussed, along with social psychology, which studies interpersonal and group processes. Personality psychology goes beyond an interest in the normally functioning individual. It provides the foundation for understanding personal problems and pathologies as well as a basis for therapeutic approaches to change personality.

In this chapter, we will examine the individual as the sum of separate processes of feelings, thoughts, and actions. We will see that people do not simply look different or respond differently to the same stimulus in a common situation. This discussion will examine what seems to be a subjective, private aspect to personality that gives coherence and order to behavior—a core aspect of each of us that we call our *self*. We begin by examining the major issues and strategies in the study of personality. Then we will survey the major theories of personality, each of which focuses on slightly different aspects of human individuality.

Strategies for Studying Personality

Think of someone you really trust. Now think of someone you know personally who is a role model for you. Imagine the qualities of a person with whom you would like to spend the rest of your life—and then of someone you can't stand to be around. In each case, what springs to mind immediately are personal attributes, such as honesty, reliability, sense of humor, generosity, outgoing attitude, aggressiveness, moodiness, or pessimism. Even as a child, you probably developed and used your own system for appraising personality. You tried to determine which new acquaintances would be friend or foe; you worked out ways of dealing with your parents or teachers based on how you read their personalities. You have probably spent a great deal of time trying to get a handle on who *you* are—on what qualities distinguish you from others, which ones to develop, and which ones to discard.

In each case, your judgments were, in fact, naive personality assessments reflecting your *implicit personality theory*. They were based largely on intuition and limited observations. Such naive judgments can often be accurate, but they are also open to many sources of error. For example, think of some of the people whose personalities you feel you understand. Now consider the narrow range of situations in which you have observed them. We tend to have one-dimensional impressions of many people because we see them in only a few kinds of situations. Often, their behavior is strongly influenced by features of those situations. You yourself may elicit certain reactions from them that they do not usually make with others. Your impressions of others may be biased by these and other factors, leading you to interpret their personalities in ways with which they and others may not agree. For example, if you have just received

Children develop their own styles of assessing the personalities of others.

disappointing news—such as a poor grade on a test—when you first meet a bright classmate, you may unfairly judge her to be arrogant or "stuck up," simply because you feel incompetent or depressed.

Personality researchers are interested in many different aspects of personality. Their data come from subjects' self-reports, as well as observers' reports of subjects' behavior. Observers and interviewers can record specific instances of people's behavior, as well as biographical details and life events. Finally, special instruments make it possible to record physiological data about subjects' bodily processes, including heart rate, hormone levels, and brain chemistry. Researchers interpret the data they collect using either of two approaches: the *idiographic approach* or the *nomothetic approach.*

The **idiographic approach** is *person-centered,* focusing on the way unique aspects of an individual's personality form an integrated whole. It assumes that traits and events take on different meanings in different people's lives. The **nomothetic approach** is *variable-centered,* assuming that the same traits or dimensions of personality apply to everyone in the same way; people simply differ in the *degree* to which they possess each characteristic. Nomothetic research looks for relationships between different personality traits in the general population. Researchers and practitioners who study individuals favor the idiographic approach, focusing on what makes a given person similar to, yet different from, others. In contrast, researchers interested in particular qualities—such as aggressiveness, or stress-management styles—prefer the nomothetic approach, learning all they can about the qualities that seem to describe most people, or the "average" person.

idiographic approach Method of studying personality that emphasizes individual uniqueness rather than common dimensions.

nomothetic approach Method of studying personality that emphasizes identifying universal traits and patterns.

Personality Theorizing

Theories of personality are hypothetical statements about the structure and functioning of individual personalities. They help us achieve two of the major goals of psychology: *understanding* the structure and development of personality, and *predicting* behavior and life events based on what we know about personality. Different theories make different predictions about the way people will respond and adapt to certain conditions.

Why are there so many different—often competing—theories of personality? Theorists differ in their approaches to personality by varying their starting points and sources of data and by trying to explain different processes. Some are interested in the structure of individual personality and others in how that personality develops in one's life. Some are interested in what people do, while others study how people feel about their lives. Finally, some theories try to explain individuals with problems, while others focus on healthy individuals. In the next section we examine the most important and influential personality theories. Each theory can teach us something about personality, but together they can teach us even more about human nature.

SUMMING UP

The implicit theories we use to understand and predict people's behavior may be biased because they are based on only limited information. We often make judgments about people after seeing them in only one type of situation. Personality psychologists draw their theories from systematic observations of individuals across many situations. They interpret data according to either an idiographic (person-centered) or nomothetic (variable-centered) approach. The personality theories we will examine in this chapter are based on different types of data and aim to explain different types of phenomena.

Personality Theories

 Theoretical approaches to understanding personality can be grouped into six categories: *type, trait, psychodynamic, humanistic, learning,* and *cognitive.* **Table 10.1** lists the six categories, their major concepts, and examples (approaches) of each theory.

Table 10.1 Summary of Personality Theories

CATEGORY	MAJOR CONCEPT	SPECIFIC APPROACHES AND KEY IDEAS
Type Theories	Personalities can be classified into a limited number of groups or types.	*Hippocrates' Four-Humors Theory:* blood, phlegm, black bile, and yellow bile *Sheldon's Somatotypes:* endomorph, mesomorph, and ectomorph *Myers-Briggs Type Indicator:* introversion-extroversion, sensing-intuiting, thinking-feeling, and judgment-perception
Trait Theories	Human behavior can be organized by labeling and classifying observable personality characteristics.	*Allport's Trait Approach:* cardinal traits, central traits, and secondary traits *Eysenck's Type-Trait Hierarchy:* extro-version-introversion, neuroticism (stability-instability), and psychoticism *The Big Five Personality Dimensions:* extroversion, agreeableness, conscientiousness, emotional stability, openness to experience
Psychodynamic Theories	Personality is shaped and behavior is motivated by inner forces.	*Sigmund Freud: Psychoanalysis:* psychic determinism; early development; drives and instincts; unconscious processes *Freudian Personality Theory:* personality structure; ego defense mechanisms *Alfred Adler: Lifestyle Adequacy:* search for adequacy and competence; overcompensation for feelings of inferiority *Carl Jung: Analytic Psychology:* collective unconscious; archetypes
Humanistic Theories	Personality is driven by self-actualization.	*Carl Rogers's Person-Centered Approach:* need for self-actualization vs. need for approval from self and others; unconditional positive regard
Social-Learning and Cognitive Theories	Personality is shaped by environment and/or styles of thinking.	*George Kelly's Personal Construct Theory:* personal constructs influence behavior; new situations demand new constructs
Cognitive Social-Learning Theories		*Cognitive Social-Learning Theories:* Mischel: situational influence Bandura: reciprocal determinism

Type Theories

One of the oldest approaches to describing personality involves classifying people into a limited number of distinct types. In our everyday lives, we continually group people into a small number of categories according to some distinguishing features. These features may include college class, major, sex, race, and qualities such as honesty or shyness. Some personality theorists also group people according to their **personality types**—distinct patterns of personality characteristics used to assign people to categories. These categories do not overlap; if a person is assigned to one category, he or she is not in any other category within that system. When you remark that a new acquaintance seems to be "the shy type," you are expressing the assumption that all people either do or don't belong in this category—that everyone must be either shy or non-shy.

Early personality typologies (classification systems) were designed to specify a connection between a simple, highly visible characteristic and behavior that can be expected from people of that type. If fat, then jolly; if an engineer, then conservative; if female, then sympathetic. Such systems have traditionally had much popular appeal and still do in the mass media; they simplify a very complicated process of understanding the nature of personality.

personality types Patterns of behavior and characteristics used to assign people to categories.

Four-Humors Theory. One of the earliest type theories was proposed in the fifth century B.C. by **Hippocrates,** the Greek physician who gave medicine the Hippocratic oath. He theorized that the body contained four basic fluids or *humors,* each associated with a particular *temperament.* An individual's personality depended on which humor was predominant in his or her body. Hippocrates paired body humors with personality temperaments according to the following scheme:

- Blood = sanguine temperament: cheerful and active
- Phlegm = phlegmatic temperament: apathetic and sluggish
- Black bile = melancholy temperament: sad and brooding
- Yellow bile = choleric temperament: irritable and excitable

Hippocrates' four-humors system was popular for centuries, although today we know it is baseless: Personality and moods are not driven by bodily fluids. Nonetheless we still see references to it in our language. For example, *bilious* means both "bile-filled" and "ill-tempered." Our culture retains hints of four-humors theory in ideas and words that imply a biological origin to problematic moods and personalities. However, not since the Middle Ages have barber-surgeons or other professionals treated mood-afflicted patients with surgical bloodletting and leeches to remove the "bad blood."

somatotype Descriptive category that classifies a personality pattern according to physical characteristics.

Hippocrates theorized that the body contained four essential fluids, or humors, each associated with a particular temperament. Clockwise: melancholy patient suffers from an excess of black bile; blood impassions a sanguine lutist to play; a maiden, dominated by phlegm, is slow to respond to her lover; choler, too much yellow bile, makes an angry master.

Somatotypes. Another interesting type theory of personality was advanced by **William Sheldon** (1942), a U.S. physician who related physique to temperament. He assigned each individual to one of three categories based on the person's **somatotype,** or body build: *endomorphic* (fat, soft, round), *mesomorphic* (muscular, rectangular, strong), or *ectomorphic* (thin, long, fragile). The typology specified relationships between each physique and particular personality traits, activities, and preferences.

According to Sheldon, endomorphs are relaxed, fond of eating, and sociable. Mesomorphs are physical people, filled with energy, courage, and assertive tendencies. Ectomorphs are brainy, artistic, and introverted; they would rather think about life than consume it or act upon it.

Sheldon's theory is intriguing, but not substantiated. It has proven to be of little value in predicting an individual's behavior (Tyler, 1965). In addition, people come in many different shapes—certainly more than three—and not all can be assigned readily to one of Sheldon's three somatotypes.

William Sheldon related physique to temperament by assigning people to categories based on their somatotypes. Endomorphic people are fat, soft, and round. Mesomorphic people are muscular, rectangular, and strong. Ectomorphic people are thin, long, and fragile.

trait Relatively stable personality tendency.

cardinal trait Trait around which people organize their lives.

central trait Major trait assumed to explain an individual's pattern of behavior.

secondary trait Trait that indicates enduring personal qualities but is not assumed to explain general behavior patterns.

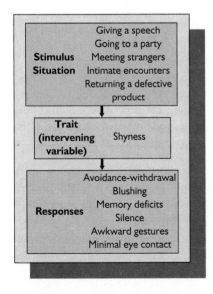

Stimulus Situation	Giving a speech Going to a party Meeting strangers Intimate encounters Returning a defective product

↓

Trait (intervening variable)	Shyness

↓

Responses	Avoidance-withdrawal Blushing Memory deficits Silence Awkward gestures Minimal eye contact

Figure 10.1 Shyness as a Trait
Traits may act as intervening variables, relating sets of stimuli and responses that might seem, at first glance, to have little to do with each other.

The MBTI Typology. A popular modern typology is derived from Carl Jung's theory of personality types (1953). (See "In Focus: The Post-Freudians" on p. 386.) Using the *Myers-Briggs Type Indicator* (MBTI), people's self-reported preferences are used to measure four dimensions: extraversion-introversion (E or I), sensing-intuition (S or N), thinking-feeling (T or F), and judgment-perception (J or P). If you took this test, you would be assigned to only one pole of each dimension, and the combination of dimensions would determine which of the 16 possible types best describes you. For example, people of type ENFP (for Extroverted-Intuitive-Feeling-Perceiving) are said to be enthusiastic innovators who are skillful in handling people but hate uninspired routine. The Myers-Briggs is a type system because its categories are distinct or discontinuous, and people of one type are supposed to be very much like each other in ways that distinguish them from the other types (Myers, 1987).

The MBTI typology is widely used because people who take the test find the types easy to understand. Opponents of the system believe that, while the four dimensions are informative, people should be described according to their actual scores on each dimension instead of being collapsed into types.

Trait Theories

The practice of identifying personality *traits* is about as ancient as the type approach to personality. Labeling and classifying the many personality characteristics we observe may help us organize human behavior, but it is no simple task. In fact, a dictionary search by psychologists Gordon Allport and H. S. Odbert (1936) found over 18,000 adjectives in the English language to describe individual characteristics!

Type theories presume that there are separate, *discontinuous categories* into which people fit. In contrast, trait theories propose *continuous dimensions,* such as intelligence or warmth, that vary in quality and degree. A **trait** is a general action tendency; people are assumed to possess traits in varying degrees. Traits describe what is consistent about a person's behavior in different situations and times. For example, if you possess the trait of "honesty," you may demonstrate it one day by returning a lost wallet and demonstrate it another day by not cheating on a test. Some trait theorists think that traits *cause behavior,* but more conservative theorists argue that traits merely *describe or predict patterns* of behavior.

Allport's Trait Approach. Gordon Allport (1937, 1961, 1966) was one of the most influential personality theorists. He is the best known of the idiographic trait theorists who believe that each person has some unique characteristics, as well as some common ones, that together form a unique combination of traits. Allport viewed traits as the building blocks of personality and the source of individuality. Traits connect and unify a person's reactions to a variety of stimuli, as shown in **Figure 10.1.**

Allport identified three kinds of traits. A **cardinal trait** is a trait around which a person organizes his or her life; most people have more than one. Howard Hughes organized his life around power and achievement. For Mother Teresa of Calcutta (awarded the 1979 Nobel Peace Prize), a cardinal trait might be self-sacrifice for the good of others. Not all people develop cardinal traits, however. A **central trait** is a trait that represents a major characteristic of a person, such as honesty or optimism. A **secondary trait** is a specific, personal feature that helps us predict the individual's behavior, but is less useful for understanding an individual's personality. Food or dress preferences are examples of secondary traits. According to Allport, these traits form the structure of the personality—which, in turn, determines an individual's behavior.

Eysenck's Type-Trait Hierarchy. Hans Eysenck (pronounced I-zenk), a leading trait theorist, proposed a model that links types, traits, and behavior into a

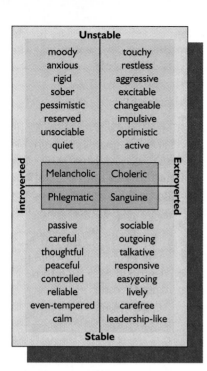

Unstable	
moody	touchy
anxious	restless
rigid	aggressive
sober	excitable
pessimistic	changeable
reserved	impulsive
unsociable	optimistic
quiet	active
Melancholic	**Choleric**
Phlegmatic	**Sanguine**
passive	sociable
careful	outgoing
thoughtful	talkative
peaceful	responsive
controlled	easygoing
reliable	lively
even-tempered	carefree
calm	leadership-like
Stable	

(Introverted / Extroverted labels on sides)

Figure 10.2 The Four Quadrants of Eysenck's Personality Circle (redrawn here as a quadrangle)

The Big Five Five basic dimensions underlying the traits used to describe people's behavior: Extroversion; Agreeableness; Conscientiousness; Emotional Stability; and Openness to Experience.

single hierarchical system (1947, 1990). At the lowest level of Eysenck's hierarchy are single *responses* like actions or thoughts. Regularly occurring responses form *habits,* and related habits form *traits.* From his test data, Eysenck concluded that there are three broad personality dimensions: *extroversion* (outgoingness), *neuroticism* (stability or instability), and *psychoticism* (realistic or unrealistic thinking).

Eysenck believes that personality differences on his three basic dimensions are caused by genetic and biological differences between people. He feels that his hierarchy can be used in combination with other trait models to provide new insights into personality. For example, he has related extroversion-introversion and neuroticism (stability-instability) to the physiological-personality types of Hippocrates, as shown in **Figure 10.2.**

Eysenck's theory is not a strict typology, so people can fall anywhere in the quadrangle, ranging from very introverted to very extroverted and from very unstable (neurotic) to very stable. The traits listed around the circle describe people with each combination of scores. For example, a person who is very extroverted and somewhat unstable is likely to be impulsive.

The Big Five.   One hazard of trait psychology is that different researchers study many different traits, design many different ways to measure them, and sometimes create their own idiosyncratic names for the dimensions they measure. This "free enterprise" system creates a difficult climate for scientific progress. The confusion over terminology can make it hard to know whether the empirical results of different studies even agree—or if they can be compared. For example, criminal behavior in adolescence can be predicted from either high Psychoticism scores, as measured by Eysenck's scale (1982), or from low Socialization scores, as measured by the California Psychological Inventory (Gough, 1968). Paradoxically, the more research we consult, the more confusing the picture seems.

The Search for Synonyms.   This emerging confusion led to a search for common dimensions of meaning that would link together the wealth of information in personality psychology. The goal of the search was to develop a common language that all personality psychologists could use to compare their measures and results. The search began by examining trait terms found in natural language. The hope was that, over time, people would have developed words to describe the important dimensions they perceived in themselves and others.

Several research efforts started with a list of all the traits in the English language that Allport and Odbert (1936) had extracted from the dictionary. The traits were then reduced to about 200 synonym clusters that were used to form bipolar (two-ended) trait dimensions, such as "responsible-irresponsible." People rated themselves and others on these dimensions, and their ratings were analyzed to identify relationships among clusters of synonyms. The startling conclusion of researchers using this method was that there are only *five basic dimensions* underlying all the traits people use to describe themselves and others (Norman, 1967; Tupes & Christal, 1961).

Five Common Dimensions.   The five dimensions are very broad, because each category includes many traits that have unique connotations but a common theme. These five dimensions are known as **The Big Five.** In the following list of The Big Five, you'll notice that each dimension is *bipolar* although it has a one-word label; the name of the dimension describes the "high" pole, while an opposite term describes the "low" pole.

1. *Extroversion*—talkative, energetic, and assertive vs. quiet, reserved, and shy.
2. *Agreeableness*—sympathetic, kind, and affectionate vs. cold, quarrelsome, and cruel.

3. *Conscientiousness*—organized, responsible, and cautious vs. careless, frivolous, and irresponsible.
4. *Emotional Stability*—stable, calm, and contented vs. anxious, unstable, and temperamental.
5. *Openness to Experience*—creative, intellectual, and open-minded vs. simple, shallow, and unintelligent.

The Big Five are not meant to replace the many specific trait terms that carry their own nuances and shades of meaning. Rather, these five dimensions outline a taxonomy (an organizing list or glossary) that demonstrates the relationships between traits, theories, and actual behavior.

As a descriptive system, The Big Five is comprehensive; almost any trait imaginable can be related to one or a few of the dimensions. The dimensions are easy to understand because they were derived from natural language. They are very flexible and can accommodate many scientific approaches. Most importantly, the same five dimensions have been rediscovered with many different subject samples, with many different types of data, and have been translated to several languages.

The Consistency Paradox. Both trait theory and type theory presume that personality characteristics influence behavior across different types of situations. However, in the 1920s several researchers set out to observe trait-related behaviors in different situations. They were surprised to find little evidence of consistent behavior across situations. For example, two behaviors presumably related to the trait of honesty—lying and cheating on a test—were only weakly correlated among school children (Hartshorne & May, 1928).

The Illusion of Stability. If trait-related behaviors are not cross-situationally consistent—that is, if an individual's behavior changes in different situations—how can people perceive their own and others' personalities as relatively stable? Research shows that the personality ratings of observers who see an individual in one situation do correlate with the ratings of observers who see that individual in another situation (Bem & Allen, 1974; Norman & Goldberg, 1966). The observation that personality ratings across time and among different observers *are consistent,* while behavior ratings of individuals across situations are *not consistent,* is called the **consistency paradox** (Mischel, 1968).

The Need for Consistency. Implicit theories of personality and cognitive biases may contribute to, but cannot entirely explain, our stable and consensual perceptions of personality. For example, if someone thinks a trait applies to herself personally, she becomes more likely to see it as consistent in others' behavior too. Consistency may be a quality people find in their observations precisely because they *need* to find it.

Alternatively, people may interpret traits as consistent—even when they are really inconsistent because they make so few observations. For example, if you have heard a classmate described as "generous," and subsequently observe her on only one occasion, you may look for (and find) "proof" that she is indeed generous. A scientist might then ask: Does she behave generously in other situations? If you don't observe other situations and occasions, you cannot answer that question, and so you have no information about consistency over time. In fact, researchers who studied collections of behaviors, making many observations of an act in every situation, were able to confirm that some traits are consistent *over time* (Epstein, 1979).

Coherence Versus Consistency. The consistency debate forced personality researchers to rethink traits in a more exact way—to outline precisely what classes of behavior *should* be related to personality traits and under what conditions. It seems now that personality is not a matter of behavioral consistency at

consistency paradox Observation that personality ratings made by different observers at different times are similar while behavior ratings across situations are not.

all. Instead, personality produces patterns of behavioral *coherence*. A trait may be expressed through different behaviors in different situations and at different ages, but as long as the theory of a trait predicts the *range* of behavioral expressions, the pattern is coherent.

For example, one study found that boys who were very shy as children later seemed reluctant to take on new social roles; they lagged 3 to 4 years behind their non-shy peers in getting married, having children, and entering stable careers (Caspi et al., 1988). In other words, shy boys did not consistently behave shyly, as boys and later as men, in the same ways; but they did act in ways that cohered (or fit together) as part of a "more shy pattern" overall.

The Power of Situations. Situations are also important in the expression of personality. In one sense, the details of a situation influence what you will do at any given time. However, research shows that situations differ in the extent to which personality is likely to be expressed in behavior. Personality *traits* are expressed most often when *situations* are novel, ill-defined (and thus open to interpretation), or stressful (Caspi & Bem, 1990).

On the other hand, your personality influences the situations you're likely to get into. Sometimes you deliberately select certain types of situations, like going to many different parties, or never raising your hand to answer a question in order to avoid speaking in front of your entire class. Other times, your personality influences the nature of a situation because you evoke certain responses from others. For example, if you talk often, and loudly, people might contribute less to a conversation with you than they usually do with others. And so you judge those people you talk with as reticent or quiet. (See "Cross-cultural Perspective: Explanations for Behavior.")

Criticizing Types and Traits. Type and trait theories have been criticized as inadequate because they do not *explain* the causes or development of personality. Instead, they merely identify and describe characteristics that are correlated with behavior. Trait theories typically portray a *static*, or at least stabilized, view of personality structure as it currently exists. In contrast, *dynamic* theories of personality emphasize conflicting forces within the individual and fast-paced environmental challenges. Together, these forces lead to continuous change and development within the individual. In the next section, we'll examine how dynamic personality theories differ from type and trait theories.

Sometimes your personality influences the situations you get into. For example, a competitive person, like this swimmer, would seek out and participate in competitive events.

Cross-cultural Perspective   Explanations for Behavior

All over the world, people are frequently faced with the task of explaining why individuals, including themselves, behave the way they do. For example, if a politician wants our vote or support and makes promises, people are likely to ask whether the politician is sincere or whether he will simply promise anything to get elected. Cross-cultural researchers (for example, Miller, 1984; Shweder & Sullivan, 1993) have asked, "Do people in different parts of the world explain behavior in ways that emphasize different types of reasons?" As the text notes, one reason that people behave in certain ways is that they have certain traits. Another reason for behavior is that various social situations pressure individuals to behave in particular ways. The distinction between traits and social situations can be shown in the following incident.

Assume that you have studied intensely Friday night and most of Saturday and feel that you need a break. You look at a newspaper and see that your favorite female vocalist is in town. She has recently joined a well-established band and is making one of her first public appearances with this new group. You go to the concert, but find that most of her performance consists of back-up vocals. Most of the lead vocals are taken by a tall, athletic male who has a pleasant but not outstanding voice. The concert is OK, but you are disappointed that you heard so little from your favorite singer. How do you explain the behavior of the people in the band?

If you are like many members of the American middle-class Anglo culture, your explanation attributes behavior to individuals' traits. You are likely to say things like "The male singer is domineering and so he hogged all the vocals." You may have been less likely to focus on aspects of the social situation (sometimes called social context) that could have influenced the behavior. Perhaps the female singer had a recent bout with a flu that settled in her throat. Perhaps this fact meant that she could not handle any lead vocals. Or, perhaps she only recently joined the group and did not know the lyrics to all the songs in the band's repertoire.

In discussing cross-cultural research on moral development (in Chapter 4), we introduced the concepts of individualism and collectivism. If a culture emphasizes individualism, as does the American middle-class culture, behavior is understood within the context that people pursue their own goals. As a result, people come to view themselves and others in their culture as *individual actors* who are responsible for their own behavior. The reasoning is that if people pursue their own goals, they must take advantage of their own resources. If they want to have friends, they will take advantage of the trait of being "sociable." If they want to do well in college, they will take advantage of their trait of being "hardworking." In contrast, people in collectivist cultures are more likely to take the goals of others into account when making decisions about their own behavior. These people view themselves and others as actors who are part of a larger social context. A major part of this social context is the long-term presence of others. When explaining behavior, people in collectivist cultures (like those in Asia and Latin America) are more likely to draw upon aspects of the social context in which people find themselves.

Joan Miller (1984) studied explanations of behavior in a collectivist culture (the Mysore in Southern India) and in an individualistic culture (in Chicago, in the United States). As predicted, she found that Americans were more likely to focus on people's traits when explaining behavior, and these Indians were more likely to focus on aspects of the social context. Miller asked respondents to present examples of behaviors that led to something good for another person and to discuss behaviors that the respondent thought wrong. For example, one of the Indian respondents talked about hiring a man to do construction work on his house. The respondent gave the man 1500 rupees, but the man did no work and did not return the 1500 rupees. How did the respondent explain the man's behavior? He referred to social context. "The man is unemployed. He is not in a position to give [back] that money" (Miller, 1984, p. 968). When Americans discussed similar stories about deviant behavior involving money, they were more likely to refer to the person's traits. Trait explanations, of course, would focus on words like "dishonest" and "crooked."

Cross-cultural psychologists do not want to question all explanations of behavior based on personality traits or all uses of tests that measure traits. They do, however, emphasize that there are other reasons for behavior besides traits and that people in other parts of the world often focus on these other reasons. This discussion brings up an intriguing issue. At one time or another, you may have taken a personality test and have received the results, which were phrased in the language of traits. You might have been told that you are "introverted or extroverted," "stable," or "responsible." Personality testing developed in individualistic countries, such as the United States and countries in Western Europe. If it had developed in a collectivist country such as Japan, China, or India, would assessment tests focus more on aspects of the social context in which people find themselves? Would people receive the results of assessment tests in terms that describe social context, such as "opportunities given socioeconomic status," "pressures given time demands," or "behavior in public vs. behavior in private?" We believe that the answer is "yes," and that a major focus of research from now into the twenty-first century will combine the contributions of trait research with analyses of social context.

Psychodynamic Theories

By the end of the nineteenth century, Charles Darwin had made the world aware of the common bonds between human beings and animals. Psychologists were quick to borrow Darwin's concept of instinct—as an explanation for animal behavior—and apply it to human action. However, a reliance on instincts to *identify* the sources of action does not help *explain* the action. Saying that someone is stingy because he has a "miserly instinct" does not really explain *why* one person possesses that instinct more than another. Ultimately, the instinct approach to personality was not particularly helpful.

Sigmund Freud provided a new approach. Freud broadened the notion of instinct in analyzing human behavior. All **psychodynamic personality theories,** which are based on Freud's work, share the assumption that personality is shaped and behavior is motivated by powerful inner forces.

psychodynamic personality theories
Any models that share assumptions that inner forces shape personality and motivate behavior.

Freudian Psychoanalysis. According to psychoanalytic theory, at the core of personality are experiences within a person's mind that motivate behavior. We may be aware of some of these motivations, but some motivation operates at an unconscious level. The emphasis on inner sources of energy characterizes this approach as *psychodynamic* (which means "mind energized"). For Freud, *all behavior was motivated.* All acts are *determined* by motives, not by chance. Every human action has a cause and a purpose that can be discovered through psychoanalysis—analysis of thought associations, dreams, errors, and other behavioral clues to inner passions.

The primary data for Freud's hypotheses about personality came from his observations and case studies of patients in therapy. Curiously, he developed a theory of normal personality from his intense study of those with mental disorders. Although there are serious problems validating many of Freud's ideas, his early concepts of personality structure have endured a century of criticism and are worth a careful review. The core of the psychodynamic approach is based on four core concepts: *psychic determinism,* early developmental *experience, drives and instincts,* and *unconscious processes.* Together they provide a conceptually rich perspective on the development and functioning of personality.

Psychic Determinism. **Psychic determinism** is the assumption that all mental and behavioral reactions (symptoms) are determined by earlier experiences. Freud believed that symptoms were related in a meaningful way to significant life events.

psychic determinism Assumption that mental and behavioral reactions are caused by earlier experience.

In the late 1800s, physicians recorded many cases of hysteria, physical ailments for which no adequate physical explanations could be found. The afflicted (who were mostly women) would experience impaired bodily functioning—paralysis or blindness, for example—and yet they had intact nervous systems and no obvious organic damage to their muscles or eyes. As a young physician, Freud became interested in treating the bizarre symptoms of this disorder. His experiences with hysteria influenced his later theories.

Freud observed that the particular physical symptom often seemed related to an earlier forgotten event in a patient's life. For instance, under hypnosis, a "blind" patient might recall seeing her parents having intercourse when she was a small child. As she becomes an adult, she may anticipate her first sexual encounter, which might arouse powerful feelings associated with that upsetting memory. The young woman's blindness might represent an unconscious attempt to undo her vision of the original event—and to deny her own sexual feelings. Blindness would also bring her attention, comfort, and sympathy from others. Her inner psychic motives thus determine her condition.

Early Experience. Freud assumed a continuity of personality development from "the womb to the tomb." He believed that experiences in infancy and early childhood had the most profound impact on personality formation and adult

psychosexual stages Freudian concept of successive phases—oral, anal, phallic, latency, and genital—of development in which a child associates pleasure with different bodily regions.

oral stage First phase of psychosexual development, in which the mouth is the region associated with greatest gratification.

anal stage Second phase of psychosexual development, in which elimination and retention of feces is associated with greatest gratification.

phallic stage Third phase of psychosexual development, in which stimulation of genitals is associated with greatest gratification.

latency stage Fourth phase of psychosexual development, in which bodily gratification is less important than acquiring skills and relating to peers.

genital stage Fifth phase of psychosexual development, in which sexual relations with a partner are associated with greatest gratification.

fixation Freudian hypothesis that excessive stimulation or frustration in early psychosexual stages causes arrested development.

behavior patterns. Freud described a progression of **psychosexual stages,** which are successive patterns of satisfying instinctual biological urges through stimulation of different areas of the body and different times of life:

1. During the **oral stage,** from birth through the first year of life, an infant experiences gratification primarily through stimulation of the *mouth*. A baby not only takes in nourishment orally, but also makes contact with the environment by mouthing and sucking on objects, toys, and fingers.
2. The **anal stage** follows at about age 2, when a child experiences pleasure in eliminating or retaining feces. Society demands toilet training, and the child must learn to control and suppress anal stimulation.
3. From about ages 3 to 5, during the **phallic stage,** a child explores and stimulates his or her own body, discovering the pleasure associated with the penis or clitoris. During this same stage, a child develops unconscious feelings of possessive love toward the opposite-sex parent, and must resolve feelings of conflict and anxiety by identifying more closely with the same-sex parent.
4. By about age 6, a child begins formal schooling and begins to pay more attention to friends and peers than to parents and family. During this **latency stage,** unconscious associations of pleasure with bodily stimulation become "latent" (less obvious), while the child concentrates on learning and competence.
5. As the child experiences puberty, he or she enters the **genital stage** (from about age 12 or 13 through part or all of adolescence), associating physical pleasure with personal relationships rather than self-stimulation or possessive fantasies.

According to Freud, either too much stimulation or too much frustration at any of the early psychosexual stages leads to **fixation**—an inability to progress normally to the next stage of development. For example, oral fixation allegedly leads to dependency on others, overeating, drug addiction, and even tendencies toward verbal fluency and sarcasm. Anal fixation is presumed to result in a stubborn, compulsive, stingy, excessively neat pattern of behavior.

Some clinicians treating patients with certain mental disorders have found Freud's concept of psychosexual stages useful. On the other hand, Freud never actually studied children—only adults' recollections of childhood experiences. Nonetheless, his emphasis on early experience helped to make the scientific study of infant and child behavior respectable.

During the phallic stage, a child must resolve feelings of conflict and anxiety by identifying more closely with the same-sex parent.

Freud suggested that the primitive urge, Thanatos, drives people toward aggressive and destructive behaviors.

Eros Freudian concept of life instinct that energizes growth and survival.

libido Freudian concept of psychic energy that drives individuals to experience sensual pleasure.

Thanatos Freudian concept of death instinct, theorized to energize destructive and aggressive behavior.

Unconscious Psychoanalytic concept of psychic domain that stores repressed and primitive impulses; unconscious processes repress impulses that motivate thoughts, feelings, and actions.

"All right, deep down it's a cry for psychiatric help—but at one level it's a stick-up."

Drives and Instincts. As a result of his medical training as a neurologist, Freud argued that human motivation was powered by biological, psychic energy found within each individual. Psychoanalysis focused on how this energy was exchanged, transformed, and expressed. Each person was assumed to have inborn drives that were created by bodily organs and could be expressed in many ways. For example, when activated, the sex drive could be directly expressed through sexual activity, or indirectly expressed through joking or creative activities.

Freud originally postulated two basic drives. One he saw as involved with *self-preservation.* The other he called **Eros,** which is the driving force related to sexual urges and preservation of the species. Freud greatly expanded the notion of human sexual desires to include not only the urge for sexual union, but also all additional attempts to seek pleasure or to make physical contact with others. He used the term **libido** to identify the source of energy for sexual urges—a psychic energy that drives people toward sensual pleasures of all types.

Clinical observation of patients who had suffered traumatic experiences during World War I led Freud to add to his theory a third drive called **Thanatos**—the death instinct or "death wish." Thanatos was a negative force that drove people toward *aggressive* and destructive behaviors. Freud found that many patients continued to relive their wartime traumas in nightmares and hallucinations, which Freud could not work into his self-preservation or sexual drive theories. He suggested that Thanatos was part of the tendency for all living things to follow the *law of entropy*—a physical principle of the disintegration of matter into energy—and return to an inorganic state.

Unconscious Processes. Freud put the concept of the **Unconscious** at center stage in the human drama. He believed that behavior can be motivated by drives of which we are not aware. We may act without knowing the true cause of our actions. This repository of drives, feelings, and thoughts that is part of the mind but unavailable for reflection is the Unconscious. Today, many psychologists consider this concept of the Unconscious to be Freud's most important contribution to the science of psychology.

The meaning of neurotic (anxiety-based) symptoms, dreams, and slips of the tongue are found at the unconscious level of thinking and information processing. According to Freud, impulses within us that we find unacceptable still strive for expression. A *Freudian slip* occurs when accidental speech or behavior reveals an unconscious desire. For example, as you leave a boring social function, you may tell your host, "I have to go now, but I had a terrible—I mean *terrific*—time." Similarly, being consistently late for a date with a particular person is no accident; it is an expression of the way you really feel.

The concept of unconscious motivation adds a new dimension to personality by allowing for greater complexity of mental functioning. The notion of an unconscious mind is threatening to those who want to believe they are in full command of their mind and will at all times.

Freudian Personality Theory. Freud assembled his basic concepts into specific theories about the structure of personality, and he described how its parts and processes work together to produce the behavior patterns of personality. In this section we first examine Freudian personality structure, then the concept of defense mechanisms. Finally, we consider what the critics said about Freud's ideas.

Personality Structure. In Freudian theory, personality differences arise from the different ways in which people deal with their fundamental drives. To explain these differences, Freud pictured a continuing battle between two antagonistic parts of the personality, the *id* and the *superego,* that are moderated by a third aspect of the self, the *ego.*

id Freudian concept of primitive, unconscious personality structure that operates irrationally, impulsively, and selfishly.

superego Freudian concept of personality structure that embodies society's values, standards, and morals.

ego Freudian concept of self, the personality structure focused on self-preservation and appropriate channeling of instinctual drives.

repression Freudian defense mechanism, underlying all other defense mechanisms, in which unacceptable thoughts, feelings, or memories are excluded from consciousness.

ego defense mechanisms Freudian concept of mental strategies used to reduce conflict or anxiety.

anxiety Intense, negative emotional reaction to the threat of becoming conscious of a repressed conflict.

The **id** is the primitive, unconscious part of the personality; it is the storehouse of the fundamental drives. The id acts on impulse and pushes for immediate gratification—especially sexual, physical, and emotional pleasures—to be experienced here and now without concern for consequences.

The **superego** is the storehouse of an individual's values, including moral attitudes learned from society. The superego corresponds roughly to our common notion of *conscience*. It develops as a child develops values based on the prohibitions of parents and other adults against socially undesirable actions. It is the inner voice of "oughts" and "should nots." The superego also includes the *ego ideal,* an individual's view of the kind of person he or she should strive to become.

As you might imagine, the superego is often in conflict with the id. The id wants to do what feels good, while the superego insists on doing what is right. The **ego** is the part of the self that resolves the conflict between id and superego. The ego represents an individual's personal view of physical and social reality. Part of the ego's job is to choose actions that will gratify id impulses without undesirable consequences. For example, the ego would block an impulse to cheat on an exam because of concerns about getting caught, and it would substitute the resolution to study harder the next time or ask the teacher for help. When the id and superego are in conflict, the ego arranges a compromise that at least partially satisfies both. However, as id and superego pressures intensify, it becomes more difficult for the ego to work out optimal compromises.

Ego Defenses. Sometimes this compromise between id and superego involves "putting a lid on the id." Extreme desires are pushed out of conscious awareness into the privacy of the unconscious. **Repression** is the psychological process that protects an individual from experiencing extreme anxiety or guilt about unacceptable or dangerous impulses, ideas, or memories. The ego remains unaware of both the mental content that is censored and the process by which repression works. Repression is considered to be the most basic of the ego defense mechanisms. For example, a student who suspects she failed an important test may "forget" to attend class the day the graded tests are returned. This unconscious "memory lapse" protects her from feeling upset or anxious—at least temporarily.

Ego defense mechanisms are the mental strategies with which the ego defends itself in the daily conflict between id impulses that seek expression and the superego's demand to deny them. By using these mechanisms, a person can maintain a favorable self-image and sustain an acceptable social image. For example, if a child has strong feelings of hatred toward her father—which, if acted out, would be dangerous—repression may take over. The hostile impulse is then no longer consciously pressing for satisfaction or even recognized as existing. Although the impulse is not seen or heard, it is not gone; these feelings continue to play a role in personality functioning. Repressed childhood memories can have effects on the lives of adults. Women who were sexually abused as children by men often repress these memories. Such unrecognized repression can interfere with the later development of trusting relationships with adult men. For a summary of some of the major ego defenses, see **Table 10.2** on the next page.

In Freudian theory, **anxiety** is an intense emotional response triggered when a repressed conflict is about to emerge into consciousness. Anxiety is a danger signal: "Repression is not working! Red alert! More defenses needed!" Anxiety signals the need for a second line of defense—one or more additional ego-defense mechanisms that will relieve the anxiety and send the distressing impulses back into the Unconscious. For example, a mother who did not want her child might use *reaction formation* which transforms her unacceptable impulse into its opposite: "I don't want my child" becomes "I love my child. See how I smother him with love?"

Table 10.2   Major Ego Defense Mechanisms

Denial	Protecting self from unpleasant reality by refusing to perceive its meaning
Displacement	Discharging pent-up feelings, usually of hostility, on objects less dangerous than those that initially aroused the emotion
Fantasy	Gratifying frustrated desires in imaginary achievements ("daydreaming" is a common form)
Identification	Increasing feelings of worth by identifying self with another person or institution, often of illustrious standing
Isolation	Cutting off emotional charge from hurtful situations or separating incompatible attitudes into logic-tight compartments (holding conflicting attitudes that are never thought of simultaneously or in relation to each other); also called *compartmentalization*
Projection	Placing blame for one's difficulties upon others or attributing one's own "forbidden" desires to others
Rationalization	Attempting to prove that one's behavior is "rational" and justifiable and thus worthy of the approval of self and others
Reaction Formation	Preventing dangerous desires from being expressed by endorsing opposing attitudes and types of behavior and using them as "barriers"
Regression	Retreating to earlier developmental levels involving more childish responses and usually a lower level of aspiration
Repression	Pushing painful or dangerous thoughts out of consciousness, keeping them unconscious; this is considered to be *the most basic of the defense mechanisms*
Sublimation	Gratifying or working off frustrated sexual desires in substitutive nonsexual activities socially accepted by one's culture

Useful as they are at times, ego mechanisms of defense are ultimately self-deceptive. When overused, they create more problems than they solve. Some forms of mental illness may result from excessive reliance on defense mechanisms to cope with anxiety, as we shall see when we examine mental disorders in Chapter 13.

Criticizing Freudian Theory. Freud's ideas have had an enormous impact on the way many psychologists think about normal and abnormal aspects of personality. However, more psychologists today would probably criticize Freudian concepts than support them. What is the basis of some of their criticisms?

First, psychoanalytic concepts are vague. Because they lack clear operational definitions, much of the theory is difficult to evaluate scientifically. How can the concepts of libido, the anal stage, or repression be studied in any direct fashion? How is it possible to predict whether an overly anxious person will use projection, denial, or reaction formation to defend a threatened ego?

A second, related criticism is that Freudian theory is good history but bad science. It does not reliably *predict* what will occur; it is applied *retrospectively*—after events have occurred. By overemphasizing historical origins of current behavior, the theory directs attention away from current events that may be inducing and maintaining the behavior.

Freud's theory was developed from speculation about clinical patients in therapy, almost all of them women with similar symptoms. Thus, another criticism is that the theory has little to say about healthy life-styles, which are not primarily defensive or defective. Instead, it offers the pessimistic view that human nature develops out of conflicts, traumas, and anxieties. It does not fully acknowledge the positive side of our existence nor offer any information about healthy personalities striving for happiness and realization of their full potential.

From the beginning, critics of Freudian theory have offered alternative explanations of personality structure and function. As you can see in "In Focus: The Post-Freudians" on the next page, some of Freud's early colleagues ultimately proposed theories very different from his, although they based them on psychoanalytic concepts and assumptions.

To end this discussion on a more positive note, a recent critical evaluation of Freud's ideas has validated many of his theories about how personality and psychopathology may develop in one's life (Fisher & Greenberg, 1985). Whether or not people accept Freud's theories, most recognize that Freud changed the way we think about the human mind, its complex possibilities, and its variations.

Humanistic Theories

Humanistic approaches to personality focus on concern for an individual's personal and conscious experience and growth. Humanistic personality theorists believe that the motivation for behavior comes from a person's unique biological and learned tendencies to develop and change positively toward *self-actualization*. **Self-actualization** is a constant striving to realize one's inherent potential—to fully develop one's capacities and talents. This innate striving toward self-fulfillment and the realization of one's unique potential is a constructive, guiding force that moves each person toward generally positive behaviors and enhancement of the self. Humanistic theories, in contrast to the psychodynamic approach, are optimistic about human nature.

self-actualization Humanistic concept of an individual's lifelong process of striving to realize his or her potential.

Several perspectives characterize humanistic theories. First, they explain an individual's separate acts in terms of the entire personality; an individual is not simply the sum of discrete traits that each influence behavior in different ways. Humanistic theories also focus on the innate qualities within a person that exert a major influence over the direction behavior will take. Situational inputs are often seen as constraints and barriers, like strings that tie down balloons. Once people are freed from negative situations, the actualizing tendency should actively guide them to choose life-enhancing situations. Humanistic theories emphasize an individual's frame of reference and subjective view of

THE POST-FREUDIANS

Some of those who came after Freud retained his basic representation of personality as a battleground on which unconscious primal urges fight with social values. However, many of Freud's intellectual descendants were also dissidents who made major adjustments in the psychoanalytic view of personality. In general, the post-Freudians made the following changes:

- They put greater emphasis on ego functions, including ego defenses, development of the self, conscious thought processes, and personal mastery.
- They view social variables (culture, family, and peers) as playing a greater role in shaping personality.
- They put less emphasis on the importance of general sexual urges, or libidinal energy.
- They have extended personality development beyond childhood to include the entire life span.

Two of the most important of Freud's followers were also severe critics, Alfred Adler and Carl Jung. **Alfred Adler** (1929) accepted the notion that personality was directed by unrecognized wishes: "Man knows more than he understands." However, he rejected the significance of Eros and the pleasure principle. Adler believed that as helpless, dependent, small children we all experience feelings of inferiority. He argued that our lives become dominated by the search for ways to overcome those feelings. We compensate to achieve feelings of adequacy or, more often, overcompensate for inferiority feelings by

attempting to become superior. Personality is structured around this underlying striving, and people develop life-styles based on particular ways of overcoming their basic, pervasive feelings of inferiority. Personality conflict arises from the incompatibility between external environmental presssures and internal strivings for adequacy, rather than from competing urges within the person.

Carl Jung (1959) greatly expanded the concept of the Unconscious. For him, the Unconscious was not limited to an individual's unique life experiences but was filled with fundamental psychological truths shared by the whole human race. The concept of **collective unconscious** predisposes us all to react to certain stimuli in the same way. It is responsible for our intuitive understand-

ing of primitive myths, art forms, and symbols, which are the universal archetypes of existence. An **archetype** is a primitive symbolic representation of a particular experience or object. Each archetype is associated with an instinctive tendency to feel and think about it or experience it in a special way. Jung postulated many archetypes from history and mythology: the sun god, the hero, the earth mother. *Animus* was the male archetype, while *anima* was the female archetype, and all men and women experienced both archetypes in varying degrees. In reacting to those of the opposite sex, then, we react to their particular characteristics as well as to *our own* male or female archetype. The archetype of the self is the *mandala* or magic circle; it symbolizes striving for unity and wholeness (Jung, 1973).

Jung saw the healthy, integrated personality as balancing opposing forces, such as masculine aggressiveness and feminine sensitivity. This view of personality, as a constellation of compensating internal forces in dynamic balance, was called **analytic psychology.** Although he was chosen by Freud as the "crown prince" of the psychoanalytic movement, Jung led a palace revolt by rejecting the primary importance of libido—so central to Freudian sexual theory. To the basic urges of sex and aggression Jung added two equally powerful unconscious instincts: the need to create and the need to self-actualize. Jung's views became central to the emergence of humanistic psychology in America (Jung, 1965).

collective unconscious Jungian concept of inherited, unconscious ideas and forces common to all members of a species.

archetype Jungian concept of universal symbols of human experience as part of a collective unconscious.

reality—not the objective perspective of an observer or therapist. Finally, humanistic theories have been described by theorists such as Rollo May (1975) as having an *existential perspective.* These theories focus on higher mental processes that interpret current experiences and enable people to meet or be overwhelmed by the everyday challenges of existence. A unique aspect of these theories is the focus on human *freedom;* this aspect separates these theories from the more deterministic behaviorist and psychoanalytic approaches.

analytic psychology Jungian view that the healthy personality is an integrated balance of opposing forces.

Rogers's Person-Centered Approach.
Carl Rogers (1947, 1951, 1977) developed the practice of *client-centered therapy*, in which it was up to the *client* to determine the therapeutic goals and the direction the therapy should take to achieve those goals. Later, Rogers called his therapy *person-centered* because it was an approach for dealing with clients—and with individuals in general—as "people," not merely as patients. Rogers's advice was to listen to what people said about themselves—to their concepts and to the significance they attach to their experiences. As we have noted, at the core of this theoretical approach is the concept of self-actualization.

The drive for self-actualization at times conflicts with the need for approval from the self and others, especially when the person feels that certain obligations or conditions must be met in order to gain approval. Thus, Rogers stressed the importance of *unconditional positive regard* in raising children. He meant that children should feel they will always be loved and approved of, in spite of any of their mistakes and misbehavior—in other words, that children should not have to earn their parents' love. For example, when a child is punished for hitting his sister, his parents should reassure him that they love *him* even though they dislike what he *did*—loving a person is not the same as approving of what the person does. When people know that they are loved and accepted unconditionally, they need not worry about how to win approval from those important to them. Instead, people can concentrate on being the best they can, achieving their potential, and giving love and approval to others. (See "Time Out for Critical Thinking.")

Such an upbeat view of personality was a welcome treat for many therapists who had been brought up on a diet of bitter-tasting Freudian medicine. Humanistic approaches focus directly on improvement—on making one's present and future life more palatable, rather than dredging up painful memories of an unalterable past. Client-centered therapists encourage clients to write their own recipes for improvement, deciding which aspects of their lives they would like to change and what ingredients should go into such change.

➡ TIME OUT . . . FOR CRITICAL THINKING

Unconditional positive regard is important in adulthood as well as in childhood, because worrying about approval interferes with self-actualization. As adults, we need to give and receive unconditional positive regard from those to whom we are close. Most importantly, we need to feel unconditional positive *self-regard,* or acceptance of ourselves, in spite of the weaknesses we might be trying to change. The pop psychology common to many support groups and self-improvement programs recommends that we learn to appreciate ourselves, reward ourselves, and forgive ourselves. Is this a reasonable approach to healthy living? Is it always possible to admire and support yourself? Consider how you would answer the following questions:

- What are your best qualities as a person, student, friend? Who appreciates these qualities in you?

- What have you achieved lately? Why are you proud of these accomplishments?

- When you are happy with your own work or behavior, how do you usually reward yourself?

- What was the last thing you did that you regret? How did you seek to compensate or make amends?

- Are there things you could do—or have done—that you feel do not deserve forgiveness, either your own or others'? What guides you in making such a judgment?

Criticizing Humanistic Theories. Humanistic theories have been questioned from many different perspectives in psychology. Behaviorists question and criticize humanistic concepts for being fuzzy: What exactly is self-actualization? Is it an inborn tendency or is it created by one's culture? Experimental psychologists contend that too many of the concepts in humanistic psychology are so unclear that they defy testing in controlled research settings. Other psychologists note that humanistic psychologists neglect the influence of important environmental variables by emphasizing the role of the self in behavior. Last but not least, psychoanalytic theorists criticize the humanistic emphasis on present conscious experience. They argue that this approach does not recognize the power of the Unconscious.

The criticism of humanistic theories shows how unlikely it is that a single theory of personality will satisfy psychologists' many different concerns. Perhaps psychologists should develop an *eclectic* point of view, collecting and appreciating the parts of each approach that seem to work best and make the most sense.

Social-Learning and Cognitive Theories

All of the theories we have reviewed so far emphasize hypothetical inner mechanisms—traits, instincts, impulses, self-actualizing tendencies—that propel behavior and establish a functioning personality. Psychologists with a *learning theory* orientation have a different focus. They look for environmental contingencies (reinforcing circumstances) that control behavior. From this perspective, behavior and personality are shaped primarily by the outside environment.

This narrow behaviorist conception of personality was first developed by a team of Yale University psychologists headed by John Dollard and Neal Miller (1950). This theory was considerably expanded by Albert Bandura and Walter Mischel into a meaningful integration of core ideas from the learning-behavioral tradition and newly emerging ideas from social and cognitive psychology.

Dollard and Miller showed that one could learn by *social imitation*—by observing the behavior of others without actually performing the response first. This idea broadened psychologists' perceptions of the ways that both effective and destructive habits are learned. Personality emerges as the sum of these learned habits.

Bandura and Mischel emphasized the importance of learned behavioral patterns based on social learning, including observation of others and social reinforcement from others. They went one critical step further to emphasize the importance of cognitive processes as well as behavioral ones, returning a thinking mind to the acting body.

Cognitive theories of personality point out that there are important individual differences in the way people think about and define situations. Cognitive theories stress the mental processes through which people turn their sensations and perceptions into organized impressions of reality. They emphasize that people actively *choose* their own environments to a great extent. Thus, even in influential environments, people are not merely passive reactors. Individuals weigh alternatives and select the settings in which they act and are acted upon. People choose to enter those situations that they expect to be reinforcing and to avoid those that are unsatisfying and uncertain. One reason for the common observation that members of minority ethnic groups "stick together" on college campuses is that members are uncertain about whether they would be accepted if they ventured into different ethnic friendships. They avoid relationships that they anticipate as unsatisfying by not attempting to start them and by continuing with familiar ones instead.

The relationship between situational variables and cognitive variables in regulating behavior is found in several personality theories. In this section, we will review the *personal construct theory* of George Kelly, the *cognitive social-learning* theories of Walter Mischel and Albert Bandura, and the relevant criticisms that have been offered of social and cognitive theories.

Personal Construct Theory. **George Kelly** (1955) developed a theory of personality that places primary emphasis on each person's active, cognitive construction of his or her world. He argued that no one is ever a victim of either past history or the present environment. All events are open to alternative interpretations; people can always reconstruct their past or define their present difficulties in different ways.

personal construct George Kelly's theoretical concept of an individual's unique system for interpreting reality.

Kelly argued that all individuals function as amateur scientists. People want to be able to predict and explain the world around them—especially their interpersonal world. They build theories about the world from units called *personal constructs*. Kelly defined a **personal construct** as a person's belief about what two objects or events have in common and what sets them apart from a third object or event. For example, if you have been hurt by broken relationships in the past, the qualities of loyalty and fidelity might be particularly relevant to you at this point in your life. Perhaps you can even "sort" the people you know according to whether or not they can be trusted to make and keep commitments. Thus your personal construct—this concept of the importance of faithfulness in friendship—is important in how you see and judge others and form relationships with them.

You have many different personal constructs that you can apply to understanding any person or situation. All of your constructs are combined into an integrated belief system that influences the way you interpret and react to each situation you encounter. Personal constructs influence the way you evaluate information and form impressions of others.

Adapting to new situations requires that an individual's construct system be open to change. When someone has trouble understanding or predicting the course of events, it is helpful to find new ways to interpret them. Kelly believed that people differ in their readiness to change their constructs. He also felt that they can run into trouble either by rigidly refusing to change their old, ineffective constructs or by nervously changing their constructs every time the wind turns in a new direction.

Cognitive Social-Learning Theories. Two somewhat different theories combine an emphasis on cognitive processing with a focus on social-learning processes. The first theory has been proposed by a personality researcher and the second by a learning researcher.

Mischel's Theory. **Walter Mischel** (pronounced mish-ELL) questioned the utility of describing personality according to traits. As an alternative, he proposed a cognitive theory of personality that also draws on principles from social-learning theory. In his view, much of what we do and many of our beliefs and values are not best thought of as emerging properties of the self.

He sees them instead as *responses* developed, maintained, or changed by our observation of influential models and by specific stimulus-response pairings in our own *experience*.

According to Mischel, your response to a specific environmental input depends on several factors: your abilities; your information processing style; your expectancies; your values; and your rules and plans. Each of these factors is distinctive for you, as a result of your particular experiences and influences. The combination of these distinct factors makes your response pattern unique. This pattern filters your experiences so that you see the world differently from anyone else. People respond differently to the same environmental input because of differences in these person-based variables (Mischel, 1973).

Mischel argued that, because people are so sensitive to situational cues, features of situations are as important as features of people in our attempts to understand human behaviors. Person variables, he suggested, will have their greatest impact on behavior when cues in the situation are *weak* or *ambiguous*. When situations are strong and clear, there will be less individual variation in response. For example, when riding in an elevator, most of us tend to behave pretty much the same in response to the strong, silent situational demands. However, at a party, where many behaviors are appropriate, person variables will lead to large differences in behavior.

Bandura's Theory. Through his theoretical writing and extensive research with children and adults, **Albert Bandura** (1986) has become an eloquent champion of a social-learning approach to personality. This approach combines principles of learning with an emphasis on human interactions in social settings. Human beings are driven by neither inner forces nor environmental influences but rather by monitoring the impact of their behavior on other people, on the environment, and on themselves.

Because we can manipulate symbols and think about external events, we can foresee the possible consequences of our actions without having to actually experience them. In addition to learning from our own experience, we learn *vicariously* by observing other people. We can also evaluate our own behavior according to personal standards and provide ourselves with reinforcements, such as self-approval or self-reproach. We are capable of *self-regulation,* but we often gauge our own behavior according to imposed standards. Someone who accepts an external standard as a behavioral guide will react differently than someone who has developed his or her own personal standard. For example, if you prefer to type your class papers even though some professors accept handwritten work, you may feel disappointed in yourself when you fail to complete an assignment in time to type it before you turn it in.

Bandura's theory points to a complex interaction of individual factors, behavior, and environmental stimuli. Each factor can influence or change the others, and the direction of change is rarely one-way; it is *reciprocal* or bidirectional. To appreciate this concept of social-learning theory called **reciprocal determinism** (Bandura, 1981a), it is necessary to examine all components, including human behavior, personality, and social ecology (see **Figure 10.3**). For example, if you would rather read novels than attend sports events, you may frequent local bookstores instead of attending or watching games on weekend afternoons. If you are also extroverted, you will start conversations with the store's staff and with fellow customers, making the bookstore a socially attractive environment for future visits. This is one instance of the reciprocal determinism between person (extroverted book-lover), place (bookstore), and behavior (browsing instead of watching sports).

Perhaps the most important contribution of Bandura's theory is its focus on **observational learning** as the process by which a person changes his behavior based on observations of another person's behavior. Through observational learning, children and adults acquire an enormous range of information about their social environment—what gets rewarded and what gets pun-

reciprocal determinism Albert Bandura's social-learning theory concept of the mutual influence between person, behavior, and environment.

observational learning Process of learning new responses by watching others' behavior.

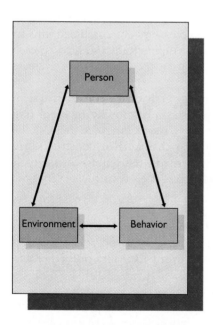

Figure 10.3 Reciprocal Determinism In reciprocal determinism, the individual, the individual's behavior, and the environment all interact.

Children develop a clearer sense of identity by observing how men and women behave in their culture.

self-efficacy Albert Bandura's concept of an individual's set of beliefs that he or she can perform adequately in a particular situation.

ished or ignored. Skills, attitudes, and beliefs may be acquired simply by watching what others do and the consequences that follow. Even personality traits like altruism can be learned by observing models, whether those are live and immediate or viewed indirectly through books, movies, and television (Straub, 1974).

Finally, Bandura has elaborated on the concept of *self-efficacy* as a central theme of social-learning theory (1986). **Self-efficacy** is a belief that one can perform adequately in a particular situation. Your sense of self-efficacy influences your perceptions, motivation, and performance in many ways. You probably don't even try to do things or take chances when you expect to be ineffectual. You avoid situations where you don't feel adequate. Even when you do, in fact, have the ability, you may not take or maintain the required action if you think you lack what it takes. For example, if you have not bowled since you were a child, you may decline an invitation to a bowling party, despite the fact that you are probably more coordinated and self-confident today than you were years ago. While it is no tragedy to pass up the chance to go bowling, your poor sense of self-efficacy in this situation leads you to miss the opportunity to meet new people, spend time learning a new activity, and simply have fun.

Expectations of failure—and a corresponding decision to stop trying—may, of course, be based on the perception that a situation is unresponsive, punishing, or unsupportive instead of on a perception of one's own inadequacy. Such situational assumptions are called *outcome expectations*. Perception of one's own inadequacy leads to *efficacy expectations*. (See **Figure 10.4** on p. 392.) The person who believes that responding is useless because of low self-efficacy must develop competencies that will boost self-perception of efficacy. On the other hand, when a person believes that responding is useless because of outcome expectancies, then the environment, and not the person, may need to change so that reinforcements will follow competent responding. If you are having trouble using a friend's computer, is it because *you* are "doing it wrong" or because there is something wrong with the computer itself? If you believe the former, you must develop your skill and your efficacy. If you believe the latter, perhaps someone should fix the computer.

Evaluating Learning and Cognitive Theories. Is personality all about stimulus variables or living people? If personality is built upon the learned repetition of previously reinforced responses, what is the origin of new behavior—such as

Albert Bandura

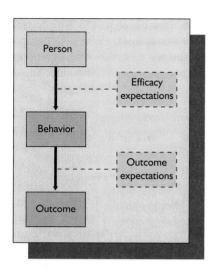

Figure 10.4 Bandura's Self-Efficacy Model The model positions efficacy expectations between the person and his or her behavior; outcome expectations are positioned between behavior and its anticipated outcomes.

creative achievements, innovative ideas, inventions, and works of art? Critics argue that much of the learning that behaviorists study is reinforced because an organism is in a state of tension due to some deficiency, and because other actions and reinforcements are not available. In contrast, your own experience may tell you that you don't have to be in a state of need or desperation to try something new or explore different forms of self-expression.

Some critics argue that cognitive theories generally overlook *emotion* as an important component of personality. These theories emphasize rational information-processing rather than emotions, which are viewed as mere by-products of thoughts and behavior. For those who feel that emotions are central to the functioning of human personality, this cognitive perspective has a serious flaw. Feelings may themselves be important determinants of cognitive content and structure.

Other critics focus on the vague explanations given for how personal constructs and competencies are created. Cognitive theorists have little to say about the developmental origins of adult personality. Their focus on the individual's perception of the current behavior setting obscures the individual's history.

Despite these criticisms, cognitive personality theories have made significant contributions to modern thought. Kelly's theory has influenced many cognitive therapists. Bandura's ideas have improved the way we educate children and help them to achieve. Mischel's awareness of situational variables has brought about a better understanding of the interaction between what the person brings to a behavior setting and what that setting draws out of the person.

It is also important to appreciate the interaction between person and situation if you are to understand *yourself*. As you see in "In Focus: Self Theories," much of what you know—or *think* you know—about yourself is a product of cognitive processes, not of behavioral observation. Common sense dictates that we consider personality theories of both the inner and outer person in understanding people.

Comparing Personality Theories

There is no unified theory of personality that a majority of psychologists can endorse. In our survey of the various theories, several differences in basic assumptions have come up. It may be helpful to recap the five most important differences in assumptions about personality, and the approaches that advance each assumption.

1. *Heredity versus environment.* This difference is also referred to as *nature vs. nurture.* Which is more important: genetic and biological factors or influences from the environment? Freudian theory depends heavily on heredity; humanistic, learning, cognitive, and self theories all emphasize either environment or interaction with the environment as sources of personality development and differences.

2. *Learning processes versus innate laws of behavior.* Should emphasis be placed on *modifiability* or on the view that personality development follows an internal timetable? Freudian theory has favored the inner determinant view, while humanists believe that people change as a result of their experiences. Learning, cognitive, and self theories clearly support the idea that behavior and personality change as a result of learned experiences.

3. *Emphasis on past, present, or future.* Trait theories emphasize past causes, whether innate or learned. Freudian theory stresses past events in early childhood. Learning theories focus on past reinforcements and present contingencies. Humanistic theories emphasize present interpretations or future goals. Cognitive and self theories emphasize past and present; and when goal-setting is included, these theories stress the future as well.

self-concept Individual's awareness of his or her continuing identity as a person.

self-esteem Evaluation of oneself that affects moods and behavior.

self-handicapping Manufacturing a preferred or acceptable excuse for anticipated failure, other than personal fault.

behavioral confirmation Process of acting in ways that elicit expected responses from others, which then validate those expectations.

In Focus:

SELF THEORIES

When cognitive social-learning theories reopened the mysterious mind to scientific scrutiny after decades of behaviorism had discouraged talk of things unseen, they readmitted the *self* to the study of personality. Although the cognitive approach to the self was new, a foundation of self theory had already been laid by philosophers, sociologists, analytic, and humanistic psychologists.

The strongest advocate for self theory was **William James** (1890). James identified three components of self-experience: the *material me* (one's body and personal possessions); the *social me* (one's awareness of his or her social reputation); and the *spiritual me* (the self that monitors private thoughts and feelings). James believed everything associated with one's identity became a part of self. For example, when our friends or family members are insulted, we react as though we have been attacked because a part of ourselves has been threatened. We likewise take pride in possessions like cars and special collections, which are really extensions of our "selves" (Belk, 1988).

Self-Concept

Some self theorists distinguish between the *knower* and the *known*. The *knower* refers to the part of you that experiences thoughts, feelings, and perceptions—the part that guides behavior. The *known* refers to what Carl Rogers and others have called the **self-concept**—that is, all the conscious or potentially conscious thoughts, ideas, and evaluations you have of yourself. The self-concept is a dynamic mental structure that motivates, organizes, and regulates intrapersonal and interpersonal behaviors. Your self-concept influences the way you process information about yourself. Research indicates that the self-schemas—concepts you use to interpret your own behavior—influence the way you process information about other people as well (Markus & Smith, 1981; Cantor & Kihlstrom, 1987). The salient aspects of self-concept change with development: Very young children think of themselves in terms of physical characteristics, gradually incorporate moods and preferences, and finally focus on their interpersonal traits, morals, and life philosophies (Damon & Hart, 1986; Livesley & Bromley, 1973).

Self-Esteem

A person's **self-esteem** is a generalized *evaluation* of the self, which can strongly influence our thoughts, moods, and behavior. Interestingly, belief in the impact of self-esteem on performance has generated a congressional appropriation in California (1987) to establish a Self-Esteem Commission. The commission's task is to discover ways to enhance self-esteem to benefit both individuals and society.

Most people go out of their way to maintain self-esteem and to sustain the integrity of their self-concept (Steele, 1988). For example, when experiencing self-doubt about their ability to perform a task, people sometimes engage in **self-handicapping** behavior: They deliberately sabotage their performance! They do this to have a ready-made excuse for failure that does not implicate *lack of ability* (Jones & Berglas, 1978). For example, if you are afraid to find out whether you have what it takes to excel academically, you might decide to party instead of studying the night before an important exam. That way, if you fail, you can blame it on bad judgment or poor effort instead of incompetence or lack of intelligence.

Private and Public Selves

Most of the time, people engage in *self-verification*, trying to know themselves better. Sometimes, when confronted by self-doubt, people prefer to remain in the dark about personal problems and engage in *self-enhancement* processes instead. In self-enhancement, people deny or distort information—manipulate their private selves—in order to sustain a desired self-image (Swann, 1990).

When you deliberately manipulate your public self to create a particular impression on another person, you are engaging in *impression management*. Sometimes you may manage your public self without even realizing it, by maintaining an impression that agrees with how you see yourself. In this process, known as **behavioral confirmation,** your beliefs about yourself control your behavior (source) in the presence of particular others (target) (Snyder, 1984). Target people are then more likely to react according to the behavioral context established and confirm the original belief about what kind of person you really are. In this way, beliefs create reality. For example, people who are extroverted bring out extroverted behaviors in others (Fong & Markus, 1982); those who are anxious cause anxiety in others (Riggs & Cantor, 1981); and those who feel depressed provoke depressed, hostile feelings in others (Strack & Coyne, 1983).

The Interpersonal Self

Some theorists believe we must ultimately return to an integrated (or unified) conception of self. These theorists promote a conception of the *interpersonal self*, in which behavior is directed not by an invisible *homunculus* (Latin for "little man") within the person but by the social context in which the person lives (Rosenberg, 1988). **Hazel Markus** believes that the self is a dynamic construct, deriving its meaning only in interpersonal contexts; without others there can *be* no self (Markus & Cross, 1990). There are no obvious distinctions between public and private aspects of the self or between what *we* think of ourselves and what we think *others* think of us. All of our interpersonal behavior becomes incorporated into the self. In addition, much of our behavior is scripted by the social roles we play, and the behaviors we characteristically display in different roles become worked into the self as well.

4. *Consciousness versus unconsciousness.* Freudian theory emphasizes unconscious processes. Humanistic, learning, and cognitive theories emphasize conscious processes. Trait theories pay little attention to either consciousness or unconsciousness; self theories are unclear on this specific issue.

5. *Inner disposition versus outer situation.* Learning theories emphasize situational factors. In contrast, humanistic, cognitive, social learning, and self theories allow for an interaction between personal and situational variables.

Students sometimes wonder why personality theorists cannot "agree" on a single approach. Isn't there one reality underlying the psychologists' different interests and interpretations? The answer is no. Each type of theory makes different contributions to our understanding of human personality. No single theory competes for the power of providing "one true answer." Rather, the strength of the theories comes from their diversity, since each one emphasizes different ideas. Together they provide a rich and enormously useful explanation of human personality.

SUMMING UP

Type theories use personal characteristics to sort people into discrete groups or types, and attempt to predict behavior on the basis of a person's type. Trait theories describe people according to continuous dimensions of personality, predicting behavior from the degree to which a person possesses certain traits. Among all traits, The Big Five dimensions of personality—Extroversion, Agreeableness, Conscientiousness, Emotional Stability, and Openness to Experience—are the common themes or dimensions that underlie the various descriptive systems.

The observation that personality ratings are consistent across time and across observers, while specific behaviors are usually not consistent across situations, is the consistency paradox. Because personality traits summarize behavior, they are better for predicting general patterns of behavior than specific behavior.

Freud's psychodynamic theory of personality identifies unconscious motives and conflicts as determinants of behavior. He proposed that personality develops through five psychosexual stages: oral, anal, phallic, latency, and genital. Excessive gratification or frustration at any early stage leads to fixation in adult behavior. Freud argued that personality conflicts occur between three structural parts: the id, superego, and ego. In solving these conflicts and reducing anxiety, the ego often resorts to defense mechanisms. After Freud, later psychodynamic theories put greater emphasis on ego functions and social variables, and less emphasis on sexual urges. These later themes also conceptualized personality development as a lifelong process that continues in adult life. Adler proposed that life-style compensates for feelings of inferiority. Jung emphasized the ideas of the collective unconscious and archetypes, and the basic need to create.

Humanistic theories emphasize self-actualization, a basic tendency to develop one's potential for creativity and growth. These theories serve to explain the whole personality, including innate qualities, subjective feelings, and the challenges of existence. Carl Rogers's person-centered therapy permits the client to guide the goals and direction of treatment. A necessary ingredient for self-actualization is unconditional positive regard, from the self and significant others.

Learning theories view behavior as caused by combined environmental stimuli and reinforcements. Dollard and Miller added learned drives, inhibition of responses, and habits to Freudian concepts. Bandura emphasized that social and cognitive factors—especially observational learning, reciprocal determinism, and self-efficacy—influence behavior. Kelly suggested that personal constructs influence information processing. Mischel has combined social-learning theory with a cognitive approach, emphasizing that people adapt flexibly to changes in environments and reinforcements. In applying personality theories to the self, a distinction is made between the self that is doing the knowing and the self that is known. Research has distinguished and clarified the processes of self-concept, self-esteem, and the interpersonal self.

Personality theories can chiefly be distinguished by their varying emphases on five issues: heredity vs. environment; the power of learning vs. innate factors; emphasis on past, present, or future; consciousness vs. unconsciousness; and inner dispositions vs. outer situations.

Assessing Personality

Beyond their interest in the shape and development of human personality, psychologists wonder how to measure the attributes that characterize an individual, set one person apart from others, or distinguish people in one group from those in another. Personality assessment tries to answer such questions.

Two assumptions are basic to these attempts to understand and describe human personality: First, the personal characteristics of individuals give coherence to behavior and, second, those characteristics can be assessed or measured. Psychologists use special tests designed to reveal important personal traits and the way those characteristics fit together in particular individuals. This information may be used in psychological research, individual therapy, career counseling, or personnel selection and training. The many different types of personality tests can be classified as either objective or projective.

Objective Tests

The administration and scoring of objective tests of personality are relatively simple procedures that follow standardized, objective rules. The final score is usually a number along a single dimension (such as "adjustment vs. maladjustment") or a set of scores on different traits (such as masculinity, dependency, or extroversion) reported relative to some comparative group.

A *self-report inventory* is an objective test in which individuals answer a series of questions about their thoughts, feelings, and actions. A person taking a **personality inventory** reads a series of statements and indicates whether each one is true for herself. On some inventories the person is asked to assess how frequently each statement is true or how well each describes her own typical behavior, thoughts, or feelings.

personality inventory Self-report questionnaire used for personality assessment.

The most famous test of this type is the *Minnesota Multiphasic Personality Inventory,* or MMPI (Dahlstrom et al., 1975). It is used by clinical psychologists as an aid in the diagnosis of patients and as a guide for their treatment. After reviewing the MMPI, we will briefly discuss three personality inventories that are used widely with nonpatient populations: the *California Psychological Inventory* (CPI), the *NEO Personality Inventory* (NEO-PI), and the *Myers-Briggs Type Indicator* (MBTI).

The MMPI. The MMPI was developed at the University of Minnesota during the 1930s by psychologist Starke Hathaway and psychiatrist J. R. McKinley. It was first published in the 1940s (Hathaway & McKinley, 1940, 1943). Its basic purpose is to diagnose individuals according to a set of psychiatric labels. The first test consisted of 550 items, each of which the subject judged as being "true," "false," or "cannot say." From that item pool, scales were developed that related to the kinds of problems patients showed in psychiatric settings. Standards for response patterns were established for both psychiatric patients and normal subjects.

The MMPI has 10 *clinical scales,* each constructed to differentiate a special clinical group (such as schizophrenics or paranoids) from a normal control group. The test is scored by adding up the number of items on a particular scale that a person answered in the same way as the clinical group; the higher the score, the more the person is like the clinical group and unlike the normal group. This type of scale development is called *empirical* because items are chosen not because they are theoretically related or relevant to some category, but because they are answered in a particular way by a given clinical group. The test also includes scales that detect suspicious response patterns, such as blatant dishonesty, carelessness, defensiveness, and evasiveness. A respondent's score on these scales is considered by the tester before the clinical scale answers are interpreted. The pattern of the scores—which ones are highest, how they differ—forms the "MMPI profile" (see **Figure 10.5**).

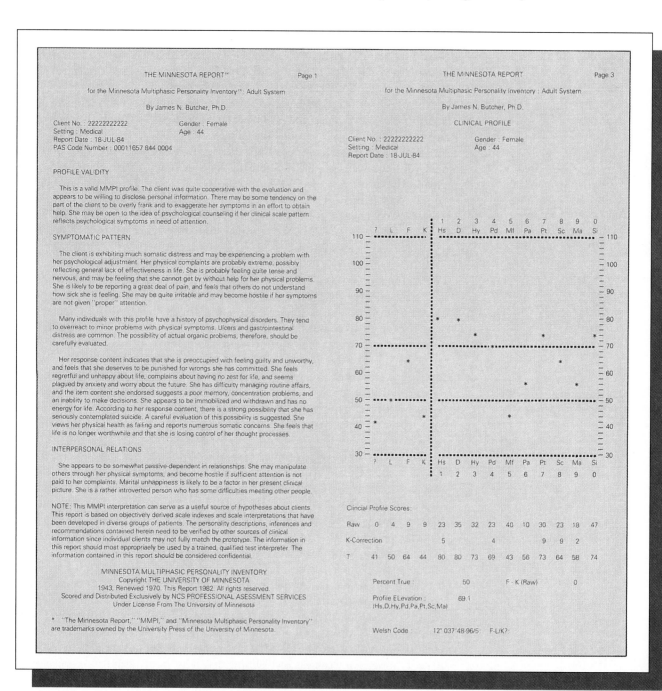

Figure 10.5 A Computerized Printout of an MMPI Profile

Recently, the MMPI has undergone a major revision, and it is now called the *MMPI-2* (Dahlstrom et al., 1989). Some items have been dropped, new ones added, and others rewritten to remove sexist language and themes that are no longer culturally relevant. The most dramatic change is the addition of 15 new *content scales*. For each of 15 clinically relevant topics (such as anxiety or family problems), items were selected on two bases: if they seemed theoretically related to the topic area and if each scale measures a single, unified concept. The MMPI-2's clinical and content scales are given in **Table 10.3** on the next page. You'll notice that most of the clinical scales measure several related concepts and that the names of the content scales are simple and self-explanatory. The benefits of the MMPI include its established strengths as a test, its ease and economy of administration, and its usefulness for research. However, the MMPI is not without its faults. Its clinical scales have been criticized because they measure several things at once, and because the scale names are confusing and do not correspond to what they measure. Another shortcoming of the MMPI is that it has little to do with normal personality; the items were selected to measure clinical problems, so the inventory is not well-suited to measure personality in nonpatient populations.

The CPI. **Harrison Gough** (1957) created the California Psychological Inventory (CPI) to measure individual differences in personality among people who are more or less normal and well adjusted. Its personality scales measure "folk concepts"—behavioral qualities that lay persons can easily understand, such as Dominance, Self-Control, Tolerance, and Intellectual Efficiency. All the scales are presented on a profile sheet that shows how a person scored on each scale relative to same-sex norms.

The most recent version of the CPI contains 20 folk scales. Over the years, the CPI has been administered to thousands of people all over the world and has been the subject of many research studies, generating valuable archives of data.

The CPI has been used to study personality structure in healthy adults and to evaluate characteristic personality structures of various groups, such as people in different occupations. Studies employing the CPI have helped psychologists understand how personality develops and how personality traits in young adulthood are related to life events.

Like the MMPI, the CPI has been criticized because many of its scales measure several different things at once, and because certain scales seem to measure overlapping concepts. However, unlike the MMPI, the CPI scales are easy to understand, because the names have been changed to reflect what the scales measure.

NEO-PI: The Big Five Inventory. The NEO Personality Inventory (NEO-PI) was also designed to assess personality characteristics in normal adults. It measures the five-factor model of personality, sometimes called *The Big Five*, which we discussed earlier in this chapter. If you took the NEO-PI, you would receive a profile sheet that showed your standardized scores relative to a large comparison group on each of the five major dimensions: Neuroticism (N), Extroversion (E), Openness (O), Agreeableness (A), and Conscientiousness (C).

The NEO is used to study personality stability and change across the life span as well as the relationship of personality characteristics to physical health and various life events, such as career success or early retirement. The NEO may be useful in career counseling—to help people select jobs that are right for them. However, it has never been validated for making decisions about hiring or promoting employees.

The Myers-Briggs Type Indicator. This popular personality test, based on Carl Jung's typology theory (1923, 1971), assigns people to one of sixteen cate-

Table 10.3 MMPI-2 Clinical and Content Scales, 1989

CLINICAL SCALES AND DESCRIPTIONS	CONTENT SCALES
Hypochondriasis (Hs): Abnormal concern with bodily functions	Anxiety
Depression (D): Pessimism; hopelessness; slowing of action and thought	Fears Obsessiveness
Conversion Hysteria (Hy): Unconscious use of mental problems to avoid conflicts or responsibility	Depression
Psychopathic Deviate (Pd): Disregard for social custom; shallow emotions; inability to profit from experience	Health Concerns Bizarre Mentation
Masculinity-Femininity (Mf): Differences between men and women	Anger Cynicism
Paranoia (Pa): Suspiciousness; delusions of grandeur or persecution	Antisocial Practices Type A (workaholic)
Psychasthenia (Pt): Obsessions; compulsions; fears; guilt; indecisiveness	Low Self-Esteem
Schizophrenia (Sc): Bizarre, unusual thoughts or behavior; withdrawal; hallucinations; delusions	Social Discomfort Family Problems
Hypomania (Ma): Emotional excitement; flight of ideas; overactivity	Work Interference
Social Introversion (Si): Shyness; disinterest in others; insecurity	Negative Treatment Indicators (negative attitudes about doctors and treatment)

gories or types. Developed by Peter Myers and Isabel Briggs, the test attempts to find "an orderly reason for personality differences" or the ways people perceive their world and make judgments about it (Myers, 1962, 1976, 1980).

Basic differences in perception and judgment are assumed to result in corresponding differences in behavior. Both Perception (P) and Judgment (J) are subdivided into dual ways of perceiving—by direct sensing (S) and unconscious intuition (N)—and dual ways of judging—by thinking (T) and feeling (F). The added factor in the Myers-Briggs test is preferences for Extroversion (E) or Introversion (I). This factor is based on Jung's idea that people focus on either their inner or outer worlds. Sixteen types emerge from the combination of these preferences, such as extroverts who judge thinking with intuition, or introverts who perceive by sensing with feeling.

A major use of this test is relating type to occupation—showing that certain preferences for perceiving, thinking, and extroversion or introversion influence occupational choice and job satisfaction (McCaulley, 1978). Its appeal lies in its ability to categorize people into a small number of types that simplify the enormous complexity of personality differences between individuals.

Projective Tests

Have you ever looked at a cloud and seen a face or the shape of an animal? If you shared your interpretations with friends, you probably found that they saw different images. Psychologists rely on a similar phenomenon when they use projective tests for personality assessment.

In a **projective test,** a person is given a series of stimuli that are purposely ambiguous, such as abstract patterns, incomplete pictures, and drawings that can be interpreted in many ways. The person may be asked to describe the patterns, finish the pictures, or tell stories about the drawings. Because the stimuli are vague, responses to them are determined by what the person brings to the situation—namely, inner feelings, motives, and conflicts that are *projected* onto the situations.

Projective tests were first used by psychoanalysts who hoped that such tests would reveal their patients' unconscious personality dynamics. For example, to uncover emotionally charged thoughts and fears, Carl Jung studied subjects' **word associations** to common words ("What is the first thing brought to mind by the word *house*?").

Two of the most common projective techniques in use today are the Rorschach test and the Thematic Apperception Test (TAT).

The Rorschach. In the Rorschach test, developed by Swiss psychiatrist **Hermann Rorschach** in 1921, the ambiguous stimuli are symmetrical inkblots (Rorschach, 1942). Some are black and white and some are colored (see **Figure 10.6**). A respondent is first shown an inkblot and asked, "Tell me what you see, what it might be to you. There are no right or wrong answers." The tester first records verbatim what the subject says, how much time she takes to respond, the total time she takes per inkblot, and the way she handles the inkblot card. In a second phase called an *inquiry,* the respondent is reminded of the previous responses and asked to elaborate on them.

Interpreting a person's scores into a coherent portrait of personality dynamics is a complex, highly subjective process that relies on clinical expertise and skilled intuition. The Rorschach has questionable soundness as a testing instrument because it is based on untestable psychodynamic concepts, such as "unconscious drives." Nonetheless, it is recommended as an indirect way to identify sources of information, such as sexual interests or aggressive fantasies that people may resent being questioned about or will lie about on objective tests (Levy & Orr, 1959). The Rorschach is gaining renewed popularity among clinicians interested in using it in combination with other forms of objective personality assessment.

The TAT. In the Thematic Apperception Test (TAT), developed by U.S. psychologist **Henry Murray** in 1938, respondents are shown pictures of ambiguous scenes. For each one they are asked to generate a story, describing what the people in the scenes are doing and thinking, what led up to each event, and how each situation will end. In theory, the respondent perceives the elements in the actual picture and further *apperceives* (or fills in) "obvious" interpretations and explanations. These apperceptions are not in the picture, but are really products of the respondent's own thoughts and feelings.

The psychologist administering the TAT evaluates the structure and content of the stories, as well as the behavior of the individual telling them, in an attempt to discover some of the respondent's major concerns, motivations,

projective test Personality assessment technique in which respondent is asked to interpret ambiguous stimuli.

word associations Personality assessment techniques in which individual generates responses triggered by common words.

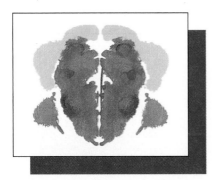

Figure 10.6 A Sample Rorschach Inkblot What do you see? Does your interpretation of this inkblot reveal anything about your personality?

and personality characteristics. For example, an examiner might evaluate a person as "conscientious" if his stories concerned people who lived up to their obligations and if he told them in a serious, orderly way. The test can be used with clinical patients to reveal emotional problems, or with normal individuals to reveal dominant needs, such as needs for power, affiliation, and achievement (McClelland, 1961).

Can Personality Be Tested? Some scholars refer to personality tests as "techniques" or "assessment" instruments. Unlike the kinds of tests you encounter in school, personality tests don't test how *much* personality you have, but rather they assess the measurable *qualities* of that personality. In essence, the goal of personality instruments is description, not evaluation.

The most effective and useful personality assessments are based on one or more major personality theories. With theory as a guiding system, professional psychologists are able to collect information that might not be readily available. More importantly, psychologists are able to interpret and apply that information more precisely and fairly than if they had to rely on impressions, hunches, and "intuitions" about people.

SUMMING UP

Personality tests are either objective or projective. Objective tests such as the MMPI-2, the CPI, and the NEO-PI are very reliable and valid for specific purposes. All three are valuable research tools, in part because of the enormous archives of data available about them. In applied settings, the MMPI-2 is good for making rough clinical diagnoses and forming hypotheses about clients. The CPI and NEO-PI are good for finding out about a person's preferences, values, interpersonal style, and level of functioning. They can be used to plan treatment programs or aid in self-understanding. In addition, the CPI measures various cognitive and social skills, which makes it especially useful for career counseling. Similarly, the Myers-Briggs test, which identifies 16 different types of people, has been useful in vocational and career counseling.

On the other hand, projective techniques such as the Rorschach and the TAT depend heavily on the clinician's subjective judgment and are not as reliable or valid for revealing personality characteristics. The Rorschach involves having a respondent interpret the visual design of an inkblot, while the TAT asks subjects to tell stories about what they see depicted in pictures. Both techniques rely on the assumption that inner motives and themes will be projected onto the ambiguous test stimuli. These tests are best used as therapeutic icebreakers and as sources of preliminary clinical hypotheses to be confirmed by more objective techniques.

The Psychology of the Person *How is personality defined? How do researchers study it? How do personality theories meet the goals of psychology?*

Personality is what characterizes an individual—what is unique about a person across different situations and over time. Personality theorists study the whole person as the sum of the separate processes of feelings, thoughts, and actions. The focus of the idiographic approach is the organization of the unique person. The nomothetic approach attempts to understand all people in terms of individual differences along common dimensions.

Key Terms
  personality, p. 371
  idiographic approach, p. 372
  nomothetic approach, p. 372

 Personality Theories *What are the six major personality theories? How do they resemble each other? How do they differ?*

Some theorists categorize people by all-or-none types and assume that the types are related to particular characteristic behaviors. Examples include Hippocrates' four-humors theory, Sheldon's somatotypes, and the Jungian types of the Myers-Briggs test.

Other theorists view traits as the building blocks of personality. Allport differentiated cardinal, central, and secondary traits, while Eysenck combined the type and trait approaches and explored the relationship between personality and physiological characteristics. The Big Five factors describe the central themes among all trait words and personality concepts. Traits are difficult to employ accurately because specific behaviors are not consistent across different situations. However, the consistency paradox is resolved by showing that traits do predict general behavioral coherence.

Freud's psychodynamic theory accepted Darwin's emphasis on instinctive biological energies as sources of all human motivation. Basic concepts of Freudian theory include psychic determinism, the power of early experiences, psychic energy, and powerful unconscious processes. During the oral, anal, phallic, latency, and genital stages of psychosexual development, children associate pleasure with different ideas and regions of bodily stimulation. Personality structure consists of the id, superego, and the ego. Unacceptable impulses are repressed and ego defense mechanisms are developed to lessen anxiety and bolster self-esteem. Post-Freudians such as Alfred Adler and Carl Jung have put greater emphasis on lifelong development, ego functioning, and social variables.

Humanistic theories focus on the growth potential of the individual. Humanistic theories are characteristically more optimistic than psychoanalytic concepts. At the core of Rogers's person-centered personality theory is the concept of self-actualization, a constant striving to realize one's potential and to develop one's talents.

Social-learning theorists focus on understanding individual differences in behavior and personality as a consequence of different histories of reinforcement. Cognitive theorists emphasize individual differences in the perception and subjective interpretation of the environment. Bandura's cognitive social-learning theory combines principles of learning with an emphasis on social interactions. Reciprocal determinism, observational learning, and self-efficacy are concepts that are critical in the analysis of person-behavior-situation interactions.

Applying personality theories to the self involves developing an understanding of the self-concept—a dynamic mental structure that motivates, organizes, and regulates interpersonal behaviors. Different personality theories vary in their assumptions about the fundamental structure and function of human nature.

Key Terms

personality types, p. 374
somatotype, p. 374
trait, p. 375
cardinal trait, p. 375
central trait, p. 375
secondary trait, p. 375
The Big Five, p. 376
consistency paradox, p. 377
psychodynamic personality theories, p. 380
psychic determinism, p. 380
psychosexual stages, p. 381
oral stage, p. 381
anal stage, p. 381
phallic stage, p. 381
latency stage, p. 381
genital stage, p. 381
fixation, p. 381
Eros, p. 382
libido, p. 382
Thanatos, p. 382
Unconscious, p. 382
id, p. 383
superego, p. 383
ego, p. 383
repression, p. 383
ego defense mechanisms, p. 383
anxiety, p. 383
self-actualization, p. 385
collective unconscious, p. 386
archetype, p. 386
analytic psychology, p. 386
personal construct, p. 389
reciprocal determinism, p. 390
observational learning, p. 390
self-efficacy, p. 391
self-concept, p. 393
self-esteem, p. 393
self-handicapping, p. 393
behavioral confirmation, p. 393

Major Contributors

Hippocrates, p. 374
Sheldon, William, p. 374
Allport, Gordon, p. 375
Eysenck, Hans, p. 375
Freud, Sigmund, p. 380
Adler, Alfred, p. 386
Jung, Carl, p. 386
Rogers, Carl, p. 387
Kelly, George, p. 389
Mischel, Walter, p. 389
Bandura, Albert, p. 390
James, William, p. 393
Markus, Hazel, p. 393

3 **Assessing Personality** *What are the two major approaches to personality assessment? What are the major personality inventories in use today? How are projective tests thought to reveal personality?*

Personality characteristics are assessed by both objective and projective tests. The MMPI is a personality inventory used to diagnose clinical problems. The CPI is an inventory intended for use with normal populations. The NEO-PI measures five major dimensions of personality: Neuroticism, Extroversion, Openness, Agreeableness, and Conscientiousness. The Myers-Briggs Type Indicator identifies 16 personality types based on Jung's type theory, organized along four dimensions: perceiving-judging; intuiting-sensing; thinking-feeling; and introversion-extroversion. All four inventories have been used in studies of personality structure and applied in career counseling and psychotherapy.

Projective tests of personality involve having subjects interpret or respond to ambiguous stimuli. Many of these techniques are less reliable than objective inventories because they rely on untestable concepts. In clinical use they are usually combined with other assessment techniques. One popular projective test is the Rorschach test, in which respondents interpret inkblots. In Murray's TAT, the test subject composes a story about an ambiguous picture. In both cases, themes and patterns in responses are assumed to indicate concerns or motives that are important to subjects.

Key Terms

personality inventory, p. 395
projective test, p. 399
word associations, p. 399

Major Contributors

Gough, Harrison, p. 397
Rorschach, Hermann, p. 399
Murray, Henry, p. 399

Chapter 10: Personality

For each of the following items, choose the single correct or best answer. Correct answers, explanations, and page references appear in the Appendix.

1. Implicit personality theories are usually based on _____ .
    A. case studies
    B. aggregated case studies
    C. personality inventory scores
    D. intuition and limited observations

2. Your new teacher announces in class: "In my experience, I've found that all students have a certain degree of laziness. Some have a lot, and others have only a little. But everyone has some." This teacher seems to favor the _____ approach to understanding personality.
    A. idiographic
    B. nomothetic
    C. humanistic
    D. psychodynamic

3. "I don't like thin people," your friend remarks, explaining why a new classmate is not attractive, "they're too nervous!" This assumption reveals that your friend favors a _____ theory of personality.
    A. trait
    B. type
    C. humanistic
    D. social-learning

4. Which of the following personality dimensions is *not* one of The Big Five factors common to all traits?
    A. Intelligence
    B. Emotional Stability
    C. Conscientiousness
    D. Openness to Experience

5. According to Freud, the _____ is the part of the personality that corresponds roughly to our notion of the conscience.
    A. id
    B. ego
    C. superego
    D. libido

6. A unique aspect of humanistic theories is their focus on _____ , which sets them apart from the determinism that characterizes psychodynamic theories.
    A. instincts
    B. freedom
    C. the unconscious
    D. sexuality

7. _____ developed a cognitive social-learning theory whose key concepts include observational learning, reciprocal determinism, and self-efficacy.
    A. Alfred Adler
    B. Hans Eysenck
    C. George Kelly
    D. Albert Bandura

8. Self- _____ refers to a generalized evaluative attitude toward the self, which can strongly influence one's thoughts, moods, and behavior.
    A. concept
    B. esteem
    C. handicapping
    D. efficacy

9. Which of the following personality assessment techniques does *not* belong with the others?
    A. CPI
    B. TAT
    C. NEO-PI
    D. MMPI-2

10. Which of the following is *not* one of the dimensions assessed by the Myers-Briggs Type Indicator?
    A. thinking vs. feeling
    B. sensing vs. intuiting
    C. stable vs. unstable
    D. extroverted vs. introverted

IF YOU'RE INTERESTED . . .

Freud. (Video: 1962, black-and-white, 120 minutes). Directed by John Huston; starring Montgomery Clift, Susannah York, Larry Parks.

Intriguing, engrossing story of Sigmund Freud's early work and theories, based on his use of hypnosis and dream analysis in treating hysteria. Interesting story-in-a-story dramatizes influences on Freud's own personality, and his efforts to understand himself.

Gay, P. (1990). *Freud: A life for our time.* New York: W. W. Norton and Co.

A comprehensive but engaging and detailed biography by historian Peter Gay, with stories of Freud's influences and relationships, and photographs of the people and places important to the development of psychoanalytic theory.

Lust for life. (Video: 1956, color, 122 minutes). Directed by Vincente Minnelli; starring Kirk Douglas, Anthony Quinn, James Donald, Pamela Brown.

Moving and visually stunning adaptation of Irving Stone's biography of French impressionist painter Vincent Van Gogh, who sold but one work in his lifetime, and died of a self-inflicted gunshot wound. Strong images of the influences and anguish that moved this great artist.

Maclean, H. N. (1993). *Once upon a time: A true story of memory, murder, and a trial.* New York: HarperCollins.

The story of Eileen Franklin-Lipsker, whose recollection of long-repressed memories led to the reopening of a 20-year-old unsolved murder case, and the conviction of her own father for the murder of her childhood friend.

Patton. (Video: 1970, color, 169 minutes). Directed by Franklin Schaffner; starring George C. Scott, Karl Malden, Stephen Young, Michael Strong.

Wonderful screen biography of brilliant, tempestuous General George Patton, Allied commander of mechanized forces in European and Mediterranean conflicts of World War II. Poignant, vivid scenes illustrate the influences, consistencies, and surprises assembled within this one powerful personality.

Rogers, C. R. (1980). *A way of being.* Boston: Houghton-Mifflin.

Invitation to the person-centered view of personality by Carl Rogers, founder of that approach within psychology.

Skinner, B. F. (1982). *Beyond freedom and dignity.* New York: Bantam/Vintage.

By the late, great behaviorist, this work is an appeal for an alternative understanding of human action, rooted in science and applied to improving the human condition.

Trillin, C. (1993). *Remembering Denny.* New York: Farrar, Straus & Giroux.

Eloquent essayist Calvin Trillin's reflections on the life and times of his late friend Denny Hansen, a promising fellow member of Yale's Class of 1957 who somehow never became a superstar as his friends predicted. Trillin speculates on the stressors that shaped Denny's life and led to his recent death by suicide.

Chapter 11   **Individual Differences**

Preview Questions

1. Why do we assess individual differences? What are the historical origins of assessment? What goals do formal and informal assessment have in common? What qualities make an assessment technique effective? On what kinds of information do psychologists base assessments?

2. What is intelligence? How was intelligence testing originally developed? What do IQ tests measure? How do different theories account for intelligence? How do biology and environment combine to influence an individual's intelligence?

3. How can vocational interests and abilities be assessed to support career planning? What are the components of a job analysis? What qualities are important to make testing fair and meaningful?

At the age of 37, newspaper and magazine columnist Bob Greene started to suspect that he "was dumber than [he] had been in high school" (Greene, 1985). At 17 he had been able to add, subtract, and multiply without using a calculator. Twenty years later, those skills seemed to have disappeared completely. To see if he could still make the grade, Greene decided to retake the Scholastic Aptitude Test (SAT), the three-hour examination of verbal and mathematical abilities that many colleges use to select students for admission. Greene sent in his fee, and on the designated Saturday morning, he showed up at his local high school with six sharpened No. 2 pencils in his pocket. After one hour, "all of us looked dazed, unhappy, and disoriented, although I believe that I was the only student to go to the water fountain and take an Inderal for his blood pressure" (Greene, 1985).

The SAT was designed as a standardized measure of high-school students' academic performance. Admissions officers had had difficulty interpreting grade-point averages from thousands of high schools with different standards and grading policies. Although the tests were intended to be objective evaluations, they have been accused of bias, and despite many revisions over the years, it has been difficult to quell those accusations. Across all ethnic groups, average SAT scores increase as family income goes up. Whites and Asian Americans consistently outperform Mexican Americans, Puerto Ricans, and African Americans (Hacker, 1986). Men on the average score higher than women (Gordon, 1990).

However, the SAT is changing. Consider the use of calculators. When the SAT was introduced in 1941, pocket calculators did not exist. When Greene took the test for the second time, the proctor instructed that "Calculators or wristwatches with calculator functions may not be used." In 1994, students will be permitted to use calculators for the first time and 20 percent of the math questions will require students to produce their own response rather than select from a set of multiple-choice alternatives. Test-takers will have to come up with their own answers for questions such as "If the population of a certain country is increasing at the rate of one person every 12 seconds, by how many persons does it increase every half hour?" (Educational Testing Service, 1990).

When Greene's test results finally arrived in the mail, his hands were shaking. He felt ridiculous. After all, he already had a college degree and a successful career. Nevertheless, he nervously ripped open the envelope. Greene's verbal score had gone up 56 points, not surprising for a writer. In math, over the two decades, his score had nose-dived by 200 points! Just as it is difficult to know why some groups perform better than others on the SAT, it is impossible to know with certainty why Bob Greene's math score plummeted. Wasn't the test supposed to measure his basic aptitude for math—what he understood and not just what he had learned? Had his math aptitude decreased because in his work he doesn't often use the math skills that he once practiced regularly in high school? Would Greene have improved his score if he had signed up for a course that prepared him for the test? Had he just been watching too much TV where the only numbers he needed to know were the channels of his favorite stations?

Introduction

Some people consider the use of psychological tests to assess differences between individuals' mental abilities to be "one of psychology's unquestioned success stories" (Tyler, 1988). That "success" is determined in several ways. Psychological tests compare people on various dimensions according to objective standards that are not open to the biases of subjective interpreters. They are supposed to be fair comparisons of the mental capacities of all individuals taking the same test under the same conditions. These tests have been perceived as "tools of democracy," allowing selection of individuals for education and employment to be based on what the individuals know and can show, rather than on *whom* they know and what their family can show (Sokol, 1987).

Any test can be said to work if it accurately predicts performance in future situations. Test results, such as those from the SAT, are generally good predictors of later academic grades, just as tests for personnel selection predict some types of job performance. When a person's aptitudes, interests, attitudes, and personality are all taken into account, the chances of improving the "fits" between person and school or person and job greatly increase—to the benefit of all concerned.

Psychological testing is big business. Many psychologists spend a great deal of time on the construction, evaluation, administration, and interpretation of psychological tests. Testing is a multimillion-dollar industry; thousands of children and adults regularly take some form of the many tests distributed by more than 40 major U.S. test publishers. Virtually everyone in our society who has attended school, gone to work, joined the military services, or registered in a mental health clinic has undergone some kind of psychological testing.

There's another side to this success story. Despite the widespread use of standardized psychological tests, some psychologists believe that testing is psychology's worst embarrassment. These critics argue that many of the tests are not objective measures of native ability and basic capacity. The tests may overcome the biases of teacher and employer evaluations, but they are themselves biased in more fundamental ways because they are based, in part, on specific learning experiences that vary with social class, cultural background, and personal experiences.

Writer Bob Greene's SAT scores show that people improve in the tasks they practice and worsen in the tasks they neglect. Similarly, practicing test-taking actually can improve performance. The Educational Testing Service, which designs and distributes the SAT, markets courses for high schools and how-to-succeed books for the general public. Because scores can be improved with practice, schools have been accused of "teaching the test" rather than enabling students to master the material on which they will be tested. Some students additionally pursue private "prep courses" that they hope will improve their performance on specific tests. Such practices underscore the role of tests not only in planning life decisions, but as goals in themselves.

In this chapter, we will examine the foundations and applications of psychological assessment. We will review the contributions psychologists have made to our understanding of individual differences in intelligence and vocational ability. Our focus will be on what makes any test useful, how tests work, and why they may not always do the job they were intended to do. We will conclude by considering the role of psychological assessment in our personal and professional lives.

Assessing Individual Differences

The most damning criticism of psychological tests comes from those who believe that testing mental ability contributes to *elitism;* these tests play up the importance of *differences* between people while most of the rest of psychology focuses on similarities. Some people use test scores as evidence of innate mental abilities. Then the evidence is used to justify discrimination against the disadvantaged poor, women, minorities, and immigrants in educational and career opportunities and in formulating public policy (Gould, 1981; Hirsch et al., 1990; Kamin, 1974). For example, if inner-city students attend poorly equipped, understaffed schools, they will not perform as well as students in wealthier suburban neighborhood schools. Suppose most inner-city students are minority students. A local private school might try to keep minority students out by admitting only students who perform well on an admissions test and meet a minimum standard—a cut-off level that is hard for students from minority backgrounds to meet.

psychological assessment Use of specified procedures to evaluate people's abilities, behaviors, and personal qualities.

Psychological assessment is the use of specified testing procedures to evaluate the abilities, behaviors, and personal qualities of people. Assessment contributes to an individual's understanding of herself so that she can make more informed decisions about current problems or future choices (Maloney & Ward, 1976). Psychological assessment is often referred to as the measurement of individual differences, since the majority of assessments specify how an individual is different from or similar to other people on a given dimension. "In Focus: The Individual Differences Perspective" on the next page focuses on this distinction between individual differences and shared experiences—an essential distinction in scientific psychology.

The use of *objective* assessment procedures to evaluate a person's abilities and skills eliminates the need for the subjective and sometimes biased evaluations of authority figures. As we saw in Chapter 10, assessment is especially valuable in helping clinical psychologists detect problems that may require special counseling or treatment. Keep in mind that assessment in general makes assumptions about whether and how to compare individuals and scrutinize differences between them.

When psychologists try to understand the causes of a given behavior, they search for variables in one of two places: inside the person or outside in the situation. In the next chapter we will explore how social psychologists study the power of situations to influence our behavior. In this chapter, we examine how personality psychologists investigate the inner determinants of human performance. How and why do people differ from each other—in the same situation or on the same task? Let's review some milestones in the history of assessment and examine how individual differences have been identified and evaluated.

History of Assessment

The development of formal tests and procedures for assessment is a relatively new enterprise in psychology, coming into wide use only in the early 1900s. Long before Western psychology began to devise tests to evaluate people, assessment techniques were commonplace in ancient China. In fact, China employed a sophisticated program of civil service testing over 4,000 years ago. Officials were required to demonstrate their competence every third year at an oral examination. Two thousand years later, during the Han Dynasty, written civil service tests were used to assess competence in the areas of law, the military, agriculture, and geography. During the Ming Dynasty (1368–1644), public officials were chosen on the basis of their performance at three stages of an objective selection procedure, involving several days of examinations and written work. China's selection procedures were observed and described by British diplomats and missionaries in the early 1800s. Modified versions of China's system were soon adopted by the British and later by the Americans for the selection of civil service personnel (Wiggins, 1973).

In Focus:

THE INDIVIDUAL DIFFERENCES PERSPECTIVE

Psychological assessment brings into focus a basic tension in psychology: *individual differences* versus *situational influence*. The two perspectives are interwoven, and an appreciation of this tension is necessary to assess individual differences.

Everyone Is Different

The **individual differences** perspective focuses on identifying the differentiations among people, the characteristics and patterns that distinguish one person from others. For example, personality psychology favors an individual differences approach, whether it is idiographic (person-centered) or nomothetic (trait-centered) in emphasis.

People who know little or nothing about psychology assume that *all* of psychology is about individual differences. For example, newspapers and magazines include features on "Are You Commitmentphobic?" and "How to Tell If Your Friends are Loyal." Talk shows and pop "psychologists" explore different "personality types": procrastinators, pathological liars, teenagers who are obsessed with their looks, or men who like older women. A barrage of such "pseudoscience" can leave you with the impression that, to know yourself and others, you must first figure out what *kind* of person acts in certain ways. This notion is tempting because it is so simple; the problem is that it may also be simplistic.

Individual differences are fascinating and get lots of attention from researchers. But researchers repeatedly find that the differences in people's characteristics do not explain the differences in their behavior. For example, what

kind of person will be most likely to help a stranger in need? Perhaps measures of traits such as generosity, altruism, or religiousness could be taken; high scorers should be more likely than low scorers to respond in a helpful way when they get the chance. Such measures are a common model for research on individual differences. Unfortunately, the highest correlation researchers find between a given trait and appropriate behavior is only .30 (Ross & Nisbett, 1991). (Since .30 is much closer to zero—no correlation—than to a perfect correlation of 1.00, you can see that this statistic does not indicate a very impressive connection between traits and actions.) Although it seems desirable to be able to predict people's behavior from their distinctive qualities, human behavior is not that simple.

Everyone Is the Same

Why do we think in terms of individual differences if such differences don't predict behavior very well? For one thing, as we shall consider in the next chapter, when we watch others, we notice *them*—not their circumstances. This biased perspective causes us to overlook a powerful source of influence: the *situation*. Individual differences in important qualities—such as intelligence, extroversion, and emotional stability—will influence and show up as general behavioral differences. But specific situations also influence how people behave. *Where* you are may matter as much as *who* you are.

For example, will you stop to help a stranger in distress? If you are especially friendly or "good," perhaps these qualities will motivate you to stop. But as we

will see in the next chapter, all those helpful qualities may not be enough to overcome the situation if the circumstances do not cooperate. For example, if there would be real danger to you if you interfered, or you are in a hurry and cannot stop or slow down to assist a person in need, or if there are many others around, you will probably *not* intervene, regardless of your virtues (Darley & Batson, 1973; Ross & Nisbett, 1991). Situations have power, and it shows up in behavior.

The individual differences approach does not deny situational forces, but it minimizes the power of situations and concentrates on the ways in which people differ and how these differences show up in our actions. In contrast, the *situationist perspective* sees behavior as influenced by external as well as internal factors. **Situationism** is the principle that situations and circumstances outside oneself have the power to influence behavior (Ross & Nisbett, 1991). Some situations are so powerful, in fact, that almost anyone—regardless of unique qualities and personality traits—will respond to them in the same ways. For example, you may think of yourself as a free spirit, more independent than most of your classmates, but if your instructor were to suddenly order the class to "Raise your right hands," you would most likely comply quickly, along with everyone else. Quickly obeying a direct order from a respected authority figure does not prove you are a weak-minded conformist—does it? It does show that some situations are compelling and leveling, affecting people similarly despite their differences.

---

individual differences Distinctions and variations among people's characteristics and behavior patterns.

situationism View that our actions are more influenced than we realize by factors in our settings rather than by personal qualities.

The key figure in the era of modern intelligence testing was an upper-class Englishman, **Sir Francis Galton.** His book *Hereditary Genius* (published in 1869) greatly influenced subsequent thinking on the methods, theories, and practices of testing. Galton (who was a half-cousin to Charles Darwin) attempted to apply Darwinian evolutionary theory to the study of human abilities. He was interested in how and why people differ in their abilities. He wondered why some people were gifted and successful while many others were not.

Sir Francis Galton (1822–1911)

eugenics Movement that advocated improving the human species by encouraging biologically superior people to interbreed while discouraging biologically inferior types from having offspring.

Galton was the first to postulate that differences in intelligence were *quantifiable* in terms of degrees of intelligence, and that these differences were *normally distributed* in the population, meaning that few people possessed extremely high or low intelligence while most people clustered in the middle. Galton also believed that intelligence could be measured by objective tests, and that the precise extent to which two sets of test scores were related could be determined by a statistical procedure he called *co-relations,* now known as *correlations.* These ideas proved to be of lasting value.

Unfortunately, Galton also believed that genius was inherited. He argued that talent (or eminence) passed through generations of families; nurture had only a minimal effect on intelligence. Then Galton went one big step further in his assumption: Galton believed that intelligence was somehow related to moral worth. Galton attempted to base public policy on the concept of genetically superior and inferior people. He coined the term **eugenics**, and started a movement that advocated improving the human species by applying evolutionary theory to family planning. Biologically superior people were encouraged to interbreed, while biologically inferior people were discouraged from having offspring. Galton wrote, "There exists a sentiment, for the most part quite unreasonable, against the gradual extinction of an inferior race" (Galton, 1883, p. 200).

These controversial ideas were endorsed and later expanded by many who argued forcefully that the intellectually superior race should propagate at the expense of those with inferior minds. Among the proponents of these ideas were American psychologists Henry Goddard and Lewis Terman and, of course, Nazi dictator Adolf Hitler. The horrors of the Nazi Holocaust of the 1930s and 1940s, in which millions of people were exterminated for being "inferior" to the ideals of the Aryan race, made racist notions of "natural" superiority even more gruesome.

In the United States, the eugenics movement never became a powerful motive for mate selection and family decisions, primarily because Americans value their civil rights and individual freedom when making such personal choices. Unfortunately, many other communities still wage battles of "ethnic cleansing"—the murder and exile of unwanted people. Among today's battles are those involving the Serbs, Croatians, and Muslims of the former Yugoslavia. Nonetheless, most countries are less tolerant than ever before of persecutions motivated by baseless claims of racial superiority.

Purposes of Assessment

Most people do not use their interest in individual differences to justify racism. The assessment of individual differences has practical, everyday goals. The goals of formal assessment resemble your own concerns when you size up another person. You may want to know how smart, trustworthy, creative, responsible, or dangerous a new acquaintance is; you may attempt to evaluate these qualities with whatever evidence you can gather informally.

Scientific psychology attempts to formalize the procedures by which accurate predictions about individual behavior can be made. Assessment begins with the measurement of a limited number of individual attributes and samples of behavior. This narrow body of personal information in a testing situation forms the basis of predictions about the individual's reactions at another time in a real-life situation that is not identical to the test situation. Psychologists use assessment techniques to understand individuals and how they differ from one another. The science of assessment is also used to test psychological theories and concepts, such as personality structure or intelligence.

While a clinical psychologist uses testing to make predictions about a *particular* client, a research psychologist tries to discover the regularities in personality in the *general* population that indicate behavior patterns or life events. For example, a research psychologist might test to see if there are certain ages at which children acquire a certain skill, such as self-disclosure or conflict resolution.

When certain questions arise about an individual's behavioral or mental functioning, the individual is referred to a psychologist who is trained to make an assessment that might provide some answers. A judge may want to know if a confessed murderer is capable of understanding the consequences of such actions, or a teacher may want to know why a child has difficulty learning. A mental health worker may want to know the extent to which a patient's problems result from psychological disorders or from physical, organic disorders. When a psychologist's judgment have a profound impact on a person's life, a *complete* assessment must involve more than just psychological testing. Tests may be very helpful, but results should be interpreted in light of *all* available information about a person, including medical history, family life, previous difficulties, or noteworthy achievements (Matarazzo, 1990).

Assessment Methods

There are important differences between our own *informal* assessments of self and others and the *formal* assessments of professionals. Formal psychological assessments are developed more systematically, applied in a more organized way, and used for carefully specified purposes.

We will first consider the characteristics that make professional assessments *formal*. We will then examine some of the techniques and sources of information psychologists use to make assessments. While some techniques are derived from particular *theoretical* perspectives, others are based on purely *empirical* grounds. Empirically constructed techniques are guided only by data; they are built to make specific predictions and, therefore, utilize the items or questions that do the job regardless of whether or not they make theoretical sense. For example, students might be asked to indicate their views on the importance of sexual intimacy in maintaining a personal relationship. If males consistently differ from females in their scores on this measure—for example, by expressing much greater permissiveness and emphasis on sex—then these data could be used as one test of gender differences, even without offering any theory about why the two groups differ.

Formal Assessment. To effectively classify individuals or select those people with particular qualities, an assessment procedure should meet three requirements. The assessment instrument should be *reliable, valid,* and *standardized.* If it fails to meet these requirements, researchers cannot be sure whether the conclusions of the assessment can be trusted.

Reliability. A test is *reliable* if it measures something consistently. **Reliability** is the extent to which an assessment instrument can be trusted to give consistent scores, either on retests or when different raters judge the same performance. If your bathroom scale gives you a different reading each time you step on it (even though you haven't eaten or changed your clothing and little time has passed between testings), the scale is not doing its job. You would call the instrument *unreliable* and throw it out, because you could not count on it to give consistent results.

One straightforward way to determine whether a test is reliable is to calculate its **test-retest reliability.** This measure indicates the correlation between the scores of the same subjects on the same test given at two different times. If subjects achieve the same or a similar score as one they earned previously, we can conclude that the test is reliably measuring the same thing—behavior, ability, or any other element.

A second way to assess reliability is to administer alternate, **parallel forms** of a test that measure the same thing using different words or examples instead of giving exactly the same test twice. By presenting parallel forms, the

reliability Degree to which an assessment method yields the same score each time an individual is measured; consistency.

test-retest reliability A measure of the correlation between the scores of the same people on the same test given at two different times.

parallel forms Different versions of the same test, used to assess test reliability.

researcher reduces the effects of direct practice of the test questions, and memorization of the test questions. Parallel tests also remove any test-taker's efforts to appear consistent from one version of a test to the next. Reliable tests yield comparable scores on parallel forms of the test. For example, what is the answer to the following multiple-choice question?

> If a test yields consistent scores each time an individual is retested, the test is considered _____.
> A. valid
> B. reliable
> C. formal
> D. standardized

If you understand the concept of reliability and answer this item correctly, you should likewise be able to answer the following question:

> True or false? A test is considered valid if it yields consistent scores each time an individual is retested.

These two parallel items test for the same knowledge in a similar way. If you answer B to the first question, you will probably answer "false" to the second one.

internal consistency Degree to which different components of the same test yield similar scores; a measure of reliability.

The third measure of reliability is the **internal consistency** of responses on a single test. For example, we can compare a person's score on the odd-numbered items of a test to the score on the even-numbered items. A reliable test yields the same score for each of its halves. The test is then said to have high internal consistency on *split-half reliability*—which is obtained by splitting the test's items and assessing reliability between the two halves. These halves should be the same or very similar if the test is indeed reliable.

Although a reliable test tends to give the same test scores when it is repeated, obtaining different test scores does not necessarily mean that a test is unreliable. Sometimes the variable being measured actually changes from one testing to the next. For example, if you took the same test on theories of personality before and after reading Chapter 10, you would do better the second time—because you knew more. In addition, besides the quality or skill being tested, many other variables may affect test scores. You may have different scores on different occasions because of changes in your mood, fatigue, and level of effort you put out. These extraneous variables will alter the desired test performance, giving a false picture of your ability. Similarly, a teacher may grade an essay differently if he or she is tired after reading many student essays. In such a case, the test itself would not be unreliable, but the scoring procedure would be.

validity Extent to which a test measures what it is intended to measure.

Validity. The **validity** of a test is the degree to which it measures what an assessor intends it to measure. A valid test of intelligence measures a person's intelligence and predicts performance in situations where intelligence is important. Scores on a valid measure of creativity reflect actual creativity, not drawing ability or moods. In general, then, validity is not a property of the test itself, but a feature of the test's ability to make accurate predictions about outcomes. Validity answers the basic question, "What is the test good for?"

criterion validity Degree to which test scores indicate a result that is consistent with another standard of the same characteristic.

To assess the **criterion validity** of a test, we compare a person's score on the test to his or her score on some other standard, or *criterion*. This other performance should be theoretically associated with what was measured by the test. For example, we would compare someone's score on a typing *test* to how well (for example, how quickly and accurately) the subject actually *types* on the job. Typing performance is the criterion or standard the test is intended to predict. Ideally, scores on the criterion directly reflect a personal characteristic or behavior that is related to, but not the same as, that assessed by the test. For example, if an aptitude test is designed to predict success in college, then college grades would be an appropriate criterion. If the test scores correlate highly with college grades, then the test has criterion validity. A major task of test developers is finding appropriate, measurable criteria to determine the validity of their tests.

For many personal qualities that interest psychologists, there is no ideal criterion. For example, no single behavior or objective measure of performance can tell us how anxious, depressed, or aggressive a person is. Psychologists have theories or *constructs* about these abstract qualities. Constructs are ideas about what affects personal qualities, and the ways these show up in behavior and relate to other variables. Although there may be no perfect, direct measure of a given construct, there might be several tests or criteria that each tap into a part of the construct. For example, this chapter explores different test items and how they tap into constructs of intelligence.

A particular construct can usually be measured in more than one way. For example, a construct like "anger" could be measured by observing a person's angry behaviors or by having him complete a self-report questionnaire on frequency of angry feelings. The **construct validity** of a particular test is the degree to which it correlates positively with all the other data that represent valid measures of the construct (Loevinger, 1957). Construct validity is a subjective evaluation of the appropriateness of the available evidence for measuring a given construct. *Construct validation* is the process of combining what we know about a large set of related measures—such as different tests, judges' ratings, and observed behaviors—to determine whether a theoretical construct is useful for understanding the data. Once we have determined that a construct is a good working model that explains a large body of data, we can examine separately each of the measures of the construct. The conditions under which a test is valid may be very specific, so it is always important to ask about a test, "For what purpose is it valid?"

For example, suppose you design a test to measure the ability of medical students to cope with stress, and you find that scores on it correlate well with students' ability to cope with classroom stress. You presume your test will also correlate with students' ability to deal with stressful hospital emergencies, but you discover it does not. Since you have demonstrated some validity, the important question is not *whether* the test is valid, but *when* it is valid, and *for what purpose*. (See "Time Out for Critical Thinking.")

Validity has something in common with reliability. While reliability is measured by the degree to which a test correlates with itself (administered at different times or using different items), validity is measured by the degree to which the test correlates with something external to it (another test, a behavioral criterion, or judges' ratings). Usually, a test that is not reliable is also not valid, because a test that cannot predict *itself* will be unable to predict anything else. For example, if your class took a test of aggressiveness today and scores were uncorrelated with scores from a parallel form of the test tomorrow (demonstrating unreliability), it is unlikely that the scores from either day would predict which students had fought or argued most frequently over a week's time. The two sets of test scores cannot even make the same prediction, so it is unlikely that either form of test is valid.

Standardization and Norms. To be most useful, a measuring device should be standardized. **Standardization** is the administration of a testing device to all persons in the same way under the same conditions. Through this method, we can establish a **norm,** or statistical standard for a test that allows each individual's score to be compared with the scores of others in a defined group.

Suppose you get a score of 18 on a test designed to reveal how depressed you are. What does "18" mean? Are you a little depressed, not at all depressed, or depressed to an average degree? You need to compare your individual score to typical scores of other students. To do so, you would check the *test norms*

construct validity Degree to which test scores based on a specific characteristic correlate with other measures of the same characteristic (for example, other test scores, judges' ratings, or behaviors).

standardization Uniformity of procedures in applying treatments or recording data; in test construction, specifying population and conditions for establishing norms.

norm Standard or value based on measurements of a large group of people; in social psychology, the group standard for approved behavior.

to see what the usual range of scores is and what the average is for students of your age and sex. You have probably encountered test norms when you received your scores on aptitude tests such as the SAT. The norms told you how your scores compared to those of other students and helped you interpret how well you had done relative to that *normative population*.

Group norms are most useful when the standardization group shares important qualities with the individuals tested (such as age, social class, and experience). The group norms are a useful measure against which an individual's score can be interpreted. So whenever you are given your results on any psychological test, the first question you should ask is, "Compared to what?" What norms were used to interpret *relative* performance? For example, a student who receives a score of 46 on a psychology test may be worried about her performance until she learns that the highest score possible was 50, that her classmates' scores

A psychologist may administer a battery of tests to determine the person's level and quality of functioning in different areas.

interview Face-to-face conversation between a respondent and a researcher or counselor, for purposes of gathering information about the respondent.

life history Information about an individual's experiences based on school or military records, personal accounts, and medical data.

archival data Previously published or documented findings available in public records or cultural artifacts.

psychological test Instrument used to measure an individual's standing relative to others on some mental or behavioral characteristic.

situational behavior observations First-hand study of an individual's actions and performance in one or more settings.

ranged from 21 to 47, and that the average score was 36. In a sense, any particular score is meaningless—*until* comparative information is provided.

Sources of Information

Psychological assessment methods make use of interviews, life history or archival data, tests, and situational observations to gather information about a person. These methods also distinguish information according to the person who is supplying the information: the person being assessed or other people reporting on the person being assessed. When the person being assessed is providing the information, the methods are called *self reports;* when others are supplying the data, the methods are called *observer reports.*

We will first examine assessment techniques, and then the two reporting methods. Keep in mind that a complete assessment should use as many different techniques and sources of information as are available.

Four Assessment Techniques. An **interview** is a very direct approach to learning about someone. The interview content and style may be casual and unstructured, and tailored to fit the person being interviewed. On the other hand, interviews can be highly structured or standardized, asking very specific questions in a very specific way. Counselors find unstructured interviews useful in planning individualized treatment programs. Structured interviews are preferred for job interviews and psychological research, when it is important that many people be assessed accurately, completely, consistently, and without bias.

A well-trained interviewer must be able to accomplish five goals: put the respondent at ease; elicit the desired information; maintain control of the direction and pace of the interview; establish and maintain rapport with the respondent; and finally, bring the interview to a satisfactory conclusion.

Interview data may be supplemented with **life history** or **archival data**, information about a person's life taken from different types of available records, especially those of different time periods and in relation to other people. This information may include school or military records, written work (stories and drawings), personal journals, medical data, photographs, and videotapes.

A **psychological test** can measure virtually all aspects of human functioning, including intelligence, personality, and creativity. Unlike interviews, tests provide *quantitative* characterizations of an individual by using normative comparisons with others. In other words, tests can convert your performance to a number or set of numbers that can be directly compared to a standard. For example, if an instructor tells you that your score on a test was at the "75th percentile" for the class, this means that 25 percent of your classmates (100 – 75 = 25) earned higher scores than you—regardless of how many items were on the test. Thus a percentile score is a convenient single-number summary of test performance and class standing.

Tests are economical, easy to use, and provide important normative data in quantitative form, but they are not always useful for finding out what a person actually *does,* especially when a person cannot objectively judge or report his or her own behavior. Psychologists use **situational behavior observations** to assess behavior objectively in laboratory or real-life settings. In this procedure, an observer watches an individual's behavioral patterns in one or more situations, such as at home, at work, or in school. The goal here is to discover the determinants and consequences of the various responses and habits of the individual. To plan and evaluate therapy, direct situational observations are especially useful for finding the conditions in which problem behaviors occur. These observations are also useful for observing job applicants' behavior in a "joblike" situation, and for determining whether what people say corresponds to what they do; these observations serve to validate test and interview data.

self-report methods Popular research techniques, in which respondents are assessed by their answers to a series of questions.

Reporting Methods. **Self-report methods** require respondents to answer questions or give information about themselves. This information may be gathered from an interview, a test, or a personal journal. One very easily administered self-report is the *inventory*—a standardized, written test with a multiple choice, true-false, or rating format. The MMPI, discussed in Chapter 10, is an example of a true-false inventory.

Self-report measures are valuable because they tap into an individual's personal experiences and feelings. They are convenient because they do not require trained interviewers and they are generally easy to score. The greatest shortcoming of self-report measures is that sometimes people are not in touch with their feelings or can't objectively report their own behavior. Thus, psychologists often use methods that rely on observers' reports.

observer-report methods Evaluation of some aspect of an individual's behavior by another person.

Observer-report methods involve a systematic evaluation of some aspect of a person's behavior by another person, called a rater or judge. Observer reports may consist of very specific situational behavior observations or more generalized ratings. For example, teachers' aides may observe a preschool class and record the number of times each child performs particular behaviors—such as talking, shoving, hitting, or sharing a toy—during a particular period.

rating Quantitative judgment of the degree to which some characteristic is present or influential.

While situational behavior observations are typically made *on-line*—at the time the behavior is performed—a **rating** or quantified judgment of behavior is typically made *after* an observation period. Sometimes judges are asked to first record specific behaviors and then make overall ratings based on them. Often, ratings are made according to detailed guidelines. At other times, the guidelines are less precise, allowing for spontaneous reactions and informal impressions.

What drawbacks could result from such ratings? One drawback is that ratings may tell more about the *judge* or about the judge's relationship with the person than about the true characteristics of the person being rated. If you like someone, you may tend to judge him favorably on nearly every dimension. For example, if you think one of your professors is an interesting and enjoyable lecturer, you may rate other aspects of the class as high also, such as the quality of class discussions or the suitability of the required text. This type of rating bias—in which an overall positive or negative feeling about the person is extended to the specific dimensions being evaluated—is referred to as a **halo effect.** A different type of bias occurs when a rater thinks most people in a certain category (for example, Republicans, Arabs, the unemployed) share certain qualities. The rater may "see" those qualities in any individual who happens to be in that category. This type of bias is called a **stereotype effect.** For example, if a student thinks professors who are middle-aged or older are "absent-minded" or "boring," she may expect to be uninspired by a new instructor who appears to be an older adult.

halo effect Bias in which an observer's judgment of a single characteristic affects judgments of most or all other qualities.

stereotype effect Bias in which judge's beliefs about most people in a social category influence how a particular individual in the category is perceived.

Rating biases can be reduced by phrasing rating items in terms of behaviors, not inferences. For example, "keeps to himself" is a less biasing description than "withdrawn." Specific rules can also be established for each rating level, such as "if the person does X, give a rating of 10." Finally, several raters can be employed so that the bias introduced by each judge's unique point of view is canceled out by the other judges.

interjudge reliability Degree to which different observers agree about a particular individual or case.

Whenever you use more than one observer, you can calculate the **interjudge reliability**—the degree to which the different observers make similar ratings or agree about what the target person did during an observation period. Typically, interjudge reliability will be highest when judges record the specific behaviors observed in a specific situation rather than general impressions of behavior. A judge who watches you as you shop for groceries in one store will probably agree with the ratings of another judge who watches you shop in a different store. Two judges are less likely to agree on how they might rate your "bargain-hunting skills," since that is an impression they must form, not a specific behavior you display.

Assessment, the controlled measurement of individual differences, is used to understand and predict the behavior of individuals. Assessment assumes an individual differences perspective on behavior, rather than a situationist perspective. The tradition of assessment for job placement can be traced back 4000 years to civil service exams in China. Galton proposed important early ideas about the measurement of intelligence but extended his theory to make moralistic social-political recommendations. Modern-day assessments are used for a variety of research and applied purposes, measuring attributes such as general knowledge, cognitive capabilities, attitudes and interests, particular skills, and personality traits. The goal of assessment is to use samples of behavior to predict future behavior. Information gathered from systematically assessing a large number of people can improve understanding of the reasons why people differ on certain attributes and traits that are of theoretical interest to researchers.

The most important qualities of any assessment method are its reliability, validity, and standardization. Reliability means that a technique gives consistent scores on different occasions, on different test items, and with different observers. Validity means that a technique measures what it is supposed to measure, as shown by its correlation with a related technique or with a large body of relevant data. Finally, standardization means that a test is always administered and scored in the same way, so that a person's score may be compared to the norms of other, similar people (of the same age and sex) who took the same test.

The information used in assessments can come from many sources. Self-report or observer-report information may be gathered through interviews, life history data, and psychological tests. Observer reports can also be gathered through situational behavior observations and ratings. A comprehensive assessment should include data from as many different sources as possible.

Assessing Intelligence

Scientists continue to consider how to define intelligence. They have yet to agree on a single definition, but most would include in their measure of intelligence at least three types of skills:

1. Adapting to new situations and changing task demands
2. Learning or profiting from experience or training
3. Thinking abstractly, using symbols and concepts (Phares, 1984)

More specific ways of defining intelligence are linked to theories of human adaptation and intellectual functioning. These theories have emerged from all walks of psychology, including neurology-biology, learning theory, and human development.

We will define **intelligence** as the complex capacity to profit from experience—to go beyond what is perceived and imagine symbolic possibilities. Intelligence is a hypothetical construct, usually equated with higher-level, abstract thought processes. Not directly observable, intelligence is verified only by the operations (tests) used to measure it and by how it functions in criterion situations that are developed to validate it. Human intelligence provides us with a distinct advantage for survival in our world. Intelligence enables us to respond flexibly and imaginatively to environmental challenges; it is the reason our species has survived and prospered so well in so many different environments throughout the planet.

intelligence Global capacity to profit from experience and go beyond given information.

The way we think about intelligence and mental functioning influences the way we try to assess it. Some psychologists believe intelligence can be quantified as a score, while others argue that assessment should reflect the complexities and components of intelligence (Hunt, 1984; Sternberg, 1985). Is intelligence a *unitary attribute* (like height)—can people be assessed in terms of how smart they are? Or is it instead a collection of several mental competencies (like athletic abilities), involving different "intelligences" for different kinds of tasks? Some people believe that assessment of intellectual abilities is one of psychology's most significant contributions to society, but others maintain that it is a systematic attempt by elitists to weed out undesirables (Gould, 1981). Before we examine some evidence for these conflicting claims, we first need a bit more history to set the stage.

Historical Context

The movement to measure intelligence began in France as an attempt to identify children who were unable to learn in school. Soon, however, intelligence testing crossed the Atlantic to become an all-American enterprise.

Binet's Test of Mental Age. The year 1905 marked the first published account of a workable intelligence test. French psychologist **Alfred Binet** had responded to the call of the French Minister of Public Instruction to develop a way to more effectively teach developmentally disabled children in the public schools. Binet and his colleague, Théodore Simon, believed that it was necessary to measure a child's intellectual ability in order to plan an instructional program. Their radical proposal argued that education should fit the child's level of competence and not that the child be fit to a fixed curriculum.

Binet tried to devise an objective test of intellectual performance that could be used to classify and separate developmentally disabled from normal schoolchildren. He hoped that such a test would reduce the school's reliance on the more subjective, and perhaps biased, evaluations of teachers.

mental age (MA) Average age at which normal individuals achieve a particular score on a measure of intelligence.

chronological age (CA) Number of months or years since an individual's birth.

Binet's Approach. There are four important features of Binet's approach. First, he interpreted scores on his test as an estimate of *current performance* and *not* as a measure of *innate intelligence*. Second, he wanted the test scores to be used to identify children who needed special help and not to stigmatize them. Third, he emphasized that training and opportunity could affect intelligence and he wanted to identify areas of performance in which special education could help these children. Finally, he constructed his test empirically—based on how children were observed to perform—rather than tying it to a particular theory of intelligence.

Quantifying Intelligence. To *quantify* intellectual performance, Binet designed age-appropriate problems or test items on which many children's responses could be compared. The problems on the test were chosen so that they could be scored objectively, could vary in content, were not heavily influenced by differences in children's environments, and tested judgment and reasoning rather than rote memory (Binet, 1911).

Children of various ages were tested, and the average score for normal children at each age was computed. Then, each individual child's performance was compared to the average for other children of that age. Test results were expressed in terms of the average age at which normal children achieved a particular score. This measure was called the **mental age (MA).** When a child's scores on various items of the test added up to the average score of a group of 5-year-olds, the child was said to have a *mental age* of 5, regardless of his or her actual **chronological age (CA)**. *Retardation* was then defined operationally by Binet as being two mental-age years behind chronological age.

Alfred Binet (1857–1911)

As he conducted longitudinal tests of the children (they were tested repeatedly at intervals), Binet found that those assessed as developmentally disabled at one age fell further behind the mental age of their birth cohorts (other children their age) as they grew older. A child of 5 who performed at the level of 3-year-olds might, at the age of 10, perform at the level of 6-year-olds. Although the *ratio* of mental age to chronological age would be constant (3/5 = 6/10), the total number of mental-age years of retardation would have increased from two to four.

American Intelligence Testing. Due to a unique combination of historical events and social and political forces, Binet's successful development of an intelligence test had great impact in the United States. At the beginning of the twentieth century, the United States was a nation in turmoil. Global economic, social, and political conditions resulted in millions of immigrants entering the country. New universal education laws flooded schools with students. When World War I began, millions of volunteers marched into recruiting stations. These events—world conditions, new education laws, and World War I—all resulted in large numbers of people needing to be identified, documented, and classified. Some form of assessment was needed to facilitate these tasks (Chapman, 1988). At the time, "Intelligence test results were used not only to differentiate [among] children experiencing academic problems, but also as a measuring stick to organize an entire society" (Hale, 1983, p. 373). Assessment was seen as a way to inject order into a chaotic society and as an inexpensive, democratic way to separate those who could benefit from education or military leadership training from those who could not.

In 1917, when the United States declared war on Germany, it was necessary to establish quickly a military force led by competent leaders. Recruiters needed to determine which of the many draftees could learn quickly and benefit from special leadership training to become officers. New nonverbal, group-administered tests of mental ability were used to evaluate over 1.7 million recruits. Incidentally, a group of famous psychologists, including Lewis Terman, Edward Thorndike, and Robert Yerkes, designed these new tests in only one month's time (Lennon, 1985).

One consequence of this large-scale group testing program was that the American public came to accept the idea that intelligence tests could differentiate people in terms of leadership ability, intelligence and other socially important characteristics. This acceptance led to the widespread use of tests in schools and industry. Another, more unfortunate, consequence was that the tests reinforced prevailing prejudices, because the army reports indicated that differences in test scores were linked to race and country of origin (Yerkes, 1921). Of course, the same statistics *could* have been used to demonstrate that environmental disadvantages limit the full development of people's intellectual abilities. Instead, these statistics fueled racist ideology. Immigrants to America with limited facility in English or even little understanding of how to take such tests were found to be "morons," "imbeciles," and worse. Immigrants from Northern Europe did much better than those from Southern Europe. Consider whether that surprises you, given the differences in their educational levels and familiarity with English.

IQ Testing

Despite the risks of unfairness and the difficulties of refining novel testing techniques, the assessment of intelligence clearly had many practical applications, and this spurred further research and test development. After Binet began the standardized assessment of intellectual ability, statistics-minded U.S. psychologists took the ball from him and ran. U.S. psychologists modified Binet's scoring procedure, improved the reliability of the tests, and studied the scores of enormous normative samples of people who took the new tests. They

intelligence quotient (IQ) Index derived from standardized tests of intelligence.

also developed the IQ (**intelligence quotient**). The IQ was a standardized, numerical measure of intelligence, obtained from an individual's score on an intelligence test. Two sorts of individually administered IQ tests are used widely today: the Stanford-Binet scales and the Wechsler scales.

The Stanford-Binet Intelligence Scale. Stanford University's **Lewis Terman,** a former public school administrator, adapted Binet's test questions for U.S. schoolchildren, standardizing its administration and its age-level norms. In 1916 he published the Stanford Revision of the Binet Tests, commonly referred to as the *Stanford-Binet Intelligence Scale* (Terman, 1916).

With his new test, Terman provided a base for the concept of the **intelligence quotient,** or IQ (coined by Stern, 1914). The IQ was the ratio of mental age to chronological age (multiplied by 100 to eliminate decimals):

$$IQ = MA/CA \times 100$$

A child with a CA of 8 whose test scores revealed an MA of 10 had an IQ of 125 *(10/8 × 100 = 125)*, while a child of that same chronological age who performed at the level of 6-year-olds had an IQ of 75 *(6/8 × 100 = 75)*. Individuals who performed at the mental age equivalent to their chronological age had IQs of 100, considered to be the average or normal IQ.

The new Stanford-Binet test soon became a standard instrument in clinical psychology, psychiatry, and educational counseling. Unlike Binet, Terman believed that intelligence was an inner quality, that it was largely hereditary, and that IQ tests could measure this inner quality throughout the range of abilities that make up intelligence. His implicit message was that IQ reflected something essential and unchanging about human intelligence.

Charles Spearman of England, the leading assessment theorist of the 1920s, influenced Terman's beliefs. Spearman had concluded that all mental tests were a combination of an innate general intellectual ability, the **g-factor,** and some specific abilities as well (Spearman, 1927). "It was almost universally assumed by psychologists and by the general public in these early years that individual differences in intelligence were innately determined. One's intellectual level was a characteristic one must accept rather than try to change" (Tyler, 1988, p. 128).

g-factor General intelligence factor, assumed to be the individual's inherited basic intelligence, to which s-factors (specific kinds of intelligence) are added.

IQ scores are no longer derived by dividing mental age by chronological age. If you took the test today, your score would be added up and directly compared to the scores of other people your age. An IQ of 100 (average) indicates that 50 percent of those your age earned lower scores. Scores between 90 and 110 are now labeled normal, above 120 are superior, and below 70 are evidence of developmental disability (see **Figure 11.1** on page 422).

The Stanford-Binet scales were criticized because the subtests used to measure IQ at different ages focused on different types of skills. For example, 2- to 4-year-olds were tested on their ability to manipulate objects, whereas adults were tested almost exclusively on verbal items. As the scientific understanding of intelligence increased, psychologists found it increasingly important to measure *several* intellectual abilities at *all* age levels. A recent revision of the Stanford-Binet now provides different scores for several mental skills, but it has not been widely accepted (Vernon, 1987).

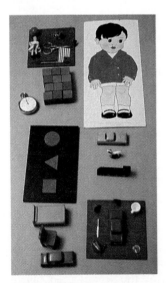

A psychologist administers an intelligence test to a 4-year-old child. The performance part of this test includes a block design task, an object completion task, and a shape identification task.

The Wechsler Intelligence Scales. **David Wechsler** of Bellevue Hospital in New York set out to correct the dependence on verbal items in the assessment of adult intelligence. In 1939, he published the Wechsler-Bellevue Intelligence Scale, which combined verbal subtests with nonverbal or performance subtests. Thus, in addition to an overall IQ score, subjects were given separate estimates of verbal IQ and nonverbal IQ. After a few changes, the test was retitled the Wechsler Adult Intelligence Scale—the WAIS in 1955, and the revised WAIS-R today (Wechsler, 1981).

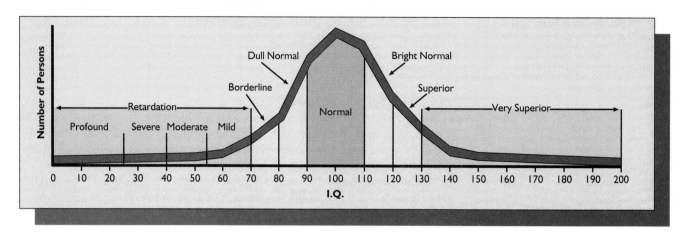

Figure 11.1 Distribution of IQ Scores Among a Large Sample

There are six *verbal* subtests of the WAIS-R (pronounced wayce-AHR): Information, Vocabulary, Comprehension, Arithmetic, Similarities (stating how two things are alike), and Digit Span (repeating a series of digits after the examiner). These verbal tests are both written and oral.

The WAIS-R's five *performance* subtests involve manipulation of materials and have little or no verbal content. In the Block Design test, for example, a subject tries to reproduce designs shown on cards by fitting together blocks with colored sides. The Digit Symbol test provides a key that matches 9 symbols to 9 numeric digits, and the task is to write the appropriate digits under the symbols on another page. Other performance tests involve Picture Arrangement, Picture Completion, and Object Assembly. If you were to take the WAIS-R, you would perform all 11 subtests, and receive 3 scores: a verbal IQ, a performance IQ, and an overall or full-scale IQ.

The WAIS-R is designed for people 18 years or older, but similar tests have been developed for children. The Wechsler Intelligence Scale for Children—Revised (WISC-R [1974], pronounced wisk-AHR or whisker) is suited for children ages 6 to 17, and the *Wechsler Preschool and Primary Scale of Intelligence* (WPPSI, pronounced WHIP-see) for children ages 4 to 6½ years. Some subtests were specially created for use with children, but most have a direct counterpart in the WAIS-R.

The WAIS-R, the WISC-R, and the WPPSI form a family of intelligence tests that yield a verbal IQ, a performance IQ, and a full-scale IQ at all age levels. In addition, they provide comparable subtest scores that allow researchers to track the development of even more specific intellectual abilities. For this reason, the Wechsler scales are particularly valuable when the same individual is to be tested at different ages.

Group Tests of Intelligence. In addition to the individually administered Stanford-Binet and Wechsler scales, there are many other tests that are given to groups. If you went through a U.S. school system, chances are you took several of these; some students take as many as 20 standardized group tests before graduating from high school (Seligman, 1988). Because these tests are restricted to written items that can be scored easily, they measure a narrowly defined type of intellectual functioning, often called *school ability* or *scholastic aptitude*.

Two of the most popular group tests of intelligence are the Cognitive Abilities Test (CAT; Thorndike and Hagen, 1978) and the School and College Ability Tests (SCAT, Series III; Educational Testing Service, 1980). They provide separate verbal and quantitative (math) scores, and the CAT also provides a nonverbal score. They are valid predictors of school achievement, and are as reliable as the Stanford-Binet and the Wechsler tests.

One of the tests adults can take is the WAIS-R.

In these examples from the WISC-R for children, subjects are asked to put the frames in order so they make a story.

The primary benefits of group tests are that they require no special training to administer, they can be administered to a large group in relatively little time, and they are quickly and accurately scored by computer. These tests are ideal when a large number of people must be tested in an economical way. However, individualized tests can provide rich, clinical detail that group tests cannot. For example, a psychologist providing counseling or planning a treatment may wish to observe firsthand how a person deals with a frustrating test problem or note the tasks a person most enjoys (Lennon, 1985).

Theories of Intelligence

IQ scores, by themselves, do not tell how much children know or what they can do. A high-school student with an IQ of 100 has knowledge and skills that a fourth-grader with a higher IQ of 120 does not have. In addition, people labeled "developmentally disabled" on the basis of their IQ scores vary considerably in what they can do and how much they can learn. Similarly, elderly subjects may perform more poorly than the young on test items where speed is important, but they still have greater measurable *wisdom* in many domains (Baltes, 1990). Thus, an operational definition such as "intelligence *is* what intelligence tests *measure*," does not cover all that we mean by the concept of human intelligence. We will examine several theories that attempt to explain what intelligence is.

psychometrics   Field of psychology that specializes in mental testing.

Psychometric Theories.   **Psychometrics** is the field of psychology that specializes in all areas of mental testing, including personality assessment, intelligence evaluation, and aptitude measurement. Psychometric approaches to intelligence study the *statistical relationships* between different measures—how one set of scores is related to another set. One common approach uses a technique called *factor analysis*—a statistical procedure that locates a smaller number of dimensions, clusters, or factors from a larger set of independent variables or items on a test. (Reducing many thousands of trait terms into the Big Five personality factors, as reviewed in the last chapter, is one example of what factor analysis can do.) The goal of factor analysis is to identify a small number of factors that represent the basic psychological dimensions being investigated.

Cattell's Analysis of Intelligence.   **Raymond Cattell** (1963), using advanced factor analytic techniques, determined that general intelligence can be broken

crystallized intelligence   Knowledge a person has already acquired and the ability to use that knowledge.

fluid intelligence   Ability to perceive complex relationships and solve problems.

down into two relatively independent components he called *crystallized* and *fluid* intelligence. **Crystallized intelligence** is the knowledge a person has already acquired and the ability to access that knowledge. Crystallized intelligence is measured by tests of vocabulary, arithmetic, and general information. **Fluid intelligence** is the ability to see complex relationships and solve problems. Fluid intelligence is measured by tests of block designs and spatial visualization in which the background information needed to solve a problem is included or readily apparent.

Recent investigations indicate that both crystallized and fluid intelligence are partly inherited and partly learned. In addition, some psychometricians believe there may be no such thing as general intelligence. Instead, four or five relatively independent characteristics of people may influence their performance on different intellectual tasks. These characteristics might be fluid, crystallized, verbal, and auditory intelligence and speediness (Horn, 1985).

Guilford's Structural Model.   **J. P. Guilford,** another psychometrician, used factor analysis to examine the demands of many intelligence-related tasks. His structure-of-intellect model specifies three features of intellectual tasks: the *content,* or type of information; the *product,* or form in which information is represented; and the *operation,* or type of mental activity performed. For example, answering the question, "What important event in American history took place on November 22, 1963?" involves searching your semantic memory for that knowledge (the operation), the knowledge itself (the content), and writing or saying, "The assassination of President John F. Kennedy" (the product).

The structure-of-intellect model, shown in **Figure 11.2,** indicates five kinds of content (visual, auditory, symbolic, semantic, and behavioral); six kinds of products (units, classes, relations, systems, transformations, and implications); and five kinds of operations (evaluation, convergent production, divergent production, memory, and cognition). Each task performed by the intellect can be identified according to the particular types of content, prod-

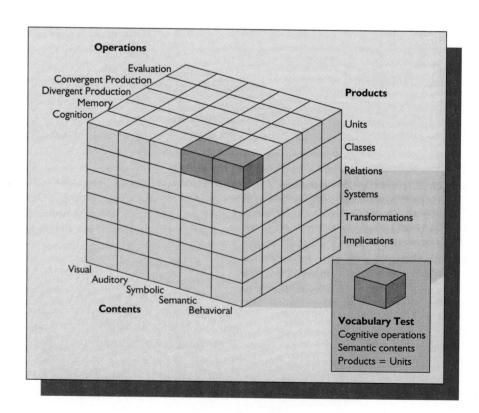

Figure 11.2 J. P. Guilford's Model of the Structure of Intellect

ucts, and operations involved. Further, Guilford believes that each content-product-operation combination (each small cube in the model) represents a distinct mental ability.

There are 150 possible combinations of contents, products, and operations. That is, any of the five types of content may take the form of any of the six products ($5 \times 6 = 30$), and on these 30 resulting kinds of information, any of the five types of operations may be performed ($30 \times 5 = 150$). For example, a test of vocabulary would assess your ability for *cognition* of *units* with *semantic content*, while learning a dance routine requires *memory* for *behavioral systems*.

Guilford's theoretical model is analogous to a chemist's periodic table of elements. By using such a systematic framework, researchers can postulate intellectual factors before they are discovered. That is, the framework tells psychologists what to look for before they have observed examples. In 1961, when Guilford proposed his model, nearly 40 intellectual abilities had been identified. Researchers have since accounted for over 100 (Guilford, 1985).

Cognitive Science Approaches. Since Guilford created his model, many psychologists have broadened their conceptions of intelligence to include much more than performance on traditional IQ tests. While Guilford defined mental abilities in terms of the features of the *tasks* people confronted, cognitive scientists focus on the different *cognitive processes* or mental activities we use when we learn new things or find a novel solution to a problem.

Hunt's Problem-Solving Intelligence. **Earl Hunt** (1983), one proponent of the cognitive processes view, believes that the interesting individual differences in people's intelligence are not to be found in test scores but in the way different individuals go about solving a problem. He identifies three ways cognitive processes may differ in individuals: choice about the way to internally (mentally) *represent* a problem; strategies for *manipulating* mental representations; and the abilities necessary to *execute* whatever basic information-processing steps a strategy requires.

Using Hunt's model, scientists can design special tasks to observe individual differences in the way people represent problems. For example, a subject may mentally picture a calendar in order to remember an upcoming appointment. They can also observe the way individuals encode material, and the way information is transferred in their working memories. This approach encourages scientists to see the flexibility and adaptiveness of human thinking.

Sternberg's Three Components. Yale psychologist **Robert Sternberg** (1986) also stresses the importance of cognitive processes in problem solving. He identifies three types of *components* that are central to his model of information processing:

1. Knowledge acquisition components, for learning new facts
2. Performance components, for problem-solving strategies and techniques
3. Metacognitive components, for selecting a strategy and monitoring progress toward success

These three components tell only part of the story of intelligence. In addition to this *componential intelligence,* which is reflected in IQ scores and college grades, Sternberg identifies two other important types of intelligence: *experiential* and *contextual.*

Experiential intelligence is reflected in creative accomplishments. It involves the ability to picture the external world using alternate types of internal representations, and the ability to combine very different experiences in unique and original ways. For example, artists captivate audiences by repre-

senting commonplace things in unusual ways, while scientists use their experiential intelligence to develop provocative scientific theories.

Contextual intelligence is reflected in the practical management of day-to-day affairs. It involves your ability to adapt to new and different contexts, make the most of your available resources, and effectively shape your environment to suit your needs. For example, if you have the insight that your new roommate's moodiness reminds you of the way your brother or sister behaved after a painful breakup, you keep that context in mind as you interact with your roommate. Contextual intelligence is what people sometimes call *street smarts* or *business sense*. Keep in mind that contextual and experiential intelligence would be overlooked if we examined only IQ scores.

Gardner's Seven Intelligences. Researcher **Howard Gardner** (1983) has proposed a somewhat different theory of intelligence. He defines intelligence in terms of numerous abilities, each of which is equally important. The value of any of the abilities is culturally determined, according to what is needed by, useful to, and prized by a given society. (See "Cross-cultural Perspective: Defining Intelligence in Terms of Culture" on p. 428.) Gardner identifies seven intelligences, as follows:

1. Linguistic ability
2. Logical-mathematical ability
3. Spatial ability (navigating in space, using mental images)
4. Musical ability
5. Bodily-kinesthetic ability
6. Interpersonal ability (understanding others)
7. Intrapersonal ability (understanding oneself)

All these seven intelligences are aspects of human potential and promote survival and adaptation. Gardner argues that Western society promotes the first two intelligences, while other societies value others. For example, in small island societies, people place a value on getting along with others (number 6, above). In these restricted social settings, there is no place to go if people have an intense quarrel and want to escape or part ways. People cannot move 100 miles away if they live on an island 10 miles in diameter. In such societies, people avoid intense quarrels by recognizing potential problems at an early stage and by modifying behaviors to solve problems quickly (emphasizing the last two intelligences on the list).

Howard Gardner (*Discovering Psychology,* 1990, Program 16)

One of Gardner's seven intelligences is bodily-kinesthetic intelligence, the ability to coordinate one's body movements with grace and control, as demonstrated by dancers.

Assessing these kinds of intelligence demands more than paper-and-pencil tests and simple quantified measures. Gardner's tests of intelligence require that the subject be observed and assessed in a variety of life situations as well as in the artificial samples of life depicted in traditional intelligence tests. The theory is sound, but the way to operationally verify it through valid, reliable tests is still in the process of being developed.

The Origins of Intelligence

The use of tests to assess intelligence (and other personal attributes) has had an extensive impact on industry, society, and individual lives. But where does intelligence come from? What are the primary factors that contribute to your intelligence? We now return to a familiar debate, the nature-nurture controversy.

Heredity Versus Environment. There is no question that heredity *influences* those elusive mental qualities that we call intelligence. Many different lines of research have shown there is a strong genetic basis to a variety of human attributes. Research to assess the genetic contribution given to a function compares identical twins with same-sex fraternal twins and sometimes with siblings. Significant genetic effects have been found on attributes as diverse as heart functioning (Brown, 1990); personality traits (Tellegen et al., 1988); and hypnotizability (Morgan et al., 1970). So it is reasonable to believe that there is also a genetic basis to intellectual functioning. The question is how much basis there is.

The Genetic Basis for Intelligence. Psychologists have also compared performances of twins and siblings who have been reared together or apart. **Table 11.1** (on p. 429) compares IQ scores of individuals on the basis of their degree of genetic relationship (from bottom to top, scores are listed from the lowest to the highest). The greater the genetic similarity the greater the IQ similarity. The correlation between IQ scores increases as we move up in degree of heredity from cousins to siblings to fraternal twins to identical twins. It is also greater between biological parent and child than between foster parent and adopted child. Environment also makes its contribution, revealed in the greater IQ similarities among those who have been reared together.

Most psychologists agree that heredity plays an important part in variance of IQ scores. It is difficult to determine the relative roles of genetics and environment in the development of intelligence or other aspects of mental functioning (Plomin, 1989; Scarr, 1988; Stevenson et al., 1987). Children who

Whenever we consider traditional views of intelligence, we must keep in mind that they were developed by educators and psychologists from North America and Western Europe. In addition, as seen in the review of Alfred Binet's work in France, work on intelligence has long been associated with the skills children need to succeed in schools. If you have reached the point in your education where you are taking a college level psychology course, you have been exposed to skills traditionally considered part of "intelligence." You have learned general information useful for solving various problems, such as the difference between a teaspoon and a tablespoon, or between a yard and a meter. You have a good vocabulary in your native language. You are able to read material and can comprehend its meaning. You can multiply and divide numbers. You can see similarities in objects (considered familiar in their culture), and can answer questions such as, "How are a sparrow and a squirrel alike?" People have these intellectual skills because they have been socialized in a culture that places a value on them. If people have been socialized in another culture, would they be expected to acquire different skills to be considered "intelligent?"

Cross-cultural psychologists are interested in the answers to these questions (Vernon, 1969; Rogoff, 1990). For example, John Berry (1992) has studied the behaviors considered necessary for intelligence among Native Americans. Berry worked among the Cree in Northern Ontario, Canada. He asked 60 Cree adults (32 males, 28 females) to give him various words in the Cree language that dealt with thinking. To begin the interviews, Berry used examples such as "smart," "intelligent," or "wise." After the adults responded, Berry asked them to give the opposites of the various terms, as well as to describe the meaning of the Cree words as fully as possible.

After gathering twenty different Cree words, Berry asked the respondents to sort the words based on their similarity. The results of a sorting task like this begin to give insights into the way that the Cree organize *their* thinking about intelligence. Some of the results are very intriguing and force us to think about the behaviors necessary for success in different cultures. The most frequently mentioned terms suggested by the Cree translate roughly as "wise, thinks hard, and thinks carefully." Closely related were terms that related to "smartness displayed at school" and that translate as "understands new things" and "accumulated knowledge." Berry suggests that the Cree recognize the importance of these aspects of intelligence given that Cree children attend schools introduced by the dominant Anglo culture. However, the Cree distinguish between this "school" intelligence and the "good thinking" valued in traditional Cree culture.

Another term the Cree used was "respectful." One respondent explained that part of intelligence ". . . is being respectful in the Indian sense. You need to really know the other person and respect them for what they are. When the Creator created the animals He showed respect to His Creation. When He created Adam and Eve He instructed them to guard the land and to show respect to the land and the animals that He created" (Berry, 1992, p. 79). The element of "respect for others" is widespread in Native American cultures.

One of the terms that is the opposite of intelligence among the Cree translates as "lives like a white." This term refers to behaviors that the Cree have observed among some Anglo people. In analyzing reasons for this negative term, Berry (1992) points to the fact that the Cree place the term for "lives like a white" close to the terms for "stupid" and "backwards knowledge." A stupid person does not know the necessary skills for survival in Cree culture and does not learn properly by observing and listening to respected elders. "Backwards knowledge" refers to wisdom that people use to disrupt smooth relationships and to create disharmony. At times, outsiders who work in the Cree culture can be disruptive without any intent or awareness. Anglo teachers may introduce skills in their classroom that have no place in traditional culture. For example, teachers in an English class may ask students to write an essay or to give a speech that has the goal of *persuading others* to change certain behaviors. The concept "persuading others," however, may interfere with the traditional Cree value of "respecting others *as they are*." Encouraging children to disagree openly with adults on some issues (which is common in Anglo culture) can be disruptive. There may be some Anglo wisdom involved, but it is backward in Cree views of intelligence.

One good class exercise to encourage an understanding of concepts from other cultures is to draw on the experiences of students who have interacted in more than one culture. People who are expected to learn another culture's concepts find the experience especially memorable (Brislin, 1993). In one class, a Navajo student remembered a time when she lived with an Anglo family during her early adolescence. Her duties around the house (such as cleaning her room and emptying the garbage) were written down and the list put on the refrigerator with a magnet. This may seem reasonable from an Anglo viewpoint, but it conflicted with the Navajo student's concept of intelligent behavior. She reported: "This interfered with the Navajo idea of respect for others. This wouldn't happen in Navajo culture. There, people are expected to be smart enough to see that the garbage needs emptying. No one would insult other Navajos by telling them to do something obvious or to write it down on paper!"

Table 11.1	IQ and Genetic Relationship
	CORRELATION
Identical Twins	
Reared together	0.86
Reared apart	0.72
Fraternal Twins	
Reared together	0.60
Siblings	
Reared together	0.47
Reared apart	0.24
Parent/Child	0.40
Foster Parent/Child	0.31
Cousins	0.15

live in the same family setting do not necessarily share the same critical, psychological environment. You probably are aware of this fact if you have siblings with interests and lifestyles that differ from yours.

Counterarguments to Inherited Intelligence. There are problems with comparing group IQ scores to make inferences about genetic differences in intelligence. First of all, if one group is more environmentally advantaged, it will do better on tests that are responsive to such influences. Those who focus on genetic explanations typically ignore the environmental, situational determinants of mental and behavioral functioning. Those people who are stigmatized by genetic inferiority theories suffer by believing they cannot improve their fated genetic destiny. For example, if a young woman believes that students with her ethnic heritage "typically" do worse on medical school admissions examinations than white students or men, she may withhold effort that might have proved successful in reaching her goal of becoming a physician.

Another reason that genetic makeup does not appear to be responsible for group differences in IQ has to do with the relative sizes of the differences. For example, even though some studies show that the group average of IQ for African Americans is as much as 10 to 15 IQ points below the group average for U.S. whites, there is much overlapping of scores. The difference *between* groups is small compared to the differences among the scores of individuals *within* each group (Loehlin et al., 1975). In fact, geneticist **Stephen Jay Gould** (1981) argues that for human characteristics in general, the differences between the gene pools of different racial groups are minute compared to the

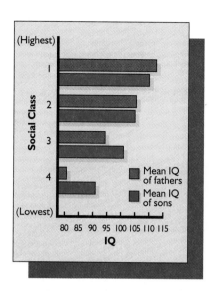

Figure 11.3 The Relationship Between Heredity, Environment, and IQ
This chart shows evidence for the contribution of heredity and environment to IQ scores. We see similar IQs for fathers and sons (influence of heredity), but the IQs of both fathers and sons are related to social class (influence of environment).

genetic differences among individual members of the same group (see also Zuckerman, 1990).

A third argument against the genetic interpretation of group differences is that many other variables are *confounded* with race, each of which can influence IQ scores (see **Figure 11.3**). For example, in a large-scale, longitudinal study of more than 26,000 children, the best predictors of a child's IQ at age 4, for both black and white children, were the family's socioeconomic status and the level of the mother's education (Broman et al., 1975).

Environmental Factors in Intelligence. There is ample evidence that environments influence intellectual development. Poverty can affect intellectual functioning in many ways. Researchers have traced poor health during pregnancy and low birth weight to low mental ability in children. So too, poor nutrition, a lack of books and other materials for verbal stimulation, and a job schedule that leaves parents little time or energy to play with and intellectually stimulate their children can be detrimental to performance on tasks such as those on standard IQ tests (for example, vocabulary or sentence comprehension). A significant proportion of children with low IQs were adversely affected by "environmental insults," such as lead-based paint chips peeling from walls (Needleman et al., 1990).

Environmental factors, such as the cognitive complexity and intellectual demands of one's job, can influence IQ throughout adulthood (Dixon et al., 1985). Most adult IQs are stable over many years simply because the adults remain in environments that provide a constant level of intellectual stimulation. Recall that columnist Bob Greene's verbal SAT scores increased while his math SAT scores plummeted—in part due to his use of verbal skills and his disuse of math skills.

The best way to summarize these and other relevant findings is to say that *both* heredity and environment affect intelligence. Heredity plays a big role in differences between individuals but not in differences among groups. Environmental factors play important roles in creating differences between individuals and between groups. Although heredity may make learning easier for some people than for others, genetic makeup alone does not determine level of intellectual achievement. Intervention programs and enriched learning environments can help overcome the disadvantages of poverty and discrimination.

The personal attention children receive can affect their intelligence. In the "separate but equal" schoolroom of 1950s Tennessee shown at left, African-American children received little attention. In contrast, the parents shown at right are deeply involved in their children's education.

IQ, Race, and Society. Faulty assumptions about intelligence can lead even well-intentioned persons to misuse tests or misinterpret results. As reviewed in "In Focus: The Seeds of Intellect" on the next page the debate that began a century ago has had lasting repercussions for intelligence testing policy today.

In the United States today, African Americans and Latinos score (on the average) lower than Asian Americans and whites on standardized intelligence tests. Of course, there are individuals in all groups who score at the highest (and the lowest) extremes of the IQ scale. How should we interpret IQ scores, and what is the source of these group differences? Genetics, environment, and test bias play different roles in these differences and each leads to important social consequences.

The Genetic Argument. The genetic position claims that IQ tests measure inherent intellectual ability, and that some racial or cultural groups score lower because they are genetically inferior. Group differences are used to justify racist views. In the extreme, racist interpreters of the genetic argument support eugenics programs (which promote the propagation of "superior," not "inferior," races) to limit "breeding" by undesirable groups, laws restricting the immigration of certain groups, and legal inequality that favors the group in power. This position, at the least, feeds intergroup conflict, encourages school segregation and discriminatory hiring practices, and argues against funding for intervention programs that help minorities. William Shockley, who won the Nobel Prize in Physics for co-inventing the transistor, supported the genetic position. He alleged that the lower IQ test scores of African Americans and Latinos in the United States are "hereditary and racially genetic in origin and thus not remedial to a major degree by practical improvements in environment" (Shockley, 1986, p. 67). However, in our pluralistic culture, composed of diverse but interwoven subcultures, it is difficult to determine how much of the variation in intellectual performance on any standard test can be assigned to hereditary factors and what proportion is attributable to environmental influences—or, indeed, why there is so much variation.

The Environmental Argument. The environmental position interprets IQ scores as a measure of current functioning and alleges that low scores often reflect social factors. Group differences in IQ scores are believed to be a symptom of larger social problems. In the United States the minority groups with the lowest average IQ scores are those for whom poverty, illiteracy, and hopelessness are most widespread. Supporters of the environmental position claim that racism and discrimination initially landed many minorities in the impoverished inner cities, and these same factors continue to keep them there today.

Proponents of the environmental view support equal opportunity legislation, better schools, and intervention programs, such as Head Start, which helps disadvantaged children build self-confidence and learn the skills necessary to succeed in school.

The Problem of Bias. Proponents of the third view are also interested in protecting the civil rights of minority group members. They believe that group differences in IQ scores are caused by systematic bias in the test questions. As a result, the questions are invalid and unfair for minorities. There are significant dialect differences between whites and blacks, for example, that could affect an African-American person's verbal scores on a standardized test with a bias toward standard English. Proponents of this view also believe that remedial classes do more harm than good for those minority children who are incorrectly assigned to them on the basis of unfair IQ tests. These classes stigmatize the students and encourage their distaste for the school experience. Minority students, however, have shown great progress when taught in non-biased classes and labs. Children from privileged backgrounds often have far more experi-

In Focus:

THE SEEDS OF INTELLECT

In the early 1900s, psychologist **Henry Goddard** endorsed the IQ scale as a fixed measure of the mind. He advocated mental testing of all immigrants and the *selective exclusion* of those who were found to be "mentally defective." With some encouragement from assessment-minded psychologists, Congress passed the 1924 Immigration Restriction Act designed to bar those immigrants "proven" to be inferior on the basis of their low IQ test score. Thus it became national policy to administer intelligence tests to immigrants as they arrived at Ellis Island in New York harbor. Vast numbers of Jewish, Italian, and Russian immigrants were classified as "morons" on the basis of IQ tests. Some psychologists interpreted these statistical findings as evidence that immigrants from southern and eastern Europe were genetically inferior to those from the hardy northern and western European stock. However, these groups were also least familiar with the dominant language and culture because they had immigrated most recently. (Within a few decades, these group differences completely disappeared from IQ tests—but the theory of racially inherited differences in intelligence did not.)

Goddard (1917) and others then went beyond merely associating low IQ with hereditary racial and ethnic origins. They added moral worthlessness, mental deficiency, and immoral social behavior to the mix of negatives related to low IQ. They found support for their view in the case studies of two infamous families: the **Juke Family** and the **Kallikak Family**. These families allegedly were traced for many generations to show that "bad seeds" planted in family genes yield defective human offspring. Reportedly, by the year 1875 over 2,000 members of a New York state family with "Juke's blood" had been traced because the fam-

ily had such a notorious record of developmental disability, delinquency, and crime. Of these family members, 458 were found to be developmentally disabled in school performance, 171 classified as criminals, and hundreds of their kin were labeled as "paupers, intemperates, and harlots." The conclusion reached was that heredity was a dominant factor in the disreputable development of members of this family (and presumably others similar to it).

Goddard drew the same conclusion from his case study of a family with one "good seed" side and one "bad seed" side to its family tree. (In his study, Goddard renamed the family "Kallikak," which means *good-bad* in Greek.) Martin Kallikak was a revolutionary war soldier who had an illegitimate son with a woman who would be described today as developmentally disabled. Their union eventually produced 480 descendants. Goddard classified 143 of them as "defective," and only 46 as normal. He found crime, alcoholism, mental disorders, and illegitimacy common among the rest of the family members. By contrast, when Martin later married a "good woman," their union produced 496 descendants, only three of whom were classified as "defective." Goddard also found that many offspring from this quality union had become "eminent"— recognized as talented and productive members of society (Goddard, 1912).

Goddard came to believe that heredity determined intelligence, genius, and eminence on the positive side and delinquency, alcoholism, sexual immorality, developmental disability, and maybe even poverty on the negative side (McPherson, 1985). A critical analysis of Goddard's arguments would reveal many sources of error and bias in reliance on these family "case studies." Because many people found Goddard's

conclusions compatible with their own preexisting assumptions about race and intelligence, these ideas found wide acceptance despite methodological and logical weaknesses.

Goddard's genetic superiority argument was further reinforced by the fact that on the World War I Army Intelligence tests, African Americans and other racial minorities scored lower than the white majority. Louis Terman responded to the intelligence test data he had helped collect on U.S. racial minorities as follows: "Their dullness seems to be racial. . . . There seems no possibility at present of convincing society that they should not be allowed to reproduce, although from a eugenics point of view, they constitute a grave problem because of their unusually prolific breeding" (Terman, 1916, pp. 91–92).

These ideas of "bad seeds" and "racial inferiority" are difficult to understand today. Take a critical thinking approach to understanding the ideas promoted by Henry Goddard and others, and ask yourself these questions:

- In the 19th and early 20th centuries, where would educated people get the idea that racial and ethnic differences were important?
- Which racial and ethnic groups would most want to believe in the concept of racial superiority or inferiority? Which would least want to believe it? Why?
- What are some modern examples of belief in racial superiority? What factors might make such beliefs popular today?
- How is racial "pride" different from the pride you take in your work or your achievements? How can emotions and beliefs bias our efforts to study human psychology?

ence taking tests and may score higher because of "test wiseness," rather than knowing more about what the test is supposed to measure.

Several suggestions have been made in response to the test bias position. For example, some people assert that test makers should try to improve their

Juke family American family allegedly studied as an example of how "bad" bloodlines or heritage may produce generations of defective offspring.

Kallikak family Name given to American family allegedly studied as evidence that "bad seeds" planted in family genes produce generations of defective offspring, while "good seeds" produce normal and eminent offspring.

tests to make them *culture fair*. Also, some suggest that courts restrict the use of IQ tests so that they can no longer be used to assign minority children to special classes; this suggestion has been carried out in some states. However, when test bias is seen as the sole cause for group differences, legislators may pretend that racial injustice in the larger society is not a serious problem, and thereby work to reduce incentives for remedial action programs.

Toward Fairer Testing Practices. Along with affirmative action legislation, the movement to ensure fair testing practices seeks to remove discriminatory practices in our society. Unfortunately, sometimes when standardized tests are forbidden, educators and employers must revert to more expensive, less valid, and perhaps *more* discriminatory assessment procedures—such as interviews that rely on the subjective impressions of teachers or supervisors. The rights and interests of many people must be considered. Otherwise, poor decisions will be made, with negative consequences for both the institution (the school or business) and the individual (the student or job applicant). The decision to use a test should always be based on the validity and fairness of the test as compared to other selection methods.

SUMMING UP

The construct of intelligence has been defined and measured in many ways. Today, the most popular individually administered tests of intelligence are the Stanford-Binet and the Wechsler scales (the WAIS-R, the WISC-R, and the WPPSI). Group tests of intelligence, though more convenient and inexpensive, offer somewhat narrower results because they are restricted to written items.

Psychometric analyses of IQ, which are based on statistical relationships between mental measurements, suggest that there are several types of abilities that contribute to IQ scores, such as separate fluid and crystallized intelligence. Cognitive science approaches encourage us to conceive of and measure intelligence broadly by assessing the skills and insights people use to solve all the types of problems they encounter. Cognitive scientists claim that IQ tells only a small part of the story; a fuller scenario must include many different components of intellectual functioning.

Because some racial and cultural groups score lower on IQ tests on the average than other groups, some critics believe that IQ doesn't (or shouldn't) "tell the story" at all. Although IQ differences between groups are sometimes blamed on genetic differences between groups, the evidence suggests that group differences reflect both environmental disadvantages and cultural bias in the tests themselves. Some argue that group differences in IQ can be reduced, and in time probably eliminated, by improving public education for minority groups and through early special intervention programs to give disadvantaged children an advantaged intellectual foundation.

Issues in Assessment

As a college student, you may be struggling with decisions about the kind of job you would like to have when you finish school. In our final section, we will first discuss the role of assessment in vocational counseling. Then we will address some of the political and ethical issues posed by the widespread use of formal assessment procedures in our society today.

Vocational Interests and Aptitude

Have you already decided on a career path? Are you still undecided, or thinking of leaving a present job? Many assessment instruments can help people learn which vocations best fit their personalities, values, interests, and skills—or, in some cases, can show them that the career they have chosen may not be the wisest choice.

Assessing Interests. Even if you do not yet know what careers you might like best, you would probably want a job that suits your interests and serves goals that you consider worthwhile. However, you may be unsure about what your major interests and abilities are. Furthermore, you may have little idea of what people in many occupations actually *do,* and you may not really know how their job activities relate to your personal situation. A number of tests have been designed to help people identify major interests, abilities, and appropriate career directions.

The most widely used test for measuring vocational interests is the Strong-Campbell Interest Inventory, which was constructed in 1927 by psychologist **Edward Strong.** The test is based on an empirical approach similar to that used later for the MMPI. In developing this test, Strong studied groups of men in different occupations who answered items about activities they liked or disliked. The answers of those who were successful in particular occupations were then compared with the answers of men in general to create a scale. Subsequent versions of the test have added scales relevant to women and to newer occupations. If you took this test, a vocational counselor could tell you what types of jobs are typically held by people with interests such as yours, since these are the jobs that are likely to appeal to you.

aptitude test Test designed to measure an individual's potential for acquiring various skills.

achievement test Standardized test designed to measure an individual's current level of competence in a given area.

job analysis Study of a specific job, focusing on skills required, effort demanded, worker's responsibilities, and job-related stressors.

Assessing Abilities. Even if a job appeals to you and it suits your personality and fits your values and interests, you are unlikely to be satisfied with it unless you can do it well. Your employer will certainly not be satisfied with you if you are unable to do the job for which you were hired.

To recommend a career path for you, therefore, a vocational counselor will want to assess your abilities as well as your interests. Ability has two components: aptitude and achievement. An **aptitude test** measures your potential for acquiring various skills—not necessarily how well you can perform tasks now but how well you will be able to in the future, with adequate training. An **achievement test,** on the other hand, measures your current level of competence. A test of how well you can speak a foreign language or program a computer would be an example of an achievement test.

With knowledge of not only what you like to do but also what you can do well, a counselor is in a good position to predict your suitability for different jobs (Anastasi, 1975; Sundberg & Matarazzo, 1979; Tyler, 1974). Tests of ability are also used by companies seeking new employees. If you apply for a specific job, you may be asked to take tests involving the abilities and skills required for that job. If a job involves using a computer, you may be given a test of your familiarity with software or word-processing. If it involves hard physical labor like lifting and stacking heavy but fragile stock, you may be given a test of strength. If managing and directing salespeople will be an important part of the job, your ability to assert yourself or resolve conflicts may be assessed. The goal of such tests is to match people with the jobs for which they are best suited, thereby increasing the satisfaction of both employees and their employers.

Career counselors help individuals match their abilities with potential careers.

Assessing Jobs. Organizations often invest substantial time and money in personnel selection. They rely not only on an assessment of an applicant's characteristics but also on a careful identification and analysis of the requirements of the job. In a **job analysis,** a specific job is carefully examined first to determine the nature and degree of *skill* required, the amount of *effort* demanded, and the extent to which an individual is *responsible* for decisions that affect company resources or personnel, and second to identify any other types of *stress* the job may entail (Tenopyr & Oeltjen, 1982). The results of job analyses are used not only in selecting personnel but also in determining the pay scale for different jobs.

Job assessment is performed in many ways. Workers, supervisors, and specially trained job analysts are asked to provide information about the abilities required for particular jobs. Subject-matter experts rate the relevance of knowledge, skills, and abilities. An inventory of appropriate requirements, tasks, and duties can then be prepared for each occupation. One such inventory that has been developed—the Occupational Analysis Inventory—provides information about a wide spectrum of occupations and can be very helpful to a job seeker (Pass & Cunningham, 1978).

Some companies supplement other assessment methods with *realistic job previews*. They show applicants what will be expected of them on the job through films, tapes, employee checklists of most- and least-liked aspects of a job, and simulations of critical incidents likely to arise (Wanous, 1980). These previews give applicants a clearer picture of what will be expected of them if they take the job, and help them decide how well the job fits their abilities and interests.

How well one person does in a job often depends on more than knowledge and hard work. Among the other variables affecting job performance might be assertiveness, social skills, appearance, and general congruence or fit with a company's picture of its ideal supervisor, manager, or executive. When these types of characteristics are important, personality tests such as the CPI can be used in employee selection—but *only* for those jobs for which a test has been specifically validated.

Political and Ethical Issues

The primary goal of psychological assessment is to reduce errors of judgment that bias accurate assessments of people. This goal is achieved by replacing subjective judgments of teachers, physicians, employers, and other evaluators with more objective measures that have been carefully constructed and are open to critical evaluation. This is the goal that motivated Alfred Binet in his pioneering work. Binet and others hoped that testing would help democratize society and minimize decisions based on arbitrary criteria of sex, race, nationality, or physical appearance. Despite these lofty goals, there is no area of psychology more controversial than assessment. Three unresolved issues central to the controversy are the *fairness* of test-based decisions, the utility of tests for *evaluating education*, and the implications of using test scores as *labels*.

Fairness. Critics concerned with the fairness of testing practices argue that the costs or negative consequences may be higher for some test-takers than for others. The costs are quite high, for example, when low scores on certain tests are used to keep people from minority groups out of certain jobs. For example, in some cities, applicants for civil service janitor jobs must pass a verbal test, rather than a more appropriate test of janitorial manual skills.

Even when tests are valid predictors of job performance, they should not be used as an excuse to ignore the special needs of some specific groups in society. For example, some allegedly valid employment tests predict performance in training sessions but *not* performance on the job. People with less education or experience who have difficulty in training might, with a few extra training sessions, learn to perform a job as proficiently as people who already had the necessary skills when they were hired (Haney, 1982). Though still in school, for example, a college student could learn a mental hospital's jargon and policies well enough to work as a psychiatric aide before she completes work on her college degree. In addition, reliance on testing may all too often make personnel selection too often an automatic attempt to fit people into available jobs. Sometimes we might benefit more by changing the job descriptions to fit the needs and abilities of people.

Evaluating Education. Testing not only helps evaluate students; it also plays an indirect role in education. The quality of school systems and the effectiveness of teachers are frequently judged on the basis of how well their students score on standardized achievement tests. Local support of the schools through tax levies and even individual teacher salaries may ride on test scores.

These test scores, however, may not accurately reflect what students really know. Since the same tests are used for several years between revisions, teachers come to know what is on the test and prepare their students for those items. Scores improve, but the norms are not immediatey updated, so students in each district *appear* to be doing better and better each year until a revision comes out that makes them look inept in comparison to the previous year's students with their inflated scores. Students may be made to feel overly anxious about their performance by teachers who spend more time teaching them to be "test-wise" than to think for themselves (Leslie & Wingert, 1990).

Tests as Labels. We are a nation of test-takers and we sometimes forget that our test scores are, at best, statistical measures of our current functioning. Instead, we imbue the scores with an absolute significance that is not limited to appropriate normative comparisons. People too often think of themselves as *being* "an IQ of 110" or "a B student" as if the scores were labels stamped on their foreheads. Such labels may become barriers to advancement as people come to believe that their mental and personal qualities are fixed and unchangeable—that they cannot improve their lot in life.

This tendency to give test scores a sacred status has societal as well as personal implications. When test scores become labels that identify qualities *within* an individual, people begin to think about the "abnormality" of individual children rather than about educational systems that need to modify programs to accommodate all learners. Labels put the spotlight on deviant personalities rather than on problems in the environment. Human assessors need to recognize that what people are now is a product of where they've been, where they think they are headed, and what situation is currently influencing their behavior. Such a view can help to unite different assessment approaches and theoretical camps as well as lead to more humane treatment of those who do not fit the norm.

Assessing Our Lives

We conclude on a personal note, one that may have some inspirational value to students who do not do well on objective tests. Although we, your text authors, have gone on to have successful careers as professional psychologists, relevant tests and assessments earlier in our schooling might have predicted otherwise. One of us (P.G.Z.), despite being an Honors undergraduate student, got his only C grade in Introductory Psychology, a course in which grades were based solely on multiple-choice exams. He was initially rejected for graduate training at Yale University, then became an alternate, and finally was accepted—reluctantly, in part because his GRE math scores were below the Psychology Department's cut-off level. Your second author (A.L.W.) had taken psychology in high school, and "tested out" of Introductory Psychology in college, going directly to sophomore-level courses. (Note the irony of having a text author who never took the college course for which she is now writing.) Later she got her only relatively poor college grade in a course on Psychological Statistics. Later, in graduate school, she was "assessed" as being perhaps in the wrong field, and sent by her advisor for career counseling. The moral of our two stories is that isolated assessments—a surprisingly low test score, condemning judgment, or a poor rating—cannot possibly tell an individual's story fairly or completely. We made it in our careers despite the dire predictions about our being "misfits."

As we know now, successful performance in a career and in life requires something more than the abilities recognized by standardized tests, or the impressions sought by scrutinizing interviewers. While the best tests can predict how well people will do on the average, there is always room for error when desire, ambition, imagination, self-esteem, or personal pride get in the way, for better or worse. Perhaps you should learn to know when to believe more in yourself than in the results of any one evaluation. Further, when you yourself are in a position to evaluate others' potential for work or school, keep your human limitations in mind, and let your humility remind you how complex human abilities really are.

SUMMING UP

Assessment instruments have been developed to identify people's vocational interests. In measuring work-related abilities, aptitude tests identify learning potential, while achievement tests reflect current competency levels. In job analysis, the skill, effort, responsibilities, and stresses associated with a particular job are assessed.

Political and ethical issues associated with applied assessment include developing fair tests and using tests to evaluate the effectiveness of educational programs. Test-takers as well as administrators often mistakenly see test results as unchangeable labels indicating individuals' worth. Because isolated test scores and assessment experiences cannot tell one's whole story, it is important to have faith in oneself and others beyond the results of any single evaluation.

CHAPTER REVIEW

Assessing Individual Differences *Why do we assess individual differences? What are the historical origins of assessment? What goals do fomal and informal assessment have in common? What qualities make an assessment technique effective? On what kinds of information do psychologists base assessments?*

The purpose of psychological assessment is to describe or classify individuals in ways that will be useful for prediction or treatment. The individual differences perspective assumes that people are different from each other in measurable ways; in contrast, a situationist perspective assumes that different people still respond similarly to the same situations. A wide variety of personal characteristics can be assessed, including intelligence, traits, interests, skills, and behaviors.

A useful assessment tool must be reliable, valid, and standardized. A reliable measure gives consistent results on different testings. A valid measure assesses the attributes for which the test was designed. A standardized test is always administered and scored in the same way; norms allow a person's score to be compared to the averages of similar others.

Formal assessment is carried out through interviews, reviews of life histories, and observations. These important sources of information can come from either self-reports or other-reports. Self-reports may be subjectively distorted, while other-reports may be biased by halo and stereotype effects.

Key Terms
psychological assessment, p. 409
individual differences, p. 410

Major Contributor
Galton, Sir Francis, p. 410

2 Assessing Intelligence

What is intelligence? How was intelligence testing originally developed? What do IQ tests measure? How do different theories account for intelligence? How do biology and environment combine to influence an individual's intelligence?

Binet began the tradition of objective intelligence testing in France in the early 1900s. His test was designed to separate developmentally disabled from normal schoolchildren in order to plan special training programs. Scores were given in terms of mental ages and were meant to represent children's current level of functioning.

Terman created the Stanford-Binet Intelligence Scale and the concept of IQ. Wechsler designed special intelligence tests for adults, children, and preschoolers; each test consists of 11 different subtests and gives separate verbal, performance, and Full-Scale IQs at each age level. Highly efficient group tests of intelligence, which measure a narrower conception of intelligence, are widely used in education and business.

Psychometric analyses of IQ suggest that several basic abilities, such as fluid and crystallized aspects of intelligence, contribute to IQ scores. Cognitive science approaches conceive of and measure intelligence very broadly by considering the skills and insights people use to solve the many types of problems they encounter.

IQ tests are controversial because, on the average, some racial and cultural groups score lower on the tests than other groups. Instead of genetic differences, environmental disadvantages and test bias seem to be responsible for the lower scores of certain groups. Research shows that these group differences can be corrected through educational interventions.

3 **Issues in Assessment** *How can vocational interests and abilities be assessed to support career planning? What are the components of a job analysis? What qualities are important to make testing fair and meaningful?*

Vocational assessment includes assessment of an individual's interests, aptitudes, and current level of achievement. The Strong-Campbell Interest Inventory compares an individual's interests with those of people who are successful in various occupations. The Occupations Analysis Inventory provides information about the requirements of various jobs.

Assessment is prevalent in many areas of our lives, but it also has become highly controversial. Though often useful for prediction and as an indication of current performance, test results should not be used to limit an individual's opportunities for development and change. When the results of an assessment will touch an individual's life, it is important to be sure that the techniques used are reliable and valid for that individual and for the purpose in question, and that the assessment is as thorough as possible.

Key Terms
    aptitude test, p. 434
    achievement test, p. 434
    job analysis, p. 434

Major Contributor
    Strong, Edward, p. 434

PRACTICE TEST

Chapter 11: Individual Differences

For each of the following items, choose the single correct or best answer. Correct answers, explanations, and page references in the Appendix.

1. Despite widespread use of standardized psychological tests, some psychologists believe such testing is an embarrassment because _____ .
   A. no tests are objective
   B. no tests can overcome teachers' or employers' biases
   C. all tests are based in part on experiences that vary for different individuals
   D. None of the above.

2. Which of the following best expresses the opinion of early supporters of eugenics movement?
   A. Only the fittest and brightest individuals in a species should be encouraged to reproduce.
   B. A supportive, stimulating environment can overcome even a genetically inferior start in life.
   C. It is immoral for superior races to contribute to the extinction of inferior ones.
   D. A person's eminence is more a product of luck and circumstance than of inherited endowments.

3. A testing entrepreneur has invented Big Toe Intelligence Test. To obtain a gauge of your intellectual ability, he measures your left big toe in centimeters, multiplies that figure by 10, and adds your age. This, he says, yields your IQ. Given your knowledge of testing, you know this test is _____ .
   A. not reliable
   B. reliable but not valid
   C. valid
   D. probably standardized for abnormal but not normal populations

4. By establishing _____ , we are able to standardize the use and administration of a given test.
   A. norms
   B. validity
   C. reliability
   D. internal consistency

5. The major advantage of using _____ as a strategy for collecting information about a subject is that this approach provides *quantitative* characterizations of the individual being studied.
   A. a psychological test
   B. an interview
   C. situational behavior observation
   D. a life history

6. Intelligence is defined in your text as _____ .
   A. the sum of an individual's acquired knowledge, including episodic, semantic, and procedural information
   B. an individual's aptitude for collecting new knowledge regardless of past patterns of function
   C. all cognitive abilities, including memory, problem-solving, logical functions, and perception
   D. the ability to profit from experience by going beyond perceptions to imagined possibilities

7. A child who takes an IQ test has a chronological age of 12 and is found to have a mental age of 15. According to Terman's mathematical formula for intelligence quotient, the child's IQ must be _____ .
   A. 150
   B. 125
   C. 120
   D. 103

8. The intelligence theory developed by _____ argues that intelligence is broken into five kinds of content, six kinds of products, and five kinds of operations, for a total of 150 possible unique combinations of content and form, best represented by a cube.
   A. David Wechsler
   B. R. B. Cattell
   C. J. P. Guilford
   D. Howard Gardner

9. According to Robert Sternberg, there are three kinds of intelligence, one of which is _____ intelligence, also known as business sense or street smarts.
   A. performance
   B. contextual
   C. componential
   D. experiential

10. The Strong-Campbell Inventory is an example of a test that _____ .
    A. assesses vocational interests
    B. conducts a job analysis
    C. measures aptitude in general subject areas
    D. identifies an individual's level of achievement in a particular subject

IF YOU'RE INTERESTED . . .

Anastasi, A. (1982). *Psychological testing, 5th edition*. New York: Macmillan.

Not a sit-down-and-read-it book, but a respected reference worth thumbing through to gain a familiarity with the many qualities and abilities that are measurable, and the tests and instruments developed to assess them.

Charly. (Video: 1968, color, 103 minutes). Directed by Ralph Nelson; starring Cliff Robertson, Claire Bloom, Lilia Skala, Leon Janney.

Engrossing film based on Daniel Keyes' short story, "Flowers for Algernon," about a retarded man who volunteers for experimental surgery that transforms him into a genius. Effective, if slightly stereotyped, portrayals of how intelligence influences personality and relationships.

Competition, The. (Video: 1980, color, 129 minutes). Directed by Joel Oliansky; starring Richard Dreyfuss and Amy Irving.

Simple but well-done story of what happens when two gifted pianists, competing for the same prize, fall in love. Nice treatment of the centrality of achievement and ability in personal and social identity.

Gould, S. J. (1981). *The mismeasure of man*. New York: Norton.

Readable, engaging, fascinating review of the efforts of people to assess themselves and each other, whether for noble or nefarious purposes. By Stephen Jay Gould, the bestselling author of numerous popular presentations of cultural anthropology.

Jensen, A. R. (1980). *Bias in mental testing*. New York: Free Press.

Complex but worth looking at, a review of the controversies surrounding the question of group, racial, and cultural biases in intelligence testing, by Arthur Jensen—not an "unbiased" source but one who has had much to say.

Chapter 12 **Social Psychology**

1. How can social situations affect task performance? What processes teach us about the rules that operate in our social environments? What two motives have been proposed to explain conformity? How does Milgram's study of obedience to authority demonstrate the power of situations? Which factors best predict whether a bystander will help in a crisis?

2. How can a person's expectations affect what happens? What major everyday task underlies social perception? What are the two main lessons of social psychology?

3. What is social psychology's ultimate goal? What is the irony of experiencing close relationships? What does peace psychology seek to accomplish?

On a summer Sunday in California, a siren shattered the serenity of college student Tommy Whitlow's morning. A police car screeched to a halt in front of his home. Within minutes, Tommy was charged with a felony, informed of his constitutional rights, frisked, and handcuffed. After he was booked and fingerprinted, Tommy was blindfolded and transported to the Stanford County Prison, where he was stripped, sprayed with disinfectant, and issued a smock-type uniform with an I. D. number on the front and back. Tommy became Prisoner 647. Nine other college students were also arrested and assigned numbers.

The prison guards were not identified by name, and their anonymity was enhanced by khaki uniforms and reflector sunglasses—Prisoner 647 never saw their eyes. He referred to each of his jailers as "Mr. Correctional Officer, Sir"; to them, he was only number 647.

The guards insisted that prisoners obey all rules without question or hesitation. Failure to do so led to the loss of a privilege. At first, privileges included opportunities to read, write, or talk to other inmates. Later on, the slightest protest resulted in the loss of the "privileges" of eating, sleeping, and washing. Failure to obey rules also resulted in the assignment of menial, unpleasant work such as cleaning toilets with bare hands, doing push-ups while a guard stepped on the prisoner's back, and spending hours in solitary confinement. The guards were always devising new strategies to make the prisoners feel worthless. Every guard Prisoner 647 encountered engaged in abusive, authoritarian behavior at some point during his incarceration. The main difference among the guards was in the frequency and regularity of their hostility toward the prisoners.

Less than 36 hours after the mass arrest, prisoner 8412, one of the ringleaders of an aborted prisoner rebellion that morning, began to cry uncontrollably. He experienced fits of rage, disorganized thinking, and severe depression. On successive days, three more prisoners developed similar stress-related symptoms. A fifth prisoner developed a psychosomatic rash all over his body when the Parole Board rejected his appeal.

At night, Prisoner 647 tried to remember what Tommy Whitlow had been like before he became a prisoner. He also tried to imagine his tormentors before they became guards. He reminded himself that he was a college student who had answered a newspaper ad and agreed to be a subject in a two-week experiment on prison life. He had thought it would be fun to do something unusual, and he could always use some extra money.

In the Stanford Prison Experiment, the participants learned never to underestimate the power of a bad situation to overwhelm the personalities and good upbringing of even the best and brightest individuals.

social psychology Branch of psychology that studies the effect of social variables on individual behavior, cognitions, and motives, as well as group and intergroup processes.

social context Part of the environment that includes real and imagined other people, interactions, the interactive setting, and guidelines for how people relate to each other.

Everyone in the prison, guard and prisoner alike, had been selected from a large pool of student volunteers. On the basis of extensive psychological tests and interviews, the volunteers had been judged as law-abiding, emotionally stable, physically healthy, and "normal-average." In this mock prison experiment, assignment of participants to "guard" or "prisoner" roles had been *randomly determined* by the flip of a coin. The prisoners lived in the jail around the clock and the guards worked standard eight-hour shifts.

As guards, students who had been pacifists and "nice guys" behaved aggressively—sometimes even sadistically. As prisoners, psychologically stable students soon behaved pathologically, passively resigning themselves to their unexpected fate of learned helplessness. The power of the simulated prison situation had created a new *social reality*—a real prison—in the minds of the jailers and their captives.

Because of the dramatic and unexpectedly emotional and behavioral effects the researchers observed, those prisoners with extreme stress reactions were released early from their pretrial detention in this unusual prison, and the psychologists had to terminate their two-week study after only six days. Although Tommy Whitlow said he wouldn't want to go through it again, he valued the personal experience because he learned so much about himself and about human nature. Fortunately, he and the other students were basically healthy, and they readily bounced back from that highly charged situation. Follow-ups over many years revealed no lasting negative effects. The participants had all learned an important lesson: Never underestimate the power of a bad situation to overwhelm the personalities and good upbringing of even the best and brightest among us (Haney & Zimbardo, 1977; Zimbardo, 1975; replicated in Australia by Lovibond et al., 1979).

Introduction

Suppose YOU had been a subject in the Stanford Prison Experiment. Would you have been a "good" guard? A "model" prisoner? Could you have resisted the powerful pressures and stresses of your bizarre circumstances? We'd all like to believe we would be good guards and heroic prisoners, but the best predictor for the way you might react in such a setting is the way some typical students, like yourself, actually behaved. The results of this study indicate that, despite our optimistic beliefs, most of us would fall on the negative side of the good-bad, hero-victim dichotomy. The results do not offer an upbeat, positive message. However, it is a message that social psychologists feel obliged to pass along in the hope that such knowledge may deter mindless submission to the powerful situational forces that subtly and pervasively shape human behavior.

Welcome to the study of *social psychology*, which investigates how individuals affect each other. **Social psychology** is the study how individuals' thoughts, feelings, perceptions, motives, and behavior are influenced by interactions and transactions between people. Social psychologists try to understand behavior within its *social context*. Defined broadly, the **social context** includes the real, imagined, or symbolic *presence* of other people; the *activities and interactions* that take place between people; the *settings* in which behavior occurs; and the *expectations and norms* governing behavior in a given setting (C. Sherif, 1981).

The Stanford Prison Experiment conducted by **Philip Zimbardo** underscores the *power of social situations* to control human behavior—a major theme to emerge from innovative research social psychologists have conducted over the past 50 years. In the first part of this chapter, we will consider a large body of research that shows how minor features of social settings can have a significant impact on what we think and how we act.

A second theme of social psychology is that situations matter not so much in their objective features but in their *subjective* nature—in the way that people perceive, interpret, and find meaning in them. We will study this second theme, the *construction of social reality*, by investigating how people create social realities for themselves and others.

Finally, we will look at a third theme of social psychology: the determination to solve *social problems* by applying information about social processes. Social psychologists are at the forefront of work in such applied fields as health psychology, relationship studies, environmental psychology, psychology and law, and peace psychology. On this dimension of *social relevance*, abstract theory meets the stern test of practicality: Does the theory make a difference in the lives of people and society?

The Power of the Situation

Social psychologists believe that the primary determinant of individual behavior is the nature of the social situation in which that behavior occurs. They argue that social situations exert significant control over individual behavior, often dominating one's personality and past history of learning, values, and beliefs. Situational aspects that appear trivial to most observers—labels, rules, social roles, the mere presence of others—can powerfully influence how we behave. Often, subtle situational variables affect us without our awareness. In this section, we will review some classic research and recent experiments that explore **situationism,** or the effect of these subtle situational variables on people.

situationism View that, to a greater extent than we realize, forces in behavior settings determine our behavior more than personal qualities do.

Social Facilitation

The earliest demonstration that the *mere presence* of other people has a measurable impact on individual behavior was conducted by **Norman Triplett** in 1897. As an avid cyclist, Triplett had noticed that bicycle racers had faster times when they were racing with other people than when they were racing against a clock. To determine whether this effect held true for other activities, Triplett had children perform the task of winding fishing reels. Sure enough, the children performed faster when another child was present in the room than when they were alone.

This speedy-reeling effect was not simply the result of competition; later studies found that it occurred also when an individual performed in front of an audience. The effect was also found in a *coacting group*—a group of people engaged in the same behavior but not interacting with each other. This improvement of individual performance brought about by the presence of other people is called **social facilitation.**

The social facilitation effect turned out to be more complicated than it first seemed. Subsequent researchers found that sometimes the presence of others *interfered* with performance. Standing up before an audience, for example, may cause stage fright. One explanation for these apparently contradictory findings is that the presence of other people has the general effect of increasing an individual's level of *arousal*. High arousal will facilitate performance when a person is engaging in behavior that is well-learned. However, if the responses are relatively new and not well-learned, then the increased arousal can be disruptive. In such cases, the individual becomes tense, and the drive fostered by this tension will interfere with optimal performance (Zajonc, 1976). For example, if you are used to making class presentations or understand your subject well, the attention of your classmates will probably help you give a better talk. In contrast, if you lack confidence about your speaking ability or your knowledge of the topic, the attentiveness of your audience may make you so nervous that you choke up and perform poorly.

social facilitation Amplifying effect that the presence of others can have on individual performance.

Have you ever participated in a group task, and found yourself tempted to give less effort since your individual contributions would not be taken into account? Aren't there times when working with other people seems to encourage goofing off? This phenomenon occurs often enough to be viewed as the flip side of social facilitation. **Social loafing** is defined as the unconscious ten-

social loafing Unconscious tendency to withhold effort when performing in a group.

dency to slack off when performing in a group, regardless of whether the task is interesting or meaningful (Latané, 1981). The negative effects of social loafing are that people not only work less, but they take less responsibility for what they are doing. For example, business administration students assigned to work in teams may find their motivation suffers when they know the instructor plans to assign not individual grades but one group grade per team. Each team member may withhold her best effort, fearful of being exploited by her teammates, and some members may drop out in hopes of taking a "free ride" at the others' expense.

The social loafing effect is attributed to the person's reduced self-attention as he or she must process more external inputs from other group members. When self-attention diminishes, so do the usual self-imposed controls of surveillance on behavior. People become less concerned about matching their own behavior to group goals or their own past history. They tend to go with the slower flow of the group (Carver & Scheier, 1981; Mullen & Baumeister, 1987). An employee newly assigned to a new planning committee might take his cue from the casual pace of the group instead of working at his usual speed or worrying about the project deadline.

Social facilitation, interference, and loafing effects demonstrate the power of even the simplest social situation—the mere presence of other people. Most groups, however, involve more dynamic and direct interactions among their members. Let's examine these sources of social power.

Roles, Rules, and Norms

rules Behavioral guidelines for how to act in certain situations.

To promote social interaction and to achieve the desired outcomes of those in the majority or in power, situations are characterized by the operation of **rules**—behavioral guidelines for certain settings. Some rules are explicitly stated in signs ("Don't Smoke," "No Eating in Class") or in socialization practices ("Respect the elderly," "Never take candy from a stranger"). Other rules are implicit; they are learned through transactions with others in particular settings. How loud you can play your stereo, how close you can stand to another person, when you can call your teacher or boss by a first name, and how you should react to a compliment or a gift all depend on the situation. For example, the Japanese do not open a gift in the presence of the gift-giver for fear of not showing sufficient appreciation; foreigners not aware of this unwritten rule will misinterpret the behavior as rude instead of sensitive.

The situations in which you live and function also determine the roles available to you. Being a college student diminishes the likelihood that you will become a warrior, drug pusher, shaman, or prisoner, for example. Because you have college experience, numerous other roles (such as manager, teacher, and politician) are available to you.

social role Socially defined pattern of behavior expected of a person when functioning in a given setting or group.

Social Roles. Situations help define the social meaning that each role will have for the people who have assumed it. A single action can be interpreted in many different ways, depending on the meaning different people assign to it. For example, defying authority can be interpreted as admirable and heroic, foolish and troublemaking, or dangerous and deviant. A **social role** is a socially defined pattern of behavior that is expected of a person when functioning in a given setting or group. People play many different social roles in the various situations in which they usually operate.

For example, at the conclusion of the Stanford Prison experiment, guards and prisoners differed from one another in virtually every observable way; yet, just a week before, their role identities (college students) had been interchangeable. Chance, in the form of random assignment, had decided their roles, and these roles created status and power differences that were validated

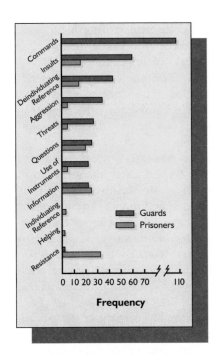

Figure 12.1 Guard and Prisoner Behavior During the Stanford Prison Experiment, the assigned roles of prisoners and guards drastically affected subjects' behavior. The observations recorded in this 6-day interaction profile show that across 25 observation periods, the prisoners engaged in more passive resistance, while the guards became more dominating, controlling, and hostile!

social norms Group's expectations regarding what is appropriate and acceptable for its members' attitudes and behaviors.

in the prison situation. The social context induced a host of differences in the way those in each group thought, felt, and acted (see **Figure 12.1**).

No one taught the participants to play their roles. Each student had the capacity to become either a prisoner or a guard by calling upon stored structures of knowledge about those roles. In our schemas and scripts, a "guard-type" is someone who uses *coercive rules* to limit the freedom of "prisoner-types." Prisoners can only *react* to the social structure of a prison-like setting created by those with power. Rebellion or compliance are the primary options of the prisoners. Some prisoners resign themselves to helplessness; they passively wait until the situation changes.

The student participants had already experienced such power differences in many of their previous social interactions: parent-child; teacher-student; doctor-patient; boss-worker; male-female. The participants merely refined and intensified their improvised scripts for this particular setting. Each student could have played either role. Many students in the guard role were surprised at how easy it was for them to enjoy controlling other people, and how just putting on the uniform transformed them from college-student research subjects into prison guards ready to manage inmates (*Discovering Psychology*, Program 18).

Social Norms. In addition to developing expectations about role behaviors, groups develop many expectations for the ways their members should act. Expectations for socially appropriate attitudes and behaviors that are embodied in the stated or implicit rules of a group are called **social norms.** Social norms can be broad guidelines, such as ideas about which political or religious attitudes are considered acceptable. Social norms can also embody specific standards of conduct, such as allowable actions or duties. Norms can guide conversation, as when they restrict discussion of sensitive or taboo subjects in certain company. Finally, norms can define habits, such as dress codes for group members, whether requiring uniforms or outlawing inappropriate attire.

Adjustment to a group typically involves discovering the set of social norms that regulates desired behavior in the group setting. Individuals experience this adjustment in two ways: by noticing the *uniformities* in certain behaviors of all or most members and by observing the *negative consequences* when someone behaves in a nonnormative way, violating a social norm. For example, a child whose parents move her from a public school to a private academy sees that her new classmates all wear the same outfits and behave in very similar ways during class or when talking with the teacher. If a child dresses "wrong" one day, the others laugh at her, and misbehavior such as talking out of turn is quickly penalized.

Norms serve several important functions. Awareness of the norms operating in a group orients members and regulates their social interaction. Each participant can anticipate the way others will enter the situation—the way they will dress, what they are likely to say and do, as well as what type of behavior will be expected of them and gain approval. Adhering to the norms of a group is the first step in establishing *identification* with the group. Such identification allows an individual to have the feeling of sharing in whatever prestige and power the group possesses. For example, a young man visits his best friend's church and notes that others his age are dressed more formally than his own jeans and T-shirt, that they claim not to drink, and that their taste in music is different from his own. When invited to visit again, he dresses more conservatively, avoids mentioning a drinking party he attended, and listens politely to music he would normally reject as bland. To his pleasure, he finds his new friends are more interesting than he thought, and treat him as if he "belongs."

In exchange for adhering to group norms, some *tolerance for deviating* from the standard is also part of the norm—wide in some cases, narrow in others. Members are usually able to estimate how far they can go before experiencing the coercive power of the group in the form of the three painful

Social norms can define rigid dress codes for group members.

reference group Formal or informal group from which an individual derives norms and seeks information, direction, and life-style support.

R's: *ridicule, reeducation,* and *rejection.* The young man visiting his friend's church, for example, finds that as he spends time with his new friends, he is better able to relax—as long as he does not break any important rules. Good-natured joking keeps him in line when he says or does something that offends others (ridicule). Some church members take him aside to explain religious doctrine and urge him to join (reeducation). He knows that if he "goes too far"—disagrees too much with accepted beliefs or customs—his new friends will no longer welcome him (rejection).

Norms emerge in a new group through two processes: *diffusion* and *crystallization.* When people first enter a group, they bring with them their own expectations, previously acquired through other group memberships and life experiences. These various expectations are diffused and spread throughout the group as the members communicate with each other. As people talk and carry out activities together, their expectations begin to converge or crystallize into a common perspective. For example, as members of a new landscaping crew work together, they learn to understand and speak each other's language, soon referring to plants and tools by the same set of terms and using these to agree on their goals and tasks.

Once norms are established in a group, they tend to perpetuate themselves. Current group members exert social pressure on incoming members to adhere to the norms, and they in turn put direct or indirect pressure on successive newcomers to conform to the norms. Norms can be transmitted from one generation of group members to the next and can continue to influence people's behavior long after the original group that created the norm no longer exists (Insko et al., 1980). In natural groups like families, group *rituals* often serve the purpose of transmitting symbols, history, and values important to the group from old to new members. Social clubs conduct initiation ceremonies for new members, just as initiates to a church undergo baptism and military recruits must survive basic training. Such experiences are often personally poignant and memorable, and can strengthen one's loyalty to the group.

Gordon Allport (1937; 1985), a major contributor to both personality theory and social psychology, has argued that social psychological researchers face two profound questions: How does one generation impose its culture and thought forms on the next? Second, what happens to the mental life of the individual when he or she enters into association with others? The first question is addressed by studies on norm crystallization—the process by which group standards are established—and by the research of cultural anthropologists and sociologists. The second question is studied in depth through the analysis of group processes and the nature of social influence.

Group norms have a strong impact on an individual's behavior as long as the individual values the group. If the person comes to value and identify with a new group, then he or she will change to follow the norms of the new group. **Reference group** is the term for a formal or informal group from which an individual derives attitudes and standards of acceptable and appropriate behavior and to which the individual refers for information, direction, and support for a given life-style. For example, when you started college, you probably left behind many or most members of your high-school reference group, but eventually came to identify with a new reference group of college campus acquaintances.

Bennington's Liberal Norms. Often, the process of being influenced by group norms is so gradual and so subtle that an individual does not perceive what is happening. Some insights into this process are provided by a classic study conducted in a small New England college for women in the late 1930s. Researcher **Theodore Newcomb** studied the shifts in political and social attitudes experienced by these students during their four years at Bennington College. He then followed up the observed effects 20 years later to determine if these effects were enduring.

The prevailing norm at Bennington College was one of political and economic liberalism, as encouraged by its young, dynamic, politically committed, and liberal faculty. On the other hand, most of the students had come from privileged, conservative homes and brought conservative attitudes with them. Newcomb's study examined the impact of the college's liberal atmosphere on the attitudes of individual students. The conservatism of the new students steadily declined as they progressed through college, so that by their senior year most had been converted to a clearly liberal position.

Newcomb accounted for this change in terms of the powerful reference group norms that were operating. The women belonged to a close-knit, self-sufficient social community. The strong sense of school spirit included activist concerns and support for the norm of liberalism. Politically active liberal students were most likely to be chosen for positions of leadership and for friendship. Pressures to conform to particular attitudes and political actions were enforced by greater social acceptance and implied threats of rejection. These values became *internalized* (personally accepted) by those individuals for whom their Bennington classmates had become the primary reference group. Students who *resisted* this pervasive norm and retained their conservatism were either part of a small, close-knit, isolated group or had maintained strong ties with their conservative families, conforming to their family's standards rather than the school's (Newcomb, 1943).

Twenty years later, the marks of the Bennington experience were still evident. Most women who had left as liberals were still liberals; those who had resisted had remained conservatives, and the rest were "middle of the roaders." Most had married men with values similar to their own, thus creating a supportive home environment. In the 1960 presidential election, the Bennington allegiance was evident when about 60 percent of the 1935–1939 graduates voted for John F. Kennedy, compared to less than 30 percent support for Kennedy among graduates of comparable colleges (Newcomb et al., 1967).

Situational Norms. The force of social norms depends on the extent to which group members are in a *total situation*. A **total situation** is one in which group members have no access to contrary points of view and in which sources of information, social rewards, and punishments are all highly controlled by group leaders. The more people rely on social rewards from a group for their primary sense of self-worth, the greater will be the social influence that the group can bring to bear on them.

Social situations also include the operation of roles, rules, and norms, which can be powerful agents of change. They can affect people in socially prescribed ways or inhibit and restrain them from changing in socially inappropriate or situationally unacceptable ways. In this way, people take on different roles in different contexts: They may become liberals or conservatives in American politics, supporters of apartheid in South Africa, revolutionary nationalists in a former communist-bloc country, or extremists willing to bomb abortion clinics if they belong to pro-life groups.

As exemplified at the beginning of this chapter, social psychologists have attempted to demonstrate the power of situational forces by devising experiments that reveal the ease with which smart, independent, rational, good people can be led into behaving in ways that are dumb, compliant, irrational, and even evil. Although social psychologists have shown the *serious* consequences of situational power, it is equally possible to demonstrate this principle with *humor*. Indeed, "Candid Camera" scenarios, created by the television program's producer and intuitive social psychologist **Allen Funt,** have been demonstrating the power of situational forces for over 40 years. Funt showed how human nature seems to follow a situational script. Millions in his TV audiences laughed when a diner stopped eating a hamburger whenever a "Don't Eat" counter light flashed; when pedestrians stopped and waited at a red traffic light above the *sidewalk* on which they were walking; when highway

total situation Environmental conditions in which people are isolated from contrary points of view, and in which group leaders control distribution of information, rewards, and punishments.

In this 1960s "Candid Camera" scenario, the woman with three legs asks the man if he would like to go dancing. Would you?

drivers turned back upon seeing a road sign that read "Delaware is Closed"; and when customers jumped from one white tile to another in response to a store sign that instructed them not to walk on black tiles, for no reason. One of the best "Candid Camera" illustrations of the subtle power of implicit situational rules is the "elevator caper." A person riding a rigged elevator first obeyed the usual silent rule to face the front, but when a group of other passengers all faced the rear, the hapless victim followed the new *emerging group norm* and faced the rear as well.

In these slice-of-life episodes, we see the minimal situational conditions needed to elicit unusual behaviors in ordinary people. We laugh when people similar to ourselves behave foolishly and act irrationally in odd situations, and we distance ourselves from them by assuming we would not act that way. The lesson of social psychological research is that (more than likely) we would behave exactly as others if we were placed in the same situation.

➡ How would you behave if you found yourself in a situation that pressured people to act in evil, foolish, or irrational ways? The wise reply appears to be, "I don't know; it depends on how powerful the situation is." Researchers can predict your behavior by knowing the rate or extent of compliance of others in that situation and making the conservative assumption that you would probably behave as the majority did. It is the heroes among us who are able to behave otherwise—to resist and overcome situational forces—and there are fewer heroes than followers in everyday life. (See "Time Out for Critical Thinking.")

instructor who has not noticed the cheater? What if the cheater had been copying answers from your exam?

- In the cereal aisle of the local grocery store, you watch in horror as a screaming child, throwing an unsuccessful tantrum, is repeatedly struck by his angry mother. The screams only get louder, but other shoppers act as though they do not even notice the abuse. Do you walk on and "mind your own business," or do you attempt to intervene? Why or why not?

- Your cab driver insists on telling you a racist joke he thinks is really funny. Do you tell him you don't want to hear it? Do you listen and laugh to be polite? Do you tell him you find it offensive, and show your displeasure by not tipping him? What factors determine your behavior?

Some situations may be easier to ignore than others, because you "don't care" and your actions seem unimportant. What circumstances seem to prompt you to break away from the flow or complacency of your surroundings? In contrast, what conditions tend to keep you "in your place" and lull you into remaining silent or inactive? Why is it important to become a "hero" and break with the norms of a group? Have you ever done it? What were the consequences of your deviation?

Conforming

In the Bennington Study, conformity to the group norm had clear adaptive significance for the students; they were more likely to be accepted, approved of, and recognized for various social rewards if they adopted the liberal norm. However, in the Candid Camera vignettes, the subjects were not part of a reference group that controlled vital social reinforcements and punishments. Their conformity to the norm of a transient group was not based on *normative pressures* but rather on other needs, such as the need for cognitive clarity about one's world. When uncertain, we typically turn to others in the situation to satisfy *information needs* that will help us understand what is happening (Deutsch & Gerard, 1955). Two processes that explain why people conform to group pressures and comply with pressures from individuals are **normative influence**—wanting to be liked, accepted, and approved of by others—and **informational influence**—wanting to be correct and to understand how best to act in a given situation (Insko et al., 1985).

normative influence Effect of a group on an individual who strives to be liked, accepted, and approved of by others.

informational influence Effect of a group on an individual who desires to be correct and understand how best to act in a given situation.

Of Lines and Lies: The Asch Effect. Even if you were caught in the act of "being yourself" in a Candid Camera scene, you could rationalize your compliance by insisting that these are only habits of action, not matters of life and death or right and wrong. But what if your dilemma really were a matter of fact, not merely opinion? In other words, what if you were part of a group asked to judge some aspect of physical reality, and you found that the rest of the group saw the world differently—*wrongly*, in fact—from you? This situation was created by one of the most important social psychologists, **Solomon Asch** (1940; 1956). Asch believed that the constraints of physical reality on perception would be stronger than the power of the social context to distort individual judgments. He was wrong, but his studies led to a significant psychological finding. The **Asch effect** describes the influence of a unanimous group majority on the judgments of individuals even under unambiguous conditions. The Asch effect has become the classic illustration of **conformity**—the tendency for people to adopt the behavior and opinions presented by other group members.

Asch effect Pattern of conformity in which, even when conditions are not ambiguous, a unanimous group majority influences individuals' judgments.

conformity Tendency for people to adopt the behaviors, attitudes, and values of other members of a reference group.

In Asch's study, groups of seven to nine male college students were told they would be participating in a study of simple visual perception. They were shown cards with three lines of differing lengths and asked to indicate which of the three lines was the same length as a separate, standard line (see **Figure 12.2**). The lines were different enough so that mistakes were rare, and their relative sizes changed on each series of trials.

On the first three trials, everyone agreed on the correct comparison. However, the first person to respond on the fourth trial reported an obviously wrong answer, seeing as equal two lines that were clearly different. So did the next person and so on, until all members of the group but the remaining one unanimously agreed on a judgment that conflicted with the perception of that final student. That student had to decide whether he should go along with everyone else's view of the situation and conform, or rather remain independent, standing by what he clearly saw. That dilemma was repeated on 12 of the 18 trials. Unbeknownst to this last subject, all of the others were experimental confederates who were following a prearranged script. Their script allowed for

Figure 12.2 Conformity in the Asch Experiments
In this photo from Asch's study, it is evident that the naive subject, number 6, is worried by the unanimous majority's erroneous judgment. The typical stimulus array is shown at top right. At top left, the graph illustrates conformity across 12 critical trials when solitary subjects were grouped with a unanimous majority, as well as their greater independence when paired with a dissenting partner. A lower percentage of correct estimates indicates the greater degree of an individual's conformity to the group's false estimate.

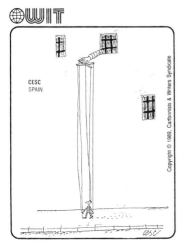

Social influence without awareness

no communication other than calling out the perceptual judgment. The genuine subject showed signs of disbelief and discomfort when faced with a majority who saw the world so differently from the way he did. What did he and others in his position finally do?

In Asch's complete series of trials, only one-fourth of these real subjects remained completely independent. In various related studies, between 50 and 80 percent of the subjects conformed with the majority's false estimate at least once, while a third of the subjects yielded to the majority's wrong judgments on half or more of the critical trials. In other words, the fact that subjects were judging matters of fact—not merely personal opinions—did not make most of them immune to conformity pressures.

Group Conformity. In other studies, Asch varied three factors: the size of the unanimous *majority,* the presence of a *partner* who dissented from the majority, and the size of the *discrepancy* between the correct answer and the majority's position. He found that strong conformity effects were elicited with a unanimous majority of only three or four people, but no conformity effect was obtained with only one confederate. Giving the naive subject one ally who dissented from the majority opinion sharply reduced conformity, as shown in **Figure 12.2.** With such a "partner," the subject was usually able to resist the pressures to conform to the majority.

Remarkably, a certain proportion of individuals continued to yield to the group even under the most extreme stimulus circumstances. All who yielded underestimated the influence of the social pressure and the frequency of their conformity; some even claimed that they really had *seen* the lines as the majority had claimed (Asch, 1955, 1956).

Numerous studies of conformity have confirmed these results. The power of the group majority depends on its unanimity. Once that is broken in any way, the rate of conformity drops dramatically. A person is also more likely to conform when a judgment task is difficult or ambiguous, the group is cohesive, the members are perceived as competent, and the person's responses are made public. For example, when you vote in a group election, you are more likely to go along with the majority if the issue being decided is complex (difficult) or confusing (ambiguous); if most others present are friends of yours (cohesive group); if they seem to know what they are talking about (are perceived as competent); and if you must vote by raising your hand instead of casting an anonymous ballot (public response). In many cases, people conform without awareness that they have been affected, maintaining an *illusion* of freedom and independence that is unwarranted by their actions.

Social Conformity. In society, the majority tends to be the defender of the *status quo* (the existing state of affairs), while the force for innovation and change comes from the minority members or individuals either dissatisfied with the current system or able to visualize new options and creative alternatives for dealing with current problems. For example, issues of protecting the natural environment are still viewed as "special interests" in many regions of North America. However, through persistence and flexibility, environmentalists in many communities have succeeded in winning broad-based support for such innovations as recycling, waste control, and wildlife conservation. The conflict between the entrenched majority view and the dissident minority perspective is an essential precondition of innovations that can lead to positive social change. An individual is constantly engaged in a two-way exchange with society—adapting to its norms, roles, and status prescriptions but also acting upon society to reshape those norms (Moscovici, 1985). Perhaps the greatest challenges for social psychologists to understand are the dynamics of group forces that influence individual behavioral and mental processes, and those individual factors that maintain or change group functioning.

Obeying Authority

So far, we've seen how groups influence individuals, but certain individuals—such as leaders and authorities—influence groups by exerting considerable power on group behavior. The ultimate demonstration of this effect was seen in the 1930s with the emergence of Adolf Hitler in Germany and Benito Mussolini in Italy. These dictators were able to transform rational citizens into mindless masses with unquestioning loyalty to a fascist ideology bent on world conquest. Their authoritarian regimes threatened democracies and freedom everywhere. Curiously, modern social psychology developed out of this crucible of fear, war, and prejudice. The early concerns of social psychology focused on the nature of the authoritarian personality behind the fascist mentality (Adorno et al., 1950), the effects of propaganda and persuasive communications (Hovland et al., 1949), and the impact of the group on its members. Later research by **Stanley Milgram** extended these studies to focus on how individuals become so blindly obedient to the commands of authorities.

The Question of Obedience. What made "good" German citizens as well as fanatical Nazis willing to send millions of Jews to the gas chambers merely a few decades ago? Did a character defect lead them to carry out orders blindly, even if the orders violated their own values and moral principles? More recently, why did nearly 100 members of the Branch Davidian religious sect join their leader, David Koresh, in defying federal agents who charged their compound in Waco, Texas? After a standoff of several weeks during the spring of 1993, cult members apparently set fire to their quarters rather than surrender to authorities; scores of men, women, and children perished in the resulting blaze. How can we explain the 1978 mass suicide-murders of the members of the Peoples Temple? Over 900 American citizens belonging to the cult willingly administered cyanide poison to their children and to themselves because their leader, Reverend Jim Jones, told them to commit "revolutionary suicide."

➡ Let's get personal: How about YOU? Would you electrocute a stranger if a respected authority figure asked you to? Are there any conditions under which you would blindly obey an order from a religious leader to poison others and then commit suicide? Could you imagine participating on one afternoon in the American military massacre of hundreds of innocent civilians in the Vietnamese village of My Lai (pronounced me-LYE)—merely on the orders of the young commanding officer (Hersh, 1971; Opton, 1970, 1973)?

Your answer is most likely, "No! What kind of person do you think I am?"—as if your actions are determined by the "kind" of person you happen to be. After reading this next section, you may be more willing to answer, "Maybe I would obey orders to harm others. I don't know for sure." Depending on the power of the social forces operating on your moral judgment and weakening your will to resist, you might do what others have done in those situations, however horrible and alien their actions may seem outside that setting. The study of obedience brings into critical focus the tension between the power of individual differences and that of situations.

The most convincing demonstration of situational power was created by Stanley Milgram, a student of Solomon Asch (and a high school classmate of Philip Zimbardo). Milgram's research (1965, 1974) showed that the blind obedience of Nazis was less a product of dispositional characteristics (their unusual personality or German national character) than it was the outcome of situational forces that could engulf anyone—even you and me. How did he demonstrate this "banality of evil," that evil deeds could be engaged in by good people for what they felt were noble purposes (Hannah Arendt, 1963, 1971)? Milgram's obedience research is one of the most controversial in psychology both because of the ethical issues it raises and its significant implications for real world phenomena (Miller, 1986; Ross & Nisbett, 1991).

After a standoff of several weeks during the spring of 1993, members of the Branch Davidian cult apparently set fire to their quarters rather than surrender to authorities.

The Obedience Paradigm. To separate the variables of personality and situation, which are always entangled in natural settings, Milgram used a series of controlled laboratory experiments involving more than 1000 subjects. Milgram's first experiments were conducted at Yale University with Yale college students and then with male residents of New Haven who received payment for their participation. In later variations, Milgram set up a storefront research unit in Bridgeport, Connecticut, recruiting through newspaper ads a broad cross section of the population. Subjects eventually included both sexes and varied widely in age, occupation, and education. Volunteers were told they were participating in a scientific study of memory and learning.

In the basic experimental paradigm, individual subjects delivered a series of what they thought were extremely painful electric shocks to another person. Subjects were led to believe that the purpose of the study was to discover how *punishment* affects memory so that learning and memory could be improved through the proper balance of reward and punishment. In their *social roles* as *teachers,* the subjects were to punish each error made by someone playing the role of *learner* (unbeknownst to the subjects, this was always the same actor). The major *rule* they were to follow was to increase the level of shock by a fixed amount each time the learner made an error until the learning was errorless. The white-coated experimenter acted as the *legitimate authority* figure; he presented the rules, arranged for the assignment of roles (by a rigged drawing of lots), and ordered the *teachers* to do their jobs whenever they hesitated or dissented.

The *dependent variable* was the final level of shock a subject delivered. Shocks were measured on a "shock generator" that went from 15 to 450 volts in 15-volt steps. The initial study was simply a demonstration of the phenomenon of obedience; there was no manipulation of an independent variable. Later versions varied many situational factors, such as the physical distance between the *teacher* and the *authority* and the *learner*. Milgram did not use a formal control or comparison group that received no treatment. As with the Stanford prison simulation, the comparison group was implicit—typical readers of the research who had beliefs about the way they themselves *would have behaved* under such circumstances (you and other ordinary people).

The Test Situation. Each *teacher* had been given a sample shock of about 75 volts to feel the amount of pain it caused. Thus Milgram's study was staged to make a subject think that he or she was causing pain and suffering and perhaps even killing an innocent person by following orders. The part of the *learner* was played by a pleasant, mild-mannered man, about 50 years old, who mentioned having a "heart condition" but was willing to go along with the procedure. He was strapped into an "electric chair" in the next room and communicated with the teacher via an intercom. His task was to memorize pairs of words, then choose the correct response for each stimulus word from a multiple-choice listing. The learner soon began making errors, and the teacher began shocking the learner. The protests of the victim rose with the shock level. At 75 volts, he began to moan and grunt; at 150 volts he demanded to be released from the experiment; at 180 volts he cried out that he could not stand the pain any longer. At 300 volts he insisted that he would no longer take part in the experiment and must be freed. He cried out about his heart condition and refused to reply any further. What would the teacher do?

If a teacher hesitated or protested delivering the next shock, the experimenter said, "Teacher, you have no other choice; you must go on! Your job is to punish the learner's mistakes." As you might imagine, the situation was stressful for the subjects. Most teachers complained and protested, insisting they could not continue. Subjects protested to the unwavering experimenter: "He can't stand it! I'm not going to kill that man in there! You hear him hollering? He's hollering . . . I mean, who is going to take the responsibility if anything happens to that gentleman?" Protesting all the way, the teachers spoke as though the experimenter were extracting each shock from them:

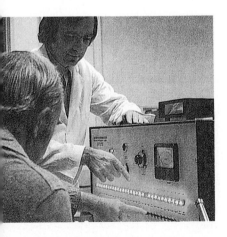

An experimenter shows the "teacher" how to use the shock generator. How would you behave in this situation?

"Aw, no. You mean I've got to keep going up with that scale? No sir, I'm not going to kill that man! I'm not going to give him 450 volts!" (1965, p. 67).

When the learner simply stopped responding to the teacher's questions, some subjects called out to him, urging him to get the answer right so they would not have to continue shocking him. All the while they protested loudly to the experimenter, but the experimenter *insisted* that the teacher continue. "Rules are rules!" Even when there was only silence from the learner's room, the teacher was ordered to keep shocking him more and more strongly, all the way up to the button that was marked "Danger: Severe Shock XXX (450 volts)."

Results and Reasons. ➡ Did they obey? How far do you think the average subject in Milgram's experiment actually went in administering the shocks? What percentage do you estimate went all the way up to the end of the shock scale in blindly obeying authority? Suppose for a moment that you were the subject-teacher. How far up the scale would you go? At which level of shock would you absolutely refuse to continue?

Psychiatrists asked to predict the performance of Milgram's subjects estimated that most would not go beyond 150 volts. In their professional opinions, fewer than 4 percent of the subjects would still be obedient at 300 volts and only one-tenth of 1 percent would continue to 450 volts. The psychiatrists presumed that only those few individuals who were "abnormal" in some way—the sadists—would blindly obey orders to harm another person in an experiment. Do you agree with these experts?

If so, you are both wrong! The psychiatrists based their evaluations on presumed *dispositional* qualities of people who would engage in such abnormal behavior; they overlooked the power of this special *situation* to influence the thinking and actions of most people caught up in its social context. *The majority of subjects obeyed the authority fully!* Nearly two thirds delivered the maximum 450 volts to the learner. The average subject did not quit until about 300 volts. No subject who got within five switches of the end ever refused to go all the way. By then, their resistance was broken; they had resolved their own conflicts—and just tried to get it over with as quickly as possible. It is important to note that most people *dissented* verbally, but the majority did not *disobey* behaviorally. From the point of view of the victim, that's a critical difference.

To assuage your concerns about psychological research, without lessening the meaning and poignancy of Milgram's results, we remind you that *no actual shocks were ever delivered to the learner.* The "victim" of this torture was an accomplished actor who congenially chatted with his "tormentor" after the experiment, and assured him he was fine and had never felt any shocks at all. In Milgram's research, no one was actually hurt by the subjects' obedience. Consider whether this makes a difference in terms of what these research findings mean.

Why Do We Obey Authority? From the many variations Milgram conducted on his original study, we can conclude that the obedience effect is strongest under the following conditions, shown in **Figure 12.3:**

- With the social influence of a peer who first models obedience
- When there is great remoteness of victim from subject
- When there is direct surveillance of the subject by the authority
- When a subject acts as an *intermediary bystander* assisting another person who actually delivers the shock
- When the relative status of the authority figure to the subject is greater (Milgram, 1965, 1974; Rosenhan, 1969).

If you carefully review these conditions, you can see that the obedience effect is due to situational variables and not personality variables. In fact, per-

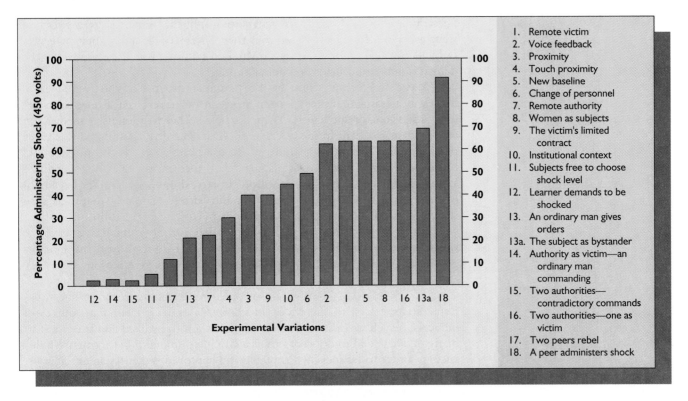

1.	Remote victim
2.	Voice feedback
3.	Proximity
4.	Touch proximity
5.	New baseline
6.	Change of personnel
7.	Remote authority
8.	Women as subjects
9.	The victim's limited contract
10.	Institutional context
11.	Subjects free to choose shock level
12.	Learner demands to be shocked
13.	An ordinary man gives orders
13a.	The subject as bystander
14.	Authority as victim—an ordinary man commanding
15.	Two authorities—contradictory commands
16.	Two authorities—one as victim
17.	Two peers rebel
18.	A peer administers shock

Figure 12.3 Obedience in 18 Experiments
The graph shows a profile of weak to strong obedience effects across Milgram's 19 (one experiment has two variations) experimental variations.

sonality tests administered to the subjects did *not* reveal any traits that differentiated those who obeyed from those who refused, nor identify any psychological disturbance or abnormality in the obedient punishers. These findings enable us to rule out the role of personality in obedient behavior.

Belief in the Consequences of Obedience. So why did they do it? One possibility is that the subjects did not really believe the "cover story" of the experiment, and knew that the victim was not really getting hurt. This guess was ruled out by an independent replication (replay of Milligram's scenario) that made the effects of being obedient vivid, immediate, and direct for the subjects.

In the replication, college students were asked to train a puppy on a discrimination task by punishing it with increasing levels of shock whenever it made an error. They could see it jumping around on an electrified grid when they pressed a switch. Actually, the puppy received only a low level of shock—just enough to make it squeal but not hurt it. The students dissented, complained, and became upset—some even cried. Then, at a given point, an odorless, colorless anesthetic was secretly released into the puppy's enclosed chamber. The dog wobbled and finally fell asleep, but the subjects thought they had killed the puppy. Then the experimenter reminded them of the *situational rule:* Failure to respond is a punishable error; they must continue to give shocks.

Three-fourths of all students delivered the maximum shock possible. Every one of the female subjects proved to be totally obedient despite her dissent (Sheridan & King, 1972). In this case, subjects could have no doubt that their compliance with orders had harmful and distressing consequences. In light of these findings, it is unlikely that the obedience of Milgram's subjects was fostered by a rationalization that they were not really causing anyone harm.

demand characteristics Cue in an experimental setting that influences subjects' perceptions of how they are expected to behave.

Demand Characteristics. Another explanation for subjects' behavior is that the effect is limited to the **demand characteristics** of the experimental situation.

Sometimes cues in the experimental setting influence subjects' perceptions of what is expected of them; these cues then systematically affect their behavior. Is blind obedience to authority in Milgram's study merely a response to the demands of the unusual experimental setting?

Consider the results of a field experiment that tested the obedience of nurses in a hospital setting. In this study, a nurse received a telephone call from a staff doctor she had never met, who told her to administer medication to a particular patient in the doctor's absence. The dose he ordered was twice the maximum dosage indicated on the drug container, as the nurse could plainly see. Would the nurse violate standard medical practices by following a stranger's orders without authorization? In fact, almost every nurse obeyed: 20 of the 22 subjects began to administer the "drug" (actually a harmless substance) before being stopped by a researcher (Hofling et al., 1966). Thus even when there are good reasons to hesitate or defy authority, the demands of the situation are so scripted and well-learned that it is hard to resist them. Doctors give orders, and nurses obey—with little room for error or question.

The Rules of Influence. Two reasons people obey authority in compelling situations can be traced to the effects of *normative* and *informational* sources of influence, which we discussed earlier. People want to be liked and they want to be right. They tend to do what others are doing or requesting (normative influence) in order to be socially acceptable and approved. When in an ambiguous, novel situation, people rely on others for cues as to the appropriate and correct way to behave (informational influence). They are more likely to do as they are told when experts or credible communicators tell them what to do.

A third factor in the Milgram paradigm is that subjects were probably confused about *how to disobey;* nothing they said in dissent satisfied the authority. They did not know how to exit without suffering the "exit costs" of confronting the authority figure. Had they known a simple, direct way out of the situation—for example, by pressing a "quit" button—it is likely more people would have disobeyed (Ross, 1988).

Finally, obedience to authority in this experimental situation is part of an *ingrained habit* that is learned by children in many different settings: Obey authority without question (Brown, 1986). This heuristic (rule of thumb) can serve us well when authorities are legitimate and deserving of our obedience. The problem is that the rule gets overapplied, just as when children first learn the grammatical rules for past tense and add -ed to all verbs even when it is wrong to do so. Blind obedience to authority means obeying any and all authority figures simply because of their status, regardless of whether they are unjust or just in their requests and commands.

What does obedience research signify to you personally? Recall the image of a lone man standing before tanks in Beijing's Tiananmen Square during the rebellion of Chinese students in June 1989. We must ask ourselves if we would do the same. What choices will you make when faced with moral dilemmas throughout your life? Many of the scandals exposed at the highest levels of government, the military, and business involve authorities who expect their subordinates to behave in unethical and illegal ways. Even people who should "know better" because they enjoy positions of favor and status will find it hard to "rock the boat" by questioning the very authorities who have exalted them. When the president of a company invites his advisors to speak candidly about what he is doing wrong, for example, few will believe he wants to hear criticism. No one likes to be the bearer of bad news—especially to the boss. People prefer, perhaps, to keep silent and hope things will work out, or at least that they will not get too much worse.

➡ We ourselves are subject to the same circumstantial pressures as these research subjects. Resisting situational forces requires first being aware of and accepting the fact that they can be powerful enough to affect almost anyone, even you. Second you need to analyze the situation mindfully and critically for

the details that don't fit, flaws in the "cover story," or the rationales that don't make sense upon careful analysis. For example, imagine that someone you work for—a teacher, artist, or politician whom you respect and admire—asks you for help. Suppose this person has done something wrong or made a mistake, confides in you, and requests your assistance in dealing with the problem. Initially you might be flattered to be singled out as a trusted advisor. But are you being asked to do something incriminating or unethical? Ask yourself why the authority figure needs *you* to do the dirty work. Perhaps you are really being set up to take the fall—pay the consequences—in case something goes wrong and a scapegoat is needed. In that case, is it still desirable—is it your *duty*—to follow orders without qualm or question? At what point must you refuse to comply and instead think for yourself?

Disobeying authority is seldom easy, because our socialization emphasizes the value of respecting role models and doing as we are told. Remember these important strategies for resisting all compliance-gaining situations:

- Leave the situation.
- Take a "time out" to think things over.
- Never sign on the dotted line the first time.
- Be willing to admit you have made a mistake or let others think you are a "poor team player."

Like the Stanford prison study, obedience research challenges the myth that evil lurks in the minds of evil people—that the bad "they" are different dispositionally from the good "us" who would never do such things. The purpose in recounting these findings is not to debase human nature nor to excuse evil deeds, but to make clear that even normal, well-meaning individuals are subject to the human potential for giving in to strong situational and social forces to do wrong. As TV's kindly neighbor, Mr. Rogers, tells his little viewers, "Sometimes even nice people do bad things." What he doesn't add, but you now know, is that "It all depends on the power of the situation."

Helping

Consider a different perspective on Milgram's obedience situation: If you were a *bystander* to the teacher-learner transaction, would you intervene to help one of the distressed subjects disobey the authority and exit from the situation? When would you be more likely to intervene: if you were the only bystander on the scene, or if you were one of several observers? Before answering, you might want to reflect on what social psychologists have discovered about the nature of **bystander intervention** and the way it reflects another aspect of situational forces.

Consider a news event that stunned the nation and triggered years of research into the apparent problem of bystander apathy:

> For more than half an hour, 38 respectable, law-abiding citizens in Queens, New York, watched a killer stalk and stab a woman in three separate attacks. Two times the sound of the bystanders' voices and the sudden glow of their bedroom lights interrupted the assailant and frightened him. Each time, however, he returned and stabbed her again. Not a single person telephoned the police during the assault; only one witness called the police after the woman was dead (*The New York Times,* March 13, 1964).

This newspaper account of the murder of Kitty Genovese shocked a nation that could not accept the idea of such apathy on the part of its responsible citizenry. In a similar case, an 18-year-old secretary was beaten, choked, stripped, and raped in her office. She finally broke away from her assailant and, naked and bleeding, she ran down the stairs of the building to the doorway screaming, "Help me! Help me! He raped me!" A crowd of 40 persons gathered on the busy street and watched passively as the rapist dragged her back upstairs. Only the chance passing of the police put an end to further abuse and possibly murder (*The New York Times,* May 6, 1964).

Would you have called the police to help Kitty Genovese, or intervened in some way to help the woman being raped? The temptation is to say, "Yes, of course." However, we must be careful to resist overconfidence about the way we would react in an unfamiliar situation. Why don't bystanders help in cases such as these? What would make them more likely to do so?

Abandoned in the Laboratory. Social psychologists **Bibb Latané** and **John Darley** conducted a classic series of studies of the bystander intervention problem soon after the Kitty Genovese murder. The psychologists ingeniously created in the laboratory an experimental analogue of the bystander-intervention situation. A college student, placed in a room by himself with an intercom, was led to believe that he was communicating with one or more students in adjacent rooms. During the course of a discussion about personal problems, the subject heard what sounded like one of the other students having an epileptic seizure and gasping for help. During the "seizure" it was impossible for the subject to talk to the other students or to find out what, if anything, they were doing about the emergency. The dependent variable was the speed with which he reported the emergency to the experimenter. The major independent variable was the number of people he believed were in the discussion group with him. It turned out that the likelihood of intervention depended on the number of bystanders he thought were present. The more there were, the slower he was in reporting the seizure, if he did so at all. As you can see in **Figure 12.4,** all subjects in a two-person situation intervened within 160 seconds, but nearly 40 percent of those who believed they were part of a larger group never bothered to inform the experimenter that another student was seriously ill (Latané & Darley, 1968).

Personality tests showed no significant relationship between particular personality characteristics and speed or likelihood of intervening. The best predictor of bystander intervention is the situational variable of *size of the group* present. The likelihood of intervention *decreases* as the group *increases* in size, probably because each person makes the assumption that others will help, so he or she does not have to make that commitment.

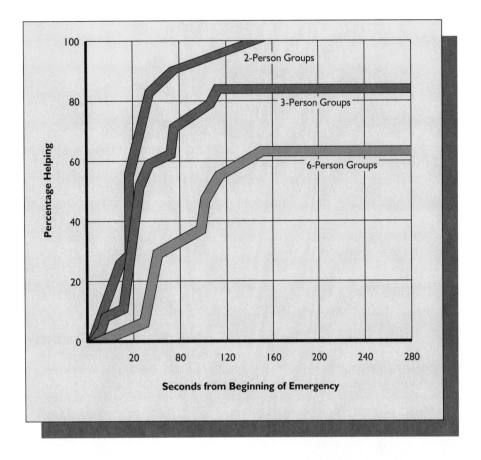

Figure 12.4 Bystander Intervention in an Emergency
The more other people present, the less likely any one bystander will intervene. Bystanders act most quickly in two-person groups.

Rescued in the Real World. When similar studies of bystander intervention are carried out in *field situations* rather than in the laboratory, a victim's chances of getting help increase significantly. Consider what researchers learned from the following staged series of events: A man on a moving New York subway train suddenly collapsed and fell to the floor. A number of bystanders witnessed this event. The experimenters manipulated the situation by varying the characteristics of the "victim"—an invalid with a cane, a drunk smelling of liquor, or, in a companion study, a disabled person apparently bleeding (or not bleeding) from the mouth. The researchers unobtrusively recorded the bystander's responses to these emergency situations. One or more persons responded directly in most cases (81 out of 103) with little hesitation. Help was slower when the apparent *cost* of intervening was higher (that is, slower for a bloody victim who might require a greater degree of involvement than for a victim who simply collapsed), but it still usually came (Piliavin & Piliavin, 1972; Piliavin et al., 1969).

 Why don't students help as much in a laboratory situation as citizens do in a natural setting? Intervention in the laboratory setting may be inhibited because the college students have already adopted the *passive* role of "subject," and they assume that the experimenter is responsible and "in charge." Laboratory subjects often do not actually see the victim-in-distress, and even when they do, they are severely restricted by their obedience to an unstated rule of the laboratory setting: "Remain in your seat; stay put and follow instructions until you are told you can get up." In unstructured, informal settings, none of these conditions hold, and the decision to intervene is based more on an observer's weighing of the personal costs of intervening against the consequences of not doing so.

Further, as reviewed in "In Focus: Research: The Good Samaritan—If There's Time" (on the next page), this weighing process may be more difficult and time-consuming than effective help can allow. Even if you would do the

Research   THE GOOD SAMARITAN — IF THERE'S TIME

The presence or absence of other people is one situational factor that apparently affects bystander intervention. In addition, if a bystander is in a hurry to do something else, he or she is less likely to offer help. In the biblical tale of the Good Samaritan (See Luke 10:30–37), several important people are too busy to help a stranger in distress. He is finally assisted by a man who has plenty of time on his hands. Could the failure of the important people to help really be due to time pressures rather than their personal dispositions? A research team recreated the story of the Good Samaritan.

Students at the Princeton Theological Seminary were the subjects of an experiment that they thought involved evaluation of their sermons, one of which was to be about the parable of the Good Samaritan. Before they left the briefing room to have their sermons recorded in a nearby building, they were each told something about the time they had available to get to the studio. Some were randomly assigned to a *late condition,* in which they had to hurry to make the next session; others to an *on-time condition,* in which they would make the next session just on time; and a third group to an *early condition,* in which they had a few spare minutes before they would be recorded.

When each seminarian walked down an alley between the two buildings, he came upon a man slumped in a doorway, in obvious need of help. On their way to deliver a sermon about the Good Samaritan, these seminary students now had the chance to practice what they were about to preach. Did they? Of those who were in a hurry, only 10 percent helped. If they were on time, 45 percent helped the stranger. Most bystander intervention came from those who were not in any time bind—63 percent of these seminarians acted as Good Samaritans (Darley & Batson, 1973).

The situational manipulation of time had a marked effect on the altruism of these young men, increasing it sixfold between the late and early conditions, when all else was held constant. We can hardly attribute the lack of intervention of those in the late condition to their callousness or other dispositions since they were randomly assigned to that condition and had chosen a career based on helping others. It is likely that, while fulfilling their obligation to the researcher to hurry and not be late for their appointment, their single-minded purpose blinded them to "irrelevant events" that might interfere with that obligation. Some of those who did not help may not have noticed the man in distress, others might have misinterpreted what they saw as a man merely resting.

In applying these results to your own life, consider that helping is more a matter of taking the right actions than of thinking the right thoughts. Carrying scriptural aphorisms in your head will not enable you to do good if the stresses of daily life—feeling hurried, harried, or worried—crowd out your awareness of what is really important in life. It is possible that we will overlook our own values because we are caught up in the demands or inertia of our situations.

If you wish to break free of these numbing, dulling constraints, change your habits, stay alert—be mindful, not "mindless"—and look for ways to be helpful *in spite of* pressures against it. Keep change in your pocket so you will always be ready to contribute to a worthy cause or needy stranger, without having to slow your pace or reach for your wallet. Determine what you need to know about causes—is it nonpartisan? does most of the profit go toward helping people?—so that you can ask questions on the spot to decide whether to contribute. Memorize the phone numbers of police and ambulance services, and the location of pay telephones in your neighborhood. Such resolutions will improve your chances of acting on your values, so that when a crisis erupts, you will be less distracted, and more efficient at deciding whether—and *how*—to help.

right thing eventually, a genuine victim in distress likely needs the help sooner rather than later, and cannot afford the delay caused by a would-be helper's crisis of conscience. It is all the more important, therefore, to identify the circumstances that prompt or inhibit helping responses, so that we can give help when others need it, and get it when we do.

Seek and Ye Shall Find. To demonstrate the positive effects of situational power, social psychologist **Tom Moriarity** (1975) arranged two fascinating experiments. In the first study, New Yorkers watched as a thief snatched a woman's suitcase in a restaurant when she left her table. In the second, they watched as a thief snatched a portable radio from a beach blanket when the owner left it for a few minutes. What did these onlookers do? Some did nothing, letting the thief go on his merry way. What were the conditions under which some did help and others did not?

In each experiment, the would-be theft victim (the experimenter's accomplice) had first asked the soon-to-be observer of the crime either "Do you have the time?" or "Will you please keep an eye on my bag (radio) while I'm gone?" The first interaction elicited no personal responsibility, and the bystander stood by idly as the theft unfolded. However, of those who had agreed to watch the victim's property, almost every bystander intervened. They called for help, and some even tackled the runaway thief on the beach.

The encouraging message is that we can convert apathy to action and transform callousness to kindness just by asking for it. The act of requesting a favor forges a special human bond that involves other people in ways that materially change the situation. It makes them responsible to you, and thereby responsible for what happens in your shared social context.

SUMMING UP

We have explored the basic theme of social psychology—the power of situational variables to influence individual behavior. Controlled laboratory experiments and field studies both strongly support the generalization that human thought and action are affected by situational influences to a far greater extent than we realize.

The mere presence of others can facilitate and intensify reactions under some circumstances. Being assigned to social roles, even in artificial settings such as a mock prison, can modify individual reactions dramatically in ways contrary to one's personal values, beliefs, and dispositions. Other influential situational variables include behavioral rules, signs, symbols, and uniforms.

Social norms function within groups to direct and shape members' behavior. Informational influence leads to conformity and compliance when the situation is ambiguous and the person wants to be right and act correctly. The Bennington studies pointed to the power of social norms to affect students' basic attitudes and values, sometimes for a lifetime. Even in highly structured situations, perceptions can be influenced by conformity pressures, as demonstrated in the Asch situation.

One of the most powerful and controversial demonstrations of situational power was Milgram's series of studies on obedience to authority, in which many good people typically behaved in evil ways with the best of motives. The final proof of the significance of situational forces came from studies in which bystander intervention decreased as the number of observing bystanders increased and as bystanders' sense of time urgency increased. The positive effects of situational power showed up in research that indicates we can induce altruism in others by simply asking for it.

Constructing Social Reality

Even if you accept the logical conclusions of the research reviewed in the last section, you may experience discomfort with the idea that situations can so easily overwhelm you. You have values, after all, and you do your best to act on them. How, then, could you yield to situational pressure—and still be an honorable or healthy human being? The answer lies in understanding how situations come to wield such influence in so many human endeavors.

To understand how the situation matters, we need to discover how the behavioral setting is perceived and interpreted by those people in it and what meanings they attribute to its various components. This second lesson of social psychology thus emphasizes the nature of *the subjective reality* that individuals construct from a situation's objective features. An actor's view of the circumstances sets in motion certain psychological processes. These processes change the situation itself, so that it fits the actor's other perceptions, values, and attitudes. It is not so much the physical, objective features of a situation that control individual and group behavior; it is the *mental representations of the person in the situation* that matter most.

For the social psychologist, an adequate account of any behavior includes three basic components: the *features* of the current situation, the specific *content* and *context* of the observed behavior, and the actor's subjective *interpretations* of the important elements in the behavioral setting. This type of behavior analysis is complicated when we realize that different people often interpret shared events in different ways. When members of a group reach a common interpretation of an event, activity, or person, their shared perspective is known as *social reality*. **Social reality** is the consensus of perceptions and beliefs about a situation generated by group members' social comparisons.

In this section, we will see the power of situations in a slightly different light, as it is filtered through a person's mind. After reviewing studies that illustrate how our subjective constructions of reality operate, we will outline several theoretical approaches that social psychologists have taken to help them make sense of the ways people think about and perceive their social world. It will become apparent that a strong cognitive orientation is at the core of much social psychology.

social reality The consensus of perceptions and beliefs about a situation that is derived from social comparisons among group members.

Guiding Beliefs and Expectations

Have you ever disagreed with a friend about what *really* took place at some event you both experienced? People's beliefs can lead them to view the same situation from different vantage points and to make contrary conclusions about what "really happened." One example of these contrary conclusions comes from a study of a famous football game that took place some years ago between two Ivy League teams. The undefeated Princeton team played Dartmouth in the final game of the season. Ultimately won by Dartmouth, the game was rough, filled with penalties and serious injuries to both sides. After the game, the newspapers of the two schools offered very different accounts of what had happened. A team of social psychologists surveyed students at both schools, showed them a film of the game, and recorded their judgments.

Nearly all Princeton students judged the game as "rough and dirty," none saw it as "clean and fair," and most believed that Dartmouth players started the dirty play. In contrast, the majority of Dartmouth students thought both sides were equally to blame for the rough game, and many thought it was "rough, clean, and fair." When viewing the same film, Dartmouth students "saw" both sides commit the same number of penalties (Hastorf & Cantril, 1954). Clearly, a complex social occurrence, such as a football game, cannot be observed in an objective fashion. In this case, people *looked* at the same activity, but they *saw* two different games—based on what they believed, felt, and wished.

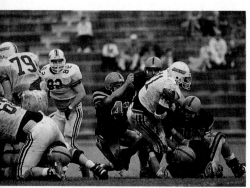

The thrill of victory or the agony of defeat? What you see here depends on which team you are rooting for.

Fulfilling Prophecies. Can beliefs and expectations actually shape social reality? Much research suggests that the very nature of some situations can be modified significantly by the beliefs and expectations people have about them. Such *social expectancy effects* are similar to placebo effects—beliefs that medical treatment will work can *make* it work for about one-third of all people. For example, ordinary students or underachievers can be transformed into high achievers if their teachers believe they are "special," or if the students are led to think so.

In Greek mythology, the sculptor Pygmalion created—and then fell in love with—a statue of his ideal woman, naming her Galatea. With the intervention of the goddess of love, Pygmalion's creation came to life, fulfilling the wish from which he had first sculpted her. In honor of this classic tale of wishes that come true, the influence of social expectancy has been dubbed the *Pygmalion effect*. This effect was re-created in an experiment by psychologist **Robert Rosenthal** (in conjunction with school principal Lenore Jacobson).

Some elementary school teachers in Boston were led to believe that particular students of theirs were "intellectual bloomers" who would show unusual gains during the coming year. In fact, there was no objective basis for that prediction; the names of these rapid bloomers had been chosen *randomly*. By the end of that school year, 30 percent of the arbitrarily labeled "spurters" had gained an average of 22 IQ points. Almost all of them had gained at least 10 IQ points. Their gain in intellectual performance was significantly greater than that of their control group classmates. In absolute terms, their improvement is remarkably significant for any known kind of enriched education program over such a short time, and these were students in ordinary classes (Rosenthal & Jacobson, 1968a, 1968b).

How did the false expectations of the teachers get translated into such positive student performance? In some way, the teachers must have used influence strategies that motivated the targeted students to work harder and more efficiently. These strategies were probably communicated in many nonverbal ways, perhaps even nonconsciously, through the teachers' facial expressions and body language. Rosenthal points to several processes that were activated by the teachers' expectations. They acted warmer and more friendly to the chosen students, even while they were putting greater demands on their performance. They gave more immediate feedback about the selected students' performance. Finally, the teachers created more opportunities for the special students to respond, "show their stuff," and be reinforced in class.

In one sense, this research put some students on the fast track. The opposite happens when students are assigned to slow learner or learning disability tracks; they often become slower when they have been identified in this way. Negative teacher expectations may be responsible for poorer performance by females and some minority students in science and mathematics courses even at the college level.

self-fulfilling prophecies One's private expectations of how others will act that influence them to behave in the predicted manner.

Self-fulfilling prophecies (Merton, 1957) are predictions about some future behavior or event that modify its outcome so as to produce what is expected. Social reality can be changed in several ways by such "prophecies." A shy student has the expectation that he won't have a good time at an upcoming dance. An extroverted student predicts the same dance will be fun and enjoyable. Whatever the dance is "really" like, both students experience what they expected.

➡ In earlier chapters, we noted the positive effects on health and well-being of an optimistic outlook on life (Seligman, 1991). Optimism is a general system of beliefs that gets translated into actions affecting someone's health and well-being. Social perception mediates between those general beliefs and specific actions. Research has shown that our wishes and hopes for how life will turn out can actually have some influence on the way it does. Motivated reasoning comes to determine the kind of evidence we focus on in making our self-predictions, the methods we use to make those predictions, the confidence we invest in our predictions, and our insensitivity to contrary evidence that might disconfirm our predictions (Kunda, 1990). Optimists assume setbacks are temporary, and, they persevere in the face of adversity until they reach their goals. For example, you can probably think of something you do well today that you once did far less competently, such as an athletic activity, playing a musical instrument, painting, typing, or cooking. Think how different your life would be now if, when you experienced early discouragement, you had not persisted in thinking—perhaps optimistically, even unrealistically—that you could do better.

behavioral confirmation Process of acting in ways that another person expects, thus validating those expectations.

Confirming Expectations. **Mark Snyder** (1984) uses the term **behavioral confirmation** for the process by which an observer's expectations about another person influence that other to behave in ways that confirm the observer's hypothesis.

In a series of studies, students were led to expect that they would interact with another person who was described in particular terms (not necessarily true) such as *introvert, extrovert, depressed,* or *intelligent.* After interacting with the target person, the subject rated the person on a variety of dimensions. Typically, the target person was more likely to act in whatever way the subject expected him or her to behave. The subjects as well as observers (who did not know what the expectation was) agreed that those hypothesized to be outgoing were indeed very sociable, that the introverted target people behaved unsociably, and so forth (Kulik, 1983; Snyder & Swann, 1978). How were these impressions confirmed? The extroverted target person was likely to be asked how she would liven up a party, while the shy target person was asked why it's hard to open up to others. Different questions elicited different responses that guided the evaluation. The evaluator was not aware that the question had a strong role in creating and distorting social reality.

A recent incident shows how expectations can lead to false conclusions and regrettable actions. Two California police officers used their batons to beat a blind man who was standing at a bus stop. Why? They mistakenly thought that the folding cane in his pocket was an illegal martial arts weapon and they "demanded that he hand over the contents of his pockets." The man believed he was being robbed because the police officers did not identify themselves; they assumed he could see their uniforms. When the blind man tried to defend himself from being mugged by reaching for his cane, the police felt his behavior confirmed their suspicions and they began to hit him (*The New York Times,* May 17, 1989).

Creating and Reversing Prejudices. Few human weaknesses are more destructive to the dignity of the individual and the social bonds of humanity than prejudice. The Supreme Court's 1954 decision to outlaw segregated public education was, in part, based on research, presented in federal court by social psychologist **Kenneth Clark,** which showed the negative impact on black children of their separate and unequal education (Clark & Clark, 1947).

prejudice Negative attitude and feelings about a group and its members.

Prejudice is a prime example of social reality gone awry—a situation created in the minds of people that can demean and destroy the lives of others. **Prejudice** is defined as a learned attitude toward a target object, involving negative affect (dislike or fear), negative beliefs (stereotypes) that justify the attitude, and a behavioral intention to avoid, control, dominate, or eliminate those in the target group. Prejudiced attitudes serve as biasing filters that influence the way individuals are perceived and treated once they are categorized as members of a target group. Once formed, prejudice exerts a powerful force on the way pertinent information is selectively processed, organized, and remembered.

Although prejudice has many origins and serves a variety of needs (Allport, 1954; Pettigrew, 1985; Sarnoff & Katz; 1954), one of its most basic purposes is to simplify a complex environment and increase other individuals' predictability by categorizing them in certain ways. The simplest and most pervasive form of categorizing involves individuals determining whether other people are like themselves. This categorization results in an *in-group bias,* an evaluation of one's own group as better than others (Brewer, 1979).

social categorization Process by which people organize their social environment by classifying themselves and others into groups.

Social categorization is the process by which people organize their social environment by categorizing themselves and others into groups (Wilder, 1986). This categorization has been shown to have the following consequences: perception of similarity of those within one's group (the in-group) and dissimilarity of those who are not members (the out-group); failure to distinguish among individuals in the out-group; reduced influence of out-group

members on the in-group; and hostile attitudes toward and beliefs in the inferiority of the out-group (Tajfel, 1982; Tajfel & Billig, 1974). These consequences developed regardless of limited exposure to the out-groups and despite the contradictory experience of their individual members with any other out-group category (Park & Rothbart, 1982; Quattrone, 1986). For example, if your softball team were matched with a new team for a single game, despite your lack of familiarity with the other team and its individual members, you could readily think of them as "the opponents" and assure yourself that your team and teammates are superior.

Does there need to be a kernel of truth in the basis for categorization that leads to prejudiced attitudes and discriminatory actions? The answer is no; all that is necessary is any salient cue on which individuals can be sorted into exclusive categories. A third-grade teacher, **Jane Elliott,** wanted her pupils from an all-white, rural Iowa farm community to experience how prejudice and discrimination felt to those in minority groups. She devised an activity to provide her students with that experience. One day she arbitrarily designated brown-eyed children as "superior" to the "inferior" blue-eyed children. The superior, allegedly more intelligent, brown-eyes were given special privileges, while the inferior blue-eyes had to obey rules that enforced their second-class status. Within a day, the blue-eyed children began to do more poorly in their schoolwork and became depressed, sullen, and angry. The brown-eyed superiors mistreated their former friends, called them "blue-eyes," refused to play with them, got into fights with them, and worried that school officials should be notified that the blue-eyes might steal things.

The second day of the activity, Elliott told the class that she had been wrong. It was really the blue-eyed children who were superior and the brown-eyed ones who were inferior. The brown-eyes now switched from their previously positive self-labels to derogatory labels similar to those used the day before by the blue-eyes. Their academic performance deteriorated, while that of the new ruling class improved. Old friendship patterns between children temporarily dissolved and were replaced with hostility—until the experiment was ended (Elliott, 1977).

Sadly, in many schoolrooms throughout the country, students are made to feel inferior through their negative interactions with other pupils or their teachers. These students often begin to act in ways to confirm this prejudiced belief and come to internalize their sense of academic inadequacy. When competing for the scarce resource of teacher's attention and affection, the more

Jane Elliott's experiment measured overt changes in prejudicial behavior among children and changes in their schoolwork. She obtained measures of their feelings toward each other by asking the children to draw pictures of the way they felt. The picture on the top was drawn by a child who felt "on top," confident, and capable because he had the superior eye color. Nonetheless, the children were generally delighted when the experiment—and discrimination—ended.

social perception   Process of recognizing the personal attributes of oneself and others.

cognitive dissonance   According to theory developed by Leon Festinger, motivating state of tension produced by inconsistency or contradiction between an individual's feelings, beliefs, or actions.

verbal, advantaged students take charge; the others back off, fearing failure and further rejection. In many schools, teachers respond more to "take-charge" students. Often these dominant students tend to be the Caucasian males in the class. Females and members of minority groups consequently receive less attention and less support from teachers. This system fosters a situation for out-group members that is characterized by envy, competitiveness, suspicion, self-derogation, and disidentification with school and academics.

Forming Cognitive Frameworks

How do people construct their views of others and understand their transactions within a shared social context? They do so by observing the ways that they and others behave in various settings and over time. The general process by which we come to perceive and know the personal attributes of ourselves and others is called **social perception.**

A major task of everyday social perception involves figuring out what behavior "means," forming accurate impressions, and making sound predictions about what we and others are likely to do. We constantly try to make sense of our world by applying old knowledge and beliefs to new events and assimilating the new to the familiar. For example, if a new friend suddenly acts distressed and upset, you may try to remember what caused old friends to act in similar ways, and how you successfully helped them. If these rehearsed tactics succeed, you will learn how to help your new friend; if they fail, you must experiment with other strategies, and add them to your interpersonal skills.

Social psychology is understood as *cognitively oriented*. In its analysis of human behavior, social psychology has always included the role of subjective perceptions, symbolic causal stimuli and imagined results, and above all, a thinking organism that tries rationally to make sense of the workings of the social world and physical environment. In other words, social psychology conceives of the individual as an active agent in the social world—a person who is always collecting information about people and events, thinking about what is happening and what to do, and organizing these thoughts and data into lessons about knowledge and meaning.

Dissonance Theory: Self-justification.   People prefer consistency in their social perceptions and cognitions. That is, we like new information to agree with or fit into old beliefs and assumptions. Several theories have been proposed to explain why and how people seek to maintain consistency in their thoughts and experiences. The most influential of these approaches is the theory of **cognitive dissonance,** as developed by **Leon Festinger** (1957), a student of Kurt Lewin. Cognitive dissonance is the state of conflict someone experiences after making a decision, taking an action, or being exposed to information that is contrary to prior beliefs, feelings, or values. It is assumed that when cognitions about one's behavior and relevant attitudes are dissonant—they clash and contradict each other—an unpleasant tension arises that the individual is motivated to reduce. Dissonance-reducing activities modify this unpleasant state and achieve consonance among one's cognitions.

For example, suppose the two dissonant cognitions are some self-knowledge ("I smoke") and a belief about smoking ("Smoking causes lung cancer"). To reduce the dissonance involved, you could take one of several different actions. For example, you could change your belief ("The evidence that smoking causes lung cancer is not very convincing"); change your behavior (stop smoking); reevaluate the behavior ("I don't smoke very much"); or add new cognitions ("I smoke low-tar cigarettes") that make the inconsistency less serious.

Cognitive dissonance motivates people to make discrepant behaviors—contradictory actions or statements—seem more rational, as if they followed naturally from personal beliefs and attitudes. If you can't deny that you took

Leon Festinger (1920–1989) was the protegé of Gestalt theorist Kurt Lewin. Festinger became a leading theorist in social psychology, noted especially for his theories in social comparison and cognitive dissonance.

attribution theory System of explanations for individual and social causes of behavior.

an action, you might change your attitudes to make them fit your action. You then internalize your attitude change to make acceptable what otherwise appears to be "irrational behavior." Hundreds of experiments and field studies have shown the power of cognitive dissonance to change attitudes and behavior (Wicklund & Brehm, 1976).

According to dissonance theory, under conditions of high dissonance (for example, when one has just done something that completely contradicts a previously-stated attitude), an individual acts to justify his or her behavior after-the-fact, engages in self-persuasion, and often becomes a most convincing communicator and convinced target audience. The principle of cognitive dissonance can be deftly applied by those who wish to influence your actions and beliefs. For example, a young woman smoking a cigarette is asked by a friend why she doesn't quit. The smoker believes that smoking does cause cancer, emphysema, heart disease, and other life-threatening diseases. She knows that her family has a history of circulatory ailments, and that she may be at risk if she continues to smoke. She experiences cognitive dissonance because she must consciously confront two conflicting self-cognitions: "I keep smoking" but "I know smoking is bad for my health." Fortunately (for reducing dissonance), tobacco advertisements have taught the smoker many rationalizations for her behavior. Why doesn't she quit? The young woman insists, "I know it's probably not good for me, but smoking makes me feel good, and it calms me down when I feel nervous. I just enjoy smoking too much to quit right now." By convincing herself that she *thoroughly enjoys* smoking, the smoker temporarily ignores health worries, justifies her behavior, and reduces cognitive dissonance.

Attribution Theory. One of the most important inferential tasks for social perceivers is determining the causes for events. We want to know the "whys" of life. Why did my girlfriend break off the relationship? Why did he get the job and not I? Why did my parents divorce after so many years of marriage? All such why's lead to an analysis of possible causal determinants for some action, event, or outcome. **Attribution theory** is a general approach to describing the ways the social perceiver uses information to generate causal explanations for events. Attribution theory has come to play an important role not only in social psychological thinking but in many other areas of psychology, because it focuses on a basic aspect of human functioning—the way individuals make causal attributions for achievement (Weiner, 1986), depression (Abramson et al., 1978), and other life domains.

The Intuitive Psychologist. The origin of attribution theory came from the writings of **Fritz Heider** (1958). Heider argued that people continually make causal analyses as part of their attempts to comprehend the social world. Such causal understanding helps predict and control future events. If you know what makes your roommate upset, then you may be able to reduce or induce that reaction by manipulating those causal conditions.

Heider believed that most attributional analyses focus on two questions: Is the cause for the behavior found in the *person* (internal causality) or in the *situation* (external causality)? Who is responsible for the outcomes? A woman kills her husband; her defense is that he had battered her for years. She feared for her life and her children's when he was drunk, which was becoming more frequent. The case rests largely on determining what caused the woman's admitted crime, given the mitigating circumstances. The defense argues that she was the victim, driven to act in self-defense. The prosecution insists that she committed murder willfully and must pay for her crime. To decide the case, the jurors must agree on their attributional analysis of what happened, and why.

Heider suggested that instead of developing theories about how people are supposed to think and act, psychologists should discover the personal theo-

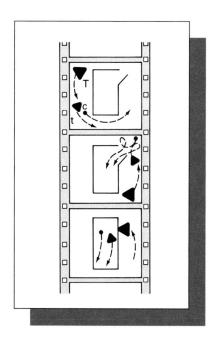

Figure 12.5 Heider's Demonstration of the Natural Tendency to Make Causal Attributions

These geometric figures were stimuli in a convincing demonstration of the fact that we infer rather than observe personal characteristics and causes. When subjects were shown a film in which the geometrical forms simply moved in and out of the large rectangle at different speeds and in different patterns, they attributed underlying "motivations" to the "characters." They often "saw" the triangles as two males fighting over a female (the circle). The large triangle was "seen" as being aggressive, the small triangle as being heroic, and the circle as being timid. In the sequence shown here, most observers reported seeing T chase t and c into the house and close the door.

intuitive psychologists Laypersons who rely on their personal theories about personality, behavior, and motivation.

covariation principle Inferring causes of events through the observation of co-occurrences of two events.

ries (belief systems) that ordinary people themselves use to make sense of the causes and effects of behavior. After all, he argued, aren't we all **intuitive psychologists** who try to figure out what people are like and what causes their behavior, just as professional psychologists do for a living? Heider used a simple film to demonstrate the tendency for people to leap from observing actions to making causal inferences and attributing motives to what they see. The film involved three geometric figures that moved around an object without any prearranged plan. Research subjects, however, always made up scripts that animated the action, turning the figures into actors and attributing personality traits and motives to their causal actions (see **Figure 12.5**).

The Covariation Principle. Attribution theory was given a boost by the contributions of **Harold Kelley** (1967) who focused on the issue that often we make causal attributions for events under conditions of uncertainty. We may not have sufficient or precise information, our self-confidence may be low, or our capacities limited. We seek out additional information and are susceptible to social influence from peers and experts. When we have access to information about multiple events, we tend to employ the **covariation principle** to infer the causes of events—by observing co-occurrences of two events. People will attribute a behavior to a causal factor if that factor was present whenever the behavior occurred, but was absent whenever it didn't occur.

For example, in trying to figure out why you had insomnia one night, you would compare the events and activities that were present on the night you couldn't sleep with those present on nights you sleep well. Caffeine becomes a likely causal candidate if you had late night coffee, something you usually don't drink. However, many potential causes are lurking in the analytical woods. Suppose you had also just gotten a new mattress, you were upset about failing a test, you were excited about a big competition the next morning, and there was a noisy party next door. Which factor was "the" culprit? Obviously the multiple events make this a more complex attributional analysis.

Kelley formalized Heider's line of thinking by specifying the variables that people use to make their attributions. People assess covariation information across three dimensions relevant to the person whose acts they are trying to explain: *distinctiveness, consistency,* and *consensus. Distinctiveness* refers to whether the entity or event is unique—whether the effect occurs only when it is present. *Consistency* refers to whether the effect occurs each time and across different situations when the entity is present. *Consensus,* or normativeness, refers to whether other people also experience the same effect with respect to the entity. We use these three sources of information to determine if some experience or effect is due to a cause in another person or in ourselves (a dispositional attribution) or comes from something external (a situational attribution).

An attractive person pays you a great compliment, and after replying, "Thanks, I needed that," you wonder what really caused that behavior (the complimenting). First, if the behavior is distinctive (no one else ever compliments you), you might attribute it to the kind of person he or she is, such as a mindless flatterer or a hustler. Second, if the person always compliments you over many situations, his or her consistency tells you about the person paying the compliment, not the one receiving it (you). Third, if the person acts this way with others, the high consensus of the behavior means you make a dispositional attribution about the person and not about the situation that you hoped motivated the compliment—your deserving appearance or actions.

Thousands of studies have been conducted to refine and extend attribution theory (Fiske & Taylor, 1991). These studies reveal the conditions under which the search for causal explanations proceeds rationally—and also when the social thinker is more rationalizing than rational. You can probably imagine wanting to believe that it is something special about you that elicited a compliment. If so, you might not want to find out if the attractive person's reaction to you was common and, in fact, "nothing personal." By distorting your attributional search, through selective questioning ("You don't pay some compliments to everyone, do you?") or by limiting your observations (deciding not to notice the complimenter has moved on to flatter the person sitting next to you), you could end up with the desired conclusion: "That compliment was sincerely meant just for me!"

When personal goals, motives, and attitudes get in the way of the systematic analysis of causes, the attributional process is biased. One class of attributional biases is known as the **self-serving bias,** in which people tend to take credit for their successes while denying responsibility for their failures. Self-serving biases are quite robust, occurring in many situations for most people and even across cultures (Fletcher & Ward, 1988). We tend to make dispositional attributions for success and situational attributions for failure: "I *earned* a B in Economics because I worked hard, but my Political Science instructor dislikes me and *gave* me a D." This is an instance of the motivated tactician at work to protect the self-esteem of the social thinker.

self-serving bias Attributional pattern in which one takes credit for success but denies responsibility for failure.

Learning Social Psychology's Lessons

The two main lessons that emerge from the social psychological tradition are the power of the situation and the construction of social reality by the person as a social perceiver in a behavior setting. Taken together, these two principles lead to a significant conclusion with important action implications for action: People are basically similar in their biological and psychological processes. Whenever this principle is violated—someone seems or acts different from us—we should base our subsequent actions on the awareness of two possibilities—first, that their *situation is different* from ours or has changed in some way we don't notice, and second, that their *perception of the situation* differs from our perception in an important way that we may not recognize.

The source of much human misunderstanding and social conflict between groups and nations is the belief that "we," as reasonable people, perceive the world or some vital part of it accurately—the only rational way it could be seen. "They," the other side who sees it differently, are wrong. Obviously, however, *we* are *they* to them. Each group or nation attributes negative dispositions to other groups and nations and positive ones to itself, all the while ignoring the situational determinants of the differences that, if changed, can reverse its perceptions and actions. By learning to recognize how situations shape us—for example, by imagining ourselves in others' circumstances, growing up in their cultures, and surroundings—we can take a step toward eliminating the prejudice that threatens to destroy our society. In our quest for meaning, we may impose a framework or label on the world we encounter that is not only inaccurate, it is dangerously distorted or unfair to others. We would do well to remember that just as wishing does not make it so, judging does not make us right.

SUMMING UP

To understand the way situations can exert powerful influences on behavior, social psychologists analyze the way people perceive, interpret, and give meaning to the features of behavior. In doing so, each person constructs a version of social reality. This is the second lesson, or principle, of social psychology. Research evidence illustrates the way beliefs and expectations can guide actions and shape aspects of the behavioral setting. People use predictions as self-fulfilling prophesies that lead to desirable outcomes, such as improved student achievement; these predictions change the way the relevant behavioral actors view the situation. Our expectancies can be confirmed by our verbal and nonverbal actions which induce in others the actions we expect them to show. The cognitive tendency to simplify information by categorizing individuals can contribute to prejudice and discrimination.

Many social psychologists have long endorsed the use of cognitive frameworks to understand social phenomena. They have been interested in issues of social perception and social cognition, to learn how people construct mental representations of their world. Dissonance theory accounts for the self-justification that people engage in when they have behaved in ways that are discrepant from their internal states. The tension that is created by cognitive dissonance is reduced by changing some aspect of the situation or of oneself. Attribution theory is a general attempt to describe the ways in which people find the causes for the behavior they observe in others and themselves. Some attributional rules lead to explanations that are based on the traits of the actor and others on the nature of the situation. Important social and political implications follow the tendency to blame people for their failures and negative life outcomes rather than to examine their life situations.

Solving Social Problems

Many social psychologists are motivated by psychology's ultimate goal: to improve the human condition. This concern is expressed in two major ways. First, studies by social psychologists are often carried out in natural field settings—in housing projects, at dances, in nursing homes, or in factories, for example—as well as in laboratory recreations of those natural settings (Rodin, 1985). Efforts are made to include elements of real-world settings. Second, the knowledge obtained from basic research and theories is used to explain social phenomena and systematic attempts are made to apply that knowledge to remedy a range of social problems (Deutsch & Hornstein, 1975). The Society for the Psychological Study of Social Issues (SPSSI) is a major organization of social psychologists dedicated to just that principle.

The focus on solving social problems moves us a long way from the traditional view of psychology as the study of individual actions and mental processes. We become aware of the person as only one level in a complex system that includes social groups, institutions, cultural values, historical circumstances, political and economic realities, and specific situational forces. Modern social psychologists have expanded the domain of their inquiry to include this broader network of interactive elements. Many new areas of application have opened up to both the curious investigator and to the psychologist as agents of social change (Fisher, 1982). For example, "Cross-cultural Perspective: Accepting the Importance of Diversity" reviews how the lessons of social cognition (processes such as social perception and attribution) can be applied when individuals from different cultural background come into contact with each other.

The expansion of psychology's relevance to life problems provides great opportunities and challenges to psychologists just beginning their professional careers. Among the exciting liaisons of social psychology and its research paradigms and perspectives are psychology and such fields and issues as law, education, health care, counseling, interpersonal relations, politics (including international relations, terrorism, conflict, and public policy), consumerism, business, the environment, and the promotion of world peace (see Oskamp [1984] and Rodin [1985] for more applications of social psychology to everyday life). We dealt at length with health psychology in Chapter 9. Here we will look at close relationships and peace psychology.

Cross-cultural Perspective   Accepting the Importance of Diversity

Part of people's socialization into their own culture involves developing the concept that "We behave in reasonable ways in all kinds of social situations." For example, people learn to meet others for the first time, learn to give an acceptable presentation of their ideas to a group, and learn how much emotion they should show when presenting their ideas. Given the amount of time and effort they put into mastering skills such as these, they develop the ethnocentric concept that everyone should possess these skills. They find it odd and sometimes objectionable that people from other cultural backgrounds have learned a different set of skills. Recall the discussion of culture and intelligence in Chapter 11. Anglo-Americans often develop the skill of persuading others that their ideas are best. Reasonably enough, these same people may feel that everyone should know how to present their ideas in a persuasive manner. This skill, however, is not universal. Native Americans believe that others should be respected as they are, and that making direct attempts at persuasion interferes with this respect.

Cultural differences can cause difficulties when people from different cultural backgrounds come into extensive contact (Barna, 1991; Hofstede, 1991). Cultural contact has become an everyday fact of life given social changes such as global economics, affirmative action, international travel, immigration policies, attention to cultural diversity on college campuses and the movement of international students. If people in one culture receive different rules for behavior than people in another, misunderstandings can result. Assume that Anglo-American students interact with Native Americans on a college campus. If the students are expected to share their opinions, Anglo-Americans may present their views in a direct, forceful manner. If the Native Americans do not respond in a similar manner, the Anglos may make attributions such as "uninformed," "dull in discussion," "uninterested in sharing ideas with us" and

so forth. Native Americans, on the other hand, will have other attributions. They may conclude that the Anglos are rude, obnoxious, and perhaps foolish since they are not using their knowledge in a wise manner. If people from different cultural backgrounds make negative attributions like these, they are not likely to seek out interactions in the future. Under such circumstances, the enriching possibilities of intercultural interactions, with their strong potential to stimulate people's thinking, do not occur.

Various programs have been established that prepare people for intercultural contact. The goals of these programs, most frequently called "cross-cultural training," include giving people information about cultural differences so that they are prepared to use the information in their actual intercultural interactions (Brislin, 1993). One approach to training (Bhawuk, 1990) takes advantage of research on attribution, discussed earlier in this chapter. Various critical incidents are presented involving interactions among members of different cultural groups. One set of materials is based on 100 such incidents (Brislin et. al., 1986). In each incident, some kind of misunderstanding occurs. Readers are asked to suggest reasons for the misunderstandings, based on their now increasing knowledge of culture and cultural differences. Often, the misunderstandings are based on *different* attributions about the *same* behavior. For example, versions of the following incident (first analyzed by Foa and Chemers, 1967) are frequently used.

Andrea, an Anglo American from Oregon was in the same college class as Juanita, a Hispanic American from Texas. Juanita had been born in Mexico and moved to the United States with her family three years ago. The class had only 12 students and the professor expected a good deal of student participation. Andrea and Juanita seemed to "hit it off" and began spending some of their free time together. One day in class, Juanita presented some ideas she had on a class

assignment. Andrea disagreed with one of Juanita's ideas, basing her disagreement on research presented in two recent books. After the seminar, Juanita left without speaking to Andrea. Juanita appeared very upset. Can you suggest reasons, based on people's cultural backgrounds, that can help explain this incident?

Explanations should include analyses of attributions made by Andrea and Juanita. The cultural differences stem from the relative emphasis on individualism and collectivism (see Chapter 4). In Andrea's individualistic culture, friends can disagree in public and still be friends. Andrea's attribution might be, "I'm a college student who is expected to give my views. Surely Juanita will feel the same way." In Juanita's collective culture, it is hard for friends to also serve as public critics. Friends are supposed to be supportive and helpful, and Juanita felt that Andrea withdrew her friendship in the seminar. Juanita's attribution might be, "I thought Andrea and I were friends since we were spending so much time together. Friends don't disagree in front of others."

If people learn to understand the attributions others are likely to make, they will not always interpret behaviors as personally directed. They will be able to say, "Well, I don't behave that way, but I realize that's the way they do things in their culture and it's OK from their viewpoint." People will also learn to modify their behavior so that it is more acceptable from the other's viewpoint. In this incident, Juanita might learn to speak up in small classes given that the cultural norms are Anglo. Or Andrea might submit her ideas in private to the professor, realizing that Juanita might be upset with a public presentation. If people are motivated to become culturally sensitive, there is a great deal of guidance available for putting their desires into action (Triandis, 1989; Bhawuk, 1990; Hofstede, 1991; Brislin, 1993).

Close Relationships

Social psychological processes such as self-fulfilling prophecies, behavioral confirmation, and attribution are certainly interesting in themselves (especially to social psychologists), but may be all the more relevant to you because they help to explain relationships with other people. An important quality of social psychology is its assumption that people live in a social world, not a vacuum, and that we are motivated to seek out others, interact with them, and understand them. We reach outside ourselves, affiliate with others, become particularly attracted to a few of those we meet, and work to establish and maintain intimacy. Closeness is desirable but certainly not automatic; it does not "come naturally."

This irony—that close relationships are important but difficult to sustain—is apparent to anyone who has suffered the loss of a loved one, whether family or friend, through death or breakup. To become close to anyone is to risk the complex pains of loss—grief and bereavement, loneliness and depression, the anger and humiliation of being rejected. To judge from themes in popular literature, music, and films, most of us are hungry for information about how to find love, resolve conflicts, and make up after breakups. If intimacy is so important to well-being and happiness, why is it so hard to find? And if we are not the first to ask these questions, why are there so few answers, beyond the questionable opinions of columnists, cartoonists, and television characters?

From Attraction to Interaction. One social psychologist has wryly observed that his discipline has been the last to arrive at the "party" of those interested in liking and loving—long after poets, journalists, and the lovers themselves (Rubin, 1973). However, for over four decades, social psychologists have been slowly but steadily assembling the data necessary to draw some conclusions about how people might best form and strengthen intimate bonds. The earliest work on relationships focused on interpersonal attraction, and identified key factors that determine whom we like: similar attitudes, physical attractiveness, shared values and history, compatibility of needs, and fair exchange of resources (for example, see Hendrick & Hendrick [1992] for a summary). Laboratory studies of these processes—for example, whether receiving a compliment would increase a subject's liking for someone—were usually restricted to short-term interactions between strangers. How well might their results predict the course of long-term relationships among intimates?

Although the study of existing relationships—real people interacting with their friends and lovers—is a messier, less precise business than manipulating encounters in the lab, it is essential for an understanding of genuine intimacy. Social psychologists **Ellen Berscheid** and **Elaine Hatfield** published the first text on interpersonal attraction in 1969 (see Berscheid & Hatfield, 1969; 1978). Among other topics they explored, Berscheid and Hatfield tackled a basic mystery—the nature of love. Why is it that people in so many cultures expect a special emotional experience (romantic or passionate love) to signal that they have found their life partner? And further, if love is the key to a successful intimate relationship, why do so many relationships end in breakup or divorce? The questions Berscheid and Hatfield asked three decades ago may seem reasonable and worthwhile to us today, but when they first proposed their work, the two social psychologists had to defy both popular derision and political pressure in order to conduct their research. Despite the difficulties of this endeavor, Berscheid, Hatfield, and other investigators persisted in exploring the psychology of the human heart, identifying patterns not only in how people become attracted and fall in love, but also in how relationships develop, are maintained, and often break down (Hatfield & Rapson, 1993).

By the early 1970s, social psychologists began to share their interests and findings with relationship researchers in other disciplines—communication, sociology, counseling, and anthropology. Since then scholars have occasionally left the lab to study meeting, mating, and dating in the "field," including singles bars and personal ads (Harrison & Saeed, 1977; Pennebaker et al., 1979). Their scrutiny of people's relationships has been intensified by what has been referred to as the "divorce epidemic" (Brehm, 1992). In a nutshell, if current rates hold, approximately half of all today's first marriages—and up to 60 percent of second marriages—will end in divorce. Divorces and presumably nonmarital breakups as well constitute a social problem for several reasons:

- When relationships end, families (the functional units of society) are disrupted, especially the children of divorcing parents (for example, Hetherington, 1987, 1988; Wallerstein & Blakeslee, 1989; Wallerstein & Kelly, 1980).
- The process of breaking up or divorcing typically causes individuals to experience extreme financial, physical, and emotional stress (for example, Bloom, Asher & White, 1978; Somers, 1981; Weitzman, 1985).
- At the very least, loss of an intimate relationship represents loss of access to the social support, care, and happiness a partner provides (for example, Campbell, 1981; Weingarten, 1985; Weiss, 1975).

In the last decade, researchers' interest has shifted to the processes by which people actually maintain and develop their relationships *beyond* initial attraction. As a result of efforts by scholars in many different disciplines, we can identify what some of those processes are (for a review, see Brehm [1992], Duck [1992], and Hatfield & Rapson [1993]). For example, we know that the *social exchange* of resources between partners must be rewarding and *equitable*. *Communication* between partners must be open, ongoing, and mutually validating. *Conflicts* must be faced early and resolved fairly and effectively. Ultimately, each partner must take *responsibility* for his or her own identity, self-esteem, and commitment to the relationship—rather than unrealistically expecting the partner to engage in mindreading or self-sacrifice.

Applying Relationship Lessons. Though young compared to its parent disciplines, the field of close relationships has already yielded some benefits in addressing social concerns. Teachers familiar with research findings can now inform their students about the basic principles of healthy relationships with friends and partners. Therapists apply these principles in advising clients on how to communicate with partners, negotiate the terms of their relationships, and resolve inevitable conflicts. And, as considered in "In Focus: Application: Using Accounts in Coping with Loss" (on the next page), research and theory have developed effective ways to cope with loss and move on when relationships end.

Peace Psychology

Just as social psychology can throw light on interpersonal relationships, it can likewise illuminate the complexities and conflicts of interpersonal relations. Psychologists for Social Responsibility is an organization of psychologists who not only study various aspects of the complex issues involved in war and peace but conduct educational programs on these topics for professionals, schoolchildren, and the lay public. In addition, they try to have input in relevant political decision-making policies at the state and national levels. This organization is just one example of the dual roles that many psychologists have chosen to play as dedicated, objective scientists and, at other times, as committed, impassioned advocates of social-political action.

Attempting to *help* resolve the dilemmas of superpower competition or, for that matter, many of the domestic and international problems that we now face poses challenges that psychology is uniquely equipped to study. **Peace psychology** represents an interdisciplinary approach to prevention of nuclear

peace psychology Interdisciplinary approach to the prevention of nuclear war and the promotion and maintenance of peace.

In Focus:

USING ACCOUNTS IN COPING WITH LOSS

Two social psychologists attending a conference on personal relationships discussed how they might best present their work the next day to their 200 colleagues. Their paper dealt with the fact that many people, in dealing with the breakup of a relationship, seem to formulate stories about their experiences. As time passes these stories pass into memory, and are related less frequently in explaining the loss to others—but they are always available, and easily retrieved. This process is interesting, but it might not come across that way if presented as yet another dust-dry, prosaic analysis. If only they could provide a live example of the process. . . . That was it! They would go out and find a "real" person with such a story.

Walking from the conference center into the summer sunshine, the two divided their task, one choosing to scout likely subjects while the other would approach each target person in search of an interview. Several likely candidates sat in the city square, enjoying the July weather: a man strumming a guitar, a couple in intense conversation, a young woman selling earrings arranged on a blanket. The interviewer approached the young woman, who looked away from her earrings occasionally to glance behind her at a quilted basket, in which a baby lay sleeping. After a brief introduction—and the approving nod of her colleague across the square—the interviewer chatted with the woman about relationships, breakups, and stories.

Had the woman ever lost a relationship, one she remembered particularly well?

"Oh, yes! There was this architect I met when I first finished school. I thought we'd be together forever, but that's not how it turned out, of course."

Had the woman ever considered what happened and why, and come up with an explanation or conclusion about what went wrong?

"Oh, yes! See, he was basically very materialistic, and I was not into 'things' that much. I thought—"

Wait! Would the woman be willing to tell her story on tape, so we could use it as an example during this conference?

"Well, sure. Ready? Okay, like I said, he was basically a very materialistic guy, but I was not really into having 'things' as much as he was. At first I didn't think it was a problem. But over time we argued more and more . . ."

The young woman chattered into the small tape recorder, earnestly relating her **account,** the story of her relationship, its demise, and what she learned from that loss. She later admitted she had not told anyone her story in a long time. But her story was there, close to the surface of her memory, easy to retrieve and recount, even to a stranger.

Research indicates that people formulate accounts in the wake of traumatic experiences such as relationship loss, crime, or injury (Harvey, Weber & Orbuch, 1990). When you tell your story, almost automatically relating your experiences and trying to explain what has happened and why, you may even be promoting your own healing. According to Harvey et al. (1990), your ultimate goal in the process of *account-making* is to make sense of your traumatic experience, helping you to get over it and go on with your life. Your account assembles attributions, self-concepts, emotions and memories into an orderly chronicle. At the end of this process, you have worked through much of your grief and fear, and have achieved a new sense of purpose and identity.

For example, a woman is devastated when the man she has been seeing breaks off their relationship without a word of explanation. He does not answer her letters or phone calls, and effectively disappears from her social circle. At first her account is full of holes—something must have happened, perhaps he met someone else, or became bored or afraid of commitment. Over time she is less emotional, more reflective; she can now remember other times when he did not explain his behavior reasonably to her, or did things that seemed hurtful or selfish. His disappearance is less of a surprise (or disappointment). Eventually, when asked what ever became of him, she is able to explain their breakup as if she had "known all along" their relationship would not last. She no longer wonders if she bored or frightened him, and accepts that he is no longer part of her world. Her story makes sense to her, comforts her, and frees her to leave her old questions behind and get on with her life.

Accounts represent one way we cope with loss. According to therapists, grief is not a single emotion but a process involving several tasks—facing the loss, expressing sadness and pain, healing, and reentering one's now-changed life and world (Davidsen-Nielsen & Leick, 1991; Rando, 1988). Their recommendations are consistent with theories of how relationship experiences lead to breakups in the first place. Researcher **Steve Duck** (1982) suggests that the termination of relationships progresses through four phases:

- An *intrapsychic phase,* in which one partner feels dissatisfied with the relationship and privately reviews justifications for withdrawing
- The *dyadic phase,* begun when the complaining partner makes his or her dissatisfaction known to the other, and they discuss whether to reconcile or part
- The *social phase,* during which both partners arrange to part ways, and inform their friends and families of the impending change and the reasons for it
- Finally, the *grave-dressing phase,* in which the now-ended relationship is mourned, and retrospective accounts of its history and its demise are recounted.

The challenge of work on account-making and other coping strategies lies in the fact that people's real-life experiences are so hard to sort, analyze, and study objectively. On the other hand, difficult as it may be to disentangle the threads woven into stories of loss, this research reveals the richness of people's efforts to find meaning in pain, and hope in sadness.

account The story of one's experience, especially of a trauma or loss, including attributions of blame, social perceptions, beliefs, memories, and emotions.

war and maintenance of peace (Plous, 1985). Psychologists committed to contributing their talents and energies to this vital element of our future draw upon this work of investigators in many areas. Among them are political scientists, economists, physicists, mathematicians, computer scientists, anthropologists, climatologists, and physicians.

Some peace psychologists are conducting research that examines the basis for false beliefs, misperceptions, and erroneous attributions on issues germane to nuclear arms, military strength, risk, national security, and even language. They study the fears of children and the anxieties of adults about nuclear war. To explore the individual and cultural forces that create war and promote peace, peace psychologists study propaganda and media images that glorify war and violence and demonize the enemy. Although most cultures oppose individual aggression as a crime, nations train millions of soldiers to kill. Part of this mass social influence involves dehumanizing the soldiers of the other side into "the enemy"—nonhuman objects to be hated and destroyed. This dehumanization is accomplished through political rhetoric and through media (for example, movies and cartoons) and popular culture (for example, anti-enemy "jokes"). A dehumanized enemy—a subhuman or even a nonhuman—can be killed without guilt. The problem of military psychology is to convert the act of murder into patriotism (Keen, 1986), and this is most effectively accomplished by giving every soldier not a gun but an exaggerated, internalized view of the hated enemy (see **Figure 12.6** on the next page). In recent years, Americans have been urged by politicians, journalists, cartoonists, and entertainers to loathe and ridicule the people of Iran, Grenada, Panama, Iraq, and the former Yugoslavia. A major challenge to peace psychology is that humans can readily and vividly imagine many different kinds of people as "enemies."

Peace psychologists have taken several different directions in their work. For quite some time, social scientists have been investigating arms negotiations, international crisis management, and conflict resolution strategies. They have developed experimental gaming studies to test the utility of different models of the nuclear arms race, using the players' responses as clues to the motivations and political decisions of national leaders. Arms negotiations or international crises are simulated to resemble historical situations. Participants communicate and make decisions in teams with different power structures (Guetzkow et al., 1963). By varying factors such as arrangements of the problem or the participants, researchers can observe which structures and strategies work best. Such simulations also generate new negotiating strategies and techniques for crisis management (Bazerman, 1990).

Some psychologists believe that to affect policy-making toward nuclear war, it is necessary to study the way those in authority have handled past nuclear crises. By learning how decision makers have made sense of events that could have led to nuclear war, psychologists can offer more fully formed decision rules that minimize the cognitive and motivational biases of policymakers. This work may prevent future crises through an understanding of past and current crisis management (Blight, 1987).

From a psychodynamic perspective, the nuclear arms race is driven by the quest for personal power among national leaders (Frank, 1987). Superpower leaders may possess a constellation of personality traits—toughness, persuasiveness, suspiciousness, optimism, and competitiveness—that can lead to predictable errors in judgment. For example, only a strong, independent person is likely to reach a high level of power, but strength and independence may isolate such a leader from sensible advice just when he or she needs it most. Psychologists realize how difficult it is to change the very traits that have made leaders successful in many aspects of their jobs. Consequently, they urge leaders to become aware of superordinate goals on which they can agree. Alternatives to violence as the ultimate expression of power must also be identified.

Figure 12.6 Faces of the Enemy
Notice how the propagandists have created images of the enemy that are fearsome, monstrous, or dehumanized.

Finally, many peace psychologists focus their attention on the sociopsychological effects of nuclear war—the way people perceive and respond to its threat and the reason citizens who are fearful of nuclear destruction do not get involved in activities to promote peace (Allen, 1985; Fiske, 1987).

The New (Psychological) World Order? Psychologists have a new role in the revolution that is sweeping away entire political systems and economic orders throughout the world. The transition of hundreds of millions of people from a totalitarian to a democratic mentality and from a central collectivist society to a free-market economy is a change of unprecedented proportions. Generations of formerly Communist citizens have never experienced the freedoms and responsibilities of democratic ideas and practices. Democracy is more than a political system; it is a unique way of thinking about the significance of the individual and the role of oneself in shaping shared societal goals. Those who have lived with some sense of security in government-controlled economy and state-run industries, such as in the former Soviet Union, must learn to cope with the risks and uncertainties of competitive market economies. Additionally, individuals and whole communities need help in dealing with decades of abuses by totalitarian regimes—exiles, imprisonments, forced labor, displacement, and ecological catastrophes. This psychological help involves education, research, therapy, and social policy-planning. The Center for the Psychology of Democracy is a newly formed organization of psychologists committed to assisting people and societies in reshaping their lives and country within the framework of democratic principles and practices (Balakrishnan, 1991).

This brief discussion of peace psychology barely touches on the many new directions that researchers and social change agents are taking to reduce the threat of war and increase the prospects for peace. (See *Discovering Psychology,* Program 24 for other illustrations of peace psychology in action.) For example, what can the world community do about the deep-seated hatreds and fears that have so long held sway in Northern Ireland? Or consider Bosnia, the battle-torn province in the former Yugoslavia. What can be done for nations emerging from decades of Communist oppression only to take up arms against each other to renew long-buried grudges and feuds with their neighbors—to destroy human beings through the systematic extermination euphemistically called "ethnic cleansing"? The umbrella of peace psychology must grow larger to accommodate this latest challenge to the world community. The basic research and theories we have been discussing can be applied to solve the urgent problems facing us. Our goal in this is to improve the qualify of life for individuals, societies, and the planet.

SUMMING UP

A strong motivating goal for many social psychologists is the desire to improve the human condition. Teachers, therapists, and laypersons alike benefit from research on close relationships. Early work identified influential factors in interpersonal attraction, while more recent research has suggested processes important to developing and maintaining healthy relationships, and coping with loss.

Peace psychology endeavors to understand the nature of international competition and conflict so that problems can be defused before they pose a nuclear threat. Peace psychologists have found that hostilities are based in prejudices, misperceptions, and dehumanizing images of "the enemy." By learning how to avoid such costly errors in social thinking, we can transform our energies into constructive commitments between peoples and nations.

CHAPTER REVIEW

The Power of the Situation. *How can social situations affect task performance? What processes teach us about the rules that operate in our social environments? What two motives have been proposed to explain conformity? How does Milgram's study of obedience to authority demonstrate the power of situations? Which factors best predict whether a bystander will help in a crisis?*

Human thought and action are affected by situational influences. Being assigned to play a social role, even in artificial settings, can cause individuals to act contrary to their beliefs, values, and dispositions. Social norms shape the behavior of group members, as demonstrated by the Asch experiments and the Bennington study. Milgram's studies on obedience are a powerful testimony to the influence of situational factors. Bystander intervention studies show that, when among part of a large group of people or when in a hurry, individuals are less likely to aid a person in distress. Directly asking for help is an effective way of promoting altruism.

Key Terms	**Major Contributors**
social psychology, p. 444	Zimbardo, Philip, p. 444
social context, p. 444	Triplett, Norman, p. 445
situationism, p. 445	Allport, Gordon, p. 448
social facilitation, p. 445	Newcomb, Theodore, p. 448
social loafing, p. 445	Funt, Allen, p. 449
rules, p. 446	Asch, Solomon, p. 451
social role, p. 446	Milgram, Stanley, p. 454
social norms, p. 447	Latané, Bibb, p. 460
reference group, p. 448	Darley, John, p. 460
total situation, p. 449	Moriarity, Tom, p. 462
normative influence, p. 451	
informational influence, p. 451	
Asch effect, p. 451	
conformity, p. 451	
demand characteristics, p. 457	
bystander intervention, p. 460	

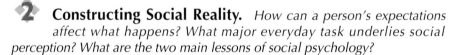

2 Constructing Social Reality. *How can a person's expectations affect what happens? What major everyday task underlies social perception? What are the two main lessons of social psychology?*

Everyone constructs a personal social reality that is shared by his or her social group. Beliefs and expectations can guide actions and shape outcomes in any behavioral setting. Prejudice develops as an outcome of the desire to simplify complex information through categorization. Even minimal cue differences are a sufficient basis for social categorizations. Social psychologists often use cognitive frameworks to understand social phenomena. Theories using cognitive frameworks include dissonance theory and attribution theory.

Key Terms	**Major Contributors**
social reality, p. 464	Rosenthal, Robert, p. 465
self-fulfilling prophecies, p. 465	Snyder, Mark, p. 466
behavioral confirmation, p. 466	Clark, Kenneth, p. 466
prejudice, p. 466	Elliott, Jane, p. 467
social categorization, p. 466	Festinger, Leon, p. 468
social perception, p. 468	Heider, Fritz, p. 469
cognitive dissonance, p. 468	Kelley, Harold, p. 470
attribution theory, p. 469	
intuitive psychologists, p. 470	
covariation principle, p. 470	
self-serving bias, p. 471	

3 **Solving Social Problems.** *What is social psychology's ultimate goal? What is the irony of experiencing close relationships? What does peace psychology seek to accomplish?*

Many social psychologists strive to improve the human condition by applying psychological principles to various social problems. The study of close relationships applies research on attitude formation, social influence, social perception, and attribution. The study of grief teaches us how to cope with loss and move on with our lives.

Peace psychologists look for ways to help resolve international competition and hostilities. They conduct research that examines the basis for false beliefs, misperceptions, and erroneous attributions in areas related to national security and nuclear arms. They also study fears about war among children and adults. Psychologists have assembled organizations to develop programs that can promote the transition from totalitarian to democratic forms of government. In issues ranging from intimate relationships to international relations, social psychology aims to be both practical and theoretical.

Key Terms	Major Contributors
peace psychology, p. 475	Berscheid, Ellen, p. 474
account, p. 476	Hatfield, Elaine, p. 474
	Duck, Steve, p. 476

PRACTICE TEST

Chapter 12: Social Psychology

For each of the following items, choose the single correct or best answer. Correct answers, explanations, and page references in the Appendix.

1. Which of the following social psychological themes is underscored by the Stanford Prison experiment and its findings about its participants' behavior?
   A. Social situations have the power to control human behavior.
   B. Experiences are not socially real unless the group is unanimous about their interpretation.
   C. Everyone is different, and no two people respond to social stimulation in the same way.
   D. Even in healthy circumstances, disturbed people will behave in unhealthy ways.

2. An instructor assigns all members of your class to work in project teams. Everyone in the team will get the same grade, no matter what individual members contributed or failed to do. In these circumstances, your own actions are most likely to be affected by the power of social _____ .
   A. roles
   B. facilitation
   C. loafing
   D. interference

3. According to your text, *ridicule, reeducation,* and *rejection* are the most common examples of _____ .
   A. behavior by deviants or nonconformists
   B. causes of cognitive dissonance
   C. how Asch's subjects behaved in his classic research
   D. coercive tactics to encourage group conformity

4. Theodore Newcomb's study of the attitudes of Bennington College students showed that, twenty years after they were first studied, _____ .
   A. all the women had gradually shifted to more conservative attitudes
   B. all the women had gradually shifted to more liberal attitudes
   C. the liberals were still liberal, and the conservatives still conservative
   D. None of the above.

5. Which of the following is *not* a condition that breeds greater conformity in research on the Asch effect?
   A. a difficult or ambiguous judgment task
   B. each group member votes privately and anonymously
   C. the group is extremely cohesive
   D. the group's members are perceived as highly competent

6. Which of the following statements about the findings of Milgram's studies of obedience to authority is true?
   A. Even though subjects knew they were participating in a study of obedience, they were unable to resist following the authority figure's orders.
   B. Subjects delivered shocks of increasing intensity until the learner complained of a heart condition, at which point they were afraid to go on.
   C. Although most subjects dissented and complained, the majority did not disobey behaviorally.
   D. None of the above.

7. According to research on helping, the best predictor of bystander intervention is _____ .
   A. an individual's score on a scale of altruism
   B. an individual's belief in Christian values
   C. the situational variable of the size of the group
   D. the situational variable of victim appearance

8. Marianne meets a friend of her roommate's in the dining hall. Mistakenly believing he is someone her roommate described as a music student, Marianne steers the conversation to an upcoming concert, and notes how interested he is in the topic. Later her roommate is surprised to learn of the mixup, insisting that Marianne's new friend is an engineering major, not a music student. Marianne's misperceptions illustrate a process known as _____ .
   A. behavioral confirmation
   B. self-fulfilling prophecy
   C. social categorization
   D. self-serving biases

9. Which of the following experiences is most likely to produce cognitive dissonance?
   A. A young man believes he is overweight, so he joins a new fitness club to work off the extra pounds.
   B. As much as she likes the new car the salesman is showing her, a woman realizes she cannot afford it and declines his price offer.
   C. After rearranging her work schedule to allow her to take a difficult new course, a woman decides the class is boring and not what she had hoped it would be.
   D. A business executive, tired of travel and long hours, takes a cut in pay to work a lighter schedule and spend more time with his family.

10. In the _____ phase of relationship dissolution, the dissatisfied partner confides his or her doubts to the other, and they decide either to work on their relationship or part ways.
    A. intrapsychic
    B. dyadic
    C. social
    D. grave-dressing

IF YOU'RE INTERESTED . . .

Brehm, S. S. (1992). *Intimate relationships,* 2nd edition. New York: McGraw-Hill.

Interesting and comprehensive text, covering the stages and issues typical of close personal relationships—attraction, love, sexuality, communication, power, jealousy, conflict, breakups, therapy, research, and popular culture.

Challenger. (Video: 1990, color, 150 minutes). Directed by Glenn Jordan; starring Karen Allen, Barry Bostwick, Joe Morton, Peter Boyle.

Pretty good story, originally a TV movie, chronicling the disastrous explosion of the space shuttle Challenger in January 1986. The script includes documentation of the group processes involved in deciding whether to launch the shuttle during questionable weather conditions.

Cialdini, R. B. (1993). *Influence: Science and practice,* 3rd edition. New York: HarperCollins.

Interesting and practical summary of research on social and interpersonal influence, by master scholar in this area.

Duck, S. (1983). *Friends, for life.* New York: St. Martin's Press.

Brief introductory text to the multidisciplinary field of personal relationships, including attraction, love, friendship, intimacy, and conflict, by a top scholar in the field.

Starting Over. (Video: 1979, color, 106 minutes). Directed by Alan J. Pakula; starring Burt Reynolds, Jill Clayburgh, Candice Bergen, Charles Durning, Austin Pendleton.

Funny story of a man's ambivalences about the end of his marriage and the beginning of his relationship with a new partner. Fairly accurate representation of attraction and relationship processes, including the trials of dating, loneliness, commitment, and conflict.

Twelve Angry Men. (Video: 1957, black-and-white, 95 minutes). Directed by Sidney Lumet; starring Henry Fonda, Lee J. Cobb, E. G. Marshall, Ed Begley, Jack Klugman, Jack Warden.

Gripping real-time story of jurors deliberating the outcome of a murder trial, in which one man argues for acquittal. Illustrates such processes as conformity, authoritarian personality, group influence, and reconstructive memory.

Chapter 13 **Psychopathology**

Preview Questions

1. What qualities or experiences indicate abnormality? How have attitudes toward abnormal behavior changed in the course of human history? What are the major approaches in psychopathology today? Of what use is a diagnostic classification system of psychological disorders?

2. How is a personality disorder different from other mental disorders? What class of disorders is someone suffering from who has a "split personality"? What experience do phobias and panic have in common? Which affective disorder accounts for a majority of all mental hospitalizations? What are the major types of eating disorders? What are the different types of schizophrenia?

3. What evidence suggests that clinicians have difficulty making objective judgments? What are the dangers of stigmatizing those who suffer from any of the forms of psychopathology presented in this chapter?

"I want to let you know what it is like to be a functional scitzophrenic in these days and times and what someone with my mental illness faces.

"I live by myself and am 30. I live on SSI and work part-time as I go through college. Im not allowed to go into Nursing despite past patient care experience and college classes, because of my illness. Im majoring in Human Services to help others with problems, because when I first was sick, I suffered bad and can relate with the suffering.

"I live pretty normal and no one can tell Im mentally ill unless I tell them. . . . My sister (not a twin) has this illness too, for 12 years, and wont take her medicine because she refused to understand she has this illness. Ive had mine for 5 years. I became convinced the 1st year through my suffering by reading the book, "I Never Promised You a Rose Garden." So I improved, thanks to the antipsychotic medicine availible. The patient and public, in my opnion needs to be educated about mental illness, because people ridicule and mistreat, even misunderstand us at crucial times. Like how family, husband, friends, or social services react to what they don't know about us. The medicine works good on some of us.

"I can tell the difference between a noise of my illness and a real noise, because Ive studied myself reading about it. There is a common sense rule I use. I just try hard to remember what the world and people are really like. The illness picks such silly nonsense to bother the mind with. The medicine is strong with me and my body chemistry so I don't have too many illness symptoms bothering me.

"The delusions before I got my medicine picked any storyline it chose, and changed it at will. As time went by before help, I felt it was taking over my whole brain, and I'd cry wanting my mind and life back. . . .

"Every person that comes down with an illness is going to be different in handling it. The things that are consistant are the usual symptoms that come along with the illness.

"I hope my letter fits in with some pattern that you see in other scitzophrenics. If they can master it with medicine, medical help, and recognize the illness in themselves, they can live pretty normal lives if given the *opportunity,* which isn't easy to be lucky enough to have.

"Everyone that wants to succeed in life needs opportunities for them to prove themself. Im a person besides just a person with an illness. . . .

"I hope this letter does some good, it was nagging my mind to write a letter about this illness to you, Dr. Zimbardo.

Much Respect and Thanks,

Cherish (fictitious name)"

Introduction

What are your reactions as you read this young woman's letter? It would be reasonable for you to feel a mixture of sadness at her plight, delight in her willingness to do all she can to cope with the many problems her mental illness creates, anger toward those who stigmatize her because she may act differently at times, and hope that, with medication and therapy, her condition may improve. These are but a few of the emotions that clinical psychologists and psychiatrists feel as they try to understand and treat mental disorders. While clinical psychologists are on the frontlines, working directly with individuals suffering from the many forms that mental illness can take, an army of researchers in university laboratories, clinics, hospitals, and government-sponsored research centers is investigating the causes, correlates, and consequences of mental disorders.

This chapter focuses on the nature and causes of psychological disorders: what they are, what they look like, why and how they develop. The next, and final, chapter builds on this knowledge to describe strategies for treating and preventing mental illness.

The Nature of Psychological Disorders

Have you ever worried excessively, felt depressed or anxious without really knowing why, been fearful of something you knew rationally could not harm you, believed you were not living up to your potential, had thoughts about suicide, or used alcohol and drugs to escape a problem? Almost everyone will answer "yes" to at least one of these questions. Occasional periods of worry, self-doubt, sadness, and escapism are all part of normal life. But taken to

psychopathology Abnormality or disorder in patterns of thought, emotion, or behavior.

excess, such experiences endanger healthy functioning and are considered abnormal. This chapter looks at the range of psychological functioning that is considered unhealthy or abnormal, often referred to as *psychopathology* or *psychological disorder*. **Psychopathology** involves disrupted emotions, behaviors, or thoughts leading to personal distress or inability to achieve important goals. The field of abnormal psychology is the area of psychological investigation most directly concerned with understanding individual pathologies of mind, mood, and behavior.

Psychopathology touches the daily lives of millions of us, directly and indirectly. It can be insidious, working its way into many situations and diminishing our emotional and physical well-being. It can be devastating, destroying the effective functioning of individuals and their families. It can create an enormous financial burden through lost productivity and the high costs of prolonged treatment. A recent study estimates that as many as 32 percent of all Americans have suffered from a form of identified psychological disorder at some point in their lives (Regier et al., 1988). Statistics on the most dreaded mental disorder, *schizophrenia,* are frightening. One of every 100 Americans is likely to become afflicted. By the year 2000, over 2 million people in the United States will suffer from schizophrenia (the worldwide data are comparable). About one-third of the victims of schizophrenia will never fully recover, even with therapy.

Throughout this chapter, as we present more statistics, discuss categories of psychological disorders, and consider theoretical models that help us understand these problems, try to envision the real people, who live with a psychological disorder every day. Remember Cherish: Her words convey the personal distress and struggles that accompany psychopathology.

What Is Abnormal?

Experts in the field of abnormal psychology do not agree completely about what behaviors constitute psychological disorders. The judgment that someone has a mental disorder is typically based on the evaluation of the individual's *behavioral* functioning by people who have special authority or power. The terms used to describe these phenomena—*mental disorder, mental illness,* or *abnormality*—depend on the particular perspective, training, and cultural background of the evaluator; on the situation; and on the status of the person being judged. In some cases, judgments of abnormality are confused with evaluations of morality. For example, our culture frowns upon hallucinations, because they are taken as signs of mental disturbance; other cultures value hallucinations, because they are interpreted as mystical visions from spirit forces.

The first step in classifying someone as having a psychological disorder is making a judgment that some aspect of the person's functioning is *abnormal.* A **psychological diagnosis** serves to identify, classify, and categorize the observed behavior pattern within an approved diagnostic system of disorders, syndromes, and other conditions.

psychological diagnosis Identifying and explaining mental disorders according to clinical interview and observation, testing, and analysis of mental and behavioral development.

Diagnosing Abnormality. The evidence for diagnosis comes from interpretations of a person's actions. Consider what it means to say someone is *abnormal* or *suffering from a psychological disorder*. How do psychologists decide what is abnormal? Is it always clear when behavior moves from the normal to the abnormal category? Judgments about abnormality are far from being clear cut; mental disorder is best thought of as a *continuum,* as shown in **Figure 13.1** on the next page. The definition of *abnormality* is not very precise; there are no fail-safe rules for identifying abnormality.

No single definition can summarize a widely accepted meaning of "abnormality." Instead, most clinicians judge a possible abnormality according to the presence of six indicators (Rosenhan & Seligman, 1989).

Figure 13.1 Mental Disorder Continuum

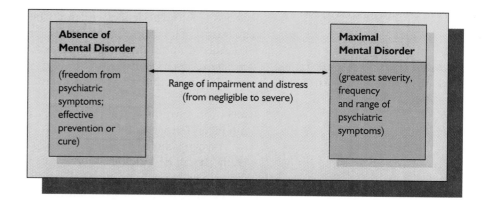

1. *Distress*: personal distress or intense anxiety.
2. *Maladaptiveness*: acting in ways that interfere with goals, personal well-being, and the goals and needs of society.
3. *Irrationality*: acting or talking in ways that are irrational or incomprehensible to others.
4. *Unpredictability*: behaving unpredictably or erratically from situation to situation, as if experiencing a loss of control.
5. *Unconventionality and Statistical Rarity*: behaving in ways that are statistically rare and violate social standards of what is morally acceptable or desirable.
6. *Observer Discomfort*: creating discomfort in others by making them feel threatened or distressed in some way.

Most of these indicators of abnormality are not immediately apparent to all observers; in other words, they involve a large degree of judgment. At the end of this chapter we will consider the negative consequences and dangers associated with such judgments.

Is the presence of just one indicator "enough" to demonstrate abnormality? In fact, psychologists are more confident in labeling behavior as "abnormal" when two or more of the six indicators are present and valid. The more extreme and prevalent the indicators are, the more confident psychologists can be about identifying an abnormal condition.

None of these six criteria is a *necessary* condition shared by all cases of abnormality. And not one of these criteria, by itself, is a *sufficient* condition that distinguishes all cases of abnormal behavior from normal variations in behavior. The distinction between normal and abnormal is not so much a difference between two independent types of behaviors as it is a matter of the *degree* to which a person's actions resemble a set of agreed-upon criteria of abnormality. When making judgments of normality, it is important to operate from a *mental health* perspective as well as from a *mental illness* perspective. As shown in **Figure 13.2**, one's mental health is not simply either good or bad, but can rather be described as some point on a continuum between optimal (best possible) mental health and minimal (worst) mental health. To be healthy, one must be more than just illness-free—one must be functioning in a way that secures and maintains healthiness beyond present conditions.

Before we consider specific examples of abnormality that are classified as psychological disorders, we will look at some historical views of psychological problems. We will then illustrate how these perspectives have contributed to our current understanding of psychological disorders.

Perspectives on Psychopathology

Throughout history, humans have feared psychological disorders, often associating them with evil. Because of their fear, people have reacted aggressively

Figure 13.2 Mental Health Continuum

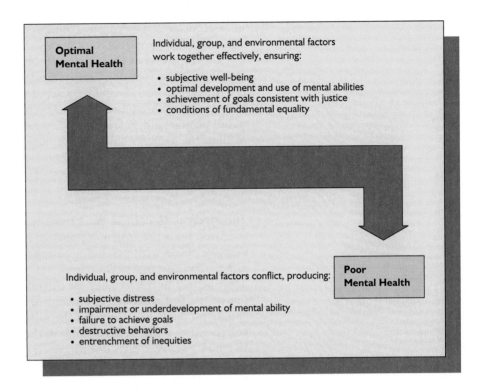

and decisively to any behaviors they perceived as bizarre or abnormal. Not until very recently have people begun to accept the notion that psychological disorders are a form of illness that is very often treatable.

Ages and Attitudes. Attitudes about the link between mental illness and evil may be as old as human history. Archaeologists have found prehistoric skulls with surgical holes drilled in them. These discoveries might indicate that our ancestors believed such holes would allow the escape of demons that had possessed a loved one.

Through the Middle Ages, concepts of mental and physical illness were intertwined and primitively blended with superstition and religious fantasy. Bodily functions were only understood in the simplest mechanical terms, and the complexities of the nervous system were completely undeciphered. For example, the syndrome termed **conversion disorder,** in which psychological causes lead to physical afflictions like paralysis or blindness, was originally called **hysteria** (from the Greek *hustera,* "womb"). This is because it was thought to afflict only women in whom the uterus—under the devil's control—interfered with healthy body functions.

During the Renaissance (about 1350–1630 A.D.), intellectual and artistic enlightenment flourished. Oddly enough, amid this intellectual fervor, fear of the devil peaked as the Roman Catholic Church launched a campaign of trials and torture to weed out evil and all nonbelievers. The Inquisition led to the torture and execution of thousands.

In early 1692 in the Massachusetts town of Salem Village, several girls and young women began experiencing convulsions, nausea, and weakness. They reported sensations of being pinched, pricked, or bitten. Many became temporarily blind or deaf; others reported visions and sensations of flying through the air. Such strange symptoms sparked a frantic search for an explanation. Many people theorized that the symptoms were the work of the devil who, through the efforts of earthbound witches, had taken over the minds and bodies of the young women. These theories led to a witchcraft panic and to the execution of over 20 men and women believed to be witches. A recent analysis strongly suggests that the "bewitched" Salem women may have been suffering

conversion disorder   Type of psychological disorder in which there is loss of motor or sensory function without corresponding organic cause.

hysteria   Archaic term for mental illness characterized by clusters of painful or paralyzing symptoms without clear physical cause.

from ergot poisoning; *ergot,* a fungus that grows on rye, is a source of LSD (Caporeal, 1976; Matossian, 1982).

Until the end of the eighteenth century, the mentally ill in Western societies were perceived as mindless beasts who could be controlled only with chains and physical discipline. They were not cared for in hospitals but were incarcerated with criminals. A society cannot deal with what it cannot understand; people tend to fear what they cannot explain. For this reason the treatment of the mentally ill has always depended on the state of the science of psychology. Modern approaches are a vast improvement over the demonic nightmares and persecutions of past centuries, but we are still a long way from knowing all we need to know.

The Medical Model. In the latter part of the eighteenth century, a new perspective about the origins of abnormal behavior emerged. People began to perceive those with psychological problems as *sick* (suffering from illness), rather than as possessed or immoral. A number of reforms were gradually implemented in the facilities for the insane. **Philippe Pinel** (1745–1826) was one of the first clinicians to attempt to develop a classification system for psychological difficulties based on the idea that disorders of thought, mood, and behavior are similar in many ways to the physical, organic symptoms of illness. In Pinel's system, each disorder is seen as having a group of characteristic symptoms that distinguishes it from other disorders and from healthy functioning. Disorders are classified according to the patterns of symptoms, the circumstances of onset, their usual course of development, and their response to treatment. Classification systems, such as Pinel's, are created to help clinicians identify common disorders more easily, and are modeled after the biological classification systems naturalists use.

In 1896, **Emil Kraepelin** (1855–1926), a German psychiatrist, was responsible for creating the first truly comprehensive *classification system* of psychological disorders. Psychiatrists continue to draw from his terminology and perpective when they speak of *mental illness* and *treating* mental *patients* in the hope of *curing* their *diseased* brains. The medical model also tends to be based on the perspective that mental illness is caused by deficits in structure or neurobiological functioning.

Salem witchcraft trials, Salem, Massachusetts, 1692

Psychological Models. An alternative perspective to the medical approach focuses on the psychological causes and treatment of abnormal behavior. This perspective began to emerge most clearly at the end of the eighteenth century, helped along by the dramatic work of **Franz Anton Mesmer** (1734–1815). Mesmer believed that many disorders, including hysteria, were caused by disruptions in the flow of a mysterious force that he called *animal magnetism*. He unveiled several new techniques to study animal magnetism, including one originally called *mesmerism* that was later termed *hypnotism* (from its use of *hypnosis*). Mesmer's animal magnetism theory was discredited by scientists, but his hypnotic techniques were adopted by many researchers, including a prominent French neurologist, **Jean-Martin Charcot** (1825–1893). Charcot found that some of the symptoms of hysteria, such as paralysis of a limb, could be eliminated when a patient was under hypnosis. Hypnosis even had the power to *induce* the symptoms of hysteria in healthy individuals, dramatically illustrating the potential of *psychological factors* to cause problems that were once thought to have an exclusively physical basis.

One of Charcot's students, Sigmund Freud, continued to experiment with hypnosis. Freud used his experiments to elaborate on his own theories of personality and abnormality that influence current theories of the nature and causes of psychopathology today. Eventually Freud developed psychoanalysis as a more effective system for explaining and treating psychological disorders, and abandoned the use of hypnosis to reveal unconscious conflicts.

All psychological models are based on the perspective that there is no known *organic* disorder responsible for the symptoms of mental illness. These models identify learning, reinforcement, motivation, cognitions, cultural factors, family systems, and other psychological processes as contributing to mental disorders.

Psychopathology Today

Knowing why the disorder occurs, what its origins are, and how it affects thought and emotional and behavioral processes may lead scientists to new ways of treatment and, ideally, prevention. Approaches to understanding the causal factors in psychopathology can be grouped into two major categories: biological and psychological.

Biological Approaches. Building on the medical model, modern biological approaches assume that psychological disturbances are directly attributable to underlying biological factors, most often linked to the brain or nervous system.

The brain is a complex organ whose interrelated elements are held in delicate balance. Subtle alterations in the brain's tissue or in its chemical messengers—the neurotransmitters—can have significant effects. Genetic factors, brain injury, and infection are a few of the causes of these alterations. Technological advances in brain scanning techniques, such as PET scans, have enabled biologically oriented researchers to discover links between psychological disorders and specific brain abnormalities. For example, extreme violence has been linked to brain tumors located in an area of the brain (in the limbic system) associated with aggressive behavior. Biochemical approaches to psychopathology include studies showing how drugs can alter the normal reality of the mind and how drug therapies can alleviate certain symptoms of psychological disorders (Bowers, 1980; Papolos & Papolos, 1987). Advances in the field of behavioral genetics have improved researchers' abilities to identify the links between specific genes and the presence of psychological disorders (Joyce, 1989; Tsuang & Vandermey, 1981). However, despite the promise of these approaches, there are still many unknowns about the connections between biology, genes, and psychopathology.

Psychological Approaches. Psychological approaches focus on the causal role of psychological or social factors in the development of psychopathology. These approaches perceive personal experiences, traumas, conflicts, and environmental factors as the roots of psychological disorders. The three dominant psychological approaches to abnormality are the *psychodynamic, behaviorist,* and *cognitive* models.

Psychodynamic. The psychodynamic model holds that the causes of psychopathology are forces inside the person. According to Sigmund Freud, who developed this model, these internal causal factors are psychological rather than biological. Freud developed psychoanalytic theory to explain apparently irrational and senseless behavior in a rational way. He believed that many psychological disorders developed from the extension of "normal" processes of psychic conflict and ego defense. In the psychodynamic model, early childhood experiences and personal development shape both normal and abnormal behavior in life.

Symptoms of psychopathology have their roots in *unconscious conflict* and thoughts. If the unconscious is in conflict and tension-filled, a person will be plagued by anxiety and other disorders. Individuals attempt to avoid the pain caused by conflicting motives and anxiety with *defense mechanisms,* such as repression or denial. For example, a woman who has been through a humiliating breakup may defend against her grief and anxiety by avoiding the people and places she associates with the lost relationship. However, defenses can become overused, distorting reality or leading to self-defeating behaviors. The woman who spends so much energy avoiding unpleasant associations may find she has fewer and fewer "safe" havens and relationships. When psychic energy is bound up in attempts to defend against the emergence of repression-bound anxiety, little is left for a productive and satisfying life. (For a review of defense mechanisms, consult **Table 10.2** on page 384).

A therapist relying on the psychodynamic perspective will pay attention to the patterns in the client's past actions and relationships, and will try to identify the unconscious conflicts that lie at the heart of present difficulties. For example, if a woman enters therapy because she is grieving over a lost relationship, a psychoanalyst will encourage her to talk about past relationships and losses in order to unearth insights into unconscious wishes and fears about intimacy. The psychodynamic perspective assumes that insight into the origins of one's problems is essential to making successful adjustments.

Behavioral. Freudian notions gained ready acceptance among clinical psychologists and psychiatrists. However, you will recall that American research psychology from the 1930s to the early 1970s was dominated by a behavioristic orientation. Those who insisted that only observable responses could be acceptable psychological data had no use for hypothetical psychodynamic processes.

Behavioral theorists argue that abnormal behaviors are acquired in the same fashion as healthy behaviors—through learning and reinforcement. They focus not on internal psychological phenomena or early childhood experiences, but rather on one's *current* behavior and the *current* conditions or reinforcements that sustain it—whether it is adaptive or not. The symptoms of psychological disorders arise because an individual has learned self-defeating or ineffective ways of behaving. By discovering the environmental contingencies that maintain any undesirable, abnormal behavior, an investigator or clinician can then recommend treatment to change those contingencies and extinguish the unwanted behavior (Emmelkamp, 1986). Behaviorists rely on both classical and operant conditioning models to understand the processes that can result in maladaptive behavior.

For example, a behavioral therapist treating a woman grief-stricken over a broken relationship will focus primarily on the immediate problems associated with the woman's bereavement and pain. Is she unable to work because she is depressed or unable to concentrate? Does she dread being alone at night because she expects to feel lonely and abandoned? Behavioral therapy will emphasize identifying problem behaviors, analyzing the contingencies (conditions) that keep those in place, and identifying ways to encourage and reinforce changed behavior. Instead of investigating the past origins of the client's disorder, the behavioral perspective examines the lessons and associations that presently determine her experience.

Cognitive. The cognitive perspective on human nature that has evolved over the last several decades is often used to supplement behavioristic views. The cognitive perspective suggests that we should not expect to discover the origins of psychological disorders in the *objective reality* of stimulus environments, reinforcers, and overt responses. Rather, we must look at how we *perceive* or *think* about ourselves and our relations with other people and our environment. Some of the cognitive variables that can guide (or misguide) adaptive responses are our perceived control over important reinforcers, beliefs in our own ability to cope with threat, and patterns of attributing causes of behavior to either situational or personal factors (Bandura, 1986).

For example, a cognitive therapist whose client has suffered a painful relationship loss will question the client's assumptions about the experience. Did her partner really "reject" her or were there signs that the relationship was not likely to last? Was the breakup a genuine "catastrophe" or merely a hurtful disappointment that she will ultimately survive? Was he truly "the only one" for her or is she likely to have other chances for satisfying personal relationships? The woman must examine her own thoughts and perceptions, and question how rational or realistic they are. According to the cognitive perspective, her grief and disorientation will be magnified if she sustains irrational ideas about the breakup. By correcting these beliefs, she can develop more constructive, positive feelings and behaviors.

The cognitive approach views psychological problems as the result of distortions in the reality of a situation or of ourselves, faulty reasoning, or poor problem solving. Whether they help us or harm us, our personal cognitions are our own way of dealing with the complexities and uncertainties of everyday life (Ellis & Grieger, 1986). For example, a woman may be fooling herself by believing that she initiated a recent breakup, but this may be preferable (and easier for her to live with) than the "truth" that it was her partner who rejected her.

Today researchers increasingly view psychopathology as the product of a complex *interaction* between a number of biological and psychological factors (Cowan, 1988). For example, genetic predispositions may make a person vulnerable to a psychological disorder by affecting neurotransmitter levels or hormone levels, but psychological or social stresses or certain learned behaviors may be required for the disorder to develop fully. Why does one person seem to get over a relationship breakup fairly quickly, while another suffers prolonged grief and distraction? The first survivor may have recovered quickly because the relationship had lasted only a brief time, so both partners had few expectations from the start. Additionally, the first survivor may be genetically equipped to deal better with stress, while the latter may be predisposed to depression no matter what circumstances trigger its onset. If no single factor or set of factors (such as the environment or one's inherited constitution) "causes" disordered behavior, therapists must develop various combinations of treatments to address the different factors involved.

Classification Systems

Whichever approach we subscribe to, it is essential to have a system with a record of observed patterns of disordered behavior that clinicians can consult when identifying and treating new cases. However, a number of challenges confront the clinician who wishes to catalogue observations. A number of distinctly different approaches exist for explaining psychological disorders. Thus, the diagnosis of a disturbed person often has as much to do with the theoretical orientation of the clinician as it does with the actual symptoms presented (Franklin, 1987). To create greater consistency among clinicians and greater coherence in their diagnostic evaluations, psychologists have developed a system of diagnosis and classification that provides precise descriptions of symptoms to help clinicians decide whether a person's behavior is evidence of a particular disorder.

Goals of Classification. To be most useful, a diagnostic system should provide common, concise language; an explanation of causes and development; and a recommended course of treatment. Our discussion will consider how difficult each is to achieve, and the advantages of each.

Common Shorthand Language. To facilitate understanding among clinicians or researchers working in psychopathology, it is helpful to have a common set of terms with agreed-upon meanings. A diagnostic category, such as *depression,* summarizes a large and complex collection of information, including characteristic symptoms and the typical course of a disorder. Mental health professionals in clinical settings can use such a diagnostic system to communicate more effectively about the people they are helping. For example, a clinical psychologist developing a treatment program for a new client can consult with a distant colleague by phone or mail based on his description of the client's presenting (immediately apparent) symptoms. Researchers can use a classification system to design studies of different aspects of disorders and to evaluate their treatment. For example, researchers may discover that a particular type of therapy is more effective and generates fewer dropouts among patients with one type of eating disorder than among those with another, because the two disorders are distinguished by an accepted system of classification (see Van Strien et al., 1992).

Understanding Origins. Ideally, diagnosis of a specific disorder should suggest the causes of the symptoms. A thoroughly researched classification system permits a clinician to look up diagnoses appropriate for certain symptoms and case histories, and then goes on to suggest typical etiology (origins and development) as well as commonly recommended treatments. Unfortunately, because there is substantial disagreement or lack of knowledge about the causes of many psychological disorders, this goal is difficult to meet. The key to providing information about origins and development in a classification system is first collecting ample data from experienced professionals.

Treatment Plans. A diagnosis should also suggest what types of treatment to consider for particular disorders. Researchers and clinicians have found that certain treatments or therapies work most effectively for specific kinds of psychological disorders. For example, drugs that are quite effective in treating schizophrenia do not help and may even hurt people with depression.

Cataloguing Disorders. In the United States, the most widely accepted classification scheme is one originally developed by the American Psychiatric Association. It is called the *Diagnostic and Statistical Manual of Mental Disorders.* A revision of the third edition of the manual was published in 1987, and is known by clinicians and researchers as **DSM-III-R.** It classifies, defines, and describes over 200 mental disorders. "In Focus: Updating DSM-III-R" explains how this classification system builds a continually updated catalogue of disorders and what is known about them, for use by both clinicians and researchers in psychopathology.

DSM-III-R Diagnostic and Statistical Manual of Mental Disorders, Third Edition, Revised; American Psychiatric Association's catalogue that classifies, defines, and describes over 200 mental disorders.

neurotic disorder Mental disorder characterized not by irrational thinking or violation of norms but by personal distress, especially anxiety; archaic term.

psychotic disorder Severe mental disorder characterized by impaired reality-testing due to difficulties in thought, emotional, or perceptual processes; archaic term.

In Focus:

The American Psychiatric Association regularly publishes updated editions of a reference book titled *Diagnostic and Statistical Manual of Mental Disorders,* affectionately abbreviated DSM. The latest edition in use is the revision (R) of the third edition (III). In DSM-III-R, each of the mental disorders described is seen as a behavioral or psychological syndrome that occurs within the person and that is associated with either present distress (a painful symptom), the risk of future distress; impairment in one or more important areas of functioning, or with an important loss of freedom (DSM-III-R, 1987).

DSM-III-R emphasizes the *description* of patterns of symptoms and courses of disorders rather than theories of causation or treatment strategies. The purely descriptive terms allow clinicians and researchers from different backgrounds to use a common language to describe these psychiatric problems. There is still much disagreement about which theories best explain particular problems.

The first version of DSM (DSM-I), which appeared in 1952, listed several dozen mental illnesses. Introduced in 1968, DSM-II revised the diagnostic system to make it more compatible with another popular system, the World Health Organization's International Classification of Diseases (ICD). A committee is currently hard at work on a fourth edition of DSM (DSM-IV) that is scheduled to be introduced sometime in 1994, at about the same time as the tenth version of the ICD.

Changes and Revisions

The diagnostic categories and the methods used to present them have shifted with each edition of DSM. These shifts reflect changes in the opinions of most mental health experts about what constitutes a psychological disorder and where the lines between different types of disorders should be drawn. They also reflect changing perspectives among the public about what constitutes *abnormality.*

The revisions for DSM-III-R were based on the judgments of over 200 mental health experts who worked on advisory panels in specific areas of psychopathology. In the revision process of each DSM, some diagnostic categories are dropped and others are added. For example, with the introduction of DSM-III in 1980, the traditional distinctions between *neurotic* and *psychotic* disorders were eliminated. A **neurotic disorder** (or *neurosis*) was originally conceived of as a relatively common psychological problem in which a person did not have signs of brain abnormalities, did not display grossly irrational thinking, and did not violate basic norms. He or she did, however, experience subjective distress or a pattern of self-defeating or inadequate coping strategies. A **psychotic disorder** (or *psychosis*) was thought to differ in both quality and severity from neurotic problems. It was believed that psychotic behavior deviated significantly from social norms and was accompanied by a profound disturbance in rational thinking and general emotional and thought processes. The DSM-III-R advisory committees felt that the terms *neurotic disorders* and *psychotic disorders* had become too general in their meaning to have much usefulness as diagnostic categories—so the official distinction in the original terminology was dropped.

The committee currently producing the fourth edition of DSM has examined how to make the document more politically sensitive as well as more useful in clinical diagnosis. For example, DSM-IV listings for some disorders will describe how culture or ethnicity can influence the expression of symptoms. The committee has received hundreds of suggestions for new diagnostic categories, based on patterns clinicians have encountered and tried to diagnose. Some candidates for new diagnostic categories seem to reflect the stresses and strains of modern culture ("Revising Psychiatric Diagnoses," 1993):

- Caffeine withdrawal
- Mild cognitive disorder (found among HIV-positive patients)
- Binge eating disorder (overeating without purging)
- Telephone scatalogia (making obscene phone calls)

Listing a diagnostic category in DSM is intended not just to label an observable pattern of symptoms, but to help clinicians make diagnoses for some time to come. Therefore the revisers are being conservative about which patterns qualify for inclusion in DSM-IV.

Is DSM-III-R Effective?

In order for a diagnostic system to become a shorthand language for communicating, its users must be able to agree reliably on what the criteria and symptoms are for each disorder and what the diagnoses would be in specific cases. *Reliability* has improved substantially with the introduction of the more descriptive and precise *DSM-III-R* (Klerman, 1986), although it is still far from complete, especially for certain categories of disorders. Improved reliability has helped facilitate research efforts to improve understanding of psychopathology and its treatment.

Some practitioners have raised concerns about the *validity* of DSM-III-R. Validity in descriptions and diagnoses of mental disorders is a complex concept. It involves, in part, fulfilling the second and third goals of classification systems: identifying causes and recommending treatments. For example, is it valid to consider disorders with some common features as different *versions* of the *same* disorder—or rather as completely *different* disorders? This issue has plagued researchers and clinicians who study and treat those with schizophrenic disorders: Is it one mental disease or many different disorders? (Heinrichs, 1993)? These are ongoing questions and criticisms, and so DSM is more a work in progress than the "last word" on psychopathology. Even though it has its critics, *DSM-III-R* continues to be the most widely used classification system in clinical practice and is frequently used in training new clinicians.

Psychologists classify behavior as psychopathological by making a judgment about whether the behavior is abnormal. Abnormality is judged by the degree to which a person's actions resemble a set of indicators including distress, maladaptiveness, irrationality, unpredictability, unconventionality, and observer discomfort. Throughout history, people have tried to explain the origins of psychopathology. Early views regarded psychopathology as the product of evil spirits or weak character. In the late eighteenth century, emerging modern perspectives considered psychopathological functioning to be a result of psychological or bodily disturbances.

Today, biological approaches to mental illness concentrate on structural abnormalities in the brain, biochemical processes, and genetic influences. Among psychological approaches, the psychodynamic model focuses on early childhood experiences, unconscious conflicts, and defenses. The behavioral perspective focuses on overt behavioral reactions and environmental conditions that create and maintain them. In the cognitive model, distortions in an individual's beliefs and perceptions of self and the world are at the heart of psychological disorders. Interactionist approaches combine these psychological and biological views.

Any diagnostic and classification system of psychological disorders should seek to provide a common shorthand language about types of psychopathology in order to facilitate clinical and research work, and offer information about causes and treatment. DSM-III-R is the most widely accepted diagnostic and classification system used by psychologists and psychiatrists.

DSM-III-R (soon to be updated as DSM-IV) emphasizes description of symptom patterns rather than identifying causes or treatments. The continually evolving diagnostic categories of the DSM system reflect the shifting views of mental health experts and the public about what is or is not abnormal and about how best to describe particular categories of abnormality. The reliability of diagnosing psychological disorders has improved substantially with the more descriptive and precise DSM-III-R. However, some critics have raised concerns about the limited usefulness of DSM-III-R for making treatment decisions or helping people understand the causes of psychological disorders.

Major Psychological Disorders

We now turn to a more detailed analysis of several prominent categories of psychological disorders. For each category, we will begin by describing what sufferers experience and how they appear to observers. Then we will consider how the biological and psychological approaches explain the development of these disorders.

We will look closely at six categories of disorders: personality disorders, dissociative disorders, anxiety disorders, depressive disorders, eating disorders, and schizophrenia. Once again, because of space limitations, our treatment of these disorders will be brief. At the end of this section, we will describe several additional categories of disorders that merit attention—although they can only be mentioned briefly in an introductory text discussion.

Personality Disorders

personality disorder Chronic, inflexible, maladaptive pattern of perception, thought, and behavior that seriously impairs an individual's ability to function personally or socially.

A **personality disorder** is a long-standing (chronic), inflexible, maladaptive pattern of perceiving, thinking, or behaving. These patterns can seriously impair an individual's ability to function in social or work settings and can cause significant distress. They are usually recognizable by the time a person reaches adolescence. There are many types of personality disorders (twelve types are recognized in DSM-III-R). We will discuss two of the better known forms: *narcissistic personality disorder* and *antisocial personality disorder*.

narcissistic personality disorder
Personality disorder marked by exaggerated sense of self-importance, preoccupation with success or power fantasies, and need for constant attention or admiration.

People with a **narcissistic personality disorder** have a grandiose sense of self-importance, a preoccupation with fantasies of success or power, and a need for constant attention or admiration. These people often respond inappropriately to criticism or minor defeat, either by acting indifferent to criticism or by overreacting. They have problems in interpersonal relationships; they tend to feel entitled to favors without obligations, exploit others selfishly, and have difficulty recognizing how others feel. For example, an individual with narcissistic personality disorder might express annoyance—but not empathy—when a friend has to cancel a date because of a death in the family.

antisocial personality disorder
Personality disorder in which symptoms include absence of conscience and lack of sense of responsibility to others.

Antisocial personality disorder is marked by a longstanding pattern of irresponsible behavior that hurts others without causing feelings of guilt for oneself. Lying, stealing, and fighting are common behaviors of this disorder. People with antisocial personality disorder often do not experience shame or intense emotion of any kind; they can "keep cool" in situations that would arouse and upset normal people. Violations of social norms begin early in their lives—disrupting class, getting into fights, and running away from home. Their actions are marked by indifference to the rights of others. Although sufferers of this disorder can be found among street criminals and con artists, they are also well represented among successful politicians and businesspeople who put career, money, and power above everything and everyone. Two to three percent of the population in the United States is believed to have antisocial personality disorder. Men are four times more likely to be so diagnosed than women (Regier et al., 1988).

2 Personality disorders as a group are among the least reliably judged of all the psychological disorders and are the most controversial. Psychologists even disagree about whether personality disorders can be said truly to exist, and whether it is possible to diagnose a personality disorder independently of the contexts—the social and cultural factors—in which an individual's behavior is seen to develop.

The term *narcissistic personality disorder* is derived from the mythological character Narcissus who was enchanted with his own reflection.

Dissociative Disorders

dissociative disorder Psychological reaction in which an individual experiences sudden, temporary alteration of consciousness through severe loss of memory or identity.

psychogenic amnesia Memory loss involving inability to recall important personal information, caused not by physical damage but by psychological distress.

multiple personality disorder (MPD) Dissociative disorder in which different aspects of a personality function independently, creating the appearance of two or more distinct personalities within the same individual.

A **dissociative disorder** is a disturbance in the integration of identity, memory, or consciousness. It is important for us to see ourselves as whole selves, in control of our own behavior. Psychologists believe that, in dissociated states, individuals escape from their conflicts by giving up this precious consistency and continuity—in a sense, disowning part of themselves. Not being able to recall details of a traumatic event—amnesia without the presence of neurological damage—is one example of dissociation. Psychologists have only recently begun to appreciate the degree to which such memory dissociation accompanies instances of sexual and physical childhood abuse. The forgetting of important personal experiences caused by psychological factors in the absence of any organic dysfunction is termed **psychogenic amnesia.** The story of Eileen Franklin presented in Chapter 7 is an example of psychogenic amnesia. Only as an adult did she remember that when she was a young child her own father had sexually molested her and murdered her girlfriend. In her case, the horror of what she had experienced and witnessed led to the psychological self-defense of forgetting associated events and information.

Multiple personality disorder (MPD) is a rare dissociative disorder in which two or more distinct personalities exist within the same individual. At any particular time, one of these personalities is dominant in directing the individual's behavior. MPD has been popularized in fact-based books and movies, such as *The Three Faces of Eve* (Thigpen & Cleckley, 1957) and *Sybil* (Schreiber, 1973). Multiple personality disorder is popularly known as *split personality,* and sometimes mistakenly described as *schizophrenia,* a disorder in which personality often is impaired but is not "split" into multiple versions. In MPD, although the original personality is unaware of the other personalities, *they* are conscious of *it* and often of each other. Each of the emerging personalities contrasts in some significant way with the original self; they might be outgoing if the person is shy, tough if the original personality is weak, and sex-

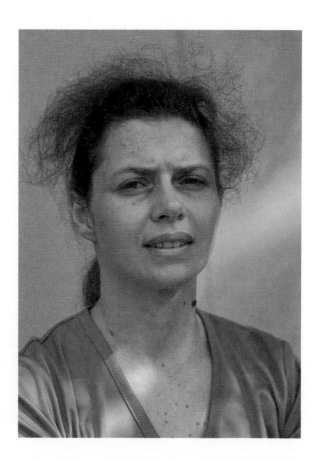

When found in a park in Florida, this woman (dubbed "Jane Doe" by authorities) was emaciated, incoherent, and near death. She was suffering from a rare form of psychogenic amnesia in which she had lost the memory of her name and her past and the ability to read and write.

These two paintings by Sybil, a multiple personality disorder victim, illustrate differences between the personalities. The painting on the left was done by Peggy, Sybil's angry, fearful personality. The painting on the right was done by Mary, a home-loving personality.

ually assertive if the other is fearful and sexually naive. Each personality has a unique identity, name, behavior pattern, and even characteristic brain-wave activity. In some cases, dozens of different characters emerge to help the person deal with a difficult life situation. The emergence of these alternate personalities, each with its own consciousness, is sudden and typically precipitated by stress.

➡ Consider the factors that might account for such a drastic fracturing of the self. Research has indicated that for many patients, MPD is a defensive "strategy" spun out of control; different personalities are developed within one's consciousness to defend against a traumatic or hostile environment. Typically, MPD victims are women who were severely abused mentally or physically by family members or close others during their childhood. MPD victims may have been beaten, locked up, or abandoned by those who were supposed to love them—those on whom they were so dependent that they could not fight them, leave them, or even hate them. Instead, they have fled their terror symbolically through dissociation. One questionnaire survey of several hundred clinicians who had treated MPD cases (see **Table 13.1** on the next page) found an almost universal incidence among female patients of being abused at a very early age, starting around 3 years old and continuing for more than a decade (Schultz et al., 1989).

Psychologists believe that multiple personalities develop to serve a vital survival function. Individuals in horrifying situations may protect their egos by creating stronger internal characters to help them cope with the ongoing traumatic situation and also to relieve their pain by numbing the dominant personality to the abuse. As a leading researcher in the study of multiple personality disorder, **F. W. Putnam** (1989) has found that in the typical case there are many different alter egos of different ages and even of both sexes within the mind of the troubled person. Until recently, information on multiple personality disorder had come from single cases treated by one therapist over an

Table 13.1 Responses to Inquiries Regarding Abuse: Comparing Multiple Personality Disorder and Depression

QUESTIONNAIRE ITEM	MPD (N = 355) %		MAJOR DEPRESSION (N = 235) %		SIGNIFICANCE
Abuse incidence	98		54		p<.0001
Type(s)					
Physical	82		24		p<.0001
Sexual	86		25		p<.0001
Psychological	86		42		p<.0001
Neglect	54		21		p<.0001
All of above	47		6		p<.0001
Physical and sexual	74		14		p<.0001
	Mean	S.D.	Mean	S.D.	
Beginning age of abuse	3.3	2.6	7.5	8.7	p<.0001
Ending age of abuse	17.3	7.5	22.6	15.6	p<.001
Gender					
Female	90.0		73.0		p<.001
Male	10.0		27.0		

extended period of time. However, newer research being conducted with the collaboration of the National Institute of Mental Health and other institutions is enabling clinicians to get a more complete picture of this remarkable disorder that puts too many actors on stage for any one director to manage (Putnam, 1984).

Anxiety Disorders

Everyone experiences anxiety or fear in certain life situations. The feelings of uneasiness that characterize anxiety and fear are often accompanied by physical reactions, such as a sweaty brow or clammy palms, and may include a sense of impending harm. For some people, anxiety interferes with their ability to function effectively or enjoy everyday life. It has been estimated that 15 percent of the general population has, at some time, experienced the symptoms that are characteristic of various anxiety disorders recognized in DSM-III-R (Regier et al., 1988). While anxiety plays a key role in each category, the disorders differ in the extent to which anxiety is experienced, the severity of the anxiety, and the situations that trigger the anxiety.

Types of Anxiety Disorders. We will review four major categories of anxiety: generalized anxiety disorder, panic disorder, phobic disorder, and obsessive-compulsive disorder. (In Chapter 9 we discussed a fifth kind of anxiety disorder, posttraumatic stress disorder).

generalized anxiety disorder
Disorder in which an individual experiences anxiety that persists for at least one month and is not focused on a specific object or situation.

panic disorder   Anxiety disorder characterized by recurrent episodes of intense anxiety, feelings of unpredictability, and symptoms of arousal usually lasting several minutes.

fear   Rational emotional reaction to a clear, external danger that may induce a person to flee or attack in self-defense.

phobic disorder   Maladaptive pattern of behavior in which anxiety is associated with a specific external object or situation that the individual seeks to avoid.

agoraphobia   Extreme fear of being in public places or distant from familiar surroundings.

Being part of such a crowded scene would cause many agoraphobics to panic.

Generalized Anxiety Disorder. When, for at least a six-month period, a person feels anxious or worried most of the time, though not specifically threatened, a **generalized anxiety disorder** is diagnosed. The anxiety might focus on specific life circumstances, such as unrealistic concerns about finances or the well-being of a loved one, or it just might be a general apprehensiveness about impending harm. The specific symptoms vary from person to person, but the common symptoms include *body tension, physical arousal,* and *vigilance* (hyper-attentiveness to events and one's reactions to them). If you ever found yourself unable to relax or get to sleep at night because of worries that are keeping you awake, you will recognize the form and effects of anxiety.

A chronically anxious person may continue to function with only a mild impairment of work or social life, but the constant physical and psychological drain takes a toll that may show up as greater susceptibility to common ailments like colds, headaches, and infections.

Panic Disorder. Sufferers of **panic disorder** experience unexpected but severe attacks of anxiety that may last only minutes. These attacks occur at least several times a month and typically begin with a feeling of intense apprehension, fear, or terror. Accompanying these feelings are physical symptoms of anxiety such as rapid heart rate, dizziness, faintness, or sensations of choking or smothering. As one sufferer described the experience of a panic attack, "It feels, I just get all, like hot through me, and shaky, and my heart just feels like it's pounding and breathing really quick. . . . It feels like I'm going to die or something" (Muskin & Fyer, 1981, p. 81).

Because of the unexpected nature of these "hit and run" attacks, *anticipatory anxiety* often develops as an added complication in panic disorders. The dread of the next attack and of being helpless and suddenly out of control can lead a person to avoid public places yet fear being left alone.

Phobic Disorders. **Fear** is a rational reaction to an objectively identified external danger (such as a fire in one's home or being mugged) that may induce a person to flee or attack in self-defense. In contrast, a person with a **phobic disorder,** or *phobia,* suffers from a persistent and irrational fear of a specific object, activity, or situation that creates a compelling desire to avoid it. Phobic disorders, like panic disorders, are based in the experience of anxiety, not fear.

Many of us have irrational fears of spiders or snakes (or even multiple-choice tests). Such fears become phobic disorders only when they interfere with our adjustment, cause significant distress, or inhibit necessary action toward goals. Consider the following example. Edith is afraid of writing her name in public. When placed in a situation where she might be asked to sign her name, Edith is terrified, and she experiences muscle tension, rapid heart rate, and apprehension—the common symptoms of anxiety. Edith's phobia has far-reaching effects on her life. She can't use checks or credit cards to shop or to eat in a restaurant. She no longer can play golf because she can't sign the golf register. She can't go to the bank unless all transactions are prepared ahead of time in her home. She can't sign any papers that require approval of a notary public, and she can't vote because she can't sign the voting register.

Phobias are a relatively common psychological problem. Recent studies suggest that 12.5 percent of Americans suffer from some form of phobia at some point in their lives (Regier et al., 1988). Almost any stimulus can come to generate a phobic avoidance reaction (see **Table 13.2** on the next page), although some phobias are much more common than others. Two of the most common phobic disorders are *agoraphobia* and *social phobia.*

Agoraphobia is an extreme fear of being in public places or open spaces from which escape may be difficult or embarrassing. Individuals with agoraphobia fear places such as crowded rooms, malls, buses, and freeways. They are often afraid that, if they experience some kind of difficulty outside the home,

Table 13.2 The Common Phobias

	APPROXIMATE PERCENT OF ALL PHOBIAS	SEX DIFFERENCE	TYPICAL AGE OF FIRST OCCURRENCE
Agoraphobias (fear of places of assembly, crowds, open spaces)	10–50	Large majority are women	Early adulthood
Social Phobias (fear of being observed doing something humiliating)	10	Majority are women	Adolescence

The Specific Phobias
Animals
    Cats (allurophobia)
    Dogs (cynophobia)
    Insects (insectophobia)
    Spiders (arachnophobia)
    Birds (avisophobia)
    Horses (equinophobia)
    Snakes (ophidiophobia)
    Rodents (rodentophobia)
	5–15	Vast majority are women	Childhood

Inanimate Objects or Situations
    Dirt (mysophobia)
    Storms (brontophobia)
    Heights (acrophobia)
    Darkness (nyctophobia)
    Closed spaces (claustrophobia)
	20	None	Any age

Illness-Injury (nosophobia)
    Death (thanatophobia)
    Cancer (cancerophobia)
    Venereal disease (venerophobia)
	15–25	None	Middle age

social phobia Category of phobic disorders in which an individual irrationally fears engaging in public action or display; extreme form of shyness.

help might not be available or the situation will be embarrassing to them. These fears deprive individuals of their freedom, and, in extreme cases, agoraphobics become prisoners in their own homes. They cannot hold a job or carry on normal daily activities because their fears restrict contact with the outside world.

Social phobia is a persistent, irrational fear that arises in anticipation of a public situation in which one can be observed by others. Like Edith who is afraid of writing her name in public, a person with a social phobia fears that he or she will act in ways that could be embarrassing. The person recognizes that the fear is excessive and unreasonable yet he is compelled by the fear to avoid situations in which public scrutiny is possible. The fear of choking on food when eating in front of others and the fear of trembling embarrassingly when speaking in public are examples of social phobias. Sometimes the phobia is more general and may include fears about acting foolishly in social situations.

Obsessive-Compulsive Disorders. Because fear and anxiety are similar, it seems obvious that phobias are a form of anxiety disorder. Less obvious are *obsessive-*

obsessive-compulsive disorder
Mental disorder characterized by patterns of obsessions (persistent, unwanted thoughts) and compulsions (undesired, repetitive actions).

compulsive patterns, which seem not fearful, but driven—in fact, driven by anxiety. Just last year, 17-year-old Jim seemed to be a normal adolescent with many talents and interests. Then, almost overnight, he was transformed into a lonely outsider, excluded from social life by his psychological disabilities. Specifically, he developed an obsession with washing. Haunted by the notion that he was dirty—in spite of what his senses told him—Jim began to spend more and more of his time cleansing himself of imaginary dirt. At first, his ritual ablutions were confined to weekends and evenings, but soon they began to consume all his time, forcing him to drop out of school (Rapoport, 1989). (If Jim's pattern seems familiar, recall that in Chapter 10 we discussed the case of millionaire Howard Hughes, whose anxiety about cleanliness and hygiene forced him to become increasingly reclusive prior to his death.)

Jim is suffering from a condition known as **obsessive-compulsive disorder** that is estimated to affect 2.5 percent of Americans at some point during their lives (Regier et al., 1988). *Obsessions* are thoughts, images, or impulses that recur or persist despite a person's efforts to suppress them. Obsessions are experienced as an unwanted invasion of consciousness, seem to be senseless or repugnant, and are unacceptable to the person experiencing them. Frequently, the individual avoids the situations that relate to the content of the obsessions. For example, a person with an obsessive fear of germs may avoid using bathrooms outside his or her home or refuse to shake hands with strangers. As is the case with Jim, behavior driven by obsessive thinking can increasingly interfere with other aspects of one's life.

You probably have had some sort of mild obsessional experience, such as petty worries ("Did I really lock the door?"; "Did I turn off the oven?") or the persistence of a haunting melody that kept running through your mind. The thoughts of obsessive-compulsive people are much more compelling, cause much more distress, and may interfere with the social or role functioning of the affected individuals.

Compulsions are repetitive, purposeful acts performed according to certain rules or in a ritualized manner in response to an obsession. Compulsive behavior is intended to reduce or prevent the discomfort associated with some dreaded situation, but it is either unreasonable or clearly excessive. Typical compulsions include irresistible urges to clean, to check that lights or appliances have been turned off, and to count objects or possessions.

People with obsessive-compulsive disorder initially resist carrying out their compulsions. When they are calm, they view the compulsion as senseless. When their anxiety rises, however, the power of the compulsive behavior ritual to relieve tension seems irresistible—and the action must be performed. Part of the pain experienced by people with this problem is that they are frustrated by the irrationality of their obsessions but cannot eliminate them.

Causes of Anxiety Disorders.   Each of the four approaches that we have outlined—psychodynamic, behavioral, cognitive, and biological—emphasizes different factors. Let's analyze how each adds something unique to our understanding of anxiety disorders.

Psychodynamic Approaches.   The psychodynamic model begins with the assumption that the symptoms of anxiety disorders and obsessions and compulsions come from underlying psychic conflicts or fears. The symptoms are attempts to protect the individual from psychological pain.

In anxiety disorders, intense pain attacks and phobias are the result of unconscious conflicts bursting into consciousness. The unconscious conflicts are seen as having their roots in early childhood experiences. For example, perhaps a child is punished by being isolated in a small room or closet until she agrees to behave. In her later life, enclosed spaces remind her of her early shame and guilt, and she avoids closets and phone booths to escape this anxiety. Instead of developing healthy self-esteem and overcoming her discomfort over her childhood experiences, she takes the unconscious "short cut" of just avoiding cramped spaces. Unfortunately, this claustrophobic behavior increasingly intrudes on her ability to lead a normal life. Ironically, her phobic efforts to avoid remembering childhood anxiety seem to guarantee that she will be haunted by reminders.

In obsessive-compulsive disorders, the obsessive pattern is an attempt to displace anxiety created by a related but far more feared desire or conflict. By substituting an obsession that symbolically captures the forbidden impulse, a person gains some relief. For example, obsessive fears of dirt may have their roots in conflict about having "dirty" (sexual) thoughts. Compulsive performance of a minor ritualistic task also allows the individual to avoid the issue that creates unconscious conflict, or the task may seem intended to undo feelings of guilt over real or imagined sins.

Behavioral Approaches. Behavioral explanations of anxiety focus on how symptoms of anxiety disorders are reinforced or conditioned. A previously neutral object or situation becomes a stimulus for a phobia by being paired with a frightening experience. For example, a woman calls home while away on her first overnight camping trip only to receive the painful news that a loved one has suddenly died. Now she may develop a phobia of camping or visiting wilderness sites. After this experience, whenever she approaches a campground or even discusses going on wilderness excursions with friends she may experience a wave of fear and dread that cannot be relieved. By avoiding the phobic situation—deciding she does not like camping, or parks or scenic routes—the individual reinforces the phobia with the reward of feeling relief.

Cognitive Approaches. Cognitive perspectives on anxiety concentrate on the perceptual processes or attitudes that may distort a person's estimation of the danger that he or she is facing. Faulty thinking processes, such as a tendency to *catastrophize* (to focus selectively on the worst possible outcomes in a situation) are at the heart of anxiety disorders. In the case of panic attacks, for example, a person may attribute undue significance to minor distress, such as shortness of breath after some physical exertion. A vicious cycle is initiated when a person mistakenly interprets the distress as a sign of impending disaster (like a heart attack), leading to increased anxiety and aggravated physical sensations (Beck & Emery, 1985). (See "Time Out for Critical Thinking" on p. 505.)

Biological Approaches. Various investigators have suggested that anxiety disorders have biological origins. Certain phobias seem to be more common than others. For example, a fear of spiders or heights is more common than a fear of electricity, possibly because the former stimuli (spiders or heights) represent ancient threats from our evolutionary past. Perhaps humans are born with a predisposition to fear whatever is related to sources of serious danger in our distant past. This *preparedness hypothesis* suggests that we carry around an evolutionary tendency to respond quickly and "thoughtlessly" to once-feared stimuli (Seligman, 1971).

The fact that certain drugs can relieve and others can produce symptoms of anxiety offers evidence of a biological role in anxiety disorders. Studies also suggest that abnormalities in sites within the brainstem might be linked to panic attacks. Currently, work is under way to investigate how these abnormalities may influence obsessive-compulsive symptoms.

Each of the major approaches to anxiety disorders may explain part of the puzzle, but continued research on each approach is needed to further our understanding of the most important factors.

Biological explanations of the origins and development of anxiety disorders offer the promise of medical treatments. If a problem can be traced to a biochemical imbalance, for example, drug therapy might be an effective prospect. But is a biological explanation necessarily a "better" explanation than a more complex explanation, such as those provided by a cognitive theory? For each of the following situations, consider the pros and cons of developing "simple" explanations of origins and development.

- Your best friend has been moody, sad, and angry for over a year. If a drug would make your friend feel better but would not explain the problem, should you recommend your friend to take it—or discourage your friend from taking it? Why?

- You feel anxious whenever you are about to take a test, even when you have prepared and studied adequately. Do you want to understand *why* you feel anxious, or would you be happy simply to make the nervous sensations go away by "popping a pill"?

- A family member becomes upset or angry whenever plans have to be changed, whether the change is due to uncontrollable factors like the weather or more controllable ones like other people's preferences. Are you curious about how your family member became so plan-conscious in the first place, or would you be satisfied merely to have this person become less inflexible and more spontaneous?

- A friend of yours has emotional problems and confides in you about how desperate she sometimes feels. When might it be appropriate for you to seek outside assistance for her? When would such action be considered meddlesome, so that you are accused of not "minding your own business" and could even risk losing the friendship? If you did decide to seek assistance, where in your community could you go for help?

To some extent, your own curiosity and need to know will lead you to seek a variety of explanations for the causes and courses of behavioral disorders. However, it is also true that, in order to solve or treat some problems, we must first understand them. Biological explanations tell only part of the story, since we ourselves experience life on more than just the biological level.

Affective Disorders

affective disorder   Class of disorders in which primary symptoms are associated with disturbances of mood and emotion.

An **affective disorder** is a mood disturbance, such as excessive depression or depression alternating with mania. There are three well-known affective disorders: manic episodes, bipolar disorders, and unipolar depression.

manic episode   A period of *mania,* during which an individual generally acts and feels unusually elated and expansive.

Manic Episodes. A person experiencing a period of *mania,* which is referred to as a **manic episode,** generally acts and feels unusually elated and expansive. Sometimes the individual's predominant mood is irritability rather than elation, especially if the person feels thwarted in some way. Other symptoms, such as inability to concentrate or impulsive behavior, often accompany these highly charged mood states which typically last from a few days to months.

During a manic episode, a person often experiences an inflated sense of self-esteem or an unrealistic belief that he or she possesses special abilities or powers. The person may feel a dramatically decreased need to sleep and may engage excessively in work or in social or other pleasurable activities. The individual may speak faster, louder, or more often than usual and his or her mind may be racing with thoughts. Caught up in this manic mood, the person shows unwarranted optimism, takes unnecessary risks, promises anything, and may give away everything. Ironically, the manic episode may set in place circumstances that are increasingly difficult to rationalize or accept. To continue to live in the fantasy world he has constructed, the manic person must withdraw further and further from real events, real people, and personal responsibility.

Bipolar Disorder. It is not unusual for people in manic episodes to spend their life savings on extravagant purchases and to engage promiscuously in a number of sexual liaisons or other potentially high-risk actions. When the mania begins to diminish, they are left trying to deal with the damage and predicaments they have created during their frenetic period. Those who have manic episodes will almost always also experience periods of severe depression. This condition is called **bipolar disorder,** or manic-depressive disorder, to signify the experience of both types of mood disturbance—the two "poles" or extremes of emotion.

bipolar disorder Type of affective disorder in which individual's behavior alternates between periods of mania and depression.

The duration and frequency of the mood disturbances in bipolar disorder vary from person to person. Some people experience long periods of normal functioning punctuated by occasional, brief manic or depressive episodes. A small percentage of unfortunate individuals go right from manic episodes to clinical depression and back again in continuous, unending cycles that are devastating to them, their families, their friends, and their co-workers.

Unipolar Depression. Depression has been characterized as the "common cold of psychopathology" because it occurs so frequently and almost everyone

Almost everyone has experienced elements of depression; in some people, however, it becomes a full scale disorder.

unipolar depression Category of affective disorder involving intense, extended depression without interruption by manic periods; also called *clinical depression*.

has experienced elements of the full-scale disorder at some time in life. We have all, at one time or another, experienced grief after the loss of a loved one or felt sad or upset when we failed to achieve a desired goal. These sad feelings are only one symptom experienced by people suffering from a clinical **unipolar depression** (see Table 13.3). As opposed to victims of bipolar depression, those who suffer from unipolar depression do not also experience manic highs.

Novelist William Styron (1990) has written a moving story about his own experience with severe depression. The pain he endured convinced him that clinical depression is much more than a bad mood; it is best characterized as "a daily presence, blowing over me in cold gusts" and "a veritable howling tempest in the brain" that can begin with a "gray drizzle of horror" and result in death (*Darkness Visible*, Random House, 1990).

People diagnosed with unipolar depression differ in terms of the severity and duration of their depressive symptoms. While many individuals only struggle with clinical depression for several weeks at one point in their lives, others experience depression episodically or chronically for many years. It is estimated that about 20 percent of females and 10 percent of males suffer a major unipolar depression at some time in their lives. Bipolar disorder is much rarer, occurring in about 1 percent of adults and distributed equally between males and females.

Unipolar and bipolar disorders take an enormous toll on those afflicted, their families, and society. In the United States, depression accounts for the majority of all mental hospital admissions, but it is still believed to be underdiagnosed and undertreated (Bielski & Friedel, 1977; Lichtenstein, 1980;

Table 13.3 Characteristics of Clinical Depression

CHARACTERISTIC	EXAMPLE
Dysphoric Mood	Sad, blue, hopeless; loss of interest or pleasure in almost all usual activities
Appetite	Poor appetite; significant weight loss
Sleep	Insomnia or hypersomnia (sleeping too much)
Motor Activity	Markedly slowed down (motor retardation) or agitated
Guilt	Feelings of worthlessness; self-reproach
Concentration	Diminished ability to think or concentrate; forgetfulness
Suicide	Recurrent thoughts of death; suicidal ideas or attempts

Robins et al., 1991). For example, according to a 1983 NIMH survey, 80 percent of those suffering from clinical depression never receive treatment.

Causes of Affective Disorders. Because it is more prevalent, unipolar depression has been studied more extensively than bipolar depression. We will look at it from the cognitive, psychodynamic, behavioral, and biological approaches.

Cognitive Approaches. Two theories are at the center of the cognitive approach to unipolar depression. One theory suggests that **negative cognitive sets** lead people to take a negative view of events in their lives for which they feel responsible. The *learned helplessness* model proposes that depression arises from the belief that one has little or no personal control over significant life events. According to **Aaron Beck,** a leading researcher on depression, depressed people seem to have three types of negative cognitions. Beck calls these three the *cognitive triad* of depression: negative views of *themselves,* negative views of ongoing *experiences,* and negative views of the *future* (Beck, 1983; 1985; 1988). This pattern of negative thinking clouds all experiences and produces the other characteristic signs of depression. An individual who always anticipates a negative outcome is not likely to be motivated to pursue any goal, leading to the *paralysis of will* that is prominent in depression.

In the learned helplessness view, individuals learn that they cannot control future outcomes that are important to them. This conclusion creates feelings of helplessness that lead to depression (Abramson et al., 1978; Peterson & Seligman, 1984; Seligman, 1975). The learned helplessness theory suggests that individuals who attribute failure to *internal, stable* (unchangeable), and global causes are vulnerable to depression. A study of college students supports the notion that depressed people have a negative type of attribution style. Depressed students attributed failure on an achievement test to an internal, stable factor—their lack of ability—while attributing successes to luck. In comparison, on an achievement test, nondepressed students took more credit for successes and less blame for failures than they were due, blaming failures on an external, unstable (changeable) factor—bad luck (Barthe & Hammen, 1981).

There is considerable debate over the key proposition of the cognitive model of depression—that cognitive factors play a *causal* role in the development of depression. Despite the appeal of the model, it remains plausible that the negative cognitive patterns are, in fact, a *consequence* rather than a *cause* of depression.

Research has confirmed what many people already believed about depression—that major changes in one's life, especially those that involve a loss such as the death of a loved one, divorce, or loss of a job, often precede the onset of depression. "Loss" events are important precipitators of depression, according to both the behavioral and psychodynamic approaches. However, each perspective interprets loss events in distinct ways.

Psychodynamic Approaches. In the psychodynamic approach, unconscious conflicts and hostile feelings that originate in early childhood play key roles in the development of depression. Freud was struck by the degree of self-criticism and guilt that depressed people displayed. He believed that the source of this self-reproach was anger, originally directed at someone else, that had been turned inward against the self. Losses, real or symbolic, in adulthood trigger hostile feelings that were originally experienced in childhood. The anger that is reactivated by a later loss is now directed toward the person's own ego, creating the self-reproach and guilt that characterize depression.

Behavioral Approaches. Rather than searching for the roots of depression in past relationships or for the unconscious meaning of a recent loss experience, one behavioral approach focuses on the effects of the amount of positive rein-

negative cognitive set Consistently pessimistic and self-blaming views of one's experiences.

forcement and punishments a person receives (Lewinsohn, 1975). In this view, depressed feelings result from a lack of sufficient positive reinforcement and from many punishments in the environment following a loss or other major life change. For example, after he and his wife separate, a young man may spend less time in social activities, because he feels awkward about running into friends who will be curious or perhaps accusatory about the breakup. By withdrawing from others, he also misses out on the pleasures of social life, so he begins to feel sad and sorry for himself, and isolates himself even further. Old friends who initially offered support and company grow tired of his self-pitying and make themselves less available to him—so that the young man becomes even lonelier and more depressed. A similar cycle of reduced reinforcement can be set in motion because a mood-disordered person *lacks the skills* to obtain social reinforcements—for example, when a shy woman has not learned effective ways of making conversation with new acquaintances relocates to a *new environment* with a different, as-yet-unknown social network. Research confirms that depressed people give themselves fewer rewards and more punishment than others (Rehm, 1977; Nelson & Craighead, 1977).

Biological Approaches. The ability of certain drugs such as lithium (a salt compound) to relieve the symptoms of depression supports a biological view of unipolar depression. Reduced levels of two chemical messengers in the brain, called serotonin and norepinephrine, have been linked with depression. Drugs that are known to increase the levels of these neurotransmitters are commonly used to treat depression. However, the exact biochemical mechanisms of depression have not yet been discovered.

While our overall understanding of the cause of bipolar disorder remains similarly limited, there is some growing evidence that it is influenced by genetic factors. Because family members usually share the same environment, similarities among family members do not prove that the cause of a psychological disorder is hereditary. To separate the influence of heredity from environmental or learned components in psychopathology, researchers study twins and adopted children.

Studies of identical twins (twins who have the same genetic material) show that when one twin is afflicted by bipolar disorder, there is an 80 percent chance that the second twin will have the disorder. Studies of adopted children with bipolar disorder show a higher incidence of the same disorder among biological parents than among the adoptive parents. More direct evidence of this role seemed to come from a 1987 study that linked bipolar disorder to a specific gene in a unique population. In this study, the pattern of transmission of bipolar disorder was traced among the Amish community in Pennsylvania (Egeland et al., 1987). Researchers isolated a piece of DNA that was present in all bipolar members of one extended Amish family. Localized at the tip of chromosome 11 the defective gene was passed on to children half of the time, and of those who received it, 80 percent had at least one manic episode in their lives.

This result was hailed as a real breakthrough—until the predictions made from this genetic analysis to other Amish relatives failed to be supported. When a team of independent researchers checked out the procedures, they were forced to declare there was no convincing proof (Kelsoe et al., 1989). Either the gene for manic depression is not on chromosome 11, or the Amish have two such genes, only one of which may be in that chromosome location (Barinaga, 1989).

The biological approach to understanding one type of psychological disorder has shed new light on an unusual form of depression. Some people regularly become depressed during the winter months; this is especially apparent for people living in the long Scandinavian winters (see **Figure 13.3**). This disturbance in mood has been appropriately named *seasonal affective disorder (SAD).* An internal body rhythm involving the hormone melatonin, which is

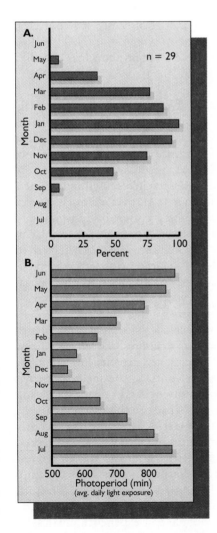

Figure 13.3 Seasonal Affective Disorder

Research on the Amish in Pennsylvania has investigated a proposed link between a particular gene and bipolar disorder, a pattern of mood swings between depression and mania.

secreted by the pineal gland into the blood, has been linked to SAD. In most species, including humans, the level of melatonin rises after dusk and falls at or before dawn. Melatonin is implicated in sleep processes as well as circadian (24-hour) rhythms that set the body's biological clock. While it is not clear that disrupted melatonin cycles *cause* the depressive symptoms of SAD, it does appear that a biological intervention that "resets" their abnormal circadian rhythm is an effective treatment (Lewy et al., 1987).

Sex Differences in Depression. Psychologists have been challenged to explain the finding that women are twice as likely to experience unipolar depression as men (Boyd & Weissman, 1981). According to **Susan Nolen-Hoeksema** (1987) the response styles of men and women once they begin to experience negative moods may account for the difference. In this view, when women experience sadness, they tend to think about the possible causes and implications of their feelings. In contrast, men attempt to distract themselves from depressed feelings, either by focusing on something else or by engaging in a physical activity that will take their minds off their current mood state. This model suggests that the more *ruminative* response of women—characterized by a tendency to obsessively focus on problems—increases women's vulnerability to depression. From a cognitive approach, paying attention to one's negative moods can increase thoughts of negative events which eventually increase the quantity and/or intensity of negative feelings.

The response styles of both men and women can be seen as a product of socialization. In the United States and many other cultures, the female schema includes being passive, paying attention to feelings, and experiencing emotions fully as well as sharing them with others. In contrast, the male schema is focused on being tough, physical, and nonemotional and on not displaying signs of weakness by talking about one's moods—bad or otherwise.

A task force of the American Psychological Association has recently reviewed research on the origins of sex differences in rates of unipolar depression (McGrath et al., 1990). Their report suggests that higher risk for depression among women can be understood as the product of an interaction between a number of psychological, social, economic, and biological factors. Many of these factors relate to the experience of being female in many cultures, such as a greater likelihood that women will experience physical or sexual abuse, that they will live in poverty, and that they will be the primary

On July 20, 1993, Vincent W. Foster, Jr.— White House deputy counsel and lifelong friend of President Bill Clinton—was found dead of a gunshot wound in a park outside Washington, DC. Foster, 48, had seemed happy and successful, and associates were unable to explain his apparent suicide. Later a note was found in Foster's handwriting, confessing "mistakes" and expressing pain at being victimized by political attacks and media criticism: "I was not meant for the job or the spotlight of public life in Washington. Here ruining people is considered sport" (*The New York Times*, 8/11/93, p. A-9).

eating disorder Loss of appetite behavior in which one deprives oneself of food or prevents food from being digested.

anorexia nervosa Pattern of self-starvation with psychological rather than physical causes.

caregivers for children and elderly parents. Another issue that women face frequently and can contribute to depression is the difference between their own goals and limited opportunities in society. Women may prepare themselves for important careers in the business world, for example, but they can become frustrated if they encounter the "glass ceiling"—invisible but insuperable prejudices and policies that keep them from rising to positions of greater power and authority. The causes of depression may be a complex combination of factors; there are multiple paths from "normal" behavior to depression.

Psychologists focus so much attention on depression not only because depression itself is a horribly painful experience, but also because it represents a risk of suicide. "In Focus: Depression and Suicide" on the next page shows how the connection between depression and suicide has given us a window into this otherwise inscrutable tragedy. The more we can learn about depression and all affective disorders, the better able we will be to help ourselves and those we love.

Eating Disorders

When you think of examples of abnormal behavior, it may be easiest to imagine self-defeating patterns that are somehow beyond the individual's control or awareness—overwhelming anxiety that terrifies a person and keeps her from going out, or paralyzing depression that cannot be explained. Surely no one would willingly take on such difficult or uncomfortable behavior if it could be helped. Less easy to understand are disorders that seem to involve deliberate acts of self-destruction. For example, since eating is necessary to survival, and good food provides satisfaction and pleasure, why do some people willingly starve themselves?

This is the riddle of an **eating disorder,** patterns of abnormal behavior in which a person starves herself, prevents her body from digesting food, or combines starvation with purging. The deadly result of such unnatural habits is dangerous weight loss and a severely disordered metabolism. Technically, DSM-III-R classifies eating disorders with syndromes (patterns of symptoms) that develop and are diagnosed during childhood and adolescence rather than later adulthood. Like drug addiction, an eating disorder seems to "take over" the individual's body, so that she cannot resume normal eating behavior without great difficulty. For example, an eating-disordered individual may feel "full" after eating only a bite or two, or may spontaneously vomit after a meal, thus risking malnourishment and sickness. Eating disorders are most prevalent in cultures in which hunger is not a widespread problem. These disorders are especially likely to develop among middle-class and upper-middle-class young women, which is why we tend to use feminine pronouns to describe a typical case. Psychological research has brought to light new understanding of the causes, associations, and effective treatments of eating disorders. Here we examine the two best known eating disorders: *anorexia nervosa* and *bulimia.* Both afflict many high school and college women.

Anorexia Nervosa. It is normal behavior to eat when hungry, as we reviewed in Chapter 8, but there are times when people refrain from eating even when they want to eat, such as when they are dieting or fasting for health or religious reasons. The general condition of *anorexia* (persistent lack of appetite) may develop as a consequence of certain physical diseases or conditions, such as shock, nausea, or allergic reactions. However, when loss of appetite that endangers an individual's health stems from emotional or psychological reasons rather than from these organic causes, the syndrome is called **anorexia nervosa** ("nervous anorexia"). A person suffering from anorexia nervosa may act as though she is unconcerned with her condition, although she is visibly undernourished and emaciated. In contrast, a familiar problem for normal

In Focus:

DEPRESSION AND SUICIDE

"The will to survive and succeed had been crushed and defeated. . . . There comes a time when all things cease to shine, when the rays of hope are lost" (Shneidman, 1987, p. 57). This sad statement by a young suicidal man reflects the most extreme consequence of any psychological disorder—suicide. While most depressed people do not commit suicide, most suicides are attempted by those who are suffering from depression (Shneidman, 1985). Depressed people commit suicide at a rate 25 times higher than nondepressed people in comparison groups (Flood & Seager, 1968). In the general population, the number of suicidal deaths is estimated to run as high as 100,000 per year, with attempted suicides estimated to reach up to half a million yearly in the United States alone. Based on data compiled by the National Center for Health Statistics (1989), the following patterns hold for suicide:

Suicide in the United States, 1987

Day and rate data are rounded. Rate is the number of suicides by group divided by the population size of the group and multiplied by 100,000.

	NUMBER	PER DAY	RATE
Nation	30,796	84	13
Males	24,272	66	20
Females	6,524	18	5
Whites	28,217	77	14
Nonwhites	2,579	7	7
Blacks	1,963	5	7
Elderly (65 +)	6,464	18	22
Young (15–24)	4,924	14	13

- It is the eighth leading cause of death in the United States, the third among the young, and the second among college students.
- An average of one person commits suicide every 17 minutes.
- Five million living Americans have attempted to kill themselves.
- For every completed suicide there are 8 to 20 suicide attempts.

Suicide is most often committed by older white males who are unemployed, living alone, in poor health, and divorced. The breakdown of suicides in the United States by sex, age, and race is shown in the table above. Despite these high numbers, suicide is underreported since single-car fatal accidents and other deaths that may be suicidal are not listed as such without the evidence of a suicide note, and because the potential stigma leads family members to deny suicide when it occurs.

Given women's greater frequency of depression than men's, it is not surprising to find that women *attempt* suicide about three times more often than men do; attempts by men, however, are more successful. This difference is largely because men use guns more often, and women tend to use less lethal means, such as sleeping pills (Perlin, 1975; Rosenhan & Seligman, 1989).

One of the most alarming social problems in recent decades is the rise of youth suicide. Every nine minutes a teenager attempts suicide; and every 90 minutes a teenager succeeds. In one week, 1000 teenagers will try suicide and 125 will succeed in killing themselves. In the last two decades, the suicide rate among American teenagers has jumped by 300 percent (Coleman, 1987).

What life-style patterns are most commonly associated with youth suicides? Among males, the majority of suicides are found in those who abuse drugs and are seen as aggressive and unruly. The next most common pattern is the hard-driving male perfectionist who is socially inhibited and overly anxious about many social or academic challenges. Among females, depression ranks as the primary predictor of youth suicide. The symptoms of depression reflect serious emotional disorders that often go unrecognized or untreated. A survey of students who reported past suicidal thoughts or intentions revealed that while some cited specific fears or issues (for example, grades, parents, or money), the majority blamed negative mood (hopelessness, depression) or interpersonal problems (loneliness) (Westerfeld & Fuhr, 1987).

Several precipitating factors can trigger suicidal actions. The breakup of a close relationship is the leading traumatic incident for both sexes. Other significant incidents that create shame and guilt—such as being assaulted, raped, or arrested for the first time—can overwhelm immature egos and lead to suicide attempts. Suicide is an extreme reaction to these acute stressors that occurs especially when adolescents feel unable to cry out to others for help.

Youth suicide is *not* a spur-of-the-moment impulsive act, but typically occurs as the final stage of a period of inner turmoil and outer distress. The majority of young suicide victims have talked to others about their intentions or have written about them. Thus, talk of suicide should always be taken seriously (Shafii et al., 1985). Because girls are more often part of a social support network than are boys, they are more able to confide in others about their distress (Holden, 1986a, 1986b). Recognizing the signs of suicidal thinking and the experiences that can start or intensify such destructive thoughts is a first step toward prevention. For almost 40 years, **Edwin Shneidman** has studied and treated people with suicidal tendencies. He concludes that "Suicide is the desperate act of a perturbed and constricted mind, in seemingly unbearable and unresolvable pain. . . . The fact is that we can relieve the pain, redress the thwarted needs, and reduce the constriction of suicidal thinking" (1987, p. 58). Being sensitive to signs of suicidal intentions and caring enough to intervene are essential to save the lives of both youthful and mature people who have come to see no exit for their troubles except total self-destruction.

You (yes, *you*) should be aware of the clues to suicidal intentions. As we have seen, suicidal despair may be indicated by depression—lethargy (persistently sluggish or sleepy behavior), expressing hopelessness, social withdrawal or isolation, or expressing the fear that one's problems cannot be solved. Some people planning suicide make telltale, exaggerated gestures, such as "generously" giving away prized possessions, or impulsively acting in a dangerous or risky manner. Contrary to the myth that those who talk suicide don't actually do it, people who discuss committing suicide—whether they openly joke about it or privately confide in someone—are most at risk for going through with their plans (Shneidman, 1985). Suppose you recognize these signs in someone you care about, what can you do? While most suicidal people want help, you cannot simply talk them out of their depression. Equip yourself with names and numbers so you can get professional help. Start by calling your campus counseling center, community mental health center, or the hotline sponsored by the International Association for Suicide Prevention (in Los Angeles, California): (213) 381-5111.

bulimia Disorder characterized by pattern of bingeing (overeating) and purging (vomiting or using laxatives to prevent digestion).

dieters is their desire for food and their exaggerated awareness of their calorie intake.

What causes anorexia nervosa? Most anorexics are young white females from middle-class homes. They have backgrounds of good behavior and academic success, but they "starve" themselves to become acceptably thin and attractive (Gilbert & DeBlassie, 1984; Brumberg, 1988). While cultural ideals of feminine beauty change over time, in recent decades mass media—including fashion magazines and MTV—have promoted images of unrealistically slim models and celebrities. Especially during adolescence, people tend to evaluate themselves in terms of physical attractiveness, judging themselves harshly for failing to live up to cultural ideals (Conger & Petersen, 1984). A victim of anorexia typically holds a distorted body image, believing herself to be unattractively fat, and rejects others' reassurances that she is not overweight (Bruch, 1980; Fallon & Rozin, 1985). In an effort to lose imagined "excess" weight, the anorexic rigidly suppresses her appetite, feeling rewarded for such self-control when she does lose pounds and inches—but never feeling quite thin enough.

Despite the vivid cultural fantasy that thinness equals success and happiness, most adolescent girls do not develop eating disorders, regardless of their disappointment or social anxieties about their bodies. What is it that pushes a desperate few (about one percent of adolescents) over the edge into anorexia nervosa? Situational explanations for many cases of this eating disorder blame problems in family interactions. One hypothesis is that overdependence on their parents leads some girls to fear becoming sexually mature and independent. Extreme self-starvation interrupts sexual development, causes cessation of menstruation, and retains a childish, immature body shape—in this sense, then, a girl can "keep from growing up." Thus this life-threatening condition may develop for personal reasons stemming from combinations of family and social pressures (Polivy & Herman, 1985). Unfortunately, as most anorexics discover, being thin and unhealthy is not the same as remaining young.

Bulimia. Somewhat more complex than anorexia nervosa is the behavior pattern involved in **bulimia** (pronounced boo-LEE-me-uh), a "binge-and-purge" syndrome in which the sufferer indulges in episodes of overeating (binges) followed by efforts to lose weight (purging) by means of self-induced vomiting, laxative use, or fasting. Bulimics, who usually keep their disorder inconspicuous, may be supported in their behavior patterns by peers and by

Eating disorders may result from real or imagined pressure to be thin. Successful and celebrated people are not immune—and may even be at some risk as a result of life under public scrutiny. Diana, Princess of Wales (pictured at top with singers Paul and Linda McCartney), may have suffered from bulimia, according to one biographer. Actress Traci Gold (lower photo), star of TV's "Growing Pains," has been called a victim of anorexia by some tabloid newspapers. Does such speculation call needed attention to real problems, or could it actually make matters worse?

competitive norms in their academic, social and athletic lives (Rodin et al., 1985; Squire, 1983).

To the normal population, a secret life of bingeing-and-purging to the point of being unable to resume normal eating behavior seems obviously unnatural and disordered. How could such a habit go undetected or unchallenged? One answer is suggested in the following anecdote by psychologist James Pennebaker (1990), explaining his early research on *active inhibition* (deliberate strategies for behavior change):

> In the late 1970s, I intended to begin to study inhibition by surveying people to get an idea of the ways they dieted and the relative effectiveness of their weight-loss techniques. Before the project started, however, my plans changed after some discussions with my students.
>
> It was 1979 and one of my students was complaining about her roommate, who was eating tremendous quantities of food each night and then vomiting what she had eaten. I told this story to a group of my researchers with the air of you'll-never-believe-this. Over the next week, at least half of my research team spoke privately with me and admitted that they, too, binged and purged food on a regular basis. Here was a phenomenon that I had never heard of that was apparently affecting a respectable number of college students. Who were these people and why were they doing it? (pp. 24-25)

In subsequent research, Pennebaker and his colleagues surveyed more than 700 university women about their eating behavior and dieting experiences (see Pennebaker, 1990). Somewhat unexpectedly, the researchers found that, before they developed the disorder, bulimic women were no different from other women in terms of their backgrounds, body images, and food preferences. The major difference between normal and disordered women was that bulimic women had tried and failed with more different weight-loss programs. In other words, for these women, bulimia appeared to be "an extreme form of dieting" (Pennebaker, 1990, p. 25). Other research indicates that bulimics rely on local norms—standards of behavior among their immediate circle of friends and classmates—with an emphasis on thinness and an acceptance of bingeing-and-purging to attain the ideal (see, for example, Johnson & Connors, 1987). Pennebaker found that bulimic women were not as worried about the threat to their health as they were stressed by the practical difficulties of concealing their "secret lives" from family and friends. Time spent with others interfered with their need to binge-and-purge, and they constantly ran the risk of being "discovered." For some women, the solution was to sever social ties with those who might disapprove of their bulimic behavior. By associating only with other bulimics, each woman could convince herself that her habit was relatively normal and acceptable—at least among her circle of bulimic friends. But this isolation led to loneliness and depression, which in turn led to more eating and overeating, so that the disorder took on a momentum of its own.

Researchers have also found that eating disorders are often associated with other forms of psychopathology. For example, there may be common risk factors for both bulimia and major depression (Walters et al., 1992). Further, while hungry normal people look forward to eating and enjoy a good meal, eating-disordered individuals do not associate pleasure with food, and may even dread having to eat. In comparison with control subjects, bulimic patients in one study took longer to begin eating a scheduled meal, ate more slowly, and reported significantly more negative affect during eating (Hetherington et al., 1993). Whatever their original rationale might have been to lose weight, anorexics and bulimics apparently take little joy in their slimmer states. Ironically, the negative affect these individuals exhibit may eventually help them, by attracting the attention of friends and family members who can urge them to seek professional treatment for their disorder.

Approaches to Eating Disorders. Psychodynamic approaches to understanding eating disorders primarily examine family interactions and origins, as cited above. Disordered eating behavior may represent an unconscious wish to remain young, dependent, or vulnerable.

Behavioral approaches focus on the life-threatening habits that must be changed if the disordered individual is to recover. One strategy for behavior change is to remove the individual from the environment or social arrangement that may be tolerating or encouraging her habit. Anorexics have been found to resist cooperating with such programs more than bulimic patients (Van Strien et al., 1992). Perhaps self-starvation reflects a greater need for control than does the binge-and-purge habit of bulimics. Effective behavioral strategies must take into account the importance of control and self-determination in maintaining the pattern of disordered behavior.

Cognitive approaches to eating disorders analyze how the individual sees herself and thinks about food, eating, and weight. Anorexics may exhibit more mental rigidity (less flexibility in their thinking) than normal individuals (Korkina et al., 1992). Bulimics who purge more often have been found to suffer interference in performing certain cognitive tasks (Cooper & Fairburn, 1993). Research results such as these suggest that eating-disordered individuals have distorted ways of perceiving and thinking. Accordingly, many successful treatments of eating disorders are based on cognitive strategies that focus first on building up self-esteem and self-efficacy (Baell & Wertheim, 1992).

Treatment. Considering the personal, social, and cultural factors in their development, it's not surprising to find that eating disorders are difficult to treat. Both anorexia nervosa and bulimia have a high rate of relapse; those who have been successfully treated remain at some risk for the same disorder (Kennedy & Garfinkel, 1992). Victims of anorexia nervosa may resist admitting that they have a problem in the first place. Those who suffer from bulimia may have become so secretive that they are reluctant to confide in a friend or therapist.

Confiding is important. Although therapists have difficulty agreeing on reliable treatments for eating disorders, those surveyed in one study overwhelmingly favored "talking therapy" for both anorexia and bulimia patients (Herzog et al., 1992). Support groups (especially in clinical settings) can help treat bulimia by bringing together sufferers who sympathize with and accept each other, and relieve each other of the need to go on "hiding" (Garfinkel & Garner, 1982; Pennebaker, 1990). Students surveyed about their preferences favor psychologically based treatment, such as counseling and behavior change, instead of medical approaches such as drugs (Sturmey, 1992). Does your school have such support services to help overcome eating disorders? Find out so that you can recommend them to friends in need—including, perhaps, your best friend: you.

Researchers have sought to inform and reassure health care professionals about the importance of identifying and treating anorexia nervosa and bulimia (Herzog, 1992). Still, a major hurdle for psychologists is our diet-obsessed culture, whose imagery undercuts therapists' efforts to have their clients start eating and regain lost weight. After all, how readily can you name an "attractive" media personality, celebrity, or heroic figure—other than a comic entertainer—who is also clearly overweight? As long as "fat" is a dirty word, self-conscious individuals will worry about their weight, and risk their mental and physical well-being in the impossible quest to be "perfect."

Schizophrenic Disorders

Everyone knows what it is like to feel depressed or anxious, even though few of us experience these feelings severely enough to be disordered. *Schizophrenia*

schizophrenic disorder Severe disorder characterized by the breakdown of personality functioning, withdrawal from reality, distorted emotions, and disturbed thought.

(pronounced skits-a-FREE-nee-a), however, is a disorder that represents a qualitatively different experience from normal functioning (Bellak, 1979). A **schizophrenic disorder** is a severe form of psychopathology in which personality seems to disintegrate, perception is distorted, emotions are blunted, thoughts are bizarre, and language is strange. Schizophrenia is the disorder we usually mean when we refer to "madness," psychosis, or insanity.

Between two and three million living Americans at one time or another have suffered from this most mysterious and tragic mental disorder (Regier et al., 1988). Schizophrenic patients currently occupy half of the beds in this nation's mental institutions. For as yet unknown reasons, the first occurrence of schizophrenia typically occurs for men before they are 25 and for women between 25 and 45 years of age (Lewine et al., 1981).

Mark Vonnegut, son of novelist Kurt Vonnegut, was in his early 20s when he began to experience symptoms of schizophrenia. In *Eden Express* (1975), he tells the story of his break with reality and his eventual recovery after being hospitalized twice for acute schizophrenia. Once, while pruning some fruit trees, he hallucinated—creating distorted perceptions and a different reality:

> I began to wonder if I was hurting the trees and found myself apologizing. Each tree began to take on personality. I began to wonder if any of them liked me. I became completely absorbed in looking at each tree and began to notice that they were ever so slightly luminescent, shining with a soft inner light that played around the branches. And from out of nowhere came an incredibly wrinkled, iridescent face. Starting as a small point infinitely distant, it rushed forward, becoming infinitely huge. I could see nothing else. My heart had stopped. The moment stretched forever. I tried to make the face go away but it mocked me. . . . I was holding my life in my hands and was powerless to stop it from dripping through my fingers. I tried to look the face in the eyes and realized I had left all familiar ground (1975, p. 96).

During the weeks after the pruning experience, young Vonnegut's behavior went out of control more often and more extremely. He would cry without reason. His terror would evaporate into periods of ecstasy, with no corresponding change in his life situation. For 12 days he ate nothing and slept not at all. One day, while visiting friends in a small town, he stripped off his clothes and ran naked down the street. Suicidal despair nearly ended his young, once promising life.

Symptoms of Schizophrenia. In the world of schizophrenia, *thinking* becomes illogical; associations among ideas are remote or without apparent pattern. Language may become incoherent—a "word salad" of unrelated or made-up words—or an individual may become mute. *Emotions* may be flat, with no visible expression, or they may be inappropriate to the situation. *Psychomotor behavior* may be disorganized (grimaces, strange mannerisms), or posture may become rigid. Even when only some of these symptoms are present, deteriorated functioning in work, social relations, and self-care is likely. *Interpersonal relationships* are often difficult as individuals withdraw socially or become emotionally detached. These same symptoms of schizophrenia are found in many different cultures (Draguns, 1980, 1990). There appears to be more similarity among schizophrenics in all parts of the world than among people who suffer from other major psychological disorders.

hallucination False sensory or perceptual experience.

Schizophrenics often experience **hallucination,** involving imagined sensory perceptions (sights, smells, sounds, usually voices) that are assumed to be real. For example, a person may hear one voice that provides a running commentary on his or her behavior, or several voices in conversation.

delusion False belief maintained despite contrary evidence and lack of social support.

Delusion is also common in schizophrenia; these are false or irrational beliefs maintained in spite of clear evidence to the contrary. Delusions are often patently absurd, such as the belief that one's thoughts are being broadcast, controlled, or taken away by aliens. In other cases, delusions may not seem so outlandish, but they are still not realistic or true. For example, a man may experience delusions that his sexual partner is not being faithful, or that he is being persecuted.

Psychologists divide these symptoms into two categories, positive and negative. During *acute phases* of schizophrenia, the "positive" symptoms—hallucinations, delusions, incoherence, and disorganized behavior—are prominent. At other times, the "negative" symptoms—social withdrawal and flattened emotions—become more apparent. Some individuals, such as Mark Vonnegut, just experience one or a couple of acute phases of schizophrenia and recover to live normal lives. Others, often described as chronic sufferers, experience either repeated acute phases with short periods of negative symptoms or occasional acute phases with extended periods marked by the presence of negative symptoms. Even the most seriously disturbed are not acutely delusional all the time (Liberman, 1982).

Major Types of Schizophrenia. Investigators consider schizophrenia a constellation of separate types of disorders. The four most commonly recognized subtypes are outlined in **Table 13.4.**

Disorganized Type. In this subtype of schizophrenia, a person displays incoherent patterns of thinking and grossly bizarre and disorganized behavior. Emotions are flattened or inappropriate to the situation. Often, a person acts in a silly or childish manner, such as giggling for no apparent reason. Language can become so incoherent, full of unusual words and incomplete sentences, that communication with others breaks down. Delusions or hallucinations are common, but are not organized around a coherent theme.

Catatonic Type. The catatonic person seems frozen in a stupor. For long periods of time, the individual can remain motionless, often in a bizarre position, showing little or no reaction to anything in the environment. When the indi-

Table 13.4 Types of Schizophrenic Disorders

TYPE OF SCHIZOPHRENIA	MAJOR SYMPTOMS
Disorganized	Inappropriate behavior and emotions; incoherent language
Catatonic	Frozen, rigid, or excitable motor behavior
Paranoid	Delusions of persecution or grandeur with hallucinations
Undifferentiated	Mixed set of symptoms with thought disorders and features from other types

vidual is moved, he or she freezes in a new position, assuming the waxy flexibility of a soft plastic toy.

Catatonic negativity sometimes involves motionless resistance to instructions, or doing the opposite of what is requested. For the catatonic person, stupor sometimes alternates with excitement. During the excited phase, motor activity is agitated, apparently without purpose, and not influenced by external stimuli.

Paranoid Type. Individuals who suffer from this form of schizophrenia experience complex and systematized delusions focused around specific themes. Individuals suffering *delusions of persecution* feel that they are being constantly spied on and plotted against and that they are in mortal danger. Those with *delusions of grandeur* believe that they are important or exalted beings—millionaires, great inventors, or religious figures such as Jesus Christ. Delusions of persecution may accompany delusions of grandeur: An individual may believe he is a great person who is continually opposed by evil forces.

Individuals may suffer *delusional jealousy,* becoming convinced that their mates are unfaithful, and contriving data to "prove" the truth of the delusion. Finally, those suffering *delusions of reference* misconstrue chance happenings as being directed at them. A paranoid individual who sees two people in earnest conversation readily concludes that they are talking about him. Even lyrics in popular songs or words spoken by radio or TV actors are perceived as having some special message for the individual, or exposing some personal secret.

The onset of symptoms in paranoid schizophrenic individuals tends to occur later in life than it does in other schizophrenic types. Paranoid schizophrenic individuals rarely display obviously disorganized behavior. Instead, it is more likely that their behavior will be intense and quite formal.

Undifferentiated Type. This "grab bag" category of schizophrenia describes a person who exhibits prominent delusions, hallucinations, incoherent speech, or grossly disorganized behaviors that fit the criteria of more than one type, or of no clear type. The hodgepodge of symptoms experienced by these individuals does not clearly differentiate among various schizophrenic reactions.

Causes of Schizophrenia. Different models point to very different initial causes of schizophrenia, different developmental pathways, and different avenues for treatment. A review of several of these models can help us understand how a person may develop a schizophrenic disorder.

Genetic Approaches. It has long been known that schizophrenia tends to run in families (Bleuler, 1978; Kallmann, 1946). Persons related genetically to someone who has been schizophrenic are more likely to become affected than those who are not (Kessler, 1980). The risk is greater for first-degree relatives (siblings and children), greater in families with many affected relatives, and greater where schizophrenic reactions are severe (Hanson et al., 1977). In fact, for all close relatives of a diagnosed *index case* of schizophrenia, the risk factor may be as great as 46 times higher than for the general population (see **Figure 13.4**).

The most compelling evidence for the role of genetic factors in the etiology of schizophrenia comes from adoption studies. When the offspring of a schizophrenic parent are reared by a normal parent in a foster home, they are as likely to develop the disorder as if they had been brought up by the biological parent (Heston, 1970; Rosenthal et al., 1975). In addition, adoptees who are schizophrenic have significantly more biological than adoptive relatives with schizophrenic disorders (Kety et al., 1975).

While there is certainly a strong relationship between genetic similarity and the risk of schizophrenia, even in the groups with the greatest genetic similarity, the risk factor is less than 50 percent. This indicates that, although genes

Figure 13.4 Genetic Risk for Schizophrenic Disorder

Out of a sample of 100 children of schizophrenic parents, from 10 to 50 percent will have the genetic structure that can lead to schizophrenia. Of these, about 5 percent will develop schizophrenia early and 5 percent later in life. It is important to note that as many as 40 percent of the high-risk subjects will not become schizophrenic.

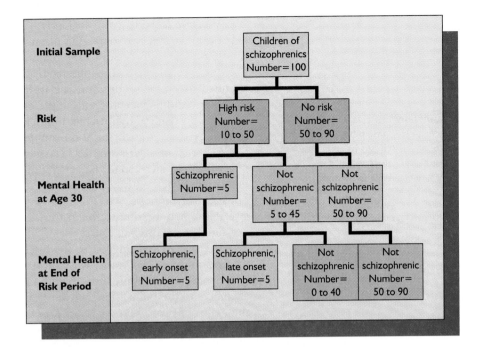

play some role, schizophrenia is a complex disorder that involves other contributing factors.

The genetics of schizophrenia is still undetermined. Critics of the genetic hypothesis of schizophrenia argue that the available evidence is weak for all types of schizophrenia except for *chronic* forms of the disorder. They point out that 90 percent of the relatives of schizophrenics do not have schizophrenia (Barnes, 1987). Taken as a whole, research suggests that genetic factors may contribute to schizophrenia but may not by themselves be sufficient for the development of schizophrenia (Nicol & Gottesman, 1983).

One widely accepted hypothesis for causes of schizophrenia is the **diathesis-stress hypothesis.** (The word *diathesis* refers to a predisposition or physical condition that makes one susceptible to disease.) This hypothesis suggests that genetic factors place the individual at risk, but environmental stress factors must impinge for the potential risk to be manifested as a schizophrenic disorder. Thus, individuals who are genetically predisposed to develop schizophrenia may never do so if they do not experience certain damaging conditions or stressors that push them "over the edge."

diathesis-stress hypothesis
Predisposition to develop a particular disorder as a result of interaction between stressful demands and personal traits.

These four genetically identical women each experience a schizophrenic disorder, which suggests that heredity plays a role in the development of schizophrenia. For each of the Genain quadruplets, the disorder differs in severity, duration, and outcome.

Neurochemicals and Brain Structure. Are the brains of individuals who are genetically at risk for schizophrenia unusual in some way? Particular neurotransmitters and processes in the brain have been associated with the production and reduction of schizophrenic reactions. The most promising line of biochemical research focuses on the influence of a specific neurotransmitter, dopamine, and its receptor sites in the brain.

The **dopamine hypothesis** holds that schizophrenia is associated with a relative excess of the chemical dopamine at specific receptor sites in the central nervous system (Carlsson, 1978; Snyder, 1986). Schizophrenic symptoms result from an increase in the activity of nerve cells that use dopamine as their neurotransmitter. Although impressive evidence has been accumulated for the dopamine hypothesis, we still must be cautious. It is possible that dopamine availability may be one factor in the sequence of development of schizophrenia, but not the original cause.

Another area of interest in the biology of schizophrenia is the association of schizophrenic symptoms with subtle brain abnormalities, such as reduced brain volume in specific areas of the brain or enlarged ventricles (fluid-filled chambers in the brain). Further research comparing structure and functions of the brains of twins who are *discordant* for schizophrenia (one has the disorder, the other does not) and normal control twins has been conducted by an interdisciplinary research team headed by Irving Gottesman and **E. Fuller Torrey** using brain scanning and other assessment techniques (see *Discovering Psychology*, 1989, Program 21; Gottesman, 1991).

Although it is unlikely that one single "biological" silver bullet will ever be found to explain the wide range of schizophrenic symptoms, increasingly refined methods will ultimately clarify our understanding of the genetic, biochemical, and anatomical factors at work in schizophrenia.

Psychodynamics and Family Interaction. Sociologists, family therapists, and psychologists all study the influence of family role relationships and communication patterns in the development of schizophrenia. From a psychodynamic view, schizophrenia is a regression to an infantile stage of functioning and is marked by a fragile ego that has difficulty distinguishing between the self and the outside world. One psychodynamic model developed by **Margaret Mahler** (1979) traces the schizophrenic individual's difficulty in differentiating between self and external world to an early, intense *symbiotic attachment* between mother and child. She believes the two failed to differentiate themselves from each other, were highly dependent on one another, intruded on each other's lives, and had difficulty separating.

Researchers have provided some evidence to support theories that deviations in parental communication influence the development of schizophrenia (Liem, 1980). One such deviation is a family's inability to share a common focus of attention. Another is indicated when parents have difficulty taking other family members' perspectives or communicating clearly and accurately. Studies suggest that the speech patterns of families with a schizophrenic member show less responsiveness and less interpersonal sensitivity than those of normal families. It may be that *having* a schizophrenic member contributes to families' interaction problems. But results also support the conclusion that schizophrenia is somewhat fostered by poor communication, confusion, and double messages (for example, a parent saying, "Come give Mommy a hug" and then pushing her child away because the child's hands are sticky).

Deviant communication in families may contribute to the child's distortion of reality by concealing or denying the true meaning of an event or by injecting a substitute meaning that is confusing (Wynne et al., 1979). Anthropologist **Gregory Bateson** used the term **double bind** to describe a situation in which a child receives from a parent multiple messages that are contradictory and cannot all be met. A mother may complain that a son is not affectionate and yet reject his attempts to touch her for some reason. Torn

dopamine hypothesis Explanation proposing relationship between many schizophrenic symptoms and relative excess of the neurotransmitter dopamine at specific brain receptor sites.

double bind Conflict situation in which individual receives multiple, contradictory messages from a significant other.

E. Fuller Torrey

between these different verbal and nonverbal meanings (between demands and feelings), a child's grip on reality may begin to slip. The result may be that the child will see his or her feelings, perceptions, and self-knowledge as unreliable indicators of the way things really are (Bateson et al., 1956).

There is not sufficient evidence to rally confidence in the hypothesis that family factors play a causal role in the *development* of schizophrenia. However, there is reliable evidence that family factors do influence the functioning of an individual *after* the first symptoms appear. When parents reduce their criticism, hostility, and intrusiveness toward schizophrenic offspring, the recurrence of acute schizophrenic symptoms and the need for rehospitalization is also reduced (Doane et al., 1985).

Cognitive Processes. The hallmarks of schizophrenia include abnormalities in attention, thought, memory, and language. Some cognitive psychologists argue that these abnormalities may play a role in causing schizophrenia instead of being consequences of the disorder. One view focuses on the role of attentional difficulties. *Attentional deficits* may involve ignoring important environmental or cultural cues that most people use to socially regulate or "normalize" their behavior. For example, in order to "fit in" and not disturb others if you arrive late to class, you glance quickly around the room to see what's going on, and how your classmates are behaving. If you do not or cannot notice that the others are working very quietly, you draw reproving glances as you enter in your usual noisy manner. A pattern of such social errors makes it difficult for someone to win acceptance and social support.

The speech of some schizophrenic individuals seems to be under the control of immediate stimuli in the situation. The incoherence of schizophrenic speech is due, in part, to bizarre *intrusions* by thoughts that are not directly relevant to the statement being uttered—intrusions that the person cannot suppress. Normal speaking requires that a speaker remember what has just been said (past), monitor where he or she is (present), and direct the spoken sentence toward some final goal (future). This coherence between past, present, and future may be difficult for some schizophrenic individuals, accounting for their inability to maintain long strings of interconnected words. What comes out is often termed "word salad," wildly tossed semantic confusion.

According to the cognitive approach taken by psychologist **Brendan Maher** (1968), the bizarre speech of schizophrenic individuals may be a result of deviant processing whenever a person comes to a "vulnerable" word—one that has multiple meanings to him or her. At that point, a personally relevant but semantically inappropriate word is used. For example, a patient may say, "Doctor, I have pains in my chest and hope and wonder if my box is broken and heart is beaten." *Chest* is a vulnerable word; it can mean a *respiratory cage* or a *container* such as a *hope* chest. *Wonder* could mean *Wonder Bread*® that is kept in a bread *box*. Hearts *beat* and are *broken*.

Reality testing is also impaired in schizophrenia. While most of us evaluate the reality of our inner worlds against the external world, individuals with schizophrenic disorders typically *reverse* this usual reality-testing procedure. Their inner experiences are the criteria against which they test the validity of outer experience (Meyer & Ekstein, 1970). Theirs is a world in which thinking it makes it so—as in the fantasy world of children or the dream world of adults. By carefully listening to schizophrenic speech, it is often possible for a clinician to decode the sense in what appears at first to be pure nonsense (Forest, 1976).

Other Categories of Disorders

We will not be able to examine closely other categories of psychopathology, simply because of space limitations. However, some other important disorders are worthy of mention.

- *Sexual disorders* involve problems with sexual inhibition or dysfunction and deviant sexual practices.
- *Organic mental disorders* are psychological or behavioral abnormalities associated with temporary or permanent brain damage or malfunction. They may be a product of aging of the brain, disease, accidents, or excessive ingestion of substances, such as alcohol, lead, and certain drugs such as barbiturates, amphetamines, and opiates.
- *Substance-use disorders* include both dependence on and abuse of alcohol and drugs.
- *Somatoform disorders* involve physical (from Greek *soma,* "body") symptoms, such as paralysis or pains in a limb, that arise without a physical cause. This category includes the symptoms of *conversion disorder,* which used to be called *hysteria.*
- *Disorders that typically arise in infancy or childhood* include retardation, stuttering, or behavior problems. Included within this group is the subset referred to as *eating disorders,* such as anorexia and bulimia, which were examined earlier. Eating disorders are categorized with other childhood-onset disorders because they typically occur in adolescence or young adulthood.

As you read about the symptoms and experiences that are typical of the various psychological disturbances, you may begin to feel that some of the characteristics apply to you—at least part of the time—or to someone you know. Some of the disorders that we have considered here are not uncommon, so it would be surprising if they sounded completely alien. Many of us have some human frailties that appear on the list of criteria for a particular psychological disorder. Recognizing this familiarity can be a useful way of furthering your understanding of abnormal psychology, but remember that a diagnosis for any disorder depends on a number of criteria and requires the judgment of a trained mental health professional. Please *resist the temptation* to use this new knowledge to diagnose friends and family members as pathological! On the other hand, being sensitive to others' needs for counsel and social support in times of personal trouble is always appropriate.

SUMMING UP

Personality disorders are long-standing, inflexible, maladaptive patterns of perceiving, thinking, or behaving that seriously impair an individual's functioning or cause significant distress. Two of the better known personality disorders are narcissistic personality disorder and antisocial personality disorder.

Dissociative disorders involve a basic disruption of the integrated functioning of memory, consciousness, or personal identity. In cases of multiple personality, two or more separate identities emerge to cope with the trauma of childhood sexual and physical abuse experienced by those who develop this disorder, most of whom are women.

Anxiety disorders affect 15 percent of the population of the United States at some time in their lives. The four major types of anxiety disorders include generalized anxiety disorder, panic disorder, phobic disorders, and obsessive-compulsive disorder.

Affective disorders involve disturbances in mood. One main type of affective disorder is unipolar depression, the "common cold of psychopathology," characterized by sad feelings as well as other symptoms. Bipolar disorder is much rarer and is marked by the alternating occurrence of depression and periods of mania during which a person experiences intense elation or irritability and other cognitive and motivational symptoms. Least common are "pure" manic episodes, without the balancing pole of depression. Explanations for the greater incidence of unipolar depression in women support the notion that the causes of affective disturbances may be a complex combination of factors and that it is likely that there is more than one path from "normal" behavior to depression. Most suicides are attempted by people suffering from depression. More women than men attempt suicide, but men are more likely to complete the suicidal act. In recent years, there has been an alarming increase in youth suicide.

Eating disorders, categorized with a larger class of disorders that develop in childhood and adolescence, are characterized by deliberately refusing to eat or preventing digestion. In anorexia nervosa, the individual starves herself, whereas a bulimic binges (overeats) and then purges (prevents digestion by vomiting or using laxatives). Both disorders are related to unrealistic body images, and are difficult to treat.

Schizophrenia is a severe form of psychopathology affecting about one percent of the population. Someone with a schizophrenic disorder experiences extreme distortions in perception, thinking, emotion, behavior, and language. Hallucinations and delusions are common, and there may be a disintegration of the coherent functioning of personality. Psychologists have identified four subtypes of schizophrenia: disorganized, catatonic, paranoid, and undifferentiated.

Evidence for the cause of schizophrenia has been found in genetic factors, biochemical and brain abnormalities, family structure and communication, and faulty cognitive processes. Each of the systematic attempts to make sense of the origins of schizophrenia offers only a partial explanation, because the development of most cases of psychopathology is likely to be influenced by a number of interacting complex factors.

DSM-III-R includes many categories of disorders that were not examined here. Among these are sexual disorders, organic mental disorders, substance-use disorders, somatoform disorders, and childhood-onset disorders.

Judging People as Abnormal

Although diagnosis and classification yield benefits for research and clinical purposes, these same processes can have negative consequences. The task of actually assigning a person the label "psychologically or mentally disordered" remains a matter of human judgment—thus open to bias and error. The labels of mental illness, insanity, or psychological disorder can be acquired in a number of ways other than by the diagnosis of a trained clinician. When psychologically untrained people are in a position to judge the mental health of others, their decisions are often vulnerable to biases based on expectations, status, gender, prejudice, and context. Too often those identified as psychologically disordered suffer from stigma, as we saw in the letter from Cherish at the beginning of the chapter.

The Problem of Objectivity

The label "mentally ill" is typically assigned because the person is under some form of *care*. Influential members of the community or family agree that the person's behavior is *dangerously maladjusted*, the person's scores on psychological tests *deviate* from standards of normality, the person declares himself or herself to be *"mentally sick,"* and/or the person's public behavior is *dangerous* to himself or herself or to others.

The criteria psychologists and psychiatrists use to make diagnostic decisions also influence judgments of the legal system and of the insurance and health care businesses. The legal determination of **insanity** carries with it serious implications regarding a defendant's competence to stand trial and to be held responsible for criminal indictments.

insanity Legal designation for the state of an individual judged to be irresponsible or incompetent.

The decision to declare someone psychologically disordered or insane is always a *judgment* about behavior. It is a judgment made by one or more people about another individual who often has less political power or socioeconomic status than those making the judgment.

Research has shown that clinicians in the United States use a double standard to assess the maladjustment of men and women. In one study, both male and female clinicians ascribed more positive characteristics to males and less desirable characteristics to normal, healthy females (Broverman et al., 1972). Other research shows that clinicians tend to judge females as maladjusted when they show behaviors that are incongruent with their gender role. When women act "like men"—use foul language, drink excessively, or exhibit uncontrollable temper—they are seen as neurotic or self-destructive. Moreover, clinicians reflect the biases of their society when they regard masculinity as more important than femininity. In one study, male behavior that was incongruent with the male gender role was rated as a more serious violation than was female gender-role incongruity (Page, 1987).

Labeling Behavior.

We have seen throughout our study of psychology that the meaning of behavior is jointly determined by its *content* and by its *context*. The same act in different settings conveys very different meanings. A man kisses another man: it may signify a gay relationship in the United States, a ritual greeting in France, and a Mafia "kiss of death" in Sicily. Unfortunately, the diagnosis of a behavior as abnormal can depend on where the behavior occurs—even professionals' judgments may be influenced by context. Is it possible to be judged as sane if you are "a patient" in an insane place? This question was addressed in a classic study by **David Rosenhan** (1973, 1975).

Rosenhan and seven other sane people (colleagues and friends who collaborated with him) gained admission to different psychiatric hospitals by pretending to have a single symptom: hallucinations. All eight of these *pseudopatients* were diagnosed on admission as either paranoid schizophrenic or manic-depressive. Once admitted, they behaved normally in every way. When a sane person is in an insane place, he or she is likely to be judged insane, and any behavior is likely to be reinterpreted to fit the context. When the pseudopatients discussed their situation in a rational way with the staff, they were reported to be using "intellectualization" defenses, while the notes they made of their observations were evidence of "writing behavior." The pseudopatients remained on the wards for almost three weeks, on the average, and not one was identified by the staff as sane. When they were finally released—only with the help of spouses or colleagues—their discharge diagnosis was still "schizophrenia" but "in remission"; that is, their symptoms were not active (Fleischman, 1973; Lieberman, 1973).

The Context of Mental Illness.

Rosenhan's research challenged the former system of classifying mental disorders, but it also raised basic issues about the validity of judgments of abnormality in other people, about how dependent such judgments may be on factors other than behavior itself, and about how difficult psychological labels are to remove once they are "stuck" on a person. In the view of radical psychiatrist **Thomas Szasz,** mental illness does not even exist; it is a "myth" (1961, 1977). Szasz argues that the symptoms used as evidence of mental illness are merely medical labels that sanction professional intervention into what are social problems—deviant people violating social norms. Once labeled, these people can be treated for their "problem of being different," with no threat of disturbing the existing status quo.

Few clinicians would go this far today, but there is a movement of psychologists who advocate a *contextual* or *ecological model* in lieu of the classic medical model (Levine & Perkins, 1987). In an ecological model, abnormality is viewed as a product of an interaction between individuals and society.

David Rosenhan

Abnormality is seen as a mismatch between a person's abilities and the needs and norms of society. For example, schools typically demand that children sit quietly for hours at desks and work independently in an orderly fashion. Some children are not able to do this and are often labeled "hyperactive." The abilities of these children do not conform to the needs of most school settings and they quickly come to the attention of school authorities. However, if these same children were placed in an alternative school setting where they were free to roam around the classroom and talk to others as part of their work, the mismatch would not exist and these children would not be labeled in this negative, stigmatizing way.

The Problem of Stigma

Psychopathology is not statistically so abnormal: It has been estimated that 32 percent of Americans have struggled with some kind of psychopathology—making the experience at least relatively normal (Regier et al., 1988). In practice, being *deviant* connotes moral inferiority and brings social rejection. In addition, the term *deviant* implies that the whole person "is different in kind from ordinary people and that there are no areas of his personality that are not afflicted by his 'problems' " (Scott, 1972, p. 14). There is little doubt that in our society to be *mentally disordered* is to be publicly degraded and personally devalued. Society extracts costly penalties from those who deviate from its norms (see **Figure 13.5**).

People who are psychologically disordered are stigmatized in ways that most physically ill people are not. A **stigma** is a mark or brand of disgrace. In the psychological context, a stigma is a set of negative attitudes about a person that sets him or her apart as unacceptable (Clausen, 1981). Negative attitudes toward the psychologically disturbed come from many sources. Prominent

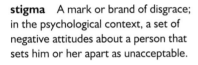

stigma A mark or brand of disgrace; in the psychological context, a set of negative attitudes about a person that sets him or her apart as unacceptable.

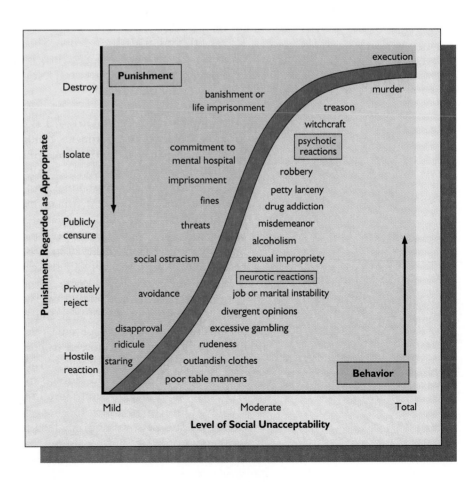

Figure 13.5 "Let the Punishment Fit the Crime"
This figure illustrates a continuum of behaviors that are deemed increasingly unacceptable and are responded to with increasing severity. Basically, each reaction is a punishment for deviance, so behavior toward those who act neurotically or psychotically can be seen to resemble behavior toward criminals or other deviants.

Although 1 in every 100 Americans is diagnosed as schizophrenic, 60 percent receive no treatment. Federal funds for research amount to only $17 per patient per year.

among these sources are mass media portrayals of psychiatric patients as prone to violent crime, jokes, family denial of the mental distress of one of its members, an individual's fear of loss of employment if others discover his or her distress or former mental health care, and legal terminology that stresses mental incompetence (Rabkin et al., 1980). The stigmatizing process discredits a person as "flawed" (Jones et al., 1984).

At a 1986 congressional hearing, the director of the National Institute of Mental Health reported on several aspects of the national neglect of schizophrenia. Although in 1986 one in every 100 Americans were diagnosed as sufferers of this insidious disease, only $17 in federal funds per year and per schizophrenic victim were being spent on research. In comparison, $300 were being spent for each cancer victim. Nearly 60 percent of all schizophrenia sufferers received no treatment.

Our negative attitudes toward psychologically disturbed people bias our perceptions of and actions toward them and also influence their behavior toward us. A series of experiments conducted in laboratory and naturalistic settings demonstrates the unfavorable influences of the social situation on both the behavior of a person perceived to be a mental patient (even when not so) and the behavior of the person making that judgment.

When one member of a pair of male college students was falsely led to believe the other had been a mental patient, he perceived the pseudo expatient to be inadequate, incompetent, and not likable. When one of a pair of interacting males falsely believed he was perceived by the other as stigmatized, he behaved in ways that actually caused the other naive subject to reject him (Farina, 1980; Farina et al., 1971).

Our growing understanding of psychopathology does more than enable society to reclaim its "familiar strangers," such as the young woman whose personal account of schizophrenia opened this chapter. In making sense of psychopathology, we are forced to come to grips with basic conceptions of normality, reality, and social values. (See "Cross-cultural Perspective: Culture and Abnormality.") A mind "loosed from its stable moorings" does not just go on its solitary way; it bumps into other minds, sometimes challenging their stability. In discovering how to understand, treat, and ideally, to prevent psychological disorders, we not only help those who are suffering and losing out on the joys of living, but we also expand the basic understanding of our own human nature.

Cross-cultural Perspective   Culture and Abnormality

The ecological model of abnormality starts with the assumption that people need certain skills to meet the norms of the society in which they live. If people do not have the necessary skills, they may exhibit unusual psychological symptoms that are obvious to others; consequently they receive the label of "abnormal." For example, most people in the middle-class American culture obtain their food through purchases in a grocery store. The necessary skills for obtaining food are to have a job that pays a salary, to set aside a certain amount of the salary for food purchases, to enter the grocery store and fill one's cart with a variety of nutritional foods, and so forth. Among the Cree, people obtain food through hunting. They have to develop skills in finding sites where game animals live, approaching game without being seen, and so forth. If people do not have the skills considered necessary in their society, they risk being seen as abnormal by others. Given this label, they may be stigmatized by others in their culture and denied opportunities to gain the benefits available to respected members of the culture.

Abnormality can also result from an *overemphasis* on skills considered useful in a culture. Juris Draguns (1973; 1990) believes that some mental problems can be viewed as exaggerated versions of behaviors considered normal and useful in a culture. He suggests that people think about "the exaggeration of the normal" by imagining themselves visiting a carnival or amusement park. In many carnivals,

there is a funhouse with several warped mirrors. When people look into the mirrors, they recognize themselves, but their images are distorted. Their head, legs, and arms look like exaggerated versions of their normal selves.

Some mental health difficulties can be understood through the analogy of the funhouse mirror, for example. When people become overinvolved with their jobs and exaggerate the usefulness of hard work, they risk becoming workaholics. Along with feeling the stress that results from overwork, workaholics run the risk of neglecting their families. Or consider the usefulness of suspicion. It is a useful skill to be suspicious of salespeople who have a deal that is "too good to be true." Taken to a more extreme level, however, suspicion can lead to paranoia and the feeling that "everyone is plotting against me." In some cultures, contact with the spirit world is considered normal and can occur frequently. However, respected elders in these cultures can recognize abnormality when people appeal to spirits too frequently or in an incorrect manner (Draguns, 1980).

The relationship between culture and normal skills can become problematic when people move across cultural boundaries. Many times, the skills necessary for success in one culture clash with the skills considered useful in another. This clash can be especially problematic for women moving from cultures where there are many restrictions on their behavior to cultures where there are fewer restrictions.

Moghaddam and his colleagues (1990) interviewed immigrant women from India who were living in Montreal, Canada. These women came from backgrounds where strong societal norms encouraged them to accept the roles of homemaker, wife, mother, and caretaker for elderly parents. In Canada, they were exposed to norms that allowed them to consider many more roles. However, many women did not have the necessary skills to take advantage of their increased choices. In many cases, however, they were forced to accept nontraditional roles, given that both husbands and wives had to work outside the home to bring in sufficient income. Over time, many women accepted and appreciated their increased choices. Their acceptance led to other changes such as the desire to increase their skills for the job market, an unwillingness to pass on traditional gender roles to children, and the desire for more equality in relationships with their husbands. Stress resulted, however, when the women did not receive support for these desires from other family members. One problem identified in other research among Indian families by Sinha (1990) is that men enjoy having the extra money brought in by their wives, but they do not enjoy sharing decision-making power concerning use of the money. The stress experienced by Indian women led to various psychological problems such as feelings of depression, anxiety, and the inability to get enough sleep.

SUMMING UP

Labeling a person as mentally disordered is a process of human judgment. The criteria professionals use to make such judgments also have influence on legal and social status. Research by David Rosenhan has shown that clinical labels bias the perceptions people form of patients. Behavior patterns may be labeled as psychopathological merely because they are mismatched with one's culture or social expectations. Another problem with labeling abnormality is the stigma it attaches to labeled persons. Until education helps society to be both informed and fair, disordered individuals may suffer misunderstanding and prejudice.

CHAPTER REVIEW

◆ The Nature of Psychological Disorders
What qualities or experiences indicate abnormality? How have attitudes toward abnormal behavior changed in the course of human history? What are the major approaches in psychopathology today? Of what use is a diagnostic classification system of psychological disorders?

Abnormality is judged by the degree to which a person's actions resemble a set of indicators that include distress, maladaptiveness, irrationality, unpredictability, unconventionality, and observer discomfort. In the past, psychopathology was considered to be the result of evil spirits or weak character. Today, psychologists use a number of approaches to studying the origins of psychopathology. The biological approach concentrates on abnormalities in the brain, biochemical processes, and genetic influences. The psychological approach includes the psychodynamic, behavioral, and cognitive models. The interactionist approach combines these views.

Classification systems for psychological disorders should provide a common shorthand for communicating about general types of psychopathology and specific cases. The most widely accepted diagnostic and classification system is DSM-III-R. It emphasizes descriptions of symptom patterns and encourages mental health professionals to consider psychological, physical, and social factors that might be relevant to a specific disorder.

Key Terms
psychopathology, p. 487
psychological diagnosis, p. 487
conversion disorder, p. 489
hysteria, p. 489
DSM-III-R, p. 494
neurotic disorder, p. 495
psychotic disorder, p. 495

Major Contributors
Pinel, Philippe, p. 490
Kraepelin, Emil, p. 490
Mesmer, Franz Anton, p. 491
Charcot, Jean-Martin, p. 491

◆ Major Psychological Disorders
How is a personality disorder different from other mental disorders? What class of disorders is someone suffering from who has a "split personality"? What experience do phobias and panic have in common? Which affective disorder accounts for a majority of all mental hospitalizations? What are the major types of eating disorders? What are the different types of schizophrenia?

Personality disorders are patterns of perception, thinking, or behavior that are long-standing and inflexible and that impair an individual's functioning. Dissociative disorders involve a disruption of the integrated functioning of memory, consciousness, or personal identity. The four major types of anxiety disorders are generalized anxiety, panic, phobic, and obsessive-compulsive disorders.

Affective disorders involve disturbances of mood. Unipolar depression is the most common affective disorder while bipolar disorder is much rarer. Suicides are most frequent among people suffering from depression. There are two common patterns of eating disorders: anorexia nervosa (self-starvation) and bulimia (bingeing-and-purging). Both are related to unrealistic, negative body images and are difficult to treat.

Schizophrenia is characterized by extreme distortions in perception, thinking, emotion, behavior, and language. The four subtypes of schizophrenia are disorganized, catatonic, paranoid, and undifferentiated. Evidence for the causes of schizophrenia has been found in a variety of factors including genetics, biochemical and brain abnormalities, family environment and communication, and faulty cognitive processes.

Key Terms	Major Contributors
personality disorder, p. 496	Putnam, F. W., p. 499
narcissistic personality disorder, p. 497	Beck, Aaron, p. 508
antisocial personality disorder, p. 497	Nolen-Hoeksema, Susan, p. 510
dissociative disorder, p. 498	Shneidman, Edwin, p. 513
psychogenic amnesia, p. 498	Torrey, E. Fuller, p. 520
multiple personality disorder (MPD), p. 498	Mahler, Margaret, p. 520
generalized anxiety disorder, p. 501	Bateson, Gregory, p. 520
panic disorder, p. 501	Maher, Brendan, p. 521
fear, p. 501	
phobic disorder, p. 501	
agoraphobia, p. 501	
social phobia, p. 502	
obsessive-compulsive disorder, p. 503	
affective disorder, p. 505	
manic episode, p. 505	
bipolar disorder, p. 506	
unipolar depression, p. 507	
negative cognitive set, p. 508	
eating disorder, p. 511	
anorexia nervosa, p. 511	
bulimia, p. 513	
schizophrenic disorder, p. 516	
hallucination, p. 516	
delusion, p. 516	
diathesis-stress hypothesis, p. 519	
dopamine hypothesis, p. 520	
double bind, p. 520	

3 **Judging People as Abnormal** *What evidence suggests that clinicians have difficulty making objective judgments? What are the dangers of stigmatizing those who suffer from any of the forms of psychopathology presented in this chapter?*

The task of labeling someone psychologically or mentally disordered is ultimately a matter of human judgment. Even professional judgments can be influenced by context and biased by prejudices. Those with psychological disorders are often stigmatized in ways that most physically ill people are not. Understanding psychopathology enables us to help those who are suffering from mental illness and to improve our understanding of human nature.

Key Terms	Major Contributors
insanity, p. 523	Rosenhan, David, p. 524
stigma, p. 525	Szasz, Thomas, p. 524

PRACTICE TEST

Chapter 13: Psychopathology

For each of the following items, choose the single correct or best answer. Correct answers, explanations, and page references appear in the Appendix.

1. Which of the following is *not* one of the six indicators of possible abnormality agreed upon by psychologists?
   A. chronic physical illness
   B. observer discomfort
   C. unconventionality
   D. irrationality

2. DSM-III-R refers to _____ .
   A. a personality inventory
   B. the most widely used diagnostic system
   C. the neurochemical implicated in anxiety disorders
   D. a class of psychoactive drugs effective in the treatment of schizophrenia

3. A young woman wanders into a hospital, claiming not to know who she is, where she came from, or how she got there. Her symptoms indicate that she might be suffering from a(n) _____ disorder.
   A. anxiety
   B. affective
   C. personality
   D. dissociative

4. Which of the following statements about phobic disorders is true?
   A. Any irrational fear, such as of spiders or multiple-choice tests, is considered a "phobia."
   B. The "preparedness hypothesis" is suggested by biological explanations for common human fears.
   C. Phobias represent one form of affective disorders.
   D. All of the above.

5. _____ has been called the "common cold of psychopathology" because it occurs so frequently, and almost everyone has experienced elements of the disorder at some time in life.
   A. Obsessive-compulsive disorder
   B. Bipolar disorder
   C. Unipolar depression
   D. Paranoid schizophrenia

6. Which of the following statements about suicide is *false*?
   A. More women than men attempt suicide.
   B. The typical suicide is committed by an older white, unemployed male living alone.
   C. The most common triggering event to suicide is the breakup of a close relationship.
   D. Youth suicide tends to be an impulsive, spur-of-the-moment tragedy prompted by imagined problems.

7. A person who suffers from _____ cannot eat normally, but engages in a ritual of "bingeing"—overeating fattening foods—followed by "purging" with induced vomiting or use of laxatives.
   A. anorexia
   B. bulimia
   C. inhibition
   D. mania

8. The _____ type of schizophrenia is characterized by delusions of persecution, grandeur, jealousy, and reference.
   A. disorganized
   B. paranoid
   C. catatonic
   D. undifferentiated

9. Somatoform disorders are psychological disorders that involve _____ .
   A. physical symptoms
   B. substance abuse
   C. delusional thinking
   D. uncontrollable changes or extremes in mood

10. A common problem experienced by those diagnosed with mental illness is _____ , referring to the sense of disgrace and deviance with which the rest of society has branded them.
    A. hysteria
    B. diathesis
    C. stigma

IF YOU'RE INTERESTED . . .

Caine Mutiny, The. (Video: 1954, color, 125 minutes). Directed by Edward Dmytryk; starring Humphrey Bogart, Jose Ferrer, Van Johnson, Fred MacMurray, E. G. Marshall.

Based on Herman Wouk's prizewinning novel, the story of a U.S. Navy court martial and the events that led to it. Humphrey Bogart is outstanding as the paranoid Captain Queeg, whose nervous habits and delusional thinking frighten his officers into taking mutinous action.

Duke, P. & Hochman, G. (1992). *A brilliant madness.* New York: Bantam.

A vivid, poignant account by actress Patty Duke of her struggle with manic-depressive (mixed bipolar) disorder.

Endler, N. S. (1982). *Holiday of darkness: A psychologist's personal journey out of his depression.* New York: Wiley.

Sad, but informative first-hand account of one of the most common and devastating disorders, as related by one of our colleagues.

One Flew Over the Cuckoo's Nest. (Video: 1975, color, 133 minutes). Directed by Milos Forman; starring Jack Nicholson, Louise Fletcher, Brad Dourif, Will Sampson, Danny DeVito, Christopher Lloyd, Scatman Crothers.

Captivating film based on Ken Kesey's novel, about the confrontation embodied in a criminal's entry into a psychiatric hospital and his relationships with voluntary patients. Won Oscars for Best Picture, Actor, Actress, Director, and Screenplay.

Seidenberg, R. & DeCrow, K. (1983). *Women who marry houses.* Cambridge, MA: McGraw-Hill.

Interesting review of what is known and not yet known about disorders like agoraphobia, an anxiety disorder that keeps its victims imprisoned by their fear of the outside world.

Sheehan, S. (1982). *Is there no place on earth for me?* New York: Vintage.

Originally published as a series in *The New Yorker*, Sheehan reports on her impressions of a young schizophrenic woman, "Sylvia Frumkin," with whom she lived and spent time in order better to understand the nature of thought disorders and the difficulties of treating them.

Styron, W. (1990). *Darkness visible: A memoir of madness.* New York: Random House.

The author of *Sophie's Choice* documents his own plunge into clinical depression and his gradual progress back to the light.

Three Faces of Eve, The. (Video: 1957, black-and-white, 91 minutes). Directed by Nunnally Johnson; starring Joanne Woodward, Lee J. Cobb, David Wayne.

Based on fact, the story of a woman found to have at least three distinct personalities, and the efforts she and her therapists make to find the source—and the resolution—of her disorder.

Vonnegut, M. (1975). *The Eden express.* New York: Bantam.

First-person account of his own experiences with schizophrenia by Mark Vonnegut, son of novelist Kurt Vonnegut.

Chapter 14   **Psychotherapies**

1. What are the two main kinds of therapy for mental disorders? Most often, why do people enter therapy? What are the primary goals of therapy?

2. What is the task of the psychoanalyst in most psychodynamic therapies? According to behavior therapists, how can most psychopathological behaviors be understood and modified? What is the underlying assumption of cognitive therapy? What concept is at the core of both humanistic and existential therapies?

3. What is the best known and most frequently used form of psychosurgery? For what class of disorders has electroconvulsive therapy been found to be especially effective? What kinds of drugs primarily are used today in chemotherapy programs?

4. With what questions are most psychotherapy researchers concerned today? How does the public-health model view the individual afflicted with a psychological disorder?

Sharon felt overwhelmed by a sense of impending doom. Nothing in her childhood or her current life explained her anxiety. Her therapist, Dr. José Stevens, suggested that Sharon focus her attention inward to discover what part of her body was most affected by these feelings. After Sharon identified the area just above her solar plexus, Dr. Stevens asked her to breathe deeply into that place, allowing her body to move spontaneously, expressing any images that came to her. This is how Dr. Stevens described Sharon's experience:

"As she began to stir, I accompanied her movements with soft drumbeats. She began to curl up, then abruptly she straightened and circled the room in a gliding movement that ended with some low guttural sounds. The dance continued with many flying gestures, sounds, and much emotional intensity, coming to a resolution and completion after some time. She was quite out of breath, but her eyes were clear and bright; her face was flushed with excitement. . . .

"She explained she had begun with an image of a dark cave deep in her body at the place where she had focused. This cave felt familiar but filled her with dread. She cried for help and a bird appeared who lifted her on his back and circled out above a strange landscape. There she could look down and see a double of herself hurriedly leading a group of others toward the cave. Before the group could make it, they were overtaken by an avalanche, and all were buried except her double who lay dying, pinned under a tree. The bird swooped with her down to where the people lay; she climbed off and rushed to the side of her dying double. She was able to comfort her, explaining to her double that the avalanche was not her fault, but an act of nature, and that her life and the lives of the others had come to an end in the natural course of events. With this done, the bird swept her up and returned her to the cave which now felt bright and homelike, without the former feeling of dread. The bird then told her a number of things that were to be kept in absolute confidence until many days later. The dance ended there" (Stevens, 1986, p. 48).

After this therapy session, Sharon's vague sense of dread disappeared. She felt more powerful and decisive, and she started using her leadership skills, taking responsibility without feeling guilty when plans didn't work out. "Her previous, limiting feelings were literally worked out of her system in the concentrated and intense healing dance with her guardian spirit" (Stevens, 1986).

When traditional western "talk therapy" did not help Sharon, Dr. Stevens turned to **shamanism,** an ancient and powerful spiritual tradition that has been practiced for close to 30,000 years. *Shamanism* originally referred to the religion of the Ural-Altaic peoples of Siberia. It was characterized by belief in demons, gods, and ancestral spirits. According to Native American psychologist Leslie Gray, in the shamanistic tradition "all forms of suffering and disease are diagnosed as powerlessness. The remedy is to regain power for the patient by restoring a vital soul, retrieving a guardian spirit, or instructing in ceremonial practices that return power" (Gray, 1989). Drumming, chanting, and other rituals are used to inspire awe and induce altered states of consciousness that facilitate the quest for knowledge and empowerment (Walsh, 1990).

Recently, the medical, psychiatric, and psychological professions have begun to work with shamans (pronounced SHAH-munz) in an effort to integrate Western psychotherapies that involve self-analysis with the therapies of collectivist societies that view the individual within the current communal context. These attempts at integration will make therapies more culturally appropriate to a wider range of clients (Kraut, 1990). (For an excellent analysis of shamanism, consult Mircea Eliade's book *Shamanism: Archaic Techniques of Ecstasy*, 1964.)

Introduction

shamanism Ancient spiritual tradition, still practiced in Native American cultures, combining healing with making contact with the spirit world.

How has the treatment of psychological disorders been influenced by historical, cultural, and social forces? What can be done to influence a mind ungoverned by ordinary reason to modify uncontrolled behavior, to alter unchecked emotions, and to correct abnormalities of the brain and even genes themselves? These are some of the formidable questions that we will address in this final chapter of our journey through *Psychology*.

This chapter surveys the major types of treatments currently used by health care providers, and examines the way these treatments work. In this chapter, we will also evaluate the validity of claims about the success of any particular type of therapy.

The Context of Therapy

Why seek therapy? There are many reasons why people seek help—and why others who need it do not. The purposes or goals of therapy, the settings in which therapy occurs, and the kinds of therapeutic helpers vary. Regardless of the differences between therapies, however, all are *interventions* into a person's life, designed to change that person's functioning in some way.

Treatment of physical illness and mental illness is determined by the severity of illness. Some illnesses, such as cancer or schizophrenia, are so serious that they require long-term, intensive treatment by highly trained professionals in special institutional settings. Relatively minor problems, whether occasional head colds or a mild phobia of escalators, do not usually require any treatment. Illnesses between these two extremes may be short-term but intense, but not long lasting or mild; they may be disturbingly repetitive; and they may vary in the degree to which they interfere with the daily life of the afflicted person.

Overview of Major Therapies

biomedical therapy Any of several treatments of psychological disorders that change biological or physical mechanisms.

Using the computer as a metaphor for the brain, we can say that mental problems may occur either in the brain's *hardware* (physical components) or the *software* (programs). The two main kinds of therapy for mental disorders focus on either that hardware or software.

Biomedical therapy focuses on changing the hardware—the mechanisms that run the central nervous system, endocrine system, and the metabolism. Biomedical therapies try to alter brain functioning with chemical or physical interventions. Only psychiatrists and specialists with M.D. (Doctor of Medicine) degrees can legally administer biomedical therapies.

"OF COURSE I'VE BECOME MORE MATURE SINCE YOU STARTED TREATING ME. YOU'VE BEEN AT IT SINCE I WAS 14 YEARS OLD."

psychotherapy Treatments for psychological disorders that work by changing behaviors, thoughts, perceptions, and emotions.

Psychological therapies, which are collectively called **psychotherapy,** focus on changing the software—the faulty behaviors we have learned and the words, thoughts, interpretations, and feedback that direct our daily strategies for living. There are four major types of psychotherapy: psychodynamic, behavioral, cognitive, and existential-humanistic.

The *psychodynamic approach* views adult neurotic suffering as the outer symptom of inner, unresolved childhood traumas and conflicts. The best-known psychodynamic treatment is *psychoanalysis,* the so-called "talking cure" in which a therapist helps a person develop insights about the relationship between the overt symptoms and the unresolved hidden conflicts that presumably caused those symptoms.

Behavior therapy treats the behaviors themselves as disturbances that must be modified. Disorders are viewed as learned behavior patterns rather than as the symptoms of some underlying mental disease. Behavior therapists believe that changing the problem behavior corrects the disorder.

Cognitive therapy tries to restructure how a person thinks by altering the often distorted self-statements a person makes about the causes of a problem. Cognitions (such as thoughts) are viewed as changeable behaviors.

Therapies emerging from the *existential-humanistic tradition* emphasize the *values* of patients. Existential-humanistic therapies are directed toward self-actualization, psychological growth, the development of more meaningful interpersonal relationships, and the enhancement of freedom of choice.

Before we examine the conceptual rationale for and methods of each of these types of therapeutic intervention, let's start at the beginning of the process—with a troubled person who enters some form of therapy.

Entering Therapy

Why does anyone go into therapy? Most often, people enter therapy when their everyday functioning violates societal criteria of normality or their own sense of adequate adjustment. They may seek therapy on their own initiative after trying ineffectively to cope with their problems, or they may be advised to do so by family, friends, doctors, or co-workers. Psychotherapy can help with problems associated with long-term illnesses that drastically affect the person's life. Sudden life changes due to unemployment, death of a loved one, or divorce may trigger or worsen one's psychological problems. Students often seek therapy from college mental health facilities because of their difficulties in interpersonal relationships and concerns about academic performance. Finally, those whose behavior is judged as dangerous to self or others can be involuntarily committed by a state court to a mental institution for a limited period of time for treatment, testing, or observation.

Why *don't* people seek therapy? Many people who might benefit from therapy do not seek it. Sometimes it is inconvenient for them to do so. People also often lack community mental health facilities, are ignorant of available resources, lack the money or mobility, fear stigmatization, or have prejudices against seeking help from a psychologist. (See "Time Out for Critical Thinking.")

One's ability to get help can be affected even by the psychological problems themselves. The person with agoraphobia finds it hard, even impossible, to leave home to seek therapy; a paranoid person will not trust mental health professionals. Extremely shy people cannot call for an appointment or go to an initial diagnostic interview precisely because of the problem for which they desire help. In many communities, it is still much easier to get help from a medical doctor for physical health problems than it is to find a qualified mental health worker who has time to provide needed, affordable psychological help.

People who do enter therapy are usually referred to as either *patients* or *clients*. The term **patient** is used by professionals who take a biomedical approach to the treatment of psychological problems. The term **client** is used by professionals who think of psychological disorders as "problems in living" and not as mental illnesses (Rogers, 1951; Szasz, 1961).

patient An individual with medical problems; term used in biomedical approach to treatment of psychological disorders.

client Person receiving treatment for psychological problems; term used by therapists who see disorders as problems in living, not as mental illness.

➡ *TIME OUT . . . FOR CRITICAL THINKING*

Is therapy for *you*? Would you personally benefit from what therapy has to offer, either now or sometime in your life? Consider the factors involved in making decisions about these situations and experiences:

- Do you have at least one close friend with whom you could discuss almost anything? Is there any problem you would *not* be willing or able to discuss with such a close friend? If so, and if you had such a conflict, how would you find sympathy or assistance?

- Have you ever wanted to change anything about your own behavior or habits? If you have been successful in such efforts, what do you think did the trick? If you have not had success, what would it take to accomplish your goals?

- In you personal relationships—with family members, romantic partners, or valued friends—have you encountered problems or conflicts that were difficult to resolve? When the person you usually confide in is part of the problem, in whom could you then confide about the situation?

- When you want information or new ideas to help you solve problems or achieve goals, what resources do you consult? At which times is another person a more effective source of help or information than a book, class, or television program?

- Do you ever feel that family, teachers, friends, or employers do not give you the breaks you deserve—to the point that you wonder if life is even worth living? What circumstances usually bring on such feelings?

There is no single or "correct" way to decide whether you personally should seek the services of a psychotherapist. A good guideline to keep in mind is that you "ought" to ask for counseling if and when you *think* you "ought" to.

More importantly, consider how to integrate therapy into your life. Your therapist will keep your relationship strictly confidential; you may wish to do the same, not revealing to friends or family that you are in counseling. On the other hand, keeping your therapy a "secret" from others may be a difficult or stressful process—or may subtly convince you that it is appropriate to feel embarrassed or ashamed of seeking therapy.

Remember that whatever assistance or information you seek, it is ultimately *you* who will make the difference in changing your behavior and your life. To become the person you want to be, you need the help of many other people—a supportive family, accepting friends, effective teachers and doctors. No one would think it reasonable to "go it alone" if that meant rejecting all these relationships. If psychotherapy would make your life better, your counselor or therapist would be one more person among the many who are already important and even necessary at some point in your life.

The Therapeutic Relationship

The therapeutic process can involve the following four primary tasks or goals:

1. Diagnosis. Reaching a *diagnosis* about what is wrong, possibly determining an appropriate psychiatric (DSM-III-R) label for the presenting problem, and classifying the disorder.
2. Etiology. Proposing a probable origin or history of the problem, identifying the *etiology* of the disorder—its probable origins of the disorder and the functions being served by its symptoms.
3. Prognosis. Making a *prognosis*, or estimate, of the course the problem will take with and without any treatment.
4. Treatment. Prescribing and carrying out some form of *treatment*, a therapy designed to minimize or eliminate the troublesome symptoms and, perhaps, also their sources.

Therapy is conducted in a variety of different settings: hospitals, clinics, schools, and private offices. Newer community-based therapies that aim to take the treatment to the client may operate out of local store fronts or church facilities. Therapists who practice *in vivo* **therapy** work with clients in the life setting that is associated with their problem. For example, they work in airports and airplanes with people who suffer from flying phobias, or in shopping malls and other busy, public places with people who have social phobias.

***in vivo* therapy** Therapeutic approach in which professionals treat clients in settings associated with clients' disorders.

Professional Therapists. When psychological problems arise, most of us initially seek out informal counselors who operate in familiar settings. Many people turn to family members, close friends, physicians, lawyers, or favorite teachers for support, guidance, and counsel. Those with religious affiliations may seek help from a religious advisor. Others get advice and a chance to talk by "opening up" to neighborhood bartenders, beauticians, cab drivers, or other people willing to listen. In our society, these informal therapists carry the bulk of the daily burden of relieving people's pent-up frustration and conflict.

Although more people seek out therapy now than in the past, people usually turn to trained mental health professionals only when their psychological problems become severe or persist for extended periods of time. When they do, they usually turn to one of six main types of therapists: counseling psychologists, psychiatric social workers, pastoral counselors, clinical psychologists, psychiatrists, and psychoanalysts. We'll consider briefly what distinguishes each type.

Cathy ☐ Cathy Guisewite

counseling psychologist Professional psychologist specializing in providing guidance in solving problems of normal adjustment.

Counseling Psychologists. The term **counseling psychologist** describes a member of the general category of professional psychologists who provides guidance in areas such as vocation selection, school problems, drug abuse, and marital conflict. Typically, these counselors work in community settings related to the problem areas—within a business, a school, a prison, the military service, or a neighborhood clinic—and use interviews, tests, guidance, and advice to help individuals solve specific problems and make decisions about future options.

psychiatric social worker Mental health professional trained in social work with emphasis on the social context of individuals' problems.

Psychiatric Social Workers. A **psychiatric social worker** is a mental health professional whose specialized training in a school of social work prepares her or him to work in collaboration with psychiatrists and clinical psychologists. However, unlike psychiatrists and psychologists, these counselors are trained to consider the *social contexts* of people's problems, so they may involve other family members in the therapy or at least become acquainted with clients' home and work settings.

pastoral counselor Member of a religious order who specializes in treating psychological disorders, often combining spiritual guidance with practical problem-solving.

Pastoral Counselors. A **pastoral counselor** is a specially trained member of a religious order or ministry who specializes in the treatment of psychological disorders. Often these counselors combine spiritual and practical problem-solving directions. In a sense, shamanistic healing ceremonies (as described in our opening case on Sharon) represent a "pastoral-religious" approach to healing mental disorders—even though they may not resemble mainstream American religious traditions.

clinical psychologist Professional psychologist (with training and degree in psychology) specializing in assessing and treating psychological disorders.

Clinical Psychologists. A **clinical psychologist** has concentrated his or her graduate school training in the assessment and treatment of psychological problems, completed a supervised internship in a clinical setting, and earned a Ph.D. (Doctor of Philosophy degree). These psychologists tend to have a broader background in psychology, assessment, and research than do psychiatrists; however, the day-to-day work of psychologists and psychiatrists may be similar.

psychiatrist Physician (with training and degree in medicine) specializing in treatment of mental and emotional disorders.

Psychiatrists. A **psychiatrist** has completed all medical school training for an M.D. degree and also has some postdoctoral specialty training in dealing with mental and emotional disorders. Psychiatrists' training lies more in the biomedical base of psychological problems, and they are the only therapists who can legally prescribe medications or physically based therapy.

Psychoanalysts. A **psychoanalyst** is a therapist with either an M.D. or Ph.D. degree. Psychoanalysts complete specialized postgraduate training in the

Freudian approach to understanding and treating mental disorders. We will discuss the details of psychoanalytic treatment in a later section when we describe the basic features of the major psychotherapies. Before that discussion, we will review the history of psychological treatment; some forms of treatment for mental problems have been practiced for centuries in different cultures.

Historical and Cultural Context. What kind of treatment might you have received in past centuries if you suffered from psychological problems? If you lived in Europe or the United States, chances are the treatment would not have helped and could even have been harmful. In other cultures, treatment of psychological disorders has usually been seen within a broader perspective that includes religious and social values. This point of view has resulted in kinder treatment of those with aberrant behavior.

Treatment in the Western World. Population increases and migration to big cities in fourteenth-century Western Europe created unemployment, poverty, and social alienation. These conditions led to crime and psychological problems. Special institutions were soon created to warehouse European society's three emerging categories of misfits: the poor, criminals, and the mentally disturbed.

In 1403, a London hospital—St. Mary of Bethlehem—admitted its first patient with psychological problems. For the next 300 years, mental patients of the hospital were chained, tortured, and exhibited to an admission-paying public. Over time, "Bedlam"—a mispronunciation of *Bethlehem*—came to mean *chaos* because of the horrible confusion reigning in the hospital and the dehumanized treatment of patients there (Foucault, 1975).

In fifteenth-century Germany, the mad were assumed to be possessed by the Devil who had deprived them of reason. As the Inquisition's persecutory mania spread throughout Europe, mental disturbances were "cured" by painful death or prosecuted as evidence of witchcraft.

During the late eighteenth century the perception of psychological problems as *mental illness* emerged in Europe. The French physician **Philippe Pinel** wrote in 1801, "The mentally ill, far from being guilty people deserving

The engraving at right depicts the chaotic conditions that existed in the 1730s at Bethlehem.

of punishment, are sick people whose miserable state deserves all the consideration that is due to suffering humanity. One should try with the most simple methods to restore their reason" (Zilboorg & Henry, 1941, pp. 323–24).

In the United States, psychologically disturbed citizens were confined for their own protection and for the safety of the community, but they were given no treatment. However, by the mid-1800s, when psychology as a field of study was gaining some credibility and respectability, "a cult of curability" emerged throughout the country. Eventually, madness came to be viewed as a social problem to be cured through mental hygiene, just as contagious physical diseases were being treated by physical hygiene. This was the perspective of the disease model.

One of the founders of modern psychiatry, German psychiatrist **J. C. Heinroth,** helped provide the conceptual and moral justification for the disease model of mental illness. In 1818, Heinroth wrote that madness was a complete loss of inner freedom or reason depriving those afflicted of any ability to control their lives. Others who "knew best" what was good for the patient would have to be put in charge of care (Szasz, 1979). Initially the state had an interest in confining the mentally ill, to protect them as well as society. However, from Heinroth's time to the present, with the assistance of the mental health profession, this initial interest has been "transformed into a power . . . to treat . . . the mental disorder thought to be the basis of the problem" (White & White, 1981, p. 954).

Heinroth's work heralded a change. One of his former mental patients, **Clifford Beers,** carried on the work of a *mental hygiene movement* in the 1900s. Beers' 1908 book, *A Mind That Found Itself,* helped to make the welfare of the mentally ill a matter of public concern and social action. Eventually, the confinement of the mentally ill assumed a new *rehabilitative* goal. The *asylum* then became the central fixture of this social-political movement. The disturbed were confined to asylums in rural areas, far from the stress of the city, not only for protection but also for treatment (Rothman, 1971). Unfortunately, many of the asylums that were built became overcrowded. Then the humane goal of rehabilitation was replaced with the pragmatic goal of *containing* strange people in remote places.

Philippe Pinel frees the insane.

Curing in Cultural Context. Modern Western views and practices regarding psychological disorders emphasize competition, independence, survival of the fittest, a mastery over nature, the uniqueness of the individual, and personal responsibility for success and failure. Both demonology and the disease model are consistent with modern views in one respect—regarding mental disorder as something that happens *inside* a person, as an outcome of some type of failure.

Many other cultures do not share this view (Triandis, 1990). For example, the African view emphasizes groupness, commonality, cooperation, interdependence, tribal survival, unity with nature, and collective responsibility (Nobles, 1976). Treatment of mentally ill individuals by *removing* them from society is *contrary* to the thinking of many non-European cultures. Among the Navajo and African cultures, for example, healing always takes place in a social context, involving a distressed person's beliefs, family, work, and life environment. The African use of group support in therapy has been expanded into a procedure called "network therapy," where a patient's entire network of relatives, co-workers, and friends becomes involved in the treatment (Lambo, 1978). (See "Cross-cultural Perspective: Universals in Therapy" on the next page.)

In many cultures, the treatment of mental and physical disease is bound up with religion and witchcraft; certain persons are assumed to have special mystical powers to help in the transformation of their distressed fellow beings. Common to all folk healing ceremonies are the important roles of symbols, myths, and ritual (Levi-Strauss, 1963). **Ritual healing** ceremonies infuse special emotional intensity and meaning into the healing process. They heighten patients' suggestibility and sense of importance, and, combined with the use of symbols, they connect the individual sufferer, the shaman, and the society to supernatural forces to be won over in the battle against madness (Devereux, 1981; Wallace, 1959).

Some of these non-Western views have begun to work their way into Western practices. The influence of the social-interactive concept and the focus on the *family context* and *supportive community* are evident in newer therapeutic approaches that emphasize social support networks and family therapy.

ritual healing Ceremonial process of infusing emotional intensity and meaning into treating illness by heightening patients' suggestibility and sense of importance.

SUMMING UP

People enter therapy for help with mental or emotional problems that are causing suffering, dysfunctional behavior, or social problems. Biomedical therapies affect physiological processes; psychological therapies try to change thoughts, feelings, or behaviors. Four major types of psychotherapy are the psychodynamic approach, behavioral therapy, cognitive therapy, and existential-humanist therapies.

The therapeutic process involves four tasks: diagnosing what is wrong; figuring out the source of the problem; making a prognosis about probable outcomes with or without treatment; and carrying out a specific kind of treatment. Various kinds of professionals provide therapy, including counseling psychologists, psychiatric social workers, pastoral counselors, clinical psychologists, psychiatrists, and psychoanalysts.

Historically, conceptions of disease and deviant behavior were influenced by religious, social, and political agendas of different cultures in different eras. Emerging conceptions of the afflicted person as mentally ill led to more humane treatment and hospitalization in mental institutions.

Western psychological views of mental disorder and therapy have been extended to reveal a broader social-religious context. Folk healing typically involves a blend of "magic," myth, and ritual practiced by a healer or shaman, who depends on the patient's total belief in that cultural system of cure.

At times, people will seek help from family members and close friends for their problems. At other times, they will seek help from individuals outside their families who have a reputation for skillfulness in helping people. In different cultures, these helpers can be clinical psychologists, psychiatrists, counselors, native healers, medicine men, herbalists, religious figures, shamans, or social workers. Do people who seek help share common experiences regardless of who provides that help? Various researchers have concluded that there are indeed common experiences called "universals" that characterize the relationship between help-seeker and help-giver (Torrey, 1986; Draguns, 1980, 1990; Ponterotto & Benesch, 1988).

We will discuss six universals here, and we'll use the general term "therapist" for the person with the reputation or role-expectation for offering help.

1. *Therapists apply a name to the problem people have.* When people learn that a problem has a name, they come to believe that others may have experienced the same difficulties and that there may be some solutions.

2. *The qualities of the therapist are important.* The therapist must be seen as caring, competent, sensitive, and able to find solutions to problems. While all therapies are solution-oriented, people in some cultures *expect to be told what to do.* With this expectation, they are less comfortable examining many possibilities and developing *their own* solutions. Researchers in the United States have offered the generalization that people from various culturally diverse groups (Asian Americans, Hispanic Americans) expect some relief from their problems early in therapy. The long, "talk-oriented" therapies favored by some Anglo Americans (as in person-centered therapy) are not as popular with such groups. If people from these culturally diverse groups

do not receive some immediate relief, they will terminate therapy after one or a few sessions (Locke, 1992). When the therapist comes from one cultural background and the help-seeker from another, therapy can be effective if the help-giver can demonstrate cultural sensitivity (Sue, 1988). For example, many African Americans believe that their cultural experiences include a history of rejection due to prejudice and discrimination. If therapists are Anglo Americans, they must demonstrate an understanding about and sensitivity toward this viewpoint (Locke, 1992).

3. *Therapists have to establish their credibility.* This can be done by using the symbols of status that are well-known in a culture. In middle-class American culture, an attractive office and diplomas on the wall can establish the therapist's credibility. In other cultures, such impression management can include ceremonial robes that can be worn only by people who have served a long apprenticeship. In any culture, credibility is aided when therapists benefit from positive "word of mouth." If one person is helped and tells many others, the therapist's positive reputation will spread.

4. *Therapists place the help seeker's problem and their interventions into a framework that will be familiar to the help-seeker.* If the help-seeker believes in spirits, the therapist may introduce an intervention to drive out or to appease the spirits. In some cultures, this intervention involves symbolic cutting of the skin, which draws blood but does not invade the body, so that any evil left by the spirits can be removed. Within a complex culture, such as the United States, there will be vast differences in the framework that the therapist intro-

duces. In many cases, the decision concerning frameworks will be made by the help seeker. If a person thinks that today's problems stem from the childhood of 30 years ago, he or she may seek a psychoanalyst. If a person wants to *change* the actual behaviors that are causing problems (hostile actions toward superiors at work, words or gestures that are ineffective in establishing romantic relationships), he or she may find one of the cognitive or behavior therapies attractive.

5. *Therapists apply a set of techniques that are meant to address the problem and to bring eventual relief.* Again, specific techniques will either be familiar to help-seekers, or the therapist will educate the help-seekers about their importance. There are many specific techniques; mastery of even a limited number of such techniques demands years of study and (or) apprenticeship.

6. *The actual therapy occurs at a specific time and in a special location.* Setting aside a special time and place gives people a chance to deal with their problems in an intense, emotionally charged manner, away from their day-to-day lives. Examples of special places for therapy include well-furnished offices, hospitals, churches, and in tribal villages, huts that are taboo except when used for healing ceremonies.

People seek help from therapists either because they feel overwhelmed by problems they perceive as beyond their control, or because they are so rebellious or deviant that *others* in their culture demand that they seek help. The goal of therapy, no matter where it occurs, is to bring relief to people and to contribute to harmonious relationships within a culture. When therapy is successful, there is typically a better "fit" between the person and his or her life setting and culture.

Psychological Therapies

Psychological techniques of therapy emphasize the application of psychological processes—such as learning, development, and communication—to influence individual experience and well-being. Although some psychotherapists specialize in a particular theory or tradition, most adopt an *eclectic* approach, choosing and applying concepts and strategies from different perspectives. They use a mixture of ideas and techniques borrowed from several approaches, according to what a particular client seems to need. The four perspectives we will review here are the psychodynamic, behavioral, cognitive, and existential-humanistic therapies.

Psychodynamic Therapies

Psychodynamic therapies assume that a patient's problems have been caused by the psychological tension between unconscious impulses toward certain actions and the constraints of the individual's life situation. **Psychoanalytic therapy,** as developed by **Sigmund Freud,** is the premier psychodynamic therapy. It is an intensive and prolonged technique for exploring unconscious motivations and conflicts in neurotic, anxiety-ridden individuals. The major goal of psychoanalysis is "to reveal the Unconscious."

Of central importance to a therapist is understanding the way a patient uses the process of *repression* to handle conflicts. Symptoms are considered to be messages from the unconscious that something is wrong. A psychoanalyst's task is to help a patient bring repressed thoughts to consciousness and to gain *insight* into the relationship between the current symptoms and the repressed conflicts. In this psychodynamic view, therapy works and patients recover when they are "released" from repression established in early childhood (Munroe, 1955). Because a central goal of a therapist is to guide a patient toward discovering insights between present symptoms and past origins, psychodynamic therapy is often called **insight therapy.**

The goals of psychoanalysis are ambitious. They involve not just the elimination of the immediate symptoms of psychopathology but a total personality

psychoanalytic therapy
Psychodynamic therapy developed by Sigmund Freud, involving intensive, prolonged exploration of patients' unconscious motivations and conflicts.

insight therapy Treatment in which therapist guides patient (or client) toward perceiving relationships between present symptoms and past origins.

Sigmund Freud's office at Bergasse No. 19 in Vienna, where he lived and worked for over 40 years. The famous couch is on the right.

reorganization. Because traditional psychoanalysis is an attempt to reconstruct long-standing repressed memories and then work through painful feelings to an effective resolution, it is a therapy that takes a long time (several years at least, with as many as five sessions a week). It also requires introspective patients who are verbally fluent, highly motivated to remain in therapy, and willing and able to bear considerable expense (for example, a typical hourly fee might be about $100).

The Talking Cure. Psychoanalysts use several techniques to bring repressed conflicts to consciousness and to help a patient resolve them (Langs, 1981; Lewis, 1981). These techniques include *free association,* analysis of *resistance, dream analysis,* and analysis of *transference and countertransference.*

Free Association. The principal procedure used in psychoanalysis to probe the unconscious and release repressed material is called **free association.** A patient, sitting comfortably in a chair or lying in a relaxed position on a couch, lets his or her mind wander freely and gives a running account of thoughts, wishes, physical sensations, and mental images as they occur. The patient is encouraged to reveal every thought or feeling, no matter how personal, painful, or seemingly unimportant. For example, a patient might say, "It's nice to relax. I hope I don't fall asleep. I couldn't sleep well last night and I'm really tired. I kept tossing and turning. Remember that song about 'tossing and turning all night'? I hated that song, but I love music. I miss dancing. I wish I had someone to dance with. Sometimes I feel so lonely, it's like a pain inside." One statement may lead to another statement, or the patient's thoughts might seem to ramble, but these free associations are all important clues for the psychoanalyst's investigative work.

Freud maintained that free associations are *predetermined*, not random. The task of an analyst is to track the associations to their source and identify the significant patterns that lie beneath the surface of the words. The patient is encouraged to express strong feelings (usually toward authority figures) that have been repressed for fear of punishment or retaliation. Any such emotional release by this or other processes is termed **catharsis.** This treatment encourages a client to face up to and talk openly about these strong repressed feelings to create a beneficial emotional purging—and healing.

Resistance. At some time during the process of free association, a patient will show **resistance**—an inability or unwillingness to discuss certain ideas, desires, or experiences. Resistance prevents repressed material from returning to consciousness. This material is often related to an individual's sexual and pleasurable feelings, or to hostile, resentful feelings toward parents. Sometimes a patient shows resistance by coming late to therapy or "forgetting" a session altogether. When the repressed material comes out in therapy, a patient may claim that it is unimportant, absurd, irrelevant, or too unpleasant to discuss. The therapist is sensitized to the likelihood that the opposite is true because the patient "protests too much." Whenever a patient shows such resistance, the psychoanalyst pays particular attention to the issues that may have prompted it.

A psychoanalyst thus attaches particular importance to subjects that a patient does *not* wish to discuss. The aim of psychoanalysis is to break down resistance and enable the patient to face these painful ideas, desires, and experiences. Breaking down resistance is a long and difficult process that is essential if the underlying problem is to be brought to consciousness where it can be resolved.

Dream Analysis. Psychoanalysts believe that dreams are an important source of information about a patient's unconscious motivations. When a person is asleep, the superego is presumably less on guard against the unacceptable

free association Principal procedure in psychoanalysis, in which patient provides a running account of thoughts, wishes, physical sensations, and mental images as they occur.

catharsis Process and outcome of expressing strongly felt emotions that are usually inhibited.

resistance Inability or unwillingness of psychoanalytic patient to discuss certain ideas, desires, or experiences.

impulses originating in the id, so a motive that cannot be expressed in waking life may find expression in a dream. Some motives are so unacceptable to the conscious self that they cannot be revealed openly, even in dreams, but must be expressed in disguised or symbolic form.

In analysis, dreams are assumed to have two kinds of content: *manifest* (openly visible) content and *latent* (hidden) content. The manifest content is what we remember upon awakening. Latent content includes the actual motives that are seeking expression but are so painful or unacceptable to us that we do not want to recognize them. Therapists attempt to uncover these hidden motives by using **dream analysis**—a therapeutic technique that examines the content of a person's dreams to discover the underlying or disguised motivations and symbolic meanings of significant life experiences and desires. For example, in one patient's dream, an elaborate dinner attended by familiar guests may really symbolize a family funeral she has recently attended. The analyst assumes that the patient's dream images of food, faces, and feelings all symbolize her unconscious motives and fears about this event and about her family in particular.

Transference and Countertransference. During the course of the intensive therapy of psychoanalysis, a patient usually develops an emotional reaction toward the therapist. Often the therapist is identified with a person who has been at the center of an emotional conflict in the past—most often a parent or a lover. This emotional reaction is called **transference.** *Positive transference* occurs when the feelings attached to the therapist are those of love or admiration. *Negative transference* occurs when the patient's feelings consist of hostility or envy. Often a patient's attitude is *ambivalent,* including a mixture of positive and negative feelings.

An analyst's task in handling transference is a difficult and potentially dangerous one because of the patient's emotional vulnerability; however, it is a crucial part of treatment. A therapist helps a patient to interpret the present transferred feelings by understanding their original source in earlier experiences and attitudes about significant others (Langs, 1981).

Personal feelings are also at work in a therapist's reactions to a patient. **Countertransference** refers to what happens when a therapist comes to like or dislike a patient who is perceived as similar to significant people in the therapist's life. In working through countertransference, a therapist may discover some unconscious dynamics of his or her own. Because of the emotional intensity of this type of therapeutic relationship and the vulnerability of the patient, therapists must guard against crossing the boundary between professional caring and personal involvement with their patients. Professional ethics do not allow therapists to become involved with their patients—although some therapists *have* violated the therapist-client relationship.

Post-Freudian Therapies. Some of Freud's followers have retained many of his basic ideas but modified certain of his principles and practices. Classical Freudian psychoanalysis emphasizes the importance of three factors: the Unconscious in motivation and conflict; the power of early childhood development; and the dynamics within one's personality. In contrast, post-Freudian theories generally have different emphases, including:

- The importance of the individual's *current* social environment
- The *ongoing influence* of life experiences beyond childhood
- The role of social and interpersonal relationships
- The significance of one's conscious *self-concept*

To get the flavor of more contemporary psychodynamic approaches of the neo-Freudians, here we will look at the work of Harry Stack Sullivan and Karen Horney. (For a look at the other members of the Freudian and post-Freudian circle, see Ruitenbeek's 1973 book, *The First Freudians.*)

dream analysis Psychoanalytic interpretation of dreams, used to achieve insight into one's unconscious motives or conflict.

transference In psychoanalysis, process in which patient attaches to therapist feelings formerly held toward another significant person associated with emotional conflict.

countertransference In psychoanalysis, process in which a therapist comes to like or dislike a patient because the patient is perceived as similar to significant people in the therapist's life.

Sullivan's Self-System. **Harry Stack Sullivan** (1953) emphasized the social dimension of a patient's life and its role in creating mental problems. He felt that Freudian theory and therapy did not recognize the importance of social relationships or a patient's needs for acceptance, respect, and love. Mental disorders, he insisted, involve not only traumatic intrapsychic processes but troubled interpersonal relationships and even strong societal pressures. A young child needs to feel secure and to be treated by others with caring and tenderness. Anxiety and other mental ills arise out of insecurities in relationships with parents and significant others. In Sullivan's view, the individual creates a self-system to hold anxiety down to a tolerable level. This self-system is derived from a child's interpersonal experiences and is organized around conceptions of the self as "good," "bad," and unacceptably "other."

Therapy based on Sullivan's interpersonal view involves observing a *patient's feelings* about the *therapist's attitudes*. The therapeutic interview is seen as a social setting in which each party's feelings and attitudes are influenced by the other's. Above all, the therapeutic situation, for Sullivan, was one where the therapist learned and taught lovingly (Wallach & Wallach, 1983).

Horney's Relationship Patterns. **Karen Horney** (pronounced HORN-eye) expanded the boundaries of Freudian theory in many ways (see Horney, 1937; 1945; 1950). She stressed the importance of environmental and cultural contexts in which neurotic behavior is expressed. Rather than viewing personality as determined solely by early childhood experiences and instincts, Horney took a more flexible view. She believed that personality involved rational coping and continual development to deal with current fears and impulses.

One of Horney's contributions to therapy was her emphasis on patterns of interpersonal relationships. Horney pointed out three *neurotic patterns* in close relationships: approaching others, attacking others, and avoiding others. Each neurotic pattern is based on a maladaptive view of the self and leads to repetitive and unsatisfying choices and behaviors. "Approachers" seek love from others to feel complete and secure; they may end up behaving passively and feeling victimized. "Attackers" earn power and respect by competing successfully against others, but risk being feared and ending up "lonely at the top." "Avoiders" withdraw from others to protect themselves from real or imagined hurt and rejection, but can end up closing themselves off from intimacy and support. By understanding these unhealthy patterns—and unraveling the neurotic self-concepts that underlie them—patients can achieve the insights necessary to forge new habits and constructive relationships.

Although psychoanalytic therapy and Freud's theories have been widely criticized (Fisher & Greenberg, 1985), there are still many enthusiastic supporters, especially in many Western European countries and in large urban centers in the United States. But the pragmatics of expense and limits on available time have led to more short-term psychodynamic therapies and approaches that focus on changing symptoms, not the whole personality.

Behavioral Therapies

While psychodynamic therapies focus on presumed inner causes, behavior therapies focus on observable outer behaviors. Behavior therapies apply the principles of conditioning and reinforcement to modify undesirable behavior patterns associated with mental disorders. This orientation rejects the medical model along with all assumptions about "patients" suffering from mental "illness" that is *cured* by therapy.

Behavioral therapists argue that abnormal behaviors are acquired in the same way as normal behaviors—through a learning process that follows the basic principles of conditioning and learning. These therapists assert that all pathological behavior, except where there is established organic causation, can be best understood and modified by focusing on the behavior itself rather than by attempting to alter any underlying pathology.

Karen Horney (1885–1952)

behavior modification In behavioral psychotherapy, approach that applies operant conditioning and classical conditioning to change client's behavior.

Behavior modification is defined as "the attempt to apply learning and other experimentally derived psychological principles to problem behavior" (Bootzin, 1975). The terms *behavioral therapy* and *behavior modification* are often used interchangeably. Both refer to the systematic use of principles of learning to increase the frequency of desired behaviors and/or decrease the frequency of problem behaviors. Behavioral therapy is used to treat an extensive range of deviant behaviors and personal problems, including fears, compulsions, depression, addictions, aggression, and delinquent behaviors. In general, behavioral therapy works best with specific rather than general types of personal problems. For example, it is more effective in treating a phobia than an inadequate personality.

Behavioral therapies are based on classical conditioning, operant conditioning, or a combination of the two. The development of irrational fears and other undesirable *emotional* reactions is assumed to follow the paradigm of classical conditioning. Therapy to change these negative responses uses principles of **counterconditioning,** substituting a new response for the inadequate one. In **contingency management,** behavior is changed by modifying its consequences. In this way, operant conditioning principles are used to accomplish the therapeutic task of reinforcing desired actions or decreasing undesired habits. For example, a student who usually puts off studying for a test by pursuing various distractions can be trained and rewarded for concentrating on deadlines and organizing his study materials. Special adaptations also have been developed for *social learning,* in which clients learn from looking at the behavior of others. In this section, we will first outline how classical conditioning principles have been adapted for behavioral therapies and next how operant conditioning is being applied.

counterconditioning Therapeutic technique which uses conditioning to substitute a new response for an inadequate one.

contingency management General treatment strategy for changing behavior by changing its consequences.

Counterconditioning. Why does someone become anxious when faced with a harmless stimulus, such as a fly, a nonpoisonous snake, an open space, or a social contact? Is the anxiety due to simple conditioning principles we reviewed earlier? From our discussion of classical conditioning, we know that *any* neutral stimulus may acquire the power to elicit strong condition reactions on the basis of prior association with an uncondition stimulus. However, not everyone who is exposed to situations that are alarming, dangerous, or traumatic develops long-lasting conditioned fears that become *phobias* that lead to avoidance of those situations. In fact, it is surprising that relatively few people do develop such fears.

Strong emotional reactions that disrupt a person's life "for no good reason" are often conditioned responses that the person does not recognize as having been learned previously. To weaken the strength of negative learned associations, behavior therapists use the techniques of systematic desensitization, implosion, and aversive learning.

Systematic Desensitization. The nervous system cannot be relaxed and agitated or anxious at the same time because different incompatible processes can't be activated simultaneously. This simple notion was central to a *theory of reciprocal inhibition* developed by South African psychiatrist **Joseph Wolpe** (1958, 1973) who used it to treat fears and phobias. He taught his patients to *relax* their muscles, and then to *imagine* visually their feared situation. They did so in gradual steps that moved from initially remote associations to direct images of it. Psychologically confronting the feared stimulus while being relaxed and doing so in a *graduated* sequence is the therapeutic technique known as **systematic desensitization.**

systematic desensitization Behavioral therapy technique in which client learns to relax in order to prevent anxiety arousal.

Desensitization therapy involves three major steps. The client identifies the stimuli that provoke anxiety and arranges them in a *hierarchy* ranked from weakest to strongest. For example, a student suffering from severe test anxiety constructed the hierarchy in **Table 14.1** on p. 548. Note that she rated immediate anticipation of an examination as more stressful than taking the exam

Table 14.1 Hierarchy of Anxiety-producing Stimuli for a Test-anxious College Student

1. On the way to the university on the day of an examination.	(Most)
2. In the process of answering an examination paper.	
3. Before the unopened doors of the examination room.	
4. Awaiting the distribution of examination papers.	
5. The examination paper face down.	
6. The night before an examination.	
7. One day before an examination.	
8. Two days before an examination.	
9. Three days before an examination.	
10. Four days before an examination.	
11. Five days before an examination.	
12. A week before an examination.	
13. Two weeks before an examination.	
14. A month before an examination.	(Least)

itself. Next, the client is trained in a system of progressive deep-muscle relaxation. Relaxation training requires several sessions in which the client learns to distinguish between sensations of tension and relaxation and to let go of tension to achieve a state of physical and mental relaxation. Finally, the actual process of desensitization begins: The relaxed client vividly imagines the *weakest* anxiety stimulus on the list. If the stimulus can be visualized without discomfort, the client goes on to the next stronger one. After a number of sessions, the client can imagine the most distressing situations on the list without anxiety—even situations that she could not face originally (Lang & Lazovik, 1963). A number of evaluation studies have shown that this behavior therapy works remarkably well with most phobic patients and better than any other form of therapy (Smith & Glass, 1977). Desensitization has also been successfully applied to a diversity of human problems, including such generalized fears as stage fright, impotence, and frigidity (Kazdin & Wilcoxin, 1976).

Implosion and Flooding. **Implosion therapy** uses an approach that is the opposite of systematic desensitization. At the start of implosion therapy, a client is exposed to the most frightening stimuli at the top of the anxiety hierarchy but in a safe setting. The idea behind this procedure is that the client is not allowed to deny, avoid, or otherwise escape from the anxiety-arousing stimulus situations. He must discover that contact with the stimulus does not actually have the anticipated negative effects (Stampfl & Levis, 1967).

To expose the client to contact with the feared stimulus, the therapist *describes* an extremely frightening situation relating to the client's fear, such as snakes crawling all over his body. The therapist then urges the client to *imagine* it fully, experiencing it through all the senses as intensely as possible. Such imagining is assumed to cause an explosion of panic. Because this explosion is an inner one, the process is called *implosion;* hence the term *implosion therapy.* As the situation happens again and again, the stimulus loses its power to elicit anxiety. When anxiety no longer occurs, the maladaptive behavior previously used to avoid it disappears.

Flooding is similar to implosion except that it places clients, with their permission, in the actual phobic situation. Whereas implosion requires imagining the dreaded stimulus, the client experiencing flooding makes contact with the real thing. A claustrophobic might sit in a dark closet, or a child with a fear of water get into a pool. A therapist might choose to "work up to" flooding by first stimulating the imagination. For example, the phobic client may be required to listen to a tape that describes the most terrifying version of her phobic fear in great detail for an hour or two. Once her terror subsides, the client is then taken to the feared situation, which, of course, is not nearly as frightening as she just imagined. Flooding is more effective than systematic desensitization in the treatment of behavior problems such as agoraphobia, and treatment gains are shown to be enduring for most clients (Emmelkamp & Kuipers, 1979).

Aversion Therapy. The forms of exposure therapy just discussed help clients deal directly with stimuli that are not really harmful. What can be done to help those who are *attracted* to stimuli that *are* harmful or illegal? Drug addiction, sexual perversions, and uncontrollable violence are human problems in which deviant behavior is elicited by tempting stimuli. **Aversion therapy** uses counterconditioning procedures of aversive learning to pair these stimuli with strong noxious stimuli (such as electric shocks or nausea-producing drugs). In time, through conditioning, the same negative reactions are elicited by the conditional tempting stimuli, and the person develops an aversion for them that replaces her former desire.

For example, the drug Antabuse is sometimes prescribed for alcoholics who wish to control their drinking. The drug has no side effects—unless the patient drinks even a small amount of alcohol; then he or she becomes severely nauseous. By anticipating such aversive consequences, the patient can significantly strengthen her resolve *not* to take a drink by making the single daily decision to take the prescribed Antabuse.

In the extreme, aversion therapy resembles torture, so why would anyone submit voluntarily to it? Usually people do so only because they realize that the long-term consequences of continuing their behavior will destroy their health or ruin their careers or family lives. They may also be coerced to do so by institutional pressures, as in some prison treatment programs. Many critics are concerned that the painful procedures in aversion therapy give too much power to the therapist, can be more punitive than therapeutic, and are most likely to be used in situations where people have the least freedom of choice

implosion therapy Behavioral therapy technique in which a client is exposed to the most anxiety-provoking stimuli in order to extinguish anxiety associated with the class of stimuli.

flooding Therapy for phobias in which clients agree to be exposed to stimuli they consider most frightening, in order to force them to test reality.

aversion therapy Behavioral therapy technique in which individuals are presented with a pairing of the attractive stimuli with unpleasant stimuli in order to condition a negative reaction.

In Stanley Kubrick's film *A Clockwork Orange*, the subject, a violent criminal, is trained to feel sick at the sights and sounds of violence. Here his eyes are forced open so he must view scenes like his own past crimes.

about what is done to them. The movie *A Clockwork Orange* (1971), based on Anthony Burgess's novel (1962), depicted aversion therapy as an extreme form of mind control in a police state. In recent years, use of aversion therapy in institutional rehabilitation programs has become regulated by state laws and ethical guidelines for clinical treatment. The hope is that, under these restrictions, it will be a therapy of choice rather than coercion.

Contingency Management. The operant conditioning approach of **B. F. Skinner** to developing desirable behavior is simple: Find the reinforcer that will maintain a desired response, apply that reinforcer (contingent upon the appropriate response), and evaluate its effectiveness. If it works, continue using it; if it doesn't, search for other reinforcers and then apply those. The two major techniques of contingency management in behavior therapy are *positive reinforcement strategies* and specific *extinction strategies.*

Positive Reinforcement Strategies. When a response is followed immediately by a reward, the response will tend to be repeated and will increase in frequency over time. This central principle of operant learning becomes a therapeutic strategy when used to modify the frequency of a desirable response in place of an undesirable one. The application of positive reinforcement procedures to the behavior problems of children with psychiatric disorders has met with dramatic success. For example, combative children can learn to cooperate with others when reinforced with privileges, and victims of abuse can be encouraged to talk about their experiences if they are rewarded with praise, sympathy, and acceptance.

Extinction Strategies. Why do people continue to do something that causes pain and distress when they are capable of doing otherwise? The answer is that many forms of behavior have multiple consequences—some negative and some positive. Often, subtle positive reinforcements keep a behavior going despite its obvious negative consequences. Just as positive reinforcement can increase the incidence of a behavior, *lack* of desirable consequences can decrease its incidence. By removing the rewards—or removing the individual from a rewarding situation when he or she is manifesting the unwanted behavior—the therapist can weaken and ultimately extinguish the problem behavior. For example, a child who no longer receives attention when he throws a tantrum, or who is placed in a "time-out" room when he misbehaves, will eventually cease his ineffective displays. The "trick" of extinction strategies is to correctly identify the reinforcers for the problem behavior, and remove those quickly and consistently.

Extinction is useful in therapy when dysfunctional behaviors have been maintained by unrecognized reinforcing circumstances. Those reinforcers can be identified through a careful situational analysis and then a program can be arranged to withhold them in the presence of the undesirable response. When this approach is possible, and everyone in the situation who might inadvertently reinforce the person's behavior cooperates, extinction procedures work to diminish the frequency of the behavior and eventually to eliminate the behavior completely.

For example, a woman complains that her husband expresses anger violently, by threatening to strike her or the children, or by noisily breaking things. After each episode he apologizes and promises to express himself calmly next time, but his destructive behavior persists. With the help of a therapist, the couple discover that although the wife hates violent behavior, she only listens to her husband when he threatens or destroys. She has inadvertently reinforced his outbursts with her attention. By leaving the situation each time a new incident begins, she takes away his "audience," and his exaggerated rage is extinguished. He learns to express himself calmly before he becomes angry, and she reinforces this preferred behavior by immediately paying attention to him and validating his concerns.

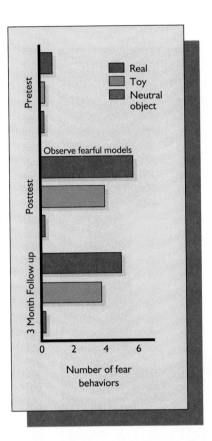

Figure 14.1 Fear Reactions in Monkeys After young laboratory-raised monkeys observe unfamiliar adult monkeys showing a strong fear of snakes, they are vicariously conditioned to fear snakes with an intensity that persists over time.

social-learning therapy Treatment system based on theory that behavior is influenced by observation and imitation of others.

participant modeling Therapeutic technique in which a therapist demonstrates, and encourages client to imitate, desired behavior.

cognitive therapy Psychotherapeutic approach to changing problem feelings and behaviors by changing how clients perceive or think about significant experiences.

Social Learning Therapy. Social learning theorists point out that humans learn—for better or worse—by observing the behavior of other people. **Social learning therapy** is designed to modify problematic behavior patterns by arranging conditions in which the client will observe models being reinforced for the desired response. This vicarious learning process has been of special value in overcoming phobias and building social skills.

When discussing phobias, we noted that one way such fears could be learned was through vicarious conditioning—through the transmission of fear displayed by others, such as from mother to child. An interesting series of studies with monkeys illustrates this imitation of modeled behavior.

In one study, young monkeys were reared in the laboratory where they never saw a snake. These monkeys observed their parents who had been raised in the wild and who reacted fearfully to real snakes and toy snakes. The young monkeys promptly showed a strong fear of snakes. The more disturbed the parents were at the sight of the snakes, the greater the fear in their offspring (Mineka et al., 1984). In a follow-up study, young, laboratory-raised rhesus monkeys observed the fearful reactions of adult monkeys who were strangers to them. **Figure 14.1** shows the young monkeys revealed little fear in the initial pretest; however after observing models that reacted fearfully, they did also, both to the real and toy snakes. This fear persisted but was less strong and more variable than that of the other young monkeys who had observed their own parents' fearful reactions (Cook et al., 1985).

Many new responses, especially complex ones, can be acquired more readily if a person can observe and imitate another person performing the desired behavior and be reinforced for doing so. If fear of snakes can be learned by observing others with fearful reactions, then it should be possible for people with snake phobias to unlearn them through imitation of models. In treating a phobia of snakes, a therapist will first demonstrate fearless behavior, such as approaching a caged snake, then touching the snake, and so on. The client is urged and helped to imitate each modeled behavior. At no time is the client forced to perform any behavior. Resistance at any level is overcome by having the client return to a previously successful, less threatening approach behavior.

The power of this **participant modeling** can be seen in research comparing the participant modeling technique with symbolic modeling, desensitization, and a control condition (see **Figure 14.2** on the next page). In *symbolic modeling therapy,* subjects who had been trained in relaxation techniques watched a film in which several models fearlessly handled snakes; the subjects could stop the film and relax themselves whenever a scene made them feel anxious. In the control condition, no therapeutic intervention was used. Participant modeling was clearly the most successful of these techniques. Snake phobia was eliminated in 11 of the 12 subjects in the participant modeling group (Bandura, 1970).

Social learning therapy extends the lessons of the "life laboratory"—the influences that shape all our behaviors as we seek to reach our goals, please others, and deal well with the circumstances of our lives. "In Focus: Learning Social Skills" (p. 553) notes that such therapy can also redo or enhance mislearned lessons about how to interact successfully with other people.

Before turning to cognitive therapies, take a few minutes to review the major differences between the two dominant psychotherapies outlined thus far—the psychoanalytic and the behavioral—as summarized in **Table 14.2** on p. 554.

Cognitive Therapies

Cognitive therapy attempts to change problem feelings and behaviors by changing the way a client *thinks* about significant life experiences. The underlying assumption of such therapy is that abnormal behavior patterns and emotional distress start with problems in *what* we think (cognitive content) and *how* we think (cognitive process). As cognitive psychology has become more

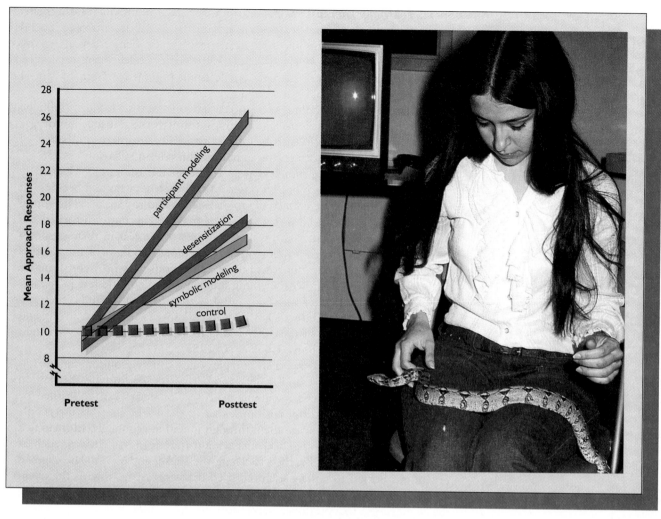

Figure 14.2 Participant Modeling Therapy

The subject shown in the photo first watched a model make a graduated series of snake-approach responses and then repeated them herself. She eventually was able to pick up the snake and let it crawl about on her. The graph compares the number of approach responses subjects made before and after receiving participant modeling therapy (most effective) with the behavior of those exposed to two other therapeutic techniques and a control group.

prominent in all areas of psychology, therapies based on cognitive principles have proliferated. These therapies focus on different types of cognitive processes and different methods of cognitive restructuring. The two major forms of cognitive therapy involve cognitive behavior modification and alteration of false belief systems.

Cognitive Behavior Modification. We are what we tell ourselves we can be, and we are guided by what we believe we ought to do. These assumptions initiate the process of **cognitive behavior modification.** This therapeutic approach combines the cognitive emphasis on thoughts and attitudes with the behaviorist emphasis on reinforcement to modify performance. Unacceptable behavior patterns are modified by changing a person's negative *self-statements* into constructive coping statements.

In this therapeutic approach, the therapist and client must discover the way the client thinks about and expresses the problem for which therapy is sought. Once both therapist and client understand the kind of thinking that is leading to unproductive behaviors, they can develop new self-statements that

cognitive behavior modification
Therapeutic technique that combines emphasis on thoughts and attitudes with strategies for changing performance by altering reinforcement contingencies.

LEARNING SOCIAL SKILLS

Many difficulties arise for someone with a mental disorder, or even just a person with an everyday problem, if he or she is socially inhibited, inept, or unassertive. A major therapeutic innovation encouraged by social learning therapists involves training people with inadequate social skills to be more effective (Hersen & Bellack, 1976).

Identifying Social Skills

Social skills are sets of responses that enable people to effectively achieve their social goals when approaching or interacting with others. These skills include knowing *what* to say and do (content) in given situations, in order to elicit a desired response (consequences), *how* to say and do it (style), and *when* to say and do it (timing). One of the most common social skill problems is lack of assertiveness—inability to state one's own thoughts or wishes in a clear, direct, non-aggressive manner (Bower & Bower, 1991).

To help people overcome such a problem, many social learning therapists recommend **behavioral rehearsal**—visualizing how one should behave in a given situation and the desired positive consequences. Rehearsal can be used to establish and strengthen any basic skill, from personal hygiene to work habits to social interactions. Behavioral rehearsal procedures are being widely used in social skills training programs with many different populations (Yates, 1985).

Isolated Children

Adult pathology has often been preceded by deficits in social skills in childhood (Oden & Asher, 1977). A considerable amount of research and therapy is currently directed at building competence in shy and withdrawn disturbed children (Conger & Keane, 1981; Zimbardo & Radl, 1981).

One study demonstrated that preschool-age children diagnosed as *social isolates* could be helped to become sociable in a short training period (Furman et al., 1979). Twenty-four subjects were randomly assigned to one of three play conditions: with a same-age peer, with a peer 1 to 1½ years younger, or with no partner (control condition). The pairs were brought together for ten play sessions, each only 20 minutes long, over a period of about a month. Their classroom behavior before and after this treatment was recorded, and it revealed that the intervention had a strong effect. The opportunity to play with a *younger* playmate doubled the frequency with which the former social isolates interacted later on with other classmates—bringing them up to the average level of the other children.

Playing with a *same-age* peer also increased children's sociability, but not nearly so much. The researchers concluded that the one-on-one play situation had offered the shy children safe opportunities to be socially assertive. They were allowed to practice leadership skills that were likely to be approved by the nonthreatening, younger playmates (Furman et al., 1979).

In another study (Matson et al., 1980), social skills training with a group of hospitalized emotionally disturbed children changed both verbal and nonverbal components of their behavior in social settings. The children were taught to give appropriate verbal responses in various social situations (giving help or compliments, making requests). They were also taught to display appropriate affect (for example, to smile while giving a compliment) and to make eye contact and use proper body posture (face the person being talked to). These improved social skills were generalized to "untreated" situations outside of training. The children also put them into practice on their own when on the ward. These positive effects continued even months later.

Social Skills in Everyday Life

Even people educated in psychology sometimes forget that those who make a poor social impression have probably learned their maladaptive behaviors—or at least have not yet learned effective alternative ways to act with others. When others make a "bad impression" on us, we are well advised to consider whether that bad impression might be due to poor social skills. It might be worthwhile to take time to encourage and help an acquaintance to interact more successfully. The other individual's poor social skills don't have to prevent us from befriending a good person.

behavioral rehearsal   Procedures used to establish and strengthen basic skills by requiring client to mentally practice a desirable sequence of action.

are constructive and minimize the use of self-defeating ones (Meichenbaum, 1977). For example, they might substitute the negative self-statement "I was so boring at that party that I'll never get invited back" with constructive criticism: "Next time, to be more interesting, I will plan some effective opening lines, practice telling a good joke, and respond to other people's stories." Instead of dwelling on negatives in past situations that are unchangeable and part of past history, the client is taught to focus on positives in the future that can be realized.

Building *expectations of being effective* increases the likelihood of behaving effectively. It is through setting attainable goals, developing realistic strategies

Table 14.2 Comparison of Psychoanalytic and Behavioristic Approaches to Psychotherapy

ISSUE	PSYCHOANALYSIS	BEHAVIOR THERAPY
Basic human nature	Biological instincts, primarily sexual and aggressive, press for immediate release, bringing people into conflict with social reality.	Similar to other animals, people are born only with the capacity for learning, which follows similar principles in all species.
Normal human development	Growth occurs through resolution of conflicts during successive stages. Through identification and internalization, mature ego controls and character structures emerge.	Adaptive behaviors are learned through reinforcement and imitation.
Nature of psychopathology	Pathology reflects inadequate conflict resolutions and fixations in earlier development, which leave overly strong impulses and/or weak controls. Symptoms are defensive responses to anxiety.	Problematic behavior derives from faulty learning of maladaptive behaviors. The *symptom* is the problem; there is no *underlying disease*.
Goal of therapy	Psychosexual maturity, strengthened ego functions, and reduced control by unconscious and repressed impulses are attained.	Symptomatic behavior is eliminated and replaced with adaptive behaviors.
Psychological realm emphasized	Motives, feelings, fantasies, and cognitions are experienced.	Therapy involves behavior and observable feelings and actions.
Time orientation	The orientation is discovering and interpreting past conflicts and repressed feelings in light of the present.	There is little or no concern with early history or etiology. Present behavior is examined and treated.
Role of unconscious material	This is primary in classical psychoanalysis and somewhat less emphasized by neo-Freudians.	There is no concern with unconscious processes or with subjective experience even in the conscious realm.
Role of insight	Insight is central; it emerges in "corrective emotional experiences."	Insight is irrelevant and/or unnecessary.
Role of therapist	The therapist functions as a *detective*, searching basic root conflicts and resistances; detached and neutral, to facilitate transference reactions.	The therapist functions as a *trainer*, helping patients unlearn old behaviors and/or learn new ones. Control of reinforcement is important; interpersonal relationship is minor.

for attaining them, and evaluating feedback realistically that people develop a sense of mastery and *self-efficacy* (Bandura, 1986). **Figure 14.3** outlines the four major sources of efficacy expectations and the specific means by which each of them develops. For example, different types of modeling influence different efficacy sources, just as different types of desensitization do.

Changing False Beliefs. Some cognitive behavior therapists argue that many psychological problems arise because of the way we think about ourselves in relation to other people and the events we face. Faulty thinking can be based on three kinds of unhealthy cognitive elements.

1. *Unreasonable attitudes.* Problems are caused by irrational or extreme attitudes: "Being accurate is the only important trait for a student to have," or "To attract a romantic partner, I must be physically perfect and totally unselfish."
2. *False premises.* Some self-statements are based on false premises: "If I do everything people want me to, then I'll be popular," "If I never complain and always do as they ask, my employers will surely promote me," or "If I refuse to have sex with my boyfriend, he'll stop loving me and I'll never find anyone else."
3. *Rigid rules.* These rules put behavior on "automatic pilot," so that prior patterns are repeated even when they have not worked. Examples of such statements include: "I must obey authorities" and "Being honest always hurts other people's feelings."

Do any of these examples have the ring of familiarity for you? It is believed that emotional distress is caused by misunderstandings and by the failure to distinguish between current reality and one's imagination (or expectations). A cognitive therapist induces a patient to correct faulty patterns of thinking by applying more effective problem-solving techniques. She might remind a client that giving in to a boyfriend's demands just so she can "keep him" is really dishonest and manipulative—and carries no guarantee that the relationship will last. When the client examines her own beliefs and assumptions, such thoughts become less automatic and powerful, and she can begin to reconstruct a more rational, effective view of the world.

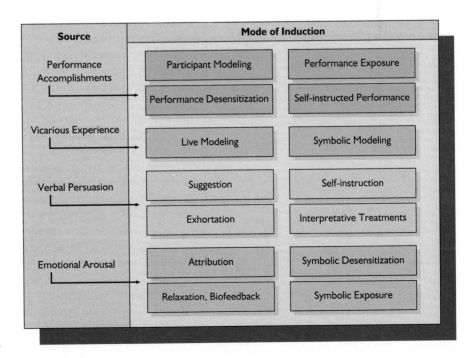

Figure 14.3 Efficacy Expectations According to Bandura (1989), each of the four major sources of efficacy information that an individual can utilize has a specific mode of treatment that operates to induce it.

Cognitive Therapy for Depression. **Aaron Beck** has successfully pioneered the application of cognitive therapy to the problem of *depression*. Beck states the formula for treatment in simple form: "The therapist helps the patient to identify his warped thinking and to learn more realistic ways to formulate his experiences" (1976, p. 20). For example, depressed individuals may be instructed to write down negative thoughts about themselves, figure out why these self-criticisms are unjustified, and come up with more realistic (and less destructive) self-cognitions.

Beck believes that depression is maintained because depressed patients are unaware of the negative automatic thoughts that they repeat to themselves, such as "I will never be as good as my brother"; "Nobody would like me if they really knew me"; and "I'm not smart enough to make it in this competitive school."

Given the insidious nature of these unhealthy thinking habits, a cognitive therapist relies on specific tactics to change the cognitive foundation that supports the depression. These tactics include the following:

- Evaluating the evidence the patient has for and against these automatic thoughts
- Reattributing blame to situational factors rather than to the patient's incompetence
- Openly discussing alternative solutions to the problem
- Challenging the client's basic assumptions. (Beck et al., 1979)

This therapy is similar to behavior therapies in that it centers on the present state of the client. Regardless of how problem thinking got to be so firmly established, the cognitive behavior therapist focuses on the client's current thinking, and how best to realign it so that it is more realistic and healthy.

One of the worst side-effects of being depressed is having to live with all the negative feelings and lethargy associated with depression. Becoming obsessed with thoughts about one's negative mood cues memories of all the bad times in life, which further worsens the depressive feelings. By filtering all input through the dark lens of depression, depressed people see criticism where there is none and hear sarcasm when they listen to praise—further "reasons" for being depressed (Diamond, 1989). Therapy can direct the client so that he doesn't become further depressed about depression itself (Teasdale, 1985).

Rational-Emotive Therapy. One of the earliest forms of cognitive therapy was the **rational-emotive therapy** (RET) developed by **Albert Ellis** (1962, 1977). RET is a comprehensive system of personality change based on transforming irrational beliefs that cause undesirable emotional reactions, such as severe anxiety. Clients may have core values *demanding* that they succeed and be approved, *insisting* that they be treated fairly, and *dictating* that the universe be more pleasant. A therapist teaches clients how to recognize the "shoulds," "oughts," and "musts" that control their actions and prevent them from choosing the lives they want.

A therapist attempts to break through a client's closed-mindedness by showing that an emotional reaction that follows some event is really the effect of unrecognized beliefs about the event. For example, behaving in a possessive and clingy way toward a romantic partner when that partner seems less interested or distracted may be an emotional overreaction, triggered by an irrational fear of abandonment. Signs that the other person is pulling away are unreasonably interpreted to mean, "My partner will leave me if I don't take emergency action." Experiencing a real breakup may prompt the irrational thought that "Without this person to love me, I'll have no one in my life at all!" In RET, these beliefs are openly disputed through rational confrontation and examination of alternative reasons for the event. For example, a distracted partner may have worries about school, work, or family concerns that have

rational-emotive therapy (RET)
System of personality change developed by Albert Ellis, based on changing irrational beliefs that cause problematic emotional reactions such as anxiety.

nothing to do with the relationship. Such cognitive techniques are followed by a variety of others—those used in behavior modification, humor, and role-playing to replace dogmatic, irrational thinking with rational, situationally appropriate ideas.

Rational-emotive therapy aims to increase an individual's sense of self-worth and the potential to be self-actualized by getting rid of the faulty belief system that blocks personal growth. As such, it shares much with humanistic therapies, which we consider next.

Existential-Humanistic Therapies

The primary symptoms for which many college students seek therapy include general dissatisfaction, feelings of alienation, and failure to achieve all they feel they should. Problems in everyday living, the lack of meaningful human relationships, and the absence of significant goals to strive for are common *existential crises*. These critical life dilemmas focus on one's very existence, according to proponents of humanism and existentialism. These orientations on human nature have been combined to form a general type of therapy addressing the basic problems of existence common to all human beings.

The *humanistic movement* has been called a "third force in psychology" because it grew out of a reaction to the two dominant forces that held a pessimistic view of human nature: early psychoanalytic theory and the mechanistic view offered by early radical behaviorism. When the humanistic movement was forming in the United States, similar viewpoints had already gained acceptance in Europe; these viewpoints came to be known collectively as *existentialism*. One of the first American therapists to embrace existentialism was **Rollo May** (1950; 1969; 1972). May's popular books and therapy are designed to combat feelings of emptiness, cynicism, and anomie (social alienation), by emphasizing basic human values, such as love, creativity, and free will.

At the core of both humanistic and existential therapies is the concept of a *whole person* who engages in the continual process of changing and of becoming. Despite the restrictions of environment and heredity, we always remain free to choose what we will become by creating our own values and committing ourselves to them through our decisions. Along with this *freedom to choose*, however, comes the *burden of responsibility*. Since we are never fully aware of all the implications of our actions, we experience anxiety and despair. We also suffer from guilt over lost opportunities to achieve our full potential.

Existential and humanistic psychotherapies attempt to help clients define their own freedom, value their experiencing selves and the richness of the present moment, cultivate their individuality, and discover ways of realizing their fullest potential.

Person-Centered Therapy. As developed by **Carl Rogers** (1951; 1977), the primary goal of **person-centered therapy** is to promote the healthy psychological growth of the individual. This approach begins with the assumption that all people share the basic tendency to self-actualize; that is, to realize one's potential. Healthy development is hindered by faulty learning patterns in which a person accepts the evaluation of others in place of those provided by his or her own mind and body. A conflict between one's naturally positive self-self-image and negative external criticisms creates anxiety and unhappiness.

The task of Rogerian therapy is to create an environment that allows a client to learn how to behave in order to achieve self-enhancement and self-actualization. People are assumed to be basically good. The therapist's task is mainly to help remove barriers that limit the expression of this natural positive tendency and help the client clarify and accept his or her own feelings. This is accomplished within an atmosphere of *unconditional positive regard*—nonjudgmental acceptance and respect for the client, with no strings attached and no performance evaluations. The therapist allows his or her own feelings and

person-centered therapy
Humanistic approach to treatment developed by Carl Rogers, emphasizing individuals' tendency for healthy psychological growth through self-actualization.

Carl Rogers (1902–1987)

thoughts to be transparent to the client. In addition to maintaining this *genuineness*, the therapist tries to experience the client's feelings. Such total empathy requires that the therapist care for the client as a worthy, competent individual—not to be judged or evaluated but to be assisted in discovering his or her individuality (Meador & Rogers, 1979). Unlike practitioners of other therapies who interpret, give answers, or instruct, the client-centered therapist is a supportive listener who reflects and, at times, restates the client's evaluative statements and feelings. Person-centered therapy strives to be *nondirective* by having the therapist merely facilitate the patient's search for self-awareness and self-acceptance and never direct it.

Rogers believes that individuals have the potential to lead themselves back to psychological health once they are freed to relate to others openly and to accept themselves. This optimistic view and the humane relationship between therapist-as-caring-expert and client-as-person has influenced many practitioners (Smith, 1982).

Gestalt therapy Psychological treatment emphasizing the union of mind and body to make the person whole.

Gestalt Therapy. **Gestalt therapy** focuses on ways to unite mind and body to make a person whole (recall the Gestalt school of perception described in Chapter 5). Its goal of self-awareness is reached by helping participants express pent-up feelings in a group and to recognize unfinished business from past conflicts that is carried into new relationships and must be finished for growth to proceed. **Fritz Perls** (1969), the originator of Gestalt therapy, asked participants to act out fantasies concerning conflicts and strong feelings and also to recreate their dreams, which were seen as repressed parts of personality.

In Gestalt therapy workshops, therapists borrow from Zen teachings a focus on immediate experience, so that the client is aware of emerging feelings, attitudes, and actions. Like some Eastern philosophies, Gestalt therapy uses paradox to instruct: "Change is possible only when we accept who we are at the moment, and awareness is itself the cure" (Thompson, 1988).

An example of a Gestalt therapy technique that you might attempt on your own is the "empty chair" exercise. In this technique, imagine that someone important to you—someone you need to interact with, whether available or not—is seated in a real chair before you. Imagine her in that chair and talk to the chair, emphasizing the feelings you need to express and the ideas you may have kept to yourself. Then imagine her response; listen to it in your imagination, and respond honestly and fairly. You may surprise yourself with the words you say and the feelings you admit. Although this is an imaginary role-play exercise, it can help you clarify what you really feel and assume now—and clarify how these personal experiences shape your life.

Group Therapies. All the treatment approaches we have discussed thus far are primarily designed as one-to-one relationships between a patient or client and therapist. However, there are many reasons that group therapy can have value and benefit for a variety of concerns. Some of the benefits of group therapy are feelings of belonging and acceptance; opportunities to observe, imitate, and be socially rewarded; the chance to experience the universality of human problems, weaknesses, and strengths; and the experience of recreating scenes of one's original family system, allowing people to relive and correct basic emotions and relationships (Klein, 1983).

Group therapy can be designed to accommodate a variety of goals.

The most dramatic development in therapy has been the surge of interest and participation in *self-help groups.* It is estimated that there are 500,000 such groups, which are attended by 15 million Americans every week (Leerhsen, 1990). These group support sessions are typically free, especially when they are not directed by a health care professional, and they give people a chance to meet others with the same problems who are surviving and sometimes thriving. Alcoholics Anonymous pioneered the application of the self-help concept to community group settings, but the women's consciousness-raising movement of the 1960s helped to extend self-help beyond the arena of alcoholism.

Today, support groups deal with four basic categories of problems: addictive behavior problems, physical and mental disorders, life transition or other crises, and the traumas experienced by friends or relatives of those with specific types of problems. Virtually every community now has a self-help clearinghouse you can phone to find out where and when a local group that addresses a given problem meets. (You can call the National Self-Help Clearinghouse at [212] 642-2944.)

Group therapy has contributed valuable applications and techniques to the situations of terminally ill patients. The goals of such therapy are to help patients and their families live lives as fulfilling as possible during their illnesses; to cope realistically with impending death; and to adjust to the terminal illness (Adams, 1979; Yalom & Greaves, 1977). One general focus of such support groups for the terminally ill is helping them learn "how to live fully until you say goodbye" (Nungesser, 1990).

Group therapies can provide social support or acceptance to individuals whose problems would otherwise isolate them and prevent them from reaching help. However, sometimes the problems for which we seek therapy *are* our relationships, or they *begin* with our group memberships. An otherwise skilled and confident worker, for example, may find himself tongue-tied and intimidated by supervisors or groups of colleagues who seem to be "ganging up" on him. Or a woman may be weary of making poor choices in romantic partners, and suspect that she is incapable of attracting a partner who will treat her with respect and sensitivity. In such cases, we cannot solve our problems purely by seeking help for ourselves. We must involve our loved ones in the therapeutic process, and win their cooperation if we are to change our thoughts and behavior patterns. Fortunately, as we explore in "In Focus: Marital and Family Therapy" (page 561) relationship therapies offer well-established strategies for resolving the tensions and conflicts that are a normal part of intimacy and interaction with others.

SUMMING UP

Sigmund Freud's psychoanalytic therapy is the main form of psychodynamic therapy. One of Freud's main contributions was postulating the dynamic role of unconscious processes in normal and pathological reactions. The goal of psychoanalysis is to reconcile these conflicts into a stronger ego that mediates these drives. Important concepts in psychodynamic therapy include repression of unacceptable impulses, free association that allows repressed material to surface in undirected speech, resistance of a patient to discuss significant feelings and experiences, and dream analysis to reveal latent meaning in manifest con-

It is estimated that in the United States there are 500,000 self-help groups attended by 15 million people every week (Leerhessen, 1990).

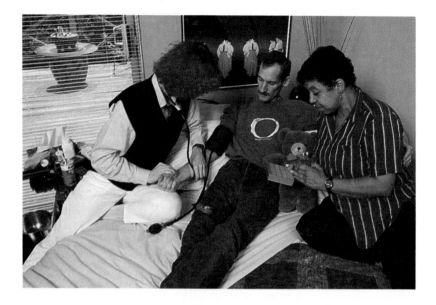

Home care and outpatient programs must absorb some of the caseload of people with AIDS. Hospice workers visit patients at home, giving them physical and emotional support. Many hospitals and clinics now offer group therapy for these patients.

tent. Neo-Freudians, such as Harry Stack Sullivan and Karen Horney, differ from classic Freudian psychoanalysts in their emphasis on the patient's current social situation, interpersonal relationships, and self-concept.

Behavior therapy views abnormal behavior as a set of learned responses that can be modified with principles of reinforcement and conditioning. Counterconditioning includes systematic desensitization, implosion, flooding, and aversive learning. Contingency management uses operant conditioning to modify behavior. This conditioning primarily involves the introduction of positive reinforcement strategies and extinction strategies. Social learning therapy, developed by Bandura, uses imitation of models and social skills training to make individuals feel more confident about their abilities.

Cognitive therapy seeks to change a person's behavior by altering negative or irrational thought patterns about oneself and social relationships. Cognitive behavior modification involves discovering how the client thinks about a problem, learning more constructive thought patterns, and applying these new techniques to other situations. Two popular types of cognitive therapy are Aaron Beck's treatment for depression and Albert Ellis's use of rational-emotive therapy (RET) to change the irrational beliefs that prevent people from living the lives they want. (See "Cross-cultural Perspective: Universals in Therapy" on p. 542.)

Existential-humanist therapies focus on the process of becoming more fully self-actualized. Client-centered therapy, developed by Carl Rogers, emphasizes the therapists' unconditional positive regard for the client. The therapist strives to be genuine and nondirective in helping the client to establish congruence between naturally positive self-image and external criticisms. Gestalt therapy, developed by Fritz Perls, attempts to combine body and mind to make a person more whole and able to experience the present moment.

Group therapy can be used as immediate social support, for example, with terminally ill patients. In marital and family therapy the unit of analysis is no longer the individual but a distressed couple or an entire nuclear family. These therapies focus on situations that the couple or group can change or minimize instead of treating the dispositional tendencies of the individuals involved.

People seek and provide therapy everywhere in the world. Six universal criteria have been identified in therapy: therapists name clients' problems; the therapist must possess appropriate qualities to be effective; therapists must establish their credibility; the client's problem must be placed in a familiar context; therapeutic techniques address problems and bring relief; and therapy itself occurs at a special time and place separate from clients' daily lives.

Much group therapy consists of strangers coming together periodically to form temporary associations from which they may benefit. However, some individuals who are experiencing problems with spouses or other family members need to address the issues directly with those significant others. Therapy for couples and for families is expanding in scope and influence throughout the United States.

Couples Counseling

Couples counseling for marital and relationship problems seeks to clarify the typical communication patterns of the partners and then to improve the quality of their interaction. By seeing a couple together (and sometimes videotaping and playing back their interactions) a therapist can help both partners appreciate the verbal and nonverbal styles they use to dominate, control, or confuse each other. Each party is taught how to reinforce desired responses in the other and withdraw reinforcement for undesirable reactions; they are also taught nondirective listening skills to help the other person clarify and express feelings and ideas. Couples therapy is more effective in resolving marital problems than is individual therapy with only one partner, and it has been shown to reduce marital crises and keep marriages intact (Cookerly, 1980; Gurman & Kniskern, 1978).

Family Therapies

In family therapy, the "client" is an entire nuclear family, and each family member is treated as a member of a system of relationships. A family therapist works with troubled family members to help them perceive the issues or patterns that are creating problems for one or more of them. The focus is on altering the psychological "spaces" between people and the interpersonal dynamics of people acting as a unit, rather than on changing processes within maladjusted

individuals (Foley, 1979). This therapy considers the synergy or joined power of the group as its members interact and stimulate each other, which is absent in solitary individuals.

Family therapy can reduce tensions within a family and improve the functioning of individual members by helping clients recognize the positives as well as the negatives in their relationships. **Virginia Satir** (1967), an innovative developer of family therapy approaches, notes that the family therapist plays many roles, acting as an interpreter and clarifier of the interactions that are taking place in the therapy session and as influence agent, mediator, and referee. Unlike laypersons, who might tend to blame personalities, most family therapists assume that the problems brought into therapy represent situational difficulties between people or problems of social interaction rather than dispositional aspects of an individual. These difficulties may develop over time as members are forced into or accept unsatisfying roles. Situations are easier to "fix" or change than long-established dispositions. Nonproductive communication patterns may be set up in response to natural transitions in a family situation: loss of a job, a child's going to school, dating or getting married, or having a baby. As family members recognize how situations affect their lives, they can learn to be more tolerant of each other and more flexible in their responses.

In a structured family therapy approach, the family is seen as the system that is creating disturbances in the individuals rather than the other way around (Minuchin, 1974). The therapist focuses on the way the family interacts in the present in order to understand its organizational structure, power hierarchy, channels of communication, and who gives and gets blame for what goes wrong. Like a consultant to an organization, a family therapist actively (but not always directly) tries to help the family

reorganize its structure and work to function better to meet the needs of its members and the demands imposed on it. Family therapists can also help forge harmonious relationships between generations within a family, as in the case of grandparents and their grandchildren whose parents have divorced (see Nichols, 1984).

Individuals Within Systems

To understand how family or relationship therapy can work in your own life, consider how you behave when you return home for a holiday visit, or make a date to spend time with an old friend. In the time you have been away, you have grown and changed. But "going back" to earlier relationships—especially if you are also returning to familiar scenes—can trigger old patterns of behavior you thought were long outgrown. For example, you might become too easily angered by a sibling's silly teasing. Or you may feel guilty about refusing your mother's home cooking, despite your reasonable wish to eat sensibly and adhere to a healthier diet. And even though years have passed, a few minutes with a former romantic partner might "push your buttons" and revive old feelings of jealousy, inadequacy, or insecurity.

To change such patterns, or be less susceptible to the circumstances that seem to trigger them, you must "relearn" your assumptions and interactions with the other people involved. This may not be a practical solution, especially if you have moved away or do not expect many reunions. Most of us resign ourselves to never quite overcoming the quirks and ironies of old relationship patterns. If the patterns are not that old and the people are more accessible, the ideal solution is to endeavor to rework entire relationships—not just our private, individual contributions to them.

Biomedical Therapies

The ecology of the mind is held in delicate balance. It can be upset by mishaps in the workings of our genes, hormones, enzymes, and metabolism. Behavior, thinking, and emotions are end products of brain mechanisms. When something goes wrong with the brain, we see the consequences in abnormal patterns of behavior and peculiar cognitive and emotional reactions. Environmental, social, or behavioral disturbances—such as certain kinds of pollution, drugs, and violence—can also alter brain chemistry. Just consider how your moods and outlook change when you have a cold or the flu, and then you are once more ready to appreciate how moods, thoughts, and actions are tied to our biology.

One approach to correcting upset biology has been to change the functioning of the brains of disturbed people by either precise neurosurgery or electroshock stimulation of the brain's neural activity. The most dramatic modern biomedical development is *chemotherapy*, the use of drugs to alter mood and mental states.

Biomedical therapies treat mental disorders as "hardware problems" in the brain and in the nervous, hormonal, and endocrine systems. These therapies emerge from a medical model of abnormal mental functioning that assumes an organic basis for mental illnesses and treats schizophrenia, for example, as a disease.

Psychosurgery

The headline in the *Los Angeles Times* read, "Bullet in the Brain Cures Man's Mental Problem" (February 23, 1988). The article revealed that a 19-year-old man suffering from severe obsessive-compulsive disorder had shot a .22 caliber bullet through the front of his brain in a suicide attempt. Remarkably, he survived, his pathological symptoms were cured, and his intellectual capacity was not affected—although some of the underlying causes of his problems remained.

This case illustrates the potential effects of one of the most direct biomedical therapies: intervention in the brain. Such intervention involves lesioning connections between parts of the brain, removing small sections of the brain, and subjecting the whole brain to intensive electrical stimulation. These therapies are often considered methods of last resort to treat psychopathologies that have proven intractable with other, less extreme forms of therapy. There is an ongoing, heated controversy about their usefulness and their side effects, as well as the ethics of taking such drastic measures to change behavior.

psychosurgery Surgical procedures that alter brain tissue in order to alleviate psychological disorders.

Psychosurgery is the general term for surgical procedures performed on brain tissue to alleviate psychological disorders. In medieval times, psychosurgery involved "cutting the stone of folly" from the brains of those suffering from madness, as shown vividly in many engravings and paintings from that era (there is, of course, no such "stone"). Modern psychosurgical procedures include severing the fibers of the corpus callosum to reduce violent seizures of epilepsy (as we saw in Chapter 2), severing pathways through the limbic system, and performing *prefrontal lobotomy*.

The best-known and most frequently used form of psychosurgery is the prefrontal lobotomy—an operation that severs the white-matter nerve fibers connecting the frontal lobes of the brain with the diencephalon, especially the fibers of the thalamus and hypothalamus. The procedure was developed by neurologist **Egas Moniz,** who in 1949 won a Nobel Prize for this treatment which seemed to transform the functioning of mental patients.

The ideal candidates for lobotomy were agitated schizophrenic patients and patients who were compulsive and anxiety ridden. The effects of this psychosurgery were dramatic; a new personality emerged, without intense emotional arousal and thus without overwhelming anxiety, guilt, or anger. In part, this positive effect occurred because the operation disconnected present func-

In medieval times, those suffering from madness were sometimes treated by cutting "the stone of folly" from their brains.

tioning from memory for past traumas and conflicts and also from future concerns. However, the operation permanently destroyed basic aspects of human nature. Lobotomized patients lost something special—their unique personality. Specifically, the lobotomy resulted in inability to plan ahead, indifference to the opinions of others, childlike actions, and the intellectual and emotional flatness of a person without a coherent sense of self. Because the effects of psychosurgery are permanent, the negative effects are severe and common, and the positive results are less certain, the continued use of psychosurgery is limited to special cases (Valenstein, 1980).

Electroconvulsive Therapy

Electroconvulsive therapy (ECT) is the use of electroconvulsive shock for certain psychiatric disorders. It is designed to produce a temporary upheaval in the central nervous system, by scrambling the brain's own electrical circuits. The technique consists of applying weak electric current (20–30 milliamps) to a patient's temples for a fraction of a second until a *grand mal* seizure occurs (loss of consciousness and strong bodily convulsions, followed by a brief coma-like sleep). Patients are prepared for this traumatic intervention by sedation with a short-acting barbiturate and muscle relaxant which minimize the violent physical reactions (Malitz & Sackheim, 1984). The use of these relaxants and sedatives is important. Contrary to the imagery provoked by the inappropriate term "shock therapy," properly administered ECT does *not* cause painful electrical shocks or wrenching physical jolts to a conscious, anxious patient.

ECT produces temporary disorientation and a variety of memory deficits, most of which are permanent. After a typical series of ECT treatments (every other day), some patients are calmer and more susceptible to psychotherapy when it is available. Today, ECT is often administered to only one side of the brain—the nondominant hemisphere—so as to reduce the possibility of speech impairment. Such unilateral (one-sided) ECT is reported to be an effective antidepressant (Scovern & Kilmann, 1980).

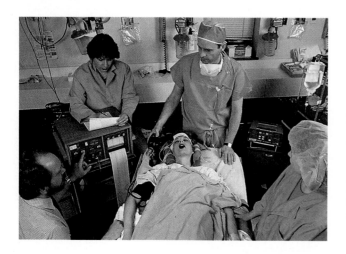

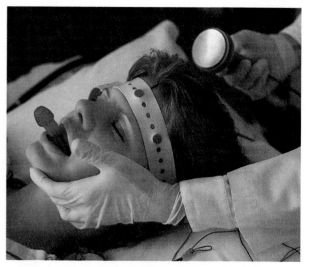

Electroconvulsive therapy has been effective in cases of severe depression. However, there is considerable controversy about its therapeutic value.

The effects of ECT were initially hailed as unparalleled in the history of psychiatry. ECT has been especially effective in cases of severe depression; but no one knows exactly why it works. It may increase available norepinephrine and other neurotransmitters or induce a strong psychological reaction, such as determination to avoid another treatment or feeling sufficiently punished to get rid of guilt over an imagined wrong (Fink, 1979). Because the technique involves so many physical reactions, it is unlikely that a single key ingredient can be isolated (Squire, 1986).

In 1985, a National Institutes of Health panel concluded that ECT "is demonstrably effective for a narrow range of severe psychiatric disorders" that include depression, mania, and some schizophrenias. ECT is often used as emergency treatment for suicidally depressed patients, especially those who do not respond to antidepressant drugs or can't tolerate the drugs' side effects. It is effective in reducing the symptoms of patients who have had a recent onset of schizophrenic symptoms, although it does not change the cognitive problems that are central to schizophrenia (Salzman, 1980).

Critics of ECT are especially fearful that it will be used without control or justification in large, understaffed mental institutions merely to punish patients or make them more manageable (Breggin, 1979). For some patients the side effects of ECT include impairments in language and memory and subsequent loss of self-esteem. With repeated ECT treatments, signs of personality deterioration may appear. The debate continues as to whether ECT's faults outweigh its utility (Diamond, 1989). Because it is a cost-effective procedure for mental hospitals, critics worry that ECT may become overly and capriciously prescribed (Frank, 1978; Squire, 1988).

Chemotherapy

In the history of the treatment of mental disorder, nothing has ever rivaled the revolution created by the discovery of drugs that could calm anxious patients, restore contact with reality in withdrawn patients, and suppress hallucinations in psychotic patients. This new therapeutic era began in 1953 with the introduction of tranquilizing drugs, notably *chlorpromazine* (the U.S. brand name is Thorazine), into mental hospital treatment programs.

Chemotherapy is a general term for any form of therapy that treats disorders with drugs and chemicals. You are probably familiar with references to

chemotherapy Any use of drugs to treat mental, behavioral, or physical disorders.

"chemotherapy" in the treatment of cancer. The application of chemotherapy to psychological disorders was first developed by researchers in the field of psychopharmacology. It gained almost instant recognition and status as an effective therapy for transforming patient behavior. When they had received appropriate chemotherapy, unruly, assaultive patients became cooperative, calm, and sociable. Thought-disordered patients who had been absorbed in their delusions and hallucinations began to be responsive to the real physical and social environment around them. No longer did mental hospital staff have to act as guards, putting patients in seclusion or straitjackets; staff morale improved as rehabilitation replaced mere custodial care of the mentally ill (Swazey, 1974).

Another profound effect of the chemotherapy revolution was its impact on the nation's mental hospital population. Over half a million Americans were living in mental institutions in 1955, staying an average of several years. The introduction of chlorpromazine and other drugs reversed the steadily increasing numbers of patients. By the early 1970s, it was estimated that less than half the country's mental patients actually resided in mental hospitals; those who did were institutionalized for an average of only a few months.

Categories of Drugs. Three major categories of drugs are used today in chemotherapy programs: *antipsychotic, antidepressant,* and *antianxiety* compounds. As their names suggest, these drugs chemically alter specific brain functions that are responsible for psychotic symptoms, depression, and extreme anxiety, respectively.

Antipsychotic Drugs. Antipsychotic drugs alter the psychotic symptoms of delusions, hallucinations, social withdrawal, and occasional agitation. Chlorpromazine, derived from the compound *phenothiazine,* is an antipsychotic drug. Patients treated with such drugs become calm and tranquil but remain alert. Many of these patients are then able for the first time to be treated with psychotherapy.

There are several negative side effects of long-term administration of antipsychotic drugs. *Tardive dyskinesia* is an unusual disturbance of motor control (especially of the facial muscles), caused by antipsychotic drugs. *Agranulocytosis* is a rare blood disease that develops in two percent of patients treated with Clopazine—an antipsychotic drug that is sometimes used to control schizophrenic symptoms.

Antidepressant Drugs. The two basic antidepressants are the *tricyclics,* such as Tofranil and Elavil, and the *monoamine oxidase (MAO) inhibitors.* Now a third generation of antidepressants is used that consists mostly of tetracyclics. One of these third-generation antidepressants is Prozac—touted by its developers as a drug whose therapeutic effects are more potent than its competitors.

Another remarkable chemical is *Lithium salt,* the extract of a rock, which can influence the uniquely subtle property of mind that regulates mood. It has proven effective in the treatment of manic disorders. People who experience uncontrollable periods of hyperexcitement—when their energy seems limitless and their behavior extravagant and flamboyant—are brought down from their state of manic excess by doses of lithium. Regular maintenance doses of lithium can help break the cycle of recurring episodes of mania and/or depression. Lithium also allows a person to be alert and creative (Ehrlich & Diamond, 1980). Given that lithium is only a "salt of the earth," it qualifies as a miracle medicine for natural healing of severe mental mood disturbances.

Antianxiety Drugs. To cope with everyday hassles, untold millions of Americans take pills to reduce tension and suppress anxiety. In general, these antianxiety drugs work by sedating the user.

There are three classes of such antianxiety compounds: *barbiturates, propanediols,* and *benzodiazepines.* Barbiturates have a relaxing effect, but they can be dangerous if taken in excess or in combination with alcohol. Propanediol drugs, such as Miltown and Equanil, reduce the tension that accompanies agitated anxiety. Benzodiazepine drugs, such as Valium and Librium, are effective in reducing generalized fears and anxiety without affecting a person's ability to pay attention or process information. A new class of antianxiety drugs, such as *busparin*, appears to have fewer negative side effects than other antianxiety drugs.

Caution: Being on "Good" Drugs. Because these tranquilizers work so well, it is easy to become psychologically dependent on them or physically addicted to them. Many people choose chemical treatments to cope with conflicts or emotional distress rather than confronting their problems, trying to solve them, or accepting pain and grief as part of the human experience.

In 1975, Valium was the most frequently prescribed drug in the United States. Since then its sales have fallen somewhat, but the eight to nine million Americans who still take doses of Valium every day make it the nation's most popular tranquilizer. Valium has a high *abuse potential* and is being overly relied upon to handle the emotional chores of modern life. Critics argue that it is self-defeating for people to believe that pills control their stress rather than their own actions. Unfortunately, drug therapy is often given in place of, and not as an adjunct to, the psychotherapy a person may need to learn how to cope effectively with life's recurring hassles.

Here are some *cautions* to bear in mind about tranquilizers—the drugs that students are most likely to take:

1. Benzodiazepines should not be taken to relieve anxieties that are part of the ordinary stresses of everyday life.
2. When used for extreme anxiety, they should not be taken for more than four months at a time, and their dosage should be gradually reduced by a physician. Abrupt cessation can lead to *withdrawal symptoms,* such as convulsions, tremors, and abdominal and muscle cramps.
3. Because these drugs depress the central nervous system, they can impair driving, operating machinery, and tasks that require alertness (such as studying or taking exams).
4. In combination with alcohol (also a central nervous system depressant) or with sleeping pills, benzodiazepines can lead to unconsciousness and even death (Hecht, 1986).

As an introductory student in psychology, you are now in a better position to make informed decisions about how best to face life's problems, and to advise those you love as they deal with those decisions for themselves.

SUMMING UP

Biomedical therapies try to change the physiological aspects of mental illness. These therapies now rely primarily on a range of psychoactive drugs to alleviate the pathological symptoms of behavioral and mental disorders. However, they do not cure the disorder.

Psychosurgery, such as the prefrontal lobotomy (once a popular medical treatment), is used infrequently because of the irreversible nature of its negative side effects.

Electroconvulsive therapy is undergoing a resurgence of use for severely depressed patients. Current techniques have neither the aversiveness nor the same negative consequences as earlier forms of ECT.

Chemotherapy includes antipsychotic medication for schizophrenics. Antidepressants, such as tricyclics and MAO inhibitors, are used to chemically control depression. Lithium is used to treat bipolar mental disorders. Antianxiety medication is used to reduce tension and sometimes to promote sleep. Antianxiety drugs include barbiturates, propanediols, and benzodiazepines. Such medication is particularly susceptible to abuse because it is readily prescribed, is self-administered, and has calming, reinforcing effects for millions of normal people suffering from the ordinary stress of living.

Does Therapy Work?

Do these therapies work? The answer to that simple question is complex and unresolved. There are many methodological issues involved in evaluating therapeutic success. Although these questions are currently being examined by both researchers and clinicians, there is not yet full agreement about which therapies work best, for whom they work, or why.

Many conceptual and practical issues make it difficult to assess whether any given therapy is effective or is more effective than other forms of treatment. For example, if we restrict the evaluation of therapy to just one type of mental disorder—such as depression—it is still staggeringly complex. One expert notes that "there may be a dozen kinds of depression . . . it's not one disorder, like measles . . . and it's carried within the person's personality or within their character. The treatment for depression for one person may look quite different from the effective treatment of depression with another. So it depends on the person as well as the disorder that they're suffering from" (Coyne, 1990; *Discovering Psychology*, Program 22).

Certain general factors seem related to the success of therapy, however; some of these are listed in **Table 14.3** on the next page.

Evaluating Therapy

British psychologist **Hans Eysenck** (pronounced I-zenk) created a furor some years ago by declaring that psychotherapy does not work at all (Eysenk, 1952). He reviewed the effects of various therapies and found that patients who received no therapy had just as high a recovery rate as those receiving psychoanalysis or other forms of insight therapy. His claim was that roughly two-thirds of all people with neurotic problems will recover spontaneously within two years of the onset of the problem.

Does therapy *really* help—or do clients only improve because they hope and expect to receive special help? If the latter is true, then therapy is a kind of *placebo*, a behavioral sugar pill that only "works" because the individual wishes it to be effective. Many psychologists and psychiatrists believe that the key placebo ingredients in any therapy's success are a patient's *belief* that therapy will help and a therapist's social influence in conveying this suggestion (Fish, 1973). Psychiatrist **Jerome Frank** (1961) has compared the processes that take place in modern psychotherapy, religious revivalism, native healing ceremonies, and Communist thought-reform programs. He argues that "belief is really crucial to all of these processes because without the belief the person does not participate in any real way. . . . Nothing happens unless they really believe that this could help them" (Frank, 1990). As the discussion of "Universals in Therapy" notes, people's belief that they will be helped is central to all relationships between help-seekers and therapists worldwide.

Most psychotherapy researchers agree with Eysenck that it is important to show that psychotherapy is more effective than spontaneous recovery or client expectations. However, they criticize his findings because of many methodological problems in the studies he reviewed. A later evaluation of nearly a hundred therapy-outcome studies found that psychotherapy *did* lead to greater improvement than spontaneous recovery in 80 percent of the cases (Meltzoff & Kornreich, 1970). Thus, we begin to feel a little more confident that the therapeutic experience itself is a useful one for many people much of the time.

Table 14.3 Factors Affecting the Success of Psychotherapy

FACTORS*	CONDITIONS LEADING TO SUCCESS	CONDITIONS MAKING SUCCESS LESS LIKELY
Disorder	Neurotic, especially anxiety	Schizophrenic; paranoid
Pathology	Short duration; not severe	Serious chronic disturbance
Ego strength	Strong; good	Weak; poor
Anxiety	Not high	High
Defenses	Adequate	Lacking
Patient's attitudes	Motivated to change Realistic expectations for therapeutic change	Indifferent Unrealistic or no expectations for change
Patient's role in therapy	Active; collaborative; involved; responsible for problem solving	Passive; detached; makes therapist responsible
Therapeutic relationship	Mutual liking and attraction	Unreciprocated attraction
Therapeutic characteristics	Personally well adjusted; experienced	Poorly adjusted

*No differences in outcome and no inconsistencies were found for these factors: age, sex, social class, and race. (Adapted with permission from Gomes-Schwartz, Hadley, & Strupp (1978), *Annual Review of Psychology*, vol. 29, copyright © 1978 by Annual Reviews, Inc.) See also Coyne & Downey (1991) regarding social factors in coping.

A general model of the way theory, clinical observation, and research all play a role in the development and evaluation of any form of treatment (for mental and physical disorders) is shown in the flowchart in **Figure 14.4.** It demonstrates that systematic research is needed to help clinicians discover if their therapies are having the impact that their theories predict.

One well-controlled study compared patients who had undergone psychoanalytic or behavior therapy with patients who had simply been on a waiting list for therapy. Both types of therapy turned out to be beneficial, with behavior therapy leading to the greatest overall improvement. The researchers also concluded that the improvement of patients in therapy was "not entirely due either to spontaneous recovery or to the placebo effect of the nonspecific

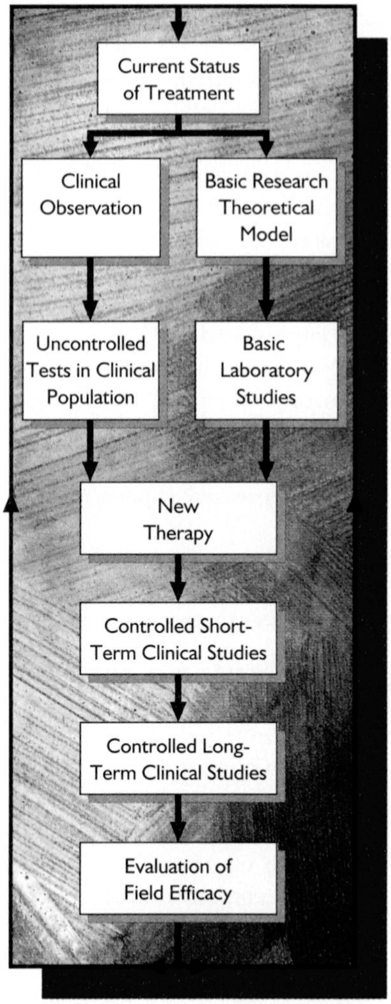
Current Status of Treatment
Clinical Observation
Basic Research Theoretical Model
Uncontrolled Tests in Clinical Population
Basic Laboratory Studies
New Therapy
Controlled Short-Term Clinical Studies
Controlled Long-Term Clinical Studies
Evaluation of Field Efficacy

Figure 14.4 Drug Therapy and Psychotherapy
Flowchart of stages in the development of treatments for mental/physical disorders.

aspects of therapy, such as arousal of hope, expectation of help, and an initial cathartic interview" (Sloane et al., 1975, p. 224). Because of such findings, current researchers are less concerned about asking *whether* psychotherapy works and more concerned about asking *why* it works and whether any one treatment is most effective for any particular problem and for certain types of patients (Goldfried et al., 1990).

According to recent research, some of the confounding variables found to account for the effectiveness of different therapies include the following: differences in therapist experience; duration of therapy; accuracy of the initial diagnosis; type of the disorder; differences in the severity and types of patient difficulties; the kinds of outcome measures used; the fit between a patient's expectations and the type of therapy offered; and length of follow-up times (Kazdin, 1986; Kazdin & Wilson, 1980; Smith et al., 1980; Smith & Glass, 1977).

We might also wonder whether a combination of therapies is better than a single one for some kinds of disorders. According to research with acutely depressed patients, the answer is *yes* (see **Figure 14.5** on the next page).

Prevention Strategies

> Two friends were walking on a riverbank. Suddenly, a child swept downstream in the current. One of the friends jumped in the river and rescued the child. Then the two friends resumed their stroll. Suddenly, another child appeared in the water. The rescuer jumped in and again pulled the victim to safety. Soon, a third drowning child swept by. The still-dry friend began to trot up the riverbank. The rescuer yelled, "Hey, where are you going?" The dry one replied, "I'm going to get the bastard that's throwing them in." (Wolman, 1975, p. 3)

The moral of this story is clear: *Preventing* a problem is the best solution. All of the traditional therapies that we examined here focus on changing a person who is already distressed or disabled. They begin to do their work only *after* the problems show up and the suffering starts. By the time a person enters therapy, it is often too late to keep the psychological disorder from "settling in" and having disruptive effects on one's daily functioning, social life, or work.

The *prevention* of psychological problems is being practiced by a number of community mental health centers under the general direction of the National Association for Mental Health. To meet this goal, mental health workers use systematic methods for combatting psychological problems. These methods include reducing the *severity* of existing disorders (using traditional therapies); reducing the *duration* of disorders through new programs for early identification and prompt treatment; and reducing the *incidence* of new cases among the unaffected, normal population that is potentially at risk for a particular disorder (Klein & Goldston, 1977).

4

A medical approach to psychological health involves treating people who are afflicted. In contrast, a *public health model* includes identifying and eliminating the sources of disease and illness that exist in the environment. In this approach, an affected individual is seen as the host or carrier—the end-product of an existing process of disease. Change the conditions that breed illness and there will be no need to change people later with expensive, extensive treatments. The dramatic reduction of many contagious and infectious diseases, such as tuberculosis, smallpox, and malaria, has come about through this approach. With psychopathology, too, many sources of environmental or organizational stress can be identified; plans can then be made to alleviate them, thus reducing the number of people who will be exposed to them. The new field of **clinical ecology** expands the boundaries of biomedical therapies by relating disorders (such as anxiety and depression) to environmental irritants (such as chemical solvents, noise pollution, seasonal changes, and radiation) (Bell, 1981).

clinical ecology Field that relates disorders to environmental irritants and sources of trauma.

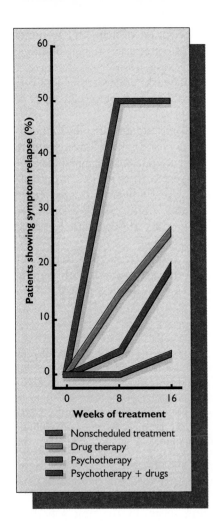

Figure 14.5 Depression Symptom Relapse
For treating severely depressed patients,
drugs used in combination with psychotherapy and cognitive therapy are very effective in
preventing the return of symptoms of
depression.

These newer mental health approaches are directing attention toward the *precipitating* factors—origins and triggers—in a person's current environment and focusing on practical ways to change *what is* rather than reinterpreting *what was*. In recognizing that certain situations are likely to foster psychopathology—when people are made to feel anonymous, rejected, isolated, or abused—new approaches instruct people in ways to avoid or modify these noxious life situations individually or through community action. These newer approaches often target members of culturally diverse groups (such as African Americans and Hispanics) who have been denied access to society's opportunities because of prejudice and discrimination.

The prevention of mental disorders is a complex and difficult task. It involves not only understanding the relevant causal factors but also overcoming individual, institutional, and governmental resistance to change. Educational efforts directed at the public and government would serve to demonstrate the long-range utility of prevention and the community mental health approach to psychopathology—and justify the necessary expense of prevention.

SUMMING UP

Hans Eysenck and other critics have charged that therapy may not be any more effective than the healing effects of the normal passage of time. Some critics have suggested that therapy's strongest influence may be a placebo effect. While belief is an important component to therapeutic cooperation, there is also evidence that therapy is objectively useful when applied expediently and appropriately.

Prevention strategies may be more effective than treatment that begins only after a problem is established. Public health and clinical ecology models focus on controlling the factors that precipitate and develop mental disorders.

A Personal Endnote

We come to the end of our long journey through *Psychology.* Upon reflection, and, ideally, when you take your final examination, you will realize just how much you have learned on the way. Yet we have barely scratched the surface of the excitement and challenges that await students of psychology, those curious people-watchers who choose to continue on to the next phase of the journey into more advanced realms of this discipline.

We hope you will be among them, and that you may even go on to contribute to this dynamic enterprise as a scientific researcher or a clinical practitioner or by applying what is known in psychology to the solution of social and personal problems.

Playwright Tom Stoppard reminds us that "Every exit is an entry somewhere else." We would like to believe that the entry into the next phase of your life will be facilitated by what you have learned from *Psychology* and from your introductory psychology course. In that next journey, may you infuse new life into the study of human nature, while strengthening the human connections among all people you encounter. *Bon voyage!*

The Context of Therapy *What are the two main kinds of therapy for mental disorders? Most often, why do people enter therapy? What are the primary goals of therapy?*

Therapeutic tasks involve diagnosing the problem, finding the source of the problem, making a prognosis about probable outcomes with and without treatment, and carrying out treatment. A variety of professionals work under this model. In earlier times, treatment for those with mental problems were usually harsh and dehumanizing. Only recently in history have people with emotional problems been treated as individuals with illnesses to be cured. This view of mental illness has led to more humane treatment of patients. Many cultures have their own ways of understanding and treating mental disorders, although some "universals" hold true for all forms of therapy.

Key Terms

shamanism, p. 533
biomedical therapy, p. 534
psychotherapy, p. 535
patient, p. 536
client, p. 536
in vivo therapy, p. 537
counseling psychologist, p. 538
psychiatric social worker, p. 538
pastoral counselor, p. 538
clinical psychologist, p. 538
psychiatrist, p. 538
psychoanalyst, p. 538
ritual healing, p. 541

Major Contributors

Pinel, Philippe, p. 539
Heinroth, J. C., p. 540
Beers, Clifford, p. 540

2 Psychological Therapies *What is the task of the psychoanalyst in most psychodynamic therapies? According to behavior therapists, how can most psychopathological behavior be understood and modified? What is the underlying assumption of cognitive therapy? What concept is at the core of both humanistic and existential therapies?*

Psychodynamic therapies grew out of Sigmund Freud's psychoanalytic theory. Free association, repression, resistance, and dream analysis are all important components of this therapy. Neo-Freudians place more emphasis on the patient's current social situation, interpersonal relationships, and self-concept.

Behavior therapy attempts to apply the principles of learning and reinforcement to problem behaviors. Counterconditioning and systematic desensitization are two categories of techniques commonly employed. Contingency management uses operant conditioning to modify behavior, primarily through positive reinforcement and extinction strategies. Social learning therapy involves the use of models and social skills training to help individuals gain confidence about their abilities.

Cognitive therapy concentrates on changing negative or irrational thought patterns about oneself and social relationships. The client must learn more constructive thought patterns in reference to a problem and apply the new technique to other situations. Rational-emotive therapy helps clients recognize that their irrational beliefs about themselves interfere with life, and to help them learn how to change those thought patterns.

Existential-humanist therapies focus on individuals becoming more fully self-actualized. Therapists strive to be nondirective in helping their clients establish a positive self-image that can deal with external criticisms. Group therapy has many applications including community self-help groups and support groups. Gestalt therapy focuses on the whole person—body, mind, and life setting. Family and marital therapy concentrate on situational difficulties and interpersonal dynamics as a total system in need of improvement.

Key Terms	Major Contributors
psychoanalytic therapy, p. 543	Freud, Sigmund, p. 543
insight therapy, p. 543	Sullivan, Harry Stack, p. 546
free association, p. 544	Horney, Karen, p. 546
catharsis, p. 544	Wolpe, Joseph, p. 547
resistance, p. 544	Skinner, B. F., p. 550
dream analysis, p. 545	Beck, Aaron, p. 556
transference, p. 545	Ellis, Albert, p. 556
countertransference, p. 545	May, Rollo, p. 557
behavior modification, p. 547	Rogers, Carl, p. 557
counterconditioning, p. 547	Perls, Fritz, p. 558
contingency management, p. 547	Satir, Virginia, p. 561
systematic desensitization, p. 547	
implosion therapy, p. 549	
flooding, p. 549	
aversion therapy, p. 549	
social-learning therapy, p. 551	
participant modeling, p. 551	
cognitive therapy, p. 551	
cognitive behavior modification, p. 552	
behavioral rehearsal, p. 553	
rational-emotive therapy (RET), p. 556	
person-centered therapy, p. 557	
Gestalt therapy, p. 558	

3 Biomedical Therapies
What is the best known and most frequently used form of psychosurgery? For what class of disorders has electroconvulsive therapy been found to be especially effective? What kinds of drugs primarily are used today in chemotherapy programs?

Biomedical therapies concentrate on changing the physiological aspects of mental illness. Psychosurgery has lost popularity in recent years because of its radical, irreversible side effects. Electroconvulsive therapy is undergoing a resurgence of use with depressed patients, but it remains controversial. Chemotherapy includes antipsychotic medicine for schizophrenics as well as antidepression and antianxiety drugs. Antianxiety medication is particularly susceptible to abuse and should not be used by people suffering from the ordinary stress of living.

Key Terms	Major Contributor
psychosurgery, p. 562	Moniz, Egas, p. 562
electroconvulsive therapy (ECT), p. 563	
chemotherapy, p. 564	

4 **Does Therapy Work?** *With what questions are most psychother-apy researchers concerned today? How does the public-health model view the individual afflicted with a psychological disorder?*

Some researchers have argued that therapy for mental illness does not work any better than the passage of time or nonspecific placebo treatment. Research shows that behavior therapy and psychotherapy are effective for specific types of disorders, but the reasons for this are not clear. Innovative evaluation projects are helping to answer the question of what makes therapy effective. Prevention strategies have become especially important in the new public health model.

Key Term

clinical ecology, p. 569

Major Contributors

Eysenck, Hans, p. 567
Frank, Jerome, p. 567

PRACTICE TEST

Chapter 14: Psychotherapies

For each of the following items, choose the single correct or best answer. Correct answers, explanations, and page references appear in the Appendix.

1. Despite the differences between various types of therapy, all therapeutic strategies are designed to _____ .
   A. make the client feel better about herself
   B. help the individual fit better into her society
   C. change the individual's functioning in some way
   D. inform and educate but not interfere with the person's usual patterns of behavior

2. While professionals with somewhat different training and orientations can provide similar forms of therapy, only _____ are qualified to prescribe medications for the treatment of mental or behavioral disorders.
   A. psychiatrists
   B. psychiatric social workers
   C. psychoanalysts
   D. All of the above.

3. Because a central goal of a therapist is to guide a patient toward understanding the connections between past origins and present symptoms, psychodynamic therapy is often called _____ therapy.
   A. insight
   B. cognitive
   C. existential
   D. rational-emotive

4. A psychoanalyst finds herself feeling personally fond of a young client who reminds her of her son when he was that age. If the therapist has difficulty separating her own feelings from the needs of her patient, this may be an example of the psychoanalytic process known as _____ .
   A. resistance
   B. transference
   C. countertransference
   D. negative transference

5. Leni has an irrational fear of speaking in front of others. With the support of her instructor and her entire psychology class, Leni confronts her fear by standing alone in front of her classmates and talking about her phobia. This strategy of placing the individual in the dreaded situation is called _____ .
   A. systematic desensitization
   B. catharsis
   C. implosion
   D. flooding

6. To teach his young daughter not to be afraid to swim, a man tells her to "Watch me!" as he wades into the surf, then rolls with the waves, and finally invites her to join him if she wants to try. In behavioral therapy, this technique is known as _____ .
   A. clinical ecology
   B. counterconditioning
   C. behavioral rehearsal
   D. participant modeling

7. Which of the following problems might best be corrected through rational-emotive therapy (RET)?
   A. An addicted smoker wants to quit.
   B. A young man pursues a difficult, unenjoyable career because it is the only work his father approves of.
   C. An average-weight woman diets constantly, believing that she must be thin in order to have anyone love her.
   D. None of the above.

8. Which of the following statements about electroconvulsive therapy (ECT) is true?
   A. Proper ECT applies a very strong electric current to a patient's brain without the interference or insulation of sedatives or anesthetic medication.
   B. ECT has been found to be especially effective in the treatment of severe depression.
   C. It is known to work by increasing the stimulation of a particular neurotransmitter in the brain.
   D. It works best with manic patients.

9. Valium, a drug with a high "abuse potential," is classified as an _____ medication.
   A. antianxiety
   B. antidepressant
   C. antipsychotic
   D. antihistamine

10. Psychiatrist Jerome Frank argues that, like religious and political indoctrination programs, healing processes rely on a common crucial element: _____ .
    A. deception
    B. fear of authority
    C. rejection of culture
    D. belief in the experience

IF YOU'RE INTERESTED . . .

Amadeus. (Video: 1984, color, 158 minutes). Directed by Milos Forman; starring Tom Hulce, F. Murray Abraham, Elizabeth Berridge, Jeffrey Jones.

Absorbing (and musically astounding) film based on Peter Shaffer's play about the psychological rivalry between 18th century composer Antonio Salieri and Wolfgang Amadeus Mozart, the young musical genius who seemed to be favored by God. Told in flashbacks, the story is framed by Salieri's retrospective confession from his asylum cell, surrounded by powerful scenes of the "therapies" of the day—the cages and restraints shackling the mentally ill, suicidal, and eccentric citizens of early modern Europe.

Eliade, M. (1964). *Shamanism: Archaic techniques of ecstasy.* Pantheon.

A classic review of the healing arts in non-Western cultures and traditions.

Goleman, D. and Spaeth, K. R. (Eds.). (1982). *The essential psychotherapies.* New York: New American Library.

Good, clear, readable collection of introductory reviews of different psychotherapeutic techniques.

Kaysen, S. (1993). *Girl, interrupted.* New York: Turtle Bay Books.

Susanna Kaysens's frank and vivid account of her two years, beginning in 1967 when she was 18, in McLean Hospital, a psychiatric hospital with a ward for teenage girls. Dark, funny stories of herself, her jumbled thinking, and the other patients are interspersed with pages from her medical record.

May, R. (1969). *Love and will.* New York: Norton.

An excellent introduction to the existential-humanistic perspective on human nature, motivation, modern life, and relationships.

Ordinary People. (Video: 1980, color, 123 minutes).
Directed by Robert Redford; starring Donald Sutherland, Mary Tyler Moore, Judd Hirsch, Timothy Hutton.

Powerful film version of Judith Guest's novel about an upper-middle-class family's struggles to cope with the death of their older son, including the suicidal guilt of his surviving younger brother. Appealing portrayal of a psychotherapist as an important relationship in a troubled life.

Snake Pit, The. (Video: 1948, black-and-white, 108 minutes).
Directed by Anatole Litvak; starring Olivia de Havilland, Mark Stevens, Leo Genn.

Affecting film portrayal of a young woman's acute schizophrenia and gradual recovery through psychotherapy. Powerful images of what mental institutions were like in most of this country before the development of effective chemotherapy.

Spellbound. (Video: 1945, black-and-white, 111 minutes).
Directed by Alfred Hitchcock; starring Gregory Peck, Ingrid Bergman, Leo G. Carroll.

Classic Hitchcock mystery, blending psychoanalytic jargon and techniques with old-fashioned detective skills in solving the dilemma of an amnesiac suffering from a guilt complex. Compelling dream sequences were appropriately designed by surrealist artist Salvador Dali.

Valenstein, E. S. (1986). *Great and desperate cures.* New York: Basic Books.

Fascinating reading, a review of efforts to treat mental illness with techniques adapted from medicine—and with variable results.

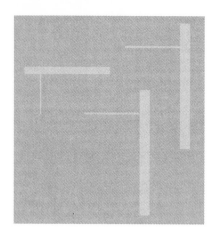

Appendix

Answer Keys to Practice Tests

A Practice Test is provided in the Chapter Review that concludes each chapter in *Psychology*. Each Practice Test consists of ten multiple-choice questions, designed to help you review both the depth and breadth of the material covered. Answers to those items are provided in this appendix.

For each correct answer, we have provided both a page reference for the location of the material that answers the item and a brief explanation of how you might reach the correct answer. For greatest benefit, please (1) refer to the page references and look up the original text discussion of tested material; and (2) look up the items you answered *correctly* as well as those you answered *incorrectly*. This process will reinforce your understanding of the material you are already beginning to comprehend as well as correct any misconceptions about items that are still challenging you.

There is some overlap of coverage between the material reviewed by the Practice Tests (in the Chapter Reviews) and that assessed in the Mastery Tests (in a separate section of this text). Most items refer to the same general discussions and issues, and a very few items cover the same points. However, in preparing for course tests and examinations, *only your instructor* can identify the specific topics and concepts with which you are expected to be familiar. Be sure to collaborate with your instructor in studying, writing, applying course material, and preparing for evaluations.

Chapter 1: Mind, Behavior, and Science

1.   C (page 5): Science is a method of collecting information and solving problems. The first step in scientific investigation is collecting empirical evidence, data that are available to the senses of the observer.

2.   A (page 8): A "scientific prediction" is based on an understanding of how events are related, and by what mechanisms. A more common form of prediction is based on the assumption that people's past actions are a good indicator of their future behavior.

3.   B (page 8): The discipline of psychology has five scientific goals: describing what happens, explaining what happens, predicting what will happen, controlling what happens, and improving the quality of life. Of these, control may reflect a particularly Western bias among world cultures.

4.   A (page 10): German psychologist Wilhelm Wundt established the first psychological laboratory in Leipzig, Germany, in 1879.

5.   A (page 12): The school of functionalism emphasized the importance of understanding the purpose or function of a behavior. Of the other two historic influences in early psychology—structuralism and evolutionism—evolutionism is more sympathetic to the value of function in making a species adaptable. However, evolutionism applies a scale of millions of years—as the human species evolves—rather than focusing on a specific action.

6.   D (page 14): The psychodynamic perspective, originally developed by Sigmund Freud, emphasizes the influence of unconscious conflicts among inner forces and motivations and societal restrictions on individual behavior.

7.   B (page 17): The evolutionary approach emphasizes the importance of adaptive behavior in promoting gene survival. In contrast, conflict between individual and society is a concept of the psychodynamic approach, information processing is a cognitive concept, and personal-cultural integration is a humanistic goal.

8.   C (page 10): Clinical, counseling, and community psychology are all applied areas of professional psychology, focusing on delivery of services and treatment to individuals, groups, and communities. Social psychology is a research specialty focusing on individual behavior in its social and situational context.

9.   A (page 22): A hypothesis is a testable explanation or guess about the relationship among variables being studied. In contrast, a theory is a set of principles explaining a broad phenomenon. A model is a system or analogy used to explain a process. A paradigm is a way of thinking about the world and how to study it.

10.   D (page 26): This is an example of an experiment, not a correlational study. The researcher manipulates the independent variable (type of stories)—giving the experimental group scary stories and the control group a variety of non-scary stories—and measures the dependent variable (the children's preference for group activities). In contrast, correlational research studies naturally occurring relationships among variables.

Chapter 2: Biopsychology

1.   B (pages 37–38): Field and Schanberg's research shows that preemies thrive when they are stimulated by gentle physical massage. Human touch has powerful effects on biological and psychological health.

2.   C (page 40): Natural selection is affected by environment, variation, and competition. Variation refers to individual differences in an individual's inherited traits (genotypes) and their expression (phenotypes).

3.   C (pages 40–41): Bipedalism (walking upright) and encephalization (increased brain size and development) are two adaptations natural selection favored in human evolution. The capacity for language stemmed directly from encephalization.

4.   A (page 44): French scholar René Descartes originally developed the idea that the body is an "animal machine" that responds reflexively to the environment. His writings in the early seventeenth century laid the foundation for modern research in biopsychology.

5.   A (page 46): Brain researchers may be able to study the results of accidental brain damage, or they may prefer to carefully control such research by lesioning (removing or destroying) specific tissue. They also learn about the brain by studying the effects of electrical stimulation and recording (for example, the EEG), and using noninvasive techniques like CT-scanning, PET-scanning, and MRI imaging.

6.   D (pages 45, 50): The central core includes the medulla, pons, reticular formation, thalamus, and cerebellum. The limbic system includes the amygdala, hippocampus, and hypothalamus. The cerebral cortex is divided into four lobes—frontal, parietal, temporal, and occipital—which include the somatosensory, motor, auditory, visual, and association cortices (cortexes).

7.   C (page 56): The autonomic nervous system sustains basic life processes that are not normally under conscious control, such as respiration, digestion, and arousal.

8.   B (page 59): When a neuron is sufficiently stimulated, it is depolarized, and its electrical charge relative to the outside environment changes from slightly more negative to slightly more positive.

9.   C (page 63): The left hemisphere controls verbal functions, while the right hemisphere is more involved in visual-spatial processing.

10.   D (page 64): The brain is a "behaving brain" because it processes information and controls action. It is also "responsive" in the sense that it receives and is affected by stimulation from the external environment.

Chapter 3: States of Mind

1. C (page 74): From the research of Michael Gazzaniga and Roger Sperry came the perspective of emergent-interaction theory, a modern form of dualism that asserts that brain and mind interact but are not one and the same.

2. C (page 75): Think-aloud protocols involve describing strategies as you work. In experience-sampling, subjects are signaled randomly and asked to record their conscious experiences at those moments. Dichotic listening involves receiving two different messages and dividing attention between them. All three are more reliable variations on the classical method of introspection.

3. B (page 75): Three functions of consciousness are restricting attention to relevant experience; selecting stimuli for attention, perception, and memory; and enabling one to imagine and plan for alternative actions and events.

4. A (page 77): Repressing thoughts or ideas that make you anxious is a part of your unconscious. Nonconscious processes are bodily functions of which you are normally unaware. Preconscious memories are accessible but not recalled unless we are interrupted or need to instruct others. Subconscious processes attend to events we are not aware of on a more conscious level.

5. D (page 79): The sleep cycle consists of four stages of increasingly deep sleep plus one stage (Stage 5) of REM or rapid eye movement sleep, in which one is most likely to experience and spend time in vivid dreams.

6. A (page 83): Insomnia is any chronic failure to get adequate sleep. Narcolepsy is characterized by compulsive daytime sleeping accompanied by cataplexy (loss of muscle control). Sleep apnea is an upper respiratory disorder in which one stops breathing while asleep, wakens, and then resumes breathing and sleeping. Excessive daytime sleepiness is a common physiological disorder brought on by various stressors.

7. D (pages 85–86): Hypnosis is wrongly named after the god of sleep, since it is not a form of sleep. Not anyone can be hypnotized; it takes a particular talent or ability to accept and imagine the hypnotist's suggestions. Hypnotizability is not correlated with gullibility, intelligence, or conformity.

8. D (page 87): Advocates of regular meditation claim its benefits are increased physical and mental relaxation, as well as greater mindfulness and peace.

9. D (page 88): Hallucinations may be induced by hallucinogenic drugs like LSD or mescaline. They are also experienced by severe alcoholics undergoing alcohol withdrawal. The brain's need for stimulation may lead to hallucinations as a result of sensory deprivation and isolation.

10. A (page 92): Stimulants can heighten energy, alertness, arousal, self-confidence, and euphoria. In contrast, depressants slow down bodily and mental processes. Opiates dull sensitivity to stimulation and pain. Hallucinogenics distort perceptual experience and thought.

Chapter 4: Psychological Development

1. B (page 100): In most studies of developmental psychology, the independent variable is age and the dependent variable is the behavior of interest. Thus we examine the effects of age on the experience or ability in question.

2. A (page 101): The empirical view that the mind at birth is a blank slate (*tabula rasa*) was originally developed by British philosopher John Locke at the end of the eighteenth century. In contrast, French essayist Jean Rousseau proposed the nativist view that people at birth are "noble savages," corrupted by their contact with society.

3. D (pages 105–106): The neonate (newborn) is born alert, turning and reaching in general directions. Babies are born with prejudices favoring particular tastes and smells while rejecting others. Vision is less well developed; babies are born "legally" blind, but they quickly develop visual detection.

4. B (page 110): Normative investigations compare research subjects with established standards of behavior. The most ambitious design is longitudinal, which involves following the same group of subjects over time to chart their development. Cross-sectional designs are somewhat easier to manage and compare several different age groups simultaneously. A compromise may be the sequential design, in which small groups of different ages are studied for limited periods.

5. B (page 116): Overregularization occurs as a child learns the rules of grammar, and overapplies them. "Foots" and "handses" overapply the rule of adding an s to make a plural, when "feet" and "hands" are actually correct. "Bababababa" illustrates babbling. The other two utterances illustrate telegraphic speech.

6. C (page 119): Conservation is the concept that objects and quantities remain the same even if their appearance has changed. Ice cream may look like "more" because it fills the bottom of a dish, but a child who understands conservation knows that the amount has not increased. Object permanence involves knowing objects exist even when they are unavailable. Egocentrism is a rigid self-focused perspective. Animistic thinking involves thinking of objects as if they had life and intentions.

7. A (pages 121–122): Harlow gave baby monkeys a choice between a wire dummy that gave milk and a terrycloth dummy that did not. The babies preferred the soft dummy, clinging to it for rest and reassurance when they were not feeding. These studies confirmed the general finding that physical contact is critical to healthy early development.

8. C (page 124): Trust versus mistrust is the crisis of infancy and attachment. Autonomy versus doubt is the crisis of tod-

dlerhood and early self-control. Initiative versus guilt is the crisis of preschool experience. In early elementary school, children confront the crisis of competence versus inferiority, in which they must develop their skills and compare themselves favorably to their peers.

9. C (page 129): Freud claimed that adult development is driven by basic needs for love and work. In different terms, Erikson also confirms that early adulthood involves a crisis of intimacy while later adulthood focuses on the crisis of generativity.

10. C (page 138): Hearing loss may cause an older person to imagine others are whispering or deliberately excluding him or her from interaction. Paranoia may develop because isolation is blamed on the talkers' behavior rather than on one's own reduced sensitivity.

Chapter 5: Sensation and Perception

1. C (page 150): In transduction, one form of energy is transduced (literally "led across") to another processing system and a different form of energy. Sensory adaptation is the process whereby receptors fade out repetitive or continuous stimulation. Psychophysics is the field that studies the relationship of physical stimulation to psychological experience. Kinesthesis is the sense of bodily motion.

2. B (pages 151–153): According to the signal detection theory, sensation is a function of both sensitivity and judgment; judgment can be affected by expectations, such as Marcus's fear that his brother's car might break down any minute. Classical absolute threshold theory argues that sensation depends strictly on signal strength, not judgment. Weber's law explains the detection of difference thresholds. Hallucinations and delusions are characteristic of altered states of consciousness.

3. A (page 156): The eye's crystalline lens becomes thick or thin to accommodate the nearness of the viewed object and keep it in focus. The ganglion cells carry impulses from the retina to the visual cortex via the optic nerve. On the way, information is processed by the LGN for patterning.

4. B (page 167): Place theory argues that the location of greatest stimulation on the basilar membrane determines the pitch perceived. Frequency theory argues that the rate of neural firing determines pitch. Pitch is the perception of how high or low a sound is, determined by the frequency of sound waves that stimulate the auditory system.

5. D (page 166): Smell or olfaction is processed in the rhinencephalon, a structure in the oldest part of the brain. Some species communicate by means of pheromones, chemical signals about danger, food, territory, or sex.

6. B (page 172): The three stages of the perceptual process are sensation, perception, and identification/recognition. In the last stage, meaning is assigned to percepts so they can be identified (for example, labeled) and recognized (compared with information in memory).

7. A (page 176): An illusion is a perception of a pattern that is demonstrably incorrect. At the sensory level illusions result from signals that confuse sensory processing. At the perceptual level illusions result from ambiguous or distorted patterns.

8. B (page 179): The approach of von Helmholtz argues that perception is a function of personal experience. That of Gibson credits the development of perceptual processes to evolution and adaptation to a stimulus-filled environment. The Gestalt psychologists argued that perception involves a brain-based quest for meaning. The AI or artificial intelligence approach focuses on the operations involved in sensing and interpreting sensations.

9. B (page 183): We selectively give our attention to the most demanding stimuli. In this example, louder sounds such as a loudly speaking newcomer would distract Liza and cause her to lose information in the conversation to which she is trying to attend.

10. A (page 185): By grouping stimuli according to similar features—seeing large, dark spots as belonging together as part of the figure, while small, light spots belong together as part of the background—your perception is relying on the law of similarity. Grouping by nearness is the law of proximity. Grouping by direction or orientation is the law of common fate. The principle of closure leads to a tendency to see incomplete figures as whole.

Chapter 6: Learning

1. A (page 199): Unlike simpler species, humans have not inherited instincts or specific behavior tendencies, but our survival is supported by an inherited capacity to learn. All humans have a similar capacity for learning, but we have different life experiences and so learn different lessons.

2. D (pages 200–201): John B. Watson, the founder of behaviorism, argued that only observable, measurable change and behavior should be the focus of scientific psychology. This led to the development of behavior analysis, which carefully studies and explains the processes of learning.

3. C (page 203): The cat naturally oriented to and sniffed for her food when it was present in the dish. After several pairings of the noisy can opener (CS) with the cat food (UCS), the cat's response (running and orienting to the food) was elicited by the sound of the can opener alone.

4. B (pages 207–208): Research by Rescorla has shown that a CS must seem to reliably predict a UCS that is contingent on it. Further work by Kamin indicates that the CS must appear to provide distinctive information about the UCS in order for the stimulus-stimulus connection to be learned.

5. A (page 209): According to Thorndike's work with cats in puzzle boxes, behaviors (like successfully escaping from the box) increase in frequency if they have satisfying consequences, and eventually become the dominant response when the organism is placed in that environment.

6. C (page 212): A consistent relationship between an outcome or consequence, such as a paycheck, and a response, such as a full week's work, indicates that the paycheck is contingent on working a full week.

7. B (page 213): If the best part of a beach vacation is its power to prevent or eliminate stress and other painful experiences, then your friend's beach-going behavior will increase, indicating the effects of reinforcement. Because the reinforcement works by removing noxious stimuli, it is considered negative reinforcement.

8. B (page 214): Effective punishment must be limited in intensity. Other conditions include that it must be swift and brief, immediately administered, focused on the response instead of the behaver's character, limited to the situation where the behavior occurs, unambiguous, and administered in the form of penalties rather than physical pain.

9. D (page 216): According to the Premack principle, a more preferred activity can be used to reinforce a less preferred one, as when a child who would rather read is allowed to do so only after first doing household chores.

10. D (pages 220–221): Biological constraints on learning indicate that there are limitations to what members of a species can learn. Learned helpless results when an organism learns that none of its responses are effective. Fear conditioning is the process of classically conditioning new stimuli to be associated with those that trigger fear. Spontaneous recovery is the partial recurrence of a conditional response that has been extinguished.

Chapter 7: Cognitive Processes

1. A (page 234): The information processing model of cognition proposes that processes such as sensation, perception, memory, reasoning, and problem-solving operate at distinct stages in a hierarchical arrangement of processes. These are more distinct than in a continuum. "Procedural" describes a type of memory, while "logical" describes the reasoning involving induction or deduction.

2. D (page 235): Think-aloud protocols employ a modern version of introspection. Other methods for studying cognitive processes include measuring reaction time to stimuli, analyzing errors, and objectively observing behavior.

3. A (page 237): Thinking, the process of forming new representation by transforming available information, has three features: it cannot be directly observed but can be inferred from observable behavior; it manipulates knowledge in a person's cognitive system; and it is directed toward solving one's problems.

4. C (page 238): A concept is a category linking items with common features. In contrast, a schema is a cluster of ideas and preconceptions about related items. A heuristic is a rule of thumb that generally works to solve some problem. And a memory is the product of the process of encoding and storing a sensory and cognitive experience.

5. B (pages 242–243): A script is an event schema, a cluster of knowledge about a sequence of activities. In contrast, schemas in general may be about objects, persons, or roles. An algorithm is a problem-solving strategy that guarantees a solution. A mental map is an image that stores and organizes spatial and locational information.

6. B (page 247): The syllogism is a common form of deductive reasoning. In contrast, inductive reasoning is typical of scientific research, in which particular findings are built upon to establish general theories or truths. An algorithm is a guaranteed but sometimes tedious problem-solving method, while a heuristic is a rule of thumb that may be easier though it cannot guarantee a solution.

7. D (pages 248–249): In information-processing terms, a problem has three parts: an initial state, a goal state, and a set of operations. A prototype is an ideal or most representative example of a concept. A concept is a category whose members share recognizable features. Assimilation is a process of incorporating new information into familiar ways of thinking.

8. B (page 251): An algorithm is a guaranteed strategy for solving a problem, although a less-reliable heuristic may be faster or easier. A prototype is an ideal example of a concept. A syllogism is a common form of deductive reasoning. A mnemonic is a verbal strategy for memorizing complex material.

9. A (pages 264–265): Procedural memory involves remembering "how to" do things. Semantic memory is memory of facts or ideas. Sensory memory is a brief prolongation of a sensory impression to facilitate processing. Constructive memory is a form of long-term memory in which information is added to the material being recalled.

10. C (page 271): In proactive interference, old memories act in a forward-moving direction to distort new knowledge. In retroactive interference, later memories cause us to forget earlier ones. Some early psychologists thought memories could decay over time, though there is little evidence for this. In cases of emotional or traumatic memories, our conscious may be unable to access repressed information.

Chapter 8: Motivation and Emotion

1. A (page 283): Five uses of the concept of motivation include the following: to account for behavioral variability; to relate biology to behavior; to infer private states from public acts; to assign responsibility for actions; and to explain perseverance despite adversity. Human social behavior is not theorized to have instinctive origins.

2. C (page 284): In this example, deprivation of the substance is one form of stimulus input. This is presumed to cause a motivational state, an intervening variable between stimulus and response. And the animal's behavior is one form of response output. The animal is rewarded, not punished, so no aversive experience is involved.

3. D (page 294): James, McDougall, and Freud all offered forms of instinct theories of motivation. James saw instincts as purposive, while McDougall defined instincts as inherited dispositions that are energizing, active, and goal-directed. Freud thought that instincts had neither conscious purpose nor predetermined direction, and that one could learn many ways to satisfy them.

4. B (page 298): Attachment needs are needs to belong, to affiliate with others, to love and be loved.

5. D (page 307): In humans, sexuality is more dependent on psychological factors than it is in animals. For humans and nonhumans alike, sexuality is not essential to survival, may be accompanied by other motivations, and motivates a wide variety of behaviors and psychological processes.

6. A (page 314): TAT stands for Thematic Apperception Test, in which a subject creates a story about each of a series of pictures. The subject's needs are theorized to appear in the themes of the stories.

7. D (pages 314–315): The need for achievement (*n Ach*) has been found to be associated with individuals' efforts to persist on impossible tasks, whereas those low in *n Ach* persist on easy tasks, and with upward mobility. Members of achievement-motivated cultures also value working autonomously or independently.

8. C (page 316): Research by Mark Lepper confirms that when an extrinsic reward is given for intrinsically enjoyable tasks the motivation becomes extrinsic and the task seems less enjoyable—relying solely on external reward.

9. D (pages 288–289): The reticular activating system controls emotional arousal. The autonomic nervous system prepares the body for emotional reactions. The limbic system and hypothalamus are old-brain control systems for emotions.

10. B (page 320): According to the Cannon-Bard theory, physiological arousal and the subjective awareness of experiencing emotion are independent processes—both set in motion by the same central processes and triggered by the original emotional stimulus.

Chapter 9: Stress, Coping, and Health

1. A (page 334): Getting married is one of the top ten most stressful life changes, according to the Student Stress Scale. The other stressors—car trouble, arguments, a change of major—rank lower and are associated with less likelihood of stress-related illness. A life change is stressful because it demands adaptation, whether it means something positive or negative in the long run.

2. D (page 336): Societal stressors include society-wide problems like overpopulation, economic recession, pollution, epidemics, and the threat of war. An earthquake is a catastrophic event. A jail term is considered a stressful life change. Being stuck in traffic is an example of a hassle.

3. B (page 337): A stress moderator variable filters or modifies how stressors will affect one's reactions. A defense mechanism is an automatic coping strategy that protects one's self or self-esteem. Cognitive appraisal is a process of evaluating stressors and one's abilities to respond. A life change is caused by an event that requires adaptation.

4. A (pages 337–338): Hardiness is an ability to welcome change as a challenge instead of as a threat. The Type-A personality is highly prone to stress. The Type-T profile involves risk-taking and thrill-seeking. Learned helplessness indicates a complete loss of perceived control.

5. C (page 339): The fight-or-flight response is governed by the autonomic nervous system. PTSD stands for post-traumatic stress disorder. PNI refers to psychoneuroimmunology. The GAS is the general adaptation syndrome for responding to stress.

6. B (page 341): The three stages of the GAS are alarm, resistance, and exhaustion. Withdrawal is not a stage in the adaptation to severe stress.

7. A (page 343): Different reactions have been identified for mild, moderate, and severe stress. Mild stress can increase alertness and responsiveness, although unresolved mild stress can cause maladaptive behavior. Moderate stress disrupts behavior, and severe stress may lead to immobility. Chronic stress recurs, while acute stress is event-related.

8. C (page 350): Judith Rodin and Ellen Langer found their nursing home patients thrived on perceived control when the patients were assigned tasks like plant care and allowed to make choices such as which movies to watch.

9. C (page 356): The "war on lifestyle" involves preventing diseases of civilization by encouraging people to change unhealthy behaviors and develop healthier action patterns.

10. B (page 361): Research by James Pennebaker confirms the value of talking it out. Keeping it in or seeking distractions can prolong stress and recovery. Accepting too much help can lead to learned helplessness.

Chapter 10: Personality

1. D (page 371): Implicit personality theories are the theories laypersons form about people, based on their interactions and impressions. Scientific personality theories are based on case studies, inventory scores, and other systematic research techniques.

2. B (page 372): The nomothetic approach is variable-centered, assuming that the same traits or dimensions can be used to describe everyone, while people differ in the degree to which they possess each trait. The idiographic approach is person-centered, assuming that traits mean different things to different people. Humanistic and psychodynamic theories focus on personality development, not traits.

3. B (page 374): Assuming that thin people are nervous fits with type theories, like Sheldon's theory of somatotypes. Sorting people into categories (for example, thin) favors a type theory rather than a trait theory. Judging people on their appearance does not involve humanistic assumptions, and it does not have any obvious social-learning connection.

4. A (pages 376–377): The Big Five include Extroversion, Agreeableness, Conscientiousness, Emotional Stability, and Openness to Experience.

5. C (page 383): The superego includes both the processes of the conscience and the ego ideal (one's concept of what one wishes to be like).

6. B (page 386): Humanistic theories emphasize that human action and growth are free, healthy, and directed toward self-actualization. In contrast, Freudian theory proposes that behaviors are motivated by unconscious instincts like life (sexuality) and death (aggression).

7. D (page 390): Bandura's theory combines principles of learning with an emphasis on social interactions. George Kelly's theory focuses on the concept of the personal construct. Eysenck combined type and trait theories in his model. Adler was a post-Freudian theorist.

8. B (page 393): Self-esteem refers to one's esteem or estimation of one's value. Self-concept includes all the concepts, thoughts, and ideas one has about oneself. Self-handicapping involves sabotaging one's own efforts in order to create a more acceptable excuse for failure. Self-efficacy refers to one's belief that one can perform adequately in a particular situation.

9. B (page 399): The TAT is the only projective technique listed; the others are all objective personality tests.

10. C (pages 397–399): Stable-unstable is a dimension in Eysenck's type-trait theory. The Myers-Briggs includes the following dimensions: judging-perceiving; thinking-feeling; sensing-intuiting; extroverted-introverted.

Chapter 11: Individual Differences

1. C (page 408): A problem with tests is the degree to which results indicate experiences that vary widely from one individual to another. Some tests are objective, and some can employ strategies to reduce or overcome evaluators' biases.

2. A (page 411): The eugenics movement promoted selective breeding to promote the reproducing of the best, brightest, and fittest qualities among humans. Eugenicists believed superior races existed and would eventually overwhelm and replace inferior ones. They did not accept the value of environmental over hereditary influence.

3. B (pages 412–414): The size of a person's left toe will not vary over situations and sessions, so the score yielded by this "test" will be consistent, thus reliable. However, big toe size is obviously unrelated to intelligence, so it is not valid.

4. A (page 414): To be useful, a test must be reliable, valid, and standardized. Standardization is accomplished by establishing norms, statistical standards for how a test is to be administered, who should administer it, and under what conditions.

5. A (page 416): A major advantage of tests over other assessment techniques—such as interviews, life histories, and situational behavior observations—is that psychological tests provide quantitative information by characterizing an individual in terms of the normal comparisons derived for the test.

6. D (page 418): The text defines intelligence as the capacity to profit from experience—to go beyond what is perceived to imagine symbolic possibilities.

7. B (page 421): Terman's equation is MA/CA x 100 = IQ. Using this formula, 15/12 x 100 = 125.

8. C (page 424): It was Guilford who designed the 5 x 6 x 5 "cube" representing the structure of intellect. Wechsler developed the intelligence scales that include both verbal and performance subscales. Cattell distinguished between verbal and performance abilities. And Gardner identified seven kinds of intelligence abilities.

9. B (page 426): Contextual intelligence is reflected in one's ability to shape his or her context and available resources to meet his or her needs. Experiential intelligence is reflected in creative intelligence, while componential intelligence involves knowledge acquisition, problem solving, and metacognition. Performance ability is an aspect of Wechsler's assessment of intelligence, and not one of Sternberg's three types of intelligence.

10. A (page 434): The Strong-Campbell Interest Inventory is the most widely used instrument for measuring vocational interests. It was developed by matching the answers of men in different occupations with those of men in general.

Chapter 12: Social Psychology

1.   A (page 444): The prison simulation underscores the principle that social situations are powerful shapers of human action. It does not emphasize the power of individual differences (choices C and D). Moreover, although the study's participants had different ideas about prisons, they did not need to be unanimous in order for the prison situation to influence their thoughts and behavior.

2.   C (pages 445–446): Social loafing occurs when group members withhold maximum effort in pursuing group goals. This contrasts with social facilitation (enhancement of performance by the presence of others) and social interference (interruption of performance by arousal caused by others' presence). Social loafing is the result of group context, not specific social roles or rules.

3.   D (pages 447–448): The so-called "three R's" are examples of the coercive power of the group. They are the penalties for deviating from or refusing to conform with the group.

4.   C (page 449): The marks of their Bennington experience were still evident 20 years later: those who left college as liberals were still liberal, those who resisted remained conservative, and the rest were middle-of-the-roaders.

5.   B (page 453): Besides unanimity of the majority, several conditions that breed conformity are a difficult or ambiguous task, a cohesive group, the perception that the group's members are competent, and having to make responses in public rather than privately.

6.   C (page 456): The majority of subjects obeyed the authority fully, despite verbal protests and discomfort. They believed they were participating in a study of the effects of punishment on learning, not of obedience to authority. The learner's complaint of a heart condition elicited protests and concerns, but did not reduce obedience.

7.   C (page 460): Laboratory studies of bystander intervention show that the best predictor of intervention is the size of the group present. The larger the group, the less likely any individual is to feel responsible for intervening. No personality variable has been found to be related to individuals' likelihood of intervening.

8.   A (page 466): Behavioral confirmation is the process by which someone's expectations about another—such as assuming someone is a music major—actually influence the person to act in ways that confirm those expectations. In contrast, self-fulfilling prophecies are predictions about future behavior that later produce what the predictor expected. Social categorization involves sorting people into groups, but not necessarily interacting with them. Self-serving biases concern the ways we interpret our own behaviors and outcomes.

9.   C (page 468): Cognitive dissonance is experienced as tension caused when two cognitions clash with or contradict each other. Making an effort to take a class which then turns out to be disappointing would cause dissonance. In the other examples, the two cognitions involved support or do not contradict each other.

10.   B (page 476): Relationship breakdown starts with the intrapsychic phase, when one partner keeps his or her dissatisfaction private. Problems are discussed openly in the dyadic phase. If they decide to break up, the couple enters the social phase and informs their friends. After the breakup, they remember the relationship during the grave-dressing phase, and try to make sense of their experiences.

Chapter 13: Psychopathology

1.   A (page 488): The six indicators of possible abnormality are distress, maladaptiveness, irrationality, unpredictability, unconventionality and statistical rarity, and observer discomfort. Chronic physical illness is not one of them.

2.   B (page 494): DSM-III-R stands for Diagnostic and Statistical Manual, Third Edition, Revised. Developed by the American Psychiatric Association, it classifies, defines, and describes over 200 mental disorders.

3.   D (page 498): Dissociative disorders include disturbances in the integration of identity, memory, or consciousness. Among these rare disorders are included psychogenic amnesia and multiple personality disorder.

4.   B (page 504): Irrational fears are only considered phobias if they interfere with our adjustment and achievements. Phobias are one kind of anxiety (not affective) disorder. One biological explanation for anxiety disorders is that certain fears are common to our evolutionary past, and phobias represent a pattern of being ready to respond to such ancient threats.

5.   C (page 506): Almost everyone has experienced the sadness, pain, and lethargy of unipolar depression after suffering a loss or disappointment. People diagnosed with unipolar depression suffer from longer-lasting and more severe symptoms than those of us who experience only mild depression.

6.   D (page 512): Youth suicide typically occurs as the final stage of a period of inner turmoil and outer distress, and most victims have talked or written about their intentions prior to making the attempt.

7.   B (page 513): Bulimia is characterized by a binge-and-purge pattern of symptoms. Anorexia resembles self-starvation. Inhibition generally refers to changing or reducing unwanted behaviors. Mania is the term for elated mood.

8.   B (page 518): Paranoid schizophrenia involves complex delusions focused around specific themes. The most common delusions involve grandeur (believing oneself to be very important), persecution (thinking that others are out to hurt you),

delusional jealousy (believing one's spouse is unfaithful), and delusions of reference (misconstruing chance happenings as directed at oneself).

9. A (page 522): From the Greek word *soma*, for "body," the classification of somatoform disorders includes problems with physical symptoms, including conversion disorders which were formerly referred to as "hysteria."

10. C (page 525): Stigma refers to the brand or mark of disgrace that accompanies a deviant label. It involves a set of negative attitudes about a person that sets him or her apart as unacceptable.

Chapter 14: Psychotherapies

1. C (page 534): All therapies are interventions into a person's life, designed to change that person's functioning in some way. Not all forms of therapy will make one feel good about himself or herself at a given moment, or shape the individual to fit better into his or her society.

2. A (page 538): Psychiatrists are trained in medicine with some special focus on treating mental and emotional disorders. They are the only therapists who can prescribe medications, to the exclusion of all psychologists (trained in psychology), social workers, psychoanalysts, and other counselors.

3. A (page 543): Psychoanalysis is called *insight therapy* because it seeks to help a patient gain insights into the unconscious conflicts that underlie his or her symptoms. Cognitive therapies—including rational-emotive therapy—regard thought processes as behaviors that can be changed by applying learning principles. Existential-humanist therapies emphasize the here-and-now more than the client's past.

4. C (page 545): Transference refers to a patient's emotional identification of the therapist with a significant personal relationship. In countertransference, the therapist feels this involvement with the patient. Negative transference is transference of emotions like hate or envy. Resistance involves denying or avoiding feelings and ideas the therapy is revealing.

5. D (page 549): In flooding, the client is put into the phobic situation. Systematic desensitization pairs phobic imaginings gradually with relaxation exercises. Implosion therapy involves imagining the worst phobic situation first instead of building up to it. Catharsis is a psychoanalytic concept of intense emotional release.

6. D (page 551): Participant modeling treats phobias by first demonstrating (modeling) the feared behavior, and then inviting the client to imitate the model. Counterconditioning refers to behavior modification to undo or reverse maladaptive lessons. Behavioral rehearsal involves visualizing acting in desirable ways. Clinical ecology is a specialty relating behavioral disorders to environmental stressors.

7. C (page 556): The goal of RET is to increase a person's self-worth by getting rid of faulty beliefs like "I must be thin before anyone will love me." Behavior therapies work well with changing problem behaviors like smoking. Person-centered therapy focuses on self-actualization by providing acceptance and unconditional positive regard for persons who fear harsh judgments, such as parental disapproval.

8. B (page 563): ECT is effective in treating severe depression, although the reasons for its effectiveness are unknown. Properly applied ECT always prepares the patient with sedatives and muscle relaxants to minimize violent physical reactions.

9. A (page 566): Like other antianxiety drugs, Valium reduces tension by sedating the user. Antidepressant drugs include Tofranil and Elavil, and the anti-manic extract Lithium. Antipsychotic drugs like Thorazine reduce schizophrenic symptoms. An antihistamine drug reduces allergic symptoms.

10. D (page 567): Frank has argued that "belief is really crucial to all the healing processes. . . . Nothing happens unless they really believe that this could help them." If a client believes in therapy, he or she will be more willing to cooperate in making the desired changes.

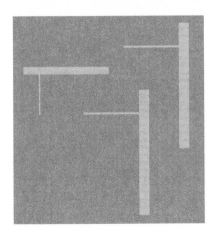

Glossary

A

absolute threshold (p. 151) Minimum amount of physical energy needed to stimulate a sensory system.

accommodation (p. 118) A process that restructures or modifies the child's existing schemes so that new information is better understood.

account (p. 477) The story of one's experience, especially of a trauma or loss, including attributions of blame, social perceptions, beliefs, memories, and emotions.

achievement test (p. 434) Standardized test designed to measure an individual's current level of competence in a given area.

acquisition (p. 204) Stage of classical conditioning when conditional response is first elicited by the conditional stimulus.

activation-synthesis theory (p. 82) Theory that all dreams begin with random electrical discharges from deep within the brain.

acute stress (p. 338) Temporary pattern of arousal, with clear onset and offset.

addiction (p. 90) Physical state in which withdrawal occurs if a certain drug is not present in the body.

adolescence (p. 125) The stage of life that begins at the onset of puberty and continues until adulthood.

affective disorder (p. 505) Class of disorders in which primary symptoms are associated with disturbances of mood and emotion.

afferent systems (p. 150) Sensory systems that process information coming into the brain.

ageism (p. 137) Prejudice against older people.

aggression (p. 28) Physical or verbal behavior with the intent to hurt or destroy.

agoraphobia (p. 501) Extreme fear of being in public places or distant from familiar surroundings.

AI approach (p. 179) Artificial intelligence approach to studying cognitive processes that studies perception at three levels of analysis: neurophysiological mechanisms, perceptual processes, and perceptible properties of the world.

AIDS (p. 360) Acquired Immune Deficiency Syndrome, a lethal condition caused by virus that damages the body's immune system.

algorithm (p. 251) Problem-solving procedure that guarantees reaching a correct outcome by reviewing every possible strategy.

Alzheimer's disease (p. 140) Chronic, organic brain disorder, characterized by gradual loss of cognitive abilities and memory, and deterioration of personality.

amygdala (p. 50) Limbic system structure involved in aggression, eating, drinking, and sexual behaviors.

anal stage (p. 381) Second phase of psychosexual development, in which elimination and retention of feces is associated with greatest gratification.

analytic psychology (p. 386) Jungian view that the healthy personality is an integrated balance of opposing forces.

anorexia nervosa (p. 511) Pattern of self-starvation with psychological rather than physical causes.

anticipatory coping (p. 346) Efforts made in advance of a potential stressor to balance perceived demands with available resources.

antisocial personality disorder (p. 497) Personality disorder in which symptoms include absence of conscience and lack of sense of responsibility to others.

anxiety (p. 383) Intense, negative emotional reaction to the threat of becoming conscious of a repressed conflict.

aptitude test (p. 434) Test designed to measure an individual's potential for acquiring various skills.

archetype (p. 386) Jungian concept of universal symbol of human experience, part of collective unconscious.

archival data (p. 416) Previously published or documented findings available in public records or cultural artifacts.

Asch effect (p. 451) Pattern of conformity in which, even when conditions are ambiguous, a unanimous group majority influences individuals' judgments.

assimilation (p. 118) A process that modifies new environmental information to fit into what is already known.

association cortex (p. 52) Part of the cortex where processes such as planning and decision-making occur.

attachment (p. 121) The intense, enduring, social-emotional relationship between a child and a parent or other regular caregiver.

attribution theory (p. 469) System of explanations for individual and social causes of behavior.

auditory cortex (p. 51) Part of the cortex that processes auditory information. (p. 165) Area of temporal lobes in brain that receives and processes sound information.

auditory nerve (p. 165) Bundle of axons from inner-ear cells carrying sound information to the brain.

autistic thinking (p. 247) Distinctive, personal cognition involving fantasy, daydreaming, unconscious processes, and untestable ideas.

automaticity (p. 183) Apparently effortless, involuntary processing conducted without intention.

autonomic nervous system (ANS) (p. 56) Subdivision of the PNS which sustains basic life processes.

availability heuristic (p. 255) Cognitive strategy that estimates probabilities based on personal experience.

aversion therapy (p. 549) Behavioral therapy technique in which individuals are presented with a pairing of the attractive stimuli with unpleasant stimuli in order to condition a negative reaction.

axon (p. 58) A single, extended fiber that conducts information about stimulation along its length, usually from neuron cell body to terminal buttons.

B

bait shyness (p. 222) Aversion to novel foods or to familiar foods in novel environments or conditions.

base rate (p. 8) A statistic that identifies the most common frequency or probability of a given event.

basic level (p. 240) Optimal level of categorization for an object to be mentally represented; level most quickly accessed by memory and most efficiently used.

basilar membrane (p. 165) Thin membrane (tissue) that runs through the cochlea; hair cells on the basilar membrane are activated by sound (vibration) energy.

behavior (p. 5) Observable action; the means by which organisms adjust to their environment.

behavior modification (p. 547) In behavioral psychotherapy, approach that applies operant conditioning and classical conditioning to change client's behavior.

behavioral confirmation (pp. 393, 466) Process of acting in ways that another person expects, thus validating those expectations.

behavioral data (p. 6) Reports of observations about the behavior of organisms and the conditions under which the behavior occurs or changes.

behavioral measures (p. 25) Techniques used to study overt, observable, and recordable actions.

behavioral rehearsal (p. 553) Procedures used to establish and strengthen basic skills by requiring client to mentally practice a desirable sequence of action.

behaviorism (p. 15) Assertion that only the overt behavior of organisms is the proper subject of scientific study.

behavioristic approach (p. 15) Approach that focuses on overt behaviors that can be objectively recorded and manipulated.

biased assimilation (p. 254) Collecting data without careful attention because the information supports one's preexisting beliefs.

Big Five (p. 376) Five basic dimensions underlying the traits used to describe people's behavior: Extroversion; Agreeableness; Consciousness; Emotional Stability; and Openness to Experience.

biological approach (p. 13) Approach that searches for the causes of behavior in the functioning of genes, the brain, the nervous system, and the endocrine system.

biological constraints on learning (p. 220) Limitation on an organism's capacity to learn that is caused by inherited capabilities of the species.

biomedical therapy (p. 534) Any of several treatments of psychological disorders that change biological or physical mechanisms.

biopsychosocial model (p. 352) New view of body-mind interaction which examines the health consequences of links among factors in the nervous system, immune system, behavior, cognition, and environment.

bipedalism (p. 40) The ability to walk upright.

bipolar cell (p. 157) Nerve cell, with one dendrite and one axon, that combines impulses from many receptors and transmits them to ganglion cells.

bipolar disorder (p. 506) Type of affective disorder in which individual's behavior alternates between periods of mania and depression.

blind (p. 24) Uninformed about the purpose of a research study.

body image (p. 127) The way one views one's appearance.

bottom-up processing (p. 173) Processing in which incoming stimulus information is perceived as coming from sensory data and is sent upward to the brain for analysis and interpretation.

brightness (p. 160) Perceived intensity of light.

bulimia (p. 513) Disorder characterized by pattern of bingeing (overeating) and purging (vomiting or using laxatives to prevent digestion).

bystander intervention (p. 460) Act of assisting those who need help in unfamiliar or critical circumstances.

C

cannabis (p. 91) Drug, derived from hemp plant, whose psychoactive effects include altered perception, sedation, pain relief, and mild euphoria.

Cannon-Bard theory of emotion (p. 320) Theory, developed independently by Walter Cannon and Philip Bard, that arousal and emotional experience do not cause each other but are both produced by an emotional stimulus.

cardinal trait (p. 375) Trait around which people organize their lives.

catharsis (p. 544) Process and outcome of expressing strongly felt emotions that are usually inhibited.

central core (p. 45) Area of the brain that contains five structures that collectively regulate the internal state of the body.

central nervous system (CNS) (p. 55) Subsystem of the nervous system composed of all the neurons in the brain and spinal cord.

central trait (p. 375) Major trait assumed to explain an individual's pattern of behavior.

centration (p. 119) Thought pattern characterized by inability to take into account more than one factor at a time.

cerebellum (p. 47) Structure of the brain at the base of the skull, which organizes bodily motion, posture, and equilibrium.

cerebral cortex (p. 50) Area of the brain that regulates the brain's higher cognitive and emotional functions.

cerebral dominance (p. 63) Tendency of each hemisphere of the brain to dominate the control of different functions.

cerebral hemispheres (p. 50) Two nearly symmetrical halves of the cerebral cortex.

chemotherapy (p. 564) Any use of drugs to treat mental, behavioral, or physical disorders.

chronic stress (p. 338) Continuous state of arousal, in which demands are perceived to be greater than resources available to deal with them.

chronological age (CA) (pp. 100, 419) Number of months or years since an individual's birth.

chronological approach (p. 101) Understanding of behavior and mental processes by focusing on the orderly sequence of development over time.

chunk (p. 263) Meaningful unit of information.

chunking (p. 263) Recording information into a single meaningful unit.

circadian rhythms (p. 79) Patterns that repeat approximately every 24 hours.

classical conditioning (p. 201) Form of learning in which two stimuli become associated so that one acquires the power to elicit the same behavioral response as the other.

client (p. 536) Person receiving treatment for psychological problems; term used by therapists who see disorders as problems in living, not as mental illness.

clinical ecology (p. 569) Field that relates disorders to environmental irritants and sources of trauma.

clinical psychologist (p. 538) Professional psychologist (with training and degree in psychology) specializing in assessing and treating psychological disorders.

closure (p. 184) Organization process leading to perception of incomplete figures as complete.

cognition (p. 232) Processes of knowing, including attending, remembering, and reasoning; contents of cognitive processes, including concepts and memories.

cognitive appraisal (p. 337) Recognition and evaluation of stressor to assess the threat, demand, resources available to deal with it, and appropriate strategies.

cognitive approach (p. 16) View that emphasizes human thought and all the processes of knowing as central to the study of psychology.

cognitive behavior modification (p. 552) Therapeutic technique that combines emphasis on thoughts and attitudes with strategies for changing performance by altering reinforcement contingencies.

cognitive bias (p. 255) A systematic error in the sequence of inference, judgment, and decision.

cognitive development (p. 116) The study of the processes and products of the mind as they emerge and change over time.

cognitive dissonance (p. 468) According to theory developed by Leon Festinger, motivating state of tension produced by inconsistency or contradiction between an individual's feelings, beliefs, or actions.

cognitive economy (p. 238) Minimizing time and effort required to process information.

cognitive map (p. 224) (p. 245) Mental representation of physical space.

cognitive model (p. 234) An explanatory metaphor that describes how information is detected, stored, and used by people and machines.

cognitive psychology (p. 233) The scientific study of mental processes and mental structures.

cognitive science (p. 234) An interdisciplinary field that studies the variety of systems and processes that manipulate information.

cognitive therapy (p. 551) Psychotherapeutic approach to changing problem feelings and behaviors by changing how clients perceive or think about significant experiences.

collective unconscious (p. 386) Jungian concept of inherited, unconscious ideas and forces common to all members of a species.

complementary colors (p. 160) Colors opposite each other on the color circle.

concept (p. 238) Mental representation of categories of items or ideas, based on experience.

conditional response (CR) (p. 203) In classical conditioning, response elicited by previously neutral stimulus that has become associated with the unconditional stimulus.

conditional stimulus (CS) (p. 203) In classical conditioning, previously neutral stimulus that comes to elicit the conditional response.

conditioned reinforcers (p. 215) In operant conditioning, a formerly neutral stimulus that has become a reinforcer.

conditioning (p. 15) The process of learning and modifying behavior by pairing stimulus events in specific patterns.

cones (p. 157) Photoreceptors concentrated in and near the fovea of the retina that detect wavelength (color) and function best in bright light.

conformity (p. 451) Tendency for people to adopt the behaviors, attitudes, and values of other members of a reference group.

confounding variables (p. 24) Factors that could be confused with the independent variable in a research study and thus distort the results.

consciousness (p. 75) Awareness of the general condition of one's mind, awareness of particular mental contents, or self-awareness.

conservation (p. 119) The understanding that physical properties of an object do not change when nothing is added or taken away, even though its appearance changes.

consistency paradox (p. 377) Observation that personality ratings made by different observers at different times are similar while behavior ratings across situations are not.

constitutional factors (p. 104) Basic physical and psychological tendencies that remain fairly constant throughout a person's lifetime.

construct validity (p. 414) Degree to which test scores based on a specific characteristic correlate with other measures of the same characteristic (for example, other test scores, judges' ratings, or behaviors).

contact comfort (p. 122) Reassurance derived from physical touch and access of caregiver.

context of discovery (p. 21) Initial phase of research during which an investigator comes up with a new idea or a different way of thinking about phenomena.

context of justification (p. 23) Second phase of research, in which results are tested and prepared for useful communication with the scientific community.

contingency management (p. 547) General treatment strategy for changing behavior by changing its consequences.

control condition (p. 27) Condition in which research subjects are not exposed to the experimental treatment in a controlled experiment; contrasted with experimental condition.

controlled experiment (p. 26) Observations of specific behavior made under systematically varied conditions, in which subjects have been randomly assigned to experimental and control (non-treatment) conditions.

conversion disorder (p. 489) Type of psychological disorder in which there is loss of motor or sensory function without corresponding organic cause.

coping (p. 345) Means of dealing with a situation perceived to be threatening.

corpus callosum (p. 50) Thick mass of nerve fibers that connects the two hemispheres of the cerebral cortex.

correlation coefficient (p. 25) A statistical measure used to determine the precise degree of correlation between two variables; symbolized as r.

counseling psychologist (p. 538) Professional psychologist specializing in providing guidance in solving problems of normal adjustment.

counterconditioning (p. 547) Therapeutic technique which uses conditioning to substitute a new response for an inadequate one.

countertransference (p. 545) In psychoanalysis, process in which a therapist comes to like or dislike a patient because the patient is perceived as similar to significant people in the therapist's life.

covariation principle (p. 470) Inferring causes of events through the observation of co-occurrences of two events.

criterion validity (p. 413) Degree to which test scores indicate a result that is consistent with another standard of the same characteristic.

critical feature (p. 238) Quality that is a necessary and sufficient condition for including a concept in a category.

critical period (p. 106) A sensitive time in an organism's development when it will acquire a particular behavior if certain stimuli and experiences occur.

critical set point (p. 303) Level on an internal, biological scale that alerts the central nervous system about the body's fat content; when fat cell composition drops below this level, the brain triggers eating behavior.

cross-sectional design (p. 110) A type of investigation in which groups of subjects of different chronological ages are observed and compared at a given time.

crystallized intelligence (p. 424) Knowledge a person has already acquired and the ability to use that knowledge.

CT scanning (p. 47) The process of computerized tomography, which creates a computerized image of X-rays passed through various angles of the brain.

D

daydreaming (p. 78) Mild form of consciousness alteration, in which attention shifts away from the immediate situation.

debriefing (p. 28) Procedure conducted with subjects at the end of an experiment, in which researcher explains hypothesis, reveals deception, and provides emotional support.

decibels (dB) (p. 164) Units of physical intensity of sound.

decision making (p. 253) Choosing between alternatives; selecting or rejecting available options.

declarative memory (p. 265) Memory for explicit information; also known as *fact memory.*

deductive reasoning (p. 247) Drawing a conclusion intended to follow logically from two or more statements (premises).

deficiency motivation (p. 297) Motivation to restore physical or psychological equilibrium (balance).

delusion (p. 516) False belief maintained despite contrary evidence and lack of social support.

demand characteristics (p. 457) Cue in an experimental setting that influences subjects' perception of how they are expected to behave.

dendrites (p. 58) Branched fibers that extend outward from the cell body and take information into the neuron.

dependent variable (p. 8) Any behavioral variable whose values result from or depend upon changes in one or more independent variables.

depressants (p. 92) Drugs that slow down the mental and physical activity of the body by inhibiting CNS transmission of nerve impulses.

determinism (p. 10) Doctrine that physical, behavioral, and mental events are not random but rather are determined by specific causal factors.

developmental age (p. 100) The chronological age at which most children show a particular level of physical or mental development.

developmental disabilities (p. 43) Genetically based disorders that affect the development of some behavior or process.

developmental psychology (p. 100) The branch of psychology that is concerned with the changes in physical and psychological functioning that occur, from conception across the entire life span.

developmental stages (p. 106) Periods during which physical or psychological functioning differs from earlier or later functioning.

diathesis-stress hypothesis (p. 519) Predisposition to develop a particular disorder as a result of interaction between stressful demands and personal traits.

dichotic listening task (p. 75) Experiment where a subject listens through stereo earphones to two different channels of input while being instructed to attend to just one channel.

difference threshold (p. 154) Smallest recognizable difference between two stimuli, also known as the *just noticeable difference (JND).*

dishabituation (p. 112) Recovery from habituation; occurs when novel stimuli are presented.

dissociative disorder (p. 498) Psychological reaction in which an individual experiences sudden, temporary alteration of consciousness through severe loss of memory or identity.

distal stimulus (p. 173) Object in environment that is source of external stimulation; contrasted with *proximal stimulus.*

distraction (p. 179) Inability to perceptually process available stimuli due to interference.

dopamine hypothesis (p. 520) Explanation proposing relationship between many schizophrenic symptoms and relative excess of the neurotransmitter dopamine at specific brain receptor sites.

double bind (p. 520) Conflict situation in which individual receives multiple, contradictory messages from a significant other.

double-blind control (p. 24) A control strategy that employs both uninformed experimenters and uninformed subjects.

dream analysis (p. 545) Psychoanalytic interpretation of dreams, used to achieve insight into one's unconscious motives or conflict.

drive (p. 283) Biologically instigated motivation.

DSM-III-R (p. 494) Diagnostic and Statistical Manual of Mental Disorders, Third Edition, Revised; American Psychiatric Association's catalogue that classifies, defines, and describes over 200 mental disorders.

dual-code model (of memory) (p. 267) Memory coding theory that proposes both visual and verbal codes are used to store information.

dualism (p. 73) Theory that the mind is fundamentally different from and independent of the brain: the mind and the brain are two distinct but interwoven aspects of human nature.

E

eating disorder (p. 511) Loss of appetite behavior in which one deprives oneself of food or prevents food from being digested.

echo (p. 262) Auditory memory, lasting several seconds.

efferent systems (p. 150) Motor systems or systems that process information from the brain to muscles and glands.

ego (p. 383) Freudian concept of self; the personality structure focused on self-preservation and appropriate channeling of instinctual drives.

ego defense mechanisms (p. 383) Freudian concept of mental strategies used to reduce conflict or anxiety.

egocentrism (p. 119) Self-centered focus; the inability to distinguish mental from physical worlds.

eidetic imagery (p. 267) Uncommon memory process by which some individuals can store detailed, whole pictorial representations of scenes or patterns for some periods of time.

elaboration (p. 260) Relating new input to previously acquired information or to relevant goals or purposes.

elaborative rehearsal (p. 263) Repetition of incoming information to analyze and relate new material to previously stored knowledge.

electroconvulsive therapy (ECT) (p. 563) Medical therapy in which mild electric current is briefly applied to patient's brain to influence central nervous system function.

electrode (p. 46) A thin wire passing mild electrical current, usually into a brain site.

electroencephalogram (EEG) (p. 46) An amplified tracing of the brain's electrical activity used to study the brain during states of arousal.

emergent-interaction theory (p. 74) Theory that brain activities give rise to mental states, but these mental states are not the same as and not reducible to brain states.

emotion (p. 286) Complex pattern of changes in response to situation perceived as personally significant, including physiological arousal, feelings, thoughts, and behaviors.

emotion wheel (p. 292) Theorist Robert Plutchik's model of innate emotions, involving eight basic emotions made up of four pairs of opposites: joy-sadness, fear-anger, surprise-anticipation, and acceptance-disgust.

empathy (p. 134) The condition of feeling someone else's emotion.

empirical investigation (p. 21) Research that relies on sensory experience and observation as research data.

encephalization (p. 40) Increases in brain size.

encoding (p. 259) Converting information into a code that can be communicated.

encoding specificity principle (p. 267) Assumption that information retrieval is enhanced if cues received at time of recall are consistent with those present at time of encoding.

endocrine system (p. 53) A network of glands that manufacture and secrete chemical messengers called hormones into the bloodstream.

episodic memory (p. 265) LTM component that stores autobiographic information coded for reference to a time frame for past occurrences.

Eros (p. 382) Freudian concept of life instinct that energizes growth and survival.

eugenics (p. 411) Movement that advocated improving the human species by encouraging biologically superior people to interbreed while discouraging biologically inferior types from having offspring.

evolution (p. 39) The theory that over time organisms originate and adapt to their unique environments.

evolutionary approach (p. 17) Approach that assumes that human mental abilities, like physical abilities, evolved over millions of years to serve particular adaptive purposes.

evolutionism (p. 12) Theory that all species are ever-changing as successful features survive and are passed on genetically to successive generations.

experience-sampling method (p. 74) Research technique where subjects wear electronic pagers and record what they are feeling and thinking whenever the pager signals.

experimental condition (p. 27) Condition in which research subjects are exposed to the independent variable or treatment in a controlled experiment; contrasted with *control condition*.

extinction (p. 206) In learning, the weakening of a conditioned association in the absence of unconditional stimulus or reinforcer.

extrinsic motivation (p. 315) Desire to engage in activity to achieve external consequences.

F

false memory syndrome (FMS) (p. 273) A pattern of thoughts, feelings, and actions based on mistaken or distorted recollection of experiences the rememberer claims to have previously repressed.

fear (p. 501) Rational emotional reaction to a clear, external danger that may induce a person to flee or attack in self-defense.

fight-or-flight syndrome (p. 339) Sequence of internal activities preparing organism for struggle or escape, triggered when a threat is confronted.

figure (p. 184) Object-like region in forefront of visual field, distinguished from *ground*.

fixation (p. 381) Freudian hypothesis that excessive stimulation or frustration in early psychosexual stages causes arrested development.

fixed action pattern (pp. 198, 294) Unlearned set of responses triggered within a given species by a specific stimulus.

flooding (p. 549) Therapy for phobias in which clients agree to be exposed to stimuli they consider most frightening, in order to force them to test reality.

flow (p. 316) Near-ecstatic state achieved by total, present focus on activity, increasing creative ability.

fluid intelligence (p. 424) Ability to perceive complex relationships and solve problems.

fovea (p. 157) Central focal region of retina, densely packed with cones, that provides sharpest vision.

free association (p. 544) Principal procedure in psychoanalysis, in which patient provides a running account of thoughts, wishes, physical sensations, and mental images as they occur.

frequency theory (p. 167) Explanation for pitch perception; claims that neural firing rate along basilar membrane is caused by a tone's frequency, and that pitch is neurally coded for different firing rates.

frustration (p. 27) State assumed to exist when goal-directed activity is blocked in some manner.

functional fixedness (p. 250) Inability to perceive a new use for an object associated with a different purpose; limits problem solving and creativity.

functionalism (p. 12) School that gave primary importance to learned habits that enabled organisms to adapt to their environment and to function effectively.

G

g-factor (p. 421) General intelligence factor, assumed to be the individual's inherited basic intelligence, to which s-factors (specific kinds of intelligence) are added.

ganglion cell (p. 158) Nerve cell that integrates impulses from many bipolar cells into a single rate of firing.

general adaptation syndrome (GAS) (p. 341) Pattern of nonspecific bodily mechanisms activated in response to a continuing threat by almost any serious stressor.

generalized anxiety disorder (p. 501) Disorder in which an individual experiences anxiety that persists for at least one month and is not focused on a specific object or situation.

genes (p. 42) Functional units of the chromosomes; genes influence heredity by directing protein synthesis.

genetics (p. 42) The study of heredity—the inheritance of physical and psychological traits from ancestors.

genital stage (p. 381) Fifth phase of psychosexual development, in which sexual relations with a partner are associated with greatest gratification.

genotype (p. 40) Genetic structure inherited from one's parents.

Gestalt (p. 178) German word, meaning whole configuration, from which the name for Gestalt psychology is derived.

Gestalt psychology (p. 178) School of psychology that maintains that psychological phenomena can only be understood when viewed as organized, structured wholes, not when broken down into component elements.

Gestalt therapy (p. 558) Psychological treatment emphasizing the union of mind and body to make the person whole.

glia (p.59) Cells that bind neurons to each other.

grammar (p. 115) A language's set of rules about how to combine—and not combine—words, word units, and order to make understandable sentences.

ground (p. 184) Background areas of visual field against which figures stand out.

growth motivation (p. 297) Motivation to help oneself beyond what one has been and done in the past; central to humanistic theories.

H

habituation (p. 112) Decrease in response to any repeatedly presented event.

hallucinations (pp. 88, 516) Vivid perception that occurs in the absence of objective stimulation.

hallucinogens (psychedelics) (p. 90) Drugs that alter perceptions of the external environment and inner awareness.

halo effect (p. 417) Bias in which an observer's judgment of a single characteristic affects judgments of most or all other qualities.

hardiness (p. 337) Quality resulting from the three C's of health: challenge (welcoming change), commitment (focused involvement in purposeful activity), and control (internal guide for actions).

health (p. 352) Condition in which body and mind are sound and vigorous as well as free from illness or injury.

health psychology (p. 330) Field of psychology devoted to understanding how people stay healthy, why they become ill, and how they respond when ill.

heredity (p. 39) The biological transmission of traits from parents to offspring.

hertz (Hz) (p. 164) Unit of sound frequency, also expressed as cycles per second (cps).

heuristic (p. 251) Cognitive strategy or "rule of thumb," used as a shortcut to solve a complex mental task.

hippocampus (p. 47) Limbic system structure that is involved in memory.

HIV (p. 360) Human Immunodeficiency Virus, a virus that attacks white blood cells (T-lymphocytes) in human blood, thus weakening immune system functioning.

homeostasis (p. 50) The body's internal balance or equilibrium.

hormones (p. 53) Chemical substances secreted into the bloodstream.

hue (p. 160) Perceived color, corresponding to wavelength of light.

human behavior genetics (p. 43) New field that unites geneticists and psychologists interested in determining the genetic basis of behavioral traits and functioning, such as intelligence, mental disorders, and altruism.

human sexuality (p. 307) Combination of humans' physical characteristics and capacities for sexual behaviors; psychosexual learning, values, norms, and attitudes about sexual behaviors.

humanistic approach (p. 16) View that the main task for human beings is to strive for growth and development of their potential.

hypnosis (p. 85) An induced alternate state of awareness characterized by deep relaxation and heightened suggestibility.

hypnotizability (p. 85) The degree to which an individual is responsive to standardized hypnotic suggestions.

hypothalamus (p. 50) Limbic system structure that regulates the physiological processes involved in motivated behavior (including eating, drinking, temperature regulation, and sexual arousal).

hypothesis (p. 22) A tentative and testable explanation of the relationship between two or more events or variables.

hysteria (p. 489) Archaic term for mental illness characterized by clusters of painful or paralyzing symptoms without clear physical cause.

I

icon (p. 262) Visual memory, lasting about one half-second.

id (p. 383) Freudian concept of primitive, unconscious personality structure that operates irrationally, impulsively, and selfishly.

identification and recognition (p. 172) Two processes in which meaning is assigned to percepts.

idiographic approach (p. 372) Method of studying personality that emphasizes individual uniqueness rather than common dimensions.

illness (p. 353) Pathology or damage to the structure or function of bodily systems.

illness prevention (p. 354) General and specific strategies to reduce or eliminate the risk that one will become sick.

illusion (p. 174) Demonstrably incorrect experience of a stimulus pattern, shared by others in the same perceptual environment.

immediate memory span (p. 263) Brief, limited (between five and nine chunks of information) storage capacity of working memory.

implosion therapy (p. 549) Behavioral therapy technique in which a client is exposed to the most anxiety-provoking stimuli in order to extinguish anxiety associated with the class of stimuli.

imprinting (p. 121) Primitive learning in which some infant animals follow and form an attachment to the first moving object they see and hear.

in vivo **therapy** (p. 537) Therapeutic approach in which professionals treat clients in settings associated with clients' disorders.

incentive motivation (p. 286) Motivation aroused by external stimuli.

incentives (p. 286) External stimuli that arouse motives.

independent variable (p. 8) The stimulus condition that can vary independently of other variables in the situation; presumed to predict or influence behavior.

individual differences (p. 410) Distinctions and variations among people's characteristics and behavior patterns.

inductive reasoning (p. 248) Drawing a conclusion about the probability of an event or condition based on available evidence.

inference (p. 253) Logical assumption or conclusion based, not on direct observation, but on samples of evidence or prior beliefs and theories.

information-processing model (p. 234) Model that proposes that thinking and all other forms of cognition can be understood by analyzing them into parts.

informational influence (p. 451) Effect of a group on an individual who desires to be correct and understand how best to act in a given situation.

initiation rites (p. 125) Rituals (or rites of passage) that usually take place around puberty and serve as a public acknowledgment of the transition from childhood to adulthood.

insanity (p. 523) Legal designation for the state of an individual judged to be irresponsible or incompetent.

insight therapy (p. 543) Treatment in which therapist guides patient (or client) toward perceiving relationships between present symptoms and past origins.

insomnia (p. 83) Chronic failure to get adequate sleep characterized by an inability to fall asleep quickly, frequent arousals during sleep, and/or early morning awakening.

instinctual drift (p. 221) Tendency over time for learned behavior to relapse and resemble instinctual behavior.

intelligence (p. 418) Global capacity to profit from experience and go beyond given information.

intelligence quotient (IQ) (p. 421) Index derived from standardized tests of intelligence.

interjudge reliability (p. 417) Degree to which different observers agree about a particular individual or case.

internal consistency (p. 413) Degree to which different components of the same test yield similar scores; a measure of reliability.

interneurons (p. 58) Neurons that relay messages from sensory neurons to other interneurons or to motor neurons.

intervening variables (p. 7) Hypothetical conditions that are assumed to function as the links between observable stimulus input and measurable response output.

interview (p. 416) Face-to-face conversation between a respondent and a researcher or counselor, for purposes of gathering information about the respondent.

intimacy (p. 129) The capacity to make a full commitment—sexual, emotional, and moral—to another person.

intrinsic motivation (p. 315) Desire to engage in activity for its own sake.

intuitive psychologists (p. 470) Laypersons who rely on their personal theories about personality, behavior, and motivation.

J

James-Lange theory of emotion (p. 319) Theory, developed independently by William James and Carl Lange, that emotional stimulus triggers behavioral response that sends sensory and motor feedback to the brain and creates feeling of a specific emotion.

job analysis (p. 434) Study of a specific job, focusing on skills required, effort demanded, worker's responsibilities, and job-related stressors.

job burnout (p. 363) Pattern of symptoms—including emotional exhaustion, depersonalizing others, and sense of failure—that afflicts human service professionals.

judgment (p. 253) Process of forming opinions, reaching conclusions, and making evaluations based on available material; the product of the judgment process.

Juke family (p. 432) American family allegedly studied as an example of how "bad" bloodlines or heritage may produce generations of defective offspring.

just noticeable difference (JND) (p. 154) Difference threshold (above).

K

Kallikak family (p. 432) Name given to American family allegedly studied as evidence that "bad seeds" planted in family genes produce generations of defective offspring, while "good seeds" produce normal and eminent offspring.

kinesthetic sense (p. 165) Sense of body position and movement of body parts relative to each other (also called *kinesthesis*).

L

language acquisition device (LAD) (p. 114) Biologically predetermined mental structure that facilitates the comprehension and production of speech.

latency stage (p. 381) Fourth phase of psychosexual development, in which bodily gratification is less important than acquiring skills and relating to peers.

lateralization of emotion (p. 289) Different influences of the two brain hemispheres on various emotions, with the left hemisphere assumed to influence positive emotions (for example, happiness) and the right hemisphere to influence negative emotions (for example, anger).

law of common fate (p. 185) Grouping law that asserts that elements moving in the same direction and at the same rate are grouped together.

law of effect (p. 209) Basic law of learning that states that the power of a stimulus to evoke a response is strengthened when the response is followed by a reward and weakened when it is not followed by a reward.

law of forward conduction (p. 58) Principle that neurons transmit information in only one direction: from the dendrites through the soma to the axon to the terminal buttons.

law of Prägnanz (p. 185) Gestalt principle of meaningfulness, which asserts that the simplest organization requiring the least cognitive effort will emerge.

law of proximity (p. 185) Grouping law that asserts that nearest stimuli are grouped together.

law of similarity (p. 185) Grouping law that asserts that stimili are grouped together on the basis of common elements.

Lazarus-Schachter theory of emotion (p. 320) Theory, developed independently by Richard Lazarus and Stanley Schachter, that emotional experience is the joint effect of physiological arousal and cognitive appraisal, which determines how an ambiguous inner state will be interpreted.

learned helplessness (p. 218) Pattern of not responding to noxious stimuli after an organism learns its behavior has no effect.

learning (p. 199) Process based on experience that results in a relatively permanent change in behavior or behavior potential.

lesions (p. 46) Carefully inflicted destruction of tissue at specific brain areas.

libido (p. 382) Freudian concept of psychic energy that drives individuals to experience sensual pleasure.

life-change units (LCU) (p. 333) Measures of stress caused by different kinds of change experienced during a specific time period.

life history (p. 416) Information about an individual's experiences based on school or military records, personal accounts, and medical data.

life-span developmental psychology (p. 125) Study of personality, mental functioning, and behavior as they develop and change throughout the entire life cycle.

limbic system (p. 47) Brain system that processes motivated behaviors, emotional states, and certain kinds of memory.

locus of control orientation (p. 300) General belief about whether one's actions are controlled by internal or external factors.

long-term memory (LTM) (p. 264) Memory processes associated with preserving information for retrieval at any later time; theorized to have unlimited capacity.

longitudinal design (p. 110) A type of investigation in which researchers repeatedly observe and test the same individuals over time.

loudness (p. 164) Perceived intensity or amplitude of sound energy.

M

maintenance rehearsal (p. 263) Active repetition of information to enhance subsequent access to it.

manic episode (p. 505) A period of mania, during which an individual generally acts and feels unusually elated and expansive.

maturation (p. 103) Systematic changes occurring over time in bodily functioning and behavior, influenced by physical factors that are the same for all members of a species.

meditation (p. 86) A form of consciousness change designed to enhance self-knowledge and well-being by reducing self-awareness.

medulla (p. 45) The center for breathing, waking, sleeping, and the beating of the heart. Nerve fibers connecting the brain and the body cross over at the medulla.

memory (p. 234) Mental capacity to store and later retrieve previously experienced events.

menarche (p. 126) The onset of menstruation in women.

mental age (MA) (p. 419) Average age at which normal individuals achieve a particular score on a measure of intelligence.

mental set (p. 251) Tendency to respond to a new problem in the manner used for a previous problem.

mnemonics (p. 266) Strategies or techniques that use familiar associations in storing new information to be more easily retrieved.

monism (p. 73) Theory that mind and brain are one—that mental phenomena are the products of brain activity.

morality (p. 132) A system of beliefs, values, and underlying judgments about the rightness or wrongness of human acts.

motherese (p. 114) An exaggerated, high-pitched intonation adults use when speaking to young children.

motivation (p. 282) Process that starts, directs, and maintains physical and psychological activity, including activity preference, strength, and persistence.

motive (p. 283) Psychologically and socially instigated motivation, assumed to be at least partially learned.

motor cortex (p. 51) Part of the cortex that controls the actions of the body's voluntary muscles.

motor neurons (p. 58) Also called *efferent neurons,* nerve cells that carry messages away from the central nervous system toward the muscles and glands.

MRI (p. 47) Magnetic resonance imaging process used to reveal whether brain cells are functioning normally by using radio waves to glimpse the effects of magnetic pulses of energy.

multiple personality disorder (MPD) (p. 498) Dissociative disorder in which different aspects of a personality function independently, creating the appearance of two or more distinct personalities within the same individual.

N

narcissistic personality disorder (p. 497) Personality disorder marked by exaggerated sense of self-importance, preoccupation with success or power fantasies, and need for constant attention or admiration.

narcolepsy (p. 83) Sleep disorder characterized by a periodic compulsion to sleep during the daytime.

natural selection (p. 39) The theory that the forces of nature select the organisms—and the features of those organisms—that will survive, reproduce, and pass their advantageous traits to the next generation.

nature-nurture controversy (p. 101) A long-standing debate among scholars over the relative importance of heredity and learning.

need for achievement (*n Ach*) (p. 314) Concept developed by Henry Murray and David McClelland of basic human drive to meet a wide variety of goals.

needs hierarchy (p. 298) Abraham Maslow's theoretical sequence of needs motivating human behavior, from the most primitive level to higher needs only satisfied after lower ones are achieved.

negative cognitive set (p. 508) Consistently pessimistic and self-blaming views of one's experiences.

negative reinforcer (p.213) Stimulus that increases the probability of a response when it is terminated or avoided after that response.

nervous system (p. 53) A massive network of nerve cells that relays messages to and from the brain.

neuron (p. 57) Nerve cell specialized to receive, process, and/or transmit information to other cells within the body.

neurotic disorder (p. 495) Mental disorder characterized not by irrational thinking or violation of norms but by personal distress, especially anxiety; archaic term.

neurotransmitters (p. 53) Chemical messengers that relay messages to and from the brain. (p. 60) Biochemical substances that stimulate other neurons and the endocrine system.

nomothetic approach (p. 372) Method of studying personality that emphasizes identifying universal traits and patterns.

non-REM sleep (NREM) (p. 79) The time when a sleeper is not showing REM.

nonconscious processes (p. 76) Information that is not represented in consciousness or memory but that still influences fundamental bodily or mental activities.

norm (p. 414) Standard or value based on measurements of a large group of people; in social psychology, the group standard for approved behavior.

normative influence (p. 451) Effect of a group on an individual who strives to be liked, accepted, and approved of by others.

normative investigations (p. 110) A type of investigation in which researchers describe a characteristic of a specific age or developmental stage.

O

object permanence (p. 119) The perception that objects exist independently of one's own actions or awareness.

observational learning (pp. 223, 390) Process of learning new responses by watching others' behavior.

observer-report methods (p. 417) Evaluation of some aspect of an individual's behavior by another person.

obsessive-compulsive disorder (p. 503) Mental disorder characterized by patterns of obsessions (persistent, unwanted thoughts) and compulsions (undesired, repetitive actions).

olfactory bulb (p. 166) Brain site of olfactory processing, below frontal lobes, where odor-sensitive receptors send their signals.

operant (p. 211) Behavior that can be characterized in terms of its effects on the environment.

operant extinction (p. 213) Withholding a positive reinforcer to extinguish an operant behavior.

operational definition (p. 23) Definition of a concept in terms of how the concept is measured or what operations produce it.

opiates (p. 91) Class of drugs, derived from opium, that suppresses physical sensation and response to stimulation.

optic nerve (p. 158) Bundled axons of ganglion cells carrying information from the eyes to the brain.

optimal arousal (p. 296) Level of arousal at which people best perform tasks of different levels of difficulty.

oral stage (p. 381) First phase of psychosexual development, in which the mouth is the region associated with greatest gratification.

overregularization (p. 116) Applying a grammatical rule too widely and creating incorrect forms.

P

pain (p. 169) Bodily sensation of noxious stimuli intense enough to threaten or cause tissue damage.

panic disorder (p. 501) Anxiety disorder characterized by recurrent episodes of intense anxiety, feelings of unpredictability, and symptoms of arousal usually lasting several minutes.

paradigm (p. 22) A model of the functions and interrelationships of a process; a "way of thinking" about the world and how to study it.

parallel forms (p. 412) Different versions of the same test, used to assess test reliability.

parasympathetic division (p. 57) Division of the the autonomic nervous system (ANS) that monitors the routine operation of the body's internal functions, and returns it to calmer functioning after sympathetic arousal.

parental investment (p. 309) Time, energy, and resources parents must spend raising their offspring.

partial reinforcement effect (p. 217) Principle that behavioral responses acquired through intermittent reinforcement resist extinction more than those continuously reinforced.

participant modeling (p. 551) Therapeutic technique in which a therapist demonstrates, and encourages client to imitate, desired behavior.

pastoral counselor (p. 538) Member of a religious order who specializes in treating psychological disorders, often combining spiritual guidance with practical problem-solving.

patient (p. 536) An individual with medical problems; term used in biomedical approach to treatment of psychological disorders.

patient nonadherence (p. 359) Patient's failure to abide by medical guidelines or follow physicians' recommendations for treatment.

peace psychology (p. 475) Interdisciplinary approach to the prevention of nuclear war and the promotion and maintenance of peace.

percept (p. 172) The experienced outcome of the process of perception.

perception (pp. 149, 172) Processes that organize sensory information and interpret it in terms of its environmental origins.

perceptual grouping (p. 185) Process of perception in which sets of stimuli are judged to belong together; focus of several Gestalt princples of perception.

perceptual organization (p. 184) Putting sensory information together to create coherence.

performance (p. 199) External behavior that reveals that learning has occurred, although it may not reveal all that has been learned.

peripheral nervous system (PNS) (p. 55) Subsystem of the nervous system composed of all the neurons forming the nerve fibers that connect the CNS to the rest of the body.

person-centered therapy (p. 557) Humanistic approach to treatment developed by Carl Rogers, emphasizing individual's tendency for healthy psychological growth through self-actualization.

personal construct (p. 389) George Kelly's theoretical concept of an individual's unique system for interpreting reality.

personality (p. 371) Unique qualities and distinctive behavior patterns of an individual across time and situations.

personality disorder (p. 496) Chronic, inflexible, maladaptive pattern of perception, thought, and behavior that seriously impairs an individual's ability to function personally or socially.

personality inventory (p. 395) Self-report questionnaire used for personality assessment.

personality types (p. 374) Patterns of behavior and characteristics used to assign people to categories.

PET scan (p. 47) Positron emission tomography used to measure neural functioning by tracking the movement of radioactive substances in the active regions of the brain.

phallic stage (p. 381) Third phase of psychosexual development, in which stimulation of genitals is associated with greatest gratification.

phenotype (p. 40) Observable features by which individuals are recognized.

pheromones (pp. 167, 305) Chemical signals released by organisms to communicate with other members of their species; often a sexual attractor.

phobic disorder (p. 501) Maladaptive pattern of behavior in which anxiety is associated with a specific external object or situation that the individual seeks to avoid.

phonemes (p. 113) Smallest meaningful units of sound in a language.

photoreceptors (p. 157) Light-sensitive cells in the retina that convert light energy to neural responses.

physiological measures (p. 25) Data based on subjects' biological responses to stimuli.

pitch (p. 164) Perceived frequency of sound.

pituitary gland (p. 54) Gland that secretes hormones that influence the secretions of all other endocrine glands, as well as a hormone that influences growth.

place theory (p. 167) Explanation for pitch perception; claims that different frequencies produce maximum neural activity at different locations on basilar membrane, and that pitch is neurally coded for these different places.

placebo control (p. 24) A control strategy where researchers compare those who received actual treatment with those who received only attention or a "dummy drug."

pons (p. 47) Part of the brain involved in dreaming and waking from sleep.

positive reinforcer (p. 212) Stimulus, received after a response, that increases the probability of that response.

postformal thought (p. 132) A more dynamic, less abstract way of thinking that can accept inconsistencies and contradictions.

posttraumatic stress disorder (PTSD) (p. 343) Reaction in which individual involuntarily reexperiences emotional, cognitive, and behavioral aspects of past trauma.

preattentive processing (p. 180) Processing that operates on sensory inputs from receptors before they are attended to.

preconscious memories (p. 77) Memories accessible to consciousness only after something calls attention to them.

prejudice (p. 466) Negative attitude and feelings about a group and its members.

Premack principle (p. 216) Principle developed by David Premack that a more preferred activity can be used to reinforce a less preferred activity.

primary appraisal (p. 337) First stage of cognitive appraisal of stress, in which a situation or its seriousness is evaluated.

proactive interference (p. 271) Memory process in which stored information prevents learning similar new information.

problem solving (p. 248) Moving from an initial state (the problem) to a goal state (the solution) by means of a set of mental operations.

procedural memory (p. 264) Long-term memory (LTM) component that stores memory for how things are done.

projective test (p. 399) Personality assessment technique in which respondent is asked to interpret ambiguous stimuli.

proposition (p. 267) Expression of relationship between concepts, objects, or events.

prototype (p. 239) Most representative example of a category.

proximal stimulus (p. 173) Sensory system's impression of external stimulation, for example, image on the retina; contrasted with *distal stimulus.*

pseudomemory (p. 240) Form of memory in which one confidently believes a new stimulus was experienced previously because several of its features have been remembered.

psychiatric social worker (p. 538) Mental health professional trained in social work with emphasis on the social context of individuals' problems.

psychiatrist (p. 538) Physician (with training and degree in medicine) specializing in treatment of mental and emotional disorders.

psychic determinism (p. 380) Assumption that mental and behavioral reactions are caused by earlier experience.

psychoactive drugs (p. 90) Chemicals that affect mental processes and behavior by temporarily changing conscious awareness.

psychoanalyst (p. 538) Individual (physician, psychologist, or layperson) who is trained and qualified in practicing Freudian approach to assessing and treating mental disorders.

psychoanalytic therapy (p. 543) Psychodynamic therapy developed by Sigmund Freud, involving intensive, prolonged exploration of patients' unconscious motivations and conflicts.

psychodynamic approach (p. 14) Approach that views behavior as driven or motivated by powerful mental forces and conflicts.

psychodynamic personality theories (p. 380) Any models that share assumptions that inner forces shape personality and motivate behavior.

psychogenic amnesia (p. 498) Memory loss involving inability to recall important personal information, caused not by physical damage but by psychological distress.

psychological assessment (p. 409) Use of specified procedures to evaluate people's abilities, behaviors, and personal qualities.

psychological dependence (p. 90) Pervasive desire to obtain or use a drug; not based on physical addiction.

psychological diagnosis (p. 487) Identifying and explaining mental disorders according to clinical interview and observation, testing, and analysis of mental and behavioral development.

psychological test (p. 416) Instrument used to measure an individual's standing relative to others on some mental or behavioral characteristic.

psychology (p. 5) The scientific study of the behavior of individuals and their mental processes.

psychometrics (p. 423) Field of psychology that specializes in mental testing.

psychoneuroimmunology (PNI) (p. 330) Research specialty that investigates effects of stress on systems and functions of the body, particularly the immune system.

psychopathology (p. 487) Abnormality or disorder in patterns of thought, emotion, or behavior.

psychophysics (p. 150) Study of correspondence between physical stimulation and psychological experience.

psychosexual stages (p. 381) Freudian concept of successive phases—oral, anal, phallic, latency, and genital—of development in which a child associates pleasure with different bodily regions.

psychosocial dwarfism (p. 122) Syndrome in which children's normal development is inhibited by traumatic living conditions.

psychosocial stages (p. 122) According to Erikson, successive developmental crises that focus on an individual's orientation to self and others.

psychosurgery (p. 562) Surgical procedures that alter brain tissue in order to alleviate psychological disorders.

psychotherapy (p. 535) Treatments for psychological disorders that work by changing behaviors, thoughts, perceptions, and emotions.

psychotic disorder (p. 495) Severe mental disorder characterized by impaired reality testing due to difficulties in thought, emotional, or perceptual processes; archaic term.

puberty (p. 126) Attainment of sexual maturity (ability to reproduce).

punisher (p. 214) Aversive stimulus that decreases the probability of the preceding response.

R

randomization (p. 27) Assignment of subjects so that every subject has an equal chance of ending up in any of the conditions, experimental or control.

rapid eye-movement (REM) (p. 79) Eye movements that occur at periodic intervals during sleep.

rating (p. 417) Quantitative judgment of the degree to which some characteristic is present or influential.

rational-emotive therapy (RET) (p. 556) System of personality change developed by Albert Ellis, based on changing irrational beliefs that cause problematic emotional reactions such as anxiety.

reaction time (p. 235) Time elapsed between stimulus presentation and organism's response; used to measure time required by mental processes.

realistic thinking (p. 247) Fitting one's ideas to situational demands, time limits, rules of operation, and accurate evaluation of one's personal resources; contrasted with *autistic thinking.*

reasoning (p. 247) Realistic thinking process that draws a conclusion from a set of facts; goal-directed thinking.

recall (p. 260) Retrieval method in which one must reproduce previously presented information.

reciprocal determinism (p. 390) Albert Bandura's social-learning theory concept of the mutual influence between person, behavior, and environment.

recognition (p. 260) Retrieval method in which one must identify present stimuli as having been previously presented.

reference group (p. 448) Formal or informal group from which an individual derives norms and seeks information, direction, and life-style support.

reflex (p. 202) Unlearned response elicited by specific stimuli that are biologically relevant to the organism.

reinforcement contingency (p. 212) Consistent relationship between a response and the changes it produces in the environment.

relapse (p. 353) Reverting to former behavior patterns that have been changed.

reliability (p. 412) Degree to which an assessment method yields the same score each time an individual is measured; consistency.

remembering (p. 236) Retaining or recalling experiences.

representative heuristic (p. 256) Cognitive strategy that assigns items to categories based on whether items possess some characteristics representative of the category.

repression (p. 272) In Freudian theory, basic defense mechanism that excludes painful thoughts, feelings, or memories from consciousness. (p. 383) Freudian defense mechanism, underlying all other defense mechanisms, in which unacceptable thoughts, feelings, or memories are excluded from consciousness.

residual stress pattern (p. 344) Chronic pattern in which symptoms of posttraumatic stress disorder persist over time.

resistance (p. 544) Inability or unwillingness of psychoanalytic patient to discuss certain ideas, desires, or experiences.

reticular formation (p. 47) Dense network of nerve cells situated between the medulla and pons that arouses the cerebral cortex to attend to new stimulation and keeps the brain alert.

retina (p. 157) Layer of cells at the back of the eye containing photoreceptors.

retrieval (p. 259) Recovery of stored information from memory.

retrieval cues (p. 268) Available internal or external stimuli that help in recovering information from memory.

retroactive interference (p. 271) Memory process in which newly learned information prevents retrieval of previously stored, similar material.

ritual healing (p. 541) Ceremonial process of infusing emotional intensity and meaning into treating illness by heightening patients' suggestibility and sense of importance.

rods (p. 157) Photoreceptors abundant in periphery of retina that detect presence/brightness of light and function best in dimness.

rules (p. 446) Behavioral guidelines for how to act in certain situations.

S

saturation (p. 160) Perceived purity or vividness of color.

schedules of reinforcement (p. 217) In operant conditioning, patterns of delivering and withholding reinforcement.

schema (p. 241) Collected knowledge and expectations about topics.

schemes (p. 118) In Piaget's theory, cognitive structures that develop as a child learns to adapt sensorimotor sequences to environmental conditions.

schizophrenic disorder (p. 516) Severe disorder characterized by the breakdown of personality functioning, withdrawal from reality, distorted emotions, and disturbed thought.

scientific method (p. 5) A set of orderly steps used to analyze and solve problems by relying on objective research data; also an open-minded yet cautiously skeptical attitude toward evidence and conclusions.

script (p. 242) A cluster of knowledge about sequences of interrelated, specific events and actions expected to occur in a certain way in particular settings.

secondary appraisal (p. 337) Second stage of cognitive appraisal of stress, in which individual evaluates personal and social resources needed to respond and determines action to take.

secondary trait (p. 375) Trait that indicates enduring personal qualities but is not assumed to explain general behavior patterns.

self-actualization (p. 385) Humanistic concept of an individual's lifelong process of striving to realize his or her potential.

self-awareness (p. 76) Cognizance that personally experienced events have an *autobiographical* character.

self-concept (p. 393) Individual's awareness of his or her continuing identity as a person.

self-efficacy (p. 391) Albert Bandura's concept of beliefs an individual has that he or she can perform adequately in a particular situation.

self-esteem (p. 393) Evaluation of oneself that affects moods and behavior.

self-fulfilling prophecies (p. 465) One's private expectations of how others will act that influence them to behave in the predicted manner.

self-handicapping (p. 393) Manufacturing a preferred or acceptable excuse for anticipated failure, other than personal fault.

self-report measures (p. 25) Verbal answers to researchers' questions.

self-report methods (p. 417) Popular research techniques, in which respondents are assessed by their answers to a series of questions.

self-serving bias (p. 471) Attributional pattern in which one takes credit for success but denies responsibility for failure.

semantic memory (p. 265) LTM component that stores memory for basic meanings of words and concepts.

sensation (p. 149) Process of converting physical energy into stimulation of receptor cells (for example, converting light energy into visual stimulation).

sensory adaptation (p. 155) Loss of responsiveness in receptor cells after stimulation has remained unchanged.

sensory memory (p. 261) Initial process that preserves brief impressions of stimuli; also *sensory register*.

sensory modalities (p. 148) Separate sensory systems that take in information.

sensory neurons (p. 58) Also called *afferent neurons,* nerve cells that carry messages from sense receptor cells toward the central nervous system.

sensory processes (p. 148) Sense organ functions that put nervous system in direct contact with sources of stimulation.

sensuality (p. 148) State or quality of appreciating sensory pleasures.

sequential design (p. 112) A type of investigation in which subjects who span a certain, small age range are grouped according to their birth years and observed repeatedly over several years.

set (p. 186) Temporary readiness to perceive or react to stimulus in a particular way.

sex chromosomes (p. 42) Chromosomes that contain genes for the development of male or female anatomy.

sexual arousal (p. 307) Motivational state stimulated by physiological and cognitive reactions to erotic stimuli.

sexual reproduction (p. 305) Production of offspring by means of sexual interaction, so that germ cells (for example, sperm, eggs) combine to form unique genetic combinations.

sexual scripts (p. 310) Socially learned programs of sexual interpretation and responsiveness.

shamanism (p. 533) Ancient spiritual tradition, still practiced in Native American cultures, combining healing with making contact with the spirit world.

shaping (p. 216) Also training by successive approximations, operant learning technique in which a new behavior is produced by reinforcing responses that approach the desired performance.

short-term memory (STM) (p. 262) See *working memory*.

situational behavior observations (p. 416) First-hand study of an individual's actions and performance in one or more settings.

situationism (pp. 410, 445) View that, to a greater extent than we realize, forces in behavior settings determine our behavior more than personal qualities do.

skin senses (p. 168) Sensory systems for processing reception and experience of pressure, warmth, and cold.

sleep apnea (p. 83) Upper respiratory disorder in which the person stops breathing while asleep.

social categorization (p. 466) Process by which people organize their social environment by classifying themselves and others into groups.

social context (p. 444) Part of the environment that includes real and imagined other people, interactions, the interactive setting, and guidelines for how people relate to each other.

social facilitation (p. 445) Amplifying effect that the presence of others can have on individual performance.

social-learning therapy (p. 551) Treatment system based on theory that behavior is influenced by observation and imitation of others.

social loafing (p. 445) Unconscious tendency to withhold effort when performing in a group.

social norms (p. 446) Group's expectations regarding what is appropriate and acceptable for its members' attitudes and behaviors.

social perception (p. 468) Process of recognizing the personal attributes of oneself and others.

social phobia (p. 502) Category of phobic disorders in which an individual irrationally fears engaging in public action or display; extreme form of shyness.

social psychology (p. 444) Branch of psychology that studies the effect of social variables on individual behavior, cognitions, and motives, as well as group and intergroup processes.

social reality (p. 464) The consensus of perceptions and beliefs about a situation that is derived from social comparisons among group members.

social role (p. 446) Socially defined pattern of behavior expected of a person when functioning in a given setting or group.

social support (p. 349) Resources, materials, sympathy, or information provided by others to help a person cope with stress.

socialization (p. 121) The life-long process of shaping an individual's behavior patterns, values, standards, skills, attitudes, and motives to conform to those regarded as desirable in a particular society.

soma (p. 58) The cell body containing the nucleus of the cell and the cytoplasm that sustains its life.

somatic nervous system (p. 56) Subdivision of the PNS that regulates the actions of the body's skeletal muscles.

somatosensory cortex (p. 51) Part of the cortex that processes information about temperature, touch, body position, and pain.

somatotype (p. 374) Descriptive category that classifies personality pattern according to physical characteristics.

SPECT (p. 47) Single-photon emission computerized tomography, used as a brain scanning process that tracks cerebral blood flow, which is a sign of activity in specific brain areas.

spontaneous recovery (p. 206) Reappearance of an extinguished conditional response after a rest period.

SQUID (p. 47) Superconducting quantum interference device which senses tiny changes in the brain's magnetic fields that depict the pattern of neural activity in a three-dimensional portrait.

standardization (p. 23) Second phase of research, in which results are tested and prepared for useful communication with the scientific community. (p. 414) Uniformity of procedures in applying treatments or recording data; in test construction, specifying population and conditions for establishing norms.

stereotype effect (p. 417) Bias in which judge's beliefs about most people in a social category influence how a particular individual in the category is perceived.

stigma (p. 525) A mark or brand of disgrace; in the psychological context, a set of negative attitudes about a person that sets him or her apart as unacceptable.

stimulants (p. 92) Drugs that increase CNS activity, speeding up both mental and physical activity.

stimulus discrimination (p. 206) In conditioning, responding differently to stimuli that differ from the conditional stimulus.

stimulus generalization (p. 206) Making conditional responses to similar stimuli that have never been paired with the unconditional stimulus.

storage (p. 259) Retaining encoded information over time.

strain (p. 330) Organism's reaction to external stressors.

stress (p. 330) The pattern of specific and general responses made by an organism to stimulus events that disturb the organism's equilibrium and tax or exceed its ability to cope.

stress moderator variables (p. 337) Variables that change the impact of a stressor on a particular reaction.

stressor (p. 330) Internal or external stimulus event that induces stress.

structuralism (p. 12) The study of the structure of mind and behavior, including elements and components.

subconscious awareness (p. 77) The processing of information not currently in consciousness but retrievable from memory by special recall or attention-getting procedures.

subjective contours (p. 184) Edges or boundaries perceived in proximal stimulus that do not exist in distal stimulus.

superego (p. 383) Freudian concept of personality structure that embodies society's values, standards, and morals.

syllogism (p. 247) Form of deductive reasoning with a major premise, a minor premise, and a logical conclusion.

sympathetic division (p. 56) Division of the ANS that governs responses to stress in emergencies.

synapse (p. 60) Space between neurons that provides a junction for information transfer.

synaptic transmission (p. 60) Process in which information is relayed from one neuron to another across the synaptic gap.

systematic desensitization (p. 547) Behavioral therapy technique in which client learns to relax in order to prevent anxiety arousal.

T

taste buds (p. 168) Receptors for taste, located primarily on upper side of the tongue.

taste-aversion learning (p. 222) Biological constraint on learning in which an organism learns in one trial to avoid a food when eating it is followed by illness.

temperament (p. 104) Individual's specific manner of behaving or reacting.

terminal buttons (p. 58) Swollen, bulblike structures, located at the far end of the axon, through which stimulation passes to nearby glands, muscles, or other neurons.

test-retest reliability (p. 412) A measure of the correlation between the scores of the same people on the same test given at two different times.

thalamus (p. 47) Relay station that channels incoming sensory information to the appropriate area of the cerebral cortex, where that information is then processed.

Thanatos (p. 382) Freudian concept of death instinct, theorized to energize destructive and aggressive behavior.

Thematic Apperception Test (TAT) (p. 299) Projective test in which an individual tells stories about each of a series of ambiguous pictures.

theory (p. 21) A body of interrelated principles used to explain or predict some psychological phenomenon.

theory of signal detection (TSD) (p. 151) Theory that a perceptual judgment combines sensation and decision-making processes.

think-aloud protocols (p. 74) Reports used to document the mental strategies of subjects and analyze their awareness of using them. (p. 235) Reports of mental processes subjects make while working on tasks.

thinking (p. 237) Mental process that transforms available information to form a new mental representation.

timbre (p. 164) Perceived complexity of sound wave.

top-down processing (p. 173) Processing in which perceiver's past experience, knowledge, expectations, motivation, and background influence analysis and interpretation of perceived stimuli.

topical approach (p. 101) Approach to developmental psychology that examines each topic or task as a distinct, lifelong process.

total situation (p. 449) Environmental conditions in which people are isolated from contrary points of view, and in which group leaders control distribution of information, rewards, and punishments.

trait (p. 375) Relatively stable personality tendency.

transduction (p. 150) Transformation of one form of energy into another (for example, tranformation of vibration energy into neural impulses later interpreted as sound).

transference (p. 545) In psychoanalysis, process in which patient attaches to therapist feelings formerly held toward another significant person associated with emotional conflict.

Type-A behavior syndrome (p. 362) Pattern of angry, competitive, and perfectionistic behavior in response to stress; assumed to increase risk of coronary heart disease.

Type-T personality (p. 338) Behavior pattern of taking risks, seeking thrills, stimulation, and excitement.

U

unconditional response (UCR) (p. 203) In classical conditioning, the response elicited by an unconditional stimulus without prior learning.

unconditional stimulus (UCS) (p. 203) In classical conditioning, the stimulus that elicits an unconditional response.

Unconscious (p. 77) Mental processes that keep out of conscious awareness any information that would cause extreme anxiety. (p. 382) Psychoanalytic concept of psychic domain that stores repressed and primitive impulses; unconscious processes repress impulses that motivate thoughts, feelings, and actions.

unipolar depression (p. 507) Category of affective disorder involving intense, extended depression without interruption by manic periods; also called *clinical depression*.

V

validity (p. 413) Extent to which a test measures what it is intended to measure.

vestibular sense (p. 165) Sense of body orientation with respect to gravity.

visual cortex (pp. 52, 158) Region of occipital lobes in back of brain where visual information is processed.

W

Weber's law (p. 154) Assertion that the size of the difference threshold is proportional to the intensity of the standard (background) stimulus.

wellness (p. 353) Optimal health, including full, active functioning in the physical, intellectual, emotional, spiritual, and social domains.

wisdom (p. 138) Knowledge, practical experience, and judgment.

withdrawal symptoms (p. 90) Painful physical symptoms experienced when, after addiction, level of drug is decreased or drug is eliminated.

word associations (p. 399) Personality assessment techniques in which individual generates responses triggered by common words.

working memory (p. 262) Memory processes that preserve recently perceived events or experiences; also *short-term memory*.

Y

Yerkes-Dodson law (p. 296) Correlation between task difficulty and optimal level of arousal; as arousal increases, performance of difficult tasks decreases, while performance of simple tasks increases, to form an inverted-U function.

References

A

Abelson, R. P. (1981). Psychological status of the script concept. *American Psychologist, 36*, 715–729.

Abramson, L. Y., Garber, J., Edwards, N., & Seligman, M. E. P. (1978). Expectancy changes in depression and schizophrenia. *Journal of Abnormal Psychology, 87*, 102–109.

Abramson, L. Y., Seligman, M. E. P., & Teasdale, J. (1978). Learned helplessness in humans: Critique and reformulation. *Journal of Abnormal Psychology, 87*, 32–48.

Ackerman, D. (1990). *A natural history of the senses.* New York: Random House.

Adams, J. (1979). Mutual-help groups: Enhancing the coping ability of oncology clients. *Cancer Nursing, 2*, 95–98.

Adler, N. E., David, H. P., Major, B. N., Roth, S. H., Russo, N. F., & Wyatt, G. E. (1990). Psychological responses after abortion. *Science, 248*, 41–44.

Adler, N. T. (1978). On the mechanisms of sexual behaviour and their evolutionary constraints. In J. B. Hutchison (Ed.), *Biological determinants of sexual behavior* (pp. 657–694). New York: Wiley.

Adorno, T. W., Frenkel-Brunswick, E., Levinson, D. J., & Sanford, R. N. (1950). *The authoritarian personality.* New York: Harper.

Affleck, G., Tennen, H., Pfeiffer, C., & Fifield, J. (1987). Appraisals of control and predictability in adapting to a chronic disease. *Journal of Personality and Social Psychology, 53*, 273–279.

Agnati, L. F., Bjelke, B., & Fuxe, K. (1992). Volume transmission in the brain. *American Scientist, 80*, 362–373.

Ahern, G. L., & Schwartz, G. E. (1985). Differential lateralization for positive and negative emotion in the human brain: EEG spectral analysis. *Neuropsychologia, 23*, 744–755.

Allen, B. P. (1985). After the missiles: Sociopsychological effects of nuclear war. *American Psychologist, 40*, 927–937.

Allison, T., & Cicchetti, D. (1976). Sleep in mammals: Ecological and constitutional correlates. *Science, 194*, 732–734.

Allport, G. W. (1937). *Personality: A psychological interpretation.* New York: Holt, Rinehart & Winston.

Allport, G. W. (1954). *The nature of prejudice.* Cambridge, MA: Addison-Wesley.

Allport, G. W. (1961). *Pattern and growth in personality.* New York: Holt, Rinehart & Winston.

Allport, G. W. (1966). Traits revisited. *American Psychologist, 21*, 1–10.

Allport, G. W., & Odbert, H. S. (1936). Trait-names, a psycho-lexical study. *Psychological Monographs, 47*(1, Whole No. 211).

Anastasi, A. (1982). *Psychological testing* (5th ed.). New York: Macmillan.

Anderson, J. R. (1976). *Language, memory, and thought.* Hillsdale, NJ: Erlbaum.

Anderson, J. R. (Ed.). (1981). *Cognitive skills and their acquisition.* Hillsdale, NJ: Erlbaum.

Anderson, J. R. (1982). Acquisition of cognitive skill. *Psychological Review, 89*, 369–406.

Anderson, J. R., & Bower, G. H. (1973). *Human associative memory.* Washington, DC: Winston & Sons.

Antelman, S. M., & Caggiula, A. R. (1980). Stress-induced behavior: Chemotherapy without drugs. In J. M. Davidson & R. J. Davidson (Eds.), *The psychobiology of consciousness* (pp. 65–104). New York: Plenum.

Antelman, S. M., Rowland, N. E., & Fisher, A. E. (1976). Stimulation bound ingestive behavior: A view from the tail. *Physiology and Behavior, 17*, 743–748.

Antoni, M. H., Schniederman, N., Fletcher, M. A., Goldstein, D. A., Ironson, G., & Laperriere, A. (1990). Psychoneuroimmunolgy and HIV-1. *Journal of Consulting and Clinical Psychology, 58*, 38–49.

Antrobus, J. (1991). Dreaming: Cognitive processes during cortical activation and high afferent thresholds. *Psychological Review, 98*, 96–121.

Arendt, H. (1963). *Eichmann in Jerusalem: A report on the banality of evil.* New York: Viking Press.

Arendt, H. (1971). Organized guilt and universal responsibility. In R. W. Smith (Ed.), *Guilt: Man and society.* Garden City, NY: Doubleday Anchor Books.

Aronson, E., & Mills, J. (1959). The effect of severity of initiation on liking for a group. *Journal of Abnormal and Social Psychology, 59*, 177–181.

Asch, S. E. (1940). Studies in the principles of judgments and attitudes: 11. Determination of judgments by group and by ego standards. *Journal of Social Psychology, 12*, 433–465.

Asch, S. E. (1955). Opinions and social pressure. *Scientific American, 193*(5), 31–35.

Asch, S. E. (1956). Studies of independence and conformity: A minority of one against a unanimous majority. *Psychological Monographs, 70*(9, Whole No. 416).

Aserinsky, E., & Kleitman, N. (1953). Regularly occurring periods of eye mobility and concomitant phenomena during sleep. *Science, 118*, 273–274.

Ayllon, T., & Azrin, N. H. (1965). The measurement and reinforcement of behavior of psychotics. *Journal of Experimental Analysis of Behavior, 8*, 357–383.

B

Baddeley, A. D. (1986). *Working memory.* New York: Oxford University Press.

Baell, W. K., & Wertheim, E. H. (1992). Predictors of outcome in the treatment of bulimia nervosa. *British Journal of Clinical Psychology, 31*(3), 330–332.

Baillargeon, R. (1986). Representing the existence and the location of hidden objects: Object permanence in 6- and 8-month-old infants. *Cognition, 23*, 21–42.

Balakrishnan, S. (1991). Psychology of democracy. *The California Psychologist, 24*, pp. 16, 21.

Balsam, P. D., & Tomie, A. (Eds.). (1985). *Context and learning.* Hillsdale, NJ: Erlbaum.

Baltes, P. B. (1987). Theoretical propositions on life-span developmental psychology: On the dynamics between growth and decline. *Developmental Psychology, 23,* 611–626.

Baltes, P. B. (1990, November). *Toward a psychology of wisdom.* Invited address presented at the annual convention of the Gerontological Society of America, Boston, MA.

Bandura, A. (1970). Modeling therapy. In W. S. Sahakian (Ed.), *Psychopathology today: Experimentation, theory and research.* Itasca, IL: Peacock.

Bandura, A. (1981). In search of pure unidirectional determinants. *Behavior Therapy, 12,* 30–40.

Bandura, A. (1986). *Social foundations of thought and action: A social cognitive theory.* Englewood Cliffs, NJ: Prentice-Hall.

Bandura, A., Ross, D., & Ross, S. A. (1963). Imitation of film-mediated aggressive models. *Journal of Abnormal and Social Psychology, 66,* 3–11.

Banks, M. S., & Bennet, P. J. (1988). Optical and photoreceptor immaturities limit the spatial and chromatic vision of human neonates. *Journal of the Optical Society of America, 5,* 2059–2079.

Banks, W. P., & Krajicek, D. (1991). Perception. *Annual Review of Psychology, 42,* 305–331.

Barber, T. X. (1976). *Hypnosis: A scientific approach.* New York: Psychological Dimensions.

Barinaga, M. (1989). Manic depression gene put in limbo. *Science, 246,* 886–887.

Barker, L. M., Best, M. R., & Domjan, M. (Eds.). (1978). *Learning mechanisms in food selection.* Houston: Baylor University Press.

Barlett, D. L., & Steele, J. B. (1979). *Empire: The life, legend, and madness of Howard Hughes.* New York: Norton.

Barna, L. (1991). Stumbling blocks in intercultural communication. In L. Samovar & R. Porter (Eds.), *Intercultural communication: A reader* (6th ed., pp. 345–352). Belmont, CA: Wadsworth.

Barnes, D. M. (1987). Biological issues in schizophrenia. *Science, 235,* 430–433.

Baron, A., Perone, M., & Galizio, M. (1991). Analyzing the reinforcement process at the human level: Can application and behavioristic interpretation replace laboratory research? *The Behavior Analyst, 14.*

Baron, L., & Straus, M. A. (1989). *Four theories of rape in American society: A state-level analysis.* New Haven, CT: Yale University Press.

Barthe, D. G., & Hammen, C. L. (1981). The attributional model of depression: A naturalistic extension. *Personality & Social Psychology Bulletin, 7*(1), 53–58.

Bartlett, F. C. (1932). *Remembering: A study in experimental and social psychology.* Cambridge: Cambridge University Press.

Basseches, M. (1984). *Dialectical thinking and adult development.* Norwood, NJ: Ablex.

Bateson, G., Jackson, D. D., Haley, J., & Weakland, J. H. (1956). Toward a theory of schizophrenia. *Behavioral Science, 1,* 251–264.

Baum, A. (1990). Stress, intrusive imagery, and chronic distress. *Health Psychology, 9,* 653–675.

Bazerman, M. H. (1990). *Judgment in managerial decision making* (2nd ed.). New York: Wiley.

Beardslee, W. R., & Mack, J. E. (1983). Adolescents and the threat of nuclear war: The evolution of a perspective. *Yale Journal of Biological Medicine, 56*(2), 79–91.

Beck, A. T. (1983). Cognitive theory of depression: New perspectives. In P. J. Clayton, & J. E. Barrett (Eds.), *Treatment of depression: Old controversies and new approaches* (pp. 265–290). New York: Raven Press.

Beck, A. T. (1985). Cognitive therapy. In H. I. Kaplan & J. Sandock (Eds.), *Comprehensive textbook of psychiatry* (4th ed.). Baltimore: Williams & Wilkins.

Beck, A. T. (1988). Cognitive approaches to panic disorders: Theory and therapy. In S. Rachman & J. D. Maser (Eds.), *Panic: Psychological perspectives.* New York: Guilford Press.

Beck, A. T., & Emery, G. (1985). *Anxiety disorders and phobias: A cognitive perspective.* New York: Basic Books.

Beck, A. T., Rush, A. J., Shaw, B. F., & Emery, G. (1979). *Cognitive therapy of depression.* New York: Guilford Press.

Beck, J. (Ed.). (1982). *Organization and representation in perception.* Hillsdale, NJ: Erlbaum.

Begg, I., & Paivio, A. V. (1969). Concreteness and imagery in sentence meaning. *Journal of Verbal Learning and Behavior, 8,* 821–827.

Begley, S. (1992, April 20). The Brain: Science opens new windows on the mind. *Newsweek* (pp. 66–70).

Belk, R. W. (1988). Possessions and the extended self. *Journal of Consumer Research, 15,* 139–168.

Bell, A. P., Weinberg, M. S., & Hammersmith, S. K. (1981). *Sexual preference.* Bloomington: Indiana University Press.

Bellak, L. (Ed.). (1979). *Disorders of the schizophrenic syndrome.* New York: Basic Books.

Bem, D. J., & Allen, A. (1974). On predicting some of the people some of the time: The search for cross-situational consistencies in behavior. *Psychological Review, 81*(6), 506–520.

Benedict, R. (1959). *Patterns of culture.* Boston: Houghton Mifflin.

Bennett, B. M., Hoffman, D. D., & Prakash, C. (1989). *Observer mechanics: A formal theory of perception.* NY: Academic Press.

Benson, H. (1975). *The relaxation response.* New York: Morrow.

Berkman, L. F., & Syme, S. L. (1979). Social networks, host resistance, and mortality: A nine-year follow-up study of Alameda County residents. *American Journal of Epidemiology, 109,* 186–204.

Berlyne, D. E. (1960). *Conflict, arousal, and curiosity.* New York: McGraw-Hill.

Bernard, L. L. (1924). *Instinct.* New York: Holt, Rinehart & Winston.

Berndt, T. J. (1979). Developmental changes in conformity to peers and parents. *Developmental Psychology, 15,* 608–616.

Bernstein, I. L. (1988). What does learning have to do with weight loss and cancer? *Proceedings of the Science and Public Policy Seminar of the Federation of Behavioral, Psychological and Cognitive Sciences.* Washington, DC.

Bernstein, I. L. (1990). Salt preference and development. *Developmental Psychology, 26,* 552–554.

Berry, J. (1992). Cree conceptions of cognitive competence. *International Journal of Psychology, 27,* 73–88.

Berscheid, E., & Hatfield, E. (1969). *Interpersonal attraction.* Reading, MA: Addison-Wesley.

Berscheid, E., & Hatfield, E. (1978). *Interpersonal attraction,* 2nd edition. Reading, MA: Addison-Wesley.

Bhawuk, D. P. S. (1990). Cross-cultural orientation programs. In R. Brislin (Ed.), *Applied cross-cultural psychology* (pp. 325–346). Newbury Park, CA: Sage.

Bianchi, A. (1992, September–October). Dream chemistry. *Harvard Magazine,* (pp. 21–22).

Biederman, I. (1989). Higher-level vision. In D. N. Osherson, H. Sasnik, S. Kosslyn, K. Hollerbach, E. Smith, & N. Block (Eds.), *An invitation to cognitive science.* Cambridge, MA: MIT Press.

Bielski, R. J., & Friedel, R. O. (1977). Subtypes of depression, diagnosis and medical management. *Western Journal of Medicine, 126,* 347–352.

Billings, A. G., & Moos, R. H. (1982). Family environments and adaptation: A clinically applicable typology. *American Journal of Family Therapy, 10,* 26–38.

Binet, A. (1911). *Les idées modernes sur les enfants.* Paris: Flammarion.

Bitterman, M. E. (1975). The comparative analysis of learning. *Science, 188,* 699–709.

Blacher, R. S. (1987). General surgery and anesthesia: The emotional experience. In R. S. Blacher (Ed.), *The psychological experience of surgery* (pp. 9–14). New York: Wiley.

Blass, E. M. (1990). Suckling: Determinants, changes, mechanisms, and lasting impressions. *Developmental Psychology, 26,* 520–533.

Blass, E. M., & Teicher, M. H. (1980). Suckling. *Science, 210,* 15–22.

Bleuler, M. (1978). The long-term course of schizophrenic psychoses. In L. C. Wynne, R. L. Cromwell, & S. Mattysse (Eds.), *The nature of schizophrenia: New approaches to research and treatment* (pp. 631–636). New York: Wiley.

Blight, J. G. (1987). Toward a policy-relevant psychology of avoiding nuclear war: Lessons for psychologists from the Cuban missile crisis. *American Psychologist, 42,* 12–19.

Block, R. I., Ghoneim, M. M., Sum Ping, S. T., & Ali, M. A. (1991). Efficacy of therapeutic suggestions for improved postoperative recovery presented during general anesthesia. *Anesthesiology, 75,* 746–755.

Bloom, B., Asher, S. J., & White, S. W. (1978). Marital disruption as a stressor: A review and analysis. *Psychological Bulletin, 85,* 867–894.

Bolger, N., DeLongis, A., Kessler, R. C., & Schilling, E. A. (1989). Effects of daily stress on negative mood. *Journal of Personality and Social Psychology, 57,* 808–818.

Bond, C. F., & Brockett, D. R. (1987). A social context-personality index theory of memory for acquaintances. *Journal of personality and social psychology, 52,* 1110–1121.

Bongiovanni, A. (1977). *A review of research on the effects of punishment in the schools.* Paper presented at the Conference on Child Abuse, Children's Hospital National Medical Center, Washington, DC.

Bootzin, R. R. (1975). *Behavior modification and therapy: An introduction.* Cambridge, MA: Winthrop.

Bootzin, R. R., & Nicasio, P. M. (1978). Behavioral treatments for insomnia. In M. Hersen, R. Eisler, & P. Miller (Eds.), *Progress in behavior modification.* New York: Academic Press.

Borkovec, T. D. (1982). Insomnia. *Journal of Consulting and Clinical Psychology, 50,* 880–985.

Borod, C., Koff, E., Lorch, M. P., Nicholas, M., & Welkowitz, J. (1988). Emotional and non-emotional facial behavior in patients with unilateral brain damage. *Journal of Neurological and Neurosurgical Psychiatry, 5,* 826–832.

Bower, G. H. (1972). A selective review of organizational factors in memory. In E. Tulving & W. Donaldson (Eds.), *Organization of memory.* New York: Academic Press.

Bower, G. H. (1981). Mood and memory. *American Psychologist, 36,* 129–148.

Bower, S. A., & Bower, G. H. (1976/1991). *Asserting yourself: A practical guide for positive change.* Reading, MA: Addison-Wesley. (Original work published 1976).

Bowers, K. S. (1976). *Hypnosis for the seriously curious.* New York: Norton.

Bowers, M. B., Jr. (1980). Biochemical processes in schizophrenia: An update. In S. J. Keith & L. R. Mosher (Eds.), *Special Report: Schizophrenia, 1980.* Washington, DC: U.S. Government Printing Office.

Bowlby, J. (1973). *Attachment and loss: Vol. 2. Separation, anxiety and anger.* London: Hogarth.

Boyd, J. H., & Weissman, M. M. (1981). Epidemiology of affective disorders: A reexamination and future directions. *Archives of General Psychiatry, 38,* 1039–1046.

Braine, M. D. S. (1976). Children's first word combinations. *Monographs of the Society for Research in Child Development, 41* (Serial No. 164).

Bransford, J. D., & Franks, J. J. (1971). The abstraction of linguistic ideas. *Cognitive Psychology, 2,* 331–350.

Bransford, J. D., & Johnson, M. K. (1972). Contextual prerequisites for understanding: Some investigations of comprehension and recall. *Journal of Verbal Learning and Verbal Behavior, 11,* 17–21.

Breggin, P. R. (1979). *Electroshock: Its brain disabling effects.* New York: Springer.

Brehm, S. S. (1992). *Intimate relationships, 2nd edition.* New York: McGraw-Hill.

Breland, K., & Breland, M. (1951). A field of applied animal psychology. *American Psychologist, 6,* 202–204.

Breland, K., & Breland, M. (1961). A misbehavior of organisms. *American Psychologist, 16,* 681–684.

Brenner, M. H. (1976). *Estimating the social costs of national economic policy: Implications for mental and physical health and criminal violence.* Report prepared for the Joint Economic Committee of Congress, Washington, DC: U.S. Government Printing Office.

Brett, J. F., Brief, A. P., Burke, M. J., George, J. M., & Webster, J. (1990). Negative affectivity and the reporting of stressful life events. *Health Psychology, 9,* 57–68.

Brewer, M. B. (1979). In-group bias in the minimal intergroup situation: A cognitive-motivational analysis. *Psychological Bulletin, 86,* 307–324.

Brim, O. G., & Kagan, J. (1980). *Constancy and change in human development.* Cambridge: Harvard University Press.

Brislin, R. (1974). The Ponzo illusion: Additional cues, age, orientation, and culture. *Journal of Cross-Cultural Psychology, 5,* 139–161.

Brislin, R. (1993). *Understanding culture's influence on behavior.* Fort Worth, TX: Harcourt Brace Jovanovich.

Brislin, R., Cushner, C., Cherrie, C., & Yong, M. (1986). *Intercultural interactions: A practical guide.* Newbury Park, CA: Sage.

Broadbent, D. E. (1954). The role of auditory localization in attention and memory span. *Journal of Experimental Psychology, 47,* 191–196.

Brody, R. V. (1986). Pain management in terminal disease. *Focus: A Review of AIDS Research, 1,* 1–2

Broman, S. H., Nichols, P. I., & Kennedy, W. A. (1975). *Preschool IQ: Prenatal and early developmental correlates.* Hillsdale, NJ: Erlbaum.

Broverman, I. K., Vogel, S. R., Broverman, D. M., Clarkson, F. E., & Rosenkrantz, P. S. (1972). Sex-role stereotypes: A current appraisal. *Journal of Social Issues, 28*(2), 59–78.

Brown, A. M. (1990). *Human universals.* Unpublished manuscript, University of California, Santa Barbara.

Brown, C. C. (Ed.). (1984). *The many facets of touch.* Skillman, NJ: Johnson & Johnson.

Brown, G. W., & Harris, T. O. (Eds.). (1989). *Life events and illness.* New York: Guilford.

Brown, J. S. (1961). *The motivation of behavior.* New York: McGraw-Hill.

Brown, R. (1986). *Social psychology: The second edition.* New York: The Free Press.

Brownell, K. D. (1982). Obesity: Understanding and treating a serious, prevalent, and refractory disorder. *Journal of Clinical and Consulting Psychology, 50,* 820–840.

Bruch, H. (1978). *The golden cage: The enigma of anorexia nervosa.* Cambridge, MA: Harvard University Press.

Brumberg, J. J. (1988). *Fasting girls: The history of anorexia nervosa.* New York: Plume.

Bruner, J. S. (1973). *Beyond the information given.* New York: Norton.

Bruner, J. S., Olver, R. R., & Greenfield, P. M. (1966). Studies in cognitive growth. New York: Wiley.

Bulman, J. R., & Wortman, C. B. (1977). Attribution of blame and coping in the "real world": Severe accident victims react to their lot. *Journal of Personality and Social Psychology, 35,* 351–363.

Burrows, G. D., & Dennerstein, L. (Eds.). (1980). *Handbook of hypnosis and psychosomatic medicine.* New York: Elsevier/North Holland Biomedical Press.

Buss, D. M. (1989). Sex differences in human mate preferences: Evolutionary hypotheses tested in 37 cultures. *Behavioral and Brain Sciences, 12,* 1–14.

Butler, R. N., & Lewis, M. I. (1982). *Aging and mental health: Positive psychosocial and biomedical approaches* (3rd ed.). St. Louis: Mosby.

Byrne, D. (1971). *The attraction paradigm.* New York: Academic Press.

Byrne, D. (1981, August). *Predicting human sexual behavior.* G. Stanley Hall Lecture presented at the meeting of the American Psychological Association, Los Angeles, CA.

C

Cairns, R. B., & Valsinger, J. (1984). Child psychology. *Annual Review of Psychology, 35,* 553–577.

Campbell, A. (1981). *The sense of well being in America: Patterns and trends.* New York: McGraw-Hill.

Campos, J. J., Barrett, K. C., Lamb, M. E., Goldsmith, H. H., & Stenberg, C. (1983). *Socioemotional development* (Vol. 2). New York: Wiley.

Cann, A., Calhoun, L. G., Selby, J. W., & Kin, H. E. (Eds.). (1981). Rape. *Journal of Social Issues, 37* (Whole No. 4).

Cannon, W. B. (1927). The James-Lange theory of emotion: A critical examination and an alternative theory. *American Journal of Psychology, 39,* 106–124.

Cannon, W. B. (1929). *Bodily changes in pain, hunger, fear and rage* (2nd ed.). New York: Appleton-Century-Crofts.

Cannon, W. B. (1934). Hunger and thirst. In C. Murchison (Ed.), *A handbook of general experimental psychology.* Worcester, MA: Clark University Press.

Cannon, W. B., & Washburn, A. L. (1912). An explanation of hunger. *American Journal of Physiology, 29,* 441–454.

Cantor, N., & Kihlstrom, J. F. (1987). Social intelligence: The cognitive basis of personality. In P. Shaver (Ed.), *Review of personality and social psychology, Vol. 6* (pp. 15–34). Beverly Hills, CA: Sage.

Cantor, N., & Mischel, W. (1979). Traits as prototypes: Effects on recognition memory. *Journal of Personality and Social Psychology, 35,* 38–48.

Caplow, T. (1982). *Middletown families: Fifty years of change and continuity*. Minneapolis: University of Minnesota Press.

Caporeal, L. R. (1976). Ergotism: The Satan loosed in Salem? *Science, 192,* 21–26.

Carey, S. (1978). The child as word learner. In M. Halle, J. Bresnan, & G. A. Miller (Eds.), *Linguistic theory and psychological reality* (pp. 265–293). Cambridge, MA: MIT Press.

Carlsmith, J. M., & Gross, A. (1969). Some effects of guilt on compliance. *Journal of Personality and Social Psychology, 11,* 232–240.

Carlsson, A. (1978). Antipsychotic drugs, neurotransmitters, and schizophrenia. *American Journal of Psychiatry, 135,* 164–173.

Carmichael, L. (1970). The onset and early development of behavior. In P. H. Mussen (Ed.), *Carmichael's manual of child psychology* (3rd ed., Vol. 1). New York: Wiley.

Carpenter, G. C. (1973). Differential response to mother and stranger within the first month of life. *Bulletin of the British Psychological Society, 16,* 138.

Carstensen, L. L. (1987). Age-related changes in social activity. In L. L. Carstensen & B. A. Edelstein (Eds.), *Handbook of clinical gerontology* (pp. 222–237). New York: Pergamon Press.

Carstensen, L. L. (1991). Selectivity theory: Social activity in life-span context. In K. W. Schaie (Ed.), *Annual Review of Geriatrics and Gerontology* (Vol. 11). New York: Springer.

Cartwright, R. D. (1978). *A primer on sleep and dreaming*. Reading, MA: Addison-Wesley.

Cartwright, R. D. (1982). The shape of dreams. In *1983 yearbook of science and the future*. Chicago: Encyclopaedia Britannica.

Cartwright, R. D. (1984). Broken dreams: A study of the effects of divorce and depression on dream content. *Psychiatry, 47,* 251–259.

Carver, C. S., & Scheier, M. P. (1981). *Attention and self-regulation: A control theory approach to human behavior*. New York: Springer-Verlag.

Carver, C. S., Scheier, M. F., & Weintraub, J. K. (1989). Assessing coping strategies: A theoretically based approach. *Journal of Personality and Social Psychology, 56,* 267–283.

Caspi, A., & Bem, D. J. (1990). Personality continuity and change across the life course. In L. A. Pervin (Ed.), *Handbook of personality theory and research* (pp. 549–575). New York: Guilford Press.

Caspi, A., Elder, G. H., Jr., & Bem, D. J. (1988). Moving away from the world: Life-course patterns of shy children. *Developmental Psychology, 24,* 824–833.

Cattell, R. B. (1963). Theory of fluid and crystallized intelligence: A critical experiment. *Journal of Educational Psychology, 54,* 1–22.

Chamberlain, K., & Zika, S. (1990). The minor events approach to stress: Support for the use of daily hassles. *British Journal of Psychology, 81,* 469–481.

Chapman, P. D. (1988). *Schools as sorters: Lewis M. Terman, applied psychology, and the intelligence testing movement, 1890–1930*. New York: New York University Press.

Cherry, E. C. (1953). Some experiments on the recognition of speech, with one and with two ears. *Journal of the Acoustical Society of America, 25,* 975–979.

Chilman, C. S. (1983). *Adolescent sexuality in a changing American society* (2nd ed.). New York: Wiley.

Chomsky, N. (1957). *Syntactic structures*. The Hague: Mouton.

Chomsky, N. (1965). *Aspects of a theory of syntax*. Cambridge, MA: MIT Press.

Chomsky, N. (1975). *Reflections on language*. New York: Pantheon Books.

Churchland, P. S. (1986). *Toward a unified science of the mind-brain*. Cambridge, MA: MIT Press.

Clark, H. H., & Clark, E. V. (1977). *Psychology and language: An introduction to psycholinguistics*. New York: Harcourt Brace Jovanovich.

Clark, K., & Clark, M. (1947). Racial identification and preference in Negro children. In T. M. Newcomb & E. L. Hartley (Eds.), *Readings in social psychology*. New York: Holt.

Clausen, J. A. (1981). Stigma and mental disorder: Phenomena and mental terminology. *Psychiatry, 44,* 287–296.

Cleek, M. B., & Pearson, T. A. (1985). Perceived causes of divorce: An analysis of interrelationships. *Journal of Marriage and the Family, 47,* 179–191.

Coates, T. J., Temoshok, L., & Mandel, J. (1984). Psychosocial research is essential to understanding and treating AIDS. *American Psychologist, 39,* 1309–1314.

Cobb, S. (1976). Social support as a moderator of stress. *Psychosomatic Medicine, 35,* 375–389.

Cohen, R. E., & Ahearn, F. L., Jr. (1980). *Handbook for mental health care of disaster victims*. Baltimore: Johns Hopkins University Press.

Cohen, S. (1988). Psychosocial models of the role of social support in the etiology of physical disease. *Health Psychology, 7,* 269–297.

Cohen, S., & McKay, G. (1983). Social support, stress, and the buffering hypotheses: A theoretical analysis. In A. Baum, S. E. Taylor, & J. Singer (Eds.), *Handbook of psychology and health* (Vol. 4). Hillsdale, NJ: Erlbaum.

Cohen, S., & Syme, S. L. (Eds.). (1985). *Social support and health*. Orlando, FL: Academic Press.

Coleman, L. (1987). *Suicide clusters*. Winchester, MA: Faber & Faber.

Collier, G., Hirsch, E., & Hamlin, P. (1972). The ecological determinants of reinforcement. *Physiology and Behavior, 9,* 705–716.

Conger, J. C., & Keane, S. P. (1981). Social skills intervention in the treatment of isolated or withdrawn children. *Psychological Bulletin, 90,* 478–495.

Conger, J. J., & Peterson, A. C. (1984). *Adolescence and youth,* 3rd edition. New York: Harper & Row.

Conrad, R. (1964). Acoustic confusions in immediate memory. *British Journal of Psychology, 55,* 75–84.

Cook, M., Mineka, S., Woklenstein, B., & Laitsch, K. (1985). Observational conditioning of snake fear in unrelated rhesus monkeys. *Journal of Abnormal Psychology, 94,* 591–610.

Cookerly, J. R. (1980). Does marital therapy do any lasting good? *Journal of Marital and Family Therapy, 6,* 393–397.

Cooper, M. J., & Fairburn, C. G. (1993). Demographic and clinical correlates of selective information processing in patients with bulimia nervosa. *International Journal of Eating Disorders, 13*(1), 109–116.

Coren, S., & Girgus, J. S. (1978). *Seeing is deceiving: The psychology of visual illusions*. Hillsdale, NJ: Erlbaum.

Coren, S., & Ward, L. M. (1989). *Sensation and perception* (3rd ed.). San Diego: Harcourt Brace Jovanovich.

Cosmides, L., & Tooby, J. (1987). From evolution to behavior: Evolutionary psychology as the missing link. In J. Dupre (Ed.), *The latest on the best: Essays on evolution and optimality* (pp. 277–306). Cambridge, MA: MIT Press.

Cousins, N. (1979). *The anatomy of an illness as perceived by a patient: Reflections on healing and rejuvenation*. New York: Norton.

Cousins, N. (1983). *The healing heart*. New York: Norton.

Cousins, N. (1989). *Head first: The biology of hope*. New York: Dutton.

Cowan, P., & Cowan, P. A. (1988). Changes in marriage during the transition to parenthood. In G. Y. Michaels & W. A. Goldberg (Eds.), *The transition to parenthood: Current theory and research*. Cambridge: Cambridge University Press.

Cowan, P. A. (1988). Developmental psychopathology: A nine-cell map of the territory. In E. Nannis & P. A. Cowan (Eds.), *Developmental psychopathology and its treatment: New directions for child development* (No. 39, pp. 5–29). San Francisco: Jossey Bass.

Cowan, W. M. (1979). The development of the brain. In *The brain* (pp. 56–69). San Francisco: Freeman.

Cowles, J. T. (1937). Food tokens as incentives for learning by chimpanzees. *Comparative Psychology Monographs, 74,* 1–96.

Coyne, J. (1990). In *Discovering Psychology*, Program 22 [PBS video series]. Washington, DC: Annenberg/CPB Project.

Coyne, J. C., Wortman, C. B., & Lehman, D. R. (1988). The other side of support: Emotional overinvolvement and miscarried helping. In B. Gottlieb (Ed.), *Marshalling social support* (pp. 305–330). Newbury Park, CA: Sage.

Craik, K. (1943). *The nature of explanation*. Cambridge: Cambridge University Press.

Cranston, M. (1991). *The noble savage: Jean-Jacques Rousseau, 1754–1762*. Chicago: University of Chicago Press.

Crapo, L. (1985). *Hormones: The messengers of life*. Stanford, CA: Stanford Alumni Association Press.

Crick, F., & Mitchison, G. (1983). The function of dream sleep. *Nature, 304,* 111–114.

Crosby, F. J. (1982). *Relative deprivation and working women*. New York: Oxford University Press.

Csikszentmihalyi, M. (1990). *Flow: The psychology of optimal experience*. New York: Harper & Row.

Csikszentmihalyi, M., Larson, R., & Prescott, S. (1977). The ecology of adolescent activity and experience. *Journal of Youth and Adolescence, 6,* 281–294.

Cumming, E., & Henry, W. E. (1961). *Growing old: The process of disengagement*. New York: Basic Books.

D

Dackman, L. (1986). Everyday illusions. *Exploratorium Quarterly, 10,* 5–7.

Dahlstrom, W. G., Welsh, H. G., & Dahlstrom, L. E. (1975). *An MMPI handbook, Vol. 1: Clinical interpretation*. Minnesota: University of Minnesota Press.

Dakof, G. A., & Taylor, S. E. (1990). Victims' perceptions of social support: What is helpful from whom? *Journal of Personality and Social Psychology, 58,* 80–89.

Damon, W., & Hart, D. (1986). Stability and change in children's self-understanding. *Social Cognition, 4,* 102–118.

Darley, J. M., & Batson, C. D. (1973). From Jerusalem to Jericho: A study of situational and dispositional variables in helping behavior. *Journal of Personality and Social Psychology, 27,* 100–108.

Darwin, C. J., Turvey, M. T., & Crowder, R. G. (1972). The auditory analogue of the Sperling partial report procedure: Evidence for brief auditory stage. *Cognitive Psychology, 3,* 255–267.

Davidsen-Nielsen, M., & Leick, N. (1991). *Healing pain: Attachment, loss and grief therapy*. New York: Routledge.

Davidson, J. M. (1980). The psychobiology of sexual experience. In J. M. Davidson & R. J. Davidson (Eds.), *The psychobiology of consciousness* (pp. 271–331). New York: Plenum.

Davidson, R. (1984). Hemispheric asymmetry and emotion. In K. Scherer & P. Ekman (Eds.), *Approaches to emotion*. Hillsdale, NJ: Erlbaum.

Davis, I. P. (1985). *Adolescents: Theoretical and helping perspectives*. Boston: Kluwer-Nijhoff Publishing.

DeCasper, A. J., & Fifer, W. P. (1980). Of human bonding: Newborns prefer their mothers' voices. *Science, 208,* pp. 1174–1176.

De Charms, R. C., & Muir, M. S. (1978). Motivation: Social approaches. *Annual Review of Psychology, 29,* 91–113.

Deci, E. L. (1975). *Intrinsic motivation*. New York: Plenum.

Deci, E. L., & Ryan, R. M. (1987). The support of autonomy and the control of behavior. *Journal of Personality and Social Psychology, 53,* 1024–1037.

Delgado, J. M. R. (1969). *Physical control of the mind: Toward a psychocivilized society*. New York: Harper & Row.

Delisi, C. (1988). The human genome project. *American Scientist, 76,* 488–493.

Dembroski, T. M., Weiss, S. M., Shields, J. L. et al. (1978). *Coronary-prone behavior*. New York: Springer-Verlag.

Dembrowski, T. M., & Costa, P. T., Jr. (1987). Coronary prone behavior: Components of the Type A pattern and hostility. *Journal of Personality, 55,* 211–235.

Dement, W. C. (1976). *Some watch while some must sleep*. San Francisco: San Francisco Book Co.

Deregowski, J. B. (1980). *Illusions, patterns and pictures: A cross-cultural perspective* (pp. 966–977). London: Academic Press.

DeRivera, J. (1984). Development and the full range of emotional experience. In C. Malastesta & C. Izard (Eds.), *Emotion in adult development* (pp. 45–63). Beverly Hills: Sage.

Deutsch, J. A., & Deutsch, D. (1963). Attention: Some theoretical considerations. *Psychological Review, 70,* 80–90.

Deutsch, M., & Gerard, H. B. (1955). A study of normative and informational social influence. *Journal of Abnormal and Social Psychology, 51,* 629–636.

Deutsch, M., & Hornstein, H. A. (1975). *Applying social psychology*. Hillsdale, NJ: Erlbaum.

Devereux, G. (1981). Mohave ethnopsychiatry and suicide: The psychiatric knowledge and psychic disturbances of an Indian tribe. *Bureau of American Ethology* (Bulletin 175). Washington, DC: Smithsonian Institution.

Diamond, D. (1989, Fall). The unbearable darkness of being. *Stanford Medicine*, pp. 13–16.

Diamond, J. (1990). The great leap forward. *Discover* (Special Issue), pp. 66–77.

Dickman, H., & Zeiss, R. A. (1982). *Incidents and correlates of post-traumatic stress disorder among ex–Prisoners of War of World War II*. Manuscript in progress. Palo Alto, CA.: Veterans Administration.

Dietrich, N., & Thomas, B. (1972). *Howard: The amazing Mr. Hughes*. Greenwich, CT: Fawcett.

Dillon, K. M., & Totten, M. C. (1989). Psychological factors affecting immunocompetence and health of breastfeeding mothers and their infants. *Journal of Genetic Psychology, 150,* 155–162.

Dixon, R. A., Kramer, D. A., & Baltes, P. B. (1985). Intelligence: A life-span developmental perspective. In B. B. Wolman (Ed.), *Handbook of intelligence* (pp. 301–352). New York: Wiley.

Doane, J. A., Falloon, I. R. H., Goldstein, M. J., & Mintz, J. (1985). Parental affective style and the treatment of schizophrenia. *Archives of general psychiatry, 42,* 34–42.

Dohrenwend, B. P., & Shrout, P. E. (1985). "Hassles" in the conceptualization and measurement of life stress variables. *American Psychologist, 40,* 780–785.

Dohrenwend, B. S., & Dohrenwend, B. P. (1974). *Stressful life events: Their nature and effects*. New York: Wiley.

Dollard, J., & Miller, N. E. (1950). *Personality and psychotherapy*. New York: McGraw-Hill.

Donnerstein, E. (1980). Aggressive erotica and violence against women. *Journal of Personality and Social Psychology, 39,* 269–277.

Donnerstein, E., & Berkowitz, L. (1981). Victim reactions in aggressive erotic films as a factor in violence against women. *Journal of Personality and Social Psychology, 41,* 710–724.

Donnerstein, E., Linz, D., & Penrod, S. (1987). *The question of pornography*. London: The Free Press.

Draguns, J. (1973). Comparison of psychopathology across cultures: Issues, findings, directions. *Journal of Cross-Cultural Psychology, 4,* 9–47.

Draguns, J. (1980). Psychological disorders of clinical severity. In H. Triandis & J. Draguns (Eds.), *Handbook of cross-cultural psychology, Vol. 6: Psychopathology* (pp. 99–174). Boston: Allyn & Bacon.

Draguns, J. (1990). Applications of cross-cultural psychology in the field of mental health. In R. Brislin (Ed.), *Applied cross-cultural psychology* (pp. 302–324). Newbury Park, CA: Sage.

Driver, J., & Tipper, S. (1989). On the nonselectivity of "selective" seeing: Contrasts between interference and priming in selective attention. *Journal of Experimental Psychology: Human Perception and Performance, 15,* 304–314.

Drosnin, M. (1985). *Citizen Hughes*. New York: Holt, Rinehart & Winston.

Duck, S. (1982). A topography of relationship disengagement and dissolution. In S. Duck (Ed.), *Personal relationships 4: Dissolving personal relationships*. London: Academic Press.

Duck, S. (1992). *Human relationships,* 2nd edition. Newbury Park, CA: Sage.

Duncker, K. (1945). On problem solving. *Psychological Monographs, 58* (No. 270).

Dunkel-Schetter, C., Folkman, S., & Lazarus, R. S. (1987). Correlates of social support receipt. *Journal of Personality and Social Psychology, 53,* 71–80.

Dutton, D. G., & Aron, A. P. (1974). Some evidence for heightened sexual attraction under conditions of high anxiety. *Journal of Personality and Social Psychology, 30,* 510–517.

E

Ebbinghaus, H. (1908/1973). *Psychology: An elementary textbook*. New York: Arno Press. (Original work published 1908).

Edwards, A. E., & Acker, L. E. (1962). A demonstration of the long-term retention of a conditioned galvanic skin response. *Psychosomatic Medicine, 24,* 459–463.

Efron, R. (1990). *The decline and fall of hemispheric specialization*. Hillsdale, NJ: Erlbaum.

Egeland, J. A., Gerhard, D. S., Pauls, D. L., Sussex, J. N., Kidd, K. K., Allen, C. R., Hostetter, A. M., & Housman, D. E. (1987). Bipolar affective disorder linked to DNA markers on chromosome 11. *Nature, 325,* 783–787.

Eger, E. E. (1990). Auschwitz at 16, Auschwitz at 61. *California State Psychologist,* pp. 6–9.

Ehrlich, B. E., & Diamond, J. M. (1980). Lithium, membranes, and manic-depressive illness. *Journal of Membrane Biology, 52,* 187–200.

Eich, E., Reeves, J. L., & Katz, R. L. (1985). Anesthesia, amnesia, and the memory/awareness distinction. *Anesthesiology and Analgesia, 64,* 1143–1148.

Ekman, P. (1984). Expression and the nature of emotion. In K. R. Scherer & P. Ekman (Eds.), *Approaches to emotion.* Hillsdale, NJ: Erlbaum.

Ekman, P., & Friesen, W. V. (1975). *Unmasking the face: A guide to recognizing emotions from facial clues.* Englewood Cliffs, NJ: Prentice-Hall.

Ekman, P., & Friesen, W. V. (1986). A new pan-cultural facial expression of emotion. *Motivation and Emotion, 10,* 159–168.

Eliade, M. (1964). *Shamanism: Archaic techniques of ecstasy.* New York: Pantheon.

Elliott, J. (1977). The power and pathology of prejudice. In P. G. Zimbardo & F. L. Ruch, *Psychology and life* (9th ed., Diamond Printing). Glenview, IL: Scott, Foresman.

Ellis, A. (1962). *Reason and emotion in psychotherapy.* New York: Lyle Stuart.

Ellis, A., & Grieger, R. (1986). *Handbook of rational emotive therapy* (Vol. 2). New York: Springer.

Eme, R., Maisiak, R., & Goodale, W. (1979). Seriousness of adolescent problems. *Adolescence, 14,* 93–99.

Emmelkamp, P. M. (1986). Behavior therapy with adults. In S. L. Garfield & A. E. Bergin (Eds.), *Handbook of psychotherapy and behavior change* (pp. 385–442). New York: Wiley.

Emmelkamp, P. M. G., & Kuipers, A. (1979). Agoraphobia: A follow-up study four years after treatment. *British Journal of Psychology, 134,* 352–355.

Emmons, C. A., Joseph, J. G. et al. (1986). Psychosocial predictors of reported behavior change in homosexual men at risk for AIDS. *Health Education Quarterly, 13,* 331–345.

Engle, G. L. (1976). The need for a new medical model: A challenge for biomedicine. *Science, 196,* 129–136.

Epstein, S. (1979). The stability of behavior: 1. On predicting most of the people much of the time. *Journal of Personality and Social Psychology, 37,* 1097–1126.

Ericsson, K. A., & Simon, H. A. (1984). *Protocol analysis: Verbal reports as data.* Cambridge, MA: MIT Press.

Erikson, E. H. (1963). *Childhood and society* (2nd. ed.). New York: Norton.

Erikson, E. H. (1968). *Identity: Youth and crisis.* New York: Norton.

Evans, C., & Richardson, P. H. (1988). Improved recovery and reduced post-operative stay after therapeutic suggestions during general anesthesia. *Lancet, 2,* 491–493.

Evans, R. I., Rozelle, R. M., Mittelmark, M. B., Hansen, W. B., Bane, A. L., & Havis, J. (1978). Deterring the onset of smoking in children: Knowledge of immediate physiological effects and coping with peer pressure, media pressure, and parent modeling. *Journal of Applied Social Psychology, 8,* 126–135.

Eysenck, H. (1990). Biological dimensions of personality. In L. A. Pervin (Ed.), *Handbook of personality theory and research* (pp. 244–276). New York: Guilford Press.

Eysenck, H. J. (1947). *Dimensions of personality.* London: Routledge and Kegan Paul.

Eysenck, H. J. (1952). The effects of psychotherapy: An evaluation. *Journal of Consulting Psychology, 16,* 319–324.

F

Fallon, A., & Rozin, P. (1985). Sex differences in perceptions of desirable body states. *Journal of Abnormal Psychology, 84,* 102–105.

Fanslow, C. A. (1984). Touch and the elderly. In C. Caldwell Brown (Ed.), *The many facets of touch* (pp. 183–189). Skillman, NJ: Johnson & Johnson.

Fantz, R. L. (1963). Pattern vision in newborn infants. *Science, 140,* 296–297.

Farah, M. J. (1984). The neurological basis of mental imagery: A componential analysis. *Cognition, 18,* 245–272.

Farina, A. (1980). Social attitudes and beliefs and their role in mental disorders. In J. G. Rabkin, L. Gelb, & J. B. Lazar (Eds.), *Attitudes toward the mentally ill: Research perspectives* (pp. 35–37). Rockville, MD: National Institute of Mental Health.

Farina, A., Gliha, D., Boudreau, L. A., Allen, J. G., & Sherman, M. (1971). Mental illness and the impact of believing others know about it. *Journal of Abnormal Psychology, 77,* 1–5.

Farley, F. (1990, May). The Type T personality, with some implications for practice. *The California Psychologist, 23,* 29.

Farquhar, J. W., Maccoby, N., & Solomon, D. S. (1984). Community applications of behavioral medicine. In W. D. Gentry (Ed.), *Handbook of behavioral medicine* (pp. 437–478). New York: Guilford Press.

Fechner, G. T. (1860). *Elemente der Psychophysik.* Germany: Breitkopf und Hartel.

Fernald, A., Taeschner, T., Dunn, J., Papousek, M., De Boysson-Bardies, B., & Fukui, I. (1989). A cross-cultural study of prosodic modification in mothers' and fathers' speech to preverbal infants. *Journal of Child Language, 16,* 477–501.

Fernald, R. (1984). Vision and behavior in an African cichlid fish. *American Scientist, 72,* 58–65.

Ferrare, N. A. (1962). *Institutionalization and attitude change in an aged population.* Unpublished doctoral dissertation, Western Reserve University.

Ferster, C. B., & Skinner, B. F. (1957). *Schedules of reinforcement.* New York: Appleton-Century-Crofts.

Festinger, L. (1957). *A theory of cognitive dissonance.* Stanford, CA: Stanford University Press.

Field, T. (1990). In *Discovering Psychology,* Program 4 [PBS video series]. Washington, DC: Annenberg/CPB Project.

Field, T. F., & Schanberg, S. M. (1990). Massage alters growth and catecholamine production in preterm newborns. In N. Gunzenhauser (Ed.), *Advances in touch* (pp. 96–104). Skillman, NJ: Johnson & Johnson Co.

Fink, M. (1979). *Convulsive therapy: Theory and practice.* New York: Raven Press.

Fischer, S., & Greenberg, R. P. (1985). *The scientific credibility of Freud's theories and therapy.* New York: Columbia University Press.

Fish, J. M. (1973). *Placebo therapy.* San Francisco: Jossey-Bass.

Fisher, S., & Greenberg, R. P. (1985). *The scientific credibility of Freud's theories and therapy.* New York: Columbia University Press.

Fiske, S. (1987). People's reactions to nuclear war: Implications for psychologists. *American Psychologist, 42,* 207–217.

Fiske, S. T., & Pavelchak, M. A. (1986). Category-based versus piecemeal-based affective response: Developments in schema-triggered affects. In R. M. Sorrentino & E. T. Higgins (Eds.), *The handbook of motivation and cognition: Foundations of social behavior* (pp. 167–203). New York: Guilford Press.

Fiske, S. T., & Taylor, S. E. (1991). *Social cognition.* New York: McGraw-Hill.

Flavell, J. H. (1985). *Cognitive development* (2nd ed.). Englewood Cliffs, NJ: Prentice-Hall.

Fleischman, P. R. (1973). [Letter to the editor concerning "On being sane in insane places"]. *Science, 180,* 356.

Fletcher, G. J. O., & Ward, C. (1988). Attribution theory and processes: A cross-cultural perspective. In M. H. Bond (Ed.), *The cross-cultural challenge to social psychology* (pp. 230–244). Newbury Park, CA: Sage.

Flood, R. A., & Seager, C. P. (1968). A retrospective examination of psychiatric case records of patients who subsequently committed suicide. *British Journal of Psychiatry, 114,* 433–450.

Flora, J. A. (1991, May). AIDS prevention among young people. *California Psychologist,* pp. 14, 18.

Foa, U., & Chemers, M. (1967). The significance of role behavior differentiation for cross-cultural interaction training. *International Journal of Psychology, 2,* 45–57.

Fodor, J. (1983). *The modularity of mind.* Cambridge, MA: MIT Press.

Foley, V. D. (1979). Family therapy. In R. J. Corsini (Ed.), *Current psychotherapies* (2nd ed., pp. 460–469). Itasca, IL: Peacock.

Folkman, S. (1984). Personal control and stress and coping processes: A theoretical analysis. *Journal of Personality and Social Psychology, 46,* 839–852.

Fong, G. T., & Markus, H. (1982). Self-schemas and judgments about others. *Social Cognition, 1,* 191–204.

Ford, C. S., & Beach, F. A. (1951). *Patterns of sexual behavior.* New York: Harper & Row.

Forest, D. V. (1976). Nonsense and sense in schizophrenic language. *Schizophrenia Bulletin, 2,* 286–381.

Foucault, M. (1975). *The birth of the clinic.* New York: Vintage Books.

Fowler, H. (1965). *Curiosity and exploratory behavior.* New York: Macmillan.

Fowler, R. D. (1986, May). Howard Hughes: A psychological autopsy. *Psychology Today,* pp. 179–185.

Frank, J. (1987). The drive for power and the nuclear arms race. *American Psychologist, 42,* 337–344.

Frank, J. (1990). In *Discovering Psychology,* Program 2 [PBS video series]. Washington, DC: Annenberg/CPB Project.

Frank, L. R. (Ed.). (1978). *The history of shock treatment.* (Available from L. R. Frank, San Fransisco, CA).

Franklin, D. (1987, January). The politics of masochism. *Psychology Today,* pp. 52–57.

Freeman, F. R. (1972). Sleep research: *A critical review.* Springfield, IL: Charles C Thomas.

Freud, S. (1904/1914). *The psychopathology of everyday life.* New York: Macmillan. (Original work published 1904).

Freud, S. (1915). Instincts and their vicissitudes. In S. Freud, *The collected papers.* New York: Collier.

Freud, S. (1923). *Introductory lectures on psycho-analysis* (J. Riviera, Trans.). London: Allen & Unwin.

Frey, W. H., & Langseth, M. (1986). *Crying: The mystery of tears.* New York: Winston Press.

Frey, W. H., II, Hoffman-Ahern, C., Johnson, R. A., Lydden, D. T., & Tuason, V. B. (1983). Crying behavior in the human adult. *Integrative Psychiatry, 1,* 94–98.

Fridlund, A. J. (1990). Evolution and facial action in reflex, social motive, and paralanguage. In P. K. Ackles, J. R. Jennings, & M. G. H. Coles (Eds.), *Advances in psychophysiology.* Greenwich, CT: JAI Press.

Friedman, H. S. (Ed.). (1990). *Personality and Disease.* New York: Wiley.

Friedman, H. S., & Booth-Kewley, S. (1987). The "disease-prone personality": A meta-analytic view of the construct. *American Psychologist, 42,* 539–555.

Friedman, H. S., & Booth-Kewley, S. (1988). Validity of the Type A construct: A reprise. *Psychological Bulletin, 104,* 381–384.

Friedman, M., & Rosenman, R. F. (1974). *Type A behavior and your heart.* New York: Knopf.

Friedman, M., Thoresen, C. E., Gill, J. J., Ulmer, D., Powell, L. H., Price, V. A., Brown, B., Thompson, L., Rabin, D. D., Breall, W. S., Bourg, E., Levy, R., & Dixon, T. (1986). Alteration of Type A behavior and its effect on cardiac recurrences in post-myocardial infarction patients: Summary results of the Recurrent Coronary Prevention Project. *American Heart Journal, 11,* 653–665.

Frijda, N., Kuipers, P., & Peter Schure, E. (1989). Relations among emotion, appraisal, and emotional action readiness. *Journal of Personality and Social Psychology, 57,* 212–228.

Fromm, E., & Shor, R. E. (Eds.). (1979). *Hypnosis: Developments in research and new perspectives* (2nd ed.). Hawthorne, NY: Aldine.

Fry, W. F., Jr. (1986). Humor, physiology, and the aging process. In L. Nahemow, K. A. McCluskey-Fawcett, & P. E. McGhee (Eds.), *Humor and aging* (pp. 81–98). Orlando: Academic Press.

Fuller, J. L. (1982). Psychology and genetics: A happy marriage? *Canadian Psychology, 23,* 11–21.

Furman, W., Rahe, D., & Hartup, W. W. (1979). Rehabilitation of socially withdrawn preschool children through mixed-aged and same-sex socialization. *Child Development, 50,* 915–922.

Furnham, A., & Bochner, S. (1986) *Culture shock: Psychological reactions to unfamiliar environments.* London: Methuen

Furstenberg, F., Jr. (1985). Sociological ventures in child development. *Child Development, 56,* 281–288.

G

Gagnon, J. H. (1977). *Human sexualities.* Glenview, IL: Scott, Foresman.

Gallagher, J. M., & Reid, D. K. (1981). *The learning theory of Piaget and Inhelder.* Monterey, CA: Brooks/Cole.

Galluscio, E. H. (1990). *Biological psychology.* New York: Macmillan.

Galton, F. (1869). *Hereditary genius.* London: Macmillan.

Galton, F. (1884). Measurement of character. *Fortnightly Review, 42,* 179–185.

Garcia, J. (1990). Learning without memory. *Journal of Cognitive Neuroscience, 2,* 287–305.

Garcia, J., & Garcia y Robertson, R. (1985). Evolution of learning mechanisms. In B. L. Hammonds (Ed.), *Psychology and learning: 1984 Master Lecturers* (pp. 187–243). Washington, DC: American Psychological Association.

Gardner, H. (1983). *Frames of mind.* New York: Basic Books.

Gardner, H. (1985). *The mind's new science: A history of the cognitive revolution.* New York: Basic Books.

Gardner, L. I. (1972). Deprivation dwarfism. *Scientific American, 227*(7), 76–82.

Garfinkel, P. E., & Garner, D. M. (1982). *Anorexia nervosa: A multidimensional perspective.* New York: Brunner/Mazel.

Garmezy, N. (1976). Vulnerable and invulnerable children: Theory, research, and intervention. *Journal Abstract Supplement Service. Catalog of Selected Documents in Psychology, 6,* 96.

Gay, P. (1988). Freud: *A life for our time.* New York: Norton.

Gazzaniga, M. (1970). *The bisected brain.* New York: Appleton-Century-Crofts.

Gazzaniga, M. S. (1985). *The social brain.* New York: Basic Books.

Gelles, R. J. (1980). Violence in the family: A review of research in the family. *Journal of Marriage and the Family, 42,* 873–885.

Ghoneim, M. M., & Block, R. I. (1992). Learning and consciousness during general anesthesia. *Anesthesiology, 76,* 279–305.

Gibson, J. J. (1966). *The senses considered as perceptual systems.* New York: Houghton-Mifflin.

Gibson, J. J. (1979). *An ecological approach to visual perception.* New York: Houghton-Mifflin.

Gilbert, E. H., & DeBlassie, R. R. (1984). Anorexia nervosa: Adolescent starvation by choice. *Adolescence, 19,* 839–853.

Gilligan, C. (1982). *In a different voice: Psychological theory and women's development.* Cambridge, MA: Harvard University Press.

Glass, A. L., Holyoak, K. J., & Santa, J. L. (1979). *Cognition.* Reading, MA: Addison-Wesley.

Glass, D. C. (1977). *Behavior patterns, stress, and coronary disease.* Hillsdale, NJ: Erlbaum.

Goddard, H. H. (1912). *The Kallikak family. A study of the heredity of feeble-mindedness.* New York: Macmillan.

Goddard, H. H. (1917). Mental tests and immigrants. *Journal of Delinquency, 2,* 243–277.

Goldfried, M. R., Greenberg, L., & Marmar, C. (1990). Individual psychotherapy: Process and outcome. *Annual Review of Psychology, 41,* 659–688.

Goodkind, M. (1989, Spring). The cigarette habit. *Stanford Medicine,* 10–14.

Gordon, L. (1990, September 2). Proposal to overhaul SAT to consider relevance, bias. *The Seattle Times/Post-Intelligencer.*

Gottesman, I. I. (1991). *Schizophrenia genesis: The origins of madness.* New York: Freeman.

Gottlieb, G. (1983). The psychobiological approach to developmental issues. In M. M. Haith & J. J. Campos (Eds.), *Handbook of child psychology: Infancy and developmental psychobiology* (pp. 1–26). New York: Wiley.

Gottlieb, B. H. (Ed.). (1981). *Social networks and social support.* Beverly Hills, CA: Sage.

Gough, H. G. (1957). *California psychological inventory manual.* Palo Alto, CA: Consulting Psychology Press.

Gough, H. G. (1968). An interpreter's syllabus for the California Psychological Inventory. In P. McReynolds (Ed.), *Advances in psychological assessment, vol. one* (pp. 55–79). Palo Alto, CA: Science and Behavior Books.

Gould, S. J. (1981). *The mismeasure of man.* New York: Norton.

Gray, C. R., & Gummerman, K. (1975). The enigmatic eidetic image: A critical examination of methods, data, and theories. *Psychological Bulletin, 82,* 383–407.

Gray, L. (1989, June). Quoted in M. Knaster, Paths to power. *East West,* pp. 42–50.

Green, D. M., & Swets, J. A. (1966). *Signal detection theory and psychophysics.* New York: Wiley.

Greene, B. (1985). A testing time. In B. Greene, *Cheeseburgers* (pp. 56–61). New York: Ballantine.

Greenfield, P. M., & Smith, J. H. (1976). *The structure of communication in early language development.* New York: Academic Press.

Guetzkow, H., Alger, C. F., Brody, R. A., Noel, R. C., & Snyder, R. C. (1963). *Simulation in international relations.* Englewood Cliffs, NJ: Prentice-Hall.

Guilford, J. P. (1985). The Structure-of-Intellect model. In B. B. Wolman (Ed.), *Handbook of intelligence.* New York: Wiley.

Guilleminault, C. (1989). Clinical features and evaluation of obstructive sleep apnea. In M. Kryser, T. Roth, & W. C. Dement (Eds.), *Principles and practice of sleep medicine* (pp. 552–558). New York: Saunders Press.

Guilleminault, C., Dement, W. C., & Passonant, P. (Eds.). (1976). *Narcolepsy.* New York: Spectrum.

Gummerman, K., Gray, C. R., & Wilson, J. M. (1972). An attempt to assess eidetic imagery objectively. *Psychonomic Science, 28,* 115–118.

Gunzenhauser, N. (Ed.). (1990). *Advances in touch: New implications in human development.* Skillman, NJ: Johnson & Johnson Co.

Gurman, A. S., & Kniskern, D. P. (1978). Research on marital and family therapy: Progress, perspective, and prospect. In S. L. Garfield & A. E. Bergin (Eds.), *Handbook of psychotherapy and behavior change: An empirical analysis* (2nd ed.). New York: Wiley.

H

Hacker, A. (1986, February 13). The decline of higher learning. *The New York Review.*

Hale, R. L. (1983). Intellectual assessment. In M. Hersen, A. E. Kazdin, & A. S. Bellack (Eds.), *The clinical psychology handbook* (pp. 345–376). New York: Pergamon.

Haney, C. (1982). Employment tests and employment discrimination: A dissenting psychological opinion. *Industrial Relations Law Journal, 5,* 1–86.

Haney, C., & Zimbardo, P. G. (1977). The socialization into criminality: On becoming a prisoner and a guard. In J. L. Tapp & F. L. Levine (Eds.), *Law, justice and the individual in society: Psychological and legal issues* (pp. 198–223). New York: Holt, Rinehart & Winston.

Hanson, D., Gottesman, I., & Meehl, P. (1977). Genetic theories and the validation of psychiatric diagnosis: Implications for the study of children of schizophrenics. *Journal of Abnormal Psychology, 86,* 575–588.

Harlow, H. F. (1965). Sexual behavior in the rhesus monkey. In F. Beach (Ed.), *Sex and behavior.* New York: Wiley.

Harlow, H. F., & Zimmerman, R. R. (1958). The development of affectional responses in infant monkeys. Proceedings of the *American Philosophical Society, 102,* 501–509.

Harris, B. (1979). Whatever happened to Little Albert? *American Psychologist, 34,* 151–160.

Harris, G., Thomas, A., & Booth, D. A. (1990). Development of salt taste in infancy. *Developmental Psychology, 26,* 534–538.

Harrison, A. & Saeed, L. (1977). Let's make a deal: An analysis of revelations and stipulations in lonely hearts advertisements. *Journal of Personality and Social Psychology, 35,* 257–264.

Hart, R. A., & Moore, G. I. (1973). The development of spatial cognition: A review. In R. M. Downs & D. Stea (Eds.), *Image and environment.* Chicago: Aldine.

Hartmann, E. (1989). Boundaries of dreams, boundaries of dreamers: Thin and thick boundaries as a new personality measure. *Psychiatric Journal of the University of Ottawa, 14,* 557–560.

Hartmann, E. L. (1973). *The functions of sleep.* New Haven, CT: Yale University Press.

Hartshorne, H., & May, M. A. (1928). *Studies in the nature of character, Vol. 1: Studies in deceit.* New York: Macmillan.

Harvey, J. H., Weber, A. L., & Orbuch, T. L. (1990). *Interpersonal accounts: A social psychological perspective.* Cambridge, MA: Basil Blackwell.

Harvey, P. H., & Krebs, J. R. (1990). Comparing brains. *Science, 249,* 140–146.

Hass, A. (1979). *Teenage sexuality: A survey of teenage sexual behavior.* New York: Macmillan.

Hastorf, A. H., & Cantril, H. (1954). They saw a game: A case study. *Journal of Abnormal and Social Psychology, 49,* 129–134.

Hatfield, E., & Rapson, R. L. (1993). *Love, sex, and intimacy: Their psychology, biology, and history.* New York: HarperCollins.

Hatfield, E., & Sprecher, S. (1986). *Mirror, mirror. The importance of looks in everyday life.* New York: State University of New York Press.

Hathaway, S. R., & McKinley, J. C. (1943). *The Minnesota Multiphasic Personality Inventory.* Minneapolis: University of Minnesota Press.

Hayes-Roth, B., & Hayes-Roth, F. (1979). A cognitive model of planning. *Cognitive Science, 3,* 275–310.

Haygood, R. C., & Bourne, L. E., Jr. (1965). Attribute and rule-learned aspects of conceptual behavior. *Psychological Review, 72,* 175–195.

Haynes, S. G., & Feinleib, M. (1980). Women, work, and coronary heart disease: Prospective findings from the Framingham Heart Study. *American Journal of Public Health, 70,* 133–141.

Hebb, D. O. (1980). *Essay on mind.* Hillsdale, NJ: Erlbaum.

Hecht, A. (1986, April). A guide to the proper use of tranquilizers. *Healthline Newsletter,* pp. 5–6.

Heider, F. (1958). *The psychology of interpersonal relationships.* New York: Wiley.

Heinrichs, R. W. (1993). Schizophrenia and the brain: conditions for a neuropsychology of madness. *American Psychologist, 48,* 221–233.

Henderson, N. D. (1980). Effects of early experience upon the behavior of animals: The second twenty-five years of research. In E. C. Simmel (Ed.), *Early experiences and early behavior: Implications for social development* (pp. 39–77). New York: Academic Press.

Hendrick, S. S., & Hendrick, C. (1992). *Liking, loving, and relating,* 2nd edition. Pacific Grove, CA: Wadsworth.

Hersen, M., & Bellack, A. J. (1976). Assessment of social skills. In A. R. Ciminero, K. R. Calhoun, & H. E. Adams (Eds.), *Handbook of behavioral assessment* (pp. 509–554). New York: Wiley.

Hersh, S. M. (1971). *My Lai 4: A report on the massacre and its aftermath.* New York: Random House.

Herzog, D. B. (1992). Eating disorders: New threats to health. *Psychosomatics, 33*(1), 10–15.

Herzog, D. B., Keller, M. B., Strober, M., Yeh, C. et al. (1992). The current status of treatment for anorexia nervosa and bulimia nervosa. *International Journal of Eating Disorders, 12*(2), 215–220.

Hetherington, E. M. (1987). Family relations six years after divorce. In K. Pasley & M. Ihinger-Tallman (Eds.), *Remarriage and stepparenting* (pp. 185–205). New York: Guilford.

Hetherington, E. M. (1988). Parents, children, and siblings: Six years after divorce. In R. A. Hinde & J. Stevenson-Hinde (Eds.), *Relationships within families* (pp. 311–331). Oxford: Clarendon Press.

Hetherington, E. M., & Parke, R. D. (1975). *Child psychology: A contemporary viewpoint.* New York: McGraw-Hill.

Hetherington, M. M., Spalter, A. R., Bernat, A. S., Nelson, M. L. et al. (1993). Eating pathology in bulimia nervosa. *International Journal of Eating Disorders, 13*(1), 13–24.

Hilgard, E. R. (1968). *The experience of hypnosis.* New York: Harcourt Brace Jovanovich.

Hilgard, E. R. (1973). The domain of hypnosis with some comments on alternative paradigms. *American Psychologist, 28,* 972–982.

Hilgard, E. R. (1980). Consciousness in contemporary psychology. *Annual Review of Psychology, 31,* 1–26.

Hilgard, E. R. (1986). *Psychology in America: A historical survey.* San Diego, CA: Harcourt Brace Jovanovich.

Hinton, G. F., & Anderson, J. A. (1981). *Parallel models of associative memory.* Hillsdale, NJ: Erlbaum.

Hirsch, J., Harrington, G., & Mehler, B. (1990). An irresponsible farewell gloss. *Educational Theory, 40,* 501–508.

Hirst, W., Spelke, E. S., Reaves, C. C., Charack, G., & Neisser, U. (1980). Dividing attention without alternation of automaticity. *Journal of Experimental Psychology: General, 109,* 98–117.

Hobson, J. A. (1988). *The dreaming brain.* New York: Basic Books.

Hoffman, M. (1986). Affect, cognition, and motivation. In R. Sorrentino & E. Higgins (Eds.), *Handbook of motivation and cognition: Foundations of social behavior* (pp. 244–280). New York: Guilford.

Hoffman, M. L. (1987). The contribution of empathy to justice and moral judgment. In N. Eisenberg & J. Strayer (Eds.), *Empathy and its development* (pp. 47–80). New York: Cambridge University Press.

Hofling, C. K., Brotzman, E., Dalrymple, S., Graves, N., & Pierce, C. M. (1966). An experimental study in nurse-physician relationships. *Journal of Nervous and Mental Disease, 143*(2), 171–180.

Hofstede, G. (1986). Cultural differences in teaching and learning. *International Journal of Intercultural Relations, 10,* 301–320.

Hofstede, G. (1991). *Cultures and organizations: Software of the mind.* London and New York: McGraw-Hill.

Holahan, C. J., & Moos, R. H. (1987). Personal and contextual determinants of coping strategies. *Journal of Personality and Social Psychology, 52,* 946–955.

Holden, C. (1978). Patuxent: Controversial prison clings to belief in rehabilitation. *Science, 199,* 665–668.

Holmes, D. S. (1984). Meditation and somatic arousal: A review of the experimental evidence. *American Psychologist, 39,* 1–10.

Holmes, T. H., & Masuda, M. (1974). Life change and stress susceptibility. In B. S. Dohrenwend & B. P. Dohrenwend, (Eds.), *Stressful life events: Their nature and effects* (pp. 45–72). New York: Wiley.

Holmes, T. H., & Rahe, R. H. (1967). The social readjustment rating scale. *Journal of Psychosomatic Research, 11*(2), 213–218.

Homme, L. E., de Baca, P. C., Devine, J. V., Steinhorst, R., & Rickert, E. J. (1963). Use of the Premack principle in controlling the behavior of nursery school children. *Journal of the Experimental Analysis of Behavior, 6,* 544.

Hopson, J. L. (1979). *Scent signals: The silent language of sex.* New York: Morrow.

Horn, J. L. (1985). Remodeling old models of intelligence. In B. B. Wolman (Ed.), *Handbook of intelligence* (pp. 267–300). New York: Wiley.

Horney, K. (1937). *The neurotic personality of our time.* New York: Norton.

Horney, K. (1939). *New ways in psychoanalyses.* New York: Norton.

Horney, K. (1945). *Our inner conflicts: A constructive theory of neurosis.* New York: Norton.

Horney, K. (1950). *Neurosis and human growth.* New York: Norton.

Horowitz, R. M. (1984). Children's rights: A look backward and a glance ahead. In R. M. Horowitz & H. A. Davidson (Eds.), *Legal rights of children* (pp. 1–9). New York: McGraw-Hill.

Hovland, C. I., Lumsdaine, A. A., & Sheffield, F. D. (1949). *Studies in social psychology in World War II—Vol. 3, Experiments in mass communication.* Princeton, NJ: Princeton University Press.

Hull, C. L. (1943). *Principles of behavior: An introduction to behavior theory.* New York: Appleton-Century-Crofts.

Hull, C. L. (1952). *A behavior system: An introduction to behavior theory concerning the individual organism.* New Haven, CT: Yale University Press.

Hume, D. (1748/1951). In L. A. Selby-Bigge (Ed.), *Inquiries concerning the human understanding and concerning the principles of morals.* London: Oxford University Press. (Original work published 1748).

Humphrey, T. (1970). The development of human fetal activity and its relation to postnatal behavior. In H. W. Reese & L. P. Lipsitt (Eds.), *Advance in child development and behavior* (Vol. 5). New York: Academic Press.

Hunt, E. (1983). On the nature of intelligence. *Science, 219,* 141–146.

Hunt, E. (1984). Intelligence and mental competence. *Naval Research Reviews, 36,* 37–42.

Hunt, J. M. (1982). Toward equalizing the developmental opportunities of infants and preschool children. *Journal of Social Issues, 38*(4), 163–191.

Hunt, W. A., Matarazzo, J. D., Weiss, S. M., & Gentry, W. D. (1979). Associative learning, habit, and health behavior. *Journal of Behavioral Medicine, 2,* 111–123.

Hurlburt, R. T. (1979). Random sampling of cognitions and behavior. *Journal of Research in Personality, 13,* 103–111.

Hyman, I. A., McDowell, E., & Raines, B. (1977). Corporal punishment and alternatives in the schools: An overview of theoretical and practical issues. In J. H. Wise (Ed.), *Proceedings: Conference on corporal punishment in the schools* (pp. 1–18). Washington, DC: National Institute of Education.

I

Insel, P. L., & Roth, W. T. (1985). *Core concepts in health.* Palo Alto, CA: Mayfield.

Insko, C. A., Smith, R. A., Alicke, M. D., Wade, J., & Taylor, S. (1985). Conformity and group size: The concern with being right and the concern with being liked. *Personality and Social Psychology Bulletin, 11,* 41–50.

Insko, C. A., Thibaut, J. W., Moehle, D., Wilson, M., Diamond, W. D., Gilmore, R., Solomon, M. R., & Lipsitz, A. (1980). Social evolution and the emergence of leadership. *Journal of Personality and Social Psychology, 39,* 431–448.

Irwin, M., Daniels, M., Smith, T. L., Bloom, E., & Weiner, H. (1987). Impaired natural killer cell activity during bereavement. *Brain Behavior Immunology, 1,* 98–104.

Isen, A. (1984). Toward understanding the role of affect in cognition. In R. Wyer & T. Srull (Eds.), *Handbook of social cognition* (pp. 174–236). Hillsdale, NJ: Erlbaum.

Itard, J. M. G. (1962). *The wild boy of Aveyron* (G. & M. Humphrey, Trans.). New York: Appleton-Century-Crofts.

Izard, C. E. (1977). *Human emotions.* New York: Plenum.

Izard, C. E. (Ed.). (1982). *Measuring emotions in infants and children.* New York: Cambridge University Press.

J

Jacobs, B. L. (1987). How hallucinogenic drugs work. *American Scientist, 75,* 386–392.

Jacoby, L. L., Baker, J. G., & Brooks, L. R. (1989). Episodic effects of picture identification: Implications for theories of learning and theories of memory. *Journal of Experimental Psychology: Learning, Memory & Cognition, 15,* 275–281.

James, W. (1890). *The principles of psychology* (2 vols.). New York: Holt, Rinehart & Winston.

James, W. (1902/1958). *The varieties of religious experience.* New York: Mentor Books. (Original work published 1902).

Janis, I. L. (1958). *Psychological stress.* New York: Wiley.

Janis, I. L. (1982). Decisionmaking under stress. In L. Goldberger & S. Breznitz (Eds.), *Handbook of stress* (pp. 69–87). New York: Free Press.

Janis, I. L., & Frick, F. (1943). The relationship between attitudes toward conclusions and errors in judging logical validity of syllogisms. *Journal of Experimental Psychology, 33,* 73–77.

Janowitz, H. D., & Grossman, M. I. (1950). Hunger and appetite: Some definitions and concepts. *Journal of the Mount Sinai Hospital, 16,* 231–240.

Janz, N. K., & Becker, M. H. (1984). The health belief model: A decade later. *Health Education Quarterly, 11,* 1–47.

Jenkins, C. D. (1976). Recent evidence supporting psychologic and social risk factors for coronary disease. *New England Journal of Medicine, 294,* 987–994, 1033–1038.

Jenkins, J. G., & Dallenbach, K. M. (1924). Oblivescence during sleep and waking. *The American Journal of Psychology, 35,* 605–612.

Johnson, C., & Connors, M. (1987). *The etiology and treatment of bulimia nervosa.* New York: Basic Books.

Johnson, J. E. (1983). Psychological interventions and coping with surgery. In A. Baum, S. E. Taylor, & J. E. Singer (Eds.), *Handbook of psychology and health* (Vol. 4). Hillsdale, NJ: Erlbaum.

Johnson, J. H., & Sarason, I. B. (1979). Recent developments in research on life stress. In V. Hamilton & D. M. Warburton (Eds.), *Human stress and cognition: An information processing approach* (pp. 205–233). Chichester, England: Wiley.

Johnson-Laird, P. (1983). *Mental models.* Cambridge, England: Cambridge University Press.

Johnson-Laird, P. N., & Byrne, R. M. J. (1989). Only reasoning. *Journal of Memory and Language, 28,* 313–330.

Johnston, L. D., O'Malley, P. M., & Bachman, J. G. (1989). *Drug use, drinking, and smoking: National survey results from high school, college, and young adult populations, 1975–1988.* Rockville, MD: U.S. Department of Health and Human Services.

Jones, E. E., & Berglas, S. (1978). Control of attributions about the self through self-handicapping strategies: The appeal of alcohol and the role of underachievement. *Personality and Social Psychology Bulletin, 4,* 200–206.

Jones, E. E., Farina, A., Hastod, A. H., Markus, H., Miller, D. T., & Scott, R. A. (1984). *Social stigma: The psychology of marked relationships*. New York: Freeman.

Joseph, G. H., Kessler, R. C. et al. (1988). *Psychosocial predictors of symptom development in HIV-infected gay men*. International Conference on AIDS, Stockholm, Sweden.

Joseph, J. G., Montgomery, S. B., Emmons, C. A., Kirscht, J. P., Kersler, R. C., Ostrow, D. G., Wartman, C. B., O'Brien, K., Eller, M., & Eshleman, S. (1987). Perceived risk of AIDS: Assessing the behavioral and psychosocial consequences in a cohort of gay men. *Journal of Applied Social Psychology, 17,* 231–250.

Joyce, L. (1989, Fall). Good genes, bad genes. *Stanford Medicine,* pp. 18–23.

Julesz, B. (1982). Textons, the elements of texture perception and their interaction. *Nature, 290,* 91–97.

Jung, C. G. (1936/1959). The concept of the collective unconscious. In *The archetypes and the collective unconscious, collected works* (Vol. 9, Part 1, pp. 54–74). Princeton, NJ: Princeton University Press. (Original work published 1936).

Jung, C. G. (1965). *Memories, dreams, reflections*. New York: Random House.

Jung, C. G. (1923/1971). Psychological types [Bollingen Series XX]. *The collected works of C. G. Jung* (Vol. 6). Princeton: Princeton University Press. (Original work published 1923).

Jung, C. G. (1973). *Memories, dreams, reflections* (Rev. ed., A. Jaffe, Ed.). New York: Pantheon Books.

K

Kagan, J., & Klein, R. E. (1973). Cross-cultural perspectives on early development. *American Psychologist, 28,* 947–961.

Kagan, J., Reznick, J. S., & Snidman, N. (1986). Temperamental inhibition in early childhood. In R. Plomin & J. Dunn (Eds.), *The study of temperament: Changes, continuites, and challenges*. Hillsdale, NJ: Erlbaum.

Kagan, J., & Snidman, N. (1991). Infant predictors of inhibited and uninhibited profiles. *Psychological Science, 2,* 40–44.

Kahneman, D. (1973). *Attention and effort*. Englewood Cliffs, NJ: Prentice-Hall.

Kahneman, D., Slovic, P., & Tversky, A. (Eds.). (1982). *Judgment under uncertainty: Heuristics and biases*. Cambridge, MA: Cambridge University Press.

Kahneman, D., & Snell, J. (1990). Predicting utility. In R. Hogarth (Ed.), *Insights in decision making*. Chicago: University of Chicago Press.

Kalat, J. W. (1984). *Biological psychology*. (2nd ed.). Belmont, CA: Wadsworth.

Kalish, R. A. (1985). The social context of death and dying. In R. H. Binstock & E. Shanas (Eds.), *Handbook of aging and the social sciences* (pp. 149–172). New York: Van Nostrand Reingold.

Kallmann, F. J. (1946). The genetic theory of schizophrenia: An analysis of 691 schizophrenic index families. *American Journal of Psychiatry, 103,* 309–322.

Kamin, L. J. (1969). Predictability, surprise, attention, and conditioning. In B. A. Campbell & R. M. Church (Eds.), *Classical conditioning: A symposium*. New York: Appleton-Century-Crofts.

Kamin, L. J. (1974). *The science and politics of IQ*. Potomac, MD: Erlbaum.

Kasl, S. V., & Cobb, S. (1966). Health behavior and illness behavior: I. Health and illness behavior. *Archives of Environmental Health, 12,* 246–266.

Kastenbaum, R. (1986). *Death, society, and the human experience*. Columbus, OH: Merrill.

Kay, D. W. K., & Bergman, K. (1982). Epidemiology of mental disorders among the aged in the community. In J. E. Birren & R. B. Sloane (Eds.), *Handbook of mental health and aging* (pp. 34–56). Englewood Cliffs, NJ: Prentice-Hall.

Kazdin, A. E. (1986). Comparative outcome studies of psychotherapy: Methodological issues and strategies. *Journal of Consulting and Clinical Psychology, 54,* 95–105.

Kazdin, A. E., & Wilcoxin, L. A. (1976). Systematic desensitization and nonspecific treatment effects: A methodological evaluation. *Psychological Bulletin, 83,* 729–758.

Kazdin, A. E., & Wilson, G. T. (1980). *Evaluation of behavior therapy: Issues, evidence, and research strategies*. Lincoln: University of Nebraska Press.

Keats, J. (1966). *Howard Hughes*. New York: Random House.

Keen, S. (1986). *Faces of the enemy: Reflections of the hostile imagination*. New York: Harper & Row.

Keesey, R. E., & Powley, T. L. (1975). Hypothalamic regulation of body weight. *American Scientist, 63,* 558–565.

Kelley, H. H. (1967). Attribution theory in social psychology. In D. Levine (Ed.), *Nebraska Symposium on Motivation* (Vol. 15). Lincoln, NE: University of Nebraska Press.

Kelly, G. A. (1955). *A theory of personality: The psychology of personal constructs* (2 vols.). New York: Norton.

Kelsoe, J. R., Ginns, E. I., Egeland, J. A., Gerhard, D. S., Goldstein, A. M., Bale, S. J., Pauls, D. L., Long, R. T., Kidd, K. K., Conte, G., Housman, D. E., & Paul, S. M. (1989). Re-evaluation of the linkage relationship between chromosome 11p loci and the gene for bipolar affective disorder in the Old Order Amish. *Nature, 342,* 238–243.

Kennedy, S. H., & Garfinkel, P. E. (1992). Advances in diagnosis and treatment of anorexia nervosa and bulimia nervosa. *Canadian Journal of Psychiatry, 37*(5), 309–315.

Kessler, S. (1980). The genetics of schizophrenia: A review. In S. J. Keith & L. R. Mosher (Eds.), *Special report: Schizophrenia, 1980* (pp. 14–26). Washington, DC: U.S. Government Printing Office.

Kety, S. S., Rosenthal, D., Wender, P. H., Schulsinger, F., & Jacobsen, B. (1975). Mental illness in the biological and adoptive families of adopted individuals who have become schizophrenic: A preliminary report based on psychiatric interviews. In R. R. Fieve, D. Rosenthal, & H. Brill (Eds.), *Genetic research in psychiatry* (pp. 147–165). Baltimore: Johns Hopkins University Press.

Kiecolt-Glaser, J. K., & Glaser, R. (1987). Psychosocial moderators of immune function. *Annals of Behavioral Medicine, 9,* 16–20.

Kiecolt-Glaser, J. K., Glaser, R., Shuttleworth, E. C., Dyer, C. S., Ogrocki, P., & Speicher, C. E. (1987). Chronic stress and immunity in family caregivers of Alzheimer's disease victims. *Psychosomatic Medicine, 49,* 523–535.

Kihlstrom, J. F., & Harackiewicz, J. M. (1982). The earliest recollection: A new survey. *Journal of Personality, 50,* 134–148.

Kihlstrom, J. F., Schacter, D. L., Cork, R. C., Hurt, C. A., & Behr, S. E. (1990). Implicit and explicit memory following surgical anesthesia. *Psychological Science, 1,* 303–306.

Kintsch, W. (1981). Semantic memory: A tutorial. In R. S. Nickerson (Ed.), *Attention and performance* (Vol. 8). Hillsdale, NJ: Erlbaum.

Klag, M. J., Whelton, P. K., Grim, C. E., & Kuller, L. H. (1991). The association of skin color with blood pressure in U.S. blacks with low socioeconomic status. *Journal of the American Medical Association, 265,* 599–602.

Klein, D. C., & Goldston, S. E. (Eds.). (1977). *Primary prevention: An idea whose time has come*. Washington, DC: U.S. Government Printing Office.

Klein, R. H. (1983). Group treatment approaches. In M. Hersen, A. E. Kazdin, & A. S. Bellack (Eds.), *The clinical psychology handbook*. New York: Pergamon Press.

Kleinginna, P. R., & Kleingigna, A. M. (1981). A categorized list of motivation definitions with a suggestion for a consensual definition. *Motivation and Emotion, 5,* 263–291.

Klerman, G. L. (1986). Historical perspectives on contemporary schools of psychopathology. In T. Millon & G. L. Klerman (Eds.), *Contemporary directions in psychopathology: Toward the DSM-IV* (pp. 3–28). New York: Guilford Press.

Klinger, E. (1987, May). The power of daydreams. *Psychology Today,* pp. 37–44.

Kobasa, S. O. (1984). How much stress can you survive? *American Health, 3,* 64–77.

Kobasa, S. O., Hilker, R. R., & Maddi, S. R. (1979). Who stays healthy under stress? *Journal of Occupational Medicine, 21,* 595–598.

Kochman, T. (1981). *Black and white styles in conflict and communication*. Chicago: University of Chicago Press.

Kohlberg, L. (1964). Development of moral character and moral ideology. In M. L. Hoffman & L. W. Hoffman (Eds.), *Review of child development research* (Vol. 1). New York: Russell Sage Foundation.

Kohlberg, L. (1981). *The philosophy of moral development.* New York: Harper & Row.

Kolata, G. (1985). Why do people get fat? *Science, 227,* 1327–1328.

Kolb, B. (1989). Development, plasticity, and behavior. *American Psychologist, 44,* 1203–1212.

Kolb, L. C. (1973). *Modern clinical psychiatry.* Philadelphia: Saunders.

Konner, M. J. (1977). Research reported in J. Greenberg, The brain and emotions. *Science News, 112,* 74–75.

Korkina, M. V., Tsivil'ko, M. A., Kareva, M. A., & Zhigalova, N. D. et al. (1992). Clinico-psychological correlations of mental rigidity in anorexia nervosa. *Journal of Russian and East European Psychiatry, 25*(2), 21–28.

Korn, J. W. (1985). Psychology as a humanity. *Teaching of Psychology, 12,* 188–193.

Koss, M. P. (1985). The hidden rape victim: Personality, attitudinal, and situational characteristics. *Psychology of Women Quarterly, 9,* 193–212.

Kosslyn, S. M. (1983). *Ghosts in the mind's machine: Creating and using images in the brain.* New York: Norton.

Kraft, C. L. (1978). A psychophysical contribution to air safety: Simulator studies of visual illusions in night visual approaches. In H. Pick, H. W. Leibowitz, J. R. Singer, A. Steinschneider, & H. W. Stevenson (Eds.), *Psychology from research to practice* (pp. 363–385). New York: Plenum.

Krasner, L. (1985). Applications of learning theory in the environment. In B. L. Hammonds (Ed.), *Psychology and learning: 1984 master lecturers* (pp. 51–93). Washington, DC: American Psychological Association.

Kraut, A. M. (1990). Healers and strangers: Immigrant attitudes toward the physician in America—A relationship in historical perspective. *Journal of the American Medical Association, 263,* 1807–1811.

Kübler-Ross, E. (1969). *On death and dying.* Toronto: Macmillan.

Kübler-Ross, E. (1975). *Death: The final stage of growth.* Englewood Cliffs, NJ: Prentice-Hall.

Kuhn, T. S. (1970). *The structure of scientific revolutions* (2nd ed.). Chicago: University of Chicago Press.

Kulik, J. A. (1983). Confirmatory attribution and the perpetuation of social beliefs. *Journal of Personality and Social Psychology, 44,* 1171–1181.

Kunda, Z. (1990). The case for motivated reasoning. *Psychological Bulletin, 108,* 480–498.

Kurtines, W., & Greif, E. B. (1974). The development of moral thought: Review and evaluation of Kohlberg's approach. *Psychological Bulletin, 8,* 453–470.

L

Labouvie-Vief, G. (1985). Intelligence and cognition. In J. E. Birren & K. W. Schaie (Eds.), *Handbook of the psychology of aging* (2nd ed., pp. 500–530). New York: Van Nostrand Reingold.

Lachman, R., Lachman, J. L., & Butterfield, E. C. (1979). *Cognitive psychology and information processing: An introduction.* Hillsdale, NJ: Erlbaum.

Lackner, J. R., & Garrett, M. (1973). Resolving ambiguity: Effects of biasing context in the unattended ear. *Cognition, 1,* 359–372.

Lambo, T. A. (1978). Psychotherapy in Africa. *Human Nature, 1*(3), 32–39.

Lang, P. J., & Lazovik, D. A. (1963). The experimental desensitization of a phobia. *Journal of Abnormal and Social Psychology, 66,* 519–525.

Langer, E. J., & Rodin, J. (1976). The effects of choice and enhanced personal responsibility for the aged: A field experiment in an institutional setting. *Journal of Personality and Social Psychology, 34,* 191–198.

Langs, R. (Ed.). (1981). *Classics in psychoanalytic technique.* New York: Jason Aronson.

Latané, B. (1981). The psychology of social impact. *American Psychologist, 36,* 343–356.

Latané, B., & Darley, J. M. (1968). Group inhibition of bystander intervention in emergencies. *Journal of Personality and Social Psychology, 10,* 215–221.

Lazarus, R. S. (1976). *Patterns of adjustment* (3rd ed.). New York: McGraw-Hill.

Lazarus, R. S. (1981, July). Little hassles can be hazardous to your health. *Psychology Today,* pp. 58–62.

Lazarus, R. S. (1982). Thoughts on the relations between emotion and cognition. *American Psychologist, 37,* 1019–1024.

Lazarus, R. S. (1984a). On the primacy of cognition. *American Psychologist, 39,* 124–129.

Lazarus, R. S. (1984b). Puzzles in the study of daily hassles. *Journal of Behavioral Medicine, 7,* 375–389.

Lazarus, R. S. (1991). Progress on a cognitive-motivational-relational theory of emotion. *American Psychologist, 46,* 819–834.

Lazarus, R. S., & Folkman, S. (1984). *Stress, appraisal, and coping.* New York: Springer.

Leask, J., Haber, R. N., & Haber, R. B. (1969). Eidetic imagery in children: II. Longitudinal and experimental results. *Psychonomic Monograph Supplements, 3* (3, Whole No. 35).

Leerhsen, C. (1990, February 5). Unite and conquer: America's crazy for support groups. *Newsweek,* pp. 50–55.

Leger, D. (1991). *Biological foundations of behavior: An integrative approach.* New York: HarperCollins.

Leiter, M. P., & Maslach, C. (1988). The impact of interpersonal environment on burnout and organizational commitment. *Journal of Organizational Behavior, 9,* 297–308.

Lenneberg, E. H. (1969). On explaining language. *Science, 164,* 635–643.

Lennon, R. T. (1985). Group tests of intelligence. In B. B. Wolman (Ed.), *Handbook of intelligence* (pp. 825–847). New York: Wiley.

Lepper, M. R. (1981). Intrinsic and extrinsic motivation in children: Detrimental effects of superfluous social controls. In U. A. Collins (Ed.), *Aspects of the development of competence: The Minnesota Symposium on Child Psychology* (Vol. 14, pp. 155–214). Hillsdale, NJ: Erlbaum.

Lepper, M. R., & Greene, D. (Eds.). (1978). *The hidden costs of reward.* Hillsdale, NJ: Erlbaum.

Lepper, M. R., Greene, D., & Nisbett, R. E. (1973). Undermining children's intrinsic interest with extrinsic reward: A test of the overjustification hypothesis. *Journal of Personality and Social Psychology, 28*(1), 129–137.

Lerner, R. M., Orlos, J. R., & Knapp, J. (1976). Physical attractiveness, physical effectiveness and self-concept in adolescents. *Adolescence, 11,* 313–326.

Leslie, C., & Wingert, P. (1990, January 8). Not as easy as A, B, or C. *Newsweek,* pp. 56–58.

LeVay, S. (1991). A difference in hypothalamic structure between heterosexual and homosexual men. *Science, 253,* 1034–1037.

Leventhal, H. (1980). Toward a comprehensive theory of emotion. In L. Berkowitz (Ed.), *Advances in experimental social psychology* (Vol. 13, pp. 139–207). New York: Academic Press.

Levi, P. (1985). *A quiet city: Moments of reprieve.* New York: Simon & Schuster.

Levi-Strauss, C. (1963). The effectiveness of symbols. In C. Levi-Strauss (Ed.), *Structural anthropology.* New York: Basic Books.

Levine, M. (1987, April). *Effective problem solving.* Englewood Cliffs, NJ: Prentice-Hall.

Levine, M., & Perkins, D. V. (1987). *Principles of community psychology: Perspectives and applications.* New York: Oxford University.

Levine, M. W., & Shefner, J. M. (1981). *Fundamentals of sensation and perception.* Reading, MA: Addison-Wesley.

Levinson, B. W. (1967). States of awareness during general anesthesia. In J. Lassner (Ed.), *Hypnosis and psychosomatic medicine* (pp. 200–207). New York: Springer-Verlag.

Levinson, D. L. (1978). *The seasons of a man's life.* New York: Knopf.

Levinson, D. L. (1986). A conception of adult development. *American Psychologist, 41,* 3–13.

Lewin, R. (1987). The origin of the modern human mind. *Science, 236,* 668–670.

Lewine, R. R., Strauss, J. S., & Gift, T. E. (1981). Sex differences in age at first hospital admission for schizophrenia: Fact or artifact? *American Journal of Psychiatry, 138,* 440–444.

Lewinsohn, P. M. (1975). The behavioral study and treatment of depression. In M. Hersen, R. M. Eisler, & P. M. Miller (Eds.), *Progress in behavior modification* (pp. 19–64). New York: Academic Press.

Lewis, C. (1981). The effects of parental firm control: A reinterpretation of findings. *Psychological Bulletin, 90,* 547–563.

Lewy, A. J., Sack, R. L., Miller, S., & Hoban, T. M. (1987). Antidepressant and circadian phase-shifting effect of light. *Science, 235,* 352–354.

Liberman, R. P. (1982). What is schizophrenia? *Schizophrenia Bulletin, 8,* 435–437.

Lichtenstein, E. (1980). *Psychotherapy: Approaches and applications.* Pacific Grove, CA: Brooks/Cole.

Lieberman, L. R. (1973, April 3). [Letter to *Science* concerning "On being sane in insane places"]. *Science, 179.*

Lieberman, M. A. (1982). The effects of social support on responses to stress. In L. Goldberger & S. Breznitz (Eds.), *Handbook of stress* (pp. 764–783). New York: Free Press.

Liem, J. H. (1980). Family studies of schizophrenia: An update and commentary. In S. J. Keith & L. R. Mosher (Eds.), *Special report: Schizophrenia, 1980* (pp. 82–108). Washington, DC: U.S. Government Printing Office.

Liem, R., & Rayman, P. (1982). Health and social costs of unemployment: Research and policy considerations. *American Psychologist, 37,* 1116–1123.

Lindsley, D. B. (1951). Emotion. In S. S. Stevens (Ed.), *Handbook of experimental psychology.* New York: Wiley.

Linton, M. (1975). Memory for real-world events. In D. A. Norman & D. E. Rumelhart (Eds.), *Explorations in cognition* (Chapter 14). San Francisco: Freeman.

Lipsitt, L. P., Reilly, B., Butcher, M. G., & Greenwood, M. M. (1976). The stability and interrelationships of newborn sucking and heart rate. *Developmental Psychobiology, 9,* 305–310.

Livesley, W. J., & Bromley, D. B. (1973). *Person perception in childhood and adolescence.* London: Wiley.

Locke, D. (1992) *Increasing multicultural understanding: A comprehensive model.* Newbury Park, CA: Sage.

Loehlin, J. C., Lindzey, G., & Spuhler, J. N. (1975). *Race differences in intelligence.* San Francisco: Freeman.

Loevinger, J. (1957). Objective tests as instruments of psychological theory. *Psychological Reports, 3,* 635–694.

Loftus, E. F. (1979). *Eyewitness testimony.* Cambridge, MA: Harvard University Press.

Loftus, E. F. (1984). The eyewitness on trial. In B. D. Sales & A. Alwork (Eds.), *With liberty and justice for all.* Englewood Cliffs, NJ: Prentice Hall.

Logan, G. (1980). Attention and automaticity in Stroop and priming task: Theory and data. *Cognitive Psychology, 12,* 523–553.

London, K. A., Mosher, W. D., Pratt, W. F., & Williams, L. B. (1989, March). *Preliminary findings from the National Survey of Family Growth, Cycle IV.* Paper presented at the annual meeting of the Population Association of America, Baltimore, MD.

Loomis, A. L., Harvey, E. N., & Hobart, G. A. (1937). Cerebral states during sleep as studied by human brain potentials. *Journal of Experimental Psychology, 21,* 127–144.

Lynch, J. J. (1979). *The broken heart: The medical consequences of loneliness.* New York: Basic Books.

M

Maccoby, N., Farquhar, J. W., Wood, P. D., & Alexander, J. K. (1977). Reducing the risk of cardiovascular disease: Effects of a community-based campaign on knowledge and behavior. *Journal of Community Health, 3,* 100–114.

MacLean, P. (1977). On the evolution of three mentalities. In S. Arieti & G. Chrzanowki (Eds.), *New directions in psychiatry: A world view* (Vol. 2). New York: Wiley.

Maddi, S. (1980). *Personality theories: A comparative analysis.* Homewood, IL: Dorsey.

Maher, B., & Ross, J. S. (1984). Delusions. In H. E. Adams & P. B. Sutker (Eds.), *Comprehensive handbook of psychopathology* (pp. 383–987). New York: Plenum.

Maher, B. A. (1968, November). The shattered language of schizophrenia. *Psychology Today,* pp. 30ff.

Mahler, M. S. (1979). *The selected papers of Margaret S. Mahler* (2 vols.). New York: Jason Aronson.

Maier, N. R. F. (1931). Reasoning in humans: II. The solution of a problem and its appearance in consciousness. *Journal of Comparative Psychology, 12,* 181–194.

Maier, S. F., & Seligman, M. E. P. (1976). Learned helplessness: Theory and evidence. *Journal of Experimental Psychology, 105,* 3–46.

Majewska, M. D., Harrison, N. L., Schwartz, R. D., Barker, J. L., & Paul, S. M. (1986). Steroid hormone metabolites are barbiturate-like modulators of the GABA receptor. *Science, 232,* 1004–1007.

Malamuth, N. M. (1984). Aggression against women: Cultural and individual causes. In N. M. Malamuth & E. Donnerstein (Eds.), *Pornography and sexual aggression* (pp. 19–52). Orlando, FL: Academic Press.

Malamuth, N. M. (1984). Aggression against women: Cultural and individual causes. In N. M. Malamuth & E. Donnerstein (Eds.), *Pornography and sexual aggression.* Orlando, FL: Academic Press.

Malamuth, N. M. (1986). Predictors of naturalistic sexual aggression. *Journal of Personality and Social Psychology, 50,* 953–962.

Malamuth, N. M. (1989). The attraction to aggression scale: Part one. *Journal of Sex Research, 26,* 26–49.

Malitz, S., & Sackeim, H. A. (1984). Low dosage ECT: Electrode placement and acute physiological and cognitive effects. *American Journal of Social Psychiatry, 4,* 47–53.

Maloney, M. P., & Ward, M. P. (1976). *Psychological assessment: A conceptual approach.* New York: Academic Press.

Mandler, G. (1984). *Mind and body: The psychology of emotion and stress.* New York: Norton.

Manfredi, M., Bini, G., Cruccu, G., Accornero, N., Beradelli, A., & Medolago, L. (1981). Congenital absence of pain. *Archives of Neurology, 38,* 507–511.

Manschreck, T. C. (1989). Delusional (paranoid) disorders. In H. I. Kaplan & B. J. Sadock (Eds.), *Comprehensive textbook of psychiatry* (pp. 816–829). Baltimore: William & Wilkins.

Markus, H., & Cross, S. (1990). The interpersonal self. In L. A. Pervin (Ed.), *Handbook of personality theory and research* (pp. 576–608). New York: Guilford Press.

Markus, H., Cross, S., & Wurf, E. (1990). The role of the self-system in competence. In R. J. Sternberg & J. Lollgian, Jr. (Eds.), *Competence considered* (pp. 205–225). New Haven, CT: Yale University Press.

Markus, H., & Smith, J. (1981). The influence of self-schemas on the perception of others. In N. Cantor & J. F. Kihlstrom (Eds.), *Personality, cognition, and social interaction* (pp. 233–262). Hillsdale, NJ: Erlbaum.

Marshall, G. D., & Zimbardo, P. G. (1979). Affective consequences of inadequately explained physiological arousal. *Journal of Personality and Social Psychology, 37,* 970–988.

Martin, J. A. (1981). A longitudinal study of the consequences of early mother-infant interaction: A microanalytic approach. *Monographs of the Society for Research in Child Development, 46* (203, Serial No. 190).

Martin, R. J., White, B. D., & Hulsey, M. G. (1991). The regulation of body weight. *American Scientist, 79,* November–December, 528–541.

Maslach, C. (1979). Negative emotional biasing of unexplained arousal. *Journal of Personality and Social Psychology, 37,* 953–969.

Maslach, C. (1982). *Burnout: The cost of caring.* Englewood Cliffs, NJ: Prentice-Hall.

Maslach, C., & Florian, V. (1988). Burnout, job setting, and self-evaluation among rehabilitation counselors. *Rehabilitation Psychology, 33,* 135–157.

Maslow, A. H. (1970). *Motivation and personality* (Rev. ed.). New York: Harper & Row.

Mason, J. W. (1975). An historical view of the stress field: Parts 1 & 2. *Journal of Human Stress, 1,* 6–12, 22–36.

Masters, W. H., & Johnson, V. E. (1966). *Human sexual response.* Boston: Little, Brown.

Masters, W. H., & Johnson, V. E. (1970). *Human sexual inadequacy.* Boston: Little, Brown.

Masters, W. H., & Johnson, V. E. (1979). *Homosexuality in perspective.* Boston: Little, Brown.

Matarazzo, J. D. (1980). Behavioral health and behavioral medicine: Frontiers for a new health psychology. *American Psychologist, 35,* 807–817.

Matarazzo, J. D. (1984). Behavioral immunogens and pathogens in health and illness. In B. L. Hammonds & C. J. Scheirer (Eds.), *Psychology and health: The Master Lecture Series, Vol. 3* (pp. 9–43). Washington, DC: American Psychological Association.

Matarazzo, J. D. (1990). Psychological assessment versus psychological testing: Validation from Binet to the school, clinic, and courtroom. *American Psychologist, 45,* 999–1017.

Matossian, M. (1982). Ergot and the Salem witchcraft affair. *American Scientist, 70,* 355–357.

Matson, J. L., Esveldt-Dawson, K., Andrasik, F., Ollendick, T. H., Petti, T., & Hersen, M. (1980). Direct, observational, and generalization effects of social skills training with emotionally disturbed children. *Behavior Therapy, 11,* 522–531.

Matthews, K. A. (1988). Coronary heart disease and Type A behavior: Update on an alternative to the Booth-Kewley and Friedman (1987) quantitative review. *Psychological Bulletin, 104,* 373–380.

May, R. (1969). *Love and will.* New York: Norton.

May, R. (1972). *Power and innocence: A search for the sources of violence.* New York: Delta.

May, R. (1975). *The courage to create.* New York: Norton.

Mayer, R. E. (1981). *The promise of cognitive psychology.* San Francisco: Freeman.

McCaulley, M. H. (1978). *Application of the Myers-Briggs Type Indicator to medicine and health professions* [Monograph 1]. Gainesville, FL: Center for Applications of Psychological Type.

McClelland, D. C. (1961). *The achieving society.* Princeton, NJ: Van Nostrand.

McClelland, D. C. (1985). *Human motivation.* Glenview, IL: Scott, Foresman.

McClelland, D. C. (1985). *Human motivation.* New York: Cambridge University Press.

McClelland, D. C., Atkinson, J. W., Clark, R. A., & Lowell, E. L. (1976). *The achievement motive* (2nd ed.). New York: Irvington.

McCoy, E. (1988). Childhood through the ages. In K. Finsterbusch (Ed.), *Sociology 88/89* (pp. 44–47). Guilford, CT: Duskin.

McDougall, W. (1908). *An introduction to social psychology.* London: Methuen.

McGaugh, J. L., Weinberger, N. M., Lynch, G., & Granger, R. H. (1985). Neural mechanisms of learning and memory: Cells, systems and computations. *Naval Research Reviews, 37,* 15–29.

McGinnis, J. M. (1991). Health objectives for the nation. *American Psychologist, 46,* 520–524.

McLintock, T. T. C., Aitken, H., Dowie, C. F. A., & Kenny, G. N. C. (1990). Post-operative analgesic requirements in patients exposed to positive intraoperative suggestions. *British Journal of Medicine, 301,* 788–790.

McNeil, B. J., Pauker, S. G., Sox, H. C., Jr., & Tversky, A. (1982). On the elicitation of preferences for alternative therapies. *New England Journal of Medicine, 306,* 1259–1262.

McPherson, K. S. (1985). On intelligence testing and immigration legislation. *American Psychologist, 40,* 242–243.

Mead, M. (1939). *From the South Seas: Studies of adolescence and sex in primitive societies.* New York: Morrow.

Meador, B. D., & Rogers, C. R. (1979). Person-centered therapy. In R. J. Corsini (Ed.), *Current psychotherapies* (2nd ed., pp. 131–184). Itasca, IL: Peacock.

Mehrabian, A. (1971). *Silent messages.* Belmont, CA: Wadsworth.

Meichenbaum, D. (1977). *Cognitive-behavior modification: An integrative approach.* New York: Plenum.

Meier, R. P. (1991). Language acquisition by deaf children. *American Scientist, 79,* 60–70.

Meltzoff, J., & Kornreich, M. (1970). *Research in psychotherapy.* New York: Atherton.

Menzel, E. M. (1978). Cognitive mapping in chimpanzees. In S. H. Hulse, H. Fowler, & W. K. Honzig (Eds.), *Cognitive processes in animal behavior* (pp. 375–422). Hillsdale, NJ: Erlbaum.

Merton, R. K. (1957). *Social theory and social structures.* New York: Free Press.

Mervis, C. B., & Rosch, E. (1981). Categorization of natural objects. *Annual Review of Psychology, 32,* 89–115.

Meyer, M. M., & Ekstein, R. (1970). The psychotic pursuit of reality. *Journal of Contemporary Psychotherapy, 3,* 3–12.

Milgram, S. (1965). Some conditions of obedience and disobedience to authority. *Human Relations, 18,* 56–76.

Milgram, S. (1974). *Obedience to authority.* New York: Harper & Row.

Miller, A. G. (1986). *The obedience paradigm: A case study in controversy in social science.* New York: Praeger.

Miller, G. A. (1956). The magic number seven plus or minus two: Some limits on our capacity for processing information. *Psychological Review, 63,* 81–97.

Miller, J. (1984). Culture and the development of everyday social explanation. *Journal of Personality and Social Psychology, 46,* 961–978.

Miller, J., Bersoff, D., & Harwood, R. (1990). Perceptions of social responsibilities in India and the United States: Moral imperatives or personal decisions? *Journal of Personality and Social Psychology, 58,* 33–47.

Miller, J. D. (1987, Sept. 27). Ignoramus Americanus. *San Francisco Examiner-Chronicle,* This World Section, p. 7.

Miller, P. Y., & Simon, W. (1980). The development of sexuality in adolescence. In J. Adelson (Ed.), *Handbook of adolescent psychology.* New York: Wiley.

Mineka, S., Davidson, M., Cook, M., & Keir, R. (1984). Observational conditioning of snake fear in rhesus monkeys. *Journal of Abnormal Psychology, 93,* 355–372.

Minuchin, S. (1974). *Families and family therapy.* Cambridge, MA: Harvard University Press.

Mischel, W. (1968). *Personality and assessment.* New York: Wiley.

Mischel, W. (1973). Toward a cognitive social learning reconceptualization of personality. *Psychological Review, 80,* 252–283.

Moar, I. (1980). The nature and acquisition of cognitive maps. In D. Cantor & T. Lee (Eds.), *Proceedings of the international conference on environmental psychology.* London: Architectural Press.

Moghaddam., F., Ditto, B., & Taylor, D. (1990). Attitudes and attributions related to psychological symptomatology in Indian immigrant women. *Journal of Cross-Cultural Psychology, 21,* 335–350.

Moncrieff, R. W. (1951). *The chemical senses.* London: Leonard Hill.

Montague, A. (1986). *Touching: The human significance of the skin.* New York: Harper & Row.

Moore, P. (1990). In *Discovering Psychology,* Program 18 [PBS video series]. Washington, DC: Annenberg/CPB Program.

Morgan, A. H., Hilgard, E. R., & Davert, E. C. (1970). The heritability of hypnotic susceptibility of twins: A preliminary report. *Behavior Genetics, 1,* 213–224.

Moriarity, T. (1975). Crime, commitment and the responsive bystander: Two field experiments. *Journal of Personality and Social Psychology, 31,* 370–376.

Moscovici, S. (1985). Social influence and conformity. In G. Lindzey & E. Aronson (Eds.), *Handbook of social psychology* (3rd ed.). (pp. 347–412). New York: Random House.

Mowrer, O. (1960). *Learning theory and symbolic processes.* New York: Wiley.

Muehlenhard, C. L., & Cook, S. W. (1988). Men's self-reports of unwanted sexual activity. *The Journal of Sex Research, 24,* 58–72.

Mullen, B., & Baumeister, R. F. (1987). Group effects on self-attention and performance: Social loafing, social facilitation, and social impairment. In C. Hendrick (Ed.), *Review of personality and social psychology.* Beverly Hills, CA: Sage.

Mullin, P. A., & Egeth, H. E. (1989). Capacity limitations in visual word processing. *Journal of Experimental Psychology: Human Perception and Performance, 15,* 111–123.

Munroe, R. L. (1955). *Schools of psychoanalytic thought.* New York: Dryden.

Murnen, S. K., Perolt, A., & Byrne, D. (1989). Coping with unwanted sexual activity: Normative responses, situational determinants, and individual differences. *The Journal of Sex Research, 26,* 85–106.

Murray, J. P., & Kippax, S. (1979). Children's social behavior in three towns with differing television experience. *Journal of Communication, 28,* 19–29.

Muskin, P. R., & Fyer, A. J. (1981). Treatment of panic disorder. *Journal of Clinical Psychopharmacology, 1,* 81–90.

Myers, D. G. (1987). *Social psychology* (2nd ed.). New York: McGraw-Hill.

Myers, I. B. (1962). *The Myers-Briggs type indicator.* Palo Alto, CA: Consulting Psychologists Press.

Myers, I. B. (1976). Introduction to type (2nd ed.). Gainesville, FL: Center for Applications of Psychological Type.

Myers, R. E., & Sperry, R. W. (1958). Interhemispheric communication through the corpus callosum: Mnemonic carry-over between the hemispheres. *Archives of Neurology and Psychiatry, 80,* 298–303.

N

Natsoulas, T. (1981). Basic problems of consciousness. *Journal of Personality and Social Psychology, 41,* 132–178.

Nauta, W. J. H., & Feirtag, M. (1979). The organization of the brain. *Scientific American, 241*(9), 88–111.

Navon, D., & Gopher, D. (1979). On the economy of the human processing system. *Psychological Review, 86,* 214–255.

Needleman, H., Schell, A., Belinger, D., Leviton, A., & Allred, E. (1990). The long-term effects of exposure to low doses of lead in childhood: An 11-year follow-up report. *New England Journal of Medicine, 322,* 83–88.

Neese, R. M. (1990). Evolutionary explanations of emotions. *Human Nature, 1,* 261–289.

Nelson, R. E., & Craighead, W. E. (1977). Selective recall of positive and negative feedback, self-control behaviors and depression. *Journal of Abnormal Psychology, 86,* 379–388.

Newcomb, T. M. (1943). *Personality and social change.* New York: Holt.

Newell, A., Shaw, J. C., & Simon, H. A. (1958). Elements of a theory of human problem solving. *Psychological Review, 65,* 152–166.

Newell, A., & Simon, H. A. (1972). *Human problem solving.* Englewood Cliffs, NJ: Prentice-Hall.

Nguyen, T., Heslin, R., & Nguyen, M. L. (1975). The meanings of touch: Sex differences. *Journal of Communication, 25,* 92–103.

Nichols, M. P. (1984). *Family therapy: Concepts and methods.* New York: Gardner Press.

Nicol, S. E., & Gottesman, I. I. (1983). Clues to the genetics and neurobiology of schizophrenia. *American Scientist, 71,* 398–404.

Nisbett, R. E. (1972). Hunger, obesity and the ventromedial hypothalamus. *Psychological Review, 79,* 433–453.

Nisbett, R. E., & Ross, L. (1980). *Human inference: Strategies and shortcomings of social judgment.* Englewood Cliffs, NJ: Prentice-Hall.

Nissen, M. J., & Bullimer, P. (1987). Attentional requirements of learning: Evidence from performance measures. *Cognitive Psychology, 19,* 1–32.

Nobles, W. W. (1972). African psychology: Foundations for black psychology. In R. L. Jones (Ed.), *Black psychology.* New York: Harper & Row.

Nobles, W. W. (1976). Black people in white insanity: An issue for black community mental health. *Journal of Afro-American Issues, 4,* 21–27.

Nolen-Hoeksema, S. (1987). Sex differences in unipolar depression: Evidence and theory. *Psychological Bulletin, 101,* 259–282.

Norman, D. A., & Rumelhart, D. E. (1975). *Explorations in cognition.* San Francisco: Freeman.

Norman, W. T., & Goldberg, L. R. (1966). Raters, ratees, and randomness in personality structure. *Journal of Personality and Social Psychology, 4,* 681–691.

Nungesser, L. G. (1986). *Epidemic of courage: Facing AIDS in America.* New York: St. Martin's Press.

Nungesser, L. G. (1990). *Axioms for survivors: How to live until you say goodbye.* Santa Monica, CA: IBS Press.

Nuttin, J. (1985). *Future time perspective and motivation: Theory and research method.* Hillsdale, NJ: Erlbaum.

O

Oberg, K. (1960). Cultural shock: Adjustments to new cultural environments. *Practical Anthropology, 7,* 177–182.

Oden, S., & Asher, S. R. (1977). Coaching children in social skills for friendship making. *Child Development, 48,* 495–506.

Offer, D., Ostrov, E., & Howard, K. I. (1981). *The adolescent: A psychological self-portrait.* New York: Basic Books.

O'Leary, K. D. (1988). Physical aggression between spouses: A social learning theory perspective. In V. B. Van Hasselt, R. L. Morrison, A. S. Bellack, & M. Hersen (Eds.), *Handbook of family violence* (pp. 31–55). New York: Plenum.

Olson, J. M., & Zanna, M. P. (1981). *Promoting physical activity: A social psychological perspective.* Report prepared for the Ministry of Culture and Recreation, Sports and Fitness Branch, 77 Bloor Street West, 8th Floor, Toronto, Ontario M7A.2R9, Canada (November).

Olton, D. S. (1979). Mazes, mazes, and memory. *American Psychologist, 34,* 583–596.

Oppel, J. J. (1854–55). Ueber geometrisch-optische Tauschungen. *Jahresbericht des physikalischen Vereins zu Frankfurt a. M.,* 34–47.

Opton, E. M. (1970). Lessons of My Lai. In N. Sanford & C. Comstock (Eds.), *Sanctions for evil.* San Francisco: Jossey-Bass.

Opton, E. M., Jr. (1973). "It never happened and besides they deserved it." In W. E. Henry & N. Sanford (Eds.), *Sanctions for evil* (pp. 49–70). San Francisco: Jossey-Bass.

O'Reilly, C. A. (1991). Organizational behavior: Where we've been, where we're going. *Annual Review of Psychology, 42,* 427–458.

Orne, M. T. (1980). Hypnotic control of pain: Toward a clarification of the different psychological processes involved. In J. J. Bonica (Ed.), *Pain* (pp. 155–172). New York: Raven Press.

Ornstein, R., & Sobel, D. (1989). *Healthy pleasures.* Reading, MA: Addison-Wesley.

Ornstein, R. E. (1986a). Multimind: *A new way of looking at human behavior.* Boston: Houghton-Mifflin.

Ornstein, R. E. (1986b). *The psychology of consciousness* (Rev. ed.). New York: Penguin Books.

Oskamp, S. (1984). *Applied social psychology.* Englewood Cliffs, NJ: Prentice-Hall.

Oskamp, S. (Ed.). (1985). International conflict and national public policy issues. *Applied Social Psychology Annual, 6.*

P

Page, S. (1987). On gender roles and perception of maladjustment. *Canadian Psychology, 28,* 53–59.

Paivio, A. (1983). The empirical case for dual coding. In J. C. Yuille (Ed.), *Imagery, memory and cognition* (pp. 307–332). Hillsdale, NJ: Erlbaum.

Paivio, A. (1986). *Mental representations: A dual coding approach.* New York: Oxford University Press.

Palmer, S. (1981). The psychology of perceptual organization. In J. Beck (Ed.), *Organization and representation in perception* (pp. 269–339). Hillsdale, NJ: Erlbaum.

Papolos, D. F., & Papolos, J. (1987). *Overcoming depression.* New York: Harper & Row.

Pappas, A. M. (1983). Introduction. In A. M. Pappas (Ed.), *Law and the status of the child* (pp. xxvii–lv). New York: United Nations Institute for Training and Research.

Park, B., & Rothbart, M. (1982). Perception of out-group homogeneity and levels of social categorization: Memory for the subordinate attributes of in-group and out-group members. *Journal of Personality and Social Psychology, 42,* 1051–1068.

Pass, J. J., & Cunningham, J. W. (1978). Occupational clusters based on systematically derived work dimensions: Final report. *Journal of Supplemental Abstract Service: Catalogue of selected documents: Psychology, 8,* 22–23.

Paul, S. M., Crawley, J. N., & Skolnick, P. (1986). The neurobiology of anxiety: The role of the GABA/benzodiazepine complex. In P. A. Berger & H. K. H. Brodie (Eds.), *American handbook on psychiatry: Biological psychology* (2nd ed.). New York: Basic Books.

Pavlov, I. P. (1928). *Lectures on conditioned reflexes: Twenty-five years of objective study of higher nervous activity (behavior of animals)* (Vol. 1, W. H. Gantt, Trans.). New York: International Publishers.

Paykel, E. S. (1973). Life events and acute depression. In J. P. Scott & E. C. Senay (Eds.), *Separation and depression* (pp. 215–236). Washington, DC: American Association for the Advancement of Science.

Penfield, W., & Baldwin, M. (1952). Temporal lobe seizures and the technique of subtotal lobectomy. *Annals of Surgery, 136,* 625–634.

Pennebaker, J. W. (1990). *Opening up: The healing power of confiding in others.* New York: Avon Books.

Pennebaker, J. W., Dyer, M. A., Caulkins, R. J., Litowitz, D. L., Ackerman, P. L., Anderson, D. B., & McGraw, K. M. (1979). Don't the girls get prettier at closing time: A country and western application to psychology. *Personality and Social Psychology Bulletin, 5,* 122–125.

Pennebaker, J. W., & Harber, K. D. (1991, April). *Coping after the Loma Prieta earthquake: A preliminary report.* Paper presented at the Western Psychological Association Convention, San Francisco, CA.

Pennick, S., Smith, G., Wienske, K., & Hinkle, L. (1963). An experimental evaluation of the relationship between hunger and gastric motility. *American Journal of Physiology, 205,* 421–426.

Perlin, S. (Ed.). (1975). *A handbook for the study of suicide.* New York: Oxford University Press.

Pert, C. B., & Snyder, S. H. (1973). Opiate receptor: Demonstration in the nervous tissue. *Science, 179,* 1011–1014.

Peterson, C., & Seligman, M. E. P. (1984). Explanatory style and depression: Theory and evidence. *Psychological Review, 91,* 341–374.

Peterson, C., Seligman, M. E. P., & Vaillant, G. E. (1988). Pessimistic explanatory style is a risk factor for physical illness: A thirty-five year longitudinal study. *Journal of Personality and Social Psychology, 55,* 23–27.

Pettigrew, T. F. (1985). New patterns of racism: The different worlds of 1984 and 1964. *Rutgers Law Review, 37,* 673–706.

Phares, E. J. (1984). *Clinical psychology: Concepts, methods, and professionals* (Rev. ed.). Homewood, IL: Dorsey.

Piaget, J. (1954). *The construction of reality in the child.* New York: Basic Books.

Piaget, J. (1977). *The development of thought: Equilibrium of cognitive structures.* New York: Viking Press.

Pifer, A., & Bronte, L. (Eds.). (1986). *Our aging society: Paradox and promise.* New York: Norton.

Piliavin, I. M., Rodin, J., & Piliavin, J. A. (1969). Good Samaritanism: An underground phenomenon? *Journal of Personality and Social Psychology, 13,* 289–300.

Piliavin, J. A., & Piliavin, I. M. (1972). Effect of blood on reactions to a victim. *Journal of Personality and Social Psychology, 23,* 353–361.

Pilisuk, M., & Parks, S. H. (1986). *The healing web: Social networks and human survival.* Hanover, NH: University Press of New England.

Pittenger, J. B. (1988). Direct perception of change. *Perception, 17,* 119–133.

Plomin, R. (1989). Environment and genes: Determinants of behavior. *American Psychologist, 44,* 105–111.

Plomin, R., & Rende, R. (1991). Human behavioral genetics. *Annual Review of Psychology, 42,* 161–190.

Plous, S. (1985). Perceptual illusions and military realities: A social-psychological analyses of the nuclear arms race. *Journal of Conflict Resolution, 29,* 363–389.

Plutchik, R. (1980). *Emotion: A psychoevolutionary synthesis.* New York: Harper & Row.

Plutchik, R. (1984). Emotions: A general psychoevolutionary theory. In K. Scherer & P. Ekman (Eds.), *Approaches to emotion.* Hillsdale, NJ: Erlbaum.

Polivy, J., & Herman, P. (1985). Dieting and bingeing: A causal analysis. *American Psychologist, 40,* 193–201.

Pomerleau, O. F., & Rodin, J. (1986). Behavioral medicine and health psychology. In S. L. Garfield & A. E. Bergin (Eds.), *Handbook of psychotherapy and behavior change,* 3rd edition. New York: Wiley.

Ponterrotto, J., & Benesch, K. (1988). An organizational framework for understanding the role of culture in counseling. *Journal of Counseling and Development, 66,* 237–241.

Poon, L. W. (1985). Differences in human memory with aging: Nature, causes, and clinical implications. In J. E. Birren & W. K. Schaie (Eds.), *Handbook of the psychology of aging* (pp. 427–462). New York: Van Nostrand Reinhold.

Posner, M. I. (1982). Cumulative development of attentional theory. *American Psychologist, 37,* 168–179.

Posner, M. I. (1988). Structures and functions of selective attention. In T. Boll & B. Bryant (Eds.), *Master lectures in clinical neuropsychology* (pp. 173–202). Washington, DC: American Psychological Association.

Posner, M. I. (1990). In *Discovering Psychology,* Program 10 [PBS video series]. Washington, DC: Annenberg/CPB Project.

Powell, L. H., & Eagleston, J. R. (1983). The assessment of chronic stress in college students. In E. M. Altmaier (Ed.), *Helping students manage stress—new directions for student services* (Vol. 21, pp. 23–41). San Francisco: Jossey-Bass.

Premack, D. (1965). Reinforcement theory. In D. Levine (Ed.), *Nebraska Symposium on Motivation* (pp. 128–180). Lincoln, NE: University of Nebraska Press.

Price, R. (1953/1980). *Droodles.* Los Angeles, CA: Price/Stern/Sloan.

Putnam, F. W. (1984, March). The psychophysiologic investigation of multiple personality disorder [Symposium on Multiple Personality]. *The Psychiatric Clinics of North America, 7*(1), 31–40.

Q

Quattrone, G. (1986). On the perception of a group's variability. In S. Worchell & W. Austin (Eds.), The psychology of intergroup relations (Vol. 2, pp. 25–48). New York: Nelson-Hall.

R

Rabkin, J. G., Gelb, L., & Lazar, J. B. (Eds.). (1980). *Attitudes toward the mentally ill: Research perspectives* [Report of an NIMH workshop]. Rockville, MD: National Institutes of Mental Health.

Rachman, S. (1966). Sexual fetishism: An experimental analogue. *Psychological Record, 6,* 293–296.

Rahe, R. H., & Arthur, R. J. (1978, March). Life change and illness studies: Past history and future directions. *Journal of Human Stress,* pp. 3–15.

Rakic, P. (1985). Limits of neurogenesis in primates. *Science, 227,* 1054–1057.

Rando, T. A. (1988). *Grieving: How to go on living when someone you love dies.* Lexington, MA: Lexington Books.

Rapoport, J. L. (1989, March). The biology of obsessions and compulsions. *Scientific American,* pp. 83–89.

Regier, D. A., Boyd, J. H, Burke, J. D., Rae, D. S., Myers, J. K., Kramer, M., Robins, L. N., George, L. K., Karno, M., & Locke, B. Z. (1988). One-month prevalence of mental disorders in the United States. *Archives of General Psychiatry, 45,* 977–986.

Rehm, L. P. (1977). A self-control model of depression. *Behavior Therapy, 8,* 787–804.

Reisenzein, R. (1983). The Schachter theory of emotion: Two decades later. *Psychological Bulletin, 94,* 239–264.

Reiser, B. J., Black, J. B., & Abelson, R. P. (1985). Knowledge structures in the organization and retrieval of autobiographical memories. *Cognitive Psychology, 17,* 89–137.

Rescorla, R. A. (1966). Predictability and number of pairings in Pavlovian fear conditioning. *Psychonomic Science, 4,* 383–384.

Rescorla, R. A. (1972). Information variables in Pavlovian conditioning. In G. Bower (Ed.), *The psychology of learning and motivation* (Vol. 6). New York: Academic Press.

Rescorla, R. A., & Wagner, A. R. (1972). A theory of Pavlovian conditioning: Variations in the effectiveness of reinforcement and nonreinforcement. In A. H. Black & W. F. Prokasy (Eds.), *Classical conditioning, II: Current research and theory* (pp. 64–94). New York: Appleton-Century-Crofts.

Rest, J. R., & Thoma, S. J. (1976). Relation of moral judgment development to formal education. *Developmental Psychology, 21,* 709–714.

"Revising Psychiatric Diagnoses." (1993, 11 June). *Science, 260,* 1586–1587.

Richardson-Klavern, A., & Bjork, R. A. (1988). Primary versus secondary rehearsal in an imaginary voice: Differential effects recognition memory and perceptual identification. *Bulletin of Psychonomic Society, 26,* 187–190.

Riddle, D., & Morin, S. (1977). Removing the stigma from individuals. *American Psychological Association Monitor, 16,* 28.

Riggs, J. M., & Cantor, N. (1981). *Information exchange in social interaction: Anchoring effects of self-concepts and expectancies.* Unpublished manuscript, Gettysburg College.

Ripps, L. (1988). Deduction. In R. J. Sternberg & E. E. Smith (Eds.), *The psychology of human thought* (pp. 118–152). Cambridge: Cambridge University Press.

Robins, L. N., Locke, B. Z., & Regier, D. A. (1991). An overview of psychiatric disorders in America. In L. N. Robins & D. A. Regier (Eds.), *Psychiatric disorders in America: The epidemiologic catchment area study.* New York: Free Press.

Rodin, J. (1983, April). Behavioral medicine: Beneficial effects of self control training in aging. *International Review of Applied Psychology, 32,* 153–181.

Rodin, J. (1985). The application of social psychology. In G. Lindzey & E. Aronson (Eds.), *Handbook of social psychology* (3rd ed., Vol. 2, pp. 805–882). New York: Random House.

Rodin, J. (1986). Aging and health: Effects of the sense of control. *Science, 233,* 1271–1276.

Rodin, J. (1990). In *Discovering Psychology,* Program 23 [PBS video series]. Washington, DC: Annenberg/CPB Program.

Rodin, J., & Janis, I. J. (1982). The social influence of physicians and other health care practitioners as agents of change. In H. S. Freidman & M. R. DiMatteo, *Interpersonal issues in health care* (pp. 33–49). New York: Academic Press.

Rodin, J., Striegel-Moore, R. H., & Silberstein, L. R. (1985, July). A prospective study of bulimia among college students on three U. S. campuses. Unpublished manuscript. New Haven: Yale University.

Rogers, C. R. (1947). Some observations on the organization of personality. *American Psychologist, 2,* 358–368.

Rogers, C. R. (1951). *Client-centered therapy: Its current practice, implications and theory.* Boston: Houghton-Mifflin.

Rogers, C. R. (1977). *On personal power: Inner strength and its revolutionary impact.* New York: Delacorte.

Rogers, R. W. (1984). Changing health-related attitudes and behavior: The role of preventive health psychology. In J. H. Harver, J. E. Maddux, R. P. McGlynn, & C. D. Stoltenberg (Eds.), *Social perception in clinical and consulting psychology* (Vol. 2, pp. 91–112). Lubbock, TX: Texas Tech University Press.

Rogoff, B. (1990). *Apprenticeship in thinking: Cognitive development in social context.* New York: Oxford University Press.

Rorschach, H. (1942). *Psychodiagnostics: A diagnostic test based on perception.* New York: Grune & Stratton.

Rosch, E. H. (1973). Natural categories. *Cognitive Psychology, 4,* 328–350.

Rosch, E. H., Mervis, C. B., Gray, W. D., Johnson, D. M., & Boyes-Braem, P. (1976). Basic objects in natural categories. *Cognitive Psychology, 8,* 382–439.

Roseman, I. J. (1984). Cognitive determinants of emotions: A structural theory. In P. Shaver (Ed.), *Review of personality and social psychology: Vol. 5, Emotions, relationships, and health* (pp. 11–36). Beverly Hills, CA: Sage.

Rosenberg, S. (1988). Self and others: Studies in social personality and autobiography. In L. Berkowitz (Ed.), *Advances in experimental social psychology* (Vol. 21, pp. 57–95). New York: Academic Press.

Rosenhan, D. L. (1969). Some origins of concern for others. In P. Mussen, J. Langer, & M. Covington (Eds.), *Trends and issues in developmental psychology.* New York: Holt, Rinehart & Winston.

Rosenhan, D. L. (1973). On being sane in insane places. *Science, 179,* 250–258.

Rosenhan, D. L. (1975). The contextual nature of psychiatric diagnoses. *Journal of Abnormal Psychology, 84,* 462–474.

Rosenhan, D. L., & Seligman, M. E. P. (1989). *Abnormal Psychology* (2nd ed.). New York: Norton.

Rosenthal, D., Wender, P. H., Kety, S. S., Schulsinger, F., Weiner, J., & Rieder, R. (1975). Parent-child relationships and psychopathological disorder in the child. *Archives of General Psychiatry, 32,* 466–476.

Rosenthal, R., & Jacobson, L. F. (1968a). *Pygmalion in the classroom.* New York: Holt.

Rosenthal, R., & Jacobson, L. F. (1968b). Teacher expectations for the disadvantaged. *Scientific American, 218*(4), 19–23.

Rosenzweig, M. R. (1984b). Experience, memory, and the brain. *American Psychologist, 39,* 365–376.

Ross, L. (1988). Situational perspectives on the obedience experiments. [Review of The obedience experiments: A case study of controversy in social science]. *Contemporary Psychology, 33,* 101–104.

Ross, L., & Lepper, M. R. (1980). The perseverance of beliefs: Empirical and normative considerations. In R. A. Shweder & D. Fiske (Eds.), *New directions for methodology of behavioral science: Fallible judgments in behavioral research* (pp. 17–36). San Francisco: Jossey-Bass.

Ross, L., & Nisbett, R. E. (1991). *The person and the situation: Perspectives of social psychology.* New York: McGraw-Hill.

Roth, T., Roehrs, T., Carskadon, M. A., & Dement, W. C. (1989). Daytime sleepiness and alertness. In M. Kryser, T. Roth, & W. C. Dement (Eds.), *Principles and practice of sleep medicine* (pp. 14–23). New York: Saunders.

Rothman, D. J. (1971). *The discovery of the asylum: Social order and disorder in the new republic.* Boston: Little, Brown.

Rotter, J. B. (1954). *Social learning and clinical psychology.* Englewood Cliffs, NJ: Prentice-Hall.

Rozin, P. (1976). The evolution of intelligence and access to the cognitive unconscious. In J. M. Sprague & A. A. Epstein (Eds.), *Progress in psychobiology and physiological psychology* (pp. 245–280). New York: Academic Press.

Ruback, R. B., Carr, T. S., & Hopper, C. H. (1986). Perceived control in prison: Its relation to reported crowding, stress, and symptoms. *Journal of Applied Social Psychology, 16,* 375–386.

Rubin, J. Z., Provenzano, F. J., & Luria, Z. (1974). The eye of the beholder: Parents' views on sex of newborns. *American Journal of Orthopsychiatry, 44,* 512–519.

Rubin, Z. (1973). *Liking and loving.* New York: Holt, Rinehart & Winston.

S

Saarinen, T. F. (1987). *Centering of mental maps of the world: Discussion paper.* Tucson: University of Arizona, Department of Geography and Regional Development.

Sacks, O. (1985). *The man who mistook his wife for a hat and other clinical tales.* New York: Summit.

Salmon, D. P., Zola-Morgan, S., & Squire, L. R. (1987). Retrograde amnesia following combined hippocampus-amygdala lesions in monkeys. *Psychobiology, 15,* 37–47.

Salter, S. (1993). "Buried Memories/Broken Families," *San Francisco Examiner,* April 4, pp. A1ff.

Salzman, C. (1980). The use of ECT in the treatment of schizophrenia. *American Journal of Psychiatry, 137,* 1032–1041.

San Francisco Chronicle (1993). "Bad habits, violence raise health costs." February 23.

San Francisco Chronicle (1993). "Exercise slashes risk of heart disease." February 25, p. A20.

Sapolsky, R. (1990). In *Discovering Psychology,* Program 4 [PBS video series]. Washington, DC: Annenberg/CPB Project.

Sapolsky, R. M. (1990). Adrenocortical function, social rank, and personality among wild baboons. *Biological Psychiatry, 28,* pp. 1–17.

Sarbin, T. R., & Coe, W. C. (1972). *Hypnosis: A social psychological analysis of influence communication.* New York: Holt, Rinehart & Winston.

Sarnoff, I., & Katz, D. (1954). The motivational basis of attitude change. *Journal of Abnormal and Social Psychology, 49,* 115–124.

Satir, V. (1967). *Conjoint family therapy* (Rev. ed.). Palo Alto, CA: Science and Behavior Books.

Scarr, S. (1988). Race and gender as psychological variables: Social and ethical issues. *American Psychologist, 43,* 56–59.

Schachter, S. (1959). *The psychology of affiliation.* Stanford, CA: Stanford University Press.

Schachter, S. (1971). *Emotion, obesity and crime.* New York: Academic Press.

Schachter, S., & Gross, L. (1968). Manipulated time and eating behavior. *Journal of Personality and Social Psychology, 10,* 98–106.

Schachter, S., & Singer, J. (1962). Cognitive, social and physiological determinants of emotional state. *Psychological Review, 69,* 379–399.

Schacter, D. L. (1989). Modality specificity of implicit memory for new associations. *Journal of Experimental Psychology: Learning, Memory, and Cognition, 15*, 3–12.

Schanberg, S. M. (1990). In *Discovering Psychology*, Program 4 [PBS video series]. Washington, DC: Annenberg/CPB Project.

Schanberg, S. M., Kuhn, C. M., Field, T. M., & Barolome, J. V. (1990). Material deprivation and growth suppression. In N. Guzenhauser (Ed.), *Advances in touch* (pp. 3–10). Skillman, NJ: Johnson & Johnson Co.

Schank, R. C., & Abelson, R. (1977). *Scripts, plans, goals and understanding: An inquiry into human knowledge and structures.* Hillsdale, NJ: Erlbaum.

Scherer, K. R. (1984). On the nature and function of emotion: A component process approach. In K. R. Scherer & P. Ekman (Eds.), *Approaches to emotion* (pp. 293–317). Hillsdale, NJ: Erlbaum.

Schleifer, S. J., Keller, S. E., Camerino, M., Thornton, J. C., & Stein, M. (1983). Suppression of lymphocyte stimulation following bereavement. *Journal of the American Medical Association, 250*, 374–377.

Schreiber, F. (1973). *Sybil.* New York: Warner Books.

Schultz, R., Braun, R. G., & Kluft, R. P. (1989). Multiple personality disorder: Phenomenology of selected variables in comparison to major depression. *Dissociation, 2*, 45–51.

Schulz, R., Tompkins, C., Wood, D., & Decker, S. (1987). The social psychology of caregiving: The physical and psychological costs of providing support to the disabled. *Journal of Applied Social Psychology, 17*, 401–428.

Schwartz, B., & Lacey, H. (1982). *Behaviorism, science, and human nature.* New York: Norton.

Schwartz, G. E. (1975). Biofeedback, self-regulation, and the patterning of physiological processes. *The American Scientist, 63*, 314–324.

Schwartz, S. (1990). Individualism-collectivism: Critique and proposed refinements. *Journal of Cross-Cultural Psychology, 21*, 139–157.

Scott, J. P. (1963). The process of primary socialization in canine and human infants. *Monographs of the Society for Research in Child Development, 28*, 1–47.

Scott, R. A. (1972). A proposed framework for analyzing deviance as a property of social order. In R. A. Scott & J. D. Douglas (Eds.), *Theoretical perspectives on deviance.* New York: Basic Books.

Scovern, A. W., & Kilmann, P. R. (1980). Status of electro-convulsive therapy: Review of outcome literature. *Psychological Bulletin, 87*, 260–303.

Segall, M., Campbell, D., & Herskovits, M. (1966). *The influence of culture on visual perception.* Indianapolis: Bobbs-Merrill.

Selfridge, O. G. (1955). Pattern recognition and modern computers. *Proceedings of the Western Joint Computer Conference.* New York: Institute of Electrical and Electronics Engineers.

Seligman, K. (1988, October 9). Educators are alarmed over testing frenzy. *San Francisco Examiner*, pp. B-1, B-5.

Seligman, M. E. P. (1971). Preparedness and phobias. *Behavior Therapy, 2*, 307–320.

Seligman, M. E. P. (1975). *Helplessness: On depression, development, and death.* San Francisco: Freeman.

Seligman, M. E. P. (1991). *Learned optimism.* New York: Norton.

Seligman, M. E. P., & Maier, S. F. (1967). Failure to escape traumatic shock. *Journal of Experimental Psychology, 74*, 1–9.

Selye, H. (1956). *The stress of life.* New York: McGraw-Hill.

Shafii, M., Carrigan, S., Whittinghill, J. R., & Derrick, A. (1985). Psychological autopsy of completed suicide in children and adolescents. *American Journal of Psychiatry, 142*, 1061–1064.

Shapiro, D. H. (1985). Clinical use of meditation as a self-regulation strategy: Comments on Holmes's conclusions and implications. *American Psychologist, 40*, 719–722.

Shatz, M., Wellman, H. M., & Silber, S. (1983). The acquisition of mental verbs: A systematic investigation of the first reference to mental state. *Cognition, 14*, 301–321.

Shaw, R., & Turvey, M. T. (1981). Coalitions as models for ecosystems: A realist perspective on perceptual organization. In M. Kubovy & J. R. Pomerantz (Eds.), *Perceptual organization* (pp. 343–346). Hillsdale, NJ: Erlbaum.

Sheehy, G. (1976). *Passages: Predictable crises of adult life.* New York: Dutton.

Sheingold, K., & Tenney, Y. J. (1982). Memory for a salient childhood event. In U. Neisser (Ed.), *Memory observed.* San Francisco: Freeman.

Sheldon, W. (1942). *The varieties of temperament: A psychology of constitutional differences.* New York: Harper.

Shepard, R. N. (1984). Ecological constraints on internal representation: Resonant kinematics of perceiving, imagining, thinking and dreaming. *Psychological Review, 91*, 417–447.

Sheridan, C. L., & King, R. G. (1972). Obedience to authority with an authentic victim. *Proceedings of the 80th Annual Convention, American Psychological Association, Part 1, 7*, 165–166.

Sherif, C. W. (1981, August). *Social and psychological bases of social psychology.* The G. Stanley Hall Lecture on social psychology, presented at the annual convention of the American Psychological Association, Los Angeles, CA.

Shiffrin, R. M., & Schneider, W. (1977). Controlled and automatic human information processing: II. Perceptual learning, automatic attending, and a general theory. *Psychological Review, 84*, 127–190.

Shirley, M. M. (1931). *The first two years.* Minneapolis: University of Minnesota Press.

Shneidman, E. (1985). *At the point of no return.* New York: Wiley.

Shneidman, E. (1987, March). At the point of no return. *Psychology Today*, pp. 54–59.

Shweder, R., & Sullivan, M. (1993). Cultural psychology: Who needs it? *Annual Review of Psychology, 44*, 497–523.

Siegel, B. (1988). *Love, medicine & miracles.* New York: Harper & Row.

Siegel, J. M. (1990). Stressful life events and use of physician services among the elderly: The moderating role of pet ownership. *Journal of Personality and Social Psychology, 58*, 1081–1086.

Silver, R., & Wortman, E. (1980). Coping with undesirable life events. In J. Garber & M. E. P. Seligman (Eds.), *Human helplessness: Theory and application.* New York: Academic Press.

Simmel, E. C. (1980). *Early experiences and early behavior: Implications for social development.* New York: Academic Press.

Sinclair, J. D. (1983, December). The hardware of the brain. *Psychology Today*, pp. 8, 11, 12.

Singer, J. (1990). *Seeing through the visible world: Jung, Gnosis, and chaos.* New York: Harper & Row.

Singer, J. L. (1966). *Daydreaming: An introduction to the experimental study of inner experience.* New York: Random House.

Singer, J. L. (1975). Navigating the stream of consciousness: Research in daydreaming and related inner experience. *American Psychologist, 30*, 727–739.

Singer, J. L., & Antrobus, J. S. (1966). *Imaginal processes inventory.* New York: Authors.

Singer, J. L., & McCraven, V. J. (1961). Some characteristics of adult daydreaming. *Journal of Psychology, 51*, 151–164.

Singer, M., Candida, F., Davison, L., Burke, G. et al. (1990). SIDA: The economic, social, and cultural context of AIDS among Latinos. *Medical Anthropology Quarterly, 4*(1), 72–114.

Sinha, D. (1990). Interventions for development out of poverty. In R. Brislin (Ed.), *Applied cross-cultural psychology* (pp. 77–97). Newbury Park, CA: Sage.

Sjorstrom, L. (1980). Fat cells and body weight. In A. J. Stunkard (Ed.), *Obesity.* Philadelphia: Saunders.

Skinner, B. F. (1938). *The behavior of organisms.* New York: Appleton-Century-Crofts.

Skinner, B. F. (1981). Selection by consequences. *Science, 213*, 501–504.

Skinner, B. F. (1990). Can psychology be a science of mind? *American Psychologist, 45*, 1206–1210.

Skolnick, A. (1986). Early attachment and personal relationships across the life course. In P. B. Baltes, D. M. Featherman, & R. M. Lerner (Eds.), *Lifespan development and behavior* (Vol. 7, pp. 173–206). Hillsdale, NJ: Erlbaum.

Sloane, R. B., Staples, F. R., Cristol, A. H., Yorkston, N. J., & Whipple, K. (1975). *Psychotherapy versus behavior therapy.* Cambridge, MA: Harvard University Press.

Slobin, D. (1979). *Psycholinguistics* (2nd ed.). Glenview, IL: Scott, Foresman.

Slovic, P. (1984). *Facts vs. fears: Understanding perceived risk.* Presentation at a Science and Public Policy Seminar. Federation of

Behavioral, Psychological, and Cognitive Sciences, Washington, DC.

Smith, C. A., & Ellsworth, P. C. (1985). Patterns and cognitive appraisal in emotion. *Journal of Personality and Social Psychology, 48,* 813–838.

Smith, D. (1982). Trends in counseling and psychotherapy. *American Psychologist, 37,* 802–809.

Smith, E. E., & Medin, D. L. (1981). *Cognitive Science Series: 4. Categories and concepts.* Cambridge, MA: Harvard University Press.

Smith, M. L., & Glass, G. V. (1977). Meta-analysis of psychotherapy outcome studies. *American Psychologist, 32,* 752–760.

Smith, M. L., Glass, G. V., & Miller, T. I. (1980). *The benefits of psychotherapy.* Baltimore: Johns Hopkins University Press.

Snarey, J. (1985) Cross-cultural universality of social-moral development: A critical review of Kohlbergian research. *Psychological Bulletin, 97,* 202–232.

Snyder, M. (1984). When beliefs create reality. In L. Berkowitz (Ed.), *Advances in experimental social psychology, Vol. 18* (pp. 247–305). New York: Academic Press.

Snyder, M., & Swann, W. B., Jr. (1978a). Behavioral confirmation in social interaction: From social perception to social reality. *Journal of Experimental Social Psychology, 14,* 148–162.

Snyder, M., & Swann, W. B., Jr. (1978b). Hypothesis-testing processes in social interaction. *Journal of Personality and Social Psychology, 36,* 1202–1212.

Snyder, S. H. (1986). *Drugs and the brain.* New York: Scientific American Books.

Sokol, M. M. (Ed.). (1987). *Psychological testing and American society, 1890–1930.* New Brunswick, NJ: Rutgers University Press.

Solso, R. L. (1991). *Cognitive psychology* (3rd ed.). Boston: Allyn and Bacon.

Solso, R. L., & McCarthy, J. E. (1981). Prototype formation of faces: A case study of pseudomemory. *British Journal of Psychology, 72,* 499–503.

Somers, A. R. (1981). Marital status, health, and the use of health services: An old relationship revisited. In P. J. Stein (Ed.), *Single life: Unmarried adults in social context* (pp. 178–190). New York: St. Martin's Press.

Sorenson, R. C. (1973). *Adolescent sexuality in contemporary America.* Cleveland: World.

Spearman, C. (1923). *The nature of "intelligence" and the principles of cognition.* London: Macmillan.

Spearman, C. E. (1927). *The abilities of man.* London: Macmillan.

Sperling, G. (1960). The information available in brief visual presentations. *Psychological Monographs, 74,* 1–29.

Sperling, G. (1963). A model for visual memory tasks. *Human Factors, 5,* 19–31.

Sperry, R. W. (1968). Mental unity following surgical disconnection of the cerebral hemispheres. *The Harvey Lectures,* Series 62. New York: Academic Press.

Sperry, R. W. (1976). Changing concepts of consciousness and free will. *Perspectives in Biology and Medicine, 20,* 9–19.

Sperry, R. W. (1987). Consciousness and causality. In R. L. Gregory (Ed.), *The Oxford companion to the mind* (pp. 164–166). New York: Oxford University Press.

Spiegel, D., Bloom, J. R., Kraemer, H. C., & Gottheil, E. (1989, October 14). Effect of psychosocial treatment on survival of patients with metastatic breast cancer. *The Lancet,* pp. 888–891.

Spiro, R. J. (1977). Remembering information from text: The "state of schema" approach. In R. C. Atkinson, R. J. Spiro, & W. E. Montague (Eds.), *Schooling and the acquisition of knowledge.* Hillsdale, NJ: Erlbaum.

Squire, L. R. (1986). Memory functions as affected by electroconvulsive therapy. *Annals of the New York Academy of Sciences, 462,* 307–314.

Squire, L. R. (1992). Memory and the hippocampus: A synthesis from findings with rats, monkeys, and humans. *Psychological Review, 99,* 195–231.

Squire, S. (1983). *The slender balance: Causes and cures for bulimia, anorexia, and the weight loss/weight gain seesaw.* New York: Putnam.

Squire, S. (1988, January 3). Shock therapy. *San Francisco Examiner-Chronicle,* This World Section, p. 16.

Stampfl, T. G., & Levis, D. J. (1967). Essentials of implosive therapy: A learning theory-based psychodynamic behavioral therapy. *Journal of Abnormal Psychology, 72,* 496–503.

Steele, C. M. (1988). The psychology of self-affirmation: Sustaining the integrity of the self. In L. Berkowitz (Ed.), *Advances in experimental social psychology* (Vol. 21, pp. 261–302). New York: Academic Press.

Stern, W. (1914). The psychological methods of testing intelligence. *Educational Psychology Monographs* (No. 13).

Stern, W. C., & Morgane, P. S. (1974). Theoretical view of REM sleep function: Maintenance of catecholamine systems in the central nervous system. *Behavioral Biology, 11,* 1–32.

Sternberg, R. (1985). *Beyond IQ.* Cambridge, MA: Cambridge University Press.

Sternberg, R. (1986). Inside intelligence. *American Scientist, 74,* 137–143.

Stevens, J. (1986, Fall). The dance of the tonal. In *Shaman's Drum* (pp. 47–52).

Stevenson, J., Graham, P., Fredman, G., & McLoughlin, V. A. (1987). Twin study of genetic influences on reading and spelling ability and disability. *Journal of Child Psychiatry, 28,* 229–247.

Storms, M. D. (1980). Theories of sexual orientation. *Journal of Personality and Social Psychology, 38,* 783–792.

Storms, M. D. (1981). A theory of erotic orientation development. *Psychological Review, 88,* 340–353.

Strack, S., & Coyne, J. C. (1983). Social confirmation of dysphoria: Shared and private reactions to depression. *Journal of Personality and Social Psychology, 50,* 149–167.

Straub, E. (1974). Helping a distressed person: Social, personality, and stimulus determinants. In L. Berkowitz (Ed.), *Advances in experimental and social psychology* (Vol. 7). New York: Academic Press.

Stroebe, W., Stroebe, M. S., Gergen, K. J., & Gergen, M. (1982). The effects of bereavement on mortality: A social psychological analysis. In J. R. Eiser (Ed.), *Social psychology and behavioral medicine* (pp. 527–560). New York: Wiley.

Strube, M. J. (Ed.). (1990). *Type A behavior.* Corte Madera, CA: Select Press.

Sturmey, P. (1992). Treatment acceptability for anorexia nervosa: Effects of treatment type, problem severity and treatment outcome. *Behavioural Psychotherapy, 20*(1), 91–93.

Styron, W. (1990). *Darkness visible: A memoir of madness.* New York: Random House.

Sue, S. (1988). Psychotherapeutic services for ethnic minorities: Two decades of research findings. *American Psychologist, 43,* 301–308.

Suedfeld, P. (1980). *Restricted environmental stimulation: Research and clinical applications.* New York: Wiley.

Sullivan, H. S. (1953). *The interpersonal theory of psychiatry.* New York: Norton.

Suls, J., & Marco, C. A. (1990). Relationship between JAS- and FTAS-Type A behavior and non-CHD illness: A prospective study controlling for negative affectivity. *Health Psychology, 9,* 479–492.

Suls, J., & Sanders, G. S. (1988). Type A behavior as a general risk factor for physical disorder. *Journal of Behavioral Medicine, 11,* 201–226.

Sundberg, N. D., & Matarazzo, J. D. (1979). Psychological assessment of individuals. In M. E. Meyer (Ed.), *Foundations of contemporary psychology* (pp. 580–617). New York: Oxford University Press.

Swann, W. B., Jr. (1990). To be adored or to be known?: The interplay of self-enhancement and self-verification. In R. M. Sorrentino & E. T. Higgins (Eds.), *Handbook of motivation and cognition* (Vol. 2). New York: Guilford Press.

Swazey, J. P. (1974). *Chlorpromazine in psychiatry: A study of therapeutic innovation.* Cambridge, MA: MIT Press.

Swets, J. A., & Bjork, R. A. (1990). Enhancing human performance: An evaluation of "new age" techniques considered by the U.S. Army. *Psychological Science, 1,* 85–96.

Szasz, T. S. (1961). *The myth of mental illness*. New York: Harper & Row.

Szasz, T. S. (1977). *The manufacture of models*. New York: Dell.

Szasz, T. S. (1979). *The myth of psychotherapy*. Garden City, NY: Doubleday.

T

Tajfel, H. (Ed.). (1982). *Social identity and intergroup relations*. New York: Cambridge University Press.

Tajfel, H., & Billig, M. (1974). Familiarity and categorization in intergroup behavior. *Journal of Experimental Social Psychology, 10,* 159–170.

Targ, R., & Harary, K. (1984). *The mind race: Understanding and using psychic abilities*. New York: Villard Books.

Taylor, S. E. (1986). *Health psychology*. New York: Random House.

Taylor, S. E. (1990). Health psychology: The science and the field. *American Psychologist, 45,* 40–50.

Taylor, S. E. (1992). *Health psychology* (3rd. ed.). New York: Random House.

Taylor, S. E., & Brown, J. D. (1988). Illusion and well-being: A social psychological perspective on mental health. *Psychological Bulletin, 103,* 193–210.

Teasdale, J. D. (1985). Psychological treatments for depression: How do they work? *Behavior Research and Therapy, 23,* 157–165.

Tellegen, A., Lykken, D. T., Bouchard, T. J., Wilcox, K. J., Segal, N. L., & Rich, S. (1988). Personality similarity in twins reared apart and together. *Journal of Personality and Social Psychology, 54,* 1031–1039.

Temoshok, L., Sweet, M. D., & Zick, J. (1987). A three city comparison of the public's knowledge and attitudes about AIDS. *Psychology and Health: An International Journal.*

Tenopyr, M. L., & Oeltjen, P. D. (1982). Personnel selection and classification. *Annual Review of Psychology, 33,* 581–618.

Terman, L. M. (1916). *The measurement of intelligence*. Boston: Houghton-Mifflin.

Thigpen, C. H., & Cleckley, H. A. (1957). *Three faces of Eve*. New York: McGraw-Hill.

Thompson, K. (1988, Oct. 2). Fritz Perls. *San Francisco Examiner-Chronicle,* This World Section, pp. 14–16.

Thompson, R. F. (1986). The neurobiology of learning and memory. *Science, 233,* 941–944.

Thoresen, C. E., & Eagleston, J. R. (1983). Chronic stress in children and adolescents [Special edition: Coping with stress]. *Theory into Practice, 22,* 48–56.

Thorndike, E. L. (1898). Animal intelligence. *Psychological Review Monograph Supplement, 2* (4, Whole No. 8).

Thorndike, R. L., & Hagen, E. (1978). *The cognitive abilities test*. Lombard, IL: Riverside.

Thorndyke, P. W., & Hayes-Roth, B. (1979). *Spatial knowledge acquisition from maps and navigation*. Paper presented at the Psychonomic Society Meeting, San Antonio, TX.

Timko, C., & Moos, R. H. (1989). Choice, control, and adaptation among elderly residents of sheltered care settings. *Journal of Applied Social Psychology, 19,* 636–655.

Tipper, S. P., & Driver, J. (1988). Negative priming between pictures and words in a selective attention task: Evidence for semantic processing of ignored stimuli. *Memory and Cognition, 16,* 64–70.

Titchener, E. B. (1898). The postulates of structural psychology. *Philosophical Review, 7,* 449–453.

Tolman, E. C. (1932). *Purposive behavior in animals and men*. New York: Appleton-Century-Crofts.

Tolman, E. C. (1948). Cognitive maps in rats and men. *Psychological Review, 55,* 189–208.

Tolman, E. C., & Honzik, C. H. (1930). "Insight" in rats. *University of California Publications in Psychology, 4,* 215–232.

Tomkins, S. (1981). The quest for primary motives: Biography and autobiography of an idea. *Journal of Personality and Social Psychology, 41,* 306–329.

Torrey, E. (1986). *Witchdoctors and psychiatrists: The common roots of psychotherapy and its future*. New York: Harper & Row.

Treisman, A. (1988). Features and objects: The fourteenth Bartlett Memorial Lecture. *The Quarterly Journal of Experimental Psychology, 40,* 201–237.

Treisman, A. M. (1964). Verbal cues, language and meaning in selective attention. *American Journal of Psychology, 77,* 206–219.

Triandis, H. (1989). The self and social behavior in differing cultural contexts. *Psychological Review, 96,* 506–520.

Triandis, H. (1990). Cross-cultural studies of individualism and collectivism. In J. Berman (Ed.), *Nebraska Symposium on Motivation, 1989* (pp. 42–133). Lincoln, NE: University of Nebraska Press.

Trinder, J. (1988). Subjective insomnia without objective findings: A pseudodiagnostic classification. *Psychological Bulletin, 103,* 87–94.

Trivers, R. L. (1972). Parental investment and sexual selection. In B. Campbell (Ed.), *Sexual selection and the descent of man* (pp. 139–179). Chicago: Aldine.

Tronick, E., Als, H., & Brazelton, T. B. (1980). Moradic phases: A structural description analysis of infant-mother face to face interaction. *Merrill-Palmer Quarterly, 26,* 3–24.

Tulving, E. (1983). *Elements of episodic memory*. Oxford: Clarendon Press.

Tulving, E. (1985). Memory and consciousness. *Canadian Psychology, 26,* 1–12.

Tulving, E., & Pearlstone, Z. (1966). Availability versus accessibility of information in memory for words. *Journal of Verbal Learning and Verbal Behavior, 5,* 381–391.

Tulving, E., & Thomson, D. M. (1973). Encoding specificity and retrieval processes in episodic memory. *Psychological Review, 80,* 352–373.

Tupes, E. G., & Christal, R. C. (1961). *Recurrent personality factors based on trait ratings* (Tech. Rep. No. ASD-TR-61-97). Lackland Air Force Base, TX: U.S. Air Force.

Tversky, B. (1981). Distortions in memory for maps. *Cognitive Psychology, 13,* 407–433.

Tyler, L. (1988). Mental testing. In E. R. Hilgard (Ed.), *Fifty years of psychology* (pp. 127–138). Glenview, IL: Scott, Foresman.

Tyler, L. E. (1965). *The psychology of human differences* (3rd ed.). New York: Appleton-Century-Crofts.

Tyler, L. E. (1974). *Individual differences*. Englewood Cliffs, NJ: Prentice-Hall.

U

Uleman, J. S., & Bargh, J. A. (1989). *Unintended thought*. New York: Guilford Press.

V

Valenstein, E. S. (Ed.). (1980). *The psychosurgery debate*. New York: Freeman.

Van Strien, D. C., Van der Ham, T., & Van Engeland, H. (1992). Dropout characteristics in a follow-up study of 90 eating-disordered patients. *International Journal of Eating Disorders, 12* (3), 341–343.

Van Wagener, W., & Herren, R. (1940). Surgical division of commissural pathways in the corpus callosum. *Archives of Neurology and Psychiatry, 44,* 740–759.

Vernon, P. (1969). *Intelligence and cultural environment*. London: Methuen.

Vernon, P. E. (1987). The demise of the Stanford-Binet Scale. *Canadian Psychology, 28,* 251–258.

von Hofsten, C., & Lindhagen, K. (1979). Observations on the development of reaching for moving objects. *Journal of Child Psychology, 28,* 158–173.

Vonnegut, M. (1975). *The Eden express*. New York: Bantam.

W

Waldvogel, S. (1948). The frequency and affective character of childhood memories. *Psychological Monographs, 62* (Whole No. 291).

Wallace, A. F. C. (1959). Cultural determinants of response to hallucinatory experience. *Archives of General Psychiatry, 1,* 58–69.

Wallach, M. A., & Wallach, L. (1983). *Psychology's sanction for selfishness*. San Francisco: Freeman.

Wallerstein, J. S., & Blakeslee, S. (1989). *Second chances: Men, women, and children a decade after divorce*. New York: Tickner & Fields.

Wallerstein, J. S., & Kelly, J. B. (1980). *Surviving the breakup: How children and parents cope with divorce*. New York: Basic Books.

Wallis, C. (1984, June 11). Unlocking pain's secrets. *Time,* pp. 58–66.

Walsh, R. N. (1990). *The Spirit of Shamanism*. Los Angeles: J. P. Tarcher.

Walters, C. C., & Grusec, J. E. (1977). *Punishment*. San Francisco: Freeman.

Walters, E. E., Neale, M. C., Eaves, L. J., Heath, A. C. et al. (1992). Bulimia nervosa and major depression: A study of common genetic and environmental factors. *Psychological Medicine, 22*(3), 617–622.

Wanous, J. P. (1980). *Organizational entry: Recruitment, selection, and socialization of newcomers*. Reading, MA: Addison-Wesley.

Watson, J. B. (1919). *Psychology from the standpoint of a behaviorist*. Philadelphia: Lippincott.

Watson, J. B., & Rayner, R. (1920). Conditioned emotional reactions. *Journal of Experimental Psychology, 3*, 1–14.

Webb, W. B. (1974). Sleep as an adaptive response. *Perceptual and Motor Skills, 38*, 1023–1027.

Wechsler, D. (1981). *Manual for the Wechsler Adult Intelligence Scale—revised*. New York: Psychological Corp.

Weil, A. T. (1977). The marriage of the sun and the moon. In N. E. Zinberg (Ed.), *Alternate states of consciousness* (pp. 37–52). New York: Free Press.

Weinberger, M., Hiner, S. L, & Tierney, W. M. (1987). In support of hassles as a measure of stress in predicting health outcomes. *Journal of Behavioral Medicine, 10*, 19–31.

Weiner, B. (1986). *An attributional theory of motivation and emotion*. New York: Springer-Verlag.

Weingarten, H. R. (1985). Marital status and well-being: A national study comparing first-married, currently divorced, and remarried adults. *Journal of Marriage and the Family, 47*, 653–662.

Weinstein, N. D. (1980). Unrealistic optimism about future life events. *Journal of Personality and Social Psychology, 39*, 806–820.

Weisenberg, M. (1977). Cultural and racial reactions to pain. In M. Weisenberg (Ed.), *The control of pain*. New York: Psychological Dimensions.

Weiss, R. S. (1975). *Marital separation*. New York: Basic Books.

Weissman, W. W. (1987). Advances in psychiatric epidemiology: Rates and risks for depression. *American Journal of Public Health, 77*, 445–451.

Weitzman, L. J. (1985). *The divorce revolution: The unexpected social and economic consequences for women and children in America*. New York: The Free Press.

Wener, R., Frazier, W., & Farbstein, J. (1987, June). Building better jails. *Psychology Today*, 40–49.

Wertheimer, M. (1923). Untersuchungen zur lehre von der gestalt, II. *Psychologische Forschung, 4*, 301–350.

Westerfeld, J. S., & Fuhr, S. R. (1987). Suicide and depression among college students. *Professional Psychology: Research and Practice, 18*, 119–123.

Whitbourne, S. K., & Hulicka, I. M. (1990). Ageism in undergraduate psychology texts. *American Psychologist, 45*, 1127–1136.

White, M. D., & White, C. A. (1981). Involuntarily committed patients' constitutional right to refuse treatment. *American Psychologist, 36*, 953–962.

Wicklund, R. A., & Brehm, J. W. (1976). *Perspectives on cognitive dissonance*. Hillsdale, NJ: Erlbaum.

Wiggins, J. S. (1973). *Personality and prediction: Principles of personality assessment*. Reading, MA: Addison-Wesley.

Wilder, D. A. (1986). Social categorization: Implications for creation and reduction of intergroup bias. *Advances in Experimental Social Psychology, 19*, 291–355.

Wills, T. A. (1986). Stress and coping in early adolescence: Relationships to substance use in urban school samples. *Health Psychology, 5*, 503–529.

Wilson, E. D., Reeves, A., & Culver, C. (1977). Cerebral commissurotomy for control of intractable seizures. *Neurology, 27*, 708–715.

Wilson, M. (1959). *Communal rituals among the Nyakusa*. London: Oxford University Press.

Wingerson, L. (1990). *Mapping our genes*. New York: Dutton.

Wise, S. P., & Desimone, R. (1988). Behavioral neurophysiology: Insights into seeing and grasping. *Science, 242*, 736–740.

Wolman, C. (1975). Therapy and capitalism. *Issues in Radical Therapy, 3*(1).

Wolpe, J. (1958). *Psychotherapy by reciprocal inhibition*. Stanford, CA: Stanford University Press.

Wolpe, J. (1973). *The practice of behavior therapy* (2nd ed.). New York: Pergamon.

Woodworth, R. S. (1918). *Dynamic psychology*. New York: Columbia University Press.

Workman, B. (1990, December 1). Father guilty of killing daughter's friend in '69. *San Francisco Examiner-Chronicle*, pp. 1, 4.

Wundt, W. (1896/1907). *Outlines of psychology* (7th ed., C. H. Judd, Trans.). Leipzig: Englemann. (Original work published 1896).

Wyatt, G. E., Peters, S. D., & Guthrie, D. (1988). Kinsey revisited, Part I: Comparisons of the sexual socialization and sexual behavior of white women over 33 years. *Archives of Sexual Behavior, 17*, 201–239.

Wynne, L. C., Roohey, M. L., & Doane, J. (1979). Family studies. In L. Bellak (Ed.), *The schizophrenic syndrome*. New York: Basic Books.

Y

Yates, B. (1985). *Self-management*. Belmont, CA: Wadsworth.

Yerkes, R. M. (1921). Psychological examining in the United States Army. In R. M. Yerkes (Ed.), *Memoirs of the National Academy of Sciences: Vol. 15*. Washington, DC: U.S. Government Printing Office.

Yerkes, R. M., & Dodson, J. D. (1908). The relation of strength of stimulus to rapidity of habit formation. *Journal of Comparative Neurology and Psychology, 18*, 459–482.

Z

Zadeh, L. A. (1965). Fuzzy sets. *Information Control, 8*, 338–353.

Zahn-Waxler, C., & Radke-Yarrow, M. (1982). The development of altruism: Alternative research strategies. In N. Eisenberg-Berg (Ed.), *The development of prosocial behavior* (pp. 109–138). New York: Academic Press.

Zajonc, R. B. (1976). Family configuration and intelligence. *Science, 192*, 226–236.

Zanchetti, A. (1967). Subcortical and cortical mechanisms in arousal and emotional behavior. In G. C. Quarton, T. Melnechuk, & F. O. Schmitt (Eds.), *The neurosciences: A study program*. New York: Rockefeller University Press.

Zilboorg, G., & Henry, G. W. (1941). *A history of medical psychology*. New York: Norton.

Zimbardo, P. G. (1975). On transforming experimental research into advocacy for social change. In M. Deutsch & H. Hornstein (Eds.), *Applying social psychology: Implications for research, practice and training*. Hillsdale, NJ: Erlbaum.

Zimbardo, P. G. (1990). *Shyness: What it is, what to do about it* (Rev. ed.). Reading, MA: Addison-Wesley. (Original book published 1977).

Zimbardo, P. G., & Leippe, M. (1991). *The psychology of attitude change and social influence*. New York: McGraw-Hill.

Zimbardo, P. G., & Montgomery, K. D. (1957). The relative strengths of consummatory responses in hunger, thirst, and exploratory drive. *Journal of Comparative and Physiological Psychology, 50*, 504–508.

Zimbardo, P. G., & Radl, S. (1981). *The shy child*. New York: McGraw-Hill.

Zubeck, J. P., Pushkar, D., Sansom, W., & Gowing, J. (1961). Perceptual changes after prolonged sensory isolation (darkness and silence). *Canadian Journal of Psychology, 15*, 83–100.

Zuckerman, M. (1979). Sensation seeking and risk taking. In C. E. Izard (Ed.), *Emotions in personality and psychopathology*. New York: Plenum.

Zuckerman, M. (1983). *Biological bases of sensation-seeking impulsivity and anxiety*. Hillsdale, NJ: Lawrence Erlbaum Associates.

Zuckerman, M., Buchsbaum, M. S., & Murphy, D. L. (1980). Sensation seeking and its biological correlates. *Psychological Bulletin, 88*, 187–214.

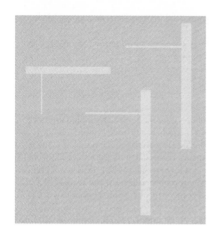

Acknowledgments

Photo Credits

Unless otherwise acknowledged, all photographs are the property of Scott, Foresman. Page abbreviations are as follows: (T) top, (C) center, (B) bottom, (L) left, (R) right.

Cover Musee National d'Art Moderne/Giraudon/Art Resource, NY

Chapter 1
2	Santrock/Insight Magazine
7	Richard Lord/The Image Works
9	Sidney Harris
11T	Archives of the History of American Psychology, University
11B	Bettman Archive
12	From *Puck's Almanack for 1882*/Puck
13	Pete Turner/The Image Bank
14	Bettman Archive
21	Sidney Harris
22	Sidney Harris
23	Elizabeth Crews
24	Sidney Harris
25L	Larry Mulvehill/SS/Photo Researchers
25R	Howard Sochurek
29	Hank Morgan/Rainbow

Chapter 2
36	Hank Morgan/Rainbow
38	Courtesy WGBH, Boston
39	By permission of the Darwin Museum, Down House
42T	Jerry Jacka Photography
42B	Rainbow
42C	Dan Bosler/Tony Stone Images
44T	Vol. 238, 1989, SCIENCE
44B	Giraudon/Art Resource, NY
45TL	Howard Sochurek
45TC	Monte S. Buchsbaum, M.D.
45TR	Monte S. Buchsbaum, M.D.
45BR	Dan McCoy/Rainbow
45BL	Hank Morgan/Rainbow

Chapter 3
70	Mike Maple/Woodfin Camp & Associates
72	John W. Verano, National Museum of Natural History/Smithsonian Institution
73	Bettman Archive
78T	Benn Mitchell/The Image Bank
78B	Rhoda Sidney/The Image Works
79	© 1977 J. Allan Hobson and Hoffman-LaRoche, Inc. Courtesy *Dreamstage* Scientific Catalog
83	Comstock Inc.
89	Mike Maple/Woodfin Camp & Associates
90T	David Young-Wolff/Tony Images
90C	Arnold Hinton/Monkmeyer Press Photo Service
90B	Mark Lawrence/The Stock Market

Chapter 4
98	Kindra Clineff/AllStock Inc.
102	Bibliotheque Nationale, Paris
104T	Greenlar/The Image Works
104B	From *A Child Is Born,* New York: Dell, 1977, p. 42
106	Diana O. Rasche
107	Courtesy Dr. Lew Lipsitt
109L	The Prado, Madrid, Erich Lessing/Art Resource, NY
109R	The Louvre/Erich Lessing/Art Resource, NY
114	Santrock/Insight Magazine
117TL	Zefa/H. Armstrong Roberts
117TR	Gerard Lacz/*Animals Animals*
117BL	John Eastcott/Yva Momatiuk/The Image Works
117BR	Robert Maier/*Animals Animals*
118T	Peter Menzel/Stock Boston
118C	George Godwin/Monkmeyer Press Photo Service
118B	Robert Mayer/Tony Stone Images
119T	Kevin Smith/Monkmeyer Press Photo Service
119B	Kevin Smith/Monkmeyer Press Photo Service
120All	Marcia Weinstein
121T	Bob Daemmrich/The Image Works
121	Nina Leen/Life Magazine/Time Warner Inc.
122	Martin Rogers/Tony Stone Images
128	Judith Canty/Stock Boston
129	Genaro Molina from *A Day in the California*
130B	Harley Schwadron
134L	Michael Newman/PhotoEdit
134R	Myrleen Ferguson/PhotoEdit
140	Bob Daemmrich/The Image Works
141T	Picture Group
141B	Dorothy Littell/Stock Boston

Chapter 5
146	Jim Cummins/AllStock Inc.
148	Courtesy WGBH, Boston
149	Stephen Dalton/Oxford Scientific/*Animals Animals*
160T	National Portrait Gallery, London
160B	Comstock Inc.
161	Fritz Goro © 1944/Life Magazine/Time Warner Inc.
168	J. Adanson/Sygma
170	Fuji Photos/The Image Works
175T	"Gestalt Bleue" by Victor Vasarely. Courtesy of the artist.
175BL	Cordon Art-Baarn-Holland, M. C. Escher Heirs, Collection of C. V. S. Roosevelt, Washington, D.C.
175BR	"Slave Market with the Disappearing Bust of Voltaire," oil, 1940, Salvador Dali Museum, St. Petersburg, Florida
179	NASA
183B	Peter Frunk/Tony Stone Images
183T	Joe Sohm/The Image Works

Literary Credits

Name Index

Subject Index

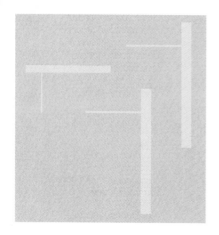

Mastery Tests

In this section of the text, Mastery Tests are provided to permit assessment of students' mastery of text material beyond that provided in each chapter's Practice Test.

Each chapter's Mastery Test consists of two parts: 20 multiple choice items, and 5 short answer items. Answers are provided in a special section of the Instructor's Manual.

How should the Mastery Tests be used? Instructors may choose to administer Mastery Tests as reviews of chapter and lecture comprehension, or as either graded or non-graded "rehearsals" for formal examinations. Alternatively, students may be asked to complete Mastery Tests as homework assignments, or may choose to complete specific Mastery Tests on their own and request scoring by the instructor.

How should Mastery Tests be graded? Because only instructors have access to answer keys, performance on Mastery Tests can only be assessed through student-teacher collaboration. In the Answer Key, page references are provided for every answer, and guidelines are provided for the best answers to short answer items.

We have included these Mastery Tests in a special section of this text so that every student gets the most from using *Psychology,* and every instructor has ample opportunity to assess students' mastery of the material. Let us know how you use the Mastery Tests, and what *we* can do—in future editions of this text—to correct errors, improve the material and its organization, and make more creative recommendations. Please send your comments, complaints, and constructive criticism to:

Ann L. Weber, Ph. D.
Department of Psychology
University of North Carolina at Asheville
Asheville, NC 28804

You are also welcome to make contact via electronic mail: **weber@unca.edu.** We look forward to hearing from you! Thanks for your input, and best wishes in getting the most out of *Psychology.*

Mastery Test

Chapter 1: Mind, Behavior, and Science

Name _____ Date _____

Multiple Choice Items

1. Which of the following concepts is *not* part of the formal definition of psychology?
   A. scientific
   B. normality
   C. behavior
   D. mental processes

2. Because psychology analyzes the causes and consequences of people's actions, it is considered a _____ science.
   A. social
   B. cognitive
   C. biological
   D. behavioral

3. The psychologist conducting basic research has four goals. Which of the following is a goal of applied psychology, *not* of basic psychological research?
   A. to explain behavior
   B. to improve human life
   C. to control behavior
   D. to predict how individuals will behave

4. The first task in psychology is carefully observing and objectively describing _____.
   A. animals
   B. behavior
   C. social institutions
   D. symptoms of abnormality

5. Which of the following would be an example of what psychologists call an intervening variable?
   A. hunger
   B. a public speech
   C. a large crowd
   D. short reaction time

6. An experimenter gives different sets of instructions to students solving written problems to see whether some strategies work better than others. In this research, the students' problem-solving performance is the _____ variable.
   A. intervening
   B. external
   C. dependent
   D. independent

7. Early psychologist Hermann Ebbinghaus once observed that psychology has a long _____ but a short _____.
   A. history; memory
   B. history; past
   C. past; history
   D. future; past

8. Early psychologists including Wilhelm Wundt and Gustav Fechner advocated _____, the doctrine that physical, behavioral, and mental events result from specific causes.
   A. determinism
   B. functionalism
   C. behaviorism
   D. humanism

9. Both Edward Titchener and Wilhelm Wundt favored the approach known as _____, which presumed that mental experience is composed of combinations of simpler elements.
   A. evolutionism
   B. determinism
   C. empiricism
   D. structuralism

10. Evolutionism questions whether the behavior patterns and mental processes of an entire species _____.
    A. are composed of simpler elements
    B. can be explained in terms of stimulus-response connections
    C. help each individual to become fully developed and happy
    D. have adaptive value

11. The _____ approach to psychology is associated with the work of the early twentieth-century theorist Sigmund Freud.
    A. biological
    B. behavioristic
    C. psychodynamic
    D. cognitive

12. If you wanted to study anger in accordance with the approach supported by John B. Watson and B. F. Skinner, your research should concentrate on _____.
    A. angry behaviors such as shouting or hitting
    B. the unconscious origins of anger
    C. the physiological changes that accompany angry emotions
    D. the evolutionary purpose of anger

13. From the cognitive perspective, people act a certain way because of how they _____.
    A. are driven by inner forces and motivations
    B. are stimulated by environmental conditions
    C. are biologically designed to act
    D. think

14. Bonita thinks of herself as overweight, and believes that this makes her unattractive to others. In trying to understand Bonita, a humanistic psychologist would focus on _____.
    A. her observable behaviors, not her thoughts and feelings
    B. Bonita's personal view of what is real in her life
    C. identifying Bonita's most adaptive behaviors
    D. helping her to lose weight so she will be more attractive

15. A psychologist is working in the context of _____ when her research is in the initial phase, and her data, beliefs, and knowledge lead her to think about an idea or event in a new way.
    A. investigation
    B. discovery
    C. justification
    D. measurement

16. In a 1959 experiment by Aronson and Mills, women who wished to join a group discussion about sex were first required to read aloud either a difficult list (with embarrassing, obscene words) or an easy list (with inoffensive words). Although the discussion afterwards was scripted to be boring, women who _____ thought it was very interesting.
    A. read the easy list
    B. read the difficult list
    C. were permitted to join the group
    D. were not allowed to join the group

17. A person's mood, quality of performance, and body temperature are all examples of _____, because each process changes with different times and conditions.
    A. biases
    B. stimulus events
    C. hypotheses
    D. variables

18. A scientist announces that his latest research has changed the way he thinks about the world and how it should be studied. In other words, his _____ has shifted.
    A. theory
    B. context
    C. paradigm
    D. operational definition

19. A psychologist administers a self-report scale of shyness to a college class. After scoring the forms, he classifies everyone who scored 30 or higher as "high" in shyness, and those who scored below 10 as "low." This illustrates the procedure known as _____.
    A. operationalization
    B. reliability
    C. random assignment
    D. placebo control

20. Citizens' groups complain that television violence is related to children's aggressive behavior. Television executives argue that aggressive children watch aggressive programs. The only way to determine whether television violence is causing aggressive behavior is to _____.
    A. do a correlational study
    B. conduct an experiment
    C. complete self-report measures
    D. collect physiological measures

Short Answer Items

Briefly define or explain each term.

21. base rate

22. independent variable

23. functionalism

24. behaviorism

25. double-blind control

Chapter 2: Biopsychology

Name _____   Date _____

Multiple Choice Items

1. According to research by psychologist Tiffany Field and biologist Saul Schanberg, premature infants who _____ gained more weight, were more active and alert, and later showed greater cognitive, emotional, and motor development than infants in a control group.
   A. were fed a high-sugar formula
   B. received periodic massages
   C. were housed in a colorful environment
   D. listened to tapes of their biological mothers' voices

2. According to Charles Darwin's theory of evolution, organisms which inherit biological characteristics that are not adaptive to their environment will _____.
   A. develop new, more adaptive traits
   B. compensate by procreating at a greater rate
   C. behave in frustrated and aggressive ways
   D. eventually become extinct

3. Sasha's mother has blue eyes, but Sasha has brown eyes like her father. The color of Sasha's eyes is an example of _____.
   A. her genotype
   B. her phenotype
   C. encephalization
   D. a maladaptive trait

4. Human beings live in more geographical locations and greater environmental extremes of the world than most other species. This extensive migration and relocation is a result of the evolutionary adaptation known as _____.
   A. bipedalism
   B. encephalization
   C. variation
   D. competition

5. A hunger researcher carefully applies electrical current to a minute portion of a rat's brain in order to destroy the cells thought to be responsible for eating behavior. This technique is an example of conducting brain research by studying _____.
   A. brain damage
   B. electrical stimulation
   C. lesioning
   D. brain scanning

6. In the deepest recesses of the brain is a region known as the _____, which includes structures involved with processes such as heart rate, breathing, swallowing, and digestion.
   A. frontal lobe
   B. cerebral cortex
   C. limbic system
   D. central core

7. Marcel feels thirsty, and looks for something to drink. The structure in Marcel's brain triggering these feelings and actions is the _____.
   A. hippocampus
   B. hypothalamus
   C. cerebellum
   D. corpus callosum

8. Your nose itches, so you scratch it. The sensations of itching are processed by the _____ lobe of your brain, whereas scratching movements are controlled by the _____ lobe.
   A. frontal; parietal
   B. frontal; temporal
   C. parietal; frontal
   D. temporal; occipital

9. Processes such as planning and decision making take place in the _____ cortex, which is not located in any single lobe.
   A. association
   B. auditory
   C. motor
   D. somatosensory

10. Hormones are manufactured and secreted by the _____.
    A. medulla
    B. endocrine glands
    C. transmitting neuron
    D. somatic nervous system

11. The pituitary gland is considered part of the _____.
    A. central core of the brain
    B. cerebral cortex
    C. peripheral nervous system
    D. endocrine system

12. The _____ nervous system consists of the brain and spinal cord, while the _____ nervous system is made up of all the nerve fibers connecting to the rest of the body.
    A. autonomic; peripheral
    B. autonomic; somatic
    C. central; somatic
    D. central; peripheral

13. After the stress of dealing with a family emergency, Sonya feels exhausted, sleepy, and almost faint. Her behavior at this point is influenced by the _____ division of her nervous system.
    A. somatic
    B. sympathetic
    C. parasympathetic
    D. peripheral

14. Which of the following is *not* a structure in a typical neuron?
    A. terminal button
    B. nucleus
    C. axon
    D. glia

15. According to the law of forward conduction, neurons only transmit information in which direction?
    A. from the dendrites to axon
    B. from the axon to the dendrites
    C. from the soma to the dendrites
    D. from the axon to the soma

16. As you take notes in class, neurons send messages from your brain to the muscles in your arm and hand to guide your handwriting. These neurons are classified as _____.
    A. sensory neurons
    B. afferent neurons
    C. efferent neurons
    D. interneurons

17. Which of the following is *not* one of the neurotransmitters identified in your text?
    A. serotonin
    B. dopamine
    C. GABA
    D. CNS

18. The _____ is the part of the brain responsible for the experience of consciousness.
    A. cerebral cortex
    B. limbic system
    C. central core
    D. cerebellum

19. Which of the following statements best summarizes the findings of research on cerebral dominance?
    A. The two hemispheres have completely different functions.
    B. The hemispheres' functions oppose each other.
    C. Hemispheric differences are not very obvious, and usually work together.
    D. Hemispheric differences are caused by gender differences.

20. Scientists say the brain is _____ because it is changed by the behavior it generates and by environmental stimulation.
    A. responsive
    B. behaving
    C. controlling
    D. static

Short Answer Items

Briefly define or explain each term.

21. natural selection

22. reticular formation

23. visual cortex

24. volume transmission

25. split-brain surgery

Mastery Test

Chapter 3: States of Mind

Name _____ Date _____

Multiple Choice Items

1. "Everything that exists is made of physical matter. Even mental states are actually the result of chemical reactions." This statement agrees with the view of reality known as _____.
   A. emergent-interactionism
   B. activation-synthesis
   C. dualism
   D. monism

2. A subject in a study of consciousness talks into a tape recorder to describe his thoughts while he solves various problems. This illustrates the _____ method of research.
   A. think-aloud protocol
   B. experience-sampling
   C. emergent-interaction
   D. dichotic listening

3. From a biological perspective, consciousness probably evolved because it helped individuals to _____.
   A. understand and use environmental information effectively
   B. express themselves clearly to others
   C. understand the meaning of existence
   D. experience pleasure

4. When you talk about things you have personally experienced, you realize that these events have an autobiographical character. This demonstrates the level of consciousness known as _____.
   A. self-awareness
   B. nonconsciousness
   C. preconsciousness
   D. the Unconscious

5. Although she was startled awake by a late-night telephone call, Hannah is soon able to relax and go back to sleep. Her body's automatic adjustments reflect the operation of _____.
   A. preconscious processes
   B. nonconscious processes
   C. subconscious processes
   D. unconscious processes

6. Which of the following illustrates the functioning of a circadian rhythm?
   A. If Janise doesn't go for a run every other day, she feels uncoordinated and out of shape.
   B. At least once a week, Mariko gets a craving for sweets.

C. Jonas finds that he does his most careful, alert work every morning from about 9 o'clock until noon.
   D. All of the above illustrate circadian rhythms.

7. Which of the following statements about sleep is *false?*
   A. If sleepers are awakened during REM, they report having dreams.
   B. In Stage 5 sleep, the sleeper's EEG is the same as during Stage 4.
   C. Personal problems and worries have been found to shorten the duration of individuals' sleep.
   D. According to research, the more one dreams, the more waking fantasies and obsessive thoughts one will have.

8. According to _____ theory, the content of our dreams is the result of random stimulation in our brains, with meaning added as an afterthought.
   A. Freudian
   B. activation-synthesis
   C. placebo-response
   D. mindful-awareness

9. One of the most common and undisputed values of hypnosis is its effect on _____.
   A. intelligence
   B. accurate remembering
   C. the experience of pain
   D. problem-solving ability

10. Buddhist traditions view meditation as a life-long exercise in learning to think imaginatively and without distraction, while Western science views meditation as _____.
    A. a loss of consciousness
    B. an altered state of consciousness
    C. identical to light sleep
    D. an addictive practice that can limit mental function

11. Sam sees a terrifying visual image of something that really isn't there. Sam is experiencing _____.
    A. a hallucination
    B. an illusion
    C. withdrawal
    D. meditation

12. Which of the following can cause hallucinations?
    A. migraine headaches
    B. psychoactive drugs
    C. sensory isolation
    D. All of the above

13. A person who has developed _____ to a drug will suffer painful withdrawal symptoms—such as shakes, sweats, or nausea—if he or she is deprived of the substance.
    A. addiction
    B. tolerance
    C. psychological dependence
    D. physiological dependence

14. Which of the following is *not* technically classified as a hallucinogenic drug?
    A. mescaline
    B. morphine
    C. PCP
    D. LSD

15. Drugs such as heroin and codeine that suppress physical sensation and responsiveness to stimulation are known as _____.
    A. barbiturates
    B. depressants
    C. stimulants
    D. opiates

16. Oliver is suffering from anxiety, so his physician has prescribed _____, which can help Oliver to feel calm without sedating him or making him sleepy.
    A. cannabis
    B. depressants
    C. benzodiazepines
    D. barbiturates

17. A diagnosis of alcoholism is appropriate when _____.
    A. a person drinks every day
    B. each drink a person takes contains at least 15% alcohol
    C. the drinker exhibits slurred speech or muscle incoordination
    D. drinking impairs one's job, health, and relationships

18. Heavy users of _____ develop paranoid delusions, such as believing that others intend to harm them.
    A. stimulants
    B. depressants
    C. cannabis
    D. opiates

19. In terms of mortality and medical costs, the total negative impact of _____ on health is greater than that of all other psychoactive drugs combined.
    A. nicotine
    B. caffeine
    C. marijuana
    D. cocaine

20. Human intelligence and consciousness evolved as a result of competition with the most hostile force in the environment: _____.
    A. natural elements such as weather and terrain
    B. the scarcity of food
    C. predatory animals
    D. other humans

Short Answer Items

Briefly define or explain each term.

21. dichotic listening task

22. the Unconscious

23. hypnotizability

24. tolerance

25. conscious mind

Mastery Test

Chapter 4: Psychological Development

Name _____   Date _____

Multiple Choice Items

1. In studies of development, the usual independent variable is _____.
    A. intelligence
    B. education
    C. gender
    D. age

2. Which of the following questions illustrates the nature-nurture controversy?
    A. Who usually mature faster, boys or girls?
    B. Is intelligence influenced more by education or inherited ability?
    C. What mental skills must a child acquire before developing language?
    D. On the average, at what age do children begin to walk?

3. Which of the following is *not* an example of what developmental researchers call constitutional factors?
    A. Five-year-old Carly has a shy temperament.
    B. Four-year-old Matt copies his father's facial expressions.
    C. Marta has always had a thin, fragile body shape.
    D. Devon is very susceptible to digestive illnesses.

4. A female infant monkey is raised by human caretakers after her mother dies. The baby grows up healthy but has no contact with other monkeys. When she is an adult, she is placed in a refuge with other monkeys. Which of the following is true?
    A. She will not mate or rear children normally.
    B. Mating will come naturally, but childrearing will not.
    C. Mating and childrearing will develop more slowly, but both will be normal and effective.
    D. Both mating and childrearing will develop instinctively in the same time and manner as for other monkeys.

5. In studying how children develop a sense of humor, a researcher tells the same jokes to children who are 5, 7, and 9 years old, and observes the reactions of each age group. This illustrates the use of _____ in developmental research.
    A. a longitudinal investigation
    B. a cross-sectional design
    C. a sequential investigation
    D. internal processes

6. Developmental psychologists believe that, without infants' basic interest in _____, there would be no motivation for children to learn language.
    A. comfort
    B. colors
    C. social interaction
    D. self-control

7. Psycholinguist Noam Chomsky argues that _____ plays a major role in children's language learning.
    A. overregularization
    B. object permanence
    C. the LAD
    D   synchronicity

8. Which of the following is an example of telegraphic speech?
    A. "I can dress myself."
    B. "Mikey hitted me!"
    C. "Want drink milk."
    D. "Mamama."

9. The mental programs that guide basic sensorimotor sequences such as sucking, grasping, and pulling are called _____.
    A. schemes
    B. scaffolds
    C. morphemes
    D. imprints

10. According to Piaget's theory of cognitive development, by the time a child enters the _____ stage, he or she has usually acquired the concept of conservation.
    A. sensorimotor
    B. preoperational
    C. concrete operational
    D. formal operational

11. According to the information-processing approach to development, children's thinking differs from that of adults because _____.
    A. children cannot think in symbols
    B. adults take in information more frequently than children do
    C. adults are not as open-minded as children are
    D. children are restricted by limited memory capacity

12. Harry Harlow studied the behavior of infant monkeys who had been separated from their mothers and provided with artificial mother models. What conclusion did the baby monkeys' behavior support?
    A. that attachment is based on contact comfort
    B. that attachment is based on imprinting
    C. the cupboard theory of attachment
    D. Erikson's theory of psychosocial development

13. Two-year-old Jessica cannot tie her own shoes, but she complains that she wants to do it herself and does not want others' help. According to Erikson's theory, which psychosocial stage of development does Jessica's behavior demonstrate?
    A. competence versus inferiority
    B. autonomy versus self-doubt
    C. initiative versus guilt
    D. trust versus mistrust

14. Which of the following is considered to be the central task of adolescence?
    A. achieving competence in one's chosen field
    B. forming an intimate relationship
    C. separating from parents and family
    D. establishing an integrated identity

15. Which of the following statements about adolescence is *not* true?
    A. Shyness reaches its highest level during the early teenage years.
    B. Females are less likely than males to give in to social pressure to behave antisocially.
    C. Adolescents talk to their peers four times as much as adults talk to theirs.
    D. Teenagers rely on their friends for structure and support, and no longer look to their families for these resources.

16. Which of the following is an example of the psychosocial crisis of generativity versus stagnation?
    A. An adolescent boy is depressed about breaking up with his girlfriend.
    B. Now that her children are older and less dependent on her, a woman in her 40s wants to do something more meaningful with her life.
    C. A young woman believes that once she and her fiance get married they will live happily ever after.
    D. A successful executive loves his work, but wishes he had someone special in his life.

17. According to the "doctrine of two spheres" that influenced gender roles a generation ago, men ruled in the world of _____ while women ruled in the world of _____.
    A. war; peace
    B. words; feelings
    C. work; home
    D. money; property

18. In Stage 1 of Kohlberg's theory of moral development, a child's "moral" behavior is motivated by a desire to _____.
    A. gain acceptance and avoid disapproval
    B. promote the welfare of society
    C. avoid painful punishment
    D. obey the rules

19. According to Erikson's theory of psychosocial development, the greatest danger of old age is that, instead of achieving ego-integrity, the individual will experience _____.
    A. despair
    B. inferiority
    C. stagnation
    D. isolation

20. Which of the following is *not* one of the emotional stages in Kübler-Ross's theory of coping with death?
    A. anger
    B. denial
    C. dementia
    D. depression

Short Answer Items

Briefly define or explain each term.

21. maturation

22. habituation

23. motherese

24. initiation rites

25. postformal thought

Mastery Test

Chapter 5: Sensation and Perception

Name _____ Date _____

Multiple Choice Items

1. _____ is the process by which a stimulated receptor cell creates neural impulses that result in an awareness of conditions in or outside the body.
   A. Sensation
   B. Sensuality
   C. Perception
   D. Kinesthesis

2. Which of the following is not an important subject of research in psychophysics?
   A. the just noticeable difference
   B. the AI approach
   C. signal detection theory
   D. absolute thresholds

3. After your roommate agrees to turn the television down, you notice the volume has not been turned down "enough." You and your roommate disagree about a sensory judgment abbreviated as _____.
   A. AI
   B. LGN
   C. TSD
   D. JND

4. Leaving a darkened theater after seeing a movie, Yolanda walks outdoors and is briefly blinded by the bright sunlight. Soon, however, because of the process known as _____, she can see clearly enough to resume walking into the parking lot.
   A. sensory adaptation
   B. saturation
   C. transduction
   D. automaticity

5. In vision, the _____ is the structure that carries information from the eye to the brain.
   A. bipolar cell
   B. retina
   C. fovea
   D. optic nerve

6. Brian squints from the glare of sunlight on the car in front of his, as he tries to blink away the sun-like flashes that seem imprinted on his eyes. What is interfering with Brian's vision?
   A. afterimages
   B. color blindness
   C. the blind spot
   D. perceptual instability

7. Hertz or cycles-per-second is a measurement of _____.
   A. color intensity
   B. loudness of sound
   C. frequency of sound
   D. chemical concentration

8. Where in the ear is sound energy transformed into neural activity?
   A. the eardrum
   B. the hammer, anvil, and stirrup
   C. the basilar membrane
   D. the pinna

9. Pheromones are stimuli that are best detected by which sensory process?
   A. the vestibular sense
   B. the kinesthetic sense
   C. olfaction
   D. gustation

10. Which of the following statements about human sensitivity to pain is *false*?
    A. Pain is a purely physical process that is unaffected by psychological factors.
    B. Research shows that pain can be influenced by one's gender role.
    C. People born with an insensitivity to pain are at greater risk for illness, injury, and early death.
    D. About one-third of Americans are estimated to suffer from persistent or recurring pain.

11. The process of perception is actually made up of three sequential processes: sensation, perception, and _____.
    A. motion
    B. automaticity
    C. correct rejection
    D. recognition and identification

12. Alonso sits at his desk by the window, looking outside at his little boy who is playing in the yard. In this example, the distal stimulus is _____.
    A. the window
    B. the little boy
    C. the image of the little boy on Alonso's retina
    D. the yard and other outdoor scenery

13. A woman visiting an art gallery gazes at the abstract painting on the wall and remarks to her companion, "This is very ambiguous." She means that the painting _____.
   A. could be interpreted in more than one way
   B. distorts her visual perception
   C. is easy to analyze
   D. has no meaning

14. "People see and remember whole experiences, rather than breaking them down into separate parts." This statement agrees with which approach to explaining perception?
   A. Helmholtz's theory of experience-based inference
   B. Gibson's theory of environmental adaptation
   C. the Gestalt approach
   D. the AI approach

15. Sorting his laundry, Jamal must separate white socks from light blue socks. Because the socks differ in this single simple feature—their color—the difference will "pop out," which is a sign of _____ processing.
   A. selective
   B. preattentive
   C. bottom-up
   D. figure-ground

16. Nilda's friend whispers some gossip to her during a lecture. As a result, Nilda misses hearing what the professor was saying at the same time. Nilda's experience illustrates the _____ function of attention.
   A. sensory filter
   B. response selection
   C. perceptual grouping
   D. gateway-to-consciousness

17. Because she worked several years as a secretary, Ann can type up to 90 words a minute, sometimes while doing other tasks like watching television or talking on the phone. For Ann, typing meets the conditions of _____.
   A. automaticity
   B. perceptual set
   C. limited capacity
   D. region segregation

18. In the passing zone of a highway, the yellow center line is dotted rather than solid, but it is still seen as a line rather than as a series of dashes. This illustrates the organizational process known as _____.
   A. region segregation
   B. figure-ground distinction
   C. subjective contours
   D. closure

19. A children's map of a zoo is illustrated with small symbols for buildings and trees along the pathway. Even though the symbols are all the same size, a child reading the map sees the trees as "belonging with" the other trees. Which principle of perceptual grouping does this illustrate?
   A. Weber's law
   B. the law of common fate
   C. the law of proximity
   D. the law of similarity

20. Aaron recently got a speeding ticket. Now, even though his driving does not exceed the speed limit, he notices every police car and state trooper on the road. Aaron's readiness to detect the presence of traffic police is an example of _____.
   A. sensory adaptation
   B. selective attention
   C. the law of common fate
   D. perceptual set

Short Answer Items

Briefly define or explain each term.

21. transduction

22. false alarm

23. timbre

24. illusion

25. Prägnanz

Chapter 6: Learning

Name _____ Date _____

Multiple Choice Items

1. When certain pet lizards see their reflection in a mirror, they behave as if confronted by another lizard, striking a pose that is normally part of mating or defending territory. Such a built-in, unlearned set of responses is an example of _____.
   A. spontaneous recovery
   B. a conditioned reflex
   C. instinctual drift
   D. a fixed-action pattern

2. When your cat is hungry, she walks to her food dish, sits, and waits. She has learned that when you see her, you will put food in the dish. This illustrates operant conditioning, because the cat's behavior has become associated with _____.
   A. the stimuli that provoked it
   B. the sight of the food dish
   C. its purpose
   D. its consequences

3. Based on how *learning* is defined, which of the following is *not* an example of a learned behavior?
   A. After weeks of practice, a gymnast is able to perform a series of leaps and turns without making an error.
   B. When she poses for a photograph, a child facing bright sunlight reflexively squints and smirks.
   C. Now that he has memorized the Presidents' initials in order, Marcus can recite all their names.
   D. Although Tamara now drives a car with an automatic transmission, she can still drive a vehicle with a standard transmission when she has to.

4. A learning researcher deprives a rat of food, and then trains it to press a lever by delivering a food pellet every time the rat does so. According to a behaviorist, which of the following is *not* an explanation of the rat's actions?
   A. hunger
   B. food deprivation
   C. food pellets
   D. environmental consequences

5. During classical conditioning, an organism learns a new association between _____.
   A. two stimuli
   B. two responses
   C. an old stimulus and a new response
   D. an old environment and a new reflex

6. In his original research on classical conditioning, Pavlov studied _____ behavior.
   A. maternal
   B. emotional
   C. reflexive
   D. aggressive

7. When five-year-old Jesse's father acts angry, Jesse feels afraid. Jesse's father usually slams the door if he is in an angry mood when he returns home. Now Jesse starts to feel afraid any time he hears a door slam. In this example of classical conditioning, the conditional response is _____.
   A. acting angry
   B. feeling frightened
   C. slamming a door
   D. returning home

8. After taking a cherry-flavored medicine while she was sick, Vanessa found that any kind of cherry flavoring made her feel ill. Later she associated sickness with other fruit flavors besides cherry. Vanessa's experience is an example of _____.
   A. spontaneous recovery
   B. stimulus generalization
   C. stimulus discrimination
   D. extinction

9. According to Leon Kamin's research on why we form certain CS-CR connections, of the many stimuli we encounter in our experiences, we pay particular attention to those that provide _____.
   A. sensory pleasure
   B. comfortable levels of arousal
   C. distraction from our worries
   D. important information about the environment

10. E. L. Thorndike's research with cats escaping from puzzle boxes led him to conclude that learning is a process of acquiring habits or _____ connections through trial and error.
    A. UCS-CS
    B. S-R
    C. reflexive
    D. positive-negative

11. Literally, an "operant" is any behavior that _____.
    A. is elicited by an environmental stimulus
    B. affects the environment
    C. elicits a response
    D. is reflexive

12. Which of the following illustrates the use of negative reinforcement?
   A. When Lizzie throws a tantrum, her parents ignore her, so eventually Lizzie calms down and stops misbehaving.
   B. Each time Keenan's cat scratches the furniture, Keenan squirts him with a water pistol to discourage him.
   C. Whenever Ed makes himself a sandwich, he makes one for his roommate too, to prevent him from nagging Ed for a sandwich.
   D. Whenever Ellie's boyfriend compliments her, she thanks him warmly to encourage him to do it more often.

13. Which of the following is *not* one of the recommendations researchers make for using punishment effectively?
   A. Administer punishment immediately after the unwanted response occurs.
   B. Punishment should be limited in intensity.
   C. Punish the person, not just the bad behavior.
   D. Penalties are a more effective punishment than pain.

14. Talia would rather study for her psychology course than for her history course. She promises herself she can work on her psychology only after she finishes reading her history assignment. Talia's self-discipline is an example of _____.
   A. shaping
   B. instinctual drift
   C. conditioned reinforcement
   D. the Premack principle

15. Which of the following would best be achieved by the technique known as shaping?
   A. teaching drivers to pull over at the sound of a siren
   B. training children to trust adults who wear uniforms
   C. training a puppy to sit and hold up a paw on command
   D. discouraging schoolchildren's misbehavior by punishing the entire class whenever one child breaks a rule

16. Learned helplessness results when an individual _____ after receiving prolonged, noncontingent, inescapable punishment.
   A. stops responding
   B. increases responding
   C. behaves aggressively
   D. finally makes the desired response

17. Instead of finishing his class reading assignments ahead of time, Travis puts off working until just before the deadline, which is characteristic of a _____ schedule of reinforcement.
   A. fixed-ratio
   B. variable-ratio
   C. fixed-interval
   D. variable-interval

18. Rae got sick while on a vacation in an ocean-side town famous for its fresh seafood. Now eating any type of seafood makes her nauseous. Rae's experience shows the effects of _____.
   A. observational learning
   B. instinctual drift
   C. taste aversion
   D. bait shyness

19. "Children should not see violence on television, because it teaches them to copy aggressive models." This statement draws conclusions from research on the power of _____.
   A. learned helplessness
   B. appetitive conditioning
   C. continuous reinforcement
   D. observational learning

20. An inner representation of the learning situation as a whole is _____.
   A. an operant
   B. a fixed action pattern
   C. a reinforcement contingency
   D. a cognitive map

Short Answer Items

Briefly define or explain each term.

21. acquisition

22. law of effect

23. conditioned reinforcers

24. partial reinforcement effect

25. bait shyness

Mastery Test

Chapter 7: Cognitive Processes

Name _____   Date _____

Multiple Choice Items

1. After reading about concentration-camp survivor Dr. Edith Eger, we might extend Descartes' original statement on human nature so that we now say, "I am human, therefore I must _____."
   A. survive
   B. forget
   C. think
   D. die

2. Among the following names, who is *not* specifically associated with developing the modern, computer-modeled approach to understanding cognitive processes?
   A. John von Neumann
   B. Hermann Ebbinghaus
   C. Allen Newell
   D. Herbert Simon

3. "I believe the best way to understanding cognitive processes is to organize them into their component parts." This statement indicates support for the _____ model.
   A. information-processing
   B. language-acquisition
   C. functional-fixedness
   D. cognitive-economy

4. The human brain is more flexible and complex than computer programs, because the brain can conduct _____ processing of several messages, while computers rely on _____ processing.
   A. long-term; short-term
   B. sensory; semantic
   C. deductive; inductive
   D. parallel; serial

5. From the perspective of cognitive psychology, thinking has three general features. Which of the following is *not* one of them?
   A. Thinking is directed toward solving an individual's problems.
   B. Thinking is limited by an individual's experience, and cannot by itself overcome biased information.
   C. Thinking manipulates knowledge with one's cognitive system.
   D. Thinking occurs in the mind but can be inferred from observable behavior.

6. When Marla finds a kitten to adopt at the animal shelter, she picks it up and holds it the way she has learned with other cats. In other words, though she has never seen this particular kitten before, her behavior toward it is guided by her _____.
   A. concept of cats
   B. sensory register
   C. inductive reasoning
   D. cognitive map

7. When hurrying to pack for a beach vacation, Leon forgets his sunglasses. "I was in a hurry to pack things I usually wear," he explains, "but I only thought of clothes like shirts and pants, and forgot things I wear on my face." In other words, _____.
   A. sunglasses lack the critical features of "things to wear"
   B. sunglasses resemble the prototype of "things to wear"
   C. Leon's cognitive economy has no room for "sunglasses"
   D. None of the above

8. A script is defined as a schema for a particular _____.
   A. event
   B. language
   C. age-group
   D. relationship

9. Of the following questions, which one would probably require relying on visual mental imagery for the answer?
   A. How many quarts are in a gallon?
   B. What are the colors of your state flag?
   C. Is the gas tank of your car located on the driver's side or the passenger's side?
   D. How long does it take you to get home after school?

10. Which of the following is an example of autistic thinking?
    A. calculating the steps necessary to solve a math problem
    B. imagining a landscape you would like to paint
    C. planning to assemble ingredients to bake a cake
    D. using available data to draw a conclusion about something

11. In information-processing terms, which of the following is not one of the three parts of a problem?
    A. an initial state
    B. a goal state
    C. a conflict or crisis
    D. a set of operations

12. Corbett can't find his recipe for pancakes, and is not sure how many eggs it requires. Corbett experiments with the ingredients, methodically making pancakes with one egg, two eggs, and three eggs, until he gets it right. Corbett has solved his problem by using _____.
    A. a heuristic
    B. inductive reasoning
    C. an algorithm
    D. inference

13. _____ is the process of choosing between alternatives, selecting and rejecting available options.
    A. Realistic thinking
    B. Judging
    C. Deciding
    D. Chunking

14. Before inviting a new friend to attend a basketball game with you, you wonder whether or not she is a sports fan. To decide, you judge whether she resembles most other sports fans you know. In other words, you are relying on _____.
    A. the representativeness heuristic
    B. the availability heuristic
    C. pseudomemory
    D. mental set

15. A TV commercial for a pain reliever claims that "nothing works faster!" But a consumer magazine reporting on the same product concludes that "all products tested were equally fast." The same information is presented in both statements, but it is _____ differently.
    A. retrieved
    B. biased
    C. framed
    D. reasoned

16. Which of the following statements about Ebbinghaus's early research on memory is *not* true?
    A. He used the savings method to evaluate memory.
    B. The subject performed a serial learning task.
    C. The stimuli presented were nonsense syllables.
    D. Subjects had better recall for more meaningful stimuli.

17. Studying for a psychology test, Adrienne tries to think of links between new information and knowledge she already possesses. This encoding process is known as _____.
    A. elaboration
    B. recognition
    C. biased assimilation
    D. syllogistic reasoning

18. _____ is an impression formed from input of any of the senses.
    A. Short-term memory
    B. Pseudomemory
    C. Working
    D. Sensory

19. You are most likely to rely on chunking to retain information in _____ memory.
    A. working
    B. long-term
    C. sensory
    D. episodic

20. According to the _____ theory of forgetting, trying to remember one set of information can prevent other lessons from being retained.
    A. motivated
    B. interference
    C. retrieval-failure
    D. decay

Short Answer Items

Briefly define or explain each term.

21. cognitive economy

22. schema

23. realistic thinking

24. chunk

25. false memory syndrome

Chapter 8: Motivation and Emotion

Name _____   Date _____

Multiple Choice Items

1. _____ refers to needs that are primarily biological, while _____ refers to learned psychological and social needs.
   A. Goal; incentive
   B. Motivation; emotion
   C. Drive; motive
   D. Instinct; goal

2. Researcher C. J. Warden studied the relative strength of various drives influencing rats' behavior by means of _____.
   A. an obstruction box
   B. a Skinner box
   C. an operant chamber
   D. a puzzle box

3. Alden's grades are suffering because he is taking so many classes during his last semester of college. He would rather take a lighter load now, and finish up in the summer. But his parents want to attend the graduation ceremony this spring, and he doesn't want to disappoint them. Alden's behavior is affected by a negative form of _____.
   A. intrinsic motivation
   B. incentive motivation
   C. achievement motivation
   D. optimal arousal

4. Which of the following is *not* one of the brain structures involved in the physiology of emotion?
   A. reticular activating system
   B. hypothalamus
   C. thalamus
   D. limbic system

5. The emotion wheel developed by _____ proposes an innate set of eight emotions, made up of four pairs of opposites.
   A. W. B. Cannon
   B. Robert Plutchik
   C. Carroll Izard
   D. Stanley Schachter

6. Today, what used to be called instincts in animals are usually studied as _____, unlearned patterns of behavior triggered by identifiable stimuli.
   A. primary drives
   B. scripts
   C. deficiency motives
   D. fixed-action patterns

7. Which of the following motivation theorists did *not* support the concept of instinct as an explanation for human behavior?
   A. Abraham Maslow
   B. Sigmund Freud
   C. William James
   D. William McDougall

8. When Jade is doing something simple, like writing a letter home, she seems to do a better job when she has the additional stimulation of conversation or listening to the radio. But when Jade is doing something difficult like writing a paper for school, such stimuli distract her and hurt her efforts. Jade's behavior is explained by _____.
   A. the hierarchy of needs
   B. the concept of flow
   C. the Yerkes-Dodson law
   D. the Lazarus-Schachter theory

9. According to the theory of Maslow's hierarchy of needs, of the following, the highest level of needs are the _____ needs.
   A. esthetic
   B. attachment
   C. esteem
   D. safety

10. If a hungry person is asked to complete the Thematic Apperception Test, she will probably _____.
    A. not be able to do so until she has something to eat
    B. compose stories with themes related to eating and food
    C. compose stories about everything *except* eating and food
    D. compose stories similar to those of non-hungry persons

11. According to Julian Rotter's social learning theory, the probability that you will engage in a given behavior—such as studying for an exam tomorrow—depends on _____.
    A. who else will be engaging in the same behavior
    B. how strongly you want to succeed in school
    C. whether you have met more basic needs in the hierarchy
    D. whether you expect to achieve a valued goal by doing so

12. Which of the following statements about hunger and eating is true?
    A. Modern research has concluded that all eating behavior originates in a brain region that acts as a "hunger center."
    B. The "critical set point" is the minimum number of calories needed in a given meal.
    C. Only social customs—such as mealtimes—prevent humans from eating all the time, whatever the circumstances or emotions.
    D. People who are born with more fat cells than others may be biologically "programmed" to be obese.

13. Sex is considered a unique source of human motivation because it _____.
    A. can be aroused by almost any type of stimulus
    B. is essential to both the species and the individual
    C. motivates only a narrow range of behaviors
    D. All of the above

14. According to Masters and Johnson's research on human sexual response, during the _____ phase, a maximum level of arousal is reached, with rapid increases in bodily responses.
    A. excitement
    B. plateau
    C. orgasm
    D. resolution

15. According to your text, crimes such as date rape may be the result of confusion over _____.
    A. sexual orientation
    B. sexual scripts
    C. evolutionary rules
    D. sex roles

16. Sigmund Freud is credited with saying that the secret to a healthy life involves two goals: _____.
    A. love and work
    B. work and play
    C. life and death
    D. power and pleasure

17. _____ activities have been described as producing a special state of mind called "flow."
    A. Achievement-oriented
    B. Extrinsically motivating
    C. Intrinsically motivating
    D. Emotionally arousing

18. One day your professor behaves out of the ordinary by arriving just in time for class, abruptly beginning to lecture, not smiling, and answering only a few questions. You decide your professor is probably angry, so you plan to wait until later to ask for an extension on a project. This example illustrates the _____ function of emotions.
    A. arousing
    B. amplifying
    C. communication
    D. socially-regulating

19. According to the Lazarus-Schachter theory of emotion, emotion is the result of two factors: _____.
    A. bodily arousal and a mental label
    B. bodily arousal and social regulation
    C. social regulation and subjective evaluation
    D. subjective feelings and evolutionary adaptation

20. _____ plays a role in determining how emotions are displayed, when it is appropriate to express them, to whom, and how.
    A. Evolution
    B. Biology
    C. Instinct
    D. Culture

Short Answer Items

Briefly define or explain each term.

21. lateralization of emotion

22. deficiency motivation

23. lateral hypothalamus (LH)

24. *n Ach*

25. James-Lange theory

Chapter 9: Stress, Coping, and Health

Name _____   Date _____

Multiple Choice Items

1. An organism's reaction to external stressors is _____.
   A. adaptation
   B. burnout
   C. coping
   D. strain

2. Researchers Holmes and Rahe have developed the Social Readjustment Rating Scale for evaluating the degree of adjustment required by various _____ that many people experience.
   A. illnesses
   B. life changes
   C. catastrophic events
   D. hassles

3. Researchers have found that people's response to disasters occurs in five stages. Which of the following summarizes them correctly?
   A. shock; effort; letdown; numbness; resignation
   B. confusion; action; focus; completion; recovery
   C. shock; automatic action; effort; letdown; recovery
   D. effort; automatic action; shock; recovery; letdown

4. The personality quality known as hardiness is characterized by the "three C's": _____.
   A. challenge, commitment, and control
   B. cognition, competition, and creativity
   C. coping, competence, and companionship
   D. calm, concern, and community

5. _____ is a state of enduring arousal, continuing over time, in which demands are perceived as greater than one's resources for coping with them.
   A. Societal stress
   B. Chronic stress
   C. Residual stress
   D. Relapse

6. At the center of the fight-or-flight response is the _____, referred to as the "stress center" because it controls the autonomic nervous system and activates the pituitary gland.
   A. reticular formation
   B. limbic system
   C. medulla
   D. hypothalamus

7. Grief-stricken at the sudden death of his wife, an elderly man becomes physically less able to fight illness and risks his own premature death. This is an example of _____.
   A. immunosuppression
   B. residual stress
   C. anticipatory coping
   D. secondary appraisal

8. In a coping strategy with a _____ focus, one's goal is not to confront the problem directly, but rather to lessen the discomfort associated with experiencing stress.
   A. problem-solving
   B. primary-appraisal
   C. emotion-regulation
   D. residual-stress

9. Arvid's humanities grades have been so low he may fail. Though he is worried, Arvid puts off confronting the problem or talking to his professor. He tells himself it would do no good to complain—it might only make things worse. Arvid is using the ego defense mechanism known as _____.
   A. denial
   B. repression
   C. rationalization
   D. projection

10. For a person in a stressful setting, thinking differently and more constructively about the situation is a way of achieving _____ control.
    A. information
    B. cognitive
    C. decision
    D. behavioral

11. Which types of social support are most helpful for specific events? Research by Shelley Taylor and her colleagues indicates that the answer depends on _____.
    A. the victim's relationship with the person providing it
    B. the victim's anxiety level
    C. the victim's physical health
    D. whether the provider has professional training

12. Space program researchers have found that they can help astronauts cope with the stress of long-duration space travel by _____.
    A. training them in the use of peer counseling techniques
    B. prescribing a diet high in fiber and vitamins
    C. designing the space capsule to be a relaxing environment
    D. teaching them to use meditation and biofeedback

13. According to health psychologists, a _____ is a behavior pattern that operates automatically—without extrinsic reinforcement or incentives—and that contributes directly to your overall well-being.
    A. general adaptation syndrome
    B. healthy habit
    C. Type-A syndrome
    D. Type-T personality

14. Health psychologists have identified four elements that determine that someone is likely to change from unhealthy to healthy behavior. Which of the following is *not* one of them?
    A. believing one's health is severely threatened
    B. feeling one's likelihood of developing the disorder is high
    C. feeling unable to perform the threat-reducing response
    D. believing it is not too late to change to healthy habits

15. Which of the following would not be considered a "disease of civilization"?
    A. heart disease
    B. automobile accidents
    C. cirrhosis
    D. smallpox

16. Research on who exercises and when indicates that people are most likely to exercise regularly if _____.
    A. their doctors have advised them to do so
    B. they want to lose weight
    C. it is easy and convenient to do so
    D. other family members do so

17. _____ represents a problem that makes AIDS resistant to intervention because individuals at risk incorrectly believe they cannot be harmed.
    A. Relapse
    B. Anticipatory coping
    C. Patient nonadherence
    D. The illusion of vulnerability

18. The result of maintaining positive illusions about one's well-being is likely to result in _____.
    A. adaptive, health-maintaining behavior
    B. taking unnecessary risks with one's health
    C. a feeling of learned helplessness
    D. a higher risk of stress-related disorders

19. Which of the following would *not* describe an individual who fit the Type-A profile?
    A. impatient
    B. depressed
    C. aggressive
    D. hostile

20. A teacher who used to love her work now feels exhausted, unappreciated, exploited, and often angry at her students. Her symptoms suggest she may be suffering from _____.
    A. relapse
    B. burnout
    C. nonadherence
    D. immunosuppression

Short Answer Items

Briefly define or explain each term.

21. cognitive appraisal

22. PTSD

23. denial

24. biopsychosocial model

25. patient nonadherence

Chapter 10: Personality

Name _____   Date _____

Multiple Choice Items

1. Psychologists define personality in many different ways, but common to all of them are two basic concepts: _____.
   A. positive and negative influences
   B. genetic heritage and experiential or educational factors
   C. the push of the past and the pull of the future
   D. uniqueness and characteristic patterns of behavior

2. The nomothetic approach to personality is said to be _____-centered, because it assumes that the same personality traits apply to everyone in the same way.
   A. variable
   B. person
   C. situation
   D. theory

3. "I just took the Myers-Briggs personality test at the Career Center," your roommate announces, "and it turns out I'm an 'ENTJ.' This explains so much about my personality!" Your roommate apparently favors _____ theories of personality.
   A. trait
   B. type
   C. psychodynamic
   D. social-learning

4. According to Gordon Allport, a _____ trait is one around which a person organizes his or her life, the way Howard Hughes pursued lifelong goals of power and achievement.
   A. maximal
   B. cardinal
   C. central
   D. primary

5. _____ is the assumption that all mental and behavioral reactions are determined by earlier experiences.
   A. Radical behaviorism
   B. Reciprocal determinism
   C. Psychic determinism
   D. Social-learning theory

6. According to Freudian theory, during the _____ stage of psychosexual development, a child explores his or her own body, and discovers the pleasure associated with self-stimulation of the genitals.
   A. latency
   B. oral
   C. genital
   D. phallic

7. Julio has a test in the morning and he should spend the evening studying for it. However, he has also been invited to attend a party tonight. According to Freudian theory, if Julio gives in to the urging of his _____, he will attend the party instead of studying.
   A. id
   B. ego
   C. libido
   D. superego

8. In humanistic theory, _____ is a constant striving to realize one's inherent potential, to fully develop one's potential and talents.
   A. psychic determinism
   B. self-actualization
   C. self-efficacy
   D. the ego ideal

9. The post-Freudian theorist _____ proposed that people's lives are dominated by the search for ways to overcome feelings of inferiority and inadequacy.
   A. Carl Jung
   B. Carl Rogers
   C. Alfred Adler
   D. Albert Bandura

10. An important concept in person-centered therapy is that children should be raised with an emphasis on _____, so they know they will be loved and accepted regardless of their mistakes.
    A. unconditional positive regard
    B. conditional positive reinforcement
    C. self-actualization
    D. self-efficacy

11. In their social-learning theory of personality, John Dollard and Neal Miller argued that one can learn a behavior pattern through a process of _____.
    A. classical conditioning
    B. trial-and-error
    C. social imitation
    D. ego defense

12. According to theorist Walter Mischel, "person variables" will have their greatest impact on behavior when _____.
    A. the individual is high in Extroversion
    B. fixation has occurred early in psychosexual development
    C. situational forces are equally powerful
    D. cues in the situation are weak or ambiguous

13. Which of the following illustrates the concept of self-efficacy?
    A. After her husband leaves her, a young woman believes she herself will be able to fill the household roles he once filled.
    B. A man who likes pornographic materials publicly announces his support for censorship and laws to ban such materials.
    C. A child who has lived in a series of foster homes sees most families as unstable and unreliable.
    D. A battered wife has given up trying to change her husband's behavior, and no longer seeks to escape her circumstances.

14. Marnie likes to run for fitness, so she meets other people who run on the same route. Because she spends more time with these people, she spends more time talking and thinking about being fit. This circular relationship of traits and forces illustrates the process Bandura calls _____.
    A. self-efficacy
    B. reciprocal determinism
    C. observational learning
    D. reaction formation

15. Critics of cognitive theories of personality have argued that such theories generally overlook _____ as an important aspect of personality.
    A. thoughts
    B. beliefs
    C. emotions
    D. expectations

16. A person's self-_____ is a generalized self-evaluation of the self, which can strongly influence our thoughts, moods, and behavior.
    A. concept
    B. enhancement
    C. handicap
    D. esteem

17. Of the following categories of personality theories, which places the *least* emphasis on past causes or influences in determining individuals' behavior?
    A. psychodynamic
    B. learning
    C. trait
    D. humanistic

18. The _____ is a personality inventory based on the Big Five model of personality.
    A. NEO-PI
    B. MMPI
    C. MBTI
    D. CPI

19. As part of a personality assessment, Giles examines a series of drawn stimuli, and makes up stories about them. Which of the following techniques is being used?
    A. NEO-PI
    B. TAT
    C. MMPI
    D. CPI

20. The most effective and useful personality assessments are based on _____.
    A. close observations of an individual over several months
    B. interviews with family and friends of the subject
    C. data about the groups to which the subject belongs
    D. one or more major personality theories

Short Answer Items

Briefly define or explain each term.

21. idiographic approach

22. The Big Five

23. anxiety

24. personal construct

25. projective technique

Mastery Test

Chapter 11: Individual Differences

Name _____ Date _____

Multiple Choice Items

1. Psychological assessment is often referred to as the measurement of _____, since the majority of assessments specify how a person compares or contrasts with others.
   A. situationism
   B. fluid intelligence
   C. individual differences
   D. psychometrics

2. Which of the following is *not* one of the arguments put forth by Sir Francis Galton?
   A. Evolutionary theory should be applied to family planning.
   B. Differences in intelligence can be quantified and measured.
   C. Differences in intelligence are randomly distributed in the population.
   D. Biologically inferior people should not produce offspring.

3. A clinical psychologist typically uses testing _____.
   A. to make predictions about a population
   B. to make predictions about a particular client
   C. as a substitute for direct observation of an individual
   D. to discover regularities in personality that indicate patterns of behavior or life events

4. If a test yields the same results consistently but does not measure what its users intend it to measure, it is _____.
   A. neither reliable nor valid
   B. reliable but not valid
   C. valid but not reliable
   D. both valid and reliable

5. A test developer identifies several kinds of data that measure a personal quality she calls "fussiness." She develops a test of individual fussiness, and finds that test scores correlate positively with the data she has identified. This means her test is high in _____ validity.
   A. construct
   B. criterion
   C. test-retest
   D. split-half

6. The process of standardization is necessary to establish _____, test performance standards to which individual scores can be compared.
   A. g-factors
   B. constructs
   C. aptitudes
   D. norms

7. Which of the following is the most direct approach to learning about a given individual?
   A. a personality inventory
   B. archival data
   C. an interview
   D. a psychological test

8. Positively impressed with the good looks and self-assured manner of the young man she interviews for her company's position, Stephanie interprets all his traits in a positive way. This illustrates a type of bias called the _____ effect.
   A. halo
   B. stereotype
   C. interjudge
   D. g-factor

9. Human intelligence provides us with a distinct advantage for survival in our world, because it enables us to _____.
   A. outsmart our enemies, whatever they might be
   B. repeatedly use the same effective problem-solving strategies
   C. calculate the limits and possibilities for our personal achievement
   D. respond to environmental challenges with flexibility and imagination

10. Which of the following is *not* one of the four features that distinguished Alfred Binet's approach to testing mental age?
    A. He interpreted test scores as a measure of innate intelligence.
    B. He meant the test to identify children who needed help.
    C. He believed training and opportunity could affect intelligence.
    D. He based the test on how children were observed to perform.

11. Which of the following social and political forces made it most necessary for American psychologists to quickly develop nonverbal, group-administered tests of mental ability?
    A. America's entry into World War I
    B. passage of new universal education laws
    C. a wave of immigrants entering the United States
    D. the discovery that intelligence is largely inherited

12. The Stanford-Binet Intelligence Scale was developed by _____.
    A. Alfred Binet
    B. Leland Stanford
    C. Lewis Terman
    D. Raymond Cattell

13. According to the formula for calculating IQ, a person with chronological age of 20 and a mental age of 25 has an IQ of _____.
    A. 80
    B. 105
    C. 120
    D. 125

14. The intelligence scales developed by David Wechsler include two types of subtests: _____.
    A. verbal and spatial
    B. verbal and performance
    C. performance and insight
    D. internal and external

15. Group tests of intelligence measure a narrowly defined type of intellectual functioning often called school ability or _____.
    A. mental age
    B. crystallized intelligence
    C. scholastic aptitude
    D. factor analysis

16. Young Jared is better than most children his age at seeing complex relationships and solving problems. He would probably score high in what researcher Raymond Cattell calls _____ intelligence.
    A. crystallized
    B. fluid
    C. semantic
    D. componential

17. An intelligence expert claims that there are many different kinds of intelligence, distinguished by three features: the content of one's knowledge, the product that represents it, and the operation one performs on it. This expert agrees with the model of intelligence originally proposed by _____.
    A. Henry Goddard
    B. Howard Gardner
    C. Earl Hunt
    D. J. P. Guilford

18. Which of the following reflects what psychologist Robert Sternberg calls "contextual intelligence"?
    A. practical skills and adaptability to daily living
    B. artistic or creative endeavors
    C. IQ scores and college grades
    D. manipulating mental representations in problem solving

19. Psychologists' studies of the Juke and Kallikak families were originally undertaken to demonstrate that extremes of intelligence were powerfully determined by _____.
    A. educational opportunity
    B. socioeconomic status
    C. heredity
    D. gender differences

20. Luann is taking a test of her current level of competency in German language. This would be an example of a(n) _____ test.
    A. aptitude
    B. achievement
    C. vocational
    D. job analysis

Short Answer Items

Briefly define or explain each term.

21. eugenics

22. parallel forms

23. stereotype effect

24. g-factor

25. aptitude test

Mastery Test

Chapter 12: Social Psychology

Name _____   Date _____

Multiple Choice Items

1. One social psychological explanation for the behavior of the "guards" and "prisoners" in Zimbardo's prison simulation is that _____ had created a new social reality for the participants.
   A. personalities susceptible to violence
   B. individuals with behavior disorders
   C. the power of the prison situation
   D. None of the above

2. The earliest demonstration that the mere presence of others has an impact on individual behavior was an experiment on the phenomenon of _____.
   A. conformity
   B. social facilitation
   C. prejudice
   D. demand characteristics

3. Members of a group are usually able to estimate how much they may deviate before they experience coercion through the three "painful R's." Which of the following is *not* one of them?
   A. rejection
   B. reinforcement
   C. reeducation
   D. ridicule

4. According to research by Theodore Newcomb, students at Bennington College in the late 1930s were most influenced in their later social attitudes by _____.
   A. their parents
   B. their romantic partners
   C. their reference group
   D. world events

5. The Asch effect describes the influence of _____ on an individual's judgments, even when conditions are unambiguous.
   A. a lone opponent
   B. unpopular social opinions
   C. an oppressed minority
   D. a unanimous group majority

6. Stanley Milgram's research showed that blind obedience to authority is more a matter of _____ than of _____.
   A. situational forces; personality
   B. situational forces; powerful circumstances
   C. dispositional characteristics; personality
   D. dispositional characteristics; situational influence

7. Which of the following best summarizes the results of Milgram's study of obedience, in which teachers were ordered to administer "shocks" to a learner?
   A. None of the subjects obeyed to the highest shock level.
   B. None of the subjects obeyed to the midpoint level of shock.
   C. Most subjects refused to go on after the learner first complained about pain.
   D. Most subjects obeyed to the highest level of shock.

8. According to the "rules of influence," people are subject to normative influence because they want to be _____, and to informational influence because they want to be _____.
   A. right; informed
   B. right; liked
   C. liked; right
   D. liked; appreciated

9. Latané and Darley created a laboratory version of bystander intervention, in which individual subjects overheard another student having a "seizure." The more witnesses the subject believed could overhear the crisis, _____.
   A. the slower the subject was to respond to the emergency
   B. the faster the subject was to respond to the emergency
   C. the more likely the subject was to ask them for help
   D. None of the above

10. In Darley and Batson's "Good Samaritan" experiment, seminarians on their way to keep an appointment were most likely to offer help to a needy stranger if they _____.
    A. were in a hurry
    B. were not in a hurry
    C. were on time for the appointment
    D. had just evaluated a sermon about helping others

11. According to research by Tom Moriarity, if you find yourself in need of assistance, the best way to get help from the strangers around you is to _____.
    A. demand it
    B. ask for it
    C. promise a reward for it
    D. pretend you do not need it

12. _____ is the consensus of perceptions and beliefs about a situation created by group members' social comparisons.
    A. A norm
    B. Social reality
    C. The total situation
    D. Covariation

13. The Pygmalion effect refers to the influence of _____.
    A. social expectancies
    B. group pressure to conform
    C. self-serving bias
    D. cognitive dissonance

14. Diego has been told that Carmen is very shy. Meeting her at a party, he talks about school instead of asking her about herself, and invites her to sit at a quiet table instead of asking her to dance. As a result of _____, Carmen acts as shyly as Diego expects her to.
    A. social loafing
    B. social facilitation
    C. self-serving bias
    D. behavioral confirmation

15. _____ is a learned attitude toward a target, involving negative feelings, negative beliefs, and negative intentions toward the target.
    A. Attribution
    B. Social categorization
    C. Prejudice
    D. Covariation

16. Third-grade teacher Jane Elliott was able to generate hostility toward minority-group members in her classroom simply as a result of _____.
    A. the Asch effect
    B. the placebo effect
    C. social categorization
    D. demand characteristics

17. Attribution theory is a general approach to the way individuals ask and answer questions about _____.
    A. who they are
    B. how to get along with others
    C. what they should do
    D. why events and actions occur

18. According to Fritz Heider, we are all "intuitive psychologists" because each one of us tries to _____.
    A. understand other people and their actions
    B. analyze others so we can control what they do
    C. develop close relationships with others
    D. help people when they are suffering

19. When her team wins a game, the coach brags, "We worked hard and it paid off!" When the team loses, she rationalizes, "Because we've had to sideline our best players due to injuries, we could not overcome our opponents' tactics." This pattern of explanations reflects the operation of _____.
    A. the self-serving bias
    B. demand characteristics
    C. social perception
    D. the covariation principle

20. Although most cultures frown on individual aggression, nations encourage military aggression against their opponents by a process of _____.
    A. social categorization
    B. dehumanization
    C. bystander intervention
    D. situationism

Short Answer Items

Briefly define or explain each term.

21. social loafing

22. demand characteristics

23. self-fulfilling prophecies

24. cognitive dissonance

25. account

Mastery Test

Chapter 13: Psychopathology

Name _____   Date _____

Multiple Choice Items

1. Which of the following descriptions would *not* be considered an indicator of abnormality, as outlined in the text?
   A. acting in ways that interfere with personal well-being, personal goals, and society's goals
   B. experiencing periods of worry, self-doubt, anxiety, and escapism
   C. acting or talking in ways that are irrational or incomprehensible to others
   D. making others feel uncomfortable by causing them to feel threatened or distressed

2. Which of the following is true of the "medical model" of abnormal behavior?
   A. Mental disorders are considered to be caused by processes such as learning, cognitions, and cultural factors.
   B. It adopts the perspective that no known organic disorder is known to be responsible for causing mental illness.
   C. Afflicted individuals are considered to be sick, and are treated as patients who must be cured.
   D. None of the above

3. According to the psychodynamic model of mental illness, the symptoms of psychopathology have their roots in _____.
   A. unconscious conflict
   B. maladaptive reinforcement patterns
   C. irrational or unrealistic thinking
   D. structural or functional problems in the nervous system

4. To be most useful, a good system of classifying forms of psychopathology should meet several goals. Which of the following is *not* one of them?
   A. to suggest how best to treat certain types of problems
   B. to demonstrate that there is no such thing as abnormality, since everyone fits in at least one of the categories
   C. to establish an agreed-upon language for clinicians and researchers to use in discussing mental illness
   D. to suggest the causes of the symptoms of any particular case

5. Jake, an inmate in a federal prison, has a history of breaking laws and hurting people since childhood, and seems indifferent to the feelings or rights of others. Jake's symptoms suggest that he might be diagnosed with _____.
   A. a dissociative disorder
   B. a social phobia
   C. narcissistic personality disorder
   D. antisocial personality disorder

6. Which of the following is *not* an example of an anxiety disorder?
   A. psychogenic amnesia
   B. panic disorder
   C. obsessive-compulsive disorder
   D. agoraphobia

7. Lorena is abnormally worried about cleanliness and hygiene, and sometimes feels she has to wash her hands dozens of times before they feel clean enough. This repetitive handwashing behavior is an example of a(n) _____.
   A. social phobia
   B. manic episode
   C. compulsion
   D. obsession

8. The two "poles" in bipolar disorder are _____.
   A. rational and irrational thinking
   B. obsession and compulsion
   C. neurosis and psychosis
   D. mania and depression

9. According to Aaron Beck, depressed people seem to have a "cognitive triad" of negative views, focused on three aspects of their lives. Which of the following is *not* one of the three?
   A. themselves
   B. other people
   C. ongoing experiences
   D. their future

10. The biological view of unipolar depression is supported by the ability of _____ to relieve depressive symptoms.
   A. psychoanalysis
   B. cognitive therapy
   C. lithium
   D. environmental change

11. Which of the following statements about suicide is *not* true?
    A. Most suicides are attempted by those suffering from anxiety disorders.
    B. Suicide is most often committed by unemployed, older, white males.
    C. Women attempt suicide about three times more often than men.
    D. The leading traumatic incident that triggers suicide for both sexes is the breakup of a close relationship.

12. Which of the following statements about individuals suffering from anorexia nervosa is true?
    A. The typical victim maintains a distorted body image, believing herself to be unattractively fat.
    B. Anorexics alternate between episodes of overeating and efforts to lose weight by vomiting, fasting, or using laxatives.
    C. Anorexic symptoms include an end to menstruation and keeping an immature, "childish" body shape.
    D. None of the above

13. Which of the following is *not* one of the symptoms of schizophrenia?
    A. flat or inappropriate emotions
    B. unexpected, severe anxiety attacks
    C. disorganized or rigid psychomotor behavior
    D. hallucinations

14. A schizophrenic patient claims she knows about secret plans by the CIA to support an invasion from Mars, and that because of this she is being persecuted both by space aliens and government officials. This patient is most likely suffering from the _____ type of schizophrenia.
    A. undifferentiated
    B. catatonic
    C. disorganized
    D. paranoid

15. According to the _____ hypothesis of schizophrenia, genetic factors place a particular individual at risk for the disorder, but environmental factors provide the pressure that causes the individual to manifest the symptoms of schizophrenia.
    A. double-bind
    B. diathesis-stress
    C. dopamine
    D. DSM-III

16. According to psychologist Brendan Maher, the "word salad" typical of some schizophrenics' speech is caused by processing difficulties whenever the speaker utters a(n) _____ word.
    A. vulnerable
    B. abstract
    C. stigmatized
    D. antisocial

17. _____ disorders involve physical symptoms such as pain or paralysis that arise without a physical cause.
    A. Organic
    B. Substance-use
    C. Psychogenic
    D. Somatoform

18. Although many people suffer from psychopathological symptoms, the label "mentally ill" usually only gets applied to an individual if that person _____.
    A. has attempted to harm himself or others
    B. is under some form of care
    C. violates civil or criminal law
    D. is diagnosed with a problem of organic origin

19. Which of the following is true of Rosenhan's study in which pseudopatients falsely gained admission to psychiatric hospitals?
    A. Though all were admitted to the hospitals, none was able to be diagnosed.
    B. Though some fellow patients were fooled, all of the hospital staff members recognized that the pseudopatients were sane.
    C. Though healthy when they were admitted, the pseudopatients soon developed symptoms like those of patients around them.
    D. None of the above

20. According to the cross-cultural discussion, the ecological model of abnormality starts by assuming that people must _____ in order to meet the norms of the society in which they live.
    A. repress unconscious motivations
    B. experience regular reinforcement
    C. be of at least average intelligence
    D. develop certain necessary skills

Short Answer Items

Briefly define or explain each term.

21. conversion disorder

22. MPD

23. catastrophizing

24. bulimia

25. delusion

Name _____   Date _____

Multiple Choice Items

1. The therapeutic tradition of _____ combines healing prac-
   tices with belief in spirits.
   A. psychoanalysis
   B. rationale-emotive therapy
   C. shamanism
   D. Gestalt therapy

2. _____ therapy views disordered behavior as the result of
   _____.
   A. Behavior; faulty self-statements
   B. Biomedical; malfunctioning body systems or
       metabolism
   C. Psychodynamic; learned patterns
   D. Behavior; unresolved traumas and conflicts

3. The therapeutic process can involve four primary tasks or
   goals: diagnosis, etiology, _____, and treatment.
   A. prescription
   B. prognosis
   C. prediction
   D. psychoanalysis

4. Of the following types of mental health professionals, only
   the _____ is likely to have earned an advanced degree in
   psychology rather than social work, ministry, or medicine.
   A. psychoanalyst
   B. psychiatrist
   C. clinical psychologist
   D. pastoral counselor

5. In the late eighteenth century, the French physician
   Philippe Pinel advocated the position that the mentally
   ill _____.
   A. were afflicted by moral corruption
   B. were sick and should be treated
   C. had lost their reason and must be cared for by others
   D. should be rehabilitated by their social communities

6. One universal feature of therapy is the fact that therapists
   must establish _____. This can be done by using the status
   symbols that are already well-known in a culture.
   A. how long a disorder has been developing
   B. the organic bases of the disorder
   C. the incompetency of the patient
   D. their own credibility

7. _____ is also known as "the talking cure."
   A. Psychoanalysis
   B. Behavior modification
   C. Participant modeling
   D. Person-centered therapy

8. Marina had a dream in which she had to open a series of
   drapes and curtains to find her mother. Marina thinks this
   dream was really about her difficulty in talking to her
   mother. In dream analysis, the story of the curtains represents the _____ content while the story of Marina's relationship with her mother represents the _____ content.
   A. hidden; visible
   B. latent; open
   C. manifest; latent
   D. realistic; symbolic

9. Dion's therapist reminds Dion of his father, with whom
   he does not get along. Sometimes Dion expresses anger
   toward his therapist that is really meant for Dion's father.
   This is an example of the Freudian concept of _____.
   A. transference
   B. countertransference
   C. counterconditioning
   D. flooding

10. Post-Freudian theorist Karen Horney identified three
    types of neurotic patterns in interpersonal relationships.
    Which of the following is *not* one of them?
    A. approaching
    B. ambivalent
    C. avoiding
    D. attacking

11. In the behavioral technique known as _____, behavior is
    changed by modifying its consequences.
    A. counterconditioning
    B. contingency management
    C. rationale-emotive therapy
    D. resistance

12. Toni is afraid of flying. With her permission, Toni's thera-
    pist accompanies her on a short airplane trip, helping her
    to cope directly with her most dreaded fear. Toni's experi-
    ence is an example of the treatment strategy known as
    _____.
    A. aversion therapy
    B. systematic desensitization
    C. social-learning therapy
    D. flooding

13. "My coworker Jed always whistles at me when he walks by my desk. It makes me so mad, and I know he just does it to irritate me," complains Carla. Her friend Alice suggests, "Stop acting irritated, and just ignore him. When he realizes he's not bothering you any more, he'll quit whistling." Alice is recommending that Carla use _____ to change Jed's behavior.
   A. symbolic modeling
   B. cognitive behavior modification
   C. negative transference
   D. an extinction strategy

14. In a study of social learning, researchers showed live snakes to young laboratory-raised rhesus monkeys, and observed that the greatest fear was shown by monkeys who _____.
   A. had never seen a real snake before
   B. had not seen how their own parents reacted to a snake
   C. had seen their own parents display fear of snakes
   D. had previously acted fearless with toy snakes

15. In cognitive behavior therapy, clients develop a sense of _____ by setting attainable goals, developing realistic strategies to attain them, and evaluating feedback realistically.
   A. self-efficacy
   B. self-actualization
   C. unconditional positive regard
   D. catharsis

16. Rational-emotive therapy is a comprehensive system of personality change based on transforming _____.
   A. unconscious conflicts
   B. free association
   C. irrational beliefs
   D. negative transference

17. At the core of _____ is the concept of a whole person who engages in the continual process of changing and becoming.
   A. humanistic and existential therapies
   B. family therapies
   C. in vivo therapy
   D. insight therapies

18. As part of her therapy, Eva sometimes imagines her brother, who died when she was young, seated in an empty chair. She finds it helpful to talk to the chair as if she were talking to her brother, and to imagine how he might respond. The use of this technique suggests that Eva is involved in _____ therapy.
   A. person-centered
   B. Gestalt
   C. cognitive behavior
   D. aversion

19. Couples counseling generally focuses on clarifying and improving _____ in the partners' relationship.
   A. individual self-esteem
   B. communication
   C. rational thinking
   D. synergy

20. Much controversy and research was stimulated by the assertion by psychologist _____ that therapy does not work at all.
   A. Egas Moniz
   B. Jerome Frank
   C. Hans Eysenck
   D. Virginia Satir

Short Answer Items

Briefly define or explain each term.

21. etiology

22. insight therapy

23. implosion therapy

24. chemotherapy

25. clinical ecology